CRITICAL ACCLAIM FOR DIARMAID MACCULLOCH'S

THOMAS CRANMER

'... a passionate, committed biography... [MacCulloch] gets as much under his subject's skin as it is possible for a biographer to do'
– Gerald Hammond, *London Review of Books*

'... marvellous – extremely good to read as well as being a definitive biography'
– Robert Harris, *The Times*

'... constantly absorbing... surely definitive... Only rarely can the biographer of a major figure in history hope to make such a difference to our knowledge of a life'
– Patrick Collinson, *Times Literary Supplement*

'... an enthralling new study' – David Walker, *Financial Times*

'Four centuries and more since his death, Cranmer has at last received the biography he deserves... formidable... a model study'
– C. D. C. Armstrong, *Spectator*

'Magisterial' – P. D. James, *Sunday Times*

'A massive, powerful and unexpectedly moving reappraisal of the man whose position as the patron saint of the English language has often been overshadowed by his dramatic last-minute recantation before being burned at the stake... A model biography, wise, revealing and wholly absorbing'
– Miranda Seymour, *Independent*

'... lucidly written, deeply researched and surprisingly accessible'
– Allen D. Boyer, *New York Times Book Review*

'Diarmaid MacCulloch's *Thomas Cranmer* brings a figure fixed for most of us in exam-answers instantly and agonisingly to life'
– Jackie Wullschlager, *Financial Times*

'Could well be the biography of the year... everyone concerned with Church-State relationships *must* read it' – John Munsey Turner, *Methodist Recorder*

'Diarmaid MacCulloch's phenomenal familiarity with so much new, as well as all the old, manuscript, and even topographical material, holds one clamped to his 650 pages' – *Country Life*

'... massive, balanced and without doubt enduring'
– Philip Caraman, *Literary Review*

'MacCulloch's magnificent biography, scrupulously researched... deserves to find a place wherever the dialogue between Protestants and Catholics continues on a scholarly level' – *The Tablet*

'... a superb biography. The reader is amazed at MacCulloch's learning and entranced by his literary skill' – *Expository Times*

'... one of the best biographies of the year' – Kevin Sharpe, *The Times*

'A work of massively persuasive scholarship...not to be missed by anyone wanting to understand the English Reformation' – *English Churchman*

'... a superb source of information and insight; it is also a rippingly good read'
– *Christianity*

'What a wonderful book this is! MacCulloch knows the sources like a woodsman who knows every tree in the forest. He writes with a narrative drive and an ability to capture scenes that make us turn the pages with eager anticipation to see what happens next. He handles an enormous cast of characters with the aplomb of one who seems to have conversed with all of them' – Richard Marius, *Guardian*

'At last we have the truth about Archbishop Cranmer, the most controversial bigwig in the history of the English Church' – A. L. Rowse, *Evening Standard*

'Definitive... An intellectual biography of a man whose most dramatic personal moments, despite the blood-letting all around him, took place in his mind and soul' – Stuart Ferguson, *Wall Street Journal*

'MacCulloch's ability to depict both the man and his times with such clarity and dynamism marks this as a work of rare quality'
– William L. Sachs, *Christian Century*

'... scholarly but gripping... Cranmer stands at the heart and root of Englishness, a source of both its most enduring institutions and of its familiar speech. With both changing fast, we need to know much more about the intellectual godfather who oversaw their birth' – Boyd Tonkin, *Independent*

'a work of majestic breadth and magisterial authority...impressive erudition, great psychological insight, and considerable narrative skill'
– R.A. Houlbrooke, *English Historical Review*

'MacCulloch has given us an extraordinary biography of Archbishop Cranmer and, with him, of the English Reformation. Impeccably researched, with absolute mastery of an overwhelming body of source material and subsequent scholarship, engagingly written, the book is a remarkable achievement'
– Marc M. Arkin, *New Criterion*

THOMAS CRANMER

Thomas Cranmer

A Life

Diarmaid MacCulloch

YALE UNIVERSITY PRESS · NEW HAVEN & LONDON

FOR MARK ACHURCH

Designed by Patty Rennie

Set in Garamond by Best-set Typesetter Ltd, Hong Kong
Printed and bound in Great Britain by the Bath Press

Library of Congress Cataloging-in-Publication Data

MacCulloch, Diarmaid.
Thomas Cranmer: a life/Diarmaid MacCulloch
Includes bibliographical references and index.
ISBN 0-300-06688-0 (hbk: alk. paper)
ISBN 0-300-07448-4 (pbk)
1. Cranmer, Thomas, 1489–1556. 2. Great Britain—History—Tudors, 1485–1603—Biography. 3. Statesmen—Great Britain—Biography. 4. Theologians—England—Biography. 5. Bishops—England—Biography.
I. Title.
DA317.8.C8M34 1996
283'.092—dc20
[B] 95-49593
CIP

A catalogue record for this book is available from the British Library

10 9 8 7 6 5 4

Contents

Illustrations

Abbreviations

All primary and secondary works cited in footnotes are abbreviated with reference to the bibliography, by title or author: the catchword for primary source abbreviations is capitalized in the bibliography. Likewise, see the bibliography for full bibliographical descriptions of specific works mentioned in the table below.

A.C.	*Archaeologia Cantiana*
A.C.C.	*Alcuin Club Collections*
A.P.C.	*Acts of the Privy Council*, with date
A.R.G.	*Archiv für Reformationsgeschichte*
A.S.T.	Archives Municipales, Strasbourg, Archives du Chapitre de St Thomas de Strasbourg
B.I.H.R.	*Bulletin of Historical Research* (see also *H.R.*)
B.L.	British Library
Bodl.	Bodleian Library, Oxford
C.C.C.C.	Corpus Christi College Cambridge, Library
Ch.Hist.	*Church History*
C.J.	*Journals of the House of Commons*
Cox	*Works of Archbishop Cranmer*, ed. J.E. Cox
C.P.R.	*Calendar of Patent Rolls*
C.Q.R.	*Church Quarterly Review*
C.S.	Camden Society
C.S.P.	*Calendar of State Papers*
C.U.L.	Cambridge University Library
D.N.B.	*Dictionary of National Biography*
E.H.R.	*English Historical Review*
E.T.	*Epistolae Tigurinae*
Foxe	J. Foxe, *Acts and Monuments*, ed. Cattley and Townsend
H.M.C.	Historical Manuscripts Commission
H.J.	*Historical Journal* (formerly *Cambridge Historical Journal*)
H.R.	*Historical Research* (formerly *Bulletin of Historical Research*)
H.T.R.	*Harvard Theological Review*
H.W.R.O.	Hereford and Worcester Record Office
J.Eccl.Hist.	*Journal of Ecclesiastical History*
J.T.S.	*Journal of Theological Studies*
Lambeth	Lambeth Palace Library
L.J.	*Journals of the House of Lords*
L.P.	*Letters and Papers . . . Henry VIII*
N.A.	*Norfolk Archaeology*
N.Q.	*Notes and Queries*
N.S.	New Series
O.L.	*Original Letters*
P.C.C.	Prerogative Court of Canterbury wills, P.R.O.
P.R.O.	Public Record Office, London
Proc.P.C.	*Proceedings and Ordinances of the Privy Council*, ed. Nicolas
P.S.	Parker Society
R.H.S.St.Hist.	Royal Historical Society Studies in History
R.S.T.C.	*Short Title Catalogue*, revised by W.A. Jackson and F.S. Ferguson and completed by K.F. Pantzer
S.C.J.	*Sixteenth Century Journal*
ser.	series
St.Ch.Hist.	Ecclesiastical History Society: *Studies in Church History*
St.P.	*State Papers* (see bibliography)
T.R.P.	*Tudor Royal Proclamations*
Tr.Bristol & Glos. Arch.Soc.	*Transactions of the Bristol and Gloucestershire Archaeological Society*
Tr.R.H.S.	*Transactions of the Royal Historical Society*
Tr.Thoroton Soc.	*Transactions of the Thoroton Society of Nottinghamshire*
U.P.	University Press

Acknowledgements

THE FIRST PERSON TO BE thanked is Dr Virginia Murphy, who suggested the project of a biography of Cranmer to me precisely at the moment when I was wondering where my research should go next, and who encouraged the early stages of the work. With her no doubt innocent enquiry, she shaped nearly a decade of my life, and the direction of my career, and at a later stage she made valuable comments on drafts of the text. Subsequently, I have received much help from various sources. I am very grateful to the Leverhulme Trust for awarding me a Fellowship during 1990–91, and to the Wingate Trust for a similar scholarship during 1993–5, both in order to carry out research on this book; I am also indebted to the British Academy for generous help with travel expenses. I thank my former colleagues at Wesley College, Bristol for taking the trouble to arrange for my sabbatical leave at the beginning of this project; my especial thanks are extended to Dr John Farrell, librarian of Wesley College, and to his staff, for their generosity and friendship in providing extended loans of material in the Library's holdings.

The Vicar of the Cranmer Group of Parishes (the Revd D. Bridge-Collyns) and local historian Mr Tom Greasley welcomed me to Aslockton and Whatton in Nottinghamshire and made my visits thoroughly constructive. I have also much appreciated the helpfulness and courtesy of staff at the following institutions: Bristol University Library; Cambridge: Corpus Christi College Library, University Library; the Archivist, Hatfield House; Hereford and Worcester Record Office; London: British Library, Institute of Historical Research, Lambeth Palace Library, Public Record Office; Oxford: All Souls College Library, Bodleian Library; Nottinghamshire County Record Office; Paris, Bibliothèque Ste-Geneviève; St Andrews University Library; Strasbourg: Archives Municipales, Bibliothèque Nationale et Universitaire de Strasbourg. Crown copyright documents in the Public Record Office are quoted by permission of the Controller of Her Majesty's Stationery Office, documents in the British Library by permission of the Trustees, those in the care of Cambridge University Library by permission of the Syndics, and those in the Bodleian Library with its permission. I am grateful to Faber and Faber Ltd for permission to quote from T. S. Eliot's *The Love-Song of J. Alfred Prufrock*.

Many friends and acquaintances, former students and academic colleagues, have greatly improved this book along the way, especially the late Sir Geoffrey Elton. I am only sorry that he did not live to see the final result. I am grateful to those who contributed comments at various seminars when I was gathering and considering my material; I am especially indebted to my former research student Dr Ashley Null, whose insights on and knowledge of Cranmer's theology I can never hope to rival, and who was kind enough to give me a copy of his dissertation at a crucial moment of final tidying-up. I am also indebted not only to the two anonymous readers for Yale University Press, but also to Dr Andrew Pettegree, who read through the entire text and offered useful comments; additionally I must thank Drs Paul Ayris and Rory McEntegart for permission to quote from their unpublished theses. In the latter stages of production, I have received invaluable help and encouragement from Robert Baldock and his colleagues at Yale University Press. Chiefly I have to thank Mark Achurch, who for many years has accepted a *ménage à trois* with a dead Archbishop. I hope that he enjoys the outcome.

DIARMAID MACCULLOCH
ST CROSS COLLEGE, OXFORD
DECEMBER 1995

Introduction

THIS BOOK TELLS A man's life-story, and tries to do it as far as possible in sequence. It is selective in what it tells of the story, although readers may find that hard to believe in what has ended up as an extensive text. Certainly, it is not an impartial narrative: as I have written the tale, I have afforded myself the luxury of having opinions about the actions, motives and influence of one who attracted controversy and wildly polarized comment in his life and in the manner of his death. Ever since he was burned at the stake in Oxford in 1556, Thomas Cranmer's story has frequently been told in two completely contrasting ways: he has been portrayed as a hero or as a villain. In either case, the narrator's prime intention has been to comment on a larger story, that of the Church of England: to legitimize the Church or to dismiss it, to present it as Catholic or as evangelical in character. There is good reason for doing this. It is impossible to disentangle Cranmer's career from the confused manoeuvres which led to the birth of one strand of world Christianity, the Anglican Communion.

Cranmer's own reticence encourages this identification of his own story with the larger narrative of public affairs. He was a very private man, who habitually hid his emotion, as his admiring servant and early biographer Ralph Morice tells us:

> He was a man of such temperature of nature, or rather so mortified, that no manner of prosperity or adversity could alter or change his accustomed conditions: for, being the storms never so terrible or odious, nor the prosperous estate of the time never so pleasant, joyous or acceptable, to the face of [the] world his countenance, diet or sleep commonly never altered or changed, so that they which were most nearest and conversant about him never or seldom perceived by no sign or token of countenance how the affairs of the prince or the realm went. Notwithstanding privately with his secret and special friends he would shed forth many bitter tears, lamenting the misery and calamities of the world.[1]

Those friends have not betrayed their confidence, and Cranmer's private face remains for the most part inscrutable. A telling instance of his own

1 *Narratives of the Reformation*, pp. 244–5.

separation of the public and private is that in more than three hundred letters of his which survive, there is only one mention of his second wife and children, for whom he had risked his career in the Church: the silence persists even in the days under Edward VI when he openly displayed his family as his pride and joy. That single reference comes in a letter to Martin Bucer, another married theologian who had come to play a central role in his thinking, and who might count as one of the 'secret and special friends'.[2] If one compares Cranmer's correspondence with the undisciplined yet sparkling flow of words from his lifelong rival Stephen Gardiner, his letters are controlled and circumspect, and they contain few jokes. The margins of the surviving books from his great library (clearly one of his passions) are frequently covered in his notes, but with a few exceptions which I will explore, they are part of his elaborate classified filing-system for research, and they studiously avoid expressing opinions except under the interrogation of the most keen-eyed researcher. For the most part, therefore, this life-story will be of the public man: often the reader will feel that it is a recital of decisions and events in Parliament and the Council Chamber, with Cranmer as a passive spectator. Often that probably reflects reality.

One relentlessly repeated usage in the text may strike some readers as eccentric: in common with many Tudor historians today, I use the word 'evangelical' to describe the religious reformism which developed in England during the 1520s and 1530s, excluding terms like 'Protestant' or 'Lutheran' which create problems at this early stage in the English Reformation. 'Protestant' as a usage did not become naturalized in England until the reign of Mary, after 1553: 'Lutheran' unacceptably narrows the sources for reformist views in Henry VIII's England, and both of them give undue precision to people's outlooks amid a countless number of individual rebellions (often confused and sometimes temporary) against the traditional Church and its assumptions. 'Evangelicalism' is the religious outlook which makes the primary point of Christian reference the Good News of the *Evangelion*, or the text of scripture generally; it is a conveniently vague catch-all term which can be applied across the board, except to the very small minority of English religious rebels who proceeded further towards Continental radicalism. In the nineteenth century the word was appropriated in the English-speaking world to describe a party within Protestantism and within the Church of England, but it can be liberated once more to perform a useful task for the religious history of Tudor England.[3]

Similarly, some readers may object to my characterization of the religion of Sir Thomas More, Bishop John Fisher and the vast majority of the population

2 New College Oxford MS 343 f. 41, and cf. below, Ch. 11, p. 481.

3 For more detailed discussion of the usage, see D. MacCulloch, 'Henry VIII and the early Reformation', in MacCulloch (ed.), *Reign of Henry VIII*, pp. 168–9; and for wise discussion of the imprecision of early reformist stances, see Ives, 'Anne Boleyn and the early Reformation', p. 393.

of England up to the late 1540s as 'conservative' or 'traditionalist'. I am well aware that there is a Whiggish ring to these usages, and that viewed from the perspective of Erasmian humanism in the 1500s or 1510s, they are incomprehensible. They are not meant to imply that the religion of Cranmer and his reformist colleagues was in some way more progressive or more modern than that of More, Fisher or Erasmus, although it is noticeable that the supporters of the late medieval version of Catholicism were fond of terming their opponents 'men of the New Learning'. To term the late medieval Western Church 'Catholic' without further explanation begs too many questions, and the usage would certainly have infuriated Thomas Cranmer in the second half of his career. One can hardly deny that in the struggles over religion from the beginning of the 1520s up to the death of the Archbishop in 1556, the dynamic of events was that of an old world of devotion struggling to conserve and maintain its identity against a new religious outlook which aimed to destroy it and replace it with something 'reformed'. Unsatisfactory as the labels 'conservative' and 'traditionalist' may seem, they are the best which a narrative of early Tudor England can do without lapsing into anachronism and partisanship.

With the consciousness of discordant voices in the past, I do not seek to make Thomas Cranmer into either a hero or a villain; like most of us, he could be both (although in his mature evangelical theology, he would violently have disagreed that one could be both saint and sinner: all are sinners until rescued by God). Frequently Cranmer's actions can legitimately be assessed in sharply contrasting ways. Yet readers should be aware that I retain a wary affection for the Church of England of which he was Primate for more than twenty years, and which has shaped my own identity. If there is bias in this narrative, it is sympathy for a man who was frequently confused and who confused others; and there is also admiration for the way in which he struggled to a final gesture of certainty in his last hour. As I have looked at what we know of Cranmer, I have also concluded that those who told the hero-narrative generally distorted fewer elements of the evidence than those who told the villain-narrative. It is for readers now to decide whether they agree with me.

All quotations in text and footnotes and most titles of contemporary books have been modernized. As far as possible I have rendered place and personal names in a consistent modern form according to the language from which they come. One notable exception is Strasbourg, which I have called 'Strassburg' throughout; it seems pointless to use the French form for a city which was overwhelmingly Germanic in its dominant class and cultural stance in the sixteenth century. Names of Continental figures with a very common English equivalent have been rendered in the English form, and certain academics who adopted Latinized forms of their surnames are referred to in that form.

Part I

ACADEMIC PRELUDE

No! I am not Prince Hamlet, nor was meant to be;
Am an attendant Lord, one that will do
To swell a progress, start a scene or two,
Advise the prince; no doubt, an easy tool:
Deferential, glad to be of use,
Politic, cautious, and meticulous;
Full of high sentence, but a bit obtuse;
At times, indeed, almost ridiculous –
Almost, at times, the Fool.

T.S. Eliot, *The Love-Song of J. Alfred Prufrock*

CHAPTER 1

Simple esquire: 1489–1503

ASLOCKTON IN NOTTINGHAMSHIRE DOES its secular and sacred best to commemorate its most famous child: one of the two pubs in the centre of the little village has been christened The Cranmer Arms, with a sign proudly displaying the family heraldry. When the Victorians built a new parish church here, three centuries after the Reformation disposed of the chapel which Cranmer had known, they dedicated the building to St Thomas: a delicate gesture fraught with characteristic Anglican ambiguity. The prime dedicatee was the apostle who is the patron saint of the intellectually curious, but behind him were the shadows of two archbishops of Canterbury who died defying their monarch in the name of conscience, Thomas Becket and Thomas Cranmer. There are hints of all three in the stained glass installed in the church in 1989 to commemorate the fifth centenary of Cranmer's birth.

St Thomas's, an economical 1890s essay in Early English by Sir Reginald Blomfield, is thus a decorous icon of doubt and scruples of conscience. It also serves as a sentinel at the approach to the site of Cranmer's first home, a large expanse of meadow enclosed by trees and containing a series of grassy hummocks. The small motte known as Cranmer's Mound is probably Norman; most prominent among the complex series of earthworks around it are two rectangular ditched platforms to its east, on which probably stood the late medieval house. The Cranmers had arrived in Aslockton from Sutterton on the Wash in Lincolnshire seven or eight decades before the future Archbishop was born; they came through the marriage of Thomas's great-grandfather Edmund with the heiress of the Aslockton or Haslerton family. It was a good match for Edmund Cranmer, for the Aslocktons were of knight's degree; bolstered by this descent, Thomas's father, Thomas senior, styled himself esquire in his will, although his wealth was probably dangerously modest to claim such a status.[1]

Neither the township of Aslockton nor the Cranmer family were of great account by themselves. Aslockton did not have its own parish church; its little

1 *Testamenta Eboracensia*, pp. 194–5; Payling, *Political Society*, p. 228. The best pedigree of the Cranmers is to be found in Pollard, but *Nottingham Visitations 1569 and 1614*, pp. 70–71 is also useful. For a brief discussion and plan of the earthworks, see Gould, 'Some Nottinghamshire Strongholds', p. 61.

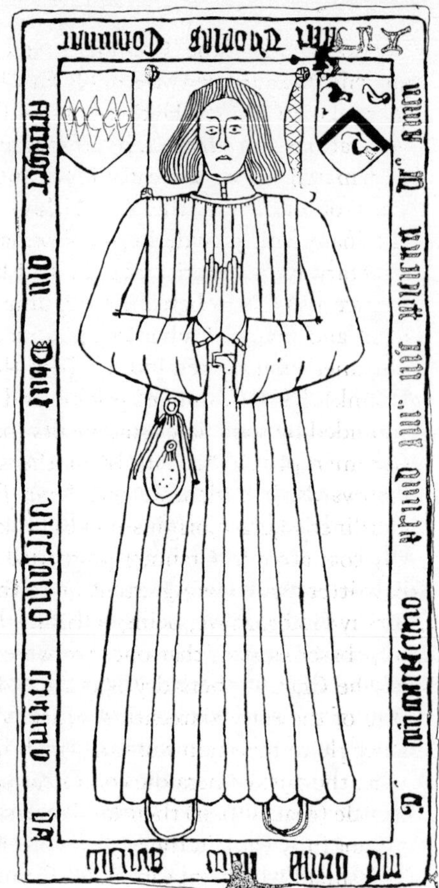

1 The tomb-slab of Archbishop Cranmer's father, d. 1501, Whatton Church, Nottinghamshire, drawn by John Graham Wallace. The inscription, transcribed and translated by Peter Newman Brooks, reads *Hic iacet Thomas Cornmar {sic} armiger qui obiit vicesimo septimo die mensis maii anno D'n'i D millesimo qui'gentesimo primo cuius anime propicietur Deus Amen* (Here lies Thomas Cranmer, esquire, who died on the 27th day of the month of May in the year of the Lord 1501; may God have mercy on his soul. Amen).

medieval chapel of Holy Trinity is now rather amorphously represented in the stonework of a cottage in the village main street. The building used to be known as 'Cranmer's Mission House'; a secular age has toned this down to 'Cranmer's Cottage', the name which it now bears on a plaque. Thomas Cranmer senior dutifully bequeathed half a mark to Holy Trinity chapel, but he was buried in the much grander parish church at Whatton, of which parish the township of Aslockton formed a part. Whatton church was no more than a quarter-mile's walk from Aslockton if two stream-courses were not in flood, and the Cranmers clearly appreciated a burial-place beside the stately earlier tombs of knights and clergy. The family chose not to compete too brashly with the armoured effigies and tomb-chests of Hugh de Newmarch and Sir Richard de Whatton, for they bought an incised limestone slab for Thomas, and had him portrayed (not very elegantly) in civilian clothes: a double admission that there were limits to their purse and to their current social pretensions.

Nevertheless, the Cranmers were determined to make their claim to ancient lineage: the two shields on Thomas senior's slab ignored not only his marriage to Agnes Hatfield, but all the other fifteenth-century Cranmer generations, and instead, beside the arms of Cranmer was placed the shield of Newmarch, as on the early fourteenth-century tomb-chest of Hugh. In his years of greatness, the Archbishop would continue this heraldic sign of obstinate family pride in his Newmarch ancestry, and he emphasized to his secretary Ralph Morice that he had been educated in gentlemanly pursuits. Morice also remembered him arguing in 1540 with a roomful of Henry VIII's legal and financial advisors about the education of the humble; he recalled Cranmer robustly reminding them that all present were 'gentlemen born (as I think)'.[2] The Cranmers' prickly and precarious self-esteem would have been wounded by some later statements that the Archbishop was of yeoman stock. Cranmer placed his family in the social order very precisely many years afterwards, in a delicate put-down for Bishop Stephen Gardiner; although Gardiner's family origins in a Suffolk market town had not bequeathed him any coat armour, Cranmer pretended to assume a common social origin with his bitter foe. Drawing attention to their episcopal titles, the Archbishop said 'I pray God that we, being called to the name of lords, have not forgotten our own baser estates, that once we were simple squires'.[3]

The Cranmer heraldry is more problematically varied than for most families of the early sixteenth century, variations which must reflect the family struggle to maintain a status which its present circumstances made dubious. Even the normal heraldic complications caused by the need of Archbishops to impale (that is, pair) their family arms with the arms of the see of Canterbury cannot fully explain the vagaries of Thomas Cranmer's heraldic achievements. The shield which appears as the Cranmer arms on Thomas senior's tomb-slab from 1501 is a chevron between three cranes, and it is this which appears on his illustrious son's signet or personal seal, duly impaled with Newmarch, and then quartered with the coat of the Archbishop's Hatfield mother. The simple and therefore impressively ancient Cranmer coat also appears on his prerogative seal as Archbishop (see below, Ch. 6, pl. 19), but very soon after he became Archbishop, Cranmer decided to alter his personal arms, apparently wanting something which was distinctively his own. The birds (apparently cranes, in a typical heraldic pun on the family name) were changed to pelicans, to give the symbolism of that bird's legendary willingness to feed its young with its own blood; this typology of Christ's blood-shedding for humanity on the cross appealed to the evangelicalism which the Nottinghamshire squire's son had now embraced. The Archbishop's heraldic alteration

2 *Narratives of the Reformation*, pp. 239, 274.

3 Cox 1, p. 275. On Cranmer's supposed yeoman origins, cf. e.g. Smyth, *Cranmer*, p. 43, and also the hostile contemporary comments of *Cranmer's Recantacyons*, p. 2. On Gardiner, see MacCulloch, 'Two Dons in Politics', pp. 2–3 and nn.

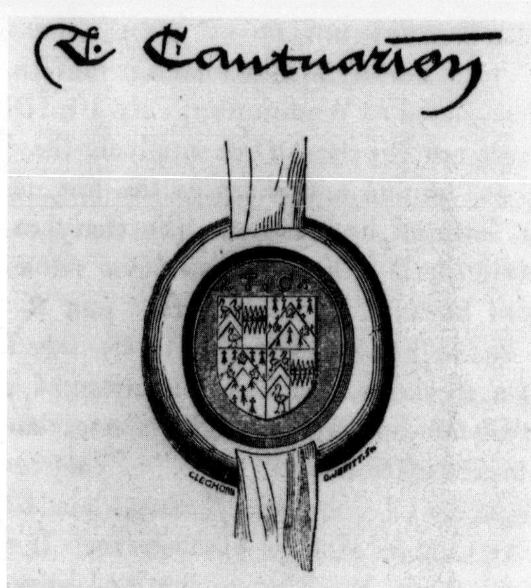

2 Cranmer's personal seal, from a wax impression with his signature above: Cranmer (ancient) impaling Newmarch quarters Hatfield.

3 Archbishop Cranmer's arms in modishly Renaissance style on a glass panel, probably from one of his palaces: See of Canterbury impaling Cranmer with pelicans (as Archbishop) quartering unknown coat (probably Aslockton) and Newmarch, all with a crescent for difference. Cranmer's motto NOSCE TEIPSUM ET DEUM is mis-spelt NOSCE TE IPSUM IT DEUM.

4 Cranmer's first official seal used for his personal action as Archbishop. Note the arms at the dexter (*bottom left*): See of Canterbury impaling Cranmer (as Archbishop). At the sinister Newmarch impales Aslockton.

may also consciously have sought to contrast with the action of his predecessor but one in the see of Canterbury, Henry Deane (1501–3), who had also adopted birds in his coat-armour. However, Deane had taken the unprecedented step of referring to the symbol of Thomas Becket, three choughs or beckets, in the coat which he bore – Cranmer's opinion in the 1530s would have been that Deane had thus identified himself with a traitor to the English Crown. Additionally Cranmer added the three cinquefoils from his mother's arms to the family chevron, and then his new coat was complete, together with a punctiliously added crescent to show that he was a younger son.[4]

This revised heraldry appears first on the seal which Cranmer hastily cannibalized from a matrix used by his predecessor Archbishop Warham, using it to authenticate his official actions undertaken in person, as soon as he was made Archbishop in 1533.[5] It can be seen identifying the Archbishop on the title-page of the Great Bible of 1539 (see below, Ch. 7, pl. 20), and it also occurs in stained glass which must have adorned one of his homes in the

4 Gorham, *Gleanings*, pp. 13–14, although Gorham is wrong in stating (ibid., p. 9) that Cranmer had assumed the earlier arms. Cf. *Narratives of the Reformation*, pp. 238, 250–51. On Deane, see Collinson, Ramsay and Sparks (eds), *Canterbury Cathedral*, p. 487.

5 This is the seal wrongly identified by Gorham, *Gleanings*, pp. 8–10, as Cranmer's first faculty seal; for its true identification, see below, Ch. 4, p. 117 n. 120.

1540s. In good feudal fashion, it seems to have been the model for the coats of arms assumed by at least two of his household servants, Peter Hayman and John Sandford.[6] Yet Cranmer did not altogether forget the older family coat, with its claim to ancient blood. The heraldry on his signet and on his faculty seal continued to display the old design, without any crescent, and additionally the faculty seal conjured up from the past in its quartering, the six lions of the Aslocktons: remote medieval knightly splendours recalled amid Renaissance clerical splendour (see below, Ch. 4, pl. 12).

The Cranmers were not the clients of any great noble family. The occupants of Belvoir Castle a few miles to the south-east of Whatton dominated the surrounding countryside both earlier and later, but in Cranmer's boyhood the castle was a derelict shell; it was abandoned after the fifteenth-century civil wars, and subsequently 'the timber of the roofs uncovered rotted away, and the soil between the walls at the last grew full of elders'. Nottinghamshire county politics under Henry VII was dominated by a few great gentry families, in particular Sir Henry Willoughby of Wollaton near Nottingham.[7] If we want to gauge the important people in the young Thomas's life, we must turn first to his father Thomas's will. This was a fairly brief document, dated on the day of his death as recorded on his tomb, 27 May 1501; the elder Thomas had probably made most of the necessary arrangements elsewhere. There are no signs in the will of any looming family disagreements over the inheritance of the heir, his son John.

Thomas senior made no elaborate provisions for masses, but the will shows every sign of a household in which clergy loomed large. Whatton church was to get a new bell, and the testator's clergyman brother John was a witness; but most striking was the family's link with the great Premonstratensian Abbey of Welbeck, the patron of the living of Whatton. Abbot Thomas Wydur of Welbeck was to be supervisor and two canons of the house were among the witnesses of the will, one of them the Vicar of Whatton, soon to be Abbot at Welbeck, Thomas Wilkinson. The family connection probably continued in later years: at Welbeck's dissolution in 1538, among the monks were William Hatfield and John Marshall, the family names respectively of Archbishop Cranmer's mother and grandmother, and the main purchaser of Welbeck, Richard Whalley, married both his sons to the daughters of Cranmer's cousin and servant Henry Hatfield.[8] Welbeck was a flourishing house in 1501. After a bad patch in the fifteenth century, Wydur and his two predecessors vigorously promoted reform, as the impressed visitor of the order

6 Sandford of Canterbury: argent on a chevron between three martlets sable, an annulet or. Hayman of Kent: argent on a chevron between three martlets sable, as many cinquefoils of the first. Papworth, *Ordinary*, pp. 503–4.

7 Belvoir: Leland 1, pp. 97–8. See also Cameron, 'Sir Henry Willoughby'; Cameron, 'Meering and the Meryng Family'.

8 Surrender: *Faculty Office Registers*, p. 144, and on the Whalley/Hatfield marriages, cf. *Nottingham Visitations 1569 and 1614*, pp. 117–18.

repeatedly attested, and in 1512, Welbeck was promoted to be the head house of the Premonstratensians in England, with Abbot Wilkinson as *ex officio* visitor-general.[9] The future Archbishop would have known English monastic life at its best when he was a boy.

Perhaps it was the Welbeck association which inspired the elder Thomas to make sure that two of his three sons, Thomas and Edmund, got a good education, the essential preparation for clerical careers (they both got modest annual allowances of 20s in their father's will). One of their sisters, Alice, went off to become a Cistercian nun at Stixwold in Lincolnshire; she was sacristan at Stixwold by 1525.[10] However, one should also consider the other clergy whom the Cranmer children would have known: Stixwold nunnery – at first sight a long way off, and a puzzling choice for Alice Cranmer – provides some of the clues. Three gentry families gave the Cranmer boys plenty of models for their eventual clerical vocations and the direction of their careers. First: the Cranmers' 'near kin' the Tamworths, a Lincolnshire family based both at Leake, near the old Cranmer home at Sutterton, and at Halstead Hall, a mile to the north of Stixwold Priory.[11] Energetic and talented, by the 1520s family members had become well entrenched in the Exchequer administration in London, but one of their most distinguished early members was the Cambridge don Dr Christopher Tamworth, Fellow of Godshouse probably from the 1490s, and a collector of ecclesiastical preferment, mostly in Lincolnshire, which culminated in the Precentorship of Lincoln Cathedral in 1538.[12]

More socially elevated were the Cliftons of Clifton near Nottingham. Here the crucial figure was Sir Gervase Clifton, who died in 1491 when Thomas Cranmer was two: one of many heads of the Clifton family called Gervase, he demonstrated his talents in successively convincing Edward IV, Richard III and Henry VII of his political indispensability in the Midlands. Sir Gervase turned his worldly success to an unmistakably fervent pious energy. Perhaps in the shadow of his relative Laurence Booth, Archbishop of York, for whom he acted as feoffee for chantry chapels in Southwell Minster, Clifton showed exuberant piety in naming some of his numerous children: he repeated the family name of Gervase, but was inspired to call a second son Protasius (Gervase's companion as proto-martyr of Milan), and his other offspring included Gamaliel, Silvanus, Elizeus and Adelina. Moreover, these children did not disappoint their father's devout expectations: four of his sons went to Cambridge, and his eldest boy, Robert, went so far as to renounce his

9 *Victoria County History: Nottinghamshire*, 2, pp. 129–38.

10 *Visitations in the Diocese of Lincoln 1517–1531* 37, p. 103. For Thomas senior's concern for the future archbishop's education, see *Narratives of the Reformation*, p. 239, and Parker, *De Antiquitate*, p. 386.

11 Cox 2, p. 368.

12 On Christopher, see Emden, *Cambridge to 1500*, pp. 575–6. Cf. P.C.C. 24 Thrower: will of Christopher's brother Thomas Tamworth of Leake, one of the royal auditors, made 26 July 1530. See also references in MacCulloch, 'Two Dons in Politics', p. 2, n. 5.

inheritance to his younger brother Gervase in order to pursue an academic career at Michaelhouse.[13]

The Cranmer connection with the prodigious Clifton dynasty is not immediately obvious, and needs to be reconstructed from fragments of evidence. Sir Gervase had been the royal receiver of the Lordships of Whatton and Aslockton since 1477, and so he would have had routine contacts with the chief gentry family of the parish, the Cranmers. The prioress of Stixwold in 1510 was Alice Clifton, although her relationship to Sir Gervase's family is not clear; however, Sir Gervase's son the Michaelhouse don Robert was also Rector of Bucknall, a church a couple of miles from Stixwold Priory and closely associated with it, and he left the fur of his gown to 'Sir Robert of Stixwold', evidently a priest attached either to the priory or the parish church there.[14] Robert's brother Gamaliel proved more of a high-flyer, pursuing his canon law studies at Turin as well as Cambridge; unfortunately we seem unable to identify the Cambridge college to which he belonged. Among Gamaliel's many east Midlands preferments was a selection of benefices around Aslockton, including from 1500 the Nottinghamshire rectory of Hawton by Newark, family home of Cranmer's cousins the Molyneux's. Archbishop Cranmer casually mentioned Dr Clifton in a letter of 1533, one of many replies to begging letters from Midlands friends and relatives which were the inevitable consequence of his sudden good fortune.[15]

The Molyneux's of Hawton were a third set of gentry relatives who might have provided a possible pattern of the future for an academically inclined boy. Dr Clifton's patron at Hawton, Sir Thomas Molyneux, was a younger son of the great family of Sefton in Lancashire; he had built himself a brilliant legal career, under Edward IV and Henry VII. One of his daughters married one of Cranmer's Hatfield relatives; of his sons (rough contemporaries of the Archbishop in age), two boys went to Oxford, one imitating Sir Thomas's legal success, the other turning an Oxford career to the church, with a fellowship of Magdalen and the rectory of the main family living at Sefton.[16] The Molyneux's were among the Cranmer relatives who approached the

13 *Nottingham Visitations 1569 and 1614*, pp. 17–18; Wood, 'Notes on the early history of the Clifton Family', pp. 32–4; and see Emden, *Cambridge to 1500* s.v. Clifton/Clyfton: Gamaliel, Robert, Silvanus, William, and MacCulloch, 'Two Dons in Politics', p. 2, n. 4.

14 Receivership: *C.P.R. 1476–85*, pp. 19, 39. Prioress Alice: *L.P.* 1 i, no. 438(4), p. 270. Will of Robert: C.U.L. UA Wills I, f. 24v. On Bucknall and Stixwold, see *Visitations in the Diocese of Lincoln 1517–1531* 37, pp. 102–3.

15 B.L. Harley MS 6148, f. 24v, pr. Cox 2, p. 248, although the name is there mistranscribed as 'Elyston'; there is no traceable Dr Elyston at the time, the original text seems to read 'Cliston', and the only Clifton with a doctorate was Gamaliel. Gamaliel's will, P.C.C. F.1 Spert, made on 19 April 1541 when he was Dean of Hereford, is a short document concerned entirely with his Hereford acquaintance; it has no mention of Cranmer.

16 Emden, *Oxford to 1540* 397–8: Anthony and Edmund Molyneux. See the pedigree in *Nottingham Visitations 1569 and 1614*, pp. 72–3.

Archbishop for help during the 1530s, when they were trying to speed up a Chancery lawsuit.[17]

Yet Cranmer's life and career pattern followed that of the Tamworths and the Cliftons rather than the Molyneux's: to Cambridge, rather than to Oxford University. Similarly, his early career suggests few links with the west and north, the alignment with Lancashire which was clearly still important to the Molyneux's of Hawton. It is noticeable that the focus of much of the clerical careers of Dr Christopher Tamworth and the clerical Cliftons was Lincoln Cathedral and Lincolnshire; it was in the Wolds east of Lincoln that Alice Cranmer chose to enter the monastic life at Stixwold. A good road runs due east from Nottingham via Whatton, across the higher country around Grantham to Boston and the fens of south Lincolnshire, from where the Cranmers had originally come. Cranmer's closest lifelong friends were both Lincolnshire men: Thomas Goodrich, from near Boston, the future Bishop of Ely and Lord Chancellor, and John Whitwell, Cranmer's personal chaplain throughout his years as Archbishop. Goodrich and Whitwell had been to school together from the age of seven, and all three boys ended up at Jesus College, Cambridge.[18] The world in which the young Thomas Cranmer grew up seems to have been structured on a triangle comprising the urban centres of Nottingham, Lincoln and Boston.

Cranmer's schooling remains a mystery. At first it was probably in the village; his early anonymous biographer talks of him learning his grammar 'of a rude parish clerk', and Archbishop Parker's biography talks of Cranmer's father encouraging him to hunt, hawk, shoot and enjoy the sports of a gentleman in order to preserve his enthusiasm for his studies; this may suggest an early education at home. Later he seems to have gone off to a grammar school, of which he had terrifying memories.[19] Perhaps it was at Southwell, or perhaps it was near his various relatives in Lincolnshire. However, at the age of fourteen, his torments at the hands of the 'marvellous severe and cruel schoolmaster' were at an end. The son of a pious family was sent off to a new college at Cambridge, to launch an academic career.

17 Cox 2, p. 295 (7 June 1534). The chancery suit is difficult to identify: it might be P.R.O., C. 1/852/58–60. The testamentary case over Henry Hatfield's will, P.R.O., C. 1/850/28, seems to be too late to be associated with this letter. The letter without address which mentions Dr Clifton, Cox 2, p. 248, may have been written to Robert Molyneux of Hawton about his son William; in it Cranmer refuses to take a son W. into his household.

18 On Goodrich and Whitwell's early career, see the testimony of Whitwell, Cranmer's Register, f. 86v. Whitwell was parson of the Jesus urban parish of All Saints during the 1520s (Venn 4, p. 397); Cranmer made him chaplain as soon as he became Archbishop (cf. Cox 2, p. 248), and parson of Lambeth when it became vacant in 1541 (Cranmer's Register, f. 379r; *Registra Gardiner et Poynet*, p. 116). For Whitwell's will and its many Lincolnshire references, see P.C.C. 18 Loftes, PROB. 11/44 f. 143v (16 March 1561, proved 10 May 1561). One of Alice Cranmer's colleagues at Stixwold in 1525 was Anne Goodrich: *Visitations in the Diocese of Lincoln 1517–1531* 37, p. 103.

19 *Narratives of the Reformation*, pp. 218, 239; Parker, *De Antiquitate*, p. 386 has a different emphasis from Morice about the gentlemanly pursuits.

CHAPTER 2

Cambridge years: 1503–29

JESUS COLLEGE, CAMBRIDGE, FOUNDED by John Alcock, Bishop of Ely, was only seven years old when Thomas Cranmer was sent there. Remotely situated by the standards of the University's other colleges, it lay east of the town centre, with spacious grounds around the convent buildings from which Bishop Alcock had evicted the last two nuns of St Radegund in 1496. From the nuns the Master and Fellows had also inherited parochial responsibilities, an unusual feature for a university college, and the conversion of the nuns' beautiful but overlarge church into the college chapel left part of the nave open for the parishioners' use, with a curate chosen from the Fellowship to look after them.[1]

The Cranmer family's choice of Jesus for their son's university studies remains to be explained: why not Christopher Tamworth's Godshouse or Robert Clifton's Michaelhouse? It might have been some personal connection with Thomas's school that led to the decision. However, it may be significant that Jesus was among that fortunate group of Cambridge colleges (also including Godshouse and Michaelhouse) which was directly benefiting from the patronage and interest of the university's greatest early Tudor benefactors: Lady Margaret Beaufort and John Fisher, the Master of Michaelhouse. Lady Margaret, the most formidably successful dynastic politician of fifteenth-century England, found the ideal partner in Fisher for an enterprise of educational funding which would give Cambridge a leading place in the northern European humanist movement during the early sixteenth century. Profiting from the University's gratitude for his spectacular success in fund-raising, not to mention his piety and scholarship, Fisher served first as Vice-Chancellor in 1501 and then from 1504 as Chancellor.[2]

Jesus's rather meagre initial endowment by Bishop Alcock was soon upstaged by the contributions of Lady Margaret, under Fisher's guidance. Fisher wrote the Jesus foundation charter of 1496, and much of the work of converting the former nunnery buildings was financed by Lady Margaret and

1 For the foundation of Jesus, and on its parish, see *Victoria County History: Cambridgeshire* 3, pp. 421–2 and Royal Commission on Historical Monuments, *City of Cambridge*, 1, p. 82.

2 For an outstanding treatment of Lady Margaret's career, see Jones and Underwood, *The King's Mother*.

5 Panoramic view of Jesus College, Cambridge in 1690, from David Loggan, *Cantabrigia Illustrata*. Note the monastic core of buildings around the cloister to the north of the cruciform chapel, all modified in sober Perpendicular style by Bishop Alcock.

her associates in the years when Cranmer was first a member of the College. Even the College's change of its name from the proposed continuation of the nunnery's dedication to St Radegund is likely to have been a compliment to, or an inspiration by, Lady Margaret; she was official patroness of the Holy Name of Jesus in England by papal grant, and she certainly influenced the later name-change of Godshouse to Christ's. Jesus's next great benefactor, and the writer of its first statutes, was Lady Margaret's stepson: James Stanley, Alcock's successor as Bishop of Ely.[3] Lady Margaret was a familiar figure at great university ceremonies in Cranmer's early Cambridge years, making frequent visits which became annual from 1505 to 1507; on this last occasion she badgered her son King Henry VII and his heir Prince Henry to attend the university Commencement with her.[4]

As a boy Cranmer made one friend who would have linked him to the Beaufort circle even before he went up to Cambridge: John Markham, who testified to this lifelong friendship in his will in 1559, when he took care to

3 Leader, *University of Cambridge to 1546*, pp. 271–3, and Jones and Underwood, *The King's Mother*, pp. 212–13. On the name of Jesus, ibid., pp. 176, 183; on Bishop Stanley, ibid., p. 235.

4 Jones and Underwood, *The King's Mother*, p. 229.

repay the late Archbishop's son an old debt owed to his father.[5] Markham was from one of Nottinghamshire's leading families, whose estates were scattered across the same belt of the Nottinghamshire–Lincolnshire landscape that Cranmer knew as a boy. He was about Cranmer's age, and they had known each other at least since they were teenagers, as the Archbishop later warmly testified to Thomas Cromwell when Markham was facing serious trouble in Nottinghamshire. Their friendship had remained strong, based on their common conversion to evangelical piety in the early 1530s, and a mark of its exceptional quality was the fact that Cranmer was prompted thus to intervene so earnestly with Cromwell in the politics of his childhood county, something which he did little during his years as Archbishop.[6] Markham was a relative of Lady Margaret's, and he entered her service before asserting his family's leading position in Midlands society by his devoted service in Henry VIII's wars.[7] Perhaps, therefore, it was the Markhams who suggested which college might be suitable for the bright young friend of their eldest boy.

One other important connection with Lady Margaret's circle persisted through Cranmer's life. It was probably during his early Cambridge years that he got to know James Morice, Lady Margaret's Clerk of the Kitchen and surveyor of her building works at Christ's and St John's – possibly at Jesus as well; James's son Ralph would later become Cranmer's trusted and long-term secretary and biographer. Once more the Lincolnshire connection is evident: James was controller of the customs at Boston, and he inevitably had much to do with the Fenland drainage schemes which so interested Lady Margaret. He also shared Lady Margaret's cultivated piety, and evidence remains of his significant devotional library.[8] Like Sir John Markham, he and his family would turn this 'high-temperature' religion to an early interest in evangelical views, but his children also sustained their prosperity on service to the great. After James's career with Lady Margaret, his son William served first Dean Pace of St Paul's and later Henry VIII; Ralph Morice was to enter Cranmer's service on the recommendation of George Lord Rochford, and in 1533 Ralph's and William's brother Philip made a spirited attempt through Cranmer to become secretary to the Duke of Richmond, before becoming Cromwell's servant.[9]

5 P.R.O., P.C.C. 50 Chayney. On Markham generally, see *History of Parliament 1509–58*, 2, pp. 568–70; their estimate of his year of birth does not quite correspond with the age of 60 years given in his deposition against Bishop Gardiner in January 1551 (Foxe 6, p. 191).

6 P.R.O., S.P. 1/98 f. 200, Cox 2, pp. 315–16 (*L.P.* 9 no. 751).

7 P.R.O., S.P. 1/127 ff. 18–19, Cox 2, p. 358 (*L.P.* 12 ii no. 1179).

8 On James and Boston, see Jones and Underwood, *The King's Mother*, p. 279, and for an indirect reference to his involvement in fen drainage at Deeping, H.M.C. *Hatfield* 1, p. 122. On his piety and books, cf. Jones and Underwood, *The King's Mother*, p. 201 and Keiser, 'Mystics and the early English printers', p. 23. For James's later Protestant convictions, cf. his will of 1555, P.C.C. 48 Wrastley.

9 Cf. *Narratives of the Reformation*, pp. 45, 235. On Ralph's entry into Cranmer's service on Rochford's recommendation, and on Philip, B.L. Harley 6148, f. 34r, pr. Cox 2, p. 259 (*LP* 6 no. 1229); for Philip's Cromwell service, Bodl. MS Jesus 74 f. 166r, and P.R.O., S.P. 1/132 f. 186.

From 1503 Cranmer entered the standard Arts course of the University. He took eight years, a surprisingly long time, to reach his BA: perhaps his admitted problems in absorbing information quickly, or even family financial worries, delayed his progress. There may be hints of trouble in two later negative comments on both the teaching and content of his early university years. In 1551 he spoke contemptuously of one of his lecturers from forty years before: 'an ignorant reader . . . who, when he came to any hard chapter which he well understood not, he would find some pretty toy to shift it off, and to skip over unto another chapter, which he could better skill of'. His anonymous biographer provided what has become a famous description of the first eight years of Cranmer's studies: 'he was nuzzled [i.e. trained] in the grossest kind of sophistry, logic, philosophy moral and natural (not in the text of the old philosophers, but chiefly in the dark riddles and quiddities of Duns and other subtle questionists)'.

However, one should remember that both these descriptions are polemical. The first was part of an attempted put-down of Cranmer's Cambridge junior, Stephen Gardiner, while the second is a perhaps conscious echo of an angry remark in William Tyndale's 1530 polemic, *The Practice of Prelates*.[10] I argue in Appendix I that Cranmer's anonymous biographer was Dr Stephen Nevinson; if so, his experience of Cambridge was forty years after Cranmer's, during which time a religious revolution had unfolded, and any perspective on older scholarship was distorted by partisanship. The biographer's description does not reveal that the BA curriculum which it so contemptuously describes was no piece of dusty medievalism, but the result of a revision only fifteen years before Cranmer embarked on his studies; older courses of lectures were abolished in 1488 and the initial Arts curriculum was shifted in emphasis away from a foundational study of logic. Thereafter the student started with study of works of classical literature (the choice initially left unspecified by the authorities), and he only went on to logic in his third year, followed by a fourth year on philosophy. The sequence was as the biographer describes – sophistry, logic, philosophy – but it was a conscious attempt by the university authorities to meet the new academic interest in direct study of the classics, an early symptom of the general English reception of humanist learning which Fisher would so encourage. Indeed, the emphasis on the classics was precisely what annoyed Tyndale in 1530, impatient as he was to turn education towards the text of the Bible.[11]

Nevertheless, the young Cranmer's embryonic library was founded on medieval scholastic textbooks which would have been familiar to generations of undergraduates, and which he often seems to have acquired second-hand in time-honoured student fashion; whatever Cranmer's later opinion of them, he

10 Cox 1, p. 305; *Narratives of the Reformation*, pp. 218–19. Tyndale: see Tyndale, *Expositions*, p. 291: 'in the universities they have ordained that no man shall look on the scripture, until he be nuzzled in heathen learning eight or nine years, and armed with false principles'.

11 Leader, *University of Cambridge to 1546*, pp. 247–50.

preserved them faithfully amid his magnificent later collections. Dr Selwyn has identified them: most prominently he points to Peter of Spain's *Summulae Logicales*, to start Cranmer off on logic, bound up with Peter Tartaret's commentary, to tackle Aristotle's logic and philosophy, both in editions of 1500. There is much else of Aristotle or commentaries on him in editions of the appropriate date, and Duns Scotus is indeed represented as the biographer suggested, with two copies of the 1497 Venice edition of his *Questiones subtilissime*.[12] Cranmer's Scotus is copiously annotated in what seems to be an early version of his hand; neatly and conscientiously he sets out responses and objections, makes notes summarizing themes and adds notes of other relevant authorities. Already he is using the Arabic numeration which he favoured throughout his later life.[13]

Cranmer's first degree was taken in the same year as several friends who became important to him in his years on the public stage. The listing of BAs in the Grace Books seems to have been done in groups of colleges: next to Cranmer in the listing of BAs was his friend at Jesus, Thomas Goodrich, and a few names below followed Richard Astall and Richard Hoore, both destined to be Cranmer's chaplains during the 1530s. Earlier in the list among the higher degrees is 'D. Boston': this is probably William Benson alias Boston, another Cranmer friend, a south Lincolnshire man like Goodrich, and the future Abbot and first Dean of Westminster. One also sees 'D. Latimer': Hugh Latimer, Cranmer's fellow-martyr. Another name in the same BA list, 'D. Nicholson', suggests a less happily-associated martyr than Latimer, for this can probably be identified with John Lambert alias Nicholson; Cranmer's association with the trial which led to Lambert's burning as a sacramentary in 1538 caused Cranmer and his later biographers much embarrassment and heart-searching.[14] A few months after the summer degree-day, another figure central to Cranmer's future entered the University for the first time: Stephen Gardiner, beginning his undergraduate career under the wing of an influential relative at Trinity Hall.[15]

Cranmer now embarked on a different course of study, for the MA. Again, the anonymous biographer put a polemical edge on his description, comparing Cranmer's work on his earlier course with a shift after 1511 to 'Faber, Erasmus, good Latin authors'. Again, we must beware any Reformation hindsight in interpreting this change in direction, and consider that it might have been as much thanks to the University curriculum as to any revulsion towards the schoolmen on Cranmer's part. It need not even be significant that Erasmus arrived for his first extended stay in Cambridge in August 1511,

12 Ayris and Selwyn (eds), *Cranmer*, pp. 63–4.

13 Cf. B.L. IB 20297.

14 *Grace Book B* 1, pp. 254–5; see below, Ch. 6.

15 On the evidence (dependent on the 1518 entries of *Grace Book A*, p. 159) for Gardiner arriving at Cambridge in 1511, see Muller, *Gardiner*, p. 340 n. 2. On the early careers of Gardiner and Cranmer compared, see MacCulloch, 'Two Dons in Politics', *passim*.

causing much excitement in the University. The Cambridge MA course which Cranmer experienced had been reformed about a decade after the BA; it had been widened to include arithmetic, music, geometry and perspective. One of the items relevant to this curriculum in Cranmer's library was a collection of mathematical treatises by the humanist polymath Jacques Lefèvre d'Etaples ('Faber'), published in 1507.[16] Besides the official subjects which Cranmer had to master, his natural progression in study may have gradually led him on to more adventurous reading. We have, after all, the testimony of those close to him that he was a methodical, even plodding scholar.[17] This time his course to his next degree showed no especial delay: he gained his MA in 1515 after twelve terms, and at some date which is still uncertain, he was elected to a Fellowship of his college. He was still a layman, but this was not uncommon among the Fellows of Jesus in its early years.[18]

One event occurred after Cranmer took his MA which nearly changed the direction of his life, and whose tragic outcome must permanently have scarred him. Cranmer married a girl named Joan. It was a decision in striking contrast to the caution normally characteristic of him in his later life, and it is only paralleled in its abrupt trespass on a conventional career pattern by his even more rash second marriage in 1532. Cranmer was clearly the marrying kind. Although he was not yet deacon or priest, he still had to forfeit his fellowship of Jesus for marriage; in its place, he eked out a living with a job which was a distinct step down in the status-conscious world of the University, and he became 'the common reader at Buckingham College' (then a Benedictine college of the university, refounded in 1542 as Magdalene).[19] Now bereft of his home in Jesus, he turned to one of his relatives in Cambridge, the landlady of one or other of two Cambridge inns called the Dolphin, to provide a lodging for his wife, while he apparently lodged elsewhere, perhaps in Buckingham College.[20] Yet alas for this apparent love-match amid heroic poverty, Joan died in her first childbirth,

16 This book was long ago disposed of by the British Museum, but is listed in MS Catalogue of Printed Books in the Old Royal Library, B.L. Department of Printed Books, p. 50. For a note on identifying the 'Faber' reference in *Narratives of the Reformation*, pp. 218–19, see MacCulloch, 'Two Dons in Politics', p. 6, n. 20. On curriculum changes, Leader, *University of Cambridge to 1546*, pp. 253–4.

17 Cf. the comments of Ridley on Cranmer's progress through scholarship: Ridley, *Cranmer*, pp. 15–16. On Erasmus in Cambridge, cf. e.g. Porter, *Reformation and Reaction in Tudor Cambridge*, pp. 21–40.

18 *Grace Book B*. ii, pp. 35–6; on Jesus fellows, *Victoria County History: Cambridgeshire 3*, p. 423.

19 *Narratives of the Reformation*, p. 240.

20 Parker, *De Antiquitate*, p. 387: '*Eius enim domus materfamilias affinis illi fuit*'. Parker the Cambridge man is more likely to have got the relationship right than John Foxe, who made the landlady a relative of Cranmer's wife: Foxe, 8, p. 4. Cobban, *King's Hall*, p. 242 n. 6 suggests that of the two Cambridge Dolphin inns, this was the one at the Bridge Street end of All Saints Passage, rather than the other situated in what is now part of Corpus Christi College.

and the child was also lost. If they had lived, Cranmer would not have been ordained, and the course of the English Reformation would have been very different.

We know little about the marriage, not even its precise date between 1515 and 1519, although it is likely to be earlier rather than later during that period. Cranmer was so reticent about it later, no doubt feeling the pain of his double loss, that we cannot even be sure of Joan's surname, although the interrogatories at his trial in 1555 seem to say that it was Black or Brown. The length of the marriage is also uncertain: Joan's death came 'within one year', according to Ralph Morice, but Archbishop Parker gave it longer than a year, perhaps with an eye to the innuendo that a hasty marriage had followed an unwise pregnancy.[21] Besides that alarming possibility, the association with the Dolphin inn would cause Cranmer's Catholic enemies a good deal of snobbishly malicious glee in later years: starting within a few months of his becoming Archbishop, the simple esquire's son was repeatedly dismissed in popular abuse as 'an ostler'.[22] At Cranmer's trial in 1555, his first wife was scornfully referred to as 'black Joan of the Dolphin'. His later admirers, John Foxe and John Strype, tried to improve her image by calling her the daughter of a gentleman, but her pedigree has not emerged from the general obscurity of the marriage.[23]

Jesus College showed its esteem for Cranmer by readmitting him to a fellowship after Joan's death; and indeed, if we follow the anonymous biographer's description without adopting his bias, it was at this time that Cranmer's studies took their decisive turn for the future. About 'the time that Luther began to write' (presumably about 1518 when the consequences of Luther's initial protest against indulgences were beginning to work themselves out on an international scale), Cranmer considered 'what great controversy was in matters of religion' and 'applied his whole study three years unto the . . . scriptures. After this he gave his mind to good writers both new and old . . . This kind of study he used till he were made Doctor of Divinity', in other words, 1526.

This is a fair description of what was entailed in Cambridge's ultimate post-graduate study, theology. If Cranmer was going to keep his hard-won Jesus fellowship, he would have little choice but to pursue this discipline, for Jesus from its foundation had discouraged its Fellows from the other major field of higher study, canon law, and encouraged them to concentrate on theology; the College was in fact standing out against the loss of theology's predominant place in the University during the 15th century.[24] The biblical

21 Parker, *De Antiquitate* p. 387: *'verum altero a nuptiis anno uxor . . . decessit'*. Foxe 8, p. 58.

22 On this abuse, see below, Ch. 5, pp. 169–70.

23 Trial: Cox 2, p. 557; cf. ibid., p. 219. Cf. Strype, *Cranmer* 1, p. 3, drawing on Foxe 8, p. 4; contrast Harpsfield's abuse of Joan in *Pretended Divorce*, p. 289.

24 Cf. e.g. Cobban, *Universities*, p. 226, for figures for the first members of the college; *Victoria County History: Cambridgeshire* 3, p. 422. On the changing status of theology, see Cobban, *Universities*, pp. 224–5, and Aston, Duncan and Evans, 'Medieval Alumni of Cambridge', p. 58 and n. 135, and pp. 61–3.

character of theological study in Jesus was underlined by the provisions of the college theology lectureship endowed for a Fellow of the College in 1512 by the civil servant Sir John Rysley: the subject matter of the lectures was restricted to the Old and New Testaments. At some stage, after his grant of his doctorate of divinity in 1526, according to Morice, Thomas Cranmer held this lectureship.[25] By 1520, he had also proceeded to holy orders, for in that year the University named him as one of the preachers whom they were entitled by papal grant to license for preaching throughout the British Isles.[26]

There is so much that is not known about Cranmer's nigh-on three decades at Cambridge that it is not surprising that his biographers have done their best to fill the gap, particularly with an eye to building up the future evangelical reformer in good time for his elevation to Canterbury. Cranmer has been portrayed as a humanist whose enthusiasm for biblical scholarship drew him naturally into the circle of those scholars fired to embrace reformism by the first years of Luther's fame in the 1520s. How much truth is there in this picture?

First, one should be wary of drawing a picture of humanist learning driving out obscurantist scholasticism in early Tudor Cambridge: events were much more ambiguous and complex than that. Notoriously, late fifteenth-century Cambridge was slower than Oxford to show interest in humanism.[27] When it did begin to make an impact on Cambridge, its effect was slow and patchy: for instance, the first endowed Cambridge lectureships in classical literature and Greek came at the very end of the 1510s.[28] Moreover, humanism was not necessarily seen as a replacement for or direct threat to the older scholastic method. After the 1530s, it was fashionable to see the relationship in terms of antagonism, particularly since government reform included the abolition of a whole section of the traditional curriculum, canon law studies, in favour of humanist learning. By then, reformers were quick to express their contempt for Scotist sophistry, while conservatives like Stephen Gardiner were equally ready to express their disillusionment with the pernicious long-term effects of Erasmus's teaching.[29] Earlier, in less confrontational days, the two approaches to learning might have seemed complementary: for instance, John Fisher's mentor and predecessor as Master of Michaelhouse, William Melton, clearly valued the volumes of Aquinas and Scotus in his library alongside those of modern humanist giants like Lorenzo Valla,

25 Leader, *University of Cambridge to 1546*, p. 273, and cf. *Narratives of the Reformation*, p. 240. Rysley's will is P.C.C. 8 Fetiplace, PROB. 11/17 ff. 60v–61. The late 1520s date for Cranmer's tenure of the lecture is reinforced by William Longforth's apparent reference to it: see below, n. 56.

26 *Grace Book B* 2, p. 77; on the licences, see Leader, *University of Cambridge to 1546*, pp. 278–80.

27 Cobban, *Universities*, pp. 243–56.

28 Ibid., pp. 250–51.

29 For Gardiner's famous remark about the relationship between Luther and Erasmus, see *Gardiner's Letters*, p. 403.

Erasmus and Pico della Mirandola, and he mentioned them equally in his will.[30]

When Cranmer was starting upon his studies at the turn of the century, what may have interested Cambridge dons as much as humanism itself was the link with the political world which had been created by the influence of John Fisher on Lady Margaret and other figures in government. Humanist learning and renaissance artistic style were part of the trappings of the world of power; were they much more than trappings at first? The University, which Fisher bestrode like a colossus, resounded to the noise of building works under the watchful eye of such worthies as James Morice: works paid for by the most powerful people in England. The happy prospect that these links between the good and the great would produce rich dividends did not end with Lady Margaret's death in 1509; within a few years Thomas Wolsey was supreme in Church and State, and he was poised to provide the same benefits. Many Cambridge dons hastened to join Wolsey's administrative machine, among them one Dr William Capon, who became Wolsey's almoner; in 1516 Capon transferred from St Catharine's to become Master of Cranmer's own college, and in 1528 he was chosen by Wolsey to be the first Dean of his grandiose Eton-style foundation in Ipswich, Cardinal College.[31]

However, Wolsey's built-in disadvantage for Cambridge men was that he had spent his academic career in Oxford. Most of his largesse would be distributed in the other place; hence the migration of some of the brightest young scholars in Cambridge to populate the staggeringly lavish new foundation of Cardinal College, Oxford during the 1520s. Cranmer, after some initial hesitation, held back from this rush to the Oxford gravy train, and his refusal was later represented by John Foxe as a principled stand which brought him danger: a strange point of view, since so many of those who went turned out to be among the earliest enthusiasts for Lutheran ideas, and they suffered severely as a result.[32] Given the sort of people who left for Oxford, one could more convincingly argue that Cranmer's change of heart showed his conservative sympathies; perhaps he was content where he was. Archbishop Parker's biography says that Cranmer was persuaded that Jesus would be a more suitable setting for a student of theology than the flashy humanist academy taking shape at Cardinal; so this was a decision about the direction of his academic career rather than anything more demonstrative.[33]

Indeed, the more one pieces together the scraps of evidence concerning Cranmer's religious outlook in his Cambridge years, the less these seem to

30 Bradshaw and Duffy (eds), *Humanism, Reform and the Reformation*, pp. 25–6; and cf. ibid., p. 30.

31 For other examples, see MacCulloch, 'Two Dons in Politics', pp. 3, 6.

32 Foxe 8, p. 5, which is clearly an attempt to improve on *Narratives of the Reformation*, p. 240.

33 Parker, *De Antiquitate*, p. 387.

point to the later reformer: they resemble more the views of his lifelong conservative rival Stephen Gardiner at the same period. One could indeed argue that Gardiner showed more signs of reformist sympathies than Cranmer. In later years, evangelicals delighted in trying to embarrass Gardiner by his early associations: in the 1520s, he had been a cautious humanist, who kept reformist friends and did them favours on occasion. For instance, in the disciplinary campaign against Lutheran sympathizers in February 1526, he did his best to help Robert Barnes to find an intellectually respectable justification for abjuring his outspoken ideas; he spoke up for George Joye when Joye was brought before Wolsey's officers in the Hall of Peterhouse, and he also warned George Stafford of impending prosecution.[34]

By contrast, there is a distinct silence about Cranmer's reforming sympathies. It was natural that his Protestant admirers should later give him respectable evangelical credentials for the 1520s, and that they should provide him with retrospective honorary membership of the famous White Horse Tavern group of Cambridge reformists; this was so Lutheran in outlook that the pub was nicknamed Little Germany. However we need to treat such well-meaning efforts with scepticism.[35] Thirty years ago Professor C.C. Butterworth pointed out that all subsequent talk of the White Horse circle has been built up from a single reference in Foxe's *Book of Martyrs*; moreover, Foxe is quite specific about which colleges provided regulars for the group, and Jesus is not among them (neither, for that matter, is Gardiner's Trinity Hall).[36]

The evidence for Cranmer's anti-papal zeal in the 1520s could hardly be less convincing. It consists, first, of a vague statement made by him when writing to Henry VIII in 1536; in this he referred to preaching a sermon the previous year, when he claimed he had prayed that he might see the power of Rome destroyed 'these many years'. He was not specific as to how many years that might have been, and he had every reason for multiplying the number to a royal correspondent who at the time was in a dangerous mood. The second supposed piece of evidence relies on a subsequent misunderstanding of a source which in any case does not inspire confidence: the bitter words of a conservative Canterbury bricklayer in 1543. His opinion was that Cranmer was then preaching in the manner of an unnamed 'worshipful prelate', who

34 Butterworth and Chester, *Joye*, pp. 30–31, 45. Cf. Gardiner's own retrospective account of his dealings with Barnes at this time: *Gardiner's Letters*, p. 166, and for another account, Foxe 5, p. 416.

35 For instance, Pollard, *Cranmer*, p. 21; Clebsch, *England's Earliest Protestants*, p. 274. For a Roman Catholic adoption of the same idea, see Hughes, *Reformation in England*, 1, p. 343. Rupp, *Protestant Tradition*, pp. 18–19, was more cautious in his phrasing, but still expansionist in his view of White Horse Tavern group membership.

36 Butterworth and Chester, *Joye*, p. 26, which provides variant readings of Foxe's text: cf Foxe 5, pp. 415–16.

'prayed seven years before the Bishop of Rome fell that the said Bishop might be expelled this realm'.[37] And that is all.

To gauge the opinions of Dr Cranmer on religious matters during the academic upheavals of the 1520s, one can find scrappy but decisive evidence in the marginal annotations that he habitually made on his books throughout his adult life: as the anonymous biographer noted, 'he was . . . a diligent marker of whatsoever he read, for he seldom read without pen in hand'.[38] In particular, there is the evidence in his copy of John Fisher's *Assertionis Lutheranae Confutatio*, published in Antwerp in 1523, Fisher's first major attack on Martin Luther: the form of the work is a refutation of Luther's major statement of his case published in 1520, *Assertio Omnium Articulorum*.[39] Cranmer, the supposed White Horse Tavern regular, might be expected to produce critical marginalia about the ultra-orthodox Fisher; and there, indeed, they are. For instance, against a quotation from John Chrysostom by Fisher suggesting that St James the Great had received his bishopric of Jerusalem from St Peter, Cranmer notes that Fisher himself has interpolated the reference to Peter into Chrysostom's text.[40] However, there are two sets of marginalia by Cranmer in this book, one in red ink and one in black, and it is the red annotations which contain these consistent criticisms of Fisher. To make interpretation even more convenient, at one point Cranmer has erased his black annotations with his red ink; thus the two sets are of different dates, and indeed they reflect a changed outlook between the earlier black set and the later red.[41]

Let us turn to the black annotations in the *Confutatio*. Here there are, to be sure, some mild criticisms of Fisher's argument,[42] but what is far more

37 Cranmer to Henry VIII, 26 Aug. 1536, B.L. Cotton MS Cleopatra E VI f. 234–5, pr. Cox 2, p. 327 (*L.P.* 11, no. 361). On Burgrave, a bricklayer, C.C.C.C. 128, p. 38 (*L.P.* 18 pt. ii no. 546, p. 303). Cf. Ridley, *Cranmer*, pp. 21–2 on these texts; he is rightly sceptical about the second text, but has not quite grasped the sense of the quotation.

38 *Narratives of the Reformation*, p. 219. In the 1980s Dr Peter Newman Brooks noted a stray from Cranmer's library, Merlin's *Quattuor Conciliorum Generalium* . . . (Paris, 1524): see below, bibliography of primary sources. For arguments that this find is not in fact relevant to Cranmer's outlook at this period, see MacCulloch, 'Two Dons in Politics', pp. 8–9 (cf. Brooks, *Cranmer in Context*, pp. 20–21).

39 Cranmer's copy is B.L. C.81.f.2. For an excellent discussion of this work of Fisher's see Rex, *Theology of Fisher*, Ch. 5.

40 B.L. C.81.f.2, f. 130v; and cf. ibid., same folio and ff. 131rv, 132rv. Cf. Rex, *Theology of Fisher*, pp. 104–5.

41 Cf. B.L. C.81.f.2, f. 132v.

42 Ibid., f. 150r, noting Erasmus's differing opinion from Fisher on the authenticity of a text of Jerome: '*Multo aliter sentit Erasm{us} super 2° tomo hieronymi f. 49*'. This refers to Erasmus's dismissal of the epistle '*Virginatis Laus*', to be found at f. 49v of Vol. 2 in the 1516 Basle edition of Erasmus's Jerome (4 vols). Cranmer's copy of this edition is Lambeth Palace *D65, although there are no relevant marginalia at that point in the text. He later possessed the 1533/4 Paris edition of Erasmus's Jerome (4 vols: B.L. 476.g. 10–13). The 1533/4 edition has an entirely different foliation, with Erasmus's remarks about '*Virginitatis Laus*' at vol. 4, f. 39rv. Cf. also a criticism of Fisher at B.L. C.81.f.2, f. 159r.

striking is Cranmer's furious and horrified condemnation of Luther's arguments, as liberally quoted in Fisher's text. Throughout the range of the black annotations, it is these quotations from Luther rather than Fisher's text itself which provoke Cranmer's greatest emotion. '*Petulanter incessit pontificem . . . Debacchatur in pontificem*', he groans: Luther wantonly attacks, and raves against, the Pontiff.[43] '*Sic crescit in malicia*' – thus his malice grows worse; '*totum concilium appellat insanum; ipse insanissimus*' – he accuses a whole council of madness; it is he who is insane! '*Sanctissimum concilium vocat impiissimum. O arrogantia hominis sceleratissimi*' – he calls a most holy council impious; oh, the arrogance of a most wicked man! When Luther concedes for a moment that he would submit to papal authority if the Pope could prove the basis for his power, Cranmer retorts sarcastically from his margin '*Sententia Christiano dignum, si hoc ex animo dicat*' – a statement worthy of a Christian, if he says this willingly. And there are a clutch of Cranmerian cheers from the sidelines as Fisher scores points against his hapless German opponent.[44]

So here is Cranmer, the papalist. These are actually some of the most candid marginalia of his career; usually his annotations in books are aide-memoires, rather than expressions of feeling. Clearly, unless we attribute a degree of baseness to him which seems implausible, these marginalia could not have been produced any later than 1532; happily, this is also suggested by Cranmer's citation of the 1516 rather than the 1533 edition of Erasmus's Jerome (see above, n. 42). By definition, the annotations are no earlier than 1523. This is the Jesus don of the mid-1520s, maybe even the late 1520s: these are no emotional jottings of a youth, but the thoughts of a man who is at least thirty-four and more probably in his late thirties. Now we see why he is absent from the attendance register at the White Horse, and why he should be struck from the list of possible early evangelical adherents produced by such commentators as A.F. Pollard, Philip Hughes or W.A. Clebsch. One might note that the same is true of another of Cranmer's contemporaries at Jesus, the Carmelite friar John Bale: Bale was a fierce champion of orthodoxy and a despiser of Lutheranism until the early 1530s.[45]

However, there is more important insight on Cranmer's views in the 1520s to be gained from his marginalia in Fisher's *Confutatio*. Shocked Cranmer may have been at Luther's insolence to the Pope, but what aroused him to the greatest bitter eloquence, as we have heard already, was his perception that Luther despised the Councils of the Church. His sharpest condemnations of Luther, already quoted, are to be found in Article 28 of Fisher's work, against the Lutheran proposition that 'It is not heretical to disagree with the Pope and a great part of the Church'. It is in fact this section on the nature of authority in the Church which earns the greatest attention from Cranmer's black-ink annotations. Fisher starts by quoting a passage in which Luther asserts that

43 Ibid., ff. 156v, 157r.

44 Ibid., ff. 158r, 158v (two marginalia applauding Fisher), 160r.

45 Fairfield, 'John Bale and Protestant Hagiography', p. 146.

ARTICVLVS VIGESIMVS OCTAVVS

neglectis interim fidei documentis pro articulis, obtrudant populo dei, non intelligimus adhuc eos, operante Satana, operationibus erroris Ecclesiam vastare? Quid enim potest esse nisi error, quod cũ necessariũ nõ sit, necessariũ arbitrio hoĩm efficitur? vt hoĩm spem ædificent sup arenã, vt credant necessariũ, quod necessariũ non est. O vos impijssimi aĩarum seductores, q̃ scelerate illuditis populo dei.

Recipit se in sua castra lutherus.

Iam id (quod & lectorem sæpius admonui) quis non aduertit. Ecce Lutherus ad conuitia se vertit, quoties efficacia defuerũt argumenta. Nihil hactenus attulit pro huius articuli roboratione. Nusq̃ enĩ probat q̃ liceat a Pontifice & a bona parte Ecclesiæ dissentire, aut q̃ non sit Pontifici cum Concilio sentienti credendum penitus. Nos vero docuimus id necessarium esse creditu, quod Pontifex cum Ecclesia decreuerit esse credẽdum, non q̃ Ecclesia quicq̃ verum, aut non verum faciat: sed q̃ id, quod ante verum fuerat, q̃q̃ a plærisq̃ dubitatum, iam explicatius & apertius verum esse diffinierit.

Igitur siue papa, siue pars, siue Concilium sic aut sic sentiat, nemini debet esse præiudicium, sed abundet quisq̃ in sensu suo, in eis rebus, quę necessariæ non sunt ad salutem.

Non possunt non esse necessariæ res ad salutem ipsę, quas Põtifex cum Concilio tales esse declarauit: non q̃ illas Pontifex efficiat salutares, sed quia pridem tales fuerant, iccirco Põtifex spiritu instructus, iam eas esse salutares diffiniuit. Præiudicatũ igitur est cuiq̃ christiano, ne diuersum sequatur sensum, hoc est, ne dissentiat ab ijs, quæ summus Pontifex vna cum concilio credenda decreuit, sed ijs oportet, & fidem, & consensum pariter adhibere. Quis enim alio pacto scire potest, quæ pro veris Euãgelijs Christi tenẽda fuerint, & quæ respuenda, nisi per Ecclesiæ decretum? Sed non ita, q̃ Ecclesia potest quicq̃ Euangelium efficere, quod non ante fuerat Euangeliũ, aut id repudiare, quod verum sit Euangeliũ: sed spiritu veritatis infallibiter edocta, quatuor nobis Euangelia tradidit, quibus nos firmã adhibere fidem oportet, atq̃ ad hunc modum de cæteris, quæ pontifex cum Ecclesia decernit, credendum est.

In libertatẽ enĩ vocati sumus, vt non sit necesse credere verũ, q͛d alius homo sentit vel dicit, contenti eis credere, quę in scripturis docti sumus.

In libertatem sane vocati sumus, sed hac abutimur libertate, quãdo licentius, aut sentimus, aut loquimur, q̃ Ecclesiæ decreta permittunt. Tũc enĩ libertas nostra, maliciæ velamen est potius q̃ libertas. Nec verũ est (quẽadmodum tu prætexis) q̃ vrgetur quiuis credere, quicquid alius quilibet credit: sed quicquicd Pontifex cum Concilio credendum decernit, id omnino credere tenetur quiuis, q̃q̃ in scripturis idipsum nõ habeatur. Nam plurima sunt (vti supra diximus) quæ tenemur credere, simul & facere

6 Folio 159v from Cranmer's copy of John Fisher, *Assertionis Lutheranae Confutatio*, Antwerp, 1523, with Cranmer's marginalia bitterly attacking the quotations from Martin Luther in the text.

even if the Pope and a great part of the Church hold one opinion and do not err in it, it is still not a sin or heresy to believe the contrary until a general Council has declared otherwise. Cranmer cautiously thinks that on this matter, Luther may have a point; in his margin he writes 'Here [Luther] seems not completely in the wrong', and he goes on to criticize Fisher for covering up a weak riposte with overblown rhetoric.[46] However, as the argument proceeds, Fisher quotes Luther again. This time Luther asserts that 'if the Pope and a Council are so foolish as to determine matters not necessary to salvation, they will waste their time and energy, and should be held and condemned as idiotic and mad, and all their conclusions as phantomlike . . .'. It is this characteristic Lutheran trenchancy which now provokes Cranmer to say that 'he grows in malice' and to accuse Luther himself of insanity for talking of madness in a Council.[47] From then on, Cranmer's sympathy for Luther is entirely gone. After two more pages, Fisher's quotations carry Luther to his climax, hurling abuse at Council and Pope for making peripheral matters into essentials: 'O impious misleaders of souls, so wickedly to mock the people of God!' It is this cry of Luther's which provokes Cranmer to fever pitch against the wicked man whose arrogance denounces a most holy Council.[48]

So the balance of emotions in these marginalia reveals Cranmer certainly as a papalist, but even more a conciliarist. One can see him already divergent from and mildly critical of Fisher's more full-blooded papalism. Fisher's discussion of such questions fairly deliberately sidestepped any discussion of the possibility of a clash between Pope and Council, both in the *Confutatio* and elsewhere.[49] Cranmer came to see the possibility of such a clash as only too real: indeed, his acceptance of such a possibility may have given him the courage to jettison his papalist belief when the times finally demanded it in 1531–33. Perhaps one might see this reverence for the authority of the General Council as the golden thread which runs through Cranmer's theological progress: the one constant to which he always returned, even when in later years his appeal for a General Council was addressed to Wittenberg, Zürich and Geneva rather than to Rome, and was conceived as a defence against the Council of Trent.[50] As Cranmer's papal loyalty fell away, this deep emotional attachment to the idea of the General Council remained

46 B.L. C.81.f.2, f. 157v: '*Videtur hic non admodum errare . . . Studet hic Roffensis argumentum pro se infirmum schematis rhetoricis obfirmare*'.

47 Ibid. f. 158v: Luther: '*Si Papa et concilium sic desiperent, ut in rebus non necessariis ad salutem determinandis, tempus et studia perderent, habendi et contemnendi essent pro fatuis et insanis, cum omnibus suis determinationibus larvalibus . . .*'. Cranmer: '*Sic crescit in malicia*'; '*totum concilium appellat insanum; ipse insanissimus*'.

48 Ibid. f. 159v: Luther: '*O vos impiissimi animarum seductores, quam scelerate illuditis populo dei*'. Cranmer: '*Sanctissimum concilium vocat impiissimum. O arrogantia hominis sceleratissimi.*'

49 Bradshaw and Duffy (eds), *Humanism, Reform and the Reformation*, pp. 119, 139; and cf. in general Dr Gogan's discussion of Fisher's ecclesiology, ibid., pp. 131–54.

50 For his letters of 1552 to Bullinger, Calvin and Melanchthon appealing for the convening of a General Council, see Cox 2, pp. 431–2, and below, Chs 11, 12.

with him all through the uncertain ecclesiological waters of the years after 1533.

Another set of marginalia also reveals Cranmer's early antipathy to Luther's ideas. These annotations are in his copy of another landmark work in the early controversy surrounding Luther, Erasmus's *De Libero Arbitrio*, in which the great humanist finally found an issue on which he felt ready to attack the reformer: the freedom of the human will. Cranmer's copy was published in Antwerp after October 1524.[51] His annotations are concentrated in the introduction, mostly mere summary notes of points which interested him (his habitual practice). However, he once ventures to express an opinion, an approving comment on a crucial aspect of Erasmus's argument. Erasmus says that Luther's arguments about the will are dangerous because they touch on the secret mysteries of God which are deliberately presented in Scripture in obscure fashion. He recommends that instead of speculating about predestination,

> we go on swiftly to better things, . . . or if we are entangled in sins, let us strive with all our might and have recourse to the remedy of penance ('*adeamus remedium poenitentiae*') . . . and what is evil in us, let us impute to ourselves, and what is good, let us ascribe wholly to divine benevolence, to which we owe our very being, and for the rest, whatever befalls us in this life, whether joyful or sad, let us believe it to be sent by him for our salvation.[52]

Against this, Cranmer has made the note '*Formula {Chri}stiane ment{is} de libero arbitrio*' – a pattern for a Christian judgement on freedom of the will. Cranmer's reverent agnosticism on the deepest meaning of scripture (echoed in his other marginalia on the book), his relaxed attitude to the question of justification, and his approval of Erasmus's commendation of sacramental penitential discipline, are all far from his later thought. In one respect, however, as in his angry comments on Luther and general councils of the Church, there is an interesting continuity with this passage in a Cranmerian pronouncement of many years later: the text of the Church of England's doctrinal article on Predestination as formulated in 1552 and preserved after Cranmer's death in 1563 in the Thirty-Nine Articles. This too discourages speculation on the subject, despite Cranmer's by then strong convictions on the truth of predestination:

> for curious and carnal persons, lacking the Spirit of Christ, to have continually before their eyes the sentence of God's Predestination, is a most dangerous downfall . . . Further, [though the Decrees of Predestination be unknown to

51 B.L. 697.b.3, bound up with another work by Erasmus and one by Cochlaeus. I am grateful to Ashley Null for drawing my attention to this volume: cf. Null Ph.D., 'Cranmer's Doctrine of Repentance', Ch. 2.

52 *De Libero Arbitrio*, sig. Aivr; Cranmer's annotation has suffered from trimming. Translation from *Luther and Erasmus*, ed. Rupp *et al.*, p. 37.

us, yet] we must receive God's Promises in such wise as they be generally set forth to us in Holy Scripture; and in our doings, that will of God is to be followed, which we have expressly declared unto us in the Word of God.[53]

In the light of the reality of Cranmer's views, even in such fleeting glimpses, what little other positive evidence we have of his ideas and acquaintance in the 1520s fits in perfectly well. While he was at Regensburg in 1532, Cranmer told the conservative humanist Johannes Cochlaeus that his chief inspiration in philosophical studies had been Dr Robert Ridley: uncle indeed of the future Bishop Nicholas Ridley, but a Cambridge don of very different outlook.[54] Robert was secretary to Bishop Cuthbert Tunstall; he was certainly a humanist, but of a very conservative and eclectic sort, exhibiting precisely the mixture of scholasticism and humanism which we have already noted as being so characteristic of early sixteenth-century Cambridge. One of the early Terence lecturers, he was a noted preacher who in 1513–14 held one of the University's general preaching licences; in one of Ridley's surviving source-books for his preaching, sermons from an eleventh-century Benedictine are followed by a piece from Lorenzo Valla. Yet on one occasion when writing to the equally reactionary Henry Gold (later to be a promoter of Elizabeth Barton, the Maid of Kent), Ridley approvingly cited Erasmus's inept French opponent Peter Sutor, an opponent of any vernacular biblical translation, in the course of condemning William Tyndale's work. He was, of course, an enthusiastic enemy of Luther.[55]

Robert Ridley's brand of humanism was eclectic indeed; so may have been that of Dr Cranmer of Jesus. One should also note that Ridley's correspondent Henry Gold was happy for Cranmer to act as his formal disputant when taking his Cambridge B.Th. degree in 1527 or 1528.[56] Another chance reference in a later letter also provides another name in Ridley's generation of senior scholars who seems to have been, at the very least, on polite visiting terms with Cranmer: William Gonell. The source is

53 Text as in Burnet 2 ii, p. 294 (Bk. 1 no. 55). The bracketed phrase of the Forty-Two Articles was omitted in the Thirty-nine Articles.

54 Cochlaeus, *Beati Isidori . . . de Officiis* (1534 edn, preface); cf. Cranmer's comments on his meeting with Cochlaeus at Regensburg, B.L. MS Cotton Vitellius B XIV f. 41, pr. *Records of the Reformation*, 2, pp. 506–7.

55 On Ridley, preaching and his notebook (C.U.L. MS Dd.5.27), see Leader, *University of Cambridge to 1546*, pp. 189–90, 251–2, 278–81. Letter to Gold, 24 Feb. 1528, B.L. MS Cotton Cleopatra E V, f. 362v (*L.P.* 4, no. 3960). For Ridley's career, see Venn 3, p. 458, and note especially the preferment in London which came to him during Tunstall's years as Bishop of London. Ridley was one of Wolsey's 1521 theological commission against Luther, and also owned a copy of Fisher's *Confutatio*: Rex, 'English Campaign against Luther', pp. 87–8.

56 P.R.O., S.P. 1/73 f. 30 (*L.P.* 5 no. 1700). The most likely academic year is 1526–7, when the list of Graces for the B.Th. is evidently incomplete: *Grace Book A*, pp. 229–30. For another, unfortunately cryptic, reference by Gold to Cranmer, see S.P. 1/73 ff. 27–8 (*L.P.* 5 no. 1698.2).

perhaps surprising: the budding evangelical humanist Richard Morison. Morison wrote from Venice in December 1533 to Cranmer, now Archbishop, trying the standard humanist ploy of turning a casual scholarly acquaintance into a potential source of patronage. He ended his letter with various attempts to jog Cranmer's memory about who he was; if the penny had not already dropped, he mentioned that Gonell had inspired him with admiration for the Jesus don, and that on Morison's visits to Cambridge in 1528, he and Gonell had twice or thrice called together on Cranmer. Gonell, a veteran Cambridge humanist who had taken his MA the year before Cranmer was born, was a friend of Erasmus and of Henry Gold, and tutor to Sir Thomas More's children; once more he was unlikely to have figured in the meetings at the White Horse Tavern.[57]

It is true that even if Cranmer was still firmly in the conformist Catholic camp, he was already a biblical humanist. John Foxe tells us that as biblical examiner in the Divinity School, he 'would never admit any to proceed in divinity, unless they were substantially seen in the story of the Bible: by means whereof certain friars, and other religious persons, who were principally brought up in the study of school authors without regard had to the authority of Scriptures, were commonly rejected by him; so that he was greatly, for that his severe examination, of the religious sort much hated, and had in great indignation'.[58] All grist to the mill for Foxe's evangelical hero; yet what seemed an obvious interpretation of Cranmer's outlook in the 1560s may not be a very good reflection of the reality of the 1520s. There was then nothing incompatible between orthodoxy and taking the Bible seriously. Ashley Null's investigations of Cranmer's intellectual background are revealing how strongly the founder of Jesus College, Bishop John Alcock, stressed the central importance of biblical authority in his sermons, writings and in the provision for his new College; we have already noted how this emphasis was reflected in Sir John Rysley's provision for the Jesus theology lecture. The most orthodox early Tudor scholars could exalt biblical authority and take a cool view of the medieval schoolmen: witness John Fisher.[59]

For that matter, there was nothing incompatible between orthodoxy and taking some delight in infuriating friars. Erasmus, after all, had set the tone here. Cranmer was later to revive what was evidently an old Cambridge joke which reflected the irritation of secular dons at the unworthiness of some

57 P.R.O., S.P. 1/81 ff. 55–6 (*L.P.* 6 no. 1582), and text pr. in Foxe 7, Appendix 5. The letter contains a reference to Morison's visits to Latimer in Cambridge, but this is much less securely tied to Cranmer than the mention of Gonell; it was probably only thrown in in the knowledge that by 1533 the two men were closely associated. On Gonell, see *D.N.B.*

58 Foxe 8, p. 5; cf. Parker, *De Antiquitate*, p. 387.

59 On Fisher, R. Rex, in Bradshaw and Duffy (eds), *Humanism, Reform and the Reformation*, p. 124, and on Fisher's comments on biblical authority and interpretation, Rex, *Theology of Fisher*, especially Ch. 9. I am most grateful to Dr Ashley Null for our conversations about Alcock.

Regulars in the University: 'at the admission of unlearned friars and monks unto their degrees in the universities . . . the doctor that presented them deposed that they were meet for the said degrees, as well in learning as in virtue. And yet that deposition in one sense was true, when indeed they were meet neither in the one nor in the other.'[60] Stephen Gardiner was later to remark that he himself 'never liked friars in his life; and he took them ever for flattering knaves; and for monks, they were but belly-gods': a striking statement from the champion of conservatism under Edward VI.[61] The great figures of Cranmer's childhood, the canons of Welbeck Abbey, were a long way away from Jesus College in the 1520s.

Cranmer at Cambridge thus remained a secular priest and academic of a conventionally traditional, if humanist, cast of mind. He loved his Bible, and he was ready to single out imprecision in his colleagues' academic arguments even when it was the great Fisher who was at fault; predictably, his admiration was reserved for Erasmus and not for Luther. This is one major correction which needs to be made to the traditional picture of his early career. However, a more startling modification of the commonly accepted interpretation comes from a recent find by Stephen Ryle in a most unexpected place: fragments of the diplomatic correspondence of the kingdom of Poland, surviving in the Czartoryski Library in Cracow. Two letters from Cranmer himself, quite apart from being his earliest surviving correspondence, shed sudden shafts of light on hitherto obscure years of his career in the late 1520s. They reveal that, far from vegetating in academic contentment, by 1527 he had already joined the flock of Cambridge dons who had been talent-spotted by Cardinal Wolsey for diplomatic purposes. This would be the making of his career, and it would lead him by a roundabout route to the throne of Augustine of Canterbury.[62]

Both Cranmer's letters were addressed to a brilliant Polish humanist scholar and writer turned diplomat, Johannes Dantiscus, and they reveal a friendship already established between the two men which was to continue into the 1530s, until it was destroyed by Cranmer's theological transformation. The letters were written just before and just after Cranmer's voyage home from Spain in early summer 1527; their content enables us to reconstruct something of the circumstances which had led to his first adventure

60 Cox 1, p. 88. For the declining role of regulars in the life of the University from the 14th century, see Aston, Duncan and Evans, 'Medieval Alumni of Cambridge', pp. 54–63.

61 Foxe 6, p. 187. For other dismissive remarks by Gardiner about the regulars, ibid., pp. 204, 222, 233. On 20 February 1533, he was the only member of the Upper House of Convocation to object to the exemption of certain regulars from the clerical subsidy: cf. Lambeth MS 751, pp. 96–7, and Lehmberg, *Reformation Parliament*, p. 176.

62 For what follows, I am much indebted to the generosity of Stephen Ryle in sharing with me his discoveries, and supplying me with photocopies of the original letters. For his own presentation of the documents, see Ryle, 'Joannes Dantiscus and Thomas Cranmer'.

abroad.[63] He was playing a minor role in the English embassy in Spain: a role indeed so minor and lacking in formal status that it appears to have left no discernible impact on official records. This Spanish embassy was led from late 1525 by Dr Edward Lee.

Perhaps Wolsey's almoner Dr Capon had drawn attention to the talents of his academic colleague at Jesus, but Lee and Cranmer are in any case likely to have been quite close. Lee was a Cambridge don who had taken his MA in 1515, the same year as Cranmer. He also shared Cranmer's special interest in biblical scholarship, and he had made his name as a humanist by launching into bitter and prolonged controversy with Erasmus about his biblical translation. Lee thus won himself the good opinions of conservative scholars who were not displeased to see the great humanist on the defensive. One of them may have been Dr Cranmer: we know that he was interested in this notorious academic dispute. In his own copy of Thomas Aquinas's Commentary on Paul's Epistles, he drew attention in the margin to disagreements between Jerome and Augustine of Hippo which lay at the heart of the row between Lee and Erasmus.[64] If Lee was indeed Cranmer's first patron in securing his appointment to the Spanish mission, it is significant, and consistent with the clues which we have already noted, to see the future evangelical leader moving in such traditionalist circles. It is also ironical, for just as with Dantiscus, the atmosphere soured later: once both men became Primates of the English Church, their relations were increasingly strained as Cranmer totally transformed his religious outlook, while Lee's conservatism was only barely contained by his reluctant acceptance of the royal supremacy.

Such was the importance of the Spanish embassy to English designs abroad that in late 1526 Lee was joined by Henry VIII's permanent representative in Rome, Jerome Ghinucci, absentee Italian Bishop of Worcester. Ghinucci proved to be another important early patron of Cranmer (below, Chapter 3). This mission was crucial because it was addressed to the Emperor Charles V himself, and it formed an essential part of the delicate balancing act which England was performing between the two great European powers, the Empire and France. The King of Poland had equally pressing dynastic and territorial concerns which led him to dispatch Dantiscus, as one of his most experienced diplomats, to shadow Charles V's travels through much of the 1520s: in the course of these journeys, Dantiscus gained first-hand knowledge of England following the Emperor's state visit in 1522. It is unlikely, however, that it was in that expedition through London and down to Plymouth that he encountered Thomas Cranmer; their meeting must have taken place in Spain. Certainly Dantiscus was in regular contact with the English mission, for on one occasion Ghinucci and Lee in a dispatch to Wolsey included information

63 The letters are Muzeum Narodowe w Krakowie, Bibl. Czartoryskich MS 1595, pp. 9–12, 13–16. They are transcripts made by a member of Dantiscus's staff.

64 The Aquinas commentary (Paris edition, 1526) is now B.L., 1215 k. 15: see f. 136v, on 2 Cor. 2. Cf. Rex, *Theology of Fisher*, pp. 52–3.

which the Polish ambassador had given them.[65] Dantiscus and Cranmer were both humanist scholars of much the same age (the Polish diplomat was four years older), and Dantiscus was notoriously good company. The blossoming of this friendship with the boisterous Pole casts a new light on the image of the austere, self-restrained scholar which posterity has foisted on Cranmer.

Cranmer's first surviving letter was written to Dantiscus in May from the Basque coast, where he was impatiently waiting for permission to join a ship home for England.[66] Ambassadors Lee and Ghinucci sent a constant stream of dispatches back to London, and it is therefore difficult to be precise about which batch of letters he was carrying back. Atrocious weather at sea had conspired to keep a large number of diplomats and imperial courtiers kicking their heels in the ports of Laredo and Bilbao, and it was perhaps boredom which inspired Cranmer to write to his Polish friend back at the imperial court to tell him that he had met some of their mutual acquaintances, including the German Melchior Rantzau and the Sieur de Longueval.[67] He also passed on greetings to a variety of distinguished acquaintances, among the Emperor's entourage at Valladolid. Jesus College was a long way away from this exotic world.

Cranmer's second letter to Dantiscus was written on 30 June, after he had arrived in London. It had been an epic journey, with the Bay of Biscay and the English Channel at their worst: he ruefully described the frenzied baling-out of the ship which had been one of the chief priorities of a thirteen-day voyage. The dangers were, however, amply compensated for by his warm reception in England: as Lee's representative, he enjoyed a journey by post-horses all the way to London, and once he arrived, was given a welcome appropriate to a VIP. This culminated in the ultimate reward for royal service, a personal half-hour-long interview with the King himself ('he is a man who is the kindest of princes', gushed Cranmer to his Polish friend). Among other presents, Henry gave him rings of gold and silver: a strange pre-echo of the royal rings

65 *L.P.* 4 ii, no. 3130 and n.

66 Stephen Ryle originally dated this letter to May 1529, thus giving Cranmer a second mission in Spain. However both the Cracow transcripts are in the same hand, somewhat unlikely if a two-year interval separated them, and the date of the May letter, though unclear, seems to be 1527. The London letter of 30 June also makes a fairly direct reference to the May letter. Cranmer's May range of greetings to members of the Imperial court would be unlikely in the frosty state of Anglo-Spanish diplomacy in 1529, but most decisive of all is Cranmer's request to Dantiscus in May to pass on greetings to the Imperial chamberlain the Sieur de Montfort at the Imperial Court. In 1529 Montfort left Spain in time to arrive in the Low Countries in April, and he was sent on from there to central Europe: cf. *L.P.* 4 iii, nos 5473 and 5499. He therefore could hardly have been in Valladolid in May 1529.

67 There is a puzzle here: Longueval is plausibly identified by Ryle with the French Master of the Household, yet Cranmer describes him as an envoy of the King of Bohemia, the Habsburg Ferdinand. Moreover, Longueval and Rantzau would well match the simultaneous arrival in Valladolid on 25 February 1527 of news from Ferdinand, and of a Prussian knight suing to the Emperor. Cf. *L.P.* 4 ii, no. 2914.

which would save Cranmer's career and indeed life in 1543 (below, Chapter 8). The gratified envoy was informative to the point of indiscretion in his letter: he had a lot to learn about the role of a diplomat. He told his friend about Cardinal Wolsey's expedition to France to negotiate for Princess Mary's marriage, and expressed his own fears about an Anglo-French royal union. His information was important enough for Dantiscus to have the letter copied for the Polish court, thus ensuring its preservation in the unlikely setting of Cracow.[68]

We have no way of knowing whether the June 1527 audience was the first meeting between the King and the future Archbishop; very probably it was. More important is the fact that we can now completely redate the relationship between the two men. They first knew each other when Cranmer was a promising minor diplomat, just before the annulment of the King's first marriage became the burning issue in English politics. When Cranmer emerged as a key player in the annulment affair in the summer of 1529, he was not an unknown voice to the King. He was one of the team of Cambridge dons who had been recruited for general diplomatic service, and who had then been directed specifically to the greatest problem to face English diplomacy at the turn of the 1520s and 1530s. He shared in the experiences of fellow-Cambridge men turned diplomats like Lee, Stephen Gardiner and Richard Sampson (whom he also complimented in his letter to Dantiscus), at a time when their evangelical colleagues in Cambridge had other concerns. A clue to this early activity on his part has long been available in the well-known source material: the account by Cranmer's anonymous biographer of how and when his involvement in the King's Great Matter had first come about. The anonymous account, always well-informed, firmly places the moment at the very beginning of the affair: that is, in the spring and summer of 1527, 'not long' after Henry VIII was first persuaded that his marriage 'was unlawful and naught'. It says that Cranmer was chosen as one of a team of twelve, six from Cambridge, six from Oxford, to debate the question. This was probably the team which we know was proposed when in late May 1527 Cardinal Wolsey abandoned the first attempt to try the validity of the royal marriage. However, the anonymous account also says that Cranmer was 'not then at Cambridge' and 'there was another chosen in his stead': an absence which would amply be accounted for by his other duties on the Spanish mission.[69] On his return to the university, says the biographer, he soon became a leading advocate of the King's case: and the cast of his career was set.

Wolsey may not have succeeded in his previous effort to tempt Cranmer away from Cambridge to Cardinal College, Oxford, but the lure of service in Wolsey's diplomatic team was more effective in diverting the theologian from

68 Ryle, 'Joannes Dantiscus and Thomas Cranmer': Dantiscus received the letter on 27 July 1527 and forwarded it to King Sigismund I of Poland on 17 August.

69 *Narratives of the Reformation*, p. 219; cf. Murphy, 'The literature and propaganda of Henry's divorce', p. 135.

his worthy academic business. Quite suddenly, as far as we can judge, he had become a cosmopolitan figure. On his return to London in June 1527 (as he told Dantiscus in his letter) Cranmer dined with members of the Polish merchant community: he would retain links with Poland throughout his career, during the 1530s even maintaining a Polish youth in his archi-episcopal household, and later on, enjoying a fruitful if tense friendship with the great Polish humanist and reformer Jan Laski. Those acquaintanceships of 1527 were thus only the beginning. Within two years of his Spanish mission, he left the university for good, and at the age of forty, he committed himself to a new, more spectacular and infinitely more dangerous life.

Part II
THE KING'S GOOD SERVANT

. . . commissioners were incontinent appointed and sent forth about this matter into several universities, as some to Oxford, some to Cambridge, some to Louvain, some to Paris, some to Orleans, some to Bologna, and some to Padua, and some to other . . . At whose return there was no small joy made of the principal parties. In so much as the commissioners were not only ever after in great estimation, but also most liberally advanced and rewarded, far beyond their worthy deserts.

(George Cavendish, *Life of Cardinal Wolsey*, 1, pp. 141–2)

Britanniae laus

Multos habet claros viros Britannia,
Habuitque semper litteris et moribus
Humanioribus: nunc esse Crammaros
Cramoëllosque habet heroas illustrissimos.
Set debui regem, optimum illum principem
Laudare primum, Henricum octavum nomine:
Quem ni venerer, feramque in coelum laudibus
Hominum omnium dicar merito ingratissimus.

Britain has many famous men
and has always had as many civilized in learning and traditions;
Now she has Cranmers and Cromwells to be her most renowned heroes.
Yet I ought first to praise the King, that most excellent prince,
Henry the Eighth by name –
Whom unless I honour and praise sky-high,
I may deservedly be called the most ungrateful of all people.

(N. Bourbon, *Nugae*, Lyon, 1538, pp. 251–2)

CHAPTER 3

Campaign to end a marriage: 1527–33

GILBERT BURNET WEARILY CALLED his own heroic effort to describe Henry VIII's struggle to end his first marriage 'an account of a tedious negotiation with the subtlest and most refined court of Christendom in all the art of human policy.'[1] In the intervening three centuries since Burnet wrote, the story has retained its capacity to confuse and intimidate: we may now have a clearer idea of the course of events and the nature of the arguments, but we have also gained a sense of the astonishing continent-wide scale of the business. In the most widely focussed survey of the King's Great Matter so far undertaken, Guy Bedouelle and Patrick Le Gal list 160 contemporary scholars and 23 European universities throughout western Europe who were drawn into consideration of the affair by the supporters of both parties: it must have been the single most lucrative source of consultancy fees for academics during the whole sixteenth century. At a more exalted level, Bedouelle and Le Gal convincingly portray the results of this activity as 'an episode in the history of ideas . . . which led to consequences of the first importance beyond the religious drama (important in itself) and the political dimension of the Affair, already so often demonstrated.'[2] Henry VIII's marital problems would affect the theory and law of marriage in the western European tradition for centuries to come.

Put briefly, the entanglement of Henry and Catherine of Aragon had begun with the death in 1502 of Prince Henry's teenage elder brother, Arthur. Henry VII, with characteristic economy, had decided to redeploy Arthur's young widow Catherine of Aragon as a potential bride for his surviving son Henry. Straight away questions were raised about how this betrothal of a man's widow to his brother might relate to the biblical prohibitions in Leviticus 18 and 20 on marriage to a deceased brother's wife, and the English and Spanish authorities naturally played safe by obtaining a papal dispensation to overcome what canon law defined as an impediment of affinity. The marriage eventually went ahead after Henry VIII's accession in 1509. Prince Henry had expressed worries about the legal feasibility of his marriage during the prolonged negotiations, and his anxieties did not entirely subside there-

1 Burnet 1 i, p. 281 (Pt 1, Bk 3).

2 Bedouelle and Le Gal (eds), '*Divorce*', p. 440 (my translation). Cf. ibid., 'Répertoire Bio-Bibliographique', and pp. 468–72 for the list of universities involved.

after; by 1514, alarmed by Catherine's series of miscarriages and stillbirths, he was so worried that his marriage was not producing an heir to the throne that he apparently made overtures to the Vatican about an annulment.[3] However, the appearance and survival of Princess Mary in 1516 prolonged Henry's hopes for a son, and it was not until the mid-1520s that he became convinced that there was something irredeemably wrong with his marriage. This conviction seems to have predated the beginning of his passion for Anne Boleyn in 1526, perhaps by as much as two years, if one accepts E.W. Ives's reconstruction of these obscure early stages of the annulment proceedings.[4]

The King now returned to the scriptural prohibitions of Leviticus, and decided that his marriage did not exist in the eyes of God: it had indeed been cursed by the prescribed biblical penalty of lack of children, a sure sign of God's anger.[5] Eagerly, perhaps with a sense of gathering panic, Henry listened to his first major advisor, the Cambridge Hebraist Robert Wakefield, who told him in 1527 that the Hebrew text of Leviticus actually said more precisely and relevantly that the punishment would be the death of sons, rather than of children in general. The King was contemptuous of those theologians (including John Fisher, quickly emerging as Catherine's main champion) who pointed to the embarrassing fact that elsewhere in Moses's law, Deuteronomy 25:5, a man was encouraged by God to marry his deceased brother's wife, to carry on the family line. For Henry, this was a monstrous irrelevance, a mere quirk of anachronistic Jewish law made all the more ridiculous because his marriage had patently failed in this purpose. Henry, always a man with a strong sense of his personal relationship as anointed monarch with God, was as desperate to escape God's pitiless wrath as was Martin Luther in his years of guilty despair in a Wittenberg convent: both viewed their personal anguish in a wider theological dimension as a cosmic struggle. Both men eventually found answers to their problems which tore apart the fabric of the medieval Western Church.

Henry's consistent aim thereafter was too obsessive, too urgent in its sense of divine anger, to be described as a strategy; Virginia Murphy has demonstrated the dangerously idealistic line from which Henry hardly ever wavered until he finally despaired of the Holy Father in Rome. From the beginning of the annulment proceedings, Henry was out to persuade the papacy to share

3 Behrens, 'Divorce project of 1514', but for reservations about this, and the possibility that a lost Vatican document referred not to Henry but to the King's sister Mary Tudor, see Scarisbrick, *Henry VIII*, p. 151.

4 Ives, *Anne Boleyn*, pp. 99–109. Technically one should not refer to the subsequent negotiations as a search for divorce, which did not exist in medieval canon law; however, the word 'divorce' was in fact frequently used at the time – cf. Bedouelle and Le Gal (eds), '*Divorce*', prefatory note 'sur l'emploi du mot "Divorce"'.

5 The best account of Henry's arguments for annulment is to be found in Murphy Ph.D., 'Debate over Henry VIII's first divorce', now summarized by Murphy, 'Literature and propaganda of Henry's Divorce'. See also Kelly, *Matrimonial Trials*, Parts 1–3.

his view that the earlier papal dispensation for the supposed marriage had been an impossible use of papal power, because it flouted an eternal prohibition of God; he ignored any easier route through the morass of canon law procedure. His task became hopeless, because he failed to persuade enough people (including the Pope and the Holy Roman Emperor) that he was right in his view of the decidedly ambiguous scriptural and theological background. Nevertheless he urged on the hapless English Lord Chancellor and legate *a latere*, Thomas Wolsey, in the prosecution of his case, and more and more University experts were called in to contribute to the cause.

As one employed in royal diplomacy from at least 1527, Cranmer was inevitably drawn into the business of the annulment, and as we have already seen (above, Chapter 2), there is a plausible early tradition that he was active in his own university as an advocate of the royal case when he returned to Cambridge from Spain that summer. For the next two years, it is likely that his life began to be divided: on the one hand, playing a worthy but not especially prominent role in university teaching and administration; on the other, acting as an occasional business agent in the affairs of Cardinal Wolsey and the King. In Cambridge, he took his turn in the annually chosen committees looking after the university accounts, filled in for a preacher called away from the University's Ash Wednesday service, and (so Parker assures us from personal memories of 1520s Cambridge) was always one of the three senior examiners for theology degrees. Edmund Ashton, one of his Jesus colleagues, caught in a fatal illness without a will, probably in spring 1529, turned to him and two other Fellows to be executors: a natural choice.[6] William Longforth, ultra-orthodox Fellow of St John's, gives us a charming glimpse of the busy don of the late 1520s trying to fit Henry Gold's disputation into his schedule:

> Mr. Dr. Cranmer is content to dispute to you what day so ever ye will choose, but ye must send him your questions before Palm Sunday or in the week after at the furthest, for he can have none other leisure but that week and Easter Week to study for the Determination that he must make of them in a solemn lecture, as you know is the manner. That lecture that he reads in Divinity and other business that he hath is the cause that he can have none other leisure but only that time to look for it.[7]

Henry Gold, the anxious candidate, later encountered Cranmer in much grimmer circumstances: he was executed during the affair of the Maid of Kent, as a result of the attack on religious conservatives in which Cranmer

6 Financial duties, 1524, 1526–8: *Grace Book A*, pp. 226, 237; *Grace Book B*, ii pp. 120, 139, 146–7. *Grace Book A*, p. 236: Cranmer preaches Ash Wednesday sermon instead of Dr Lord, 25 Feb. 1528. Cf. Parker, *De Antiquitate*, p. 387. Ashton's will, C.U.L. UA Wills 1, f. 49r: entered between wills of 28 Feb. and 9 June 1529.

7 PRO, S.P. 1/73 f. 30 (*L.P.* 5 no. 1700); for an inconclusive discussion of the date, see above, Ch. 2, n. 56.

took a major part (see Chapter 4). By that time, Cranmer's traditionalism had evaporated, and Gold and Longforth had become his bitter enemies in the dispute that would end papal authority in England.

Beyond Cambridge, the 'other business' which made Cranmer's diary so full included, for instance, a journey to London in October 1528, just at the time when the papal representative-extraordinary Cardinal Campeggio reached the capital in preparation for a special hearing of the King's case for which Henry had the highest hopes. He also travelled from London to Ipswich bearing a business letter for William Capon, the Master of his College, who doubled as Dean of Wolsey's new College at Ipswich. The agent of Wolsey who had written the letter was Thomas Cromwell. Here was yet another relationship which would shape the new pattern of Thomas Cranmer's life, once the two men had emerged from the fallen Cardinal's shadow.[8]

It was thus not entirely unexpected when, in the summer of 1529, Cranmer's role in the King's Great Matter suddenly took on a new prominence, and he began his career in politics in earnest. The precipitating factors were a crisis and a coincidence. The crisis was the disastrous end to the papal hearing of the King's case by Campeggio and the resident papal legate Wolsey, which had formally opened in the London Blackfriars on 28 May 1529 and which closed in an act of deliberate procedural sabotage by Campeggio on 30 July.[9] On that day Campeggio, probably primed by Rome to make sure no decision was taken before the Queen's appeal against the hearing had reached the Pope, finally confirmed his previous formal declaration that by Roman custom the court must adjourn until October. There was nothing that Henry could do: his confident belief that his marital troubles would be resolved had been cruelly mocked, and he was devastated. Wolsey's career never recovered from the disaster, despite all his efforts to work his old charm on the King during the summer and autumn of 1529, and the King's trust in the integrity of the Roman Pontiff had suffered a blow which would likewise prove to be fatal.[10]

The aftermath of the Blackfriars fiasco took the King and his advisers on a fretful summer progress north and west of London, and it was during these restless journeyings that the coincidental meeting took place between Cranmer and two of his Cambridge colleagues who had become deeply

8 P.R.O., S.P. 1/50/203 (*L.P.* 4 no. 4872); cf. Hall 2, p. 144. It is curious, and perhaps significant, that this early mention of Cranmer has been generally overlooked: Ridley, *Cranmer*, p. 24, garbles it.

9 For the date of Campeggio's final declaration, which seems to have come a week after the formal pronouncement on 23 July, see Hall 2, p. 153, confirmed by Harpsfield, *Pretended Divorce*, pp. 183–4; Scarisbrick, *Henry VIII*, p. 227 mistakes the date as 31 July, in an otherwise reliable account.

10 For an argument that Wolsey's future remained hopeful for longer than is often thought, see E.W. Ives, in Gunn and Lindley (eds), *Wolsey*, Ch. 11. Wolsey certainly saw the King as usual once in the summer progress, and once again in the autumn: Samman Ph.D., 'Henrician Court', p. 220.

involved in the annulment business. Cranmer avoided an outbreak of plague in Cambridge by going to stay at Waltham Holy Cross in Essex with relatives called Cressy, whose two sons he was tutoring at university.[11] He was there in the first week of August, when two men familiar to him were also lodged with the Cressys at Waltham, in the first stage of the royal progress away from Greenwich Palace: Dr Stephen Gardiner and Dr Edward Foxe.[12] Gardiner had followed a common Cambridge career pattern by entering Wolsey's service, which equally predictably brought him the Mastership of his College, Trinity Hall; he had been privy to the annulment proceedings almost from the beginning, and been sent on two missions to Rome. Adroitly abandoning Wolsey in the Cardinal's hour of peril, he had become royal principal secretary only a week or two before the Waltham meeting, in the last days of the Blackfriars hearing.[13] Foxe's career was similar: Fellow of King's, Cambridge, and secretary to Wolsey from 1527. Graham Nicholson sees Foxe as by summer 1529 the likely 'prime mover' in the work of co-ordinating the King's arguments for the annulment. One massive tribute to what Foxe owed to the Boleyn marriage is today a familiar Cambridge sight to lovers of music and church architecture: the splendid Renaissance choir screen put up in the chapel of King's in Foxe's years as Provost of the College, and covered in emblems and initials celebrating the successful end of the King's Great Matter.[14]

Probably on 2 August 1529, their first night with the Cressys after leaving Greenwich, Gardiner and Foxe told Cranmer over dinner of the impasse that the royal team had reached. Cranmer suggested switching energy in the campaign from the legal case at Rome towards a general canvassing of university theologians throughout Europe, which would prove more cost-effective, involving 'little industry and charges'; according to Morice, he was blithely confident 'that there is but one truth' in the entanglement 'which no

11 It is not clear how the Waltham Cressys were related to the Cranmers. The main Nottinghamshire line of Cressys died out in 1412, and the close Cranmer relatives the Cliftons and Markhams were the heirs of their estates in the county: Payling, 'Law and Arbitration', pp. 156–7, and Payling, *Political Society*, index, s.v. Cressy.

12 *Narratives of the Reformation*, pp. 240–41 is the basic narrative by Morice, confirmed in its timing by the note of the royal itinerary in *L.P.* 4 iii no. 5965 and Samman Ph.D., 'Henrician Court', p. 386. Foxe 8, pp. 6–7 produces a piously edited version of Morice, but there is no good reason to doubt the general veracity of these accounts. Ridley, *Cranmer*, p. 25 introduces a double journey to Waltham which is not justified either by Morice's narrative or the reference in *Grace Book B* ii p. 153 to Cranmer auditing the university accounts.

13 For further discussion of this stage of Gardiner's career, see MacCulloch, 'Two Dons in Politics', pp. 13–14, although NB that I have there followed the common error of dating the end of the Blackfriars trial to 23 July. See also Redworth, *Gardiner*, pp. 16–22.

14 Nicholson, 'Act of Appeals', pp. 25–6, and cf. *Divorce Tracts*, pp. xix–xx. Morice's mistake in *Narratives of the Reformation*, p. 241 that Foxe was royal Almoner at this time has often been repeated: the Almoner was in fact Edward Lee. On the screen, see Royal Commission on Historical Monuments, *City of Cambridge* 1, pp. 128–30.

men ought or better can discuss than the divines'. Every academic is convinced that his own discipline forms the straightest road to enlightenment. Cranmer's idea of consulting theologians was not particularly new or radical; it was in fact a humanist commonplace of the previous turbulent decade, when even leading defenders of the embattled papacy, like Dr Johann Eck and Bishop Johann Faber (let alone Erasmus and Zwingli), had suggested that Europe's theological troubles should be sorted out by referring them to leading universities. Moreover, the annulment controversy had already been picked over by plenty of university theological experts, including a straight vote about the issue at the University of Paris in October 1528, which had found for the King by a bare majority. With hindsight, we can see that the new effort of consultation would prove futile from the King's point of view: political partisanship rather than academic discipline tended to colour opinions about the absolute nature of the Levitical command, producing a Continent-wide patchwork of ideas which Hans Thieme summed up as '*cuius regio, eius opinio*'. If anything, the quest for opinions about Henry's divorce fatally discredited the pretensions of European universities to be referees of controversy.[15] Cranmer himself (according to John Foxe's later account) was so unaware that he had said anything important that he went back to Cambridge and then started out for home in Nottinghamshire; he was rather annoyed to be summoned urgently to London.[16]

However, Gardiner and Edward Foxe were desperate men, with the example of Wolsey's tottering career to demonstrate to them that their royal master paid by results. If Cranmer's idea at least sounded fresh amid a hopeless mess, then it was worth reporting to the King, and indeed Henry showed interest when they talked to him two days after the dinner at Waltham. Perhaps he remembered the minor diplomat for whom he had paraded the full resources of his royal charm two years before; perhaps Cranmer had performed other duties for him since. The sequence of the events afterwards is confused and obscure: Morice says that 'by and by' Cranmer met Henry at Greenwich, but a meeting with the King at Greenwich could not have taken place until 23 October, which seems far too late, even allowing for Cranmer's initial reluctance to make himself available.[17] Sir Thomas More subsequently remembered that Cranmer was among the theological trouble-shooters sent to present him with the latest statement of the King's case, very soon after More had replaced Wolsey as Lord Chancellor on 25 October 1529.[18]

15 On Paris, Kelly, *Matrimonial Trials*, pp. 173–4; cf. Bedouelle and Le Gal (eds), '*Divorce*', pp. 54–5. Thieme qu. ibid. p. 50, and cf. discussion of the opinions of Angers, Paris and Bourges in Kelly, *Matrimonial Trials*, pp. 177–8.

16 Foxe 8, p. 7.

17 For 23 October date, see *Divorce Tracts*, p. xxi and n. Ives is still prepared to accept an October date for the first meeting: cf. Ives, *Anne Boleyn*, p. 160.

18 *More Correspondence*, pp. 495–6. More does not mention the presence of Stokesley, which indicates that the meeting took place after Stokesley left on embassy early in October. More took the Great Seal on 25 October: Guy, *More*, p. 32.

By the time of the meeting with More, or soon afterwards, Cranmer was in high favour with the Boleyn family; he was lodged in the entourage of Anne Boleyn's father, Thomas, at Durham Place, a suitably palatial temporary residence for the parent of a prospective royal bride, conveniently available thanks to the vacancy-in-see of Durham.[19] It is also worth noting that Cranmer's old friend at Jesus College, Thomas Goodrich, was now suddenly drawn into royal favour, presumably to help with the annulment research. On 16 November 1529, Goodrich was admitted as Rector of St Peter Cheap, a London living in the gift of Wolsey as Commendatory Abbot of St Albans, and his first preferment outside Cambridge: this was probably part of Wolsey's desperate attempts to please the King by doing favours to his advisors, and soon Goodrich was granted a royal chaplaincy to indicate his new status.[20]

Cranmer's job at Durham Place was to produce arguments for the annulment, a task to which the King would send him back repeatedly over the next four years whenever he was in England. Like so much else in this first phase, it is difficult to be precise as to what he wrote. Thomas Master, researching for Lord Herbert's biography of Henry VIII in 1636, found in the Exchequer of Receipt archive a memorandum about 'a bundle of books written as is supposed by Archbishop Cranmer and [John Clerk] Bishop of Bath in defence of the King's title of Supreme Head and the divorce from his first wife Catherine and against Cardinal Pole', but this is already vague information at one remove, and it is uncertain what if anything survives from this one-time bundle. The treatise *Articuli Duodecim* ('Twelve Articles') has sometimes been credited to Cranmer's literary efforts in this period, but there are good reasons for assigning it to a later stage in the proceedings, after January 1533.[21] The only definite information that we have is that Gardiner and Foxe said that they used Cranmer's writings to good effect when they went to Cambridge in February 1530, to extort an opinion favourable to the King from the University.[22]

19 On Durham Place, lately Wolsey's, cf. Gunn and Lindley (eds), *Wolsey*, p. 78: its availability was not part of the spoils of Wolsey's downfall.

20 See D.N.B., s.v. Goodrich, Thomas.

21 Master: Bodl. MS Jesus 74, ff. 26–7; Virginia Murphy tells me that her extensive searches in Exchequer classes have not revealed any surviving material from Clerk or Cranmer. For a 1529 date for *Articuli Duodecim*, cf. Guy, *More*, p. 102, but see the arguments for a 1533 date in Kelly, *Matrimonial Trials*, p. 223 (cf. ibid., p. 162). For further discussion of the *Articuli*, see below, Ch. 4, pp. 85–6.

22 Ridley, *Cranmer*, pp. 27–8nn, is rightly sceptical about the claim in *Narratives of the Reformation*, pp. 242–3 of Cranmer's direct involvement in the discussions leading to Oxford and Cambridge's pronouncement of the divorce in February/March 1530: impossible, since he was already away on the Boleyn embassy to Italy. However, Ridley still thinks that Cranmer did attend some meeting in August to October 1529. It is more likely that Morice misunderstood the fact that Cranmer's writings had been used in persuading the universities: cf. Gardiner and Foxe's letter to Henry VIII, Feb. 1530, pr. Burnet 1 ii, pp. 124–6 (Bk 2, no. 32); *L.P.* 4 iii, no. 6247.

By then, Cranmer himself had set off with his old patron Edward Lee and his new patron Thomas Boleyn (newly ennobled as Earl of Wiltshire), on an embassy designed to tackle the Holy Roman Emperor while Charles V and the Pope were conveniently both at Bologna for the Imperial coronation; Henry had several sets of diplomats on overlapping missions at this time, reflecting his omnivorous search for a way out of his impasse.[23] Boleyn's diplomatic instructions from the King contain a glowing reference to the encouragement which Henry had taken from 'the saying of a marvellous and virtuous wise man': the King turned from French to Latin to quote from what was evidently a text written by this sage (for he broke off the quotation with an 'etc.'), rehearsing how it urged the duty of serving God rather than man, for 'one ought to be considered impious rather than pious who transgresses the master's law so that he may gratify or flatter the servant'. Here was a commentator who clearly ranked canon law below the law of God, a harmonious echo of the King's position over the previous three years: was this paragon of congenial rectitude Dr Cranmer?[24] Certainly when on 20 January 1530 the Imperial ambassador, Eustace Chapuys, gloomily observed the preparations for Boleyn's departure, he referred to the man he called 'Croma' as chaplain in ordinary to the King: Cranmer had come far in just a few months. Chapuys subsequently remains a useful if biased source of information on Cranmer's rise to the top.[25]

Cranmer did not return to England until late October 1530: as in 1527, he had no official accreditation to the Emperor, and it was probably intended from the start that he make his way to Rome for a long stay, among other things to help the other royal agents who were putting into operation his own suggested strategy of rounding up university opinions. With effect from 17 April 1530, the English government tripled his daily wage, together with that of his colleague the civil lawyer Edward Carne; it is likely that this reflects a rise in Cranmer's status to that of orator to the Apostolic See, in anticipation of the Pope's return to Rome from Bologna, and it is probably also when he was granted the complementary title of Penitentiary-General of England. The Penitentiary was traditionally appointed on a recommendation by the King of England to the Pope, and the duties involved a watching brief over papal dispensations which might affect England.[26] The move came at a

23 *British Diplomatic Representatives*, pp. 46, 75, 163, 288.

24 P.R.O., S.P. 1/56 f. 148 (*L.P.* 4 iii, no. 6111, p. 2729). My translation.

25 Chapuys to the Emperor, *C.S.P. Spanish 1529–30*, no. 252, pp. 432–3. Cranmer cannot otherwise definitely be identified as a royal chaplain until January 1532: cf. Ridley, *Cranmer*, p. 36 and n. 2, and *H.M.C., Seventh Report*, p. 601. Foxe's account of Cranmer's second interview with Henry, Foxe 8, p. 9, may have some basis in fact.

26 P.R.O., E. 101/420/11 ff. 76v, 109r (*L.P.* 5, pp. 317, 320); cf. *Trevelyan Papers*, p. 167. On Cranmer's Pensionary status, cf. Ridley, *Cranmer*, pp. 30–31; although strictly speaking the rise in Cranmer's daily expense allowance is more likely to be connected with his designation as orator. Cf. Benet's mention of the appointment of Cranmer's successor as Pensionary, P.R.O. S.P. 1/65 ff. 108f, pr. *St.P.*, 7, pp. 279–81 (*L.P.* 5 no. 68). Cranmer is called orator to the Apostolic See in his licence of 22 August 1530: see n. 28 below.

tense time, because on 7 March 1530 the Pope at Bologna had raised the stakes in the annulment crisis by citing Henry to Rome and prohibiting his remarriage, thus throwing the English Court into even greater confusion.[27] Jerome Ghinucci, permanent watchdog for English interests in Rome and Cranmer's old acquaintance from the 1527 Spanish mission, would need all the assistance he could get in promoting the King's cause.

It was in Rome that Cranmer began accumulating his first official positions outside Cambridge. His appointment as Penitentiary was simply a natural corollary of his status as an English representative in Rome, but alongside this predictable honour, it was probably at this time that he gained his first promotion in the English Church. Ghinucci gave Cranmer the Rectory of Bredon in Worcestershire, which was in his gift as Bishop of Worcester; Cranmer was called Rector of Bredon by 22 August 1530, when he took advantage of his status as Penitentiary to obtain a papal licence to hold four benefices.[28] Bredon, almost certainly Cranmer's only cure of souls before he became Archbishop, was no ordinary parish; it was one of the four wealthiest in Worcester diocese. The sight of its splendid medieval tithe barn and stately church is still one of the consolations of a drive along the M5 motorway; Bredon was a prominent part of the majestic and venerable sprawl of Worcester episcopal estates, and with medieval panache both the Bishop and the secular owners who supplanted him in the later sixteenth century retained serfs on their manor.[29] Other early sixteenth-century Rectors included Pietro Carmeliano, Latin secretary to Henry VII; the great ecclesiastical lawyer and Cranmer's future employee in Canterbury administration, Richard Gwent; and Thomas Bagard, Chancellor of Worcester diocese. Once long before, Bredon had played a role in the career of a prospective Archbishop of Canterbury: back in the eighth century, Tatwine, a monk of the monastery then on the site, had gone on to become Archbishop for three years between 731 and 734.[30]

The choice of Cranmer in this distinguished line was predictable, and no doubt it was the result of a nudge from Henry VIII to Ghinucci. The

27 *L.P.* 4 iii, no. 6256; Guy, *More*, p. 128.

28 Vatican Archivo Secreto Vaticano, Brevi Clemente VII, Arm. 40 vol. 30, f. 215: a draft only; this was a discovery of Dr Maria Dowling, and I am very grateful to her for generously letting me know of her important find. As far as we know, Cranmer never took advantage of this licence. *Narratives of the Reformation*, p. 243 indicates that the initiative in getting Cranmer a benefice came from Henry.

29 In 1552 Bredon was listed at £72.11s *per annum*, still one of the four plum livings listed in the diocese as worth over £50: P.R.O., S.P. 10/15 f. 173v. On serfs, cf. e.g. Gloucester Record Office D.2957/174(1).

30 For the collation of Carmeliano in 1506, see H.W.R.O., b.716.093-BA 2648/8(i), p. 82; the early history of the parish is outlined and other rectors are listed in Bredon Church Guide Book, which however misses Cranmer. Carmeliano, the previous known incumbent before Cranmer, died sometime before 13 January 1528: *Le Neve, Fasti 1300–1541 VI: Northern Province*, p. 29. The somewhat confused Worcester episcopal Registers of the period, H.W.R.O. b.716.093-BA 2648/8(i)(ii), 9(i)(ii), do not reveal the institution of Cranmer or any other immediate successor to Carmeliano.

7 Bredon church, Worcestershire: Cranmer's only experience of parochial responsibility. Its lavish Romanesque structure attests to the longstanding importance and wealth of the benefice.

Bishop of Worcester was now in an unenviable position in Rome, for his long and conscientious championing of Henry's cause in Italy was becoming an increasingly lonely and fruitless task. It was not surprising that he was eager to please the King and the newly arrived royal representative with the gift of a fat benefice; a parallel and contemporary case was that of John Barlow, a Boleyn client like Cranmer, who on 15 June 1530 received the rich Deanery of Westbury-on-Trym College from Ghinucci, nominated by royal signet letter. One could also compare the appointment of the radical royal protégé Hugh Latimer to West Kington in Wiltshire on 14 January 1531. Like Bredon, this was in the gift of an absentee Italian, the Bishop of Salisbury – none other than the architect of the Blackfriars disaster, Lorenzo Campeggio![31] We can also note another scrap of evidence for intimacy between Ghinucci and Cranmer during Cranmer's Roman stay: an Italian servant of Cranmer's, possibly acquired on his 1530 Italian trip,

31 On Barlow, H.W.R.O., b.716.093-BA 2648/8(ii), p. 38, and see Rupp, *Protestant Tradition*, pp. 64–5, 71. Latimer: extract from Campeggio's Register, qu. Foxe 7, pp. 773–4.

subsequently entered Ghinucci's household and became a long-term spy for Cranmer.[32]

Much of Cranmer's time in Italy was spent working with the team gathering opinions from the universities. Nicholas Harpsfield, a past-master in aphoristic sneers about the course of the English Reformation, later spoke sarcastically about 'the English angels that flew so thick among the divines and lawyers in France and Italy' in the course of this operation, and it did indeed involve a good deal of cash changing hands.[33] The letters which survive about the English team's efforts make tedious and depressing reading: the Italians who were chivvied, cajoled and bribed into agreeing with the King were rarely reliable or consistent witnesses, and the royal researchers were disastrously encumbered by Richard Croke, a self-righteous and fussy Cambridge don who was more skilled at Greek than he was at human relationships. Croke quarrelled disastrously, for instance, both with his colleague John Stokesley and with the whole family of the veteran Italian diplomat in English service, Sir Gregory Casale. It is therefore particularly impressive that in his surviving letters Croke never had a bad word to say for Dr Cranmer (despite a misreading in a *Letters and Papers* summary, compounded in Ridley's biography).[34] Indeed, after one vicious row with Stokesley in June, Croke left 'good Mr Cranmer' in Bologna to try and calm Stokesley down after Croke had accused Casale of double-dealing.[35]

It is indeed through Croke's correspondence that we catch glimpses of Cranmer, even of two of his letters to Croke. In the course of a whining piece of self-justification to Henry VIII at the end of July, Croke quoted a letter of 12 July from Cranmer at Rome, which pessimistically described the Pope's hostility to the English investigation: 'as for any favours to be had in this Court, I look for none, but to have the Pope with all his Cardinals extremely against us.'[36] Later, at the end of July or beginning of August, Cranmer was still in Rome, and still writing gloomily to Croke about the impossibility of

32 John Bianket (Bianchi or Bianchetti?), a Bolognese. Cranmer left Rome for Bologna at the end of August or beginning of September 1530: the draft licence of 22 August erases the reference to him as orator to the Apostolic See, presumably indicating that he left soon after the first preparation of the draft (above, n. 28). On Bianket, cf. B.L. Harley MS 787, f. 18, pr. Cox 2, pp. 330–32 (*L.P.* 11 no. 1100), 18 Nov 1536, and P.R.O., S.P. 1/128 ff. 86–7 (not pr. in Cox; *L.P.* 18 pt i, no. 76), 14 Feb 1538; for a mention of 'Bianchet' as ambassador Benet's host in Rome in January 1533, see *St.P.* 7, p. 416.

33 Harpsfield, *Pretended Divorce*, p. 133; cf. ibid., p. 209.

34 *L.P.* 4 iii no. 6624, p. 2986, misreads B.L. Cotton MS Vitellius B XIII f. 115 as saying that Cranmer had caused Gambara's obstructiveness; the text in fact talks of 'Mr Cranmer and I' mollifying him. Ridley 34 further misinterprets remarks about Cranmer in *L.P.* 4 iii no. 6639, B.L. Cotton MS Vitellius B XIII f. 116. Croke and Cranmer had known each since c. 1519: Cox 2, p. 547.

35 B.L. Cotton MS Vitellius B XIII f. 87, 9 June 30 (*L.P.* 4 iii no. 6446). On Croke's Italian stay generally, see Przychocki, 'Richard Croke's search for patristic MSS', and Scarisbrick, *Henry VIII*, pp. 255–8.

36 B.L. Cotton MS Vitellius XIII ff. 96–7, 28 July 1530 (*L.P.* 4 iii no. 6531).

progress in getting a suitable papal brief because the papal bureaucracy was dominated by the hostility of Cardinal Pucci of the Four Saints: 'I never knew such inconstancy in my life.' Cranmer was doing his usual meticulous best to be a subtle negotiator: he weighed up the reliability as an ally of the prominent Venetian Friar Francis, and decided that Francis's own explanation of his public neutrality could be trusted, but that it was best to 'get as much of him and utter as little unto him as I can'. Cranmer was justified in his downbeat report, for on 4 August, soon after this second letter, the Pope issued a version of the brief which Cranmer had been seeking: his Holiness made it clear that he was not going to obstruct the process of obtaining academic opinions about the annulment case, but with the pointed rider that they should not be obtained by bribery. This was a compromise between the English and Imperial representatives which pleased neither side, and it was in any case little more than a repeat of an earlier statement.[37]

Cranmer finally left Rome to reach Bologna by 16 September, and straight away walked into a diplomatic row characteristic of the English mission: the papal governor of the city, Cardinal de Gambara, had been understandably furious when it was reported to him that Stokesley had been contravening the Pope's order and doling out large cash sums to obtain opinions from Bologna University.[38] Gambara's mood had changed for the better when Croke and Cranmer went together to sweet-talk him on 16 September, although it seems unlikely, as Ridley has proposed, that Cranmer's presence was responsible for this transformation; Croke seems to suggest that Gambara had already changed his tune before the meeting.[39] In any case, this brief interval of hope at Bologna produced no further substantial results, and Cranmer was no doubt relieved to be soon on his way to rendezvous with Croke's *bête noire* Stokesley for the journey home.[40] Stokesley and Cranmer crossed from Calais to England in mid-October, their mission officially ending on the 23rd; meanwhile Croke pursued Cranmer with a fusillade of letters which, on the

37 *Records of the Reformation* 1, pp. 409–10 (*L.P.* 4 iii no. 6543); it is a copy apparently enclosed by Croke in a packet of letters for England on 5 August (cf. *L.P.* 4 iii no. 6551). Ridley, *Cranmer*, pp. 32–3 has confused Cranmer's second letter with his letter of 12 July. Cf. the Imperial ambassador Mai's comment on the brief, *L.P.* 4 iii no. 6557, and Bedouelle and Le Gal (eds), '*Divorce*', p. 52.

38 Croke was still writing to Cranmer at Rome on 12 September (*Records of the Reformation* 1 p. 421; *L.P.* 4 iii no. 6613), but Cranmer may have already set out by then; *Records of the Reformation*, 1, p. 423 (*L.P.* 4 iii no. 6619) shows him in Bologna on 16 September. This letter has the account of Gambara's anger at Stokesley.

39 *L.P.* 4 iii no. 6623 (*Records of the Reformation* 1, p. 427).

40 On Bologna's determination, see Bedouelle and Le Gal (eds), '*Divorce*', pp. 169–70. However, Lodovico Gozzadini, the most distinguished legal teacher at Bologna, did produce an opinion favourable to the King, posthumously published, and Girolamo Previdelli published his own favourable material at Bologna in November 1531: ibid., pp. 358, 406–7. Cranmer seems to have been with Stokesley by 29 September 1530: *L.P.* 4 iii no. 6644.

pretext of necessary business, badgered him to move heaven and earth in Court circles to promote Croke's reputation and financial demands, and to blacken Stokesley's name. There is no evidence that Cranmer lived up to Croke's ineptly Machiavellian hopes.[41]

The Rector of Bredon had done a reasonable job in Italy; at least he had kept on good terms with his difficult colleagues. Promoted from his previous obscurity, he had done nothing to betray the King's esteem, and on a mission which presented far more pitfalls than his earlier sojourn in Spain, he had done nothing to betray the King's esteem in a new and bewildering world. The next year in England was to improve his position still further. Straight away there was work to do on the annulment controversy, in which he was to play an increasingly prominent part. For instance, when in January 1531 Bishop Stokesley assembled a team of six royal partisans to meet a team of six opponents headed by Bishop Fisher in an unsuccessful attempt to find some compromise, Cranmer would have been an obvious name for Stokesley to include in his list. Nationally, this was a year of high drama, in which the King stepped up his campaign to intimidate the English Church authorities, initially with only limited success.[42] In the course of the year, many of those directly involved in the annulment business began to see more clearly the wider religious issues which lay behind it: among them was probably Thomas Cranmer. Although much remains obscure about this period in his life, it was crucial for his future development. Having seen the Holy Father in Rome, Cranmer next made his first recorded contacts with the evangelical reformers of Continental Europe.

During the year Cranmer may even have spent some time in his benefice of Bredon, although no doubt for the most part the parish was left to the attentions of his farmer and a flock of curates; in June 1531 a letter reveals him as waiting at Hampton Court for news from his benefice via a servant of the diocesan financial official Sir John Russell.[43] Most of his time was spent at Court, filled with congenial and profitable literary work for the King's cause in a variety of capacities. He could, for instance, be called on to vet opposition

41 P.R.O., E. 101/324/24 (*L.P.* 4 iii no. 6022 iv) is Stokesley's warrant to pay cross-Channel transport costs, 20 October 1530, and the record of the ambassadors' wages is P.R.O. E. 101/420/11 f. 133r, *L.P.* 5, p. 322; *Trevelyan Papers*, p. 172. For Croke's letters to Cranmer, see B.L. Cotton MS Vitellius B XIII ff. 122, 125rv, 131rv (*L.P.* 4 iii nos 6669, 6671, 6689, 6696, 6701).

42 Stokesley: B.L. Cotton MS Otho C X, f. 161, pr. *Records of the Reformation* 2, pp. 369–70 (for a convincing redating from 1533 to 1531 by reference to *C.S.P. Spanish 1529–33*, p. 852, *L.P.* 5 App. no. 3). For a useful general guide through these complicated events, see Guy, *More*, Chs 7–8.

43 B.L. Lansdowne MS 115, f. 1, pr. Cox 2, pp. 229–31 (*L.P.* 5, App. 10). The Rector's farmer is mentioned in a view of frankpledge for Bredon on 10 May 1530 (H.W.R.O., 009:1-BA 2636/178 (xxvii, no. 92510), a Court Roll for the episcopal manors, unfoliated). Russell should not be confused with the future Earl of Bedford: cf. *History of Parliament 1509–1558* 3, pp. 231–2.

literature; we have one surviving example in the letter already mentioned, written to the Earl of Wiltshire, which summarized and commented on a 'book' (that is, a private memorandum for Henry and his advisors) by the King's cousin Reginald Pole. In his comments on what amounted to a carpet-bombing by Pole of the royal case for the divorce, Cranmer revealed the quality for which Henry valued him so much: he gave a clear, cool analysis which realistically appraised the virtues of Pole's work. The argument, he said, 'satisfieth me very well' in all points except its major premise, 'that the King his Grace should be content to commit his great cause to the judgement of the Pope'. All through his life, Cranmer was either blessed or cursed with the ability to see his opponents' point of view: an attribute rare enough in any age, but in particularly short supply during the Reformation. The letter also testified to the intimate position which he had now achieved in royal counsels, as one of Henry's most trusted and intensively consulted academic advisors; he was to report further to Wiltshire (no doubt at London) the following day, 'if the King's Grace let [i.e. prevent] me not'.

Besides this, there was the work which the royal committee of scholars had been pursuing for several years already: what would today be known as research in primary sources. Among Cranmer's surviving private papers are very extensive collections arranging quotations from canon law which are preoccupied with the jurisdictional claims of the papacy, summarized in a clearly hostile fashion in a further shorter document; the anonymous biographer clearly places the formation of these collections before Cranmer became Archbishop, and it seems natural to regard them as part of his research in 1531.[44] However, there was also a new task. The King's team was now preparing material for publication to win hearts and minds in the kingdom and throughout Europe, and one of Cranmer's major assignments would be to edit other people's material into decent readable English. It was thus in 1531 that he began developing the skills which would bear the most lasting fruit in the greatest editorial task of his life, the Book of Common Prayer.

The research team produced two major works at this time, one for the government's private use and one for public consumption. The former was the manuscript compilation which Dr Nicholson has taught us to call the *Collectanea Satis Copiosa* ('The sufficiently abundant Collections'), a battery of historical extracts designed to embody the King's disillusionment with papal authority in the wake of the Blackfriars debacle: the idea which ran through the collection was that history proved that it was the King, not the

44 *Narratives of the Reformation*, pp. 221–2: the collections are Lambeth MS 1107 ff. 1–76 (pr. Strype, *Cranmer* Oxford edn. 3, pp. 744–883), and two copies of the summary, ibid. ff. 76–80 and C.C.C.C. MS 340, pp. 247f (pr. Cox 2, pp. 68–75). Cf. discussion of dating in Ayris and Selwyn (eds), *Cranmer*, p. 317, but I cannot agree that the fact that the collections are in a secretary's hand implies a post-1533 date; Cranmer would naturally have access to a secretary for his 1531 royal research work.

Bishop of Rome, who exercised supreme jurisdiction of all descriptions within his realm. No matter that much of the most striking evidence for this claim was the work of the twelfth-century Welsh fantasist, Geoffrey of Monmouth, whose Arthurian fables have met their nemesis in Walt Disney and Monty Python: Henry was beside himself with delight at the collections, and he spattered the surviving manuscript with his approving comments. It was the work of the *Collectanea* that was to fuel the extraordinary self-confidence of the King's break with Rome; the collections found their most explicit echo in the words of the 1533 Act in Restraint of Appeals that 'by divers sundry old authentic histories and chronicles it is manifestly declared and expressed that this realm of England is an empire . . . governed by one supreme head and king'. Edward Foxe seems to have been the co-ordinator of this effort of research; it was at its height while Cranmer was away in Rome, so that Henry was already beginning to trumpet the results to bewildered foreign observers in early autumn 1530. However, the *Collectanea* remained in need of supplementing at the time of Cranmer's return from Rome, and it is likely that he was drafted in to help with the task of completion.[45]

The other work of the committee, which ended up in print, had in fact a longer life behind it than the *Collectanea*. When it was first published in Latin for an international scholarly audience in April 1531, it was called the *Gravissimae . . . Academiarum Censurae . . .*; one of the team who had compiled it, John Stokesley, later testified that it was translated into English 'with other their addition and changings by my Lord of Canterbury'.[46] In this translated form, with Cranmer probably undertaking the whole translation and certainly making the alterations which only appear in the English, the work appeared in November 1531 as *The Determinations of the most famous and most excellent Universities of Italy and France, that it is unlawful for a man to marry his brother's wife; that the Pope hath no power to dispense therewith*. One would think from the title that the book was simply a publication of the results of Cranmer's big idea: the consultation of European universities. However, these eight opinions favourable to Henry, which had already been published separately in English in a proclamation of late 1530, were only the preliminary matter to a far longer treatise discussing the authorities throughout Scripture and the history of the Church who could be seen as supporting the King's argument.

The fearsome tedium of this work was almost deliberate, for it purported to be an abstract academic discussion of the general principles surrounding marriage to a brother's wife; the whole text achieves the remarkable feat of

45 See Nicholson's discussion in 'Appeals', a useful summary of his highly important 1977 Cambridge Ph.D. 'Nature and function of historical argument'; see also Guy, *More*, pp. 131–2. Text of Act in Restraint of Appeals conveniently available in Elton, *Tudor Constitution*, p. 353.

46 P.R.O., S.P. 1/94 f. 98 (*L.P.* 8 no. 1054).

never once mentioning Henry VIII or Catherine of Aragon after its recitation of the university opinions. Virginia Murphy has shown that it is a remodelling of the *libellus* or summary of royal arguments which Henry's lawyers had presented to the Blackfriars tribunal in late spring 1529; this *libellus* (its text beginning '*Henricus Octavus*') had itself been based on the two years of research work previously undertaken by Henry's theological advisers.[47] However, the text continued to undergo modification right up to the moment of publication, as the King's thinking evolved. The last section of *Censurae/Determinations* was the most altered, first when the published Latin text completely redrafted the latest known manuscript version of the ending, and then in Cranmer's quite extensive repositioning and clarifying of the published Latin text in the English edition. Already in the Latin edition, the changes include an appeal to individual conscience against the Pope, specifically urging the English bishops to stand up against him – in Cranmer's translation:

> it shall be the duty of a loving and a devout bishop not only to withstand the Pope openly to his face, as Paul did resist Peter, because the Pope verily is to be reprehended and rebuked, but also with all fair means and gentleness, and learning, in time and out of time ought to cry upon him to rebuke, reprove, beseech, exhort him that the persons so coupled together may forsake such marriages.[48]

As yet, this is not a declaration of independence from Rome, but there is a menacing tone which reflects the King's increasingly aggressive mood. Moreover, Cranmer in his translation twice decides to spell out with greater emphasis that the King's conscience in the matter represents a 'motion of the Holy Ghost' which is higher than mere law.[49]

This new line was sustained and extended in two other works of propaganda produced during 1531, both of which urged defiance of Rome; Cranmer probably had a hand in producing both of them, and it is likely that Chapuys was thinking of these when in January 1532 he said that Cranmer had written in favour of the divorce.[50] *The Glass of Truth* (which ran to three

47 On this major tract, see Virginia Murphy's discussion, reworked from her Ph.D. 'The debate over Henry VIII's first divorce', in *Divorce Tracts*, Introduction, especially pp. iv, viii–ix, and her introductory discussion, 'Literature and propaganda of Henry's Divorce'.

48 *Divorce Tracts*, p. 265, and Latin text, p. 264; compare with the anodyne content of the original ending in MS, B.L. Harley MS 1338, ibid., pp. 274–7. On Cranmer's alterations in the translation, cf. e.g. ibid., pp. 268 l. 24, 270 l. 2; notes on p. 445, also Introduction, pp. xxix–xxxiii.

49 Ibid., p. 267 ll. 19, 25, and notes p. 442. Note also Cranmer's significant extension of threat to the Papacy at ibid., pp. 156 l. 17, 157 l. 27 (cf. note, p. 366).

50 *C.S.P. Spanish 1531–3*, no. 888, p. 367. Chapuys refers separately to Cranmer's translation work on the *Determinations*.

editions) directly tackles the divorce question, and although it draws on the same research as the *Determinations*, it is mercifully more concise and popular in approach: it also marks yet another stage in the rapidly evolving thought of the King and his advisors, for it goes further than the *Determinations* by explicitly urging the bishops to help English people resist excommunications or inhibitions from Rome.[51] The second pamphlet, *Disputatio inter clericum et militem*, was a thirteenth-century French anticlerical dialogue which had later been circulated by the Lollards, and which was now resurrected at the initiative of the newly emerging royal servant Thomas Cromwell; the published version was edited to point up its emphasis on royal power and to add more references to the Pauline epistles. The point of this antiquarian exercise was to provide some ballast for the idea which was now surfacing in the pages of the *Collectanea* as the new emphasis of the King's campaign; as the editors expanded the original text, the *Disputatio's* Knight ordered the Cleric 'refrain your tongue, and acknowledge the king by his royal power to be above your laws, customs, privileges and liberties'. The title-page of the English *Determinations* reuses the type-face ornaments from the title-page of the *Disputatio*.[52]

Out of all these writings, only our sure knowledge that Cranmer edited and altered the *Determinations* enables us to see the future master of English prose at work. Already, in his uphill struggle to inject some life and readability into this formidably dull text, he revealed his connoisseurship of words: at the time it was not common to present an academic treatise in a vernacular language, and so Cranmer tried to make the English language work harder than it had done before, a brave and exhilarating experiment which claimed its linguistic casualties. For instance, he found it difficult to provide concise or accurate renderings of the Latin technical terms of the syllogism, and in another place his life would have been made easier if he had had the courage to make the later English formation 'context' from '*contextus*'.[53] Nevertheless, his work contained five first uses of English words earlier than those recorded in the old *Oxford English Dictionary*: 'heed, upon' for headlong, 'illighten' (enlighten), 'natural' (native), 'notificative' (designative), and 'whistle out' (dismiss in derision) – for some reason this last phrase enormously irritated Nicholas Harpsfield when he came to write his riposte to the *Determinations*. Strikingly, Cranmer's text also contained six apparent attempts to coin English words or phrases which never made it to the

51 There has been much controversy about the dating of *The Glass of Truth*. Haas, '*Glasse of Truthe*', seems substantially convincing with his 1531 date, though he there makes the serious error of confusing the *Collectanea* and the *Determinations*. P.R.O. S.P. 6/7 no. 2 (*L.P.* 8 no. 589), answer of Thomas King, has a reference to a St Albans priest reading *The Glass* on 18 February 1532 (first Monday 'in clean Lent was twelve month' before Anne Boleyn's marriage). See also discussion of the tract in *Divorce Tracts*, xxxiii–xxxvi.

52 Haas, '*Disputatio inter Clericum et Militem*', especially pp. 66, 68–9.

53 *Divorce Tracts*, pp. 184 l. 19, 185 l. 27–8; 186 l. 4, 187 l. 10 (cf. notes on pp. 386–7).

Dictionary ('caroginous', 'crudell', 'impunishment', 'sacre holy', 'like of' for alike and 'incest' for incestuous), and there were around twenty-three meanings of common English, Latinate or Norman-French words not recorded in the *OED*.[54]

Besides these verbal adventures, Cranmer made very many minor corrections, omissions or clarifications of the Latin: for instance, he repeatedly employed the device of numbering off lists of items, his sensibly tidy-minded practice in the marginalia of his own books.[55] Another habit familiar in later years, particularly in the formal prose of the Prayer Book, was his pairing of words: '*viam iustitiae*' became 'the way of justice and right, of virtue and honesty'; '*obtestationibus*' became 'by certain obtestations or affectuous and hearty desirings and prayings'. In this case, Cranmer might be thought to be providing too much of a good thing, likewise when in biblical translation the '*misericordiam*' of Matthew 12:7 became 'piety, mercy and compassion, love and charity'![56] Occasionally one has to note that his exhaustion or boredom have produced inaccuracies or wooden renderings, but the best translator can hardly avoid such lapses.

The widower Cambridge don also appeared to have some embarrassment in talking in English about sexuality, something of a handicap in a text which discusses little else. Incest seemed a particular worry for him; he repeatedly tried to translate '*incestus*' as 'unchaste', which since no subsequent usages are recorded in English was not to prove a linguistic success. In some cases, he simply omitted the word, or tried to translate it as 'filthy'.[57] Two passages in the Latin quoting from Aristotle on male homosexual incest were too much for him, one being turned back to refer to heterosexuality, the other simply left out.[58] Particularly interesting efforts came in his renderings of passages from Thomas Aquinas on the subject of marriage; he was later, in the text of the 1549 marriage service, to bring revolutionary liturgical change by asserting that marriage could be fun. In 1531, Cranmer primly added to an Aquinas quotation his current opinion about sex within marriage: 'where such pastime is to be used for necessity, and not for pleasure'. Still pursuing some private agenda of his own, soon afterwards he translated the bald phrase '*concupiscentiae repressio*' with the tortured 'repressing and quenching of bodily lust, and concupiscence, which restraint of carnal lust, though it be not the first and chief end of

54 Ibid., Glossary, pp. 461–2. Cf. Harpsfield, *Pretended Divorce*, pp. 125–6, 131.

55 E.g. ibid., pp. 64 l. 1, 65 ll. 1–2 (cf. note on p. 312) 104 l. 3–106 l. 33, 105 l. 4–107 l. 31; 158 ll. 7–21, 159 ll. 11–33; 186 ll. 8, 187 ll. 19; 220 ll. 6–7, 221 ll. 8–11.

56 Ibid., pp. 12 l. 18, 13 l. 22; pp. 44 l. 7, 45 ll. 9–10; 240 l. 9, 241 l. 17 (cf. notes pp. 289, 300, 419).

57 Ibid.: for 'unchaste', see pp. 130 l. 22, 131 l. 34 (see note on p. 348); 132 l. 17, 133 l. 27 (p. 349); 198 l. 16, 199 l. 24 (p. 398). Omissions: 188/21, 189 l. 33 (p. 389). 'Filthy': pp. 230 l. 13, 231 l. 23 (p. 416). Cranmer does use the word 'incest' on occasion: cf. pp. 130 l. 6, 131 l. 12.

58 Ibid., p. 196 ll. 9–11, 11–13; p. 197 ll. 11–15 (cf. note on p. 393).

marriage [i.e. benefit of issue], but the second, yet of itself it is an end of marriage.'[59]

Allied to his views on sex are the hints which we can pick up in the *Determinations* translation about Cranmer's religious outlook; of great significance are the first positive indications of a change away from his previous conventional humanist Catholicism towards a more radically reformist stance: we may begin to see him as an evangelical. One quirk, parallel to his sexual prudishness in using the vernacular, was his reluctance to translate literally the pagan-sounding divine title '*Deus Optimus Maximus*': on one occasion it awkwardly became 'God, most of power, and most best', but on a second it was more creatively and interestingly Christianized by adding the traditional attributes of the three persons of the Trinity: 'God, that is good, most wisest, and most of power'.[60] A new enthusiasm for an evangelical agenda was suggested by his expansion of '*usque ad evangelii promulgationem*' into 'until such time as the gospel and this happy tidings of Christ was published and openly declared unto them', or the extension of '*tempore gratiae*' into 'the time of grace, that is to say, when the law of grace and of the godspell began'.[61] Much more gratuitous were three apparent attempts to improve on a passage of Thomas Aquinas, in order to emphasize human impotence to do good without the gifts of God's law and word: we must be 'lightened by the law of God', 'lightened with the word of God' before the 'natural motion or inclination . . . to virtue', planted in our soul and reason, can turn to do only that which is 'good and virtuous'. Cranmer twice used the phrase 'lightened with/by the word of God'. Such cavalier improvement on the words of the Angelic Doctor suggests a growing sympathy with the renewed Augustinianism of the evangelicals.[62]

The work which he was also doing on the *Collectanea Satis Copiosa* might well have pushed Cranmer away from his old orthodoxy. Collaborating with Edward Foxe to survey the nature of authority in the Church, Cranmer was dealing with material which, as we have seen in Chapter 2, was of particular concern to him. One of the most important strands of the *Collectanea* was the discussion of councils and conciliar pronouncements on the independence of metropolitan churches, which could be used to justify a pronouncement on the King's marriage within the shores of England. From his old reverence for councils, Cranmer was now being led on to new thoughts about how God's will was expressed in the Church; in the tangled skein of early Church politics, there was a promising clutch of conciliar statements which could be selected to show that not the Roman Pontiff but metropolitan bishops or (later on) monarchs were entrusted with power to rule the Church. Even the first Council of Nicaea (325) could provide ammunition for such an argu-

59 Ibid., pp. 138 ll. 3, 18; 139 ll. 3–4, 29–32 (cf. notes on pp. 351–2).
60 Ibid., pp. 44 l. 5, 45 l. 8; 182 l. 11, 183 ll. 17–18 (cf. notes on pp. 300, 384).
61 Ibid., pp. 50 l. 6, 51 ll. 10–11; 148 l. 15, 149 ll. 29–30 (cf. notes on pp. 305, 356).
62 Ibid., pp. 224 ll. 16–25, 225 ll. 26–34 (cf. notes on p. 414).

ment, let alone such Councils as Carthage in 419 or Toledo in 589, which had had their own reasons for taking a cool view of Roman claims. Add to these various statements by Geoffrey of Monmouth and others about the jurisdiction of early British monarchs, which Cranmer had no reason to treat as anything other than good historical fact, and there were powerful arguments indeed for modifying his earlier opinions about the role of the Bishop of Rome in the Church.[63] A similar conclusion may be drawn from the 1531 editions of the *Disputatio* and *The Glass of Truth*, if indeed Cranmer had a hand in their production. The line which both Cranmer and his King would take, and which nerved them to accelerate the break with Rome in 1533, was an appeal to a General Council of the Church (see below, Ch. 4, pp. 105–6).

Another factor in changing Cranmer's views may have been the personal contacts which he made in 1531 with Continental evangelical reformers, including the man who so influenced him in future years, Martin Bucer of Strassburg. Here once more it was the divorce that was the spur: Henry VIII, despairing of getting any satisfaction from Rome, was turning increasingly to the various breakaway churches and theological institutions of the Empire and Switzerland to see whether they could do any better for him, now that his case had been presented in the public domain by the *Censurae*. The key figure in the contacts was a brilliant Greek scholar and humanist reformer based in Basel, Simon Grynaeus: he was possibly the first prominent foreign evangelical whom Cranmer met.

Grynaeus, a Suabian and a former monk, was already an enthusiast for the nascent evangelical reform movement when at the beginning of the 1520s he was in charge of the marvellous royal library of the doomed kingdom of Hungary at Buda; his subsequent five years at the University of Heidelberg made him impatient with the conservatism of Luther's outlook, and he found much more to admire in the more root-and-branch approach of Andreas Karlstadt. From Heidelberg Grynaeus moved to Basel in 1529, striking up a friendship with Erasmus just as the timorous humanist was making a strategic retreat to Freiburg-im-Breisgau to escape Basel's Reformation; Grynaeus quickly became the right-hand man of Johannes Oecolampadius, and he remained one of the pillars of Basel University up to his death in 1541. A complex man, he was hot-tempered and impetuous, but he clearly also had a charm and a gift for friendship (perhaps also a certain naivety?) which led him to cherish remarkably eclectic contacts made on his 1531 English visit, from Cranmer and Latimer to Cuthbert Tunstall and the circle of Thomas More. How did Grynaeus apparently charm English conservatives, given his enthusiasm for the eucharistic theology of Zwingli and Oecolampadius which apparently he made little effort to hide? He even kept up his contacts with

63 Fox and Guy, pp. 159–61.

8 Simon Grynaeus, portrayed in the frontispiece of his *Elogium* (published by Froschauer, Zürich, 1541).

More in the months after his return from England, in the face of evident worries from other reformers.[64] It is likely that his relationship with More was not nearly as good as he thought: More, then in a desperately vulnerable position as a Lord Chancellor who disagreed with his royal master's most important policies, was showing iron self-control in his courtesy to this honoured official guest. More's private opinions about Grynaeus were probably very different from what he pretended.[65]

From March into early summer 1531, Grynaeus imitated his hero Erasmus by undertaking an extended visit to England: his ostensible reason was to

64 There is no English life of Grynaeus. Useful data will be found in Pollet, *Bucer* 2, pp. 370–461; Pollet, *Bucer* heroically reduced the chaos of the surviving relevant Bucer/Grynaeus correspondence and allied material to a chronological order, letter-numbering items A-U: see Pollet, *Bucer* 2, pp. 460–61 (below, I note Pollet's letter-system in square brackets). On Grynaeus's eucharistic theology, cf. e.g. his letter to Oecolampadius, *Grynaei Epistolae*, p. 33 (Epiphany 1526), and to Zwingli (April 1526), Pollet, *Bucex* 2, p. 372 n. 8; on Grynaeus and More, Pollet, *Bucer* 2, p. 440, Grynaeus's postscript at A.S.T. 157, p. 541, i.e. Pollet, *Bucer* 2, p. 461 [O], and A.S.T. 157 f. 249c [*sic*], i.e. Pollet, *Bucer* 2, p. 461 [T].

65 Cf. Marius, *More*, pp. 391–2.

investigate the contents of English libraries, and indeed he had pestered Erasmus for a sheaf of introductions to old friends (the great humanist provided them grudgingly, and characteristically also gave Grynaeus the task of reminding Archbishop Warham to send on his pension).[66] Grynaeus enjoyed himself both socially and academically, especially in Oxford, but there was another dimension to his stay: the *Censurae* was published during his visit, with a European audience in mind, and Grynaeus was eager to see what capital might be made for the cause of the Reformation out of Henry VIII's marital difficulties. He put himself forward as an intermediary between the King and the world of Continental evangelicalism, and he seems to have been interviewed by the King in person; he left England convinced of the validity of the King's case as presented in the *Censurae*.[67] On his return to Basel in June, charged by the English authorities with gathering opinions for Henry, his enthusiastic reports of the possibilities of evangelical progress in England sparked off an agitated buzz of activity among the major reformers in Switzerland, Wittenberg and Strassburg, as they prepared material which could be construed as helpful for Henry VIII's moral dilemma.

Among the many happy if undiscriminating contacts that Grynaeus made in England, attested by his later effusive dedications of books, was his acquaintance at the Court of Henry VIII with Thomas Cranmer. When in 1534 Grynaeus dedicated his edition of a work by Plutarch to the newly made Archbishop of Canterbury, he spoke of the kindness which Cranmer had shown him, merely as one private scholar to another, three years before.[68] Nor was this warmth newly conjured up by the happy accident of a former casual acquaintance having hit on spectacularly good times: Grynaeus had repeatedly expressed the highest opinion of Cranmer immediately on his return from England in 1531, and one receptive audience for his opinion had been his friend at Strassburg, Martin Bucer.

At the end of July 1531 Grynaeus ebulliently wrote to Bucer from Basel about his English trip. He spoke of the King's genuine agonies of conscience (partly described to him by Thomas More as Lord Chancellor), and of the inevitability that Henry would go ahead with a new marriage regardless of what learned men's opinions were: he stressed the tense political state of England and Henry's moves during the spring against papal power, which made comment by the reformers an urgent matter: 'he has

66 Erasmus, *Opus Epistolarum* 10, pp. 316–17.

67 On the visit generally, see Pollet, *Bucer* 2, pp. 374–6, Bedouelle and Le Gal (eds), '*Divorce*', pp. 289–90; Erasmus, *Opus Epistolarum*, 9 pp. 262–3. For the Lutheran side of the negotiations, see McEntegart Ph.D., 'England and the League of Schmalkalden', pp. 105–6. A reference in a letter from Grynaeus to Bucer of 10 September (now apparently lost, but mentioned in Burnet 1 i, p. 59) definitely suggests a personal interview.

68 *Sitne rationis aliqua in bestiis viis . . . Plutarchi libellus . . . Simone Grynaeo interpreto* (Basel: Johann Bebel, 1534: BL copy Ac. 16778), sig. Aii.

removed all power of the Pope from the realm'. Grynaeus went on to claim that he had contacts with an influential sympathizer in the King's inner circle: since Henry 'also appropriates power in a written book, how easily you might have believed that he could be urged on in his chamber (where he has as intimate servant a most learned man sufficiently of our school), to these changes'.[69] For the moment the situation in England remained too delicate for the certainty of such movement in royal policy; the influential figure at Court also remained unnamed, but he kept recurring in the correspondence over the next few months as Grynaeus frenetically tried to orchestrate a coherent evangelical response to the King's problem. In early September, while preparing the first of what would turn out to be two supplementary missions to England by his servant Thomas, Grynaeus reassured the ministers of Strassburg about sending their interim discussion to Henry, 'because nothing is revealed in public before this King tells one particular man'; in a follow-up letter of the same day, he told them that he had changed tack, and had only sent on his own manuscript, since this particular man was due to be sent to Strassburg 'to understand the matter from you in person'.[70] Bucer was still anticipating this visit of 'an important man, suitable for the purpose' when he wrote to Grynaeus on 9 October.[71] Then in the course of a hectoring and unhappy letter to Bucer on 21 October 1531, for the first time Grynaeus quite casually names the mysterious figure: 'Cronmarus'.[72]

Cranmer was by now the key man in the negotiations, as far as Grynaeus was concerned. He confidently and eagerly anticipated Cranmer's mission abroad, which had apparently been discussed already when Grynaeus was in England; he himself had vehemently encouraged a mission by this trustworthy man, rather than leaving the English to place faith simply in his own words. Grynaeus had also sent over to Cranmer news of the unpromising pronouncements of Luther and Melanchthon by 'that man of Cologne' (possibly a coded reference to the Lutheran envoy, the disguised English ex-friar

69 '*regno ditionem papae omnem exclusit. Scripto etiam libro potestatem abrogat, in suo cubiculo, qua a nobis sat hominem doctissimum familiarem sibi habet, in istis momentis quam facile impelli posse credis{s}es*': A.S.T. 157, pp. 617–19; Pollet, *Bucer* 2, p. 460 [A]; Bedouelle and Le Gal (eds), '*Divorce*', p. 294 wrongly implies that the letter was addressed to all the ministers of Strassburg.

70 A.S.T. 157, p. 611: Pollet, *Bucer* 2, p. 460 [I]: '*Nihil enim in lucem quidquam edetur, priusquam hic virum certum res sibi habet*'; A.S.T. 157 f. 255b: Pollet, *Bucer* 2, p. 460 [J]: '*qui presens e vobis rem cognoscat*'.

71 A.S.T. 151, p. 119; Pollet, *Bucer* 2, p. 461 [N]: '*virum gravem et huic rei idoneum*'.

72 A.S.T. 157, pp. 515–17; Pollet, *Bucer* 2, p. 461 [P]. Passages relevant to following paragraph: '*Tamen spero priusquam quicquam {Rex} respondebit, mittet huc Cronmarum, sic enim consului ego, immo hortatus sum omnes ne verbis meis haberent fidem, sed dignum fide virum mitterent . . .*'; '*Scripsi enim ego per illum ipsum Coloniensem, ad Cronmarum, Lutherum et Philippum, divortium nullo pacto concedere . . .*'; '*Proinde tuum erit officium etiam atque etiam dispicere, quid simus responsuri cum illi venient, nam venturos esse certo scio, nisi fortasse tuo scripto aut meo ad Cronmarum ultimo res impedietur.*'

9 Grynaeus writes to Bucer on 21 October 1531, for the first time naming Cranmer. The bulk of the letter is in a clerk's hand, with added material written by Grynaeus himself.

Robert Barnes).[73] Moreover, by 21 October, Bucer had taken the first step in the correspondence with Cranmer that would bear much fruit later: Grynaeus was worried in case 'your or my last writing' to Cranmer might have complicated progress.

However, there were to be worse troubles than this for Grynaeus's plans. From the beginning, opinions had differed about the success of his English mission. Oecolampadius congratulated Grynaeus in July 1531 on how well he had done, but Erasmus was furious that Grynaeus used his visit to promote the evangelical cause, and a permanent rift between the two scholars developed: no doubt the doyen of humanists was worried that his own reputation in England was threatened by Grynaeus's undiplomatic enthusiasm, endangering the links with English friends which had taken more than three decades to build up.[74] Worse still than the impression which Grynaeus must have left with some conservatives in England, was the fragmented and unsatisfactory response from the leaders of the Continental Reformations; Henry's hopes had been raised in vain about the Aragon annulment.

From the moment that the King's Great Matter had become public knowledge, Luther had been sympathetic to the plight of Catherine of Aragon, whose treatment confirmed his already low opinion of Henry VIII. This, combined with his deep antipathy to divorce in general, made him advocate the drastic course of bigamy for the King. Melanchthon bizarrely added the suggestion that Henry should legitimize his bigamy with a papal dispensation – an object lesson in the fluidity of confessional lines in the early Reformation![75] These were the Lutheran responses which Robert Barnes presented to the King in December 1531. The Swiss leaders Zwingli and Oecolampadius were more sympathetic to Henry's theological arguments, but alas for themselves and for any immediate links between England and Switzerland, Zürich's military disaster of autumn 1531 left Zwingli a corpse on the battlefield of Kappel and Oecolampadius a broken man, terminally ill. Bucer, ever the mediator and a lover of nuanced (some might say chameleon-like) arguments, was at first inclined to think Henry's first marriage null and void like the Swiss, but he moved towards the Lutherans' position once he had seen their documents, much to Grynaeus's annoyance. In a letter

73 Barnes left Wittenberg with a letter of Luther's at the beginning of September 1531 (Bedouelle and Le Gal (eds), *'Divorce'*, p. 292), and it seems strange if two missions involving Wittenberg were going on in parallel with no mention of each other. Barnes dressed as a merchant on his English visit; previously in October Grynaeus referred to *'civis Coloniensis mercator'* – A.S.T. 157, p. 540, Pollet, *Bucer* 2, p. 461 [O]. However, Grynaeus could equally well be referring to the Cologne-born merchant Christoff Mont, who entered Cromwell's service in 1530–31: McEntegart Ph.D., 'England and the League of Schmalkalden', pp. 57–8.

74 Erasmus, *Opus Epistolarum* 10, pp. 316–17; Pollet, *Bucer* 2, pp. 375–6, 442 n. 1.

75 Cf. McEntegart Ph.D., 'England and the League of Schmalkalden', pp. 113–14.

to Grynaeus of 30 December 1531, Bucer and his Strassburg colleagues finally came out as rejecting the arguments of the *Censurae*, but in the course of a dissertation of sadistically Bucerian prolixity, they added in pragmatic fashion that what mattered was what the magistrate felt politic: Henry should get what he wanted, as long as he did not humiliate the blameless Catherine.[76]

This was no answer fit for the King's righteous agonies of conscience. Henry, scandalized at the monstrousness of bigamy, was no more sympathetic to reformers suggesting it in 1531 than when in desperation the Pope had raised the same idea the previous year, and Barnes's mission to the English Court in December got a boisterously hostile reception.[77] Grynaeus was appalled when he read the Strassburg document in January 1532, correctly anticipating that it would only make things worse in England, and he expressed his feelings forcibly to Bucer.[78] All Grynaeus's efforts, indeed the four separate English missions which he, his servant and Robert Barnes had undertaken throughout 1531, had produced no useful result either for the Great Matter or for the evangelical cause. Yet Grynaeus had created a link between Thomas Cranmer and the reformers of Strassburg which would never be broken. Right up to 1547, Martin Bucer was the Continental figure most consistently sympathetic with the problems of Henrician England, and he was repeatedly instrumental in pursuing alliances with Henry when all fellow-reformers despaired of the murderously eccentric monarch. The Strassburg connnection provided another enduring relationship for Cranmer; among Grynaeus's other correspondents was a cultivated and enthusiastically evangelical Dutch printer based in Strassburg, Reyner Wolfe. Cranmer was probably responsible for bringing Wolfe to England once he became Archbishop. Wolfe played a major role both in acting as an English agent abroad during Henry's reign and in printing Cranmer's books under Edward VI; he also proved a true friend to Cranmer and his family in their time of disaster under Mary.[79]

Thanks to Grynaeus, too, the Swiss reformers had established a personal tie with Cranmer, which they began exploiting in the mid-1530s. In August

76 A.S.T. 151 pp. 153–8; Pollet, *Bucer* 2 p. 461 [S], and cf. Pollet, *Bucer* 2 pp. 454–5. The whole negotiations of the Reformers with Henry are summarized in Bedouelle and Le Gal (eds), '*Divorce*', pp. 289–97, based on the definitive longer account in Pollet, *Bucer* 2, pp. 439–61. Cf. also McEntegart Ph.D., 'England and the League of Schmalkalden', pp. 105–6.

77 For the papal suggestion of September 1530, *L.P.* 4 iii, no. 6627. On the debacle of Barnes's mission, cf. *C.S.P. Spanish 1531–33*, no. 888, p. 367, with Grynaeus's interestingly similar comments on the '*nebulones*' at Court who had treated learned opinions '*tam inhumane et maligne*': A.S.T. 157 f. 249c; Pollet, *Bucer* 2. p. 461 [T]. Cf. also n. 84 below, on Gardiner.

78 Pollet, *Bucer* 2 p. 461 [T], as above.

79 On Grynaeus and Wolfe, Erasmus, *Opus Epistolarum* 11, p. 72; Pollet, *Bucer* 2, p. 376 n. 2. On Wolfe and Cranmer's family, see below, Ch. 14.

1533 Grynaeus enquired of Bucer who had succeeded Warham as Archbishop of Canterbury, and one can imagine his delight at the news that it was Cranmer; the result was his 1534 Plutarch dedication to the new Archbishop, and it cannot be coincidence that at the same time Grynaeus's publisher, Johann Bebel, also sent Cranmer a presentation copy of Polydore Vergil's *Anglica Historia*.[80] Erasmus even reported in November 1533 that Grynaeus was trying to get a pension out of Cranmer, something which horrified the aged humanist, since he had come to regard Grynaeus as a dangerous evangelical loudmouth, while still fondly believing that the Archbishop was sound in religious matters.[81] Even though Cranmer viewed askance the eucharistic views of the Swiss until the very end of Henry VIII's reign, in the end their influence, mediated through Bucer, turned his thought away from Lutheran modes of theological discourse, and these views permanently marked the character of the Church of England.

Yet one must not anticipate Cranmer's future spiritual odyssey. What happened in 1531–2 was an initial contact, through a Basel humanist reformer who was capable during 1533–34 of simultaneously dedicating his books to Cranmer, Bishop Tunstall, the son of Sir Thomas More and the conservative Oxford don John Claymond.[82] Cranmer's position before he became Archbishop can be measured by considering his colleague and rival Stephen Gardiner: always a useful relationship to watch throughout their parallel careers. Cranmer's preferment was by this time rapidly catching up with Gardiner's. Indeed, it was shadowing it in a significant way. Gardiner was Archdeacon of Worcester and had been Rector of St Michael's, Gloucester, under Bishop Ghinucci; Ghinucci had given Cranmer the Worcestershire rectory of Bredon.[83] Hardly surprisingly, Henry's permanent representative in Rome was a ready source of favours for the close-knit team of experts working on Henry's divorce. In September 1531, Gardiner won the richest royal reward yet among the divorce team, for his business as royal secretary: the Bishopric of Winchester, which took him out of Ghinucci's patronage to a position of equality with him. That meant that besides his Archdeaconry of Worcester, Gardiner relinquished his other Archdeaconry of Taunton, and his successor as Archdeacon of Taunton was Dr Cranmer. Is it too far-fetched to suppose that the appointment was on the recommendation of the previous incumbent? It was, after all, Gardiner who had brought Cranmer to the King's attention in 1529.

For until 1531, there is nothing to make us suppose that the theological opinions of Thomas Cranmer and Stephen Gardiner were notably out of step.

80 On Grynaeus's letter, 18 August 1533, Pollet, *Bucer* 2 p. 376. The Polydore Vergil is now in C.U.L: cf. *Work of Cranmer*, ed. Duffield, p. 362.

81 Erasmus, *Opus Epistolarum* 10, p. 317 (18 November 1533).

82 Grynaeus's dedications are conveniently summarized in *Grynaei Epistolae* pp. 59–61.

83 For a convenient summary of Gardiner's preferment, see Emden, *Oxford to 1540*, p. 227.

There had been nothing to suggest specifically Lutheran or even general evangelical sympathies in Cranmer at the time of his fateful meeting with Gardiner in August 1529. His patronage by the evangelical Boleyn circle could initially have meant nothing more than gratitude to a learned academic dogsbody who quickly proved his effectiveness. Cranmer and Gardiner were apparently both conservative-minded Cambridge humanists, who cheerfully accepted patronage from Italian bishops, but who had little respect for the practical reality of the papal office while the Pope sought to obstruct their royal master's wishes. Both had, at their own pace, discovered the opportunity for fame and fortune opened up by Henry VIII in his eccentric strategy for gaining a marriage annulment. Curiously enough, Gardiner himself gives us a glimpse of the two men together at Hampton Court precisely at this period, December 1531, during Robert Barnes's mission from Martin Luther; Gardiner recalled the occasion long afterwards in a pamphlet against George Joye in November 1545. The newly consecrated Bishop of Winchester happened to come face to face with Barnes at Court and seized the chance to embarrass and frighten him by referring to Barnes's unfair attack on him in print: unfortunately, Gardiner only recalls Cranmer's presence at the encounter, and not his reaction.[84]

One need not suppose that Cranmer felt any particular warmth for Barnes the Lutheran renegade friar, his Cambridge contemporary. Since Luther himself and most Lutherans (notably including their most celebrated English-born sympathizer, William Tyndale) were opposed to the divorce, there was little incentive for any member of the divorce team to feel well-disposed to Lutheran ideas; even the evangelical Grynaeus found Luther's high moral tone about the King's Great Matter hard to cope with.[85] Cranmer, with memories of his first unfortunate encounters with Luther's works, may have found the humanist Grynaeus, and the Swiss Reformation which he represented, a more attractive initial introduction to what was going on in central Europe than an encounter with a Lutheran. One much later and perhaps dubious piece of evidence from a hostile witness may reinforce this picture of a conservative don who was becoming cautiously interested in some varieties of Continental reform, but who was not as yet definitely associated with it. Dr Cranmer, on the eve of his appointment as Archbishop, is pictured as to outward appearances a thoroughly traditional cleric: the speaker is Bishop Brooks, the judge at Cranmer's trial in 1555. 'Who was thought as then more devout? who was more religious in the face of the world? who was thought to have more conscience of a vow-making, and observing the order of the church, more

84 *Gardiner's Letters*, pp. 166–7.

85 Cf. Richard Croke's remarks on Lutheran hostility to the divorce in his letter to Henry VIII, B.L. Cotton MS Vitellius B XIII f. 91, pr. Burnet 1 pt. ii, pp. 128–9 (Bk. 2, no. 33; *L.P.* 4 iii no. 6491); or Robert Wakefield's hostile remarks about Luther in a sermon of 1534 – Rex, 'Luther', pp. 91–2.

earnest in the defence of the real presence of Christ's body and blood in the sacrament of the altar, than ye were?'[86]

During 1532, Cranmer indeed went on his long-planned mission, but after the disappointments provided by the reformers, the official emphasis was changed: he was to address himself principally to the Holy Roman Emperor. Cranmer was to replace Sir Thomas Elyot as ambassador to the Emperor, since Henry VIII considered Elyot unsound on the question of the divorce – with good reason, since Richard Rex convincingly suggests that Elyot can be credited with the authorship of a major attack on the *Censurae* which was produced with startling speed in May 1531.[87] On his mission, Cranmer was left with plenty of time abroad in which to acquaint himself better at first hand with the Continental Reformation, and it was at this time that he and Gardiner definitely parted ideological company. In 1532, both men made decisions which could have ruined their careers, and which thus for the first time revealed them as having religious convictions not coincident with convenience. These decisions also took them in precisely opposite directions. During spring 1532, Stephen Gardiner boldly and unexpectedly, if eventually in vain, led the defence of the Church's liberties against Henry VIII, a rash stand which probably cost him his chance of becoming Archbishop of Canterbury, and which left permanent doubts in the King's mind about his trustworthiness. That spring was the moment that the arch-opponent of further reform in the English Church, John Foxe's arch-villain 'Wily Winchester', was born.[88] By contrast, during summer 1532, Cranmer did something even more crazy than Gardiner; he got married. What happened?

Cranmer was already out of England by the time that the parliamentary row over the Supplication against the Ordinaries heralded the assault on church liberties in which Gardiner played such a leading part. He was sent to central Europe at the end of January 1532, taking with him a chaplain who unfortunately cannot be identified, although we know Cranmer retained him in later years; perhaps it was John Whitwell, but Nicholas Heath is another possibility.[89] We can reconstruct something of their route from a highly informative letter of 14 March 1532 from Sir Thomas Elyot to the Duke of Norfolk; Elyot, forced in the interests of royal diplomacy to swallow whatever

86 Foxe 8, p. 46.

87 Fox and Guy, *Reassessing the Henrician Age*, pp. 46, 59–63. Rex, *Theology of Fisher*, pp. 179, 266, and cf. Bedouelle and Le Gal (eds), '*Divorce*', pp. 383–6: this was the work *Non esse . . . prohibitum . . . adversus aliquot academiarum censuras . . . Apologia sive Confutatio.*

88 For Gardiner's clash with Henry during 1532, see MacCulloch, 'Two Dons in Politics', pp. 19–20.

89 There are two references to Cranmer's chaplain, both in relation to a meeting with Johannes Cochlaeus at Regensburg: *Scopa Joannis Cochlaei Germani, in Aranea Ricardi Morysini* (Leipzig, 1538), sig. Gii, and Cranmer's letter to Henry VIII, Pocock 2 p. 506, B.L. Cotton MS Vitellius B XIV 41, 43 (undated, but probably 1538, arising from this book of Cochlaeus, although LP 8, no. 1126 dates it to 1535).

resentment he felt towards his successor, travelled with Cranmer in the wake of the Emperor up from the Low Countries.[90] The envoys travelled down the Rhine to Worms and Speyer, from where they could travel due east, to reach the free Imperial city of Nuremberg in early March; by 14 March they had made the comparatively short journey from there to Regensburg (Ratisbon) to try to address themselves to Charles V. At Lutheran Nuremberg, for the first time Cranmer had a chance to see for himself at leisure the effects of the Reformation launched by the man who had so aroused his indignation a few years before; and he returned for an extended stay later in the year, since the Imperial Diet moved its deliberations there from Regensburg during the summer.

Nuremberg was the largest city of the Empire after Cologne and Erfurt, and it was one of the first to show official support for Luther, as early as 1521. Thereafter the city's leading men guided the pace of religious change, keeping a wary eye on both the Emperor and neighbouring territorial princes in order to safeguard the city's independence; their caution paid off, and Nuremberg in time 'became the vanguard of the Lutheran Reformation in the southern German area'.[91] With this guidance from the city's traditional hierarchy, change was kept within strict bounds, and expressions of sympathy with the eucharistic views of Zwingli and the Swiss were discouraged with as much firmness as Luther himself could have hoped for. The order and prosperity of the city much impressed Sir Thomas Elyot, despite his principled distaste for Lutheranism; at least it was a welcome contrast with what he regarded as contemptible anarchy in Lutheran reformations at Worms and Speyer. He described in some detail the fairly conservative liturgical arrangements which the Church in Nuremberg had developed for its revised mass, and he revealed that already Dr Cranmer was showing keen interest in these experiments: Cranmer had been using his Latin on some local worthy who was knowledgeable about the Nuremberg lectionary, and he had discovered 'that in the Epistles and Gospels they kept not the order that we do, but do peruse every day one chapter of the New Testament'.

One wonders whether Cranmer was already on this first visit talking to the preacher of the church of St Lorenz, and the leading architect of Nuremberg's religious revisions, Andreas Osiander. Over the next few months the two scholars became firm friends, and indeed Osiander was later to testify that it was Cranmer who cured the severe case of writer's block from which he had been suffering. During the 1520s Osiander had embarked on an ambitious project of pioneering scholarship, a harmony of the four Gospels, but he had despaired of finishing this huge and uncharted task. After Cranmer's arrival, the ambassador had several times invited him to the '*colloquium*' (by which

90 Elyot to Duke of Norfolk, 14 March 1532, B.L. Cotton MS Vitellius B XXI, ff. 58–9, pr. *Records of the Reformation* 2, pp. 228–30, although the writer is there wrongly identified as Augustin (cf. *L.P.* 5, no. 869). For Elyot's later feelings about Cranmer, see Ch. 4.

91 See Seebass, 'Imperial City of Nuremberg', *passim*, and p. 119.

Osiander presumably meant meetings of the Imperial Diet), and also frequently visited him at home amid his researches. It was there, during their theological discussions, that the unfinished harmony happened to appear, and Cranmer forcefully urged him to resume it, 'for it would be not only of use but indeed of ornament to the Church of Christ'. All this was recorded in the long and affectionate introduction (including, interestingly, praise of Cranmer's excellence of pedigree!) which Osiander wrote in triumph for the finished *Harmonia Evangelica* in January 1537.[92] Also during 1532, Osiander was preparing a catechism for his city, which became the basis of the catechism published in English under Cranmer's patronage much later, in 1548 (with unfortunate consequences, as will be described below; see Ch. 9).

It is noticeable that Osiander was the only major Lutheran commentator to pronounce in favour of Henry VIII's theological arguments for his annulment, although the cautious Nuremberg authorities attempted to placate the Emperor by banning the book in which he announced his opinion.[93] Very little of the correspondence between him and Cranmer has survived, but we know that as late as 1540 they were in regular contact. At Christmas 1540 the Archbishop sent a brief note of greetings to Nuremberg, but only three days later he used a moment of holiday leisure to settle down to pen a much longer and less irenic letter candidly reproaching Osiander and his fellow-Lutheran divines for collaborating with the notorious bigamous marriage of Landgraf Philipp of Hesse.[94] Thereafter, perhaps as a result of this letter, relations may have cooled. Osiander was not among those reformers who chose to take refuge in England from Charles V's Interim in 1548; instead he took the road north to Königsberg. Thereafter, his increasingly eccentric views on the theology of justification, which earned him widely based condemnation in Germany and Switzerland, would have been an additional reason for Cranmer keeping his distance. In the summer of 1552 Osiander finally did try to come to England, and Philipp Melanchthon told a friend with discreet glee that he had suffered a rebuff. This was a significant snub at a time when Cranmer was trying to gather Continent-wide support for an international Council to outface the work of Trent.[95]

Osiander's treatment in 1552 was all the more remarkable because, from 1532, Cranmer had a permanent personal debt to Osiander which far outweighed his own role as literary catalyst for the Nuremberg pastor. In his 14

92 Osiander, *Gesamtausgabe* 6, pp. 239–48, especially p. 246, 248. Cf. also Basil Hall's commentary in Ayris and Selwyn (eds), *Cranmer*, pp. 20–21, and Melanchthon's testimony to the friendship, *L.P.* 10 no. 289.

93 Ridley, *Cranmer*, p. 42, and cf. *Records of the Reformation* 2, pp. 483–6, *L.P.* 13 i no. 140.

94 Cox 2, pp. 404–8 (*L.P.* 17, no. 357).

95 *Melanchthons Briefwechsel* 6, no. 6529. On Osiander's later career and controversy, see Cameron, *European Reformation* p. 365, and on Cranmer's ecumenism, Chs 11 and 12 below.

March letter to Norfolk, Elyot pronounced himself particularly impressed by the Nuremberg Lutheran clergy's wives, whom he said 'were the fairest women of the town'. Likewise, Cranmer's interest in his new surroundings was not confined to the revised lectionary; the abolition of compulsory clerical celibacy was clearly on his mind as well. At some stage during an eventful but otherwise unproductive summer of diplomacy, probably in July, came his marriage to Margarete, the niece of Osiander's wife Katharina Preu; reportedly Osiander himself officiated. Much remains mysterious about the marriage; we know that Katharina Preu was the daughter of the brewer Heinrich Preu and Margarete his wife, née Hetzel, but we cannot be sure whether Cranmer's wife was the daughter of a sister or brother of Katharina, so the younger Margarete's maiden name remains uncertain.[96]

The experience of Lutheran Nuremberg, or indeed the future Mrs Margaret Cranmer, must have made a profound impression on Dr Cranmer for him to take this drastic step; his careful scholarship in the *Collectanea* and *Determinations* was a world away from this uncharacteristic boldness. He had, of course, married once before, but this time the stakes were much higher: at Nuremberg he set aside his priestly vow of celibacy. Perhaps his work on the *Collectanea* and the other works of propaganda on the royal supremacy helped him to square his conscience with an untidy *cuius regio eius religio* justification of what he had done: the customs of the province where he found himself justified clerical marriage, so he was entitled to take advantage of the situation.[97] At the risk of being mocked for amateur psychologizing, one might also speculate that it was actually the memory of the earlier tragedy of Joan's death and an attempt to deal with the unresolved grief of his first marriage which made him act so hastily now. Whatever Cranmer's rationalization of his marriage, his second embassy marks a watershed in his thinking.

We can reconstruct some of the very varied contacts which Cranmer made in central Europe during these adventures. As a fully fledged ambassador, he had the financial resources (or at least the credit – the English government was inclined to be stingy) to begin acquiring humanist scholars as clients; they would be useful in after years for the King to gather information from central Europe. One who later recorded that he had been recruited by Cranmer at Vienna, in the latter part of his mission in October 1532, was

96 The main evidence for the marriage is somewhat unsatisfactory, being brief accusatory statements at his trial in 1555: Cox 2, pp. 550, 557. Cranmer was in Nuremberg during July: Ridley, p. 41. He was back in Regensburg by 17 August: *St.P.* 7, p. 378. For some details of Osiander's marriages and children, see Osiander, *Gesamtausgabe* 2, p. 174 and 3, p. 450n. I am grateful to Professor Dr Gottfried Seebass for his help in correspondence about the marriage.

97 Cf. John Rogers later making use of this argument to Mary's Privy Council: Foxe 6, p. 596.

Jacobus Gislenus Thalassius, who kept in touch with successive English envoys and also monitored useful literature and translated German texts for Cranmer.[98] Among his equals in diplomatic status, Cranmer worked happily with the French ambassador, whose strategic interests England then shared.[99] He was also able to renew the friendship begun in Spain with the Polish ambassador, Johannes Dantiscus. The bond between them remained close enough for Cranmer to take on the long-term support and education of a Polish youth recommended to him by Dantiscus, and the two men argued in a friendly way about papal authority, which clearly by then Cranmer, the priest with a wife, thought to be of little value. They would correspond from time to time through the 1530s, until their religious differences became too painful for further contact.[100]

Moreover, Dantiscus seems to have known about Mrs Cranmer. Eight years later, and after a long interval, Cranmer took it into his head to write to Dantiscus, now a pillar of the Polish episcopate. It was a peculiarly dangerous and inappropriate moment to choose, at the height of the crisis over the Six Articles in June 1540. The pretext was the future of Cranmer's young Polish protégé, now ready to take his place in the world after a lavishly funded education in England and Paris, but perhaps the Archbishop was trying to divert himself from the dire circumstances in which he now found himself by recalling happy past times. If so, Dantiscus's aggressively traditionalist reply was a suitable penalty for his rashness, and out of sheer self-preservation, Cranmer hastened to reveal the letter to the King. What was particularly alarming in September 1540 in the wake of the summer's disaster for the evangelical cause and Thomas Cromwell's execution was Dantiscus's none-too-subtle enquiry about the state of clerical celibacy in England – was Cranmer leading a single life like the Apostle Paul? 'With us [Polish clergy] nothing is more pleasant and delightful than a celibate bed. I must have a joke; for while I write this I fancy that I am conversing with you, either at the table, as was our habit, or in the boat on the Danube, to which in former years you have so kindly escorted me when I was leaving Ratisbon.'[101] It was a joke which would have a sour ring in Lambeth Palace that autumn.

98 Cf. *L.P.* 13 i nos 1514–15: no. 1515 may be of 1540, since it talks of Cranmer sustaining Thalassius in Germany for eight years. On a complaint by Nicholas Hawkins about the lack of suitable silver plate on embassy, see *St.P.* 7, p. 407.

99 *St.P.* 7, p. 391.

100 Cf. the letter of 15 October 1536, calendared in fragmentary form but misdated to 1533 in *L.P.* 6, no. 1292. The full text is to be found in Uppsala, Universitetsbiblioteket MS H. 155 ff. 208–10: Ryle, 'Joannes Dantiscus and Thomas Cranmer'.

101 Cranmer's letter to Dantiscus is Uppsala, Universitetsbiblioteket MS H. 155, ff. 30r–31v, cited in Ryle, 'Joannes Dantiscus and Thomas Cranmer'. Dantiscus's reply is Cox 2, pp. 401–4. The 1536 letter (see previous note) also recalls Cranmer escorting him to the Danube.

Cranmer argued with other prominent figures about the annulment during his mission to the Emperor. The anonymous biographer tells us that Cranmer convinced Charles V's eccentric but immensely learned historiographer, Cornelius Agrippa von Nettesheim, that the royal marriage was null, although Agrippa, already under a cloud for his studies of the occult, was not prepared to court further trouble by committing himself in public.[102] By contrast, the Emperor's Lord Privy Seal, Nicolas Perrenot, Sieur de Granvelle, whom Cranmer would have first met in Spain and with whom he conducted most of his Imperial negotiations at the Imperial Court, made the remarkable statement three years later that 'when [Cranmer] was at the Imperial Court he greatly blamed that King's and his ministers' proceedings in the matter of the divorce'. Although such a surprising confession is likely to be true simply because of its unexpectedness, it is difficult to assess what Cranmer was up to. It could merely be one pirouette in his months of spinning out his talks with the Imperial authorities; it might equally well be an instance of Cranmer's habitual balancing of arguments taken to the point of reckless indiscretion, perhaps (as Jasper Ridley suggests) under the influence of expressions of disapproval of the King by German Lutherans.[103]

Unlike Cranmer's experience on the expedition to Rome, the divorce was only one concern in an embassy to Europe's greatest power. There was, for instance, the renewal of a commercial treaty to cover trade between England and the Low Countries – unfamiliar business for a theologian – which the awesome complication of Imperial administration forced the English to pursue from the Imperial government in Brussels to the Emperor in central Europe and back again.[104] However important the English may have considered this, it was a secondary matter for Charles V; his most urgent worry was the threat of Turkish invasion in the wake of the Turks' successful destruction of the kingdom of Hungary. An accommodation with his Lutheran princes was therefore a pressing necessity, and financial help from Henry VIII was highly desirable. Cranmer's role in this was to keep the Emperor's hopes up while avoiding committing Henry to any expense, and simultaneously encouraging the Lutherans in their increasing self-assertion against Charles: in collaboration with the French ambassador, and also with the separate English mission to the Lutherans under the control of William Paget, Cranmer had to do his best to delay a settlement between the two sides in an effort to win some advantage for England, preferably that the Lutherans pressurize the Emperor into changing his mind about the annulment.

Cranmer had five days of discussions at Nuremberg during July with Lutherans, including Johann Friedrich, the son of the Duke of Saxony, but

102 *Narratives of the Reformation*, p. 221.

103 *C.S.P. Spanish 1534–5*, no. 207, p. 544; cf. Ridley, *Cranmer*, pp. 43–5.

104 H.M.C. *Hatfield* 1 p. 8; Cox 2, p. 231.

they produced little result. Instead, the growing reality of the Turkish threat concentrated the minds of the Germans sufficiently for the Emperor to patch up a religious peace by the beginning of August; at last Charles was able to set out east along the Danube for Vienna.[105] It was on 28 August 1532, just as the Emperor was in a flurry of preparations to leave his headquarters at Abbach a little upstream from Regensburg, that Cranmer finally conveyed the King's blandly negative response to an Imperial request for English help against the Turk which had been made as long ago as April; Charles was furious, and it was probably a deliberate if pardonable act of spite that he made Cranmer follow him down the Danube to Linz to wait for an angry and disappointed reply.[106] Cranmer then trailed on uncomfortably in the chaotic wake of the Imperial armies; Archbishop Parker tells us that he left Mrs Cranmer in Nuremberg (as any sensible man would), until he could get back to England.[107] During October he described his squalid helter-skelter pursuit of the Emperor from Vienna to the Italian border in two successive letters, the second of which survives as a vivid testament to the horrors caused by demoralized unpaid armies and the looting, destruction and disease which they brought to whole provinces. Cranmer turned to cipher to express a low opinion of Charles, whom he saw as having produced little for all his great plans against the Turks, and he predicted rebellion against the Emperor's brother King Ferdinand. It was a revealingly frank letter from Henry's trusted servant; and on his arrival in the relative tranquillity of Italy, Cranmer learned just what that trust might imply.

Cranmer was still writing on 20 October as if he expected a long embassy following the Emperor. Anticipating more dangers on his route, he thanked God for his safety so far: 'he that conducted me safely hither, I trust he will likewise conduct me into Italy and Spain, and after to England again.'[108] However, on 22 August, far away in a country house near Canterbury, Archbishop Warham had finally died. Henry considered his various clerical servants as possible successors, and came up with a choice which made sense both to him and to the Boleyns, but to few others: Archdeacon Cranmer. The royal letter telling Cranmer of the choice, with an order to return, presumably accompanied the new ambassador Nicholas Hawkins's letters of credence to King Ferdinand dated 1 October 1532; certainly the news of his recall was made public that day, but it can only have been in the very last days of October or the beginning of November that Cranmer heard this news as he arrived with

105 McEntegart Ph.D., 'England and the League of Schmalkalden', p. 48 and n., quoting papers in the Thüringisches Staatsarchiv Weimar; Ridley, *Cranmer*, pp. 40–42; Brandi, *Charles V*, pp. 326–8. A later reference to Cranmer's discussions is at P.R.O., S.P. 1/130 f. 201 (*L.P.* 13 i 648).

106 Cf. Cox 2, pp. 231–2, Cranmer's memorandum of 28 August (*C.S.P. Spanish 1531–3*, no. 987), and Charles's response, *L.P.* 5 no. 1277. Cranmer sent this to Henry on 2 October: Cox 2, p. 233.

107 Parker, *De Antiquitate*, p. 388.

108 Cox 2, pp. 232–6, corrected from B.L. Cotton MS Vitellius B XXI f. 89.

the Emperor at Mantua.[109] On 16 November he and Hawkins were received for their change of credentials by the Emperor, who gave Cranmer the usual gracious commendation home, and he left Mantua on 19 November.[110]

Much later, at his trial in September 1555, Cranmer gave two versions of his summons home by the King, which at first sight do not tally. One was that he had prolonged his journey home by seven weeks: that fits well with receipt of the summons in early November and arrival back in England at the beginning of January. However, later in the same 1555 exchanges, Cranmer, reminiscing at greater length, suggested a six-month interval from a first initiative:

> at such time Archbishop Warham died, he was ambassador in Germany for the King, who sent for him thereupon home; and having intelligence by some of his friends who were near about the King, how he meant to bestow the same bishopric upon him, and therefore counselled him in that case to make haste home, he, feeling in himself a great inability to such a promotion, and very sorry to leave his study, and considering by what means he must have it, which was clean against his conscience . . . devised an excuse to the King of matter of great importance, for the which his longer absence, that the King would have bestowed it upon some other, and so remained there, by that device, one half year after the King had written for him to come home. But after that no such matter fell out, as he seemed to make suspicion of, the King sent for him again . . .[111]

This sounds strange, since less than half a year elapsed even between Warham's death and Cranmer's return, let alone the possibility of conveying the news out to Germany. One might dismiss the discrepancy simply as the result of confusion: the aged Archbishop was being pressured to reply about distant events in the most unfavourable possible circumstances. However, he may have been correct about this crucial sequence in his life. Henry VIII may have begun his moves to get Cranmer back home before Warham's death; it was obvious during summer 1532 that there was little time left for Warham, an old and broken man who had failed to screw up his courage and play the role of Thomas Becket in the face of royal attack on the independence of the English provinces of the Church. If so, and the summons came during the summer, Cranmer would have had plenty of legitimate excuses to prolong his stay at Regensburg and Nuremberg before it became clear that his negotiations with the Lutheran princes were going to produce little immediate

109 *Records of the Reformation* 2, 327 (*L.P.* 6 no. 1380); cf. Chapuys's knowledge of the recall, *C.S.P. Spanish 1531–3*, no. 1003, also of 1 Oct 32, pp. 529–30, and Ridley, *Cranmer*, p. 49.

110 *St.P.* 7, pp. 386–90; Imperial commendation, 18 November is P.R.O., S.P. 1/72 f. 32 (*L.P.* 5 no. 1551). Cf. the receipt of 19 November from Hawkins to Cranmer for embassy plate, *H.M.C., 7th Report*, p. 601.

111 Foxe 8, pp. 55, 65.

result; we ought therefore to read his letters to the King in September and October with the possibility in mind that he was deliberately stalling on a first command to come home.

Either way, Cranmer did not hurry back. His delay was not excessive; his successor Hawkins had taken some pride in taking just over six weeks to get from Greenwich to Mantua via Germany. However, Stephen Vaughan, Cranmer's companion in the journey home from Lyon in early December, testified that the former envoy was taking his time, being 'disposed to make small journeys'.[112] Since Cranmer had launched out on the uncharted waters of clerical matrimony in Germany, it was no doubt an unpleasant shock for him to receive Henry VIII's command that he take up the highest office in the English Church; his bewilderment at his predicament would amply account for his slow and reluctant journey home. Of course, there was more to his reluctance than the existence of Mrs Cranmer. Cranmer's own accounts of his recall, examined above, are naturally conditioned by the circumstances which gave rise to them in 1555. Although we have no reason to doubt his sincerity in what he then said, we should not look to it for a complete account of his feelings in 1532. By 1555, Cranmer's concern was to prove his consistency against charges that he had betrayed his oaths to the Pope, and so when he spoke of his reluctance to become Archbishop, he chose to highlight his scruples against receiving papal institution and induction. There is nothing implausible in his having had such scruples in 1532; the assistant editor of the *Collectanea* would have been quick to recognize the irony of his new prospects. However, his married state gave him something more immediate to worry about than papal power.

In 1532 both Cranmer and Stephen Gardiner stepped up to the brink of behaviour unacceptable for clergy in Henry VIII's eyes; yet both of them squared their consciences enough to draw back, and then go forward in their own time as major players in the politics of the new order of 1533. Gardiner exploited the King's reliance on his legal expertise to escape the consequences of his defiance over Church liberties, and he sealed his adherence to the King's cause in 1535 by writing *De Vera Obedientia*. Cranmer said goodbye to his researches, kept quiet about his German wife, and accepted the fairly dubious procedural fudges of his scruples about papal authority concocted by the King's civil lawyers; he would take the primatial see. Yet despite their respective compromises, Cranmer and Gardiner were now propelled into new and mutually antagonistic stances. Glyn Redworth has reminded us that the two men were to become joint and rival keepers of Henry VIII's Janus-like conscience, Gardiner reflecting Henry's hold on the past, Cranmer reflecting his efforts to reshape the future.[113] Their rivalry would long outlive the old King who had propelled them into politics; at Cranmer's fall in 1553, it was

112 Hawkins to the King, *St.P.* 7, pp. 386–7; Vaughan to Cromwell, P.R.O., S.P. 1/72 f. 140 (*L.P.* 5, no. 1620).

113 Redworth, *Gardiner*, pp. 190–91.

Gardiner who seized the Archbishop's river-barges from Lambeth Palace for his own use, while the last public words that Cranmer shouted before being consigned to the flames were a denunciation of the writings of the Bishop of Winchester.[114] When these two rather similar Cambridge dons found themselves launched into politics, it was the experiences of 1532 which permanently shaped their roles in the political and religious game.

114 Cf. P.R.O., E. 154/2/41, f. 11v for the inventory of Cranmer's goods in which Gardiner is given the barges. For the last speech, see below, Ch. 13.

CHAPTER 4

The reign of Queen Anne: 1533–6

SIR THOMAS ELYOT WAS an angry man in 1533, profoundly unhappy with the triumph of the Boleyn family and the humiliation of Queen Catherine; moreover, he was personally sore at his brusque recall the previous year from his embassy to the Empire and his replacement there by Thomas Cranmer, which he claimed had left him seriously out of pocket. On 6 April 1533, the day of Bishop Fisher's arrest for sedition, as Cranmer took up his duties as Primate of All England and the Lady Anne daydreamed about her coronation, Elyot wrote remarkably frankly and biliously to his former diplomatic colleague Sir John Hacket, envoy in the Low Countries. The imminent annulment of the Aragon marriage was 'a great cloud which is likely to be a great storm when it falleth'; the clergy (whose Convocation of Canterbury had finally signalled its agreement with Henry's views on annulment the previous week) 'digged the ditch that they be now fallen in, which causeth many good men the less to pity them'. Elyot's moral outrage was stiffened by his sense of financial loss and annoyance at his successor envoy's promotion:

> I beseech God . . . that truth may be freely and thankfully heard. For my part I am finally determined to live and die therein; neither mine importable expenses unrecompensed shall so much fear me nor the advancement of my successor the Bishop of Canterbury so much allure me that I shall ever decline from truth or abuse my sovereign Lord unto whom I am sworn.[1]

Elyot did not confine his feelings about the necessity of truthful counsel to private correspondence, but went into print on the subject. He was lucky, considering his flirtations with the opposition to the King's plans during the 1530s. It was apparently his long friendship with Thomas Cromwell which preserved him when other men of equal or greater reputation suffered – Fisher and More went to the scaffold, but Elyot died in his bed, honoured as England's leading humanist writer. We have noted already that Elyot was the most plausible author of the first attack on the *Censurae*, rapidly published in 1531 (see above, p. 69). In 1533 he again dangerously asserted his own injured dignity and expressed his anger at Cranmer's rise to the top by

1 P.R.O., S.P. 1/75 f. 81 (*L.P.* 6 no. 313).

writing a conversation piece with three actors, *Pasquil the Plain*, published with a pointed dedication to Henry VIII.[2]

Pasquil was an innovation in England, a borrowing of the Continental genre of satire known as the 'Pasquinade', supposedly inspired by an outspoken tailor of fifteenth-century Rome called Pasquino. It was clearly also inspired by Thomas More's *Utopia*, likewise a three-way conversation, and its theme was that of *Utopia*'s opening book: how to offer good counsel to a monarch. The work was a success: 'plain Pasquil' became a stock cliché in mid-Tudor English, and one of the dialogue's other two characters, Gnatho the flatterer, also found a niche in English literature, aided by his previous presence in *The Eunuch*, a comedy by Terence popular in school Latin courses.[3] In another dialogue published in the same year, *Of the Knowledge Which Maketh a Wise Man*, Elyot made the disclaimer familiar to modern filmgoers, that any resemblance in *Pasquil* to actual persons alive or dead was entirely coincidental: we need not treat this line with respect.[4] Pasquil, a talkative stone statue who was also an honest character, suffering serious 'damage and hindrance' by his 'railing', was clearly an image of Elyot himself. Gnatho, despite the very specific picture of him dressed half as scholar, half as gallant, ostentatiously flourishing his New Testament but with a copy of *Troilus and Cressida* in his bosom, is less easy to identify, but he may be More's replacement as Lord Chancellor, the evangelically inclined Thomas Audley (a Cambridge graduate whose promotion between 1529 and 1532 had been almost as rapid as Cranmer's). Thomas Cromwell himself is a less likely candidate for Gnatho, given his previous favours to Elyot. By contrast, there can be little doubt that the third of Elyot's characters, Gnatho's 'cousin-german' Harpocrates, was a flimsily veiled and unflattering sketch of England's new Archbishop.[5]

Harpocrates (otherwise a Greek name for the Egyptian god Horus) was described by Elyot as 'the prelate of the temple of Isis and Serapis . . . whose image is made holding his finger at his mouth, betokening silence'.[6] His Harpocrates is a royal confessor, and a clergyman with high pretensions in a fatal year of defiance against Rome: 'Peace, ye are yet no Pope, and because ye be a priest ye be exempted from being Emperor.'[7] Pasquil also comments on the name Harpocrates itself: 'that is a hard name by Jesus.' Is this a mere oath,

2 For an excellent discussion of Elyot, A. Fox, in Fox and Guy, *Reassessing the Henrician Age*, pp. 52–73, especially for his friendship with Cromwell, ibid., p. 57.

3 For an instance of 'plain Pasquils' in 1549, cf. *Latimer's Sermons*, p. 110; for Gnatho, *Joseph's Letter Book*, pp. 118–21, Gardiner, *Obedience*, ed. Janelle, p. 148, Cochlaeus, *Scopa*, sig. Fii, *Becon* 1, p. 276, *Latimer's Sermons*, p. 124.

4 Elyot, *Four Treatises*, p. xi.

5 Ibid., pp. 47, 62. Fox gives good reasons for dismissing the idea that Elyot was portraying Thomas More as Pasquil: Fox and Guy, *Reassessing the Henrician Age*, pp. 64–5: cf. also his remarks about identifying the characters, ibid., p. 69.

6 Elyot, *Four Treatises*, p. 43.

7 Ibid., pp. 66, 91, 72.

or a play on words about Harpocrates' name being near that of a Jesus don? Harpocrates himself repeats the oath 'by Jesus' later on.[8] It is Harpocrates' silence, his traditional attribute in classical mythology, which chiefly interests Elyot in the character: it is a silence which is vouched for by Cranmer's admirers like Ralph Morice, who considered it one of his great virtues. Not so Elyot. Even before he learns that Harpocrates is the King's confessor, Pasquil has started emphasizing the pernicious nature of his silence: Harpocrates insists that 'silence is surety', but is rebuked 'ye will season silence. Marry I ween my Lord should have a better cook of you than a counsellor'. Elyot goes on to make clear that this seasoning or spicing of silence is as bad as Gnatho's verbal flattery: Harpocrates admits that his silence is seasoned 'with sugar, for I use little salt'.[9] Yet this sugar is not the sugar of innocence: indeed, Harpocrates admits right at the end that he was secretly listening to the opening dialogue before he appeared on the scene, and Pasquil dismisses him with a sneer at the shallowness of his conscience: 'I ween I mought buy as much of the coster-monger for two pence.'[10]

As the argument progresses, Gnatho fades into the background, and the text becomes a fierce assault by Pasquil on Harpocrates, 'for if he can persuade me that his silence is better than my babbling, I will follow his doctrine . . .'. Pasquil scents a conspiracy against the King, of which Harpocrates may be a part, and warns him that if he does not reveal it he may be hanged, or worse, suffer 'perpetual infamy' and 'the death of the soul'. This ultimate peril threatens his master as well.[11]

> For when Gnatho with his flattery and ye with your silence have once rooted in your master's heart false opinions, and vicious affects . . . though ye after repent you, and perceive the danger, yet shall it perchance be impossible with speech to remove those opinions . . . except ye loved so well your master, that for his health ye would confess your own errors.[12]

The conversation on silence then takes a strange turn: to grace and predestination. Pasquil asks what remedy there might be for the evil which will follow if Harpocrates remains silent about his own error; Harpocrates feebly counters 'I can not tell, except it were grace'. 'I heard thee never speak so wisely', says Pasquil sarcastically, and he insists that grace is useless without the human effort of persuasion, 'unless thou thinkest, that every man shall be called of God, as Saint Paul was, who was elected.' Even then, adds Pasquil, Paul had to be specifically called by Jesus Christ speaking to him.

8 Ibid., p. 76. Since the whole work is set in Italy, it is probably fruitless to make anything of allusions to Harpocrates's time at Bologna university, or an obscure passage about the clattering complaints of stones 'at the late wars in Italy': ibid., pp. 63–4, 98.

9 Ibid., pp. 65–6, 70. Cf. Morice in *Narratives of the Reformation*, p. 244.

10 Elyot, *Four Treatises*, pp. 96, 100.

11 Ibid., pp. 69, 87–90.

12 Ibid., pp. 91–2.

Harpocrates, shocked at this assertion of the place of the human will alongside divine grace, counters (with strong echoes of the last section of Chapter 11 in the Epistle to the Romans), 'It is not for us, Pasquil, to insearch the impenetrable judgements of God; but the grace of God hath happened far above men's expectation, and where all other remedy lacked, for then the puissance of almighty God is specially proved.' There are few passages close to the text of Scripture elsewhere in *Pasquil*. Does this exchange deliberately conjure up some theological conversation of 1532 between Elyot and Cranmer in Germany, when the new ambassador contemplated the marvels of a Lutheran city for the first time, while his predecessor sneered at Lutheran innovation?[13]

In any case, this theological duel is the signal for Harpocrates' collapse in argument; he and his cousin Gnatho retire to the Court, affronted. Pasquil is left victorious, glorying in his plainness, and he defiantly celebrates the fact that his honesty means that he will 'never come unto privy chamber or gallery'. He trusts in God 'to see the day that I will not set by the best of you both a butterfly. . . . Now when these two fellows come to the Court they will tell all that they have heard of me, it maketh no matter. For I have said nothing but by the way of advertisement [i.e. warning].' Yet *Pasquil the Plain* was a paper triumph for Elyot: Pasquil had admitted defeat, in the act of preserving his moral integrity. Gnatho and Harpocrates were indeed comfortably installed at the Court of Henry VIII and Anne Boleyn, and the little part which Elyot himself was later able to play in public life would be at the behest of Thomas Cromwell. Perhaps thereafter it was no coincidence that the second edition of *Pasquil* came out in the year of Cromwell's fall, 1540.

In Elyot's eyes Cranmer owed his success to silence; nevertheless his first passport to glory was what he had been able to say and write for the Boleyn marriage. From the first public notices of him in England, Thomas Cranmer had been linked with the cause of the Boleyns; both his admirers like Ralph Morice and the many hostile commentators made the connection with the Boleyns explicit. The later poisonous anti-biography probably by Nicholas Harpsfield, *Cranmer's Recantacyons*, says specifically that Cranmer became Thomas Boleyn's chaplain, and that when Cranmer tried to thank the King for his elevation to Canterbury, Henry said 'that he ought to thank Anne Boleyn for this welcome promotion'; these statements echo comments made by Chapuys at the time, and a Venetian commentator in January 1533 called Cranmer Anne's tutor.[14] Cranmer later proved more than a fair-weather friend to the Boleyns: even though he was no more capable than anyone else of resisting the juggernaut of the King's anger which destroyed Anne Boleyn, he stood by the Earl of Wiltshire in his last broken years, and as Wiltshire's

13 Elyot, *Four Treatises*, pp. 95–7.

14 *Cranmer's Recantacyons*, pp. 2–3. Cf. Harpsfield, *Pretended Divorce*, p. 289. *C.S.P. Venetian 1527–33*, no. 846, p. 376.

executor, caused himself much hard work and trouble as he tried to sort out the tangled affairs of a fallen politician. The disputes had not finally been settled as late as the moment of Cranmer's arrest in 1553.[15]

We will have to consider what commentators referred to as Anne's 'reign' in great detail, because in the course of her three years as Queen, patterns were set which would permanently shape Cranmer's life and also create new shapes for the Church and archdiocese that he served. Even in personal terms, in the creation of his new career, Anne's importance is central. Cranmer represented the most exalted specimen of Anne's religious patronage, which characteristically and even before his emergence in the group centred on Cambridge academics; Cambridge men would take the lead in the early Reformation over Oxford, despite the powerful counter-influence at Cambridge of John Fisher.[16] The minimum list of Anne's clerical and evangelical protégés consisted of William Bettes, Thomas Cranmer, Edward Crome, Nicholas Heath, Hugh and William Latimer, Matthew Parker, Nicholas Shaxton and John Skip. Not all of them remained consistent in their evangelical views: Shaxton and Heath in particular both returned to the old faith. To expect consistency would have been asking too much of frail human beings in an age of murderous political and religious change, and of interest today is their behaviour in the reign of Queen Anne.[17] Three of these men (Crome, Shaxton and Skip) were from Gonville Hall in Cambridge, where Anne's great-great-uncle had been Master; a Gonville layman who also had close connections with Anne was Dr William Butts, who also played an important role in promoting the evangelical cause at Court after Anne's death because of his continuing closeness to the King (see below, Ch. 8).

Cranmer returned to the Court from his mission abroad at the beginning of January 1533. Events had to move swiftly, because Anne was at last pregnant, after nearly six years of keeping Henry from his heart's desire: she and the King were gambling that they would get public recognition of their married state from a tame Archbishop. The pregnancy probably followed some sort of secret marriage ceremony between Henry and Anne on their return from meeting the French King at Calais in November 1532, and this ceremony seems to have been repeated in late January 1533 (on the complexities and uncertainties of these events, see Appendix II). Chapuys said that Cranmer had not been back a week when, to general astonishment, he was appointed Archbishop. He also noted the haste with which everything happened at this time: the King was going to advance out of his own pocket the fees for the

15 For examples of Cranmer's involvement, see Cox 2 p. 369; P.R.O., C. 1/967/61; C. 1/1110/65; E. 154/2/41 (November 1553).

16 For Anne's 'reign', cf. e.g. Foxe 5, p. 420; 'Latimer's Cronickille', p. 33.

17 On Skip, see Bernard, 'Anne Boleyn's religion', pp. 15–16, but see below, pp. 154–5, for reasons to reject Bernard's arguments about him, and cf. Ives, *Anne Boleyn*, Ch. 14. NB the very interesting treatment of Crome by Wabuda, 'Equivocation and Recantation'.

papal bulls necessary for the promotion to Canterbury. That fund of malicious stories, Nicholas Harpsfield, said that the King made the offer of Canterbury to Cranmer at a bear-baiting; although this is in itself impossible, it is not impossible that some such sporting occasion was where the news became public.[18] One little incident (impossible to date precisely), preserved in a much later anecdote by the wandering Scots evangelical Alexander Alesius, is an interesting comment on the changed times that Cranmer's elevation represented: when Henry gave him the Archbishopric, he presented him with a ring that had once belonged to Cardinal Wolsey. Cranmer in turn gave it as a keepsake to Alesius when he fled England to escape the effect of the Six Articles of 1539.[19]

The Archbishop-elect was plunged into a ferment of committees thrashing out solutions to the twin problems of securing an annulment and achieving it without Roman interference. To give him a base, he was installed in lodgings at Westminster in Canon Row, the residential quarters of the Dean and Canons of St Stephen's Chapel. Perhaps he was granted some preferment in the College, although others besides the College staff lived in the buildings: certainly his friend Thomas Goodrich acquired a canonry in the College during 1533, as one of a succession of clergy associated with the annulment research team, and with Anne Boleyn generally, who were appointed to St Stephen's.[20] From Canon Row on 8 February he wrote a note to Cromwell for a favour for an old Cambridge friend, signing his letter 'Thomas Elect of Canterbury', with a large and self-conscious variant of the Gothic signature which became his trademark as Archbishop. He was clearly in constant touch with Cromwell, who was by now a key figure in the King's Council, with his own official quarters in the Palace of Westminster; Cranmer's note looked forward to their next meeting, and Chapuys said that Cromwell and Cranmer between them were responsible for the parting instructions for Edmund Bonner's mission to Rome in February.[21] Canon Row, squeezed between the palaces of Westminster and Whitehall, would have been a convenient base for a variety of committee work, and from February it would also have been useful for Cranmer's attendance at the Convocation of Canterbury in Westminster Abbey as Archdeacon of Taunton, before he could officially move across the river into Lambeth Palace.

The first glimpse of the winter's committee work comes from Ambassador Chapuys, who reported that on 5 February 'one of the principal members of the Privy Council had assembled a number of doctors, churchmen as well as

18 *C.S.P. Spanish 1531–3*, no. 1043, p. 585. Harpsfield, *Pretended Divorce*, p. 290.

19 P.R.O., S.P. 70/7 f. 11v (*C.S.P. Foreign 1558–59*, p. 533).

20 I am most grateful to Dr David Skinner for supplying me with his lists of known Canons of the College; we do not have a complete listing.

21 B.L. Cotton MS Vespasian F XIII, f. 145, Cox 2 p. 237; *C.S.P. Spanish 1531–3*, no. 1048, p. 601.

lawyers' to discuss the question of carnal copulation in Arthur's marriage to Catherine.[22] By now, as Chapuys noted in his next letter, Wiltshire and his daughter were confident of victory, and Wiltshire was openly throwing his weight behind the marriage; Anne's 'reign' had in effect already begun, but a formidable variety of tasks needed to be completed very quickly if it was to be given a legal base. A list survives in Thomas Cromwell's memoranda of a committee which indeed consists of 'doctors, churchmen as well as lawyers': headed by Cranmer as 'my Lord of Canterbury', it has twenty-four names of which there are marks beside thirteen, no doubt in order to ask them to attend.[23] As Sir Geoffrey Elton suggested, one task before the committees was probably to consider the preparations for the parliamentary legislation forbidding appeals to a power outside the realm, which would represent a decisive step in the breach with Rome.[24] Another problem which one of these committee meetings had to sort out was the quelling of Cranmer's strenuous doubts about confirming his election as Archbishop by what he regarded as usurped papal authority; he later recalled how 'the king himself called Dr Oliver, and other civil lawyers, and devised with them how he might bestow it upon me, enforcing me nothing against my conscience'.[25] Dr Oliver's name appears on Cromwell's committee list, together with other leading civil lawyers, Gwent, Tregonwell, Bedell and Corwen, paired with the churchmen who were veterans of the annulment research team: Cranmer himself, Stokesley, Edward Foxe, Thomas Goodrich and Nicholas de Burgo.

However, as Chapuys had heard, even at this late stage the prime job for the committees was to go over the intricate arguments about the annulment. The most substantial surviving piece of committee work from winter 1533 is a tract for private circulation entitled *Articuli Duodecim. . . .* 'Twelve Articles by which it is completely and plainly proved that a divorce must of necessity be made' between Henry and Catherine. Cranmer's part in the production of this is uncertain, but one of the two surviving handsome manuscripts has the clerk's notation 'Thomas Cantuariensis' which shows that it was in his library in 1553, and its arguments would be the background to his findings at the annulment trial at Dunstable later in the year. The tract had a ragbag of purposes: first to reiterate the King's conviction that unconsummated just as much as consummated marriages created an impediment of affinity subject to the eternal divine ban announced in Leviticus; second to insist in its final section that regardless of this, Arthur had indeed technically consummated

22 *C.S.P. Spanish 1531–3*, no. 1047, p. 599.

23 P.R.O., S.P. 1/74 f. 170 (*L.P.* 6 no. 150); Elton, *Studies* 2, pp. 99–100, prints and discusses the list, but omits one of the pricked names, William Repps or Rugge, Abbot of St Bene't's Hulme.

24 Elton, *Studies* 2, pp. 100–101.

25 Foxe 8, p. 66.

his marriage to Catherine, whatever the exact physical details (and the possibilities were laid out with pitiless ecclesiastical prurience). By contrast, the tract argued in its fourth and fifth articles that sexual intercourse outside marriage gave rise to a lesser impediment of affinity which was binding only by the law of the church: a clear reference to the embarrassing fact that Henry had indeed had an admitted previous sexual relationship with Anne Boleyn's sister Mary – some said with their mother as well. It would not do for the idea to circulate that the eternal Levitical prohibition applied as much to such illicit unions as to lawful marriage.[26]

Meanwhile, at the end of January the King and Anne once more privately announced their married state before a select handful of witnesses and a priest; Cranmer was certainly not present, and later told a friend that he had only heard about the event a fortnight afterwards (see Appendix II). Perhaps, in a feeble attempt at preserving the proprieties, it was felt inappropriate that the judge who would hear the annulment of one marriage should already have officiated at the celebration of the other. Other traditional proprieties were being punctiliously observed at the same time; the papal nuncio was being treated with great consideration, constantly conferring with Henry and being given an honourably prominent place on 4 February at the opening of the Parliamentary session which would later initiate the break with Rome. Under orders from Rome, the nuncio was desperately anxious to please the English, in an effort to avert a final breach; it was easy therefore for the government to arrange the bureaucratic documents for Cranmer's consecration, including the transmission of the fees for the necessary papal bulls. The nature of the pressure was made painfully clear by Edmund Bonner in a letter to Ambassador Benet in Rome: if the business of Cranmer's bulls was not expedited, 'the matter of the annates (which is in communication greatly and only stayed by the King's goodness) in my opinion should be with all celerity called upon, and things attempted therein and otherwise, that should be not a little prejudicial to the Court of Rome'. Only the previous year, Parliament had passed a conditional restraint of English annate payments to Rome, as part of the King's policy of trying to frighten the Pope.[27]

Ambassador Chapuys was furious at the nuncio's spinelessness, and he was fully aware of the threat that Cranmer represented. Writing to the Emperor on 9 February, he labelled Cranmer a Lutheran; this was his habitual catch-all term for anyone of whose religion he disapproved, but more specifically he had heard that Cranmer had taken into his service two evangelicals who had

26 Cf. discussion of this in Kelly, *Matrimonial Trials*, Ch. 13, and cf. *Records of the Reformation* 1, pp. 387–93, 394–6. For the dating to 1533 by its reference to the rediscovery of Henry VII's treaty with Spain (*C.S.P. Spanish 1531–3*, no. 1047, p. 599), see especially Kelly, *Matrimonial Trials*, pp. 162, 223. A date earlier than 1531 is in any case unlikely because of the treatise's final reference to the opinions of the universities: *Records of the Reformation* 1, p. 399.

27 *St.P.* 7, p. 410. Cf. *C.S.P. Venetian 1527–33*, p. 377; *C.S.P. Spanish 1531–3*, no. 1047, pp. 592–600.

preached against the Aragonese marriage and who had also narrowly escaped the stake the previous year.[28] One of these must have been Hugh Latimer, who had indeed been in serious trouble in Convocation during 1532 for his bold evangelical preaching in the south-west. Chapuys urged his master to persuade the Pope to delay Cranmer's bulls until the annulment proceedings had been thwarted. However, by the time that the Emperor read this entreaty, brought with maximum haste from England to Italy, it was too late. Chapuys's letter arrived in Bologna on 21 February, together with his previous letter speaking in more general terms of Cranmer's undesirability and partiality for Anne; on that very day in the same city, the formalities for the provision of Cranmer to Canterbury were completed in the Consistory. Nevertheless, the tenth of the series of eleven bulls was not finally ready and dated until 3 March, and the Emperor does not seem to have lifted a finger to stop them; the bulls, completely traditional in form, were then despatched to England.[29]

The money involved in getting the bulls and preparing the household of the Primate of All England was way beyond the resources of an Archdeacon of Taunton. Archdeacon Hawkins in Bologna outlined for the King the many thousands of ducats which the process involved, down to the pallium of fine wool, symbol of archiepiscopal office, which at a thousand ducats was one of the smallest costs.[30] According to a Spanish source which contains intermittent flashes of accuracy, the actual cash for the bulls was loaned by a Genoese resident in London, 'Arigo Salbago'; this man is likely to be one of Cromwell's associates, a Genoese merchant prominent in the City, Sebastiano de Salvago.[31] Besides this, the King loaned a thousand pounds to Cranmer after 6 February 1533, and in a gesture of extraordinary generosity in April, he backdated the restitution of the temporalities of the archdiocese to 29 September 1532, a major bonus for Cranmer's finances and a sacrifice for the royal coffers. Even so, the new Archbishop faced severe cash-flow problems, as he confided with gloomy humour to his old colleagues at Jesus College in June, and it is symptomatic of this that his earliest surviving contact with the Prior of his Cathedral is a demand for money.[32]

It took about three weeks for the bulls to arrive, some time around 26 March; at last Henry's log-jam could begin to clear with action both in the

28 *C.S.P. Spanish 1531–3*, no. 1047, pp. 598–9.

29 *C.S.P. Spanish 1531–3*, no. 1043, p. 587; 1050, 1051, pp. 606–7. Cf. Ayris and Selwyn (eds), *Cranmer*, pp. 118–19. Tenth bull: Harmer, *Specimen of Errors*, p. 28.

30 *St.P.* 7, p. 425. It is not clear how much of the payments were remitted by the papal bureaucracy; Archbishop Parker put the costs at 900 gold ducats (Parker, *De Antiquitate*, p. 382).

31 *Chronicle of Henry VIII*, p. 19. Cf. *L.P.* 4 ii nos. 3014, 3053, 3213/29; 4 iii no. 6709/10.

32 On the loan: P.R.O., S.P. 1/74 f. 169 (*L.P.* 6 no. 150); E. 101/421/9 (*L.P.* 6 no. 131); cf. Elton, *Studies* 2, p. 98. Ayris and Selwyn (eds), *Cranmer*, p. 120. Jesus: Cox 2, p. 247, B.L. Harley MS 6148, f. 24v (*L.P.* 6 no. 703). Cathedral: Cox 2, p. 260, B.L. Harley MS 6148, f. 34v (*L.P.* 6 no. 1241): ?7 October 1533. Cf. also on Cranmer's financial woes Cox 2, pp. 263–4, B.L. Harley MS 6148, f. 37r (*L.P.* 6 no. 1315).

Convocation of Canterbury and in Parliament, and with Cranmer's consecration. One can now hardly avoid a day-by-day account of events in the helter-skelter towards completing Henry's plans. Convocation had occupied itself through February with routine matters, such as the vexatious but politically uncontentious matter of the clerical subsidy, and it was actually prorogued between 2 and 17 March.[33] As Chapuys noted, Parliament also simultaneously marked time with secondary matters, and members were obstructive for more than a fortnight after the bill in Restraint of Appeals was introduced on 14 March.[34] Equally unpromisingly for the King, when the clergy of Convocation met again on 17 March, the conservatives gleefully seized on yet another outspoken sermon of Hugh Latimer to bring their second attack on him in two years; this assault on Cranmer's and the Boleyns' favourite may have led to the president imposing a further week's prorogation of Convocation on 21 March. However, the arrival of Cranmer's bulls forced an earlier meeting on 26 March, and the sudden introduction of a new topic on the agenda. Latimer still came under fierce attack, with Bishop Gardiner leading the charge, but it was symbolic of the division of purpose which would haunt religious conservatives through the 1530s that the main business to occupy Gardiner that same day was the presentation of documents about the divorce. Many of Gardiner's allies against Latimer were thrown on the defensive against the King's plans. Bitter arguments continued on 28 and 29 March.[35]

Convocation's debates were interrupted for Passion Sunday, 30 March, and for the essential next step: Cranmer's consecration as Archbishop. This took place in St Stephen's College in the Palace of Westminster, which was perhaps logical since he had been living in Canon Row all winter; however, as a royal peculiar and the monarch's private chapel, St Stephen's was also the appropriate setting for a ceremony which was to be a symbolic transition from the papal obedience to a future national Church as yet without shape. Cranmer first swore an oath of loyalty to the papacy in the College chapter-house. He immediately followed this with a solemn protestation declaring that his oath would not override the law of God and his loyalty to the King, or act to the hindrance of 'reformation of the Christian religion, the government of the English Church, or the prerogative of the Crown or the well-being of the same commonwealth', and he swore 'to prosecute and reform matters wheresoever they seem to me to be for the reform of the English Church'. Looking on during this morally dubious manoeuvre was a selection of the civil lawyers who had quieted his conscience and appealed to his idealism with these reformist phrases: Tregonwell, Bedell, Gwent, Cockes.

33 Lambeth MS 751, pp. 95–7. In all these events, one must remember that the Convocation of York usually acted only as a retrospective rubber stamp for decisions taken in the south.

34 *C.S.P. Spanish 1531–3*, no. 1053, p. 609; Lambeth MS 751, pp. 97–8. Cf. Lehmberg, *Reformation Parliament*, p. 172.

35 Lambeth MS 751, pp. 97–100; the main papers on Latimer are provided in Foxe 7 Appendix no. 9.

Cranmer then moved to St Stephen's Chapel, where the bishops Longland of Lincoln, Veysey of Exeter and Standish of St Asaph officiated at the actual consecration. Two different oaths of loyalty to Rome followed, the second after Cranmer had been vested with that exceptionally expensive woollen garment, the pallium; at each stage he referred back to his protestation in the chapter-house. This protestation was entirely different from the further short oath that he took on 19 April renouncing papal grants hurtful to the Crown; that was a customary means for petitioning for the restoration of his see's temporalities. Even in the light of more than four centuries of tensions between royal and papal jurisdiction, everyone present must have felt this consecration to be an extraordinary occasion. In a procedure which can reflect no credit on him at all, Cranmer had formally benefited from papal bulls while equally formally rejecting their authority.[36]

Now the new Archbishop could take up his presidency of Convocation, which throughout the winter had been entrusted to Bishop Standish with Bishop Stokesley as deputy, while Cranmer's own status had remained in limbo. On the Monday he entrusted the presidency to a commission (Gardiner, Stokesley and Longland), but on the Tuesday, 1 April, he was in his chair for the first time. Despite fierce opposition led by Bishop Fisher (leading to Fisher's arrest on 6 April), the next few days saw large majorities in both houses of Convocation for two essential propositions: that there was proof that Arthur had carnally known Catherine, and that the Pope had no dispensing power in the case. Convocation had then done its work, and on 8 April it was prorogued; meanwhile Parliament had stood down the previous day, after putting on a belated burst of speed to pass the Act in Restraint of Appeals, which rendered Queen Catherine's appeal to Rome illegal.[37] Cranmer was now fully armed for the divorce, after seven years of travail. Almost immediately he used his new powers as Metropolitan to forbid unauthorized preaching, ordering the bishops of his province to do the same. It was a very necessary measure after a number of furious sermons and pronouncements from Catherine's clerical partisans, particularly among the influential Observant Franciscan order, but the irony of an evangelical 'who did forbid that the word of God should be preached in the churches throughout his diocese' was not lost on a conservative chronicler at St Augustine's Abbey at Canterbury.[38]

36 These proceedings are pr. in Cox 2, pp. 559–62, and the oath for the temporalities, ibid., p. 460 (note of restoration of temporalities, *L.P.* 6 no. 578/7). Cf. Parker, *De Antiquitate*, p. 382, and discussion in Ayris and Selwyn (eds), *Cranmer*, pp. 119–21; Ayris Ph.D., 'Thomas Cranmer's Register', pp. 54, 183.

37 Lambeth MS 751, pp. 100–103; Lehmberg, *Reformation Parliament*, pp. 175–8. Cf. Parker, *De Antiquitate*, p. 382; *C.S.P. Venetian 1527–33*, no. 870, p. 392; *C.S.P. Spanish 1531–3*, nos 1057–8, pp. 625–9.

38 *C.S.P. Venetian 1527–33*, no. 878, p. 398; *Narratives of the Reformation*, p. 280. On Stokesley's ban for London diocese on 24 April, see Foxe 7 Appendix 8. NB e.g. the crop of preaching licences nearly all for friars in Worcester diocese, 13–14 May 1533, and a few more in late summer: H.W.R.O. b.716.093-BA 2648/8(ii), pp. 71–3.

Easter weekend proved momentous and busy for Cranmer. The first piece of ordinary archiepiscopal business in his register happens to be recorded for Good Friday (11 April): the collation to a Kentish benefice of Dr Hugh Price, who eventually proved so significant for the future of the Welsh Church with his establishment of Jesus College, Oxford, in 1571.[39] Of more immediate and obvious importance were the Archbishop's two letters to the King: these bore the difficult and delicate burden of accusing Henry of creating a public scandal with Queen Catherine and inviting him to ease his conscience with a hearing of his plight before a Church court. Both these letters and the King's final reply the following day had an important task even apart from the immediate aim of securing the annulment. The transaction was the first major piece of business which would reflect on the King's new *de facto* position as head of the English Church created by the Act in Restraint of Appeals. In the correspondence, primate and monarch were feeling their way to express their relationship, in an issue of sexual morality which (for all Cranmer's conventionally obsequious phrasing) threw into stark relief the relationship between fallen humanity and a just God.

The two letters of 11 April which survive from Cranmer to the King have almost identical texts, yet their purposes are different and sequential; it is incorrect to regard the second as a replacement for the first.[40] The first letter pointed out that the 'great cause of matrimony' was being discussed throughout Christendom, and that the King's poor subjects were worried about the succession; since Henry had been pleased to summon Cranmer 'albeit a poor wretch and most unworthy' to be Archbishop, and the clergy were being publicly blamed for not providing a remedy, Cranmer wanted in general terms to 'ascertain me of your Grace's pleasure in the premises, to the intent that, the same known, I may proceed for my discharge afore God' in providing such remedy. The King's response to this led to the second letter in one day from Cranmer. This played for safety by sticking closely to the general framework and phrasing of the first; but having now indeed ascertained the King's pleasure, Cranmer made a more specific request 'to license me, according to mine office and duty, to proceed to the examination, final determination, and judgement in the said great cause'. The sequence between the two letters was indicated specifically by Cranmer's new phrase at the end 'eftsoons [i.e. a second time], as prostrate at the feet of your majesty, beseeching the same to pardon me of these my bold and rude letters'; the conventional request for pardon had ended the first letter, although its obsequiousness was now intensified.

Other material changes in the text of the second letter were no doubt stipulated by Henry, and were intended to define more closely how this case

39 Cranmer's Register, f. 339r. On Price, see Emden, *Oxford to 1540*, p. 462.

40 Both versions are printed in *St.P.* 1, pp. 390–91 and Cox 2, pp. 237–9, from P.R.O., S.P. 1/75 ff. 86–90 (*L.P.* 6 no. 327), the earlier in small type; Cranmer's office copy of the second is B.L. Harley MS 6148, f. 4r.

related to the recent legislation, the week-old Act in Restraint of Appeals: Cranmer's first letter had said that 'my office and duty is, by your and your predecessors' sufferance and grants, to direct and order causes spiritual in this your Grace's realm, according to the laws of God and Holy Church'. Henry wanted more precision to identify Cranmer's office and judicial powers, so he imported the ideas of judging and determining to be found in the text of the Act. He probably also felt that this last phrase of Cranmer's sounded too much like the qualification by which the Convocation of Canterbury had held at bay his supreme headship in 1531, 'so far as the law of God allows', so it was dropped. Additionally in one significant word-change he brought Cranmer's text further into line with the vocabulary of the Act by having 'predecessors' altered to 'progenitors'; so this whole passage became 'the office and duty of the Archbishop of Canterbury, by your and your progenitors' sufferance and grants, is to direct, order, judge and determine causes spiritual in this your Grace's realm'.

Henry equally agonized about his own reply to this request for licence, which he sent to Lambeth on the following day, Easter Eve (12 April); he also spent that day aggressively parading Anne round Court as Queen for the first time.[41] Two much-altered drafts and the final fair copy of his letter survive, in general doing their best to keep Henry's royal ego under control while asserting his position as 'King and Sovereign' with 'no superior on earth but only God'.[42] The final version still made the blanket statement that 'God and we have ordained [you] Archbishop of Canterbury . . . to whose office it hath been, and is, appertaining by the sufferance of us and our progenitors, as ye write yourself, both justly and truly to order, judge and determine mere spiritual causes'. The precision of 'mere' was a refinement appearing in the second draft, and it was no doubt intended to refer to the specific procedure *ex mero officio* by which Cranmer would hear the annulment case. However, Henry's final version slightly shifted the balance from his own royal power towards the opinion of the Almighty; he added the phrase 'against God', so that he recognized that Cranmer sought to exonerate his conscience 'against God' by the trial of the case, and the King also graciously added that he must 'condignly praise you therein', rather than simply the more grudging 'we cannot, of reason, be discontented therewith'.

Most altered between first and second draft was the section which dealt with the relationship between the authorities of monarch and archbishop. Initially Henry had incautiously referred to Cranmer as 'head of our spirituality', which he hastily altered to 'the most principal minister of our spiritual jurisdiction'; both the vice-gerency and the powers of the Archbishop of

41 'Two London Chronicles', ed. Kingsford, p. 7; *C.S.P. Venetian 1527–33*, no. 870, p. 393; *C.S.P. Spanish 1531–3*, no. 1061, p. 643.

42 The version printed in *St.P.* 1, pp. 392–3 and Cox 2, pp. 238–9n is a tidied up version of the paper second draft, B.L. Harley MS 283 f. 97, omitting rejected phrases; the first draft and the final fair copy are B.L. Cotton MS Otho C X ff. 159, 158 respectively.

York might later have been in question had the King stuck to his first thoughts, and even after the alteration this jurisdictional problem did not go away, as discussed below (pp. 122–35). Henry added but then omitted at the last minute a legalistic 'our pre-eminent power and authority to us, and our successors in this behalf, nevertheless saved' from a passage in which he said that he would submit himself to and not refuse Cranmer's request to make an end to the great cause. In his added final sentence, his second thoughts also did more to remind himself of God's majesty above his own, 'For assuredly, the thing which we most covet in this world is so to proceed in all our acts and doings as may be most acceptable to the pleasure of Almighty God, our creator, and to the wealth and honour of us, our succession and posterity, and the surety of our realms and subjects within the same.'

Thus was a new procedure painfully worked out whereby a monarch who was head of the Church could be tried by his most senior clergyman; naturally, none of the exchanges mentioned the Pope, although the trial that followed would necessarily be in his name. Over the previous months, the Act in Restraint of Appeals had proved equally troublesome to get right in its successive drafts. One imagines that as in the drafting of that Act, Thomas Cromwell was at the King's side, ready with suggestions as his clerks turned the royal wishes into words, and he may well also have been rowed across to Lambeth to guide Cranmer's pen.[43] Strictly speaking, the Act in Restraint of Appeals was irrelevant to Cranmer's action: in legal form, that legislation hindered Queen Catherine in any further appeal to Rome, rather than helped the Archbishop to try the King's cause. As will be obvious from the correspondence, the trial that followed was not an appeal in any sense. Cranmer termed his tribunal 'a cause of inquisition about and upon the validity of the marriage . . . before us in judgement *ex officio mero nostro*' – that is, the normal procedure in a case initiated by the judge of a church court himself.[44] Within a fortnight, Henry and Catherine received a formal summons to appear before this inquisition in Dunstable Priory in Bedfordshire, a place chosen supposedly because it was convenient for Catherine (now exiled to the royal lodge at Ampthill, ten miles due north of Dunstable). More importantly, Dunstable was out of the way of sensation-seeking and possibly trouble-making Londoners. It is also likely to be relevant that the Prior of Dunstable, Gervase Markham, was one of Cranmer's Nottinghamshire relatives. Dunstable proved indeed 'very quiet', with 'little communication' of the sudden eruption of an archbishop and his court.[45]

43 On these, Elton, *Studies* 2, pp. 82–104. For a meeting of Rowland Lee and Cromwell with Cranmer about this time, see P.R.O., S.P. 1/75 f. 94 (*L.P.* 6 no. 333).

44 Kelly, *Matrimonial Trials*, p. 205n: my partial translation.

45 On Markham: Markham, *Markham Memorials*, p. 122. For his appointment in 1526, *L.P.* 4 i no. 2046, and his surrender of the priory, *Faculty Office Registers*, p. 211. Quietness: Thomas Bedell to Cromwell, *Records of the Reformation* 2, p. 473 (*L.P.* 6 no. 461).

The trial opened at Dunstable on 10 May, with Cranmer assisted by Bishop Longland, and in attendance the usual royal payroll of civil lawyers headed by Dr John Bell and Bishop Gardiner.[46] At no stage did Catherine deign to appear, which made Cranmer's task a good deal easier; two days into the proceedings, he could definitively pronounce her contumacious and get on at the fast pace that the arrangements for Anne's coronation required. His progress thus far won him a lawyer's slightly condescending praise from the clerk of the Royal Council, Thomas Bedell: 'my Lord of Canterbury handleth himself very well and very uprightly, without any evident cause of suspicion to be noted in him by the counsel of the said Lady Catherine, if she had had any present here'. Perhaps if such counsel had appeared, they might have found a certain symbolism in the one piece of extraneous clerical business which Cranmer managed to transact at Dunstable during the trial: the collation of Anne's cousin William Boleyn to a lucrative benefice which was an archiepiscopal peculiar in Suffolk.[47]

After 12 May, the trial proved a close-run business; besides the days set aside in the Church kalendar for Rogation and Ascension, there were aged witnesses, the Dowager Duchess of Norfolk and Lady Guildford, who had to be heard, but who refused to risk shortening their lives by toiling up to Dunstable. There was also always the danger that if there was any more publicity, Catherine might change her mind and appear, further delaying matters; Cranmer reminded Cromwell of this on 17 May, enjoining him to silence and secrecy through the days of inaction, in a letter which is depressingly reminiscent of Harpocrates.[48] The silence of Harpocrates also characterized the most intimate part of the proceedings, Dr Bell's statement of Henry's case as proctor for the King, which Cranmer read to himself wordlessly in the court. Besides this central testimony, the lawyers produced the proceedings in the Blackfriars trial – how long ago that must have seemed – and there was now much more testimony to add, including the university opinions and the recent decisions of the Convocation of Canterbury. Favourable decisions of the Convocation of York and of Cambridge University actually arrived during the course of the proceedings.

By 23 May all was ready, and Cranmer pronounced sentence; a flurry of delighted and relieved letters went to Court. To add to the black comedy, Cranmer made his pronouncement as a metropolitan who was automatically

46 The best account is Kelly, *Matrimonial Trials*, pp. 204–13, working around the record of proceedings, B.L. Arundel MS 151, ff. 342–52v; Cranmer himself provided useful details in B.L. Harley MS 6148, f. 25r, Cox 2, p. 244 (*L.P.* 6 no. 661).

47 Bedell to Cromwell, 12 May, *St.P.* 1, p. 395; Boleyn's appointment to Moulton, Cranmer's Register ff. 339v–40r (12 May 1533), and cf. B.L. Harley MS 6148, f. 77r, *L.P.* 7 no. 90 (misdated).

48 B.L. Cotton MS Otho C X f. 166; Cox 2, p. 242 (*L.P.* 6 no. 496). Cf. Bodl. MS Jesus 74, f. 247r, where the copyist Master was clearly embarrassed by this letter and made two attempts to precis it, the second shorter than the first.

papal legate ('*apostolicae sedis legatus*'), despite the silence on this point in his correspondence of 11–12 April with Henry, and he also threatened Henry with excommunication if he did not comply with the sentence.[49] Since that was an unlikely eventuality, all that remained before Anne's coronation was for a definitive judgement that Anne and Henry's marriage was valid. This time the trial was of a petition initiated by the couple themselves rather than of an *officio mero* proceeding; Cranmer returned to Lambeth Palace to hear it after the weekend, giving sentence on 28 May. It is doubtful whether the proceedings were very searching. In an additional piece of fall-out from Dunstable, a curious couple of folios survive from a draft, probably dating from the immediate aftermath of the Dunstable trial. The first folio is in the handwriting of Cranmer with additions by the King himself; the two of them are sketching out a formal statement by the Archbishop that the marriage of Arthur and Catherine had been consummated, with reference to evidence heard at Dunstable. This was probably intended to be packaged up with various documents sent off to the Emperor and Pope in the summer in a last-ditch attempt to persuade them to accept the King's *fait accompli*, but we hear nothing more of it; evidently it was felt better to let well alone on the murky issue of consummation.[50]

At last: the coronation. Eric Ives points out that this was to prove one of the two largest ceremonial displays that London witnessed during Henry's reign, the other having been the reception of the Holy Roman Emperor in 1522.[51] Festivities began on 29 May, with Anne's triumphant and noisy journey up-river from Greenwich to the Tower of London – she used Catherine of Aragon's barge, spluttered Chapuys in outrage.[52] Cranmer entered the drama on Saturday 31 May, pairing up in the cavalcade from the Tower through the City to Westminster with the French ambassador: a mutually reinforcing honour, which showed King Henry's appreciation of King Francis's measured support for his new marriage. Cranmer refrained from commenting on the popular reaction to the magnificent show, and what evidence we have for hostility or enthusiasm invariably reflects the prejudices of each commentator about Anne Boleyn. The following day, Whit Sunday 1 June, the Archbishop played the principal role in the actual coronation ceremony, praying over Anne, anointing and crowning her and delivering her the sceptre and ivory rod; afterwards his old Lincolnshire friend William Benson, the newly appointed Abbot of Westminster, took over to star as celebrant of high mass. The rest of the day was taken up

49 Ridley, *Cranmer*, p. 63; cf. the divorce sentence, pr. Cox 2, pp. 243–4n.

50 See the text, P.R.O., S.P. 1/65 ff. 13–16 (*L.P.* 5 no. 6.5), pr. and reproduced in Kelly, *Matrimonial Trials*, Appendix B, pp. 296–8, and discussed at pp. 237–8. For its reference to the proof of consummation by the admission of Catherine's own *libellus*, cf. ibid., pp. 214–15.

51 Ives, *Anne Boleyn*, p. 215, and see his account of events which follows. For Cranmer's account of the coronation, B.L. Harley MS 6148, f. 25r, Cox 2, pp. 244–7.

52 *C.S.P. Spanish 1531–3*, no. 1077, p. 700.

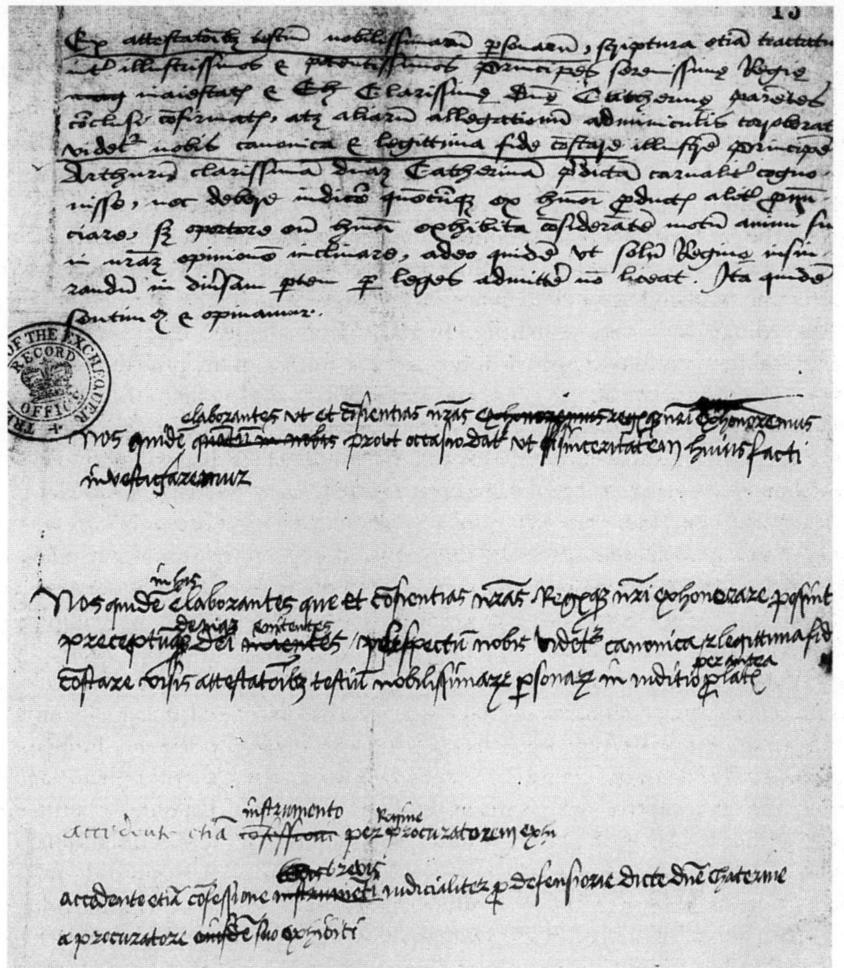

10 Draft statement on consummation of the marriage of Prince Arthur and Catherine of Aragon, in Cranmer's hand, with Henry VIII's own corrections. It was never used.

in manoeuvring the vast crowd of notables across to Westminster Hall and dividing them into honorary waiters and seated guests for the state banquet there; Cranmer was the principal male guest at the feast, exclusively sharing the same table as the new Queen (at a respectful distance), at her right hand. The two of them had the most taxing roles of the day, although the strain on Anne, who was now noticeably six months pregnant, must have been worse. Henry, who by custom was absent both from the coronation and the banquet, stared appreciatively down on proceedings above Cranmer from a specially erected private gallery, as he had already done in the Abbey.

Naturally, Pope Clement was furious at this studied defiance of his prohibitions. In the short term, he was hampered in taking decisive action by the

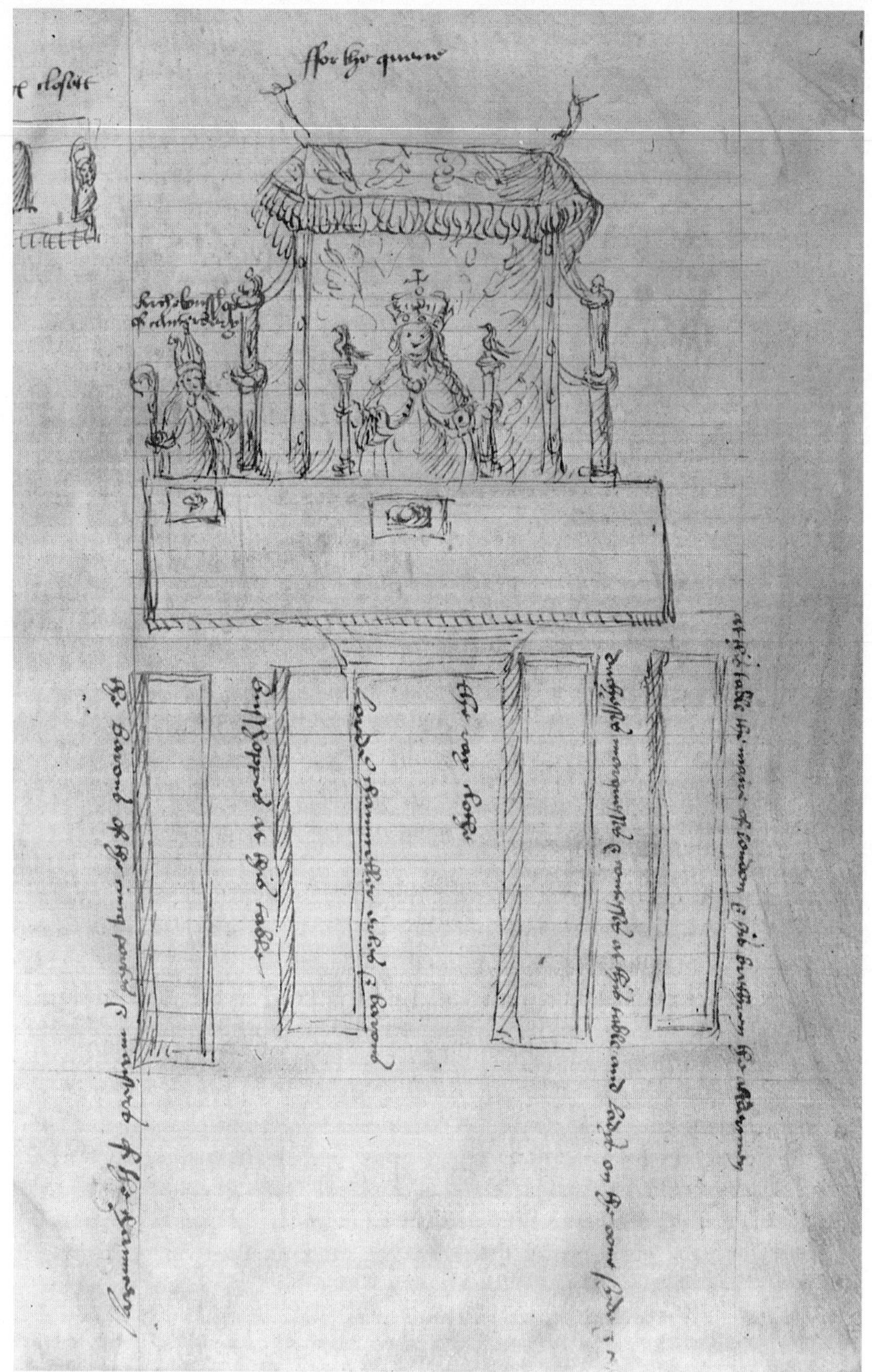

11 Sketch-plan for the Coronation banquet of Anne Boleyn: Cranmer is given the place of honour beside the Queen, while King Henry is decorously placed in an observation gallery above.

pressure on him from the King of France to avoid an irreparable breach with England, but also because of the Emperor's perplexity as to exactly how drastic a procedure would best bring Henry to heel.[53] Henry, moreover, was keeping up an agitated stream of communications with Rome, which was extra reason for the Pope to hope that the breach was not final. The King's next major move, on 30 June, was intended as a delaying tactic against any action: he prepared to give notice of an appeal about his cause of matrimony to the General Council then being planned against the Lutherans. It is noticeable that in royal instructions to Ambassador Hawkins defending the new marriage, the King said that he had acted according to 'God's word and General Councils'.[54] This strategy was cut across by the action of the Pope, who on 9 July provisionally excommunicated the King and his advisers (Cranmer included) unless he put away Anne by the end of September; intimations of this were posted in the Low Countries, a bad blow to Henry.[55]

Yet still the Pope held back from specifically excommunicating Cranmer (much to the annoyance of the Emperor and his senior advisers); still he doled out indulgences and privileges in traditional style to English royal envoys, and still English bishops were being provided by means of papal bulls: Cranmer was not the last such bishop, as is sometimes stated. At the end of August, Abbot Christopher Lord, Cranmer's own new suffragan for the diocese of Canterbury, was given bulls of provision as Bishop of Sidon (to add to the bizarre circumstances, a bureaucratic oversight thus gave him a title already held by another English suffragan!), and these bulls duly formed part of his appointment. At his consecration at Lambeth in January 1534, Lord made the same protestation about papal authority that Cranmer himself had pronounced in St Stephen's ten months before.[56] It is to this period of phoney war between the English monarchy and the papacy that we ought to ascribe an otherwise puzzling report a few years later from a London priest called George Rowland: he was a devout papalist, and described being called before the Archbishop 'for a certain business'. In the course of his examination he had said defiantly to Cranmer that he 'would pray for the Pope as the chief and principal head of Christ's Church; and the Bishop told me that it was the King's pleasure that I should not so do'. Rowland retorted that he would go on doing so 'so long as there was a memento of him in the mass' (which dates the incident before the supremacy legislation of 1534), and faced with this

53 *L.P.* 6 nos 568–70, 643, 654; *C.S.P. Spanish 1531–3*, no. 1143, p. 838.

54 P.R.O., E. 30/1026–7 (Rymer, *Foedera* 14, p. 476); *C.S.P. Spanish 1531–3*, no. 1108, pp. 760–61. Instructions for Emperor, 6 July 1533: *Records of the Reformation* 2, p. 494 (*L.P.* 6 no. 775). Cf. articles about the General Council sent to Cranmer that summer by the Bishop of Reggio, *L.P.* Add. 1 i no. 895, and *C.S.P. Spanish 1531–3*, no. 1094, p. 728.

55 *L.P.* 6, Appendix no. 3; *C.S.P. Spanish 1531–3*, no. 1111, p. 766, 1113, p. 769.

56 Ayris Ph.D., 'Cranmer's Register', p. 188. On the delay in excommunicating Cranmer, see *C.S.P. Spanish 1531–3*, no. 1120, p. 781; *L.P.* 6 no. 1104. Papal privileges: *L.P.* 6 Appendix nos 5, 6 (August 1533).

liturgical logic, Cranmer told him that he 'might pray for him secretly, but in any wise do it not openly'.[57]

The whole enterprise of the Boleyn marriage was completed with the successful end to Anne Boleyn's pregnancy on 7 September. A second daughter was not what the King had expected, but he was not going to give ammunition to sneering Aragonese partisans by seeming disappointed, and he put a brave face on matters; at least a healthy child boded well for Anne's future pregnancies. The baby was given Henry's mother's name, Elizabeth, and it was appropriate that, as at the coronation, Cranmer should take the leading role; although Bishop Stokesley, his close colleague in the annulment research, performed the actual christening, Cranmer confirmed her immediately afterwards and acted as one of her godparents. The ceremony took place in the church of the Friars Observant at Greenwich: perhaps an obvious choice near Anne's place of confinement, but also a deliberate assertion of triumph over this former centre of resistance to the Boleyn marriage. It was four years to the month since Cranmer had begun work on preparing for the marriage that had produced this child.[58]

It is difficult to assess exactly how far the new Archbishop's views had travelled by this time from the conventional piety of his Cambridge days, apart from the accumulation of imprecisely hostile remarks which we have heard from conservative commentators: the one inescapable fact demonstrating his commitment to the evangelical cause is his marriage in Nuremberg the previous year. Apart from that, there is evidence of continuity in one respect: his admiration for Erasmus. That patron saint of freelance writers was naturally concerned for the pension granted him by his old friend Archbishop Warham when a new incumbent was installed at Canterbury; indeed with sublime innocence of the new configuration of English politics, he had written twice to Thomas More as one of the people who might approach the new Archbishop to secure his money.[59] However, Erasmus was reassured by warm greetings from the new Archbishop; then, to his relief, Cranmer honoured his promises, and an instalment of the money itself arrived in autumn 1533. Erasmus did not include Cranmer in his strictures on the spread of Lutheran ideas in England.[60] Instead, with the warm ecumenism of a satisfied pensioner, he spoke of his new patron as 'a most blameless man and of a most honest disposition' ('*vir integerrimus candidissimisque moribus*'), which does not suggest that any rumours about Mrs Cranmer were travelling round the Continental humanist circuit. He went on to exclaim that 'Warham can be seen not to have been snatched away from me, but to have been reborn in

57 P.R.O., S.P. 1/102 ff. 73–4 (*L.P.* 10 no. 346).
58 Hall 2, pp. 242–4; cf. the official notarial record, C.C.C.C. MS 105, p. 274 (*L.P.* 6 no. 1111).
59 Erasmus, *Opus Epistolarum*, 10, p. 258.
60 Ibid., 10, p. 204. Cf. ibid. 10, p. 196, 233 for the negotiations.

Cranmer': a wildly inappropriate remark which would have made English conservatives wince if they had read it.[61]

Cranmer continued to be as good as his word: despite England's breach with Rome, the Canterbury pension went on finding its way to Erasmus right up to his death with only slight hitches, one of which was caused, ironically, by the fact that it was drawn from the benefice of Aldington, held by the attainted supporter of Elizabeth Barton, Richard Master. Cranmer even supplemented the amount to make up for the delay, and got Cromwell to do the same. He never lost his good opinion of Erasmus, who was the only modern writer named in the Archbishop's list of necessary books for Canterbury Cathedral Library in his visitation articles of 1550.[62] Nevertheless, a deep admiration for Europe's greatest humanist did not necessarily signify agreement with every aspect of his thought; it is unlikely that by 1533 Cranmer would have taken Erasmus's side against Luther on justification as he had once done in the margins of his copy of *De Libero Arbitrio* (see above, pp. 30–31). Everything else by this time speaks of his conscious breach with the past.

One silence in particular in Cranmer's later career becomes deafening once one notices it: his virtually complete neglect of Jesus College, the institution that had been so good to him in the grief-stricken aftermath of his first marriage, and of which he had been a Fellow for nearly two decades. Cranmer was not a good College man, once he left his Fellowship for higher things. Recorded contacts between him and the College are few: there are only two mentions of Jesus, for instance, in his surviving correspondence. The first is only a few months after he became Archbishop in 1533, when he sent Dr Capon, the Master, a buck for a College feast, with a rather nervous joke about his own lack of finance to provide a more generous present.[63] The second letter, in 1535, appears actually to be an intervention against the College, when he asked Cromwell to suspend proceedings against certain people who were supposedly troubling a College tenant.[64] One or two Jesus contemporaries of his, for instance, Bishop Thomas Goodrich, his servant and relative Francis Bassett, and his chaplain and almoner John Whitwell, remained lifelong associates; that is hardly surprising.[65] What is noticeable is the lack

61 '*ut mihi Waramus non ereptus, sed in Cronmero renatus videri queat*': Erasmus, *Opus Epistolarum*, 10, p. 318. Ridley, *Cranmer*, p. 136 has misinterpreted the reference to a Lutheran servant at ibid. 10, p. 151, which is in fact to a member of Warham's household; cf. ibid., p. 173.

62 Erasmus, *Opus Epistolarum*, 11, pp. 71, 144, 232–3, 275–8, 296, 321. For the articles, Cox 2, p. 161.

63 B.L. Harl. 6148, f. 24v, pr. Cox 2, p. 247 (*L.P.* 6 no. 703).

64 P.R.O., S.P. 1/91 ff. 207–8, pr. Cox 2 p. 302–3 (*L.P.* 8 no. 508).

65 Goodrich: Venn 2, p. 237; Bassett: Venn 1, p. 103. Whitwell: Venn 4 p. 397. He was B.A. 1515/16, M.A. 1519, and B.D. 1533/4 (a compliment to Cranmer?), besides being vicar of All Saints, Cambridge, from 1524; this was probably All Saints in the Jewry, and combined with the nominal parish of St Radegund attached to Jesus College chapel.

of further patronage to younger members of the College in his years of greatness: just one of his many chaplains, Thomas Langley, was a Jesus man from the years after Cranmer left the College.[66] This is really very strange.

The explanation is surely that while Cranmer had moved on theologically, the Fellowship of his old College had not: in particular, Cranmer's relations with William Capon are likely to have become cool. At the very beginning of the crisis of the Reformation, Capon was given a bad fright by his brief and stormy career as Wolsey's Dean of the ill-fated Cardinal College, Ipswich, which had ended with the Master of Jesus escaping back to the comparative calm of Cambridge in autumn 1530. As soon as Cranmer became Archbishop, Capon would have seen how he was going to use his influence in the drive to further religious change. Capon's views did not keep pace with his former Fellow's pursuit of reform during the 1530s, and he must have become increasingly disillusioned with the direction Henry VIII's Reformation was taking; he resigned as Master of Jesus in November 1546, leaving the College finances in a state of confusion from which they took years to recover.[67] There was probably much bitterness around the Master's departure; another veteran Fellow, Leonard Gyll, left nothing to the College when he made his will six months after Capon's departure in 1547.[68]

By the time that Capon made his own will, four years after his resignation, he in turn had lost all touch with the College over which he had presided for thirty years; there is not a single mention of it in the whole of a long will full of charitable largesse.[69] Capon was by then dividing his time between his Hampshire benefices and a lodging in Salisbury near his brother, the congenially conservative Bishop of Salisbury, and the life portrayed in the will is of an old man sadly and defiantly clinging to the traditional devotional life of the Church in a corner of England where it was still possible. Far away in Cambridge, the royal visitors of 1549 had transformed the College that he had known for so long: smashed its images, stripped it of its six altars and with it the service of God which he so clearly loved.[70] There was nothing in Cambridge left for Capon; and that was the outcome of Cranmer's Reformation. It is perhaps appropriate that the handsome modern memorial to the Archbishop in the south transept of Jesus Chapel has no comment or inscription except the single word CRANMER.

Immediately after the coronation in June 1533, Cranmer was confronted with two very different tasks of an archbishop's discipline which would define the nature of his episcopate under Henry VIII, and which also begin to provide us with indications of how his thoughts were moving. First was the embarrassing prospect of not merely disciplining an evangelical, but seeing

66 Venn 2, p. 45: student Jesus 1535–6, B.A. 1537–8.
67 *Victoria County History: Cambridgeshire* 3, p. 422.
68 C.U.L. UA Wills 1, f. 81r.
69 P.C.C. 22 Coode (26 July 1550, proved 11 October 1550).
70 C.C.C.C. MS 106, f. 490Av.

him burnt at the stake. The hopes of the evangelical party at home and abroad were the mirror-image of Chapuys's opinion of the new Archbishop: 'write to my Lord of Canterbury', the exile George Joye urged his friend Hugh Latimer a month after Cranmer's consecration, 'and animate him to his office. He is in a perilous place, but yet in a glorious place to plant the Gospel.' In view of Joye's scepticism about sacrifice and real presence in the eucharist, as expressed in his anonymous tract *The Supper of the Lord*, it was he himself who would have been in a perilous place if he had presented himself in England.[71] Instead it was Joye's friend and critic John Frith who suffered death for his denial of the real presence. Frith had been arrested in 1532 on returning to England from work with William Tyndale in the Low Countries, and in an orgy of writing while in prison in the Tower of London, he had spelled out his views on the eucharist, against Tyndale's explicit advice.[72] Now in June he was brought from the Tower first to Lambeth and then to Cranmer's Surrey house at Croydon for several examinations about his 'sacramentarian' eucharistic theology by a high-powered commission of bishops and aristocrats, before his final sentence of condemnation as a heretic in the consistory court of London. Cranmer reported on the proceedings to his friend and successor as ambassador to the Emperor, Nicholas Hawkins; he was quite clear that Frith was in serious error on the eucharist:

> whose opinion was so notably erroneous, that we could not dispatch him . . . His said opinion is of such nature, that he thought it not necessary to be believed as an article of our faith, that there is the very corporal presence of Christ within the host and sacrament of the altar, and holdeth of this point most after the opinion of Oecolampadius. And surely I myself sent for him three or four times to persuade him to leave that his imagination; but for all that we could do therein, he would not apply to any counsel.[73]

Martin Luther would have said no less. Cranmer, after his experience of Oecolampadius's colleague and successor Simon Grynaeus in 1531, knew exactly what he was talking about when discussing variants on Swiss theology, and he was evidently prepared to spend a good deal of time to argue Frith out of his views; but when he failed, the law must proceed, and as he told Hawkins without especial drama, Frith now 'looketh every day to go unto the fire'. However, the Archbishop gave the Basel reformer his Latinized academic surname, recognizing his status as an evangelical fellow-scholar; most hostile Catholic English commentators referred to Oecolampadius (if they knew of him at all) only by his original German surname, Hussgen. It may also be significant that in this account written to an intimate friend, Cranmer did not use the word 'heretic' about Frith; Luther and Lutherans,

71 P.R.O., S.P. 1/75 f. 210 (*L.P.* 6 no. 402), and see Butterworth and Chester, *Joye*, pp. 93–6. Cargill Thompson, 'Who wrote "The Supper of the Lord"?'.

72 Foxe 5, p. 133.

73 B.L. Harley MS 6148, f. 25r; Cox 2, p. 246 (17 June 1533).

having been so often called heretics themselves, tended to avoid the term as tainted, and Cranmer may have felt the same way after his experience of Lutheran Germany.[74]

Frith was burned on 4 July. His death was not of Cranmer's making; the situation was one which the Archbishop had inherited, and he can hardly be blamed for not knowing in 1533 that he would change his mind on the question of the eucharist thirteen years later. One also has to consider the politics of the Frith case against the background of the major row over Hugh Latimer's preaching which was still dragging on in Bristol; this had started back in March and had nearly got in the way of the annulment legislation in Convocation (see above, p. 88). By June, Latimer's enemies were on the defensive, thanks to sympathy for him among Bristol's secular authorities: it would be a gift to them if someone who could be associated with Latimer's evangelical circle, and who had gone so grievously off the rails in eucharistic theology, was seen to be let off the hook. As the breach with Rome widened, it was important to be firm against such 'sacramentaries' as Frith in order that Henry's regime did not lose the loyalty of conservative leaders like Bishop Stokesley, who detested Latimer to the extent of forbidding him to preach in his diocese during autumn 1533.[75]

Nevertheless, the Frith affair is not a happy story, particularly since Frith's reputation remained high among evangelicals, and his writings and Catholic refutations of them continued to be printed into the reign of Edward VI. John Foxe clearly found the whole business embarrassing; he first minimized Cranmer's role and later seized gratefully on a circumstantial account of one of Cranmer's household gentlemen vainly giving Frith the chance to escape in the woods around Brixton while they escorted him to Croydon. However, honesty compelled Foxe to narrate the story in a way that made it clear that Cranmer was not involved in this abortive act of mercy. Foxe also made the best of a bad job by suggesting that in Cranmer's *Answer* to Gardiner of 1551, Frith had been the chief source of ammunition for the Archbishop's assault on Wily Winchester: 'I doubt much whether the archbishop ever gave any more credit unto any author of that doctrine, than unto this aforesaid Frith.'[76] It may be so, and in terms of common outlook, Cranmer's eucharistic theology did eventually settle down to be much like Frith's, but unless Foxe had information otherwise lost to us, Cranmer kept his revised opinion of Frith to himself.

In July Cranmer began his involvement with a second disciplinary issue of even greater political significance, but this time one whose resolution would

74 On Luther's views on executing Christians, Levy, *Treason against God*, pp. 124–30.

75 On the Latimer affair at Bristol, see Skeeters, *Community and Clergy*, pp. 38–46, and for Cranmer's intimate involvement with the Bristol evangelicals, Cox 2, p. 275, B.L. Harley MS 6148, ff. 41Bv, 76v (*L.P.* 6 no. 1570, 7 no. 89). On Stokesley's prohibition, Foxe 7, p. 459; Appendix VII.

76 Foxe 5, p. 11; 8, pp. 697–9; 5, p. 9.

much benefit the evangelical cause. Over the previous decade the diocese of Canterbury had experienced an exceptionally spectacular case of a phenomenon not uncommon in late medieval England: a female visionary, Elizabeth Barton, who came to be known as the Maid of Kent when the fame of her visions spread. She was a servant-girl of the large Kentish village of Aldington, who had started making prophecies during an illness in 1525; she had soon linked these to the task of reviving a cult of Our Lady in a nearby free chapel at Court at Street ('Courtupstreet', as it appears in most contemporary accounts). Her master was a steward to Archbishop Warham, and the incumbent of Aldington was also a long-standing protégé of the Archbishop; so from the start, Barton found herself the object of fascinated attention by the Warham circle. The first account of her wonders was written by Edward Thwaites, a local gentleman who married as his second wife the widow of the Archbishop's nephew. Barton was consigned to a nunnery at Canterbury, St Sepulchre, under the Archbishop's patronage. She had a senior monk of the Cathedral, Edward Bocking, as her spiritual adviser, and Warham's chaplain, the former Cambridge don Henry Gold, as one of her chief promoters.[77]

In late 1528 the Maid focussed her attention on Catherine of Aragon's cause, predicting dire disasters for the King and the kingdom if Henry got his way over the annulment. With extraordinary self-confidence – there was clearly something remarkable about her – she began a series of interviews with Archbishop Warham and prevailed on him at the end of September 1528 to give her a letter of introduction to Wolsey himself; she even saw the King. Warham remained deeply impressed by her, and was swayed from his lifetime of automatic obedience to the monarch's wishes towards passive resistance to the annulment plans. In late 1529 Barton was before the King again, and even confronted Anne Boleyn, who is reliably said to have offered her a place at Court; yet the Maid was not to be diverted, and on her return from seeing the royal couple, she made a first visit which one might have thought would have happened earlier – to Bishop John Fisher. She was now fully integrated into the rearguard action of Catherine's political supporters; and her contacts continued to multiply, as the plans for the Boleyn marriage fell into place. Sir Thomas More, ultra-cautious in placing himself in the public opposition to Henry, postponed seeing her until late June 1533, after Anne's coronation.

For five years the Maid had moved in perfect freedom around Kent and the capital, exploiting to their limits both the customary latitude given to inspired women and the confused state of English treason law. By the time More saw her, her days were numbered: her words were now directed at a crowned Queen. Cranmer was the appropriate person to exercise discipline over her not simply by personal inclination but also as the Ordinary of her

77 The most comprehensive account of Barton is in Neame, *Maid of Kent*; sources are taken from there unless otherwise noted.

diocese: the King ordered him to do his duty. In July he moved for the first time over the county border to take up residence in his principal north Kent property, Otford Palace, and in a Saturday filled with correspondence, 19 July, he summoned the prioress of St Sepulchre, Canterbury, together with 'your nun which was some time at Courtupstreet' for the following Wednesday, 23 July.[78] From now on, Barton was constantly under questioning. On 11 August there is one surviving account of these interviews from Richard Gwent to Cromwell, which indicates the government's double strategy: Cranmer had been cast in the role which came easily to him, of sympathetic listener, while Cromwell was being kept as the remote, unsympathetic interrogator. The Maid evidently felt by now that she had a charmed life, and she was not prepared for a Primate who did anything else but lap up her mysticism. Gwent reported that the Maid claimed to have had her last major vision at Whitsuntide, in other words at the time of the coronation, but at that stage 'she had this answer that without fail at the next trance she shall have a determinate answer, and therefore she desired licence of my Lord to go to Courtupstreet' – obviously with the aim of being there at the major Marian feast on 15 August, the Assumption of Our Lady:

> and my Lord hath given her leave to go thither, and to repair to him again, trusting that then he shall plainly perceive her foolish dissimulation; an if your interrogatories had not been, she would have confessed nothing, for my Lord doth yet but dally with her, as [if] he did believe her every word; and as soon as he hath all he can get of her, she shall be sent to you.[79]

On Barton's return to Cranmer from the shrine, she was indeed sent to Cromwell, and it was probably at this stage, in early autumn, that Hugh Latimer joined Cranmer and Cromwell as her principal interrogator, signalling his rehabilitation at Court after the Bristol furore. Given Latimer's longstanding contempt for the more extrovert aspects of traditional religion, it is likely that the government's continuing outward pretence of treating Barton as a lady worthy of great respect now wore thin.[80] It may well have been the sudden dose of cold water provided by Latimer's withering scepticism which caused the Maid's self-confidence to collapse. Richard Morison, admittedly not a sympathetic commentator, said that the interrogators found her Achilles heel when they asked to her to divine matters that had happened in the past, about which she had no information.[81] Eventually she 'confessed all, and

78 B.L. Harley MS 6148, f. 30v; Cox 2, p. 252: the note is not dated, but occurs in a sequence of letters of 19 July. *L.P.* 6 no. 616 redates from 1534 to 10 June 1533 P.R.O., S.P. 1/76 ff. 197–8 (Cox 2, p. 296); this would put Cranmer briefly in Kent during June 1533. I see no reason to accept this redating; a 1534 date for that letter fits his movements better. For Cromwell's reference on 23 July to two letters written to Cranmer about the Maid, P.R.O., S.P. 1/78 f. 26 (*L.P.* 6 no. 887).

79 P.R.O., S.P. 1/78 fo. 119 (*L.P.* 6, no. 967).

80 Hall 2, p. 245; cf. Neame, *Maid of Kent*, p. 239.

81 Neame, *Maid of Kent*, p. 241, qu. Morison, *Apomaxis*, ff. 75–6.

uttered the very truth, which is this: that she never had vision in all her life, but all that ever she said was feigned of her own imagination, only to satisfy the minds of them the which resorted unto her, and to obtain worldly praise'. So Cranmer reported to his confidant Ambassador Hawkins in December 1533: it was a sad record of a psychological disintegration.[82] During September and October her clerical associates in Kent were rounded up and arrested, and a satisfyingly large number of incriminating papers were discovered. During November she and her principal backers were examined and humiliated by the royal Council both in private and in Star Chamber, and on 23 November they were brought to the open-air pulpit at Paul's Cross in London to hear the Maid's entire career ridiculed by Abbot John Salcot (alias Capon: the brother of the Master of Jesus, Cranmer's old college).

By now Barton's downfall was becoming part of a breach with Rome which could not be healed. In the autumn the Pope finally decided that he could no longer tolerate the spectacle of his authority in England being turned on and off like a tap by the English government; he ended the farce of providing bulls for English bishoprics, to the acute alarm of the first victim, appropriately enough John Salcot, bishop-elect of Bangor.[83] It was probably this evidence of the deteriorating situation which provoked Cranmer initially to panic about his own position; on 22 November he wrote to Henry's representative in Marseilles, Edmund Bonner, saying that he stood 'in dread, lest our holy father the Pope do intend to make some manner of prejudicial process against me and my church', and on the advice of the King and his Council, he forwarded his own appeal to a General Council.[84] He was not to know that at the beginning of the month Bonner had already made a desperate situation irretrievable at Marseilles by announcing Henry's appeal to a General Council to the Pope's face.

Nevertheless the government's nerve soon steadied: the royal Council now quickly took the decision to face out papal wrath, unleashing a full-scale campaign of preaching against the Pope as the centre-piece of an unprecedented propaganda drive to justify a complete break with a millennium of close Anglo-papal relations.[85] The Act in Restraint of Appeals was printed in December as a proclamation, apparently the first time that separate publication for an Act of Parliament had been undertaken. Additionally, a new propaganda pamphlet, the *Articles Devised by the Whole Consent of the King's most Honourable Council*, was distributed and displayed throughout the realm; this explicitly denied the power of the Bishop of Rome outside his own diocese, and asserted the authority of the General Council. The conciliar theme would have been music to Cranmer's ears, and Chapuys noted him by early Decem-

82 B.L. Harley MS 6148, ff. 40–41; Cox 2, p. 274.

83 *St.P.* 1, p. 410.

84 Cox 2, p. 268, B.L. Harley MS 6148, f. 237v (*L.P.* 6 no. 1454).

85 On Bonner, Scarisbrick, *Henry VIII*, p. 319. The Council policy document of the end of November is *St.P.* 1, pp. 411–15; cf. *C.S.P. Spanish 1531–3*, nos 1157–9.

ber as being the leader in defiance of Rome among a reluctant crew of English bishops.[86]

Central to this urgent display of the government's defiance and control of events was Cranmer's enthronement as Archbishop in Canterbury Cathedral on 3 December; this also heralded the next stage in the Maid's destruction. The enthronement was the new Archbishop's first chance to make a symbolic display of the full force of his authority. There are glimpses of the feasting in the Cathedral priory, and in Canterbury city accounts there are payments recorded for presents and a path of sand from Cranmer's lodging with the city's leading lawyer Christopher Hales, so that his barefoot procession through the streets to the Cathedral should not be too uncomfortable an act of ritual humiliation on a chilly December day.[87] Four days later the Maid and her promoters faced a repeat performance of the earlier Paul's Cross spectacle in the Cathedral precinct, where Nicholas Heath (at this stage one of Cranmer's leading assistants) 'wittily and learnedly' preached against her. The text of the sermon still exists, with corrections in Cranmer's own hand revealing that however witty and learned Heath was, he was simply preaching the same sermon that Capon had used in London a fortnight before, slightly adapted by Cranmer himself.[88] Within a week the Archbishop had begun his first visitation of his diocese, including his peculiar jurisdiction of Calais; this was another opportunity to root out supporters of the Maid (including his erstwhile Cambridge acquaintance Henry Gold) and to elicit declarations against her. Soon after came another display of his power in the county: at the beginning of 1534 he re-established the mint which by ancient right the archbishops of Canterbury maintained in their cathedral city, issuing their own version of the kingdom's silver coinage.[89]

On 20 December Cranmer relaxed after a tense and busy period by writing a satirical summary of the Maid's entire career, for the entertainment of his friend, Archdeacon Hawkins, in Spain. He even included one or two phrases lifted out of an anti-Tyndale pamphlet by Sir Thomas More, describing another modern visionary of Ipswich, and reapplied them to the Maid: evi-

86 Elton, *Studies* 3, p. 101; Fox and Guy, *Reassessing the Henrician Age*, pp. 116–17. *C.S.P. Spanish 1531–3*, no. 1158, p. 879. The *Articles* are pr. in *Records of the Reformation* 2, pp. 523–31.

87 P.R.O., S.P. 1/87 ff. 104–5, wrongly dated to 1534 because of Prior Goldwell's misdating, *L.P.* 7 no. 1520; *H.M.C., 9th Report*, p. 152.

88 Cox 2, p. 66; *Narratives of the Reformation*, p. 280. The sermon is P.R.O., S.P. 1/82 ff. 89–96, pr. with inadequate critical apparatus in 'The Sermon against the Holy Maid of Kent', ed. Whatmore.

89 *Narratives of the Reformation*, p. 281; Lambeth Cart. Misc. XII 56 (9 December 1533); on Calais, Cox 2, p. 275, B.L. Harley MS 6148, f. 41Br (*L.P.* 6 no. 1568). Cf. the declaration of Christ Church Priory, Wright, *Suppression*, pp. 19–25. On Gold, Cox 2, p. 277, P.R.O., S.P. 1/82 f. 15 (*L.P.* 7 no. 17). On the mint, Challis, *Tudor Coinage*, pp. 71–3.

dently a joke which both of them would understand.[90] Cranmer detested the Maid, for the very good reason that he was aware of her real influence on past events. 'Surely I think that she did marvellously stop the going forward of the king's marriage by the reason of her visions', even affecting Wolsey and Warham: 'with her feigned visions and godly threatenings, she stayed them very much in the matter'. In his corrections to the Salcot/Heath sermon, it was Cranmer who had made sure that the text used the word 'heretical' to describe her pronouncements, the very description which he had shied away from applying to John Frith's eucharistic views in the previous summer. He would have no compassion for Barton's fate and that of her associates: first bundled back to the Tower, and finally in April 1534 executed with the usual cruelty applied to traitors, after condemnation by the drastic short-cut of a Parliamentary attainder – there were too many risks in an open trial of her singular activities.[91]

For all the danger that the Maid represented before her arrest, once her power was broken, it became apparent how much the new Archbishop owed to her. She had achieved what probably no one else would have been able to do: the ruin or disgrace of the senior clergy and diocesan establishment bequeathed by Archbishop Warham. Every bishop needs to assert his authority and establish his staff against the previous incumbent, but the necessity was acute in the case of Thomas Cranmer. Warham had been Archbishop for nearly three decades when he died; he had set up several members of his Hampshire gentry family in the county establishment of Kent, and his clerical and lay entourage extended much further than that. As Cranmer and his associates arrived to take over the splendid and ancient power-structure which was the province and diocese of Canterbury, it would have been immediately apparent how different they were from Warham's men. There was an obvious contrast even in their university backgrounds. Warham was an Oxford man, and so were most of his servants; Cranmer was a Cambridge don who had passed up his chance to join the payroll of Cardinal College, Oxford, in the previous decade. All Canterbury's natural connections were with Oxford; the Cathedral priory actually maintained a college in the university named Canterbury College. By accidents of foundation, the Archbishop was Visitor of All Souls', Magdalen and Merton colleges, but he had no such organic links with colleges at Cambridge. Now Cranmer, faced with the daunting task of building up a great episcopal household virtually from scratch, imported his Midlands and Lincolnshire relatives and his Cambridge cronies to outface this affronted and conservative world.

90 Neame, *Maid of Kent*, p. 70, though note that he follows the misreading of Cox 2, p. 272 of 'disordered' for 'deformed': cf. B.L. Harley MS 6148, f. 40r (*L.P.* 6 no. 1546). On Anne Wentworth of Ipswich, see MacCulloch, *Suffolk and the Tudors*, pp. 143–5.

91 Elton, *Policy and Police*, pp. 274–5. On Cranmer's correction to 'heretical', apparently of a scribal error 'eternal', see first line of P.R.O., S.P. 1/82 f. 93v.

During 1533 the process of setting up a new archiepiscopal clique proceeded only slowly in the face of the entrenched Warham set; although the Archbishop had found himself overwhelmed with offers of service from eager lay relatives, the task of finding suitable local niches for his clerical protégés was harder.[92] In July 1533 he had succeeded in winkling out Warham's old secretary, Thomas Baschurch, from the wealthy Kent living of Chevening, a few miles from his palaces at Otford and Knole, in order to place his chaplain and old Cambridge friend, Richard Astall. He had a good excuse, since Baschurch had suffered a nervous breakdown a week or two after Cranmer had been consecrated Archbishop (the two events were probably connected); later the poor old man became suicidal in his despair at the religious changes of the 1530s, despite the pension which he received on resigning Chevening.[93] However, there are few other obvious significant new appointments until Elizabeth Barton's humiliation; after that, a range of senior figures were removed or put firmly in their place. Thomas Goldwell, Prior of Christ Church (that is, Canterbury Cathedral Priory) was not arrested, for he had been careful to keep his distance from the Maid: indeed he had reputedly achieved the remarkable feat of postponing his first meeting with her until November 1531. Nevertheless, Goldwell was badly frightened; among his senior priory staff, the penitentiary Dom William Hadleigh and the cellarer Dom Edmund Bocking were arrested, and Bocking was executed. Goldwell's urgent desire to please the government thereafter meant that the potentially formidable leadership of the Cathedral Priory was no threat to Cranmer before its dissolution in 1540. Another prominent potential trouble-maker, Richard Risby, the Warden of the Canterbury Observant Friars, was executed along with the Maid, and the Maid's gentleman biographer, Edward Thwaites, was nearly ruined by the confiscation of his estates.[94]

Perhaps most importantly, the destruction of the Maid gave Cranmer the chance to get rid of Archbishop Warham's Archdeacon of Canterbury, a younger William Warham, together with his clientage. Supposedly William senior's nephew, William junior is absent from the Warham family pedigree, which strengthens the likelihood that the Archdeacon was actually the Archbishop's bastard son. Archdeacons of Canterbury, as the only archdeacons in the Primate's own diocese, had taken on exceptional importance and powers, including the right to instal all bishops in the province of Canterbury; they had a castle of their own at Lympne as well as a house in Canterbury, and moreover Archdeacon Warham was Provost of wealthy Wingham College

92 Cox 2, p. 248, B.L. Harley MS 6148, f. 24v (*L.P.* 6 no. 704).

93 B.L. Harley MS 6148, f. 79r (*L.P.* 6 no. 786); cf. Cox 2, pp. 254–5, B.L. Harley MS 6148, f. 32r (*L.P.* 6 no. 885), and Cox 2, pp. 319–20, P.R.O., S.P. 1/101 f. 110 (*L.P.* 10 no. 113). Baschurch retained his London living: see a slightly inaccurate account in Brigden, *London and the Reformation*, pp. 203, 278.

94 On Goldwell and the maid, Neame, *Maid of Kent*, pp. 138–40; cf. Cox 2, p. 271, B.L. Harley MS 6148, f. 5r (*L.P.* 6 no. 1519). On Thwaites, Neame, *Maid of Kent*, pp. 345–6.

near Canterbury and rector of the important Middlesex archiepiscopal parish of Hayes.[95] The Archdeacon's registrar, Thomas Laurence, and his vicar at Hayes, Henry Gold (Warham's former chaplain), were both implicated in the Maid's treasons, and Gold was executed; this gave both good reason and occasion for Cranmer to disperse these assets into reliable hands. Who better to take them than his clerical younger brother Edmund Cranmer? During February and March 1534, the transaction was completed: Warham surrendered the archdeaconry and the provostship of Wingham to Edmund Cranmer in return for a pension totalling a handsome £80 per annum; although he seems to have kept the rectory of Hayes until his death a quarter-century later, and he retained other preferment, he became as invisible as Wolsey's bastard son Thomas Winter after the Cardinal's downfall.[96] Edmund meanwhile proved an ideal assistant for his brother, being supportive without ever trying to rival him. Theologically they were soulmates, as is first indicated by the fact that Edmund quickly emulated Thomas's rejection of clerical celibacy; by 1535 he had fathered a son (named Thomas after his brother), which implies a secret marriage in 1534.[97]

Such was the trauma of the Maid of Kent's overthrow that the conservative gentry and clergy of Kent who had been Archbishop Warham's admiring satellites were intimidated and silenced for half a decade. Only in the early 1540s did they regain enough confidence, goaded by their fury at the pace of change, to attempt a comeback and an overthrow of Cranmer's evangelical establishment; this so-called Prebendaries' Plot of 1543 then seemed for a moment as if it would achieve a reversal of Cranmer's ten-year triumph (see below, Ch. 8). But in 1534, Cranmer was riding high. Already in his first year of consecration he had set a theological course (in conjunction with Hugh Latimer) which had now thrown off any remaining doubts of his evangelical commitment. He might distance himself in good Lutheran fashion from John Frith's alarming radicalism on the eucharist, but equally, in a number of ways, he clearly signalled that he had broken with the old religion; in particular, the conservative humanist consensus which had characterized Henry's divorce research team in the later 1520s was long in the past for him.

Gradually, as Cranmer got the measure of his new fiefdom, he seized opportunities that went beyond the discountenancing of the demoralized Warham hierarchy. The diocese (as opposed to the province) of Canterbury possessed by historical accident a number of peculiars, odd islands of jurisdiction outside its main geographical block, in which the Archbishop could exercise direct influence in otherwise inaccessible places where the surround-

95 On the Archdeaconry, see Churchill, *Canterbury Administration* 1, pp. 45, 560. For a Warham pedigree, *Visitations of Kent 1530–1, 1574, 1592*, 2, p. 147.

96 Cranmer's Register, ff. 343v–44, 347r–350r; Emden, *Oxford to 1540*, p. 707.

97 B.L. Additional MS 41781 f. 107 makes the son Thomas (later Registrar of Canterbury) die in 1604, aged 69.

ing church leadership was not sympathetic to reform. We have already seen Cranmer using one fragment of this patronage in Suffolk for one of Queen Anne's relatives (see above, p. 93). Also in East Anglia was the deanery of Bocking, a scattered collection of Essex and Suffolk parishes, which could now act as a convenient evangelical fifth column in the dioceses of two conservative bishops: John Stokesley of London, and that magnificent traditionalist veteran of the episcopal bench, Richard Nix of Norwich. The most important community in the deanery of Bocking was the Suffolk town of Hadleigh, which even in the late 1520s was a notorious haunt of evangelicals, comparatively safe beyond the jurisdiction of the infuriated Bishop Nix. One of Stephen Gardiner's Fellows of Trinity Hall, little Thomas Bilney destined for martyrdom, had caused a county-wide stir in Suffolk by his preaching at Hadleigh from 1527, and soon afterwards a further evangelical pioneer, a newly arrived Devon priest called Thomas Rose, also made Hadleigh his base of operations. Cranmer undoubtedly knew of all this in his Cambridge days, not least because one of his Jesus colleagues was called over to Hadleigh as a safe man to preach down Rose's dangerous ideas: one John Bale, who subsequently came to have rather different opinions.[98]

Like Bale, Cranmer was a changed man by the time he became a bishop, and despite or because of the fact that Rose was now notorious in East Anglia for his involvement in a spectacular iconoclastic outrage in 1531/2, he offered Rose his protection. About midsummer 1533 Cranmer seems to have got Rose transferred from extremely unpleasant imprisonment by Bishop Longland; although John Foxe's narrative thereafter is not fully consistent with Cranmer's own surviving letter, they both make the same point, that Cranmer showed this aggressive evangelical every favour. Cranmer intervened in March 1534 in what was evidently a bitter religious row in Hadleigh, in which Rose's outspoken preaching on the subject of pious donations was a star item. The Archbishop sent down one of his officials as arbitrator and threw his weight behind Rose, putting an innocent gloss on his words and beseeching the angry conservatives of Hadleigh 'to accept him favourably, the rather for this my writing'.[99] Although Rose subsequently found Hadleigh too hot to hold him, he continued to receive favour from Cranmer and Cromwell, and Cranmer's interventions in Hadleigh were far from over, as we shall see (below, pp. 143–4, 353).

Even more important than Hadleigh was the 120-square mile enclave of Calais, across the English Channel, an anomalous part of the diocese of Canterbury since its conquest by the English in the fourteenth century. Despite the town's continuing shadowy place in the diocese of Thérouanne, archbishops of Canterbury exercised powers in its twenty-five parishes by a commissary, as in other peculiars. For anyone with a sensitivity to opportuni-

98 Foxe 8, pp. 581–2, and see MacCulloch, *Suffolk and the Tudors*, pp. 149–50.

99 Cox 2, p. 280, B.L. Harley MS 6148, f. 3 (*L.P.* 7 no. 355); cf. MacCulloch, *Suffolk and the Tudors*, pp. 154–5. For Hugh Vaughan the arbitrator, see *Faculty Office Registers*, p. 26.

ties for religious change it was an obvious focus of interest; with its Anglophone merchant community organized in the chartered corporation known as the Staple, it was a major route for England into Europe. Calais was therefore an English listening-post for the burgeoning variety of Continental Reformation, but it was also a showcase to bewildered foreigners for the latest religious intentions of the King of England. As one of the kingdom's very small number of garrison towns, it was also one of the few places outside London with a radical mix of the King's subjects – the thousand-strong Calais garrison spanned normal geographical divides by containing a high proportion of both Welshmen and East Anglians. One can therefore point to the town as one of the major catalysts for integration in the kingdom of England, as ex-soldiers took their experiences and newly acquired ideas back to the remotest corners of the realm. Its varied population was also uneasily split between commercial and military powers. Long-standing tensions between the two elements in the community were made worse by the economic decline that troubled the town in the early sixteenth century, and resentments were institutionalized by the town's complicated jurisdictions: a three-way split between the mayor and corporation, the Staple (both representing the merchant community), and the royal Council headed by the King's Deputy. Yet the split between civilian and military communities was not tidily reflected in a religious divide; during the 1530s, convinced conservatives and evangelicals alike emerged among the ranks of the soldiers and the other residents of the town.[100]

It would be vital for Cranmer to exercise what influence he could in this volatile and highly unusual community. As its presiding religious authority, he would naturally have to deal with the presiding secular authority, the Deputy. A new Deputy was appointed in the same month as Cranmer was consecrated Archbishop, and for seven years, their careers would intertwine in ways which would injure both of them, and which would be a major element in the ruin of Cranmer's ally Thomas Cromwell. The new appointment was Arthur Plantagenet, Lord Lisle, an illegitimate son of Edward IV; he brought with him his wife Honor Grenville. Their correspondence, accidentally preserved for us in the State Papers by Lisle's sudden fall from grace, has been magnificently edited as *The Lisle Letters* by Muriel St Clare Byrne, to produce a vivid picture of an amiable, rather weak man who nevertheless inspired strong devotion in his much more capable and strong-willed wife. Between them, the Lisles were to prove a thorn in Cranmer's side, for they had no sympathy for religious change; egged on by Lady Lisle, the Deputy harassed evangelicals whenever he dared. Yet the exchanges between Lisle and the Archbishop were always conducted in terms of the most elaborate politeness,

100 On the background, see Ayris and Selwyn (eds), *Cranmer*, pp. 135–6, and Chettle, 'Burgesses for Calais'. On the composition of the garrison, cf. Davies, 'Suffolk's Expedition to Montdidier 1523'; 'The "Enterprises" of Paris and Boulogne'; 'Boulogne and Calais from 1545 to 1550', and MacCulloch, *Suffolk and the Tudors*, p. 18.

as befitted two conscientious royal servants who had a constant round of bread-and-butter business to transact as well as fighting religious battles, and who also knew that open trouble at Calais was the surest way of arousing the fury of Henry VIII.

The first delicate skirmish came during 1534, when the Lisles decided to import to Calais two former Observant friars, Bernardine or Roger Covert, and Thomas Roche: Covert had been among the Observants who had ministered to Catherine of Aragon's circle, and Roche had been on the edge of the Maid of Kent's coterie.[101] It was probably the Deputy who obtained a royal signet letter, declaring that although certain Friars Observant had lately been detected of certain crimes, this should not mean that other virtuous members of the order should be despised, and that Covert and Roche were minded to resort to Calais 'for the shewing and declaring of the Gospel and the word of God'.[102] Cranmer was not convinced by this smokescreen of evangelical jargon, with good reason, as later events would show; he forbade Covert to preach, having heard accusations against him which have not survived, but whose general drift can be imagined. Lisle counter-attacked by lining up the Council of Calais behind a plea to the Archbishop for Covert's reinstatement, and although Cranmer kept the messenger waiting all day on 21 March for a reply, he eventually turned out a letter which was a gracious reinstatement.[103]

However, Cranmer was still not really satisfied. A week later Sir Thomas Palmer, Knight Porter of Calais, was having to assure an anxious Lisle that he would approach the Archbishop to get 'your friar . . . licence to be there for ever . . . I will show him that he made the best sermon that I heard this year'. No-one could say that the Observants were not good preachers; that was indeed the problem. It was mid-April before Palmer fulfilled his promise, once more getting the usual Cranmerian 'full gentle answer', and by 1 June Covert was writing to Lady Lisle as warden of the Canterbury Franciscans (successor to one of the Maid of Kent's executed promoters), having had a satisfactory interview with the Archbishop.[104] Nevertheless, later in the decade, Covert's Essex gentry family and ex-friar Roche would come into Cranmer's sights in collaboration with another notorious ex-Observant called Hugh Payne, and Covert ended up in the 1540s not only chaplain to the increasingly conservative Bishop Bonner of London, but accused of sedition before the Privy Council.[105] Cranmer's deep suspicion of Observants eventually ripened into outright hatred, as

101 *Lisle Letters* 2, p. 183; Neame, *Maid of Kent*, p. 280.

102 P.R.O., E. 135/2/13 (24 January 1534).

103 *Lisle Letters* 2, p. 81 (*L.P.* 7 no. 350).

104 *Lisle Letters* 2, pp. 89–90 (*L.P.* 7 no. 385); *Lisle Letters* 2, p. 129 (*L.P.* 7 no. 510); *Lisle Letters* 2, pp. 172–3 (*L.P.* 7 no. 765).

105 Cox 2, pp. 361–2, P.R.O., S.P. 1/143 ff. 30–31 (*L.P.* 14 i no. 244); *Proc. P.C.* 7, p. 182. For Covert's and Roche's clerical careers in the 1530s, see *Faculty Office Registers*, pp. 21, 39, 44, 80. See also below, Chs 5, 7, pp. 144, 282.

the cases of Payne and friar John Forest later revealed (see below, Chs 5, 6, pp. 143–4, 214).

Round one, therefore, went to the Lisles. Cranmer had to strengthen his hand in Calais, which meant getting the right official to represent him as commissary in the town. During Lent 1534, probably at the beginning of March, he replaced William Peterson, a priest appointed as commissary on Cromwell's recommendation while the see had been vacant. It was probably no coincidence that Peterson was dismissed after intervening on Ash Wednesday against an evangelical activist in the Calais garrison; his successor was a local man, John Butler.[106] This was an interesting appointment, which straight away positioned the commissary's role over against the garrison authorities, with all the usual potential for conflict inherent in the situation at Calais. Butler was one of two sons of a twice-widowed gentlewoman resident in Calais; his brother William was a merchant of the Calais Staple. Later, family and political complications arose, caused by their fraught relations with their step-brother John Banastre (their mother had married again). By 6 November 1535 Butler had the title of Royal Chaplain, probably thanks to Cranmer, although this was not enough to protect him from many conservative attacks: for what eventually proved to be especially significant about Butler's appointment was that he had more than four decades of evangelical activism in front of him. He survived many trials to die at last in 1570, secure and honoured as a prebendary of Canterbury Cathedral, still making a provisional bequest of his former property in Calais should the town ever become English again.[107]

Cranmer continued this unspectacular tinkering with his patronage in good times and bad during Henry's reign, quietly working away at putting the right men in place as the opportunity arose. What did become apparent during the rest of Henry's reign was the way in which good times led him to extend the steady drip of evangelical placements outside the areas of his immediate control; and early 1534 was among the best of times for him. In the first days of the year, no doubt to the Archbishop's delight, his assistant Nicholas Heath was singled out for a mission to Germany to renew English contacts with the Lutheran princes, this time without any of the under-the-counter overtones of Cranmer's own negotiations in 1532. The mission is

106 On Peterson's appointment, *L.P.* 5 no. 1465; he was still described as commissary in early March and his replacement by Butler was noted by Holy Week, the first days in April 1534: P.R.O., E. 36/120 ff. 147v–148 (*L.P.* 7 no. 585). See also Cranmer's letter of 16 March 1534 apparently commending his new commissary to Lord Lisle, P.R.O., S.P. 3/2 no. 74, misdated by Cox 2, pp. 320–21, corrected by *L.P.* 7 no. 320 and *Lisle Letters* 2, pp. 74–5. The dating of Butler's appointment has been confused and anticipated by misdating of Cranmer's letters to him.

107 On Lady Banastre and her family, see *Chronicle of Calais*, pp. 117, 180. Royal chaplain: *Faculty Office Registers*, p. 43. Will calendared in [Anon.], 'Kentish Wills', 5, p. 54, although probate should be read as 1570: cf. Le Neve, *Fasti*: *Canterbury, Rochester and Winchester 1541–1857*, p. 28.

likely to have been designed by Thomas Cromwell to promote the evangelical cause in the English Church. Although its immediate result was nil, it was the precedent for many subsequent initiatives.[108]

Deeply symbolic, after Heath's departure, was the Archbishop's outfacing of a former colleague in the divorce research team, Richard Sampson, Dean of the Chapel Royal, who had not moved on from conservative humanism as Cranmer had done; his conflicts with such men as Sampson, Stokesley and Gardiner become a feature of the 1530s. The Archbishop pushed two key evangelical preachers, Hugh Latimer and Nicholas Shaxton, into the plans for the Lent cycle of preaching at Court before the King and Queen. When in early January the Archbishop wrote to Sampson about this, he spelled out his motives with what was either naive tactlessness or deliberate aggression: Latimer 'for sincere preaching the word of God, hath lately been endangered, and suffered great obloquy', and so Cranmer had asked the King to place him in the pulpit on Wednesdays through Lent, while he also marked down a date for Shaxton 'the Queen's Grace's almoner'. Sampson was not pleased, and told Cranmer so in no uncertain terms. It was not just that the Dean's own arrangements were being overruled. Although Sampson was clearly reluctant directly to criticize the Queen's officer Shaxton, he was brutally frank in his low opinion of Latimer:

> his teaching moveth no little dissension among the people wheresoever he cometh, the which is either a token of new doctrine or else negligence . . . It is not unknown to your grace that he was much suspect for his preaching, before all the Convocation, of the which . . . I was and am a poor member; wherefore your grace shall be author of this matter, and I no minister.[109]

Sampson thus washed his hands of the preaching rota, admitting ungraciously that he had been outgunned by the appeal to the King. Cranmer in his triumph wrote a fascinating letter to Latimer, instructing that doyen of preachers in the art of preaching before the most discriminating ('circumspect') of royal audiences – an insight into what Henry VIII liked in his sermons. They should be based on humanist biblical exposition 'according to the pure sense and meaning thereof': the implication is that the elaborations of late medieval preaching, the exploration of layers of meaning and allegory, should be avoided. Above all Henry hated controversy: there should be no reference to Latimer's late conflicts, 'but that ye rather do seam utterly those your accusations, than now in that place any sparkle or suspicion of grudge should appear to remain in you for the same'. Magnanimity in victory! It is

108 See his record in BL Harley MS 6148, f. 81rv, unusual in this volume, of Cromwell's letter to him, and Cox 2, p. 276, P.R.O., S.P. 1/82 f. 18r (*L.P.* 7 no. 20). Cf. McEntegart Ph.D., 'England and the League of Schmalkalden', pp. 68–77 on this mission.

109 Cranmer's letter is Cox 2, p. 309, B.L. Harley MS 6148, f. 42, there misdated by the copyist from January to June (*L.P.* 7, no. 30); though note also Cox's further misdating to 1535. Sampson's reply is P.R.O., S.P. 1/82 f. 47 (*L.P.* 7, no. 32).

worth noting one Midlands farmer's son using a sheep-farming metaphor to another: 'to seam' is to dress wool with grease, and thus by analogy to gloss over.[110] However, a general evangelical tone in the sermon was permissible: 'if such occasion be given by the word of God, let none offence or superstition be unreprehended'. Above all, do not preach longer than 'an hour and an half at the most; for by long expense of time the King and the Queen shall peradventure wax so weary at the beginning, that they shall have small delight to continue throughout with you to the end'.

Cranmer was at the opening of Parliament on 15 January 1534: thereafter a freight of legislation of vital relevance to himself and his position made him, of necessity, an assiduous attender (forty-one out of forty-six possible days). His presence was in stark contrast to the complete absence of his fellow-Metropolitan of York, Edward Lee, who was clearly in turmoil about the drift of events. In fact only five other bishops turned up at all to sessions of the Lords, and one of them (most surprisingly) was the aged and ineffective Spanish confessor of Catherine of Aragon, George de Athequa, Bishop of Llandaff. It was also noticeable that the government only summoned token meetings of Convocation during the actual course of this parliamentary session, evidently loth to call up a dangerously unreliable body of clergy until all had been decided.[111] Of the four other bishops who attended the Lords, Clerk and Longland were also the most reluctant of supporters of the King's anti-papal policy, so it is likely to have been Cranmer himself, Gardiner and Stokesley who bore the burden of the rota of anti-papal preaching by bishops at Paul's Cross arranged every Sunday during Parliament time.[112]

The legislation passed was ample reinforcement for Cranmer's self-confidence. The session not only saw the condemnation of Elizabeth Barton and her promoters, but also the passage of the Act of Succession protecting the Boleyn marriage, in which Cranmer headed the commission named to gather oaths to the Succession.[113] The two absentee Italian diplomat-bishops were deprived of their sees: this was predictable enough in the case of Lorenzo Campeggio of Salisbury, the man who in King Henry's eyes had sabotaged the 1529 Blackfriars trial, but it was a cruel logic to extend the deprivation to Cranmer's old patron Ghinucci after his years of loyal defence of Henry's annulment plans. However, Ghinucci was at least quietly compensated.[114] He was bound to go, given the comprehensive assault on papal authority which ran through various other pieces of legislation, notably the permanent confir-

110 John Strype was the origin of many commentators' attempts to emend the text here because of his misunderstanding of 'seam': cf. the origin in his transcript of the letter, B.L. Lansdowne MS 1045 f. 5. Original: Cox 2, p. 308, B.L. Harley MS 6148, f. 42r (*L.P.* 7 no. 29).

111 Lehmberg, *Reformation Parliament*, pp. 38, 257; Lambeth MS 751, pp. 104–5.

112 On preaching, Hall 2, p. 260, and *C.S.P. Spanish 1534–5*, no. 9, p. 30. On Longland's unhappiness with events, *C.S.P. Spanish 1534–5*, no. 1, p. 4.

113 *L.J.* 1, p. 82.

114 *L.P.* 7, no. 701.

mation of the earlier conditional restraint of annate payments to Rome. This was the first in a series of bills enacted at the end of the session, whose untidy coverage of varied provisions testified to how much needed to be achieved in a hurry: it was not merely a financial measure, but set up a new mechanism of providing bishops for the Church in the absence of the Pope. In a curious piece of antiquarianism, the election of the bishop by members of the cathedral chapter was revived from fourteenth-century practice, but the election would now be an empty farce, since the chapter were bound by the Act to elect the man named in a royal 'letter missive'. This pointless procedure persists in the Church of England to the present day, although the modern decline in royal power has added one or two further layers of unreality to the election.

Another Act dealt with the abolition of other financial payments to the Pope, and this was seen by at least one commentator as the decisive move against his Holiness; when it passed the Commons on 20 March one MP's brother wrote back to his uncle Lord Lisle with dramatic simplicity: 'after this day the Bishop of Rome shall have no manner of authority within the realm of England'.[115] John Grenville clearly appreciated that there was again more to this Act than just financial provision, for it also destroyed the Pope's legal jurisdiction in an important practical respect, by setting up a Faculty Office for Cranmer to issue dispensations: hence the Act is usually referred as the Act of Dispensations. Now that it was clear that Roman jurisdiction was to be abrogated, it was essential to have a mechanism controlled in England for the host of useful dispensations (faculties) formerly provided by the papacy: marriage within prohibited degrees, licences for clergy to hold more benefices than the rules permitted, and so on. Wolsey as papal legate had created such an office for dispensations, and one of the curious spin-offs of his fall was extra inconvenience for England, in that his Faculty Office disappeared and once more such dispensations had to be issued in Rome, or by a variety of local papal officials.[116] Now Cranmer was empowered to issue these dispensations, but under the careful control of royal government; all dispensations costing more than four pounds would have to be confirmed and enrolled in Chancery, and there was even appeal to the King in lesser cases.

A curious last-minute proviso on the last day of the session made the proposed new faculty system seem temporary by providing that the King could abrogate the whole or any part of the bill as he thought fit; however, this addition was probably aimed less at Cranmer's new office than at the financial provisions in the legislation, which might be bargaining-chips in

115 *Lisle Letters* 2, pp. 79–80 (*L.P.* 7 no. 349).

116 *Faculty Office Registers*, pp. xvii–xviii. Cf. e.g. a marriage licence granted by Richard Gwent, still described as official of the Pope on 9 October 1533: P.R.O., E.135/7/28. Ironically, Gwent was at the time intimately involved with the destruction of Elizabeth Barton.

some deal with the Pope. It gave no pause to Cranmer's and Cromwell's bureaucrats, who under the pressure of consumer demand were already setting up the new faculty institutions in April 1534.[117] Their efficiency may have been encouraged because two of the very first beneficiaries of the Faculty Office's workings were Bishop John Salcot and Archdeacon Edmund Cranmer; but it is also noticeable that the old guard of the Canterbury provincial bureaucracy was not allowed to get its hands on this potentially important and lucrative new business. Cranmer appointed as his commissary of faculties a civil lawyer who was one of his contemporaries at Cambridge, Roger Townshend; this appointment is very reminiscent of John Butler's appointment as commissary of Calais. At least by the time that he made his will four years later, Townshend was a convinced evangelical, ordering bibles for all the churches where he was incumbent, and mentioning his book purchases from Cranmer's client bookseller and printer Reyner Wolfe; before that Townshend was a close associate of Bishop Nicholas Shaxton. Similarly Cromwell made a very unconventional appointment for Townshend's faculty counterpart in Chancery: his loyal and enthusiastically evangelical agent, Stephen Vaughan.[118]

The newly-established Faculty Office naturally needed a seal. This seal was to announce the importance of the Faculty Office, an institution which had taken on some of the usurped powers of the Pope, and also to announce a radical break with the past, just as the choice of personnel to staff the Office broke with the older Canterbury establishment. The one-sided vesica-shape and the Gothic frippery of the other seals in use by the archdiocese were entirely discarded in favour of a circular two-sided design. A first version of this seems to have been considered unsatisfactory at some later stage during the 1530s, perhaps because its inscription referred explicitly to the setting-up of the Office by the 1534 Act, and the specific date might have confused observers as time passed.[119] Both versions, however, share a nobly Renaissance format; their design and content were a marvellous showcase of evangelical iconography untainted by Popish image-worship, and were clearly carefully chosen by Cranmer himself.[120]

117 Lehmberg, *Reformation Parliament*, pp. 191–2; *Faculty Office Registers*, pp. xx–xxiii.

118 *Faculty Office Registers*, pp. 1, xxii. Ayris Ph.D., 'Cranmer's Register', p. 233 has Townshend commissioned as Cranmer's commissary of faculties on 10 April 1534. On Townshend, see also Moreton, *The Townshends and their World*, pp. 42–4.

119 First version: Birch, *Seals*, no. 1330.

120 Second version illus. in Gorham, *Gleanings*, frontispiece. Gorham, ibid., pp. 8–10, complicates matters by identifying another seal (recut from Warham's seal) as the first Faculty Seal. The deed which he quotes as bearing it (ibid., p. 9), a marriage licence, is not a Faculty Office document, and is not to be found in the *Faculty Office Registers*. Another example of this seal is on the Aragon annulment instrument (P.R.O., E. 30/1024, 23 May 1533), proving that this is not the Faculty Office seal; it is probably that used by Cranmer for direct exercise of his jurisdiction (cf. Churchill, *Canterbury Jurisdiction*, 1, pp. 130, 505–7, 587).

12 Reverse and obverse of the second state of Cranmer's Faculty Office seal, attached to his marriage licence for Henry VIII and Catherine Parr, 1543. Even in its worn state, the masterful quality of the composition is evident.

The two sides of the seal are type and antitype: serpent and cross as set out in scripture in Numbers 21:4–9 and John 3:14–15. On one side, entwined round a cross-shaped scaffold, is the brazen serpent, which Moses had set up as a protection for the Israelites after God had punished their grumbling lack of faith with a plague of fiery serpents: these noxious creatures wriggle below the scaffold, and have already claimed one victim, but Moses, clutching the tables of the law, calms the survivors' fears by pointing to his divinely commanded serpent. On the other side is the crucifixion, which as the surrounding legend from John 17:3 testifies is the true source of eternal life: the reward of faith. There was one drawback to the design: the legend identifying the seal as belonging to Cranmer's Faculty Office had of necessity to surround the serpent's scene of human lack of faith and disaster. However, in view of some of the Office's less edifying functions in issuing dispensations, the Archbishop may have felt wryly that this had a certain appropriateness.

The design and iconography of the faculty seal are of great interest. The Renaissance idiom is the norm for decorative work associated with Cranmer's patronage: the setting of his 1545 portrait by Flicke, for example (below, Ch. 8, pl. 24), or the calligraphy and surrounds to the commemorative panels at Bekesbourne of 1552 (see below, Ch. 12, pl. 35). It is also a quite precocious initiative. The faculty seal's date in the 1530s predates the move to pure Renaissance design in the Great Seals of England and Scotland, which occurred in both kingdoms in 1542. The theme of the brazen serpent is also earlier than two other nearly contemporary jewellers' representations of the same subject, one of which has clear evangelical associations with Henry VIII's Court: this is a gold cover for a devotional book, in which the design is surrounded with an English quotation from Numbers in the version of the Great Bible of 1539. The book cover has been attributed to the London-based immigrant goldsmith Hans von Antwerpen. Its treatment of the brazen serpent subject is not identical with that of the faculty seal: it lacks the antitype (and indeed it is much cruder in execution than the seal), while the design can be identified as having been taken directly from a *de luxe* Antwerp book cover dateable to c. 1539–43. It is a pity that we cannot relate the faculty seal design more closely to these two artefacts; nevertheless it is tempting to attribute the seal to the genius of Hans von Antwerpen's friend, Hans Holbein the younger, who had arrived in England in 1532.[121]

Another major Act of the 1534 Parliament introduced a further reform proposal which remained in Cranmer's thoughts for two decades to come: it confirmed the submission of the clergy of May 1532 (by which they had surrendered their legislative independence to the Crown), but it also sought to capitalize on that submission by planning the replacement of Roman canon law with a newly drawn-up English system. The initiative seems to have come from the Commons, in a petition by the Speaker directly to the King on 5 March. They were possibly prompted by their fury at the dismissive attitude of the Lords when they petitioned for redress against Bishop Stokesley for Thomas Phillips, a London evangelical long imprisoned on suspicion of heresy: Phillips's plight was distressingly reminiscent of an earlier bishop of London's treatment of another suspect, Richard Hunne, and the two cases were perfect symbols of the danger posed to the laity by Church courts. Such was the importance of this agitation for canon law reform that it prompted a joint conference of the whole of Parliament with the King, followed by a late-night sitting of the Lords alone.[122]

Cranmer is unlikely to have taken Stokesley's side in the Phillips dispute, particularly since Phillips had originally been a *bête noire* of the disgraced Sir Thomas More; More had been responsible while still Chancellor for transferring him to prison in the Tower of London. Given his previous interest in canon law (see above, Ch. 3, p. 54), the Archbishop probably welcomed the Commons initiative with enthusiasm. It is noticeable that in this same year of 1534 someone very senior encouraged the translation into English of Lyndwode's standard collection of canon law in use in the English provinces; this translation was designed specifically for the laity to be able to see what canon law actually was, and the unnamed patron had desired the translator's voluntary labour 'in his name, that might upon my

121 Starkey (ed.), *Henry VIII: a European Court*, pp. 112–14; Tait, 'Girdle-prayerbook', esp. figs 11–13. I am most grateful to John Cherry and Professor Paul Harvey for discussing the seals with me.

122 Lehmberg, *Reformation Parliament*, pp. 149–50, 186, 193.

13 Girdle prayer-book, *c.* 1539–43. Like Cranmer's Faculty seal, this takes the theme of Moses and the serpents, and the scriptural quotations proclaim an evangelical faith.

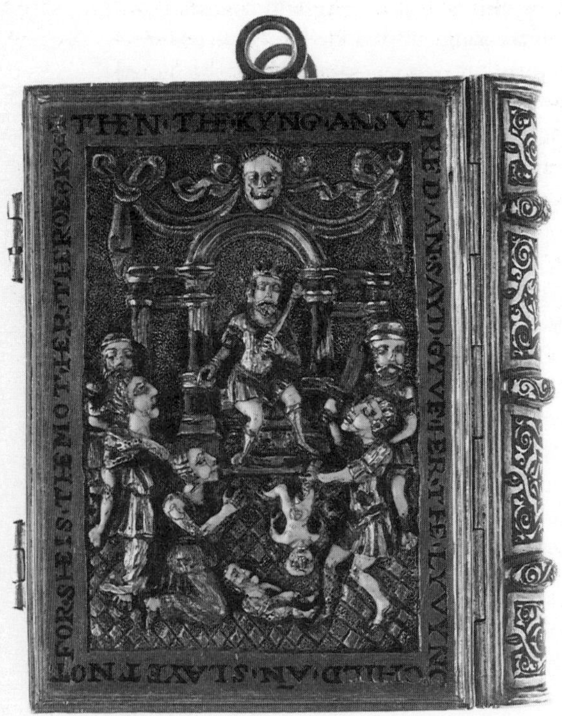

duty have commanded me in his name'. Was the patron Cromwell or Cranmer?

Like the royal demands to Convocation two years earlier which had led to the Submission, the Act which eventually emerged provided for canon law revision to be undertaken by sixteen clergy and sixteen lay representatives of Parliament; this figure of thirty-two would keep recurring in the repeated attempts to kick-start canon law reform. Other provisos again indicated the untidy genesis of the bill. There was a provision for appeals from the archbishops' courts to a commission in Chancery, which is so reminiscent of the provisions in the Faculty Office legislation that it is probably Cromwell's addition; however, the clause preserving the traditional exemption of certain great monasteries from the archbishops' jurisdiction sounds like an ill-tempered or panicky addition by the abbots present in the Lords. Within eighteen months, a sub-committee headed by Cranmer's official Richard Gwent had produced a complete draft of canon law, but, in a pattern which would become familiar to the Archbishop, work then stalled for years on end.[123]

At the end of the Parliamentary session, there remained the task of securing agreement from the Church leadership for this *fait accompli* ending papal authority. The Convocation of Canterbury was finally activated on 31 March, the day after the two Houses of Parliament had stood down, and a vote was taken on a proposition 'that the Bishop of Rome has no greater jurisdiction given him by God in holy scripture in this realm of England than has any other foreign bishop'. The vote of the lower of the two Houses is recorded as thirty-two for the motion, one doubtful and four supporting the Pope; however, the government was not satisfied with this uncertain trumpet-call for the supremacy. There exists a list of subscriptions to the same proposition for the senior clergy of the entire kingdom; eleven bishops signed, with Cranmer heading the list, and they are followed by ninety-one other names: abbots, priors, friars, archdeacons and other proctors in the convocations.[124] The way the list is set out suggests that the signatures were first collected in the Convocation of Canterbury in that session of 31 March or a day or two later, and that then during April the document was sent out to pick up the

123 *Reformation of the Ecclesiastical Laws*, ed. Spalding, pp. 19–21; Logan, 'Henrician Canons', esp. p. 100 n. 4 and p. 103.

124 B.L. Additional MS 38656, f. 3; pr. in facsimile as a fold-out frontispiece for vol. 8 of the 1849 reissue of the Townsend edition of Foxe, and in part as frontispiece to vol. 1 of Hughes, *Reformation in England* (cf. ibid., p. xiii for comment). Dating is derived from the signatures of Goodrich and Rowland Lee in their own surnames and again as bishops (consecrated 19 April 1534) and the mention of John Wakeman, Abbot-elect of Tewkesbury (royal assent to election, 27 April 1534); Salcot signs only as Abbot of Hyde (dispensation to hold bishopric, 15 April 1534). In the body of the list, there is no sense of geographical progression, and it is arranged by category of office, which suggests that for the most part it was gathered at a single meeting – no record of or indeed opportunity for such a meeting exists after 31 March.

northern bishops and other stragglers. The name of Thomas Runcorn, heading side three of the list among the last few names, conveniently gives it a *terminus post quem*, for in a letter to Thomas Cromwell of 26 April, Bishop Gardiner rounded off other business by adding 'I have caused also my chaplain, Master Runcorn, to subscribe his name to the conclusion, as ye shall perceive by the same'. During the rest of the year, the same 'conclusion' would be proffered systematically to hundreds of senior and junior clergy throughout the southern province, producing long lists, some of which still survive.[125]

At least one other significant piece of business relevant to papal authority was debated in this brief Convocation session. Four days afterwards, Cranmer issued a circular letter to both provinces of the English Church, telling them that after some argument his Convocation had decided to suspend the traditional pronunciation four times a year in each parish of a solemn curse on a sweeping list of categories of wrongdoers: the suspension was hardly surprising, since the list contained curses on those who broke 'the franchise of holy church', and even if deprived of its mention of the Pope, it was an assertion of the awesome power of the clergy, which was clearly going against the drift of events.[126] The legislation in the previous three months in Parliament provides clues to Thomas Cromwell's plans for the future exercise of the Royal Supremacy under the King, but this correspondence about the curse also makes clear why plans were abruptly changed at the end of the same year. The Faculty Office had been set up with a clumsy dual office structure between Archbishop and Chancery, and the Act for the Submission of the Clergy had created an appeals structure to Chancery: both these suggested a future in which control of the Church would be exercised by a close co-operation between the Archbishop of Canterbury and the Lord Chancellor, with the Chancellor as senior partner. This was logical on political grounds from Cromwell's point of view, because the current Lord Chancellor was Thomas Audley, a man who was increasingly obviously Cromwell's satellite, despite his nominal position at the head of England's legal system. Cromwell became Audley's theoretical deputy in Chancery on 8 October 1534, as Master of the Rolls, and he may well have contemplated persuading the King to appoint him Lord Chancellor in Audley's place.[127] On the ecclesiastical side, Cranmer was as biddable for Cromwell as Audley.

125 Gardiner to Cromwell: P.R.O., S.P. 1/83 ff. 169–70, *Gardiner's Letters*, p. 55; *L.P.* 7 no. 542; his opening remarks probably also refer to the list. See summary note on two further books of signatures, *L.P.* 7 no. 1025, though these drop the phrase referring to holy scripture present in the Convocation declarations, and in the affirmation by the Convocation of York on 5 June: Burnet 3 ii, pp. 69–70 (Bk. 2, no. 26, *L.P.* 7 no. 769).

126 Lambeth MS 751 p. 105, more likely to be accurate in its figure of 32 than the 34 of *Concilia*, ed. Wilkins, 3, p. 769; also Parker, *De Antiquitate*, p. 384. Lehmberg, *Reformation Parliament*, pp. 213–14 misses the business of the curse: cf. Cox 2, pp. 281–3, B.L. Harley MS 6148, f. 23v (*L.P.* 7 no. 435). The original makes it clear that Cox's letter no. 99 is a variant ending on letter no. 98, showing that the text is a circular; it is addressed to the official administering Salisbury diocese *sede vacante*.

127 Chambers is incorrect (*Faculty Office Registers*, p. xxi) in saying that Cromwell became Master of the Rolls in April.

However, Cranmer's circular about the suspension of the curse starkly revealed a problem in this proposed strategy for building the supremacy in the Church, which remained to be solved, and which would become more acute through the year: how could a religious revolution in two provinces of the Church be carried out through the agency of the primate of only one? Finding the right authority for most of the religious orders was relatively easy; the friars, for instance, already had their own provincial structure covering the whole of the kingdom of England, and this could now be hijacked by royal command, appointing reliable individuals as provincials and visitors. Chapuys noted that this was done for the Dominican and Austin friars: we can supply the names that he did not know, John Hilsey and George Browne.[128] There also remains the draft of a royal commission apparently dating from May or June 1534, which would have extended this process by setting up a commission of three royal visitors for those exempt religious houses that had secured their continuing privileges in the Act for the Submission of the Clergy; this was in the end not implemented, because (as we will see) a more comprehensive solution was devised.[129]

Yet the battle for the Church would be won or lost not in monastic communities, but out in the secular world: the parishes of the two provinces. Cranmer's clerk provided two alternative endings for his circular of 4 April about the suspension of the curse: one, addressed to the bishops of the Archbishop's own province, bluntly 'willed' them to order the suspension and 'with speed' to confirm to him that it had been done. The other ending, to his fellow-primate, Edward Lee of York, was necessarily more sweetly reasonable:

> I therefore pray you, my lord, that, forasmuch as it shall be meet and convenient that one conformity shall be used in your province and mine . . . that the declaration and reading of the same may be respited . . . And how ye shall be minded therein, I pray you that I may be ascertained by your letters as soon as ye may.

We have already encountered the problem in April 1533, when Henry VIII had nearly called Cranmer 'head of our spirituality', but had then thought better of it.[130] The truth was that for all the revolution wrought by the royal supremacy, an archbishop in England could only try persuasion on another archbishop, and not command.

A week later, a renewed attempt at orchestrating English pulpits further exposed the incoherence in the means available to the government to enforce change. The effort to silence conservative preachers may have been prompted

128 *L.P.* 7 no. 530 corrects the impression given by *C.S.P. Spanish 1534–5*, no. 45, p. 131, that it was Cranmer and not the King who appointed Hilsey and Browne. Cf. the protest letter of Hilsey's predecessor to Henry VIII, 17 April, P.R.O., S.P. 1/83 ff. 85–6 (*L.P.* 7 no. 495).

129 Logan, 'Thomas Cromwell and the Vice-gerency in Spirituals', p. 659.

130 Cf. B.L. Cotton MS Otho C X f. 159 with B.L. Harley MS 283 f. 97 (*St.P.* 1, pp. 392–3 and Cox 2, pp. 238–9n); above, pp. 91–2.

by a challenge at the beginning of April from a prominent supporter of Catherine of Aragon, Rowland Phillips, Hugh Latimer's old enemy and reputed his equal in preaching skills. Phillips demanded that the King grant him the opportunity to have a dispute with Latimer. Since Phillips, a survivor from the Warham years in Canterbury diocese, was defiantly sitting it out beside Cranmer's palace as Vicar of Croydon, and Latimer was the star clergyman in Cranmer's household, this was no mere innocent invitation to discussion, but Henry incautiously agreed.[131] Although details of this clash of the titans have not survived, in the week after Easter both the King and the Archbishop sent out urgent circulars about preaching.[132] The King's circular gave orders to seek out and imprison those who extolled the Pope in sermons and prayers. After a consultative meeting with Stokesley, Gardiner and Longland, the senior reliable bishops in his province, the Archbishop circularized his other fellow-bishops telling them to relicense all preachers. One might regard this double effort as a pincer movement, but it was not the most efficient means of getting things done, and once more it did not constitute a proper chain of command to cover the province of York.[133]

The enforcement of the Act of Succession at least had a straightforward basis of authority, since the Act itself had named royal commissioners to take the oaths. Yet the task of gathering the oaths was a massive one, far more ambitious than the already impressive list of senior clergy who had subscribed against the Pope: the plan was to swear every significant male in the nation. As the man who headed the list of oath commissioners, Cranmer initiated the process, summoning to Lambeth Palace a group of leading clergy (including a chastened Rowland Phillips from Croydon) and one vital layperson, Sir Thomas More, to sign on 13 April. More and Bishop Fisher refused, and remained under arrest, but it was difficult to know what to do with two men whose names carried such prestige. Characteristically Cranmer was in favour of some compromise: he advocated taking up their suggestion that they swear merely to the main text of the Act of Succession, not to its explanatory preamble with the condemnation of the Bishop of Rome and of the King's first marriage. With a revealing combination of naivety and pastoral concern, he thought that this might be an example to Catherine and Mary 'which do think that they should damn their souls, if they should abandon and relinquish their estates [that is, their royal styles]', and it would generally act as an encouragement to conservatives to conform. Yet with inept illogic, he also

131 *Lisle Letters* 2, p. 102.

132 Different versions of the King's circular with a range of dates from 12 to 21 April are B.L. Harley MS 6148, f. 81r, Burnet III ii, pp. 102–3 and *Butley Chronicle*, p. 64; Cranmer's letter is Cox 2, pp. 283–4, B.L. Harley MS 6148, f. 22r (*L.P.* 7 no. 463).

133 The instructions for bidding of the bedes (i.e. the form of English intercessions in the mass or in sermons) are probably slightly earlier than this; a MS version in C.C.C.C. MS 106, pp. 119f stipulates action before 'Easter Week next', whereas the two circulars under discussion were actually issued in Easter Week, 5–12 April 1534. Cf. pr. version, Cox 2, pp. 460–62, *L.P.* 7 no. 464.

supposed that More and Fisher could be assured that their oaths would not be given much publicity: 'their said oaths might be suppressed, but when and where his highness might take some commodity by the publishing of the same'. Cromwell and the King gave this kindly meant but unworldly advice short shrift, and soon More and Fisher were in the Tower.[134]

Events rushed on in a frenzy of activity. The two days 19–20 April 1534 provided solemn symbolic demonstrations that the Royal Supremacy had arrived. On 19 April, Cranmer for the first time consecrated bishops, at his palace at Croydon: the three men chosen were a symbol of Boleyn triumph. Two moderate evangelical members of the divorce research team were included: Thomas Goodrich went to Ely, John Salcot to Bangor, while Rowland Lee, reputedly the man who had married Henry and Anne, went to Coventry and Lichfield. A less happy part of the same sequence of events came the following day, when the Maid of Kent and five of her admirers were executed as traitors at Tyburn: a clearly deliberate prelude *pour encourager les autres* in the general launching the same day of the campaign to take oaths, with solemn swearing ceremonies in London and the dispatching of commissions to the shires.[135] Cranmer then turned his attention to yet another part of the royal schemes: a full-scale metropolitical visitation of the province of Canterbury, whereby he could directly exercise his authority through most of England and Wales. It was a huge task, and he only planned to visit certain dioceses during 1534, holding over, for instance, Winchester and Exeter until 1535; there is no surviving evidence of his visitation extending into Wales. In the end, the visitation remained unfinished, petering out in incoherence, because from the start it was bedevilled by problems: several of his diocesan bishops refused to recognize his authority to visit. Such visitations had for centuries raised tensions between archbishops and bishops, but the level of resistance that Cranmer encountered was something new, starkly revealing the weaknesses that we have already highlighted in the government's plans so far.[136]

It was natural for Cranmer to begin his visitation with the diocese of London, but it was his former annulment colleague Bishop Stokesley who proved the most effective agent in sabotaging the whole enterprise. Stokesley had the measure of Cranmer. The Bishop was present at a fraught meeting of the royal Council with Chapuys on 16 May; at this, the Archbishop left others to defend him against a sustained attack from the ambassador, who sounds to have been on exceptional form, and who indulged himself in sarcasm at the

134 Cox 2 p. 285–6, B.L. Cotton MS Cleopatra E VI f. 175 (*L.P.* 7 no. 499); for Cromwell's and Henry's opinion, P.R.O., S.P. 1/83 f. 98 (*L.P.* 7 no. 500). Marius, *More*, pp. 461–4.

135 R. Rex, 'The execution of the Holy Maid of Kent'; *Wriothesley's Chronicle* 1, p. 24; for an instance of the county commissions, see *Butley Chronicle*, pp. 62–3.

136 The best account of what follows is that by Dr Ayris, summarized in Ayris and Selwyn (eds), *Cranmer*, pp. 122–5; references are to his account unless otherwise stated, but there is also useful material in Bowker, 'The Supremacy and the Episcopate', pp. 228–33. Interpretation is my own.

expense of Cranmer's oaths to the papacy. This may have given Stokesley the idea for his own strategy.[137] Yet Cranmer clearly did not anticipate any serious difficulty in London. He took over the rota for appointing preachers at the vital pulpit of Paul's Cross, which was generally Stokesley's prerogative, and predictably he chose a selection of Cambridge men for the spring and summer. Two surviving irritated notes from him, dealing with the loss of paperwork and misunderstandings over dates, will strike a chord of weary familiarity with those who have organized programmes of speakers at a time when they have much else on their minds.[138] But worse was to follow. Stokesley orchestrated his mostly very conservative Cathedral Chapter to protest against the visitation proposal, and when the Archbishop and his officials arrived to begin work in the chapter house of St Paul's Cathedral at the end of May, they found themselves in a face-to-face confrontation with the Bishop and assembled Cathedral hierarchy.[139]

Stokesley's line of attack was simple but effective: one of the loose ends still not tied up in the winter's mapping-out of royal supremacy in the Church was Cranmer's official title, under which he was carrying out his visitation. Stokesley pointed out that in Cranmer's inhibition suspending diocesan jurisdiction, he described himself as 'Primate of All England and Legate of the Apostolic See'. It seems at first sight an astonishing piece of bureaucratic conservatism on the part of Cranmer's officials, who drew up the documentation for the visitation, but strictly speaking they had no choice: the powers of the Primate of All England had not officially been redefined – even the royal mandate of 27 April which had ordered secular authorities to assist Cranmer in his visitation spoke of him as Legate of the Apostolic See.[140] Stokesley and his Chapter punctiliously pointed out that if they accepted Cranmer's authority, they might be seen as acting 'against the Crown of our sovereign'. They had a point, since the whole clergy of England had been caught out in 1530–31 in the ancient penalties of praemunire for abetting Wolsey's legatine jurisdiction, in one of Henry VIII's more cynical practical jokes with a political purpose. Moreover, the ultra-conservative and much-respected Bishop of Norwich, Richard Nix, had only a few months before been humiliated and nearly bankrupted by an equally technical royal praemunire charge challenging a traditional exercise of his jurisdiction.[141] Stokesley wanted a decision on separating out Cranmer's powers as metropolitan from his powers as legate, and he was not prepared to drop the matter, as will become apparent.

137 *C.S.P. Spanish 1534–5*, no. 58, pp. 157–63.

138 Cox 2, p. 289, B.L. Harley MS 6148, f. 46v (*L.P.* 7 no. 616); Cox 2, pp. 292–3, B.L. Harley MS 6148, f. 46r (*L.P.* 7 no. 703). C.C.C.C. MS 106, p. 209, a letter about Cranmer's preaching rota and Cambridge men, is probably also of this time.

139 See account in Stokesley's appeal to the King of December 1534, pr. from B.L. Cotton Cleopatra F ii, Strype, *Cranmer* 2, pp. 269–71, Appendix no. 15 (*L.P.* 7 no. 1683).

140 *L.P.* 7, no. 589/7.

141 *Butley Chronicle*, p. 61.

Where Stokesley had begun, others followed during 1534: Longland of Lincoln in June, and Nix of Norwich in July. Stokesley, Nix, Longland and their suffragans even went on ordaining and instituting clergy in defiance of the Archbishop. They did not all take exactly the same line in their protests, but they had all scented the possibility of using the supremacy to strengthen their own position in relation to the primatial see; after all, since they had all been consecrated as bishops before the break with Rome, their position remained to be defined just as much as Cranmer's. Longland also seized on yet another incoherence in the Archbishop's programme; in some dioceses, such as Longland's own vast territory of Lincoln, Cranmer's officials were instructed to include the taking of the oath to the succession in their brief, but in others they were not: so unlike Longland, Stephen Gardiner was leading the oath-taking in his own diocese of Winchester, where Cranmer was not as yet visiting. Even where Cranmer was himself taking the oaths, he was puzzled as to whom he should be concerning himself with: how did his task relate to the secular commissioners gathering oaths?[142] To make matters worse, two different subscription programmes were proceeding at the same time: one gathering oaths to the Act of Succession, the other continuing to gather clerical signatures to the proposition that the Pope had no more power in the realm than any foreign bishop.

Cranmer learned one lesson from his confrontation with Stokesley in May: he only carried out in person those parts of his visitation where he would not face any embarrassing personal challenge from a resident bishop. Accordingly, in early June, he visited Rochester diocese, where the bishop was conveniently absent in the Tower of London; then he headed into the west Midlands in August and September, spending the bulk of his time in the diocese of Worcester, vacant thanks to the Act of Parliament of the previous winter. In a predictable sign of his lack of interest in his own cathedral, he did not interrupt his activity in visitation to attend what turned out to be the last-ever profession of monks at Canterbury on the feast of St Benedict in July.[143] He may have started travelling up to Leicestershire, a safely remote part of Longland's diocese, in early August; he was at Worcester in mid-August and travelled down through the Vale of Evesham and Gloucester to arrive by early September at Bristol, where a city centre church recorded the ringing of bells when he arrived.[144] We can catch a few glimpses of the content of his

142 Cox 2, p. 291, B.L. Harley MS 6148, f. 45r, *L.P.* 7 no. 702. On the succession oath, compare the identical royal letters to Richard Gwent and Peter Ligham, Bowker, *Henrician Reformation*, pp. 74–5 and *L.P.* 7 no. 876. *Gardiner's Letters*, p. 55.

143 Collinson, Ramsay and Sparks (eds), *Canterbury Cathedral*, p. 123: the feast of the deposition or translation of St Benedict is 11 July.

144 Rochester: Cox 2, p. 294, P.R.O., S.P. 1/84 f. 128 (*L.P.* 7 no. 776). Worcester, 17 August: 'Wolsey's and Cranmer's visitations', ed. Wilson, p. 419; Pershore, 23 August: P.R.O., E. 326/8961; Winchcombe, 25 August: Lambeth Cart. Misc. XI no. 56; Kingswood Abbey, Gloucs.: P.R.O., S.P. 1/94 f. 62; Bristol, 9 September: Skeeters, *Community and Clergy*, p. 229 n. 80. Several of the acknowledgements of the royal supremacy listed in *L.P.* 7 nos 1121, 1216 fit in with this itinerary.

energetic programme, and a taste of the evangelical flavour. For instance his German client Thalassius later recalled him preaching during the summer at London, Leicester and Worcester as well as Croydon and elsewhere, reprehending clerical wonder-working, avarice, belly-cheer and drunkenness. One might say that such moralizing was familiar stuff in visitation sermons, but the details of Thalassius's memories of the sermons are remarkably reminiscent of the themes which, in this same year or in late 1533, Cromwell had recommended that Cranmer issue to his clergy in pamphlet form: this too had proposed an appeal to the clergy 'to avoid clean, all pomp, all pride, all vainglory and specially all manner of covetousness . . . all ambition, all delicate fare'. Thalassius does not say whether Cranmer went on to follow this up with Cromwell's suggestive further proposed exhortation, that clergy should 'depart and dispose among the people of this realm lands, goods, money, and whatsoever other thing they now possess superfluously', but the coincidence of themes is already close enough to suggest that Cranmer had decided against print and had taken the message to the pulpit instead.[145]

Similarly, there was a new agenda in the injunctions that Cranmer issued for Worcester Cathedral Priory in February 1535; despite containing many orders that could have occurred at any time in the previous few centuries, the very first item told the monks to organize and attend a scripture reading for an hour daily throughout the year, to cover the whole of the Bible from start to finish. The injunction was the first instance of a strategy which would characterize Cranmer's career as a reformer: he appealed to the past, in this case 'the rule of your Religion' (that is, the Benedictine rule) to emphasize Bible-reading as a central precept of the monastic life, but the order came with an evangelical twist. Although the reading could be interrupted for the great festivals, Cranmer gave a specific dispensation so that it overruled community recitation of the Hours of Our Lady or the seven penitential psalms. What was particularly interesting was that he ordered that the scripture should be expounded in English 'according at least to the literal sense': this clearly relegates to a secondary place the medieval interest in exposition of the supposed allegorical layers of scripture, and is reminiscent of his recommendation to Latimer a year before to preach 'according to the pure sense and meaning' of the text. It is likely that similar injunctions went to other West Country monastic communities which he visited in person, such as Pershore, Kingswood and St Augustine's, Bristol.[146]

Elsewhere, the delegated parts of Cranmer's visitation continued to meet mixed fortunes. Nix was the easiest target to knock down, already wounded by his earlier humiliation, now in his late eighties and totally blind: he was brought to heel in September and October 1534, and was summoned into

145 Thalassius: B.L. Cotton MS Vitellius B XXI f. 124 (*L.P.* 8 no. 831). Cromwell's pamphlet: *Records of the Reformation* 2, pp. 487–9 (*L.P.* 6, no. 738); for dating and the Cromwell connection, see Elton, *Policy and Police*, p. 183.

146 'Wolsey's and Cranmer's Visitations', ed. Wilson, p. 421.

Star Chamber the following winter.[147] However, Longland and Stokesley were more formidable foes, still able to draw on their fund of goodwill with the King from the days of the annulment. In Lincoln, Cranmer's Dean of Arches, Richard Gwent, tacitly admitted defeat on 7 August, when he prorogued his visitation until 1 December; the same prorogation until December was made in London diocese in the face of Stokesley's protests.[148] Things were going badly wrong, and more was to follow in 1535.

Cranmer had been led into a fiasco through bad planning which was not really of his own making; now Cromwell had to think again about how to sort matters out. One move was to meet Stokesley's objection to the archiepiscopal title. On 11 November the Archbishop announced to a specially convened business meeting of Convocation that from now on, in addition to his title of Primate of All England, he would substitute the title of Metropolitan for that of legate of the Apostolic See: the change had an agreeable reminiscence of the early Church about it which Cranmer would have enjoyed. Yet Stokesley was not to be mollified. Remorselessly, in his appeal to the King in December 1534, he hammered away at the legatine source of Cranmer's powers, and the confusion between those powers and his jurisdiction '*jure metropolitico*'; he also gleefully threw in the red herring that many archbishops had been Chancellor of England, 'by the which authority they peradventure did enforce and maintain many things attempted against the law, as the late Cardinal did'.[149]

The only effective answer to the conservative bishops' obstruction was to clarify the operation of the Royal Supremacy, and to find a mechanism of command which would avoid the problems revealed during 1534: to explain how this was done will take us on through to 1536. The major steps were taken as part of Parliament's programme of government legislation which also began during November 1534. The Act of Supremacy passed Parliament about a week after Cranmer's change of title, together with an Act that refined the oath of succession; this was desirable since Thomas More had made cogent criticism of the previous oath tendered throughout the year, saying that its wording went beyond the terms of the Succession Act of winter 1534. The Supremacy Act did little more than recognize the *fait accompli* which the government had achieved by its activity throughout the year, except in one significant respect: a clause explicitly gave Henry the right 'to visit, repress, redress, reform, order, correct, restrain and amend all such errors, heresies . . . and enormities . . . which by any manner spiritual authority or jurisdiction ought or may be lawfully reformed . . .'.[150]

147 P.R.O., S.P. 1/89 f. 130 (*L.P.* 8 no. 159).

148 *L.P.* 7 no. 1044 iii (Lincoln). Cf. Strype, *Cranmer* 2, Appendix no. 15, p. 269: 'which [Cranmer] hath now continued until the first day of December.'

149 On Convocation, *Concilia*, ed. Wilkins, 3, p. 769; for confirmation of the date, cf. Lambeth MS 751, p. 106. Cf. Stokesley, Strype, *Cranmer* 2, Appendix no. 15, p. 270.

150 Lehmberg, *Reformation Parliament*, pp. 201–3; Elton, *Tudor Constitution*, p. 365.

Probably even before these measures had received the royal assent, the King acted on this new clarification of the royal prerogative; a draft commission dateable to mid-November or early December names three men, Cromwell and the two civil lawyers John Tregonwell and Thomas Bedell. They were to be visitors not simply to exempt religious houses but to a whole list of ecclesiastical institutions, from cathedrals downwards, which in effect meant the entire Church in England. The trio were named with titles which would resound through the Church of England for the rest of the decade: '*Vice-gerentes et vicarios nostros generales*'; among them, Cromwell was already envisaged as the senior ('*quorum te prefatum Thomam Cromwell . . . praecipuum et principaliorem esse volumus*'). Yet in the course of drafting, alterations were made to produce a final commission in January 1535 which named Thomas Cromwell as sole Vice-gerent or Vicar-general. Still the purpose of this new office remained one single royal visitation, although this apparent limitation of powers was not what it seemed. While the Vice-gerent was engaged on his visitation, all authority of the local bishops would be placed in the visitor's hands. This was to be the basis for a great expansion of the vice-gerential powers until they overshadowed those of the two archbishops themselves.[151]

Nevertheless, Dr Logan has noted the hesitancy with which this proposed structure was put into effect; months elapsed before the commission was acted upon. One can underline his point by noting the way in which Cranmer's visitation staggered on into 1535, creating more problems and embarrassments in its wake; it looks as if Cromwell had not yet decided that the archiepiscopal visitation was a lost cause. New areas of visitation were attempted; in late February or early March the aged bishop Veysey of Exeter received Cranmer's inhibition, and although he does not seem to have made a formal protest, the inhibition became tangled up with rows at two monasteries in Exeter diocese.[152] There was even an unprecedented effort to give secular backup to Cranmer's work, by placing his senior household officers on the commissions of the peace in strategic areas. This is the only plausible explanation of the sudden appearance in certain county commissions of the peace, issued in late 1534 and winter 1535, of John Goodrich, Henry Hatfield and Henry Stockwith. Goodrich, besides being Cranmer's treasurer, was elder brother to Cranmer's old friend and ally Bishop Thomas Goodrich, while the Archbishop's surveyor Hatfield and Stockwith were both also Cranmer relatives from the east Midlands.

This trio is listed together as a block in such widely-dispersed counties as Surrey and Sussex (21 December 1534), and Suffolk and Gloucestershire (20 February 1535), while Goodrich alone appears in the Norfolk commission of

151 References in this and the following paragraphs are based on Logan, 'Thomas Cromwell and the Vice-gerency in Spirituals', unless otherwise stated.

152 *L.P.* 8, no. 359; cf. ibid. no. 92.

24 November 1534.[153] Their introduction to Sussex indicates that the diocese of Chichester was also in the Archbishop's sights; Surrey was in the diocese of Winchester where he was now planning to initiate his visitation, Suffolk and Norfolk were in Norwich, where proceedings were continuing against poor Bishop Nix, and Gloucestershire was part of the diocese of Worcester, with which Cranmer had been concerned since August. Since justices of the peace were appointed by the Lord Chancellor, this is yet another instance of Archbishop and Chancery working closely together. Yet the trio of new JPs had vanished as suddenly as they had come from these various justices' benches by the time of the next surviving commissions of the peace.[154]

During this winter and into the spring, there were fresh demonstrations of defiance from Longland and Stokesley. Longland's suffragan bishop was still ignoring Cranmer's inhibition in March 1535 by holding an ordination, and Stokesley had done the same in February. It was probably also Stokesley who was responsible for yet another attack on a different aspect of Cranmer's powers, his personal Court of Audience; from this, we only have the final retort of the attacker (evidently during 1535) following two lost documents: an injured protestation of Cranmer replying to the initial assault on the Audience Court. In his retort the attacker widened his attack from the Audience Court to the province of Canterbury's appeal court, the Court of Arches, whose presence in a Canterbury peculiar in the heart of the diocese of London was of course of particular concern to Stokesley. Behind all this was still the relentless insistence on the suspect legatine element in Cranmer's powers, and there was also an adroit further widening of the argument, to enlist the Vicar-general's new powers as a challenge to the older powers of the Archbishop. Stokesley (if he was indeed the author) suggested that if the King made Cranmer 'his legate, it should peradventure derogate the power of his Grace's General Vicar. And if both should occupy, then shall the people so much the rather take occasion to think and say, that his Grace's Vicar exerciseth the power of a legate by his Grace's authority, and the Archbishop of Canterbury by authority of the Bishop of Rome.'[155]

153 P.R.O., E. 371/300 mm. 44–9; cf. the previous commissions, P.R.O., E. 371/299/42, mm. 1–15, and Bevan, 'Justices of the Peace, 1509–47', pp. 246–7. On Goodrich, Du Boulay, *Lordship of Canterbury*, p. 402, and his testimony for his brother Bishop Goodrich, Cranmer's Register f. 86v. On Hatfield, see P.R.O., S.P. 1/82 f. 182, Cox 2, p. 287 (*L.P.* 7, no. 558); on Stockwith, Du Boulay, *Lordship of Canterbury*, p. 401, and P.R.O., S.P. 1/134 ff. 210–11, Cox 2, p. 337 (*L.P.* 12 ii no. 288 and 13 i no. 1424).

154 John Goodrich did survive in Norfolk and Suffolk commissions through the later 1530s, along with his brother Henry, but here the influence of Bishop Goodrich in East Anglia provides an explanation. See MacCulloch, *Suffolk and the Tudors*, Appendices I and II.

155 B.L. Cotton MS Cleopatra F I ff. 95–6, pr. Strype, *Cranmer* 2, Appendix no. 17, pp. 275–7. For discussion of authorship, see Brigden, *London*, p. 225n and Ayris and Selwyn (eds), *Cranmer*, pp. 125–6, although I think it unlikely that the existing document is as late as October 1535. Dr Redworth chooses to see it as the work of Gardiner, without giving any strong evidence: Redworth, *Gardiner*, p. 64.

Here was good reason for Cromwell to pause and consider the best further action.

Still more trouble for Cranmer emerged. Another late flowering of protest at his visitation by Corpus Christi College, Oxford, in February 1535, was probably not unconnected with the fact that Stephen Gardiner was the College's visitor.[156] This is all the more likely because the final contretemps of the whole sorry business of visitation came in spring 1535, when Cranmer decided to try his luck and visit Stephen Gardiner's diocese of Winchester. It is puzzling that he had not staged a visitation there during 1534, since Gardiner was then very much on the defensive; Winchester's outspoken resentment of the pace of further religious change had earned him dismissal as royal secretary and exile from Court into the Hampshire heartland of his diocese in April 1534, and there he stayed probably through the rest of the year.[157] Cranmer nevertheless held off, perhaps for the honourable and compassionate reason that Winchester diocese had been visited twice before in four years; he only served a monition for visitation on the Bishop of Winchester on 20 April 1535. Gardiner then complained about this to Henry VIII.

Gardiner's gambit was a new variation on the theme of Cranmer's style and the royal supremacy: he objected to Cranmer's medieval title 'Primate of all England' as 'to the derogation and prejudice of the King's high power and authority', and he also drew attention to the financial burdens which a third visitation in five years would cause the diocese. Cranmer's reply on 12 May when Cromwell had told him the news of Gardiner's protest was as angry as the primate could get: we rarely hear him speak so frankly as in this letter to an intimate friend. Nothing could infuriate him more than a charge of disloyalty to Henry VIII, and in his letter we hear already the aggressive tones which he would use in his *Answer* to Gardiner in 1551: that useful evening meal of six years before at Waltham was in a different age. 'To be plain what I think of the bishop of Winchester, I cannot persuade with myself that he so much tendereth the King's cause as he doth his own, that I should not visit him.' The issue seemed to have hurt the Archbishop to the quick, injuring his own self-esteem at a deep level, and there tumbled out a cry of frustration which had probably been building up through twelve months of episcopal manoeuvring from his supposed colleagues:

> For I pray God never be merciful unto me at the general judgement, if I perceive in my heart that I set more by any title, name, or style that I write, than I do by the paring of an apple, farther than it shall be to the setting forth of God's word and will. Yet I will not utterly excuse me herein; for God must be judge, who knoweth the bottom of my heart, and so do not I myself; but I speak for so much as I do feel in my heart; for many evil affections lie lurking

156 *L.P.* 8, no. 316; Ayris Ph.D., 'Thomas Cranmer's Register', pp. 63–4, 265.

157 Redworth, *Gardiner*, pp. 61–3. The following details and quotations are all derived from Cranmer's letter to Cromwell, B.L. Cotton MS Cleopatra F I ff. 249–50, Cox 2, p. 304 (*L.P.* 8 no. 704).

there, and will not lightly be espied. But yet I would not gladly leave any just thing at the pleasure and suit of the bishop of Winchester, he being none otherwise affectionate unto me than he is.

In his fury, Cranmer came close to saying what he thought of Gardiner's real motives in his obstructiveness. Stokesley, Longland, Nix and Gardiner had genuine fears about their position in the wake of the momentous legislation recognizing the royal supremacy. However, to suppose that their recalcitrance was entirely about jurisdiction and their fears of praemunire penalties seems over-trusting.[158] The bishops involved were those most resistant to the evangelical programme of Cromwell and Cranmer. Nix had earned himself notoriety among evangelicals by burning Thomas Bilney in 1531. Stokesley and Gardiner had not promoted the royal annulment merely to see a fifth column of evangelicals use it to take over the Church; we have seen both of them involved in the campaign to gag or even destroy Hugh Latimer during 1532 and 1533 (see above, p. 88). It would be naive to think that two old colleagues who were such shrewd operators were not passing notes between their respective palaces at Fulham and Southwark.

Perhaps it was Cranmer's letter that finally made Cromwell realize that now was the time to change tack and activate the vice-gerency, for it was only during summer 1535 that he began exercising his new powers and started on his visitation. Even then, the structure of the vice-gerency was not quite complete. The metropolitical visitation was still staggering on in the early summer, but a decision was taken formally to end it on 1 August.[159] In September, inhibitions were issued to the two archbishops, ordering them in turn to inform the bishops in their provinces of the suspension of their authority; finally the shadow of Canterbury's legatine jurisdiction had been banished. Almost immediately the drastic practical implications of this total freezing of normal church chains of command was eased by the issuing of vice-gerential licences to bishops (including to Cranmer himself) and to others for various routine purposes: ordaining, confirming, proving wills and so on.[160] A special vice-gerential office was set up to issue these dispensations, and from January 1536 onwards there was even a vice-gerential court of probate for wills of exceptional value. The final stage in the process came in summer 1536, when Cromwell 'was made high vicar over the spirituality under the King and sat divers times in the Convocation house among the bishops as head over them'.[161] His powers had now been extended, because his visitation,

158 Cf. the comments of Bowker, *Henrician Reformation*, pp. 71–7; Ayris and Selwyn (eds), *Cranmer*, pp. 124–5.

159 B.L. Cotton MS Cleopatra E IV f. 56 (*L.P.* 8 no. 955).

160 Notes from the lost Vice-gerential archive in Harmer, *Specimen*, p. 52, and B.L. Additional MS 48022 ff. 84r, 90r, 92r, 98v; cf. also Bowker, *Henrician Reformation*, pp. 77–8.

161 *Wriothesley's Chronicle* 1, pp. 51–2. Cf. the memorandum possibly of September 1535 and probably by William Petre which mapped out most of these changes: P.R.O., S.P. 1/99 f. 231, *L.P.* 9 no. 1071, and cf. Elton, *Reform and Renewal*, p. 134.

the original reason for granting them, had run its course. By 1537 Cromwell would be calling his own vice-gerential synods, which combined clerical representatives from both provinces of Canterbury and York (see below, Ch. 6, pp. 185–96). The ultimate symbol of his new position was his promotion above the Archbishop of Canterbury in the ranking of precedence in the House of Lords, in May 1539.[162] It is only the accident of Cromwell's fall, and the loss of virtually all the archives of his activity, which have prevented us from seeing clearly the workings of this remarkable outgrowth of the royal supremacy.

By this complex evolution of institutions, the Royal Supremacy was at last given a clear structure by which it could be exercised in practice; the objections of the conservative bishops during Cranmer's 1534 visitation had been neatly outflanked by the government moving the goalposts. Dr Logan is probably correct (against many earlier commentators) in seeing the evolution as a process of *ad hoc* reactions to situations as they arose, rather than the result of planned strategy.[163] Yet one can still see the hand of Cromwell at every stage from the Act in Restraint of Appeals onwards. When it was clear in late 1533 to early 1534 that papal authority was to be ditched, Cromwell's first strategy seems to have been an unequal partnership between himself and Cranmer, in which the Archbishop should play the main public role, but under controls institutionally expressed by the various links to Chancery which the legislation of winter 1534 set up.

It was not surprising that Cromwell should think thus, for during the process of unravelling the King's first marriage in the Spring of 1533, Cranmer had indeed played the leading role in the formal business, while Cromwell directed events behind the scenes. We have already mentioned Cromwell's proposal of 1533–4 that Cranmer should publish a pamphlet addressed to the nation's clergy: this would formally defend the Archbishop's own proceedings in the divorce, and sternly exhort his clerical subordinates to exercise their ministry 'to ease the people of their burdens' rather than 'to eschew labour and travail'. 'I am very sure', Cromwell continued with an interesting blend of realism about the clergy and idealism about the laity, 'though he could never bring his purpose about, yet should he by this mean greatly content the people's minds, and make them think that they be happy thus to be rid of the Pope's oppression, and that the Archbishop is a perfect and a good bishop.'[164]

Here was a continuing vision of an evangelical archbishop on the public stage, advised by a wise statesman in the wings. Yet the woeful number of loose ends in the Supremacy, exposed by the events of 1534, led to a stage-by-stage rethink, which in the end would leave the Archbishop much more

162 *L.J.* 1, p. 107: the first listing giving Cromwell precedence is of 10 May 1539, before the full passage of the new precedence act.

163 Logan, 'Thomas Cromwell and the Vice-gerency in Spirituals', pp. 658, 667.

164 *Records of the Reformation* 2, pp. 487–9.

clearly the junior partner to the vice-gerent in spirituals. As Dr Ayris succinctly puts it, 'from 1535, Cromwell effectively eclipsed Thomas Cranmer as the principal minister of the King's spiritual jurisdiction'. Cranmer, for instance, had virtually nothing to do with the course of the dissolution of the monasteries, nunneries and friaries, one of the most permanent results of the Reformation in the 1530s, and whose story can be told virtually without reference to him.

Yet there is no evidence that Cranmer resented his position. The previous few years had revealed both his strengths and his weaknesses. He had shown himself a popular and successful diplomat, and an exceptional researcher and deviser of texts for a complex and difficult problem, but he was no politician. He lacked the political ruthlessness or deviousness to outface even clerical politicians like Stokesley and Gardiner, let alone the hardfaced noblemen on the King's Council. That was best left to Cromwell: the two men valued each other's skills, and recognized how their talents could be complementary in striving for common evangelical goals. A clear although topsy-turvy piece of evidence for Cranmer and Cromwell's special relationship is the one surviving letter-book for Cranmer's outgoing correspondence, of which we have already made much use: British Library MS Harley 6148. The remarkable feature of this book (which covers Cranmer's archiepiscopal correspondence from 1533 to 1535) is that it contains hardly a single letter from Cranmer to Cromwell, despite transcribing Cranmer's letters to other key figures including the King himself; Cranmer must have kept a separate file for his letters to his chief ally in politics. It would be the Vice-gerent who would take the lead in guiding Cranmer through the political crisis of spring 1536, which destroyed his great patroness and brought her reign to an end.

CHAPTER 5

From Anne Boleyn to Thomas Cromwell: 1535–7

THE LAST FULL YEAR of Queen Anne's 'reign' saw further evangelical advance in England, even the formation of an evangelical establishment within the central institutions of Church and State: not unchallenged or all-powerful, but for the moment keeping the initiative against the traditionalist supporters of the King's supremacy. Its membership is quite precisely indicated by the correspondence and verse dedications of Nicolas Bourbon, a fashionable French evangelical poet who carved a niche for himself at Anne's Court: Bourbon had been brought from imprisonment in France through the Queen's intercession, on the initiative of the evangelical royal physician William Butts, and he lodged with Butts while he was in England. Cromwell and Butts of course figure prominently in his poems, together with the royal family and various younger courtiers, while the clerics are Cranmer and his circle of evangelical friends: Abbot Benson of Westminster, Hugh Latimer, Thomas Goodrich and Thomas Thirlby. From Bourbon's collected works entitled *Nugae*, we have already quoted one hymn of praise to Cromwell, Cranmer and Henry VIII as the epigraph to Part II; among several other flattering references and dedications to Cranmer is one charming little poem of spring 1535, inviting the Archbishop out for a rural holiday, probably at Benson's country retreat, which, Bourbon assured the Archbishop, would seem like the spring gardens of Adonis. Noticeable among Bourbon's continental dedicatees is Cranmer's old acquaintance Simon Grynaeus.[1]

Cranmer himself now lost powers, precedence and in the end even some of his lands to the new institution of the vice-gerency. His officials may have resented the process, but there is no sign that power was ever very important to him: what mattered was the furtherance of the Gospel as he conceived it, and he may have been relieved to be rescued from the wounding fiasco of his visitation.[2] In place of the visitation came a determined Court campaign to

1 Cf. especially Bourbon, *Nugae*, pp. 82–90: for the Cranmer spring poem, ibid., p. 344. Grynaeus: ibid., pp. 428, 451. Starkey (ed.), *Henry VIII: a European Court*, pp. 109–10.

2 Note the comments of Richard Layton (a self-interested and unreliable witness) about ill-feeling from Cranmer and his officials, B.L. Cotton MS Cleopatra E IV f. 56, *L.P.* 8 no. 955. The atmosphere of co-operation between Cranmer and the Vice-gerent is most likely better reflected in the memorandum probably by William Petre, P.R.O., S.P. 1/99 f. 231, *L.P.* 9 no. 1071.

assert the Royal Supremacy and to promote evangelical advance in the Church. The consecration, on 11 April 1535, of Queen Anne's almoner, Nicholas Shaxton, to be Campeggio's successor as Bishop of Salisbury was a first step, and while evangelicals rose, traditionalists fell. Nationally respected opponents of the Supremacy were given repeated demonstrations throughout the spring and summer that they would be treated ruthlessly: between May and July, leading Carthusians, a monk of Syon Abbey and then most shockingly of all, Bishop Fisher and Thomas More, were executed. Cranmer himself was present at one of More's last major interrogations in the Tower on 3 June, but in More's description of the occasion, it is significant that he does not record anything of Cranmer's contribution: the Archbishop characteristically let Chancellor Audley and Cromwell do all the talking. Very much later, Cranmer affirmed that he had opposed More's execution, and there is no good reason to disbelieve him; we have seen already (Ch. 4, p. 124) that he had done his best to suggest a compromise for More when he was arrested in 1534. There is equally no good reason to suppose that now any more than in 1534, his opinion would have carried much weight against Henry's vicious hatred of the former Chancellor.[3]

The King's vigorous pushing of the Royal Supremacy hardly needs explanation, but rather less predictable was his decision to pursue renewed contacts with the Lutheran princes of Germany and Scandinavia, culminating in an embassy to the Germans headed by the newly consecrated Bishop Edward Foxe during autumn 1535. Henry, faced with the Emperor's hostility and seeing his former ally the French King Francis I as increasingly untrustworthy, for the moment saw the Lutheran princes as the only feasible alternative friends on the Continent; his estrangement from Francis I was completed by that monarch's horror at the deaths of Fisher and More. Henry even proposed joining the princes' Schmalkaldic League. As part of his new strategy, he became obsessed with speaking to Philipp Melanchthon in person in England, and also with diverting him from talks with the King of France (Melanchthon had only reluctantly agreed to these, and in the end he failed to meet King Francis too).[4] Melanchthon was the only Continental reformer for whom Henry VIII ever showed any genuine enthusiasm; perhaps he was attracted by the reformer's reputation as a humanist scholar who sought the middle way, characteristics that were part of Henry's own self-image. This was not Melanchthon's first official invitation to England, and it would not be the last, but he never risked the English Channel and the baffling political and

3 *More Correspondence*, pp. 555–9. The Duke of Suffolk and the Earl of Wiltshire were also present, but nothing is recorded from them either. On Cranmer's opposition, *Cranmer's Recantacyons*, pp. 80–81.

4 Burnet 3 ii, pp. 130–34 (Bk. 3, no. 42; *L.P.* 9 no. 1062). Cf. also *L.P.* 8 no. 1065; Wallop's instructions, Strype, *Ecclesiastical Memorials*, 1 ii, p. 247 (*L.P.* 10 no. 157); Foxe's instructions, *L.P.* 10 no. 213. Melanchthon's comments of 5 October: *L.P.* 9 nos 545–6. On this embassy generally, see McEntegart Ph.D., 'England and the League of Schmalkalden', Ch. 3.

theological world that lay beyond it. Nevertheless, in August 1535, he fulsomely dedicated the latest edition of his key doctrinal work the *Loci Communes* to Henry. He sent it across to England in the care of a wandering Scottish Lutheran, Alexander Alane, who had romantically transformed his surname into Alesius, 'the wanderer', and who remained in England for some years, benefiting from Cromwell's and Cranmer's patronage; we shall repeatedly make Alesius's acquaintance.[5] The Archbishop took a keen interest in what Melanchthon had to say in the *Loci Communes*.

During summer 1535, the strength of the evangelicals revealed in this diplomacy was given its most dramatic expression when Henry and Anne themselves became the leading actors in a touring pageant of the new dispensation: as Cranmer had done the previous summer, they headed into the West Country, in one of the longest and most significant progresses of Henry's reign. As the royal retinue moved slowly in a great circle from Windsor to Tewkesbury, down through the Vale of Gloucester and into Wiltshire and Hampshire, West Country evangelicals were especially rewarded by royal visits and every sign of favour; maybe Cranmer had done some research for the route on his own journey west. The extraordinary nature of the event was also emphasized by the presence of Thomas Cromwell near the King for most of the itinerary, with the new Vice-gerent taking the opportunity to visit various monasteries in person. The impact of this progress, and the King's ostentatious public backing of those promoting religious change, was probably a major factor in keeping the West quiet during the Pilgrimage of Grace in the following year.[6]

From their beginning in June, these royal journeys were marked by a barrage of propaganda about the Supremacy, with orders going out to all the bishops to lead preaching campaigns; the newly consecrated Bishop Shaxton congratulated Cromwell on prompting the King to take this action.[7] Cranmer himself carried the message into the remoter parts of his diocese and into the still unsympathetic atmosphere of his own cathedral; using the new powers of his Faculty Office, during the summer he also issued more nationwide preaching licences to his most trusted evangelical preachers. Two of them, Dr John Thyxstyll of Pembroke College, Cambridge, and John Cheke of St John's, Cambridge, were not even in deacon's orders at the time. This seems to have been the first evidence of a new group of four officially recognized preachers who were licensed to preach (naturally, in the evangelical interest) throughout the realm; three years later a foreign observer

5 *L.P.* 9 nos 222–5, and for Henry's thanks, Strype, *Ecclesiastical Memorials*, 1 i, p. 357 (*L.P.* 9 no. 166).

6 Starkey (ed.), *European Court*, pp. 118–25.

7 Letters sent out 3 June: Cox 2, pp. 306, 325–6 (B.L. Cotton Cleopatra E VI f. 234–6, *L.P.* 8 no. 820, 11 no. 361). Shaxton: Strype, *Ecclesiastical Memorials*, I ii, p. 204, *L.P.* 8 no. 821. Cf. *T.R.P.* 1 no. 158 (9 June 1535).

noted among them the prime exponent of Lutheranism in England, Dr Robert Barnes.[8]

The theatre of the royal progress culminated at Michaelmastide (late September) in a great assembly of bishops and notables at Winchester, an appropriate place, as Bishop Gardiner's cathedral city, to symbolize the united backing of evangelicals and conservatives for the King's supreme headship; it was noticeable that the hosts of the royal party in Hampshire were more conservative than on the earlier stages of the progress. The visit was therefore a sign that the King was forgiving Gardiner for his earlier recalcitrance, and was rewarding him for the two writings which he was now just completing. The Bishop's major work was *De Vera Obedientia*, generally acknowledged when it was published to be one of the most effective defences of the Royal Supremacy, and he had also produced on a smaller scale a sneering answer to the Pope's furious condemnation of the executions of Fisher and More. Cranmer came over from Kent to Winchester, partly to consult with Gardiner on the final version of the text of this latter tract.[9]

Yet Gardiner could hardly claim an unqualified victory out of these events. Cranmer had his own leading role in the Winchester pageant, because the evangelical stock on the bishops' bench was now to receive a spectacular boost: while he was there, the Archbishop consecrated John Hilsey to fill Fisher's vacant see of Rochester, Edward Foxe for Hereford, and as Ghinucci's successor at Worcester no less a figure than Hugh Latimer. Latimer's appointment was particularly outrageous, considering that only two years before the diocesan establishment of Worcester had been trying to nail him as a heretic.[10] Hilsey was nearly as symbolic a figure as Latimer, for he had been a sudden but sincere convert from traditionalism to evangelicalism during Latimer's troubles of 1533 at Bristol. Later in this year, on 20 December 1535, the Vice-gerent granted Hilsey a commission to license all preachers in the city of London, an extraordinary insult to Gardiner's like-minded colleague, the Bishop of London, John Stokesley, who only that summer had complained about Hilsey's preaching in London![11] Moreover, the price of

8 On Cranmer: Cox 2, p. 326. *Faculty Office Registers*, p. 39: Thomas Garrett (6 June), Thomas Swinnerton (8 June), Thyxstyll (20 June), Cheke (9 July): for Thyxstyll's hasty ordination two years later, see ibid., p. 107. On Barnes, Myconius's description of June 1538, qu. McEntegart Ph.D., 'England and the League of Schmalkalden', p. 233.

9 P.R.O., S.P. 1/97 f. 17, pr. Gardiner, *Obedience*, ed. Janelle, pp. xxi–xxii (*L.P.* 9 no. 442). See also Gardiner, *Obedience*, ed. Janelle, for the texts of the Pope's letter and both Gardiner's writings.

10 On the slight uncertainty of dating Latimer's consecration, see Demaus, *Latimer*, pp. 207–8.

11 B.L. Additional MS 48022 f. 87r; Stokesley to Cromwell, 17 July 1535, P.R.O., S.P. 1/94 f. 98 (*L.P.* 8 no. 1054, although Hilsey is wrongly identified as George Browne). For a (somewhat unsympathetic) treatment of Hilsey's change of heart, see Skeeters, *Community and Clergy*, pp. 40–41.

Gardiner's rehabilitation in these celebrations was what amounted to honourable exile, despite all his propaganda work for the King's cause; within a few days of the royal party leaving Winchester, he set out for a prolonged embassy to the French king, and he was thus removed from an active role in English politics for a full three years. During that time the evangelicals continued to ride high, triumphantly surviving the potentially lethal crises of the fall of Anne Boleyn and the Pilgrimage of Grace.

As always, the enclave of Calais proved a litmus test of the prevailing religious mood in politics: it is not surprising that 1535 and 1536 saw Cranmer chalking up significant victories there. In the previous year he had been outwitted by the Lisles, who had successfully imported a brace of suspect Observant friars, Covert and Roche, to preach in the town (see Ch. 4, pp. 112–13): now Cranmer made sure that convinced evangelicals from his own staff would do the job. As early as 6 January 1535, Lord Lisle's servant John Husee wrote to his master that he should 'shortly have two preachers of his Grace's own appointing', and that there were even rumours that Cranmer would come over and preach himself if he could get royal licence to do so.[12] Cranmer did not go himself in the end, but instead he repeatedly lobbied the King and Cromwell to consolidate the position of his two chosen preachers for Lent 1535 at Calais. The senior of these was Cranmer's own chaplain, Richard Hoore, a convinced evangelical (and as usual, an old Cambridge friend) who had played his part in the assault on Longland's diocese in visitation the previous summer; he held a nationwide preaching licence from the Archbishop. Hoore does not sound to have been a soulmate for the Lisles, but Cranmer seems to have prepared the ground well by securing an appointment for him from Lisle, since he talked of Hoore as 'your chaplain' when writing Lisle a letter of introduction for him.[13]

In the event Hoore seemed to go down well in Calais, and repeatedly, in April, again in May and even as late as December 1535, Cranmer went out of his way to thank the Lisles effusively for 'the well and gentle entreating' of the two preachers during that Lent.[14] This was by way of constant reminder in order to secure a repeat evangelical performance at Calais in the following Lent, 1536. The tactic worked: at the beginning of Lent, Cranmer could write a letter of introduction for his two preachers to Lisle, in which he emphasized that it was at Lisle's 'desire and request' that 'your own man Master Hoore' was returning.[15] This time Hoore's fellow-preacher was more clearly his equal, one of his close friends from Cambridge and indeed an executor of his

12 *Lisle Letters* 2, p. 372 (*L.P.* 8 no. 14).

13 P.R.O., S.P. 1/89 f. 60, Cox 2, p. 298 (*L.P.* 8 no. 85); P.R.O., S.P. 3/2/79, *Lisle Letters* 2, p. 397, Cox 2, p. 298 (*L.P.* 8 no. 172). On Hoore, see *L.P.* 7 no. 1044 iii; *Faculty Office Registers*, p. 7.

14 P.R.O., S.P. 3/2/76, Cox 2, pp. 322–3, but rightly redated to April 1535 by *L.P.* 8 no. 607 and *Lisle Letters* 2, pp. 468–70; similarly in May 1535, P.R.O., S.P. 3/2/78, Cox 2, pp. 324–5 (*L.P.* 8 no. 685). December: P.R.O., S.P. 3/2/77, Cox 2, p. 318 (*L.P.* 9 no. 996).

15 P.R.O., S.P. 3/2/75, Cox 2, p. 320, *Lisle Letters* 3, p. 284 (*L.P.* 10 no. 412).

will two years later, Robert Nicolles. Nicolles, another of Cranmer's chaplains, was one of the evangelical clique among the Fellows of Pembroke College, Cambridge, along with John Thyxstyll; like Hoore, he had additionally acquired benefices in East Anglia.[16] Once more, this formidable Cambridge team seemed to work wonders in a garrison town which may have been starved of academic stimulation: Cromwell's client John Whalley told him with cheerful indiscretion at the end of Lent 'that my Lord Deputy and my Lady his wife are well brought home with divers other which were pharisees there'. Lisle sounded quite evangelical himself when he wrote to Cranmer a fortnight later on Easter Day, 1536, to thank him for the two:

> I ensure your Grace they have done much good in these parts since their coming, and as I suppose never none heretofore did more . . . and that from henceforth it may be your Grace's pleasure to send every Lent the said Master Hoore and his associate or such other as shall be thought expedient for the good erudition of the people in these parts.[17]

Perhaps so; perhaps not. A few days after this letter, the crisis that would destroy Anne Boleyn became public, and we hear no more after that of Lisle's enthusiasm for Hoore. One might take the elaborate courtesy and positive tone of the exchanges about the preachers at face value, were it not for the survival of other evidence, which shows that during 1535 Cranmer's subordinates had been skirmishing with the Lisles about their religious conservatism. Cranmer's evangelical protégé and Calais commissary, John Butler, wrote to the Archbishop in February 1535 about the continuing reluctance of the Deputy and his Council to administer the oath ordered by Parliament the previous November, renouncing the Pope's authority. He also complained that they constantly sought 'ways to undo me', and begged the addition to the Council of some 'that were not of the papistical sort (which were hard to be found among the Council here)'.[18] Subsequently Lisle wrote indignantly to Cranmer that members of the archiepiscopal household had been noting him as a papist (it is interesting how quickly this term had caught on in English); in the same letter which thanked Lisle for being good to Hoore, the Archbishop defended Butler and patiently gave the Deputy a long lesson in what it meant to be an anti-papist. Lisle had rather naively assured him that he was habitually rude about the Pope, but Cranmer said that it was not enough to sneer at the present Bishop of Rome. It was 'the very papacy and the see of Rome, which both by their laws suppressed Christ, and set up the bishop of

16 For Nicolles in the will of the early evangelical George Stafford (19 June 1529), see C.U.L. UA Wills 1, f. 49v, and Hoore's will, P.C.C. 22 Dyngeley (P.R.O., PRO.B. 11/27 f. 175r). For his benefices, see Venn 3, p. 256, *Faculty Office Registers*, p. 78 and P.R.O., REQ. 3/16/1A, REQ. 3./4, unsorted material, Henry Watson v. Thomas Wiseman.

17 *Lisle Letters* 3, p. 326 (*L.P.* 10 no. 673(i)).

18 P.R.O., S.P. 1/102 f. 29, *Lisle Letters* 2, pp. 469–70 (*L.P.* 10 no. 292).

that see as a God of this world'. This was a very important distinction; if conservatives did not recognize the principle behind the break with Rome, and felt that loyalty to the King simply meant condemning the current pope, they clearly regarded the breach as temporary, and would easily be reconciled with the papacy once more.

Once more, Cranmer's real opinion of the Lisles and their religion was revealed in a letter to Thomas Cromwell later in 1535: Calais was a place of 'great ignorance and blindness as well of the heads now resident there, as of the common and vulgar people, in the doctrine and knowledge of scripture', and the inhabitants were 'altogether wrapt' in 'hypocrisy, false faith, and blindness of God and his Word'. His solution was to extend the idea of a pair of Lenten missionaries to a permanent presence, 'at the least two learned persons', and as a first step he recommended the appointment of Thomas Garrett, an evangelical Oxford don and client of Anne Boleyn, to St Peter's outside Calais. It was important that one local curate should not succeed in his suit for that church, 'especially in this world of reformation' – Cranmer had innocently hit on a term that would resound through later historical writing, although it does not seem to have been generally taken up at the time.[19]

In the same letter, Cranmer once more raised the case of an evangelical who was a former member of the Calais garrison, Henry Tourney: Lisle (encouraged, it was said, by Lady Lisle) had dismissed Tourney along with another evangelical during 1534, and his case was dragging on despite sympathetic support both from the Archbishop and Cromwell himself.[20] By 1535 Lisle was extremely reluctant to lose face by reinstating Tourney, and both sides again squared up for a trial of strength over the issue. The evangelicals won, for the time being. Cromwell wrote repeatedly to the Deputy about Tourney, and Cranmer used his influence directly with the King, drafting a stern letter to Lisle in Henry's name demanding Tourney's reinstatement. Lisle's final capitulation about Tourney in a letter to Cromwell did not hide his annoyance and his low opinion of Tourney, but for the moment he had no choice. Tourney was still in touch with Cranmer and Cromwell about Calais affairs two years later, and later still he was a victim of the conservative backlash there. Rows in the claustrophobic Calais enclave had a habit of surfacing and flaring up over the years, in a series of volcano-like episodes which had uncertain outcomes.[21]

The same could be said of another enclave under Cranmer's control, Hadleigh in Suffolk. Here Cranmer was on stronger ground than in Calais, for there was no rival authority of any significance for the Archbishop; already we

19 P.R.O., S.P. 1/97 f. 139v, Cox 2, p. 310 (*L.P.* 9 no. 561; 8 October 1535). On Garrett, cf. index references in Brigden, *London and the Reformation.*

20 *Lisle Letters* 2, pp. 257–63.

21 P.R.O., S.P. 1/98 f. 77, Cox 2, p. 313 (*L.P.* 9 no. 688); *Lisle Letters* 2, pp. 613–14. For Tourney in 1537, cf. P.R.O., S.P. 1/115 f. 89, Cox 2, p. 334 (*L.P.* 12 i no. 256.1), and in 1539–40, Foxe 5, pp. 498, 515.

have seen that in 1533 Hadleigh was the setting for one of Cranmer's earliest trials of strength with conservatives over the preaching of the charismatic iconoclast Thomas Rose (see above, p. 110). In 1536 trouble flared up again in Hadleigh; what is particularly intriguing is that the priest at the centre of the row was linked to earlier troubles in Calais. His name was Hugh Payne, and he was an ex-Observant friar, who had been in deep trouble as one of the Observant clique agitating for Catherine of Aragon's cause in 1533–4.[22] We have, of course, already met two of these Observants, Bernardine Covert and Thomas Roche, as preaching protégés of Lord Lisle in 1534. 'In my opinion he ought to give place to none of them in dissimulation, hypocrisy, flattery, and all other qualities of the wolfish Pharisees', Cranmer commented uncharitably on Payne when rounding up a report of the Hadleigh business to Cromwell.[23] As curate of Hadleigh, Payne had preached to such obnoxious effect during 1536 that Cranmer had summoned him, together with his distinctly more reliable rector, Dr William Rivet, and had personally ordered Payne to silence. However, the ex-Observant persisted in preaching, not just in Hadleigh but also in Cranmer's peculiar parishes in London. It is likely that there he enjoyed the patronage of the surviving members of the Warham set, clinging on to various of the benefices which the old Archbishop had given them. Such defiance could not be tolerated; it had wider implications for Cranmer's authority than simply the right instruction of the clothiers of Hadleigh.

Cranmer gave Cromwell one specimen of Payne's objectionably 'erroneous' preaching, and the example is of the highest interest: Payne 'taught openly in the pulpit there, that one paternoster, said by the injunction of a priest, was worth a thousand paternosters said of a man's mere voluntary mind: by this you may soon savour what judgement this man is of, and how sincerely he would instruct the people.'[24] Dr Ashley Null first noticed that (as Cranmer must have been perfectly aware) Payne was saying nothing shocking at all in conservative terms; he was merely quoting from a well-known fourteenth-century textbook of pastoral care, Guido de Monte Rocherii's *Manipulus Curatorum*. Indeed, he was being much more moderate than Guido, who had made the ratio of lay and clerically ordered paternosters one hundred thousand to one.[25] On this occasion Payne had clearly been preaching at Hadleigh about penance and confession, which was the context of Guido's extravagant remark; by his contemptuous rejection of Payne's message, Cranmer reveals to us that he had already by 1536 rejected medieval views of the value of auricular confession to a priest.

22 Elton, *Policy and Police*, p. 19n.

23 Details unless otherwise stated are from this letter of 28 January 1537, P.R.O., S.P. 1/115 f. 89, Cox 2, pp. 333–4 (*L.P.* 12 i no. 256).

24 Cox, and hence many other commentators, has misread the common abbreviation for 'a thousand' as 'a million', a word in any case not common in Tudor England.

25 I am very grateful to Dr Null for alerting me to his find. The reference is to the *Manipulus*, Tract 2, Pars 3 cap. 10; see also Null Ph.D., 'Cranmer's Doctrine of Repentance', pp. 55, 96.

Payne's theology was certainly much more acceptable to another power in East Anglia of different outlook to the Archbishop, for from Hadleigh the troublesome ex-friar escaped to a benefice at nearby Stoke by Nayland, a living in the gift of the Duke of Norfolk. Yet Cranmer was not thwarted; in alliance with the evangelical Suffolk magnate Thomas Lord Wentworth, he hunted Payne down, having excommunicated him when he failed to turn up on a citation. Cromwell in turn acted on the Archbishop's plea to punish the priest, and by 1537 Payne was sending pathetic pleas to the Duke of Norfolk from strict confinement in the Marshalsea Prison.[26] He never left his prison; he died there two years later, as Cranmer noted with righteous relish in another letter to Cromwell. That letter obliquely completes the circuit back to Calais and the Lisles. Payne had got himself another benefice, Great Sutton in remote south-east Essex; the patron presenting him had been one George Covert. Whatever Covert's exact relation to the ex-Observant Father Bernardine Covert, there is no doubt about the remaining link to Covert and Roche, those two Calais preachers of 1534: Cranmer, primed by an evangelical gentlewoman who had other plans for the Sutton benefice, now feared lest Payne should be succeeded at Sutton by 'one Roche, late Observant'.[27]

The whole story reveals Cranmer in an unexpectedly implacable light: Observant friars, so effectively damaging to the Gospel cause in their defence both of Catherine and of the old faith, were his particular *bête noire*. They deserved no pity, and Observants were only the worst of a corrupt organization. Friars in general were regarded by the evangelicals as a chief source of poison against their cause: a lost letter from Ralph Morice's brother, Philip, to his master, Thomas Cromwell, told him of a particularly vicious rumour about him, but he could not say whether it originated in French hatred of the Vice-gerent 'or from the friars in England'.[28] It was not surprising that at the height of his power in 1538, Cromwell made the destruction of the entire organization of the friars a priority. All the time, however, Cranmer and his fellow-members of the evangelical would-be establishment had to watch their other flank – not conservatives, but radical reformers. Conservatives and radicals equally aroused their deep hatred: one evangelical rhetorical device of abuse was to equate the different orders of monks and friars with the radicals, giving all of them the common label of 'sects'.[29]

26 P.R.O., S.P. 1/115 f. 91 (*L.P.* 12 i no. 257).

27 P.R.O., S.P. 1/143 ff. 30–31, Cox 2, p. 361 (redated to 1539 by *L.P.* 14 i no. 244). On the Covert family's links with the Duke of Norfolk, see *History of Parliament 1509–58* 1, pp. 719–20.

28 Bodl. MS Jesus 74, f. 166r, Morice to Cromwell, 4 May 1537 (there is no mention of this letter in *L.P.*).

29 Cf. *Becon* 3, pp. 40–41; for an example from William Cecil in 1582, cf. M. Thorp, 'William Cecil and anti-Catholic ideology', in M. Thorp and A.J. Slavin (eds), *Politics, religion and diplomacy in early modern Europe* (*Sixteenth Century Essays and Studies*, 27, 1994), pp. 298–9. Cranmer himself referred to the religious orders as 'sects', without making the comparison with radicals: *Homilies*, ed. Bond, pp. 110–12.

Many of those excited by the mainstream Reformation had not confined themselves to the paths of change mapped out by leading reformers such as Luther, Zwingli or Oecolampadius: to the alarm and fury of such worthies, they had begun thinking for themselves, to make their own reconstruction of Christianity. These new Christian identities are so various that modern scholarship still debates as to how they should be labelled: the term 'Radical Reformation' popularized by George Williams in the 1960s has had its critics, but it is better than the equally vague but less comprehensive description favoured by contemporary opponents of the radicals: Anabaptists ('rebaptizers'). One of the chief items on many radical agendas was indeed the rebaptism of those who as adults consciously embraced true Christian belief, but there were many other matters on which radicals shocked traditionalists and evangelicals alike. For instance, radicals scrutinized the nature of the supposedly Trinitarian relationship between Father, Son and Holy Ghost: was it one of equality, as had been decided by the leadership of the early Church after four centuries of painful debate, or was this a misreading of a divine reality in which there was only the unity of one God and no Trinity? The consequences of such a belief on one's view of Jesus Christ could lead in precisely contradictory directions for radicals: was Jesus not really human, the vision of God who only pretended to take on created flesh, or was he not God at all, simply a human being on whom God's favour peculiarly rested?

The subtleties of radical belief rarely interested evangelicals, who were outraged by any challenge to the package of Christian ideas which (as much as Catholic traditionalists) they had inherited from Christian history. Indeed, evangelicals were often more bitter about religious radicalism than traditionalists were, because it revealed the insecurity of their own position: were not the radicals seeking to capsize a boat which the evangelicals themselves were already rocking? This was especially embarrassing in England, because when Continental radicals made overtures to English Christians in the early 1530s, they did so through established Continental links to English Lollards, who had been equally hospitable to England's first contacts with Lutherans in the previous decade: contacts that had sustained the evangelicalism of which Thomas Cranmer was now the leading representative. The name 'Brethren' was one that radicals would frequently adopt, but it was also the name adopted by the shadowy activists who had linked Lollards, Continental reformers and the evangelicals, all the way up to the likes of Hugh Latimer, Thomas Cromwell and Thomas Cranmer.[30] Most radicals were peaceable, thoughtful folk, but two instances of their potential challenge to the whole fabric of western European society terrified those who kept a position within the status quo. First had been the radical inspiration of the peasants' rebellions in Germany during 1524–5, and now, during 1534, there was the

30 See Brigden, 'Thomas Cromwell and the Brethren'.

developing crisis that was sweeping the German city of Münster, and which, under the horrified gaze of Europe, developed into a lunatic Anabaptist city-state in 1535, before being destroyed by a joint expeditionary force of Lutherans and Catholics.

For such reasons, from now on throughout his career as Archbishop, Thomas Cranmer was at the forefront of efforts to counter the ideas and activities of the Anabaptists. The first big English scare broke in 1535, possibly triggered by alarm at the unfolding events in Münster, although there is evidence that a year or two before Continental radicals had made contact with Lollards in London. Dutch Anabaptists came to England during 1534, and English delegates seem to have attended a conference in Amsterdam in the winter of 1534–5.[31] The first official action against this growing cross-Channel contact was heralded by a royal proclamation, in March 1535, ordering foreign infiltrators to leave the realm within twelve days, and this was followed by arrests and examinations during April and May. Cranmer seems to have taken a leading role in examining the victims: in early June the papal nuncio in France heard that 'Doctor Chramuel' (an understandable conflation of the Vice-gerent and the Archbishop), along with other members of the Court had disputed with them.[32] A London chronicler puts the chief examination of twenty-five Anabaptists on 25 May, and it does not look like coincidence that this same day Cranmer wrote a cryptic note to Cromwell from his palace at Otford enclosing 'such thing as were noticed unto me this present Tuesday, which I cannot (observing my fidelity) keep undisclosed'. A selection of those taken, apparently all foreigners, were burnt in London and selected centres in the south-east in early June, just at the time when the siege of Münster was reaching its nightmare climax.[33]

Some of the Anabaptists were sent back from England to the Low Countries to be dealt with by the Regent, Mary, Queen of Hungary: a useful diplomatic symbol of the continuing orthodoxy of Henry's Church.[34] The English government was thus keeping cautious lines of contact open to the government of England's traditional trading partner; this was as dangerous for the evangelical cause as it was for the radicals. The potential for disaster was symbolized by the part played by English conservative agents in the Low Countries (possibly with Bishop Stokesley as paymaster), when about 21 May the translator of the Bible, William Tyndale, was arrested in Brussels; this was at much the same time as the radical prisoners sailed from England to their deaths in the Low Countries.[35] Even if Henry was not directly involved in the

31 Horst, *Radical Brethren*, pp. 49–55.

32 *T.R.P.* 1, no. 155. Bishop Pio the Nuncio: Horst, *Radical Brethren*, p. 59 and n. (*L.P.* 8 no. 846). Given the ambiguity of 'Chramuel' I think it more likely that the Archbishop than Cromwell is intended, particularly since the Vice-gerency was not fully developed at this stage.

33 'Two London Chronicles', ed. Kingsford, p. 10; P.R.O., S.P. 1/92 ff. 206–7, Cox 2, p. 306 (*L.P.* 8 no. 758). Cf. *Butley Chronicle*, p. 68.

34 *C.S.P. Spanish* 1534–5, no. 170, p. 484.

35 Mozley, *Tyndale*, Ch. 13.

sorry affair of Tyndale's imprisonment and eventual execution, he did not lift a finger to help a man whose writings he had once read with pleasure because of what they had said about royal power in the Church. Nor could Cranmer, (whose Continental agent, Thomas Theobald, gave him a detailed and angry account of English conservative meddlings in the Low Countries), do anything for Tyndale.[36] Not even Cromwell could intervene.

This was a potent symbol of the fragility of evangelical ascendancy. It came at a time when Cromwell, Cranmer and like-minded colleagues were pressing for an official translation of the Bible in English, and were also hoping for great things from renewed contacts with the Lutheran princes of Germany, promised by the embassy of Bishop Foxe.[37] Not surprisingly, in the middle of these alarms and against the background of the scare over the radicals, Queen Anne's evangelicals showed themselves extremely jumpy when, around Easter 1535, a Cambridge evangelical called Tristram Revell tried to present the Queen with his translation of a book by the radical French evangelical François Lambert, the *Farrago Rerum Theologicarum*. The personalities named in his approach are interesting in illuminating the way in which a Cambridge man might approach the evangelical Court establishment, but what is also significant is the way in which they all regarded the book as a liability to be passed on swiftly down the line. Revell first got in touch with Cranmer's brother Edmund, the Archdeacon of Canterbury, who showed the translation to the Archbishop himself; he passed it back to Edmund and to Hugh Latimer, who committed it to a monk, 'one of his doctors'; meanwhile Revell approached Queen Anne's chaplain, William Latimer, who returned it saying that Anne thanked him, but she would not trouble herself with the book. Hugh Latimer said that there were two or three extreme points in the book which rendered it objectionable; as in the case of John Frith two years before, we can guess that these were its sceptical comments on the physical presence of Christ in the eucharist.[38]

The early months of 1536 indeed gave a frightening demonstration that evangelical advance was still dependent on the right mix among those closest to the King; when the balance of influence shifted in this group, Anne Boleyn and a swathe of her close associates were destroyed. Although much remains controversial about these events, there seems no good evidence that there was any trouble before the beginning of the year; indeed, the happiest outcome of the triumphant progress of summer 1535 had been that Anne was pregnant once more.[39] The first event that would change the situation was one that superficially might have been supposed to work in the opposite direction: Catherine of Aragon died on 7 January 1536, after years of dignified misery

36 B.L. Cotton MS Galba B X ff. 119–20; Mozley, *Tyndale*, pp. 304–7; (*L.P.* 8 no. 449; mid-July–31 July 1535).

37 Cf. *L.P.* 9, no. 226.

38 P.R.O., S.P. 1/102 ff. 125–6 (*L.P.* 10 no. 371).

39 For the most soundly based and sensible account of Anne's last months, see Ives, *Anne Boleyn*, Ch. 15.

14 Anne Boleyn, a miniature identified by Sir Roy Strong, probably dateable to 1525–7. She is wearing a pendant with her badge, the falcon.

15 Jane Seymour, by an unknown artist.

made all the more bitter because she had been punctiliously surrounded by the comforts appropriate to a dowager princess.[40] Henry and Anne were both heartlessly if understandably delighted that she was finally out of the way, yet her death subtly altered the King's relationship to his second wife. While Catherine was still alive, Henry would have good emotional and political reason to cling defiantly against all opposition to the second wife who had displaced her, but now that was no longer so. Catherine's funeral took place far away from Court, at Peterborough Abbey, on 29 January; Cranmer was spared the embarrassment of going himself, being represented by Bishop Hilsey, an incongruous enough choice as Bishop Fisher's successor at Rochester. Indeed, Hilsey was given a remarkably mixed bag of his episcopal colleagues' identities to impersonate at Peterborough.[41]

However, the day of Catherine's funeral was a fateful one for Anne, because it was also the day on which she miscarried of her child – with hideous misfortune, the baby was a son. The King was reliably reported to have seen more than casual irony in this. Once more he was pulled back to the nightmare of divine prohibitions; for as he confided to one of his intimates, God did not permit him and his wife to have any male issue; he had been seduced by witchcraft into his second marriage, and it was null.[42] From this remark, probably made in the immediate shock of grief and disappointment, when frankness rather than kindness is inclined to rise to one's lips, there came a possible line of thought to take destructive shape at greater leisure. Since Henry had done all he could to put his private life in order in the sight of God, the fault must lie in someone else. The obvious person was Anne. Her high spirits, intelligence, and frequent lack of the deference to which the King felt himself automatically entitled, were dangerous qualities in a wife, however fascinating they had once been in a mistress. The King's thoughts thus prepared him to hear ill of Anne as the winter turned towards spring, and soon her enemies provided just such material. Meanwhile, only a week or two after the miscarriage, for the first time a new name appeared in Chapuys's reports: that of Jane Seymour. Seymour was everything that Anne was not: submissive, conventional – reassuringly devoid of ideas of any sort.[43]

For the moment, however, there was no reason for the evangelical establishment not to carry on consolidating its position. On 6 February 1536, two days after Parliament reconvened, Cranmer opened as the star billing in a series of weekly episcopal sermons at Paul's Cross which (as in the winter two years before) would extend through the Parliamentary session. His sermon's impor-

40 For the correct date, see *Wriothesley's Chronicle* 1, p. 32.

41 *L.P.* 10, no. 75; cf. the description of Catherine's funeral, *L.P.* 10 no. 284.

42 *C.S.P. Spanish 1536–8*, no. 13, p. 28; cf. Ives, *Anne Boleyn*, pp. 343–6. For a concise demolition of Retha Warnicke's theories built on these remarks of Henry's, see Ives in *H. J.* 34 (1991), pp. 197–200.

43 *C.S.P. Spanish 1536–8*, no. 21, pp. 39–40.

tance was signalled by the fact that it was attended by Lord Chancellor Audley and the assembled clergy of Convocation.[44] Cranmer's main theme was that the Pope was the composite biblical enemy of God Antichrist, which he proved by the methods that he and the royal research team had applied to the annulment problem, 'by scripture and by decrees of the Pope's laws . . . [and] divers expositions of holy saints and doctors for the same'. There can be little doubt that he used his extensive surviving collections from canon law as part of the ammunition for this attack, and quite possibly it was for this occasion that he made the summary extracts from his collection which have an explicitly anti-papal purpose behind them. When Latimer preached to Convocation four months later, he harked back to what Cranmer had said in this sermon in ridicule of papal jubilees and the dispensations associated with them; material on the jubilees and dispensations occurs both in the full canon law collections and in the summaries.[45] Chapuys also recorded some remarks in the same sermon in which Cranmer pointed to the Emperor's decline in power in relation to his princes, reflecting the continuing negotiations with the Lutheran Schmalkaldic League in Germany: the Archbishop was thus now rejecting two pillars of the medieval Western polity, Pope and Emperor.[46]

Cranmer was making a bold step by so uncompromisingly identifying the Pope with Antichrist. There must have been many in his audience who realized that there was only one major writer in English who had so far said this, William Tyndale, and he was currently languishing in a Low Countries dungeon. Tyndale had not always so precisely identified Antichrist, giving this terrible figure a wider and vaguer reference in his writings in the late 1520s, but by 1530 he had been prepared to make the papal identification, and he repeated it thereafter.[47] Now the Primate of all England used a major political occasion not so much to extol the Royal Supremacy but to make a root-and-branch attack on papal supremacy. The identity of the Pope with Antichrist remained with the Archbishop, probably up to his last spiritual collapse in his imprisonment under Mary. In 1549, his maverick Italian protégé, Bernardino Ochino, produced a work in dialogue form, translated by Cranmer's equally maverick chaplain John Ponet: in it Ochino represented the Archbishop as taking part in a three-way discussion also including Henry VIII and a papist, in which Cranmer constructed a knock-down case to show the identity of Antichrist with the Bishop of Rome.[48]

44 For the sequence of the sermons, and the main description, *Wriothesley's Chronicle* 1, pp. 33–4. For Convocation's presence, see *Latimer's Sermons*, p. 49.

45 *Latimer's Sermons*, pp. 49–50. On Cranmer's main notes and two copies of the summary, see above, Ch. 3, n. 44. For his material on the jubilees, cf. Strype, *Cranmer*, Oxford 1848–54 edn 3, pp. 865 and 880.

46 *L.P.* 10, no. 283.

47 Compare statements in Tyndale, *Doctrinal Treatises*, pp. 43, 147 (1526 and 1527) with Tyndale, *Answer*, pp. 102–10 (1530) and Tyndale, *Expositions* p. 183 (1532).

48 Pocock, 'Preparations for the Second Prayer Book', pp. 141–3.

Jasper Ridley has seen Cranmer's devotion to the Royal Supremacy as the key to his thinking during his mature career.[49] It may be that this is seeing the problem the wrong way round: Cranmer came to hate the papacy, and therefore he needed the Royal Supremacy to fill the chasm of authority which had opened up in his thinking as a result. This is certainly the order in which ideas are presented in another contemporary anti-papal sermon of his, given in Canterbury Cathedral, which he described to the King later in 1536: first, the history of the confidence trick that Rome had played on Christians, second, the falsity of Rome's holiness proved by its vices, and third the faults of canon law, which pretended to be identical with God's law. Only after making these three points did he end with an exhortation to obedience to the King. He said in that same sermon, 'these many years I had daily prayed unto God that I might see the power of Rome destroyed; and . . . I thanked God that I had now seen it in this realm'.[50] We have seen how Cranmer in the 1520s combined conventional respect for the papacy with a slightly problematic parallel and deeper reverence for general councils. In his work on the divorce, he had solved this theological incoherence by keeping his conciliarism, but jettisoning papal authority as a hideous confidence trick. What else had he got to hang on to in order to defend the gospel faith against papists and radicals, and to lead England towards a general council of the Church, but the authority of King Henry?

Cranmer preached a second major sermon later in the parliamentary session, on a Friday in Lent (3–31 March 1536); from a number of different glimpses of it, we can see that this was a propaganda piece backing the royal proposal before Parliament to cull the number of monasteries. Harpsfield's eye-witness reminiscence was that Cranmer preached that the people 'had no cause to be grieved with the evertion [overturning] of the abbeys' because the King would by their suppression 'gather such an infinite treasure that from that time he should have no need, nor would not put the people to any manner of payment or charge for his or the realm's affairs'. Once more, there is parallel source material about alienating ecclesiastical land in the canon law collections and summaries.[51] The London curate Thomas Dorset, in a letter to friends in Plymouth shedding a brilliant shaft of light on many details of the religious atmosphere this winter, described Cranmer saying 'that the King's Grace is at a full point for friars and chantry priests, that they shall away all that, saving they that can preach'.[52] The anonymous Spanish Chronicler, a trustworthy source when he was actually present at an event, described

49 Ridley, *Cranmer*, esp. pp. 65–6.

50 B.L. Cotton MS Cleopatra E VI ff. 234–5, Cox 2, pp. 325–8 (*L.P.* 11 no. 361); the sermon was preached in late 1535. For my comments on his prayer 'these many years', see Ch. 2, p. 25.

51 Harpsfield, *Pretended Divorce*, p. 292. Cf. Strype, *Cranmer*, Oxford 1848–54 edn 3, pp. 791–2 and 879.

52 Wright, *Suppression*, p. 38.

Cranmer's familiar theme of papal deception in this sermon directly linked to a denial of the existence of purgatory, so that the money spent on masses for the dead would be better bestowed on the poor (among 'other great heresies, which I do not repeat, to avoid scandal'). He adds that Cranmer also challenged the learned to come to his own house for a debate on the subject, which conference took place three days later; meanwhile 'nothing else was talked about in London, and as they are a very changeable people, they soon gave credit to this heresy'.[53]

This reference to a conference at Lambeth Palace might be taken as a confusion by a commentator who does not always achieve Hansard-like standards, were it not for other evidence of organized disputation at Lambeth this winter. The Palace was a hive of activity: Thomas Dorset described how when one day in February he had 'nothing to do, as an idler went to Lambeth to the Bishop's Palace, to see what news', and he found that he had spent wisely on the wherryman's fare to row him from the city.[54] One of his companions in the boat was a Cambridge don, Dr Robert Croukar, who had lately been causing a sensation in East Anglia by his rabble-rousing millenarian preaching – yet Croukar was no Anabaptist, but a sworn enemy of religious change and a fanatical Marian, whose visions of a new kingdom were fuelled by his outrage at the decline in devotion at Mary's English shrines. John Bale later placed him in a sequence of English conservative promoters of Marian visons, the previous one being, significantly, Elizabeth Barton.[55] Croukar had been summoned to Lambeth to answer for his preaching to a team of episcopal troubleshooters, Cranmer, Latimer and Shaxton, and in disputations over two days he was apparently trounced by this trio. In view of what the Spanish Chronicler reveals, it is significant that the debate turned to purgatory, on which Croukar was again routed, not before confessing that Bishop Stokesley of London had encouraged him in his line of argument, finding purgatory justified in scripture.

The same bishops would a few days later in February face another old Cambridge acquaintance who was causing trouble in a different direction: John Lambert, alias Nicholson. He had laid himself open to a heresy charge by saying that it was sinful to pray to saints, which infuriated his more moderate evangelical superiors: 'the bishops could not say that it was necessary or needful, but he might not make sin of it', and although the bishops could not back up their case with scripture, Latimer was particularly bitter against Lambert because he would not give way to argument as Croukar had done. The twin disciplinary issue was exactly that which had faced Cranmer

53 *Chronicle of Henry VIII*, pp. 87–8.

54 *Wright, Suppression*, pp. 36–9 (*L.P.* 10 no. 462).

55 Bale, *A Mystery of Iniquity*, f. 30r. For a conservative text owned by Croukar, a Fellow of Pembroke Cambridge, see Rex, 'Campaign against Luther', p. 92n. The spelling of his name is more than usually varied: I would guess that the most rational form would be 'Crewkerne'.

as soon as he had become Archbishop, with Elizabeth Barton on one flank and John Frith on the other. The evangelical establishment were constantly vulnerable to accusations of heresy, particularly so in the case of Lambert, who had been attacked by conservatives in Convocation in 1531 at the same time as Latimer.[56] Moreover, the cases of Croukar and Lambert seem to have been quite consciously paired in their East Anglian connection: it was three East Anglian aristocrats, the Duke of Norfolk, the Earl of Essex and the dowager Countess of Oxford, who were pressing for action against Lambert, while the fact that the bishops ordered Lambert to prison under Lord Chancellor Audley's care may also suggest an Essex connection. A third Cambridge man under interrogation at the same time (the end of February) was Tristram Revell, another evangelical who as we have seen had overstepped the mark in his translation of François Lambert, although it is not clear whether Revell's interrogation took place before the trio of bishops.[57]

The issues raised in the examinations of Croukar and Lambert – purgatory, and the cult of Our Lady and the other saints – also interestingly coincide with Chapuys's description of the issues raised in printed material prepared for members of Parliament, at the beginning of the session, to indicate the measures to be considered: these included 'the suppression of all Church ceremonials concerning images and the worship of saints, and likewise against those who affirm that there is a purgatory'.[58] It sounds as if Cranmer had decided that the best way to move opinion along on these questions was to pair preaching on the changes in doctrine alongside the offer of disputation about them, a common procedure of the Swiss Reformation in particular during the 1520s. Like many of those Swiss disputations, the discussion was also unfairly weighted in one direction, in this case by the disciplinary authority which the three evangelical bishops could exercise over dissent of all descriptions.

It is also very likely that the disputations in February and March were seen as part of the preliminaries for drafting the first statement of doctrine for Henry's Church, which was provided in the following summer: the Ten Articles. Chapuys noted how discussions developed later in March into full-scale meetings by the bishops 'in the Archbishop of Canterbury's rooms' to frame the articles 'as well as the reformation of church ceremonies'; once more he noted the possibility that these would not admit the existence of 'Purgatory, nor of the observance of Lent and other fasts, nor of the festivals of saints and worship of images'. The bishops were also considering interim reports on the contacts made by Bishop Foxe in his embassy to the Lutheran princes – a combination of domestic doctrine-making and diplomatic tinkering which would recur in their deliberations in the later 1530s. Alarmingly, Luther and his senior colleagues were still sticking to their opinion that the Aragonese

56 Lambeth MS 751, p. 74.
57 P.R.O., S.P. 1/101 f. 125 (*L.P.* 10 no. 371).
58 *C.S.P. Spanish 1536–8*, no. 21, p. 41; Lehmberg, *Reformation Parliament*, pp. 221–2.

marriage was valid, and regardless of whether or not this was so, that the Princess Mary was Henry's legitimate daughter. In the end, what assent they gave to the King's arguments was grudging and incomplete.[59]

However, the problem of continuing Lutheran doubts about Henry's marriages were overtaken by events which represented a far more serious danger for the cause of religious change: the developing crisis around Anne Boleyn. A gentleman of Henry's Privy Chamber, Nicholas Carew, headed the plotting of a group of conservatives at Court who had never accepted the new Queen with any more grace than was needed to avoid their own ruin. Now they exploited the King's interest in Jane Seymour; they made sure that she took a leaf out of Anne Boleyn's book and virtuously rejected Henry's advances, while mentioning the magic word marriage. However, what was fatal for Queen Anne was the breach in her previously pivotal relationship with Cromwell during March 1536, a breach whose cause is still not clear. In one of the most daring and dangerous political moves of his career, Cromwell took over the conservatives' moves against the Queen, and led her to destruction; Chapuys monitored these events with increasing excitement, and probably acted as the go-between for the union of Cromwell's plans and those of the conservatives.[60]

The degree of tension which these events quickly generated was graphically demonstrated on Passion Sunday, 2 April, when Anne's chaplain John Skip preached a long sermon in the Chapel Royal; it later landed him in deep trouble, and is such a rambling, ranting affair that it suggests that he was in a state of deep agitation on behalf of his royal mistress.[61] His text was 'Which of you convicts me of sin?', which suggests that he was aware of the rumours that were beginning to fly around the Court about Anne's supposed sexual betrayal of the King. Early on, Skip drew the audience's attention to the example of King Solomon, who in his last years spoiled his earlier achievements by 'sensual and carnal aptitude in taking of many wives and concubines', a disastrously tactless hit at both Henry and Jane Seymour. To attack Cromwell, Skip flailed around the Old Testament looking for other ill-advised kings: first Rehoboam, who ignored his wise older councillors for 'his younger councillors whom he so had promoted and dangered unto him by his gifts that for that and further promotions which they looked for, they would not advertise him to do anything but such as they perceived or thought him inclined to'. Then

59 McEntegart Ph.D., 'England and the League of Schmalkalden', pp. 121–2; *C.S.P. Spanish 1536–8*, no. 43, p. 84.

60 The crucial document here is Chapuys's despatch of 1 April 1536, *C.S.P. Spanish 1536–8*, no. 43, pp. 79–85; in general, I follow the interpretation of Ives, *Anne Boleyn*, pp. 347–57.

61 The text is P.R.O., S.P. 6/1 ff. 8–11, 6/2 ff. 1–3 P.R.O., S.P. 1/103 ff. 76–87 (*L.P.* 10 no. 615). The sermon is discussed by G. Bernard, 'Anne Boleyn's religion', pp. 12–18, and quotations will be found there. It will be apparent that I take a diametrically opposed view to Dr Bernard of the significance of Skip's sermon, but I am grateful to him for our friendly discussions about it. For further discussion, see Ives, 'Anne Boleyn and the early Reformation', pp. 395–9.

Skip hit on the perfect example, Ahasuerus of Persia, who had one evil councillor, Haman; as a well-instructed audience would know, Haman sought the Persian Queen Esther's destruction, but was himself destroyed. This story was the launch-pad for an attack on councillors who attempted 'the renovation or alteration of any old or ancient customs or ceremonies' in religion, but also of 'renovations or alterations in civil matters'. One could hardly hope for a better portrait of Sir Geoffrey Elton's Thomas Cromwell.[62]

This was a declaration of war, and it also sounds like a clumsy attempt to separate Anne and Skip's brand of reformism from a supposedly more radical and dangerous reformism in Thomas Cromwell: the sort of line which Cranmer, Latimer and Shaxton had drawn a month before between themselves and John Lambert.[63] It was hardly surprising that after this Cromwell decided to make a pre-emptive strike against Anne; he later told Chapuys that starting from 18 April he 'had planned and brought about the whole affair' of the accusations made to the King against Anne.[64] Cranmer, meanwhile, seems to have been unaware of what was going on. His two surviving notes to Cromwell during March are innocent requests for favours on minor matters; he got on with the formalities of electing Anne's chaplain William Barlow as Bishop of St David's, and in mid-April after the dissolution of Parliament he moved away from Lambeth down to Knole, just as Cromwell prepared to plunge the Court into crisis.[65] By 22 April a sudden note of urgency crept into the Archbishop's letter to the Secretary; it is a puzzling document. Cranmer evidently still did not see himself in the middle of a full-blown political crisis, for he expected Cromwell to attend to a personal grievance of the Treasurer's Remembrancer, John Smith; however, after a conventional reference to the multitude of business which the Secretary faced, he suddenly blurted out:

> I was ever hitherto cold, but now I am in a heat with the cause of religion, which goeth all contrary to mine expectation, if it be as the fame goeth; wherein I would wonder [i.e. wonderfully] fain break my mind unto you . . .

What did he mean, and what did he think was happening? Jasper Ridley is probably right in restricting his use of the word 'religion' to the monasteries and what was to happen to them. Cranmer had heard something about

62 I wrote this paragraph before reading Ives, 'Anne Boleyn and the early Reformation', and was gratified to find him coming to the same conclusion (pp. 398–9). For another comparison of Cromwell to Haman, see Cavendish, *Life of Wolsey*, 2, p. 53.

63 The supposed trump card of Dr Bernard's case for Skip's conservatism is that Skip defended traditional ceremonies as long as one explained them: Bernard, 'Anne Boleyn's religion', pp. 15–16. But this was an evangelical strategy under Henry VIII: cf. *Latimer's Remains* 2, p. 294; Cox 2 p. 349 and the Bishops' Book, ibid., p. 103; cf. also *E.T.* p. 405 (*O.L.* p. 624) and *Becon* 1, pp. 111f, 181.

64 *C.S.P. Spanish* 1536–8, no. 61, p. 137.

65 Cox 2, p. 321: P.R.O., S.P. 1/103 ff. 16, 38 (*L.P.* 10 nos 547, 557). Cf. the stages in Barlow's election, dated first from Lambeth, 12 April and then from Knole, 19 April: Cranmer's Register, ff. 205v–206v.

the trouble at Court, which made him think that there was disagreement about taking action on the parliamentary legislation just passed dissolving the smaller monasteries.[66] There is indeed evidence of confusion and delay in the process of implementing the dissolutions, first noticed three centuries ago by Gilbert Burnet, with his unerring eye for detail: the instructions for visitors to carry out the dissolution were not issued until 28 April, after the writs for an entirely new Parliament had been drawn up.[67] Eric Ives has also made out a convincing case for the view that one of the most serious issues in dispute between Anne Boleyn and Cromwell was their different views about what to do with the monastic wealth raised by the confiscations; Anne had recruited Hugh Latimer to preach before the King demanding that the windfall be spent on education and poor relief, and Ives sees a clear allusion in Skip's Passion Sunday sermon to the same theme. One can see why the issue would have excited Cranmer.[68]

Cranmer soon discovered that matters were even more serious. We can gather the evidence for the stages of Anne's doom: the secret issue of commissions of oyer and terminer to investigate treasons on 24 April, the sudden summonses to attend the first newly elected Parliament for seven years on 27 April, and on the same day a consultation with Bishop Stokesley to see whether Henry could abandon Anne. The choice of Stokesley is highly significant; it meant that Cranmer (still down at Knole) was being bypassed in favour of the bishop who had been consistently humiliated and marginalized by Cromwell and the evangelical bishops over the previous year. Eric Ives sees 27 April as the crucial day on which Henry was given the information which changed his mind on Anne's guilt and made him determined to destroy her.[69] The most dramatic description of events after this is the eye-witness reminiscence of Cromwell and Cranmer's Scottish protégé Alexander Alesius. This was written for Anne's daughter, Elizabeth, two decades later; it begins with frenzied activity on 30 April, complete with the vignette of Anne with the baby princess in her arms, pleading in vain with the implacable King, and the noise of the cannon in the Tower, thundering out for the receipt of an important prisoner, the first of Anne's associates.[70]

66 The text quoted is from P.R.O., S.P. 1/103 f. 154, Cox 2, p. 322 (*L.P.* 10 no. 705). See Ridley, *Cranmer*, p. 100.

67 Burnet 1 i, pp. 343–4; 1 ii, pp. 229–32 (Bk. 3 no. 6)

68 Ives, 'Anne Boleyn and the early Reformation', pp. 399–400.

69 Oyer and Terminer: *Wriothesley's Chronicle* 1, pp. 189–91, 205; Parliament: *L.P.* 10 no. 736; Stokesley: *C.S.P. Spanish 1536–8*, no. 47, p. 106. For Stokesley's defeat by Hilsey during the winter, see again Thomas Dorset's letter, Wright, *Suppression*, pp. 37–8 (*L.P.* 10 no. 462). Ives, *Anne Boleyn*, pp. 361–2.

70 P.R.O., S.P. 70/7/659, ff. 3–13, pr. *C.S.P. Foreign, 1558–59*, pp. 524–34. I see no reason to accept Dr Bernard's cavalier dismissal of Alesius, particularly since he himself places faith in a far more obviously gossipy and second-hand French source: Bernard, 'Fall of Anne Boleyn', pp. 596–7, 605n.

It was only on Tuesday 2 May, on the day that Anne herself was rowed from Greenwich to the Tower, that Cranmer was urgently summoned up to Lambeth by letter from Cromwell. He had been told something, but not everything; dependent on rumours and as yet unable to see Henry face to face, on the Wednesday he wrote to the King one of the most celebrated and controversial letters of his career.[71] As yet he could not accept Anne's guilt, but what he could perform was the pastoral task of ministering to the King's distress. 'In the wrongful estimation of the world, your Grace's honour of every part is so highly touched (whether the things that commonly be spoken of be true, or not) that I remember not that ever Almighty God sent unto your Grace any like occasion to try your Grace's constancy throughout.' He urged the King to patience like Job, and then entered on the most delicate and courageous part of his message:

> And if it be true, that is openly reported of the Queen's Grace; if men had a right estimation of things, they should not esteem any part of your Grace's honour to be touched thereby, but her honour only to be clearly disparaged. And I am in such a perplexity, that my mind is clearly amazed; for I never had better opinion in woman, than I had in her; which maketh me to think, that she should not be culpable. And again, I think your Highness would not have gone so far, except she had surely been culpable. Now I think that your Grace best knoweth, that next unto your Grace I was most bound unto her of all creatures living . . . And if she be found culpable, considering your Grace's goodness towards her, and what condition your Grace of your only mere goodness took her and set the Crown upon her head; I repute him not your Grace's faithful servant and subject, nor true unto the realm, that would not desire the offence without mercy to be punished to the example of all other. And as I loved her not a little for the love which I judged her to bear toward God and his gospel; so, if she be proved culpable, there is not one that loveth God and his gospel that ever will favour her, but must hate her above all other; and the more they favour the gospel, the more they will hate her . . .
>
> And though she have offended so, that she hath deserved never to be reconciled unto your Grace's favour; yet almighty God hath manifoldly declared his goodness towards your Grace, and never offended you . . . Wherefore I trust that your Grace will bear no less entire favour unto the truth of the gospel, than you did before; forsomuch as your Grace's favour to the gospel was not led by affection unto her, but by zeal unto the truth.

The hostile commentators who have read this letter as a craven piece of toadying are like those newspaper columnists who bray for churchmen to provide a firm moral lead with strong, simple answers. Cranmer's negotiation of a frightening and complex situation is a model of pastoral wisdom and courage. Knowing the King as he did, Cranmer also knew the destructive

71 B.L. Cotton MS Otho C X f. 230r, Cox 2, p. 323–4 (*L.P.* 10 no. 792).

quality of Henry's grief and anger. Yet still he chose to highlight his own esteem for Anne and his intimate association with her; still he left open the question of her guilt because he did not know the full facts, with every reference to her doings expressed conditionally. And while steadily holding the King's grief and rage in his sight, he sought to pull Henry back to patience and humility, and to shape that rage so that it did not destroy the gains of the previous three years for the evangelical cause. What is more remarkable and impressive still is the evidence of the postscript to the letter. When he had finished composing his text, a deputation of peers headed by Chancellor Audley brought him the details of the charges against Anne, with an order to cross the river for a formal hearing by the Council in Star Chamber at Whitehall. Yet Cranmer still sent his letter to the King, with all its doubts about the Queen's guilt, merely expressing his sorrow in the postscript 'that such faults can be proved by the Queen, as I heard of their relation'.

The trials of Anne and her associates were dispatched over the next fortnight, carefully organized by Cromwell to make sure that all went according to plan; yet Anne and her brother put up impressive performances at their hearings on 15 May, embarrassingly before large audiences.[72] After his moment of nobility in that letter of 3 May, Cranmer now became as much the passive vehicle of an inevitable process in the destruction of the Boleyn marriage, as he had been in its creation. He saw Anne in person in the Tower to hear her confession on 16 May, the day before he was formally to pronounce the marriage null and void and the Princess Elizabeth consequently a bastard child. We will never know what passed between Anne and Cranmer in confession; Eric Ives is probably correct that it had no bearing on the outcome of the divorce hearing the following day.[73] First there is the practical consideration that it would have been virtually impossible to incorporate information so obtained in the formal documentation for the final judgement the following afternoon; second and more important is the improbability that Cranmer would use information obtained under the seal of confession. This was not like his contradictory repudiation and affirmation of papal loyalty in March 1533, when he had already in his conscience regarded the Pope's authority as non-existent – weak and confused he could be, criminally dishonest and treacherous he was not.

His passing of the nullity judgement on 17 May at Lambeth Palace did not imply that Cranmer thought Anne guilty of lurid crimes; nullity would not be affected by sexual misbehaviour during marriage, so strictly speaking these procedures had no relevance to Anne's supposed crimes. Nevertheless, the judgement is a stain on Cranmer's reputation, the unacceptable face of his loyalty to the Supreme Head. There may have been a technical case to

72 Ives, *Anne Boleyn*, pp. 383–89.

73 Ibid., p. 405. Confession: B.L. Harley MS 283 f. 134, *Original Letters*, ed. Ellis 1st ser. 1 ii, pp. 62–3 (*L.P.* 10 no. 890); P.R.O., S.P. 1/103 f. 312 (*L.P.* 10 no. 902, misdated to 18 May).

construct for nullity through evidence of pre-contracts and the invalidity of papal dispensations; it is not now possible to say. No papers survive, hardly surprisingly in view of what they would have meant for the later Tudor succession, but in any case it was a bizarre and contradictory procedure to declare the Boleyn marriage null: if there had been no marriage, how could Anne have committed treason by her supposed sexual promiscuity? No-one, Cranmer included, seems to have pointed out this common-sense illogicality in the face both of the King's destructive fury, and of Cromwell's ferocious determination to remove his new-found enemies in the Queen's circle.[74]

On Friday 19 May, Anne died, with dignity, and without any admission of guilt. Cranmer was not there; from early morning he was walking restlessly in the gardens at Lambeth Palace, which is where his client Alesius found him. Alesius had been so troubled in his sleep by a foreboding of catastrophe that he had got up at dawn and rowed across from London to Lambeth, but it was Cranmer who told him his fears were justified: 'she who has been the Queen of England on earth will today become a Queen in heaven' was all that the Archbishop could say before he broke down in tears.[75] Clearly he did not believe that Anne was guilty of very much: that confession of 16 May had revealed no dreadful sexual secrets. Now he had much to cry about: both for his own soiled integrity, and for the uncertain future of the evangelical cause. That very day, when he was called from his garden to formal business, he signed with his own hand a dispensation from prohibitions of affinity for a marriage between the King of England and Jane Seymour.[76] Chapuys happily anticipated that most of the new bishops would now get their deserts ('*leur Saint Martin*'). Already the King's relationship with Seymour was an open secret, and preparations were being made to celebrate a new wedding; at least Cranmer seems to have been spared the misery of officiating at the private marriage ceremony at Whitehall on 30 May.[77]

In fact Cromwell's political skills meant that the Archbishop's worst fears were not to be realized: the evangelical cause, whose preservation probably provided the main motivation for his less-than-heroic behaviour during the Boleyn crisis, was not lost. Anne's conservative enemies had originally intended to rehabilitate Princess Mary, use for their own ends the pliancy of Jane Seymour, and thereby establish their own ascendancy. Instead they found themselves in political oblivion, Mary forced to admit her illegitimacy and Cromwell in a still stronger position at Court; from 18 June he was Lord Privy Seal by surrender from Anne Boleyn's father, and soon he was a peer of the realm.[78] It was not surprising that the conservatives' frustration with their

74 Ives, *Anne Boleyn*, pp. 404–6. Kelly, *Matrimonial Trials*, Ch. 14, esp. p. 250.
75 P.R.O., S.P. 70/7/659, ff. 7v–8r, *C.S.P. Foreign, 1558–59*, p. 528.
76 *L.P.* 10 no. 915.
77 *C.S.P. Spanish 1536–8*, no. 54, p. 121; Pollard, *Cranmer*, p. 101.
78 Ives, *Anne Boleyn*, pp. 414–16.

failure at Court fed into the gathering storm of resentment in the north of England to break out in rebellion in the autumn. The unexpected evangelical reprieve from disaster was reflected in Cranmer's city of Canterbury, where at the beginning of June 1536 a determined assault was made on the reformist grouping among the city's governors by conservative rivals; the evangelicals were indicted by a quarter sessions jury for radical religious opinions and for maintaining a printer of heretical texts. Those indicted were referred to the Archbishop, but he did nothing about them, and later he gave one of the victims, John Ford, an important place in his domestic staff as keeper of his Canterbury palace.[79]

Nationally, the summer was a time of careful outward religious balance, but evangelicals gained more than conservatives. When the Convocation of Canterbury opened the day after Parliament, on 9 June 1536, Bishop Stokesley celebrated the mass, but Latimer preached to the assembled clergy two Latin sermons over the day, aggressively attacking clerical immorality and ignorance, the doctrine of purgatory, shrines and devotion to images; he even ridiculed recent proceedings of convocation (which of course had included attacks on himself) and advocated the use of English in weddings and baptisms – there must have been some spluttering in clerical drinks parties that evening. These sermons were considered important enough to be reprinted the following year at Basel, with an introduction by Cranmer's friend Simon Grynaeus saying what an example of Gospel preaching England thereby gave to Switzerland.[80] Just as remarkably, a week later Cranmer granted Cromwell's lay representative, Dr William Petre, a seat beside himself in Convocation, to symbolize the Royal Supremacy exercised through the vice-gerency: the stage-by-stage construction of this new authority was complete, and Cromwell himself 'sat diverse times in the Convocation house among the bishops as head over them'. He may even have given a major address to the assembly in this session, if we are to date to this time a flattering reference to his 'good sermon' by Robert Barnes.[81]

Yet the message of the vice-gerency was that evangelical change would go at the King's measured pace. Two new bishops now succeeded at Norwich and Chichester, and these replacements for Nix and Sherburn, two great warhorses on the old episcopal bench, were both conservatives: William Repps and Richard Sampson, consecrated two days after Latimer's sermon. On Corpus Christi Day, 15 June, Sampson ('a man in very great favour with

79 B.L. Stowe MS 850, ff. 45–6; Clark, *English Provincial Society*, pp. 40–41. P.R.O., E. 315/99 f. 93: grant by Cranmer to Ford, 30 September 1538.

80 Lambeth MS 751, pp. 110–11. Sermons: *Latimer's Sermons* 33–57; *Hugonis Latimeri Anglicani Pontificis oratio*, Basel, 1537, B.L. copy Ac. Grenville 11846.

81 Lambeth MS 751, pp. 111–12; *Wriothesley's Chronicle* 1, p. 52. Barnes: P.R.O., S.P. 1/104 f. 209 (*L.P.* 10 no. 1185), though this might refer to the vice-gerential synod in 1537. A slightly garbled reference in Parker, *De Antiquitate*, p. 386 may suggest that Cromwell took his seat at the opening ceremonies on 9 June, although Parker gives the impossible date 'nonis Junii', possibly in mistake for 'novem'.

his prince') took the starring role as mass-celebrant in a carefully staged display of lavishly traditional eucharistic devotion attended by the King and new Queen, the two archbishops and an array of the nobility; Anthony Waite reported this approvingly back to Lady Lisle in Calais, who was gratified by the messages that it was designed to send.[82] This theme of balance was notably reflected in the statement produced by Convocation, which was the first attempt at defining what Henry VIII's Church now believed: the Ten Articles of religion. In their final form, published with a long approving introduction by the King, the first five articles were defined as 'principal articles concerning our faith', the second dealt with 'laudable ceremonies used in the Church'. This double structure reflects the origin of the Articles in two different discussions earlier in the year. First were the agreements worked out in Germany by conferences during winter and spring 1536 between the English ambassadors, Foxe, Heath and Barnes, and the chief German Lutherans, including Luther himself; these conferences had produced a set of seventeen numbered compromise conclusions which have been known as the Wittenberg Articles since their full text was rediscovered in 1905.[83]

Neither in Germany nor in England did the Wittenberg Articles achieve publication, but they channelled key ideas into the first five of the Ten Articles, and they themselves referred to and were shaped by the Augsburg Confession of 1530.[84] Notably, the English Church was now committed to the Lutheran position that 'the only sufficient and worthy causes' of justification (which it defined as remission of sin and accepting into God's favour) were 'the only mercy and grace of the Father, promised freely unto us for his Son's sake, Jesu Christ, and the merits of his blood and passion'. Works played no part in justification, although there followed careful discussion of how they necessarily came after it. Using the same sequence as the Augsburg Confession and the Wittenberg Articles, the Ten Articles dealt with only three sacraments (baptism, eucharist and penance) among their 'principal articles'; we know that the omission of the other four sacraments caused great offence to some of the bishops.[85] However, Article three, on penance, was one notable success for the conservatives in the first half of the Articles; it was emphatic in traditionalist vein that auricular confession to a priest was 'instituted of Christ', which would not please Cranmer, given what he had revealed of his

82 *Lisle Letters* 3, pp. 421–2 (*L.P.* 10 no. 1147).

83 Tjernagel, *Henry VIII and the Lutherans*, pp. 160–63, and text in translation, ibid., pp. 255–86. The most convenient text of the Ten Articles is in *English Historical Documents 1485–1558*, pp. 795–805. However, for scepticism about the role of the Wittenberg Articles, see McEntegart Ph.D., 'England and the League of Schmalkalden', pp. 150–51.

84 Tjernagel, *Henry VIII and the Lutherans*, pp. 163–6; Rupp, *Protestant Tradition*, pp. 112–14; Constant, 'Formularies of Faith'. For a statement of the view that the Ten Articles should be regarded as primarily conservative, see Rex, *Henry VIII and the English Reformation*, pp. 145–8.

85 *L.P.* 12 i no. 789, p. 346.

views in the row over Hugh Payne's preaching that same year (see above, p. 143). There were several other statements about penance in this Article that would not have pleased Lutherans, and that probably annoyed the Archbishop as well.

In the second part of the Ten Articles, the influence of the phrasing and ideas in the Wittenberg Articles is noticeably weaker. Instead, the second set reflected the different sequence of discussions which we have already seen proceeding at Lambeth Palace from winter 1536, in which disciplinary cases such as those of Croukar and Lambert had been integrated, and whose themes had precisely reflected the concerns of Articles six to ten: images, saints, ceremonies and purgatory. It was significant in itself that purgatory was relegated to the end of the non-essential articles: here was a central concern of late medieval religious practice, now declared in terms of 'the place . . . the name thereof, and kind of pains there, . . . uncertain by Scripture'. Yet in these second five articles, there is much evidence of compromise between conservatives and evangelicals. We are lucky to have one fragment on paper of the discussions that created the articles, which shows the way in which they evolved. This is a pair of drafts prepared by secretaries, trying to construct what would become Articles six, seven and eight on images, honouring of saints and praying to saints. Notable is the change of presentation between draft and final articles; both original drafts seem to have envisaged a continuous homily-like discussion without numbering or headings, and it may have been the arrival in England of the Wittenberg Articles with their numbered propositional format, typical of Continental confessional statements, which suggested a more systematic, user-friendly format. It was, after all, a new experience for English churchmen to have to set out measured statements of what they believed, and they learnt by trial and error how to do it.

The two drafts show us different teams of theologians trying out different efforts on their colleagues, Cranmer included. The second of the two is consistently evangelical in flavour, giving only a grudging role to images and saints, and only one phrase from it appears in the eventual text, in Article seven ('As touching the saints in heaven, they be to be honoured of all Christian men in earth, not by any religious and godly honour . . .'). More text was used from the first of the drafts, and autograph corrections on it reveal a direct tussle between Cranmer and the conservative humanist Bishop of Durham, Cuthbert Tunstall. Tunstall added to the secretary's text an affirmation that 'we may pray to our blessed Lady and John Baptist, the Apostles or any other saint particularly as our devotion doth serve us, without any superstition'; Cranmer sharply corrected the end phrase to 'so that [i.e. as long as] it be done without any vain superstition'. The combination of the two bishops' alterations arrived in the finished text. Noticeably, the elements of the first draft that were finally cut out included a long meandering introductory discussion of the limitations of images as poor men's substitutes for books, together with a rather silly list added by Cranmer ridiculing the more

16 Page from draft of the Ten Articles, 1536, with rival corrections by Cranmer and Bishop Tunstall.

esoteric calls of devotees on saints' time, including 'St Apollonia for toothache . . . St Barbara for thunder and gunshot, and such other'. The final product, as published by the King, was a far less discursive, far more focussed and dignified piece of prose; above all, it contains something to please both evangelicals and traditionalists, and something to annoy them both.[86]

Yet the double origin of the two-part articles was perceptible to those alert to such things. For instance, one Suffolk priest, who can probably be identified with that outspoken evangelical John Bale, said in early 1537 that he would 'not declare the articles the which were commanded by the King's Grace, for the one half of them were naught'; this is probably a precise statement, referring specifically to the second half on ceremonies and images, since the priest had just committed acts of iconoclastic vandalism in his own church.[87] The material on penance in the first half of the Articles, and the general tone of studied compromise in the second half, would appear most unsatisfactory to Continental Lutheran observers; their eyes and ears in England, Alexander Alesius, wrote to the Superintendent of Hamburg, Johann Oepinus, enclosing a translation and expressing his disappointment. Even so, it is remarkable that the discussions in Germany should have been preserved into Convocation's deliberations as much as they were, given that Henry had gained nothing concrete in diplomatic terms from a prolonged and expensive mission to the Lutherans; with Cromwell's backing, Cranmer and his associates saved much.[88]

We know that there was indeed much argument in Convocation leading up to the Articles' publication, so much so that the King himself claimed to have been forced to resolve the disagreement, 'to put our own pen to the book' and 'conceive certain Articles' for Convocation to agree.[89] The first sign of serious trouble was the move, on 23 June, by the Lower House of Convocation to secure a condemnation of a formidable list of erroneous quotations which sought to mix real radicalism with Lutheranism: a clear attempt by conservatives to derail proceedings.[90] The exact sequence of events after 23 June is probably significant. After the Lower House's intervention, the conservatives' list of objectionable quotations was lost from sight; Convocation turned to necessary formal business confirming the annulment, and after that there was a series of prorogations with nothing done until 11 July.

86 Lambeth Palace MS 1107 ff. 125–32. Discussion of these documents has been unnecessarily complicated by their modern editor, who for no strong reason printed them as if they were associated with a later document of 1540, and who also failed to notice that they comprised two different drafts: *Rationale of Ceremonial*, pp. 44–52.

87 B.L. Cotton MS Cleopatra E V ff. 395–6 (*L.P.* 12 i no. 818). The priest is called Sir John Gale, which is probably a simple mistake for Bale.

88 On the mission's failure, cf. Tjernagel, *Henry VIII and the Lutherans*, pp. 158–60. Ales to Oepinus, *L.P.* 11 no. 185.

89 Burnet 1 ii, p. 515, Appendix 9 (*L.P.* 11 no. 1110).

90 Lower House: Lambeth MS 751, pp. 112–13; Strype, *Ecclesiastical Memorials*, 1 ii, pp. 260–66, no. 73 (*L.P.* 10 no. 1184).

Why the gap? Cranmer and Cromwell must have been waiting for something to happen, or needed time to resolve a conflict. One new circumstance in the meantime, on 4 July, was the return of Cranmer's ally Bishop Foxe from his German embassy. It may have been as late as this that the Wittenberg Articles arrived in England in the ambassador's care; Chapuys recorded that immediately on Foxe's return from Saxony, 'a motion was made in Parliament for the reformation of the state and ceremonies of the Church in imitation of what has been accomplished in that country', which sounds very much as if Foxe presented the content of the Wittenberg Articles to the House of Lords and suggested that it be acted upon to speed up change. In the days after 4 July, what ought to have been an uncontentious bill finally extinguishing the Pope's authority mysteriously ran into severe trouble in the Lords (Cranmer was present throughout these debates), and the eventual statute contains an awkward added clause saying that the statute did not affect traditional ceremonies used in the Church.[91]

All this suggests a conflict suddenly given a new direction by Foxe's arrival home: the Lords eventually decided to keep out of the argument about ceremonies, and instead it was the Ten Articles that dealt with the question on the basis of the prepared drafts. The Wittenberg Articles could then have served as the basis for a drastic last-minute reworking of the controversial doctrinal statements, and this was the obvious time for the King's intervention with his own pen, picking out what he found acceptable in the German agreement. It was certainly Foxe who, on 11 July, formally presented the Ten Articles for subscription by Convocation.[92] Immediately all ordinary preaching was suspended until the end of September by royal order, so that the full text of the Articles could be distributed; even the contents of the 'bedes', the English prayers led by the priest during Mass, were minutely specified.[93] The King was not taking any chances with the reception of his bitterly fought-over document.

However, the bitter disagreements within Convocation over the Ten Articles had revealed the disadvantage of deciding doctrine by open debate in its two houses, and once more the problem of the two provinces must have exercised Henry and his Vice-gerent: how could the assembly of one province legislate for two? To bring the Convocation of York into any genuine decision-making role would only make matters worse, for the general tone among the clergy of the northern Convocation was even more conservative and less amenable to government pressure than in the south, as the events of the autumn would demonstrate. All subsequent doctrinal statements, during the entire course of the English Reformation up to 1563, were thrashed out in private committees of bishops and theologians, with Convocation having little or no say in them. The full development of the Vice-gerency had now

91 *C.S.P. Spanish 1536–8*, no. 76, p. 204; Lehmberg, *Later Parliaments*, pp. 26–8; *L.J.* 1, pp. 92–4.

92 Lambeth MS 751, p. 113.

93 *Concilia*, ed. Wilkins, 3, pp. 807–8; Brightman, *English Rite*, p. 1026.

revealed an alternative method of pushing change: while the Convocation of Canterbury was meeting, Cromwell was preparing injunctions which applied to the whole Church.[94] These still drew on the deliberations of Convocation; they referred to its agreement in late July to the abolition of various holy days, and also referred to the discussion of devotion to images in the Ten Articles, but they went beyond any general order so far in envisaging a basic programme of Christian education, a co-operative effort between parish clergy and heads of households to teach the Lord's Prayer, Creed and Ten Commandments. The most striking new provision was the order that by 1 August 1537 ('this side the feast of St Peter ad Vincula next coming') every parish priest should provide a copy of the Bible in Latin and English. Since the only complete English Bible had been published by Miles Coverdale less than a year before without official approval, and the bishops' own half-hearted moves to provide a translation had so far produced no result, this was a curiously impractical trumpeting of evangelical idealism, and many later copies of the injunctions omit it; nevertheless various bishops tried to follow it up in their own orders during 1537.[95]

The new relationship between the Archbishop and the Vice-gerent was poignantly symbolized for Cranmer by another event of 1536: the first assault on the great estates of the archdiocese of Canterbury to build up the position of Thomas Cromwell, now needing an income to sustain his new dignity as a peer of the realm. For a millennium the archbishopric had been the largest landowner in Kent, the flagship of a clerical estate in a county where the Church owned two-fifths of all the land.[96] Beyond that, the archbishops had also built up huge estates around London, reflecting their gradual establishment away from their original Kentish base, to become the leader of the English Church in the English capital. It was these Thames Valley lands which were first attacked, in the interests of the Surrey shearman's son from Putney. There was a first Parliamentary Act exchanging estates in February 1536, and then in a further Act, in June 1536, Cranmer surrendered Surrey estates at Wimbledon and Mortlake; Cromwell took his baron's title from Wimbledon when he was created Lord Cromwell in July, a neatly symbolic transfer from Primate of All England to Vice-gerent.[97] In return, the Archbishop got lands of the Priory of St

94 The most convenient text is in *English Historical Documents 1485–1558*, pp. 805–8.

95 The omission has caused frequent denials that Cromwell's 1536 injunctions contained the order about bibles, but several copies remain with the order, and the decisive example is provided by Rex, *Henry VIII and the English Reformation*, pp. 185–6, n. 25. The often-quoted copy in Cranmer's Register, ff. 98v–99r, may simply omit the provision by accident at the bottom of a folio. Cf. discussion by Margaret Bowker, Haigh (ed.), *English Reformation Revised*, p. 76 n. 8.

96 Du Boulay, *Lordship of Canterbury*, pp. 114, 243; Clark, *English Provincial Society*, p. 6.

97 *L.P.* 10 nos 243, 1087; the Earl of Northumberland referred to Cromwell as 'Lord of Wimbledon' on 30 March 1537 (*L.P.* 21 i no. 774), and see also *Complete Peerage* 3, p. 556nn.

Radegund near Dover, of markedly lesser value. This was the episcopal bench's first experience of the unequal property exchanges that would become a feature of Henry VIII's relations with his bishops; it was also comparatively modest compared with what Cranmer would experience over the next decade.[98]

Cranmer did his strictly limited best to preserve his estates. His old secretary Ralph Morice put up as effective a retrospective case for the defence as he could when writing to Archbishop Parker, who would have sympathized with the problems from his own experience: Morice described the pressure under which Cranmer had come as soon as he had become Archbishop-elect in 1533. For instance, he had straight away been forced to grant a ninety-nine year lease of one of the core manors of the archiepiscopal estate at Wingham, in Kent, to Anne Boleyn's vice-chamberlain Sir Edward Baynton: an extreme example of a policy of long leases which his predecessor Warham had developed.[99] At least Baynton was an evangelical, and a close friend of Hugh Latimer, but Cranmer was very unhappy at having to grant such long leases, and he instructed the Chapter of Canterbury in future not to confirm any leases granted for more than twenty-one years. Morice indeed suggested that it was this scrupulous policy that led to courtiers outflanking Cranmer by beginning the programme of disadvantageous exchanges, soon to be extended to many other ancient church estates. In any case, the good resolution was very difficult to keep; already in winter 1533–4 one can find the Prior and Chapter ratifying a thirty-year lease from the Archbishop in another part of the Wingham estate.[100] After Cromwell and the Crown initiated major exchanges of estates in 1537, Cranmer reverted to a policy of granting very long leases of many of his remaining properties, deliberately making them less attractive targets for outside interests (see below, Ch. 6, p. 202).

However, the Archbishop was handicapped in his resistance to the dispersal of his lands. He did not exhibit the keen self-protective interest in estate matters and his own financial advancement which characterized the more financially successful Tudor bishops. He said as much in 1537: 'I am the man that hath small experience in such causes, and have no mistrust at all in my prince in that behalf.'[101] Naturally, he would follow convention and not neglect the traditional rights that he possessed, as when he tried to use his feudal right of wardship in Sussex estates of the archdiocese to marry off his relative Elizabeth Cranmer to his tenant Edward Shirley; he conscientiously pursued this claim at law for a decade, although eventually with little

98 See Heal, *Of Prelates and Princes*, Ch. 5.

99 Cranmer repeated this particular ninety-nine-year lease in 1544 to Thomas Digges: *CPR Elizabeth I 1563–66*, no. 2130.

100 *Narratives of the Reformation*, p. 264; cf. Du Boulay, *Lordship of Canterbury*, p. 321. Wingham lease: *C.P.R. Elizabeth 1560–63*, p. 222.

101 P.R.O., S.P. 1/124 ff. 130–31, Cox 2, p. 348 (*L.P.* 12 ii no. 600).

success.[102] However, he was not a man to take entrepreneurial initiatives, in an age when many others were seizing the golden opportunities offered. It was noticeable that when the smaller monasteries were going down in spring and summer 1536, he made no attempt to secure any of the lands for himself, but only put forward claims on behalf of friends, relatives and servants. Morice says that the evangelical court physician, Dr Butts, in the end took pity on him and secured him a gift of Nottinghamshire monastic lands without his knowing. This initiative does not seem to have had much permanent benefit for him, however; Nottinghamshire lands did not form part of the endowment of estates that he tried to create for his family in the reign of Edward VI, after Butts was dead.[103]

Cranmer's official attitude to the Church lands question was in fact made clear in late 1535, when (rather unusually) a Kentish monastic house, a small nunnery called Davington, closed down for lack of inmates. Cranmer put forward the claim that much of its lands should escheat back to the Archbishop as feudal mesne lord, and that one of its benefices should return to his brother as Archdeacon; this brought him into conflict with the claims of the Crown. The legal situation was murky, since this was before the dissolution legislation of 1536; Cranmer perhaps disingenuously claimed to be torn between loyalty to the ancient inheritance of his see and his wish to do the will of the Supreme Head:

> I am assured that the King's Grace's mind is not to do wrong unto any subject he hath; and if I knew that it were his Grace's pleasure to have my title in the said lands, I would be more desirous to give it unto his highness, than he can be to have it. But forsomuch as I know not but his grace would that I should have it, if my title be good, I must needs make my claim and declare my title; else I must lose it, be it never so just.[104]

When he stated the case like that, it was inevitable that after the slightest pressure from the greater force, royal authority, Cranmer should yield. He was particularly vulnerable because of the debts that he had incurred from the moment of his advancement, to the King and the then Queen and also to Cromwell himself. Not just Henry but Cromwell could always be sure that Cranmer would yield to any financial favour that he might demand, as for instance in 1538, when the Archbishop made a sixty-year lease of a Sussex property to the Vice-gerent's servant Henry Polstead.[105] All Cranmer could do

102 P.R.O., C. 1/961/1, dateable between 1533 and 1538, and the final arbitration by the Duke of Norfolk in 1545, Lambeth MS Cart. Misc. XVI 11. The exact relationship of Elizabeth Cranmer to the Archbishop is not clear. Cf. Du Boulay, *Lordship of Canterbury*, pp. 91–2.

103 Ridley, *Cranmer*, pp. 96–7; *Narratives of the Reformation*, p. 263. On Cranmer's 1547 grants, see below, Ch. 9, pp. 366–7.

104 P.R.O., S.P. 1/98 f. 192v, Cox 2, p. 314 (*L.P.* 9 no. 741); cf. P.R.O., S.P. 1/98 f. 22, Cox 2, p. 312 (*L.P.* 9 no. 627).

105 *C.P.R. Elizabeth* 1578–80, no. 423 (24 April 1538; cf. Polstead's later reference to this lease, P.R.O., S.P. 1/153 ff. 17–18, *L.P.* 14 ii no. 29). See also Du Boulay, *Lordship of Canterbury*, p. 322.

was make the best of the situation and reap what advantage he could for his successors in office.

Cranmer could hardly quarrel with the King or with Cromwell, since the fortunes of the evangelical cause were tied to the continuing survival of the regime which they had constructed. This was made starkly clear by the events of autumn 1536 and 1537, when Lincolnshire and the north of England were convulsed by the series of risings collectively known as the Pilgrimage of Grace, the most serious act of opposition to government policy throughout the Tudor age, and one which came near to toppling Henry's government. Straight away in the Lincolnshire and Yorkshire risings at the beginning of October 1536, Cromwell and Cranmer were the prime targets of the rebels' fury; only a day or two after trouble began, on 3 October, Cranmer headed the list of leading evangelicals to be murdered, announced by the Lincolnshire Captain Porman at Caistor Hill. After that, the references to him in the litanies of rebel hatred are legion. It seems to have been as far away as the remote West Riding valley which sheltered Sawley Abbey that the famous rebel song denouncing 'Crim, Cram and Rich' was first heard.[106] When all was safely over in 1537, Cranmer would write with weary humour to Johann Heinrich Bullinger about the Pilgrims' demand that he himself, Latimer, Hilsey, Shaxton and all others who were thought to favour the gospel should be punished as heretics, although the rebels had never heard any of them preaching.[107]

The abuse levelled at him by the Pilgrims was no new experience for the Archbishop. As soon as he had been appointed, conservatives had quickly realized that Cranmer was their enemy: it was a chaplain to Bishop Clerk of Bath and Wells who said aloud in 1533 what his master was probably thinking, 'that he trusted to see the day that my Lord of Canterbury should be burned'.[108] The volume of hostile opinion was especially cultivated by the group around Catherine of Aragon, and then spread through all levels of society by agents such as the Maid of Kent. Cranmer was made the chief focus of resentment for the widespread popular fury about the treatment of Catherine, conveniently deflecting this anger from the King, as Cromwell pointed out.[109] The Queen herself led the attack by dismissing him as a 'shadow'; the curate to one of her chaplains called Cranmer an 'ostler' in 1533, showing that this common motif had quickly become part of the Aragonese household's repertoire of abuse.[110] Calling Cranmer an 'ostler' soon became widespread. The Elizabethan historian William Harrison recorded that 'the

106 Caistor: P.R.O., E. 36/118 f. 55 (*L.P.* 11 no. 853). Sawley: P.R.O., S.P. 1/108 f. 217r (*L.P.* 11 no. 786.3). For other examples, cf. P.R.O., S.P. 1/108 f. 50; 109 ff. 7v, 256r; S.P. 1/112 f. 27, 244–5; S.P. 1/118 f. 284; E. 36/119 ff. 17, 24v; E. 36/122 f. 28 (*L.P.* 11 nos 705, 828.v, 902.2, 1182.2, 1319; *L.P.* 12 i nos. 1021.3, 70.xii, 201.iii, 853).

107 Kessler, *Sabbata*, p. 464.

108 P.R.O., S.P. 1/79, ff. 124–5 (*L.P.* 6 no. 1192).

109 *Records of the Reformation* 2, p. 487 (*L.P.* 6 no. 738)

110 Catherine: *St.P.* 1, p. 420, and cf. ibid., p. 403; chaplain: P.R.O., S.P. 1/83 f. 184 (*L.P.* 8 no. 559).

ignorant sort of Londoners' mocked him 'when he began to preach the Gospel' (presumably meaning at the beginning of his archiepiscopate) by hanging up bundles of hay at his gate to symbolize his ostler status; Harrison, who owed his conversion to the example of Cranmer and the other great names of the early Reformation, tried to explain the phrase simply as meaning one who lived in a university hostel.[111] The Cambridge context is certainly correct, since the insult probably referred to Cranmer's brief first marriage in his early Cambridge years to Joan who lodged at the Dolphin; there is, however, no evidence that he himself had lived in one of the Cambridge hostels in his years at Jesus and Buckingham colleges.

Cranmer took such hatred philosophically, although he was well aware that (as in the case of Catherine's chaplain) 'of all sorts of men . . . priests report the worse of me'.[112] It is indeed interesting how frequently the 'ostler' phrase was used by clergy, perhaps reflecting clerical links to Cambridge gossip. One example from a parson on the Essex coast, in September 1536, also clearly demonstrates how a conservative clerical grapevine fed the north with such venom, and with other information about the evangelical hierarchy, for in the same conversation the priest talked of the rising in the north a month before it actually broke out.[113] Morice tells a pleasing extended anecdote about the fate of a northern priest who yet again repeated the 'ostler' slander, and incautiously coupled with it the expansive statement that Cranmer had 'as much learning as the goslings of the green that go yonder'. In a personal interview, the Archbishop clearly enjoyed himself, comprehensively and devastatingly demonstrating who was the more learned of the two of them, before sarcastically rebuking the man and sending him home, free but 'lamenting his folly'. Cranmer's lack of aristocratic hauteur in the face of such unrealistic abuse alarmed the politician Cromwell, but one must remember that he could react very differently if he felt his integrity genuinely threatened: witness the deep fury with which he had greeted Bishop Gardiner's insinuations of his disloyalty to the Royal Supremacy during his metropolitical visitation.[114]

While the secular aristocrats and the bishops of the north calculated where their loyalties lay in the Pilgrimage, and Cromwell and the King frenziedly improvised a strategy to defeat the rebellions, Cranmer seems to have been instructed to keep a low profile, away from the capital. There are noticeably few glimpses of him during that catastrophic autumn: he had been down beyond Canterbury at Ford in September, but he was still in Kent no nearer London than Knole Palace on 20 October, and it is probably significant that he delegated an episcopal consecration in the capital on that day. Likewise it

111 Harrison, *Description of England*, p. 79.
112 B.L. Harley MS 6148 f. 45r, Cox 2, p. 291 (*L.P.* 7 no. 702).
113 P.R.O., S.P. 1/116 f. 7 (*L.P.* 12 i no. 407): Thomas Toone of Weeley, Essex, 2 September 1536.
114 *Narratives of the Reformation*, pp. 269–72. On Gardiner, above, Ch. 4, pp. 132–3.

was from Knole that he wrote to the King on 18 November, beseeching 'the mighty Lord of Lords to strengthen and preserve your Grace ever, and to resist and suppress all your highness's adversaries with your rebels and untrue subjects'.[115]

Meanwhile trouble built up in London. At the beginning of the month (5 November) Cromwell and the King risked allowing Latimer to preach an impassioned sermon against the rebels, in which he criticized both bishops and 'certain gentlemen being justices [of the peace]' for not implementing the summer's programme of official reform (not 'new learning', as conservatives slandered it, but 'old truth').[116] However, the murder a few days later in a London street of a prominent evangelical, Robert Packington, sparked off acute tension in the city; Dr Robert Barnes was arrested for preaching a furious sermon at Packington's funeral, and four other uninhibited evangelicals were also rounded up. One of them, George Marshall, a priest who was a veteran of evangelical reform as one of the 1520s 'Christian Brethren', was lodged under Cranmer's care, first at Lambeth Palace and then down in Kent with him. This was to the disgust of one of Cromwell's more conservative henchmen, Sir John Gostwick, who wanted Marshall made an example of, to please the traditionalists of London; it was Gostwick who had been entrusted with the arrest of Robert Barnes.[117]

Gostwick's involvement is a likely hint that there was a dual strategy to these arrests. Besides keeping the evangelical activists quiet, it protected them against popular fury, but Cromwell probably also intended the action to appeal to the rebels, and conservatives generally, as a sign of government readiness to do a deal. At least two of those arrested were among the objectionably heretical writers named in a remarkably well-informed list by the rebels negotiating with the King's representatives, at Doncaster, at the beginning of December. The arrests were certainly well-publicized, news of them even reaching the ears of the Bishop of Faenza in France.[118] Similarly, it was now that Henry VIII issued a hasty circular to the bishops, putting a very different interpretation on the Ten Articles from that in Latimer's recent sermon. The sting in the letter's tail, as far as Cranmer was concerned, was its final order to enquire whether any priests had married, and if so to arrest them and send them to the King. No wonder that the aged rebel leader, Lord Darcy, hopefully wrote to the rebels' ultra-cautious fellow-traveller Archbishop Lee, in December, in the brief period of spurious peace after the King

115 Ford: B.L. Cotton MS Cleopatra E V f. 111, Cox 2, pp. 328–9 (*L.P.* 11 no. 416); Cranmer's Register, f. 197v, 20 October; 18 November: B.L. Harley MS 787 f. 18, Cox 2 pp. 330–32 (*L.P.* 11 no. 1100).

116 *Latimer's Sermons*, pp. 25–32.

117 Brigden, *London and the Reformation*, pp. 252–4, and see ibid., index refs s.v. Marshall, George. Gostwick: P.R.O., S.P. 3/3/4 (*L.P.* 11 no. 1097); S.P. 1/112 f. 68 (*L.P.* 11 no. 1220).

118 Doncaster: *L.P.* 11 no. 1246, p. 506; this list mentions Barnes and Rastell, but the Marshall it lists is probably William and not George. Faenza: *L.P.* 11 no. 1250.

had made terms at Doncaster, that the royal letter was one 'wherein all true Catholics may joy'.[119] When Latimer preached again at Paul's Cross in December, it was under strict instructions from Cromwell to preach 'unity without any special note of any man's folly', which he did at least to his own satisfaction.[120]

Bishop Clerk's chaplain, who wished to see Cranmer burnt, had a long wait after 1533. Neither did the Pilgrims succeed in destroying the Archbishop and the Vice-gerent; now comprehensively tricked by the King and his negotiators, the rebels were dispersed, and many were tempted into two more risings in winter 1537, which gave the government the excuse to destroy them. Out of a year of acute danger and tension, Cromwell had emerged triumphant, both against the spirited self-assertion of Queen Anne and also against the plans by the Aragonese to destroy everything that the reign of Queen Anne had stood for. Protected throughout by the Vice-gerent's brutal exercises in *realpolitik*, Cranmer continued to test out how much change the politicking of his brilliant lay colleague could promote, and how much their unpredictable royal master would allow.

119 Circular: *L.P.* 11 no. 1110: cf. one version of text, Burnet 1 ii, p. 515, Appendix 9. Darcy: P.R.O., E. 36/122 f. 30 (*L.P.* 11 no. 1336).

120 *Latimer's Remains*, pp. 375–7 (*L.P.* 11 no. 1374).

CHAPTER 6

A 'Reformed' Church? 1535–9

UNTIL THE MID-1530S, THE main European influences for change in the English Church had been the French reformist circles favoured by Anne Boleyn, or the Lutherans of north and central Germany. The Lutheran Reformation as Thomas Cranmer encountered it in Nuremberg in 1532 shaped his evangelical belief for a decade-and-a-half, and although Thomas Cromwell kept his exact views very carefully away from definition both then and later, it is likely that Luther's Reformation gave precision to his changing religion as well.[1] Lutheran princes and cities had established themselves as a major political force within central Europe with their formation of a defensive alliance, the Schmalkaldic League, and so it was the Lutheranism of Germany and the Scandinavian princes which was a competitor for Henry VIII's diplomatic concern, alongside France and the Empire. However, a third element in Continental evangelicalism at this time began to make itself felt within England: in the end it effectively supplanted the Lutheran style within English Protestantism, and provided the dominant religious atmosphere in the Church of England until the death of James I. It was through Archbishop Cranmer himself that a distinct evangelical stance entered England; this was eventually styled 'Reformed' Christianity, although, as we shall see, the Archbishop would resist its teaching in one important respect until the mid-1540s.

The basis of the new alignment was the crucial link to Cranmer established by Simon Grynaeus in 1531. The axis represented by Grynaeus was that of the upper Rhineland and northern Switzerland: a series of civic reformations whose prominent figures were not susceptible to Luther laying down the law (much to his annoyance); in particular, they rejected his obstinate insistence on the physical or bodily presence of Christ in the eucharistic elements. The English evangelicals were well aware of the distinction: one of Cromwell's agents interestingly characterized the Rhinelanders and northern Swiss cities as those 'which be of the evangely [i.e. use the Gospel translation] and the ceremonies and laws of Zwingli's, which be contrary to Dr. Martin Luther and

1 On the slippery evidence for Cromwell's beliefs in the 1530s, see Brigden, 'Thomas Cromwell and the Brethren', and useful comment in McEntegart Ph.D., 'England and the League of Schmalkalden', pp. 294–5, 484.

his law and constitutions'.[2] They formed an east-west chain across central Europe: from Strassburg in the west, with Martin Bucer, Johann Sturm and Wolfgang Capito, through Grynaeus's Basel and Bullinger's Zürich, to St Gall in the east, where the Reformation was directed by the unique lay reformer-scholar Joachim von Watt (Vadianus). A generation later, after mid-century, when John Calvin reigned supreme in Geneva and his disciples, such as Theodore Beza, John Knox and Andrew Melville, began forging his thought into a rock-hard basis for a confessional family of churches, this grouping would be termed 'Reformed', in contrast to the Lutheran North. The 'Reformed' label is prematurely precise in the 1530s and 1540s, and there are untidinesses in the division. Most notably, Strassburg was in fact a member of the Schmalkaldic League, and its official theology moved gradually, so that eventually the city was absorbed completely into the Lutheran camp.[3]

Nevertheless, one can already discern in the Strassburg–St Gall chain of the 1530s the distinctive outlines of the reformations which would converge later under the spell of Calvin's powerful personality. The reforming leaders of these communities kept closely in touch, monitored their always delicate relationships with the secular authorities, and scented out the possibilities of extending the work of godliness elsewhere, place by place, as had already happened piecemeal in Switzerland. England hardly looked promising territory for them, with its centralized government, its lack of civic self-assertion and its eccentric, opinionated monarch, but they boasted one great asset: that friendship established between two humanist scholars, Grynaeus and Cranmer, back in 1531, which in turn had produced the first correspondence between Cranmer and Martin Bucer. This was the basis for an ambitious and multi-faceted plan of alliance between the evangelicals of central Europe and of England in the years after 1535: to trace the complex interweaving of this plan will reveal just how closely the evangelicals of the Strassburg–St Gall network co-operated as they approached the Primate of All England.

The background was the mood of excited optimism among European evangelicals, inspired by Henry VIII's new approach to the Lutheran princes of the Schmalkaldic League in autumn 1535. It was the ministers of Strassburg, led by Bucer, who took the first initiative to widen contacts from the English–Lutheran axis; ironically, the main trigger for their action was Stephen Gardiner's freshly published *De Vera Obedientia*. Foxe and Heath almost certainly provided copies from the London print-run of this crucial work of anti-papal propaganda when they consulted with the Strassburg religious leadership on their way to northern Germany, and the result was remarkable: a new Strassburg printing of the book with a gushing preface by the ministers Capito, Hedio and Bucer. This lavished praise on Gardiner's

2 *L.P.* 10 no. 847.

3 On the changes at Strassburg, see Abray, *People's Reformation*, esp. Ch. 6.

many virtues, praise which Bucer would soon have cause to regret: more accurately from an evangelical point of view, it spoke admiringly of ambassadors Foxe and Heath, and of the goodness of God in providing England with a model archbishop in Thomas Cranmer, 'a Primate extraordinary as a man in holiness of life, in doctrine, perseverance, and zeal for the government of the Church'.[4] Bucer's intention of making this open letter the launchpad for a Continent-wide evangelical alliance embracing England was spelled out, on 17 January 1536, in a letter to Vadianus in St Gall, trying to rouse him to equal enthusiasm, and enclosing 'the oration of the English bishop' – probably already in its printed Strassburg edition.[5]

This was just the start. Bucer followed up the Gardiner preface with a further charm offensive on Cranmer, dedicating to him his commentary on the Epistle to the Romans in March 1536. This was no minor tract, but the first instalment of a planned blockbuster publishing venture from Bucer, a commentary on all the Pauline epistles; the dedication of such an important work was a huge compliment to the Archbishop. In his Preface, besides predictable flattery of Cranmer, Bucer expanded on his vision of how much England and the Continental reformations had in common in their double fight against papistry and radicalism; England (or 'Britain' as he called it – Henry VIII would enjoy the implication) was by divine providence the major bulwark against Antichrist in this dangerous time. Continental evangelicals and the English could wage war with combined forces ('*iunctis castris*') for the Church of Christ. Some months later, Bishop Foxe also got a dedication from Bucer: this work was a treatise on the eucharist prefacing a reissue of his Gospel commentary (*Enarrationes*), and it included a request to pass compliments on to Archdeacon Heath.[6]

It was not surprising, in view of this literary wooing, that the city of Strassburg's instructions to the Diet of the Schmalkaldic League at Frankfurt, in April 1536, emphasized the need for doctrinal flexibility in dealing with such an important diplomatic catch as England in its approach to the League. Bucer no doubt had some say in the city's adoption of this stance: flexibility was always his goal. Strassburg continued to push for continued negotiations with England through the summer, despite growing scepticism from most other members of the League. Simultaneously Bucer also attended to another segment of his plan: he spearheaded an effort to end the doctrinal split among European evangelicals between the Lutherans and the non-Lutheran grouping. The resulting document was a characteristic Bucerian piece of doctrinal invisible mending known as the Wittenberg Concord. It was not a success,

4 For the text, see Hopf, *Bucer*, pp. 198–200, and discussion, Gardiner, *Obedience*, ed. Janelle, pp. xxv–xxix, although Janelle is incorrect in characterizing Foxe and Heath as conservatives at this stage in their careers. Contrast useful comment in McEntegart Ph.D., 'England and the League of Schmalkalden', p. 91 n. 35.

5 Gardiner, *Obedience*, ed. Janelle, p. xxviii.

6 Hopf, *Bucer*, p. 6: dedication dated 23 August 1536.

because the Swiss felt that it was too clever by half, and many of them now began to feel doubtful about Bucer's reliability. Their doubts had some justification, since the period up to these negotiations in 1536 did pull Bucer's whole theological outlook further in Luther's direction: this new rupture grew over the next decade, causing a series of complications in Cranmer's approaches to the wider Reformation. Already the persistent problem of the eucharistic presence was raising obstacles to the vision of the grand alliance.[7]

Yet not only Bucer was making moves towards England. Hardly coincidental, and equally significant for the future of English religion, was Johann Heinrich Bullinger's initiative in 1536 to reactivate the friendship of Grynaeus and Cranmer. Bullinger was a man of astonishing energy, who acted as a one-man information network from Zürich through his European-wide correspondence; in this respect he became a reformed successor to Erasmus, albeit with a far more ideologically concentrated purpose. Within a month or so of Bucer forwarding *De Vera Obedientia* from Strassburg to St Gall, Bullinger sought to include Cranmer in his spider's web. He got in touch with Grynaeus in Basel, asking him to write to Cranmer to effect an introduction and to gain a favour for the Zürich reformer. Grynaeus obliged, but warned him against exaggerated expectations of his influence on the Archbishop.[8] In a pattern which was common in Cranmer's dealings with the Continent, the first courier was a major publisher and bookseller in Zürich, Christoff Froschauer; Froschauer's contact in England was in turn the Anglophile printer from Strassburg, Reyner Wolfe, who had already established his business in London, but who made an annual visit to the international book fair at Frankfurt, where he dealt with Froschauer. What better cover for evangelical contacts? In the heady days of Edward VI, Froschauer's nephew (also Christoff) came to Oxford to study.[9]

The likely purpose of Bullinger's initiative became apparent when three young English gentlemen, enthusiastic evangelicals, arrived in Zürich in August 1536 for an extended educational visit: John Butler, Nicholas Partridge and William Woodroffe. Partridge was a young ex-Oxford don from Lenham in Kent, and Butler may also have been a Man of Kent from the port of Sandwich (a place where Cranmer had an active interest), although he has no traceable link with the other John Butler who was Cranmer's commissary at Calais.[10] In any case, the students were all clearly protégés of Cranmer's, for they arrived 'wonderfully praising the godliness and kindness of the Bishop of

7 McEntegart Ph.D., 'England and the League of Schmalkalden', pp. 170–80; Abray, *People's Reformation*, p. 41, *Bucer*, ed. Wright, pp. 36–8, and Stephens, *Holy Spirit in Bucer*, esp. pp. 3, 8–9, 14–15.

8 17 January: Hopf, Bucer, p. 172n. Grynaeus to Bullinger, between 21 and 28 March, Zürich St.A., E II 343, 203, pr. *Bullinger Werke*, in progress (I am indebted to Dr Bruce Gordon for obtaining this for me): '*hoc erras, cum tu credis posse me tuo nomini aliquem favorem conciliare.*'

9 Smyth, *Cranmer*, pp. 81, 83n, 137.

10 On Partridge, Emden, *Oxford to 1540*, pp. 434–5. On Butler: *Visitation of Kent 1619–1621*, p. 41. Cf. also some of the data in Garrett, *Marian Exiles*, pp. 102–3.

Canterbury', as Bullinger excitedly told Vadianus in a letter at the end of the month.[11]

Bullinger had not finished: with characteristic thoroughness, he planned to pursue and extend the English contact along the north Swiss axis to Vadianus in St Gall.[12] Bullinger's letter of 22 August 1536 now urged Vadianus to join the circus of correspondence with the Archbishop: 'write in a friendly fashion to seek his friendship, and send him a copy of your *Aphorisms* as a gift in token of your friendship.' Grynaeus's name once again was the passport to Cranmer's good opinion, and Bullinger felt that by now his own name would also be a recommendation: 'the more he will rejoice, I think, when he sees from your letter that he has gained a new friend, and that on our advice.' Froschauer was again the bearer of the letters, which went off from St Gall some time during the autumn of 1536; we shall find that this particular initiative was far from being an unqualified success.

Yet the main thrust of Bullinger's plans continued to succeed brilliantly. The young Englishmen went down well in Zürich, and the ground was laid for a return of the exchange. In January 1537, Partridge returned to England as escort for an aristocratic young Züricher of similar outlook and a future leader of the Swiss Reformation, Rodolf Gualter: the first native Swiss evangelical to sample English religion, English cooking and English weather. They took with them a letter for Cranmer – and Bullinger added with complacent pride in his diary, they 'brought back the most friendly reply'.[13] This must refer to Partridge and Gualter's return to Zürich on 8 June 1537, accompanied by a further three young Englishmen, bringing the total up to six in this remarkable venture in overseas training – a seventh, Bartholomew Traheron (future librarian to Edward VI), arrived three months later. However, it is likely that even before Partridge returned, there had already been a fruitful exchange of letters between Bullinger and the Archbishop; Cranmer wrote at least twice in eminently friendly and indeed intimate terms to Bullinger during April/May 1537, and it was probably only the second of these letters which Partridge brought back.[14] Cranmer even expressed mild

11 '. . . *pietatem et humanitatem*': *Vadianische Briefsammlung*, 5, p. 351 (22 August 1536); cf. *Bullingers Diarium*, p. 25.

12 Vadianus is often credited with the influential tract *On the Old God and the New* (1521), which would make him the first mainstream Swiss reforming writer translated into English (1534), and which might have given Bullinger's approach an added point: see Clebsch, *England's Earliest Protestants*, pp. 97, 169–70, 253–4, 312. Unfortunately the evidence for his authorship is very shaky: cf. Ozment, *Reformation in the Cities*, p. 189 n. 45.

13 *Bullingers Diarium*, p. 25: '*et retulit amicissimas {litteras}*'.

14 For this and what follows, see *Kesslers Sabbata*, pp. 463–5. Cranmer's first letter is dated 8 April; the second (of which only an extract survives) can only be approximately dated to April/May. It refers obliquely to the execution of the Premonstratensian Abbot of Barlings (29 March 1537: note the reference to his black hood, '*pulla cuculla*') but not to that of the Cistercian quondam Abbot of Fountains on 25 May 1537 or the Abbot of Jervaulx on 2 June: cf. *Wriothesley's Chronicle*, 1, pp. 61–4. On the exchange visits see also Smyth, *Cranmer*, pp. 81–5.

disappointment in his first letter about not having had some feedback from Bullinger about Continental reactions to the Pilgrimage of Grace: 'it is indeed especially remarkable that you have not written anything of your own reactions, and how you have been informed by other people, and indeed whether you have been thus informed.' What is also significant is the witness to Bullinger's co-ordinating strategy which this correspondence provides: he sent Vadianus a full transcript of one of the Archbishop's letters, and edited highlights of the other. Moreover, that summer (1537) he used Vadianus as a postman to forward one of Cranmer's letters to his uncle by marriage, Andreas Osiander. This was a proof of Bullinger's seriousness about building bridges, for he was not an enthusiast for the opinionated Lutheran pastor at Nuremberg; yet Osiander's old link to Cranmer was too good to neglect, and a tie-in between him and St Gall might have its uses.[15]

Cranmer's account, on 8 April, of the Pilgrimage of Grace gives a fascinating insight into his attitude to the events, after his studied silence at home in autumn 1536; in many ways what he has to say anticipates his bitter extended comments about the later conservative rebellion in the West Country in 1549 (see below, Ch. 10, pp. 438–40).[16] Significantly, it was written for Bullinger, without inhibition, as between two evangelical leaders: the rebellion had arisen 'on account of the return of evangelical teaching from captivity to its rightful place' ('*ob doctrinam evangelicam postliminio reducendam*'). He represented the rebellion as a threeway conspiracy: 'unlearned priests and monks' wanted to continue profiting from people's ignorance, while 'many [laypeople] readily listened to them, rather turning their minds back to the fleshpots of the Egyptians, and out of dislike for the Word of God, rather reaching out to acorns and swinish food, to which once they were accustomed, than to the purest wheat'. Cranmer's remarks on the third element at work in the rebellion speak volumes for his attitude to a northern England which was a far-away country to a Cambridge-educated Midlands man:

> Added to these was a certain sort of barbarous and savage people, who were ignorant of and turned away from farming and the good arts of peace, and who were so far utterly unacquainted with knowledge of sacred matters, that they could not bear to hear anything of culture and more gentle civilisation. In its furthest regions on the Scottish border, England has several peoples (*populos*) of such a kind, who I think should rather be called devastators (*populatores*); in ancient fashion, they fight with their neighbouring clans (*gentibus*) on both sides [of the border] in perpetual battle and brigandage, and they live solely upon the pillage and plunder won from it.

Cranmer then provided a rather sunny version of that 'most merciful Prince' Henry VIII's smoothly executed and moderate suppression of the Pilgrimage, including the interesting detail not otherwise attested that the

15 Osiander, *Gesamtausgabe* 6, pp. 227–8.
16 For what follows, see *Kesslers Sabbata*, pp. 463–5.

King had rapidly raised a huge army to test out the loyalty of the rest of the nation, and then had selected only a small proportion of them to go north. The story has suspiciously scriptural overtones of the strategy of Gideon against God's enemies, recorded in the Book of Judges, but it is likely to have some basis in fact.

Cranmer's uninhibited comments on his fellow-bishops to an audience safely remote in Switzerland are one of the best surviving proofs, if any were needed, of the acutely polarized atmosphere among the Church hierarchy after the Pilgrimage of Grace. By 1537 everyone knew where they stood, at least in the eyes of the Primate of All England; there was little room for the moderate Catholic humanism which had been Cranmer's own stance in the 1520s. He saw the Pilgrimage as a turning-point in the English Reformation, and he provided a resonant Continental parallel. 'Finally may you perceive that those same bishops and presiding priests of the faction, so many as lately abounded to excess, whom we considered unbending and stiff-necked, now look humbled to the ground and oppose us less. Briefly, as that Peasants' War produced a lasting peace for you, there is hope that so will this for us.' The overtones of this remark are highly significant. The Peasants' War of 1524–5 had been a defining moment for continental evangelicals, because, through the savage repression in its wake, it had established evangelical authorities as bulwarks of stability against religious and social radicalism; this had prevented the evangelical cause being hijacked by the radicals, as traditionalists had predicted that it would be, to its lasting discredit. There is a clear vision here of a middle way, a reformism which, as Bucer had proposed in his dedicatory preface to the Romans Commentary, would destroy the old world of medieval Catholicism, but which would also establish a social stability based on the traditional authority of secular rulers. Cranmer and Bullinger were both representatives of this middle way, which was both old and new.[17]

However, after this hopeful spring of 1537, things began to go wrong. Once more, as with the Swiss doubts over Bucer's Wittenberg Concord of 1536, the stumbling-block was the eucharist. With an irony which would not have amused Bucer and his colleagues in Strassburg, the problem now came from precisely the opposite direction: the English began to panic about the eucharistic views expressed in the writings which were now showering on them from the Strassburg–St Gall axis. Evangelicals in St Gall and Strassburg found themselves rebuffed, with Cranmer acting as spokesman in both cases. First to suffer was Vadianus in St Gall. In late 1536 Cranmer had received his present from Vadianus, the published *Aphorisms*, as Bullinger had recom-

17 Cf. a similar expression of optimism, including the assertion that as a result of the Pilgrimage 'the evangelical bishops very much have the King's ear' (*'die Evangelischen bischove vill gehor bey Ko. Mat. haben'*): Sturm to Philip of Hesse, summer 1537, qu. McEntegart Ph.D., 'England and the League of Schmalkalden', p. 200. Cf. also Mont to Philip, qu. ibid. p. 215.

mended, but the Archbishop took the best part of a year (*'vertente anno'*) getting round to expressing his thanks. When his letter finally arrived in June 1537, Vadianus found that it was both friendly and aggressively critical.[18] Praising Vadianus's learning 'from which I shall not scruple to acknowledge that I have myself derived benefit', Cranmer nevertheless brutally said that the subject matter of the *Aphorisms* was 'altogether displeasing to me'; unless further explanation could be provided 'I desire to be neither patron nor supporter of that opinion of yours'. The opinion was, of course, the Swiss view that the eucharistic presence could only be expressed in spiritual and mystical terms. The proof that this cause was not a good one, said Cranmer, was that even someone of Vadianus's admirable talents did not 'appear able powerfully enough to defend and support it'. One can hardly avoid quoting at length a passage which has become a much-fought-on battleground in the long struggle over the identity of the Church of England:

> I have seen almost everything that has been written and published either by Oecolampadius or Zwingli, and I have come to the conclusion that everything of everyone's writings must be read with discrimination [*'cum delectu'*]. And perhaps one might appropriately apply to these men, the remark of the blessed Jerome respecting Origen, that 'where he wrote well, nobody wrote better', etc. – you know what follows. Indeed to the extent that they have tried to point out, confute and correct papistical and sophistical errors and abuses, I give praise and approval; would that they had confined themselves within those limits, and not trodden down the wheat together with the tares! In other words, would that they had not at the same time done violence to the authority of the ancient doctors and first writers in the Church of Christ. For however much you may exercise your ingenuity, you will certainly never convince me, nor I think any unprejudiced reader, that those ancient authors are on your side in this controversy . . . most certainly, this error (if error it be) has been handed down to us by the fathers themselves, and men of the apostolic generation, from the very beginning of the Church . . . Consequently, since this Catholic faith which we hold respecting the true presence [*'vera presentia'*] has been declared to the Church from the beginning by so open and manifest passages of scripture, and subsequently the same has also so clearly and devotedly been commended to the ears of the faithful by the first ecclesiastical writers; do not, I pray, persist to me in wishing any longer to weaken or undermine a doctrine so well rooted and supported . . . One cannot say how much such a bloody controversy as this has impeded the full course of the

18 *Vadianische Briefsammlung*, 5, pp. 462–5, or a slightly inferior text in Cox 2, pp. 342–3; I have adapted the Cox translation. This letter has been much misdated, notably by *L.P.* 15 no. 137, where it is reallocated to 1540 on no good grounds. It has also been dated to the turn of a new year by a persistent mistranslation of *'vertente anno'*, which however simply means 'in the course of a year'. The dating can be made with reference to the arrival in June of Cranmer's letters, mentioned in Bullinger's and Osiander's letters respectively of 26 June and 5 July 1537: Osiander, *Gesamtausgabe* 6, pp. 227–8.

Gospel both throughout the whole Christian world, and especially among ourselves [in England].

It is apparent that Vadianus's *Aphorisms* explored eucharistic opinions which the English evangelical establishment persisted in regarding as a threat to their whole enterprise. Vadianus praised the ninth-century theologian Ratramnus, whose eucharistic treatise had been triumphantly cited by the Swiss after its unearthing and publication at Cologne in 1531, as proof that their views on the eucharist had ancient warrant; this very mention of Ratramnus may have have alerted Cranmer's acute theological antennae, for he rightly boasted that his reading was extremely up-to-date. It is likely to have occasioned his pounding home so vehemently to Vadianus the historical point about the witness of the early Church.[19]

The irony was that Vadianus had intended the *Aphorisms* as yet another effort to bridge the gap between the Swiss and the real-presence views of Luther, parallel to Bucer's similar theological tightrope act of 1536 in the Wittenberg Concord; but just like Bucer's efforts, they now failed in their purpose.[20] Vadianus must have winced when he read Cranmer's impassioned plea 'to allow a concord to appear and knit together, to exert your whole strength in establishing it, and at length to afford to the Churches the peace of God which passes all understanding . . . We should easily convert even the Turks to the obedience of our Gospel, if only we would agree among ourselves, and unite together in some holy confederacy.' So much for Bucer's hopes; on the eucharistic question, Luther's uncompromising line was still triumphant in England. One notes the way here that the eucharistic views of the two Swiss reformers are dismissed, but also that Cranmer despises 'papistical and sophistical errors', in other words the theology of the medieval scholastic theologians, transubstantiation included. What survives is the teaching of the Church in its first five centuries (considered judiciously – so the brilliant maverick Origen, idol of many radical thinkers, gets a health warning), and also, by silent implication, the Lutheran theologians of north Germany.

Thirty years ago Peter Newman Brooks, in a brilliant piece of detective work, conclusively demonstrated this positively Lutheran phase in Cranmer's eucharistic thinking. He drew attention especially to Cranmer's careful distinction in his polemical publication of 1551 between the scholastic eucharistic theology of his early career (especially the Aristotelian-inspired language of transubstantiation), and a later phase in which he had continued to believe in the real presence in the eucharist in another fashion: this was prior to his

19 Gordon Jeanes points out the greater scepticism about the witness of the Fathers expressed in the 1537 treatise on the sacraments: Jeanes, 'Reformation treatise', pp. 165–7. However, his conclusion that this represents Cranmer's opinion is not altogether secure; and there is scepticism too in the letter to Vadianus.

20 Rupp, *Patterns of Reformation*, p. 374. Bakhuizen van den Brink, 'Ratramn's eucharistic doctrine', pp. 64–5.

last phase when he abandoned the real presence as well. In 1551 Cranmer admitted that not long before he sponsored the publication of Justus Jonas's *Catechism* (1548), 'I was in that error of the real presence, as I was many years past in divers other errors: as of transubstantiation, of the sacrifice propitiatory of the priests in the mass . . .'.[21] Transubstantiation had become distinct in his mind from the real presence in the second phase. Moreover, Brooks calls to witness the evidence of the collected quotations and commentary on the eucharist in the volumes of notes termed by Ashley Null 'Cranmer's Great Commonplaces', which were begun in the late 1530s: here Luther, Melanchthon and Brenz are specifically called in to confute the views of the Swiss. Especially notable is one passage of the notebooks where Cranmer terms the views of Zwingli 'totally unreasonable' ('*absurdum . . . omnino*'), and the specific Zwinglian view condemned is 'that the truth of the body of Christ is not in the Lord's Supper' ('*verum corporis Christi non esse in Coena Domini*').[22]

Once more, there is here a distinctive expression, 'truth', and we have heard Cranmer talk of 'true presence' to Vadianus. By using these words '*vera, verum*', he seems to be struggling to establish his own preferred theological language to express a theology distinct from both Rome and Zürich, though not from Wittenberg. The Archbishop would be well aware that in the concisely emphatic article about the Lord's Supper in the Augsburg Confession, it was precisely and exclusively the adverb *vere* which was used to describe the nature of eucharistic presence: '*corpus et sanguis Christi vere adsint*' – 'the body and blood of Christ are truly present'. The same emphasis on *vere* or 'truly' is to be found in a comment by Bucer on the Wittenberg Concord between himself and the Lutherans in 1536.[23] Another crucial instance of this same usage occurs in a letter of Cranmer's a year later in 1538: here he was sympathetically discussing the eucharistic views of the Calais evangelical Adam Damplip, who 'denieth that ever he taught or said that the very body and blood of Christ was not presently in the sacrament of the altar, and confesseth the same to be there really; but he saith, that the controversy . . . was because he confuted the opinion of the transubstantiation, *and therein I think he taught but the truth*' – to be more precise, Damplip taught only the truth of the presence, or true presence. Once actively launched in theological polemical publication a decade later, however, Cranmer would discover that 'true' was a dangerously simple word on which to fix.[24] Because of this use by Cranmer of 'true' and 'truth' in the late 1530s, I will have reason

21 Brooks, *Cranmer's Doctrine of the Eucharist*, p. 12: Cox 1, p. 374.

22 Brooks, *Cranmer's Doctrine of the Eucharist*, p. 21, and see ibid., pp. 21–37. These are the collections in B.L. Royal MS 7 B XI. On the Great Commonplaces, see below, pp. 191.

23 Augsburg Confession: *Documents of the English Reformation*, ed. Bray, p. 610. 1536: Stephens, *Holy Spirit in Bucer*, p. 254.

24 P.R.O., S.P. 1/135 ff. 86–7, Cox 2, p. 375 (*L.P.* 13 ii no. 97; my italics). On Damplip, see below, pp. 218–19.

to disagree with Dr Brooks's application of the description 'true presence' to the third phase of Cranmer's eucharistic belief after 1546; more of that below (Ch. 9).

Like Vadianus, the writers of Strassburg felt gusts of the chill breeze from England in that summer of 1537. Capito had kept up the pressure on the English. In February 1537 he sent what sounds to have been a barrage of letters across to the English Court for Cranmer, Foxe and Heath, introducing the presentation copy of a book dedicated to Henry VIII: this was his *Responsio de Missa, Matrimonio et jure Magistratus in Religionem*.[25] Cranmer handed it to the King in person, and later he joined Foxe and Cromwell in reminding Henry about it, demonstrating the importance which they all now attached to the Strassburg connection. However, it took some time for Henry to formulate his response, and when it came, it was mixed. In late July, five months after the gift, Cranmer wrote back to Capito; with more accuracy than tact, he gave an insight into the dialectical reading methods of a king who prided himself on taking the middle way in religion, yet who had also learned the value of delegation:

> The King, who is most acute and vigilant in all matters, is accustomed to hand over books of this kind that have been presented to him (especially those which he has not the patience to read himself) to one of his intimates for perusal, from whom he may afterwards learn their contents. He then takes them back, and gives them to be examined by some one else, of an entirely opposite way of thinking to the former party. Thus, when he has searched out everything from them, and sufficiently ascertained and pondered what they commend and what they find fault with, then at length he openly declares his own judgement respecting the same points.[26]

The result of this Court scrutiny had predictably raised questions for Henry about one aspect of Capito's work: Cranmer said 'while he was much pleased with many things in it, there were also several which he could by no means digest or approve. I suspect that they were the statements which you made concerning the mass.' Both Capito and Vadianus had said the wrong thing. It was noticeable that Bishop Foxe also took about a year, to autumn 1537, even to acknowledge Bucer's dedication copy of his Gospel *Enarrationes*, and in his reply he confessed that he had not read it: alongside Foxe's admittedly strong excuses of his preoccupation first with the Pilgrimage of Grace and then with the Bishops' Book, one suspects that it was the views which Bucer had expressed in the volume's

25 The original draft of Capito's letter to Heath survives in Bucer's papers, C.C.C.C. MS 119, p. 175; it is dated '12 Kal. Martii' (18 February) 1537, and since the dedication of the printed work is 9 March, the presentation copy must have been in MS if the letter was sent at this stage.

26 Cox 2, pp. 340–41; I have adapted the translation (*L.P.* 12 ii no. 315). Dating is via P.R.O., S.P. 1/123 ff. 67–8, Cox 2, p. 340 (*L.P.* 12 ii no. 314).

preface on the eucharist which caused Foxe to sidestep any comment on the volume.[27]

So, throughout the reign of Henry VIII, there remained an obstacle in the relations between England and central Europe. Primate, evangelical bishops and monarch alike, in their different ways, felt that there was a fundamental flaw in the eucharistic theology of the Strassburg–St Gall axis. Admittedly, not all was loss. The evangelicals at the English Court appreciated the warmth of Strassburg's enthusiasm for an English alliance, and valued the useful role that the city played in mediating in tricky diplomacy with the Lutheran princes of the Schmalkaldic League. Cranmer kept relations friendly, particularly in the case of Bucer, to whom he sent a warmly appreciative letter about the Romans Commentary, probably by the same post in which he wrote to Capito: Bucer's strenuous efforts to reach out to the Lutherans on the matter of the eucharist made his writings the least problematic.[28] When Foxe finally got round to sending his thanks to Bucer in late 1537, he also took the opportunity of reopening conversations with the Strassburg theologians, using the German scholar whom Cranmer had acquired as a client, Jacobus Gislenus Thalassius.[29]

Likewise, the Zürich exchange remained a spectacularly successful initiative. Not all the exchange students of 1537–8 went on to make a name for themselves, and two of the most articulate, Nicholas Partridge and Nicholas Eliot, died sadly young in the early 1540s. Yet the alumni of Zürich kept alive the Switzerland–Strassburg–England circuit, and showed the way for others to join it, with major consequences for the Church of Edward VI. Their enthusiasm for all things Swiss often became a passionately undiscriminating partisanship – characteristic of disciples: the world was divided up into goodies and baddies, with attitudes to Zürich's doctrinal purity as the litmus test. Luther was a black-hearted enemy, and even poor Bucer was an object of acute suspicion. 'There is I know not what report here, that the minds of the Bernese are somewhat inclined to Bucer's opinions', Traheron portentously wrote to Bullinger in January 1538. 'We have understood from persons of good credit here, that your influence had been much diminished by reason of that unhappy retractation of yours', Partridge loftily informed Bullinger from England later the same year, after Zürich had made yet another attempt to heal the breach with the Lutherans.[30]

27 *L.P.* 12 ii no. 410; this letter cannot be as early as July 1537 as *L.P.* suggests, since it mentions the enclosure of an English edition of the Bishops' Book, published in September 1537.

28 Bucer's reply to Cranmer's lost letter is *E.T.* pp. 340–44 (*O.L.* pp. 520–26), wrongly dated in *O.L.* to 1538, but corrected to 1537 by *E.T.* and *L.P.* 12 ii no. 969. On Strassburg and England, see ibid., pp. 205–6, n. 37.

29 *L.P.* 13 i no. 1014.

30 Traheron to Bullinger, *E.T.* pp. 210–11 (*O.L.* pp. 317–19, but see Smyth, *Cranmer*, p. 83n for the January 1538 dating); Partridge to Bullinger, 17 September 1538, *E.T.* pp. 296–8 (*O.L.* pp. 610–13; *L.P.* 13 ii no. 373).

Such callow pronouncements must have embarrassed and sometimes irritated the objects of their adulation in Zürich. Cranmer kept in touch with these intense young Englishmen, but his eagerness to keep in close contact with Bullinger had noticeably diminished. When Partridge called on the Archbishop to collect a letter for the Zürich reformer on the eve of leaving England for the Frankfurt book fair in autumn 1538, Cranmer said that he had left it at one of his other palaces fifty miles away; it would have to wait for the next postal run to the Easter Frankfurt fair, six months hence! And when that time came, in spring 1539, the looming crisis over the preparation of the reactionary Six Articles gave Cranmer ample reason to postpone writing to Bullinger yet again.[31]

This story of a promising initiative for the moment only half-fulfilled needs to be fitted against the domestic story of England from 1537, in the aftermath of the Pilgrimage of Grace: this also reveals a pattern of an evangelical advance, through doctrine-making and measures of religious change, thrown badly off course by the religious reaction of 1539. The first response of the government to the December 1536 pacification of the northern rebels was to call a Great Council on 26 January 1537; this extra-Parliamentary assembly of nobles, higher clergy and selected local dignitaries was a rare event in Henry's reign, and a measure of the emergency that the Pilgrimage had created.[32] It seems to have achieved little, and disappointment in the north at its outcome may have contributed to renewed unrest in Cumberland at the end of February. Even before the Great Council, however, a renewed rising in Yorkshire had already been easily suppressed, and it was clear that the regime was safe. The government continued to take the initiative against the disarray of its opponents by plunging the Church leadership into a fresh round of doctrinal discussion to remedy the evident inadequacy of the Ten Articles. The outcome, after months of debate and theological horse-trading, was the substantial book entitled *The Institution of a Christian Man*, informally known from its first issue as 'the Bishops' Book'.[33]

The making of the Bishops' Book was the work of another assembly called in winter 1537, soon after the dispersal of the Great Council: in this case the meeting was without exact precedent, for it was the first summoning of a vice-gerential synod for the whole Church of England, ordered by Thomas Cromwell. Papal legates had previously called legatine synods of the Church, and Cardinal Pole would do so again in the reign of Queen Mary, but this was the first time that Cromwell had fully exploited the logic of his new powers to overcome the barriers between the two provinces of

31 *E.T.* pp. 396–7, 406 (*O.L.* pp. 611–12, 626); the latter, Butler, Eliot, Partridge and Traheron to Bullinger, 8 March 1539; *L.P.* 14 i no. 466).

32 Holmes, 'Great Councils', pp. 10–11; *L.P.* 12 i no. 463.

33 This is the name scrawled on two of its drafts by Bishop Cuthbert Tunstall: cf. *L.P.* 12 i 401.1, 8.

the English Church.[34] Although no formal minutes of the synod remain, we are lucky in knowing a good deal about it in accumulations of evidence whose significance and reference have not always been recognized, often being described vaguely as working papers for the Bishops' Book.[35]

The vice-gerential synod opened some days after 18 February, at which time the bishops were still assembling for it; Cranmer would have been only unpacking his bags at Lambeth that day if he had arrived, because he was still down beyond Canterbury at Ford on 16 February.[36] The synod seems never to have been a large body; it consisted of all the bishops able to attend (there is, for instance, no evidence for the presence of the aged and passive Veysey of Exeter), plus a number of no doubt hand-picked representatives from the Lower Houses of the two Convocations of Canterbury and York. Representatives of the monasteries and friaries were notable by their absence: perhaps one indication that, at least in his own mind, Cromwell had consigned the monastic order to irrelevance if not to total oblivion by 1537. After opening around 17 or 18 February 1537, the synod settled down to committee work. The eventual signatories of the Bishops' Book in September 1537 numbered no more than the bishops and twenty-five archdeacons and academics – again, no monks or friars.[37] Theological committees of this sort continued to meet up to and beyond Cromwell's fall in 1540 for various purposes, either to contemplate the preparation or revision of the Bishops' Book or to negotiate on doctrinal matters with Lutherans.

One remarkable eye-witness snapshot of a session of the synod is provided in what is admittedly a rather self-important account by that gossipy Scottish Lutheran Alexander Alesius. This would-be Boswell to his patrons Cromwell and Cranmer published his account somewhere in Germany probably later in 1537, as part of a rambling autobiographical pamphlet attacking Bishop Stokesley.[38] In spring 1536 Alesius had been run out of Cambridge by the conservative university authorities, much to his fury, and thereafter he earned his living in London as a doctor, firing off sage advice and pleas for financial help to Cranmer and Cromwell from time to time throughout the year's

34 The date of the synod's meeting remained controversial between the winter and summer of 1537, even when its existence had finally been recognized: see Fox and Guy, *Reassessing the Henrician Age*, pp. 201–2. I am persuaded by the case for a February date set out by Holmes, 'Great Councils', pp. 10–13.

35 Cf. the material from P.R.O., S.P. 1/123 and S.P. 6 briefly described in *L.P.* 12 ii nos. 401–8. There is more material in B.L. Cotton MS Cleopatra E. V, e.g. ff. 48–52v, 139r, discussed below.

36 *Lisle Letters* 4, pp. 268–9 (*L.P.* 12 i no. 457); P.R.O., S.P. 1/116 ff. 42–3 (*L.P.* 12 i no. 436).

37 See signatures to preface (unpag.) of *Institution of a Christen Man*.

38 Alesius, *Of the Authority of the Word of God*. The account of the synod is between sigs. A v and B viii.

alarms.[39] One day, which we can be fairly certain was in February 1537, he had a lucky break:

> I did meet by chance in the street the right excellent Lord Cromwell going unto the Parliament House in the year 1537. He when he saw me, called me unto him and took me with him to the Parliament House to Westminster, where we found all the bishops gathered together; unto whom as he went and took me with him, all the bishops and prelates did rise up and did obeisance unto him as to their Vicar General; and after he had saluted them, he sat him down in the highest place, and right against him sat the Archbishop of Canterbury, after him the Archbishop of York, and then London, Lincoln, Salisbury, Bath, Ely, Hereford, Chichester, Norwich, Rochester and Worcester and certain other whose names I have forgotten. All these did sit at a table covered with a carpet with certain priests standing about them.

Cromwell's opening speech was a request in the King's name for calm debate of theological controversy, and for all argument to refer to scripture; he made it clear by implication that the Ten Articles had not been a success in settling 'unlearned people whose consciences are in doubt what they may believe'. His plea for calm was very necessary, because the first and principal item on the agenda was a discussion about the sacraments. Evidently the conservatives were still furious at the exclusion of four sacraments of the medieval seven from the Ten Articles the previous summer. Stokesley leapt in straight away with a reassertion of the whole seven, and after that the assembled bishops split on predictable party lines, Cranmer heading the evangelical group. After much furious argument, Cranmer summed up the discussion with a speech which Alesius reported at length. If we may trust this report, by implication the Primate rebuked much of the debate as playing with 'bare words' and endangering 'the unity and quietness of the Church', a clearly deliberate echo of Cromwell's opening remarks. To call the bishops to a sense of seriousness about what they were doing, he listed some of the main doctrinal disputes to be decided: they were indeed basic matters, such as whether the 'outward' performance of the sacraments 'doth justify man, or whether we receive our justification through faith'.

Despite his stress on calm discussion, the final section of Cranmer's address betrayed the fact that this was no neutral speech – after all, he was not the chairman of the debate. First, he said, the number of the sacraments must be decided, and also why 'we call baptism and the supper of the Lord sacraments of the Gospel': one notices no bracketing of penance with these two, despite the Ten Articles! His final thrust was a characteristic humanist use of patristic sources for evangelical purposes: he pointed out that the fourth-century

39 Cf. a memorandum of his to Cranmer on the Lincolnshire Rising, October 1536, P.R.O., S.P. 6/6 ff. 110–12 (*L.P.* 11 no. 987), and to Cromwell, *L.P.* 11 no. 988.

Ambrose of Milan, and other authors, 'call the washing of the disciples' feet and other things sacraments, which I am sure you yourselves would not suffer to be numbered among the other sacraments'. If anyone had any doubt about the drift of this address, Alesius's expression of delight would have enlightened them. Cromwell noticed his pleasure, and with a cavalier improvisation of protocol for his new institution, called on Alesius to give his opinion about the debate, informing the bishops by way of justification that the Scot 'was the King's scholar': this might be seen as putting him on a level with those members of the synod who had been chosen because they were senior academics.

Alesius proved to his own satisfaction (with the help of Augustine of Hippo) that there were only two sacraments, only to be interrupted by an apoplectic Stokesley. A three-way debate between the two and the establishment evangelical Bishop Foxe ensued, in which Stokesley fell back on a defence of the authority of non-scriptural Church traditions, thus fatally stepping outside the royal guidelines laid down by the Vice-gerent. This question of unwritten verities was one of the main fault-lines between evangelicals and conservatives throughout the 1530s and 1540s. At Stokesley's comments, Cromwell, Cranmer and 'the other bishops which did defend the pure doctrine of the Gospel . . . smiled a little one upon another', and Cromwell decided that perhaps it was time for lunch. The next day Alesius, spoiling for another theological scrap, turned up again with Cromwell, but 'a certain archdeacon in the name of the Archbishop of Canterbury' (Edmund Cranmer, perhaps?) took the Scot aside and told him 'that the other bishops were grievously offended with me, that I being a stranger should be admitted unto their disputation'. Cromwell thought it best to flatter their sensitivities by asking Alesius to withdraw. It was not the last time that boisterous Scottish indifference to English formalities proved a source of strain between the two cultures, as James VI and I was to discover seven decades later.

Alesius noted the major concern of the conservatives to restore the four sacraments, and this was quickly achieved; clearly it would be difficult to issue a comprehensive statement which did not talk about the whole tally of seven. The conservatives at first regarded this as a victory: very soon after debates began in mid-February Archbishop Lee was triumphantly informing his clerical staff that 'those four sacraments that were omitted be found again now, and we be concluded upon them yesternight'.[40] It is likely that the first thought was to publish a quick revision of the first doctrinal half of the Ten Articles, bumping up the number of major sacraments recognized in England from three to seven. This abortive plan may be traced in a draft address attributed by the editors of *Letters and Papers* to Cromwell's client Richard Morison: drawn up in the name of the archbishops and bishops of England, it refers back to the Ten Articles in which 'we spake long sithence' of baptism,

40 *L.P.* 12 i, no. 789, p. 346.

penance and the eucharist, and the purpose now was to speak of the other four.[41] However, this plan was abandoned, and the conservatives got less than they had hoped: when the Bishops' Book was finally published, the discussion of the four sacraments 'found again' drew a clear distinction between them and the major scriptural three, in a paragraph whose positioning at the end of the sacramental section suggests a last-minute evangelical victory. It said that while baptism, eucharist and penance were instituted of Christ, this did not apply to the other four, and so 'there is a difference in dignity and necessity between them and the other three sacraments'.[42]

We can see how this theological bush warfare proceeded through the survival of one set of preliminary theological questionnaires on the subject of confirmation, evidence of a method of consultation which was repeatedly used in the revisions of English doctrine until the early part of Edward VI's reign.[43] Once more, the contents reveal predictable party replies. Cranmer in his brief responses could find no trace in the New Testament of confirmation being instituted by Christ, only by 'acts and deeds of the apostles'; unlike his fellow-archbishop, Edward Lee, who in common with most of the conservative respondents, derived confirmation from Christ 'by tradition' unwritten but conveyed to the Apostles. We have already witnessed how Cromwell and Cranmer had sought to exclude arguments from tradition at the synod. The eventual article on confirmation in the Bishops' Book reflected Cranmer's reductionism, declaring that the sacrament was actually introduced by the early Church imitating what they had read about the practice of the Apostles. However, in his response Cranmer, with a hesitation which provides a perfect illustration of his anxiety to conform his opinions to 'unity and quietness', added the comment in his own hand 'I respond thus, subject always to the judgement of the learned and of the orthodox church'.[44]

Alesius's report suggests that what he had attended had been an early session of the synod, in which the battle-lines were still being drawn. Several surviving documents (including the final preface of the book) confirm his picture of the fairly modest numbers involved in the synod, which was really a large committee. For instance, the final draft of the Bishops' Book statement on one of the seven sacraments, holy orders, is signed by just such a roomful of people as Alesius describes: Cromwell heads the list, then Cranmer and ten of the eleven other bishops Alesius named, plus two from remote dioceses whom the metropolitan-based Scotsman would probably not have known by sight (Bangor and Durham). The 'certain priests standing about them' number twenty-three, a collection of archdeacons and of academics described as '*sacre theologie iuris ecclesiastici et civilis professores*': '*iuris ecclesiastici*' is a

41 *L.P.* 12 ii, Addenda no. 33.

42 Lloyd, *Formularies*, p. 128.

43 B.L. Cotton MS Cleopatra E. V ff. 75f, pr. Strype, *Ecclesiastical Memorials*, 1 ii, pp. 340–63, no. 88 (*L.P.* 12 ii no. 403).

44 *Hec respondeo, salvo semper eruditorum et ecclesie orthodoxe iudicio*. See Lloyd, pp. 94–6.

slightly unhappy euphemism for the Doctors of Canon Law, whose discipline Henry VIII had just abolished. The fair copy text is in the hand of Cranmer's faithful secretary Ralph Morice, and the Archbishop himself has carefully inserted a phrase where Morice's attention wandered and he had skipped from one line to another.[45]

It is noticeable that this section of the text on orders is virtually identical with that eventually published in the autumn, even though the draft itself can have been agreed no later than March.[46] An agreed version of a statement on confirmation, now separated from the holy orders statement, has a strikingly similar list of signatories, and it is clearly of much the same date in winter and early spring.[47] As Alesius has shown us, the synod thus first disposed of the contention over the sacraments festering since the previous summer. Cranmer also gives clear negative evidence that the sacramental section was finished first and early in a letter to Cromwell in the following July; in this he describes the bishops as nearly finishing their work, but he only mentions the non-sacramental subject sections of the Bishops' Book: Paternoster, Ave Maria, Creed and Commandments.[48]

Other documents of much the same date in spring reflect the work of sub-committees, often with particular axes to grind. Thus a conservative collection of bishops (Clerk, Stokesley, Longland, Tunstall, and Rugge) got together to sign a short but ringing defence of shrines and pilgrimages, which did not make it to the final text of the Bishops' Book.[49] We might even attribute to this date one unusually specialized sub-committee, Latimer's celebrated literary duel on paper with Henry VIII on the subject of purgatory, although it might equally well belong to the previous year; in this fascinating document, Henry was on top form in his marginal comments, trouncing Latimer's rather stumbling efforts to deny purgatory's existence.[50] Cranmer got a secretary to prepare (probably by personal dictation) a set of notes on the seven sacraments which probably represents the agreements reached in discussion on the sacraments; Ashley Null notes how Lutheran in tone they are, maintaining the special character of the three major sacraments although acknowledging and discussing the total of seven, just as the Bishops' Book was eventually to do. Null also points out their similarities in ideas and

45 B.L. Cotton MS Cleopatra E. V ff. 48–50r. It is conveniently dated before April 1537 by the appearance of Marmaduke Waldeby, imprisoned in the Tower in April: cf. Rupp, *Protestant Tradition*, pp. 137–8. For Cranmer's correction of the *même à même* mistake, cf. ibid., f. 49r. Cf. the description of the signatories in the preface (unpag.) of *Institution of a Christen Man*.

46 Lloyd, *Formularies*, pp. 104–5.

47 P.R.O., S.P. 6/8 f. 33r; again, Waldeby appears (*L.P.* 12 ii no. 401.1)

48 B.L. Cotton MS Cleopatra E. V, f. 55, Cox 2, pp. 337 (*L.P.* 12 ii no. 293). Gordon Rupp first noticed this point: *Protestant Tradition*, p. 138.

49 B.L. Cotton MS Cleopatra E V f. 139r, pr. Strype, *Ecclesiastical Memorials*, 1 ii, p. 388.

50 *Sermons and Remains of Latimer*, pp. 245–9, from B.L. Cotton MS Cleopatra E. V, ff. 140f.

phrasing to Melanchthon's *Loci Communes* (dedicated and presented to Henry VIII in 1535), also to the Wittenberg Articles brought back by Foxe in 1536.[51] Likewise, it may be at this time that the Archbishop's secretaries under his direction began compiling a source-book of quotations and comments on a classified list of theological questions; this now survives in the British Library as two massive volumes, which Null has christened 'Cranmer's Great Commonplaces'. They were certainly begun no later than 1538, and Cranmer and his secretarial team continued adding to them until the end of Henry VIII's reign; they became the anchor of his omnivorous theological reading.[52]

If we consider Alesius's account and the other documents which survive, we can get a reasonable picture of the procedure and the dynamics of the synod/committee as it prepared the Bishops' Book. The synod opened in the Parliament House (available because Parliament stood down throughout 1537), but once the opening debates had run their course and the broad structure of the new doctrinal statement had been agreed, it may have been thought more convenient for this comparatively small body to hold most of its meetings in a more informal atmosphere. This would perhaps be less prone to the striking of intransigent attitudes which Alesius had noted in formal debate. Meetings may have taken place either across the river at Lambeth Palace, where there would be books on hand for consultation, or in a variety of episcopal lodgings around London: one casual reference in a letter of Bishop Foxe suggests meetings in his London house.[53] At this time the synod became far more obviously a committee, and Cromwell, having much else to do, left the chairmanship and co-ordination increasingly to Cranmer and Foxe, so that in the conclusion of all the proceedings there was an evangelical bias. Cranmer's postscript memorandum on confirmation (already noted) suggests that he at least aimed for a certain public neutrality as Primate in the deliberations of the committees, but evidently Bishop Foxe did not feel that his leading role disqualified him from stridently enunciating the evangelical cause. It is not surprising that the document eventually published was full of Lutheran overtones; it made considerable textual borrowings from the evangelically-flavoured primer (lay devotional book) issued by Cromwell's favourite propaganda publisher, William Marshall, in 1535. Via this devious route there

51 Lambeth MS 1107 ff. 84, 85–92v. Null Ph.D., 'Cranmer's Doctrine of Repentance', pp. 20–23, 107–11. For dating, he notes that the text describes Erasmus as dead (so post-1536), yet it is unlikely to be associated with the 1538 negotiations with the Lutherans, since they never reached the stage of discussing the four disputed sacraments. For a rather less focussed dating, more inclined to associate the document with the 1538 negotiations with the Lutherans, see Jeanes, 'Reformation treatise', pp. 151–4.

52 B.L. Royal MS 7 B XI, XII: on dating and discussion, see Null Ph.D., 'Cranmer's Doctrine of Repentance', pp. 6–20, and for summary description, see Ayris and Selwyn (eds), *Cranmer*, pp. 312–15.

53 *St.P.* 1, pp. 556–7 (*L.P.* 12 ii no. 289).

entered disguised fragments of Martin Luther's prose into an official formulary of the Church of Henry VIII, who detested the man.[54]

In one significant and prophetic respect, however, Marshall's Primer pushed the Bishops' Book further than Lutheranism towards the theology of the Strassburg–St Gall axis. In one of its sections it renumbered the Ten Commandments, which may at first hearing sound either a drastic or a pedantic procedure. However, the renumbering had a deep theological resonance. From the beginnings of Christian commentary on the Old Testament, there had been two traditions about the opening and therefore the subsequent numbering of the Decalogue.[55] One school of thought had combined the command to have no other Gods but God with the command to make no graven images, and even argued that the graven image command was a late importation and therefore of secondary importance. This was the dominant tradition in the early and medieval western Church, not surprisingly, since it removed the embarrassing prominence of the graven image prohibition, a convenience for a religion increasingly reliant on the visual in its devotion. The other tradition, with good Jewish and patristic warrant, treated these two commandments as separate, and therefore the image prohibition became the second of the Ten Commandments in its own right. It was the sign of a religious tradition which regarded the visual as a threat to the right perception of God.

Leo Jud, Huldrych Zwingli's assistant at Zürich, first republicized this numbering in a publication of 1527; it became a distinctive feature of central European and later Reformed Christianity, rejected both by Rome and by Martin Luther, who had little quarrel with images, and who was hostile to this innovation of his fellow-reformers.[56] George Joye quickly introduced the 'Zürich' numbering to England, when he produced a pioneering evangelical English primer in 1530; a fierce treatise by Martin Bucer against images, printed in English translation by William Marshall in 1535, caused widespread English interest or alarm, according to theological taste, and gave the idea further publicity. In that same year, Marshall's Primer provided both numberings in its text, reflecting the fact that the book was a compilation, but of the two systems, it was the 'Zürich' numbering (which Marshall had taken over from Joye's Primer) which was now selected officially for the Bishops' Book, to determine the numbering of the Ten Commandments for the Church of England. There can be little doubt that it was thanks to Thomas Cranmer that this momentous choice was made.[57] England was now falteringly set on the path to the destruction of images, which would be one of the most marked features of its Reformation.

54 Rupp, *Protestant Tradition*, p. 140; Duffy, *Stripping of the Altars*, pp. 382–3. Tjernagel, *Henry VIII and the Lutherans*, pp. 172–8.

55 For an excellent treatment of this question see Aston, *England's Iconoclasts*, Ch. 7.

56 On Jud, see Aston, *England's Iconoclasts*, p. 380.

57 Aston, *England's Iconoclasts*, pp. 203–10, 239–41, 381.

Once the first formal debates were replaced by less formal committee meetings, work on the Bishops' Book went forward in sub-committees, scrutinizing individual responses to questions, and perhaps also unsolicited memoranda from individuals: one aggressively evangelical survivor from these memoranda has often misleadingly been attributed to Cranmer, when it seems to be in the hand of the much more outspoken evangelical Dean Simon Haynes.[58] Out of this mass of material were created the various messy drafts of which many fragments survive, then the final versions of these were copied fair and agreed by the whole body. Within this framework, even after bitter argument, the keynote was compromise, encouraged by the brooding personality of the King, always concerned to avoid dissension. Henry was normally only symbolically present, in the shape of Cromwell, or simply at the back of people's minds, but his own hand appears in corrections of at least one of the surviving drafts, on purgatory, and he was involved in discussions on other matters.[59] Stephen Gardiner sarcastically described the process of spatchcock ecumenism, admittedly at second hand, but unexpectedly and satisfyingly confirming Alesius's detail that bishops Stokesley and Foxe were the major combatants in the debates:

> it was shewed me that Bishop Stokesley (God have mercy on his soul) after he had stiffly withstand many things, and much stoutness had between him and the Bishop of Hereford, whose soul God pardon, then Bishop Stokesley would somewhat relent in the form, as Bishop Foxe did the like. And then, as it were in a mean, each part, by placing some words by special marks, with a certain understanding protested, the article went forth; and so to a new article, and so from one to another. There is sometime as evident contradiction as if it had been saved by a proviso.[60]

Cranmer added his own perspective on the committee's procedure, and on the way in which doctrine might in the end be decided by sheer exhaustion, when he commented, with offhand coldness about one convoluted passage of the final text on prayer in the Church, that 'this particle, I confess, I never well understood . . . but I consented thereto only because there is no evil doctrine therein contained, as far as I perceive and discern'.[61]

There seems, however, to have been other major business besides the Bishops' Book for the synod in early spring, which may account for some of the delay which occurred after the agreement on various sections of its text. Henry VIII was most alarmed at the Pope's summoning of a General Council to Mantua for May 1537, seeing that he would be dangerously isolated if the

58 B.L. Cotton MS Cleopatra E. V, ff. 51–2r, pr. e.g. in Cox 2, pp. 465–6 (*L.P.* 12 i no. 409).

59 P.R.O., S.P. 6/8 ff. 95–8 (*L.P.* 12 ii no. 401.3), part illustrated as the frontispiece in Kreider, *Chantries*; see also ibid., p. 131 for Henry's discussions. Cf. corrections by Cromwell: S.P. 6/2 ff. 315–42 (*L.P.* 12 ii no. 401.6).

60 *Gardiner's Letters*, p. 351.

61 C.C.C.C. MS 104, p. 250, Cox 2, p. 91.

King of France and the Emperor attended. The evidence suggests that it was now that he put his senior clergy to work on a document declaring why such a gathering could not be termed a General Council. This was probably intended as part of the documentation for Edmund Bonner's proposed embassy to the Emperor in Spain, and it was linked with the *Protestation* against a General Council which Henry published unilaterally in default of any combined action with the Schmalkaldic League. Once more the atmosphere of Lambeth Palace hangs round the two-paragraph document from the senior clergy: the draft of the first paragraph is in the hand of Morice with corrections by Cranmer, with either of the two paragraphs prepared and signed by a sub-committee of Cranmer and a few leading bishops before the final combined version.[62] This may well be the 'book' which Bonner said in May had been drawn out for the clergy by the Archbishop, in parallel with the King's published *Protestation*.[63] At least one of two treatises on General Councils preserved at Hatfield House can be dated to 1537, and that treatise makes direct reference to the work of the drafters of the Bishops' Book on matrimony; this Hatfield manuscript is likely to represent one of the working papers produced in the course of the synod.[64] Other incidental matters might conveniently be swept up into the remit of the meeting: even as the final touches were being put to the draft of the Bishops' Book in July, Cranmer asked Cromwell whether he should conduct the examination of Rowland Phillips, the vicar of Croydon, a veteran conservative activist, 'in this presence of the bishops and other learned men of our assembly'.[65]

Cranmer seems to have been up at Lambeth for most of the spring and summer for the discussions, apart from short escapes down to Croydon.[66] Writing to Bullinger on 3 April, as soon as he had returned to Lambeth from

62 1st paragraph (Morice's draft): Lambeth MS 1107 f. 163. 2nd paragraph: B.L. Stowe MS 141 f. 36 (pr. Burnet 1 ii, p. 259, Bk 2 no. 10). Combined version: P.R.O., S.P. 1/105 ff. 78–9, *St.P.* 1, pp. 543–4 (*L.P.* 11 no. 124.2). This is no later than the signature of Robert Aldrich without his episcopal title of Carlisle, to which he was nominated on 10 July 1537. The signature 'Wilhelmus Abbas Monasterii Sancti Benedicti' might seem to contradict my earlier observation about the lack of regulars at the synod, but this is William Repps or Rugge, Bishop of Norwich, still customarily signing himself as Abbot of St Bene't's Hulme. NB *L.P.*'s note relating this text to *L.P.* 11 nos. 83, 84, although this does not decisively push its date back to 1536.

63 P.R.O., S.P. 1/120 f. 149 (*L.P.* 12 i no. 1244). That this was about the General Council is indicated by Bonner's follow-up letter on 1 June: *St.P.* 1, p. 550, *L.P.* 12 ii no. 7. His use of the word 'book' in his letters may mislead; he simply meant a document. On the background to the *Protestation*, see McEntegart Ph.D., 'England and the League of Schmalkalden', pp. 202–3, 205.

64 See Sawada, 'Two treatises', p. 211, on 'MS 47'. There is a tradition that these treatises are associated with Cranmer, which probably merely reflects their association with the synod.

65 B.L. Cotton MS Cleopatra E. V, f. 55, Cox 2, p. 338 (*L.P.* 12 ii no. 293). The examination a week later (28–29 July) apparently took place before Cranmer only: P.R.O., S.P. 1/123 ff. 125–8, Cox 2, pp. 338–40 (*L.P.* 12 ii no. 361). On Phillips see above, p. 124.

66 E.g. he was at Croydon 31 March 1537: P.R.O., S.P. 1/117 ff. 179–80 (*L.P.* 12 i no. 776), and a summer stay, P.R.O., S.P. 1/133 ff. 22–3, Cox 2, pp. 369–70 (*L.P.* 13 i no. 1171).

an Easter break at Croydon, he looked back on the work of the synod so far and sounded ebullient; we have already heard his comments on the higher clergy, but generally the political atmosphere had unprecedented promise for the evangelicals:

> For with the rebels pacified and completely defeated, the attitude [*animus*] of the Prince himself seems to show favour to the Gospel more strongly and in earnest than ever before. And the noblemen who before were slow to believe and, if I may say so, were hardhearted [*gravicordes*], now begin to be more anxious to listen, and in all respects to be more favourable and well-disposed.

The Archbishop's description of the work of the synod itself clearly implied that, like the conservatives, he had found the previous year's compromises in the Ten Articles unsatisfactory:

> For a second time at the Prince's command we have gathered in council as bishops and learned men, to discuss the ordering of ecclesiastical matters, in which we transact everything more freely than ever before, and (I hope) will finish up with greater profit. But the result will make clear what character it has, about which you will certainly hear from me, if not from some other direction.[67]

John Husee noted on 30 April 1537 that there was still no news of 'our bishops' long sitting'.[68] Yet the bishops were still beavering away in July, notably weary by that time, and increasingly worried about the plague raging in London: 'I pray God preserve you, and send you hither shortly again, that we might end and go home into our diocese [*sic*], and do some good there', Latimer begged Cromwell in mid-July.[69] A week later, the bishops were at last getting demob-happy; Foxe and Cranmer deluged Cromwell with last-minute queries, while Latimer's letter simply expressed the accumulated frustration of a man who was not one of nature's compromisers. He incidentally provided yet more evidence of Foxe's leading role as the evangelical champion:

> This day, sir, which is Saturday, we had finished (I trow) the rest of our book, if my Lord of Hereford had not been diseased, to whom surely we owe great thanks for his great diligence in all our proceedings. Upon Monday I think it will be done altogether, and then my Lord of Canterbury will send it unto your lordship with all speed . . . As for myself, I can nothing else but pray God that when it is done it be well and sufficiently done, so that we shall not need to have any more such doings. For verily, for my part, I had liever be poor parson of poor [West] Kington again, than to continue thus Bishop of

67 *Kesslers Sabbata*, p. 464 (Cranmer to Bullinger, 3 April 1537).

68 *L.P.* 12 ii no. 1068.

69 *Sermons and Remains of Latimer*, p. 378 (15 July 1537; *L.P.* 12 ii no. 258). A suggestive trio of bishops, Cranmer, Tunstall and Foxe, was among witnesses to the new royal foundation of Stixwold Priory on 9 July 1537: Dugdale, *Monasticon* 5, pp. 725–7.

> Worcester . . . forsooth it is a troublous thing to agree upon a doctrine in things of such controversy, with judgements of such diversity, every man (I trust) meaning well, and yet not all meaning one way.[70]

Soon after this the doctrinal committee at last dispersed, leaving Foxe to the tedious task of tying up the loose ends in the book. Cranmer put as much distance as possible between himself and London, making his escape for August down to the delights of hunting and his study at Ford.[71] He was in ebullient mood, not just because of the outcome of the long discussions around the Bishops' Book, but because of a possible new initiative which would complete a yawning gap in the work of the evangelical leadership. It was illogical to stipulate, as the King had done at the outset of the doctrinal discussions in February, that all doctrine should be officially stated with reference to scripture alone, if an English Bible was not readily available to the Christians of England. There was no sign of any conclusion to the official initiative in translation agreed in the Convocation of Canterbury three years before; the delay in provision was embarrassing, particularly after the Vice-gerent's abortive attempt to order general Bible provision in his 1536 injunctions.

Cromwell and Cranmer now acted to end this anomaly. Throughout, one should note that, as in the destruction of the monasteries, it was the Vice-gerent who led the initiative, with Cranmer merely as cheerleader; their eager lieutenant was the evangelical printer Richard Grafton, who was supervising the printing in Antwerp and importation to England of the so-called 'Matthew Bible', an extension of Tyndale's incomplete translation prepared by John Rogers under the pseudonym Thomas Matthew. It is apparent from a letter of Grafton's to Cromwell in August that he was keeping in touch with both Cromwell and Cranmer separately, yet it is not clear that Cranmer realized this.[72] On 4 August the Archbishop wrote to Cromwell from Ford, sending on a copy of the new Bible with warm commendations: it was 'better than any other translation heretofore made' and with a dedicatory letter to the King 'very well done'. For the moment he was not looking to revive the order in Cromwell's injunctions, but he was hoping that if Cromwell showed the Bible to the King it could at least for the first time achieve a royal licence, until the bishops fulfilled their pledge to provide a text 'which I think will not be till a day after doomsday'.[73] A result came through remarkably

70 *Sermons and Remains of Latimer*, p. 379 (21 July 1537; *L.P.* 12 ii no. 295). Foxe's letter, 20 July: *St.P.* 1, pp. 555–7, *L.P.* 12 ii no. 289. Cranmer's letter, 21 July: B.L. Cotton MS Cleopatra E. V, f. 55, Cox 2, pp. 337–8 (*L.P.* 12 ii no. 293).

71 For Cranmer's hunting with John Hales on 8 August, P.R.O., S.P. 1/124 f. 7 (*L.P.* 12 ii no. 488).

72 Strype, *Cranmer*, App. no. 20, pp. 285–7 (*L.P.* 12 ii App. no. 35).

73 4 August 1537: P.R.O., S.P. 1/123 ff. 198–9, Cox 2, p. 344 (*L.P.* 12 ii no. 434). For a useful general survey of English bible translation at this time, see Greenslade (ed.), *Cambridge History of the Bible*, pp. 141–55.

quickly, which suggests first that Cromwell had already made his own plans for the Bible, and second, that he caught Henry at a moment of expansive generosity as Jane Seymour's pregnancy reached its last weeks. Within nine days of his first letter, Cranmer was writing his fervent thanks that the Bible had been presented to the King, approved and authorized for general sale – 'assuring your lordship, for the contentation of my mind, you have shewed me more pleasure herein, than if you had given me a thousand pound'. For an Archbishop who often had on his mind precisely such a sum in debts, this was praise indeed!

Cranmer's delight was boundless. The authorization of the Bible 'shall so much redound to your honour that, besides God's reward, you shall obtain perpetual memory for the same within this realm. And as for me, you may reckon me your bondman for the same. And I dare be bold to say, so may ye do my Lord of Worcester.' Latimer indeed showed his gratitude by immediately repeating the 1536 vice-gerential order for bibles in his own diocesan injunctions that autumn, and other bishops followed suit.[74] The Archbishop's pleasure did not diminish through August, for the first thing that came into his head when he next wrote to the Vice-gerent was to pour out more thanks for the achievement. Cranmer was also keeping in touch with Grafton, because on the same day as this last letter, Grafton quoted back to Cromwell the Archbishop's 'thousand pound' remark, although in his version Cranmer's delight had experienced inflation up to ten thousand.[75] From then on, it was still the Vice-gerent and not Cranmer who took the initiatives in the orders which envisaged a Bible in every church; Cromwell even made a major financial investment in Bible production to make this possible.[76]

It may have been because of his exuberant mood over the successful outcome of the Bishops' Book and the furtherance of the vernacular Bible that Cranmer began to take more aggressive initiatives in Kent, including a visitation of his diocese (subject now, of course, to the necessary permission of the Vice-gerent). He remained based down in south-east Kent from the autumn of 1537 until the end of March 1538, with only brief breaks for the christening of Prince Edward and the funeral of Queen Jane.[77] He had, after all, been away in London or its environs for more than five months, and by the summer the time was ripe to assert his authority in the heartland of his diocese. He was determined to end widespread recalcitrance to the evangelical programme; in winter 1537, for instance, during his previous stay in Kent, he had been alerted to the truculent conservatism among senior monks of his

74 *Sermons and Remains of Latimer*, p. 242; M. Bowker in Haigh (ed.), *English Reformation Revised*, p. 76n.

75 13 August 1537: B.L. Cotton MS Cleopatra E. V, f. 348v, Cox 2, pp. 345–6 (*L.P.* 12 ii no. 512). Cranmer and Grafton on 28 August: Cotton MS Cleopatra E. V, ff. 300, 349, Cox 2, pp. 346–7 (*L.P.* 12 ii nos. 592–3, the latter correcting Cox's 'thousand').

76 Slavin, 'Rochepot Affair'.

77 B.L. Cotton MS Cleopatra E. V, f. 55, Cox 2, p. 338 (*L.P.* 12 ii no. 293).

own cathedral at Canterbury.[78] In his absence, he continued to monitor cases of conservative resistance. The issue causing the most trouble was the abolition of various holy days, which had been one of the decisions of the 1536 Convocation, backed up by a royal proclamation; one of the misdemeanours of the Cathedral priory in February had been to stage the exposition of relics on a prohibited holy day.[79] The prohibition was the most direct government interference yet in the lives of ordinary people, yet it was more than that; clergy recognized it as a direct assault on the cult of the saints, about which there had been so much controversy during 1536. At some point when he was down in Kent in late 1536 or 1537, Cranmer had tried to give a practical example of what the change entailed by ostentatiously ignoring the fast for the eve of one of the feasts of St Thomas Becket: he ate meat in his parlour with his 'family' (that is, his household), and thereby caused a sensation in Canterbury.[80]

When he arrived back in August 1537, Cranmer was immediately struck by the widespread continued observance of the prohibited holy days, so he punished or cautioned several offenders and gave strict orders to the clergy to desist from further encouraging such disobedience. As he noted in irritation to Cromwell, his efforts were not helped by the continuing observance of the same holidays in the Court of King Henry.[81] His orders for the official abolition to be observed in the peculiars of his diocese were issued on 10 September.[82] In winter 1538 he gave the monks of Canterbury Cathedral a further practical demonstration of how evangelicals should keep a holy season by himself delivering a course of lectures in the Cathedral precinct through the first half of Lent; this was all the more pointed a gesture of innovation because the King that year for the first time suspended, by royal proclamation, the traditional Lenten ban on eating eggs and dairy produce, on the grounds that the ban was 'a mere positive law of the Church'. Cranmer's lecture theme was that favourite evangelical subject for exposition, the epistle to the Hebrews.[83]

During autumn 1537 Cranmer determined to assert himself against the conservative gentry establishment of his diocese. Predictably the Lisles in Calais were one object of his attention; he gave renewed offence to them in a severe telling-off to one of Lady Lisle's servants, and he did not refrain from repeating descriptions of the lady herself as 'a little papish'.[84] However, a new departure was the Archbishop's direct confrontation in October with one of

78 P.R.O., S.P. 1/116, ff. 42–3, Cox 2, p. 334 (*L.P.* 12 i no. 436), and cf. S.P. 1/115, ff. 85–6 (*L.P.* 12 i no. 256.2–3).

79 Lambeth MS 751, p.114; cf. Foxe 5 i, p. 164.

80 *Narratives of the Reformation*, p. 285.

81 B.L. Cotton MS Cleopatra E. V, f. 300, Cox 2, pp. 346–7 (*L.P.* 12 ii no. 592): this postscript is in his own hand.

82 *L.P.* 12 ii no. 703, and Cox 2, pp. 348–9: one survivor for the East Anglian peculiar of Bocking.

83 *Narratives of the Reformation*, p. 286. Henry's proclamation is *T.R.P.* 1, pp. 260–61.

84 Lee to Lady Lisle, 16 September 1537: *Lisle Letters* 4, p. 408 (*L.P.* 12 ii no. 705).

the most powerful men in Kent, Sir Thomas Cheyney, who was not only Lord Warden of the Cinque Ports but high steward of the archiepiscopal estates; their acrid correspondence had such potentially serious implications that the Archbishop took the precaution of copying the whole sequence of letters for the Vice-gerent.[85] The row was the culmination of years of unsatisfactory exchanges between the two men, in which Cranmer had sought Cheyney's co-operation in setting a 'good ensample' of conformity within the county: now Cranmer wrote alarmingly frankly to Cheyney, accusing him of being the chief force against allowing the people of his diocese to 'exercise themselves in the knowledge of God's laws'. In particular, the Lord Warden was undermining Cranmer's prized new achievement of the authorization of Bible-reading, for 'people dare not apply themselves to read God's word, for fear of your threats at assizes and sessions'. Cheyney's reply was not constructive; he was particularly offended by the innuendo that he was covertly encouraging disaffection just as northern magnates had done the previous autumn in Lincolnshire and the North. In reply Cranmer laid his theological cards on the table: he roundly criticized Cheyney for using his authority in quarter sessions to enforce 'mere voluntary things', rather than 'to open and set forth things requisite of necessity for our salvation as the point of justification by Christ's passion only, the difference between faith and works, works of mercy to be done before voluntary works' (by which he meant endowment of masses and the like). Once more he returned to the justices' failure to act against the notorious popular reluctance to abandon the prohibited holidays.

This open attack was a gift for a sarcastic riposte from Cheyney: he was a justice, not a preacher, he said, and he accused Cranmer of defaming royal sessions. Rather undermining his professions of theological ignorance, he aligned himself with the likes of Stokesley on the matter of unwritten verities rather than scriptural warrant alone: he snapped 'I doubt not that Almighty God accepteth to his pleasure good things done which proceed of mere devotion, though that the thing be not expressly commanded to be done by the word of God; or else all foundations of ecclesiastical things and other like perpetuities be of little reputation.' This was a shrewd thrust at a time when so many of the Church's endowments, including many of Cranmer's own estates, were under threat of confiscation. At this point, the correspondence breaks off, but we have another glimpse of Cranmer's volcanic feelings towards the gentry of Kent in an appalled letter of Brian Talbot to Cromwell a week after Cheyney's last rejoinder. He had delivered a letter of Cromwell to Cranmer; although there is no evidence that this was to do with the Cheyney row, the Archbishop belied his habitual mildness by giving Talbot 'great rebukes' and 'grievous words . . . saying unto me that I had defamed and slandered him'. When Talbot had left his Lordship's presence, he had

85 P.R.O., S.P. 6/2, ff. 86–92, in the hand of Ralph Morice: Cox 2, pp. 349–56 (*L.P.* 12 ii no. 846). The recipient is not named, but can hardly be anyone else but Cheyney. On Cheyney, see *History of Parliament 1509–58* 1, pp. 634–8.

been forced to run the gauntlet of 'delusion and scorns' from Cranmer's servants: 'pardon me for ever delivering any letters unto him again', he sniffed in outrage.[86]

There is every sign that Cheyney pulled rank on the Archbishop and emerged triumphant from their encounter; he was, after all, a lifelong courtier, and had his own good links with Thomas Cromwell. He must have used these contacts, for instance, when only a couple of months later, he secured the grant of the dissolved nunnery of Minster in Sheppey; Cranmer himself had been tussling with him for a royal grant of this for more than a year, understandably anxious to acquire it since he had previously installed his sister Alice Cranmer as prioress there.[87] Trouble continued between the two magnates: during the mid-1540s there was an interminable lawsuit between them about their respective jurisdictions over rights of wreck on the coast.[88] In the reign of Edward VI, their rivalry probably lies behind the clash over the choice of MPs at Sandwich, which was virtually the only parliamentary borough where Cranmer could exercise any control over elections, and as late as November 1552 they were still at loggerheads.[89]

Indeed, in 1537 Cranmer (with his usual combination of disinterested zeal and political misjudgement) had chosen to throw his weight about, at a moment when his own temporal power in the county was about to be drastically weakened. The royal assault on the archbishopric estates, which had begun with their northern outliers in 1536, now extended to some of their greatest central properties, and Cheyney's jibe about 'foundations of ecclesiastical things' was probably an allusion to this. In the round of losses which was being discussed in summer 1537, three of the archbishopric's great houses, Otford, Knole and Maidstone, went. Otford Palace in particular had been rebuilt by Archbishop Warham at prodigious expense, and it was not just Cranmer's biggest residence but probably the biggest house in the realm – 'one of the wonders of Britain and beyond' in the words of a modern appreciation.[90] The original proposal had only included Otford and Maidstone, but Ralph Morice was an eyewitness of the sad incident in the autumn when the King on a mischievous whim decided to take Knole as well, after Cranmer had tried to talk down its charms in order to retain it for himself.[91] The exchange was formally completed on 30 November 1537: the Arch-

86 P.R.O., S.P. 1/125 f. 204 (*L.P.* 12 ii, no. 906, and cf. nos 907–8). Talbot was the keeper of the cathedral priory's park at Westwell: *L.P.* 13 ii no. 756.

87 P.R.O., S.P. 1/106 ff. 143–4 (*L.P.* 11 no. 418); *L.P.* 12 ii no. 1311/16.

88 P.R.O., STA.C. 2/9/35; *A.P.C.* 1, p. 549.

89 *History of Parliament* 1509–58 1, p. 262, 3, p. 109; Strype, *Cranmer*, p. 495 (Cox 2, p. 441).

90 Stoyel, 'Otford Palace', p. 261.

91 *Narratives of the Reformation*, p. 266. Cranmer was still only talking in terms of losing Maidstone and Otford on 31 August 1537: P.R.O., S.P. 1/124 ff. 130–31, Cox 2, p. 348 (*L.P.* 12 ii no. 600). Du Boulay, *Lordship of Canterbury*, pp. 323–5.

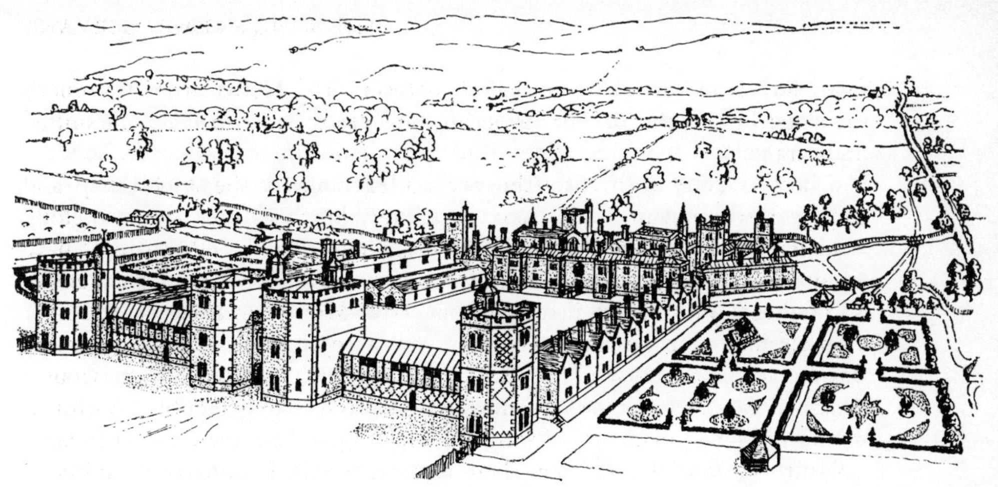

17 Conjectural reconstruction by A.D. Stoyel of Otford Palace, *c.* 1546, from the north-west, after alterations by Henry VIII.

bishop found himself in return the owner of a motley collection of lesser Kentish monastic estates and parish advowsons. At the same time came a further blow to archiepiscopal pride and prestige: Cranmer could no longer issue his own coins. His personal mint in the Close at Canterbury, an ancient privilege of his see, operative since he had first arrived in the city, seems to have closed down after a routine quality trial (the trial of the pyx) in December 1537, some years before the other ecclesiastical mints at Durham and York.[92]

There were consolations for the Archbishop amid these losses: there was a certain logic to the forced rearrangement. The royal grants to Cranmer included monastic houses which had been closely associated with the archbishopric for centuries, and he was still left with a set of four palaces, paired at either end of his normal axis of activity (Lambeth and Croydon, Canterbury and Ford). Although the programme of exchanges of Canterbury estates rolled on inexorably through the 1540s, the terms improved. As Ralph Morice pointed out in his defence of the Archbishop's policies, the exchanges were at least exchanges, at a time when 'other bishops some of them lost whole manors and lordships, withouten any exchange at all'. There was at least one substantial direct sale to the Crown, from which the archbishopric's hard-pressed finances benefited to the tune of £1200.[93] Moreover, in the 1545 phase of the Canterbury exchanges the Crown recognized their

92 Challis, *Tudor Coinage*, pp. 72–8; P.R.O., S.P. 1/126 ff. 222–3, Cox 2, pp. 357–8 (*L.P.* 12 ii no. 1168). NB the reference to the 'mint chamber' at Canterbury palace in the 1553 inventory, P.R.O., E. 154/2/39 f. 82v; however, see also the grant to Cardinal Pole of the former priory almonry building described as the former royal mint, *C.P.R. Philip and Mary* 1555–57, p. 482.

93 *L.P.* 18 i no. 258.

inequality, and provided the difference in cash.[94] The estates granted in exchange helped the concentration of lands conveniently for Cranmer's remaining palaces at the extremes of his jurisdiction at the far north, London and Croydon, and in the far south-east, around Canterbury: around them, in Morice's words, there was 'thrice so much meadow, pasture and marsh, than was left unto him' [by Warham], and Cranmer quickly rationalized their administration under close associates whom he trusted.[95] Finally in Edward VI's reign, at a time when many episcopal estates were coming under renewed pressure and many experienced very grave losses, the slimmed-down estate of the archbishopric suffered no further erosion: a remarkable achievement which must reflect Cranmer's enhanced political status in the Edwardian regimes.

Moreover, from 1537, for all his claims of financial innocence and obedience to the royal will, Cranmer began taking defensive measures to limit further damage. In a deliberate reversal of his earlier estate policy of allowing short leases only on his estates, on the advice of his team of experienced lawyers headed by James Hales, he put out his newly acquired properties on exceptionally long leases to one of his most trusted servants, his steward of household Richard Neville, to make sure that greedy courtiers would not be tempted to winkle them out of his possession.[96] He extended this new policy to his remaining ancient properties as well. One can note a sixty-year lease in 1538, fifty-year leases in 1541 and 1542, ninety-nine year leases in 1544 and 1550.[97] This was not an invariable policy: either some properties were regarded as more vulnerable than others, or occasionally the Archbishop tried to return to his earlier resolution. The year 1545 saw three much shorter leases: one of thirty years at Wingham to Cranmer's brother-in-law Henry Bingham, a twenty-one-year lease to his servant Robert Byllet, and another of thirty-two years. Similarly, there were two twenty-one-year leases in 1550, one to Ralph Morice, the Archbishop's secretary.[98]

Overall, however, the symbolism of the massive 1537 exchange for the archbishopric's position in Kent was still potent. The Archbishop's departure from his ancient estates did not appear to be much regretted by archiepiscopal

94 On the 1545 exchange, see P.R.O., E. 315/254 f. 115r–16r; *L.P.* 20 i no. 557 f. 74; P.R.O., E. 315/254 f. 116r; P.R.O., S.P. 1/204 f. 112 (*L.P.* 20 i no. 1259); cf. *L.P.* 21 i no. 149/6. Morice picked up this point about the later exchanges: *Narratives of the Reformation*, p. 267.

95 *Narratives of the Reformation*, p. 267; Du Boulay, *Lordship of Canterbury*, pp. 327–8.

96 *Narratives of the Reformation*, p. 265; Neville was inevitably from Nottinghamshire, not from the well-known Kentish Neville families. On St Gregory's Canterbury, see N. Stafford in *Antiquaries Journal* 70 (1990), p. 460, and on Dover, Churchill, *Canterbury Administration* 1, pp. 122–3.

97 *C.P.R. Elizabeth 1569–72*, no. 1112 (1550); *C.P.R. Elizabeth 1578–80*, nos 422, 423, 1733 (1538, 1541, 1542, 1544).

98 *C.P.R. Elizabeth 1575–78*, no. 819 (Bingham); *C.P.R. Elizabeth 1563–66*, no. 2126 (Byllet); *C.P.R. Elizabeth 1566–69*, no. 1551 (all these 1545). *C.P.R. Elizabeth 1566–69*, nos 564 (Morice), 1892 (Mantel).

tenants, if we are to believe Cromwell's servant Walter Hendley; the novelty value of being the King's tenants secured a record attendance at the first new sittings of the manorial courts in Knole, Otford and Maidstone in February 1538.[99] Indeed, Cranmer's lack of success in tackling Sir Thomas Cheyney reflected the fact that he had so far made little impression on the tightly knit world of Kent. The evangelical cause in Kent could already count on a number of influential native sympathizers among the laity: for instance, Sir Edward Wotton of Boughton Malherbe, who was a patron of Nicholas Partridge in Zürich, and thanks to him received the gift of a book from Bullinger in 1538. Nevertheless, the majority of the county leadership was still in the mindset of the Warham era.[100]

Only gradually did Cranmer build up useful links with evangelical gentry in Kent. His first major coup was to strike up a good relationship with the influential north Kent magnate George Lord Cobham, who much later proudly trumpeted his 'defence of the Gospel' on his tomb at Cobham; Cobham's brother, Thomas Brooke, joined Cranmer's household staff and married his niece, producing a son named Cranmer Brooke. Similarly, Edward Isaac of Well was a long-standing evangelical friend of Ralph Morice and Hugh Latimer, and he entered Cranmer's service in the 1530s.[101] Apart from these men, the most prominent Kentish name to stand out as a friend of Cranmer was Sir Edward Ringsley, of Knowlton near Dover, who made the Archbishop supervisor of his will in 1543, and who is frequently mentioned in Cranmer's correspondence.[102] Ringsley had influence in the town of Sandwich because of his property and at Calais through his office as Marshal and Controller, but in both places he may not have been the asset to Cranmer that he seemed: his relationship with Sandwich's leading men was tense, and he seems to have deserted the evangelicals of Calais in their hour of need in 1540, earning black marks from Foxe and other evangelical commentators to the extent of an accusation that he was illiterate.[103] During the 1530s, Brooke, Isaac and Ringsley were exceptional as local men who could genuinely be regarded as Cranmer clients. Otherwise the Archbishop very understandably

99 Bodl. MS Tanner 343, f. 38 (*L.P.* 13 i no. 195).

100 On Wotton, *E.T.* p. 397 (*O.L.*, p. 612). For a survey of Kentish politics in the 1530s, see Clark, *Kent*, pp. 34–56.

101 On Lord Cobham, P.R.O., S.P. 1/91 ff. 89–91, Cox 2, p. 301 (*L.P.* 8 no. 386), and on Thomas Brooke, P.R.O., S.P. 1/137 ff. 102–3, Cox 2, p. 330 (*L.P.* 13 ii no. 537); *Testamenta Vetusta*, p. 724. Isaac: *Sermons and Remains of Latimer*, pp. 221–4; P.R.O., S.P. 1/129 f. 76. Cox 2, p. 458 (*L.P.* 13 i no. 310).

102 *Testamenta Vetusta*, pp. 702–3; on Ringsley generally, see *Visitations of Kent 1530–1, 1574, 1592*, 2, p. 123; *Visitation of Kent 1619–21*, p. 39. For Cranmer's references: P.R.O., S.P. 3/2/80 (*Lisle Letters* 5, pp. 709–10); S.P. 1/123 f. 247, 1/128 ff. 176–7, 1/133 f. 174, 1/142 ff. 33–6 (Cox 2, pp. 316, 345, 361, 372, 387; *L.P.* 14 ii no. 537, 12 ii no. 473, 13 i nos. 171, 1237, 14 i no. 47).

103 On Sandwich, see Clark, *Kent*, pp. 13–14, and cf. Leland 4, p. 48; *Harpsfield's Visitation*, p. 26. Calais: Foxe 5, p. 516 and Janelle, 'Unpublished Poem', p. 93, although in both places he is styled 'Kingsley'.

continued to staff his household with imported evangelicals and trustworthy Midlands relatives and friends like Richard Neville.

Even the local structures of the Church offered Cranmer little scope decisively to infiltrate his own people into his diocese, outside his own household. He had been given some good opportunities by the Elizabeth Barton debacle at the beginning of his episcopate to clear out some of the Warham hierarchy and to put in his own brother as Archdeacon (see above, Ch. 4), but nothing very major emerged thereafter. He did make one notable appointment in 1538, when he looked beyond the veteran legal hierarchy of the province of Canterbury, to appoint as his diocesan commissary a bright young civil lawyer from Cambridge, Christopher Nevinson.[104] Nevinson was an enthusiastic evangelical who later married Cranmer's niece; he proved a faithful servant and one of the chief targets for Cranmer's enemies in 1543.[105] Yet it is significant how difficult the Archbishop found it to provide Nevinson with promotion which would provide the financial reward appropriate for such a trustworthy and sympathetic servant; he failed to get help via Cromwell, and Nevinson had to wait until a prebend in Wingham College became vacant through death in 1540 before the Archbishop could properly reward him.[106] By contrast, the wealth, power and patronage of Canterbury Cathedral Priory were in the hands of unsympathetic conservative clergy, who could be intimidated but, like most of the county gentry, could not be made enthusiastic for change. It would take time and patient work from the Archbishop, his officials and his clique of gentry sympathizers, to nurture Kent into one of the most promising strongholds of the evangelical cause.

Always in the background, too, there was the shadow of Calais, visible from the Kentish coast; many in Kent must have been aware of the none-too-discreet guerilla warfare which continued between John Butler, the Archbishop's commissary, and the conservative group of clergy and officials patronized by Lord and Lady Lisle.[107] And beyond the Lisles was yet another force, biding his time and through his Calais contacts keeping a wary eye on the process of change: the King's ambassador in France, Stephen Gardiner, an old friend of Lady Lisle's family. Just occasionally the surviving correspondence offers us glimpses of the Lisles' contacts with that episcopal champion of conservatism, and there was doubtless much more which was kept discreet.[108] There is rich symbolism in the different treatment meted out by the two prelates Cranmer and Gardiner to Lady Lisle's charming and outrageously spoiled son James Basset. Cranmer (and Cromwell) brusquely refused to co-

104 On Nevinson, Venn 3, p. 244. His appointment: Cranmer's Register, f. 17, where unfortunately the month has been omitted in the date.

105 On the marriage, C.C.C.C. MS 128, p. 155 (*L.P.* 18 ii no. 546, pp. 329–30).

106 P.R.O., S.P. 1/153 ff. 110–11, Cox 2, pp. 394–5 (*L.P.* 14 ii no. 146); Cranmer's Register, f. 375v.

107 On this, cf. e.g. P.R.O., S.P. 1/122 ff. 214–15 (*L.P.* 12 ii no. 231); *Lisle Letters* 4, pp. 156–7.

108 Cf. e.g. *Gardiner's Letters*, pp. 57, 62, 75–6, 79, 81.

operate with any scheme to find Basset a cure of souls which would provide him with a comfortable and completely undeserved little niche in the Church; Gardiner took him on as a gentleman retainer in his household. Basset became one of Gardiner's most devoted servants, and eventually married Sir Thomas More's granddaughter.[109] No wonder the miniature religious histrionics in Calais were the object of such constant concern to the Archbishop and the Vice-gerent.

One belligerent Kentish conservative, in April 1537, claimed that he and his fellows were sworn by all the justices of the peace to present evangelicals ('new fellows') for indictment at the county quarter sessions. Many Kentish JPs no doubt felt that the Archbishop would have merited inclusion in such presentments.[110] When humble evangelicals from the Wealden villages of Smarden and Pluckley were indeed indicted for unlawful assemblies at Canterbury sessions a year later, in spring 1538, Cranmer intervened on their behalf with Thomas Cromwell, lending a sympathetic ear to their claim that they were only indicted 'because they are accounted fautors [i.e. favourers] of the new doctrine, as they [i.e. conservatives] call it'.[111] Cheyney and his fellow-justices had evidently been not a whit abashed by Cranmer's attack in the autumn. The Archbishop's inconclusive confrontations in 1537–8 marked the end of a period where the debacle of the Maid of Kent's overthrow left local conservatives in disarray, and their hostility to him grew rather than diminished. During the late 1530s and 1540s, polarization mounted in the county, to reach crisis point in 1543. In that year, all the conservative forces to which we have drawn attention, within the county and beyond it, up to and including Stephen Gardiner, did their best to get their revenge on the man whom Henry styled with black humour 'the greatest heretic in Kent' (see below, Ch. 8).

While Cranmer was thus busy in Kent, poor Bishop Foxe was not being allowed to bask in Latimer's praise for his diligence over the Bishops' Book, but was stuck in London through the whole summer of 1537. He was still hammering the text into shape in late August, harassed by the disruption which the plague in the capital was causing, and by the problems of printing a text which kept growing with late last thoughts; no doubt some of the 'Observations' appended to the text in each section of the work were partly responsible.[112] Unlike Cromwell's success with the Bible licence, Foxe picked the wrong moment to get a satisfactory public endorsement from the King to preface the book, and in the end it was issued merely with a letter to Henry signed by the members of the drafting committee. The surviving draft of the King's response demonstrates why it was eventually not used: it is a

109 On Basset's marriage, *Visitations of Kent 1530–1, 1574, 1592*, 2, p. 26. On the benefice affair, *Lisle Letters* 3, pp. 510–11; 4, pp. 285, 289.

110 P.R.O., E. 36/120 f. 10 (*L.P.* 12 i no. 957).

111 P.R.O., S.P. 1/131, ff. 239–41 (*L.P.* 13 i no. 865).

112 25 August 1537: *St.P.* 1, p. 562 (*L.P.* 12 ii no. 578).

lukewarm document admitting that Henry had not got round to reading the whole volume, but saying that he would allow the printing of it on trust since the compilers were 'men of such learning and virtue, as we know you to be'.[113] Nevertheless, Cranmer exploited the King's letter when he issued the mandates about prohibited holy days for the peculiars of his diocese on 10 September; he tacked on an instruction echoing Henry's command that portions of the Bishops' Book should be read as sermons, week by week, when it appeared.[114]

The text of the Bishops' Book was indeed designed (albeit with little oratorical skill) to be read as sermons. It represents an important stage in the development of a new idea: the issuing of a collection of official sermons or homilies to guide the beliefs of the nation. This was a strategy which Cranmer and Cromwell had been considering for the last few years. In 1534 royal instructions provided detailed guidance for what priests should say in their bidding of the bedes, that is the English prayers led in the mass by the priest from the pulpit; to these instructions (which had traditional precedent) was appended for the first time a long sprawling text which was intended as material for an unstructured sermon.[115] This dealt with very limited political topics, the royal marriage and the break with Rome, and a chance to provide sermon material on wider doctrinal questions had been ducked in 1536: as we have seen (above, p. 162), the first version of the Ten Articles was also conceived as a brief collection of homilies before the Articles had been systematized on the itemized confessional model of the Continental reformations. In England the policy of issuing sermons culminated in Cranmer's supervision of a full-scale official book of homilies in 1547. The Church of Rome in England later followed suit, when Bishop Bonner published a similar collection during Mary's reign, and on a universal scale the Council of Trent ordered in 1566 that the Tridentine Catechism should be used in the same way, just as had been intended with the Bishops' Book.[116]

Cranmer's mandate of 10 September shows the Bishops' Book had still not then appeared; it can only have come out at the end of the month. Even after its publication, its status remained unhappily vague, and an atmosphere of indecision and unfinished business hung around it: this probably accounts for Cromwell's failure to issue an order for systematic nationwide catechizing using the book, a paper draft of which survives.[117] On 23 November the Dean

113 Cox 2, pp. 469–70 (*L.P.* 12 ii no. 618).

114 *L.P.* 12 ii no. 703, and Cox 2, pp. 348–9. For a Kentish example of reading it as late as 1548, see Woodruff, 'Extracts from original documents', p. 100.

115 Versions of 1534 text in C.C.C.C. MS 106, pp. 119–22, or Burnet 3 ii, p. 77 (Bk 2 no. 29), Cox 2, p. 460. On this, see above, p. 124 n133, and generally on bidding the bedes, Brightman, *English Rite*, pp. 1020–45.

116 Constant, 'Formularies of Faith', p. 163. See below, p. 224, however, for a refutation of the suggestion that Cranmer was writing homilies in 1539.

117 Tudor, 'Unpublished draft injunctions', with text from P.R.O., S.P. 6/6/20 at pp. 216–17.

of Stoke-by-Clare College, Matthew Parker, a rising evangelical star, wrote to a conservative opponent refusing to use the book as the touchstone for debating doctrine, despite its many virtues, 'until I see it have his [i.e. the King's] full perfection; which yet I know it lacketh'. Parker described it as still lacking the 'agletts' or finishing touches.[118] Others less well-disposed towards the evangelical cause seized on the undoubted ambiguities in the book's laboured presentation; one aspect of Cranmer's Kentish row with Sir Thomas Cheyney was the Archbishop's fury when, after his months of hard work on the book, he heard that Cheyney's entourage had been openly talking about it as if it overturned the Ten Articles and restored 'all things . . . to their old use, both of ceremonies, pilgrimages, purgatory and such other'. This provoked him to the strongest language: he said that he was tempted to proceed against such people 'as against heretics'.[119]

However, there were more serious travails in store for the Bishops' Book than mischievous interpretation by conservatives. Henry VIII had been speaking nothing less than the truth when he said that he had not finished reading the drafts of the book; probably the vital pregnancy of Jane Seymour, on which he was pinning so many hopes, had been distracting him throughout the spring and summer. That pregnancy ended with the birth on 12 October of a son, the legitimate male heir whom Henry had sought for so long: reason enough for his attention to remain elsewhere than the Bishops' Book. Prince Edward's christening three days later was deliberately staged as a new beginning to heal old unhappy memories of past royal marital entanglements: the godparents included the remarkable assortment of Cranmer and the Lady Mary, plus more predictably the two dukes of Norfolk and Suffolk. Also playing prominent roles were old nobility, the Earl of Essex and Marchioness of Exeter, alongside the newly ennobled Edward Seymour, and even the Boleyns were represented by that spent force, the Earl of Wiltshire, and by a cameo performance from the four-year-old Lady Elizabeth bearing the chrisom cloth. Yet this happy scene at Hampton Court, and the subsequent national rejoicing, was shatteringly interrupted by the acute post-natal illness of the Queen, which ended in her death ten days after the christening. Her Windsor funeral on 12 November and her London obsequies were entirely traditional, even though Cranmer presided and Latimer preached at Windsor; one would expect nothing else for a queen who had only four months before been named as one of the chief recipients for the prayers of the King's newly founded nunnery at Stixwold.[120]

118 *Parker Correspondence*, p. 12. This letter has often been misdated, but can only be of autumn 1537 because of this reference to 'the bishops' determinations'.

119 Cox 2, p. 351.

120 *Wriothesley's Chronicle*, 1, pp. 66–71; *L.P.* 12 ii no. 911. On Stixwold, see above, n. 69. It is difficult to make anything of the coincidence for Cranmer of this refoundation on the site of the house where his sister had been sacristan. Henry went on to refound an abbey at Bisham to pray for Jane's soul: *L.P.* 12 ii no. 1311/22.

Henry's grief for Jane was deep and genuine, but typical of the man was that his worldly desolation drove him back to contemplate theology. This was the time to finish considering the work of the bishops which he had neglected earlier in the year, and during November and December he set grimly to work scribbling improvements in the margins of the printed text of his personal copy of the Bishops' Book; this still exists, famously prefixed with the stern warning on the flyleaf that it must not be taken out of the Privy Chamber.[121] His notes extended to every part of the text except the section on purgatory, which had in any case been taken over wholesale in the Bishops' Book from the Ten Articles.[122] The accumulated royal amendments were transcribed onto other printed copies with occasional manuscript interleavings where the King's thoughts had taken wings; these were sent out for the comments of three individuals (Cranmer, Sampson the Bishop of Chichester and the common lawyer Christopher St German), plus a team headed by Nicholas Heath and presumably drawn from the former compilers. It was a typical piece of Henrician balance as Cranmer had described to Capito: Cranmer and the Heath team represented the evangelical viewpoint in their observations. Sampson and St German made up the conservative side, even though St German could be his own man, particularly in his comments on ecclesiastical jurisdiction, which were no doubt the main justification for including him.[123] Other commentators involved, to judge from a memorandum of Cromwell's about 'determinations' on the Ten Commandments, justification and purgatory, included George Day, Thomas Thirlby and John Skip: again, a varied theological selection. No one could accuse the King of selling his realm short when he decided its doctrine.[124]

Cranmer got his copy of the book in mid-January 1538 and kept his promise of making a response within a fortnight: with the courtesy of an accomplished teacher of a difficult (not to say dangerous) pupil, he accompanied his remarks with various urbane apologies:

> I trust the King's Highness will pardon my presumption, that I have been so scrupulous, and as it were a picker of quarrels to his Grace's book, making a

121 Bodl. Quarto Rawlinson 245.

122 By contrast, Henry spent a long time considering the fate of souls in purgatory some time in 1538 after he had received back the comments from Cranmer and the others: see discussion in Kreider, *Chantries*, pp. 134–7.

123 The text of the abridged and consolidated comments from these four sources survives in B.L. Royal MS 7 C XVI, ff. 199–210 (*L.P.* 13 i no. 142). It contains folio numbers relating to the printed copy of the text, as does C.C.C.C. MS 104 from p. 250, although unfortunately Cox's edition of the latter does not note these. NB also the references to material 'in fo. script.' as opposed to printed pages, C.C.C.C. MS 104, pp. 253, 264, 267, and B.L. Royal MS 7 C XVI, f. 209v. For the reference to St German's extended comments on the section on orders, see B.L. Royal MS 7 C XVI, f. 205r. For summary discussion, see Kreider, *Chantries*, pp. 132–4.

124 *L.P.* 12 ii no. 1122 ii: a remembrance written on the back of an Italian letter of 24 November 1537.

great matter of every light fault, or rather where no fault is at all; which I do only for this intent, that because the book now shall be set forth by his Grace's censure and judgement, I would have nothing therein that Momus could reprehend: and yet I refer all mine annotations again to his Grace's most exact judgement.[125]

Thus covered, he could proceed with a fairly ruthless critique of some amateurish royal doctrine-making.[126] Cranmer was on his home academic and doctrinal territory here: there is nothing craven or pussy-footing as he criticizes Henry's theological premises, his use of logic and even his grammar and style. The connoisseur of English was frequently offended: 'the preter tense may not conveniently be joined with the present tense', he rasped at one point. At another, the man who was an habitual constructor of paired nouns with a literary purpose deprecated this usage when there was no need for it: 'It is small difference between "cure" and "charge", but that the one is plain English, and the other is deducted out of the Latin.'[127] The surviving transcripts of the other participants' comments, which were combined with Cranmer's in a secretary's abridgement for the King, show that they too were capable of standing up to Henry. At one point, all the clerics achieved a rare moment of unity in condemning the obscurity of a particularly inept added phrase, while Heath's team had a number of criticisms of their own.[128] However, taking advantage of the old intimacy between the two men, Cranmer was far more confrontational with the King than his colleagues, and he also wrote at much greater length, to the despair of the abridger who when confronted with a 'long process' repeatedly referred the King back to the Archbishop's original text.

These 'long processes' opened with the Archbishop's own English translation of the Apostles' Creed, which impressed Henry, and which Cranmer later used virtually unaltered in the *Book of Common Prayer*.[129] But the material after this is even more valuable and deserves detailed consideration: Cranmer for the first time gives extended unambiguous statements of the heart of his evangelical theology, rather than the glimpses which for instance we have found in his exchanges with Sir Thomas Cheyney. The subjects which excited him to extended theological essays for the King's benefit were those at the heart of Luther's quarrel with the old Church: the contrast between two

125 B.L. Cotton MS Cleopatra E. V, f. 110, Cox 2, p. 359 (*L.P.* 13 i no. 141); the previous letter is P.R.O., S.P. 1/128 ff. 92–3, Cox 2, pp. 358–9 (*L.P.* 13 i no. 78).

126 C.C.C.C. MS 104, pp. 241–69, Cox 2, pp. 83–114.

127 C.C.C.C. MS 104, pp. 248, 252, Cox 2, pp. 86, 94.

128 Cf. B.L. Royal MS 7 C XVI, f. 200rv and C.C.C.C. MS 104, p. 249, Cox 2, p. 88: 'And shall continue as long as the world lasteth'. For examples of Heath's criticisms: B.L. Royal MS 7 C XVI, f. p. 199v on 'suffereth'; on 'before my reconciliation' B.L. Royal MS 7 C XVI, f. p. 200v, and cf. Cox 2, p. 88; on 'and so dying can not be saved', B.L. Royal MS 7 C XVI, f. 203v.

129 C.C.C.C. MS 104, p. 241, Cox 2, p. 83. Cf. Kreider, *Chantries*, p. 133.

opposed schemes of salvation. On the one hand was the Lutheran picture of humanity fallen in the disobedience of Adam, helpless and totally under condemnation until given the grace of God through faith; on the other was the prevailing late medieval view of a Christian life in which the contrite human will was capable of co-operating with God towards an individual's salvation, by the performance of good works. Repeatedly Henry revealed his wish to move the statements in the Bishops' Book back towards this late medieval view of the co-operation of the human will with God: where he found a statement of belief that a human was 'right inheritor' of the kingdom of God, he wanted to add to it 'as long as I persevere in his precepts and laws'. Where he found the statement 'we may attribute all unto thy godly will', it became 'we may attribute all to our desert'.[130]

Cranmer was having none of this. Very early on, in the fourth of his eighty-six comments, he tried to establish a ground-rule for the rest of his annotations: it was not necessary to speak, as Henry so repetitively desired to speak, of doing one's duty in relation to God, for the basic reason that the Bishops' Book 'speaketh of the pure Christian faith unfeigned'. The first presupposition of this faith was that the receiver of faith 'converteth from his sin: repenteth him that he like *filius prodigus* [the Prodigal Son] vainly consumed his will, reason, wits, and other goods, which he received of the mere benefit of his heavenly Father, to his said Father's displeasure'. Whatever good works one performed were good only because they proceeded from the once-for-all gift from God of 'very pure Christian faith and hope'. That faith should not be confused with mere intellectual assent to the propositions of Christianity, which he pointed out (in a deliberate change to James's Epistle) was a faith available to 'all devils *and wicked Christian people*'.[131] From pure faith flowed the compulsion to do good works, but they were an effect and never a cause of that great transforming act of God: justification. All was the work of God, and it was a work which could never either be reversed or improved upon by human effort. As Cranmer put it later in his series of essays, the justified man knew 'that before justification his doings were naught, nor consonant unto equity'. Pure faith involved a recognition that all human works previously performed fell into this category of wasted effort. Later still, Cranmer hammered home the essential message of his evangelical faith, when he tore apart Henry's suggested phrase 'having assured hope and confidence in Christ's mercy, willing to enter into the perfect faith'. This made no sense to him: faith was itself the assurance of Christ's mercy:

> he that hath assured hope and confidence in Christ's mercy, hath already entered into a perfect faith, and not only hath a will to enter into it. For perfect faith is nothing else but assured hope and confidence in Christ's mercy.[132]

130 C.C.C.C. MS 104, pp. 242, 259, Cox 2, p. 106.

131 C.C.C.C. MS 104, pp. 242–3, Cox 2, pp. 84–5. My italics draw attention to Cranmer's editing of James 2.19.

132 C.C.C.C. MS 104, p. 267, Cox 2, pp. 112–13.

Behind this doctrine of the all-sufficiency of Christ's mercy for salvation lurked a still larger issue: the all-powerful role of God in salvation. If humanity played no part in its own salvation, then every decision about the destiny of individuals in the afterlife was in the hands of God; in other words, everyone was predestined or elected to salvation or damnation. We have already noted Cranmer's significant extension of James's phrase about the devils' faith to include 'wicked Christian people': the visible Christian Church included the damned as well as the saved. Later, when criticizing an amendment of the text by Henry VIII, 'following Christ's steps, or when we fall repent our fault', Cranmer roundly declared that 'the elect, of whom is here spoken, will follow Christ's precepts, and repentance after falling', so the amendment was meaningless. He wanted the insertion at this point in the text of a mention of the elect.[133]

The mature Cranmer was a predestinarian; he had left far behind the free will theology of Erasmus, which once he had admired (see above, pp. 30). This should not in itself surprise us. Any theologian who reads Augustine or begins meditating on the theme of the grace and majesty of God is liable to be driven to the logic of the doctrine in considering a scheme of salvation: theologians on both sides of the Reformation gulf which opened up in sixteenth-century Western Christianity acknowledged God's overarching control of human destiny, Ignatius Loyola as much as John Calvin. Within the developing Protestant tradition to which Cranmer was now contributing, predestination was a necessary corollary of the thinking of Martin Luther on grace and faith, and it was already one of the root assumptions of the main reformers of central Europe (especially Martin Bucer and Peter Martyr) before Calvin assumed his dominant role among the Swiss.[134] From the seventeenth century, majority opinion in the Church of England echoed the distaste for Calvin and all his works which is first prominent in the writings of one of England's greatest theologians, Richard Hooker, so this essential fact about the author of the Prayer Book was thrust into obscurity. It is no coincidence that G.W. Bromiley's monograph on the theology of a sweetly reasonable and Anglican Thomas Cranmer has no reference to predestination in its index.

Cranmer may not have talked much about predestination, for the reason which he embodied in what became the Thirty-Nine Articles: it was not a subject about which one should become obsessed. Yet the margins of his books testify to his deep interest in predestination, and in particular, to his anxiety to find the expression of the doctrine in the early Fathers of the Church. It is predictably in the writings of Augustine of Hippo, particularly his anti-Pelagian tracts, and in Augustine's *plus royaliste que le roi* admirer

133 C.C.C.C. MS 104, p. 250, Cox 2, p. 92.

134 On Bucer's views, Stephens, *Holy Spirit in Bucer*, Ch. 1. Bromiley's silence on predestination can result in some comic misreadings of Cranmer's outlook: cf. Bromiley, *Cranmer, Theologian*, p. 67.

Prosper of Aquitaine, that we find Cranmer's assiduously repeated note '*predestinatio*'.[135] When reading Cranmer's comments on the doctrinal formulations of the Church of England, King Henry could not have hoped to hear a clearer exposition of the once-for-all character of justification by faith, controlled by the logic of predestination, than he did in Cranmer's annotations.

Yet Cranmer's urgent words fell on deaf ears. He could prevail with Henry on points of grammar, but he could not now, or indeed ever, win him from his steadfastly traditional view of human life as a progress towards God through the steady performance of God's commands. By contrast, it was noticeable, and in accordance with Henry's self-image as the mediator standing between opposites, that the King could be won over by the rare cross-party alliances in criticism between Cranmer and Sampson, and be persuaded into abandoning his wilder flights of fancy. One example of this came in an amusing tussle over the status of marriage. Already the compilers of the Bishops' Book had pandered to Henry's almost neurotic reverence for marriage by emphasizing the convenient commonplace of devotional teaching that it outranked the sacraments instituted in the New Testament in terms of antiquity, being in existence 'from the beginning of the world'.[136] Now Henry wanted to improve on this: in his alterations he wanted matrimony moved from the minor league to the major league sacraments, bracketing it with baptism, eucharist and penance, rather than with confirmation, orders and unction. Cranmer brutally pointed out that if this were so, it would have to conform to the stated criteria for the major sacraments, including the stipulation that it was necessary for salvation! Sampson rather nervously had to agree, even though he hastened to add that 'it seemeth that . . . matrimony is a very high sacrament'. That was the last to be heard of matrimony's chances of promotion.

Similarly, the King's attempt to edit God's prose, by adding his own words to the first of the Ten Commandments, got short shrift from both Canterbury and Chichester, although Sampson was less schoolmasterly in his criticism.[137] Together they also successfully beat off Henry's endearingly courtier-like attempt to remove criticism of tales, songs, 'gay and wanton apparel', 'surfeiting, sloth, idleness, immoderate sleep'. However, their pincer movement on this alteration was justified by significantly different criteria: Cranmer because these scandals were specifically condemned in the New Testament, Sampson on the pragmatic grounds that they were 'common occasions and furtherances of great offences'.[138] These five-way conversations

135 Cf. marginalia in Cranmer's 1531/2 Paris edition of Augustine, B.L. C.79.i–x, especially vols 4 and 7, and his 1539 Lyon Prosper, B.L. 3623 e.18, esp. pp. 90f.

136 Lloyd, *Formularies*, p. 86.

137 C.C.C.C. MS 104, p. 255, Cox 2, pp. 99–100; B.L. Royal MS 7 C XVI, f. 205v–206r. On matrimony, cf. the text of *Necessary Doctrine*, f. 44v.

138 C.C.C.C. MS 104, p. 259, Cox 2, p. 105; B.L. Royal MS 7 C XVI, f. 207v. For another example of their successful combined criticism on 'without due recompense', see ibid. and B.L. Royal MS 7 C XVI, f. 208r.

had a direct effect in shaping the second extended statement of doctrine in Henry's reign, the King's Book or *Necessary Doctrine and Erudition for any Christian Man*.

The first stage of revision was for Henry to round up what he had chosen from his experts' comments in yet another annotated copy of the Bishops' Book, which survives in the British Library's Royal Manuscripts.[139] Yet after all this meticulous activity, politics and diplomacy intervened to delay the final consideration and publication of a fully developed new statement for another five years, until 1543. For the moment, the Bishops' Book stood as the main propositions of the Henrician Church's doctrine, which would certainly have suited Cranmer and his ally the Vice-gerent. During 1538 they had a further chance to shift England into alignment with the Continental evangelicals. In January 1538, the King of France and the Holy Roman Emperor ended eighteen months of destructive war with a truce, always an event which made Henry VIII nervous, and the truce ripened into a full-scale peace in the summer. Afraid as ever of diplomatic isolation, Henry was also deeply apprehensive that the prospect of the General Council repeatedly postponed by the Pope might actually materialize.

Deploying the arts of peace as well as war, Henry plunged into a whirlwind of offers of marriage alliances to the French and the Empire; the King was, after all, a desirable widower, and the Lady Mary was also eminently marriageable. Cranmer was among those drafted in to talk to Chapuys about one of the most important of these schemes in late March 1538, but together with the whole English delegation that day, he knew that Chapuys was soon in for an unpleasant shock: secretly, the King and Cromwell were completing arrangements for detailed discussions with the Lutheran princes of Germany and Scandinavia. In fact (although Chapuys did not discover this), Henry had been seeking a new embassy from the Schmalkaldic League as early as summer 1537, and by the end of that year a Saxon ambassador was making plans for a wider embassy from Germany. In 1538, a month before the meeting with Chapuys, England's trusted agent in Germany Christoff Mont had been commissioned to open negotiations with the Elector of Saxony and the Landgraf of Hesse.[140] Cranmer's modest but significant part in preparing the ground at Court was to supply the King with an English translation of a German tract by Martin Luther on the Donation of Constantine, that ancient forgery of proof for the Pope's temporal power. The Archbishop sent this up to Henry from Kent on 16 February 1538, drawing his attention in his own hand to a passage in the manuscript in which Luther ridiculed the Pope's claim to be Lord of England. Luther went on to tell the story of the miserable end which had befallen Boniface VIII for his attempt to depose the King of

139 B.L. Royal MS 17 C XXX: for discussion, see Kreider, *Chantries*, pp. 133–8.

140 Cf. especially *C.S.P. Spanish 1536–8*, no. 223, pp. 522–7 (*L.P.* 13 i no. 756); McEntegart Ph.D., 'England and the League of Schmalkalden', pp. 190–216. On Henry's marriage proposals, see Scarisbrick, *Henry VIII*, pp. 355–61.

France. The English title of the pamphlet adroitly also drew attention to Luther's remarks about the proposed Council of Mantua: all this was nicely calculated to neutralize Henry VIII's habitual suspicion of the Wittenberg reformer.[141]

Simultaneously Cromwell, at the height of his influence, used his power to create an atmosphere of evangelical triumph in the capital and the south-east generally. Most spectacularly, from January onwards he spearheaded a campaign to destroy statues, roods and sacred objects to which cults were attached, provoking some spontaneous iconoclasm in the process; equally alarming for traditionalists was the official toleration of other examples of direct action by evangelicals, such as church services in the vernacular and open examples of clerical marriage (on this, Cranmer kept his counsel).[142] As so often in Henry's reign, the prevailing religious atmosphere was advertised by judicial murder, in this case an outspoken former partisan of Catherine of Aragon, the Observant friar John Forest; Cranmer and Latimer acted as a team on Cromwell's behalf in the proceedings which led to the friar's destruction.[143] Forest was roasted alive with unusually grotesque barbarity on 22 May, on heresy charges which amounted to the orthodoxy of a decade before; we have already heard Cranmer uninhibitedly terming traditional belief heresy when writing to Cheyney, while the Archbishop was always careful to avoid using the word for evangelicals who overstepped the mark. We have also noted Cranmer's particular hatred for the Observants, as the most effective champions of the religion which by now he regarded as a wicked confidence trick; Forest made matters worse for himself by not co-operating with the customary theatre surrounding his execution. As a result, there is a disconcerting savagery especially in Latimer's dealings with the doomed friar during April and May.[144] The burning in the presence of various dignitaries including Cranmer and Cromwell was a deeply symbolic occasion, a perfect expression of the Vice-gerent's campaign; Forest was burnt along with a wonder-working wooden image from Wales, and before the fire was lit, Latimer preached a long and bitter sermon against idolatry, one of his favourite themes.[145] He seems to have felt that he had done a good job for the evangelical cause; others may disagree.

The Germans were naturally delighted by the English diplomatic approaches. The joint delegation which they sent to England arrived on 27 May, less than a week after Forest's destruction, and was charged with the goal of securing the diplomatic and doctrinal agreement which had eluded

141 P.R.O., S.P. 1/129 ff. 64–5 (*L.P.* 13 i no. 297); the tract is now B.L. Royal MS 17 C XI, and cf. especially ff. 14v–15r.

142 Brigden, *London*, pp. 289–91; *Wriothesley's Chronicle* 1, p. 83.

143 On Forest, K. Brown in Gunn and Lindley (eds), *Wolsey*, p. 230; NB particularly his demolition of the idea that Forest had been Catherine of Aragon's confessor.

144 P.R.O., S.P. 1/131 ff. 32–3, Cox 2, pp. 364–5; *Sermons and Remains of Latimer*, pp. 391–3 (*L.P.* 13 i nos. 687, 1024); *Wriothesley's Chronicle* 1, p. 78.

145 Bodl. MS Ashmole 861 p. 335; *Wriothesley's Chronicle* 1, p. 80.

Foxe in 1535–36.[146] It was not quite as star-studded as Henry would have liked; he was still pursuing his ambition of meeting Melanchthon, the acceptable face of Lutheranism. The Germans were anxious to keep their premier league theologians at home in case of the summoning of a General Council, so Henry had to be content with some warm flattery from the great man. The embassy which came to him, distinguished enough in its way, consisted of Franz Burchard, vice-chancellor to the Duke of Saxony, the Hessian scholar-aristocrat Dr Georg von Boineburg and the superintendent of the Lutheran church in Gotha, Friedrich Myconius; Myconius thus shared with Simon Grynaeus the distinction of being the only Continental Protestant divine of any reputation to come face to face with Henry VIII.[147] There was a prompt and business-like start to the mission: the first meetings with Cranmer and Cromwell were full of warmth and optimism. The following day (2 June) Cranmer acted as chief English spokesman at a meeting with the King and Privy Council, although Henry did much of the talking himself. It was agreed to transfer discussions to Lambeth Palace under Cranmer's chairmanship to iron out theological difficulties.[148]

So far, so good; the atmosphere seemed perfect for progress, and Myconius wrote home enthusiastically praising Latimer and Cranmer and describing the great potential of the English religious situation, especially the beginnings made with evangelical preaching and the favourable reception which he saw for it in London. Thereafter, there were curious hesitations. It was only on 13 June that Cranmer wrote to Cromwell about receiving the ambassadors at Lambeth, and then it was to excuse himself from offering them hospitality because of his lack of provision at the palace.[149] This was symptomatic of a curiously lackadaisical attitude to planning which ran through the whole visit, and which increasingly infuriated the Germans. One cannot imagine Cromwell allowing things to drift in this way if he was closely involved, but he seems to have had virtually no part in the discussions, leaving no trace in the surviving discussion papers. It is likely that he was distracted from his normal meticulous preparations by the looming power struggle with his conservative enemies at Court centred on the Courtenay family: the rash of arrests and imprisonments in the so-called 'Exeter conspiracy' began in August, and the destruction of the Courtenays and Poles would in the end

146 *L.P.* 13 i nos 352–3, 367; for a narrative, cf. Tjernagel, *Henry VIII and the Lutherans*, pp. 180–82, but for a definitive treatment, McEntegart Ph.D., 'England and the League of Schmalkalden', pp. 219–85.

147 Melanchthon's letter pr. Strype, *Ecclesiastical Memorials* 1 ii no. 94, pp. 383–4 (*L.P.* 13 i no. 985).

148 McEntegart Ph.D., 'England and the League of Schmalkalden', pp. 226–30, quoting report by Burchard.

149 Report by Myconius of June 1538, qu. McEntegart Ph.D., 'England and the League of Schmalkalden', p. 233. Cranmer to Cromwell, P.R.O., S.P. 1/133, f. 28 (*L.P.* 13 i no. 1176), and cf. a similar plea by Bishop Sampson, P.R.O., S.P. 1/133, f. 250 (*L.P.* 13 I no. 1295, undated).

represent one of Cromwell's most spectacular political triumphs. However, his neglect of the German negotiations had serious consequences for the prospects of evangelical alliance.[150]

The emphasis in the Lambeth discussions with the Germans was theological: Burchard himself was no mean theologian, and the inclusion of Myconius, one of the Lutherans' leading churchmen, was significant. While in London a clerical member of the delegation, almost certainly Myconius, preached regularly at the Austin Friars, clearly thanks to Cromwell, whose London residence was in the friary precinct: it was an extraordinary development that a German Lutheran should be an honoured guest preacher in one of the chief pulpits in the city of London.[151] The chronicler Wriothesley described the mission's purpose as 'to entreat of certain acts concerning the true setting forth of God's word and the good order of the spirituality'. The Germans secured Henry's permission to attach that stormy petrel of English Lutheranism, Dr Robert Barnes, to their delegation, but the English negotiators were a team of churchmen carefully chosen on Henry's usual principle for religious balance: besides Cranmer as chairman, and Nicholas Heath (still a reliable evangelical), they comprised the conservative Bishops Sampson and Stokesley, Dr George Day (from the group at St John's, Cambridge, which had once constituted John Fisher's admirers) and Dr Nicholas Wilson, a former partisan of Catherine of Aragon. As we will see, Bishop Tunstall also played a crucial role in the later stages of negotiations, although he was not part of the actual negotiating team. Henry had in fact from the beginning chosen more conservatives than evangelicals, presumably deliberately in order that the combination of Germans, Cranmer and Heath should be effectively counterbalanced.[152] In addition there was one key absentee on the English side, a devastating loss to the English evangelicals, given his previous achievements: Bishop Foxe had died on 8 May. Something of the shock of his death can be recovered from a letter to Cromwell from Jacobus Gislenus Thalassius, German protégé of Foxe and Cranmer, who was greeted with the news on his return to London from conversations with the Strassburg leadership: 'in vain were my labours, in vain the nights and days turning German books into Latin!', he lamented.[153] There was genuine grief mixed up

150 For discussion of the Exeter conspiracy, see Elton, *Reform and Reformation*, pp. 279–81. Cf. McEntegart Ph.D., 'England and the League of Schmalkalden', pp. 238–42, although I am sceptical about his speculation that Cromwell felt out of his depth in theological discussion.

151 *L.P.* 13 ii no. 232, p. 91: one might think that this reference to 'a priest who has come in their [the ambassadors'] suite' was to Robert Barnes, but there is another reference to the Germans preaching in England in German, ibid. no. 277, p. 112.

152 *Wriothesley's Chronicle* 1, p. 81; McEntegart Ph.D., 'England and the League of Schmalkalden', pp. 244–5. On Wilson, cf. Brigden, *London*, pp. 210, 223–4, 258, 309, 313, 330, 349, 398.

153 *L.P.* 13 i no. 1014. Thalassius wrote to Cromwell from Lambeth Palace. On his patronage from Cranmer, see also ibid., nos. 1514–15, although the latter is more likely to date from 1540.

with Thalassius's natural fears for his financial future. Foxe was not replaced in the Lambeth discussions, and Cranmer would have felt the effect of his skilled and faithful colleague's absence in negotiations which eventually led nowhere.

The spirit of Foxe nevertheless hovered over the proceedings, for as drafts of proposals emerged during July, much of their text resembled the Wittenberg Articles which he had brought back to England in 1536. The German delegates still felt pleased about the way things were going in late July, when despite the length of negotiations so far Burchard wrote to his master in optimistic mood, anticipating departure from England in no more than three weeks.[154] Since the primary source of the drafts produced by the negotiators was the Augsburg Confession, the conservative members of the English delegation seemed to have a tough job on their hands, fighting against an agenda which was being set by the evangelicals on both sides, including the Archbishop as chairman. Fight they did, after the relatively uncontroversial drafts on the nature of God, original sin and two natures of Christ: Myconius recorded the bitter disagreements which lay behind the fourth article drafted on Justification, the first item which touched on a really controversial matter, and which was one matter on which the conservatives won little or no ground.[155]

After the evangelicals had successfully held the line on this admittedly important matter, the conservatives began to have more success in what was becoming a rearguard action against the tide of evangelical theology. Their efforts show up in little slippages away from the Lutheran sources in the drafts on subsequent matters discussed: at one point Cranmer revealed his impatience with conservative successes by making a whole series of alterations to a fair copy of the highly contentious text of the draft article on penance, in which he downgraded the status of auricular confession from something 'indispensable' (*summe necessariam*) to 'very appropriate' (*commodissimam*) in the Christian life. The German ambassadors, in their own working papers, noted in despair over the article on penance that Cranmer had written down their agreements with him 'in his book', but thanks to the other English negotiators the matter remained unagreed, and Cranmer's alterations to the article on penance did not survive in the final version. Martin Luther was

154 McEntegart Ph.D., 'England and the League of Schmalkalden', p. 257, quoting Burchard to Johann Friedrich, Hessisches Staatsarchiv Marburg PA 2575 ff. 131–2. McEntegart Ph.D., ibid., pp. 255–6, n. 185, argues for dropping the concept of an agreed statement of 'Thirteen Articles' which has dominated accounts of these proceedings since the analysis by Henry Jenkyns of a set of drafts (*L.P.* 13 i nos 1307–8, best presented in *Documents of the English Reformation*, ed. Bray, pp. 184–221). His decisive point is that none of the documents in the negotiations bears a signature; there was never any agreement.

155 Rupp, *English Protestant Tradition*, p. 116; McEntegart Ph.D., 'England and the League of Schmalkalden', pp. 249–51, amid his useful discussion of the surviving drafts and the level of controversy which they indicate: ibid., pp. 246–55 generally.

furious when he eventually saw the resulting text.[156] Cranmer won on this very point about penance in the Six Articles only a year later, a lonely evangelical victory achieved with Henry VIII's help, but the King does not seem to have supported him on the matter in 1538 against conservative objections. Perhaps Henry was not consulted in the arguments about penance, but we certainly find him intervening in the drafting of another article, putting his pen to some egotistical tinkerings with the discussion of the nature of the Church.[157]

Cranmer found the attitude of his conservative colleagues infuriating, but he knew that he had no choice but to work with them; when the King wanted Stokesley called away from Lambeth on other business, the Archbishop commented gloomily to Richard Morison that he 'would in no wise it were so (albeit, he saith, they might do much better if he were away): men would talk, or at the least think evil if he should be taken from their assembly'.[158] He could have said the same about any of the tortuous meetings intended to resolve England's official doctrine during the 1530s, but there were especial tensions during the summer of 1538 which badly affected the Lambeth talks: the German delegates must have been bewildered by the poisonous atmosphere, which linked in to Cromwell's developing political struggle at Court against the Courtenays and Poles. Most of the evidence has been well hidden, but one aspect of it burst to the surface at Lambeth itself through yet another row in Calais, centring on the activities of the recently arrived priest and evangelical convert, Adam Damplip. In essentials, a complex dispute pitted Damplip against John Dove, the Prior of the Calais Whitefriars, who was acting as Lord Lisle's agent: John Butler, Cranmer's commissary, rescued Damplip from his local troubles and got him sent up to Lambeth in July for examination by Cranmer.[159]

Cromwell's close involvement in the fightback on Damplip's behalf is revealed by the survival of a set of interrogatories for Dove, which in turn have a wider importance: they questioned him about his links to the chief conservative spokesmen in the Lambeth negotiations with the Germans – Stokesley and Sampson, plus their close associate Tunstall. One question sounded particularly damaging for Stokesley: had he written to Lord Lisle saying that 'he prayed that all should not perish there [i.e. Calais] as it is lost here'?[160] Cromwell wrote a savage letter of reprimand to Lisle about the affair on 14 August: alas its content is only preserved in a seventeenth-century summary, but that shows that one of the chief causes of the Vice-gerent's

156 P.R.O., S.P. 1/134 ff. 29–32, Cox 2, pp. 476–7 (*L.P.* 13 i no. 1307.8); McEntegart Ph.D., 'England and the League of Schmalkalden', pp. 250–55.

157 Cox 2, p. 474 (*L.P.* 13 i no. 1307.3); McEntegart Ph.D., 'England and the League of Schmalkalden', pp. 248–9.

158 P.R.O., S.P. 1/133 f. 251v (*L.P.* 13 i no. 1296). The other business was probably Stokesley's imminent pardon for praemunire: Elton, *Policy & Police*, p. 161.

159 The story is told clearly by Slavin, 'Cromwell, Cranmer and Lord Lisle', pp. 325–33.

160 *L.P.* 13 ii no. 248.

anger was the fact that Lisle had not stopped rumours that Stokesley was about to become Vicar-General in Cromwell's place.[161] Most unusually, Cromwell sent this diatribe to the Deputy via Cranmer at Lambeth, obviously feeling it important to keep in step with the Archbishop about one of his long-standing problems. Cranmer was delighted when he read of Lisle's humiliation and the implied put-down to Stokesley, and dashed off a second letter in a day to Cromwell to express his appreciation: he needed something to cheer him up as the conservative bishops spun out the discussions at his palace.[162]

However, this evangelical success was at the same time being steadily and fatally neutralized far away from Lambeth and Whitehall. Rory McEntegart has noted the erratic form which King Henry's summer progress took during this year; from 13 July until 24 September he was constantly on the move outside London, mainly inspecting the southern ports. Cromwell did his best to keep in touch and talk to the King, but for the most part he was back in London.[163] In this situation, with Henry keeping a close interest in the progress of negotiations at Lambeth, who would be on hand in his itinerant Court to share his reactions to progress and discuss how to reply to the delegates' proposals? The only theological adviser with Henry happened to be Cuthbert Tunstall, abruptly summoned south at the end of June from his duties as President of the Council of the North and replaced there by Bishop Holgate of Llandaff. This seems to have been an initiative of the King himself, with the specific order that Tunstall should 'remain about his person'. Henry's motives in summoning Tunstall in this way can only be guessed at; if evangelicals thought that it was a sign of royal mistrust of this notorious conservative, they were sadly mistaken. His presence with the King was to prove disastrous for chances of any progress in the German negotiations, and by the autumn he had taken the place on the Privy Council occupied by Bishop Foxe until his death.[164]

The beginning of the decline in fortunes for the Anglo-German talks came with an initiative of the German delegates on 5 August, when in an effort to speed up the interminable negotiations, they summed up their conclusions so far in a long letter addressed to Henry. They asked for responses on three abuses which particularly worried them in the English Church: the upholding of compulsory clerical celibacy, the withholding of the chalice from the laity in the eucharist, and the maintenance of intercessory or private masses for the

161 Bodl. MS Jesus 74, f. 198v. Significantly, only three days after this letter was written, Stokesley surrendered valuable property at Wimbledon and elsewhere in Surrey to Cromwell! Cf. *L.P.* 13 ii no. 119.

162 P.R.O., S.P. 1/135 ff. 118–19, Cox 2, pp. 376–7 (*L.P.* 13 ii no. 127). Note Cranmer's use of 'also' in the first sentence, which puts this letter after the other letter of 18 August, Cox 2, pp. 377–8.

163 McEntegart Ph.D., 'England and the League of Schmalkalden', pp. 258, 281.

164 *L.P.* 13 i nos 1267–8; 13 ii no. 446; McEntegart Ph.D., 'England and the League of Schmalkalden', p. 288.

dead. Directly involving the King proved to be an unwise move. While continuing with his progress through southern England, Henry plunged with alarming energy into a reply to their work, with at every stage Bishop Tunstall on hand to act as a springboard for his thoughts: the result was a devastating and thorough dismissal of many of the Germans' chief concerns about the English Church, especially on communion in one kind only and clerical marriage.[165] Perhaps after this had been delivered to the Germans, Tunstall seems to have involved himself directly with the Lambeth discussions; this is suggested by a later memory of Richard Sampson, albeit one which is not entirely securely dated. When apparently reminiscing about the background to the 1538 arguments about the articles which touched on the sacraments and liturgy, he described how Cuthbert Tunstall armed himself with a Greek liturgical book and explained 'divers places there written for that purpose' to Sampson as they rowed across to Lambeth for the discussions. Tunstall emphasized that the world of Greek Orthodoxy was a possible non-Roman source of comfort for the conservatives. Stokesley too had shared his study of 'other books of Greek' with Tunstall. This interest of Tunstall's in the Greeks has an interesting probable echo in one passage of Henry's rebuttal of the Germans' arguments: the King brushed aside their assertion that the Greek churches held only one eucharist a week with the comment that few communicated at these eucharists, 'as we have learned from those worthy of credit, who themselves have been present at Greek services'. It is likely that this crowd of experts in Greek liturgical affairs amounted to Tunstall himself, reminiscing about his experience as academic and diplomat in central and southern Europe.[166]

Even before the King's reply was complete, the conservatives had continued to build on their earlier successful stonewalling over the article about penance, turning their participation in discussions into what amounted to a filibuster; Tunstall's presence and Henry's rebuff to the Germans' letter no doubt greatly stiffened their resolve. Despite working all summer and into the early autumn, the committee never reached formal agreements. The drafts of the first phase of negotiations remained drafts only; equally there was nothing agreed on the status of the four lesser sacraments which had been a bone of contention in England since 1536, and nothing on those abuses whose survival in the English Church had been worrying the Germans since the spring 1536 discussions: compulsory clerical celibacy and vows of monks and

165 For an excellent analysis of these moves, see McEntegart Ph.D., 'England and the League of Schmalkalden', pp. 258–69. The key documents are the 5 August letter, final version B.L. Cotton MS Cleopatra E V ff. 186–22 (*L.P.* 13 ii no. 37, pr. in full, Burnet 1 ii, pp. 473–94), and Henry's reply, B.L. Cotton MS Cleopatra E V ff. 228–38 (pr. in full, Burnet 1 ii, pp. 495–514).

166 For Sampson, Strype, *Ecclesiastical Memorials*, 1 ii, no. 93, p. 381; Sampson coupled these discussions with a reference to the Bishops' Book, but he is more likely to have been talking about 1538 than 1537. Henry: Burnet 1 ii, p. 504; cf. McEntegart Ph.D., 'England and the League of Schmalkalden', pp. 273–4.

others, the withholding of the chalice from the laity, and private masses. Although papers were drawn up on these latter subjects, and on others besides, Cranmer found that his episcopal colleagues on the committee simply refused to comment on them, claiming that they might end up contradicting the documents which the King had prepared in reply to the German letter of 5 August. 'I perceive that the bishops seek only an occasion to break the concord', he confided in exasperation to Cromwell.[167]

By the end of August the German delegates were weary of these interminable discussions, despite the Archbishop's strenuous efforts, on Cromwell's instructions, to stop them going home. Cranmer even tried emotional blackmail on them, in the course of what he told Cromwell had been 'long reasoning': he begged them 'to consider the many thousands of souls in England' who might be saved if they stayed on for a further month, an interesting comment on how he viewed the prospect of the Schmalkaldic alliance.[168] He also complained to Cromwell on the Germans' behalf that they had been given miserable lodgings in the city – perhaps their growing despondency made their surroundings increasingly depressing.[169] Cromwell's efforts to cheer them up by securing them warrants to hunt deer were no more than a partial success, because the theological wrangling took up too much of their time for any extended country trips; in any case, Myconius was seriously ill for the latter part of the discussions.[170] By 1 October the Germans had all left carrying no substantial achievement back with them, apart from yet another plea from Henry VIII for a greater embassy which this time would include Melanchthon.[171]

In one respect, however, the negotiations were associated with a document which had a great bearing on the future of the Church of England: Cranmer's first traceable experiment in changing the liturgy, evidently undertaken with Cromwell's warm encouragement. This was intended to produce a single ordered scheme for the services which the Church calls offices (that is, the daily recitation of prayer, praise and readings of scripture), to distinguish them from the eucharist. These offices are principally governed by a book

167 23 August 1538: B.L. Cotton MS Cleopatra E. V, f. 225, Cox 2, pp. 379–80 (*L.P.* 13 ii no. 164). Cranmer's drafts on the abuses are P.R.O., S.P. 1/134 ff. 41–53, Lambeth 1107 ff. 116f, Cox 2 pp. 480–85, *L.P.* 13 i no. 1307.16–17; he also drew up a paper on ministerial order, P.R.O., S.P. 1/134 ff. 63–78, Cox 2, pp. 484–9 (*L.P.* 13 i no. 1307.19). Cf. the German delegates' letters of 5 August, ibid. nos 37–8.

168 P.R.O., S.P. 1/135 ff. 116–17, Cox 2, pp. 377–8 (*L.P.* 13 ii no. 126); McEntegart Ph.D., 'England and the League of Schmalkalden', p. 280, qu. Burchard to Johann Friedrich, 23 August 1538, and cf. also his quotation of a report by Boineburg, ibid., p. 280.

169 B.L. Cotton MS Cleopatra E. V, f. 225, Cox 2, pp. 379–80 (*L.P.* 13 ii no. 164). Earlier the ambassadors had seemed pleased with their lodging: McEntegart Ph.D., 'England and the League of Schmalkalden', p. 224 n. 89.

170 Morison to Cromwell, undated: *L.P.* 13 i no. 1297: Myconius to Cromwell, Strype, *Ecclesiastical Memorials*, 1 ii, no. 95, pp. 384–5 (*L.P.* 13 ii no. 298).

171 *L.P.* 13 ii no. 497.

known as the breviary, of which several different versions or 'uses' had evolved in England (as elsewhere in the West) before the Reformation. Like the later Prayer Book, therefore, the object of Cranmer's revision was to produce uniformity in the worship of the English Church. The scheme survives in a manuscript which goes on to set out an entirely different scheme of breviary revision by Cranmer; that second scheme is much more conservative than the first.[172] Attempts by both successive modern editors of the manuscript to defy source-critical common sense, by suggesting that the second section of the manuscript predated the first, were effectively refuted by Charles Smyth.[173] The explanation for the retreat from innovation is simple: the first, more adventurous scheme belonged to the more adventurous late 1530s, the second, more cautious change, to the era of more cautious change in the mid-1540s. As will become apparent, the first revision was undertaken in 1538–9.

Cranmer's sources for his 1538–9 scheme were enterprisingly ecumenical. Like General Booth, he was determined that the devil (in the form of Antichrist) should not have all the best tunes: one basic source is the revised breviary by the Spanish Cardinal Francisco de Quiñones, commissioned by Henry VIII's bitter enemy Pope Paul III as a pilot scheme for reforming and standardizing the Church's worship. Quiñones had brought out the first version of this in 1535, and heavily revised it in a second edition of 1536. Cranmer's first scheme mostly uses the 1535 edition, but there are traces of the second. Another reformist Catholic source supplied the versions of the Latin hymns which punctuate the offices: Van Clichthoven's hymn collection *Elucidatorium Ecclesiasticum*; a copy of the 1516 edition survives from Cranmer's own library. Cranmer even used one of the hymns which Clichthoven himself had composed.[174]

However, the Archbishop also drew inspiration from a very different direction: the liturgies of Lutheran northern Europe. Of all the various forms of Lutheran worship by then in use, the one which is closest to the structure of the services set out in his draft scheme is the order in use in the Church of Denmark from 1537, devised by the north German reformer Johann Bugenhagen (also known as Pomeranus). This borrowing has significance for the dating, because Henry VIII took some time to give diplomatic recognition to the Lutheran King Christian III of Denmark after Christian had finally won a Danish civil war in 1536, and good relations and communication were only firmly established in spring 1538; a Danish representative was nearly

172 BL Royal MS 7B IV, edited first by Gasquet and Bishop, pp. 311–96, then by Wickham Legg, *Cranmer's Liturgical Projects*. The best summary account is Cuming, *Godly Order*, pp. 1–23. I have deliberately been eclectic in translating passages from the text rather than simply using the slightly different wording to be found in Cranmer's 1549 version.

173 Smyth, *Cranmer*, pp. 74–7. See also further discussion of dating in Cuming, *Godly Order*, pp. 1–4.

174 Gasquet and Bishop, pp. 353–5.

included in the Lutheran delegation for the 1538 London negotiations.[175] The establishment of friendship between England and Denmark was commemorated by Bugenhagen's gift of his Church Order to Henry VIII; it probably arrived just before Henry's friendly letter of 13 March 1538 to Christian. This presentation copy, inscribed by Bugenhagen, still exists; Cranmer probably used it for his liturgical work.[176] Against this background, the first breviary scheme thus has close associations with the 1538 discussions with the Lutherans at Lambeth Palace.

The strategy behind the revised breviary plan was set out in an explanatory preface, which deplored the 'confusion of tongues almost worse than Babel' caused by the variety of older uses, naming those pioneered by the cathedrals of Salisbury, Hereford, Bangor and York. Already, like the later Prayer Books, the revision was envisaged as supplying the worshipping life of secular (non-monastic) clergy, in a Church which could do without the specialized devotional round maintained in the monasteries, now fast disappearing. It created a much simpler twofold structure for the offices, a morning and an evening service (mattins and vespers), replacing and amalgamating material from the eightfold offices of the medieval West which had originated in monastic worship. A note at the end of the orders for the two offices made it clear that no one should be obliged to recite any other services, in other words the old eightfold order. Besides setting out the new service orders, everything necessary to support the scheme was provided for: a table or kalendar of Bible readings designed to present 'the thread and order of holy Scripture' as far as possible in sequence 'entire and unbroken' through the year, and also a plan for reciting all 150 psalms each calendar month.[177] The kalendar left out saints whom Cranmer regarded as marginal, and inserted some further biblical names.

The text which has survived to us is in Latin, not in English as in the later *Book of Common Prayer*. This may at first sight suggest that Cranmer and Cromwell were not contemplating services wholly in English, an innovation which several evangelical enthusiasts were actually putting into practice in 1538. Quite apart from likely difficulties in converting Henry VIII to approving a drastic change straight away, the use of Latin in the manuscript is perfectly explicable in diplomatic terms: it meant that the finished version of this text could be submitted to Lutheran delegates in the continued negotiations which were envisaged when the deputation departed in October 1538. It might also be possible to argue that Cranmer intended at this stage to retain Latin as the main liturgical language, at least for the offices. After all, traditionally the offices had a specialist function whether performed inside or outside the setting of monasteries. Before the great Edwardian revisions, they were mainly intended for the use of the clergy, whose special duty (*officium*) it

175 *L.P.* 13 i nos 649–50, 738, 891.
176 Smyth, *Cranmer*, p. 76. Henry to Christian: *L.P.* 13 i no. 499.
177 Gasquet and Bishop, pp. 376, 363.

was, both in a traditional and an evangelical understanding of the ministry, to offer up this daily round of structured prayer and praise. In a passage added by Cranmer to the original text of Quiñones' preface, the Archbishop gave his opinion that the early Church had created the offices first to stir up the clergy to better instruction of the laity.[178]

However, one piece of evidence confirms that even as early as this, the evangelical establishment was hoping to take the plunge into a vernacular liturgy for the offices at least. This is a reference in a letter of 8 March 1539 written to Zürich by the former English exchange students: they told the Zürich clergy that Cranmer 'is now wholly employed both in instructing the people, and in devising certain prayers ("*orationes*") in English, which our clergy are to use instead of those Latin ones which they have hitherto gabbled in their churches like so many parrots'. This has always been taken as an allusion to a project to write homilies, as was later to be proposed in the Convocation of Canterbury in 1542–3 and actually finished and published in 1547. However, that reading depends on the Parker Society's misleading translation of *orationes* as 'discourses'; there is no other evidence that in 1539 Cranmer was engaged in homily writing, while we do have the evidence of the breviary text and references in other letters that he was engaged in revising the liturgy.[179] Without the Parker Society's mistranslation, the wording of the letter would hardly suggest a reference to sermons: pre-Reformation sermons in parish churches were naturally in English, not Latin, and to talk of sermons being 'gabbled . . . like parrots' hardly seems quite the appropriate shaft of abusive wit. By contrast, it would apply perfectly to the recitation of the offices.

There is no doubt that already in 1538–9 Cranmer had one eye on the presence of the laity at the revised morning and evening offices, a presence which would become such a distinctive feature of the Church of England's worship after 1552. In his preface, he immediately went on from his remark about offices and the clergy to look back to a past where the laity also 'by daily hearings of sacred scripture in holy assembly, should continually profit more and more in the knowledge of sacred matters, and be inflamed with devotion towards God'. There would always be a congregation of some sort present at the offices, and he made provision to shorten the services if a sermon was going to be preached to avoid the possibility 'that the people, kept too long and wearied by too lengthy reading, should not attend keenly enough'. In his notes to the vespers service order, Cranmer pointed out that he was giving it its own cycle of lessons 'so that the people may always undoubtedly learn something, and may return home from the churches better instructed in the word of God'.[180] This much of the service at least can only have been intended

178 Gasquet and Bishop, pp. 357–8.

179 *E.T.*, p. 406: '*qui nunc totus est in populo docendo et in excogitandis orationibus quibusdam Anglicis, quibus sacerdotes nostri vice Latinarum, quas hactenus in templis more psittacorum permurmuraverunt, usuri sint.*' Cf. translation in *O.L.*, p. 626.

180 Gasquet and Bishop, pp. 377, 373.

to be in English. There is evidence that Cromwell had already begun the process of softening up King and country for a vernacular liturgy by specifying readings of the Bible in English, which is the minimum implied by Cranmer's scheme. During 1538 he appears to have issued some general order for the epistle and gospel during mass to be read or 'declared' in English from the pulpit, because three very different bishops, Archbishop Lee of York, Shaxton of Salisbury and Veysey of Exeter, repeated the order in their own diocesan injunctions.[181]

Cranmer's preface to the breviary scheme had an especially remarkable past and future. He plagiarized it, with several of his own ideas thrown in, from both 1535 and 1536 versions of Quiñones' Breviary; it later appeared in a shortened English translation in the 1549 Prayer Book, and it is still there in the *Book of Common Prayer* today. The opening sentence, familiar to any Anglican who has whiled away sermons by starting to leaf through the Prayer Book, is a good illustration of how Cranmer was prepared to treat his literary models throughout his career as a liturgist. Quiñones in 1536 had written 'There was never anything by man so well devised which could not later be rendered more perfect by the added insight of many'. Cranmer, always theologically alert, saw that this would be a perfect proof-text for those like his difficult colleague Bishop Stokesley, who supported the authority of Church tradition (unwritten verities) alongside scripture. Ruthlessly, he therefore turned the sentence on its head: 'There was never anything by men so well devised or so surely established which in age and continuance of time has not been corrupted', and this appears with minor adjustments in 1549. One could take this weary historical insight as the motto of the English Reformation.

Cranmer did not cease work on his revision when the German ambassadors left in October 1538; in fact, the bulk of the work on the revision was probably done in the winter and spring of 1539, when he may have had more leisure than during the embassy itself. There is the evidence of the letter of 8 March already mentioned; if that is thought to be an unreliable witness, there is a passing remark, in one of his letters of 11 April 1539, which is almost certainly a reference to the fair copy of the breviary manuscript which we possess today. Writing to Cromwell, Cranmer said that he had left his chaplain, Francis Mallet, down at Ford Palace 'according to your lordship's assignment, occupied in the affairs of our Church service'; now Mallet had come up to Croydon Palace 'at the writing up of so much as he had to do' and after seeing Cromwell he should return 'for further furtherance and final finishing of that we have begun'.[182] The surviving scheme is written in two

181 Butterworth, *Primers*, p. 162.

182 P.R.O., S.P. 1/150 ff. 114–15, Cox 2, pp. 366–7 (*L.P.* 14 i no. 739). Charles Smyth first noticed the significance of this letter: Smyth, *Cranmer*, pp. 76–7. Unfortunately he accepted Cox's erroneous dating to 1538: there are good grounds for accepting *L.P.*'s redating, because Cranmer's previous letter also written from Croydon (Cox 2, p. 366, no. 222, *L.P.* 14 i no. 720) is fairly firmly dated to 1539 by its reference to monastic land not available in April 1538. The sequence of events in 1538–9 also makes redating plausible.

hands, the second of which is that of Ralph Morice; it is likely that the first hand is Mallet's. In addition to the breviary, it is more than likely that Cranmer made proposals for baptism and marriage services which he would eventually use in the 1549 *Book of Common Prayer*.[183] However, at some point after April 1539, work on the manuscript stopped. The table of lessons for half the year was never filled in. Given the traumatic events of May and June 1539, which culminated in the passage of the Six Articles, one can understand only too well why Cromwell and Cranmer dropped their scheme, and why the work of revising the liturgy was postponed.

While the German negotiations were dribbling towards their apparently unsatisfactory conclusion, the King gave dramatic, indeed destructive, support to one aspect of Cromwell's campaign of evangelical advance. The chain of circumstances is complex and has a strange beginning in an entirely different preoccupation of Henry's: he was taken up during the summer with enthusiasm for winning a French bride – almost any one would do, it seemed.[184] At the end of August he indulged his temporary Francophile passion by giving a lavish welcome in London to Madame de Montreuil, a former senior attendant of the recently deceased French-born Queen Madeleine of Scotland; her duties at an end, she was passing through England from Scotland on her way home to France, and would travel on from London to Kent. Henry decided to combine business with pleasure by making a rendezvous with her after he had inspected the defences at Dover; she was accompanied south by the French ambassador.[185] Part of Madame's tourist schedule on the way down was a stay in Canterbury, where on 31 August she made a lengthy visit to the Cathedral. She was treated by Prior Goldwell and his brethren to a special viewing of the shrine of St Thomas Becket, complete with traditional ceremonies. Her English escort, Sir William Penison, noted with interest that she refused to do reverence at the solemn exposition of the saint's head, although she was duly impressed with the staggering wealth of the shrine.[186]

Goldwell never again had a chance to show off the holy skull, and one wonders whether Madame's visit clinched a plan of action already in Henry's mind. Back in London, Cromwell was drawing up a set of draft vice-gerential injunctions, which among other new orders finally made it clear that every parish church was supposed to buy a Bible in English; these injunctions were promulgated by the archbishops and bishops during October. Cromwell's first draft notes that it was 'exhibited' on 5 September, and it is unlikely that this refers to an inspection by the Vice-gerent himself; this is surely the date on which it was shown to the King in Kent for his scrutiny. Alterations were

183 See below, Ch. 10, p. 415; this is also the conclusion of Jeanes, 'Reformation Treatise', pp. 159–60.
184 On Henry's courtship antics at this time, see Scarisbrick, *Henry VIII*, pp. 359–60.
185 *L.P.* 13 ii nos 177, 201 (*St.P.* 1, p. 582), 232, p. 90.
186 *St.P.* 1, pp. 583–4 (*L.P.* 13 ii no. 257).

made immediately after this date. When the injunctions were issued in print, they had one or two new items added at the end, all of which represented fresh attacks on devotion to the saints, and specifically on the feasts of Thomas Becket.[187]

Ever since Henry had discovered that he was Supreme Head of the Church of England, he had detested the memory of Becket, whose cult represented the triumph of the Western Church over a king of England, but this added clause of the injunctions had an urgent practical relevance. It gave backing to the destruction of Becket's shrine, and apparently even his bones, in Canterbury Cathedral, perhaps the most spectacular single piece of iconoclasm so far in the English Church: indeed, the destruction of the shrine was the primary reason stated for the papal promulgation of Henry VIII's excommunication three months later. The shrine took several days, around 8 September, to dismantle, and the scandalized ex-monk of St Augustine's, Canterbury, who recorded the atrocity also noted the simultaneous prohibition of Becket's feast-days.[188] That same night, 8 September, Cromwell's evangelical impresario and playwright John Bale staged a play before the King and Court at Canterbury, and it is hardly stretching coincidence too far to suggest that the work performed was Bale's *On the Treasons of Becket*.[189] Sometime during the next weeks Cromwell appeared at the Cathedral and ordered the monks 'to change their habits', presumably abandoning the Benedictine costume in preparation for the Cathedral Priory becoming a secular foundation, but for some reason this drastic step was postponed for another eighteen months.[190]

Who should take credit (or blame) for Becket's final annihilation? The earliest initiative was a week or two before Henry set out for Kent, when Cranmer suggested to Cromwell that it was time to have all the relics preserved in his Cathedral investigated with a sceptical eye.[191] However, typically in Cranmer and Cromwell's relationship, this was a more modest suggestion than the savage spectacle which ensued. The presence of Bale and his players at Canterbury was clearly planned, and only Cromwell could have done the planning; Wriothesley records his simultaneous unleashing of the anti-Becket campaign in London.[192] It is likely that Cromwell put the idea

187 The final text of the injunctions is available in *English Historical Documents* 5, pp. 811–14, from Cranmer's Register, ff. 99v–101r. For the draft version with the date, see *L.P.* 13 ii no. 281 and Butterfield, *Primers*, p. 169; and for the October promulgation, Elton, *Policy and Police*, pp. 254–5.

188 C.C.C.C. MS 298 Pt 4, f. 48r; this is the complete Latin original of the chronicle of which a part in English translation is printed in *Narratives of the Reformation* pp. 279–86. Cf. the excommunication of 17 December 1538: *L.P.* 13 ii no. 1087. The possibilities of what happened to Becket's bones have been entertainingly set out in Butler, *The Quest for Becket's Bones*. Burning remains their most likely fate.

189 House, 'Cromwell's message to the Regulars', p. 125.

190 *Wriothesley's Chronicle* 1, p. 86, and *L.P.* 13 ii no. 465.

191 18 August 1538: P.R.O., S.P. 1/135 ff. 116–17, Cox 2, pp. 377–8 (*L.P.* 13 ii no. 126).

192 *Wriothesley's Chronicle* 1, pp. 86–7.

into Henry's head of combining his visit to Kent with an emphatic end to the Becket cult, and then Madame de Montreuil's less than traditional reaction to the traditional splendours of the shrine clinched the King's purpose, giving Cromwell the go-ahead: hence the sudden addition to the injunctions between 5 and 8 September. The actual dismantling was performed by Richard Pollard, an agent of Cromwell and not of the Archbishop, although Cranmer was in other instances happy to lend his servants as agents in other acts of iconoclastic vandalism as the campaign against holy places and sacred images progressed during late 1538.[193] Canterbury was the first leg of Pollard's campaign of destruction, which continued at the end of the month at Winchester: another indication that Cromwell was waiting for royal approval until the last moment before unleashing his assault on the cathedral shrines of England.[194]

One direct contribution by the Archbishop to this putsch against Canterbury's chief patron was to add to Becket's symbolic oblivion by commissioning the recutting of the official seals used by the archdiocese and its prerogative court. From the twelfth century on, these had featured as their central panel Thomas Becket and his martyrdom, and Cranmer had continued this tradition when he became Archbishop. His first seal for the archdiocese was indeed simply a recutting of Warham's, adding his own family arms at the bottom and altering the legend. A second seal hardly altered this first design, which still centred on the martyrdom of Becket. From 1538, the central panel was entirely changed and the crucifixion put in the place of the death of the Archbishop; Cranmer also decided to impale the arms of the archdiocese with those of the Cathedral Priory, rather than with a version of his own family coat.[195] A similar transformation occurred on the prerogative seal: a different treatment of Becket's martyrdom was replaced in a recutting of the same matrix by the scourging of Christ.[196] Sir Thomas Cheyney, casting an unsympathetic eye over official acts of the archdiocese, would have been able to note this newly Christocentric iconography, and call to mind the Archbishop's words to him the previous

193 For Cranmer's servants and iconoclasm at Calais, see P.R.O., S.P. 1/134 ff. 233–4, Cox 2, p. 372 (*L.P.* 13 i no. 1446); and in the Midlands, Wright, *Three Chapters*, pp. 143–4 (*L.P.* 13 ii no. 244, and cf. ibid. no. 256).

194 For Pollard at Winchester, cf. *St.P.* 1, p. 621 (*L.P.* 13 ii no. 401; 21 September 1538), and for jocular references to Pollard's work at Canterbury, cf. e.g. *Lisle Letters* 5, p. 213 (*L.P.* 13 ii no. 317). For shrine destruction at Worcester Cathedral in 1538, see H.W.R.O., b.009:1-BA 2636, f. 156r.

195 First seal: Birch, *Seals*, nos 1259–60, illus. Gorham, *Gleanings*, facing p. 2. Second seal: Birch, *Seals*, no. 1261. Third seal: Birch, *Seals*, nos 1262, 1264 (dated 1540, 1544), illus. Gorham, *Gleanings*, facing p. 2. I am grateful to John Cherry for his correspondence with me about Cranmer's seals.

196 First seal: Birch, *Seals*, no. 1276 (dated 1533); Second seal: Birch, *Seals*, no. 1277 (dated January 1539); both illus. Gorham, *Gleanings*, facing p. 6. It is possible that the second state of Cranmer's Faculty Office seal (above, Ch. 4, pp. 117–18) dates from this redesign of the other seals. Might one also date his new heraldry to the time of this iconographic shake up? Cf. discussion in Ch. 1.

18 Two states of Cranmer's general seal, 1534 and 1540, showing the replacement of the martyrdom of Becket by the Crucifixion. The altered impaled coat of Archdiocese and Priory is at the bottom left (the dexter side) in the later seal.

year, that the first thing necessary for salvation was 'our justification by Christ's passion only'.

In good pantomime fashion, at this moment of symbolic evangelical triumph in September 1538, the villain entered from the wings. Stephen Gardiner had been away for a full three years on his French embassy, but he had now been recalled, and he crossed the Channel to an England much changed in his absence. His disembarkation at Dover about 26 September was an anxious moment for all concerned, particularly in view of the vicious rows which had exploded between him and his successor as ambassador in France, Edmund Bonner, at that stage a protégé of Cromwell's; hence his every move was scrutinized for signs of trouble. However, Gardiner was in expansively conciliatory mood when he arrived in Kent: he pronounced himself well satisfied with the destruction of Becket's shrine, and wished for similar action in his own cathedral (this was disengenuous; he must have known that it had just taken place). He was equally complimentary about Cromwell's injunctions, although he seized gleefully on the implication in them that 'the King's Majesty will not leave this auricular confession', an ominous indication that his co-operation with the evangelical programme would be on his own terms.[197]

197 *St.P.* 8, pp. 51–2 (*L.P.* 13 ii no. 442). Cf. Redworth, *Gardiner*, pp. 84–5.

19 Cranmer's prerogative seals, before and after alteration, 1538: Becket's martyrdom is replaced by the scourging of Christ.

Glyn Redworth, in his biography of Gardiner, has cautioned against accepting too readily the evangelical historiography which made of Gardiner the arch-villain in a cosmic struggle for the soul of Tudor England. This is a healthy warning, but it can hardly be coincidence that for the three years while he was in France, the progress of evangelical change never suffered a major reversal, progressing even in the face of Anne Boleyn's death and the explosion of the Pilgrimage of Grace. Moreover, almost from the moment of Gardiner's arrival back in London, the emphasis of royal religious policy began to change. Cromwell could not afford to resist this shift, given the precarious state of his political battle with the Courtenays and Poles; and where Cromwell led, Cranmer would follow. The keynote of the autumn was resistance to religious radicalism, a cause which the evangelical leadership could certainly not resist, and indeed could support with as good a conscience as the conservatives. After the initial flurry of persecution of Anabaptists back in 1535, the English radicals had been left in comparative peace, and had maintained their contacts with like-minded groups on the Continent, as radicalism sought to rebuild its identity in the wake of the Münster catastrophe; the English radicals, indeed, played a prominent role in Continental radical discussions.[198] Now their luck changed once more.

198 Horst, *Radical Brethren*, pp. 73–80.

One must concede to Dr Redworth that besides the presence of Gardiner, a major initial stimulus for the new line came from an entirely different direction: from the Continent via the Anglo-German contacts of 1538. The German evangelical leaders took major steps to curb radicalism in this year, and at the forefront of the action was Martin Bucer. Strassburg passed fresh legislation to curb its Anabaptists, and Landgraf Philipp of Hesse also swooped on Anabaptist gatherings: on 1 September the Duke of Saxony and the Landgraf sent to England an urgent warning letter which included alarming extracts of radical correspondence seized in Hesse. These referred in glowing terms to radical progress in England, including the publication of an English work which expressed unorthodox views about the nature of Christ.[199] One notes that the princes were desperate to dissociate such disgraceful ideas from the Lutheranism into which they hoped to entice Henry VIII: the same defensiveness affected the English evangelicals, and afforded the perfect opportunity for conservatives to sweep up opponents on the fringes of the evangelical establishment into the net of repression. The reaction of German and English government establishments to the same problem in 1538 was significantly different. In Strassburg, threats of capital punishment for obstinate radicalism remained a dead letter, while in Hesse, the Landgraf went on to invite Bucer into his territory to persuade radicals into conformity by disputation; the resulting mass conversion back to the territorial Church was virtually unique in Europe during the sixteenth century.[200] In England, with the combination of conservatives savouring the chance for a comeback plus the customary savagery of Henry VIII in reaction to religious dissent, the sequel was a good deal more ruthless.

English reaction to the German letter was remarkably swift. An English translation by Richard Morison of the German letter survives from 25 September, and within a week a vice-gerential commission had been issued against Anabaptists. Its membership was notably bipartisan, reflecting the way in which it was possible for the Anabaptists to be a unifying factor in England's religious divisions: Cranmer headed it, with Heath, Barnes and Edward Crome also representing the evangelicals, Sampson and Stokesley the conservatives, and John Skip, Thomas Thirlby and Richard Gwent more equivocal figures; one uniting factor in the group was that (whatever their chief preferment) they were mainly active in London and the south-east. During the autumn, there are records of various Anabaptists being burnt in London and Colchester, mostly Dutch refugees.[201] However, caught up in the net were a number of evangelical activists whom it was hard to prevent being

199 Ibid., pp. 81–5; cf. *L.P.* 13 ii nos 264–5. The printed work appears not to have survived.

200 Abray, *People's Reformation*, pp. 110–13; *Bucer*, ed. Wright, pp. 29–32; Williams, *Radical Reformation*, pp. 443–52.

201 Horst, *Radical Brethren*, pp. 86–9, sums up the evidence. The commission is *L.P.* 13 ii nos 427, 498.

treated in the same way as those of more radical inclinations. One burning in particular, that of John Lambert alias Nicholson, would prove a sad embarrassment for Cranmer's long-term reputation.

In some cases it was the unorthodox style of evangelical activists which attracted official suspicion: such was the case with the Lollard bricklayer from Whitechapel, John Harridance, whose gift for preaching was not inhibited by his illiteracy, nor by its improvised settings in the open air or in his own house. Such a character as Harridance was bound to infuriate the authorities, and his examination became yet another distraction for the bishops at Lambeth during the summer of 1538; despite the lack of any substantial doctrinal matters to charge him with, he ended up bearing a faggot as an abjured heretic after the alarms of the autumn.[202] However, the main Achilles heel for fringe evangelicals in the persecution remained eucharistic theology.

The extent of official evangelical sensitivity on this had been revealed by an incident in the summer, when Vice-Chancellor Burchard had made urgent representations to Cranmer and Sampson to have the penance of one Atkinson relocated from Paul's Cross to the less public setting of his parish church. We do not know what Atkinson's precise eucharistic views were, but the two bishops concurred in referring the request for Cromwell's decision, meanwhile telling Burchard that they were opposed to a concession, 'as that error of the sacrament of the altar was so greatly spread abroad in this realm'. Charles Smyth made too much of this, wrongly seeing it as conclusive evidence that Cranmer's eucharistic views never went through a Lutheran phase. In fact, all that it demonstrates is the uneasy balance of forces between an evangelical and a conservative bishop at Lambeth that summer, Cranmer's wish not to be seen stepping out of line, and the Bucerian generosity of an evangelical visitor trying to avoid undue humiliation for a harmless individual whom he favoured.[203]

The disaster which befell John Lambert well illustrates the evangelical establishment's continuing hard line on the corporal presence of Christ in the eucharist, the issue which had bedevilled relations with central Europe and Strassburg over the previous two years. What is evident from the embarrassed account in Foxe's narrative on Lambert is that it was the evangelicals who caused his downfall. Lambert began by arguing with John Taylor (Bishop of Lincoln under Edward VI) about the eucharist; Taylor called on Barnes to back him up in confuting Lambert, and he in turn decided that Cranmer ought to be brought in; after the Archbishop had examined him, Lambert was confined in Lambeth Palace. He is then said to have appealed to the King: a highly unwise move in autumn 1538. Whether or not we accept Foxe's suggestion that Gardiner orchestrated Henry's actions, it is clear that the

202 Brigden, *London and the Reformation*, pp. 273–4; *Wriothesley's Chronicle* 1, pp. 82–3.

203 P.R.O., S.P. 1/133 f. 174, Cox 2, pp. 371–2 (*L.P.* 13 i no. 1237). Smyth, *Cranmer*, pp. 56–9.

King was now taking a highly active interest in his religious policy. He decided to single out Lambert for destruction, by summoning a heresy tribunal to Westminster, over which he would preside in person as Supreme Head of the Church. It was a remarkable meeting, which given its attendance of bishops, noblemen, justices, MPs, sundry dignitaries and the King himself may be reckoned an addition to the sequence of Tudor Great Councils compiled by Dr Holmes. That in itself is a measure of the importance of the Lambert case.[204]

Lambert had become entangled in Henry's concern for national security against religious deviance, which simultaneously produced a major omnium-gatherum proclamation on a number of religious matters. A draft stage of this reveals Henry (in a highly unusual personal intervention) shifting the wording in a conservative direction. Even when the final version appeared with added material resonant of Cromwell's September reform programme, it represented a setback for the evangelical cause, which indeed suggests Gardiner and his conservative colleagues adroitly appealing to what they knew of the King's sensitivities. Cranmer would have felt highly uncomfortable at its prohibition of clerical marriage, especially at Henry's quite erroneous addition of scriptural citations suggesting that such marriages were against God's word, not just the custom of the Church. In the final version of the proclamation, there was however a crumb of comfort on this matter at least, which probably indicates one of Cromwell's rearguard amendments with the Archbishop in mind: that part of the text forbidding all clerical marriage on pain of deprivation and loss of clerical status had the small additional phrase making it apply only to marriages 'that be openly known'.[205]

This hybrid but baleful document was issued on 16 November, to coincide with the day on which Lambert's show trial was staged. Since all the leading bishops were present, it was only natural that the King should ask Cranmer to take up the questioning when he himself had finished. Cranmer concentrated on putting arguments that the body of Christ could be in two places at once, on the analogy of Christ's appearance to Paul on the road to Damascus, an approach which would have drawn the approval of Martin Luther. There is one aspect of the subsequent discussions which may be significant. If Foxe's summary of the proceedings is to be trusted, none of the first four interrogators, Henry, Cranmer, Gardiner and Tunstall, used the word 'substance' in their arguments against Lambert; it was only Stokesley, speaking fifth, who is recorded as bringing in this term and using it in a

204 Holmes, 'Tudor Great Councils', esp. p. 13. See Foxe's account of these events, 5, pp. 227–36; all details are taken from there unless otherwise stated.

205 On the proclamation, Elton, *Policy and Police*, pp. 255–7; there is useful comment in McEntegart Ph.D., 'England and the League of Schmalkalden', pp. 300–304. Strype first noticed the 'openly known' point: Strype, *Cranmer*, 1, p. 99.

scholastic sense. Nor, perhaps even more significantly, had the word 'substance' appeared in the otherwise stridently conservative language about the sacrament of the altar in the King's proclamation that day; this was all the more remarkable because Lambert himself had used the scholastic language of substance fairly freely in previous arguments, and in a eucharistic treatise which he had addressed to the King from prison in Lambeth, and at least one conservative spectator referred to the word 'substance' in his summary description of the trial.[206]

The primary eucharistic argument in the trial itself, therefore, could be regarded as being about presence, and not about the scholastic definition of the eucharistic miracle as transubstantiation. Later, after his eucharistic views had changed, Cranmer did not see this distinction as important, so that in 1555 he would say that in the Lambert trial he had 'maintained the papist's doctrine'.[207] However, that was the view of a man who had come to believe in the spiritual presence only, as Lambert had done in 1538. At the time, the Archbishop probably felt that Lambert's case was unlike that of Adam Damplip of Calais: Cranmer had defended Damplip earlier that same year for denying transubstantiation, but still upholding the 'truth' in the eucharistic presence. The analogy was rather the examination of John Frith in 1533; Lambert was going to die for his error in denying the truth of the presence, and that must have been consolation for Cranmer as the King pronounced sentence. It was also noticeable that when the watchful Lutheran princes heard about the Lambert affair, they expressed no disapproval of what had happened.[208] More straightforwardly, it may be that Foxe's account has suppressed other more embarrassing opinions of Lambert's which put him squarely in the radical camp, and which any evangelical would regard with horror: the chronicler Wriothesley records him facing charges of denying infant baptism and affirming that Christ took no human flesh of the Virgin Mary. Like the Archbishop, Cromwell was tied by the King to the act of destroying Lambert; it was from the Vice-gerent's house that he was taken to the stake on 22 November.

There was no especial reason for the evangelicals to despair at the execution of an evangelical who had overstepped the mark, or indeed at the general crackdown on radicals; rather they might note at the same time the destruction both of individuals and institutions which were their natural enemies, with the arrest and execution of the leading figures in the Courtenay and Pole circle at Court, and the removal of all the kingdom's friaries within a twelvemonth. The open excommunication of Henry at last promulgated by

206 John Husee said that Lambert denied the 'corporal substance' of the presence at his trial; that is not the same as addressing the question of transubstantiation. *Lisle Letters* 5, no. 1273 (*L.P.* 13 ii no. 854).

207 Foxe 8, p. 57.

208 Cf. a letter of Duke Johann Friedrich qu. McEntegart Ph.D., 'England and the League of Schmalkalden', p. 297 n. 22. On Damplip, see above, pp. 182, 218–19.

the Pope in December 1538 could only boost evangelical credibility in Henry's eyes, especially since he had some grounds for fearing that France and the Empire might exploit the papal condemnation to combine against him.[209] A further royal proclamation in late February 1539 had a more congenial flavour than the November proclamation that it supplemented; in something of the spirit of Bucer's work in Hesse, it proclaimed pardon for Anabaptists who repented, and it also returned to the Ten Articles of 1536 to provide a set of edifying explanations for certain ecclesiastical ceremonies whose use had been specified in November.[210] Yet hindsight would reveal that the destruction of Becket's shrine and the injunctions of September 1538 represented a significant high-water mark for the evangelical drive to transform Henry's Church. It was not the case that the conservatives steadily chalked up more triumphs, or that all change had come to an end; rather, for the rest of the reign, a series of bewildering seesaw reversals of fortune meant that up to Henry's last two months of life the further steady gains which the evangelicals made were always under threat. Throughout this, there survived at the head of the English Church one guardian of the evangelical cause (at times, indeed, appearing as little more than the caretaker of a derelict building): the Archbishop himself.

Cranmer's conduct in surviving has often attracted ridicule and contempt from purists on both sides of the Reformation religious divide. The classic riposte to these sneers was made in October 1537, during the course of events which we have already described, and it involved two of the reformers at the heart of the Strassburg–St Gall axis. On the one hand was Cranmer's first friend among the Continental evangelicals, Simon Grynaeus, the warm-hearted enthusiast for change, who had a secure base within a congenial university in a city where the Reformation's main questions had been decided. On the other was the man whom Grynaeus had introduced to Cranmer, Martin Bucer, battling to establish his vision of a godly state in one of Europe's most complex communities, placed squarely in the whirlpool of international power politics. Grynaeus had written to Cranmer bitterly criticizing the compromises which the English were making in their Reformation: probably as yet he had not seen the Bishops' Book, but he would certainly have been referring to the Ten Articles of 1536. When Bucer wrote to the Archbishop, he sought to soothe any ruffled feelings which the Primate might have suffered: he said of Grynaeus

> He is a theoretical, and not a practical divine. He conceives the perfect form of a church, and of the process by which a church ought to be reformed; and since he himself is not involved in the drama of affairs and has not had experience of what difficulties arise, when the tyranny of Antichrist is really to be destroyed, and the kingdom of Christ restored, he thinks that it is very easy to accomplish

209 Cf. the excommunication, *L.P.* 13 ii no. 1087.
210 *T.R.P.* 1 no. 188; *Lisle Letters*, 5, p. 569.

whatever he sees founded upon the word of God and therefore beneficial to humanity.[211]

Whatever obstacles had been put in the way of creating a reformed Church in England, Bucer was prepared to be patient. In the end, his patience, and his trust in Thomas Cranmer, were rewarded.

211 *E.T.* p. 342 (*O.L.* pp. 523–4), wrongly there dated to 1538, but see the redating by *L.P.* 12 ii no. 969 to 23 October 1537.

CHAPTER 7

Salvaging the cause: 1539–42

IN 1539 PARLIAMENT passed the Act of Six Articles, an abrupt change of religious direction whose motivation and development remain controversial. To understand the change and to see Cranmer's part in events, once more it will be impossible to avoid telling a wider story in which the Archbishop revealed himself an almost powerless puppet, swept along in events beyond his control and directly contrary to his hopes and plans. The first hint of a new initiative came in early March 1539, when Thomas Cromwell made one of his habitual 'remembrances' or lists of matters to be attended to: in this case, with reference to the imminent meeting of Parliament, the first for three years. One of the items which he noted was 'a device in the Parliament for the unity in religion'.[1] As yet there was little public hint as to what the shape of that unity might be. When the former English-Swiss exchange students wrote to their heroes in Zürich at much the same time as Cromwell was pondering his parliamentary agenda, they were cautiously optimistic about the future: thanks to the royal proclamation of 26 February, traditional ceremonies were provided with didactic explanations to rationalize them, and there was still no final decision on the relaxation of compulsory clerical celibacy and indeed 'there are those who have very freely preached before the King upon this subject'. Only a few months after the death of John Lambert, the view of these evangelicals was that officially 'the mass is not declared to be a sacrifice for the living and the dead, but a representation of Christ's passion.'[2]

Philipp Melanchthon, however, had his doubts about progress in England, expressed at first only obliquely in a letter to Henry, but much more vocally in the accompanying letter to Cranmer. He bitterly castigated Henry's proclamations of November 1538 and February 1539 on religion, expressing himself with particular force about February's explanations of ceremonies, which (unlike the Zürich correspondents) he assumed were a sophistical plot by Gardiner and Stokesley. In April he wrote once more to Henry, this time presuming on the King's known admiration for him to provide a full critique

1 *L.P.* 14 i no. 655; cf. Elton, *Studies* 1, p. 205.

2 John Butler and others to Conrad Pellican and others, 8 March 1539: *E.T.* p. 405 (*O.L.* p. 624, which misleadingly adds 'only' to the last phrase).

of the November proclamation. His particular concern was to knock down Henry's arguments for compulsory clerical celibacy, but he also advanced an interesting argument bearing on the German and English campaigns against Anabaptists during the previous autumn. He drew Henry's attention to the situation in the Habsburg-ruled Low Countries, where thanks to severe official persecution, toleration of idolatry and the lack of 'good teachers, many among the people are becoming open atheists; for it is a fact that there is an almost pagan license in the Low Countries, where some are superstitious by nature, and others embrace the lunatic doctrines of the Anabaptists'. It was an argument for an evangelical middle way which would have appealed to Bucer and Cranmer, but it rather missed the target of Henry VIII's own vision of the *via media*. Henry would not appreciate being lectured even by the one foreign evangelical for whom he felt deep admiration.[3]

Cromwell had his own ideas about how the important religious work contemplated in the Parliament might be shaped. He cheerfully told Henry VIII in March that he had made sure that his henchman Richard Morison (an effective and none-too-scrupulous evangelical propagandist) would be elected as an MP 'to answer and take up such as would crack or face [brag or show off] with literature of learning', and in general the elections would produce 'never more tractable parliament' for the King.[4] There was no reason to suppose that evangelical plans had been derailed; most spectacularly of all, Cromwell's greatest achievement, the first edition of a new officially authorized Bible (the 'Great Bible') appeared in April 1539, from the presses of the enthusiastically evangelical official publishers Richard Grafton and Edward Whitchurch. Its title-page, to become a familiar sight in later editions of the work, was a spectacular piece of reformist iconography, as masterfully planned in Renaissance humanist fashion as Cranmer's newly designed seals. Possibly it is another candidate for attribution to Hans Holbein. Like so many pictorial title-pages, it took advantage of the usual format to present a twofold message either side of the central title-block. However, the message was not of violently contrasted opposites, as would be the case, for instance, in the famous later title-page of Foxe's *Book of Martyrs*, where superstition and true religion fight for dominion of the human soul below the throne of God. In the Great Bible the message was one of unity: two estates, clerical and lay, harmoniously and gratefully receiving the word of God from the hands of a benevolent monarch, and drawing from it his preferred message of discipline and obedience.

The story of the title-page ran from top to bottom. At the King's right hand to receive the Bible and to lead his fellow-bishops was Cranmer (still

3 Melanchthon to Henry, 26 March 1539, Strype, *Ecclesiastical Memorials*, I ii no. 101, pp. 393–4; Melanchthon to Cranmer, 29 March 1539; Melanchthon to Henry, 1 April 1539, Burnet I ii Add. no. 6, pp. 468–72 (*L.P.* 14 i nos 613, 631, 666).

4 *St.P.* I, pp. 603–4 (*L.P.* 14 i no. 538). It is not certain which parliamentary seat was provided for Morison.

20 Title page of 'The Byble in Englyshe', 1539: a *de luxe* coloured copy in the library of St John's College, Cambridge, which is said to have belonged to Thomas Cromwell himself. Note the identifying coats of arms of Cromwell and Cranmer flanking the main inscription. This version tactfully omits the prison which in most public editions complemented the pulpit at the bottom right.

traditionally tonsured), and in the frame below he handed on the book to a clergyman, who below, out in the parishes, passed on the message from a pulpit loyally inscribed VIVAT REX. Meanwhile on the King's left hand, Cromwell the Vice-gerent also received the Bible (with a rather too accurately bored-looking set of privy councillors behind him); in the frame below, he went out personally distributing the Bible to lay people. At this level of the page, both Cranmer and Cromwell were identified by their coats of arms, although Cromwell's heraldry disappeared through political circumstances after the third edition, leaving an embarrassing blank circle in later versions of the composition. The iconography faltered below the Vice-gerent's panel, the artist clearly being unsure as to how the word of God was conveyed from the better sort among the laity to their social inferiors: while on the other side, one half of the people sat attentively below the preacher's pulpit, the rest of the population milled around confusedly but cheerfully underneath Cromwell. Yet all, whether in church or elsewhere, took up the same message from the word of God, 'VIVAT REX'! A few little children round the pulpit, not up to Latin in their schooling, did their best with 'GOD SAVE THE KING'! At the viewer's extreme lower right, opposing the loyal pulpit, there was silence from a fairly obscurely delineated set of inhabitants of a prison, no doubt a motley band of Observant friars and Anabaptists.

The Bible was not the only index of evangelical confidence. Cranmer was still working away on his liturgical reforms for vernacular offices, and the King was still scared stiff of a joint hostile alliance between the Pope, the Emperor and the King of France. The most likely conclusion to be drawn from this was that Henry would respond by paying renewed attention to his contacts with the Lutheran princes; these were indeed showing much promise. By late April Vice-Chancellor Burchard was back in England at the head of another Lutheran delegation, looking for financial help for the German princes, but also determined to build on Melanchthon's exhortations and move the King on from his disastrous reaffirmation of clerical celibacy.[5] Cromwell wrote to the King warmly commending the 'evangelic' mission, particularly on the grounds that it would annoy the Emperor.[6]

This was not a judicious note on which to finish his letter; Cromwell began to discover that Henry was now thinking along different lines. The King brooded on his threatened diplomatic isolation. There was little in the new German proposals to excite him: indeed, the Germans made more demands than offers.[7] It was no doubt particularly galling that his fervent efforts to meet Melanchthon face to face had been so rudely rebuffed: Henry was sensitive to such affronts. Accordingly, he came to the opposite conclusion to his stance in the previous year; he now preferred to concentrate on wooing

5 Tjernagel, *Henry VIII and the Lutherans*, pp. 190–93. On the diplomatic situation, see also *Castillon/Marillac*, p. 88.

6 Strype, *Ecclesiastical Memorials*, 1 ii no. 104, pp. 401–4 (*L.P.* 14 i no. 844). See also McEntegart Ph.D., 'England and the League of Schmalkalden', pp. 327–30.

7 McEntegart Ph.D., 'England and the League of Schmalkalden', pp. 324–6.

conservative opinion at home and abroad rather than the Lutherans of northern Europe. This meant that he would have to show the world what a good traditionalist Catholic he was. There can be little doubt that in the events that followed, it was Henry who was taking the initiative, and that later evangelical attempts to shift the primary responsibility to hate-figures such as Bishop Gardiner were misplaced.[8] The King began giving a calculated display of his new outlook at the season of the Church's year when it was most easy to make clear one's liturgical preferences: the ceremonies of Holy Week which climaxed in the '*Triduum*' from Maundy Thursday to Holy Saturday. No one with sensitive political antennae could fail to miss the significance of what was happening; one excited description of the King's liturgical antics in Holy Week, and in the liturgical season which followed, survives in a letter to Lord Lisle from his servant John Worth. At mass on Good Friday (4 April 1539) Henry had observed that most demonstrative act of seasonal traditional devotion, creeping to the cross, and for some Sundays after he made a point of receiving holy bread and holy water in time-honoured fashion. He celebrated Ascension Day (15 May) in great style, and also prohibited on pain of death London criticism of the controversial ceremonies.[9]

Additional evidence of Henry's thinking comes from the draft of a proclamation which was probably never issued, but which was prepared on the eve of Parliament's meeting; once more, most unusually but like the November proclamation, it bears amendments in the hand of the King himself.[10] If issued, this would have deplored the public disturbances caused by 'diversity of opinion' in religion and announced the intention of proceeding 'to a full order and resolution to extinct all such diversities of opinions by good and just laws' in Parliament. In a mood of second thoughts which might be styled benevolent, Henry had decided that 'good and just laws' read better than the original draft's 'terrible laws'. The proclamation was intended to pre-empt this lawmaking by forbidding popular religious name-calling, unauthorized preaching and also the practice of reading aloud and expounding of the Bible in churches while divine service was going on. This practice, which seems particularly to have offended Henry's sense of propriety, is of interest in reflecting surviving records of such incidents in 1538–9 from both hostile and friendly commentators: for instance in London and at Chelmsford, but perhaps more significantly still, at Calais.[11] Lay Bible-

8 This is the thrust of the argument in Redworth, 'Six Articles' (an effective presentation of the case) and also in McEntegart Ph.D., 'England and the League of Schmalkalden', pp. 319–52.

9 *Lisle Letters* 5, no. 1415, p. 478 (*L.P.* 14 i no. 967).

10 *T.R.P.* 1 no. 191, pp. 284–5. Cf. discussion in Heinze, *Proclamations of Tudor Kings*, pp. 139–41.

11 London: Foxe 5, p. 443. Chelmsford: *Narratives of the Reformation*, pp. 348–51. Calais: *Lisle Letters* 5, no. 1503 (*L.P.* 14 i no. 1351). I incline to date this letter to April rather than July as in *L.P.*; both months contain a Saturday which is the 12th of the month. Cf. P.R.O., S.P. 1/152 ff. 154–9, Cox 2, pp. 390–92, *Lisle Letters* 5, no. 1489 (*L.P.* 14 i no. 1264).

reading should be in private, and the King made it clear that the permission for vernacular scripture was not a right but a privilege, which he might easily take away.

This was the background to the opening of Parliament on 28 April; Cranmer was naturally present at the opening, but Cromwell was not. Most unfortunately for the evangelical cause, his health had given way and he was unable to appear in the Lords until 10 May; five months later, he told a further German embassy that this illness of his had given the conservative bishops their chance.[12] While he was still not fully back to health, he lodged at St James's Palace, which kept him conveniently near Parliament and also gave him the chance to talk to the German delegates.[13] However, before Cromwell had returned to the Lords' chamber, the future course of events was set, and events had slipped from his control. Dr McEntegart has pointed out that Stephen Gardiner later gave a vital clue about the origins of the Six Articles, when he reminisced about a conversation with Lord Chancellor Audley in 1543: Audley in turn was remembering the occasion on which 'our late sovereign Lord devised with him how to resist the detestable heresy against the sacrament of the altar'. On that earlier occasion, which can only have been in 1539, Audley had advised the King 'to make an act of Parliament of it'.[14] There should be no occasion for surprise in this. During the autumn of 1538, as we have seen (above, Ch. 6), the evangelical leadership showed that it experienced no problem in affirming the real presence in the eucharist and in moving against those who did not affirm it. Legislation on the sacrament of the altar was a good way of establishing consensus among leading politicians and bishops, and one imagines that Audley, never the most independent of actors among the leading evangelicals, was giving this advice to Henry with Cromwell's knowledge; this was probably the 'device . . . for the unity in religion' which the Lord Privy Seal had noted in his memoranda.

Certainly it was Audley who made a speech in the Lords on 5 May repeating Henry's concern for 'diversity of opinions'; it is likely that he drew on material from the text of the aborted royal proclamation, but now with a different plan of action attached. The Lords were to choose a committee to examine and determine doctrine. The customary attempt at a rough religious balance was observed in the composition: on the one hand, Cromwell, Cranmer, the bishops of Ely, Bangor, and Worcester, on the other Bath and Wells, York, Durham and Carlisle.[15] However, this committee had little time to do the detailed work which a thorough revision of doctrine would have

12 Lehmberg, *Later Parliaments*, pp. 55–6; McEntegart Ph.D., 'England and the League of Schmalkalden', p. 326, qu. report of Burchard and Dolzig, September 1539.

13 Cf. the reference to his lodging there and his letters dated from St James: *L.P.* 14 i, nos 967, 1029, 1060. Rupp, *English Protestant Tradition*, p. 121.

14 *Gardiner's Letters*, p. 369; McEntegart Ph.D., 'England and the League of Schmalkalden', p. 321.

15 *L.J.* 1, p. 105; cf. Lehmberg, *Later Parliaments*, pp. 57–8.

entailed; there is a startling contrast between what happened next and the previous painful long-drawn-out doctrinal battles in committee during 1537 and 1538. From now on, the speed of events was frightening for the evangelicals, who had grown accustomed to winning ground by a long process of attrition. We possess one evangelical petition to the King which can almost certainly be dated to the helter-skelter discussions of May to June 1539: it tried to point out 'how evil it hath succeeded, when in provincial, yea, or yet in general councils, men have gone about to set forth any thing as in the force of God's law, without the manifest word of God', and on these grounds it begged Henry to suspend his judgement on clerical marriage and submit the question to the universities for extended disputation.[16] Henry did no such thing.

Opinions differ as to whether or not the 5 May committee's appointment was in fact a front to disguise the fact that the King's mind was already made up about the broad shape of policy.[17] What is beyond dispute is that on 16 May the Duke of Norfolk abruptly announced in the House of Lords that the committee had not been able to agree on anything, just as (he observed sourly) some peers had predicted when it was appointed; he therefore felt it best if the Lords considered six specific doctrinal questions, which are recorded in the Lords' Journal. These were the first glimpse of the Six Articles which would eventually be embodied in an Act of Parliament, and they moved way beyond a simple concern with the sacrament of the altar.[18] The fact that the Duke of Norfolk was the agent in the announcement is itself significant; Norfolk was the embodiment of lay traditionalism. The Duke became the butt of an anecdote which circulated in Cranmer's household about the aftermath of the Six Articles debacle; in this story Norfolk acted as unwilling straight man to one of the Archbishop's more spirited evangelical protégés, Thomas Lawney, in a barbed exchange about clerical celibacy.[19]

The bald record of the House of Lords' proceedings in its Journal goes on revealing procedurally unusual occurrences which indicate that events were swinging wildly out of Cromwell's control, if not the King's. There were constant fluctuations in attendance among the churchmen in late May, probably indicating their absence in private huddles as they fought over what was happening. Henry presided in person in the Lords on 19 and 21 May, and he may also have been meeting groups of the bishops for private discussions.[20] John Husee described the same sequence of events to Lord Lisle on 21 May: 'there is great hold among the bishops for the establishment of the blessed

16 B.L. Cotton MS Cleopatra E V ff. 53–4, Cox 2, pp. 466–7 (*L.P.* 14 i no. 971). There is no reason to associate this document directly with Cranmer.

17 See Redworth, 'Six Articles', pp. 55–6.

18 *L.J.* 1, p. 109. Redworth, 'Six Articles', p. 53. McEntegart Ph.D., 'England and the League of Schmalkalden', p. 352, points out that the remaining five all relate to the concerns of the 1538 Anglo-German discussions, and this is probably significant.

19 *Narratives of the Reformation*, p. 276.

20 *L.J.* 1, pp. 109–10.

sacrament of the altar. The Lords hath sitten daily in council upon the same, and the King's Highness hath been with them sundry times in person.'[21] Cranmer is among those recorded as present every day from 19 May, and Jasper Ridley is almost certainly correct in supposing that he put up his main opposition to the Articles at this time while the King was frequently in the house. We know very little of what he said; apart from some rather vague reports in Foxe, the best summary information is in a fragment copied from a letter of one of the secular nobility present in the Lords. He gleefully recorded the evangelicals' discomfiture, including the unenthusiastic dutifulness of Chancellor Audley and Cromwell, in the face of the King's sudden decisiveness, and described the Six Articles as they stood at the end of May:

> And notwithstanding my Lord of Canterbury, my Lord of Ely, my Lord of Salisbury, my Lords of Worcester, Rochester and St David's defended the contrary long time; yet finally his Highness confounded them all with God's learning. York, Durham, Winchester, London and Chichester, Norwich and Carlisle have shewed themselves honest and well learned men. We of the temporalty have been all of one opinion, and my Lord Chancellor and my Lord Privy Seal as good as we can devise. My Lord of Canterbury and all these bishops have given their opinion, and come in to us, save Salisbury, who yet continueth a lewd fool.[22]

This result followed a further strange sequence of proceedings in Parliament. The French ambassador reported on 20 May that there was an atmosphere of general indecision; the general expectation was that once matters had been decided in religion, Parliament would either be dissolved before Whitsunday (25 May) or prorogued until the autumn.[23] Instead, there are signs of sudden activity on 20 May, even as Marillac was settling down to write. The Lords' Journal records a very odd procedure that day, which was once more entrusted to the Duke of Norfolk: he asked that there should be a mere week's recess granted around Whitsun in order to give leisure afterwards to prepare a subsidy bill for the King; Henry readily assented the following day. This was a feeble reason for a prorogation, and it was coupled with a frank piece of innovation, the stipulation that bills still in progress would not have to start afresh when Parliament met once more. The reason for all this improvisation can only have been the travails of the Six Articles.[24] John Husee wrote off gleefully to Calais the same day that 'there will be such a discreet order taken concerning the Blessed Sacrament of the altar ere this Parliament

21 *Lisle Letters* 5 no. 1422, p. 485 (*L.P.* 14 i no. 1003).

22 Strype, *Cranmer*, pp. 294–5, no. 26 (*L.P.* 14 i no. 1040). Marillac's report (next note) gives a similar description of divisions among the bishops. Cf. Ridley, *Cranmer*, pp. 178–81.

23 *Castillon/Marillac*, p. 100; see his later report of 9 June, *L.P.* 14 i no. 1091, with extracts in *Castillon/Marillac*, pp. 101–2.

24 Cf. Lehmberg, *Later Parliaments*, pp. 65–6, and Elton, *Studies* 1, p. 208.

be prorogued, that some that are now busy in scanning of the nature of the same, intending to frame so excellent a thing after their carnal judgement, will hereafter tremble in mentioning that Blessed Sacrament which they not long since hath most unreverently, against all Christian faith and religion, misused and ill spoken of'.[25] He sandwiched this cry of triumph between two pieces of information about Thomas Cromwell. Lord Lisle could be sure that the evangelicals were in serious trouble, a welcome development which was already revealing implications for his own battles, as we will see.

The week's respite from 23 to 30 May saw the final meeting between the King and the German ambassadors, on 26 May; it was an unhappy occasion, in which Henry bluntly told them that he disliked the conditions that they were offering and that he must send them home. The ambassadors were foolish enough to criticize him for letting 'some articles of religion be negotiated in the Parliament' and matters escalated out of control in an argument about clerical marriage which the Germans later described ruefully as a '*hefftige disputation*' (a violent debate). A last desperate effort by Cromwell to salvage something from the wreckage was of no avail.[26] One wonders whether news of the row reached the clerical gathering which was at the same time discussing the Six Articles. This was an enlargement of the Convocation of Canterbury (this had opened at St Paul's Cathedral a few days after Parliament) to include representatives of the province of York: the assembly could therefore claim to represent the whole Church of England. It can legitimately be regarded as the second convening of Thomas Cromwell's vice-gerential synod, since the eventual Act of Six Articles spoke of the King summoning not only Parliament but also 'a synod and convocation of all the archbishops, bishops and other learned men of the clergy of this his realm'.[27] Its first meeting may have taken place before the recess, again on 20 May, when there was a significantly large absence of prelates from the Lords, and it may well have been the decision to convene this gathering which led to Parliament's hasty prorogation at the end of the week. However, the atmosphere of the synod would be very different from the scene which Alesius had witnessed back in 1537. It is a sign of the transformed mood in politics that the abbots still remaining in the Lords took part in the synodal discussion (in sharp contrast to the 1537 synod), despite the fact that their houses would all close over the next few months.

Part of the papers containing the questions and answers put to the prelates of this synodal gathering survive, together with the results of a previous vote taken in the Lower House of the Convocation of Canterbury agreeing to abide by the decisions of the prelates; Glyn Redworth has sorted out the order of

25 *Lisle Letters* 5, no. 1421 (*L.P.* 14 i no. 990).

26 McEntegart Ph.D., 'England and the League of Schmalkalden', pp. 343–4, quoting Merriman 1, pp. 276–7.

27 The most convenient text of the Act is in *English Historical Documents 1485–1558*, pp. 814–17.

these two responses and ably analysed them.[28] The Lower House was overwhelming in its trust in the prelates: only two, Christopher Nevinson (Cranmer's commissary) and the evangelical royal chaplain John Taylor, had resisted the vote of approval, while a third dissenter, Robert Oking, had deserted them for the majority at the last moment. A host of establishment evangelicals voted on the other side, including Edward Crome, who at the end of the whole affair was one of very few senior clergy, with John Taylor, to make a brave public stand against the Act of Six Articles.[29] The prelates' responses on the big issue of transubstantiation are unfortunately lost, but two areas where the evangelical prelates chose to put up a fight were compulsory clerical celibacy and confession. Interestingly two abbots (Westminster and St Albans) joined with them in thinking that priests might marry; perhaps they had an eye to their futures in the secular world. On confession, Cranmer headed an impressive bloc of ten bishops and two abbots who thought that it was not necessary but only 'requisite and expedient'. On the question of whether the administration of communion in both kinds was necessary by the word of God, only Cranmer and Bishop Barlow were willing to stand out for this strengthened version of evangelical belief, which had no doubt been deliberately expressed by conservative draftsmen in more extreme terms than Norfolk's original wording, in order to frighten off support from it.[30]

Parliament reconvened on 30 May; by that time it was clear that the broad content of the Articles had been accepted, and that all that remained was to turn them into a statute with penalties attached for disobedience. Now two new committees of bishops were appointed from the Lords, this time separately representing opposed party views, with a canon lawyer attached to either to advise on the drafting. On the one side were Cranmer, Goodrich and Barlow, on the other Lee, Tunstall and Gardiner: Winchester's first appearance in a prominent role in the proceedings was another sign of the evangelical rout.[31]

So far we have followed a necessarily complex narrative of events in Westminster, and noted the way in which the King in person was elbowing aside Cromwell, let alone Cranmer, from the determination of policy. What had made Henry so determined on a change of direction? He was faced with much the same diplomatic situation abroad, yet he reacted to it in the opposite way to the previous year, more or less ignoring the presence of the hapless German representatives who had hoped for great things from him. Another factor

28 Redworth, 'Six Articles', pp. 59–61, especially n. 64, discussing P.R.O., S.P. 1/152 ff. 15–21 (*L.P.* 14 i no. 1065); cf. *L.P.* 14 i no. 1066. I am convinced by Dr Redworth's ordering of the sequence of these documents, although I am doubtful about the precision of his dating.

29 *Wriothesley's Chronicle* 1, p. 101.

30 A point made by Lehmberg, *Later Parliaments*, p. 68.

31 *L.J.* 1, p. 113.

must have tipped the balance in his multiform calculations of his advantage, and brought out the traditionalist side of his jackdaw-like theological outlook. The most likely candidate is that old running sore of Cranmer's diocese, the religious stand-off in Calais; for once more, religious trouble had flared up there. Part of the dispute was triggered by Cranmer's commissary John Butler; Butler was still doggedly using his jurisdiction to pursue the godly cause as he had done for half a decade, but this time a new and dangerous coincidence intervened.[32] In early spring the Earl of Hertford went to Calais on an inspection of the defences, and the Calais conservatives seized the chance to complain to him about Butler's personal version of the Church militant, and also about other 'sacramentaries'. By the time Cromwell heard of all this, the complaints had been made formally to Hertford, to Sir Anthony Browne and others at Court. Cromwell wrote on 6 May, from his convalescence, to Lord Lisle telling him to investigate. It was noticeable that he used the current royal buzzword of evil omen for the evangelicals, 'diversity of opinion'; for already the King had become involved, and 'wanted to know the truth of these matters'. Cromwell was also annoyed and alarmed that he had been bypassed in letting his royal master have this information, so potentially dangerous for his own position.[33]

Cromwell's mention of Browne is additionally significant. Sir Anthony was an influential courtier who was a good friend both of the Lisles and of Gardiner, and it was likely that he had been the conduit for the poison about Calais reaching the King. Any investigation which involved Browne was not going to be the usual whitewash for the Calais evangelicals which Cromwell and Cranmer had managed so many times; Sir Anthony also kept Lisle fully informed of what was going on in London, including the sequence of events up to 30 May which we have already surveyed. Lisle, thus secretly primed by Browne and with his own staff of informants in the capital, knew that at long last, he could hope for success if he rounded up his Calais enemies, as long as he acted with discretion – 'I beseech you' (he begged Browne on 30 May) 'keep this my letter close, for if it should comen to my Lord Privy Seal's knowledge or ear I were half undone'. He told Browne that he had written to Cromwell 'plainly' (a note of confidence which was normally absent from his dealings with the Lord Privy Seal), reminding him of no fewer than three previous letters complaining 'that I am not able to serve the King's Majesty here without obedience'. The theme of obedience was a promising line to pursue in order to secure Henry's continuing interest. Meanwhile, all through May the Calais Council (despite the opposition of its evangelical

32 See the reports on Butler's activities to Cranmer, P.R.O., S.P. 1/152 ff. 5–7 (*L.P.* 14 i nos 1057–8). McEntegart Ph.D., 'England and the League of Schmalkalden', pp. 332–3, naturally prefers to concentrate on the German dimension of events around the Six Articles; he may not have fully appreciated the extent of the evidence for the importance of the Calais factor.

33 *Lisle Letters* 5 no. 1403: not calendared in *L.P.*

sympathizers) met to gather depositions on the troubles, duly forwarded to Cromwell.[34]

John Husee, keeping his usual careful eye on events in London for Lord Lisle, noted on 21 May the appearance of 'the commissary's man' at Lambeth Palace; 'what his suits are I know not'.[35] Commissary Butler was obviously worried about the turn of events, with good reason. On 25 May he made an indiscreet and no doubt aggressively intended remark in the Pale of Calais about the blessed sacrament, which was eagerly seized on as proving that he was a sacramentary; rapidly he was presented for heresy by a Calais jury, and was thus swept further into the very net of investigation which Cromwell had been forced into ordering at the beginning of the month.[36] Immediately Cranmer faced a formal complaint from the conservatives on the Calais Council about his commissary's conduct, and they demanded Butler's replacement; a copy of this also went to Hertford.[37] Cromwell was appalled at the accelerating witchhunt. He buttonholed Hertford and tried to win him over to a sceptical view of the accusations; he tried stonewalling by keeping the depositions sent over from Calais away from the King, and he wrote to Lisle on 27 May begging him to avoid 'division' by dealing with the allegations locally and 'with charity and mild handling'. He expressed his particular sorrow that Butler had been accused on insubstantial grounds.[38] No wonder Cranmer and Cromwell were at such a disadvantage in the Six Articles discussions while the vice-gerential synod was meeting in London: the Archbishop's administration was under direct attack for the most serious form of heresy. Yet Cromwell was helpless: the juggernaut rolled on. Prisoners from Calais were now arriving for examination in the capital, together with other unfortunates rounded up in Bristol and in Cranmer's own diocese at Cranbrook; Cromwell was forced to issue a vice-gerential commission for Cranmer and a fleet of bishops and ecclesiastical lawyers to examine them on heresy charges.[39]

From now on developments in Calais and the progress of the Six Articles marched in step. The final vote on the Six Articles in the Lower House of the Convocation of Canterbury was taken on Corpus Christi day (5 June), a choice of date which is not likely to be accidental in view of the main item to be voted on, the nature of the eucharist. Two days later, the King again turned to liturgy to demonstrate his new diplomatic priorities when he orchestrated every parish of the city of London, led by St Paul's Cathedral, in an extrava-

34 *Lisle Letters* 5 no. 1435 (*L.P.* 14 i no. 1042), and cf. ibid. nos 1410, 1424 (*L.P.* 14 i nos 954, 1008).

35 *Lisle Letters* 5 no. 1422, p. 484 (*L.P.* 14 i no. 1003).

36 P.R.O., S.P. 1/150 f. 4 (*L.P.* 14 i no. 1057).

37 P.R.O., S.P. 1/152 ff. 5–7 (*L.P.* 14 i nos 1057–8).

38 *Lisle Letters* 5, nos 1428–9 (*L.P.* 14 i nos 1030, 1029).

39 *Lisle Letters* 5, no. 1438 (*L.P.* 14 i no. 1060); the commission of 3 June 1539 is recorded in Cranmer's Register, f. 68.

gant forty-eight-hour display of mourning for the death of Isabella, the wife of the Emperor Charles V. The dukes of Norfolk and Suffolk, Cranmer and most of the Privy Council were present in St Paul's over the two days, with Stokesley leading the ceremonies throughout – a congenially traditional task for him. A fortnight of mourning was decreed to follow.[40] One person who was not there to join in was Burchard, the long-suffering leader of the Lutheran delegation; he left London for home in utter fury on the first day of the ceremonies.[41] On 12 June one of the MPs for Calais, Thomas Broke, got into deep trouble for his brave but tactically misjudged and overlong attack on the Six Articles in the House of Commons, and he was soon joining those suspects under examination.[42]

There was a hesitation in the progress of the conservative bandwagon towards the end of June: 24 June was the date of the first of two minor concessions to evangelicals. The Lords and Commons agreed to a small act of pity for married clergy putting away their wives; they had been given until today to do so, but now they would have until 12 July. The second concession (27 June) narrowed the conditions under which vows of celibacy previously taken would remain binding.[43] Cromwell was now in more optimistic mood, according to an upbeat letter written from London on 24 June by an evangelical Calais priest, Cyprian Thistlethwaite; the Lord Privy Seal told Thistlethwaite that there was a generally poor opinion of Lisle's conservative witnesses and that there were good chances for the evangelical accused. The parliamentary concession made that day may have encouraged Thistlethwaite to think that the tide was turning further, for he said of the Articles that 'I think part of them will be called in again'. Nevertheless, he added that Cranmer could not perform a favour for one of the Calais evangelicals because he had 'so much business that no man can well speak with him'.[44]

One major piece of business was probably packing Mrs Cranmer's bags. It has frequently been suggested that the concession of timing about priests' wives made on 24 June was intended for the Archbishop's benefit, so that the couple could arrange for Margaret's departure with a modicum of dignity and legality, and there is no reason to dismiss the idea. We know from Archbishop Parker that Cranmer sent his wife and children abroad at this time.[45] Readers may have been wondering what had happened to Mrs Cranmer since those remote days in 1532 when the newly married English ambassador had set out

40 *Wriothesley's Chronicle* 1, pp. 97–9; cf. Duffy, *Stripping of the Altars*, p. 423.

41 On 9 June Marillac said that Burchard had gone '*depuis deux jours*': *Castillon/Marillac*, p. 102 (*L.P.* 14 i no. 1091).

42 Lehmberg, *Later Parliaments*, pp. 72–4. Cf. also *History of Parliament 1509–58* 1, p. 506; this is probably wrong about his parentage, mixing him up with the Thomas Brooke of the Cobham family who was one of Cranmer's servants.

43 Lehmberg, *Later Parliaments*, p. 82.

44 P.R.O., S.P. 1/152 ff. 98–9 (*L.P.* 14 i no. 1153).

45 Parker, *De Antiquitate*, p. 390.

for Italy, entrusting her to her relations in Nuremberg. The answer is that a complete silence envelops Cranmer's wife during the 1530s; she probably came to England quite soon after he became Archbishop, but she kept so low a profile as to be invisible. This is really quite astonishing. One would expect Cranmer's evangelical friends from Cromwell downwards to be discreet, but none of the conservative abuse about Cranmer which survives in generous quantities from the 1530s makes any reference to Margaret. In the overwhelmingly male establishment of a Tudor episcopal household, a German-speaking female cannot have been hard to spot, and noisy little children would have been even more visible (at least one daughter had arrived by this time). It is likely that Margaret remained most of the time down at Ford, the remotest of Cranmer's palaces. An inventory of Ford (admittedly taken much later, in 1553, after Cranmer was an openly married man) lists 'his wife's chamber' placed next to a room which had once been the archbishop's study: a proximity which not all scholars have welcomed in their marriages.[46]

Very soon after Cranmer's death, conservative commentators made up for their previous neglect of his marriage by publishing the splendid story that throughout Henry's reign the Archbishop had carried his wife around with him in a box equipped with breathing-holes. It seems to have been that sprightly author Archdeacon Nicholas Harpsfield who added this tale to the canon, telling it first in the Latin demolition of Cranmer's career known as *Cranmer's Recantacyons*, and again soon afterwards in his belated refutation of Cranmer's co-authored *Determinations of the Universities*. In this second version, the Archdeacon added an enjoyable anecdote about the fire at Cranmer's Canterbury palace in December 1543, by which time Mrs Cranmer had returned to England once more: the Archbishop had become particularly anxious about the saving of one chest from the flames, which contained 'this pretty nobsey'. The whole story was (not surprisingly) indignantly denied by descendants of the Cranmer family. Jasper Ridley rightly points out that the 1543 fire story is likely to be the origin of the whole canard: a Kentish joke which arose from Cranmer's desperate concern for a precious chest of papers in the burning palace. There is another explanation for his concern for a chest of papers in the wake of the 1543 Prebendaries' Plot, as will be suggested below (Ch. 8, p. 322). Nevertheless, the story of Cranmer's wife in a box was perfect material for the warehouse of sleazy stories which the Catholic recusant community built up over the years, as some compensation for losing England to the reformers. Harpsfield is likely to be more accurate in his follow-up reminiscence to the story about the fire: he said that the Archbishop's brother Edmund, Harpsfield's predecessor as Archdeacon of Canterbury, swore blind that he was not married when questioned by an official enquiry on married

46 P.R.O., E. 154/2/39 f. 77r. On the daughter Margaret, see discussion below, Ch. 9, p. 361.

clergy, entrusted in the aftermath of the Six Articles to Thomas Thirlby.[47] The question seems never to have been officially put to the Archbishop himself in King Henry's days; Thirlby was, after all, one of his old Cambridge friends.

The passage of the Six Articles Act through Parliament and the grant of the royal assent were completed by the end of June: Parliament stood down on 28 June. A day or two later, bishops Latimer and Shaxton resigned their dioceses, or were told to resign, as was inevitable given their outspoken opposition to the measure; however, Cranmer found it impossible to take the easy way out and keep his principles unsullied as they did. There are a number of glimpses of him in the immediate aftermath of the Act's passage: the most vivid comes from Alexander Alesius, once more (as in 1536) describing a scene in the garden of Lambeth Palace in the early morning, probably on 1 or 2 July 1539. Cranmer used William Paget to summon Alesius to warn him to flee, otherwise he would be compelled to give his assent to the Articles. Giving Alesius a souvenir, Wolsey's ring which the King had given to him, the Archbishop unburdened himself of his misery, confusion and shame:

> 'Happy man that you are', said he, 'you can escape! Would that I were at liberty to do the same; truly my see would not hold me back. You must make haste to escape before the island may be cut off, unless you are willing to sign the decree, as I have done, compelled by fear – for I repent of what I have done, and if I had known that my only punishment would have been deposition from the Archbishopric (as I hear that my Lord Latimer is deposed), of a truth I would not have subscribed.'[48]

It is a convincingly Cranmerian piece of self-incriminating candour; yet it is not the whole story, and there are more creditable things to be said. What weighed heavily with Cranmer was his sense of indebtedness and loyalty to Henry VIII: Henry had done so much for the kingdom, ridding it of superstition and of the tyranny of the Bishop of Rome, and there was every chance that he might do more in the future. It was particularly important that the feeling was mutual; Henry was sensitive enough to the bruised ego of his faithful servant first to offer him the opportunity to miss the final vote in the Lords (he refused this let-out), and second to try to make amends for what had happened in Parliament. This took the somewhat heavy-handed form of Henry ordering a reconciling dinner in Cranmer's honour at Lambeth Palace; the guest-list included Cromwell and the dukes of Norfolk and Suffolk 'with all the lords of the Parliament' (it is to be hoped, but it is also unlikely, that the King had the grace to foot the bill). In fact Henry's plan went badly wrong, because one of the noblemen present at the dinner (probably Norfolk)

47 Harpsfield, *Pretended Divorce*, p. 275; *Cranmer's Recantacyons*, p. 8; cf. Sander, *Schism*, p. 181. The matter is well treated in Ridley, *Cranmer*, pp. 148–51.

48 P.R.O., S.P. 70/7 f. 11v (*C.S.P. Foreign*, *1558–9*, p. 533, whose translation I have adapted).

chose to praise Cranmer by rubbishing the memory of Cardinal Wolsey. Cromwell took deep offence at this implied and possibly deliberate slur to his own old service to the Cardinal; Cranmer and others had to intervene in what became a bitter slanging-match between the two men about their former papal loyalty.[49]

Nevertheless, more happily on the same occasion, Ralph Morice overheard Cromwell say to Cranmer at the dinner table, 'You were born in a happy hour I suppose . . . for, do or say what you will, the King will always well take it at your hand. And I must needs confess that in some things I have complained of you unto his Majesty, but all in vain, for he will never give credit against you, whatsoever is laid to your charge.' It was a reassuring remark, after the fear which Cranmer had expressed to Alesius (no doubt with a morale-sapping bad night's sleep behind him), and it continued to be true. Yet another encouraging incident of the same nature reported by Morice can probably be dated to the Parliamentary debates around the Six Articles: Sir John Gostwick, knight of the shire for Bedfordshire, made accusations in the Commons about the Archbishop's sermons and lectures at Sandwich and Canterbury, only to meet a savage personal rebuke from the King. Henry furiously called him a 'varlet' and roundly declared that if he did not make a personal apology to Cranmer 'I will sure both make him a poor Gostwick, and otherwise punish him, to the example of others'.[50]

Cranmer could also consider that the evangelicals had won a number of concessions in the Six Articles. Perhaps of only symbolic value, but still extraordinary in view of the radically changed religious atmosphere, was the recurrent phrase in the Act describing Henry's Church as the 'Church and congregation of England': the word 'congregation' was surely taken from the definition of the Church in the Augsburg Confession. Second, the final version of the article on the nature of the eucharist had dropped the actual word 'transubstantiation' which had appeared in all previous versions of the article, even though the word 'substance' still appeared in its vigorous affirmation of the real presence; Cranmer could regard the article, as he had done Adam Damplip a year earlier, as teaching 'but the truth'. This was a pale shadow of a success, but the evangelicals had indeed won a material victory on confession. This article had started life as a leading question for the proposition that auricular confession was 'necessary according to the law of God'; it ended up merely stating that it was 'expedient and necessary to be retained and continued, used and frequented in the Church of God'.

The revised wording on confession struck deep at the traditional view of penance in the Church as being instituted by God himself – a view which the King had long ago affirmed in the *Assertio Septem Sacramentorum* – and therefore it struck at the foundations of the Church's authority.[51] We have already

49 Foxe 5, pp. 265, 398; 8, p. 14.
50 *Narratives of the Reformation*, pp. 258–9, 251, 253. On the true dating of the Gostwick incident, *History of Parliament 1509–58* 2, pp. 238–9.
51 *Writings of Henry VIII*, pp. 97–9.

noted the strong support among the prelates in the May vice-gerential synod for this revised point of view (the strongest agreement which the evangelicals had been able to muster), and we have also seen Cranmer making the change in one of the positional papers in the Anglo-German discussions of 1538 (see above, Ch. 6, p. 217). Henry at this time abandoned the view championed in his book, and supported the evangelicals on the issue; he openly sided with Cranmer's arguments on the matter during the debates in the Lords. When Bishop Tunstall afterwards tried to restore the more uncompromisingly traditionalist position, Henry wrote him a blisteringly angry letter, one of the longest to survive in his own handwriting, reminding him of the general agreement on the new wording which had been arrived at in the House.[52]

Overall, scrutinizing the Articles with the benefit of a good dinner and the knowledge of Henry's personal warm friendship, it was possible for a scrupulous evangelical who abhorred flamboyant gestures to argue that not very much had changed. The Articles did not overturn a single one of the concrete reforms achieved by Cromwell over the previous decade, and if they affirmed the eucharistic presence in language which Cranmer would have felt aggressively conservative, they also did no more than affirm the real presence in which he believed. Above all, he was the King's servant ('he gave me the archbishopric' as he said to Alesius in the early morning quiet of his garden), and that, as much as a pure evangelical reformation, was a valid consideration of conscience to a sixteenth-century clergyman or politician.

A comparison is worth making with another highly placed European evangelical in an uncomfortable situation: the Habsburg Mary, dowager Queen of Hungary and the Governor of the Low Countries on behalf of her brother, the Emperor Charles V, for a quarter-century from 1531. It may sound bizarre even to call Mary an evangelical, given the savage programme of repression of religious reformists over which she presided as Governor. However, B.J. Spruyt has marshalled an impressive body of evidence to demonstrate this capable and learned woman's continued sympathy throughout her years in the Low Countries for the mainstream evangelicalism which chimed with her own biblical humanist interests. It was, for instance, thanks to her that Pierre Alexandre, her ex-Carmelite chaplain, who later joined Cranmer's secretarial team, was able to make his escape from the Netherlands Church authorities in 1543. Like Cranmer, she distinguished evangelicalism from religious radicalism, which she had no hesitation in persecuting as an enemy to true religion and good government. Ultimately her first loyalty was to her family, which as a dutiful woman she served as best she could: a service which inhibited her from giving precision to her religious sympathies and on occasion confronted her with dilemmas of conscience as cruel as any which the Primate of All England faced. When finally retiring from a thankless task in

52 B.L. Cotton MS Cleopatra E V ff. 134–7 (*L.P.* 14 ii App. no. 29). On the manoeuvres around transubstantiation and confession, see useful discussion in Redworth, 'Six Articles', pp. 61–4.

1555, she expressed her sense of duty thus: 'he who governs under another must not only render account to God but also to the prince and to his subjects'. Cranmer, whose self-effacement in politics equalled that of the Emperor's sister, deserves no less sympathy than Mary of Hungary, as the conscientious servant of an anointed monarch, trying to enforce an uncongenial uniformity in an increasingly mixed religious environment.[53]

And yet, when one has seen the whole affair as Cranmer in his more cheerful moments might have seen it, the immediate reality was disaster for the hopes which he and Cromwell had cherished of pushing the evangelical cause ever onwards: all the plans which were as yet in draft, such as the liturgical revision, would have to be shelved for the time being. As far as one detached observer, the French Ambassador Marillac, was concerned, King Henry had 'taken up again all the old opinions and constitutions, excepting only papal obedience and destruction of abbeys and churches of which he has taken the revenue'.[54] The evangelical observers of northern Europe saw it the same way, Bucer viewing it quite consciously as ending the first phase of his grand design of alliance begun in 1535.[55] The English evangelical leadership (probably Cromwell and Cranmer themselves) had done their best to launch a damage limitation exercise, sending an urgent message abroad with one fugitive from the effects of the Six Articles in late August; he travelled down from Hamburg to Strassburg, where Bucer sympathetically listened to the desperate plea that a fresh Schmalkaldic embassy should be sent to England to neutralize the conservative advantage. However, the Strassburg reformer expended in vain several thousand words of his prose in lobbying other members of the Schmalkaldic League on England's behalf. Johann Friedrich of Saxony and Luther were particularly furious at what had happened, and they were not sympathetic to Bucer's entreaties.[56]

The month of July was one of unadulterated humiliation for Cranmer and his friends. Cromwell dared not see Alesius before that talkative Scotsman fled to Wittenberg. Latimer probably never went back to his diocese after the debates in Parliament, but first he unsuccessfully tried to copy Alesius by fleeing abroad, and next he was spotted in the relative safety of Lambeth Palace wearing the gown of a simple priest.[57] Bishop Hilsey's four-year control of the pulpit of Paul's Cross now became worse than an embarrassment to the poor man, with a triumphant Bishop Stokesley getting his

53 Spruyt, 'Mary of Hungary', *passim*; on Mary's resignation letter, Koenigsberger, 'Prince and States General', p. 128.

54 *Castillon/Marillac*, p. 114 (*L.P.* 14 i no. 1260).

55 See his comments on the negotiations '*iam in quintum annum*' in his letter to Cranmer, 29 October 1539, *E.T.* p. 344, *O.L.* p. 527.

56 McEntegart Ph.D., 'England and the League of Schmalkalden', pp. 353–70, with convincing arguments for Cranmer's involvement, ibid., pp. 358–9.

57 On Alesius, see account as at n. 48 above, and his letter to Cromwell from Wittenberg, *L.P.* 14 i no. 1353. Latimer: *Lisle Letters* 5, pp. 573, 577 (*L.P.* 14 i nos 1219, 1227–8).

revenge for years of snubs by meticulously listening out for unorthodox pronouncements from the nervous few whom Hilsey could persuade to open their mouths there.[58] Cranmer's own particular crucifixion all through July was the business of personally confronting evangelicals with the consequences of the Act, which involved him presiding over an examining commission at Lambeth and Croydon. Bishop Sampson was his main colleague or, more accurately, his minder on behalf of the other conservative bishops after they had gone back to their dioceses. Alesius had been luckier in his escape than another evangelical Scot, George Wishart; Wishart appeared before Cranmer and fellow-bishops before being taken back to Bristol to do repeated public penance, a preparation for the martyrdom which he later suffered in his native land.[59] A senior fellow of All Souls, Oxford, and Canon of Lincoln, Laurence Barber, had a similar experience: although (at least according to Foxe) he silenced the episcopal commission with his use of Augustine in condemnation of official eucharistic theology, the outcome was a forced recantation back in the university. Within the month the trauma had killed him – 'the good man . . . wore away', as Foxe put it.[60]

It was still Calais which rubbed especial salt into Cranmer's wounds. John Butler and the rest of the Calais radicals formed the largest group in the examinations, and their plight was reported with great satisfaction in a stream of letters back to Lord Lisle, while the Deputy and his friends found fresh charges (some of them downright absurd) to heap on their opponents.[61] One letter of 13 July in Lisle's in-tray would afford him particular delight; it was from Cranmer himself, and was the first open admission of defeat in their tangled six-year relationship. It announced that he was looking for a replacement for Butler as Commissary for Calais, and that the new Commissary would strictly enforce restrictions on preaching. At elaborate length, Cranmer agreed with Lord Lisle's complaint about people reading the Bible during divine service contrary to royal 'intent and meaning' – his phrasing about this matter was such a striking echo of the proclamation which had not been issued in April as to be beyond coincidence.[62] In an extremely revealing letter a week later, Bishop Sampson wrote privately to Lisle telling him not to gloat at his triumph: in a letter to the examining commissioners at Lambeth, the Deputy had not used any of Cranmer's titles, even 'Archbishop'. 'I write it because it is noted. Ye shall use your discretion. I would give to every man his honest degree'. Sampson, a wiser politician than Lisle, could see that since the whole religious reaction was taking place in the name of unity, discourtesy

58 Brigden, *London*, p. 308.
59 Skeeters, *Community and Clergy*, pp. 54–5.
60 Foxe 5, pp. 454–5. For correction of Foxe's misdating and the effective fixing of the date as July 1539, Emden, *Oxford to 1540*, pp. 23–4.
61 Cf. *Lisle Letters* 5, pp. 562, 564, 569, 572–4, 576–8, 580, 587–8, and discussion at pp. 562–3, 569.
62 P.R.O., S.P. 1/152 ff. 154–9, Cox 2, pp. 390–92, *Lisle Letters* 5, no. 1489 (*L.P.* 14 i no. 1264).

was the last thing which the conservative cause required.[63] But formalities apart, as the Calais evangelicals suffered imprisonment or public penance, all the Archbishop could do was to plead with Lisle not to exploit their catastrophe further in order to bring fresh charges against them.[64] Butler was banished from Calais, imprisoned in London in the Fleet with Broke the Calais MP, and he only returned to his home to face charges of heresy.[65]

Just to cap Cranmer's misery, he returned back to Croydon at the end of the month from a visit to Lambeth to find that he would have to investigate a scandal in his own home parish: a sad parody of his high-minded and decorous marriage to a theologian's niece. It was the culmination of a long-running story, which illustrated how lives could be wrecked in the state of confusion surrounding clerical celibacy in the 1530s. About August 1536 Nicholas Somer, one of the Croydon chantry priests, had started a sexual relationship with Juliana Baylie, the teenage daughter of a near neighbour; Juliana's account of the subsequent love story is more circumstantial than the priest's, and Cranmer himself clearly placed more faith in it. They had continued with regular sex, apparently as exclusive and faithful partners, for two years until Whitsun (June) 1538; Cranmer had then been informed of what was going on, and the girl herself had broken off the relationship for three months. However, the distraught Nicholas had secretly persuaded her back to his bed, up to the time of the Act of Six Articles. The three-year tragedy deepened as national events pressed in on the tormented couple. The night of 19 July was one of furtive but sultry sex before Sunday mass, then the following week there was a flaming and no doubt noisy row. With the selfishness of desperation, Nicholas bitterly blamed Juliana for his misery before they fell into bed together once more. The village watch finally decided to intervene, and the couple found themselves on Cromwell's agenda. Their fate is unknown, and Cranmer himself was at a loss about the formal procedure for their case, because the commission to examine cases of clerical incontinence under the terms of the Act had not as yet been appointed. With his farewells to his own wife less than a month old, the Archbishop's feelings can be surmised: pity, anger at the way in which this chaotic union discredited clerical partnerships, uneasy *schadenfreude*.[66]

After the initial nightmare in July, an unexpected shift in the King's mood soon signalled a general shift in the political mood, as so often in the 1530s and 1540s. Partly it may have been the fact that there were fewer conservative bishops around Henry at Court to press for consistency in religious policy. The bishops most active in the Six Articles negotiations, Tunstall, Gardiner, Rugge and Clerk, first went back to their dioceses from the beginning of July,

63 *Lisle Letters* 5, no. 1491 (*L.P.* 14 i no. 1290).
64 Cox 2, p. 393, *Lisle Letters* 5, no. 1500 (*L.P.* 14 i no. 1322).
65 *Lisle Letters* 5, no. 1492 (*L.P.* 14 i no. 1291); *Chronicle of Calais*, p. 47 (imprisoned on 10 August 1539).
66 P.R.O., S.P. 1/152 ff. 235–8 (*L.P.* 14 i no. 1333).

and then in August, in a characteristic example of his self-destructive loss of temper, Gardiner afforded the hard-pressed Cromwell the perfect excuse to secure his removal from the Privy Council; Winchester did not reappear until after Cromwell's fall. Bishop Sampson was ejected at the same time.[67] Weakening the conservative position still further, Bishop Stokesley suddenly died on 8 September, at the height of his triumph, and to great and solemn traditional mourning.[68]

The bishops' absence did not make Henry's heart grow fonder of conservatism. When Vice-Chancellor Burchard returned in September, his by now well-tuned antennae detected the surprising turnaround in the King's outlook – Henry seemed already displeased with the results of the Act and its main promulgators, and Cranmer and Cromwell (no doubt gaining credit for their hard-won co-operation) were more in favour than ever. Cromwell, quick to take advantage of the changed atmosphere, hamstrung the operation of the Six Articles by postponing the issue of commissions to make enquiries which it had authorized.[69] At the centre of Henry's change of stance was his final decision on the question of his marriage, after two years of vacillation and intricate negotiations. To Cromwell's delight, he had decided on a marriage which would ally him with a German prince, who, if not an evangelical, was certainly no great friend to Rome or the Emperor; the chosen prince was also brother-in-law to that evangelical paragon, and Burchard's master, Duke Johann Friedrich of Electoral Saxony. He was Wilhelm Duke of Cleves, and the prospective bride was his sister Anna. The marriage treaty, with Cranmer as principal English signatory and Cromwell complacently looking on, was agreed at the beginning of October 1539.[70] Now the evangelical leadership's hopes for renewed contacts with the Schmalkaldic League would be fulfilled, because delegates from the League would come over to England at the same time as the bride. All suddenly looked bright once more.

There is a significant episode recorded by Cranmer's servant, Thomas Wakefield, which forms a darkly comic prelude to the fateful Cleves marriage. At some stage probably very near the culmination of the marriage negotiations in autumn 1539, Cranmer and Cromwell had an argument about the forthcoming marriage treaty, which very clearly demonstrates their different

67 Redworth, *Gardiner*, pp. 102, 107; *L.P.* 14 ii no. 750, pp. 279–80. It is possible that Tunstall and Clerk were also excluded from the Privy Council at this time in factional conflict, but the dating is not conclusive: McEntegart Ph.D., 'England and the League of Schmalkalden', pp. 372–3.

68 *Wriothesley's Chronicle* 1, pp. 106–7.

69 *L.P.* 14 ii no. 423. Cf. McEntegart Ph.D., 'England and the League of Schmalkalden', pp. 372–3, 377–8, 399–400.

70 *L.P.* 14 ii nos 285–6. A Cleves marriage had been first mooted in November 1538: cf. *L.P.* 13 ii no. 923, and McEntegart Ph.D., 'England and the League of Schmalkalden', pp. 306–11. Cf. the King's comments on his rejection of the marriage proposal for the Duchess of Milan and Cranmer's part in the negotiation, *St.P.* 1, pp. 616–19 (*L.P.* 14 ii nos 187, 200).

priorities. There is a strong suggestion in these depositions that Catherine Howard, newly arrived at Court as a teenage maid in waiting, had already caught the King's eye, and was namelessly under discussion. Cranmer, concerned as a royal chaplain should be for Henry's personal happiness, actually opposed going further with the Cleves enterprise, despite being one of the principal negotiators for it; he said that he 'thought it most expedient the King to marry where that he had his fantasy and love, for that would be most comfort for his Grace'. Furious at this political naivety, and no doubt mindful of the appalling risks to his own fragile position if Henry chose yet another English nobleman's daughter as a wife, Cromwell snapped 'There was none meet for him within this realm'. Cranmer retorted with spirit 'that it would be very strange to be married with her that he could not talk withal'. A man with a German wife should know! In the event it was the kindly and politically clumsy Cranmer who got the King's psychology right; if only Cromwell had listened to him that day, and not placed his faith in over-ingenious portrait-painters and the arts of the Tudor advertising industry.[71]

Whatever their disagreements about the King's marital future, the two allies could now enjoy what seemed like their old advantage. A particular compensation for the Six Articles would be Henry's renewed interest in his official Bible project, their shared passionate concern. Cromwell adroitly turned round the fears about Bible-reading which Henry had expressed in his April draft proclamation to positive gain for himself, which became apparent in a new proclamation of 14 November: this put the Vice-gerent in charge of licensing all Bible translations for five years and ordered all secular authorities to give him every assistance (interestingly, nothing was said about the bishops – the Vice-gerent could presumably take care of them on his own authority). Henry had indeed changed his tune, and he had probably allowed Cromwell to be his script-writer: although he was still worried about 'wilful and heady folk' taking advantage of diverse translations, his emphasis was his interest in his people 'at all times' gaining knowledge of God's word, which he felt best effected by 'free and liberal use of the Bible in our own maternal tongue'.[72]

In this spirit of cautious permissiveness, the King also commissioned his Archbishop to write a new preface for the Great Bible which had appeared the previous April: a chance which Cranmer eagerly seized. His draft was ready for Cromwell and Henry's consideration by early November 1539, for he reminded the Vice-gerent to hurry along its royal approval on 14 November.[73] It first appeared in the second impression (April 1540) of the Great Bible, which with heroic inaccuracy has therefore been christened 'Cranmer's Bible', despite the fact that he seems to have had little more to do

71 Bodl. MS Jesus 74 f. 299v.
72 Letters patent *L.P.* 14 ii no. 619/34; *T.R.P.* 1 no. 192.
73 P.R.O., S.P. 1/154 ff. 165–6, Cox 2, p. 396 (*L.P.* 14 i no. 517).

with the rest of the enterprise than negotiating the retail price with the publishers. Nevertheless, the preface is one of Cranmer's most memorable pieces of public prose, which clearly pleased Henry VIII, since he used phrases from it in one of his most important speeches to Parliament in 1545, a speech which had the same twofold strategy as Cranmer's text.[74]

Unlike the translators of the Authorized Version seventy years later, the Archbishop did not seek to flatter his King, but instead preached what amounted to a universal sermon on the use of the Bible. It is a sermon deliberately structured in two parts, addressing two opposed audiences, a strategy neatly summarized in Cranmer's letter to Cromwell of 14 November: there he said that he trusted 'that it shall both encourage many slow readers, and also stay the rash judgements of them that read therein'. Of his 'two sundry sorts of people', 'some there are that be too slow, and need the spur: some other seem too quick, and need more of the bridle'. To both parties, he opposed the witness of history, initially by sketching out the deep roots of vernacular Bible translation in English church life. That brief discussion is itself of interest: first it referred to the beneficial spin-off from the dissolution of the monasteries, as hitherto unknown copies of Anglo-Saxon Bible translations turned up at the opening of monastic libraries. Second it acknowledged the contribution of the Lollards to biblical translation, without provoking fury among conservative churchmen by actually naming those medieval and contemporary heretics.

The witness of history continued beyond England's parochial experience, because Cranmer characteristically summoned up two great Greek fathers of the fourth-century Church, John Chrysostom and Gregory Nazianzenus, to give the burden of the two sections in his sermon: one father to encourage, the other to warn. Cranmer could not bear that people should refuse the gift of the Bible, yet he also understood what a dangerous book it could be. As he turned from Chrysostom's praise of Bible knowledge to Nazianzenus's caution about its misuse, his own words in a link passage gave more eloquent expression than Henry had done to the fears which they both shared:

> What is there here beneath, better than fire, water, meats, drinks, metals of gold, silver, iron, and steel? Yet we see daily great harm and much mischief done by every one of these, as well for lack of wisdom and providence of them that suffer evil, as by the malice of them that worketh evil . . . Wherefore I would advise you all, that cometh to the reading or hearing of this book, which is the word of God, the most precious jewel, and most holy relic that remaineth upon earth, that ye bring with you the fear of God, and that ye do it with all due reverence, and use your knowledge thereof, not to vainglory or frivolous disputation, but to the honour of God, increase of virtue, and edification both of yourselves and other.

74 See MacCulloch (ed.), *Henry VIII*, p. 175. For what follows, see the Preface text in Cox 2, pp. 118–27.

Cranmer's preface reveals another clue to the relationship between the timid lecturer and the self-righteous, God-obsessed royal bully. Cranmer became determined to give the Bible and its message to all in the kingdom; yet he was fearfully conscious that not everyone possessed his own self-discipline, his tight control over his feelings and actions. The world needed discipline to use the Gospel's message, and once the Pope had gone, who could give discipline but the King? And what a king Henry was! Only when Henry was dead and buried did Cranmer start emerging from his shadow, and a new phase of his life began, the revolutionary phase which would end in his death by fire. To the end, he struggled with the dilemmas of discipline, and what discipline might mean when God's anointed betrayed God's message in the biblical text.

In the promising situation of autumn 1539, a crucial event for the future of the evangelical cause was the filling of the vacancy in the diocese of London created by Bishop Stokesley's death, and the initiative in the choice of Edmund Bonner was without doubt Cromwell's. So far Bonner was his reliable protégé; best of all, Bonner's promotion was calculated to infuriate Stephen Gardiner, as the previous year the two men had become embroiled in poisonous and very public rows when Bonner succeeded Gardiner as ambassador to France. Hindsight tells us that Cromwell's choice was as disastrous a missed opportunity for evangelicals as his backing of the Anne of Cleves marriage: after Cromwell's fall, Bonner and Gardiner overcame their common irascibility to become rock-like allies in the defence of traditional religion.[75] Yet for the moment all seemed well with Bonner; in any case, he had no chance to prove himself either way before Cromwell's fall.

Cromwell and Cranmer seized the autumn interval, before Bonner returned from his embassy in France to be consecrated, to stamp their authority on the capital's religious affairs. Their chief scapegoat was a prominent ex-Conventual Franciscan friar, William Watts, who became the darling of London conservatism, in the aftermath of the Six Articles, with his daily preaching: hitting a man when he was down, he seems to have taken Bishop Latimer as chief target in a revivalist campaign to discredit the new learning.[76] At the beginning of October, as the Cleves negotiations reached their successful conclusion, Watts managed to say things sufficiently serious to lead to his denunciation as a heretic to the Privy Council, which led to the appointment of a commission headed by Cranmer to examine the relevant papers, forwarded from the Council by Cromwell. Even although Bishop Sampson was named to this commission, just as he had been in July, Sampson

75 Elton, *Studies* 1, p. 210. Bonner was elected on 20 October.

76 Depositions of Chaitor and Cray, P.R.O., S.P. 1/155 ff. 189r, 196 (*L.P.* 14 ii no. 750/1.i, 2). On Watts's career, see Emden, *Oxford to 1540*, p. 611. For Bale's repeated condemnations of him, see Bale, *Works* p. 510; Bale, *Epistle Exhortatory* f. 14r; Bale, *Mystery* f. 9r.

was now a spent force.[77] Unsurprisingly, Watts stayed on as a prisoner at Lambeth after his examination. His plight aroused conservative anger and demonstrations in London; the evidence for their extent is shaky, but they were sufficiently serious for Cranmer (probably on Cromwell's advice) to remove Watts out of the limelight down to Canterbury gaol, where he was still languishing in the stocks through the winter of 1540.[78] As we have noted before, Cranmer's habitual mildness deserted him when dealing with conservative friars, whom he detested as heretics even more than Anabaptists.

Once the Lambeth commission had disposed of Friar Watts, it turned its attention to the Calais affair, and the result was ludicrously predictable both as litmus test of the prevailing political atmosphere, and as contrast to the proceedings in July. Cranmer and the commissioners (Sampson included) reported back to Cromwell on 11 November, sneering at the probity of the conservative witnesses and virtually excusing all those evangelicals accused before them, among them Cranmer's long-standing Calais informant Henry Tourney; even those who could not be given an immediate clean bill of spiritual health should wait on further evidence before any decision could be made about them.[79] By the time that Lisle heard about this twist of events, he would not be in any doubt as to its cause; from mid-October he had been under instructions to make Calais respectable enough to please a royal bride from Cleves. The lady herself arrived at Calais on 11 December, and she then spent a fortnight there, doing her best to be agreeable to the King's welcoming committee, while the English Channel behaved at its worst, and the Lisles hovered discreetly in the background.[80]

Anne eventually braved the weather to land at Dover on 27 December, and she was welcomed in great style to Kent by the Archbishop and county dignitaries; she spent the next few days travelling up with Cranmer to the planned lavish reception at Greenwich. The tale has often been told of Henry's first dismayed sighting of her at Rochester on 1 January 1540, and his subsequent desperate and unsuccessful attempts to wriggle out of the wedding, at which Cranmer officiated in the Chapel Royal at Greenwich on 6 January.[81] The previous day, Cranmer and Bishop Tunstall had ended the

77 Cranmer's Register, ff. 67v–68r, 70. These are two different versions of the commissions recorded, both of 4 October, the second adding Bishops Sampson and Skip as commissioners. It is likely that the second corrected the first (which omitted Watts's Christian name) and was the one used.

78 Depositions of Chaitor and Cray, as above. John Butler to Bullinger, 24 February 1540 *E.T.* p. 406 (*O.L.* p. 627). Watts figures in Cromwell's remembrances of March 1540: *L.P.* 15 no. 438 i.

79 B.L. Cotton MS Cleopatra E V f. 387 (*L.P.* 14 ii no. 496).

80 Cf. especially *Lisle Letters* 5 no. 1571; P.R.O., S.P. 1/157, ff. 126–30 (*L.P.* 14 ii nos 347, 677).

81 Starkey (ed.), *Henry VIII: a European Court*, pp. 138–43; good contemporary accounts in *Wriothesley's Chronicle* 1, pp. 109–10; *Castillon/Marillac*, pp. 150–51.

King's efforts to find a legal bolthole by their joint conclusion that, on the evidence available, there was no reason for the marriage not to go ahead. Faced with this unwelcome candour among his advisors across the religious spectrum, the King had no choice but to proceed, 'against his will'.[82] However, the two bishops were just doing their job as honest diplomats; in reality there was only one man to blame for the disaster – Cromwell. After all theories about Cromwell's fall have been exhausted – faction, diplomacy and changing religious dynamics – the central reason remains this story-book misjudgement of his king's 'fantasy'.

For the moment, the King's volcanic misery slumbered, and Anne supposed with enviable innocence that his perfunctory kisses represented marital consummation. Perhaps because of Henry's inner turmoil, the next few months are one of the most contradictory and volatile periods in the whole reign; political and religious polarization was acute, and sacramentaries and papalists suffered shipwreck in apparently random sequence. Cranmer was generally not in the spotlight: the frontliners in controversy were on the one side Cromwell and a number of aggressive evangelical preachers, led by the veteran Lutheran spokesman Robert Barnes, and on the other the leading conservative bishops (Gardiner, Tunstall and Sampson), the preacher and royal chaplain Dr Nicholas Wilson, and traditionalist aristocrats led by the Duke of Norfolk. First success went in March to the conservatives: after a steadily escalating series of dramatic pulpit confrontations around the Court and the capital, Barnes was humiliated by Gardiner at Eastertide, and imprisoned in the Tower with equally outspoken fellow-evangelicals William Jerome and Thomas Garrett.[83] This was a chance for Gardiner to begin rebuilding his position after his humiliation the previous summer, and Cromwell hastened to mend fences with him with a long and supposedly intimate dinner party.

Calais simultaneously provided fresh possibilities of undermining Cromwell's position with a renewed assault on the usual evangelical group there, much to the delight of the Duke of Norfolk, who was keeping in touch with Lord Lisle about the way the political scene was progressing. A new royal commission set up on Norfolk's initiative reported back to the King from Calais on 5 April; it was warmly supportive of Lisle and repeatedly connected the Archbishop with the evangelicals' misdemeanours.[84] The Germans of the Schmalkaldic League did not help matters, infuriating Henry with their high moral tone towards his backsliding from the evangelical cause. Particularly at Bucer's urging, they had agreed to send yet another delegation to England in

82 *L.P.* 15 no. 824, p. 393, some of the missing material of which is supplied in Bodl. MS Jesus 74 f. 291r. Cf. *L.P.* 15 no. 850.3.

83 For a detailed consideration of these months, see Redworth, *Gardiner*, pp. 105–29, although his efforts to minimize Gardiner's initiatives in events are somewhat overdone. See also Elton, *Studies* 1, Ch. 10, and useful material in Brigden, *London*, pp. 308–15.

84 *Lisle Letters* 6 no. 1663; *St.P.* 8, p. 299 (*L.P.* 15 nos 429, 460, and cf. ibid. no. 461).

21 Anne of Cleves by Hans Holbein: the portrait which had such disastrous consequences.

spring 1540, but they committed their usual two errors: they refused to make it the high-powered theological discussion headed by Melanchthon which was one of Henry's dearest wishes, and they also adopted a stance of lofty criticism towards the erring monarch. Cranmer was drawn into this unpromising diplomatic morass when Duke Johann Friedrich of Saxony wrote to him personally. One can gauge the content of the Duke's letter (which has not survived) from the Archbishop's defensive and reproachful reply on 10 May; this emphasized everything that Henry had done for the evangelical cause in England, expelling the Pope, idolatry and monasticism, and warned Johann Friedrich not to press a learned and touchy monarch too far.[85]

While these storms raged, Cranmer was mainly occupied in the complex business of reordering his own cathedral, part of the final act in Henry's destruction of monastic life in his realm. The last monasteries closed during winter and early spring 1540 (much to evangelical satisfaction, as one can see from the Archbishop's letter to Johann Friedrich); this necessitated the remodelling of those English cathedrals which survived up to 1540 as monastic foundations, and also as some compensation for anguished conservatives it

85 McEntegart Ph.D., 'England and the League of Schmalkalden', pp. 403–7.

also entailed the retention of six more religious houses as the basis for new cathedrals and dioceses. This was one of Henry VIII's pet schemes. He took a close personal interest in the parliamentary legislation setting up the new royal foundations, which was put through at the same time as the Six Articles in 1539; he had a major hand in the preamble to the Act promising all sorts of benefits to the nation, in a purple passage which Joyce Youings has unkindly if accurately described as 'largely irrelevant jargon'.[86] In Kent, both Rochester and Canterbury cathedrals had been monastic, and they were the last monasteries in all England to surrender, between 3 and 8 April 1540. The Archbishop headed the commissioners at both institutions, and at Canterbury various local celebrities like Lord Cobham and Sir Anthony St Leger came along to watch this momentous change as the monks signed away their house.[87]

Cranmer had mixed feelings about what was happening. His relationship with Canterbury Cathedral Priory, of which he was an extremely nominal head, had been frosty. His rapport with Prior Goldwell was non-existent from the start, thanks to the Elizabeth Barton affair (see above, Ch. 4). It had not improved, as Goldwell sadly acknowledged to Cromwell when trying unsuccessfully to position himself for high office in the remodelled Cathedral: Cranmer was 'not so good Lord unto me as I would that he were'.[88] The Archbishop might be expected to view with satisfaction the dispatch of Goldwell and his black-cowled crew: the trouble was that Henry's schemes for his cathedrals inspired very different notions of the future among his churchmen and leading laypeople, depending on their religious outlook. Bishop Gardiner's blueprints for the details of the cathedral remodellings made lavish provision for staffing, based on the traditional vision of cathedrals as powerhouses of prayer and beautiful music: a vision which paradoxically survived to become a vital part of the Anglican ethos, against all the odds in the Reformation.[89]

In this respect, Cranmer was far from being an Anglican. What appealed to him (and to other evangelicals) in Henry's expansive plans was the potential benefit to education in the new foundations, whose collegiate character indeed made them very like the colleges of the universities. He was therefore not impressed when Cromwell forwarded him a draft constitution for the new Canterbury foundation in November 1539: there was too much money set aside for twelve prebendaries, a species of clergyman who in his eyes was 'neither a learner, nor teacher, but a good viander' – he considered that the

86 Youings, *Dissolution of the Monasteries*, p. 85.

87 Commission to Cranmer and others, *L.P.* 15 no. 378 (20 March 1540), and cf. P.R.O., E. 315/245 ff. 74, 76–9 (*L.P.* 15 nos 452, 474). Canterbury's actual surrender took place on Saturday 3 April: C.C.C.C. MS 298 f. 48v. Cobham was not named to the commission, but besides being present at Canterbury, he signed the account at Rochester.

88 P.R.O., S.P. 1/157 ff. 228–9, Ellis, *Original Letters*, 3 iii, pp. 277–8 (*L.P.* 15 no. 254).

89 Cf. S. Lehmberg in Guth and McKenna (eds), *Tudor Rule and Revolution*, pp. 53–4.

mere state of being a prebendary had ruined the academic promise of many learned men. Prebendaries should be completely abolished, and 'twenty divines at ten pounds apiece' could instead be supported at the Cathedral, together with 'forty students in the tongues and sciences', to take advantage of the three proposed lecturers in Greek, Hebrew and Latin, who were intended to cover theology and literature. What he was proposing was indeed a full-scale university college in a new setting, with a biblical humanist curriculum: it was not surprising that he recommended someone from Oxford or Cambridge as head of the institution, and in particular Dr Edward Crome, doubly qualified since he was a very successful former head of house at Cambridge, and also (although Cranmer did not say this in his letter) one of the few people to speak out publicly against the Act of Six Articles.[90]

It is a measure of how little effective influence Cranmer had even with his chief friend and sympathizer Cromwell that none of his suggestions was taken up, particularly his recommendation of Crome for Dean; instead, that smooth career diplomat and Kentish gentleman Nicholas Wotton was appointed, to begin a long career of non-residence with which he coupled the Deanery of York – a geographically heroic piece of pluralism designed to save the Crown money in Wotton's Continental missions. Cranmer's only consolation was the provision (unique to Canterbury) of six preachers in addition to the twelve prebendaries; he personally chose them, in line with Henry's usual obsession with religious balance, consciously to represent 'three of the New Learning, and three of the Old'.[91] Indeed, after Cranmer's November comments on the draft statutes, the Cathedral constitution actually got worse from his point of view; its educational provision was much cut down, although the school survived, and one higher lecture in theology was also maintained in the Archbishop's palace in the Close right up to 1553. After the revisions in the Canterbury foundation in 1541, a royal policy rethink in 1545 brought a virtually total retreat from the principle of higher education in a cathedral setting, something to which several other cathedrals had been initially committed: Canterbury among other cathedrals ceased to bear the obligation to support students at Oxbridge, and it also finally surrendered the dormant Canterbury College, Oxford, to form part of the new endowment for Oxford's Christ Church.[92]

90 B.L. Cotton MS Cleopatra E IV ff. 360–61, Cox 2, pp. 396–7 (*L.P.* 14 ii no. 601). Cox most unfortunately added 'and French' to 'the tongues and sciences'; this has no basis in the text. For comments on the collegiate character of the new cathedral foundations, see Knighton in Marcombe and Knighton (eds), *Close Encounters*, pp. 20–22, and MacCulloch, 'Worcester', in Collinson and Craig (eds), *The Reformation in English Towns* (forthcoming).

91 C.C.C.C. MS 128 pp. 167–70, 217–18, 295 (*L.P.* 18 ii no. 546, pp. 333–4, 345, 364).

92 Knighton in Marcombe and Knighton (eds), *Close Encounters*, pp. 26–34. On the lecture room in Canterbury Palace, see P.R.O., E. 154/2/39 f. 82r, and for Pierre Alexandre's last course of lectures in 1553, C.C.C.C. MS 126.

Many of the remaining personnel of the new Cathedral establishment provided added annoyance for the Archbishop. Even in the first list of staff produced on the surrender of the monastery, he was faced at all levels with a selection of former monks, some of whom he had criticized in the past. However, when the Cathedral establishment was completed by letters patent in 1541, the list of prebendaries had been further modified after Cromwell's fall to include one or two more stalwarts of Kentish clerical conservatism. One of these in particular, Warham's former steward of household, Richard Parkhurst, was among the Archbishop's tormentors in 1543.[93] Cranmer's experiences of that stressful time were not calculated to kindle any new affection in the Archbishop for his Cathedral; it was perhaps not without significance that he never once consecrated a bishop in the city. He used his palace in the Close at Canterbury little, even before it was damaged by fire in 1543, and although it was subsequently rebuilt in stages, mainly by Archbishop Parker, its usual occupant in Cranmer's later years seems to have been his suffragan bishop of Dover, Richard Thornden, in a caretaker role.[94] The Cathedral remained a sore disappointment to Cranmer. It may be symbolic of his attitude towards it that 1540 saw the removal of two of its chantry foundations for Archbishop Thomas Arundel and John Buckingham, Bishop of Lincoln, together with their accompanying tombs: the common factor in this precocious destruction was that these great churchmen of the turn of the fourteenth and fifteenth centuries had been great persecutors of the Lollards. The Archbishop, as chief commissioner at the dissolution of the Cathedral Priory, must have given his approval to this action, and it was not likely to endear him to the surviving Cathedral establishment.[95] Cranmer's chaplain, Nicholas Ridley, a foundation prebendary and one of his strongest supporters on the new Cathedral staff, himself later looked back with dislike and contempt on the majority of his colleagues at Canterbury; Ridley contrasted them unfavourably with the 'gentleness and obedience' which he found at little Rochester Cathedral when he became its bishop in 1547.[96]

Cranmer had better luck in the setting-up of the new school foundation at Canterbury. One small triumph occurred during the actual course of taking the surrender at Canterbury: the victory was won against his fellow-commissioners over the first choice of scholars for the school foundation at the Cathedral, a choice which inevitably set an important precedent for the future. Lord Rich and his fellows wanted entrance restricted to 'younger brethren' (that is, former Canterbury monks or novices) and gentlemen's sons. 'As for other husbandmen's children, they were more meet', they said, 'for the

93 Zell, 'Prebendaries' Plot', p. 246, comparing P.R.O., E. 315/245 ff. 76–9 (*L.P.* 15 no. 452) and *L.P.* 16 no. 779/5. On Parkhurst, cf. Du Boulay, *Lordship of Canterbury*, p. 401.

94 On Thornden's chamber in the Palace, see P.R.O., E. 154/2/39, f. 81r.

95 Collinson, Ramsay and Sparks (eds), *Canterbury Cathedral*, p. 475.

96 *Ridley's Works*, pp. 407–8.

plough and to be artificers, than to occupy the place of the learned sort.' Cranmer's donnish instincts, perhaps his memories of favourite pupils at Cambridge, were outraged; with that biting sarcasm of which he was especially capable on the subject of education, he reminded the others that 'the gifts of the Holy Ghost' were not necessarily distributed on the basis of genealogy. His *coup de grâce* was a piece of pitiless historical sociology: 'I take it that none of us all here, being gentlemen born (as I think)' – a beady eye cast at Lord Rich, perhaps? – 'but had our beginning that way from a low and base parentage; and through the benefit of learning and other civil knowledge, for the most part, all gentle ascend to their estate.' Outraged, one of his colleagues objected that 'the most part of the nobility came up by feat of arms and martial acts'. In a splendid assertion of humanist values, all the more effective for being fashionable, Cranmer sneered 'as though . . . that the noble captain was always unfurnished of good learning and knowledge to persuade and dissuade his army rhetorically, which rather that way is brought unto authority, than else his manly looks'. The collection of lawyers and career bureaucrats involved in this altercation could hardly disagree with him; perhaps they might have recognized that he was paraphrasing sentiments from Horace's *De Arte Poetica*.[97] The King's School, Canterbury, was not reserved for the well-born and well-off, at least not until the public school system subverted English education in later centuries. Another indication of Cranmer's evangelical humanist influence in the school foundation was in one detail of its curriculum: the inclusion of the Latin eclogues of the modern Italian poet Baptista Mantuanus. This was the first time that Mantuanus had received such an accolade in Tudor school statutes, but with Canterbury School setting the precedent, he later became a favourite, because of the strong attacks on papal corruption in his poetry.[98]

Immediately after the surrenders at Canterbury and Rochester, the Archbishop was plunged once more into renewed royal attempts to improve on the Bishops' Book. Just before Parliament reopened on 12 April 1540, the King appointed two committees, one a group of bishops and theologians (headed by Cranmer) to consider doctrine, the other a smaller collection of bishops to consider what liturgical ceremonies ought to be retained. Their constitution was announced in a speech to Parliament by Cromwell which followed Lord Chancellor Audley's opening oration, and which repeated the theme so familiar over the previous twelve months: the King's desire for a middle way, and the dangers of abusing scriptural knowledge. Reflecting the fevered political atmosphere, the committees were told to work intensively, occupying themselves three days a week and other afternoons when they could manage it. In practice they probably achieved little at this stage; the surviving paperwork

97 Cf. especially Horace, *De Arte Poetica*, ll. 112–13: *Si dicentis erunt fortunis absona dicta/ Romani tollent, equites peditesque, cachinnum.*

98 *Narratives of the Reformation*, pp. 273–5. Cf. Knighton in Marcombe and Knighton (eds), *Close Encounters*, pp. 24–5. Piepho, 'Mantuan's Eclogues'.

seems to date from after Cromwell's fall, and that impression is reinforced by the evidence of Ralph Morice and John Foxe.[99] Marillac spoke repeatedly in May of the bishops' fruitless disagreements, and of the King's annoyance with them for their lack of progress, though Marillac also noted in mid-June that they were still engaged in daily meetings.[100] Bishop Sampson provides another reference to the fact that the doctrine committee had 'stayed' in May, principally over their attitude to that perennial bone of contention, the validity of unwritten traditions: he also makes it clear that the deadlocks had arisen thanks to a rearguard evangelical resistance to the will of the conservative majority.[101]

The committees' slow start is understandable, given the political turmoil of the next two months. For instance, their constitution in early April coincided with a moment of conservative ascendancy in the King's inclinations, partly encouraged by the news of evangelical misdemeanours in Calais; this explains why both committees had conservative majorities. On 10 April, Ambassador Marillac reported back to France with relish that Cromwell and Cranmer 'do not know where they are', and that the Lord Privy Seal was tottering, with conservatives poised to take over. A week after it had been set up, the doctrinal committee was diverted from its allotted work in order to reconstitute itself as a commission for heresy, examining an evangelical Scots chaplain of the Duke of Suffolk, Alexander Seton: another sign of conservative pressure on Cromwell and his friends.[102] It is also at this time that one finds the first traces of the activity of commissions under the 1539 Act of Six Articles in the localities, the commissions which according to Cromwell's boasts to evangelical friends he had prevented from meeting for months after the Act had been passed.[103] Yet, in less than a fortnight after his cheerful news about evangelical travails, Marillac had to eat his words as the political wind changed abruptly once more: Cromwell had seized the chance offered by two convenient aristocratic deaths, to obtain in mid-April the ancient title of Earl of Essex, together with the noble Court office of Lord Great Chamberlain.[104] The prince of bureaucrats had thus pitchforked himself into the territory of the most blue-blooded of noblemen: thereby, ironically, he

99 Lehmberg, *Later Parliaments*, pp. 90–93. Cf. *Narratives of the Reformation*, pp. 248–9 and Foxe 8, pp. 23–4, and discussion of these stories below.

100 *Castillon/Marillac*, pp. 180, 186, 189 (*L.P.* 15 nos 651, 736, 766).

101 Strype, *Ecclesiastical Memorials*, 1 ii no. 93, pp. 381–2 (*L.P.* 15 no. 758). See below, p. 277 for a note of a possible initiative by Cromwell in Convocation on 5 May in connection with the doctrine committee.

102 *Castillon/Marillac*, p. 175 (*L.P.* 15 no. 485, and ibid. no. 486). Heresy commission recorded in Cranmer's Register, f. 69 (20 April 1540): the membership is a slightly scaled-down list of those named to the doctrinal committee.

103 Cf. a sitting of a commission on the Act at Ipswich, 28 May 1540: P.R.O., C. 244/177/19. For Cromwell's remarks, McEntegart Ph.D., 'England and the League of Schmalkalden', p. 399.

104 *Castillon/Marillac*, p. 179 (*L.P.* 15 no. 567).

may have sealed his fate, by pushing outraged snobs of ancient lineage, like the Duke of Norfolk, into joining forces with Bishop Gardiner to seek his final destruction.

Cromwell, with the concentrated energy of a desperate gambler, now moved into the offensive, aided by a sensational discovery which proved that Calais could always be relied upon to produce the unexpected. One of Lord Lisle's chaplains, Gregory Botolf, defected to Rome, and the discovery of this in mid-April also revealed that several members of the Lisle household had known what was going on.[105] It gave Cromwell the perfect excuse to turn round the situation at Calais from danger to advantage, and to bring an abrupt end to the Deputy's troubled career. Lisle was arrested for treason on 19 May, having been lured to London with the expectation of promotion in the peerage. He never regained his freedom, reputedly dying of a seizure of joy when in 1542 he was told he would be released from the Tower.[106] At the end of May, Cromwell went on to secure the arrest of the committee members Bishop Sampson and Dr Wilson, which can have done nothing to aid the concentration of their colleagues on the ceremonial and doctrinal committees. In the aftermath of Sampson's arrest, Cranmer took his place in Cromwell's flaunting of his new strength; he replaced Sampson as preacher at Paul's Cross, and he began delivering a pulpit message which the French ambassador noted as very different from that which Bishop Gardiner had put out during Lent. Marillac saw that events were reaching a final crisis: either Cromwell or his enemies must be destroyed.[107]

The result came on 10 June: Cromwell's arrest at the Council Board (a duty performed with relish by the Duke of Norfolk), and his removal straight to the Tower of London: Marillac provides us with dramatic details of these events.[108] The news was announced to a stunned House of Lords that afternoon by Chancellor Audley: was it significant that Gardiner was not there to hear it? Perhaps he had more important things to do, and people to see. The following day the House was packed, but there was no news, so they dispersed after only token business.[109] Cromwell immediately lost virtually all his friends: late on the day of his arrest, Marillac was already reporting that all the support he had left was from Cranmer, who did not dare to open his mouth, and Lord Admiral Southampton 'who for a long time has learnt well how to bend to every wind'.[110] Soon after Cromwell's arrest, Gardiner made his first appearance at the Council board for nearly a year.[111] What could Cranmer do? Probably the day after the arrest, he attended a Privy Council meeting at

105 *Lisle Letters* 6, Ch. 13, and especially no. 1672 (*L.P.* 15 no. 537).
106 *Castillon/Marillac*, p. 184 (*L.P.* 15 no. 697); *Lisle Letters* 6, p. 118.
107 *Castillon/Marillac*, p. 186 (*L.P.* 15 no. 737).
108 *Castillon/Marillac*, pp. 189–90, 193–4 (*L.P.* 15 nos 766–7, 804).
109 *L.J.* 1, p. 143 Cf. Lehmberg, *Later Parliaments*, pp. 105–7.
110 *Castillon/Marillac*, p. 190 (*L.P.* 15 no. 767).
111 *Castillon/Marillac*, pp. 193–4 (*L.P.* 15 no. 804).

which Cromwell was declared to be a traitor, and after mulling over this astonishing news for twenty-four hours, he sat down to write to the King about it. His letter is very reminiscent of his tormented defence of Anne Boleyn three years before (although its text is only preserved in fragments), and he may well have got out his 1536 files to find a model of how to write on behalf of a fallen patron and friend to whom he was devoted. The same three elements are there: warm praise of the victim, horror conditional on the charges being proved true, and pastoral concern for the King in the loss of a brilliant adviser:

> He that was such a servant, in my judgement, in wisdom, diligence, faithfulness, and experience, as no prince in this realm ever had . . . I loved him as my friend, for so I took him to be; but I chiefly loved him for the love which I thought I saw him bear ever towards your Grace, singularly above all other. But now, if he be a traitor, I am sorry that ever I loved him or trusted him, and I am very glad that his treason is discovered in time; but again I am very sorrowful; for who shall your Grace trust hereafter, if you might not trust him? . . . I pray God continually night and day, to send such a counsellor in his place whom your Grace may trust, and who for all his qualities can and will serve your Grace like to him.[112]

This was an astonishingly brave letter to write, given that Cranmer was himself now in danger. He was on his own, for the first time since he had been made Archbishop, left alone without the man who had always been able to deal with crises, to guide him through political peril. Foxe preserves a plausible story that Cranmer was also due for arrest at this time, but avoided a party waiting to buttonhole him by hastening up the 'privy stair' (the private stair to the royal apartments) to see the King in person: this gave him the vital face-to-face contact which was denied Cromwell by his enemies, thus sealing the Vice-gerent's fate. Cranmer by contrast was given the King's signet, Henry's favourite device for lending his authority to protect his intimates, which acted as a talisman to preserve the Archbishop.[113] After writing the letter, there was nothing else that he could do for Cromwell, any more than he had been able to for Anne Boleyn. He took his place in the Lords and dutifully voted through Cromwell's attainder with the rest, being absent from the deliberations on only one day in June. Cromwell was legally dead, useful now to the King only for what evidence he could provide to bolster the King's arguments about the nullity of the Anne of Cleves marriage. Once that marriage was safely ended, Cromwell would be taken from his cell in the Tower and disposed of.[114]

112 Cox 2, p. 401 (*L.P.* 15 no. 770), from Herbert's *Henry VIII*. Given the other unique material from state papers of 1540 now lost and surviving only in Thomas Master's notes for Herbert (Bodl. MS Jesus 74), there is no good reason to doubt the authenticity of this letter. I date it to 12 June, against other suggestions in Cox and *L.P.*

113 Foxe 8, p. 43.

114 *L.J.* 1, pp. 144–6; Lehmberg, *Later Parliaments*, 107–9.

The Cleves embarrassment was the real reason, indeed, why Henry had listened to the farrago of half-truths and irrelevancies which made up the conservative charges against the imprisoned Earl of Essex; yet this new quest for a royal divorce was the one good advantage which Cranmer possessed in his peril. Henry did not now merely want a new annulment, but also a new marriage. The conservatives had repeated their tactic of 1536 against Anne Boleyn and supplied an exciting new possibility for a wife: a lively little niece of the Duke of Norfolk called Catherine Howard, who had appeared at Court in autumn 1539. She may already have caught the King's eye (see above, p. 258), but the first definite evidence of his attention is a royal grant to her on 24 April 1540.[115] During the spring she was lodging with her step-grand-mother (the Duke of Norfolk's stepmother) opposite the gates of Lambeth Palace, where the King regularly visited her; Gardiner reputedly also did his share in supplying social events for the couple's entertainment a mile down the river in his Southwark palace. By midsummer (24 June), rumours of an imminent royal divorce were becoming public, and gossips would certainly have noticed when on 25 June Henry moved Anne out of the way upriver to Richmond, 'purposing it to be more for her health, open air and pleasure'.[116] The only person who could decently preside over what might be a highly embarrassing transaction would be the Primate of All England.

Even so, the preparations for the annulment and new marriage nearly plunged Cranmer into fresh disaster, thanks to the irresponsible gossip of his own servants and ecclesiastical lawyers as they prepared the necessary legal paperwork. This gossip can be dated by its content as between 25 and 29 June 1540. Most damaging were the discussions which the chief legal draftsman, Dr Richard Gwent, had with Thomas Wakefield about possible obstacles of affinity to a marriage between Catherine and the King: with astonishing tactlessness, they included the ill-omened name of Anne Boleyn. Wakefield said to Gwent that 'the King could not marry the Lady Howard, because she and Queen Anne were in the second degree of blood': Gwent countered '*in linea aequali* it is dispensable'. From this high-minded exploration of canon law, they got down to the even more enjoyable 'probabilities that the King's Grace hath been at banquet these two nights with Mistress Catherine' (a remark followed by the luridly tell-tale euphemism 'etc.'), and their other speculations included 'that the Earl of Essex . . . was sent to the Tower because he would not consent to the divorce' and 'that my Lord of Winchester procureth this divorce'. When Cranmer heard what was being said, he furiously 'charged his servants to hush it', and to save himself from being dragged down by their indiscretion, he immediately made a full report to his fellow Privy Councillors. Ralph Morice, Anthony Vaughan, Wakefield, Gwent and others from Lambeth Palace and the Court of Arches, a 'sorely terrified' set of men who ought to have known better, found themselves stammering out

115 Grant: *L.P.* 15 no. 613/12. *E.T.* p. 134 (*O.L.* pp. 201–2): Dr Redworth's scepticism about this report (*Gardiner*, pp. 119–20) seems to me excessive.

116 Hall 2, p. 307.

their stories at the Council board, and they were lucky to get away with nothing worse than a bad fright.[117]

In this very tricky situation, Cranmer got support from a surprising direction: Catherine Howard herself. According to Wakefield, she conveyed the reassuring message to the Archbishop 'that you should not care for your businesses, for you should be in better case than ever you were'. The reason for this favour was the opposition (which we have already noted) expressed by Cranmer to Cromwell's Anne of Cleves marriage project, back in autumn 1539. This background helps to explain why the Archbishop was so ready to co-operate with the King's move from wife number four to wife number five. One wonders why Lord Herbert of Chirbury never found a place in his *Life of Henry VIII* for these highly interesting depositions, which now only survive in his secretary's research notes; it is likely that he felt that they did not reflect well on Cranmer, particularly in view of the Archbishop's later role as the agent for Catherine's destruction. Earlier Herbert and his researcher had been just as embarrassed by some of the Archbishop's actions at Dunstable in the Aragon annulment proceedings (see above, Ch. 4, n. 48). Indeed, Cranmer's connivance at Henry's marital adventures reached its most dismal depth in summer 1540, with the only partial consolation that the rest of the authorities in the English Church and in Parliament were equally implicated.

The first sign of the annulment plan came fairly quietly and obliquely on 2 July, when a bill reducing the scope of marriage impediments by affinity and precontracts was introduced to the Lords; it was committed to Bishops Cranmer, Tunstall, Gardiner and Heath to examine (in fact, this is the first recorded mention of committee procedure in the House of Lords). The bill was clearly intended to help with the affinity problem raised by Gwent in his indiscretion, and among its other provisions it declared (as Gwent had done to Wakefield) that the relationship between first cousins did not constitute a divine prohibition of affinity. As an incidental result, it had a disastrous effect on the income from fees in Cranmer's Faculty Office; thereafter the Office had fewer marital obstacles which required the issue of dispensations![118] On 5 July the government went public in Parliament with what everyone knew; the following day a royal commission was issued for trying the annulment case to 'the clergy of England' – in other words, the assembly which in other days would have been Cromwell's vice-gerential synod of both provinces of the English Church. Now, with the Vice-gerent legally although not actually dead, Cranmer presided over the proceedings, while Gardiner also played a prominent part in forwarding the procedure.

117 Bodl. MS Jesus 74, f. 299. The depositions of Morice etc. were made to the Council on 29 June 1540. Gwent was prolocutor of the Lower House of Convocation and played a prominent role in the July annulment proceedings.

118 *L.J.* 1, p. 150; on the Howard connection cf. also Kelly, *Matrimonial Trials*, p. 263. On the Faculty Office, *Faculty Office Registers*, pp. xxxii, xxxv, xxxvi, lxiii–lxv.

declararetur maximo totius huius regni beneficio, id futurum,
cuius quidem regni felicitas omnis et conservatio tum in regia vestra
persona ad dei honorem et divinarum legum executionem conservanda
consistit: tum in vitandis etiam sinistris omnibus opinionibus et
scandalis que de Maiestatis vestre presentia post natam nobis ex
predicto matrimonio sobolem suborirentur; si precontractus ille de quo
diximus, et huius declaratio nulla secuta est, predicte Domine
Anne obijceretur. His itaque de causis et consideracionibus alijsque
quam multis non necessarijs que exprimantur; cum separatim singulis
tum coniunctim omnibus consideratis et perpensis, Nos Archi-
episcopi et Episcopi tum Decanis et Archidiaconis ac reliquo huius regni
clero, nunc congregato circumstantias facti eius quam veritatem, ut
ante dictum est considerantes, tum vero quid ecclesia in eiusmodi casi-
bus et possit facere et sepenumero antehac fecerit, perpendentes
tenore presentium declaramus et diffinimus Maiestatem vestram predicto matrimonio, prius utpote nullo et invalido non alligari, sed alio
desuper iudicio non expectato ecclesie sue auctoritate fretam, posse arbitrio suo ad contrahendum et consummandum matrimonium cum quavis femina
divino iure vobiscum matrimonium contrahere non prohibita procedere, ac
pretenso illo cum Domina Anna predicta matrimonio non obstante. Simi-
liter etiam Dominam Annam predictam non obstante matrimonio pretenso
cum Maiestate vestra, quod nullo pacto obstare debere determinamus
posse arbitrio suo cum quavis alia persona divino iure non
prohibita matrimonium contrahere. Hec Nos Clerum et totam
huius ecclesie Anglicane partem representantes cum vera iusta ac
honesta et sancta esse affirmamus, tum ijsdem quam perfectissime
integerrime et efficatissime ad omnem intentionem propositum et
effectum a nobis exigi potest consentimus et assentimur per
presentes. In quorum omnium et singulorum testimonium hec scripta
manuum nostrarum subscriptione communimus, utriusque etiam Ar-
chiepiscopi Sigillo apposito. Dat Westmonasterij, nono die
Mensis Julij, Anno Domini Millesimo quingentesimo quadragesimo
Presentibus tunc et ibidem ac premisse declaracioni et diffinicioni con-
sentientibus, Magistris Joanne Tregunwell et Willelmo Petre Joanne
Hughes et Willelmo Coke Legum Doctoribus, nostrum Notarijs
infrascriptis subscribentibus.

T. Cantuarien Edouardus Ebor

22 Page from the instrument of the clergy annulling the marriage of Anne of Cleves and Henry VIII, dated at Westminster, 9 July 1539. Note Cranmer's signature heading the bishops, accompanied by the signature of Edward Lee, Archibishop of York.

Within four days it was all over – depositions, discussion and voting; by 9 July, 158 members of the synod had put their names in person or by proxy to the beautifully written parchment instrument declaring that the Anne of Cleves marriage had never existed, thanks to her precontract with the Duke of Lorraine, together with Henry's inadequate consent and non-consummation once she had arrived in England.[119] The reasons for the annulment, indeed, fell over one another in protesting too much: Bishop Clerk, who had the unenviable task of travelling to tell the Duke of Cleves what had happened, initially felt that 'these two causes, viz. of precontract and no carnal knowledge etc. would weaken one another'. Dr Kelly's modern dissection of the case pitilessly reveals the inconsistencies both with the marriage law then current and with what Cranmer had done in previous royal cases.[120] Nevertheless, now there was little left to do except to see the formalities of the annulment through Parliament and prepare for the new royal wedding; this took place quietly on 28 July, the same day that Thomas Cromwell was executed, and by 8 August Catherine was being openly paraded at Hampton Court as Queen.[121] After her initial shock at the news of her imminent divorce, Anne had shown the sense to be sweetness itself about her curious situation, and she settled down to a comfortable and blameless existence on the English estates lavished on her by a grateful ex-husband. No one has ever suggested that she made the wrong decision.

One useful little by-product of Henry's ebullient mood (and perhaps also a product of Catherine Howard's reassurances to Cranmer) was a measure introduced to the Lords on the same day that the nullity decree completed its passage through the two houses: it ended the Act of Six Articles' threat of the death penalty for priests caught in sexual incontinence. The Archbishop absented himself from the Lords' discussion of this proposal! Later he attributed this modification of the Six Articles legislation specifically to royal initiative, recalling that only a year after their first passage, Henry 'was fain to temper his said laws'.[122] Similarly, a savage would-be pogrom against London evangelicals which the conservative hierarchy had unleashed in their hour of triumph in July, the first test of the effectiveness of the Six Articles legislation, was halted for good on 1 August by a royal command. Henry was in holiday mood, which was just as well for the 500 Londoners who had been rounded up in the course of a fortnight.[123]

Others were not so lucky. Cromwell's death on 28 July was followed two days later by a famously paired set of executions, the gruesome Henrician

119 Commission: *L.P.* 15 nos 843, 942/26. Annulment instrument: P.R.O., E. 30/1470 (*L.P.* 15, no. 861).

120 Kelly, *Matrimonial Trials*, pp. 264–75. Clerk's opinion is preserved in Bodl. MS Jesus 74, f. 301r.

121 Hall 2, p. 310; *Wriothesley's Chronicle* 1, p. 121.

122 Cox 2, p. 168; cf. also Richard Hilles' contemporary comments on the King's responsibility, *E.T.* p. 136 (*O.L.* pp. 205).

123 Brigden, *London*, pp. 320–22.

equivalent of a grand finale firework display to cap half a year of political mayhem. While three papalist Catholics died for treason, three clergy widely admired in evangelical circles, including Henry's former ambassador to the Lutherans, Robert Barnes, were burnt for heresy. Barnes, with admirable spirit, did his formidable best to embarrass Henry in his speech before he died. His death was widely seen as a symbol of Bishop Gardiner's triumph, but the event was symbolic in a greater sense of the to-and-fro character of politics from 1540 to 1547.[124] There was a curious ecumenism to Henry's Church of England in these years: it was probably more inclusive of English religious opinion than any phase of the established Church since, but the ecumenism also included murderous lunges against representatives of either religious wing. The conservatives were always trying to repeat the tactic which had worked to destroy Cromwell: to gather together evidence against an evangelical in order to suggest a combination of religious radicalism and subversive intent, and then if possible to extend the accusations outwards in order to suggest a wider conspiracy against the King's religious settlement. Equally, evangelicals listened out for any hint of conservative intrigue to return England to papal obedience, or to threaten the dynasty. For either wing, success was measured by convincing the King of the truth of their charges, and by how high up the social and political scale the charges could reach. These seven years were characterized by contradictory swings of influence around the monarch, in which up to mid-1543 Cranmer himself was in his enemies' sights.

Immediately, however, the Archbishop found himself thrust into a position of new political prominence, now that Cromwell was no longer there to shoulder the political burden for him. This position was both real and formal. On 10 August 1540, the Privy Council which had emerged as a small group of leading advisors to the King in the aftermath of the Pilgrimage of Grace was given a formal constitution, with minute-book and clerk. This was probably a conscious design by the great noblemen of England to stop a single figure like Cromwell or Wolsey ever again making a bid to dominate politics by accumulating his own collection of great offices at Court and in the bureaucracy.[125] First in the list of precedence, carefully established by an Act of Parliament in the previous year, was the Archbishop of Canterbury.[126] The man first named as Council Clerk was William Paget, who was available for the job since he had newly been made redundant as Queen's Secretary to Anne of Cleves. The political significance of his appointment was ambiguous. During the 1530s Paget had been in Cromwell's service, and we have already met him acting as Cranmer's messenger-boy to summon Alexander Alesius to a dangerous secret meeting

124 For an excellent account, see Brigden, *London*, pp. 315–19, 323–4.

125 On this controversial point, I find most plausible the analysis of David Starkey, as for instance summarized in his *Henry VIII: Personalities and Politics*, pp. 129–33.

126 *Proc. P.C.* 7, p. 3; *St.P.* 1, p. 646.

(see above, p. 251). However, Paget was also a former favourite Cambridge pupil of Bishop Gardiner, and the bachelor bishop long cherished an apparently unreciprocated affection for him. It is likely that in 1540 Gardiner still regarded Paget as a reliable satellite, and therefore saw his appointment as a political triumph; he was still treating Paget as an intimate friend in 1546. His impression was wholly mistaken: more dexterous than Wily Winchester, Paget in the long run repeatedly demonstrated his ingratitude towards his first patron.[127]

After the initial note in the register of the Privy Council's establishment, Cranmer is not recorded as turning up to its meetings until 23 January 1541. It is likely that he was otherwise engaged, mainly in presiding over the contentious work of the doctrine commission set up by the King at the beginning of April. In the end, neither of the April committees produced any immediate published result, probably because of the constant seesawing of political pointscoring over the next three years. The finished document produced by the committee on ceremonial survives in two slightly variant manuscripts and was only resurrected by John Strype in the late seventeenth century. It was designed in homily form, like the Bishops' Book, and was a sustained attempt to defend traditional liturgical ceremonies by giving them a didactic purpose, a conservative hijacking of an evangelical strategy of the 1530s. Yet the evangelical members of the committee, Goodrich and Holgate, secured the omission of any discussion of the eucharistic sacrifice, and the document included the alarming description of the mass as 'a remembrance of the passion of Christ, whose most blessed body and blood is there consecrated'.[128] There are also some significant variations between the two manuscripts which show signs of the committee's disagreements: the later version leans towards the evangelicals, omitting a defence of Candlemas ceremonies and including a condemnation of exorcisms which do not properly spell out the doctrine that sins are remitted exclusively through 'the merits of Christ's passion'. The fact that this evangelical version of the text is later than the other may well be an indication of why the committee never delivered the goods; perhaps the conservative members saw that it was swinging away from their control.[129]

127 On the Paget-Gardiner relationship, see Redworth, *Gardiner*, pp. 221–2, 227–30, 253–4, 292, 296, 317–21, 325–6.

128 *Rationale*, p. 15; cf. discussion in Duffy, *Stripping of the Altars*, pp. 427–8, although NB that he has been misled by the Alcuin Club's editor J.S. Cobb into associating drafts for the Ten Articles of 1536 with this document: ibid., pp. 428–9, and cf. above, p. 164, n. 86.

129 *Rationale*, pp. 32, 42; the more evangelical version is to be found in Lambeth MS 1107, the other in B.L. Cotton MS Cleopatra E V. That Lambeth MS 1107 represents a later phase is proved by the fact that it includes a final general comment mentioned in the list of contents in the B.L. MS, but not there included in the body of its text (*Rationale*, pp. 2, 43).

The committee on doctrine seems to have done the bulk of its work after Cromwell's fall; this is suggested by two different stories, one recorded by Ralph Morice and the other by John Foxe. Morice speaks of Cranmer finding out when Cromwell was in the Tower that 'the whole rabblement which he took to be his friends, being commissioners with him' deserted him for Gardiner's side; he names bishops Heath, Shaxton (probably a mistake for Skip) and Thirlby, whom he points out were 'chiefly advanced and preserved unto their dignities' by Cranmer, but also 'all other of the meaner sort'.[130] Foxe, in a passage which owes something to this anecdote and which probably relies on further information from Morice for its other material, names Heath and Skip 'having him down from the rest of the commissioners into his garden at Lambeth', and Cranmer fiercely and effectively resisting their 'persuasions'.[131] Both stories are significant in indicating the moment at which Cranmer's old friends and formerly enthusiastic evangelical fellow-travellers, Heath and Thirlby, began going back down the road to traditional Catholicism, which brought them in the end to Queen Mary's episcopal bench instead of sharing the Archbishop's imprisonment and death.

The doctrinal committee seems to have worked within a framework formed by seventeen set questions on doctrine. An enigmatic reference, preserved by John Strype, to Cromwell having visited the Convocation of Canterbury on 5 May to expound 'certain articles' should perhaps be interpreted as referring to these questions; however, very few of the surviving sets of papers can be as early as May.[132] One set of answers to the questions forms a possible exception; a note of individual opinions within it, for instance, reveals yet another argument over the necessity of auricular confession on scriptural authority, with Skip, Heath and Thirlby still at that stage supporting Cranmer against the more conservative group. So here we may have survivals from a fairly early stage in the wrangling, before the desertions of which Morice and Foxe speak. It may also be significant that unlike all the other surviving documents, these papers include the name of Bishop Gardiner, who left for his embassy abroad on 15 November. The other notable feature is their collection of marginalia from King Henry in truculently reformist mood, questioning the scriptural origins of confirmation, unction and chrism, challenging the exclusive right of bishops to ordain clergy, and wanting proof for the origins of their office.[133]

130 *Narratives of the Reformation*, pp. 248–9: NB that the name of George Day is erased in the list.

131 Foxe 8, pp. 23–4.

132 Strype, *Ecclesiastical Memorials*, 1 i, p. 553. This reference does not seem to exist in any other source: cf. *L.P.* 15 no. 921. The 'articles' may have been the questions to which the committees' sets of answers survive: cf. *L.P.* 15 no. 826.

133 B.L. Cotton MS Cleopatra E V ff. 36, 38, Strype, *Cranmer* nos 27–8, pp. 295–300 (*L.P.* 15 no. 826/22, 23).

Otherwise what survives from the committee, mainly consisting of extensive further individual responses to the seventeen questions, seems to date from autumn 1540.[134] Cranmer appears to have acted as chairman, providing summary conclusions of agreements and disagreements no doubt for the King's benefit, but naturally he also gave his own answers to the questions. On the question of sacraments, unsurprisingly he preserved his scepticism on the medieval total of seven and their exclusive claim to sacramental character. He found no supporting evidence either in scripture or in patristic writers, in contrast to plenty of evidence of a vague general use of the word '*sacramentum*' or '*mysterion*' in a whole variety of contexts; this was a point which he had made at the vice-gerential synod in February 1537. Once more he would not rank penance as a fully scriptural sacrament alongside baptism and the eucharist, he rejected any scriptural authority for the necessity of auricular confession, and he wholly rejected the medieval definition of penance, describing it simply as 'a pure conversion of a sinner in heart and mind from his sins unto God'.[135]

Cranmer's most extensive answers were made in relation to the definition of royal power in the Church, which had not been attempted in any detail by any previous doctrinal commission, and which now occupied six of the seventeen questions. He produced one of the longest responses from any committee member when he tackled the question 'Whether the apostles lacking a higher power, as in not having a Christian king among them, made bishops by that necessity, or by authority given them by God?' In this, he revealed a breathtaking scepticism about any independent character for the church. His starting point was the basic character of a Christian polity, royal supremacy in its purest form: God had delivered to 'all Christian princes . . . the whole cure of all their subjects, as well concerning the administration of God's word for the cure of souls, as concerning the ministration of things political and civil governance'. Ministers within this commonwealth were divided between those whose functions were 'civil' and those 'of God's word'. Any 'comely ceremonies and solemnities' by which they were admitted (in other words, ordination and consecration in the case of clergy) were 'only for a good order and seemly fashion', without any special conferring of grace by the 'promise of God'. This basic assumption had an important consequence for Cranmer's view of the course of Church history; it was a journey towards the righting of a wrong, the lack of proper authority in the apostolic Church, which had only been remedied when the first Christian rulers appeared, in

134 Lambeth MS 1108, ff. 69–141; P.R.O., S.P. 1/160 ff. 2–5, P.R.O., S.P. 6/6/9, ff. 77–81; B.L. Cotton MS Cleopatra E V ff. 38, 53, 113 (*L.P.* 15 no. 826). A few members of the committee named in April are not represented at all in Lambeth 1108 (Bishop Gardiner, away from 15 November, Dr Wilson, disgraced from late May, and Dr Robins) and Dr Leighton and Corwen are represented though not initially named. The mention of Thirlby as 'elect of Westminster' in Lambeth 1108 suggests a date between September and December 1540.

135 Cranmer's replies are conveniently presented in Cox 2, pp. 115–17.

third-century Armenia and the Roman Empire under Constantine the Great. The apostles of the first century AD had lacked 'remedy then for the correction of vice, or appointing of ministers' and had to make do with 'the consent of christian multitude among themselves'. There is an unmistakeable distaste in the use of the word 'multitude'; Cranmer would have sympathized with the dictum attributed to the Rev. Jabez Bunting, a great autocrat of nineteenth-century Wesleyanism, that Methodism was 'as opposed to democracy as it is to sin'.[136]

Far from holding any doctrine of apostolic succession in 1540, therefore, Cranmer saw the first Christians casting round to create makeshift structures of authority: 'they were constrained of necessity to take such curates and priests as either they knew themselves to be meet thereunto, or else as were commended unto them by other that were so replete with the Spirit of God . . . that they ought even of very conscience to give credit unto them'. Sometimes the apostles sent ministers to the people, sometimes the people chose their own. Hence he had no difficulty in assenting to the idea that Christian rulers could start the ministry off anew, creating bishops and priests, if they had no alternative; he had none of the convoluted reservations of most of his colleagues on this admittedly hypothetical case. Taking the same line as Henry VIII in one of his marginalia on the earlier paper mentioned above, Cranmer affirmed that 'princes and governors' had as much right as bishops to make a priest, or even, as he had to admit on the analogy of the early Church, 'the people also by their election [i.e. choice]'. This was going way beyond the cautious statements of the Bishops' Book about royal power in the Church, which made a distinction between the jurisdictional powers which historically had been granted by princes to clergy, and the powers conveyed independently to the Church by Christ in the sacrament of orders.[137] It was only consistent that Cranmer ended all his opinions by writing for the King's benefit 'This is mine opinion and sentence at this present, which I do not temerariously define, and do remit the judgement thereof wholly unto your majesty'. Bishop Bonner used a similar phrase to round off his contribution, despite his much more traditional views on clerical orders.

It is perhaps in this snapshot of his opinions that Cranmer is at his most remote from modern Christians. Nowhere today can one find such a theory of royal supremacy in the Christian world. His premise about the divine ordering of society through Christian princes is diametrically opposed to the Western Church's post-1789 agonizing about its links with the State. The theory of Church history which flows from his ideas is equally remote from sceptical modern accounts of the fourth- and fifth-century Church, although it does happen to coincide with the usual modern accounts of the origins of the Christian ministry in the first and second centuries. Equally, his view of

136 Qu. M. Brock, *The Great Reform Act* (1973), p. 40.
137 Lloyd, *Formularies*, pp. 101–5, 113–14.

royal supremacy as the natural condition of the Church puts an interesting question mark against a common assumption among humanist reformers: that the apostolic Church of the first generation should be the ultimate court of appeal in disputes about the nature of the contemporary Church. In Cranmer's eyes, the apostolic Church was imperfect, incomplete. Cranmer possessed the first edition of Calvin's *Institutes* of 1536, and he was also familiar with the publications of his admiring correspondent Martin Bucer. Already Bucer and Calvin were wrestling with notions about Church polity which would lead to Bucer's attempts to restructure the Church at Strassburg on scriptural lines, and to Calvin's claim that the Church of the New Testament was a clear and unequivocal guide to the perfect form of any church.

However, what probably weighed more with Cranmer than the developing theories of these eminently respectable figures was his persistent hatred for the radical reformers, an echo of which we have heard in his fastidious choice of the word 'multitude'. The radicals' constant cry was for a return to the Church of the apostles; their perception (in fact, perfectly correct) that the apostolic Church had been ambiguous in its attitude to civil government, and their frank hostility to what Constantine had done to Western Christianity, were concrete and immediate worries for the Archbishop. Such radical doctrines affronted his basic belief in the Royal Supremacy. He had to repudiate the radical threat, yet at the same time he wanted to repudiate the traditional authority of the Church, with its constant defence of error by reference to 'unwritten verities'. The neat solution was to kill two birds with one stone, by denying any independent authority or identity at all to the Church. In this case, one was then left with the authority of the Christian prince, who could be persuaded and educated in the right use of holy scripture in order to govern his kingdom correctly. That there might be theoretical drawbacks to this theory was no doubt apparent to Cranmer in 1540, and the drawbacks became painfully apparent in practice in 1553. It is likely, too, that he was influenced by Martin Bucer's arrival in England in the reign of Edward VI, and by the conversations which Cranmer and Bucer were then able to have face to face; this gave the Archbishop cause to modify the stark version of Erastian belief which he presented for the boisterous approval of Henry VIII at the beginning of the decade.

Throughout the rest of Henry's reign, however, Cranmer had every incentive to cling to Henry's authority; in successive crises, his personal relationship with the King was the only thing that saved him from the fate of Thomas Cromwell. It was a relationship based on the King's total trust in him, which meant that he could never seek to conceal anything from Henry: the King was peculiarly sensitive to the idea that he had been deceived, something which had been at the heart of the downfall of both Cromwell and Lord Lisle. Cranmer was thus punctilious in making sure that Henry should know as soon as possible when, at a bad moment, in September 1540, he received a letter from Dantiscus, the Polish Catholic bishop who had once been his friend, reproaching him for the whole course of the English Reformation during the 1530s.[138] Equally, and even more to his political advantage, he was quick to report treasonous words from his own diocese, spoken by one of his long-standing enemies among the clergy of Kent, Dr Richard Benger, a survivor from the Warham era on the staff at Wingham College.[139] Cranmer had already crossed swords with Benger about disloyal language in 1534–5; during September 1540 he was able to retail to the Council Benger's remarks made to his face about the King's abuse of taxation. The Council appointed the Archbishop to head the examining commission, the findings of which led Benger to a prison cell in the Tower of London. In the following year Benger had a remarkably lucky escape from the consequences of his habitual outspokenness, being acquitted by a jury of Kent who may have admired his stand against the combined forces of Archbishop and royal Council, but for the moment he had been put in his place, and Cranmer's position had been affirmed at a difficult time.

The conservatives begin nibbling again at the edges of the Cranmer circle in December 1540, and it is difficult to believe that there was not a certain amount of co-ordination in their actions. In London, during Advent, Nicholas Wilson provoked a pulpit war with the prominent evangelical Edward Crome, and just after Christmas Crome's enemies produced a selection of carefully edited selected highlights from his sermons, which induced the King to force him into a retraction.[140] At the same time Dr Miles Spencer and Thomas Godsalve, veteran conservative administrators in Norwich diocese, struck it rich when they were able to find a chaplain of Bishop Goodrich of Ely, Thomas Cottisford, involved in distributing an English version of Philipp Melanchthon's vituperative open letter to Henry VIII attacking the Six Articles.[141] The Privy Council's investigations of those involved led back to a friend of Cranmer's, the London printer Richard Grafton, and to the wife of the rich grocer John Blagg, Cranmer's business agent in London.[142] After these revelations, on 29 January, Bishop Bonner, now openly revealing himself as an enemy of the evangelicals, began another round of enquiries on offences against the Six Articles, in which Grafton and his fellow-printers and book-suppliers Edward Whitchurch, John Gough and John Mailer were among those harassed, and the views of Cranmer's old protégé Thomas Rose were among those of many clergy regarded as suspect. Bonner carried on his activities all through the spring.[143] In the political world two former

138 P.R.O., S.P. 1/163 ff. 1–2, 34–5, Cox 2, pp. 401–4 (*L.P.* 16 nos 4, 69); see above, Ch. 4, pp. 73–4.

139 See a full treatment of Benger's vicissitudes in Elton, *Policy and Police*, pp. 317–21. He was commissary for Warham as Chancellor at Oxford in 1522: *Canterbury College*, ed. Pantin 3, p. 262.

140 *E.T.* pp. 140–44 (*O.L.* p. 211); Brigden, *London*, pp. 330–32.

141 *Proc. P.C.* 7, pp. 97–8; Cottisford is misnamed 'Foxford' at this stage. For the text of the letter, see *L.P.* 13 ii no. 444 and Foxe 5, pp. 350–8.

142 *Proc. P.C.* 7, pp. 103–4. On Blagg, see Brigden, *London*, p. 419.

143 Foxe 8, pp. 440–54; Brigden, *London*, pp. 332–4.

Cromwellian servants, Sir Thomas Wyatt and Sir Ralph Sadler, were arrested in January: a major conservative coup, since Sadler was royal Secretary in the Privy Chamber.[144]

Yet in a pattern familiar in the 1540s, the evangelicals also capitalized on events and fought back, claiming their victims and their gains. Only two days after the Sadler and Wyatt arrests, Sir John Wallop, English ambassador in Paris and a prominent conservative, was recalled in disgrace and imprisoned on his return. It is unlikely that Cranmer was particularly sorry when in February 1541 the man whom he had been forced to appoint commissary of Calais in place of John Butler, Robert Harvey, was discovered to have spoken treasonous words and was thereafter attainted.[145] Harvey's immediate successor as commissary was an ex-Franciscan, Hugh Glazier, who was one of the new prebendaries of Canterbury Cathedral, and who seems to have been a reliable agent of the Archbishop.[146] Similarly, at the end of April, an accusation of preaching sedition brought a chaplain of Bishop Bonner first to be examined by the Privy Council, and then by Cranmer; the priest's name was Covert, and it is very likely that he can be identified with the ex-Observant friar Bernardine Covert, who long before had been a thorn in the side of the Archbishop at Calais.[147]

More positively, the first half of the year brought signs that Cromwellian reform had not ended with the Vice-gerent's death, and could even move on. Stephen Gardiner was away on his diplomatic mission to the Imperial Diet at Regensburg from autumn 1540 to autumn 1541, while from the end of February 1541 Cranmer began attending Privy Council meetings, and did so regularly all through the spring. Henry was in increasingly bad health, and in particularly low moments during the spring he was heard to turn his fury on those whom he identified as having destroyed Cromwell, 'saying that on pretexts of some trivial faults, . . . they had made several false accusations to him, as a result of which he had put to death the most faithful servant he had ever had'.[148] News in April of planned rebellions in the north of England were a reminder to the King of what conservatives had nearly achieved in the Pilgrimage of Grace; that did nothing to harm the position of the remaining evangelicals in politics.

From the end of June, when the King left unenthusiastically with Catherine Howard for the first visit of his reign to the north, the Archbishop remained in London as a member of the caretaker Council liaising with the King's advisers on the progress. It was his first major piece of responsibility outside the Church since becoming Archbishop, apart from service on the county commissions which were the lot of anyone who could be construed as

144 Starkey, *Henry VIII: Personalities and Politics*, p. 137.
145 P.R.O., S.P. 1/164 ff. 196–203 (*L.P.* 16 no. 518); *Proc. P.C.* 7, p. 140.
146 Emden, *Oxford to 1540*, pp. 233–4.
147 *Proc. P.C.* 7, p. 182. On Friar Covert and his family, see above, pp. 112, 140, 143–4.
148 *Castillon/Marillac*, p. 374 (*L.P.* 16 no. 590).

a local magnate. His chief colleagues in London were Lord Chancellor Audley and Edward Seymour, Earl of Hertford: both congenial figures for him – Henry, true to his complaints in the spring, seems to have wanted to leave a collective Cromwell behind him in London. Audley had been an unobtrusive evangelical since the early 1530s; it is difficult to know how far Hertford had already travelled towards his later enthusiasm for religious reform, but he got on well enough with Cranmer to spend the aftermath of a dinner-party at Lambeth Palace in October 1541 winning thirty-five shillings from the Archbishop at cards.[149]

The winnings for the evangelical cause were equally tangible. In May came a strengthening of Cromwell's order for Bible provision; prompted by a petition from the Great Bible's publisher, Anthony Marler, who was about to bring out a new impression, a Council meeting (with Cranmer present) agreed to arrange for a royal proclamation to enforce Cromwell's order for bibles in every church, and within less than a week this had been issued.[150] The importance of this proclamation was that for the first time it stipulated a financial penalty for parishes which did not comply with it; the evidence of surviving churchwardens' accounts is that this threat made all the difference. A chronicler at Worcester noted the proclamation as if its order for Bible provision was brand new.[151] Significantly, Grafton and Whitchurch were sufficiently delivered from their troubles earlier in the year to be commissioned to print the proclamation. Ambassador Marillac, bewildered by the sudden shift in atmosphere, also reported back to King Francis that a few days before all bishops and preachers had been ordered to preach only on the pure text of scripture, without admitting any 'opinions of doctors', that is, theologians.[152]

Later in the year, these successes continued, directed now against the world of saints and shrines which had been so important in Cromwell's attack on the religious past. In July Cranmer drew up a further modification of the number of saints' days to be observed, which was turned with the King's approval into a royal proclamation.[153] The status of St Luke's, St Mark's and St Mary Magdalene's feasts was confirmed, on the biblical humanist ground that these worthies were 'often and many times mentioned in plain and manifest scripture'; at the same time, the proclamation abolished the

149 H.M.C. *Bath* 4, p. 338. For the Council's activities, cf. e.g. *Castillon/Marillac,* p. 321 (*L.P.* 16 no. 1011), *St.P.* 1, p. 668 (*L.P.* 16 no. 1085); P.R.O., S.TAC 2/34/93.

150 *Proc. P.C.* 7, pp. 185–6; *T.R.P.* 1 no. 200.

151 H.W.R.O., 009:1-BA 2636/11 (no. 43701), f. 156v, and see MacCulloch, 'Worcester', in Collinson and Craig, *Reformation in English Towns* (forthcoming).

152 *Castillon/Marillac*, p. 301 (*L.P.* 16 no. 820). Cf. the royal order to publish a proclamation with paper schedule attached, Cranmer's Register, ff. 18r, 20r; this probably refers to this order rather than the Bible proclamation, which has no mention of an attached schedule.

153 *T.R.P.* 1 no. 203; cf. P.R.O., S.P. 1/166 ff. 114–17; *St.P.* 1, pp. 658–60 (*L.P.* 16 nos 978, 1019); Cranmer's Register, f. 21v.

ceremonials of ritual inversion held by many parishes on certain holy days, when boys were dressed up as bishops to preach and preside over mock-liturgies. Perhaps most significantly, the feast-day celebrating the Empress Helena's supposed discovery of the True Cross was abolished, together with another feast of the Exaltation of the Holy Cross. Although the abolition was justified on pragmatic grounds in relation to harvest-time and complications in the Easter law term, this was a clearly deliberately intended blow to the cult of the Rood, which was still one of the most prominent objects of devotion in churches, soaring above every chancel screen with the row of flickering candles beneath it. In the autumn the *coup de grâce* was given to the remaining shrines of England; royal letters were sent to the archbishops of both provinces ordering their destruction, an order which finally put paid to publicly tolerated cults of holy places except in the most remote parts of the kingdom.[154]

Cranmer could also seize an unusual number of opportunities to place his friends and dependents in useful positions during spring 1541, a substantial boost to his habitual preferment of evangelical clergy. Opportune deaths meant that during April he could at last appoint his intimate friend John Whitwell to the parish church beside the Palace gate at Lambeth, reward his equally long-standing friend Richard Astall with a comfortable prebend at Wingham College, and put John Gibbs into the parish of his other northern home at Croydon.[155] During May a resignation made the rich living of Great Chart available for Dr Richard Thornden, a long-standing protégé of Cranmer's, although Thornden later proved a false friend.[156] Additionally, the refoundation of Canterbury Cathedral was finally completed in April; besides some appointments which were highly unsatisfactory from his point of view, Cranmer could welcome among the twelve prebendaries his chaplains Richard Champion and Nicholas Ridley, plus his Calais commissary Hugh Glazier and Richard Thornden. Three out of the newly instituted Six Preachers were deliberately chosen by him as representatives of what conservatives scornfully termed the 'New Learning': Nicholas Ridley's cousin Lancelot Ridley, Michael Drum and John Scory. Scory started as he meant to go on by preaching in the Cathedral on 27 March 1541 about justification by faith, reportedly saying in his sermon that 'he that doth deny that only faith doth justify would deny, if he durst be so bold, that Christ doth justify'. His new

154 Order for the Northern province, 22 September 1541, Bodl. MS Jesus 74 f. 257r; for the Southern province, 4 October 1541, Cranmer's Register ff. 18–19r, 21r, Cox 2, pp. 490–91 (*L.P.* 16 no. 1262). For compliance in London, see 'London Chronicle', p. 16 and Brigden, *London*, p. 338; in Worcester Cathedral, H.W.R.O., 009:1-BA 2636/11 (no. 43701), f. 156v; in Lincoln, *Lincoln Chapter Acts 1536–47*, p. 56; in Kent, C.C.C.C. MS 128, p. 38 (*L.P.* 18 ii no. 546, p. 303).

155 Cranmer's Register, ff. 379r, 380r; on Whitwell, see also *Registrum Gardiner/Poynet*, p. 116.

156 Cranmer's Register, f. 380v. On Thornden, see below, Ch. 12, p. 551.

conservative colleagues started as they meant to go on by making notes of what he had said.[157]

It was not surprising that very quickly this uncomfortable mix of opinions among the Cathedral staff provoked major trouble, with wildly discordant messages coming out of the pulpit both in the Cathedral and surrounding parish churches. The preaching of Scory and Lancelot Ridley during May became the subject of a formal complaint to Cranmer by two conservative prebendaries, Richard Parkhurst and Arthur St Leger (former Prior of Leeds, and brother to the equally conservative Kentish magnate Sir Anthony St Leger).[158] No harm came to Scory and Ridley, and it seems to have been on this occasion that Cranmer snarled at Prebendary St Leger 'You make a band, do you? I will break your band, ywis, and I will make you leave your *mumpsimus*.'[159] The Archbishop had clearly not got over his annoyance at the defeat of his vision for the Cathedral, and the large contingent of conservatives which still infested it as a result. It would have been impossible for him to appear an honest broker in the arguments which continued to proliferate.

This became clear when, within only two months of the Cathedral's new foundation, on 12 June 1541, Cranmer felt it necessary to travel to Canterbury to sort out the arguments among the Cathedral staff. At this meeting, the Archbishop became embroiled in a row about devotion to images with two more conservatives, the new prebendary and ex-monk William Gardiner alias Sandwich, and the former Oxford don turned Six Preacher Robert Serles; this ended with Cranmer snapping at them that their distinction between a pejorative meaning of 'idol' for the Greek *eidolon* and an acceptable sense for the Latin *imago* was entirely false. The conservatives complained about the policy of exact balance in choosing the Six Preachers: 'that is a mean to set us at variance' protested Gardiner, who remained unconvinced by Cranmer's insistence that although the choice had been his, 'the King's pleasure is to have it so'.[160] This atmosphere of dissension in the Cathedral was mirrored in the city as a whole, where that same summer and perhaps at the same time, Cranmer was called on to arbitrate in a bitter argument about whether or not an alderman had been properly dismissed from office. That dispute also had a religious dimension, and the Archbishop's intervention was equally unsuccessful in ending trouble, which escalated into a Star Chamber case.[161]

Cranmer continued to look on Robert Serles as a major disaster among the new appointments, a hostility which was warmly reciprocated by a man who

157 C.C.C.C. MS 128, p. 42 (*L.P.* 18 ii no. 546, p. 304).
158 C.C.C.C. MS 128, p. 291 (*L.P.* 18 ii no. 546, p. 363).
159 C.C.C.C. MS 128, p. 125, 233, 359 (*L.P.* 18 ii no. 546, pp. 322, 349, 378).
160 C.C.C.C. MS 128, pp. 229, 263A/B, 309 (*L.P.* 18 ii no. 546, pp. 348, 356, 368).
161 P.R.O., STA.C 2/20/3; Clark, *Kent*, p. 64.

had first come to the diocese as an incumbent in a living of St Augustine's Abbey.[162] It was Serles who first tried the tactic which was used in a major campaign against the Archbishop in 1543; in September 1541 he travelled up to York to present complaints against Cranmer directly to the King. The plan backfired. Henry was kept from seeing his articles of complaint, and Serles's interview with the Council attendant on the King took a very different turn: he was charged to return to Canterbury bearing a letter to Cranmer which he was strictly ordered not to tamper with *en route*. The Archbishop's evangelical agents, such as Humphrey Churden (whom he had put in as incumbent at St Alphege's in the city), had already been monitoring Serles's preaching closely, and as a result, Serles found on his return that Cranmer haled the Preacher up before his fellow-Councillors in London, and then examined the case in his own consistory court, reputedly ignoring witnesses in Serles's favour. Serles ended up in prison and was at least temporarily expelled from the Six Preachers.[163] Meanwhile William Hunt alias Hadleigh, another new prebendary from the old guard of the Cathedral Priory (he had been sub-prior at the dissolution), had been committed to the Fleet Prison, on charges whose nature now seems unclear.[164] So far in the Cathedral's first six months of existence, two of its staff had been put in prison, two had been the subject of a formal complaint, and two others had been involved in a stand-up row with their father-in-God.

Into this promisingly explosive situation stepped Bishop Stephen Gardiner, back in early October from his mission to the Emperor and the Imperial Diet which had included face-to-face theological clashes with Cranmer's friend Osiander, his correspondent Bucer, and the all-too-familiar Alexander Alesius. Ever alert for trouble, Gardiner had been keeping his ears open while he was abroad, and he had picked up news of Canterbury, including the imprisonment of Prebendary Hunt. His visit to the Cathedral for mass on his journey back to London was therefore slightly more than casual, and after the service (which included a sermon from Prebendary Ridley) he buttonholed Prebendary Gardiner, who a year or two before had taken the opportunity provided by their common surname to write to him introducing himself.[165] The Bishop asked a leading question or two about the Canterbury stirs; thus encouraged, the Prebendary poured out his fury about the preaching of Lancelot Ridley and John Scory, and his own worries that he would suffer the fate of Serles. The Bishop listened with the gloomy relish which one reserves for particularly shocking information, gave Gardiner some advice

162 For Serles's appointment to Lenham, see Emden, *Oxford to 1540*, p. 510.

163 *Proc. P.C.* 7 p. 244; C.C.C.C. MS, 128 pp. 145, 220 (*L.P.* 18 ii no. 546, pp. 323, 346); cf. Cox 2, p. 548.

164 C.C.C.C. MS 128 pp. 193–4, 309 (*L.P.* 18 ii no. 546, pp. 339, 368); this provides the foundation for most of the following paragraph. On Hunt, see Emden, *Oxford to 1540*, p. 258.

165 *Gardiner's Letters*, p. 328. The two men were not related.

about his preaching, and remarked with the straight-faced irony which was his speciality, 'My Lord of Canterbury will look upon this, I doubt not, or else such preaching will grow into an evil inconvenience. I know well he will see remedy for it.' He also received a request for help from Prebendary Hunt's brother, made some detailed enquiries about the running of the Cathedral and finally took Nicholas Ridley aside for a quiet but severe talking-to, before passing on his way back to rejoin the politics of the capital. He had learnt much of interest for the future.

However, now a startling tragedy at Court for the time being suspended normal political life: the Queen was proved an adulteress. The whole tangled story has been well told by Lacey Baldwin Smith.[166] Catherine Howard hugely enjoyed herself spending Henry's money, but there was one element missing in the permanent party-time which she created at Court after her marriage: the series of bedroom adventures with attractive young men which had brightened up her life at the Dowager Duchess of Norfolk's home at Lambeth. Soon she summoned her lovers back, to complement her hours with her large and moody husband; her sexual liaisons became almost suicidally rash during the royal progress to the North. The most popular personality would have been on the road to disaster, but Catherine had not cared how many enemies she made. Add to this the jealousy felt by various leading aristocrats towards the Howard family for its sudden return to the King's marital circle, partly because of the religious conservatism for which the Duke of Norfolk was famed, and the Queen's downfall was just a matter of time.

It was perhaps inevitable that an evangelical should first take the risk of breaking the story to the authorities. He was a minor courtier, John Lascelles; on the prompting of his sister, who had been on the edge of Catherine's raffish world, he finally revealed in October what had become obvious to many at Court, and he chose to go to the most prominent evangelical in the government: Thomas Cranmer.[167] The King and Queen were still away, and the caretaker Councillors Cranmer, Audley and Hertford were baffled as to how and when to carry out the hideous task of telling the King. They waited until he returned, in ebullient spirits, to Hampton Court. Inevitably, they had decided that Cranmer was the one man who could get away with delivering Henry such a devastating personal blow, but even he could not face the task of presenting the news by word of mouth; he handed over a letter with the information at the All Souls' Day mass (2 November). Henry had only just given thanks for his marital bliss, and his reaction was one of stunned disbelief. After so many years of mutual trust and intimate confidences from the King, Cranmer seems to have been at his best in such moments of face-to-face emotion, and he handled the situation so skilfully as to avoid any immediate explosion of royal fury in any direction.[168] No fuss was made, but

166 Smith, *Tudor Tragedy*, for all details not otherwise referenced below.
167 The main story is told in *Proc. P.C.* 7, pp. 352–5.
168 *Narratives of the Reformation*, pp. 259–60.

straight away investigations of the story began with a desperate urgency. This was no carefully constructed plot of destruction such as had brought down Anne Boleyn and Thomas Cromwell; it all turned out to be true, and it was a thunderbolt which hit the King out of a clear sky. It was Cranmer who eventually broke Catherine's indignant denials down to an hysterical admission, and who secured her confession in writing.

After that, the details of the Catherine Howard story are hardly important. Cranmer remained at the heart of the Council investigations; there remains one long letter of his written directly to the stricken Henry in November, carefully, almost clinically setting down the details of his interviews with Catherine, like an ambassador on a negotiation of extreme delicacy, as he quietly probed for more evidence through her floods of tears and near-insane exclamations.[169] He also took good care to distance himself from attempts to revive the Cleves marriage, when the ambassador of the Duke of Cleves delivered him hopeful letters from Düsseldorf; he passed the correspondence straight over to the King with some ironical comments about its personal compliments and a detailed account of his conversation with the ambassador. Cranmer emphasized to Henry that he had said that he was the worst person to act as advocate for the marriage, 'of the which I, as much as any other person, knew most just causes of divorce'.[170] He had seen enough of Cleves marriage negotiations to last him a lifetime.

Catherine's alleged and probably actual lovers were executed in December, and she would eventually follow, along with her chief accomplice Lady Rochford, in February 1542. Despite the origins of the revelations in the denunciation by Lascelles to Cranmer, to present the affair as an evangelical triumph is misconceived: someone had to tell the King in the end. Catherine's behaviour was so beyond the conventions for a King's wife that it aroused genuine horror in her uncle the Duke as much as anyone else. Clearly Catherine's lunatic indiscretions were not going to do the Howard family any good, but none of them suffered any permanent harm as a result of the affair. On the other side, commentators as far back as Gilbert Burnet have seen the Catherine Howard era as a time of great peril for Cranmer: the narrative of events from her marriage to her death shows that this was not so in reality.[171] We now know that she helped rather than threatened the Archbishop in the crisis after Cromwell's arrest; thereafter, the brief flurry of conservative aggression against Cranmer's circle in winter 1540 to 1541 produced little result, and otherwise he was riding high throughout 1541. Catherine herself had too many trivial things on her mind to represent any religious identity, except what was conventionally on offer at Court between entertainments; the courtiers in her circle had no especially conservative

169 P.R.O., S.P. 1/167 f. 139 (*L.P.* 16 no. 1325).

170 P.R.O., S.P. 1/168 f. 144, Cox 2, pp. 409–10 (*L.P.* 16 nos 1387, 1449). On the Cleves overtures, cf. *Castillon/Marillac*, pp. 373–5 (*L.P.* 16 no. 1457).

171 Cf. Burnet's comments, 1 i, p. 441.

religious profile, and indeed they included the former right-hand man of Anne Boleyn, that veteran evangelical courtier Sir Edward Baynton. Nor is it likely that the bearer of such appalling tidings as Cranmer at that All Souls' Day mass was going to get much benefit or thanks for his pains from the devastated King Henry.

Indeed, there is every sign of acute religious polarization during 1542, both in the forum provided by the first meeting of Convocation since 1540 and also out in the country. Both sides were intent on seizing the advantage from the other, and for the moment neither gained a decisive result. When the authorities at Worcester Cathedral chose Maundy Thursday 1542 to destroy the tombs of the two much-loved local saints Oswald and Wulstan, the timing of this fulfilment of the previous autumn's royal order against shrines can only have been deliberately intended to anger and humiliate Worcestershire traditionalists. The Dean (and ex-Prior) who presumably initiated this cruel vandalism was Cranmer's old Lincolnshire friend Henry Holbeach.[172] Any issue, it seemed, would do to strike a confessional attitude in this year of troubles. In Cambridge University, an esoteric dispute during May about the pronunciation of Greek became a fierce battle about the merits of modern humanist learning; the conservatives were headed by no less a person than Bishop Gardiner, the University's Chancellor, and the 'Athenians', evangelical humanists led by John Cheke, included many friends of Cranmer and politicians of the future, such as William Cecil. The parties created by the Cambridge row thus cast a long shadow; one writer has plausibly seen it as affecting religious and political party battle-lines, both in the University and out into national politics, right into the early years of Elizabeth I's religious settlement.[173]

The biggest and most public forum for contention was the Convocation of Canterbury, which opened on 20 January 1542, a few days after Parliament. As one interprets the fragments surviving from the official record, it seems to have been one of the most disrupted and rowdy of the century. The biggest issue was the future of Cromwell's most permanent achievement and Cranmer's pride and joy, the Great Bible. The Bible had never achieved the perfection which Cranmer would have liked: one unique survival of a prefatory leaf associated with the December 1541 edition promises the provision of further critical textual apparatus once the Privy Council had 'more convenient leisure' to check it over – a rueful comment in the middle of their agonizings about what to do with the wreck of the King's marriage to Catherine Howard![174] However, now the conservatives had different ideas; many retained their long-standing conviction that an English bible on general

172 H.W.R.O. 009:1-BA 2636/11 (no. 43701), f. 156v: Thursday 6 April 1542. On Holbeach's origins, *Lincolshire Pedigrees* 3, p. 810; on his Cranmer connection, P.R.O., S.P. 1/95 ff. 93–4, Cox 2, p. 309–10 (*L.P.* 9 no. 97).

173 Hudson, *Cambridge Connection*, esp. pp. 43–57.

174 Cox 2, p. 125n.

public release was more trouble than it was worth, and all agreed that in any case the Great Bible version was full of dangerous flaws with a subversive evangelical intent. In the second session, a week after the formal opening, Cranmer announced that Henry was giving Convocation the chance to confer about errors in religion. This was in itself something of a novelty; in Cromwell's time, such consideration had largely been carried out in his synods or the associated *ad hoc* committees. The problems now to be considered included canon law revision (a perennially deferred item on the religious agenda of the 1530s) and the creation of a collection of official homilies, but also the problem that many things in the English Bible needed revision.[175]

A week later, the Archbishop formally put the question as to whether the Great Bible might or might not be retained without scandal; the majority voted for revision. On 13 February the books were doled out around the available bishops and senior clergy who could be regarded as theologians. Cranmer would no doubt remember his tart remarks in 1537 about the lack of results from a previous similar division of the job of translation among the bishops.[176] However, he had no choice; King Henry was enthusiastic for the idea. The King gave a Shrovetide banquet for the members of Convocation the following week (sadly significant that he had no one better with whom to spend his Shrove Tuesday than a gaggle of clergy!); at the feast, he waxed lyrical about the revision scheme and promised to pay the printing costs. Gardiner, too, was very busy about the project; he spent his own money on splitting up a volume of the Great Bible for distribution to those who had been assigned sections, and pored over the text in order to compile a list of words that presented particular controversial difficulties of translation.[177] The mood of Convocation towards the Cromwellian era is also indicated by the fact that on the same day it also proposed to revise the standardized English version of the Creed, Commandments and Lord's Prayer which Cromwell had promulgated.[178]

So far, all officially sounds sweetness and light, with the conservatives enjoying unruffled ascendancy. However, the session of 24 February saw Cranmer proposing the abolition of candles before images and the removal of their silk and finery, together with closer observation of the various 1530s orders about blotting out the name of the Pope and of Becket in service books. The proposal of 3 March to make the Use of Sarum the standard liturgy throughout the realm might be seen as less controversial, but trouble was already surfacing that day. The Prolocutor of the Lower House, Richard

175 For this and the following material not otherwise referenced: Lambeth MS 751, p. 115; *L.P.* 17 no. 176; Fuller 3, pp. 197–200.

176 P.R.O., S.P. 1/223 ff. 198–9, Cox 2, p. 344 (*L.P.* 12 ii no. 434).

177 *Gardiner's Letters*, p. 313. Cf. Redworth, *Gardiner*, pp. 162–3, for a correction of the notion that Gardiner was causing open confrontation at this stage; Redworth's argument is confirmed by the text of Lambeth MS 751, p. 117 (17 February 1542).

178 Cf. Butterworth, *Primers*, pp. 174–5.

Gwent, appeared before the Archbishop with a deputation of his colleagues to explain certain complaints; the Archbishop ordered them not to gossip (*ne quid effutirent!*) about what had been said.[179] A week later, on 10 March, the tensions exploded over a variety of issues.

First came a bombshell announcement from Cranmer which caused uproar. He announced that it was now the King's wish that the project of Bible revision should be taken out of the hands of the bishops and given to the universities. A sign that this came as a complete surprise to the meeting was that Dr Nicholas Wotton and Dr Edward Leighton had brought along already complete their translation of the epistles to the Corinthians, which they handed over to Gardiner after the meeting.[180] Every single bishop except Goodrich and Barlow vigorously objected to Cranmer's startling announcement, saying that biblical translation was a more suitable task for a clerical assembly than for the universities, but it was no use. The Great Bible was safe, although there would be no new edition of it until November 1546; since the universities never took any action on their new task (indeed, never seem to have been asked to do so), the Great Bible was not officially replaced until the reign of Elizabeth. Far from being the subject of drastic revision, only two days after this debate a four-year monopoly for printing it was placed by royal letters patent in the hands of the printer Anthony Marler, who seems to have bought up the old stock of John Gough. The two events, royal grant and royal change of heart on Bible translation, cannot be unconnected.[181]

After this first spat among the bishops, the same division occurred in further discussion on the translation of key phrases in the biblical text. In particular, argument centred on the translation of the Latin *Dominus*: Cranmer, Goodrich and Barlow stood out against all their fellow-bishops in their wish to translate it as 'The Lord' rather than 'Our Lord'. 'The Lord' was a form which had built up support in evangelical circles, possibly because 'Our Lord' had an unfortunate-sounding parallel in the traditionalist devotional phrase 'Our Lady'; the new usage was later to be condemned as a sectarian Protestant fad by Queen Mary's chaplain, John Christopherson. Cranmer's only marginalium in English in his copy of Erasmus's 1533 edition of the works of Jerome was his triumphant note of the phrase 'The Lord' against a passage where Jerome recommends this usage – possibly a note made as ammunition for this very debate.[182] Yet divisions had not ended on that contentious day. Cranmer's furious episcopal colleagues decided to wreck a

179 Lambeth MS 751, p. 117. Another possible translation of *effutire* is 'to blabber'.

180 Fuller, 3, p. 198, says that Bishop Salcot of Salisbury had been allotted Corinthians; perhaps Wotton and Leighton were acting on his behalf.

181 *T.R.P.* 1 no. 210 (*L.P.* 17 no. 220/45); Muller, *Gardiner*, p. 105. Cf. Butterworth, *Primers*, pp. 233, 237.

182 *Hieronymi Opera* (Paris, 1533; B.L. 476 g. 10–13) 5, f. 64r. See Marc'hadour, 'The Lord, Our Lord'. Cf. a mention of other phrases discussed in the debate: Parker, *De Antiquitate*, p. 396.

bill put into Parliament (almost certainly with his backing) which would have permitted married civil lawyers to hold positions in the ecclesiastical legal machine; this would include giving them the powers to wield the ecclesiastical penalty of excommunication. Lord Chancellor Audley had sent it across to Convocation for discussion, and the majority of bishops now sent it back as 'not worthy or convenient' to be discussed.[183] Despite this, the bill was brought up again for a first reading in the House of Lords on 15 March, and only then disappeared; Cranmer did not get it through until the Parliament of 1545.[184] It was perhaps not surprising that after this Convocation only had one business session before going through a series of adjournments for a fortnight.

Once more, one has to keep looking beyond the doors of the Convocation House to put these events into context. Down in Canterbury, the Cathedral pulpit predictably reflected the turmoil in London. Coinciding with the opening of Parliament and Convocation, Prebendary Gardiner preached on two successive Sundays in late January in no very eirenical spirit; he was still fuming about the recent demolition of the Cathedral's image of Our Lady as a result of the official orders for shrine-destruction in the previous autumn, and he concentrated his fire on those who hated images.[185] On 22 January he told the congregation that they had been the victims of 'waterlaggers' (waterbearers), who had reversed the miracle of Cana by turning 'your good wine into water that you could have no good doctrine taught ne preached unto you'. Defiant the following Sunday against protests during the week, he embroidered his metaphor, and climaxed with the cry 'they must be smoked and purged round about with fire, or else we shall never be rid of them'.[186] It was not surprising that, when in late March Cranmer first had leisure from the storms of Convocation and the very considerable complications of killing off Queen Catherine, he took the opportunity to summon up Prebendary Gardiner to Lambeth Palace to explain himself; Gardiner was not inclined to be conciliatory at the meeting, boasting of his support back in Canterbury.[187] Controversy in Kent rumbled on, with Cranmer's subordinates getting ever more aggressive in their proclamation of evangelical belief, and conservatives in their turn growing ever more convinced that something must be done to stop them.

183 *L.P.* 17 no. 176. The wording of Parker's account (*De Antiquitate*, p. 396) certainly suggests that the bill was part of Cranmer's plans.

184 *L.J.* 1, pp. 185, 275–6, 280, 282; Lehmberg, *Later Parliaments*, p. 224. Cf. the use which Cranmer made of this enactment, 28 February 1546: Cranmer's Register, f. 26.

185 C.C.C.C. MS 128, p. 311 (*L.P.* 18 ii no. 546, p. 369).

186 C.C.C.C. MS 128, p. 9–10 (*L.P.* 18 ii no. 546, p. 292).

187 C.C.C.C. MS 128, pp. 123, 240, 289–90 (*L.P.* 18 ii no. 546, pp. 322, 348, 363): 'in Passion week was twelvemonth' (26 March–1 April 1542). Cranmer was absent from the Lords between Friday 25 March and the afternoon of Monday 27 March, and this is probably when he saw Gardiner: *L.J.* 1, p. 192.

That same spring Bishop Bonner launched his own personal clean-up campaign in the capital against the evangelical printing-presses which mainly clustered round his cathedral: alone among the bishops, he sent out an index of prohibited books to his diocesan clergy, naming all the usual English objectionables, both Cromwell's followers and beyond – Frith, Roye, Joye, Tyndale, Barnes, Fish, Rastell, Marshall – but also Luther and Calvin. Curiously enough, neither Zwingli and his followers nor the radicals figured on his list, which made this an especially pointed attack on the sympathies of some of Bonner's fellow-bishops. On 22 March, five days after the last working session of Convocation that month, the capital was provided with a new commission to make enquiries under the Act of Six Articles.[188] If the conservatives could not get their way in Convocation, they could certainly use other means in other places. What was more, they could also make sure that Convocation achieved nothing to which they objected.

This was made clear at Convocation's next proper meeting, and its last, on Monday 3 April. The fact that Convocation was meeting at all was odd enough, for Parliament had been prorogued two days before; however, this was not entirely unprecedented, and it is noticeable that Parliament also had a good deal of unfinished business when it broke up.[189] What happened at the session was, however, bizarre. Cranmer opened the day with a discussion on the proposal to provide official homilies, but he then adjourned the discussion until the afternoon. At this time he sent his Vicar-General, John Cockes, to suspend from 'celebration of services and entry into the church' those prelates who had not appeared, before proroguing convocation to the conventional date of 4 November next.[190] This action against senior clergy of the Church was, to say the least, unusual, and it must reflect some major disagreement; evidently there had been a mass absence on the part of the bishops.

There is a likely explanation for what had happened. The conservatives may have agreed in principle to the preparation of homilies, but in reality they disliked the idea, given the state of doctrinal flux affecting the Church; with Parliament now ended and Easter imminent, they had decided not to turn up to discuss the proposal further. We know how much Gardiner detested the homilies project from later references in his letters, when in 1547 he fought an unsuccessful rearguard action against the issue of the series which were then being authorized. Admittedly, he claimed to have done some preliminary work on preparing a homily or two in 1542 before having been diverted onto royal business, but his version of events in the 1542 Convocation also additionally reinforces the picture of pulpit contention and divisions among the episcopate. Gardiner recalled that the bishops had agreed to make homi-

188 Brigden, *London*, p. 339.
189 Lehmberg, *Later Parliaments*, p. 171.
190 Lambeth MS 751, pp. 118–19: '*omnes prelatos non comparentes seu non licentiatos suspendebat a celebratione divinorum et ab ingressu Ecclesiae*'.

lies 'for stay of such errors as were then by ignorant preachers sparkled among the people. For other agreement there had not then passed among us.' As far as he was concerned, the project had in any case been killed by the issue of 'other agreement' in the shape of the King's Book of 1543, 'which extinguished our devices'.[191]

It is improbable that bishops of the Church of England remained effectively excommunicate for long after 3 April, but altogether the Convocation session had been a disaster. All the big plans had been lost: no biblical translation followed, no homilies, no canon law revision; no joy for married civil lawyers. The only surviving concrete outcome of the session was an order minutely specifying the menus permissible at the dinner-tables of different grades of clergy. Even this rather preposterous measure carried the agreement of both archbishops, so strictly speaking it cannot be considered a convocational act, and its effect on the dietary habits of the Church of England cannot be considered profound: a note attached to the one surviving copy says that it 'was kept for two or three months, till, by the disusing of certain wilful persons, it came to the old excess'. Parson Woodforde's table would be spared.[192] Throughout the session Cranmer had only had Goodrich and Barlow among his fellow-bishops as allies. A remarkable confirmation of this comes from an acutely observed detail in the bitter diatribe against the conservative bishops in the London polemicist Henry Brinklow's pamphlet *The Complaint of Roderick Mors*. He describes the opening of Parliament on 16 January 1542: 'What a cockatrice sight was it to see such an abominable sort of pompous bishops in lordly parliament robes . . . even to the number of eighteen, whereas three were enough to poison a whole world?' Yet there had not been only eighteen bishops there that day; the Lords' Journal confirms that there had been three more – presumably Cranmer, Goodrich and Barlow. Brinklow must have considered that they were a different species from the cockatrices.[193]

Given this episcopal obstruction, it was as if the vice-gerency had never been, and England was back to the legislative incoherence in the Church which had crippled the course of change during 1533–5. A mark of the stalemate came in the conservative attempt to secure a royal proclamation which would have comprehensively banned the works of a list of evangelical English writers, plus all biblical translations apart from the Great Bible: this was an enlargement of Bishop Bonner's diocesan order of a few months before. A draft of this proclamation survives, twenty pages in length, but there is no evidence that it was ever issued.[194] Indeed, if one can associate it with a reminiscence of Stephen Gardiner's, it was killed by ridicule:

191 *Gardiner's Letters*, pp. 296, 303, 354.

192 Cox 2, p. 491. The order is dated 1541, but this probably means Old Style months early in 1542.

193 *L.P.* 20 ii no. 733, p. 348.

194 *L.P.* 17 no. 177.

> it was moved of a good zeal that there should be no more English books of religion, but only [the King's Book] and the New Testament; which upon replication of one that would have all Latin books likewise restrained, was no more spoken of, but the Act of Parliament made after the form that passed.[195]

In other words, in place of this single proclamation, the conservatives determined to try what had not worked well enough in 1539: passing comprehensive legislation centred on a reliable revision of the Bishops' Book which would finally remove the evangelical menace. Yet they also saw clearly that one could not remove ideas without removing the people that promulgated them. Their efforts in 1543 were devoted to a far more ambitious scheme of destroying their enemies than anything so far, and its chief target was the Primate of All England.

For the meantime, attacks on Cranmer had to wait. Throughout the summer and autumn of 1542 Henry VIII was making preparations for the first war he had fought for a decade: a revival of his youthful campaigns against Scotland. The war was fought against a Scottish regime which made clear its disapproval of Henry's anti-papal religious policy, and this did no harm to Cranmer and the evangelicals at Court. Having reminded Henry of his administrative competence in 1541, the Archbishop was again at the heart of government, attending Privy Council meetings daily from the beginning of September, all through the autumn. One of those little bureaucratic details that meant so much in Henrician Court politics was the order, of 6 November 1542, that when the Archbishop was at Court in the absence of the Lord Great Master and other senior royal officers, he should be served his meals in the Council Chamber, even if there was no one else of his status to accompany him. This was a sign of particular prestige, and probably also a sign that he needed to take working lunches.[196]

Cranmer played the prominent part in the London administration of the war which this privilege would suggest. Two incidents stand out: the day after the meals order, a Scot named Douglas was committed to his charge for speaking 'lewd words'.[197] Nothing seems to be known further of Douglas, but the Archbishop received a much more important charge when the English won a crushing victory at Solway Moss on 24 November. One of the most distinguished Scottish prisoners was Gilbert Kennedy, third Earl of Cassilis, a cultured aristocrat in his late twenties who had studied at the universities of St Andrews and Paris, where he had benefited from the teaching of the great evangelical Scots humanist George Buchanan. When he was brought to London in late December, he was entrusted to Cranmer's care.[198] Cassilis

195 *Gardiner's Letters*, p. 303.
196 See the retrospective note of this privilege, *L.P.* 12 i no. 969.2.
197 *A.P.C. 1540–47*, p. 49.
198 *A.P.C. 1540–47*, pp. 66, 68 (21, 26 December 1542).

subsequently became one of the early minority among the Scottish nobility that adopted a Protestant as well as an Anglophile outlook, and it has often been asserted that this was thanks to Cranmer. Gilbert Burnet (another Scot who had taken the road south) went so far as to say that Cranmer was responsible for the Earl's conversion to evangelical belief. However, this seems to rest on a misunderstanding about the length of Cassilis's stay in England; he returned to Scotland after little more than a week, being dismissed by the Council on 29 December 1542, as part of Henry's policy to build up a fifth column within Scottish governing circles.[199] It is possible that an enjoyable Christmas holiday at Lambeth with a hospitable Archbishop influenced his later stance, but it is much more likely that the Earl's previous contacts with Buchanan had made him already receptive to alliance with an anti-papal country.

All this indicates how useful the King found Cranmer; however, the Archbishop's intense involvement in central government during the autumn had an extremely unfortunate consequence for himself. Over the previous few years, Cranmer had demonstrated a clear policy of spending the autumn in Kent whenever possible, particularly towards Christmastide, but in 1542 he had very little chance to spend any time at all in his diocese. Virtually the only evidence for him visiting Kent during the year is a Privy Council letter of April 1542, telling Lord Cobham to receive a message from the Archbishop and Sir Thomas Cheyney.[200] After September, Cranmer was continuously away at Court, and even through the January New Year festivities he was still on Council business at Hampton Court. In January and February 1543 he remained up at Lambeth, either on Council business, or latterly in attendance in the House of Lords.[201] This was just at the time when his presence was needed to monitor the build-up of trouble between his evangelical staff and the increasingly militant conservative clergy and gentry of the diocese. The consequence was that the conservatives grew increasingly confident in their plans to discredit their opponents, and their plans came to maturity during winter and spring 1543. It is to these efforts finally to force a showdown that we must now turn.

199 *L.P.* 17 nos 1243–4. On the politics of the war, cf. Scarisbrick, *Henry VIII*, pp. 434–7. Cf. Burnet 1 i, p. 495; Burnet does not give a source for his assertion. The misunderstanding may have arisen because in the Anglo-Scottish treaty of July 1543, Cassilis and other senior noblemen paid a ransom as if they were still physically captive: *L.P.* 18 i no. 805.

200 B.L. Harley MS 283 f. 249 (20 April 1542).

201 Quite apart from the attendances listed in *A.P.C. 1540–47*, cf. his signature to a Council letter from Hampton Court on 29 December, B.L. Additional MS 32648 f. 236.

CHAPTER 8

A problem of survival: 1542–6

TRADITIONALLY THE ATTACKS MADE on Cranmer in 1543 have been known as the 'Prebendaries' Plot', but as has become clear after recent detailed investigations by Michael Zell and Glyn Redworth, that label obscures the wider reference of these events.[1] One problem in understanding what happened is that some parts of the story are brilliantly illuminated by a welter of testimony which survives from Cranmer's personal papers; these are chiefly examinations of the Kentish clergy involved in the direct attack on Cranmer, and they are indeed so voluminous that they threaten the reader with archival indigestion.[2] Other equally important parts are less well-documented, and there are so many connections with other conservative initiatives at the same time that it is very difficult to sort out the dynamics of what was happening. What is clear is that not just the conservative clergy of Canterbury Cathedral were involved. Zell's treatment of the affair in 1975 highlighted the role of the gentry of Kent: Redworth's biography of Stephen Gardiner in 1989 concentrated on the Bishop's co-ordinating position, although Redworth was paradoxically concerned to discredit Gardiner's traditional evangelical stereotype as 'Wily Winchester', which in fact seems amply proved by Redworth's own meticulous analysis.

Both these interpretations proved fruitful because so many different strands of conservative opposition came together in 1543, although neither Zell nor Redworth exhausted the exposure of conservative networks, as we will see. All of the strands are interlinked; all played a part, and their complexity may well explain why the plot against Cranmer eventually failed. The essence of success would be speed. Yet no one succeeded in co-ordinating the long-drawn-out and multifaceted initiatives successfully, not even Gardiner, in contrast to the lightning success of the aristocratic coup against Cromwell three years before; ultimately Henry VIII was given time to change his mind and side with the Archbishop. To that extent, Redworth's minimizing of Gardiner's Machiavellianism has a point.

1 Zell, 'Prebendaries' Plot'; Redworth, *Gardiner*, Ch. 8.

2 These papers, C.C.C.C. MS 128, are calendared very fully and for the most part accurately in *L.P.* 18 ii no. 546.

The first traceable initiative in the whole business came at the end of 1542, a year full of trouble and contention in Kentish religious politics. One Sunday in Advent, Robert Serles rode over to Chilham church to preach for Dr John Willoughby. To make the name 'Prebendaries' Plot' all the more inexact, neither cleric was actually a prebendary of the Cathedral; Serles was a Six Preacher, and Willoughby, who had only been in the diocese for three years, had no Cathedral office, although he may have established links there because he was a medical doctor. While Serles was at Chilham, however, he talked about his traumatic experience of 1541 in trying to denounce Cranmer, and he tried to enlist Willoughby in a fresh proposal for articles of accusation against the Archbishop and his friends which 'he and his company should devise'. Willoughby showed cautious interest as long as 'they might be true and proveable'.[3] One notes already that Serles had a recognizable 'company', and not surprisingly they comprised his like-minded colleagues at the Cathedral. Serles for the moment apparently left Willoughby as a sleeping partner in the plan, and instead he concentrated with Prebendary William Gardiner on gathering material against the diocesan evangelicals. This they continued doing throughout winter 1542–3.[4]

Nearly all of the later strands of the 1543 actions are already involved in this Advent encounter. Serles was a former fellow of Merton College, Oxford, and he still held the living of St Peter in the East within the Oxford city walls; he was also (despite his trauma and temporary expulsion) still on the staff of Canterbury Cathedral. Dr Willoughby, Serles's host that Sunday, took a series of Oxford degrees rather late in life after his arrival in Kent, probably in addition to his medical degrees from elsewhere. He also had Court links as a royal chaplain, originally (ironically) because he was a cousin and doctor of Anne Boleyn, but he himself showed no evangelical leanings. Quite the contrary: Willoughby had been appointed to Chilham in 1539 by two leading conservative gentry of Kent, Sir Anthony St Leger and Edward Thwaites, the pamphleteering publicist for Elizabeth Barton the Maid of Kent. St Leger was otherwise engaged in the King's service throughout this affair, masterminding the even more complex business of converting Ireland from lordship to kingdom as Henry's Lord Deputy. Thwaites, however, was actually resident in Chilham, having saved his traditionalist skin from total disaster on Barton's fall by adroitly switching into Cromwell's service. It was probably his influence which led Willoughby to talk approvingly in his parish about Barton's now desolate cult centre of Our Lady of Court-at-Street, and also to preserve at Chilham the empty shrine of St Augustine from St Augustine's Abbey at Canterbury.[5] Thwaites, moreover, was an old friend of at least two

3 C.C.C.C. MS 128, p. 145, Strype, *Cranmer* 2, p. 314, App. 33 (*L.P.* 18 ii no. 546, p. 325).

4 C.C.C.C. MS 128, p. 101 (*L.P.* 18 ii no. 546, p. 319).

5 Willoughby's presentation: Cranmer's Register, f. 368v; on his current conservatism, C.C.C.C. MS 128, pp. 15, 37 (*L.P.* 18 ii no. 546, pp. 295, 303), and for its lifelong persistence, MacCulloch, *Suffolk and the Tudors*, p. 193. On his career, see also Emden, *Oxford to 1540*, p. 631.

of the conservative Canterbury Prebendaries, Sir Anthony St Leger's brother, Arthur, and Archbishop Warham's old secretary, Richard Parkhurst; he himself married the widow of Warham's nephew.[6]

Oxford; the shadow of Elizabeth Barton; the golden memory of Warham; ex-monks; conservative gentry; conservative courtiers – perhaps the most important unifying factor for all these strands was the former Warham connection within Kent, and the fact that it was given a natural and enduring outlet to the wider world by the strong links between the Warham-era clergy and Oxford University. This was not just because Warham himself had been an Oxford don, but because of the ancient and intimate structural connection between the archdiocese and Oxford. Partly this was through the Archbishop's role as Founder and Visitor of All Souls' College, with its many ecclesiastical lawyers who dominated the higher levels of the Canterbury courts; however, an even more important permanent link was between Canterbury Cathedral Priory and Canterbury College, Oxford, a mixed community of monastic and lay scholars dependent on the Cathedral. The College's monastic recruitment had of course been principally from Canterbury itself, but it had also drawn on other great Benedictine houses of the south-east, including Winchester Cathedral Priory. The web of relationships thus created had been torn apart by the College's dissolution in 1540; the bitterness of the dissolution must have been compounded by the fact that surviving evidence indicates the College's flourishing expansion in the early sixteenth century.[7]

The primarily conservative Fellows and members of Canterbury College would have had their sense of waste and loss in the early 1540s compounded by the consciousness of the alien clique, overwhelmingly Cambridge men, which surrounded the chief obvious villain of the closure, Archbishop Cranmer. Three former Wardens of Canterbury College (all of course ex-monks) were still on the staff of Canterbury Cathedral after its refoundation: Prebendaries William Hunt alias Hadleigh, Richard Thornden and William Gardiner alias Sandwich. The Warden for the last six years before the surrender was Gardiner alias Sandwich, whom we have met in 1541 urgently buttonholing Bishop Stephen Gardiner in Canterbury Cathedral (see above, Ch. 7, p. 286); he was already emerging in winter 1543 as one of the chief agents in the Prebendaries' Plot. One of the considerations in Prebendary Gardiner's mind in his machinations against Cranmer may even have been the restoration of Canterbury College to its former place in the University. Its final fate was not clear between 1540 and 1545, and the Cathedral Chapter was still carrying out repairs and alterations in the buildings.[8] Meanwhile, dispossessed Canterbury dons cherished their friendships with former Oxford colleagues, and during visits to the University they vented their angry feelings about changed times.

6 Zell, 'Prebendaries' Plot', pp. 250–52.

7 *Canterbury College*, ed. Pantin 1, p. vi, and cf. *Joseph Letter Book*, p. lii.

8 *Canterbury College*, ed. Pantin 4, p. 206.

In early 1543 there was still one element necessary to pull Kent, Canterbury and Oxford together, to add further ingredients and to stir up the whole poisonous brew working against the Cranmer set: this was to introduce Dr John London as a would-be *deus ex machina* to the Kentish scene. London was a flamboyant figure who makes an agreeably satisfying villain for Cranmer partisans in his 1543 troubles: a persecutor of Oxford evangelicals as early as 1528, and a papalist sympathizer in the 1530s who had nevertheless played an eager part in the dissolution of the monasteries and friaries, he eventually died in prison accused of perjury, after the plot against Cranmer had collapsed. He was also a lifelong member of the Winchester–Oxford nexus, which had taken him from schooldays at Winchester College to the Wardenship of Winchester's sister-college, New College, Oxford. Robert Serles would have been a familiar figure to him, for Serles's Oxford parish church of St Peter peers over the college wall of New College.

It is perhaps relevant that Archbishop Warham had followed precisely the same initial career path as Dr London in earlier years, but it was of even more immediate significance that the ex-officio Visitor of both Winchester College and New College was Bishop Stephen Gardiner.[9] Through John London, Gardiner was drawn (probably not unwillingly) into the web of activity against Cranmer. Gardiner seems to have been that rare bird, a Cambridge man who came to prefer the other place. He took a very active interest in Winchester and New College after becoming Bishop of Winchester, while he became very much an absentee in his continuing role as Master of Trinity Hall, Cambridge, and a notably inactive Chancellor of Cambridge University during the 1540s.[10] Perhaps the growing strength of evangelicalism in Cambridge disgusted him, in contrast with the relative evangelical weakness in Oxford. In an exercise in tracing Cranmer's and Gardiner's employees throughout their episcopal careers, I found, unsurprisingly, that Cranmer showed a clear preference for Cambridge over Oxford men: forty-four to twenty-three. A smaller-scale exercise for Gardiner showed a much less dramatic contrast: sixteen Cambridge men to thirteen Oxford, with among the Oxford men, more than half from Dr London's New College (see Appendix III).

By 1543 Dr London's pluralist empire-building had taken him in many directions beyond New College; he resigned his wardenship in 1542 to preside as dean over Oxford's new and shortlived Cathedral at Osney, but even more important for his role in the 1543 affair was the fact that two months after Thomas Cromwell's execution in 1540, he had become a canon and prebendary of St George's Chapel, Windsor. From early on in his tenure at Windsor, London had used his niche there to harass the outspoken

9 For this and other general information about London which follows, see Emden, *Oxford to 1540*, pp. 359–60.

10 It is perhaps significant that there seem to be no references to Gardiner in Trinity Hall wills of the 1540s preserved in C.U.L., UA Wills 1.

evangelicals among the Chapel staff who had been nurtured by the radically minded Dean Simon Haynes; his campaign reached a new pitch during winter 1543, when he involved Gardiner in his activities.[11] There were high stakes in this campaign; by starting with an exposure of evangelical contamination among the clergy of this famous royal foundation, Henry VIII might be infuriated enough to destroy evangelical laity at Court, as had been done in the case of Cromwell. Vulnerable courtiers indeed began to be marked out after the Windsor victims. It was all in all a very useful ploy in order to cement in place Bishop Gardiner's dearest wish and the fruits of his patient diplomacy over two years, the completion of an English alliance with the Holy Roman Emperor. This was secretly signed in February 1543 and openly acknowledged in June, to enable England to declare war on France. The intervening months would be the best of times for Gardiner, as the King ostentatiously staked out his claim to be a good Catholic ally for Charles V by his conservative domestic religious policy, and a major contributor to this turnaround in Henry VIII's religious stance was the information provided from Windsor, the Court and from Kent.[12]

One might characterize London's and Gardiner's activity, as Foxe did, simply as malicious trouble-making, but it must be set against the background of Cranmer's own simultaneous moves in the other direction. The Convocation of Canterbury was recalled in the wake of the 1543 session of Parliament, and it is probably significant that while Parliament began its active sessions on 22 January, Dr John Cockes on Cranmer's behalf prorogued Convocation for another three weeks and more. Given the fiasco of the Convocation session in winter 1542, it is likely that Cranmer wanted to take no chances in relaunching his programme of further evangelical advance, and sure enough, at the first proper Convocation meeting on 16 February, he presided over the formal presentation of the homilies which his colleagues had composed on various subjects, handing them over for filing to his registrar Anthony Hussey. The following week Cranmer set up a two-man committee with the usual religious balance (his evangelical friend Bishop Goodrich and the conservative Bishop Salcot) to examine and revise service books, with the specific aim of removing non-scriptural elements. The same day he secured agreement that at morning and evening prayer the clergy should read a sequence of New and Old Testament readings in English, a new move which was a clear supplement to the Cromwellian order of 1538 that there should be English Bible readings at the mass. Two days later, the clergy petitioned for canon law reform, a hardy perennial of Cranmer's agenda of change.[13]

It is also likely that Cranmer had been doing his best to get the right people elected for the Lower House of Convocation, in order to smooth the

11 Foxe 5, pp. 470–81.

12 Redworth, *Gardiner*, pp. 177–183.

13 Lambeth MS 751 pp. 119–20; cf. Lehmberg, *Later Parliaments*, p. 184, Bodl. MS Jesus 74 f. 23r. On the 1538 order, see Butterworth, *Primers*, p. 162.

path of his reforms. There is direct evidence of this for Canterbury diocese, where the proctors were the complaisant Dean of Canterbury, Nicholas Wotton, and the Archbishop's right-hand man, the evangelical enthusiast Christopher Nevinson. These were elected according to Dr Willoughby by a mere dozen 'of their own affinity' among the Canterbury clergy.[14] Throughout the Kentish section of the 1543 manoeuvres, Nevinson's activities in Canterbury diocese were a prime target of conservative accusations, and he was no doubt very useful to Cranmer in the Lower House. Right up till the prorogation of 17 or 18 March for Holy Week, the prevailing tone of Convocation was reformist, and this time positive action was proceeding satisfactorily along the lines which Cranmer had sought in vain a year before. Then the prorogation gave a breathing-space for the conservatives until 4 April. In this interval, something needed to be done to change the direction in Convocation away from evangelical triumph, and Gardiner and London were determined to do it. Holy Week 1543 was the crisis point.[15]

The stirs at Windsor during the winter were noted with keen interest in Kent by the very people who at Chilham in December 1542 had begun their own investigations against evangelicals. During Lent (in other words February and early March) 1543, Dr Willoughby commented to friends on what London was doing 'in the examination of the business and matters of Windsor', and he roundly declared that anyone who would co-operate 'in bolting out of this new fashion of doctrine should not only receive reward at the hand of God and thanks of the King's Majesty, but also afterward temporal profit'.[16] Dr London himself had no base in Kent, but there were two Windsor evangelicals who did; both were linked to Cranmer's circle. One, Anthony Pearson, was one of London's principal victims at Windsor, for he was eventually burnt at the stake that summer; he was encouraged by Commissary Nevinson to preach in All Hallows, Canterbury, on Palm Sunday 1543, after release from his first brief brush with London and Gardiner at Windsor, and clearly this was not his first visit to Kent.[17] The other, who was linked by the conservatives with Pearson as one who came 'out of other dioceses', was actually beneficed at Chartham near Canterbury. He was Richard Turner, who seems to have exchanged his Fellowship of Magdalen College, Oxford, for the superficially incongruous position of a cantarist at St George's Chapel, Windsor, in the last months of Anne Boleyn's life. He held this Windsor post until the dissolution of the chantry under Edward VI.

Turner owed his position at Chartham to Ralph Morice, Cranmer's secretary, and thanks to Morice he survived the conservative assault of 1543,

14 C.C.C.C. MS 128, p. 155 (*L.P.* 18 ii no. 546, pp. 329–30).

15 Lambeth MS 751, p. 121: this exhibits confusion about the date of prorogation, calling 18 March Saturday instead of Sunday, which would be a most unusual day for a convocation sitting. In itself, a Sunday sitting might be a sign of crisis, but the question remains open.

16 C.C.C.C. MS 128, p. 311 (*L.P.* 18 ii no. 546, p. 369).

17 C.C.C.C. MS 128, p. 77, 81, 245, 255 (*L.P.* 18 ii no. 546, pp. 313, 315, 353–4). Cf. Foxe 5, pp. 472–4, 487–94.

unlike Pearson; throughout his later career Turner received high favour from Cranmer.[18] Morice will recur as one of the chief architects of Cranmer's salvation during 1543. If there was a Prebendaries' Plot for the conservatives, on the other side there was a secretary's plot, in which this faithful servant of the Archbishop exploited his lifetime of family experience at Court, keeping constantly in touch with two evangelicals strategically close to the King: Sir Anthony Denny, Chief Gentleman of the Privy Chamber, and Henry's personal physician Dr William Butts. All of them had of course lifelong associations with Cambridge, and it had been the reign of Anne Boleyn which had seen them in addition cemented into the life of the royal Court.[19]

As Foxe noticed (although he misplaced the year of the incident), it was Turner who was chosen as the first victim in Kent.[20] Probably this was precisely because Turner had a triple profile as one of the suspect staff at Windsor, a Cranmer associate and a noisy evangelical in Kent, attracting large audiences to his preaching in a village strategically placed just off a main road south-west out of Canterbury. Chartham was also no more than a couple of miles from Willoughby's Chilham. Already before Passion Sunday (11 March) 1543, Willoughby and Serles repeatedly discussed denouncing Turner to the Privy Council for his preaching, using Willoughby's status as a royal chaplain to try to prevent a recurrence of the disaster which had happened to Serles before the Council in September 1541.[21] According to Morice, during the winter they formed an alliance with their conservative friends on the JPs' bench: Morice names Sir John Baker, Sir Christopher Hales and Sir Thomas Moyle. Baker turned out to be the key layman in the conservative schemes, because he was a Privy Councillor and Westminster office-holder as well as being one of Kent's leading men.[22] The conservatives chose Turner's sermon on Passion Sunday as a subject for complaint, for the good reason that Turner had exploited a coincidence of festivals to preach on a eucharistic theme, always a red rag to a bull for King Henry.

Passion Sunday that year happened to fall on the eve of the Feast of Pope Gregory the Great, and there can be little doubt that Turner took the opportunity in his sermon to scorn the so-called Trental of St Gregory or

18 For Turner's career, see Emden, *Oxford to 1540*, pp. 580–81, which usefully distinguishes him from a younger namesake. For references to his activities in Kent, C.C.C.C. MS 128 pp. 33–4, 255 (*L.P.* 18 ii no. 546, pp. 301, 354). For Morice's summary of his story, Foxe 8, pp. 31–4, which has misled commentators by being misdated to 1544 rather than 1543; cf. also his connection with the arrested John Merbecke of Windsor, Foxe 5, pp. 482–3.

19 For an excellent discussion of the role of Denny and Butts especially in the 1540s, see Starkey, *Henry VIII: Personalities and Politics*, Ch. 7.

20 Foxe 8, p. 31: 'by whose diligent preaching a great part of this heart-burning of the papists took its first kindling against the archbishop'.

21 C.C.C.C. MS 128, p. 172 (*L.P.* 18 ii no. 546, p. 335).

22 Baker's career is conveniently summarized in *History of Parliament 1509–58* 1, pp. 366–9.

'Pope Trental', an elaborate set of thirty masses said for the dead with which he would have been only too familiar, thanks to his chantry duties at Windsor. With its lurid associated legend of Pope Gregory's mother in purgatory, this had become a favourite devotion amid the luxuriance of late medieval English piety, rather to the dismay of the more austere churchmen of the period. Turner would have reason to detest it on both personal and theological grounds. In his sermon, one memorable sally which duly went into the evidence against him was that Almighty God was the soul-priest and sang the last mass of requiem, and that no other mass profited the departed: a curious angle to take on the theme of Passion Sunday unless Turner had made the connection with St Gregory. The same day Serles was back preaching with Willoughby at Chilham; they were probably expecting and indeed hoping for fireworks from the neighbouring pulpit at Chartham. Now Willoughby had the material to activate his plan to make a complaint about Turner to the King.[23]

Turner was not the only one to be attacked. Coupled with him were various other preachers, principally the outspoken former Fellow of St John's, Cambridge, John Bland, whom John's had presented to its Kentish living of Ospringe. Once there, he was taken up by Cranmer's commissary Christopher Nevinson, who had doubtless known him at Cambridge, and Bland acquired the archiepiscopal living of Adisham from Nevinson, together with responsibilities in Cranmer's administrative machine.[24] The conservative list of Bland's misdemeanours culminated in a flurry of offensive sermons throughout Kent and acts of iconoclasm in his own church at Ospringe during winter 1543; this made him the perfect subject for attack at the same time as Turner's Passion Sunday diatribe.[25] As Convocation headed towards its fortnight of prorogation around Easter, the Kentish part of the conservative trap was ready to be sprung.

The evangelicals were not passive under fire as the conservatives launched their assault. It can be no coincidence that three days after Passion Sunday Nevinson affirmed his confidence in Bland by resigning to him his prebend in Edmund Cranmer's Wingham College; Bland celebrated by a further outrageous sermon on superstitious ceremonies on Palm Sunday (18 March), a major occasion for such ceremonies.[26] We should also recall Nevinson's pointed gesture in inviting the stormy petrel of the Windsor troubles, Anthony Pearson, to preach in Canterbury that same day. Ralph Morice also

23 Foxe 8, pp. 32–3; C.C.C.C. MS 128, pp. 62, 145 (*L.P.* 18 ii no. 546, pp. 310, 325). On the trental of St Gregory, see Duffy, *Stripping of the Altars*, pp. 43, 74, 76, 293–4, 370–6.

24 Venn 1, p. 227; Cranmer's Register, ff. 53r, 362v. It is worth noting that Ralph Morice unsuccessfully tried to obtain the lease of Ospringe in 1537 (i.e. when George Day was Master of John's), while Bland was parson: Strype, *Cranmer*, 1, p. 482.

25 C.C.C.C. MS 128, pp. 7, 14, 67–9 (*L.P.* 18 ii no. 546, pp. 291, 295, 311–12).

26 Cranmer's Register, f. 387v; C.C.C.C. MS 128, p. 69 (*L.P.* 18 ii no. 546, p. 312, where the 1542 date is Old Style).

sprang into action in defence of Turner. At this stage, Turner's prospects do not seem to have been too menacing: a date was appointed for Cranmer himself to head a set of commissioners to hear the parson of Chartham's case at Lambeth after Easter. Morice went further by short-circuiting this procedure, directly intervening with Sir Thomas Moyle to let Turner preach a couple of trial sermons in Moyle's parish church at Westwell, on the Wednesday in Easter Week (28 March), and for the moment Moyle pronounced himself satisfied.

Moyle was one weak link in the conservatives' plans, either simply because he was fair-minded, or because he was too preoccupied as Speaker of the House of Commons. It was he who had been responsible for leaking the complaints about the evangelical clergy to Cranmer after Passion Sunday.[27] This priming of the enemy camp might endanger the broad sweep of London's plan to link up his Windsor complaints with those from Kent before the Council; for now Turner, having provided fuel for the flames, was small fry compared with the possible range of victims. The first was Simon Haynes, now Dean of Exeter, but more to the point London's long-standing enemy as former Dean of Windsor, who on 15 March was abruptly summoned up to the Privy Council. The following day Haynes appeared before the Council; the day after that, the courtier Thomas Weldon also appeared on charges of favouring Anthony Pearson. London noted with glee on 18 March how well his plan had worked so far: the King 'was astonied and wondered, angry both with the doers and bearers [supporters]' of the Windsor evangelicals.[28] As yet events were not completely spinning out of evangelical control; Cranmer was present at the Council Board for all the Windsor interviews, and he was armed with the knowledge of the Kentish complaints which Moyle had passed on to him. This was no doubt why Turner was for the moment given the prospect of a sympathetic hearing at Lambeth.[29]

Yet there was more to come. On the day of Weldon's appearance, 17 March, Dr London was standing outside the Council door with his fellow-Windsor Prebendary the Dean of Lichfield, Henry Williams, ready to act as principal witnesses in the Windsor affair. There the two deans spotted Serles, who had ridden up with Willoughby from Kent that day. 'You could never 'a come in better season!' London exclaimed in pleasure on seeing him, before being swept away by someone else. London and Serles later claimed that this meeting was accidental, but as Dr Redworth comments, this strains credulity. Behind all this was Bishop Gardiner, carefully noting all the different possibilities for discrediting evangelicals; one of those accused before the Council was one of his diocesan clergy from Bentworth in Hampshire, and the scribe working with London in his negotiations with the Canterbury clergy was the

27 C.C.C.C. MS 128, p. 142 (*L.P.* 18 ii no. 546, p. 325).
28 C.C.C.C. MS 128, p. 141, Strype, *Cranmer*, p. 311, App. no. 33 (*L.P.* 18 ii no. 546, p. 324).
29 *A.P.C. 1540–47*, pp. 96–7.

Bishop's nephew, Germain Gardiner.[30] Moreover, in the final form of the surviving evidence of the affair, the need for discretion and reconciliation when all the manoeuvring was over meant that Gardiner's role was obscured, but one heavily scored-out question for Dr Willoughby originally asked whether he had said to anyone 'that the Bishop of Winchester would give six thousand pounds to pluck down the Archbishop of Canterbury'.[31]

The next day, Palm Sunday, while the Council pressed on with its round-up of courtiers and Windsor evangelicals, Serles had a couple of meetings with London. One needs to remember that many senior churchmen were milling round London and Westminster in the wake of Convocation's prorogation, and that there must have been an atmosphere of frenzied gossip about what would happen next in religious politics. Thus it is noticeable that another prominent conservative theologian, and Serles's former colleague at Merton, Dr William Tresham, was sufficiently aware of what was going on to tell Serles that morning that Dr London was looking for him around Westminster. At the second meeting of the day, Serles took Willoughby along to meet the deans London and Williams; now the Kentish pair began to reveal their drawbacks as co-conspirators. Throughout the whole year, it was the Kentish component which let down the plans through hesitancy and indecision. It took a great deal of threatening from London to get Willoughby to agree to go to the Council at all, and London had to rewrite the articles that Serles had prepared that lunchtime in order to heighten the drama of their content. Having succeeded, the Dean of Osney immediately sent this altered copy over to Bishop Gardiner. As yet this set of articles contained nothing against Cranmer; it was fairly stale stuff against lesser Kentish figures. Serles himself was too nervous after his 1541 trauma to take any further part – he was, after all, still on bail from that incident – and on Monday he retreated to the comparative calm of Oxford for the next month and a half.[32]

At this point the sheer scale of the London–Gardiner–Kent enterprise began to get in the way of progress. It took two days during Holy Week before Bishop Gardiner was free enough of other business to see Willoughby, and the nearest that the increasingly nervous parson of Chilham got to the Council was to present his articles at the Council door to the Lord Privy Seal, Lord Russell, who brusquely noted that they were not signed and told him to get back to Canterbury to produce a proper set. The Prebendary reportedly had some encouragement at this stage from Bishop Gardiner's associate and fellow-Councillor, Sir Anthony Browne.[33] Nevertheless, 'with a heavy heart'

30 *A.P.C. 1540–47*, p. 97; C.C.C.C. MS 128, pp. 145, 164, 164A, Strype, *Cranmer*, p. 314, App. no. 33 (*L.P.* 18 ii no. 546, p. 325, 331, 333). Cf. Redworth, *Gardiner*, pp. 187–9.

31 C.C.C.C. MS 128, p. 157 (not calendared in *L.P.* 18 ii no. 546, p. 330).

32 C.C.C.C. MS 128, pp. 163–4 (bound in reverse), 309–10 (*L.P.* 18 ii no. 546, pp. 331–2, 368, not always reliably summarized). *A.P.C. 1540–47*, p. 97.

33 C.C.C.C. MS 128, p. 185 (marginalium of Prebendary Gardiner's deposition not included in *L.P.* 18 ii no. 546, p. 336). On Browne, see Redworth, *Gardiner*, p. 179.

and savage rebukes from Dr London for his inefficiency ringing in his ears, Willoughby rode back to Chilham on Good Friday: so far nothing was settled, and no commission according to the list prepared by Serles to examine Kentish heretics had yet been granted out. On Easter Eve (24 March) Willoughby rode into Canterbury to meet the conservative clergy, and here for the first time, if we are to believe him, he found a new set of articles (prepared by Prebendary Gardiner and Serles) which was the first of a series drawn up over the next few days listing Cranmer's misdeeds back to the rows of 1541.[34] The Kent accusations had now reached a higher target than anyone elsewhere. Prebendary Gardiner's Easter Day sermon in the Cathedral was a stormy, dramatic affair in which he mixed up accusations of anabaptism with attacks on those who criticized the cult of Mary and the role of confession: from the pulpit his shrieks of 'Heretics! Faggots! Fire!' echoed around the great building.[35] It was a declaration of war.

On 29 March Dr Willoughby bore his augmented ammunition back up to the capital and to Dr London, who saw that he had finally struck gold.[36] Throughout April the Council was shifting its attention from Windsor to the capital, and chasing up evangelical London printers and prominent people who had been breaking the regulations about eating flesh in Lent.[37] At long last, and predictably, the Council also saw the Kent articles, probably on 22 April 1543. This day's Council meeting (with Cranmer absent and Gardiner present) was crammed with business, most of which was bad news for evangelicals: among the items on the agenda were the fates of two old Calais Cranmer associates, his former commissary, John Butler, to be examined, and poor Adam Damplip, now to be executed. Besides this, articles were exhibited against Dean Haynes of Exeter and given to a committee including Sir John Baker, and it is not at all implausible in view of what happened next that at the same time the articles against Cranmer, too confidential to be noted in the Council minute-book, were also entrusted to Baker.[38] Further complaints seem to have been made to the Council by Dr London about the conduct of preachers in Cranmer's London peculiar parishes, and also about 'Dr Taller', probably Bishop Latimer's former diocesan official now in Cranmer's service, Dr Rowland Taylor.[39] The King himself saw the articles against Cranmer, probably the same night; now, in his later words, he could see who was the greatest heretic in Kent.

34 C.C.C.C. MS 128, pp. 146–50 (*L.P.* 18 ii no. 546, pp. 326–7).

35 C.C.C.C. MS 128, p. 13 (*L.P.* 18 ii no. 546, p. 294).

36 C.C.C.C. MS 128, p. 148 (*L.P.* 18 ii no. 546, p. 327). On the dating of this phase, cf. Willoughby's mention of Richard Turner with Foxe 8, p. 32.

37 *A.P.C. 1540–47*, pp. 103–4, 107, 114–15.

38 *A.P.C. 1540–47*, pp. 117–18. This is more precise than the dating of Henry's involvement in Redworth, *Gardiner*, p. 198. The date is further confirmed by the reference to the prebendaries' encounter with the Council being at the same time as the examination of Churden at Lambeth on 23 April, C.C.C.C. MS 128, pp. 150, 201 (*L.P.* 18 ii no. 546, pp. 328, 343). On Damplip and Butler, see also *A.P.C. 1540–47*, p. 123.

39 C.C.C.C. MS 128, p. 150 (*L.P.* 18 ii no. 546, p. 328).

Events began to mirror what had happened when Cranmer had delivered his denunciation of Queen Catherine Howard to Henry VIII: a highly confidential investigation needed to be set up in a very great hurry. Immediately Dean Wotton of Canterbury issued a secret and urgent summons up to the capital to his conservative prebendaries: they must bring signed copies of their articles. When the prebendaries arrived on 23 April, certain Councillors gave them much encouragement, principally Sir John Baker, their chief contact now in charge of the Kent investigation, who was liaising closely with Bishop Gardiner, and who openly told them that King Henry himself had authorized the enquiry.[40] Baker was an old associate of the Warham circle, who had already headed Morice's list of conservative Kentish JPs who had heard the accusations against Richard Turner a month before; it was perhaps Baker who had prevailed on Sir Thomas Moyle to change his mind about Turner's sermon and pursue the accusation against him in London after Easter Week.[41]

At this stage, Cranmer was naturally ignorant of the very serious turn in events represented by Baker's initiative, and in public he was still holding his own against the conservatives. When his commissioners at Lambeth did indeed meet to discuss the Turner case, they sent the parson of Chartham home with a clean bill of spiritual health, much to conservative fury.[42] Cranmer's commissioners were also investigating a parallel complaint in late April, against his protégé Humphrey Churden of St Alphege's, Canterbury, and Churden received similar sympathetic treatment from them; Prebendary Gardiner urged Sir John Baker to take control of this alarming loose end in conservative plans, and London was annoyed that Sir Thomas Moyle was still feeding the accusations sent by Kentish JPs to Cranmer's commissioners.[43] Yet the Archbishop's concern for his inferiors may have been distracting him from the mounting campaign against himself.

Meanwhile, there was a much greater distraction, indeed a major blow, for the Archbishop. When Convocation had fully reconvened on 20 April, yet another highly important front had opened in the religious battleground over the Easter break: this was at long last the revision of the Bishops' Book to provide a new doctrinal statement for the Church of England. Between 20 and 30 April successive sessions of Convocation examined the new texts proposed for the book, section by section, with Cranmer presiding over the subcommittees on the Lord's Prayer, Hail Mary, Ten Commandments, Creed and Sacraments.[44] These were no mere formal or nominal examinations: in a later

40 C.C.C.C. MS 128, pp. 150, 186–7, 221, 242 (*L.P.* 18 ii no. 546, pp. 328, 337–8, 347, 351).

41 On Baker and the Warham circle, cf. Alsop, 'Thomas Argall', pp. 229–30, and will of William Potkin, P.C.C. 15 Dyngley.

42 Foxe 8, p. 32.

43 C.C.C.C. MS 128, pp. 142, 150, 201 (*L.P.* 18 ii no. 546, pp. 325, 328, 342).

44 *L.P.* 18 i no. 365; Bodl. MS Jesus 74 f. 17.

mischievous reminiscence, Bishop Gardiner preserved an account of Cranmer's defeat in the debate on 27 April on the role of faith in salvation, a reminiscence which seems confirmed in accuracy by its outcome in the text of the book.[45] Appalled at the draft text's rejection of justification by faith alone, Cranmer in his speech tried a perhaps over-ingenious image to argue for faith's unique role: he pointed out that sight was the property of the eye, yet this did not deny the presence of the nose on the face – similarly, justification was the property of faith, which was not to deny the 'company of other virtues' with faith. Clearly failing to impress his colleagues with this, he fell back on the rather fine distinction of saying that he would accept the text denying faith 'alone', but not faith 'only', and then he made the mistake of appealing to Henry VIII as referee. With the Kent accusations fresh in his mind, the King was not disposed to be sympathetic to the greatest heretic in Kent, and the eventual text of the published statement ended up stating pitilessly that justification by faith meant 'faith neither only nor alone'.[46] On this key theological issue, Henry VIII had not moved on from his earlier insistence on the place of works in salvation against Cranmer's earnest persuasions in 1538 (see above, Ch. 6, pp. 209–12).

By the beginning of May the new statement of official doctrine was ready for publication, and on 5 May (in what must have been a rather tedious ceremony) it was solemnly read to the nobility of the realm in the Council Chamber. Once this work had been completed, Convocation stood down for the rest of the year.[47] The book was entitled *A Necessary Doctrine and Erudition for any Christian Man*, and it could be given the unambiguous nickname 'the King's Book' because its doctrine met with the King's wholehearted approval. In almost every respect it was more doctrinally conservative than the Bishops' Book, the exception being its highly dismissive treatment of purgatory.[48] Stanford Lehmberg rightly observes that the Archbishop's main contribution was probably to tidy up the literary style, for overall the book is much more concise and better arranged than its predecessor; otherwise Cranmer must have deplored the changes made in it.[49] As we will see, although for the moment he was forced to accept the royal verdict, he made his own plans to correct its faults in the future, especially on the central themes of justification, faith and works (see below, pp. 341–7).

While Cranmer was thus occupied in knotty arguments about final wordings and nuances of doctrine, it was the perfect moment for the web of conservative accusations to be woven ever more tightly, and there are complex accounts of frantic comings and goings between Bishop Gardiner, Sir John Baker, the Canterbury clergy and, in Oxford, Robert Serles, all through the

45 *Gardiner's Letters*, pp. 336–7.
46 Lloyd, *Formularies*, p. 223.
47 *A.P.C. 1540–47*, p. 127. *L.P.* 18 i no. 365; Lambeth MS 751, p. 121.
48 On this see Kreider, *English Chantries*, pp. 151–3.
49 Cf. Lehmberg, *Later Parliaments*, pp. 184–5; Rupp, *Protestant Tradition*, pp. 149–54.

later part of April and the first week of May. On 4 May Dr London predicted a general commission to extirpate heresy throughout the realm 'within short space'. Indeed Baker, in the presence of Prebendary Gardiner and Six Preacher Shether, drew up a list of thirteen names suitable for the Kent commission; they included Dr John Leffe, Master of Maidstone College. One can gauge where Leffe would have stood in the Kent stirs by salient features of his career: a Winchester College boy who had been a contemporary of Dr London at New College; a former Fellow of Canterbury College, Oxford, and vicar-general to Archbishop Warham.[50] In the event, Cranmer was present at the Privy Council meeting of 4 May at which the issue of a special commission to examine religious 'enormities' in Kent was recommended to the King for his consideration. His presence suggests a hesitation fatal for the conservatives: the King had absorbed the information about Cranmer, but he was not prepared to strike against him personally. Despite the uncertainties of the rest of the year, this may have been the moment at which Cranmer was in fact safe. Moreover, the committee set up at the same meeting to examine Dean Haynes was not unduly fearsome, containing as it did, apart from traditionalist Bishop Salcot, Haynes's old Cambridge friends the bishops Goodrich, Heath and Thirlby.

The next blow, only four days later, however, showed that the King was still deeply impressed by the information which the conservatives had fed him, and was still interested in playing the orthodox monarch for the benefit of Charles V and his diplomats. The setting of events from this time on is also significant: Convocation played little part, being repeatedly prorogued while Parliament continued to sit. Probably it had shown itself too reformist during the winter, and the new conservative programme was going to be steered more securely through Parliament, where Cranmer and his officials were deprived of the procedural control which they could exercise in the Convocation House. A bill was introduced to the House of Lords on 8 May about the printing of books, one of the chief concerns of the Privy Council during April. The title is non-committal enough, but its content was clearly controversial; Stanford Lehmberg notes the very unusual proceeding that afternoon of a separate meeting of the bishops, which can only have been convened to discuss this measure. As it progressed through its parliamentary stages, the nature of the bill became clearer; on 10 May it was described as being 'for the abolishment of erroneous books', and in its final form only two days later as an act with royal assent 'for the advancement of true religion'.

The measure was the bitterest blow yet for the evangelicals: it was the first actual turning-back of the Cromwellian tide of reforms, in a way that even the Six Articles Act had not been. It contained remarkable provisions for an attempt to restrict Bible-reading on a status basis; this central activity of the godly life was prohibited to householders under the level of yeomen, all

50 C.C.C.C. MS 128, p. 203 (*L.P.* 18 ii no. 546, p. 342); cf. Leffe's career in Emden, *Oxford to 1540*, p. 348. Cf. also C.C.C.C. MS 128, pp. 163, 242–4 (*L.P.* 18 ii no. 546, pp. 332, 351–2).

dependents and servants and all women, except (in a clause evidently hastily added after parliamentary protests) women of gentle and noble status. It makes a striking contrast with Cranmer's Convocation enactment of February for English Bible-readings at the Church's offices.[51] Even if Cranmer did not dare speak out about the measure, his Kentish subordinates were less circumspect; the very day after Parliament was prorogued with the measure passed, the evangelical Six Preacher Michael Drum stood up in Canterbury Cathedral pulpit and declared roundly that those 'who went about to take away the reading of the Bible went about to pluck Christ's words and the Holy Ghost's from the people'.[52]

The restriction of Bible-reading reflects Henry's concern about its abuse, which we have seen repeatedly surface since the first authorization of the Bible in 1538, and the whole measure was clearly a reflection of his current mood and intentions in both domestic religious policy and overseas diplomacy. Yet at the time, commentators discerned the hand of Bishop Gardiner in the enactment. Certainly only three days later, Gardiner wrote in imperious triumph to his Vice-Chancellor of Cambridge that the King 'hath, by the inspiration of the Holy Ghost, componed all matters of religion', among which he regarded his own year-old adjudication on the correct pronunciation of Greek as not the least significant. We have one record of Gardiner's direct influence on the King at this time: the accusation which he relayed to Henry from the conservative Kentish clergy that Richard Turner had transformed his journey home to Chartham from his Lambeth discharge into a triumphal progress. Only an urgent letter from Ralph Morice to his Court contacts averted the implementation of the King's angry letter to Cranmer that Turner should be ceremonially whipped out of the county.[53] There can be no doubt that we should see the Act for the Advancement of True Religion as the most lasting outcome of the great gathering of information against the evangelicals in Windsor, the capital and Kent, which Wily Winchester and Dean London had spent so much time co-ordinating.[54]

From May to August evangelicals continued to be examined and imprisoned. Of three leading evangelicals forced into a humiliating recantation in the capital at the beginning of July, two, Thomas Becon and Robert Singleton, operated mainly in Kent (Singleton possibly as an undercover agent for Cranmer's overseas business), and the third, Robert Wisdom, was a close associate of theirs, with a ministry in Essex and London.[55] One conservative magnate who seems to have begun taking an interest in the Kentish troubles

51 *L.J.* 1, pp. 229–31; Lehmberg, *Later Parliaments*, pp. 186–8.

52 Whitsunday, 13 May 1543: C.C.C.C. MS 128, p. 48 (*L.P.* 18 ii no. 546, p. 306).

53 Foxe 8, p. 32.

54 *Gardiner's Letters*, pp. 122–3. Redworth, *Gardiner*, pp. 173–4, comes to much the same conclusion, although characteristically he is concerned to minimize Gardiner's role.

55 Brigden, *London*, pp. 348–52; on Singleton (Archpriest of St Martin's Dover), Emden, *Oxford to 1540*, p. 517, and an interesting and mysterious reference to him connecting him with John Twyne, Cranmer's overseas liaison agent, C.C.C.C. MS 128, p. 267, cf. p. 153 (*L.P.* 18 ii no. 546, p. 359, cf. p. 329).

from mid-May onwards was the Duke of Norfolk; he had perhaps up till now been keeping out of the witchhunt because of the embarrassment that his own son, the Earl of Surrey, had been caught up in accusations against fashionable young men with evangelical sympathies. Soon after Whitsun (13 May), however, Norfolk was presented with one of the sets of Kentish accusations, and Cranmer's enemies were thus powerfully augmented.

Nevertheless, for the most part the Kentish denunciations continued to be fielded not by the Duke but by Bishop Gardiner and Sir John Baker, mostly via Baker's servant, Cyriac Pettit, a lifelong conservative and later founder of a Catholic recusant dynasty, who happened conveniently also to be Deputy Clerk of the Peace for Kent.[56] One of the most lurid surviving sets, however, bypassed Pettit and was addressed directly to Gardiner from the pen of Edmund Shether, Six Preacher of the Cathedral and Fellow of All Souls, Oxford. This includes a charge of bigamy against Cranmer's sister and a veiled but unmistakeable insinuation of buggery by the hated Commissary Nevinson of one of Cranmer's kitchen-boys.[57] The agenda of all this was underlined at the end of May by one of the most unpleasant incidents of the whole tale of illwill in the mother church of the province of Canterbury. Cranmer's long-standing chaplain and evangelical stalwart among the Cathedral Prebendaries, Dr Richard Champion, died in late May. At the end of his funeral in the Cathedral, the Cathedral bell-ringer seized the censer from the thurifer and poured the hot coals over the new grave, before the astonished gaze of the dispersing congregation. In his eyes, Champion was an unrepentant heretic.[58]

For a time, the accusations against Cranmer himself seem to have been put in store by his opponents: the momentum had been lost. The Archbishop was in attendance at Court and Council at frequent intervals throughout May, June and July, often involved alongside Bishop Gardiner and the Duke of Norfolk in highly important business, like the negotiations on 19 May with Ambassador Chapuys for an offensive alliance against France.[59] It was indeed this Imperial alliance which produced a bizarre royal financial experiment in which Cranmer was intimately involved. France had entered an alliance with the Turks, a cynical move which gave the Emperor and Henry the chance to present their aggressive pact as a crusade on behalf of Christendom. Henry was forced into a commitment to pay Charles V a £10,000 loan to fight the

56 C.C.C.C. MS 128, pp. 17, 255–6, 264 (*L.P.* 18 ii no. 546, pp. 297, 354, 357). On Pettit, see *History of Parliament 1509–58*, 3, pp. 96–8; Clarke, *Kent*, p. 62. On Surrey's misdemeanours, *A.P.C. 1540–47*, pp. 102, 104.

57 C.C.C.C. MS 128, p. 267 (*L.P.* 18 ii no. 546, p. 359). The addressee, 'my Lord of N.', can only be Gardiner.

58 C.C.C.C. MS 128, p. 31 (*L.P.* 18 ii no. 546, pp. 300–301). Champion made his will (entirely taken up with the evangelical cathedral staff) on 20 May: *Testamenta Vetusta*, p. 709. John Ponet was already promoted to Champion's former South Malling prebend on 31 May: Cranmer's Register, f. 388v.

59 *C.S.P. Spanish 1541–3*, no. 141, pp. 334–5.

Turks, but he decided that he would try to recoup his investment from his subjects by appealing to them for voluntary contributions towards this sum, to be raised parish by parish in church. There was no hint in the public exhortations that the money was to be a loan, and the nation's eventual response was a slap in the face for the King: less than a fifth of his expenditure was backed up by the public's gifts.[60] Yet it was Cranmer as Metropolitan who was put in the position of public relations man for this dubious enterprise, the last proclamation of a crusade in English history. On 19 July he wrote to his suffragan bishops from Croydon, giving them instructions for organizing the collection and also enclosing an 'exhortation' which is one example of the brief official homilies which were becoming a feature of the Henrician Church.[61]

There can be little doubt that Cranmer or one of his chaplains composed the exhortation, because it makes an unhappy attempt to sanitize an aspect of the world of traditional religion which the Archbishop now abhorred. Crusades were, after all, intimately connected with the origins of papal indulgences, and the text of the exhortation obliquely acknowledged this, by reminding the audience in the pews that 'ye were wont to be abused with vain tales, and for counterfeit pardons departed with your money'. Now, it hastened to make clear, the reward for a charitably intended cash gift would be 'true pardon or remission of sins, granted by him that hath purchased pardon for all penitent sinners, our Saviour and Redeemer Jesus Christ'. After this attempt to draw the congregation's eyes back to the atonement, appropriate quotations about charity followed from Luke 6 and 2 Corinthians 9. Even before this, the writer of the piece had got into a significant lather of worry about the version of a scriptural phrase 'with relieving their calamities to redeem our own sins'. It was strange that he had bothered to include this phrase in the first place: probably it had been forced on him, perhaps by the King himself. He hastily added 'which speech implieth not that we be our own redeemers, to the prejudice or derogation of the effects of Christ's passion . . . but that we, working according to the grace purchased for us by that redemption, may please God and be partakers of the same, which is called in us redeeming of sin'. This looks like an uneasy attempt to square a theological circle: to reconcile the works theology now embedded in the King's Book with a firm assertion of the unique saving work of Christ. It is what one would expect from an evangelical prelate in a vulnerable position.

Yet still Henry seemed to be keeping his distance from the Archbishop. It was surely significant that Stephen Gardiner presided at the King's wedding ceremony, on 12 July 1543, to Catherine Parr – a highly inappropriate

60 Kitching, 'Broken Angels', *passim*.

61 The text of these documents was rediscovered by Paul Ayris in the Registers of Bishops Bonner and Thirlby; he is editing them for publication, and I am most grateful to him for drawing my attention to them, and for allowing me to see his forthcoming article: P. Ayris, 'Thomas Cranmer and "devotion" money'.

officiant, given her later evangelical influence – and that Cranmer was not present at all among the household dignitaries who were invited along.[62] Cranmer's present of a buck from the new Queen on 25 July was probably just a conventional courtesy.[63] Far more indicative of the prevailing mood was a Council order made on 20 July: the campaign against the Kentish evangelicals, which had been proceeding slowly over the previous two months, suddenly took a lurch forward, going right back to its first victim, Richard Turner. More than twelve days had elapsed since the Archbishop last attended the Council Board, and now in his absence the order went out from Oatlands that Sir John Baker should search out 'one Turner, a priest dwelling about Canterbury' and send him to Court. A week later, on 28 July, Turner's fellow-sufferer Anthony Pearson and two other Windsor evangelicals were burnt at the stake in Windsor; from a safe distance in Strassburg, Richard Hilles commented with black humour to Johann Heinrich Bullinger that Henry VIII always did something like that when he got married.[64]

Turner's arrest was his third brush with the conservatives, and Ralph Morice's later letter to Butts and Denny supplies the details of what had happened.[65] Turner was now being arrested on new charges going way back beyond his arrival in Kent, including radical preaching and his composition and celebration of a vernacular mass; judging from Morice's rather uncomfortable and convoluted defence of him, the charges were probably true, and there is one excellent candidate for the accuser – Turner's former Windsor colleague, Dr London. In any case, once more it was Bishop Gardiner who was responsible for the arrest initiative – he had been present at the 20 July meeting at which the arrest warrant was issued – while Cyriac Pettit was his agent in leading Turner as a bound prisoner to London. Now the parson of Chartham found himself cast into prison, after an examination over which Bishop Gardiner presided.

Turner's misfortune is our stroke of luck, for the aftermath of his arrest as explained by Morice to Butts and Denny provides a chronological framework for subsequent events, just at the moment when the Privy Council register ends and the next volume has gone missing. John Foxe's stories of Cranmer's lucky escapes from severe peril (mostly taken from Morice's anecdotes at second hand) are totally misplaced in 1544, and Morice's anecdotes themselves are without exact dating, but we can provide an approximately accurate chronology by deduction from the casual mention in Morice's letter of the fact that after Turner was imprisoned, he was sent down to Cranmer for examination, at the time when Cranmer was 'in Kent about the trial of a conspiracy purposed against himself by the justices of the shire, and the prebendaries of Christ's Church [i.e. the Cathedral]'. So it was after Turner's arrest and the

62 P.R.O., E. 30/1472(5) (*L.P.* 18 i no. 873).

63 P.R.O., E. 315/161 no. 206.

64 *Wriothesley's Chronicle* 1 p. 143; *E.T.* p. 159 (*O.L.* pp. 241–2).

65 Foxe, 8, pp. 32–3.

final destruction of the Windsor evangelicals at the end of July, that the London/Gardiner/prebendary conspiracy finally burst on Cranmer, failed to bring him down and instead provoked the issue of a royal commission under the Archbishop himself.

Dating Cranmer's ordeal requires further intricate juggling with chronology. The crisis, which is described in one of Ralph Morice's anecdotes, involved a face-to-face meeting between the Archbishop and the King on the royal barge near Lambeth Bridge, and Henry was hardly at all at Whitehall during the end of July and August: only one brief visit is indicated, on the slightly insecure evidence of a handful of royal grants dated from Westminster on 24 and 25 August, recorded on the Patent Rolls. However, working back from the probability discussed below that the final showdown in the Kentish end of the business took place in the week following 31 October, six weeks after the issue of a commission of investigation to Cranmer, we arrive at a date for the meeting on the Thames in mid-September. Moreover, a meeting at Lambeth on 24/25 August is made slightly less likely because we can pinpoint Cranmer as being down at Croydon on 23 August.[66]

Using the same indications provided by royal grants with Westminster dates, a number of possible days emerge: 10, 14, 17, 20 and 24 September.[67] At least two scraps of evidence point very strongly to the earliest of these September dates. The first is a series of institutions to benefices in Cranmer's Register: those on 5 and 7 September are dated from Lambeth Palace, but the third, on 13 September, is dated from Canterbury; a sudden move has taken place.[68] Even more spectacular is the witness of a dispensation recorded by the Archbishop's Faculty Office: this was the first positive evangelical initiative from Cranmer since late April. On 16 September 1543, that veteran of many a battle with the papists at Calais, John Butler, now once more styled as a royal chaplain, was given a dispensation to hold a third benefice in addition to the two which he enjoyed already within the Pale of Calais. This was a radical turnaround in Butler's fortunes since his examination in the investigations at the end of April, which had resulted in the death of his old associate Adam Damplip. It sounds exactly the sort of good fortune which might result from a request made on a sunny September evening on the Thames.[69]

66 Cranmer's Register, f. 22rv; Cox 2, p. 493.

67 *L.P.* 18 ii nos. 107/45–47, 241/14–15, 21, 23, 26, 30). For what follows, the primary source is *Narratives of the Reformation*, pp. 251–58, embroidered, confused but in some useful details supplemented in Foxe 8, pp. 24–34, and Parker, *De Antiquitate*, pp. 391–4.

68 Cranmer's Register, f. 389v. While archiepiscopal acts dated at Lambeth are not necessarily significant, acts with unusual locations such as the Palace at Canterbury are strong evidence that Cranmer was actually there.

69 *Faculty Office Registers*, p. 231. Butler became commissary of Calais once more under Edward VI (Cranmer's Register, ff. 421Av–422v), but I have not ascertained when Cranmer reappointed him.

Strange as it might seem that for five months Henry had taken no action on accusations which he had first received at the end of April, it is entirely in character that he would brood on the evidence against his archbishop in private. Probably Cranmer's unheroic obedience in accepting the King's Book and the restriction of Bible reading that spring had convinced the King fairly quickly that the charges against him and his associates were not serious enough for decisive action; the Archbishop had then performed his duty as he should in the matter of the crusade appeal in July. Instead of striking Cranmer down, Henry could let conservative plans unfold, in order to observe the behaviour of his leading politicians of all shades of opinion, until he himself was ready to bring matters to a climax. Morice describes how this happened: the King was enjoying his favourite pastime of an evening's boat trip with music up the Thames from Whitehall. After Cranmer's servants had been alerted by the noise and spectacle, the Archbishop met Henry at Lambeth and was received by the King into his barge. Henry, fortunately in good spirits, chaffed him with ferocious humour, 'Ah, my chaplain, I have news for you: I know now who is the greatest heretic in Kent', and he pulled out a paper summarizing the accusations which were the fruits of Baker's labours. An investigation must be mounted, and against Cranmer's naively honest protestations, the King cheerfully told him to appoint himself as chief investigator and choose his colleagues. This was going to be a very different commission from the conservative deliberations led in late spring by Baker: the Archbishop's choice fell on his officials John Cockes, Anthony Bellasis and Anthony Hussey, and quickly he led them to Canterbury to begin enquiries.[70]

The Archbishop and his satellites were not yet home and dry. It was perhaps expecting too much of Church lawyers to mount a ruthless and destructive investigation when many of those involved were old friends and professional colleagues. Two names among the conspirators, later ferreted out by Cranmer's investigations (Edmund Shether and Edward Napper), were Fellows of All Souls College, Oxford, the most respected institution in the senior ranks of the ecclesiastical legal profession, and a college with which Cockes was associated. Moreover, Cockes had been Archbishop Warham's Chancellor before he was Cranmer's, while Bellasis had only a year before been appointed one of Dr London's canons at Osney Cathedral.[71] Cranmer himself may have acted indecisively; he had repeatedly shown himself devoid of the killer instinct if there was no one to back him up.

70 Morice (*Narratives of the Reformation*, p. 252), says that the encounter took place at 'Lambeth Bridge'. I am not clear about the location of this: it was not a bridge over the Thames. There were various bridges over the marshes around Lambeth: *Victoria County History: Surrey*, 4, p. 51.

71 On Shether and Napper, see C.C.C.C. MS 128, p. 243 (*L.P.* 18 ii no. 546, p. 351), and Emden, *Oxford to 1540*, pp. 413, 515. On Cockes, Churchill, *Canterbury Administration*, pp. 237, 243, 245, 411: Bellasis: *L.P.* 17 no. 881/3.

The first surviving dateable depositions, gathering evidence of both conservative and evangelical excesses, seem to have been gathered fairly quickly by the commissioners, for they are dated between 20 and 26 September 1543.[72] However, after that, Morice records time-wasting and concealment of evidence. The one tangible result was temporary imprisonment for three of the Six Preachers, two conservatives and one radical (Robert Serles, Edmund Shether and John Scory), after a series of mutually inflammatory sermons during the summer, but there seems little else to show for the investigations.[73] One can also find Hussey's attentions being diverted from Cranmer's enemies to a routine benefit of clergy case at Canterbury Palace during October.[74] As late as 28 October Edmund Shether, now released again from prison, was counselling Dr Willoughby that there was still not enough evidence against them, although both men were clearly now very scared, particularly because they thought that Cockes and Hussey were being sent to catch them. Shether and Willoughby were still in close touch with Bishop Gardiner, who encouraged them that the Archbishop 'could not kill them', and that 'all was against himself that [Cranmer] did'. Yet Gardiner was evidently beginning to regret trusting the Canterbury clergy; he sneered contemptuously at the news that Shether had broken down in tears when Cranmer examined him, and he called the Six Preacher a child.[75]

While Cranmer and his commissioners dithered, an ominous development for the Kent evangelicals was that the Archbishop's secular opponents tried to outflank his commission by using the Michaelmas Canterbury quarter sessions. Here, on 27 September John Bland and Richard Turner were once more indicted for their sermons before Easter; the agents in drawing up the indictment were Sir Thomas Moyle, who had originally scrutinized Turner's preaching, and Edward Thwaites, Dr Willoughby's friend and patron at Chilham.[76] Moreover, Shether was keeping in touch with his brother-in-law in the Privy Seal office: this was the power-base of Lord Russell, the Lord Privy Seal, and the Privy Councillor who had first received Willoughby's accusations back in March.[77] Something had to be done, and quickly. Once more it was Morice who took the initiative in breaking the deadlock by writing gingering-up letters to his favourite evangelical contacts close to the King, Sir Anthony Denny and Dr William Butts. This resulted in the strengthening of Cranmer's commission by the addition of Dr Thomas Legh. Legh was a chaplain of Cranmer's, and a ruthless and overbearing former

72 C.C.C.C. MS 128, pp. 40–83 (*L.P.* 18 ii no. 546, pp. 304–16).

73 C.C.C.C. MS 128, pp. 39–45, 95, 193, 269, 333–5 (*L.P.* 18 ii no. 546, pp. 303–6, 318, 339, 358, 373–4).

74 Cranmer's Register, f. 427rv, the case of William Courtenay alias Courtenall, culminating on 29 October 1543.

75 C.C.C.C. MS 128, pp. 143–4, 269, Strype, *Cranmer*, p. 313, Appendix 33 (*L.P.* 18 ii no. 546, pp. 325, 358).

76 C.C.C.C. MS 128, pp. 105–9, 135 (*L.P.* 18 ii no. 546, pp. 320–21, 323); Foxe 8, p. 33.

77 C.C.C.C. MS 128, p. 269 (*L.P.* 18 ii no. 546, p. 358).

associate of Cromwell's in the dissolution of the monasteries; he had to be sent for from duties in the north of England. None of this suggests that he shared the other Home Counties-based commissioners' tender feelings towards their old acquaintances.[78] Morice also tells us that Legh arrived in Canterbury after six weeks of indecisive sittings by the previous commissioners, and Foxe states definitely that Legh received a ring from King Henry (the mark of a personal and urgent mission) before passing down to Canterbury on All Hallows Eve, 31 October.[79]

With Legh in charge, the situation was transformed; chosen gentlemen of Cranmer's household identified likely ringleaders for him, and they immediately staged surprise night raids on selected gentry and clerical households around Canterbury. These revealed incriminating letters, which according to Archbishop Parker specifically included letters written by Bishop Gardiner's secretary, Germain Gardiner, encouraging the conspirators. Other unexpected names among those implicated included Prebendary Richard Thornden, whom Cranmer had long trusted with diocesan business, and Dr John Barber, the Official Principal of the archdiocese. Both of them had thus demonstrated that their first loyalty was to their Oxford friends, Thornden as former warden of Canterbury College, and Barber as a Fellow of All Souls. Typically, Cranmer put them through an immediate humiliation, forgave them and continued to rely on their services, even making Thornden his suffragan bishop two years later.[80]

The Kentish conservatives were thrown into complete terror by this sudden exposure of their long-drawn-out schemes, and several accounts survive of their subsequent bitter recriminations, fears and wild mood-swings in hope of exploiting Cranmer's notoriously forgiving nature, besides abject direct appeals to his mercy.[81] Most dramatic and circumstantial is the account of the panic-stricken ride of John Thatcher junior from Canterbury to the Court and Bishop Gardiner. Thatcher was Prebendary Gardiner's nephew, and with little doubt he can be identified with the John Thatcher who was one of the last undergraduates at Canterbury College; setting out on 1 November, his Paul Revere-like mission was clearly to tell Gardiner of the overnight catastrophe in Canterbury, and to try and enlist his help.[82] He took sealed letters

78 *Narratives of the Reformation*, p. 253; Foxe 8, p. 29. On Legh, cf. Knowles, *Religious Orders*, 3, index s.v. Legh, Thomas, especially pp. 272–3.

79 Foxe 8, p. 29. There is one 'rogue date' in the evidence to disturb my reconstruction: a note of an examination of Richard Parkhurst by Cranmer and Legh on 2 October. This is most probably a simple mistake for 2 November, which would fit perfectly with every other date: C.C.C.C. MS 128, p. 273 (*L.P.* 18 ii no. 546, p. 359).

80 Foxe 8, p. 30. Barber gained the rich Canterbury living of Charing on the death of Dr Cockes, and Thornden succeeded him at Wrotham on his death: Cranmer's Register, ff. 399r, 400r.

81 C.C.C.C. MS 128, pp. 240, 325, 329 (*L.P.* 18 ii no. 546, pp. 350, 371–3).

82 C.C.C.C. MS 128, pp. 313–14 (*L.P.* 18 ii no. 546, pp. 369–70). On Thatcher at Oxford, *Canterbury College*, ed. Pantin 3, pp. 270–72.

from Edmund Shether, which may have revealed the taking of Germain Gardiner's dangerous correspondence. Thatcher had to pursue the Court north of London, and when he caught up with it after two days, great was his chagrin at his unexpectedly cold reception from the Bishop. Evidently Gardiner could see that the game was up in Canterbury, and he was going to make sure that his two years of involvement with his Prebendary namesake did not cause him any more problems. 'Get you home again. What need you come so far for such a matter?' he snapped. By 6 November an exhausted and frightened Thatcher was back in Canterbury and was put under arrest.

There was one last attempt made to bring down Cranmer, this time at the Council Board itself – a scene which passed out of the pages of John Foxe into Shakespeare and Fletcher's play *Henry VIII*. The exact relationship of this to Legh's 31 October raids in Kent is annoyingly unclear. Morice's anecdote makes it the last major event in Cranmer's troubles, while Foxe makes it the first; Archbishop Parker puts it after the issue of the Hussey/Bellasis/Cockes commission but before Legh's Kentish mission. Strictly speaking, all that one can say is that this incident occurred between September and November 1543, and that it was the decisive moment when Cranmer demonstrated that he had the King's favour. However, its setting in London seems to rule out October and most of November, for we know that Cranmer was in Kent through this period, and he was still down at his house at Bekesbourne outside Canterbury on 17 November, hearing the belatedly remorseful outpourings of Prebendary Gardiner. Henry was away from London during October avoiding the plague, of which he was always terrified.[83] Further indications that this climactic incident took place after the beginning of November are provided by the letter of Ralph Morice to Sir Anthony Denny and Dr Butts written from Canterbury on 2 November, which has provided us with so much helpful material on Richard Turner. The tone of the letter is still uncertain and anxious, as if the advantage was still to be decided, even after the Hallowe'en raids. Morice was still trying to help Turner against his conservative accusers and to avert a humiliating public recantation, but Cranmer forbade him to organize a testimonial party from Chartham to go before the Privy Council, and the Archbishop himself dared 'nothing do for the poor man's delivery, he hath done so much for him already'. More to the point, 'his Grace hath told me plainly, that it is put into the King's head, that he is the maintainer and supporter of all the heretics within the realm'. This does not sound as if the Privy Councillors had yet received their humiliation for promoting these accusations.

One further tiny indication of the date of the debacle at the Council Board may be provided by the commission of the peace issued for Kent on 23

83 C.C.C.C. MS 128, pp. 227–34 (*L.P.* 18 ii no. 546, p. 347–50). It is only fair to note one institution to a benefice in Cranmer's Register (f. 389v) dated at Lambeth on 27 September 1543, and a further clutch dated at Lambeth on 9 November and every day between 15 and 18 November: ibid. f. 390rv. On plague, Lehmberg, *Later Parliaments*, p. 189.

November 1543. Most remarkably, this does not include the name of the Archbishop, who would normally have been included as a routine courtesy for this as for other counties where he held influence. Was this an oversight, or was it one small component of something more sinister? What we may be witnessing is the last effort to undermine and bring down the Archbishop in his moment of triumph, before his investigations revealed anything too incriminating about national politicians. We know that Germain Gardiner's letters had been discovered, and there may have been much else. There is a very striking comparison with the abrupt reversal of fortune of Thomas Cromwell in late spring 1540, in the moment when he seemed to be triumphing over his enemies. What is also strange is that another commission of much lesser importance, the commission of sewers for the small coastal region around Sandwich and Deal, issued only five days later on 28 November 1543, was headed by the Archbishop's name.[84] If this conjunction of changes is significant, we can join Thomas Cranmer as he waited at the door to the Council Chamber in the fourth week of November 1543.

The primary account of what happened is again Ralph Morice's. This has King Henry playing a double game. First he granted the Privy Councillors their chance to summon their colleague the Archbishop the following day to present heresy charges, 'and as they saw cause, so to commit him to the Tower', while that same night he sent Sir Anthony Denny secretly to Lambeth to summon Cranmer to his presence; once the Archbishop had arrived, the King told him what the Council planned. Morice's account of their conversation, a perfect if oblique exposition of why Cromwell had fallen, has the ring of authenticity: Henry berated Cranmer for naivety in thinking that he would get a fair hearing from his accusers once he was in the Tower and helpless to defend himself. 'Do you not think that if they have you once in prison, three or four false knaves will be soon procured to witness against you and to condemn you, which else now being at your liberty dare not once open their lips or appear before your face?'

The King then gave Cranmer his personal ring, that favourite device for demonstrating total royal trust in moments of political crisis which we have already noted in Thomas Legh's sudden mission to Kent. The following morning the Archbishop was summoned to the Council, but he was kept waiting outside the door 'amongst serving men and lackeys' more than three quarters of an hour, before once more Morice activated his usual contacts, tipping off Dr Butts about what was happening. Butts told the King, who prepared himself to burst into one of his classic rages; the affair has such an air of clockwork that it must have been sketched out beforehand. Meanwhile in the Council Chamber, Cranmer was preparing for what must have been one of the most satisfying moments of his life, allowing his Council colleagues curtly to inform him that he was under arrest before courteously delivering the

84 *L.P.* 20 i no. 622, VII, VI, pp. 316, 315.

King's ring to them. Lord Russell's belated cry 'Did not I tell you, my Lords?' expressed the feelings of the appalled Councillors as they tumbled out of the chamber into the Privy Lodging to stand before a grimly headmasterly Henry. The Duke of Norfolk did himself no favours with his mumbled piece of hypocrisy, 'we meant no manner hurt unto my Lord of Canterbury in that we requested to have him in durance; that we only did because he might after his trial be set at liberty to his more glory'. It was all over, bar some parting sarcasm from Henry, and handshakes all round.

'Nevermore after no man durst spurn [Cranmer] during the King Henry's life.'[85] The *quid pro quo* for Cranmer's victory was that his leading opponents in high places should not suffer shipwreck; their guilt was diverted to two scapegoats in the second rank, the chief go-betweens in the various strands of the 1543 plots, who both died only a month or two after the final debacle. At the beginning of 1544 Dr London died in the Fleet prison while awaiting trial on perjury charges in connection with his Windsor investigations.[86] London's death in his cell would not be unwelcome to very highly placed conservatives, and at least one associate of Cranmer's, John Ponet, later said the same of the second death: the execution for treason, in February 1544, of Bishop Gardiner's favourite nephew and servant, Germain Gardiner. Ponet's vicious remark that Germain had died 'lest he should have too much disclosed his master's art' should not be given too much weight; the Bishop was reportedly devastated at the personal loss. Germain died on strangely antiquated charges of contacts with Cardinal Pole; those who died with him also harked back to events past, for they were associates of Sir Thomas More's family. Showing the magnanimity which so infuriated Henry VIII, Cranmer actually acted as patron to one of those who was pardoned, the writer John Heywood, and asked him to write a play discussing reason and will in human beings.[87] At a safe distance, evangelicals in exile on the Continent rejoiced at the passing of London, Germain and their cronies. In a characteristically savage pamphlet of 1544, John Bale in particular linked London and Germain Gardiner to the schemes of Bishop Gardiner, whom he likened to Haman, the unsuccessful accuser of godly Queen Esther, and he directly stated that some of the More associates executed with Germain were of Gardiner's 'privy counsel'. With stingingly cruel sarcasm, William Turner speculated that 'that excellent young man Germain Gardiner' would have avoided his fate if he had been brought up in Cranmer's rather than Bishop Gardiner's household.[88]

Foxe has a story told to Cranmer later by the evangelically-inclined Charles, Duke of Suffolk, that immediately after Germain's execution, the tables were nearly turned on Stephen Gardiner as well as on his nephew. He

85 *Narratives of the Reformation*, pp. 254–8.
86 Hall 2, p. 344; Emden, *Oxford to 1540*, p. 360.
87 Redworth, *Gardiner*, p. 205. Ponet, *Treatise of politike power*, sig. I iv. On Heywood and Cranmer, see *Whythorne*, pp. 12–13, 74.
88 Bale, *Epistle* f. 9rv; Jones, *Turner*, pp. 159–60.

faced the same sort of sudden arrest after a Council examination which had threatened Cranmer a few months before, and only escaped by playing precisely the same tactic and pulling his own strings among those close to the King in the Privy Chamber to get a personal audience with Henry. It is a plausible tale, although Foxe seems unconscious of the irony of telling virtually identical stories which illustrate for him divine providence and devilish wiliness respectively.[89] Bishop Gardiner's part in the Prebendaries' Plot was eventually reduced to a few underlinings and references in Cranmer's collected depositions, some of them heavily scored through; Cranmer or his officials may also have appreciated the black humour of their humdrum administrative business with Sir John Baker over clerical taxation on 20 December 1543.[90] According to Archbishop Parker, indeed, Cranmer soon enraged Henry VIII by his innocent generosity in passing on a request for a favour for one of the Kentish gentlemen who had nearly been the architect of his own ruin; he also subsequently quietly omitted to perform Henry's boisterous order to meet with the magnate and call him a scoundrel to his face.[91]

So Cranmer had survived. Yet he suffered a personal tragedy just at the moment when he was safe; on 18 December 1543 his palace at Canterbury was virtually destroyed by fire, and one of his brothers-in-law (either Harold Rosell or Edmund Cartwright), and others of his household servants, were killed. It was this catastrophe which gave rise to the Catholic canard about Mrs Cranmer in her box, already discussed (Ch. 7, pp. 250–51). It is very tempting to suppose that the precious contents of the box which so badly needed saving from the flames were not that 'pretty nobsey', but the depositions in the Prebendaries' Plot, so many of which still exist, and which Foxe specifically tells us were brought up in a chest to Lambeth for Henry VIII's perusal just before the opening of Parliament in January 1544.[92] Yet there is also an eerie forward echo in these flames which ended Cranmer's greatest confrontation with his conservative enemies before his final disaster under Queen Mary. When that disaster came, it was not only Cranmer who burned at the stake; from among the Kentish targets of 1543, so did John Bland of Adisham, examined before he died by old adversaries from the Plot, Sir Thomas Moyle, Sir John Baker and Bishop Richard Thornden.[93] And when Cranmer faced his trial for heresy in autumn 1555, among those chosen to give evidence against him was Robert Serles, playing out the last act of the feud which he had begun with the Archbishop back in 1541.[94]

89 Foxe 5, pp. 689–91.

90 Cranmer's Register, ff. 53v–54v. Cf. Foxe's comments, Foxe 8, pp. 30–31.

91 Parker, *De Antiquitate*, p. 396.

92 Holinshed's Chronicle, qu. Harpsfield, *Pretended Divorce*, pp. 335–6; Foxe, pp. 30–31. Cf. the letter of 20 December about the fire, B.L. Harley MS 283 f. 253. Of Cranmer's three brothers-in-law in his service, only Henry Bingham can be traced any later than 1543.

93 Foxe 7, pp. 287–306.

94 Cox 2, p. 548; see below, Ch. 13.

In the wake of Cranmer's long-drawn-out vindication, winter 1543–4 marked a resumption of his restoration to both formal authority and real influence on the course of religious policy, as in the years 1541–2. In the ceremonial presentation of leading politicians, we can catch a glimpse of him on 17 February 1544 taking a joint role with the Earl of Hertford in leading the reception at Court of an important Spanish visitor, the Duke of Najera; the conjunction of Cranmer and Hertford, which was already developing at the beginning of the decade, was an increasingly important evangelical alignment in Court politics in Henry's last years.[95] From the moment in July 1544 when Henry made the painful journey to France to lead his last campaign against the French in person, Cranmer once more formally headed the Council left in London to assist Queen Catherine in her duties as Regent; his colleagues were Chancellor Wriothesley, Hertford, Bishop Thirlby and Petre. Naturally this consolidation of favour was reflected in the power balance within his diocese. In 1544 his brother Edmund's college of Wingham, an ancient satellite of the archbishopric, was finally dissolved; Edmund was allowed to get away with some spectacularly long and quite illegal last-minute leases of College property. One of these, for ninety-one years, was to the lately endangered commissary Christopher Nevinson, and the other, even more remarkably, was a ninety-year lease apparently to Edmund's clandestine wife Alice![96] In the following year, the Archbishop played an impressive part in local Kentish defence: when in August 1545 the French naval galleys, having been beaten away from Portsmouth and Sussex, threatened to make a landing at Dover, the Archbishop was there at five o'clock in the morning with a hundred horse, 'in his privy coat with his dagger at his saddle bow, his page waiting on him with his morion [helmet] and long piece [gun]'. This martial display by a man who always loved hunting and prided himself on his horsemanship may have done Cranmer's reputation in Kent more good than all the previous decade of evangelical sermons; it was certainly remembered for decades afterwards.[97]

By contrast, Bishop Gardiner was sent off for most of 1544 on worthy but essentially routine administrative supply jobs for the French campaign, a suitably harmless quarantine occupation for one whose nephew had just been executed for treason. Henry's confidence in Gardiner was only warily restored in November 1544, when the Bishop was sent on an embassy to the Emperor; he was a natural choice, as the person most likely to succeed in rebuilding an

95 *Chronicle of Henry VIII*, pp. 109–10, the general reliability of which is confirmed by Najera's diary, *L.P.* 20 i no. 296.

96 On Nevinson's lease, *C.P.R. Elizabeth 1575–78*, no. 598 (1 August 1544). On Alice's lease (4 April 1544), *C.S.P. Domestic Elizabeth 1598–1601*, p. 534; Baskerville, 'A sister of Archbishop Cranmer', p. 288, attributed this lease to Edmund and Thomas's sister Alice the ex-Prioress, but it is much more likely to have been Edmund's wife Alice.

97 B.L. Additional MS 48023 f. 359. The incident can be dated as in early to mid-August 1545 by reference to *L.P.* 20 ii nos 63, 82, 133, 136, 167.

Imperial alliance which had been shattered by mutual distrust during the summer campaigning against France. However after his return, with nothing to show for his pains, Gardiner was mostly back with his victualling during 1545; even though he was a regular attender at the Council Board for most of that year, his ability to set the political agenda had gone.[98] Two conflicts of 1545 which can be construed as attempts to square up to Cranmer and his associates are revealingly trivial.

One row which festered from January to May 1545 provides a rare instance of Gardiner intervening at Cambridge University as Chancellor: he had been infuriated by reports about the performance at Christ's College of an evangelical Latin play. This play, *Pammachius*, had been dedicated in 1538 by its German author Thomas Kirchmeyer to Cranmer, a fact which was doubtless not lost on Gardiner. However, prudence and attention to the conventional courtesies dictated that he remain silent about this dedication, and he could hardly object to the play's portrayal of the Pope as Antichrist (a favourite theme of the Archbishop). Instead, Gardiner concentrated on the reported criticisms in *Pammachius* of Lenten fasting and church ceremonies, with even darker possibilities about its reflections on the sacraments and the mass. The then Vice-Chancellor was the evangelical Matthew Parker; he courteously but firmly stood his ground under an increasingly angry barrage of letters from the Chancellor, who eventually dragged the Privy Council into the affair to command a general peace in the University and protection for Gardiner's informants. There was little end-result for the Bishop, however, apart from a lasting animus against yet another Cambridge reformer.[99]

Gardiner would have taken more satisfaction from what seems to have been a failed attempt by Cranmer to remove two conservative clergy from livings in Sussex, in favour of his own chaplains. On the pretext of non-payment of first fruits, Cranmer declared William Levet and Richard Cawarden deprived of their parishes in late spring 1545, and in their place he rapidly collated respectively his chaplains Richard Collier and John Ponet; Ponet had to be hastily kitted out in the same week with a Faculty Office dispensation for pluralism, but Collier already held one.[100] Immediately a bitter row broke out; both of the ejected clerics had friends in high places. Cawarden (who was also Dean of Chichester) was a royal chaplain; Levet was a particularly injudicious target for Cranmer in time of war, since (bizarrely for a canon lawyer, let alone a clergyman) he was one of the government's chief agents in the Sussex

98 *St.P.* 1, p. 763 (*L.P.* 20 i no. 864); cf. Redworth, *Gardiner*, pp. 208–22.

99 The correspondence is conveniently printed in *Gardiner's Letters*, pp. 129–40, *Records of Early English Drama: Cambridge*, ed. Nelson, 1, pp. 133–41, and in part, *Parker Correspondence*, pp. 20–29; *A.P.C. 1540–47*, p. 162. On the play, Wilson, *English Drama 1485–1585*, pp. 36–7.

100 Cranmer's Register, f. 395v; *Faculty Office Registers*, pp. 230, 258.

armaments industry.[101] What links Levet to Bishop Gardiner, at least in later years, is his will of 1554, which asked for Gardiner's help in distributing charitable bequests to poor scholars. A series of Privy Council meetings (with Gardiner present and Cranmer absent) probed Levet's case and resulted in the brusque ejection of Collier, while Ponet too was forced out of his newly acquired benefice after a swift royal pardon to Cawarden; it was all over by early July 1545. The collector of first fruits gathered official blame for his over-enthusiasm in provoking the affair, but Cranmer's speedy action in providing replacements for Cawarden and Levet is suspicious, to say the least.[102] Conspiracy theorists can also relish the probability that the collector involved was Peter Hayman, Cranmer's leading fiscal officer, whose daughter later married the same John Ponet.[103]

Such tussles were part of the normal small change of ill-will in the politics of a troubled decade; they were not sufficient to shake Cranmer's position. His alignment with the Earl of Hertford was of great significance for the future, but there were other useful friends. As the King grew increasingly immobile in his last years, so casual access to his person, which had always been such an important requirement for suitors who had a favour to ask, became an increasingly restricted asset. Councillors might take policy initiatives and make decisions to their own particular agenda; so conservatives such as Gardiner, Tunstall and the Duke of Norfolk were still a powerful voice at the Council board. Yet their efforts could repeatedly be undermined last thing at night amid royal domesticity, as had been shown in Cranmer's final confrontation with his enemies in 1543. His crucial allies remained William Butts and Anthony Denny, who were still in place around the King. Butts died in November 1545, but his successor as royal doctor, Robert Huicke, was also an evangelical who became a target for conservative attacks in their last effort at self-assertion in 1546. Denny was still in his place as chief gentleman of the Privy Chamber at Henry's death-bed.

Equally important was Cranmer's increasingly close relationship, in the second half of the 1540s, with the principal tutors of his godson, Prince Edward. These were Richard Cox, John Cheke and Roger Ascham. All were Cambridge men of reformist outlook (Cheke and Ascham both from St John's), and their presence around the heir to the throne reflects the quiet, patient build-up of evangelicals in the circles closest to Henry, which was steadily eroding conservative prospects of power in the event of a government

101 Cf. e.g. *A.P.C. 1540–47*, pp. 214, 218, 231, 418, 561, and Awty, 'Continental origins of Wealden Ironworkers', p. 525. Emden, *Oxford to 1540*, pp. 353–4, 668.

102 *A.P.C. 1540–47*, pp. 179, 202, 205. Cawarden's pardon: *L.P.* 20 i no. 1335/19; Ponet's resignation: Cranmer's Register, f. 396r.

103 *Visitations of Kent 1530–1, 1574, 1592*, 1, p. 63. The fragmentary correspondence of Hayman, who was imprisoned on other revenue-collecting defaults at exactly this date, may also be relevant to this incident: H.M.C. *10th Report pt. 6*, p. 82.

during a royal minority on the old King's death. One notes the godly tone of little Prince Edward's careful Latin exercise when writing a letter to his godfather, as the boy's pen was guided to praise Cranmer's promotion of 'the word of God'.[104] It was probably Butts and Denny, rather than Cranmer, who were responsible for the suggestions which led to the successive entries of the trio to royal service, beginning with Cox. Yet Cox was presented to Harrow on the Hill, one of the best livings in Cranmer's gift, in September 1544.[105] No evidence survives of any such direct favour from Cranmer to Cheke, but he was by now the dominant figure among Cambridge humanists, and he had been involved with the Cambridge–Court evangelical nexus since the time of Anne Boleyn; he wrote Butts's epitaph in Fulham parish church.[106] Ascham had some catching-up to do by comparison. He had injudiciously chosen as his initial patron the conservative Archbishop of York, Edward Lee, but early in 1545, after Lee's death, he remedied this with a successful approach to Cranmer, which earned him that humanist's dream, an *ex gratia* grant of cash. One has to record that with the canny ecumenism which we have already noted in Erasmus, Ascham made sure at the same time that Stephen Gardiner was made aware of his great merits.[107]

Curiously obscure is the relationship which ought to have mattered most to Cranmer in Henry's last years, as at last the King found marital happiness with his sixth wife, Catherine Parr. Catherine does not seem to have begun her daunting royal marriage with any great evangelical connections; indeed among her close relatives were two of the Throckmorton family, one of whom (Sir George) had been one of the most outspoken opponents of Henry VIII's policies in the 1530s, and the other of whom (Michael) was currently secretary to that condemned traitor Cardinal Pole. We have already noted that Gardiner, and not Cranmer, had officiated at the royal wedding. However, after her marriage, the Queen began to turn her piety down paths which led her from a traditionalist interest in the writings of Catherine of Siena to a royal lady with evangelical enthusiasms, Marguerite of Navarre. The result of this shift was Catherine's sponsoring of the English translation of Erasmus's biblical Paraphrase which became an official text under Edward VI, and even more unambiguously, her own devotional text entitled *The Lamentation of complaint of a sinner*, with its pointed subtitle *Bewailing the ignorance of her blind life led in superstition*. Catherine had the sense to hold this back from public release until after her unpredictable royal husband's death. She did, however, play an important role in lobbying the King for Cambridge University, at a moment when the nervous University authorities (probably wrongly) felt that

104 Cf. Edward's letter of 18 June, Cox 2, p. 413n (*L.P.* 20 i, no. 974, which places it in 1545 rather than 1544).

105 Cranmer's Register, f. 393r. Contrast a more guarded view about the choice of Edward's tutors in Rex, *Henry VIII and the Reformation*, pp. 169–70.

106 Hudson, *Cambridge Connection*, pp. 52–7; Strype, *Cheke*, p. 30.

107 Ryan, *Ascham*, pp. 44–7.

they were threatened by Henry's designs on the chantry colleges; one notes that her interest was primarily in Cambridge.[108] The precise timing of her change of views is not clear, but an interesting suggestion is that a crucial stage was during the summer of 1544, when Henry was absent on his French campaign, and she was in daily contact with Cranmer as she fulfilled her duties as regent.[109] Otherwise, evidence for the relationship between archbishop and Queen Consort is so lacking as almost to suggest deliberate discretion.

In this favourable atmosphere Cranmer could use his newly consolidated influence with the King to pursue his quiet efforts to bring reform to the English Church, at the pace which Henry would allow; reform is the religious keynote of the years 1544–5. The first area in which he chose, in January 1544, to try to move forward was canon law reform, which he had abandoned the previous winter. Only four days after Parliament resumed, a bill on the subject was introduced to the Lords, but as so often, it quickly ran into trouble: within a week, after its third reading, the Lords committed it to a group of bishops headed by Cranmer, and after a 'secret' discussion in Convocation, a new bill emerged and became law. Like all similar previous attempts, even a measure on the statute book proved abortive, for the King (for reasons best known to himself) never appointed the commission which would carry on the work of preliminary revision started nine years before.[110] Nevertheless, a further predictable sign of the changed atmosphere was that the evangelical printers Edward Whitchurch and Richard Grafton were back in official favour after their harassment the previous year; on 28 January 1544 they were given a patent for sole printing rights in service books.[111]

One significant evangelical achievement of this parliamentary session, which unlike the canon law bill had an immediate effect, was the legislation that curbed the possibilities of using the Act of Six Articles and the Act for the Advancement of True Religion. Its aim was to prevent 'secret and untrue accusations and presentments . . . maliciously conspired against the King's subjects', and it set up tight procedures for such presentments, including a forty-day time-limit on accusations about offending sermons and a year limit on other accusations. All this so closely reflected what had actually happened in Kent, London and Windsor the previous year that everyone must have been aware of its significance; throughout March the bill battled its way through Lords and Commons, with just one note of 'certain words to be put in and out of the same' colouring the bland language of the Lords' Journals with a hint

108 Swensen, 'Noble Hunters', pp. 73, 80–81, 105.
109 Ibid., p. 77, although for some reason she sees 1545 as the more significant year.
110 *L.J.* 1, pp. 238–40, 244, 250, 254; Lehmberg, *Later Parliaments*, pp. 192, 332, nn. 82–3.
111 Butterworth, *Primers*, p. 246.

of trouble.[112] Archbishop Parker fleshes this out by describing a full-scale row in the Lords: although the bill seems to have begun its passage in the Commons, Cranmer was one of its chief promoters against Bishop Gardiner's furious opposition, but he found himself deserted in mid-debate by Heath of Worcester, Day of Chichester and possibly Holbeach of Rochester, despite the fact that they had promised him their support. In the end the Archbishop won through with support from the King and the secular peers, although Parker suggests that the original measure had been an even more thoroughgoing attack on conservative legislation.[113] To complete the happy reversal of fortune for the evangelicals in Parliament, the terms of the customary enactment of a general pardon did not exclude religious offenders; the last consequences of the 1543 persecutions could finally be laid to rest.

The first vernacular service to be officially authorized in England was published on 27 May 1544. This was the processional service of intercession known as the litany. The occasion may not strike modern worshippers as especially edifying: it was designed to encourage the people of England to maximize their effort of prayer for the threatening international situation, and by implication to enlist God's aid for Henry's massive summer relaunch of his war with France.[114] Nevertheless, this first surviving specimen of Cranmer's liturgical craftsmanship in English has deep interest, for with only minor modifications it survives as the litany in the *Book of Common Prayer*. Its wonderfully sonorous language conceals the fact that, like all Cranmer's compositions, it is an ingenious effort of scissors and paste out of previous texts; the great liturgist F.E. Brightman was indeed prepared to speculate that even the passages that seem original were borrowed from sources which have not so far been identified. The sources range in date from Luther back to John Chrysostom (via a Latin translation from Chrysostom's Greek); the bulk comes from the Sarum rite which had become Cranmer's preferred text among the uses of medieval England, but Sarum's invocations of saints were drastically pruned away, and only Mary was mentioned by name.[115] Much of the original work of synthesis had in fact been done not by Cranmer, but nine years earlier by the evangelical publisher William Marshall, in his adroitly Lutheran-oriented *Goodly Primer* of 1535; as the historian of primers C.C. Butterworth noted, Marshall put a distinctly grudging preface to his

112 *L.J.* 1, pp. 252, 254, 256, 259. Lehmberg, *Later Parliaments*, p. 198; cf. Foxe 5, pp. 527–8.

113 Parker, *De Antiquitate*, p. 396. This tussle must have taken place on 1 March 1544, as Cranmer was absent for subsequent readings of the bill in the Lords: *L.J.* 1, p. 252. There is a problem with Parker's mention of Holbeach of Rochester, who is otherwise not recorded as being translated from the suffragan see of Bristol to Rochester until summer 1544.

114 See the orders for promulgation in June: Cox 2, pp. 494–5; Cranmer's Register, ff. 48v–50r; B.L. Additional Charters 8056.

115 Brightman, pp. lix–lx, lxv–lxviii. Cf. Johnson (ed.), *Cranmer*, pp. 59–60.

litany when he included this text which was to have such a distinguished future.[116]

Should the litany be regarded as a major step forward for the reformers? One has to admit that this area of liturgy chosen for vernacular experiment was the one most remote from the evangelical ideal of worship; evangelicals had a deep dislike of processions in liturgy, and the traditional litany's association with the veneration of saints was the reason why Marshall expressed negative feelings towards his composition. Nevertheless, Cranmer's text did a ruthless job in eliminating the possibility of using the litany for saint-worship, and a curious anecdote told by the Spanish Chronicler also suggests that we ought to regard the litany as one item in the resumed evangelical advance. The Chronicle is normally such an eccentric source that one would be suspicious of anything it said about high politics, but it contains an unexpected leading character who had already been revealed in Alesius's stories about Cranmer and the Six Articles in 1539 (see above, Ch. 7, p. 251). This is William Paget, who is portrayed as an evangelical with close but discreet links to Cranmer. The Chronicler has Paget (who was the King's principal secretary from May 1544) urging Henry to order the removal of all statues from churches, and when he was rebuffed, persuading Cranmer to try a different tack and suggest English services instead, a less alarming proposal which the King approved. The Chronicler's impression, as an observant and unsympathetic foreigner in London, was that there at least, the new litany was something of a popular success.[117]

The Chronicler also asserts that Paget was responsible for getting Cranmer 'to order preaching against the placing of candles before the saints and "all such idolatry", as he said'. This may be a garbled reference to the 'Exhortation to Prayer' which prefaced the litany itself from its first issue in May, or he may be referring to some order issued by Cranmer later in Henry's reign which has not otherwise been preserved. The Exhortation certainly does not contain any such direct attacks on the cult of the saints, but it is a clear attempt to meet the fears expressed by Marshall in 1535 that the litany might be misused to promote the notion that prayer was only effective if addressed 'to God by Christ' through the intercession of 'his blessed mother, and saints'. The Exhortation, intended for public reading before the procession set off, carefully analyses the nature of prayer to God without any mention of saintly intercession, and it takes up a command in the Sermon on the Mount to emphasize that prayer does not consist 'in multiplying of many words, without faith and godly devotion'. The choir waiting to sing the responses of the litany would not have been pleased to be reminded in the next sentence that 'God doth not regard neither the sweet sound of our voice, nor the great

116 Butterworth, *Primers*, pp. 110–11.

117 *Chronicle of Henry VIII*, pp. 106–7. Cf. comments on Paget's religion in Gammon, *Paget*, pp. 118–20.

number of our words' – Cranmer never showed much sign of enthusiasm for anything but the simplest of traditional church music. Altogether, the Exhortation may be counted as one of the first of Cranmer's homilies to be published, and its message does not differ from that of the Edwardian homilies of three years later.[118]

The prospect of liturgical change continued later in the year. One of Cranmer's better-known letters was written to the King on 7 October 1544, discussing the possibility of extending the reform of the litany to what he called 'certain processions, to be used upon festival days'.[119] Much confusion has been caused by this phrase. The difference from the litany that had already been published, in spring 1544, will not be obvious if one does not appreciate that in the traditional liturgy, the term 'litany' had a narrow technical reference to a penitential service of procession; in other words, a litany was only used in a time of trouble or in a spirit of sorrow for sins committed. Both these elements had been emphasized in Henry's letter of June authorizing the litany's publication. Cranmer was now referring in more general terms to the Latin service-book called the *Processionale*, and to the other processional services, besides the litany, which it contained for use on festival occasions such as saints' days and Sundays. According to a royal command which he says had been sent him via William Paget (a telling detail), the Archbishop had now 'so well as I could in so short time' produced an English version of the whole book. For once we have a direct description from Cranmer himself of the method he had adopted in tackling the Latin text. He had used 'more than the liberty of a translator', altering words, making additions and omissions, introducing new themes for procession and removing redundant saints' days – 'the judgement whereof I refer wholly unto your majesty'.

Cranmer also commented on the music appropriate to these processional services. As he noted, the English litany had already been published with a simple plainsong setting attached (in June, by Thomas Berthelet), and he wanted this now done for the rest of his proposed English *Processionale*. As usual, Cranmer put a health warning to the appropriate music: no doubt

> some devout and solemn note . . . will much excitate and stir the hearts of all men unto devotion and godliness: but in mine opinion, the song that shall be made thereunto would not be full of notes, but, as near as may be, for every syllable a note.

Cranmer thus envisaged the most basic plainsong possible as most suitable for the Church's use, citing in his letter normal unadorned choir usage in the offices and the mass. Polyphony, the giddy musical achievement of the early Tudor English Church in the works of composers like Robert Fayrfax and the early Thomas Tallis, was beyond his concern altogether: he wanted a plain-

118 The text is conveniently presented in an appendix to *Private Prayers*, pp. 565–70.

119 P.R.O., S.P. 1/208 ff. 169–70 (*L.P.* 20 ii no. 539). For comment on the content, context and dating, see Brightman, 'Litany under Henry VIII'.

song which would be functional, comprehensible to and even performable by any persevering member of a congregation. This would be the solution which would be adopted in 1550 for the Prayer Book, when in *The Book of Common Prayer noted*, John Merbecke (familiar to Cranmer as one of the Windsor evangelicals who had nearly suffered death in 1543) drew freely on traditional plainsong to produce simple syllabic musical settings, some of which are still in use in the Church of England, after their nineteenth-century revival.

The most complex plainsong to meet with Cranmer's favour in 1544 was the relatively straightforward sequence proper to the ancient festival hymn *Salve Festa Dies* ('Hail thee, festival day'): 'sober and distinct enough', in his opinion. Here the Archbishop had indeed taken the trouble to fit English words to the contours of the music, but he was pleasingly realistic about the result, which he offered 'only for a proof, to see how the English would do in song'. 'Mine English verses lack the grace and facility that I would wish they had', he admitted sadly. This was no false modesty. One probable specimen of Cranmer's 'English verses' remains: the translation of the hymn *Veni Creator Spiritus* which he provided for the ordination service (the Ordinal) of 1550. This sets out to produce a metrical version of the hymn in the up-to-date manner then being popularized by Thomas Sternhold, but the false emphases of words against the metre are grindingly inept. It is frankly a failure, and was recognized as such in 1662, when the revisers of the Prayer Book turned to the work of John Cosin to substitute the beautiful replacement setting 'Come Holy Ghost, our souls inspire'. What is impressive in the 1544 letter, however, is Cranmer's sharp craftsman-like appreciation of the limitation of his own verbal genius to prose; his realism meant that there were no other similar verse attempts left embedded in the English liturgy, where they might have done permanent damage to the English language. Indeed there is one instance in the burial service of both 1549 and 1552 Prayer Books where he turned a piece of English poetry into prose with great success. This text already had a complicated linguistic odyssey: it was Miles Coverdale's 1535 metrical translation of Martin Luther's German version of an ancient Latin liturgical text: *Media vita in morte sumus*. Cranmer turned Coverdale's verse into the solemn and seemly funereal sequence, 'In the midst of life we are in death'.[120]

For the time being, in 1544, Henry's attention was diverted from further liturgical reform, and Cranmer's English *Processionale* disappeared from history. Instead, the following year saw a substitute measure which some may regard as negative: once more, it was a detail of evangelical reform, at first sight of minor significance, which may have pleased the Archbishop more than giving the complexity of the *Processionale* a new lease of life in the vernacular. The *Processionale* was now replaced entirely by the use of the

120 See the original text of the ordinal hymn in *Liturgical Services of Edward VI*, pp. 172–4; for some charitable comments, Leaver, *Goostly Songs*, pp. 134–6. For the funeral sentences, ibid., pp. 133–4.

already published English litany. To understand the importance of this, one must again remember the distinction between the litany and other processional services. To use the penitential rite of the litany on joyful festival days like Sunday or a major saint's feast was a solecism in terms of traditional liturgy: giving the new English litany an exclusive role as the Church of England's processional rite was an attempt by evangelicals to curb the obnoxious triumphalism of the processional mode of worship.

First, the use of the English litany was reinforced during summer 1545, in what was admittedly an appropriate time of crisis, with the French threatening full-scale invasion and indeed actually landing on the south coast. Some fragmentarily surviving depositions about a quarrel at Milton parish church in Kent reveal that the Sunday use of the litany in English was already being enforced, on Cranmer's personal orders, in his own diocese, in June 1545, before the attempted French invasion had taken place. The cause of the row there was that several in the Milton congregation did not like this innovation, and refused to take part: an interesting tribute to liturgical awareness in a rural parish.[121] Perhaps as a result of this case, a Privy Council letter to Cranmer on 10 August was careful to stress that the English processions should only take place 'upon the accustomed days and none otherwise'; among the four signatories were Bishop Gardiner and his conservative ally Sir Anthony Browne.[122] However, Cranmer's extension of the litany's use had prevailed by the autumn. The London chronicler Charles Wriothesley noted that on St Luke's Day, Sunday 18 October 1545, St Paul's Cathedral choir sang the English litany 'by the King's injunction, which shall be sung in every parish church throughout England every Sunday and festival day, and none other'. The liturgically sensitive ears of the conservative staff of St Paul's would have especially appreciated F.E. Brightman's comment that this was 'something of a revolution'.[123]

It is also likely that we should date to around this phase of liturgical activity Cranmer's second scheme for revising the breviary. We have already noted him producing a scheme for the offices of the Church in 1538–9, which not only drew upon Lutheran models, but which was intended to be published for use in English (see above, Ch. 6, pp. 221–6). In the same notebook, a more conservative breviary revision project follows, a fair copy mostly in the hand of the faithful Ralph Morice; one cannot tell whether this project too was intended for an English translation, but in any case it would seem very appropriate for the 1544–45 phase of change, cautiously nibbling away at the edges of the liturgy before a main thrust against the Latin mass.[124] Its

121 P.R.O., S.P. 1/203, f. 86 (*L.P.* 20 i no. 1118). There are three ancient Kentish parishes named Milton, but this can be identified with Milton-next-Sittingbourne.

122 Cranmer's Register, f. 26v, Cox 2, p. 495–6.

123 Brightman, 'Litany under Henry VIII', p. 103. *Wriothesley's Chronicle* 1, p. 161.

124 For concise arguments for the placing of this second scheme in the 1540s, see Cuming, *Godly Order*, pp. 2–4. The text is in B.L. Royal MS 7B IV, ff. 133–59, edited first by Gasquet and Bishop, pp. 311–96, then by Wickham Legg, *Cranmer's Liturgical Projects*.

conservatism lies partly in its two drafts for a new calendar of saints' days, the second version of which has a staggering array of obscure saints of the early Church interspersed with a more predictable patriotic line-up of English saints. Yet even this is an example of Cranmer's characteristic strategy of using traditional forms to new and subversive ends; he has tried to provide an unusual scriptural dilution to this assembly by the addition of characters from the Old Testament, especially the heroes and heroines or authors of books, a new departure for the Christian liturgical year which was not to find a future. Margaret Aston points out that three of his pot-pourri of saints and worthies, the Jewish kings Hezekiah and Josiah and the grim early Church bishop Epiphanius, were best known as smashers of images, which would have provided interesting material for homilies amid the splendours of the liturgy.[125]

More basic is the abandonment for the time being, in the breviary draft, of Cranmer's earlier radical proposal for two offices only, one for the morning and one for the evening; instead, the proposal represents a much more faithful adherence to the scheme of breviary revision prepared by Cardinal Quiñones in 1535/6, which retained the eightfold offices developed in the medieval Western Church. Cranmer returned to the earlier 1538/9 twofold structure when he compiled the *Book of Common Prayer*, but in some respects he cannibalized his later more conservative work for the Prayer Book. For instance, like the second breviary scheme, the Prayer Book's provision for Old Testament readings for the offices throughout the year takes trouble to omit sections which were considered tedious or unedifying, whereas in 1538/9 Cranmer had been prepared to let the Church plough through every last phrase, Apocrypha and all.

One significant moment in the 1540s scheme occurs in the continued provisions made for the feast of Corpus Christi, one of the great liturgical innovations of the medieval Western Church. Cranmer's treatment of this feast emphasizes the reason for his difficulties with the eucharistic theology of the Strassburg–St Gall axis in the later 1530s. Even if we have seen his eucharistic views at that period carefully distanced from the theory of eucharistic transubstantiation, his liturgical material here is wholly traditional in character, and contains one tiny text apparently freshly composed which is still robustly affirmative of the real presence: an invitatory sentence for mattins: 'Come, let us adore Christ the Saviour and bread of eternal life'. He precedes this with a medieval collect inserted in his own hand, the famous eucharistic prayer often attributed to Thomas Aquinas:

> O God, who under a wonderful sacrament has left us a remembrance of your passion: grant, we beseech you, that we may so venerate the holy mysteries of your body and blood, that we may evermore perceive within ourselves the fruit of your redemption.[126]

125 Aston, *England's Iconoclasts* 1, p. 249n, although she has picked up Wickham Legg's mistaken dating of this breviary scheme.

126 Gasquet and Bishop, p. 351 and n. The translations of these texts are mine.

Cranmer may have regarded this as providing an evangelical meditation on the eucharistic presence, with its stress on remembrance, mystery, and its direction of the worshipper back to the contemplation of the cross, the only source of salvation. The relationship between passion and sacrament, so delicately expressed with the Latin '*sub*', is hard to capture in the English 'under'; it conveys the sense of nearness, something ready to be found.

Yet this was not the direction in which eucharistic thought within the reformed Tudor Church of England was destined to travel. Hardly surprisingly, the feast of Corpus Christi had no official future in the English Church, although rebellious sacramentalists would return to it in later centuries. The Cranmer of the 1550s (indeed, perhaps the Cranmer of 1546, as we will see in Chapter Nine) could not easily have used this collect, but it fits well with the irritated annotations made by the Archbishop himself to depositions of 1543 in the Prebendaries' Plot, about the wilder eucharistic statements of evangelicals in Canterbury diocese. Joan Frenche's comment that the Sacrament of the Altar 'was but a figure or memory of Christ's Passion' earned his annotation 'heresy'; despite the fact that Frenche had (no doubt unconsciously) echoed Aquinas's collect, what condemned her was clearly her emphasis that the sacrament was nothing more than a memorial or figure. Cranmer was even able still in 1543 to describe as an 'error' the opinion that 'the mass and dirige was not laudable to be said for the souls departed'.[127] No wonder that later he would see his conversion about 1546 to a new view of the eucharistic presence as the greatest watershed in his theological pilgrimage.

Like the English *Processionale*, the new breviary scheme remained unused in the obscurity of Cranmer's notebooks, yet Henry VIII's interest in liturgical reform fitfully persisted; there is evidence of a liturgical committee sitting as late as January 1546, 'to peruse certain books of service'. This was presided over by Cranmer and included bishops Heath and Day with other royal chaplains, and it nearly produced some results (see below, Ch. 9, pp. 351–2).[128] Meanwhile, during 1545, came the final innovation in worship actually to be put in place before the old king's death: a single primer in English, the first primer which was given unequivocal official backing in replacing all others. Primers for personal devotional use were one of the most important vehicles for late medieval piety: from these books, children commonly learned their alphabets and progressed on to the Church's most basic texts such as the Lord's Prayer, the Creed, Commandments and the Hail Mary, while adults would find commentary and appropriate prayers and liturgical texts both in

127 C.C.C.C. MS 128, pp. 47, 71; neither annotation is noted in the calendar of *L.P.* 18 ii no. 546, pp. 306, 312. The inclusion elsewhere (C.C.C.C. MS 128, pp. 71, 74, 83, 84) of the marginal comment 'offensive' shows that Cranmer was not merely officially noting verdicts on offences delivered by his commission of enquiry; these were his opinions of what had been said.

128 P.R.O., S.P. 1/213 ff. 144, 146–9 (*L.P.* 21 i nos 109–10).

English and Latin, by which they could enrich their participation in the Latin liturgy. Throughout the 1530s, a proliferation of printed primers had sought to capture the market in both commercial and spiritual terms, setting forward different interpretations of the Church's worship as various as the evangelical radicalism of George Joye and the traditionalism of Robert Redman; Cromwell had dabbled extensively in these waters, backing those publishers who he felt would help his programme of change.[129]

Now, from May 1545, the King proclaimed the issue of one single primer 'for the avoiding of the diversity of primer books . . . whereof are almost innumerable sorts which minister occasion of contentions and vain disputations rather than to edify'. One notes Henry's habitual detestation of arguments within his Church.[130] The publication was put in the hands of the evangelical team of Grafton and Whitchurch, and it was noticeable that a version which also included the Latin text was not brought out until the autumn, with a long additional commendatory preface whose clumsy style indicates that it is indeed, as it proclaims, the composition of King Henry himself. Here Henry declared himself anxious to be 'all things to all persons . . . that all parties may at large be satisfied'.[131]

In fact the King's Primer carried out this programme by the characteristic strategy of 1544–5: promoting reform within the shell of traditional forms.[132] There can be no doubt of Cranmer's close involvement with its compilation. It showed a significant affinity with his second abortive breviary revision; for instance, it provided modified texts for the eight traditional offices of the day. These now included eight metrical English versions and amalgamations of Latin office hymns, which were probably more examples of Cranmer's efforts at verse. As he indicated in his letter of October 1544 to Henry, most of them are designed to fit the simple syllabic plainsong of the Latin hymns, and there is evidence that they were so used; as Leaver points out, these were the first vernacular hymns to be authorized by the Church in England. Alas, if they are indeed Cranmer's, these brave pioneering efforts also reinforce his reasons for poetic modesty.[133] The King's Primer then reprints the 1544 English litany and the funeral office, the Dirige, although here it achieves the remarkable feat of omitting the psalm *Dirige Domine* which had given the office its name. By way of compensation, there follows a very generous selection from the Psalter centred on the theme of Christ's Passion, leading up to St John's narrative of the event: this was the emphasis which one would expect with the Archbishop giving the book editorial direction, but it could be represented as satisfying traditionalists' concern for the Passion as well as the evangelical agenda.

129 The standard, and excellent, treatment of these is Butterworth, *Primers*.
130 *T.R.P.* 1 no. 248; cf. ibid. no. 251.
131 Text conveniently available in Cox 2, pp. 496–8.
132 Cf. the judgement of Duffy, *Stripping of the Altars*, pp. 446–7.
133 See discussion in Leaver, *Goostly Psalms*, pp. 110–16.

Finally, forty-two folios of the Primer offer what Butterworth calls 'a large and unusual collection of prayers', beginning with six prayers on the Passion which link directly to the previous material, and which were probably specially composed by Cranmer himself. Once more, the moderate reformist agenda is clear, as much by what is missing as what is there: none of the exuberant conversations of medieval liturgy with Our Lady or the saints, and remarkably little on the eucharist. Among the sources of the prayers that are used, modern Catholic humanism is well represented by Erasmus and Juan Luis Vives, but also most remarkably one finds a substantial contribution from the Strassburg reformer and Cranmer correspondent Wolfgang Capito, via a lively translation of the English evangelical humanist Richard Taverner. Butterworth went so far as to suggest that Taverner was the general editor of the King's Primer, for besides other prayers derived directly from his compositions, there are several other verbal touches which are reminiscent of his style.[134] This former client of Thomas Cromwell deserves further recognition and investigation; as Eamon Duffy points out, some of his 1530s discourses achieved a remarkable revival under Elizabeth I, when large sections of them were incorporated in the second set of official homilies then issued to supplement Cranmer's first set, and he was a probable source of inspiration to Cranmer when he came to gather collects for the 1549 Prayer Book.[135] Whatever Taverner's and Cranmer's relationship to the Primer text, there can be no doubt about its importance for the future *Book of Common Prayer*. Perhaps Cranmer reused material from his 1538–9 drafts of vernacular services, but in any event, it was the Primer which standardized texts for the Te Deum, Benedictus, Magnificat, Nunc Dimittis and Lord's Prayer which have been used ever since, together with several other fragments salvaged from the Primer's eight offices.[136]

One other completed measure of reform in 1544–5 directly relates to that part of the Church which would have been most directly affected by Cranmer's more substantial liturgical proposals in the *Processionale*: the cathedrals of Henry's new foundation or refoundation were now given new royal statutes. It is likely that Cranmer was closely involved with this work. One of the strongest motives for the wholesale revision may well have been Henry's angry reaction to the mayhem caused by the Prebendaries' Plot and associated intrigues; quite apart from the Canterbury Cathedral stirs, 1545 saw the destruction of Dr London's former cathedral at Osney and its replacement as the cathedral of Oxford diocese by the stately ex-monastic college chapel of the King's foundation of Christ Church. Also notable, given the entanglement of Oxford with the 1543 prebendaries and the shadowy presence of Canterbury College, Oxford, in that affair, was the dismantling during 1545

134 Butterworth, *Primers*, pp. 259, 269–72.

135 Duffy, *Stripping of the Altars*, pp. 425–7, and see below, Ch. 10.

136 Convenient comparisons of these and other liturgical texts not used in 1549 are made in Cuming, *Godly Order*, pp. 32–50. Very minor adjustments were made in 1549.

of the provisions which Henry had made for cathedral involvement in university education through the provision of studentships; Canterbury College itself lost all hopes of remaining as an independent institution when, on 27 November 1545, Canterbury Cathedral's Dean and Chapter surrendered the college site to adjacent Christ Church, whose apotheosis in the form which has endured to the present day was thus complete.[137]

Henry first commissioned the team of Richard Cox and bishops George Day and Nicholas Heath to complete the devising of new cathedral statutes, and most of that work seems to have been completed during 1544. One cannot prove Cranmer's direct involvement with the committee in this first stage, but it is readily apparent in the case of the second similar line-up of clerics who subsequently recommended the dismantling of the link between cathedrals and universities: bishops Day, Heath and Thirlby. This team was staying at Lambeth Palace on 1 December 1544, when in a moment of leisure they joined with Cranmer in writing to Matthew Parker at Cambridge, asking him to do a favour for one of their friends in connection with the estates of Parker's Stoke-by-Clare College – inevitably, all the parties involved were Cambridge men and old acquaintances.[138] Like Henry, Cranmer may have been taught by his traumas of 1543 to abandon his earlier hopes that cathedrals might serve a useful purpose in higher education. Instead, the work of the bishops' committees satisfyingly tied up loose ends left from the Prebendaries' Plot.

By the end of 1544, therefore, the atmosphere had changed once again. This was apparent to interested Continental evangelicals, in particular to that perennial Anglophile Martin Bucer, who took a leading part in efforts to reopen talks between the Schmalkaldic League and England, which had remained stalled since 1540. Perhaps relying on information from Cranmer and Paget, he gave an upbeat assessment of prospects when urging new contacts on Philipp of Hesse: only the Duke of Norfolk and Bishop Gardiner were still strong voices about King Henry for the conservative cause and for an Imperial alliance, while even Norfolk's son, the Earl of Surrey, had deserted them for the evangelical camp.[139] In England, Cranmer was involved in two events symbolizing the failure of conservative hopes to unseat him within the English Church. One was personal, the other official. First, in the autumn of 1544, Prebendary William Gardiner alias Sandwich died, a year after his

137 On the remodellings of 1544–5, see C. Knighton in O'Day and Heal, *Princes and Paupers*, p. 47, and in Marcombe and Knighton, *Close Encounters*, pp. 9, 30–35. On the surrender of Canterbury College, *Canterbury College*, ed. Pantin 3 p. 156.

138 C.C.C.C. MS 114, p. 411. This letter, which has no year-date, can be fixed to 1544 by the previous and subsequent whereabouts of the signatories, and by the mention of what are clearly Parker's replies in a letter by John Mere of 26 January 1545, together with a letter on an allied Stoke theme from Queen Catherine of 24 March 1545: *Parker Correspondence*, pp. 17–20. Cf. C. Knighton in Marcombe and Knighton, *Close Encounters*, pp. 30–31.

139 McEntegart Ph.D., 'England and the League of Schmalkalden', pp. 423–32.

abject apologies and pleas for mercy to the Archbishop. His Canterbury prebend was then given, on royal presentation, to one of Cranmer's own relatives, the Cambridge academic and King's chaplain, William Devenish.[140] Second, another death that same autumn left the see of York vacant, and archbishop Lee's successor was Robert Holgate, a former Gilbertine monk whose evangelical outlook was already emerging. As part of Holgate's admission to his archdiocese, Cranmer was called on to perform the ceremony which had been one of the more expensive elements in his own consecration: the bestowal of the woollen *pallium* which was the symbol of an archbishop's authority. Its bestowal was also a symbol of the authority of the one who bestowed it: in 1533 the Pope, now the King who was Supreme Head of the Church of England, and whose agent Cranmer was – in fact, he had already once before conveyed the *pallium* to Henry's newly consecrated Archbishop of Dublin in 1536. The transformation required some judicious rewriting of the liturgy, in the typical fashion of the mid-1540s seeking to turn an old rite to new uses. A tiresomely papalist reference to the body of St Peter was removed, references to the new archbishop's obedience due to the King was added, and the pallium itself was redefined simply as a sign of the priestly office of Jesus Christ. Hardly surprisingly, such a sign was not considered necessary by the Edwardian Church, and from 1559, the English career of this garment became confined purely to archiepiscopal heraldry.[141]

In this moment of cautious triumph, Cranmer commissioned a portrait of himself from Gerlach Flicke, a German artist newly arrived in England. This has been as remarkable a success in conveying his image to posterity as Hans Holbein's carefully crafted pictorial construction of Henry VIII's persona. It is important first to confirm the picture's date, which is given as '*Anno etati* 57 *Julii* 20'. 20 July in the 57th year of a man born on 2 July 1489 fell in the calendar year 1545, not in 1546 as is often stated: a point first made by Jasper Ridley.[142] So the context of the picture is one of self-confidence and hope, not of the sudden acute anxieties amid the fresh conservative onslaught in Henry VIII's last summer of life (see below, Ch. 9, pp. 352–6). The painting, like Cranmer's seals, is a tribute to his refined and up-to-date humanist classical taste. It is a masterful work, of an almost photographic quality in its detail, so that the signet on Cranmer's finger is an exact replica of the heraldic impression which is familiar from the seals on his private correspondence. Yet this apparently straightforward, starkly simple image is in fact a complex

140 Cranmer's Register, f. 393v. For the relationship, B.L. Harley MS 6148 f. 43v, Cox 2, p. 279 (*L.P.* 7 no. 188).

141 P. Ayris in Ayris and Selwyn (eds), *Cranmer*, pp. 134–5; Cranmer's Register, ff. 306–10.

142 Ridley, *Cranmer*, frontispiece. '*Etati*', an odd dative for this position, may simply be a slightly unusual abbreviation form for *etatis*.

statement of a consistent theme, although it also continues successfully to guard some of its secrets from us.[143]

There is little doubt that the picture was conceived in relation to the image of Cranmer's predecessor as Archbishop, William Warham, whose portrait of 1527 by Holbein was then at Lambeth Palace (to which it has now returned). In his portrait, Cranmer is depicted sitting at a table in much the same disposition as Holbein's Warham, and he is dressed in strikingly similar style: black clerical cap, white rochet with over it a black chimere and fur stole. Another detail, the little paper slip or *cartellino* stuck to the window-jamb and providing the date and Cranmer's age, is an idea probably also borrowed from the Warham portrait, which is one of the earliest surviving English pictures to employ this somewhat rare device.[144] Thus far, the Flicke portrait is saying, the office of an archbishop is the same as it always was. There the resemblance ends. Warham's eyes were turned away from the spectator, and his hands rested lightly on the cushion in front of him: an old man who was using a moment of tranquillity to concentrate his thoughts on something beyond the immediate moment. The object of his contemplation was indicated by the book open beside him: a meticulously depicted litany of the saints – Warham, seventy-seven years old when the picture was painted, was reaching out very close to the holy company of heaven. His figure and personal dress might be austere, but he was flanked to right and left by the symbols of the ancient power and magnificence of his office, an intricately chased processional crucifix and a bejewelled mitre.

Cranmer, by contrast, has pulled his alert gaze back to the present and to the spectator, and his hands are occupied, opening the Epistles of Paul. One feels that he is about to speak and expound the eternal message of grace alone, carried by the Epistles, the message at the centre of his faith. In front of him are two further labelled books from his beloved library (Warham's picture also had two further books, but by contrast they were stowed behind him, and neither labelled). Directly below Paul's Epistles is a work of Paul's most celebrated Western interpreter before Luther, Augustine of Hippo – his treatise *De Fide et Operibus*; infuriatingly, the label of the second book nearest to the spectator has been badly damaged and has never satisfactorily been interpreted.[145] Cranmer's calling is therefore to expound scripture with the aid of the best of patristic scholarship. His office is not to be symbolized by liturgical books, or traditional ecclesiastical magnificence of cross and mitre, although as a position of rank within the Tudor commonwealth it is

143 I am grateful to Dr Tim Moreton of the National Portrait Gallery and to Pamela Tudor-Craig (Lady Wedgwood) for our correspondence on the portrait.

144 Cuttler, 'Holbein's inscriptions', pp. 372–3.

145 King, *English Reformation Literature*, pp. 122–3, chose like others to interpret it as '*Erasmi Testamentum*', a tempting suggestion, but frankly impossible given the surviving fragments '*E. . . . p . . . ntem*'.

23 Portrait of Archbishop Warham by Hans Holbein, 1527.

24 Portrait of Archbishop Cranmer by Gerlach Flicke, 20 July 1545.

emphasized equally emphatically by the administrative letter lying on the table in front of him, addressed in formal but business-like fashion 'To the right reverent [*sic*] Father in God and my singular good Lord my Lord the Archbishop of Canterbury his Grace, be these delivered'.

Puzzles remain in the other details of the portrait, especially the remarkable 'antique' carving in plaster, stone or wood beside the window-jamb. In itself this is not surprising; the inventory of furniture taken at Cranmer's fall reveals tapestries with classical subjects like the *Story of Virtues* and the *Story of Hercules*, which is what one would expect from the cultured humanist who had commissioned such beautiful seals for himself in the antique manner.[146] Yet even if this is a snapshot of a real room in one of Cranmer's Kentish palaces, after the evangelical intensity of the labelled books and the piece of everyday correspondence on the table, it comes as a shock to meet the stare of a naked female, saved only from total exposure by a grotesque lion's head; above her is a horned fire-breathing man who might be the Minotaur. Together with the Turkey carpet on the table, the inlay of the chair and the curtain at the window, this carving may be simply there to convey an air of modish magnificence appropriate to a member of Henry VIII's Privy Council; but there is surely more to it than that. Thoughts of the female as Mrs Cranmer in her box can be dismissed straight away. Might the setting be an Augustinian comment on the position of an evangelical statesman – a child of God and one of his elect, but also imprisoned in a fallen creation – Luther's *simul justus et peccator*?

Even if we cannot satisfactorily solve some of these enigmas, the central message of the portrait is clear. It tells of the duties of a bishop in the Church of God as an administrator, but above all, as the preacher of an evangelical message which is very clearly specified. It is the message that divine grace alone justifies humanity: the message proclaimed by Paul and pitilessly expounded by Augustine. By contrast, the early nineteenth-century commentator Henry Todd perversely seized on the detail of the portrait books in his biography of Cranmer to draw an eirenical message – this was 'a pictorial intimation, as it were, of the Archbishop's sound doctrine, that St Paul, whenever he treats of justification, insists especially upon good works, as absolutely necessary to salvation; all faith without charity being nothing'.[147]

Now it is true that one of the very few manuscript underlinings in Cranmer's own copy of Augustine's *De Fide et Operibus* is the statement that 'a good life is indeed inseparable from faith': this is a lesson that the 1547 homilies would later stress.[148] However, to regard this as a comfortable affirmation of Cranmer's essential moderation on faith and works is probably

146 P.R.O., E. 154/2/41, f. 16v.

147 Todd, *Life of Cranmer*, 1, pp. xiii–xiv, qu. R. Strong, *Tudor and Jacobean Portraits* (London, 1969), no. 535.

148 Augustine, *Opera Omnia* (Paris 1531/2; B.L. C.79 i.4), 4, f. 17v. The same quotation duly appears in Cranmer's Great Commonplaces, Royal MS 7 B XII, f. 99v.

the reverse of the meaning intended in the portrait, as a cursory acquaintance with Augustine's developed views on faith and works will reveal. It is likely that Cranmer had chosen *De Fide et Operibus* not for the content of the actual treatise, for it is in fact one of Augustine's more obscure writings, and one which the Archbishop did little to exploit. Instead, he wished to draw attention to the great theological theme embodied in the title.

The mature Augustine, in his last and greatest theological clash with the British monk Pelagius, had refined his thought on faith to the most savage affirmation of predestination; faith was a gift of God, entirely at his arbitrary disposal, and the value of any human works for justification was precisely nil. Naturally, good works flowed from justification – 'a good life is indeed inseparable from faith'. But works must be rigorously separated from faith when one was talking about the twofold human destiny: either justification, or consignment to eternal destruction, both of which lay in the predestined will of God alone. Good works by contrast were part of the deepening experience of God which was possible for the elect: the process known in theological jargon as sanctification. In Peter Stephens's useful phrase, to distinguish sanctification from justification 'is to distinguish the meaning of salvation from the means of salvation'.[149] One should recall Cranmer's clumsy but revealing image in the convocation debate on justification by faith alone in March 1543 (see above, p. 309): sight was the property of the eye, yet this did not deny the presence of the nose on the face as well as eyes. Justification was the property of faith, yet this did not deny the presence of other virtues alongside faith. They simply had other functions than justification.

Works were a part not of justification, but of sanctification. This was the main message, the truth of which Cranmer had tried to hammer home to Henry VIII back in 1538, when they were tussling over the revision of the Bishops' Book. Cranmer had failed then; and the measure of his failure had been the statements on justification and works in the King's Book of 1543. We have already drawn on Bishop Gardiner's gleeful reminder to Cranmer of the 1543 justification debate on the eve of the book's publication: the outcome was a direct defeat for the Archbishop in argument with Henry VIII. The Flicke portrait, then, can be seen as a statement that Cranmer had not given up the fight to win Henry to the truth of justification by faith alone, after his unfortunate setback in 1543. After all, he believed both in the perseverance of the predestined and in Henry's predestined role as God's agent in the realm of England; so he should be confident that God would in the end have the victory over the King's unfortunate temporary prejudices.

There is other evidence beyond the portrait that Cranmer's project in the mid-1540s was indeed to act as God's agent in bringing Henry to a right understanding of justification. This is provided by the research of Ashley Null on Cranmer's voluminous notebooks, especially the two volumes now in the

149 Stephens, *Holy Spirit in Bucer*, p. 21.

British Library, the systematic arrangement of theological sources with outline commentary which Null calls the 'Great Commonplaces'.[150] We have seen Cranmer set his secretaries to begin compiling these sourcebooks in 1537/8, about the time of the composition and revision of the Bishops' Book, yet a large part of the content of the notebooks is clearly differentiated and later in date. Very fortunately, some of the sourcebooks quoted in these later sections provide a precise date before which the sections cannot have been entered: the King's Book itself, Sir John Cheke's edition of a homily of John Chrysostom, published in August 1543, and several quotations from the controversial Catholic work *Antididagma*, published at Cologne in 1544.[151] So Cranmer was working on these notebooks after 1543–4, but the theological issues dealt with in these later sections were largely settled after 1547. Thus the notebooks were directed by the Archbishop to the religious situation in Henry's last two or three years of life.

Dr Null has acutely made a connection which gives precision to our picture of Cranmer's purpose in the wake of the 1543 debacle represented by the King's Book. Among Cranmer's papers is a manuscript treatise simply headed '*De justificatione. D. Redman*'. Null has realized that this is the fair manuscript copy of a printed treatise on the nature of justification by the leading conservative Cambridge don John Redman, posthumously published in 1555 thanks to Redman's uncle, Bishop Cuthbert Tunstall. Tunstall would have realized the value of this treatise to the work of the Marian restoration of the old faith, because it is a systematic refutation of justification by faith alone; in any case, he was anxious to refute the Protestant claim that on his deathbed in 1551 Redman had given way to the main tenets of evangelical belief.[152] In his preface to the 1555 printed edition, Tunstall explained that Redman had presented this treatise to Henry VIII, and that it had now come 'intact' into his own possession. How had this happened, and how do we now find the fair copy in Cranmer's papers? Working backwards, Null suggests that Tunstall had probably found the manuscript when Cranmer's library and papers were seized by Mary's officials in 1553. Cranmer had acquired it because Henry VIII had handed it over to him for comment, which as Cranmer himself noted was the King's habitual practice (see above, Ch. 6, p. 183).[153]

Now the importance of this is that John Redman was one of the theologians who compiled the 1543 King's Book; in fact Stephen Gardiner recalled that he had been one of the committee of six who compiled the material on justification in that work.[154] Cranmer may therefore have possessed the

150 B.L. Royal MS 7 B XI, XII: Null Ph.D., 'Cranmer's Doctrine of Repentance', p. 6, Ch. 4, passim.

151 Cf. e.g. B.L. Royal MS 7 B XI, ff. 93v, 132v, 166r–167r, Royal MS 7 B XII, f. 197v. For further discussion of the *Antididagma*, see below, Ch. 9, pp. 393, 400.

152 On Redman's deathbed, see Foxe 6, pp. 267–74.

153 Null Ph.D., 'Cranmer's Doctrine of Repentance', pp. 18–19, 130. The Redman treatise is Lambeth MS 1107 ff. 137r–162.

154 *Gardiner's Letters*, p. 365.

Redman treatise because he had argued with Henry about the statements on justification in the King's Book. What was the background which Redman had brought to his committee work, and his treatise? Redman was in high favour with Henry VIII, being chosen as the first master of his grandiose new foundation at Cambridge, Trinity College. This favour is quite surprising considering that he spent the 1530s as a fellow of St John's College, Cambridge, and that he was part of that group among the Fellowship who represented the original ethos of the College, fervently grateful to the man who had guided John's through its difficult early years: Bishop John Fisher. Gratitude had survived in St John's despite Fisher's political disgrace and execution, and Redman was one of the chief posthumous exponents of Fisher's theology, even if he had the good sense to be discreet about its source.[155] In particular, this meant that he was an exponent of Fisher's subtly drawn attempt to interpret the medieval Church's discussion on the question of justification. Fisher, like Cranmer, had meditated on the significance of Augustine of Hippo's work, but from his different situation as chief defender of the old faith, he saw his task as to reconcile Augustine with medieval views rather than to use him as chief witness for the prosecution. He was a scholar of that Cambridge generation which, as we have seen in the palmy days before the Lutheran explosion, experienced no conflict between their enthusiasms for humanism and for medieval scholasticism (see above, Ch. 2, pp. 31–2). The result, on the theme of justification as on many others, was most notably expounded in Fisher's book which had once so impressed Cranmer, the *Assertionis Lutheranae Confutatio* of 1523.

It was thus, with splendid irony, Fisher's theology of justification which was expounded in the King's Book, the final official statement of Henrician theology approved by Fisher's greatest enemy. To explain this, one can point not merely to Redman among the membership of the committee of six on justification, but also to his fellow-Johnian of the same generation and outlook (and Fisher's former chaplain), Bishop George Day. Fisher and the King's Book sought to counter the assertion of justification by faith alone by emphasizing a balance between divine and human initiative created through 'the high wisdom of God'. Of course, as the King's Book emphasized in good Augustinian fashion, God is 'the principal cause and chief worker' of justification. Nevertheless, humanity could 'refuse or receive' grace; 'man . . . shall be also a worker by his free consent and obedience to the same'. God's help was offered to humanity within the life of the Church and with the aid of its sacraments, by 'baptism, penance, and the daily spiritual renovation'. These could be defined as instruments of what was technically known as prevenient grace: grace which precedes the action of the human will.[156] Redman thus clarifies in his treatise the balance between divine initiative and human willed response:

155 Bradshaw and Duffy (eds), *Humanism, Reform and the Reformation*, p. 41.
156 Lloyd, *Formularies*, pp. 373–5.

> We understand that we are justified by grace or that everything is owed to grace alone, in the following manner: not because justification occurs in us without the movement and assent of our own will, but because God by grace alone, coming before [*praeveniens*] and preparing our will through penance and faith which is living (that is, joined to charity), effects justification in us.[157]

Cranmer would regard this as a betrayal of the principle of faith alone, because it gave back a place to human works in the once-for-all process of justification. For him, the category of prevenient grace was meaningless, because all divine grace was in effect prevenient and had no accompaniment in good works; any work, including the supposed sacrament of penance, simply obscured the uniqueness of the Passion of Christ on the cross in conveying God's grace to humanity. In response to defeat in 1543, he turned in his final gathering of scholarly ammunition in the Great Commonplaces to refute this distortion of the message of Paul and Augustine on faith and works, which he had so prominently placed in his portrait. Null's achievement has been to demonstrate in detail from the intricate and taciturn source of the Great Commonplaces how the Archbishop marshalled and commented on sources, centring on the text of Scripture and the works of Augustine, to prove his point. The conclusion was that of the late Augustine trampling over the theology of Pelagius. Justification was by faith through grace alone, within the framework of God's arbitrary predestination, without any foreseeing of individual human merit; for strictly speaking, there was no human merit, not even among the elect. All righteousness in a humanity which was utterly fallen and under destruction was that of Christ himself: an alien righteousness given to humanity by grace. Human beings could never actually be 'just' or righteous; they could only be regarded by God as just. Hence Cranmer headed one of his sections with a succinct explanatory statement of this evangelical doctrine (termed technically forensic justification): 'From this point on, "to justify" means "to pronounce, declare or exhibit as just".'[158] It does not, one notes, mean 'to make just'.

One can do no more here than outline the general strategy uncovered by Null. In an important comment, Cranmer identified what he called an invention by the 'scholastics' (Fisher was not named, but was silently included) of a 'middle grace' between the views of Augustine and of Pelagius, by the grant of which the ungodly could turn and do good works before justification: it was therefore the Archbishop's task to show that the scriptures and Augustine

157 Lambeth MS 1107 f. 144v. I am most grateful to Dr Null both for identifying this as a key text and for allowing me to draw on his translation when preparing my own: cf. Null Ph.D., 'Cranmer's Doctrine of Repentance', pp. 129–30.

158 B.L. Royal MS 7 B XII, f. 84r (cf. Cox 2, p. 8); Null Ph.D., 'Cranmer's Doctrine of Repentance', p. 149. Null, ibid., pp. 179–81, has effectively refuted the alternative view that Cranmer advocated the alternative hypothesis of factitive justification or agreed with Osiander's championing of essential righteousness: cf. ibid., p. 184, McGrath, *Iustitia Dei* 2, Ch. 8, and Collinson, 'Cranmer', pp. 96–8.

knew of no such middle grace.[159] Cranmer did the same to prove that justification was conferred freely; if justification was preceded by good works, then it would not be a free gift, but would have been earned. Similarly, he reproved the distinction in scholastic theology (repeated in the King's Book without technical language) between two sorts of faith: mere assent, which was possible before justification (*fides assensus* or *informis*) and faith which was joined to hope and charity (*fides formata*, or what Redman had called 'faith which is living'). For Cranmer, neither of these was really faith at all.[160]

Cranmer spent a good deal of effort demolishing the potential (exploited by Fisher) of the biblical story in Acts 10 of the Roman centurion Cornelius, which offered the possibility of showing that works were a preparation for faith, because God had taken notice of Cornelius's prayers and good works.[161] Naturally, he also devoted one of his sections to reconciling Paul's message with the emphasis on the value of works in the Epistle of James, which Luther had loftily called an 'epistle of straw'.[162] Complementing his exposition of the mature Augustine was also the proposition which had already been present in Cranmer's arguments with Henry VIII in 1538: predestination. In the mid-1540s, Cranmer could make the marginal comment on his excerpts from Augustine that 'no-one of the predestined can perish, and no-one not predestined can be saved'. Again, in a comment soon afterwards, any tie between human merit and the source of human fate is cut: 'God gives grace, not because we deserve it, but because he wishes to.'[163]

Most importantly, Cranmer had to face the objection which had so impressed King Henry throughout their long debates: evangelical emphasis on justification by faith alone through grace undermined the whole principle of human morality, by removing the value of good works, and thus it endangered the peace of a godly commonwealth. Null makes clear by analysis of one of the most extended commentaries in the notebooks, that as far as Cranmer was concerned this fundamental worry for the evangelical Reformation was removed by a suitable doctrine of repentance. This was now clearly separated in the Archbishop's mind from the Church's sacramental practice of penance, even if the same Latin word *poenitentia* was used for both. We have seen that already in 1540 he defined repentance simply as 'a pure conversion of a sinner in heart and mind from his sins unto God'.[164] Moreover, Cranmer further used his definition of repentance to prove that faith justified without

159 B.L. Royal MS 7 B XII, ff. 225v–226r; Null Ph.D., 'Cranmer's Doctrine of Repentance', pp. 131–6.

160 Null Ph.D., 'Cranmer's Doctrine of Repentance', pp. 136–43.

161 Null Ph.D., 'Cranmer's Doctrine of Repentance', pp. 143–5: B.L. Royal MS 7 B XII, ff. 208r–12, 224v–226r.

162 Null Ph.D., 'Cranmer's Doctrine of Repentance', p. 151; B.L. Royal MS 7 B XII, f. 106 (cf. Cox 2, p. 8).

163 Null Ph.D., 'Cranmer's Doctrine of Repentance', pp. 166–74, especially p. 171: B.L. Royal MS 7 B XII, ff. 279v–280r.

164 Cox 2, p. 116.

works. Repentance was the one authentic mark of a right will, and a right will was the only qualification for repentance; a right will was the free gift of God.[165] Repentance naturally resulted in good works, which, to use the definition of justification already spelled out, would 'exhibit [humanity] as just'; so human beings ought always anxiously to scrutinize their lives for good deeds. Thus Henry's doubts on solifidianism should have been stilled; there is no evidence that in practice they ever were. The theology expressed in the Great Commonplaces would have to wait until the old King's death before it could come into its own.

Even if this fundamental victory was denied Cranmer, the trickle of evangelical change went on through late 1545 and into early 1546, no doubt assisted by the absence from mid-October of Stephen Gardiner on yet another diplomatic mission to the Emperor. It is noticeable that Gardiner seems to have failed to pay his respects to the Archbishop while passing through Canterbury on the way to embark for the Continent. Instead Winchester contented himself with letting Secretary Paget know of Cranmer's failure to punish an incident of military indiscipline in the city![166] One can imagine what Gardiner would have said if he had been at the Council board on 24 October, when a letter was sent off to Cranmer: this intervened against those who had set up a prohibited image, also forbade a holy water custom, and ordered the removal of one of the last surviving cult images of Our Lady, which had incongruously survived in the heart of government, in the chapel of the Pew in the Palace of Westminster.[167]

In November and December, Parliament met; among those elected to the Commons was a significant number of definite evangelicals, including no fewer than seven who were also members of the King's Privy Chamber.[168] This Parliament struck a further blow at the already tottering empire of purgatory by legislation empowering the King to seize whatever chantries and intercessory institutions he liked, on the baldly pragmatic grounds that he needed the money. Although the Commons fiercely fought this measure, probably resenting this new arbitary confiscation of local assets, they also defeated a bill which was certainly intended to hurt the evangelicals. This bill against heretical books was at first vigorously promoted, but it met prolonged discussion in the Lords and was committed to a bipartisan committee over which Cranmer presided. When it was finally defeated, 'I hear not that his Majesty is much miscontented', Secretary Petre reported, and Cranmer's reaction is likely to have been the same.[169]

165 Null Ph.D., 'Cranmer's Doctrine of Repentance', pp. 156–65; B.L. Royal MS 7 B XII, ff. 225v–226v.
166 *Gardiner's Letters*, pp. 151–4.
167 *A.P.C. 1540–47*, p. 261.
168 Brigden, *London*, p. 361.
169 P.R.O., S.P. 1/212 ff. 108–10 (*L.P.* 20 ii no. 1030). Lehmberg, *Later Parliaments*, pp. 220–23.

The Archbishop appears to have been absent for the concluding ceremony of Parliament on Christmas Eve 1545, which was a pity, because he would wholeheartedly have approved of the great speech which Henry then made, the last major public statement of the old King's lifetime. This pioneer royal Christmas broadcast was the famous occasion on which Henry bewailed his subjects' lack of charity to each other: 'some be too stiff in their old mumpsimus, other be too busy and curious in their new sumpsimus'. It was an impassioned plea for unity which reduced the King himself to tears as well as his audience. Strikingly, Henry echoed the message of Cranmer's 1540 Preface to the Great Bible, which had displayed the same Janus-like strategy addressed both to those 'that be too slow, and need the spur', and those who 'seem too quick, and need more of the bridle'. He even directly borrowed one phrase from Cranmer's Preface, when he described the word of God as 'that most precious jewel', as he returned to his favourite complaint that the reading of Scripture was widely misused.[170] As the King's words drew into his own tearful emotion the Lords and Commons of England assembled in the high court of Parliament, the scene was the perfect icon of the supreme headship of the Church of England as Cranmer conceived it: it was the pictorial title-page of the Great Bible come to life. In little over a year, King Henry would be dead, and the supreme headship would be put to new purposes. Cranmer's patience in accepting his old master's theological vagaries would be vindicated, and his decade and more of planning a religious revolution would have come into its own. Yet there was one last test of survival before that consummation of his hopes.

170 Cf. Hall 2, p. 357 and Cox 2, pp. 118–25, esp. p. 122. *L.J.* 1, pp. 281–2; Lehmberg, *Later Parliaments*, pp. 229–31.

Part III

THE YEARS OF OPPORTUNITY

Lord now lettest thou thy servant depart in peace,
according to thy word,
For mine eyes have seen thy salvation,
Which thou hast prepared before the face of all thy people,
To be a light for to lighten the Gentiles, and to be the glory of thy people of Israel

(1545 Primer, incorporated with slight modifications in the 1549 Prayer Book)

Your Majesty is God's vice-gerent and Christ's vicar within your own dominions, and to see, with your predecessor Josiah, God truly worshipped, and idolatry destroyed, the tyranny of the Bishops of Rome banished from your subjects, and images removed.

(Cranmer's address to King Edward VI at his coronation, 20 February 1547)

CHAPTER 9

Welcoming King Josiah: 1546–9

THE LAST YEAR OF the old King's life is an essential part of the story of his son's brief reign; it decided the outcome of the long war of attrition which had been fought between evangelicals and conservatives at Court since the death of Thomas Cromwell, and it destroyed the balance of power so fiercely maintained by Henry VIII. When the year opened in January 1546, Cranmer seemed on the verge of securing more important changes with Paget's aid than any so far in their two years of partnership in lobbying the King. The evidence is preserved in a remarkable trio of letters: the Archbishop's letter to Henry VIII, introducing the draft of a letter to be addressed by the King to Cranmer himself, together with Cranmer's covering note to Paget telling him to check over this draft text. The King was to tell him to order the abolition of various ceremonies involving adoration of images and crucifixes, and the banning of ritual bell-ringing on All Hallows' Day; in a parenthesis rather awkwardly placed within the draft, Cranmer tried to show Henry how these ceremonies clashed with his own King's Book of 1543. Moreover, Cranmer's excited letter to Henry reveals that the King was at last showing some interest in activating the powers that he had been given by Parliament two years before to revise canon law; he had even asked to see the outline draft law-code prepared back in the 1530s.

This January initiative was a put-up job in more ways than one, demonstrating the close co-operation which now existed between the Archbishop and Secretary Paget. Cranmer wrote to Paget on 20 January and post-dated his letter to the King by three days, to allow time for the Secretary to make any changes in Henry's supposed draft and let him know about them. Foxe, relying on Ralph Morice's memories, further extends the artifice: he says that originally it was Henry's idea to prepare this draft, together with another letter tailor-made for the Archbishop of York.[1] Cranmer and Morice must have particularly enjoyed composing the clause which read like a royal afterthought, rebuking the Archbishop for not recommending the abolition of

1 Foxe 5, pp. 561–3. The correspondence is P.R.O., S.P. 1/213 ff. 124, 144v, 146–9 (*L.P.* 20 i nos 92, 109–10), and includes drafts of Cranmer's letter to Henry and of Cranmer's draft letter for Henry to sign. Main text in Cox 2, pp. 414–16, although there Cranmer's letter to the King is wrongly dated 24 and not 23 January.

creeping to the cross on Good Friday, a ceremony especially detested by evangelicals. Cranmer's original drafts of his draft and his letter to Henry have also made their way into the State Papers, and these enable us to see the Archbishop plucking up his courage as he went along. To begin with, in his ghost-writing for Henry on the subject of abolishing All Hallows' bell-ringing, he had made allowance for the retention of one peal before the Dirige service 'to give every man warning to pray for all Christian souls departed': a concession in line with the theology of the King's Book on the question of prayers for the dead.[2] Cranmer's respect for this usage of prayer, which had stayed with him precariously over the previous few years, was evidently evaporating; he struck the clause out.

It was a hopeful moment for the evangelicals, but already Gardiner's Court contacts had alerted him to the danger of change behind his back, and this triggered his intervention from abroad. Gardiner wrote from Brussels urgently to Henry that any religious changes in England would jeopardize his negotiations for an alliance with Charles V: a potent threat which at last broke through the Bishop's two years of political enfeeblement. Cranmer's drafts were 'suppressed and stopped', and on 21 March Gardiner was back at Court once more, an Imperial treaty successfully concluded.[3] He and his conservative friends, a grand coalition including the Duke of Norfolk, Lord Rich, Lord Chancellor Wriothesley and Bishop Bonner of London, now launched on their last attempt to challenge the evangelicals at Court: a contest whose stakes grew ever higher as King Henry's health grew feebler.

The tactics were little different from those of 1543: to secure the arrest of lesser evangelicals in the hope of trapping greater ones. First to feel the pressure in March was the most notorious victim of the whole campaign: a maverick evangelical gentlewoman with rather shadowy links to the Court. This remarkable lady has left us a terse but vivid diary of her sufferings embedded in the rather more self-indulgent prose of John Bale. She has been known to posterity as Anne Askew, a version of her maiden name Ayscough. This conceals the embarrassment of evangelical historiography that she ought to be remembered by her married name, Anne Kyme; she had taken the initiative in leaving her husband on account of his cruelty and conservative religious views, an irregularity which was later seized on with glee by that perceptive Elizabethan Catholic propagandist Robert Parsons. She was released after examination at the end of March, an apparent victory which may have emboldened London evangelicals to think that their two years of virtual immunity from serious trouble would continue.[4] This

2 Cf. Kreider, *Chantries*, pp. 151–3.

3 Foxe 5, p. 563; for Gardiner's return, *L.P.* 21 i no. 439. Redworth, *Gardiner*, p. 226n displays what seems to me a wholly unwarranted scepticism about Gardiner's role in this affair.

4 Bale, *Works*, p. 178. For Parsons, see the quotation from Parsons's *Third Part of a Treatise*, p. 309.

was a mistake. Soon aggressive reformist sermons were being noted, and outspoken clergy and laity were rounded up not just in the capital and at Court but in Kent and East Anglia. The month of May saw a frenzy of activity, although Anne herself was not rearrested until some time in early or mid-June.[5]

It is significant to note how many of the targeted evangelicals had links to Cranmer which were stronger than merely the acquaintance to be expected in a tightly knit ideological grouping. Of those who eventually died, Anne Ayscough was from a family with strong Court links, but also from the same Lincolnshire and Nottinghamshire gentry world as the Cranmers, and her brother Edward was one of Cranmer's servants.[6] John Lascelles was likewise from a Nottinghamshire gentry family, and was the same John Lascelles who had gone to the Archbishop in 1541 to reveal the story of Queen Catherine Howard's adultery.[7] Of those who escaped death, the courtier George Blagg, from another Lincolnshire family intimately linked in many ways with Cranmer's boyhood friend Thomas Goodrich, was the brother of the Archbishop's business agent in London.[8] Ralph Morice's elder brother William, a gentleman usher at Court, was arrested for his connection with the detained evangelical preacher Edward Crome; he was put under house arrest with Sir Richard Southwell and not released until after Henry VIII's death.[9] Cranmer's clerical friends and subordinates were as much prime targets as were his lay connections. His Suffolk peculiar of Hadleigh saw the arrest of two of his close associates: Rowland Taylor, who had been collated as rector there by the Archbishop two years before, and the former Bishop of Salisbury, Nicholas Shaxton, who had held the lease of Hadleigh parsonage even before Taylor arrived, and who acted informally in the town as a very senior curate. Both men were made to recant, Shaxton in a particularly abject manner which permanently broke his evangelical spirit and led to deep bitterness between him and Taylor.[10] Bishop Hugh Latimer was also examined by the Council, and that stormy petrel of the 1543 troubles, Richard Turner, once more found

5 For a good general account of events, see Brigden, *London*, pp. 362–77, although NB that she misdates the important Passion Sunday sermon of Edward Crome as 3 rather than 11 April (ibid., p. 363). She also probably wrongly postpones Anne's rearrest to 19 June; Anne's own account suggests that it was before she and her husband jointly met the Council on that day and it must be related to their summons at the end of May (cf. *A.P.C. 1540–47*, pp. 424, 462; Bale, *Works* pp. 198–201; *Gardiner's Letters*, p. 356). See also Wabuda, 'Crome', pp. 234–37.

6 *History of Parliament 1509–1558* 1, pp. 342–3; P.R.O., S.P. 1/156 ff. 1–2, Cox 2, p. 399 (*L.P.* 14 ii no. 751).

7 *Narratives of the Reformation*, p. 43 and n.

8 Brigden, *London*, p. 419; *Lincolnshire Pedigrees* 2, p. 415.

9 *A.P.C. 1540–47*, pp. 417, 490; *Narratives of the Reformation*, p. 45 and n.

10 Collation: Cranmer's Register, f. 392r; Shaxton's lease: will of John Davye, P.C.C. 21 Spert (I owe this reference to Dr. John Craig). On their 1546 troubles, MacCulloch, *Suffolk and the Tudors*, pp. 165, 23–4, Taylor's reference to 'tonshax', Craig, 'Marginalia of Taylor', p. 414 and n.

himself in gaol, this time in the Tower of London.[11] These conjunctions cannot have been an accident.

Cranmer was, however, by no means the only eminent target. When on 29 June Chancellor Wriothesley and Lord Rich took the legally bizarre and clearly desperate measure of personally torturing Anne Ayscough in the Tower, they were after damning information on an array of ladies at Court, including wives of the leading evangelical politicians, Lady Denny and Lady Hertford. There were even strong rumours that Queen Catherine Parr was in their sights; certainly they asked questions about her friend and champion of the godly, the Duchess of Suffolk.[12] Either by command or in an effort to keep out of involvement in the relentless official examinations of friends and acquaintances, Cranmer spent his time down in furthest Kent. His first traceable presence at Court was on 4 July, when he was summoned up to add ballast to the reception for the French ambassador. Certainly he had official duties to perform down in Canterbury, coping with the comings and goings of troops and prisoners.[13] However, he cannot have been sorry to miss subsequent moves against his friends, particularly the distressing ceremony on 16 July when Anne Ayscough, John Lascelles and two other evangelicals were burnt at the stake in Smithfield. After that, the arrests and examinations rolled on. The conservatives had made a significant breakthrough: their action was now backed by the sort of comprehensive royal proclamation against evangelical books which they had sought in vain in summer 1542, and which they had failed to secure in legislative form at Christmas 1545 (see above, Ch. 7, p. 294, Ch. 8, p. 347).[14]

The possibility must be raised that there may have been one very strong motive for Cranmer in keeping out of these events. The prime accusation against those evangelicals who became victims in 1546 was their views on the eucharist; they denied the real presence and in a variety of ways declared Christ's presence to be merely spiritual or in the remembrance of the communicant. On the theme of eucharistic presence, even evangelicals like Richard Cox, Nicholas Ridley and Simon Haynes, and their aristocratic fellow-travellers like John Dudley (Lord Lisle) and Lord William Parr, could press their accused co-religionists hard in an effort to change their minds.[15] It may be that already in 1546 Cranmer would have found it impossible to bend his conscience to do the same. The change in his views on the eucharistic presence, the final element to be put into place in his mature theology, is

11 *A.P.C. 1540–47*, p. 421.

12 Bale, *Works*, pp. 218, 220; for circumstantial stories about the Queen's troubles, Foxe 5, pp. 553–61.

13 *A.P.C. 1540–47*, pp. 406, 442.

14 For Council action, *A.P.C. 1540–47*, pp. 473, 485, 490, 492; *Selve*, p. 3. Cf. *T.R.P.* 1 no. 272 (8 July 1546) with *L.P.* 17 no. 177 and Brigden, *London*, p. 339. NB Richard Cox's description of its effect, *L.P.* 21 ii no. 321.

15 *St.P.* 1 pp. 842–5 (*L.P.* 21 i no. 790; Bale, *Works*, pp. 201, 206).

frustratingly difficult to date. We know that the agent of this change was his friend and chaplain Nicholas Ridley, because Cranmer himself said so at his trial in September 1555: Ridley persuaded him 'by sundry persuasions and authorities of doctors'.[16] This seems to be confirmed by the preface to the 1557 Latin translation of Cranmer's *Defence of the True and Catholic doctrine of the Sacrament*, which affirmed the initiative of Ridley and also put a definite date to the event: '*nimirum anno 46*'.[17]

However, the evidence is not as clear-cut as it might seem. The word *nimirum* itself carries a sliver of doubt, for as much as 'certainly' it can mean 'undoubtedly, doubtless, truly', the sort of adverb which one uses to convince oneself as well as the reader. Additionally, the writer of the preface was probably referring to the old-style year, and thus one is looking at the year March 1546 to March 1547, some of which represents the calmer waters after the old King's death. Ridley himself offers further but insufficient data by his own statement that 'the doctrine of the Lord's supper' was revealed to him while he was Vicar of Herne in Kent, through his reading of the ninth-century theologian Ratramnus of Corbie. This is a poor chronological clue, since Cranmer had given Ridley the benefice as early as 30 April 1538, and Herne was Ridley's principal home and cure until he was made Bishop of Rochester in 1547.[18] One further statement that Ridley came to his own turning-point on the eucharist in 1545 comes from an unhappily untrustworthy source, his descendant and biographer Gloucester Ridley, writing two centuries later.[19] As we will see (below, pp. 378–9), there are indications that even if Ridley and Cranmer had begun to talk about Ridley's discoveries in Ratramnus as early as the last year of Henry VIII's life, they remained hesitant about their conclusions and reluctant to cross the great theological divide between real and spiritual eucharistic presence until the first year of the new reign. Ridley, after all, was one of the team which was given the duty of examining Edward Crome during the 1546 crackdown. Only at the end of 1547 does the evidence for Cranmer's change of heart become decisive.

As in 1543, there was a diplomatic background to the conservative attack, and one with even higher stakes than the Imperial alliance which had then been concluded. Thirteen years of battling with evangelicals in the Church had begun to suggest to leading Henrician conservatives that the break with Rome had been a bad mistake, which needed to be remedied. One wonders how many people were privy to the astonishing secret that at this very moment, a mission was being launched, with French blessing and Henry's

16 Cox 2, p. 218.

17 Cox 1, 2nd pagination p. 6. This preface is attributed to Sir John Cheke, but the evidence is not decisive.

18 *Ridley's Works*, pp. 206, 407. Cf. Cranmer's Register, f. 364v.

19 Qu. Brooks, *Cranmer's Doctrine of the Eucharist*, pp. 38–9, and cf. his conclusions on this vexed question, pp. 40–41.

agreement, to see whether England could come to some arrangement with the papacy. The agent was a quixotic Anglophile Italian well known to Henry, Gurone Bertano; he arrived in London on 30 July, the first papal contact of any sort to be allowed to set foot here officially, let alone have audiences with the King, for more than a dozen years.[20] It is most unlikely that Cranmer was privy to the planning of this alarming development until the *fait accompli* of Bertano's arrival, unless that unfathomable politician and leading negotiator in the affair, Paget, revealed what he knew to him. In any case, the late spring and summer was a frightening enough time for the Archbishop without any worse news.

On 3 August, after some official hesitations, Bertano met with Henry VIII, and he found the King receptive to the idea of sending prelates and doctors to a General Council which would involve the Pope. It does not take much guesswork to narrow down the likely prelate-delegates to the leading conservative bishops Gardiner, Tunstall or Thirlby; Gardiner and Tunstall were much in evidence at the Council board at that time.[21] It was a crucial moment for the future of the Reformation in England, and once more the secret dynamic of it is locked for ever in King Henry's mind, as he meditated whether to overturn all that he had done in the previous decade and a half. Within a week, he had made his decision, and official policy made one of its dramatic about-turns, for the last time.

Perhaps it was inevitable that this monstrous egoist should draw back from such a sacrifice as the loss of exclusive authority within the English and Irish churches. One other powerful consideration may have been Henry's anger at the conservative attempts to threaten his wife; this was the opinion of Foxe and Matthew Parker.[22] In any case, a major factor must have been that Henry had already achieved peace with France without any reconciliation with the papacy or a break with the Emperor; his habitual nightmare of isolation and encirclement by hostile powers in alliance with the papacy was banished. The main architect of the French peace, and thus the beneficiary of the King's gratitude, was John Dudley, Lord Lisle, who was at best a fair-weather friend to the conservatives at Court. Lisle arrived back on 12 August; that day was also the first on which Cranmer returned to attendance at the Privy Council, and the Archbishop was not away for the rest of the month. Once more he was marked out by his office to play the leading ceremonial role in the reception

20 This remarkable venture deserves further study; it can be traced through numerous although sometimes oblique references in *L.P.* 21 i and ii and the dispatches of Ambassador de Selve. On Bertano's arrival, see *L.P.* 21 i no. 1339 and *Selve*, p. 17, and on his later career, see Bartlett, 'Papal policy and the English Crown'.

21 *Selve*, pp. 18, 20–22 (*L.P.* 21 i nos 1398, 1412).

22 Foxe 5, pp. 560–61; Parker, *De Antiquitate*, p. 397. Redworth's sceptical comments (*Gardiner*, pp. 233–4) on the relationship of Henry's feelings for Catherine to religious change are severely undermined by his own observation that a supposed candidate to replace Catherine was the Duchess of Suffolk: perhaps the most radical evangelical in aristocratic circles.

of the special French envoy to sign the treaty with France. Cranmer's evangelical ally, the Earl of Hertford, had been back from his mission abroad and increasingly regular in his Council attendance from 31 July; his would have been a powerful voice shaping Henry's thoughts.[23] Looking back at events from September, the Imperial ambassador dated the end of the persecution of evangelicals from the time when Lisle and Hertford were both back in residence at Court.[24]

The French envoy, Claude d'Annebaut, the Admiral of France, arrived at Greenwich to a massively elaborate welcome on 15 August, before passing on to London and to Hampton Court to meet the King a week later.[25] On the first night of their meeting in a specially erected banqueting-house, on 23 or 24 August, Henry talked with the Admiral in Cranmer's presence, indeed ostentatiously showing where his sympathies now lay by publicly 'leaning one arm upon the shoulder of the archbishop'. After Henry's death Cranmer confided to Ralph Morice that the proposals then discussed far exceeded 'the pulling down of roods, and suppressing the ringing of bells', which had been on the domestic agenda the previous January; the suggestions astonished the Archbishop himself. If Henry had lived, he said, the King would have finalized an agreement with Francis I 'to have changed the mass in both the realms into a communion (as we now use it)'; he was speaking of the transformed religious atmosphere in spring 1547.[26] The Archbishop, and possibly Henry, was probably over-optimistic about the intentions of the wily King Francis I, but Cranmer would hardly have mistaken the plainly expressed remarks of the King whom he knew so well. Henry confirmed this extraordinary mood-swing a week later, when he gave a friendly and positive reception to a delegation from the Schmalkaldic League, offering them the prospect of a handsome subsidy and his own leadership in their military struggle against the Emperor. Henry's aversion to the papal option had reached an unprecedented extreme in the course of the month of August 1546. Jasper Ridley plausibly suggests that this lurch in Henry's thinking was one of the major factors in Cranmer's own transition in eucharistic thought: everything was conspiring to complete his pilgrimage beyond his Lutheranism of the 1530s.[27]

23 *A.P.C. 1540–47*, pp. 508–22; Beer, *Northumberland*, pp. 37–8. For Cranmer's ceremonial role, cf. *L.P.* 21 i no. 1384.

24 *L.P.* 21 ii no. 605.

25 Bodl. MS Ashmole 861, p. 339; *Greyfriars Chronicle*, p. 51; *Wriothesley's Chronicle* 1, pp. 171–3; the sources disagree between 22 and 24 August about the reception at Hampton Court. Cf. the jaundiced comments of Ellis Gruffydd about the disruption caused by the reception, in Davies, 'Boulogne and Calais from 1545 to 1551', p. 53.

26 Foxe 5, pp. 563–4. The dating is fixed by the reference to the formal opening stage of Edward VI's royal visitation (May 1547), although it also mentions that Cranmer was at Hampton Court; I have not so far found any reference to his presence there before September 1547.

27 Ridley, *Cranmer*, pp. 256–7; on the German embassy, *L.P.* 21 I, no. 1526.

Cranmer left Court at the same time as the French ambassador, perhaps to make an immediate start on his commission from the King to draw up plans for the revision of the mass 'to be sent to the French King to consider of'; it thus may be at this point that we should look to date many of the main texts which would appear in the eucharistic rites of 1548 and 1549. He did not return to the Council board until 11 November, but in his absence Hertford and Lisle consolidated their alliance against the conservatives. Lisle showed his newly open evangelical allegiance when at one meeting of the Council in late September, he actually slapped Bishop Gardiner in a moment of fury; this act of gross indecorum earned him a month's suspension in disgrace from the Council, but it did not seriously damage the evangelicals' position.[28] Most importantly, Bertano now found that there was no follow-up to his first promising interview with the King; he was left kicking his heels in London for two months, and he was not surprised when on 30 September he received abrupt Privy Council instructions to leave England. The status and former potential of his mission were nonetheless indicated by the fact that the messengers were no less a team than Lord Chancellor Wriothesley and Lord St John the Great Master.[29]

Signs of Henry's *volte-face* continued through the autumn. One John Warne, a citizen of London, had been examined the Thursday after Anne Ayscough's burning, and imprisoned; following a personal visit by Bishop Bonner, he was condemned to the flames. However, by October Warne had been abruptly released and pardoned after approaches to Henry and evangelical courtiers; two Suffolk evangelicals were pardoned alongside him.[30] The campaign against others also petered out into accommodations and recantations, and when Bonner promoted a fresh day of burnings in London on 26 September, it was of evangelical books, not people.[31] In riposte to the July proclamation against these books, which had included the biblical translations of Tyndale and Coverdale, in November Edward Whitchurch brought out a new edition of the New Testament from the Great Bible; although of course this was legally permissible as the official translation, it represented a significant moment as the first new Bible printing in England since 1542.[32]

Throughout the autumn political tension mounted in the wake of these abrupt swings of royal mood. De Selve noted it already in early November: an

28 *Selve*, p. 51 (*L.P.* 21 ii no. 347). Lisle was back at the Council on 1 November: *A.P.C. 1540–47*, p. 546.

29 *L.P.* 21 ii nos 167, 194; *Selve*, pp. 36, 38, and cf. Bartlett, 'Papal policy and the English Crown', p. 647.

30 Foxe 7, pp. 80–81, and pardons in the October dry stamp list, *L.P.* 21 ii nos 331/66–8, where the other two (Richard Mannock and Robert Bracher) can be identified with the initiative in Hadleigh and south Suffolk. Cf. ibid., no. 648/40; Brigden, *London*, pp. 564, 658, 608, 617.

31 *St.P.* 1, pp. 866, 872, 878 (*L.P.* 21 ii nos 58, 134, 155; *Greyfriars Chronicle*, p. 52; *Wriothesley's Chronicle* 1, p. 175.

32 Butterworth, *Primers*, p. 237.

atmosphere of rumours of dissension and changes among leading politicians, with secret orders being sent out on 8 November for a national enquiry into seditious talk.[33] Then two incidents decisively and finally tipped the balance in the evangelicals' favour. The first to occur was Gardiner's final fatal miscalculation of the reign; he chose this moment to refuse a request of Henry VIII to agree to an exchange involving some of his episcopal estates. These transactions had become a feature of episcopal life since the mid-1530s; Gardiner's intransigence strikingly contrasted with Cranmer's readiness to co-operate with a further large-scale scheme of exchanges of his Kent, Sussex and Middlesex estates which had begun in 1545, and which by coincidence was just smoothly reaching its completion at the end of November 1546.[34] Henry was furious, and Gardiner's frantic efforts to calm him down at the beginning of December did not succeed. The Bishop of Winchester was removed from the list of councillors who would govern the realm for King Edward in the event of a minority, and no persuasions from his supporters, such as Sir Anthony Browne, could get the King to put him back.[35]

After Gardiner's disgrace, there rapidly followed the arrest and execution of the Earl of Surrey, on charges of treasonous claims to the throne expressed in his heraldry; with him fell his father, the Duke of Norfolk, utterly astonished at the sudden catastrophe after he had survived so many political embarrassments over the years. Surrey's proud quartering of the royal arms with his own was an even more damaging act of folly than Gardiner's, for it was a clear bid for a leading position near the throne in a new regime for Henry's son, and a still worse interpretation might be put on it. As much as Henry hated clerical disobedience, he was even more deeply paranoid about any hint of a threat to his beloved son's succession, and that is how he chose to view Surrey's action. The Duke of Norfolk, the most powerful and experienced conservative nobleman in the realm, was thus helpless just at the moment when the most prominent conservative bishop had also enraged the King. These were two extraordinary strokes of luck for the evangelical party, cementing them into the King's favour at the very time when they were already winning the struggle for his trust; they hardly needed a Machiavellian conspiracy to establish their supremacy when their enemies handed it to them on a plate.[36] As the King's health ebbed away in December and January, so did any chance of a conservative comeback. One of his last recorded encounters with a foreign

33 *Selve*, p. 55 (*L.P.* 21 ii no. 381).

34 Cranmer's final exchange can be followed though *L.P.* 20 ii no. 909/25 (November 1545); *L.J.* 1, pp. 281–2 (24 December 1545); *L.P.* 21 i no. 149/6 (4 January 1546), L.P. 21 ii nos. 200/37, 442 (24 September, 18, 25 November 1546); P.R.O., E. 328/44 (19, 25 November 1546); *C.P.R. Edward VI 1547–8*, pp. 36 ff. (31 August 1547).

35 *Gardiner's Letters*, pp. 246–9; Foxe 6, pp. 138–9 (*L.P.* 20 i no. 493); Redworth, *Gardiner*, p. 245, Ives, 'Henry VIII's will: the protectorate provisions', pp. 912–13, and cf. especially Foxe 6, pp. 164–5.

36 Cf. the excessive conspiracy theory about the last two months in Starkey, *Henry VIII: Politics and Personalities*, pp. 156–67, criticized in Ives, 'Henry VIII's will', and see subsequent debate. Also useful is Brigden, 'Henry Howard'.

representative in those last months was with a Schmalkaldic envoy, to whom in the hearing of four leading Councillors Henry reaffirmed his commitment to the evangelical cause against the Emperor.[37] While Gardiner was cast into the political wilderness and the Howard dynasty crashed to ruin, Archbishop Cranmer remained an honoured executor of the King's final will, made at the end of December.

There is no evidence that the Archbishop played any part in this political mayhem. Perhaps feeling uncomfortable in the increasingly vicious atmosphere, he stayed away from Court after one appearance for a Council meeting on 11 November.[38] On the day that Surrey and the Duke were committed to the Tower, 12 December, Cranmer was down at Croydon, peacefully writing to his cathedral chapter about the reallocation of lodgings for the prebendaries and Six Preachers.[39] Only when the issue had been decided, and it became clear that the King's death was imminent, did he return to the capital. The first definite trace of him back in London is at the reopening of Parliament on 14 January 1547, a meeting whose main purpose was to seal the fate of the Howards, and while dutifully voting through their attainder with his fellow-peers, he also remained in regular attendance at the Council. This meant that he was readily on hand to do his last duty for his old master as the King lay dying on 28 January.[40] It was Denny who persuaded Henry that he must face death, and the King asked specifically for the Archbishop to be with him. By the time that Cranmer reached him in the small hours of that morning, Henry was already incapable of speech, but reached out to his old friend.

> Then the archbishop, exhorting him to put his trust in Christ, and to call upon his mercy, desired him, though he could not speak, yet to give some token with his eyes or with his hand, that he trusted in the Lord. Then the King, holding him with his hand, did wring his hand in his as hard as he could.

Quietly playing out his calling as royal chaplain, Cranmer had won a final victory in his years of argument with the King on justification. No last rites for Henry; no extreme unction: just an evangelical statement of faith in a grip of the hand. Thus ended the most long-lasting relationship of love which either man had known.

37 Foxe 5, p. 692. This report has not been given the attention it deserves. On the last negotiations with the Schmalkaldic League, see McEntegart Ph.D., 'England and the League of Schmalkalden', pp. 466–71. Note the confidence of reports about Henry's evangelical last days in *Melanchthons Briefwechsel* 5, nos 4647, 4659.

38 *A.P.C. 1540–47*, p. 547.

39 Cox 2, p. 417 (*L.P.* 21 ii no. 536).

40 *L.J.* 1, pp. 284–7; *A.P.C. 1540–47*, p. 564. The standard account of Henry's death in Foxe 5, p. 689 (from which the quotation following is taken) claims that Cranmer was down at Croydon on the night of the King's death – a curious detail, since Parliament was still in session and he had been present on the previous day, 27 January. Burnet 1 i, pp. 537–8 took this further for the sake of Cranmer's reputation, claiming that he stayed away from London to avoid voting on the Howard attainders.

There is no doubt that Cranmer mourned the dead King. It was later said, indeed, that he made an emphatic demonstration of his grief for the rest of his life by growing a beard; it is as 'with a long beard, white and thick' that John Foxe described him in his last years, and he is thus depicted in a portrait type preserved at Lambeth Palace, which gives a very different image of him from the 1545 Flicke portrait.[41] However, this striking contrast between the two pictures is a measure of the ambiguity at the heart of Cranmer's relationship with Henry VIII. It was a break with the past for a clergyman to abandon the clean-shaven appearance which was the norm for late medieval priesthood; with Luther providing a precedent, virtually all the continental clerical reformers had deliberately grown beards as a mark of their rejection of the old Church, and the significance of clerical beards as an aggressive anti-Catholic gesture was well-recognized in mid-Tudor England.[42] Henry's death might rob the Archbishop of a deeply loved friend and cause him to mourn, but it freed him to be himself theologically and – a matter of equal importance – personally. Twice Cranmer had entered marriages in the face of powerful discouragements. The bearded man was also the family man – again, shades of Luther – and it was immediately or very soon after the accession of Edward VI that Cranmer publicly acknowledged the existence of Mrs Cranmer. As Cranmer was perfectly happy to admit at his trial in 1555, they had already begun their eventual family of a son and two daughters before the death of Henry VIII; although none of the children's ages and dates of birth is at all certain, the daughter Margaret married in or soon after 1555, and so she must have been born in the late 1530s. The son Thomas came later, probably in the reign of Edward VI: he was still described as a boy in 1559, as 'yet but young' in 1563, and the earliest traceable reference to him is in 1550.[43] In any case, the long years of subterfuge came to an end with the removal of Henry VIII from the scene, and Margaret could begin to work out the unfamiliar role of a clerical wife in the palaces at Ford, Croydon and Lambeth.

Cranmer is not recorded as present in the Lords when Henry's death was officially announced on 31 January, but he was among the executors who gathered at the Tower of London on the same day to nominate the new King's uncle, Edward Seymour, as Lord Protector, and welcome the boy king.[44] In public, nothing had changed, even if everything had changed beneath the surface: a neat metaphor for the confused state of the Henrician Church. The old King's death triggered traditional royal funeral ceremonies: his entrails were buried in the chapel at Whitehall, and his body lay in state in the privy

41 Foxe 8, p. 43.

42 For an example in 1556 from Cranmer's own diocese, see Buckingham, 'Movement of Clergy', p. 222.

43 Cox 2, pp. 550, 557; Foxe 8, p. 58. On the younger Margaret, Foxe 8, p. 44, and Fines, *Biographical Register*, s.v. Norton, Thomas. On the younger Thomas, *C.P.R. Edward VI 1549–51*, p. 321, *Zürich Letters*, 1, p. 8, and Foxe 8, p. 44.

44 *L.J.* 1, pp. 290–91; *A.P.C. 1547–50* 2, pp. 3–7; *Wriothesley's Chronicle* 1, p. 178.

25 Portrait of Archbishop Cranmer after Henry VIII's death.

chamber for five days, with masses being offered for his soul.[45] Throughout the city and its suburbs, and no doubt out into the parishes of England, diriges and requiems were chanted in traditional style, and Cranmer took his part in the magnificence of a feudal and royal funeral which would have been completely familiar to the mourners of the King's father and his forebears before him. The most prominent liturgical roles in singing diriges and masses were taken by the leading bishops who would feel most comfortable in the part, Gardiner, Bonner and the increasingly conservative Thirlby; Gardiner preached at the culminating ceremonies at Windsor on 15 February, as was his right as Prelate of the Order of the Garter. Around the coffin, banners of Our Lady and the Trinity guarded the corpse, and the most notable innovation at the funeral was hardly suggestive of imminent religious change: the addition of a banner for the saintly King Henry VI. All these were still preserved at Windsor in the early seventeenth century, protected from Protestant destruction, when so much else was lost, by the formidable residual power of Henry VIII.[46]

The new regime could afford to observe such elaborate proprieties in a ceremony which effectively buried the religious past with the monarch who had sheltered its remnants. It was only politic: there were sensibilities to be respected, powerful people to be placated. So Cranmer and his fellow-Councillors felt constrained to humour Bishop Bonner's wrath when they rebuked the parson and wardens of the city church of St Martin in Ironmonger Lane; this enthusiastic evangelical clique, even before the old King's funeral, had transformed their church interior, on the pretext of completing major fabric repairs, replacing the rood figures with the royal arms and the images of saints with biblical texts. They were ordered to replace the rood (though noticeably not the other images), and then no further harm came to them; a fortnight later Bishop Gardiner could still grumble about their wall-text which denounced images.[47] Of more lasting significance than this decorous comedy were the commissions issued a few days before, to Cranmer and then to his fellow-bishops, renewing their authority on the death of Henry VIII. Naturally they underlined the reality that all jurisdiction within the realm issued from the monarch, although the text contained a rather uncomfortable acknowledgement that there were also matters entrusted to a bishop 'divinely, from holy scripture' (*ex sacris litteris divinitus*). These matters were not specified, and the phrase remained a rather unfocussed concession to conservative or evangelical theologies of the Church's distinctive life. It was true that the commissions followed the precedent of Henry's issue of commissions to the bishops in 1535, but that did not stop Bishop Gardiner writing to

45 Strype, *Ecclesiastical Memorials*, 2 ii p. 289.

46 For a good recent analysis of the funeral, see Loach, 'Ceremonial in the reign of Henry VIII', pp. 56–68. *Wriothesley's Chronicle* 1, p. 181.

47 *A.P.C. 1547–50*, pp. 25–6; *Gardiner's Letters*, pp. 258–9; cf. Brigden, *London*, pp. 385, 399, 424.

Secretary Paget in protest at the details of their wording; he sensed that this was part of a new political and religious agenda, and Paget's vitriolic reply to his letter would have done nothing to calm his fears.[48]

The mask also began to crack in the planning of the coronation of Edward; the Privy Council's plans for it abridged some ceremonies on the pretext of avoiding strain on the boy, and although there was magnificence enough, no one who was present on 20 February could have been left in any doubt that radical change was soon to come.[49] Even the previous day, as the King was paraded from the Tower to Westminster, the city pageantry had included a boy representing Truth who proclaimed that he had been long suppressed by heathen rites and detestable idolatry; Cranmer, who paired the Imperial ambassador in icily uncomfortable silence in the cavalcade, would have enjoyed the sight, and so no doubt did his young royal master.[50] At Westminster Abbey, the Archbishop was in liturgical charge, even more so than at his previous coronation (for Anne Boleyn); displacing his old friend William Benson, who was now Dean of Westminster rather than Abbot, he sang the mass of the Holy Ghost and he presented the King to the people before the coronation proper. The sting in the tail was his address to the King when the formal ceremonies were complete: a brief but forceful statement of the Royal Supremacy and the worthlessness of the Bishop of Rome's claims on the monarchy, not to mention a fairly pointed theological put-down for the liturgy which had just been celebrated: 'the solemn rites of coronation have their ends and utility, yet neither direct force or necessity; they be good admonitions to put kings in mind of their duty to God, but no increasement of their dignity'. He emphasized that kings were God's anointed regardless of outward ceremony, his intention being to make it clear that no clergyman, be he pope or bishop, could do anything to add to the powers of a king.[51]

The last section of Cranmer's address was the most striking. Here he reminded Edward of his duty as God's vice-gerent to imitate his 'predecessor Josiah'. It was a trope familiar in King Henry's days to see the English monarchy in direct line to that of ancient Israel; the old King had liked nothing better than to identify himself with David the destroyer of Goliath or Solomon the builder of the temple.[52] However, the image of Josiah had a new

48 *Gardiner's Letters*, pp. 268–72; Paget's reply is P.R.O., S.P. 10/1/26 (*C.S.P. Domestic Edward VI* no. 24). Cf. *A.P.C. 1547–50*, pp. 13–14; Cranmer's Register, ff. 28v–29r; Ayris and Selwyn (eds), *Cranmer*, pp. 139–40.

49 Plans in *A.P.C. 1547–50*, pp. 29–33; descriptions in C.C.C.C. MS 105, pp. 235–40; *Selve*, p. 105.

50 Aston, *England's Iconoclasts*, 1, pp. 247–8; cf. ambassador Van der Delft's comments, *C.S.P. Spanish 1547–9*, pp. 46–7.

51 Cox 2, pp. 126–7. The text has no definite pedigree before Strype, and contains one oddity in referring to Paul III as 'late bishop of Rome', but its authenticity does not seem in doubt.

52 Tudor-Craig, 'Henry VIII and King David'; Ives, 'Anne Boleyn, Holbein and Tudor portraits', pp. 38–9.

resonance, not merely because, like Edward, he was a boy when he came to the throne; Cranmer had no hesitation in spelling out the full meaning. If Edward was to be 'a second Josiah', he must see God truly worshipped, destroy idolatry, the Pope's tyranny and remove images. This last item had been the particular achievement of the first Josiah.[53] As an agenda, it made a startling contrast to the reproving action taken against the parish authorities at Ironmonger Lane only ten days before. Moreover, the Archbishop kept up the pressure on the Court through his chaplain Nicholas Ridley, who only three days later, on Ash Wednesday, preached before the King about images: one of a series of very public sermons by evangelicals at this time. Ridley received a furious but vain letter of rebuke from Stephen Gardiner. This was one of the opening shots in a voluminous correspondence which Gardiner fired off against the new evangelical establishment throughout the rest of the year: letters so long, and expressed with such bitter eloquence, that he clearly intended most of them for propaganda circulation in the political elite.[54]

There was little else that Gardiner could do now. It is not too early to talk about an evangelical establishment already in being at the beginning of 1547. Cranmer and his clerical colleagues must have been working in close collaboration with Somerset, whose special power in the regime was quickly apparent; one observer of the coronation noted that the 'great number' of tipstaffs appointed for the coronation were drawn from Somerset's servants.[55] The reality of the situation was made abundantly clear when, only a fortnight or so after the show of harmony in the coronation, Somerset's most potentially threatening conservative rival on the Council, Lord Chancellor Wriothesley, was overthrown, deprived of the Great Seal on trumped-up charges of abuse of office. This was the prelude to the completion of Somerset's formal powers as Lord Protector by letters patent on 12 March; only when it was clear that the bloodless coup would not be opposed were Wriothesley's leading conservative colleagues, Arundel, Cheyney and Gage, allowed to resume a place in Council decision-making, and the Council's real authority was in any case now circumscribed by the Protector's powers.[56] Power and profit were henceforth firmly in the hands of evangelicals. It will be a central theme of my study of Cranmer's part in the regime of Edward VI that this evangelical establishment grouping knew from the start in 1547 exactly what Reformation it wanted: whatever hesitations occurred were primarily attributable to the need to disarm conservative opposition. Despite the superficial break in Edwardian politics caused by the overthrow of Somerset and his replacement by the ascendancy of John Dudley in 1549, there was an essential continuity

53 For an excellent discussion of this, see Aston, *England's Iconoclasts*, 1, pp. 249–50.

54 *Gardiner's Letters*, pp. 255–63. We know that Gardiner sent a copy of this letter to Ridley to Somerset: ibid., p. 267.

55 C.C.C.C. MS 105, p. 239.

56 Hoak, *King's Council*, pp. 231–9. On the return of conservatives, see *Selve*, p. 132; *C.S.P. Spanish 1547–9*, p. 85.

of purpose in a graduated series of religious changes over seven years. These changes were designed to destroy one Church and build another, in a religious revolution of ruthless thoroughness. Thomas Cranmer was the one man who guaranteed the continuity of the changes, and he was chiefly responsible for planning them as they occurred, although more practical secular politicians decided the pace at which they should be put into effect.

One first symbol of the new situation for Cranmer was a grant of personal estates initiated only a few days after Somerset secured his letters patent: this was a subsidiary part of the share-out of grants which were said to fulfil the verbally expressed wishes of Henry VIII before his death, and which were referred to in general terms in his will.[57] Cranmer's grant was also a logical if tacit official acknowledgement that he now had a family to support, but remarkably, it was the first personal profit which he had gained after years of self-restraint during the Henrician looting of monastic and chantry property for the benefit of England's ruling classes. The premises were oddly miscellaneous, and still an austere selection in comparison with many of the mammoth handouts to Somerset's cronies in the wake of Henry VIII's death; in any case, they were by no means a free gift, since Cranmer paid out the very substantial sum of £429.14s 2d for them. The plum among them was Kirkstall Abbey in Yorkshire; there was also a little ex-Cluniac nunnery near Kirkstall called Arthington, an obscure Kentish benefice, and a clutch of property around Cranmer's childhood home at Aslockton, including the advowson of Whatton, the church where his father lay buried. As far as the Nottinghamshire lands were concerned, Cranmer seems only to have been acting as an agent for his nephew, Thomas Cranmer of Aslockton; within a month of his grant being formalized in June, he had regranted Whatton parsonage to the younger Thomas.[58]

A second sequence of grants to the Archbishop, also in June, was a confusing amalgam of grants to him in his official capacity (completing a complex exchange in Henry VIII's last years) with personal purchases in Lancashire, Lincolnshire and Northamptonshire.[59] Cranmer kept the Lancashire properties, which were all wealthy benefices, but again in the Lincolnshire and Northamptonshire purchases, he was simply an agent for friends. The reversion of the Lincolnshire lands went to Richard and Mary Goodrich; they were

57 See Ives, 'Henry VIII's will: the protectorate provisions', pp. 902–4. Cranmer's name does not appear in the list of gifts and peerage promotions specified: *A.P.C. 1547–50*, pp. 15–22.

58 *C.P.R. Edward VI 1547–8*, pp. 105–7, pursuant to an indenture of 20 March and supposedly in fulfilment of Henry VIII's will; for the regrant to the nephew, P.R.O., C. 1/1205/75.

59 Second grant of 12 June, *C.P.R. Edward VI 1547–8*, pp. 36–9; cf. Strype, *Cranmer* 2, no. 68, p. 406. For some of Cranmer's leases of the Lancashire rectories, see Gastrell, *Notitia* 2 i p. 130 and H.M.C., *6th Report*, p. 447; these were later in the hands of the Archdiocese of Canterbury rather than the Cranmer family, thanks to an Elizabethan regrant: *C.P.R. Elizabeth 1572–75*, no. 395.

a prominent London evangelical couple long associated with Cranmer, and Richard was Bishop Goodrich's first cousin. The Northamptonshire lands went to Anthony Stringer, a minor administrator in the Court of Augmentations who would nowadays be described as a property developer, and who may have set up the deal for the Archbishop.[60] By the time that these various transactions had been completed, Cranmer was left with a personal estate worth £60 a year, or at least that is what he told Queen Mary's commissioners in 1553.[61] The reality is unlikely to have been much different, and it is still an acquisition which was modest in the extreme compared with the Archbishop's colleagues in the evangelical establishment. What is also striking is the absence of any attempt to set up Cranmer's family with an estate in his own diocese, which became the aim of many bishops with importunate relatives later in the century; indeed, it almost looks as if he deliberately chose virtually all the property which he retained because it lay outside the province of Canterbury.

Another rather curious symbol of the evangelical triumph in power was the divorce case of the Dowager Queen Catherine's brother, William Parr, newly promoted to be Marquess of Northampton in the spree of honours which followed old King Henry's death. Parr's marriage to Elizabeth Bourchier had been dead long before she had deserted him in 1542, and now he was determined to marry Elizabeth Brooke, alias Cobham, daughter of George, Lord Cobham: he lost no time in the new reign in petitioning for a commission to decide whether he might lawfully marry her. It was duly granted in April, a notably quick result, and like the rest of the honours granted to the new governing clique, it claimed to fulfil one of King Henry's last wishes.[62] Nevertheless, the composition of the commission hardly suggests Henry's habitual strategy of balance: headed by Cranmer, of its ten members, only three (Cuthbert Tunstall, John Redman and Nicholas Wilson) were not strong evangelicals. The Archbishop spent a good deal of time and effort on this case: the substantial surviving collections of sources and comments which he made about it, with opinions for and against divorce, still cry out for detailed investigation. In them, Cranmer's marginal notes frequently comment on the weakness of arguments put forward to provide a biblical basis for divorce. Yet the conclusion of the commission was in Parr's favour; and it ought to be noted that the Archbishop was hardly an impartial judge in the case. Lord Cobham was one of his chief allies in Kent, an old friend strongly like-minded in his religious outlook, while Cobham's brother, Thomas

60 On the Goodriches, *C.P.R. Edward VI 1547–8*, pp. 18–19, and Brigden, *London*, p. 419. On Stringer, *C.P.R. Edward VI 1547–8*, p. 211; *C.P.R. Edward VI 1548–9*, p. 153; *C.P.R. Elizabeth 1569–72*, nos 1159, 2371; *Stiffkey Papers* 1, p. 294 and 2, p. 53.

61 P.R.O., E. 154/2/41, f. 3v.

62 *C.P.R. Edward VI 1547–8*, pp. 137, 261 (19 April and 7 May; the second commission added Wilson), in response to Parr's undated petition, *C.S.P. Domestic Edward VI*, no. 72. On the Parr marriages, see Cokayne and Gibbs, *Complete Peerage*, 9, pp. 671–3, and Carlson, *Marriage and the English Reformation*, pp. 83–5.

Brooke, was Cranmer's servant and had married his niece, Susan Cranmer. Equally important, Parr was one of the mainstays of the evangelical cause in national government.[63]

Cranmer's admirers have been embarrassed by the Parr affair, and have said little about it; the only early historian to give it any substantial discussion was Gilbert Burnet, and even his characteristic clear-sightedness seems to have been strained by the case.[64] By taking advantage (no doubt unconsciously) of the lack of dating in the proceedings of the commission, his narrative seems to have simplified and sanitized a complex and untidy story. It was hardly surprising, given the political background which we have noted, that the commission eventually recommended that a new marriage was lawful, on the grounds of desertion by Elizabeth Bourchier; however, the exact date of this decision seems problematic. What is beyond doubt is that Cranmer showed his emphatic endorsement of the eventual outcome of the commission's deliberations when he was included among the feoffees for the Parr–Cobham marriage settlement, which took place in or before August 1547: another divorce commissioner, Bishop Henry Holbeach of Rochester, was also among the feoffees, who were generally a crop of leading evangelicals, and they were headed by Protector Somerset.[65]

However, if the divorce commissioners had already by then made their decision, it was not allowed to stand for long. Despite Parr's high-level backing, a permission for divorce was a radical decision unmistakeably taken by an evangelical coterie of clergy against all precedents of canon law, and it caused considerable alarm and controversy in political circles. Eventually, in late January 1548, Northampton found himself summoned before the Privy Council, where he was solemnly reprimanded and ordered to separate from Elizabeth Cobham; this must have been an odd occasion, because not only was Parr himself a Privy Councillor, but his marriage feoffee, Somerset, was certainly present at the meeting, and probably Cranmer was there as well.[66] Gilbert Burnet supposed reasonably enough that the divorce commission gave its favourable verdict only after this confrontation, but the Parr–Cobham marriage settlement of summer 1547 places a serious question-mark against his dating. Parr's defiant evangelical riposte to the Council that his second

63 Cranmer's notes are Lambeth MS 1108 ff. 144–81; for summary comment, see Carlson, *Marriage and the English Reformation*, pp. 83–4. On Lord Cobham, P.R.O., S.P. 1/91 ff. 89–91, Cox 2, p. 301 (*L.P.* 8 no. 386), and on Thomas Brooke, P.R.O., S.P. 1/137 ff. 102–3, Cox 2, p. 330 (*L.P.* 13 ii no. 537); *Testamenta Vetusta*, p. 724.

64 Burnet 2 i, pp. 90–93, 2 ii, pp. 175–6 (Bk 1, no. 20).

65 *C.P.R. Edward VI 1547–8*, p. 210: undated licence of alienation in a sequence of grants of July–September 1547, and immediately following on from an alienation licence to Parr of 21 August 1547. The description of Holbeach as Bishop of Rochester confirms that the settlement predates his translation to Lincoln on 20 August 1547.

66 *A.P.C. 1547–50*, pp. 164–5 (28 January 1548). There are no Council attendance lists at this time, but Cranmer can be shown to have been present at Council meetings at Somerset Place on 24 and 30 January: P.R.O., E. 101/76/35 ff. 5, 7.

marriage 'stood with the word of God' in any case did not promise a long compliance with the order for separation from Cobham, and he spent the rest of the reign pursuing the legality both of his divorce from Bourchier and of his second marriage.

In the 1548 confrontation at the Council board, Somerset and Cranmer had clearly deserted Northampton, much to the fury of his putative father-in-law, Lord Cobham, and the reasons were probably political.[67] Parr was brought before the Council at a moment when the evangelicals were piloting through a great many other controversial changes, such as the banning of seasonal ceremonies and the destruction of images, and when they had just subjected Stephen Gardiner to a lengthy spell of imprisonment. Parr's disgrace was a sign that the evangelical establishment knew that it had overreached itself in January 1548; to give an open sanction to divorce was a step too early in the programme of change. Northampton finally achieved his ambition in 1552, in a private act of Parliament which was unique at the time, and which provoked a handful of traditionalist peers and bishops to insist on registering their opposition to his bill; not surprisingly, this act was reversed under Mary. In the end, despite much discussion, the Edwardian Church never gave a general legal standing to divorce, the only Protestant Church in Europe not to do so, and Parr's marriage problems may have played their part in this failure.

The obvious way to launch religious changes on a national scale was to stage a royal visitation of the Church in both its provinces, the first such action since the death of Thomas Cromwell had killed the vice-gerency. The first formal moves were made in May, and were accompanied by a proclamation indignantly assuring the public that nothing drastic was going to happen, and ordering that all current religious legislation should be obeyed.[68] This was a smokescreen tactic which was used more than once during the Somerset years. In fact, the choice of six teams of commissioners to cover the whole country proclaimed the government's real intentions: they were as far as possible reliable evangelicals. We have a snapshot from Ralph Morice of the Archbishop briefing him as the visitation began, and the clerical and administrative component of the teams looks as if it was handpicked by Cranmer.[69] They included such stalwarts of his household as Morice (registrar of the visitation), Christopher Nevinson, Nicholas Ridley, Rowland Taylor and John Joseph, together with many of his old friends like Dean May of St Paul's, Dean Haynes of Exeter and Dean Benson of Westminster. Of these, May, Ridley, Haynes and Joseph were also Cranmer's colleagues in the Parr divorce commission.

A notable feature of the commissions was the presence of outspoken evangelical activists who had been in disgrace in the late King's reign, such as

67 *L.J.* 1, pp. 409, 413. On Cobham's feelings, Clark, *Kent*, p. 83.
68 *T.R.P.* 1 no. 281 (24 May 1547).
69 Foxe 5, p. 563.

Haynes, Joseph, John Olde and Bishop Goodrich's chaplain, Thomas Cottisford; the fact that each team had a preacher, including a Welsh speaker for the Welsh dioceses, shows that this was going to be a propaganda as well as an administrative exercise.[70] Significantly, one of the few errors in judgement made in choosing visitors was remedied when the conservatively minded Sir John Godsalve was recalled in September from his visitatorial duties in the south-east to central government work.[71] A subsidiary team for the deanery peculiar of Doncaster, in Yorkshire, reveals the same pattern of appointments; it was headed by Cranmer's boyhood friend, Sir John Markham, one of its clerical members was Edmund Farley, one of the Archbishop's right-hand men in Canterbury diocese, and its preacher was Dr Roger Tong, a long-standing chaplain of King Edward whom Gardiner bitterly characterized in May 1547 as one of the 'new men'.[72]

There was, however, a curious hesitation in beginning the work. Action on the visitation stalled for four months after the initial formalities: indeed, the bishops were quickly told in May of the postponement of action, and there is no sign of activity, even after the first issue of the visitation articles and injunctions on 31 July, until the very end of August.[73] Perhaps there was official nervousness that precipitate action would upset conservatives, particularly in view of the highly delicate matter of the Parr divorce; this is suggested by the cautionary proclamation in May, and indeed in June the French ambassador Selve noted a sudden hesitancy in the government's enthusiasm for reform.[74] On 19 and 20 June, once more the proprieties of a royal death and the courtesies of diplomacy led to a full performance of the traditional liturgy, when the death of Francis I of France led to Cranmer presiding at the dirige and requiem in St Paul's Cathedral for the deceased King, with Bishop Holbeach in the pulpit. It was true that the achievement of Francis which Holbeach particularly singled out for commendation was his provision of the Bible in the vernacular for his subjects to read, but this occasion was also the last time under Edward VI that the parishes of the capital were officially called on to carry out the full funeral rites of the old Church.[75]

Certainly, leading conservatives were on the watch for opportunities to provoke confrontation. One very high-profile row broke out in May in

70 Strype, *Cranmer* 1, p. 209.

71 *A.P.C. 1547–50*, p. 517.

72 Burnet 2 ii, pp. 176–8 (Bk 1 no. 21); *Gardiner's Letters*, p. 281. Cf. a reference by Parkyn to 'the heretic Doctor Tong' and his continuing involvement in northern ecclesiastical politics: 'Parkyn's Narrative', p. 72. On Farley, C.U.L. UA Wills 1, f. 56r; *Faculty Office Registers*, p. 143; Cranmer's Register, ff. 393r, 421Ar; Woodruff, 'Extracts from original documents', p. 97.

73 Note Gardiner's protest about the injunctions in August, *Gardiner's Letters*, p. 361. For initial moves and hesitations, see Cranmer's Register, ff. 31–2; *Registrum Gardiner/Poynet*, p. 82; *Tunstall Register*, pp. 89, 91; for date of injunctions, *T.R.P.* 1 no. 287.

74 *Selve*, pp. 151–2.

75 *Wriothesley's Chronicle* 1, p. 184; *Selve*, pp. 152–3; *Greyfriars Chronicle*, p. 54.

Gardiner's diocese, when iconoclasm in Portsmouth gave the Bishop the excuse to take his protest as far as the Privy Council, and to widen his comment into general denunciations of the direction in which official policy was going.[76] Two other prominent conservatives who presented the regime with an embarrassing challenge were the Earl and Countess of Lennox, then living in exile from Scotland at Settle, in Yorkshire. They were doubly important because of their place in Scottish politics and because of the Countess's Tudor royal blood. Born Lady Margaret Douglas, she was potentially of vital dynastic importance, despite the bitter quarrel with her uncle, Henry VIII, which had excluded her from the succession. In 1603 her grandson James did indeed become King of England. At some stage during 1547 the Lennoxes caused the arrest of their servant, John Hume (no doubt also Scots, and perhaps more accurately John Home); he was sent up to Cranmer 'for denying the sacrament . . . of the altar to be the real flesh and blood of Christ . . . saying that he would never veil his bonnet unto it, to be burned therefor' and 'that if he should hear mass, he should be damned'. This arrest may have been designed deliberately to put Cranmer on the spot, and it is not surprising in the atmosphere of religious uncertainty during 1547 that Hume disappeared quietly from the record.

Foxe links the Hume affair with a previous anecdote about another evangelical, whose public disruption of a mass celebrated in St Paul's certainly did bring about his death in the first year of Edward VI, but there are odd aspects of this story, and it may not be all it seems. The victim was Thomas Dobbe, a young ordained Fellow of St John's, Cambridge, who Foxe says was driven out of the College for wanting to challenge the rule of celibacy and marry a local girl; the puzzling aspect of this is that two of the three colleagues in St John's whom Foxe berates for persecuting Dobbe, were evangelicals both linked to Cranmer, one of them the Master of the College, John Taylor. His mind evidently unhinged by his troubles, Dobbe made his denunciation of the mass in St Paul's, was accused by the Lord Mayor before Cranmer and died of an illness contracted in the city prison in Bread Street. One suspects that the business involved a more complex College row and human tragedy than Foxe knew about or was prepared to relate; the scandal of Dobbe's death may have been one of the reasons why Taylor was forced to resign the mastership of John's in 1547.[77]

There could also have been another reason for delay in the visitation, apart from problems with conservatives and maverick evangelicals: there was a

76 *Gardiner's Letters*, pp. 273–95.

77 Both stories are told in Foxe 5, pp. 704–5, where the Earl and Countess are thinly disguised as 'Master Lewnax of Wressel . . . and Margaret Lewnax, his mistress'; she was still alive when Foxe was publishing. For Dobbe, see Venn 2, p. 47; the other fellows of John's involved were Roger Hutchinson (who dedicated a christological treatise to Cranmer in 1550) and John Pindar. The odd presentation of both stories indicates a single eccentric informant for Foxe.

further component of government policy to be completed and put in place. During summer 1547, Cranmer at last achieved his ambition of issuing a collection of homilies to remedy the grievous shortage of reliable preachers in the Church; one of the items in the visitors' list of instructions when they finally did embark on their travels was the order that all parishes should obtain a copy of the *Homilies*, which was first published at the end of July together with the royal articles and injunctions. It was the culmination of a plan which we have seen Cranmer first prepare unsuccessfully in 1542 (see above, Ch. 7); the homilies also had predecessors in the various occasional addresses issued under Henry VIII and even in the format of the 1537 Bishops' Book. Some of the twelve sermons included were indeed probably written during early 1547, but some may have been prepared in Henry's lifetime, for they were not all on themes of controversial theology. Two even achieved the remarkable feat of reappearing in a new set of homilies issued for the Marian Church under the auspices of Bishop Bonner, having actually been written by Bonner himself and by his kindred spirit and chaplain John Harpsfield.[78] A notable but not surprising absentee in 1547, given the early stages of the government's plans, was any discussion of the eucharist; one was promised in an advertisement first found in the edition of 21 June 1548, but that theme had to wait until the reign of Elizabeth.[79]

Cranmer can be associated with four of the twelve homilies. He probably composed the opening 'Exhortation to the Reading of Holy Scripture', a theme particularly dear to his heart, and one which he had already made his own in the Preface to the 1540 Great Bible. He also reserved to himself the subjects which he felt most important to get right if they were to be preserved from popish error – salvation, faith and good works: these homilies can be associated with him because of near-contemporary reminiscence, and also because of their similarities with his surviving set of notes on the theme of justification.[80] The extent to which he succeeded in his aim can be gauged from the torrent of hostile prose which his efforts elicited from Bishop Gardiner, both in anticipation of the content of the *Homilies* and after they were published. Rightly, Gardiner guessed that Cranmer's intention would be to reassert the doctrine of salvation by faith only, on which the Archbishop had been defeated in 1543; Winchester's attempt to stem the tide of evangelical doctrine included penning, for Cranmer's benefit, the sarcastic synopsis of a homily on faith which would have held the line for the doctrine in the King's Book.[81] Cranmer's only recorded reaction, as Gardiner wryly noted,

78 Duffy, *Stripping of the Altars*, pp. 535–7, is a useful discussion of the Marian homilies.

79 *Homilies*, ed. Bond, p. 201. There is an alternative possibility: that this particular promise was fulfilled in a different form by 'Richard Bonner's' eucharistic treatise of November 1548 (see below, pp. 399–403).

80 Ibid., pp. 26–8. The notes are printed from Lambeth MS 1108 ff. 58–67r, in Cox 2, pp. 203–12.

81 *Gardiner's Letters*, pp. 309–10, and see his whole long correspondence with Somerset, the Privy Council and Cranmer, ibid., pp. 296–400.

was amusement, and he was not diverted from the purpose which he had announced for those with eyes to see in the Flicke portrait, back in 1545 (see above, Ch. 8).

Once more, as in his many debates with King Henry and in the 'Great Commonplaces', the Archbishop's twin concern in the homilies was to establish the nature of salvation as God's free gift of grace by faith, while demonstrating to the person in the pew that this did not result in the collapse of morality and that good works were still an essential part of the Christian life. The whole collection of homilies is indeed arranged in a logical sequence in two pairs of six sermons, which take the hearer from matters of faith, based on the reading of scripture, through to works – in other words, the way in which everyday life should be conducted. Cranmer's trilogy (the third, fourth and fifth homilies) forms the heart of the first part, and so fundamental a statement did he feel the third homily on salvation or justification to be, that a specific reference to it was incorporated in the Forty-Two Articles of 1553, as setting the standard for discussion of the subject. Building on Harpsfield's exposition of the miseries of the human condition which was the previous sermon, Cranmer opened the 'Homily of Salvation' with a statement of human helplessness and of God's mercy. He expounded the themes which we have already met with over a decade of theological argument, with the aid of quotations from the Greek and Latin fathers amid which the name of Augustine sounded as a constant knell: remorselessly and with no particular sense of progression he returned to the contrast that 'justification is the office of God only, and is not a thing which we render unto him . . .'. After this, the 'Homily of Faith' was an attempt to distinguish the correct meaning of faith, and in particular to make clear that 'a true faith cannot be kept secret, but when occasion is offered it will break out and shew itself by good works'.[82]

Finally, the 'Homily of Good Works annexed to Faith' (again, that title hammered home the same causal relationship) was further concerned with definition. First it made clear that a good work simply did not exist without faith ('faith it is that doth commend the work to God'), and audaciously it pointed to the example of the good thief on the cross, who had no time to do good works: 'faith only saved him'.[83] After this it moved to describe counterfeit good works. These sprang from the disobedience pioneered by Adam, and significantly the recurrent characteristic of this disobedience was worship of images of false gods. After pursuing this theme through the biblical eras, for the first time Cranmer's prose became openly polemical – perhaps stirring a new interest among the less readily devout in the listening congregations. He made a bitter attack on monasticism, with words of praise for Henry VIII for suppressing it, and followed this up with a long and contemptuous list of aids to traditional devotion. The list finally consigned any notion of purgatory to the lumber room (for the first time in an official statement) along with various

82 *Homilies*, ed. Bond, pp. 83, 92–3.
83 Ibid., pp. 104, 105.

liturgical recitations such as the rosary; ceremonies such as the bearing of palms on Palm Sunday and the fire of Holy Saturday were also dismissed – sandwiched between them was a reference to 'candles' which in the context could only be a condemnation of the ceremonies of Candlemas, the Purification of Our Lady. All these observances were still perfectly legal, a point not lost on that consummate lawyer Stephen Gardiner.[84] Altogether, the list was an emphatic signpost to the consequences of believing in justification by faith, and a shifting of the goal-posts in the arguments about faith and works between evangelicals and traditionalists. Very many of the actions to which the traditional Church had pointed as good works were now proclaimed as nothing of the kind; the homilies redefined and narrowed the range of works, while still insisting on their necessary part in the Christian life.

Presentationally, this was a masterly performance. The homilies did not make any more concessions to the hearers in their prose than did the average royal proclamation, but they avoided technical theological terms beyond any which could be found in the pages of scripture, and they were very sparing in showing off classical allusions, recognizing that humanist learning would not be expected or appreciated in the backwoods. Cranmer was designing a collection to last, so the homilies avoided the preacher's refuge in anecdotes or purple passages which might entertain at first hearing, but which would become embarrassing with repetition. Quickly the authorities also realized that it would be a help to inexpert performers in the pulpit to indicate how each lengthy homily might be divided up into a series of episodes. Beginning with an edition published in 1549, twofold or threefold divisions were inserted into the twelve texts, with appropriate introductory bridge-passages to each division, to form a set of thirty-one readings. Thus in theory, like the psalter, the whole book could have been read through daily in a single month at a liturgical office, although the official recommendation was for weekly readings at the main service – to begin with, the high mass. The 1549 subdivision was done with considerable adroitness: for instance, in one of the later homilies a long meandering quotation from Paul was split by the division, so that the quotation ended and began a section in a much more effective presentation. Cranmer also ignored the criticism made by Bucer in 1551 that this scheme of subdivision produced expositions which were too short to be edifying: clearly he had the good sense to recognize that not everyone shared Bucer's addiction to producing or consuming torrents of words.[85]

Cranmer's homilies, as Ashley Null says, are 'the mature public expression of his Protestant Augustinianism'.[86] Once more, Cranmer was alarmingly eclectic in his use of sources to reach his goal. Just as he had pillaged the work

84 *Gardiner's Letters*, p. 382.

85 On the sub-division, *Homilies*, ed. Bond, pp. 194–5, although Bond has in my opinion misjudged this device: cf. ibid., note on p. 202. Cf. Bucer's criticism, *Bucer*, ed. Whitaker, pp. 46–7.

86 Null Ph.D., 'Cranmer's Doctrine of Repentance', p. 185.

of a Cardinal of the Roman Church, Quiñones, for his liturgical revision, so he built into the homily on justification material from the writings of the great Cardinal Cajetan, Luther's adversary, simply because he found that, in certain passages which he had singled out for copying in his 'Great Commonplaces', Cajetan conveniently expressed his own thoughts. More predictably elsewhere, the writings of Philipp Melanchthon provided a useful basis for his discussion of justification.[87] However, in one respect, Cranmer's pastoral instinct muffled his presentation of the great soteriological themes of Augustine of Hippo. We have seen in his private writings that the logic of his view of God's grace pointed inexorably to the doctrine of predestination. God's elect could never finally fall from grace, even if it was possible that they might temporarily fall through sin; equally, the reprobate could never attain salvation. Yet, however inescapable that assumption of predestination might be, Cranmer never felt that this was a doctrine which would bring comfort to the motley congregations which crowded the churches of England, and the Forty-two Articles would say as much in 1553 (see above, Ch. 2, p. 30). Bucer clearly agreed: he confined discussion of the signs of predestination to his biblical commentaries, rather than expound them in his preaching. The homilies of the Church of England were therefore composed as if all the hearers would be part of the elect, presumably on the principle that in any case the reprobate would be unable to benefit by listening to them; the homilies' exhortations to repentance were designed to encourage the elect to rise above any temporary stumbling into sin. In the homilies, predestination remained the doctrine that dared not speak its name.[88]

When the teams of visitors finally went out at the end of August, they were armed with the sets of royal articles of enquiry and injunctions, and they also composed their own injunctions as appropriate for the settings in which they found themselves: cathedrals, dioceses or peculiars like Doncaster. In every case, as Eamon Duffy has pointed out, these represented 'a significant shift in the direction of full-blown Protestantism', taking Henrician and Cromwellian orders from 1538 onwards and adding to them, especially making an effort to eliminate any image which had any suspicion of devotion attached to it. One of the most decisive moments of liturgical change was the injunction which ended all processions: now the English litany that Cranmer had devised for Henry VIII was going to be frozen as a static rite, within the church building. One of the traditional liturgy's greatest dramatic assets, its use of movement and its invasion of public space, was to be removed from English life for centuries, except in the brief Marian revival and in the later bowdlerized and secularized form of the parish perambulation.[89]

87 Null Ph.D., 'Cranmer's Doctrine of Repentance', pp. 185–91; cf. *Homilies*, ed. Bond, pp. 79–81, 82–4.

88 For an excellent discussion of these themes, see Null Ph.D., 'Cranmer's Doctrine of Repentance', pp. 192–206. On Bucer, Stephens, *Holy Spirit in Bucer*, p. 33.

89 Duffy, *Stripping of the Altars*, pp. 450–54.

As contemporary commentators noted, this made for rather awkward theatre when there was something to celebrate; when for instance on 20–21 September 1547 the government ordered thanksgiving for military victory in Scotland, a conservative London chronicler noted perhaps satirically that the churches 'kept a solemn procession on their knees'.[90]

Not surprisingly, this was the point when the phoney war with the conservatives ended. The royal visitation and the homilies sparked off direct conflict with Gardiner, who on 30 August pointed to the contradictions between the new legislation and the doctrinal provisions made by Henry VIII; Bishop Bonner followed suit a fortnight later, as the visitors began their work and initiated image-smashing in his cathedral and the city churches. Both bishops quickly found themselves in prison.[91] Although Bonner was soon released, Gardiner remained firm, and in a face-to-face confrontation with an evangelical delegation led by Cranmer at Dean May's house on 7 October, he chose to make Cranmer's homily on justification the centre-piece of his grievance. Cranmer was as usual magnanimous in victory, telling Gardiner that in his opinion he was 'a man meet . . . to be called to the Council again' and holding out that prospect in return for conformity: all in vain, for Gardiner chose to stay in the Fleet prison rather than betray his conscience.[92] He remained in gaol until January 1548; even then, after his release, his carefully modulated programme of legalistic foot-dragging against change inevitably resulted in his renewed arrest at the end of June, after the government had engineered a confrontation with him. Thereafter, Gardiner did not leave the Tower of London while King Edward was alive, and at last Cranmer had his old enemy where he wanted him.[93]

Winchester's strong suit in autumn 1547 was that as yet no Parliament had repealed any of the Henrician legislation; hence the urgent need to call Parliament to remedy this situation. The agenda was decided well in advance, as part of the evangelicals' rolling programme of change: at the beginning of October the clerical leadership in Strassburg had already been told by their English correspondents that the Parliamentary meeting would decide many Christian matters, after the excellent start made in the summer.[94] Parliament opened on 4 November, with Gardiner still in gaol, bitterly and accurately protesting that he was deliberately being kept from having his say in the new session. Cranmer and Nicholas Ridley carried the liturgical burden at the

90 *Wriothesley's Chronicle* 1, p. 186: see also *Selve*, pp. 205–6, who noted procession 'after the new fashion'.

91 The inhibition to Gardiner was dated 23 August: *Registrum Gardiner/Poynet*, p. 86; see *Gardiner's Letters*, pp. 368–73 for his response of 30 August. London and Bonner: *Greyfriars Chronicle*, p. 54; *A.P.C. 1547–50*, pp. 125–7, 131–2, 517; Foxe 5, pp. 743–4.

92 *Gardiner's Letters*, pp. 397–8, 403.

93 Redworth, *Gardiner*, pp. 264–81, although Redworth's interpretation of Gardiner's motives differs from my account.

94 A.S.T. 40, f. 839r, Martyr to Dryander, 5 October 1547.

parliamentary mass that day, although Bishop Bonner was prevailed on to preside at the mass for Convocation the day after. Notably, Parliament was treated to the novel experience of hearing the main parts of its mass in English, no doubt a foretaste of the texts that would appear in the 1549 *Book of Common Prayer*, and a useful piece of market testing for the legislation to come; not surprisingly, Bonner did not follow suit in his Convocation mass.[95] In Parliament, Cranmer put in his usual assiduous attendance in the Lords while the legislation dismantling the Henrician defences of traditional religion was put through. He showed himself hesitant about the very contentious act which destroyed the chantries; on 15 December he and Thomas Goodrich joined their conservative colleagues in voting against the Lords' fourth reading, but for the final reading on Christmas Eve he abandoned Goodrich and supported the bill. We have no way of knowing what aspects of the bill had caused him unease; the usual explanation, that he was reluctant to see further indiscriminate stripping of church property, is certainly plausible.[96]

In his own Convocation, Cranmer naturally played a more central role than in Parliament; he gave the keynote address, calling the clergy to discuss 'how properly to set up the true religion of Christ and bring it to the people'. Archbishop Parker's reminiscence as an eyewitness was that as an extension of that suggestive theme, Cranmer made it clear that the priority was to get rid of remaining popish abuses: the same programme which he had announced in the last of his homilies, and which was currently being vigorously prosecuted by the royal visitors.[97] Thus encouraged, the Lower House of Convocation showed itself enthusiastic for change; one wonders what pressure on elections had been brought to bear by the royal visitors and through more informal channels to secure a sympathetic representation. The lower clergy petitioned on themes dear to Cranmer's heart: discussion free from fear of the Six Articles, the introduction of general communion in both kinds, the legalization of clerical marriage and the revision of canon law. There was also a call for the draft service books produced under Henry VIII, presumably including Cranmer's drafts for breviary revision which have survived, to be produced and examined by Convocation. This was only fulfilled indirectly, for subsequent liturgical revision was put in the hands of small committees of Convocation members, with no surviving evidence of any debate in the full gathering. The only demand which produced no further action of any sort over the next few years, and of which no more was heard, was the perfectly logical request that since Convocation had surrendered its legislative independence to Henry VIII in 1532, the Lower House should now be given representation in the House of Commons, just as the bishops were represented in the Lords. This proved too alarmingly clerical a request to appeal to the

95 *Wriothesley's Chronicle* 1, p. 187; Lambeth MS 751, p. 123.

96 *L.J.* 1, pp. 293–312.

97 Lambeth MS 751 p. 124; Parker, *De Antiquitate*, p. 398.

authorities of Tudor England, and it is unlikely that Cranmer would have regarded it with much enthusiasm.[98]

One of the matters under discussion in Convocation which did result in immediate direct action in Parliament, was the enactment that henceforth communion should normally be received by all, clergy and laity, in the two kinds of bread and wine. In Convocation no one of the Lower House at least was prepared to speak against this measure, but its progress in Parliament was rather more stormy, with five conservative bishops voting against its passage in the Lords on 10 December. The government did its best to prevent conservative opposition by wrapping up the change in a good deal of angry prose about those who despised the sacrament, and including legal provisions to punish such offenders from 1 May; this sanction was some substitute for the Henrician anti-heresy legislation which was simultaneously being swept away. Yet the curb on eucharistic discussion should not be regarded simply as a piece of cynical manoeuvring on the part of the evangelical establishment.[99] There was genuine nervousness about the flood of radicalism released, particularly in south-east England, by the death of Henry VIII. This fear was revealed during the Parliamentary session by a Paul's Cross sermon on the eucharist by Nicholas Ridley (newly consecrated Bishop of Rochester). His effort proved an own goal, for his enthusiasm ran away with him, as he affirmed the notion of presence in the sacrament, and discouraged all speculation about its nature; they were, he said, 'worse than dogs and hogs, that would ask the question "How he was there present"'.[100]

Clearly the sermon was aimed against the radicals, and it was part of the official programme of legislation on the sacrament which was reinforced, at the end of December, by a royal proclamation covering the same ground as Ridley's sermon: Ridley much later explained that he was provoked by a rash of radical handbills posted around London using abusive terms about the eucharist. Significantly, he linked his memories of his sermon with a remark he had made about the eucharist to Bishop Gardiner a month or two later, when they were discussing the case of two Anabaptists in Kent: Ridley clearly regarded the two bishops' differences as unimportant compared with the gulf which separated them both from the radicals' sacramentarianism. The same explanation probably attaches to Gardiner's later malicious reminiscence of an incident before the Privy Council at the same time, when Cranmer seemed to agree with his own opinion that 'the only substance of Christ's body [was] in the sacrament'.[101] Ridley's Paul's Cross sermon was a gift to conservative

98 Lambeth MS 751, p. 125; Strype, *Cranmer* 1, pp. 220–22, from C.C.C.C. MS 121, ff. 5f. Cf. Lambeth MS 1108 ff. 2–3.

99 Cf. comment in Thomas, 'Tunstal – trimmer or martyr?', pp. 342–3.

100 Foxe 6, pp. 241–2, and cf. ibid., p. 125; the date seems to have been a Sunday in November 1547.

101 *T.R.P.* 1 no. 296. *Ridley's Works*, pp. 264–5 (and see comments by Ridley, *Ridley*, pp. 139–40, and *Cranmer's Recantacyons* pp. 21–2). *Gardiner's Letters*, pp. 448–9; the Cranmer discussion can be dated to 8 January 1548 (cf. *A.P.C. 1547–50*, p. 157).

commentators, and it was still being used as a polemical weapon by Abbot Feckenham in the 1559 Parliament. The problem for Ridley, as in Cranmer's later literary debate with Gardiner, was how best to convey a metaphorical notion of presence. If the academic language of Ridley's later attempt at recalling his expression in the sermon is anything to go by, it was not surprising that his open-air London audience did not pick up the nuances of what he said about the bread and wine: 'unto this material substance is given the property of the thing whereof it beareth the name'.[102] Ridley and Cranmer were finding it difficult to express their own changing insights in ways which would hold a distinctive and easily comprehensible line in a situation of theological flux.

Cranmer's thinking at this time can be sampled in several important fragments of his working papers and associated documents. The working papers are questionnaires which almost certainly date from the November–December Parliamentary session, because they were concerned with gauging the opinion of prominent members of Convocation on the important measures of change proposed, especially the abolition of chantries, gilds and intercessory masses and the introduction of English into the mass.[103] One set of leading questions survives with answers by four bishops who were now emerging as defenders of the traditionalist viewpoint, Bonner, Heath, Day and Skip, all of whom voted against the sacrament bill on 10 December; Cranmer then responded to their united reply with some further questions. His intention was to probe his conservative colleagues on the validity of intercessory masses by putting some absurd cases in a rather brutally literal-minded fashion: for instance, how should John's spiritual actions done in England help 'Thomas dwelling in Italy and not knowing what John in England doth'?[104] Rather pettily, he crowed at the reverent agnosticism of his colleagues' answer, which was in fact little different in kind from Ridley's plea for stilling speculation about eucharistic presence: 'why do you then affirm that to be true, which you cannot tell how, nor wherein it can be true?' Cranmer's passion against error was leading him down an unattractive path.

Another question made it clear that the Archbishop felt that a gulf had opened up on the eucharist between him and his old friends, and he was now not afraid to expose their difference: he asked what was the 'presentation of the body and blood of Christ in the mass, which *you call* the oblation and sacrifice of Christ'? 'You call' was an aggressive emendation from 'is called' in his original draft of the questions. Further questions dealt with the validity of clerical ministries which did not involve preaching, and on the desirability of

102 *Ridley's Works*, pp. 162–3. Cf. *Proceedings in Parliaments 1558–81*, ed. Hartley, p. 30.

103 See below for the main drafts, but one little-noticed further draft of questions by Cranmer at Lambeth MS 1108, f. 1 strengthens the case for dating, because it relates to the November–December 1547 Parliamentary legislation on clerical jurisdiction.

104 Cox 2, pp. 152–3, from Lambeth MS 1108, ff. 40, 44; a draft of the questions in Cranmer's own hand is in C.C.C.C. MS 105, p. 230.

having the whole mass in English. A different set of questions on the eucharist has a wider spread of replies from senior members of Convocation, and this time Cranmer gave his own responses. They included his conviction that the whole mass should be in English, 'except in certain mysteries, whereof I doubt'; what these mysteries were, he did not specify. He also bluntly dismissed intercessory masses and denied that, in the mass, 'Christ indeed is there offered and sacrificed by the priest and the people (for that was done but once by himself upon the cross) but it is so called, because it is a memory and representation of that very true sacrifice and immolation which before was made upon the cross.' To the question 'wherein consisteth the mass by Christ's institution?' his reply was both gnomic and minimalist: it 'consisteth in those things which be set forth in the Evangelists', after which followed a standard list of eucharistic passages in the synoptic gospels and Paul's account in 1 Corinthians 10–11. Already we seem very close to the doctrine which Cranmer would express in his prayer book rites and in his eucharistic writings; and we are also very close to the ideas of a man of increasing importance in the development of England's Reformation, Martin Bucer.[105]

Now it seems that the changes in Cranmer's eucharistic thinking, which we speculated may have been put in motion just before the old King's death, were coming to fruition. What is of particular importance is that just at this time he was in close correspondence with Martin Bucer and Strassburg. It is likely, indeed, that the two men had never lost contact, despite the failure of their first high hopes in the later 1530s (see above, Ch. 6). Bucer was always very conscious of his strategic position in a city of the Schmalkaldic League which was also in close contact with the Swiss evangelical leadership. His Anglophilia had put him at the centre of efforts to maintain relations between England and the Continental reformers through the 1540s, and had made him take initiatives at times when no one else on the Continent was especially enthusiastic for alliance.[106] A coincidence of circumstances now conspired to make this relationship of vital importance: the transformation in English politics, but also the disaster for Protestant fortunes on the Continent represented by the Emperor Charles V's victory at Mühlberg in April 1547. This left the kingdom of the young Josiah as one of the more reliable refuges for the godly throughout central Europe, as a triumphant Emperor prepared to impose on his dominions a conservative religious settlement which would culminate in the Augsburg Interim of 1548. Two senior evangelical theologians who were already exiles after their flight from their religious orders in Italy felt particularly vulnerable in the new situation: Peter Martyr (Pietro Martire Vermigli) and Bernardino Ochino. An English mission to Strassburg in October 1547 invited them to take refuge in England, and they arrived on 20 December, while Parliament was sitting, escorted by one of the English

105 Cox 2, pp. 150–51, distilled from Lambeth MS 1108, ff. 6–34; once more, a draft of part of the questions in Cranmer's hand is in C.C.C.C. MS 105, p. 231.

106 Cf. especially McEntegart Ph.D., 'England and the League of Schmalkalden', Ch. 6.

delegation, the merchant John Abell.[107] Cranmer gave them hospitality while the English government made arrangements for positions which would give them financial support and put their scholarly talents to good use.

Martin Bucer was host to the English delegation while it was in Strassburg, and he signalled his keen interest in the English situation by publishing a tract addressed to England and translated by Abell's colleague on the mission, Sir Thomas Hoby. This *Gratulation* on England's current moves to evangelical reformation began with an enthusiastic commendation of Cranmer's contribution to the *Homilies*, but the brevity of this compliment revealed that the first section of the work was a hasty last-minute addition to a previously written and bitter attack on Bishop Gardiner. No doubt the English envoys had told Bucer that there could be no surer way of annoying his old enemy Gardiner than praising Cranmer's theology of justification. Bucer reminisced in this work about his contacts during 1546 with Henry VIII, who he said had dissuaded him from open attack on Gardiner until a general European conference of evangelicals could be arranged in England which would bring 'a godly concord and unity in religion . . . and a further instauration [i.e. renovation] of the churches'; the bulk of the rest of Bucer's tract was clearly that same attack resurrected.[108] However, Bucer's contacts with Cranmer were not limited to public praise. On the eve of Martyr and Ochino's departure from Strassburg at the end of November, Bucer wrote Cranmer a letter. The two Italian refugees clearly brought this to England with them on their journey, since it contained a commendation for them, besides an encouragement to Cranmer to issue a further invitation to another Italian exile in Strassburg, the Hebrew scholar Emmanel Tremellio, who arrived in England the following year. Comparatively concise for the man whom Luther styled 'the chatterbox', the letter was almost wholly devoted to a careful exposition of what Bucer and those whom he trusted at Strassburg did and did not believe about the eucharist.[109]

This letter, which is dated 28 November 1547, is of the highest significance. It reveals that at this crucial juncture in the development of his theology, the Archbishop had turned to the Strassburg reformer to discuss the question of the eucharist, for Bucer was replying to a letter of Cranmer's (now lost) about eucharistic theology. Bucer set out his carefully nuanced views about presence and the benefits of the sacrament: 'We acknowledge that the bread and wine do not change in their nature, but that they become signs . . . by which signs [Christ] indeed with his own benefits and gifts may be offered to everyone. . . . We do not consider that Christ descends from heaven, nor that he is joined with the symbols, nor that he is included in

107 See *Travels and Life of Hoby*, pp. 3–6 for this and next paragraph; see also Abell's expenses claim of 20 December, pr. Gorham, *Gleanings*, p. 38. *Selve*, p. 258 confirms the date of their arrival.

108 Bucer, *Gratulation*, sigs Biv–Bv.

109 Paris, Bibliothèque Ste-Geneviève MS 1458, ff. 173v–175.

them.' This was a dig at orthodox Lutheranism as much as Catholic theology, which Bucer followed further on with even more predictable condemnations of transubstantiation and adoration of the elements. Meanwhile, however, he resumed with an affirmation that Christ 'is Lord, and he remains in the heavens until he will show himself openly to all as judge'. And repeatedly Bucer emphasized his own form of receptionism; only the faithful received Christ in the eucharist: 'But by means of the holy meal, he who fitly participates is drawn up by faith to heaven and receives his own Christ, as celestial food, by which he may have more fully his own citizenship in Heaven.' The contrast between the false view of Christ being drawn down to earth in the eucharist and the contrary truth of the believer being drawn up to heaven is typical of Bucer's thinking, and in his wake, also characteristic of John Calvin's eucharistic views.[110] Curiously, however, Bucer consistently refused to move on from this image to embrace the standard reformed argument that the local presence of Christ in heaven effectively excluded presence elsewhere; more than once he rejected this approach as undermining the believer's consciousness of Christ's presence through faith.[111] The fact that Cranmer was already using this particular argument in the debate in the Lords on the eucharist in 1548 (see p. 406 below) shows that the Archbishop was soon to move beyond the ground which Bucer had painstakingly defined for himself; another statement of the argument can be found in Article 29 of the Forty-Two Articles of 1553. Yet what Bucer said in his letter was likely, in 1547, further to corrode any remaining notion of the real or true presence which we have seen Cranmer maintain during the 1530s.

Another piece of the jigsaw was provided by Peter Martyr. When he came to England that November, he brought with him a manuscript copy of an epistle, *Ad Caesarium Monachum*, by John Chrysostom, which he had discovered in Florence before fleeing Italy. The epistle contained a passage on the eucharist which provided a perfect patristic basis for a non-realist eucharistic theology, including as it did the statement that 'the nature of bread doth still remain' after consecration. The discovery much excited Cranmer and Ridley: as Ridley later recalled, their 'conference' with Martyr was an important confirmation for Ridley's prior discovery of Ratramnus. Cranmer gleefully quoted the relevant passage from the Chrysostom epistle in his 1550 *Defence*, only to face the reasonable objection in Bishop Gardiner's counterblast that the passage was only found in Martyr's copy, together with the insinuation

110 On Calvin and Bucer's influence on his eucharistic thought, cf. F. Wendel, *John Calvin* (1965), pp. 346–55.

111 Cf. Bucer's condemnation in 1549 or 1550 of incautious use of the argument that Christ's body is locally circumscribed in heaven, at the same time as re-emphasizing that we are 'conveyed [to heaven] by faith': *Bucer*, ed. Wright, pp. 390–91 (and *C.S.P. Domestic Edward VI*, no. 296, propositions 26–7). Another good exposition, of 15 May 1550, is *E.T.* pp. 354–5 (*O.L.* pp. 543–5); and cf. Hopf, *Bucer*, p. 48.

that Cranmer had mistranslated much of the rest of the Chrysostom text.[112] Nevertheless, this was a coup for the Archbishop: precisely the sort of reward which he expected from his hospitality to distinguished foreign theologians. Chrysostom was in the major league among the Greek Fathers, being described in 1536 by Bucer as the most distinguished of biblical commentators in the early Church.[113] Such a witness was welcome ballast for Cranmer and Ridley's now fully developed non-realist eucharistic theology, and they were not the only Edwardian evangelicals to use the passage from Martyr's manuscript. Later John Ab Ulmis would report back to Bullinger, in Zürich, that Jan Laski had much influenced Cranmer on the eucharist when he arrived in England in autumn 1548. The Zürich party in England, however, were not always reliable observers, and were inclined to give their friends credit where it was not due. It is unlikely that by the second half of the year, well after his transactions with Ridley, Bucer, Martyr and the long-dead Ratramnus and Chrysostom, Cranmer still needed much more influencing in his shift in perspective on the eucharist.[114]

There were other changes to set in motion now. At the end of January 1548, at the same time that Parr was humiliated before the Privy Council because of his second marriage, Cranmer saw one promise of his homilies fulfilled, when he was able to announce to the bishops of his province that Candlemas candles, Ash Wednesday ashes and Palm Sunday palms would henceforth be banned. Despite the short notice, there is evidence of the command being carried out on Candlemas Day as far from London in the province of Canterbury as Worcester; even in the province of York, which did not officially receive the order until three weeks after Candlemas, the conservative parson Robert Parkyn gloomily recorded that candles had not been allowed on 2 February. The whole country had been well primed about official policy.[115] In a pattern that was becoming usual in the Somerset regime, this change was swiftly followed by a royal proclamation forbidding private innovation. Yet even some versions of this, distributed to the bishops, contained an added proviso, making it clear that the innovation forbidden did not extend to Cranmer's letters about the abolished ceremonies. The proviso suggests that some barrack-room lawyer among the conservatives had tried to turn the proclamation on the Archbishop, and that there had been a hasty effort to remedy the embarrassment.[116]

112 Cox 1, pp. 273–5, 287. Cf. Anderson, 'Rhetoric and Reality', pp. 457–9.

113 Foxe 6, p. 477; Bucer, *Metaphrasis* f. vr.

114 *E.T.* p. 253 (*O.L.* p. 383). For various uses of the Chrysostom quotation, see *Ridley's Works*, p. 34 and cf. note B, pp. 509–10; *Grindal's Remains*, p. 72; *Bradford* 1, p. 87.

115 Cox 2, p. 417; Heylyn 1, pp. 113–14; HWRO 009:1-BA 2636/11 (no. 43701), f. 157r, and for further comment, MacCulloch, 'Worcester'. On York, 'Parkyn's Narrative', p. 66; and for the order to the Province issued on 20 February, Bodl. MS Tanner 90 art. 38 f. 135, qu. Pocock, 'Preparations for the First Prayer Book', p. 41.

116 *T.R.P.* 1 no. 299.

In any case, subsequent moves both by the Privy Council and Cranmer himself showed how little intention there was of maintaining the status quo. At the end of February, Cranmer saw his coronation admonition to the young Josiah fulfilled when the Council ordered that all images should be removed from churches, on public order grounds, since (its letter somewhat disingenuously argued) the removal of only selected images by the royal injunctions the previous autumn had caused arguments and contention. The Primate would have forwarded this order to his diocesan bishops with relish.[117] In his own diocese, he then seems blithely to have ignored the prohibition of private innovation, for he appears to have issued his own orders drastically modifying the ceremonies of Holy Week 1548: banning the setting up of Easter sepulchres on Maundy Thursday and the use of fire and hallowed water which so distinguished the performance of the traditional Holy Saturday liturgy. No national ban was issued, and indeed there is evidence of the old ceremonies going ahead without official interference in Winchester and Worcester dioceses. Nevertheless, a ban in Canterbury diocese is strongly suggested by the articles of inquiry in Cranmer's diocesan visitation of summer 1548, when he sharply questioned his Kentish parishes as to whether they had performed these Holy Week ceremonies, along with questions about the ceremonies which had been banned in January. The summer visitation in Kent was itself a measure of his ruthless determination to enforce change, coming as it did immediately on the heels of the royal visitation in the previous year.[118]

These measures were the prelude to an even more significant break with the past: the first general modification in the central act of worship of the Church, the mass. Another royal proclamation on 8 March announced Parliament's enactment about communion in both kinds, introduced a liturgical form to put this into effect and promised 'from time to time' further official 'travail for the reformation and setting forth of such godly orders as may be most to God's glory, the edifying of our subjects, and for the advancement of true religion'. Attentive ears would have noticed that at no point did this proclamation use the word 'mass'; it was in fact the first time that the phrase 'Holy Communion', so familiar in later Anglican usage, became the preferred official description of the service.[119] The liturgy itself was called 'the Order of the Communion', but this was strictly accurate, because it concerned itself solely with that part of the mass which was the actual partaking of communion by the laity. The official starting point of the new order was Easter Day, 1 April 1548, explicitly (as the Council explained in a circular to the bishops) to give time for the liturgical forms to be distributed and reluctant clergy to be persuaded or bullied into using them. An enterprising publisher had also got

117 Cox 2, pp. 509–11.

118 Cox 2, pp. 154–9, especially pp. 157–8. On Winchester and Worcester, see MacCulloch, 'Worcester'. There seems also to have been a ban in York diocese: 'Parkyn's Narrative', p. 67.

119 *T.R.P.* 1 no. 300.

copies of the English text to the spring Frankfurt book fair within a fortnight of the initial royal proclamation; Cranmer and his colleagues were clearly anxious for international publicity for their efforts. A Latin translation of the order was published for the Continental trade by a certain 'A.A.', almost certainly Cranmer's old friend, the irrepressible Scottish Lutheran Alexander Alesius, who undertook translations of successive prayer books.[120]

It is worth pausing to scrutinize this first intimation of a revolution in England's official eucharistic theology. The experience of the mass would now be that the traditional rite proceeded in Latin until after the celebrant himself had communicated. He then suddenly broke into English, with an exhortation to those present to 'be partakers of the communion': 'dearly beloved in the Lord', it began, with an evangelical informality which must have seemed shocking after the ancient and familiar texts and liturgical actions. There followed a series of texts, short exhortation, confession, absolution, 'comfortable words' for frightened sinners, prayer of humble access, administration and blessing.[121] These passed into the 1549 Prayer Book virtually unaltered, an indication that Cranmer's work on the communion section of the liturgy was already well advanced; indeed, as we have already noted (see p. 358 above), he may have prepared these texts for Henry VIII in summer 1546. Their wording and the ideas which lay behind the rite were partly drawn from medieval liturgy, but also from the *Pia Deliberatio* of Archbishop Hermann von Wied; this work was a Latin translation made in 1545 of von Wied's 1543 German Church Order, which he had unsuccessfully proposed for the archdiocese of Cologne, and in the preparation of which Bucer had played a major part. Von Wied was probably much on Cranmer's mind at this time, as we will see (below, pp. 393, 400).[122]

Two final rubrics gave some further hints about the agenda behind the change: the first stipulated that every consecrated wafer should be broken at least in two before being distributed, and it spelled out that 'men must not think less to be received in part, than in the whole, but in each of them the whole body of our Saviour Jesu Christ'. One might think that this was a needless piece of pedantry, were it not for the testimony from Kent that, when the new rite was introduced at Deal, the conservative rector ministered the bread whole to those whose confessions he had heard, 'and to other that were not confessed, he ministered the same broken'.[123] There were other good reasons for insisting on the breaking of all the bread: it was a reflection of the

120 Council circular is P.R.O., S.P. 10/4/2 f. 3 (*C.S.P. Domestic Edward VI* no. 97). There are variant texts and lists of Council signatories in *Concilia*, ed. Wilkins, 4, p. 31, and Foxe 5, p. 719, suggesting a major and hastily organized effort in circularizing the bishops. On Frankfurt and Alesius, *Coverdale's Remains*, p. 525 and n.

121 A convenient version of the text is in *Liturgical Services of Edward VI*, pp. 3–8.

122 See analysis in Brightman, *English Rite* 1, pp. lxxii–lxxvi, and discussion in Cuming, *Godly Order*, pp. 73–81.

123 Woodruff, 'Extracts from original documents', pp. 96–7.

Gospel narratives in which Christ broke the bread which he distributed, and probably it was also an attempt to undermine the symbolism of the Fraction of the priest's wafer which was an integral part of the Roman canon of the mass. It was important to emphasize that there was no difference in kind between priest's and people's communion, and the ceremonial Fraction disappeared altogether in 1549. Nevertheless, the rubric's attempt to quell superstitious anxieties about the breaking of the wafers was rather ham-fisted, and later Stephen Gardiner delighted in teasing Cranmer about it, insinuating with his usual perverse ingenuity that it was a sure indicator of real presence doctrine.[124] The second rubric provided for an additional consecration of wine (it would be much easier to miscalculate the wine than the number of wafers), which should be done with the Latin consecration text, but 'without any levation or lifting up'. This might simply reflect a practical sense of theatre: it would be confusing to have the elevation of the cup in the middle of the laity's communion, for the elevation of the consecrated bread was the high point of the old mass and (still in the 1548 pattern) had already taken place at the first moment of consecration. However, perhaps a more important consideration was that Cranmer had no intention of further encouraging the ceremony of elevation, for which he (or his team of literary assistants) was expressing open contempt by 1550.[125]

Overall, the clear purpose of the Order of the Communion in text and rubric was to attack the notion of real presence, and it also made a first assault on the Church's traditional power of the keys in confession. Our attentive listener would have noticed that in the first exhortation, the statement that 'we receive the holy sacrament' was immediately qualified by the parenthesis 'for then we spiritually eat the flesh of Christ, and drink his blood'; he or she would also have noticed that in the earlier exhortation which gave notice of the date on which a communion was to be celebrated, confession to a priest as preparation was made optional. As we have seen at Deal, many took advantage of the new freedom to opt out of confession straight away. Several clergy in Cranmer's own diocese were certainly quite clear that the intention behind the alteration was to alter its theology: the rectors of Deal and Sandhurst got into trouble not only because they refused to follow the Communion order's instructions, but because they openly said that there remained no material bread after the consecration. Only a few months before, they would have been expressing the orthodoxy of the realm, and could have made trouble for parishioners who had contradicted them.[126]

A further publication a few months later, this time only semi-official, was to prove a grave embarrassment to Cranmer when later he had to defend

124 Cox 1, pp. 63–4, 142–3, 145–6, 325, 327; cf. Proctor and Frere, *Book of Common Prayer*, pp. 444, 460.

125 Cf. Cranmer, *Defence*, p. 442; the obvious relationship of this to a passage in *Becon's Works* 3, pp. 270–71 may suggest that Becon had a hand in writing the original.

126 Woodruff, 'Extracts from original documents', pp. 96–7.

himself against charges of inconsistency in his eucharistic doctrine. This was the *Catechism* which came out probably in June 1548 and went through three editions up to the autumn: it was a free translation with some additions and significant modifications of a work which had first been published in German at Nuremberg in 1533. The original principal author had been Cranmer's own relative by marriage, Andreas Osiander; Osiander produced a work for children which consisted of a series of sermons based on Martin Luther's *Small Catechism* of 1529. Osiander's work had become widely popular in Germany, and gained even further circulation when the Wittenberg reformer Justus Jonas (Jodocus Koch) translated it into Latin in 1539. There is every likelihood that Osiander was already working on the text when Cranmer was in Nuremberg in 1532 and that he discussed it with him; however, it was the Latin version by Jonas which the Archbishop seems to have used as the basis of the English translation. Jonas's son, also known as Justus Jonas, seems to have arrived in England at the same time as Martyr and Ochino in December 1547, and was certainly being given hospitality by Cranmer himself by spring 1548. Thus the book which Cranmer adapted was the one purely Lutheran devotional work to take any official place in the English Reformation.[127]

The extent of Cranmer's participation in the work is uncertain, for it is most unlikely that he would have had the time at such a busy period of change amid other greater priorities. Dr Selwyn carefully reviews the possible ghost writers or team assistants: Cranmer's chaplains, John Ponet, Thomas Becon and Rowland Taylor, or even the Dutch evangelical publisher of the work, Walter Lynne.[128] Nevertheless, since Cranmer put his name to the work and its dedicatory preface to his godson, King Edward, he must take responsibility for its contents. It was a handsome volume, which unlike most English Reformation literature had no fear of illustrations: the child readership could be beguiled by a number of woodcuts, including some deriving from the work of the great Hans Holbein the younger. One delightful example deftly put a polemical twist on the parable in Luke 18 of the Pharisee and the publican, which depicted the pompous self-satisfied Pharisee as a tonsured religious praying at an altar.[129] However, the text shows every sign of a rushed final stage of production, which led to unfortunate inconsistencies and second thoughts. The most substantial addition can be shown actually to have been added to the text while the first edition was being printed: a long sermon against imagery with a very specific English reference. This was against both the spirit and the letter of the original text: conservative Lutherans like

127 *Catechism*, ed. Selwyn, Introd., pp. 25–31, and for detailed discussion of the date of the English edition, Selwyn, 'Neglected Edition', pp. 90–91. On the younger Jonas, see *C.S.P. Spanish 1547–9*, p. 238, and Gorham, *Gleanings*, pp. 42–5. The *Pia Deliberatio* of Hermann von Wied discussed elsewhere in this chapter drew heavily on Lutheran sources, but could not be regarded as a purely Lutheran work in the same sense.

128 *Catechism*, ed. Selwyn, Introd., pp. 56–65.

129 Ibid., Introd., pp. 87–90.

26 Preface picture in Cranmer's 1548 Catechism: King Edward gives the Bible to bishops, lesser clergy, nobility and commons. The general format is that of the title-page of the Coverdale Bible of 1535.

Osiander did not in any case share Cranmer's hatred of traditional sacred images, but additionally the English editors did not correct the inconsistency of retaining the Lutheran and traditional numbering of the Ten Commandments, which omitted the divine prohibition against graven images as a separate commandment. It was the third edition before this anti-image text was even added to the quotation of the Lutheran first commandment.[130]

Besides this, there were very many minor modifications of the text, mostly with the aim of shortening or clarifying it. In some respects, however, the adaptation of the text did not go far enough to reconcile it with what we know of Cranmer's views elsewhere, which is in itself a strong indication that Cranmer did not have a chance to work on the detailed adaptation himself. First, in the arcane technicalities of the theology of salvation, Osiander increasingly stood apart from most other reformers in believing that Christ's

130 *Catechism*, ed. Selwyn, Introd., pp. 38–9, text, pp. 16–30; cf. above, Ch. 6, p. 192.

Thou shalt haue none other Goddes but me.

Exo.xxxii

A declaration of the fyrst commaundement.

27 The worship of the Golden Calf, prefacing the inserted sermon on prohibiting idolatry in the 1548 Catechism. Note that it was the priest Aaron who had encouraged this disobedience to God.

28 The Pharisee (shaven, with tonsure) and the Publican (a layman, with beard).

Of prayer. Fol.clxvi.

Luke.xviii

righteousness was actually imparted to justified believers, in contrast to the forensic theory of justification, which saw righteousness merely being imputed or attributed to fallen humanity by a loving God. We have seen in his supervision of the 'Great Commonplaces' (see above, Ch. 8, pp. 341–7) that Cranmer explicitly embraced the forensic viewpoint; yet traces of Osiander's distinctive perspective are strong in the phrasing of the *Catechism*.[131] Much more serious, because Cranmer's conservative enemies and indeed some reformers seized on the point, was the robustly realist language about eucharistic presence which characterized the work, and proclaimed its uncompromisingly Lutheran position. Already in the first edition of the *Catechism*, some effort was indeed made to deal with this. For instance, in a passage which recited the words of Christ so often emphasized by Luther, 'This is my body . . . this is my blood', the Latin original went on to say 'therefore we ought to believe that his body and blood are truly there'. The English text emended this to 'Wherefore we ought to believe, that in the sacrament we receive truly the body and blood of Christ'. This shifts the reader's attention from local presence to the experience of reception, which was precisely what Cranmer understood to be the thrust of Bucer's doctrine. As he wrote testily against Gardiner in 1551, Bucer 'denieth utterly that Christ is really and substantially present in the bread, either by conversion or inclusion, but in the ministration he affirmeth Christ to be present' – and Cranmer then added in 1551, 'so do I also'.[132]

However, not enough was done to keep Lutheran real presence language at bay from the *Catechism* text in 1548. Already on 18 August 1548 Bullinger's disciple, John Ab Ulmis, wrote to Zürich from London expressing his disgust at the eucharistic doctrine of the *Catechism*, in which the Archbishop 'has all but consented to that foul and sacrilegious transubstantiation of the papists in the holy supper of our Saviour; all the rest of Luther's dreams seem to him to be sufficiently well-grounded, evident and plain.'[133] Despite the rhetorical exaggeration of this complaint, it was not unique; such views were deeply embarrassing for the Cranmer circle, and may even account for the very odd feature of the third and some copies of the second edition of the *Catechism* that they conceal the identity of the printer, the Dutchman Nicholas Hill or van den Berghe.[134] Cranmer himself specifically acknowledged his own embarrassment two years later, although like many modern politicians complaining about their treatment at the hands of the media, he blamed the public for their lack of sophistication in appreciating his message:

131 *Catechism*, ed. Selwyn, Introd., pp. 43–47. Cf. Bucer's characteristic hedging of his bets on this issue: Stephens, *Holy Spirit in Bucer*, p. 49.

132 Cox 1, p. 225; cf. Brooks, *Cranmer's Doctrine*, pp. 43–4.

133 *E.T.* p. 251 (NB the bad inaccuracy of *O.L.* p. 381). Cf. the hostile comments about Cranmer from Bartholomew Traheron, *E.T.* p. 211 (*O.L.* p. 320).

134 *Catechism*, ed. Selwyn, Introd., pp. 90–91.

> And in a catechism by me translated and set forth, I used like manner of speech, saying, that with our bodily mouths we receive the body and blood of Christ. Which my saying divers ignorant persons, not used to read old ancient authors, nor acquainted with their phrase and manner of speech, did carp and reprehend for lack of good understanding.[135]

Something would have to be done. In the third edition of the *Catechism*, there were a number of changes (ingeniously done so as to minimize the necessity of resetting the typeface), including apparent attempts to give a rationale for clerical marriage and to downgrade the role of auricular confession. However, of greater significance were no fewer than six alterations to eucharistic passages. One place modified 'under the form of bread and wine' to 'under bread and wine', an inelegant attempt to remove an opportunity for reading transubstantiation into the text, which an injudicious first edition alteration to the Latin text had made possible. Elsewhere, there were simple direct contradictions of the original text, as one can see from comparing the two versions of the very passage which figured in Cranmer's reminiscence: 'For he doth not only with his bodily mouth receive the body and blood of Christ, but he doth also believe the words of Christ . . .' became 'For he doth not with his bodily mouth receive the body and blood of Christ, but he doth believe the words of Christ . . .'.[136] Richard Smith seized on this particular alteration with delight in 1550, and in a slightly garbled form it was alluded to by Dr Martin at Cranmer's trial in 1555, with devastating effect on the Archbishop's morale. On that occasion, he made no effort to deny his responsibility for the change, and the memory of the apparent inconsistency was clearly a painful one.[137]

The 1548 *Catechism* was a fiasco, and it is notable that nothing from it was reused in the 1549 Prayer Book: the very short catechism provided there as part of the structure of the confirmation service was derived entirely from English official teaching materials of the previous decade, including Hilsey's 1539 Primer and the 1543 King's Book.[138] Far from attesting to Cranmer's continuing belief in the eucharistic real presence, the whole sorry business of the Justus Jonas translation is strong evidence that by summer 1548 Cranmer's eucharistic theology had decisively crossed the Rubicon. First under the influence of Ridley (perhaps in 1546), with his highlighting of the respectable antiquity of figurative eucharistic discussion by Ratramnus, and later after correspondence with Bucer and discussions with the immigrants

135 Cox 1, p. 226; interestingly, this passage was omitted in the 1557 Latin translation of the *Defence*.

136 *Catechism*, ed. Selwyn, Introd., pp. 78–81, text, pp. 212–13 and list of textual variants; see also Selwyn, 'Neglected edition'.

137 Selwyn, 'Neglected edition', pp. 76–7, 83–4, and Foxe 8, p. 57. Cf. also Sander, *Schism*, pp. 181–2.

138 See the analysis in Brightman, *English Rite* 2, pp. 778–86.

from Strassburg, he had moved to the final phase of his eucharistic belief, which he would set out at such length between 1550 and 1551 first in the *Defence* and then in the *Answer*. By 28 September 1548, there is definite evidence that Cranmer's change of stance was in the public domain, at least for the group of English reformers who were the correspondents of the leaders in Zürich and who were always grimly on the watch for doctrinal deviation. Bartholomew Traheron, formerly one of Cranmer's most poisonous critics, now wrote in delight to Bullinger that Hugh Latimer 'has come over to our opinion respecting the true doctrine of the eucharist, together with the Archbishop of Canterbury and the other bishops, who before this seemed to be Lutherans'.[139] This new attitude may well have resulted from a careful perusal of the revised version of Cranmer's *Catechism* by Traheron and his friends.

The problem now for Cranmer was how to find appropriate language in which to present his new eucharistic belief acceptably in English to the public and to his episcopal colleagues, and the habitual intricacy of Bucer's thought and Latin expression would have not been of great help in this task. All the time there was the equally acute worry which had so preoccupied Ridley in his pronouncements on the eucharist in late 1547 and early 1548: how to keep one's views distinct from the hated radical 'Anabaptists'. To recast the official eucharistic theology of the Church was to tread a perilous path. It is almost as difficult for us to work out a simple system of labelling the evolution of Cranmer's eucharistic views for our own use. The splendid survey by Peter Newman Brooks is flawed by his decision to label the final phase of the Archbishop's beliefs 'true presence'; Brooks uses this in conjunction with the label 'spiritual', against the earlier 'real or corporal presence' years.[140] Above, in Chapter Six (pp. 181–3), I have tried to show that the 'true presence' label is better applied to the views of Cranmer's more-or-less Lutheran years after 1532; it was a phrase which at that time he seems to have used almost in a technical sense. In his last years, in fact he rarely talked of 'true presence', and the passage which Dr Brooks quotes from the *Answer* to justify the usage is quite exceptional.[141] More characteristic was the emphasis also to be found in that passage (and moreover, so frequently in Bucer): that the presence of Christ in the eucharist was to be associated with the gift of the Holy Spirit. It is therefore much safer to describe Cranmer as holding a 'spiritual presence' view of the eucharist from at least 1548, and that will be the usage which I adopt.

A further and increasingly important dimension for Cranmer as he struggled to create acceptable formulae for the English Church, was his preoccupa-

139 *E.T.* p. 212 (*O.L.* p. 322). Cf. *E.T.* p. 211 (*O.L.* p. 320).

140 Cf. e.g. index refs in Brooks, *Cranmer's Doctrine of the Eucharist*, s.v. 'Presence, eucharistic mode of'.

141 Brooks, *Cranmer's Doctrine of the Eucharist*, p. 93; Cox 1, p. 61. Cf. similar criticisms by David Selwyn in *J.T.S.* N.S. 17 (1966), p. 231.

tion with establishing English doctrine as a standard acceptable to the whole spectrum of evangelical truth on the Continent, from the Lutherans to the Swiss. Perhaps the germ of this idea came to him from the downfall of the great Archbishop Hermann von Wied of Cologne: after two decades of trying to establish a central evangelicalism which would remould rather than destroy the traditional Church, von Wied had finally succumbed to his conservative enemies after being formally deposed by the Pope in August 1546, and during the following year he had lost power in his archdiocese. Von Wied had been the friend and patron of numerous prominent evangelicals, including Philipp Melanchthon and Martin Bucer, who had worked closely with him on doctrinal and liturgical reform. Cranmer was well aware of the literary feud between von Wied and his conservative cathedral canons. He owned at least one copy of the *Pia Deliberatio*, the Latin version of von Wied's proposed Church Order, and (as already noted) he used it extensively in his liturgical constructions, while his 'Great Commonplaces' included extracts from the canons' 1544 publication the *Antididagma*, a bitter criticism of the Church order.[142] In 1545 Bucer prepared a robust reply to the *Antididagma*, the *Constans Defensio*, and although its first appearance in print was as late as 1613, we will find this work playing a significant role in England's eucharistic disputes in 1548 (see below, pp. 399–403). In addition, a complete but patently rushed English translation of the *Pia Deliberatio* appeared from John Day's press in October 1547, and ran to a corrected second edition in 1548, while also in that year there was a different English translation of the baptismal section; the example of the Archbishop of Cologne was much in the minds of English evangelicals.[143]

It would be entirely in character if Cranmer saw the failure of one reforming metropolitan of the Universal Church as a call to action for himself, who held the equivalent office in England. He remained an admirer of von Wied, and seems to have been in touch with the fallen archbishop right up to the year of his death in 1552.[144] Nevertheless, furthering the unity of Protestantism was a task in which a host of theologians of good will had so far

142 Cranmer's use of the *Antididagma* was first noted by Brightman, 'Capitulum Coloniense', although NB that his theory that Cranmer approved of its content has no basis in fact, and has had malign consequences for interpretation of the 1540s. A good summary account of von Wied's reforming career is Cuming, *Godly Order*, pp. 68–73, but see D. Selwyn's modification of Cuming's reference to Cranmer's *Pia Deliberatio* preserved at Chichester Cathedral, Ayris and Selwyn (eds), *Cranmer*, p. 62 and n. 105. See nn. 154, 160 below.

143 Cuming, *Godly Order*, pp. 71–2, 88–90, although Dr J.M. Blatchly convinces me that Richard Rice, the author of the baptism translation, was not Abbot of Conwy but (much more logically) an ex-Norwich Carmelite and future incumbent of Kirton, a few miles from the translation's place of publication at Ipswich.

144 Cox 2, p. 437 (better text in Strype, *Cranmer* 2, pp. 404–5). Cranmer refers merely to 'the B. of Cologne's letters', but it is unlikely that he is talking about von Wied's successor.

ignominiously failed; if one wants any justification for Cranmer's often-criticized doctrinal hesitations during 1547–8, one should remember this daunting international history of the previous two decades. The Archbishop's unhappy tinkering with the Justus Jonas Catechism may have been one small first attempt to heal the wounds of Protestant Europe; certainly, it was published in the wake of the correspondence which he resumed with Philipp Melanchthon involving the son of Justus Jonas, a correspondence which provides the first public trace of Cranmer's new guise as international doctrinal referee. Melanchthon had already suggested to the Archbishop (probably at the beginning of 1548) that a general 'summary of necessary doctrine' ought to be compiled and published in conscious opposition to the deliberations of the Council of Trent, whose first two years of meetings had ended the year before. In a follow-up letter to Cranmer in May, prompted by correspondence from the younger Jonas, Melanchthon suggested that Cranmer should make this his especial task 'in order that an illustrious testimony of doctrine, delivered with grave authority, may be extant among all nations, and that posterity may have a rule to follow'.[145] This was a compliment indeed from Europe's most distinguished living Lutheran to the Primate of All England, and it hit on the most constant idea in Cranmer's theology through all his years of dramatic changes of heart: his fervent belief in the potential of a General Council.

Back in the 1520s, Cranmer had raged against Luther for apparently treating the authority of a Council with contempt (see above, Ch. 2). Now the idea that he himself might organize the first true General Council since the centuries of the early Church gave an urgent purpose to his hospitality to foreign refugee evangelicals, which had probably begun simply as an emergency gesture of humanitarian aid. Accordingly, one finds this agenda increasingly stressed in the Archbishop's overseas correspondence. He was so excited by Melanchthon's idea of a Council to rival Trent that he plundered the Wittenberg reformer's May letter for ideas and phrases (including those quoted above) when in July he composed two letters to overseas divines, urging them to come to England, and it is quite likely that if other invitations survived, the same verbal recycling could be detected. One of these letters was addressed to the Bremen leader Albrecht Hardenberg, the other to Hardenberg's friend, the distinguished Polish exile at Emden, Jan Laski (John à Lasco). It was no doubt significant that Hardenberg had been a close associate of that great failed ecumenist, Archbishop von Wied; certainly Cranmer referred to 'the venerable elector of Cologne' in his letter to Bremen. Both men were told to persuade Melanchthon to come across at least for a temporary visit, the same constant cry that had gone up from Henry VIII all through the later 1530s.[146]

145 Gorham, *Gleanings*, pp. 42–6; *Melanchthons Briefwechsel* 5, no. 5103 dates the first of the letters pr. by Gorham to just before 26 March 1548 rather than c. 1 April.

146 Cox 2, pp. 420–23.

However, Melanchthon was evidently not prepared to follow up his own initiative; Wolfgang Musculus of Augsburg (also invited to England in 1548) found an easier refuge in Berne, and Hardenberg postponed his visit to England for two years. Even Laski was initially hesitant, but when it became clear that he was under threat in Emden in the aftermath of Charles V's Interim, he took up Cranmer's invitation with relief, and he was in London by the end of October 1548 for a visit which lasted several months until his permission of absence from the East Frisian authorities expired.[147] A further refugee arrival from Strassburg earlier in the month was the former Carmelite friar Pierre Alexandre, lately an evangelical protégé of the Regent Mary of Hungary in the Netherlands: he got a warm welcome from Cranmer, and became one of his principal secretaries, alongside Ralph Morice. Alexandre was an admirer of Martin Bucer, and strongly identified with his views on the eucharist. His new position at Lambeth Palace was a token that Cranmer still pursued the greatest prize of all: the arrival of Bucer himself. Bucer's position in Strassburg was becoming ever more desperate as the city authorities came under greater pressure from the Emperor: his tone in a letter of 3 September to Cranmer was brave, but showed that he was resigned to the fact that a quarter-century of ministry was about to be ruined, and that he would have no alternative but to take refuge in England. Cranmer's response was swift, warm and welcoming: 'nothing can be more gratifying or pleasing to us than the presence of Bucer'.[148] Slightly later, Hugh Latimer's enthusiastic anticipation of the meeting would verge on the blasphemous: Pierre Alexandre told Bucer that 'he earnestly desires to embrace you, and the like of you, as Simeon did Christ'. Yet Cranmer and Latimer would have to wait until April 1549 before they could sing their *Nunc Dimittis*.[149]

As this panorama of international ecumenical possibilities unfolded, equally momentous preparations were being made at home for the publication of a complete uniform liturgy for the English Church, building on all the work that Cranmer had begun in 1538–9 and that had been revealed in part over the subsequent decade. In fact, all through 1548, after the precedent set by the opening of Parliament in November 1547, there had been increasing use of English in the offices and even at the eucharist in key churches where the authorities were sympathetic or could be bullied by the government into compliance: evidence remains, for instance, for the Chapel Royal, St Paul's, Westminster and Lincoln cathedrals and for Cambridge University, to say

147 For Laski's arrival, *E.T.* p. 417 (*O.L.* p. 644). Cf. Hall, *John à Lasco*, pp. 29–30. A letter noted in Cox 2, p. 460n. about these transactions supposedly of 11 October 1547 should probably belong to 1548. For excuses of Melanchthon and Musculus, see Parker, *De Antiquitate*, p. 399, and cf. *E.T.* pp. 221–2 (*O.L.* pp. 334–6).

148 On Alexandre's troubles and arrival, *C.S.P. Spanish 1547–9*, p. 299, and Spruyt, 'Mary of Hungary', esp. pp. 299–301. *E.T.* pp. 346–8 (*O.L.* pp. 531–33); Cox 2, pp. 423–4; cf. Smyth, *Cranmer and the Reformation*, pp. 156–9. On Alexandre's eucharistic views and Bucer, see Gorham, *Gleanings*, pp. 148–50.

149 Gorham, *Gleanings*, p. 76.

nothing of the minority of advanced parishes which set their own agenda of change. No doubt most versions of the officially encouraged experiments derived from Chapel Royal practice (as was certainly the case at Cambridge), and they may have been drafts of the Prayer Book, being tested to iron out faults and perhaps even to gauge consumer reaction.[150] However, if the new liturgy was going to obtain authorization without embarrassing scenes in Parliament, it would be necessary to achieve something like a general acceptance from the Church's leadership. Notably this was not done through Convocation, but through *ad hoc* meetings, first among the bishops and some senior theologians in September, and then for the membership of the entire House of Lords in December.

The September meeting was held in an interestingly unconventional setting, the remnant of the half-demolished abbey at Chertsey, on the Thames between Hampton Court and Windsor Castle, and a mile or two from Oatlands Palace, where King Edward was lodging until his move to Windsor in mid-month. The Chertsey venue may have simply have been chosen because of the general disruption then caused by an outbreak of plague, or perhaps Oatlands was simply too small to accommodate both the Court and a liturgical committee; however, it may also have been thought useful to hold the gathering in a place which had no associations with previous argumentative meetings, in order to have a better chance of achieving an atmosphere of consensus. Sessions at Chertsey seem to have lasted all month, and at some stage a sub-committee went upstream to Windsor to interview the King, probably towards the end when an apparently satisfactory result had been achieved; hence subsequent references (including from Cranmer himself) to the gathering which produced the *Book of Common Prayer* as having met at Windsor.[151] Exactly who attended the Chertsey committee can only be tentatively reconstructed; the seventeenth-century historian Peter Heylyn, who had access to sources now lost, said that it was the same team that had prepared the earlier Order for the Communion. A plausible core list of nine bishops and theologians can be found in attendance at the Chertsey consecration of Bishop Ferrar of St David's on 9 September, while another seventeenth-century commentator, Thomas Fuller, could gather a list of thirteen names.

The quest for consensus at Chertsey can be seen from the fact that a number of those in either list were now identified as conservatives: bishops Day, Skip and Thirlby, Dr Robertson and Dr Redman. Cranmer would later recall this when he reminisced about the meeting: of the 'best learned men reputed within this realm' who were convened, there were 'some favouring the old,

150 *Lincoln Chapter Acts 1547–59*, pp. 14–15 (anthems and incidentals only); *Wriothesley's Chronicle* 2, p. 2 (Westminster and St. Paul's); C.C.C.C. MS 106 f. 493a (Cambridge and Chapel Royal). Cf. comments by Gasquet and Bishop, p. 147.

151 The evidence for the Chertsey and Windsor meetings is well summarized in Page, 'First Book of Common Prayer', pp. 56–61.

some the new learning'.[152] According to Heylyn, the meeting began with a royal letter defining their task of preparing a public liturgy for the offices of the Church, 'together with a form of ministering the Sacraments and Sacramentals, and for the celebrating of all other public offices which were required by the Church of good Christian people'. It may be significant that one of these 'public offices' which actually took place during the meeting, Ferrar's consecration in the setting of an English communion service, was not incorporated in the Prayer Book that came out in 1549: the ordination services for deacons and priests and the consecration of bishops would have to wait until the 1550 Ordinal. The two conservative bishops, Skip and Day, did not attend Ferrar's consecration, and it may have proved impossible to secure their agreement to the authorization of the new ordination rites. Nevertheless, Cranmer tells us that by this stage there was at least unanimous agreement that 'the service of the church should be in the mother tongue'. The English rite which would be the Archbishop's great legacy to history had passed one vital hurdle.[153]

An ingenious piece of detective work by David Selwyn may have retrieved for us one of the documents which also secured general agreement at Chertsey, for the time being, among evangelicals and conservatives; if he is right, he has hit on a vital piece of evidence for the Somerset regime's long-term strategy on securing change in the Church.[154] Two copies survive of a short English treatise on the eucharist, a longer version in the Bodleian Library and a shorter version at Corpus Christi College, Cambridge, in a volume (MS 102) which interestingly also contains notebook material from Cranmer's collections dateable to 1547–9. The additional Bodleian material ends with sections arguing a conservative case for adoration of the eucharistic elements and a moment of oblation in their consecration, even affirming that Christ 'is also daily offered in this sacrament'. The whole work is cast as a commentary to a eucharistic liturgy, to which it makes frequent reference; it is notable not only for its close affinity with phraseology in the communion service of the 1549 *Book of Common Prayer*, but also for the markedly conservative flavour of its doctrine. Now subsequent to Chertsey, there took place the crucial week-long debate on eucharistic doctrine in the House of Lords in December 1548, which is considered in detail below (pp. 404–8). In this debate, much was made by the conservative bishops of a 'book . . . touching the doctrine of the Supper', whose present state, when it was read to the House at the beginning of the December debate, caused them considerable annoyance. Bishop

152 Cox 2, p. 450: Cranmer here referred to the meeting as taking place at Windsor.

153 Ibid. Ferrar's consecration: Cranmer's Register, ff. 327v–328; cf. Heylyn 1, pp. 132–3.

154 On what follows, Selwyn, 'Vernacular tract' (which gives the full text) and Selwyn, '"Book of Doctrine"'. Criticisms by Brooks, *Cranmer's Doctrine of the Eucharist*, pp. 171–2, do not seriously address Selwyn's arguments. As will be seen from my account, I take a different view from Selwyn on the timing of Cranmer's own change of belief: cf. Selwyn, '"Book of Doctrine"', pp. 452–6. The Bodley text is MS Add. c. 197.

Tunstall said angrily that 'adoration is left out of the book', while Bishop Thirlby was even more explicit: he said that the book 'was not agreed on among the bishops, but only in disputation', and he made this point 'lest the people should think dishonesty in them to stand in argument against their own deed that they hands unto' (presumably a slip for 'they had set their hands unto'). The following day, Thirlby further complained that 'also there was in the book, oblation, which is left out now'.[155]

Previous commentators have simply assumed that these complaints referred to the text of the communion service in the draft *Book of Common Prayer*, without reflecting on how badly these references to a book of doctrine fit a liturgical book. Selwyn very plausibly suggests that what Thirlby and Tunstall were complaining about was that at their 'disputation', that is, in the discussions at Chertsey, they had indeed 'agreed' a statement of eucharistic doctrine, but that between September and December a betrayal of trust had taken place: the statement had been cut down, just as Selwyn has observed between the Bodleian and Cambridge versions of the tract, to omit the final sections discussing adoration and oblation. Adoration of the elements had been condemned by Bucer in his letter to Cranmer of 28 November 1547, and Cranmer had already made it clear that he had personally jettisoned the doctrine of oblation in his questionnaire to the conservative bishops in November/December 1547 (see above, pp. 379–80).

All this may suggest a coherent and deliberately cumulative strategy by the Somerset regime. Until autumn 1548, the aim was to keep agreement alive among senior churchmen on the most vexed issue remaining in doctrine: the nature of the eucharist. Thus in the December debate, Protector Somerset retorted to Thirlby's first complaint, in reference to the Chertsey meeting, that 'the bishops' consultation was appointed for unity'.[156] The area of uncertainty had moved on from the theology of justification, ever since the homilies had been imposed in 1547 over the protests of Bishop Gardiner, effectively supplanting the definitions of justification achieved in 1543. After that, the big issue to be decided had been the eucharist (which one notes had been entirely ignored in the homilies); this was a very difficult matter to resolve, given the markedly conservative tone of the great majority of the replies from senior churchmen to Cranmer's questions on the eucharist in late 1547. It was noticeable that when Gardiner was told in June 1548 by Protector Somerset to preach the trial sermon on doctrine which in fact led to his arrest, he was specifically instructed to keep away from discussing the eucharist, which 'with the pleasure of almighty God, shall be in small time, by public doctrine and authority, quietly and truly determined'.[157]

155 BL Royal MS 17 B XXXIX, ff. 1r, 5r, 6v (Gasquet and Bishop, pp. 397, 403, 405). As always, one should remember that in Tudor usage, a 'book' could refer to a very brief document, even of a page length.

156 BL Royal MS 17 B XXXIX, f. 5v, badly set out in Gasquet and Bishop, p. 404 which at first sight makes it appear that Thirlby was speaking.

157 Selwyn, '"Book of Doctrine"', pp. 449–50.

The question had indeed been tackled straightaway in Cranmer's *Catechism*, but in a fumbling and indecisive manner which only compounded confusion. It had then been brought to some agreement in the 'book' at Chertsey, at the same time as the text of the new prayer book had been finalized. During the autumn, however, the government's evangelical clique moved on from the misjudgement represented by the *Catechism* to grow more self-confident, perhaps because thanks to Chertsey they had secured agreement to the final draft of the prayer book. This new mood of aggression was shown by the official assault on reservation of the blessed sacrament (the focus for eucharistic adoration) which then took place in some of the most visible churches in the land: for instance, in Worcester Cathedral, the reserved sacrament was removed from the altar in October, and in York Minster, the hanging pyx was taken down in November. At St Paul's Cathedral, the newly consecrated Bishop Ferrar of St David's marked the resumption of Paul's Cross sermons on 10 November by attacking 'all manner of things of the Church and the sacrament of the altar'.[158] These moves quite deliberately broke any consensus which had been decided by the eucharistic statement at Chertsey, and if we accept Dr Selwyn's argument, by December the evangelicals felt able unilaterally to truncate the agreed document.

The autumn also saw a campaign of evangelical propaganda against traditional eucharistic theology which deserves careful consideration. To begin with, we need to consider an intriguing literary puzzle. On 14 November, a certain priest named Richard Bonner completed the preface to a devotional and polemical work entitled *A treatise of the right honouring and worshipping of our Saviour Jesus Christ in the sacrament of bread and wine*, which was published soon afterwards. One should note straight away that not only was this dedicated to Cranmer by Bonner, who described himself in his dedication as the Archbishop's 'obedient diocesan [*sic*] and daily orator', but that the book came from the same publisher and printer as Cranmer's *Catechism*, Walter Lynne and Nicholas Hill, and in fact it even reused the elaborate border of the *Catechism* title-page.[159] A major concern of this treatise, as will be apparent from its title, was precisely the question of adoration of the sacrament. Not long before publishing the book, this Richard Bonner had apparently been in correspondence with Bucer about the eucharist, receiving a very extended surviving reply from him on 4 September, the day after Bucer had written to Cranmer; both letters no doubt went by the same post from Strassburg.

Bucer's letter to Bonner was an extended argument that the recitation of the Lord's own words were sufficient for a complete celebration of the eucharist: precisely the point which Cranmer had made in his late 1547 reply to the question 'wherein consisteth the mass by Christ's institution?' Bucer's letter to Bonner was specifically aimed against a contrary statement on the

158 HWRO 009:1-BA 2636/11 (no. 43701), f. 157r; 'Parkyn's Narrative', pp. 68–9; *Greyfriars Chronicle*, p. 57.

159 *Catechism*, ed. Selwyn, Introd., p. 87; Hopf, *Bucer*, p. 10. Puzzlingly, the *Treatise* bears the date 12 November 1548 on its title-page, two days before the date of the preface.

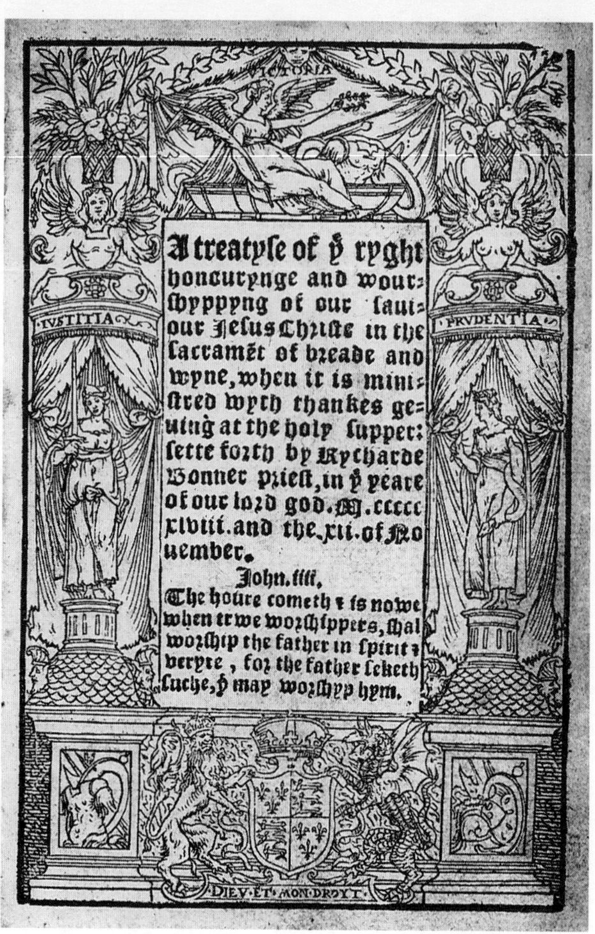

VICTORIA

IVSTITIA

PRVDENTIA

A treatyse of ẏ ryght honourynge and wourshyppyng of our sauiour Jesus Christe in the sacramẽt of breade and wyne, when it is ministred wyth thankes geuĩg at the holy supper: sette forth by Rycharde Bonner priest, in ẏ yeare of our lord god. M.ccccc xlviii. and the .xii. of Nouember.

John. iiii.

The hoũre cometh & is nowe when trwe worshippers, shal worship the father in spirit & verytе, for the father seketh suche, ẏ may worshyp hym.

DIEV ET MON DROYT

29 Title-page of Richard Bonner's *Treatise of the right honouring of the sacrament* (1548).

normative character of the Roman eucharistic prayer made by what he called 'the sophists of Cologne': that is, the conservative canons of Cologne Cathedral who had published their view as part of their swingeing attack on Archbishop von Wied in the 1544 *Antididagma*. Bucer's answer to this work, the 1545 *Constans Defensio*, was only circulating in manuscript in 1548; yet analysis of Richard Bonner's printed *Treatise* reveals that it contains (without acknowledgement) free translations of extensive portions of this defence of von Wied on eucharistic adoration.[160] The tract thus takes its place beside the one complete and one partial English translation of von Wied's *Pia Deliberatio*

160 Bucer's letter to Bonner is C.C.C.C. MS 113, pp. 315–24; for Bucer's letter to Cranmer, *E.T.* p. 348 (*O.L.* p. 531). Cf. Hope/Hopf, 'English version of Bucer's Reply', although NB that this is flawed by Hope's theory that Bonner was writing to persuade Cranmer away from his supposed approval of the *Antididagma*. This idea has no foundation, and is based on wishful thinking about Cranmer's outlook by Brightman, 'Capitulum Coloniense', esp. p. 437.

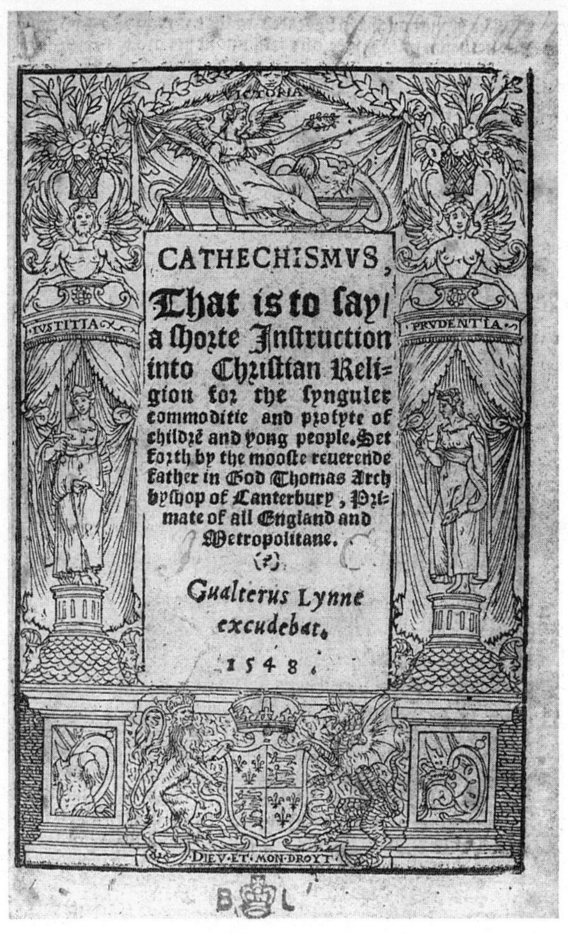
VICTORIA

IVSTITIA

PRVDENTIA

CATHECHISMVS,

That is to say/ a shorte Instruction into Christian Religion for the synguler commoditie and profyte of childre and yong people. Set forth by the mooste reuerende father in God Thomas Archbyshop of Canterbury, Primate of all England and Metropolitane.

Gualterus Lynne excudebat.

1548.

DIEV ET MON DROYT

30 Title-page of Cranmer's 1548 Catechism.

published in England in 1547 and 1548. To make a tangled set of associations even more claustrophobic, a complete contemporary manuscript copy of Bucer's *Constans Defensio* is, like Selwyn's 'Chertsey' treatise, to be found in the Bodleian Library.[161]

Richard Bonner said that he wrote about the exact form which eucharistic adoration should take, not because he thought that Cranmer was 'ignorant of the same' or 'would not provide (as much as in you lay) the truth in all things to be known', but so that his doctrine might be examined and corrected by the Archbishop's 'godly judgement'. He used very positive but also carefully controlled language about the eucharistic presence: he spoke of 'the holy sacrament of his body, and blood, by the which I have said, that our Lord Christ (though through his heavenly spirit also) offereth and presenteth unto

161 Bodl. MS Add. c. 97: cf. C. Hope/Hopf, 'An English version of parts of Bucer's Reply to the Cologne *Antididagma* of 1544', *J.T.S.* N.S. 11 (1960), pp. 95–6.

us his very body and blood', and soon after that, he re-emphasized that Christ's presence was 'by his mighty and most heavenly spirit and by this holy sacrament'. Christ's passion was 'but once for all', and justification was by means of passion, resurrection and ascension, 'by means whereof . . . this sacrament is *called* the body and blood of Christ' (my italics).[162] This careful Bucerian balance of presence with the work of the spirit in bringing it to the believer was the preliminary to defining the nature of appropriate adoration: this should be done 'in spirit and verity'. Outward signs of respect, such as doffing the cap and bowing, were as appropriate to the sacrament as to worldly rulers, but they should be preceded by 'faith and trust in the bodily passion and true resurrection of Christ'; there should be no non-communicating mass at which the congregation merely adored the sacrament, and no elevation of the host. Bonner/Bucer also argued against reservation of the consecrated elements, on the grounds that the presence of Christ was only associated with the holy supper when the words of institution were spoken: 'so can we not say that we do reserve Christ amongst us after the supper, but by the applying of our whole lives to his holy will'.[163]

The likelihood of Richard Bonner ever having existed is small. No trace of him has ever been discovered apart from the documents quoted above, and it is likely that his name was a pseudonym intended to annoy the arch-conservative Bishop Bonner of London. Let us take stock of the web of associations just catalogued. At a supremely delicate moment of Cranmer's public disclosure of his change in eucharistic thinking, we have an unknown individual writing about the eucharist to Cranmer's greatest ally on the Continent, Bucer, with whom the Archbishop had been in constant contact for at least the previous year. Bucer wrote replies to Cranmer and that same unknown correspondent by the same post: this major figure of the Continental Reformation addressed the mysterious priest in terms of remarkable warmth and familiarity, referring to him as 'most dear Richard' and twice as 'brother'. Immediately afterwards, Richard Bonner produced a treatise closely associated with Cranmer, clandestinely incorporating eucharistic discussion by Bucer on the matter of adoration of the elements. The question of adoration was to be a particular point of controversy in the autumn discussions between conservative and evangelical bishops, and it led to accusations of bad faith from the conservatives in the December debate in the Lords. The chances of Cranmer not being involved in this covert propaganda operation are already remote.[164]

However, one can go even further. Phrases and ideas from Bonner's work are actually to be found redeployed in the *Book of Common Prayer* of both 1549 and 1552 for instance, the 1549 emphasis that there should be no elevation 'or

162 Bonner, *Treatise*, sigs Aiii–Aiv.

163 Ibid., sigs Av–Avii, Bii, Eiv–Fiv, Fvii.

164 Cf. the less suspicious-minded account in Selwyn, '"Book of Doctrine"', pp. 456–8. Selwyn has been swayed by the wholly inaccurate view of Bonner's motives in Hope/Hopf, 'English version of Bucer's Reply', pp. 94–8, noted above (n. 160) as originating with Brightman.

shewing the sacrament to the people'. Moreover, one of the prominent themes in Bonner's *Treatise* is the analogy in nature and effect of the eucharistic sacrament with the sacrament of baptism. Considering this theme, the modern scholar who first properly resurrected Bonner's work innocently and accurately remarked that 'the similarity of thought here with Cranmer is remarkable', and he cited a section of Cranmer's *Answer* to Gardiner of 1551 to prove his point.[165] The strong suspicion begins to take shape that the writer 'Richard Bonner' was one of the fleet of chaplains of the Primate of All England, and that his personality slid into that of Cranmer himself. If so, the first reason for his invention was to provide a cover for eucharistic discussion between Cranmer and Bucer in the search for material which might undo the unfortunate effects of the Jonas Catechism. At such a crucial moment, it would not do to run the danger of a correspondence about the eucharist between Bucer and Cranmer being intercepted by the Emperor's agents, especially after the proclamation of the Interim in the Empire at the end of June 1548. After that date, there is significantly no mention of the eucharist in Cranmer and Bucer's correspondence while Bucer was still in Strassburg and at risk. The likelihood is that 'Richard Bonner' was afterwards sustained by Lambeth Palace as a useful fictional front-man who could introduce Bucer's eucharistic ideas to the English reading public.

The work of 'Bonner' was not alone: there was an orchestration of propaganda in preparation for the Lords' Debate. Besides Ferrar's Paul's Cross sermon in November and a stream of more or less aggressive evangelical eucharistic tracts, Selwyn points out two books in particular from 1548 which are products of the government's evangelical circle. One was by the prominent young Cambridge don Edward Guest, and was dedicated to Cranmer's friend John Cheke; again it gave prominent place to a hostile discussion of eucharistic adoration. The other was an English manuscript translation of a treatise by Peter Martyr, who had been lecturing on the eucharist at Oxford University during 1548. The significance of this work is that it is dated 1 December, just before the Lords' debate on the eucharist, and that one of its surviving copies is directly associated with the summary account of that debate, even bearing annotations in the same handwriting: despite the moderation of its language there can be little doubt that it was intended to make the issues clear for Protector Somerset to consider and perhaps enunciate in the debate. This was the careful establishment of a party line for English evangelicals by one of the major figures of the European Reformation. Once more, the Martyr tract made a point of condemning adoration of the elements.[166]

165 Hope/Hopf, 'English version of Bucer's Reply', pp. 100–101, citing Cox 1, pp. 180–81; cf. also Cox 1, pp. 41, 160–61. On elevation, cf. *Liturgical Services of Edward VI*, p. 89.

166 Selwyn, '"Book of Doctrine"', pp. 458–61; cf. annotations in the copy of Martyr's treatise, BL Royal MS 17C V, ff. 49v, 50r, 54v, with the text of BL Royal MS 17 B XXXIX, ff. 1–31. The treatise may have been translated by Somerset's chaplain William Turner. For other 1548 eucharistic tracts, see Pocock, 'Preparations for the First Prayer Book', pp. 53–60.

It was not surprising that there was this careful preparation for what would be a unique occasion: the debate on the eucharist which took place in the Lords in December 1548. The old problem of the Royal Supremacy had returned: how to secure the appearance of public consent for a vital theological change in the face of widespread public suspicion and hostility. Henry VIII had secured changes through various combinations of Parliamentary legislation and action in Convocations and vice-gerential synod. Yet there was now no vice-gerency, and the Church was still divided into two provinces, with their Convocations shackled to the Supremacy since 1532. Cranmer's own Convocation had shown alarming signs of asserting itself again in 1547, but it was only representative of one province, and the smaller Convocation of York was perhaps then still far more conservative; it remains a completely unknown quantity to us at this date. There is no record of any meeting of the Convocation of Canterbury during the Parliamentary session of 24 November 1548 to 14 March 1549, in which the December debate took place, apart from the final prorogation after the session had ended; however, one indication that there probably were at least token meetings of Convocation is the fact that throughout this Parliament the Lords generally avoided meeting on Fridays, the normal Convocation day. Amid this silence, there is no way of knowing whether Convocation gave any form of consent to the new draft prayer book during autumn 1548 or winter and spring 1549.[167]

Those involved in the December debate included the available bishops (the most significant absentee being Stephen Gardiner, still in the Tower of London), plus certain leading councillors; assistants revealed by the record included Sir Thomas Smith, Principal Secretary, who was not merely there as note-taker, since he played an active part in discussion. We have little information about the rest of the attendance or audience, beyond the attendance register of the *Lords' Journals* and the knowledge that members of the Commons were regular and interested spectators. The gathering had its nearest parallel in the Great Councils which had been a feature of medieval decision-making, and which as we have seen were still called for specific purposes in the 1530s (see above, Chs 6, 7). Yet its unprecedented feature was that it took place in the middle of a parliamentary session, and it is probably unwise to try to give it any constitutional label.[168] It was a chance for the most powerful people in the realm to air their opinions on a central question of their salvation, although the events of the autumn already considered show that the result was not going to be left to chance by the evangelical establishment.

167 Cranmer's Register, f. 12v, prorogation on 15 March 1549. It was not unusual for convocation to be prorogued later than Parliament, although NB that the date is wrongly described as Friday; it should be Monday.

168 The relevant sections of the *Lords' Journal* record meetings of the Lords on each day of the debate, without however recording any business: *L.J.* 1, pp. 324–6.

The debate began on Saturday 14 December and extended over four days. The record of it is idiosyncratic, consisting of an abbreviated minute of the discussion, probably composed for the benefit of Protector Somerset, but it is a great improvement on our knowledge of very many key moments in the English Reformation. The Protector began by attempting to set the agenda, ordering the bishops to stick to the question of 'whether bread be in the sacrament after the consecration or not'. The form of the proposition is an indication that the decision had been taken at Chertsey to include a definite moment of consecration in the liturgy of the eucharist; this appeared in the eventual 1549 Order even to the extent of including printed crosses in the text to indicate the manual actions. Although this was a clear concession to conservative sensibilities, Cranmer by now regarded the consecration as of figurative significance only, as he made clear at the end of the debate: it was a sign that the bread was 'separated to another use' – a definition which he would provide again in his eucharistic treatise, the *Defence*. When he first intervened early in the debate, he immediately made a distinction between 'the spiritual and corporal body of Christ'. Further on in the Saturday debate, after his old friend Nicholas Heath had quoted '*Hoc est corpus meum*' to prove the real presence (with a stark simplicity which would have appealed to Luther as much as to any medieval Catholic), Cranmer shifted the subject in a significant manner. He opened up the topic of the *manducatio impiorum*: that is, the question as to whether the unworthy or the unregenerate consume the body of Christ in the eucharist, in the same manner as true Christians.[169]

The *manducatio impiorum* issue was the great gulf between on the one hand medieval and orthodox Lutheran belief, and on the other the churches of south Germany and central Europe which would coalesce into the Reformed tradition. Anyone who believed that only the faithful consume the body of Christ had clearly left behind any notion of real or corporal presence, whatever notion of presence or lack of presence they put in its place. Cranmer made it quite clear in what he said that by now he had moved into the 'Reformed' camp. He took up Heath's quotation, and turned it round: 'All men eat not the body in the Sacrament. *Hoc est corpus meum*. He that maketh a will bequeaths certain legacies, and this our legacy, remission of sins, which those only receive that are members of his body.'

In other words, 'This is my body' was a statement of ownership or identity on the part of Christ, and it was his right as owner to bequeath his property within his own family and no further. Moreover, even before making this remarkable analogy, Cranmer had detached membership of the body of Christ from eucharistic fellowship: 'The eating of the body is to dwell in Christ, and this may be though a man never taste the sacrament.' The underlying agenda of this was once more predestination. Cranmer's long speech on the *manducatio*

169 BL Royal MS 17 B XXXIX, ff. 31r, 1v, 3r (Gasquet and Bishop, pp. 442, 398, 400), for this and the following paragraph. Cf. Cranmer, *Defence*, p. 413.

impiorum was controversial enough to hold the debate to this topic for the rest of the day, with various conservatives intervening against him, until Thirlby (apparently fuming in silence up till now) broke in with his angry complaint about his dissent from the book of doctrine. Since this in turn provoked a furious riposte from John Dudley, Earl of Warwick, it was evidently thought best to end Saturday's debate there and then in order to cool tempers.

Monday began with a reading by Sir Thomas Smith of the 'book of [the bishops'] agreements'; this is likely to have been the Chertsey document. Thirlby returned to the theme of adoration about which Tunstall had complained on Saturday as being omitted from 'the book'; he renewed Tunstall's complaint, and quoted from a passage from Augustine which the paragraph on adoration in the extended Bodleian eucharistic document also cites.[170] Thirlby then made an additional protest because of the omission of 'oblation', and the atmosphere was once more incandescent. Cranmer's first intervention, late in that day's debate, was to support Nicholas Ridley after he had once more raised the subject of the *manducatio impiorum*, with a blunt statement that 'the evil man cannot receive the body'. The Archbishop spelled out again that 'I believe that Christ is eaten with heart. The eating with our mouth cannot give us life. For then should a sinner have life. For eating of his body giveth life.' He was thus making the point that his experience of the eucharist was centred on a true encounter with the presence of Christ, but one which was spiritual and not corporeal. It is also notable that he went on from this point to use the argument about eucharistic presence which Bucer found so dangerous, that Christ's body was locally present 'on the right hand' of the Father in heaven.

As the Archbishop emphasized in a second intervention, the right understanding of language was all-important: 'Scriptures and doctors prove that *Hic calix* [this cup] is figurative, which he often used and *significabat vinum* [commonly signified wine].'[171] This was one of the recurring emphases in his reconstructed eucharistic theology: a plea for sensitivity in distinguishing direct language from metaphor. Cranmer's concern for language had profound resonances for his view of the nature of Christ: he accused those who did not distinguish between metaphor and reality of abolishing the reality of Christ's body, and thus joining with the ancient Manichean dualists in their hatred of the physical. A later intervention further showed how deeply he now felt separated from the Lutheran idea of the ubiquity of Christ's body which had once been the cornerstone of his real presence ideas: equally this led to christological heresy, because now he felt that ubiquity was comparable to the views of fifth-century monophysites whose views had undermined Christ's true humanity. 'Christ is in the world in his divinity, but not in his humanity.

170 BL Royal MS 17 B XXXIX, f. 6rv (Gasquet and Bishop, pp. 404–5, and cf. Selwyn, 'Vernacular Tract', p. 228 and n. 57).

171 BL Royal MS 17 B XXXIX, ff. 15rv (Gasquet and Bishop, pp. 418, 420, the first quotation there incomplete).

The property of his Godhead is everywhere, but his manhood is in one place only. These heretics denied that he was very man.'[172] It was not surprising that Cranmer's thoughts should be turning repeatedly to deviant christology; only a fortnight after these remarks in the debate, he took powers as royal 'commissary' to hold his first full-scale heresy trial of the reign, for John Ashton. Ashton was no obscure eccentric, but a scholarly and well-connected unitarian clergyman, a Cambridge man and chaplain to peers. His lapse from orthodoxy was a terrible reminder of how easily heresy could threaten the central ground within the Church.[173]

The debate in the Lords ended on Wednesday 19 December, and the same day the Commons began debating the bill to introduce the *Book of Common Prayer*; the government was not going to hesitate in its plans.[174] As in most such theological encounters during the Reformation, it is unlikely that any of the debate's major participants had been induced to shift their views, and there is plenty of evidence that the conservative bishops were not in the least cowed by what had been said. However, both they and the other spectators must have been impressed by the evident solidarity of Somerset, Warwick, Cranmer, Ridley and their few like-minded colleagues on the episcopal bench; the evangelical establishment was now clearly determined to push forward its programme regardless of further opposition. For evangelicals, the debate does seem to have been the first occasion on which they realized that Cranmer had decisively changed his mind; this was a point made by several commentators. Among the Zürich-inclined group who had previously criticized the Archbishop, Bartholomew Traheron had words of surprised praise for him to Bullinger: Cranmer 'contrary to general expectation, most openly, firmly and learnedly maintained your opinion', and he noted that among the Archbishop's arguments had been the proposition that 'the body of Christ was taken up from us into heaven'. A correspondent of Sir Edward Bellingham, the Lord Deputy of Ireland, made the point about the public shift in views, also noting the same statement which would not have pleased Martin Bucer: 'Part of our bishops that have been most stiff in opinions of the reality of his body there now leaveth his body sitting on the right hand of his Father, as our common creed testifieth.'[175] When sending his own enthusiastic report to Bucer of the Archbishop's conduct in the debate, Peter Martyr tactfully

172 BL Royal MS 17 B XXXIX, ff. 23r, 29v–30r: NB the reference to Vigilius Thapsensis against Eutyches (Gasquet and Bishop, pp. 431, 440). Cf. Cranmer's comments on ubiquity at the 1538 trial of John Lambert: above, Ch. 7, p. 233.

173 The trial is in Cranmer's Register, f. 73v (the 1549 trial of John Champneys before this is wrongly dated to 1548). For Ashton's previous career and family connections, see *Faculty Office Registers*, pp. 22, 115, 159, 262; Cranmer's Register, f. 406r and *Grace Book A*, pp. 323–4, 345. Cf. Davies, 'Commonwealth', p. 35, Horst, *Radical Brethren*, p. 136, and a probable reference to Ashton in *Latimer's Remains*, p. 96.

174 *C.J.* 1, p. 5.

175 *E.T.* p. 213 (*O.L.* p. 323); Pocock, 'Preparations for the First Prayer Book', p. 56. Cf. Ochino's comments on Cranmer, *E.T.* p. 223 (*O.L.* p. 337).

glossed over the actual content of what had been said, apart from the fairly obvious point that 'transubstantation . . . is now exploded' – indeed, Martyr did not always see eye to eye on the eucharist with Bucer, having moved, like Cranmer, rather further away from real presence ideas than his former Strassburg colleague.[176]

After Christmas, the parliamentary session proceeded in a more conventional form. Not only the Act of Uniformity which backed the Prayer Book was passed, but also at long last the legislation that legalized clerical marriage, in a remarkably grudging spirit, two years after the Convocation of Canterbury had given their consent to the idea. Still the conservative bishops exercised their right to vote against the changes, together with a handful of lay peers.[177] From now on the episcopate was hopelessly split, with evangelicals displaying open contempt for the conservative bishops. The most remarkable expression of this came from a sermon preached in Whitehall in front of King Edward by Hugh Latimer, on 15 March 1549, the day after Parliament had ended: it was one of the most viciously political sermons which survives from him, and it gave widespread offence for which its author showed not the slightest sign of contrition.[178] First came a swingeing attack on Lord Thomas Seymour, under sentence of death because of his intrigues against his brother the Protector; Latimer ruthlessly encouraged the authorities to proceed with the execution, using an extended biblical metaphor which involved casting Lord Thomas's eminently respectable and lately deceased wife, Catherine Parr, as King David's whore Abishag. However, equally pointed were his attacks on Stephen Gardiner (again historically disguised as one of his fifteenth-century predecessors as Bishop of Winchester) and his dismissal of the traditionalist bishops generally: Latimer said that they were neglecting to enforce the new order, and that the ex-abbots among them had only been made bishops 'to save and redeem their pensions' – this did not say much for Henry VIII's probity or judgement, although Latimer did not say so! In a remarkable declaration of war, Latimer appealed to the King directly to 'make them quondams, all the pack of them', and he even recommended their replacement by suitable laymen to be ordained *per saltum*, singling out with little concealment the government's reliable spokesman, Sir Thomas Smith.[179]

Over the next few years, Latimer's call would be heeded: of those who led the conservative cause in the eucharist debate of December 1548, Bonner, Day, Heath and Rugge all lost their dioceses, and Thirlby survived only by being promoted to a see where he did virtually nothing during his episcopate.

176 *E.T.* pp. 310–11 (*O.L.* pp. 469–70).

177 *L.J.* 1, pp. 331, 343.

178 *Latimer's Sermons* 1, pp. 112–28, and cf. ibid., pp. 131, 134, 154, 160–63. His subsequent sermon after Lord Thomas's execution is also said to have aroused popular anger: B.L. Additional MS 48023 f. 351r.

179 *Latimer's Sermons* 1, pp. 122–3.

The English Church reached a watershed when Parliament ended in March 1549. Now it was on the verge of adopting a fully vernacular liturgy, its clergy could legally marry, and its metropolitan had openly declared his allegiance to an unmistakeably Reformed eucharistic theology. Yet this was only a beginning, as was perceptively noted by the Spanish evangelical exile in Oxford, Francis Dryander (Francisco Encinas), when writing to Bullinger: the English government's object had been 'not to form a complete body of Christian doctrine' but was 'entirely directed to the right ordering of public worship in churches'.[180] William Paget, that patron saint of deviousness, recommended minimizing the significance of the changes to England's dangerously uncertain and suspicious ally, the Holy Roman Emperor: 'seem to yield to him, to dally with him, to win time of him by putting him in hope that you will give ear to him'.[181] It is doubtful, however, that Charles V or his seasoned advisors would have been any less able than Dryander to perceive the events of early 1549 as a revolution. Another newcomer in Oxford was Peter Martyr; despondently facing a hostile and unfamiliar world as he began his lectures in a largely conservative university, he both praised Cranmer and sounded daunted at the task which still lay ahead of him:

> Our most Reverend [Archbishop] fights strenuously, and with the highest commendation of all good men . . . I see that there is nothing more difficult in the world than to found a church. The stones are generally rough and very unpolished; hence, unless they are rendered plane and smooth by the Spirit, the Word, and examples of holy life, they cannot easily be made to fit each other. May the Lord grant that among us there may be rightly planted a vine which in due time may produce fruit delicious both to men and to God.[182]

Cranmer now had just over four years left in which to plant the vine more securely.

180 *E.T.* p. 231 (*O.L.* pp. 349–50).
181 'Letters of Paget', p. 24.
182 Gorham, *Gleanings*, p. 74 (15 January 1549). For Martyr's unhappiness in Oxford, cf. A.S.T. 40 f. 883 (1 February 1549). Cf. Bucer's remarks of 1537 qu. at the end of Ch. 6 above, from *E.T.* p. 342 (*O.L.* pp. 523–4).

CHAPTER 10

1549: Commotion in Church and commonwealth

OFFICIALLY THE USE OF the new Prayer Book was not compulsory until Pentecost or Whitsunday, 9 June 1549. However, even before Parliament had been prorogued on 14 March and the royal assent given to the new legislation, St Paul's Cathedral, together with various evangelical parish strongholds in London and beyond, began using the new book; the earliest dated edition is from 7 March. During the next two months, its use spread slowly across the country; Worcester Cathedral, for instance, waited to complete its already truncated cycle of traditional Holy Week ceremonies before going over fully to English on Easter Tuesday (23 April).[1] Cranmer and the Lord Mayor planned a culmination to this gradual takeover with a commemorative Whitsunday service and sermon before the assembled city worthies in St Paul's, followed by a sequence of Paul's Cross sermons on the following days by star evangelical preachers (Coverdale and the Vice-Chancellor of Cambridge). The festivities were somewhat dampened by the failure of Cranmer's chosen Whitsunday preacher to turn up, and by disagreement about whether the Wednesday which was no longer a feast-day in the new book should be commemorated at all; in the end, the Wednesday sermon was abandoned.[2]

The Prayer Book's contents were avowedly conciliatory to conservative opinion, but it was emphasized to evangelical insiders that the conciliation was purely temporary: the book was not intended to last long in its initial form. Martin Bucer, having met Cranmer for the first time in April, was straightaway assured about this point, and retailed the information back to Strassburg:

> I gather that some concessions have been made both to a respect for antiquity, and to the infirmity of the present age; such as, for instance, the vestments commonly used in the sacrament of the eucharist, and the use of candles; so

1 *Wriothesley's Chronicle* 2, p. 9, which talks of use 'in the beginning of Lent'; Brightman, p. lxxviii; on Worcester, HWRO 009:1-BA 2636/11 (no. 43701), f. 157r.

2 *Wriothesley's Chronicle* 2, p. 14: the missing preacher 'Mr. Lydall' may have been Henry Syddall of Christ Church Oxford, to match the Cambridge Vice-Chancellor, but in any case there were two men of this name: Emden, *Oxford to 1540*, p. 551.

> also in regard to the commemoration of the dead, and the use of chrism . . . They affirm that there is no superstition in these things, and that they are only to be retained for a time, lest the people, not yet thoroughly instructed in Christ, should by too extensive innovations be frightened away from Christ's religion, and that rather they may be won over.[3]

Later, when giving his opinion on the revision of the book, Bucer would also acknowledge the difficulties which the compilers of 1549 had faced with conservatism, expressing his admiration that their communion service had been so true to evangelical principles 'particularly considering the time at which it was done'.[4] The 1549 book gave witness to a characteristic Cranmerian principle: one should make haste slowly, and be sensitive to the prejudices of those Christians who had not yet been made conscious of their elect status, but one should never abandon the eventual goal of reform.[5] It was indeed a strategy which had served the Archbishop well in the last decade of the old King's life, but it contained acute dangers for evangelical change. Cranmer was always slow to appreciate that ceremonies and imagery which he confidently reinterpreted purely as educational symbols might retain a very different significance for others, and thus prove a barrier to the evangelical understanding which he was trying to create. Admittedly, he was already aware that he was walking a tightrope in what he was doing in the 1549 book, and that both friends and enemies could misunderstand the outward traditionalism of much within its covers. Witness to this was the last item in the Prayer Book: a careful exposition in homily form (almost certainly from Cranmer's pen) 'of ceremonies: why some be abolished and some retained'. This was evidently rather hastily tacked on to the text, probably reflecting last-minute jitters about what conclusions might be drawn from the liturgical possibilities still on offer, and in 1552 it was moved from the end to the Preface.

In this homily, in the same fashion as in his 1540 preface to the official Bible, Cranmer spoke Janus-like both to those who were 'addicted to their old customs' and to those who were 'so new fangle [*sic*] that they would innovate all thing, and so do despise the old that nothing can like them, but that is new'. Mindless innovation was far from the writer who could resort to his favourite early father, Augustine, in order to criticize the proliferation of medieval ceremonial; yet who also explained the retention of some ceremonies 'for a discipline and order'. Cranmer prudently also put down a marker for the future: these ceremonies 'upon just causes may be altered and changed'. Some might be abolished if it appeared 'from time to time' that they were those

3 *E.T.* pp. 349–50 (*O.L.* pp. 535–6). Dryander echoed the point about the concessions being temporary: *E.T.* p. 231 (*O.L.* p. 350).
4 *Bucer*, ed. Whitaker, pp. 44–5.
5 Cf. my discussion of Cranmer's exchange with William Morice in *Narratives of the Reformation*, pp. 246–7: MacCulloch, 'Cranmer: consensus and tolerance'.

'most abused, as in men's ordinances it often chanceth diversely in divers countries'. The new shape of the Prayer Book was thus avowedly on trial, and as had been made clear to Bucer and Fagius, the criterion for its revision would not be consumer satisfaction, but conformity with 'the setting forth of God's honour and glory'.[6]

For the moment, as the star of an enthusiastic welcome to an English spring, Bucer decided to declare himself well pleased with the underlying principles of the English reform. 'It much refreshed us', he added as a comforting rider to his previous rather apprehensive remarks, 'that everything in the churches is read and sung in the vernacular tongue, that the doctrine of justification is purely and soundly taught, and the eucharist is administered according to Christ's ordinance, private masses having been abolished.' Yet even though private masses had gone, the liturgy's concessions to the past did include the restoration of the (by now extremely suspect) word 'mass' to the title of the communion service, after it had been completely dropped from official pronouncements during 1548: so the service was now entitled 'The supper of the Lord and the holy communion, commonly called the mass'. This was as grudging as it could be without being insulting; it was presumably the only way of avoiding a total breach with the conservative bishops in the aftermath of Chertsey and the December 1548 debate, or – equally important – allaying conservative fears in the House of Commons. Dryander, who had a reliable line to Cranmer through his older friend, and Oxford colleague, Peter Martyr, said as much in a letter to Bullinger: 'The bishops could not for a long time agree among themselves on this part, and it was a long and earnest dispute among them whether transubstantiation should be established or rejected.'[7]

The rite of communion which emerged from these disputes was in fact very far from transubstantiation in its theological intention. It might be dressed up with the old forms, but its liturgical engineering was designed to present the eucharistic theology which we have seen Cranmer develop over the previous two or three years (see above, Ch. 9). This fact has been obscured by later disputes in the Church of England which would have surprised and probably distressed Cranmer; he would not have approved of Anglo-Catholic use of his 1549 rite as a safe haven from the implications of his 1552 rite, and indeed one can only understand the substitutions of 1552 as designed to end precisely this sort of misuse of his first eucharistic essay. The very great liturgist F.E. Brightman did his Anglo-Catholic best to misunderstand Cranmer's outlook in general, and in particular his intentions in 1549; it has taken the work of Geoffrey Cuming and others to disentangle subsequent confusion.[8] The issues were the same as those on which the evangelical

6 Brightman, *English Rite*, pp. 38–45. On the 1540 Bible preface, see above, Ch. 7, pp. 258–60.

7 *E.T.* p. 232 (*O.L.* p. 351).

8 Cf. especially Cuming, *Godly Order*, pp. 91–107, and cf. discussion in Ch. 9 above about Brightman and Cranmer's use of the *Antididagma*.

establishment had fought the conservatives in the months after Chertsey: adoration of the eucharistic elements of bread and wine and their offering to God in the mass. Cranmer was determined to suppress such ideas. The measure of his success was the perception of the 1549 Prayer Book by an intelligent conservative far away from London in Yorkshire, Robert Parkyn: he angrily noted the prohibition of elevation of the elements 'or adoration, or reservation in the pyx'.[9]

At the heart of the 1549 eucharistic rite was a prayer of consecration which elsewhere in the Prayer Book text Cranmer once incautiously referred to as the 'Canon'; he thus revealed the prayer's kinship with the Sarum version of the Canon of the Mass which he had probably taken at the beginning of his work on the eucharist and translated into English. Even after modification the Sarum Canon still provided much of the prayer's framework.[10] Cranmer's end-product had a threefold structure. Its first element was prayer to God for king, clergy and people, which was kept quite separate from the ensuing material, culminating as it did in the petition 'grant this, O Father, for Jesus Christ's sake, our only mediator and advocate'. One can imagine some over-eager congregations of 1549 hastening to fill the ensuing silence with 'Amen', but instead the rite moved straight on to consecration of the elements (emphasized to the extent of crosses printed in the text at the crucial moments of blessing and sanctifying), and it was completed by a statement of the offering of priest and congregation to God.

Brightman pointed out that the old canon of the mass contained a fourfold offering, as set out, for instance, in the stridently orthodox statements of the *Antididagma*: offering was made of eucharistic elements, of thanksgiving, of Christ and of the whole Church. However, he then took Cranmer's revised prayer as still containing a threefold offering: of Christ 'once offered' on the cross, of thanksgiving, and of the whole Church. Cuming usefully corrected this assumption: Cranmer himself made clear in his *Defence* of 1550 that the offering of thanksgiving and the offering of the whole Church were one and the same, and so his 'canon' contained only two quite distinct forms of offering, the first of which was the recalling of a sacrifice on the cross which could never be repeated. In Colin Buchanan's pithy phrase, 'What Jesus did "there" is wholly different from what we do "here".'[11] Even without this clarification of Cranmer's intentions, it is clear that he was determined to remove all association of offering from the elements of bread and wine themselves, a connection with which, as Cuming remarks, 'the Canon of the Mass is obsessively concerned'; various small changes in wording of the Sarum

9 'Parkyn's Narrative', pp. 69–70.

10 *Liturgical Services of Edward VI*, p. 142.

11 Buchanan, *What did Cranmer think he was doing?*, p. 18. Cf. discussion of Cranmer's *Defence*, below, Ch. 11, pp. 464–5. On the *Antididagma*, see Couratin, 'The service of Holy Communion, 1552–1662', p. 434.

text removed the possibility of making such an assumption.[12] In Cranmer's eyes, there is really nothing which humanity can offer God, except itself.

One interesting detail of the 1549 rite emphasizes this separation of the elements from the sacrifice of Christ. This occurs in the rubrics (instructions) accompanying the celebration of communion for the sick. Here the priest was told that if anyone was seriously ill or otherwise prevented from receiving communion, the distressed would-be communicant should be instructed that given true repentance and steadfast belief that 'Jesus Christ hath suffered death upon the cross for him, and shed his blood for his redemption, earnestly remembering the benefits he hath thereby, and giving him hearty thanks therefore, he doth eat and drink spiritually the body and blood of our Saviour Christ, profitably to his soul's health, although he do not receive the sacrament with his mouth'. This makes an interesting contrast with the stance of an important private document which Cranmer would vividly have remembered from eleven years before, Henry VIII's devastating response to the German ambassadors' letter of 1538 on English ecclesiastical abuses. Here Henry had set out four possible modes of making a eucharistic communion, and (exercising some theological originality) he had asserted that one possibility of the four was for someone who was not physically capable of receiving the elements to be shown them, 'so that by seeing them, he may more readily bring to mind the death of Christ his redeemer and make a spiritual communion with a penitent heart'. The obvious difference between these two statements is that the requirement for the elements to be shown to the communicant has disappeared from the 1549 rubric: their presence or absence makes no difference to the communion. Cranmer would go further in 1552 by making a vital omission of the word 'spiritually' from the text of the rubric quoted above: no doubt he feared that otherwise he might be taken as suggesting that such a communion was different from and inferior to the physical reception of the elements. It was important for him to maintain that all communions were spiritual only.[13]

The Archbishop was not the sort of man to advertise his own work, and it remains difficult to know how much of 'Cranmer's Prayer Book' is actually Cranmer's personal composition. The most straightforward task, albeit one which has required an heroic effort of detective work by generations of liturgical scholars, is to track down the sources that he used. One major model already noted was the Sarum rite which had been the most usual liturgical variant in medieval England; this Cranmer used in creative tension with Archbishop von Wied's *Pia Deliberatio*, which itself synthesized many of the reconstructed liturgical texts of Germany and central Europe. To sort out these borrowings entails meeting many familiar names in complex relationships to each other. In particular, von Wied and Bucer had borrowed gener-

12 Cuming, *Godly Order*, pp. 92–3; cf. Cox 1, p. 346.

13 Brightman, *English Rite*, pp. 846–7: cf. Henry's letter, Burnet 1 ii, p. 500 (Addenda, no. 8).

ously in their work from the Church Order of Brandenburg and Nuremberg. This Brandenburg–Nuremberg rite was one of the more conservative Lutheran liturgies, and it was partly from the pen of Andreas Osiander (who, it will be remembered, was related to Cranmer by marriage, and who produced the German ancestor of Cranmer's 1548 *Catechism*). Occasionally there is the evidence from verbal correspondences that Cranmer used Brandenburg–Nuremberg directly; one possible example is the prayer on the theme of the flood (originally composed by Luther) which forms the first prayer in the 1549 baptism service. Similarly, the rite of private baptism seems to be taken directly from the original text of an Order for Albertine Saxony constructed in 1539 and 1540 by the same Justus Jonas who had produced the Latin predecessor of the 1548 *Catechism* out of Osiander's original German text. The 1549 marriage rite, despite its general Sarum framework, also shows verbal relationships to Lutheran rites which predate the publication of the *Pia Deliberatio*. Such features, as Geoffrey Cuming suggested, may indicate that in these sections of the Prayer Book we are looking at drafts which were done in the earliest phase of Cranmer's liturgical work before the *Deliberatio*'s publication, some even as early as the 1539 phase of drafting. However, a very high proportion of correspondences between German rites and Cranmer's text can be accounted for by redeployment of Brandenburg–Nuremberg and other German sources in von Wied's work, which acted as a middleman to England.[14]

There are a few traces of more exotic sources. The 1549 book retained a monthly rite of changing and blessing the baptismal water in the font, and in this there is a sequence of prayers which can be traced to the ancient and formidably elaborate Mozarabic liturgy which was even then becoming rare in the churches of Spain; in the precise form used in 1549 this sequence can only have reached Cranmer via some Spanish manuscript now lost, perhaps in the hands of the refugee Spaniard Francis Dryander. Cranmer clearly liked the Mozarabic prayers very much, for when he jettisoned the regular blessing of water in the 1552 revision, he transferred part of the sequence to the public baptism service. Probably he enjoyed it for the vivid verbal imagery which it contained; this went some way to compensate for the impact of the old visual ceremonies which he was jettisoning from the baptismal rite. Like the people of the Old Law, evangelicals had much less fear of verbal than visual extravagance.[15]

Another source of inspiration which has sometimes been suggested in Cranmer's work is Eastern Orthodox liturgy: one suspects that for some

14 Cuming, *Godly Order*, pp. 72–85; Jeanes, 'Reformation treatise', pp. 161–2. On Lutheran elements in the marriage service, see Stevenson in Ayris and Selwyn (eds), *Cranmer*, p. 196; Ratcliff, *Liturgical Studies*, p. 191.

15 *Liturgical Services of Edward VI*, pp. 118–19, 288; cf. Boone Porter, 'Hispanic influences', pp. 175–6 and nn.; Sykes, in Johnson (ed.), *Cranmer*, pp. 137–8; Pollard, *Cranmer*, pp. 221–2.

commentators, this possibility of one eminently respectable liturgical lineage for the Prayer Book has been a welcome refuge from the dismaying contemplation of Cranmer's theological radicalism with regard to the western rite. Cranmer certainly had Greek liturgical texts in his library, but their effect on his thinking seems to have been minimal: the prayer of St Chrysostom which graced first the 1544 litany, and later in 1662 also the service of mattins, was derived from a 1528 Latin translation, as a misreading of the Greek in both Latin and English confirms. More generally, K.J. Walsh in his detailed consideration of Cranmer's interest in the early fathers came to the conclusion that the Archbishop had 'a somewhat retarded and fragmentary interest in Eastern patristic writing', since most of its theological concerns held little interest for him.[16] Principally and most significantly, the suggestion of eastern influence on his liturgical work has been made about the central moment of Cranmer's 1549 eucharistic 'canon', when the celebrant asks God the Father 'with thy holy Spirit and Word vouchsafe to bl+ess and sanc+tify these thy gifts and creatures of bread and wine, that they may be unto us the body and blood of thy most dearly beloved Son Jesus Christ'.

This wording does sound very like the *epiklesis* or invocation of the Holy Spirit which is a feature of Eastern and other early liturgies; Brightman first suggested that it originated in a similar phrase in the liturgy of St Basil, but later with commendable honesty he retracted the idea, putting forward a number of ancient Western precedents about which Cranmer would have known. More to the point, as Bryan Spinks points out, is that such phrases about the Holy Spirit are characteristic of Bucer's, and also of Peter Martyr's, eucharistic theology; Martyr was actually staying with Cranmer during the preparation of the final drafts of the Prayer Book. When Bucer was later asked to criticize the book for revision, he showed himself unhappy with the fact that this particular part of the prayer could be taken as indicating a change in the eucharistic elements, but he wrote that he would be content if it was redirected to blessing and sanctifying the congregation rather than the elements through Word and Spirit. In the end, Cranmer drastically modified it in 1552, dropping altogether the key phrases about Word and Spirit, blessing and sanctifying.[17]

A rather more problematic task than source reconstruction is to gauge how Cranmer worked on the book and what assistance he had. Very occasionally one can hear echoes in the Prayer Book of probable collaborators, notably Cranmer's chaplain Thomas Becon: for instance, in the final notes about ceremonies, the affirmation of the harmlessness of various forms of outward devotion such as 'kneeling, crossing, holding up of hands, knocking upon the breast, and other gestures' echoes two passages in a work of Becon's from

16 Brightman, *English Rite*, p. lxviii; Walsh, 'Cranmer and the Fathers', p. 235.

17 Spinks, in Johnson (ed.), *Cranmer*, pp. 94–102; Hopf, *Bucer*, pp. 77–8; cf. comments in Buchanan, *What did Cranmer think he was doing?*, p. 16 n. 2.

1542. Similarly, the prayer of thanksgiving after receiving communion, which seems to have no liturgical ancestor, has considerable resemblance to a prayer of Becon's composed for the purpose in another of his 1542 tracts.[18] More startling is to note the passage ending the proper preface for Whitsun in the eucharistic 'canon': 'whereby we are brought out of darkness and error, into the clear light and true knowledge of thee'. This has no apparent precedent apart from a sentence in a work by William Barlow, his *Dialogue on the Lutheran Factions*. By 1549 Barlow was Bishop of Bath and Wells and a staunch evangelical, but he had written the *Dialogue* in 1531 under conservative pressure (probably under Thomas More's supervision) as a bitter attack on the evangelicals. There can be no better proof of Cranmer's extraordinarily omnivorous pursuit of a good phrase which could be captured from the enemy and put to a godly use.[19]

Whatever help of this sort Cranmer received, he should take credit for the overall job of editorship and the overarching structure of the book. There is little doubt that we owe him the present form of the sequence of eighty-four seasonal collects and a dozen or so further examples embedded elsewhere in the 1549 services: no doubt either that these jewelled miniatures are one of the chief glories of the Anglican liturgical tradition, a particularly distinguished development of the genre of brief prayer which is peculiar to the Western Church. Their concise expression has not always won unqualified praise, especially from those who consider that God enjoys extended addresses from his creatures; but they have proved one of the most enduring vehicles of worship in the Anglican communion. They exhibit the characteristic threefold nature of Cranmer's liturgical compilations: adaptation of ancient examples in his own English translation (sixty-seven collects with origins in the Sarum rite alone), refinement of existing translations and new texts from contemporaries, and straightforward original composition, the last element being the smallest proportion. These twenty-four purely original collects include the first two in the seasonal sequence, Advent 1 and Advent 2, and overall the marked characteristic of the new compositions is their emphasis on the Bible, either directly by exhortations to read it (as in Advent 2, which fixes on human need to 'read, mark, learn, and inwardly digest' the Bible), or by an unprecedented degree of borrowings of scriptural phrases. Altogether, J.A. Devereux found thirty quotations from the Bible in the new collects, apart from the allusions to particular incidents and persons which would be demanded by the seasonal form of the prayer.[20]

18 Cf. *Liturgical Services of Edward VI*, p. 157 with *Becon's Works* 1, pp. 132, 164, and *Liturgical Services of Edward VI*, p. 95, Brightman, *English Rite*, p. 708, with *Becon's Works* 2, p. 120.

19 *Liturgical Services of Edward VI*, p. 86 and Barlow, *Dialogue*, ed. Lunn, p. 72 and n.; on Barlow's authorship and More, see McLean, 'William Barlow and the *Lutheran Factions*', esp. p. 179 n. 19.

20 Devereux, 'Reformed doctrine', p. 65; Cuming, *Godly Order*, p. 61.

However, very generally the rest of the collects are witnesses to Cuming's acute general observation that Cranmer 'does seem to require an external stimulus to release the flow of creative activity'; very few collects are redeployed from elsewhere without alteration to improve on the verbal rhythm or shift the theology.[21] Various authors of contemporary English primers brought Cranmer inspiration. Some phrases and even whole collects can be traced right back to the evangelical maverick George Joye, with his pioneering primer *Hortulus anime* of 1530. A number of collects translated from Latin originals derived from a 1541 English primer published by the evangelical printer Edward Whitchurch; these had possibly been translated by Richard Taverner, who had also been so important for the official 1545 Primer. Much was gathered up in that 1545 text from earlier compilations. However, central to the evolution of many collects and other liturgical texts was the fairly conservative primer, drawing closely on the Sarum use, which first appeared from the press of Robert Redman in 1535. It is worth considering one example of this influence in detail.

Among Redman's translations was an English version of one of the collects which would become most familiar to Anglicans: what is now the prayer for peace at evensong. Its Latin ancestor was among the eighth-century texts collectively known as the Gelasian Sacramentary, but in 1535 Redman had already developed and elaborated the Latin original:

> O God, from whom all holy desires, all good counsels and all just works do proceed, give unto us the same peace which the world cannot give, that our hearts being obedient to thy commandments (and the fear of our enemies taken away) our time may be peaceable through thy protection. By Christ our Lord.

This was the basis for Cranmer's text, but it has been modified partly using phrases which can successively be found in other essays at translating the Latin original: so 'us' became 'us thy servants' in an even more conservative English–Latin primer published in Rouen in 1536. The 1541 Whitchurch primer, in a new version of the collect retranslated closely to the Latin, pointed the linking of the last two clauses in the Latin (et . . . et) by 'that both . . . and also'. The 1545 Primer created more emphasis for 'the same peace' by rewording to 'that same peace'. All these new thoughts persisted in the 1549 text, although Cranmer trimmed 'same' from 'that same peace': 'same' was a piece of verbal pedantry pointing out repetition for which he showed little enthusiasm in his formal prose. The further he progressed through the little text, the more radical he grew in his restructuring: again a characteristic feature of his editorial work throughout the Prayer Book. One change indicates doctrinal concern: it was important to sustain the struggle against the idea that human initiative had any place in salvation, so human

21 Cuming, *Godly Order*, p. 77. Cf. also excellent discussion by B. Spinks in Ayris and Selwyn (eds), *Cranmer*, pp. 175–88, esp. p. 180.

hearts must not merely be obedient, but passively 'set to obey' God's commands. Other changes are primarily aesthetic. The latter part of Redman's text untidily placed a past participle ('taken away') following a present participle ('being obedient'); Cranmer transformed the present participle into a strong verb ('that our hearts may be set to obey'). Then 'peaceable' seemed inadequate to convey the profoundness of peace, so Cranmer's habitual pairing of nouns lit up two different facets of a single adjective: 'rest and quietness'. Finally, the favourite evangelical stress on Christ's merits should plead the whole collect before the Father, but to avoid two agents (the Father's protection and Christ's merits) appearing in succession, the Father's protection was placed earlier and reduced to the phrase 'by thee', perhaps also with the intention of describing the Father's power in more absolute terms. This had the pleasing result of bringing a repetition and assonance of long 'e' sounds, which in public recitation would create a dramatic slowing of pace before the introduction of the central idea of defence from the congregation's fear of its enemies. The result can now be set out with italicization of its new material neither present in Latin nor in previous English texts – relatively minor innovations as a proportion of the text, but together with the reordering, a vital contribution to a marvellously tightly constructed text:

> O God, from whom all holy desires, all good counsels and all just works do proceed: give unto thy servants that peace which the world cannot give, that both our hearts may *be set to obey* thy commandments, and also that *by thee*, we being defended from the fear of our enemies, may pass our time in *rest and quietness*, through *the merits of* Jesu Christ our *saviour*.[22]

Elsewhere, Cranmer's intricate scrutiny of both English and Latin prototypes revealed an equally anxious attention to redirecting his material towards his evangelical programme. In this he had the advantage that many early collects were composed in the period following Augustine's clash with the Pelagians, and were therefore concerned to express Augustine's twin emphasis on the majesty of God and on human frailty; this was precisely the right theme for a theological programme which sought to bring England to a lively awareness of justification by faith. However, Cranmer altered texts to heighten this emphasis: for instance, he censored phrases containing the Latin verb *mereri*, which could dangerously be translated 'to merit' and thus suggest a doctrine of works. So in the collect for purity at the beginning of the eucharist, the Sarum text has *ut te perfecte deligere et digne laudare mereamur*, which Cranmer shifts in direction to create 'that we may perfectly love thee and worthily magnify thy holy name'. The possibility of 'merit' has disappeared, and instead the idea of praise has blossomed into a complete phrase. Equally, one finds in the collects changes which seem to reflect that constant

22 Cf. Brightman, *English Rite*, p. 164; Cuming, *Godly Order*, p. 51; Butterworth, *Primers*, pp. 227–8. In the following discussion, Brightman's text provides the easiest means to make comparisons of successive versions.

theme which we have met with in Cranmer's discussions of justification since the 1530s, the importance of defining the right relationship of works to faith. An example may be found in the collect for the twenty-fifth Sunday after Trinity, which from its opening line has given the day the cheerful nickname 'Stir Up Sunday'. In the original Latin of the seventh- or eighth-century Gregorian sacramentaries, the collect asks that the faithful *divini operis fructum propensius exsequentes, pietatis tue remedia maiora percipiant* ('following more eagerly the advantage of the divine work, may lay hold of the greater saving graces of thy mercy'). Cranmer seized on the word 'work' and directed it away from divine to human works. Now 'the wills of thy faithful people' are to be stirred up by God to bring forth the fruit of faith, that is, works. The resulting passage read 'that they plenteously bringing forth the fruit of good works, may of thee be plenteously rewarded'.[23]

In the collects, the saints were to prove a particular challenge of revision. The Prayer Book retained a number of major saints' days, with collects and their own sets of scripture readings for the eucharist, yet it was important that all idea of saintly intercession should be removed from these prayers. Several saint's-day collects are brand-new, and those older texts which have not been completely jettisoned have been altered, although one of the most striking alterations with this agenda comes from a collect not for a holy day but for a winter Sunday, Sexagesima. The Gregorian sacramentary's original had called on *doctoris gentium protectione*: the protection of the teacher of the Gentiles, that is the Apostle Paul. Now Cranmer firmly replaced this 'by thy power': the power of God. Elsewhere in the collects for the saints, references to their life or character are strictly based on information provided in the Bible, with the exception of a detail about St Andrew, his crucifixion: tellingly, this was removed in the 1552 revision. Such information was provided merely by way of example to those being led in prayer, to provide some aspect of the Christian life on which their minds could dwell.[24]

One of the most interesting parts of the new Prayer Book was the marriage service: here the first married Archbishop of Canterbury was scrutinizing a rite devised by generations of medieval celibate clergy. At first sight, the result is a conservative rendering into English of the Sarum rite, but throughout there are small changes and expansions to bring a new warmth and humanity into the service. For instance, a peculiarity of the Sarum rite was that it repeatedly blessed the woman and not the man: this was now remedied, and the groom included.[25] At the heart of the service were vows of the parties which for obvious reasons had always been in the vernacular. Cranmer for the most part respected these words which still endure as one of the most ancient English texts in common use, but he made two significant alterations from Sarum. First, he removed the wife's promise to be 'bonner and buxom in

23 Devereux, 'Reformed doctrine', pp. 50–53; Cuming, *Godly Order*, p. 57.

24 Devereux, 'Reformed doctrine', pp. 55–6, 64–5.

25 Brightman, *English Rite*, pp. 806–7, 812–13.

bed and at the board'; perhaps already the phrase sounded a little racy for humanist ears, although its retention might have stemmed the slide of the word 'buxom' down the scale of respectability. However, he newly added the promise by the groom 'to love and to cherish', and by the wife 'to love, cherish and obey', as the climax of their vows to each other. And for the first time in an official liturgical marriage text, marriage was announced as being 'for the mutual society, help and comfort, that the one ought to have of the other, both in prosperity and adversity'. Few medieval theologians would have extended the reasons for marriage beyond the avoidance for sin and the begetting of children; the classical list of Thomas Aquinas was *fides, proles, sacramentum,* and no mention of enjoyment. However, the Archbishop had at least sixteen years' experience of Margaret Cranmer's society, help and comfort in prosperity and adversity when he and his drafting team finalized these words. This was an innovation which his married friend Martin Bucer greatly approved, so much so that when Bucer was suggesting his revisions for the 1549 rite, he unsuccessfully urged that it should be moved to appear as the first of the three stated reasons for marriage.[26]

We have met Cranmer the adventurous connoisseur of words as long ago as 1531, when he had been set the task of turning the *Censurae* into the *Determinations* (see above, Ch. 3). One of his greatest achievements in the 1549 and 1552 Prayer Books was to exercise a fine discrimination in keeping at bay the worst excesses of humanism in colonizing the English language with Latin or Greek formations. Tudor prose has attracted much praise, often from those who use it as a stick with which to beat modern linguistic practice, but the truth is that prose was as mixed a bag then as at any period in the development of the English language, and that it could be pompous, broken-backed and laden with the showy Latinate jargon of humanism. Cranmer rarely descended to the depths of pedantry, although no one can deny that as a busy man amid other cares he made misjudgements. One can hardly blame him for the subsequent linguistic wanderings of the verb 'prevent', which has caused entertainment for generations of young enquiring minds in the collect 'Prevent us O Lord in all our doings'; for him the theology of prevenient grace was an urgent concern, and worth repeated emphasis in his liturgical work.[27] Less forgivable was his decision when compiling the 1550 Ordinal to retain Sarum's Latin adjective '*immarcescibilem*' in an exhortation to newly consecrated bishops to work to 'receive the immarcescible crown of glory'; perhaps he felt that Oxbridge-educated leaders of the Church would appreciate an elevated style. It took the revisers of 1662 to calm this down to 'the never-fading crown of glory'.[28]

In March 1549, at the same time that the bill authorizing the Prayer Book was getting the royal assent, the city of Strassburg's reaction against the

26 *Bucer*, ed. Whitaker, pp. 120–21.
27 Devereux, 'Reformed doctrine', pp. 53–4.
28 Brightman, *English Rite*, pp. 1014–15.

evangelicals reached its height, and Martin Bucer and the Hebrew scholar Paul Fagius were finally told to leave. Bucer could resist Cranmer's blandishments no longer, and he and Fagius responded swiftly and with relief to the excited invitations and promises of jobs in the English universities conveyed from the Archbishop in Pierre Alexandre's letters. The pair set out from Strassburg on 6 April, and within twelve days were receiving a warm official welcome at Calais, where Alexandre was waiting before escorting them to Lambeth Palace. At last, on 25 April, Cranmer and Bucer met face to face, after eighteen years of correspondence.[29] It was a sign of how much the English evangelical establishment valued this great name of the Continental Reformation that it was prepared to risk the anger of the Emperor and offer shelter to one of the most notorious opponents of the Interim. Unfortunately, the government, plunged into almost permanent crisis from May to December, was slow to give the two great names their due; it was December before Bucer was officially appointed to a professorial Chair at Cambridge, much to Cranmer's embarrassment. In the meantime, the Archbishop bore the financial burden of supporting the two men, and it was a kindly thought of that friend of his youth, the wealthy evangelical Dean of Westminster, William Benson, to make Bucer and Fagius generous bequests when Benson lay dying in September 1549. In fact, Fagius had very little time to make a contribution to the Edwardian Reformation; he fell ill during the summer and died at Cambridge University in mid-November, to the united shock and grief of the evangelical world.[30]

For the moment Cranmer had small leisure to relax with his guests, because he was in the middle of a new official campaign against radical religion. The old heresy laws had been abolished in 1547, and the inevitable consequence had been to free debate and to encourage adventurous religious minds. By 1549 the government had decided that something must be done, but its actions show signs of improvisation and a panicky return from persuasion to coercion. A description by Fagius the day after his arrival at Lambeth suggests that the evangelicals had begun by arranging a series of public disputations in churches against radicals; he particularly noted with approval that these would be conducted in the vernacular, 'so that the people may detect the impostures of Satan in his instruments'. However, sweet reasonableness had failed to overawe the radicals, and Fagius noted that from now on the disputations would be conducted behind closed doors in the presence of those 'appointed by the King for that purpose'.[31] Although he was writing a

29 Gorham, *Gleanings*, pp. 75–80; *E.T.* pp. 217–19 (*O.L.* pp. 329–32).

30 Benson's will is P.C.C. 38 Populwell (made 10 September, proved 23 September); Cranmer was supervisor, and his household officers were executors with Hugh Latimer. Cf. Cranmer's letter to Bucer on Fagius's death, Cox 2, pp. 426–8. Fagius's will is C.U.L. UA Wills I, f. 84v.

31 Gorham, *Gleanings*, p. 79.

31 Portrait of Martin Bucer, from Boissard, *Icones quinquaginta virorum* (1560). The writing-tablet notes the burning of his bones and his recent rehabilitation in Cambridge.

fortnight after the issue of the royal commission against heresy, Fagius's picture of a nervous reaction to unexpected defiance is perhaps confirmed by the fact that on the same day that the commission was issued, 12 April, we have a record of its commissioners sitting in the Lady Chapel of St Paul's under Cranmer's chairmanship; this is indeed speedy action. It looks as if what had begun by being an informal gathering of champions of orthodoxy had hurriedly been given *ad hoc* official standing to act as a legal tribunal.

A notable feature of the 12 April commission is that bishops Heath, Thirlby and Day were named to it, together with the conservative academics John Redman and Richard Croke; out of these, there is evidence that at least Thirlby was at some stage an active participant. The government was perhaps hoping that it might be possible to use the radical challenge to mend fences and draw the chief conservative bishops into action alongside evangelicals against a common enemy. However, the abiding conservative memory of the spring 1549 trials was the fact that the scaffolding for the tribunal had been erected directly over the Lady Altar of St Paul's, so that Cranmer was standing and sitting as judge on top of a still-consecrated altar: in their eyes, a disgrace and a blasphemy as bad as the views of the radicals, even if it had been Bishop

Bonner's officers who had determined on the choice rather than Cranmer himself.[32] The first sitting of the improvised heresy court on 12 April was not a success; the victim in front of it was Joan Bocher, the formidable veteran radical whose christological views seem to have developed dramatically away from orthodoxy in the opening years of Edward's reign, and who seems to have been arrested and imprisoned during 1548.[33] Joan may single-handedly have prompted the move towards excluding the public from later heresy proceedings.

Cranmer had better results to report to his new guests from Strassburg on 27 April, when John Champneys recanted his published views on the sinlessness of those who were regenerate in Christ. An interesting survival among the Cranmer and Bucer papers at Corpus Christi College, Cambridge, is a paper which begins with a proposition in Cranmer's hand about the inevitable condemnation of the sinful, and which goes on in another hand to argue against this, and to discuss other characteristic radical positions; this may well represent a stage in the attempt to win back Champneys by reasoned discussion, perhaps even with the newly arrived visitors taking part, which produced good results. However, Champneys's subsequent career represented an ambiguous success for the evangelicals; he was ordained in Edward's Church, but ironically his reaction against his former determinist views on salvation led him to publish fierce criticisms of predestinarians which were still causing fury to the godly in the reign of Elizabeth.[34] In any case, Champneys was the only one completely convincing official catch out of the campaign of spring 1549. Of two further recantations at Paul's Cross by Anabaptists in May, one penitent behaved in so unsatisfactory a manner that Cranmer forced him to repeat the ordeal. Joan Bocher remained obstinate and contemptuous of her official condemnation at the end of April, and she was reconsigned to prison while the government dithered about how to handle such an embarrassingly awkward would-be martyr.[35] The spring offensive against the radicals did little to curb their militancy. During the summer large numbers of them took delight in attending the lectures given in a London church by John Hooper (newly returned from exile in Zürich), and

32 *Cranmer's Recantacyons*, p. 15; Foxe 8, p. 73. The commission is *C.P.R. Edward VI 1548–9*, p. 406, and a record of proceedings, Cranmer's Register, f. 74v; for Thirlby, see Heylyn 1, p. 153. The commission of 1548 to try John Ashton has not survived, but is reflected in the wording of Cranmer's Register, f. 73v, where Cranmer is described as a 'commissary' of the Crown.

33 A flurry of letters from the Privy Council to the Lord Warden and Sir Anthony St Leger in Kent between 9 and 11 April 1549 may represent orders to bring Bocher up to London: P.R.O., E. 101/76/35, 1st foliation f. 6r.

34 On Champneys, Heylyn 1, p. 153; Ayris in Ayris and Selwyn (eds), *Cranmer*, pp. 149–50 (although he has followed the mistaken dating to 1548 in Cranmer's Register, f. 71v); *Greyfriars Chronicle*, p. 58. The paper is C.C.C.C. MS 105, pp. 233–4.

35 Davis, 'Joan of Kent', pp. 231–3; Cranmer's Register, ff. 74v–75v. Recantations: ibid., pp. 58–9; *Wriothesley's Chronicle* 2, pp. 12–13.

annoying him with their forthright opinions; Hooper felt constrained to publish his arguments against them as a brief tract on the incarnation, brought out on the semi-official press of Edward Whitchurch.[36]

Radical religion remained a problem to be solved, but there was the other religious front to be considered as well. The membership of the heresy commission overlapped with two further commissions for royal visitation which set out during May to tackle the two universities; the authorities must have decided that combatting conservatism was a more pressing need than continued action against the radicals, and the relevant heresy commissioners left London to carry out their new task. It was noticeable that, unlike the heresy commission, there was no attempt in either university commission at a bipartisan approach: no outspoken conservatives were named. Moreover, there was a striking imbalance in both commissions between Oxford and Cambridge men. There was no one on either commission with a purely Oxford background. On the Oxford team, there were only two Oxford graduates, one of whom, Principal Secretary William Petre, does not seem to have exercised his commission, and the other of whom, Richard Morison, had in any case become an early escapee to Cambridge: the most prominent active commissioner visiting Oxford was the evangelical immigrant to Oxford from Cambridge, Richard Cox. Altogether this was going to be a fitting Cambridge evangelical revenge for the leading Oxford role in the Prebendaries' Plot back in 1543.

The new move was co-ordinated to make an impact in both universities at once: the Cambridge commission had been appointed as long ago as 12 November 1548, but it did not arrive in the University until 6 May 1549, two days before the commission for Oxford and St George's Chapel, Windsor, was issued.[37] Both commissions would, in addition to the predictable work of visiting colleges, be responsible for staging a major disputation on doctrine with leading conservative academics, rather as in the initial proceedings against the radicals. Here, however, the topic to be debated would be the nature of eucharistic presence, rather than the problems of christology; the main issues which divided evangelicals from what they regarded as the two extremes were different on either flank. In Oxford, the champion of the now reasonably united evangelical stance for spiritual presence and against transubstantiation was Peter Martyr, who far outranked any native evangelical talent in the University; in Cambridge a homegrown team was capable of performing the task. In Cambridge, the opening day of the disputation was pointedly chosen as Corpus Christi, 20 June. Both disputations aroused widespread national interest, as they were of course intended to do, and at

36 *E.T.* pp. 41–3 (*O.L.* pp. 65–6); the tract is *Later Writings of Hooper*, pp. 2–18, representing a lecture given five days before Hooper's letter. Cf. also *E.T.* p. 232 (*O.L.* p. 351).

37 *C.P.R. Edward VI 1548–9*, pp. 369, 406; C.C.C.C. MS 106, unpaginated insertion after p. 490, s.v. 6 May 1549. For Petre's non-participation in the Oxford commission, see Emmison, *Tudor Secretary*, p. 72.

Cambridge this was symbolized during some of the debate by the presence of William Parr, Marquess of Northampton.[38]

Cranmer was the only leading heresy commissioner not to be involved with the university commissions, although he kept in touch with Ridley at Cambridge over the mushrooming of a serious row about Protector Somerset's proposal to amalgamate two of the smaller colleges, Trinity Hall and Clare Hall. Besides being occupied with Privy Council attendance at intervals in late May and early June, he had other, more congenial plans to enjoy the company of his Strassburg guests and start them to work on an ambitious task. This was nothing less than a plan to create a new Latin text of the Bible to act as the basis for a definitive English translation: he had the obvious team with which to do this in Fagius and Bucer, as outstanding scholars on respectively the Old and New Testaments. Each man would also provide a commentary, summaries and notes of parallels. With this in mind he moved them down to Croydon Palace, which had become his favourite summer retreat, and from where he could join the Privy Council at Greenwich when necessary. Indeed, on one of these occasions, 5 May, he took Bucer and Fagius with him up to Greenwich to be presented to the King, and both men came back highly impressed: Bucer took up Cranmer's old description of Edward as Josiah when he wrote about the boy to one of his friends in Strassburg. It is likely that this was the occasion on which Cranmer revealed the Bible translation plan to his guests, using the additional persuasive power of the young King and Protector Somerset.[39]

Fagius told his correspondent that he was daunted by the scale of the translation proposal, and it appears that to accommodate such worries the team was widened. The proof is in a volume of Bucer's papers now at Corpus Christi College, Cambridge, which contains fragments of the great enterprise: what survives is the draft of a joint commentary by Bucer and Cranmer on the first eight chapters of Matthew's Gospel, plus a translation into rather idiosyncratic English of the same Gospel and the beginning of Luke by Sir John Cheke. It may be for this purpose that Cheke left the Court for his duties as Provost of King's College, Cambridge, that May, not (as John Strype surmised) because he was under a political cloud. A further commentary on Mark by Pierre Alexandre in the same volume at Corpus is also likely to be part of the enterprise, for Ashley Null has noticed that tipped into it is another fragment of Cranmer's commentary on Matthew. This indicates that he did

38 Oxford (late May 1549): summary account in Foxe 6, pp. 298–305. Cambridge: Foxe 6, pp. 305–35. Cf. also C.C.C.C. MS 106 f. 490(b)rv. For Martyr's and Bucer's efforts to reconcile their teaching after the disputations, cf. Pollet, *Bucer*, 1, pp. 263–72; Gorham, *Gleanings*, pp. 80–92.

39 *E.T.* pp. 220–21 (*O.L.* pp. 333–4). For Cranmer and Cambridge, P.R.O., S.P. 10/7/30 (*C.S.P. Domestic Edward VI* no. 272). Council warrants signed by him, May/June: P.R.O., E. 101/76/35 ff. 68, 76, 78, 81, 84, 87 (5, 26, 28, 30 May, 3 June 1549). Cf. Bucer's letter to Catherine Zell from Croydon, Pollet, *Bucer*, 2, pp. 251–6.

more work on Matthew, although it is now lost.[40] This new Bible would have been the ultimate triumph of international evangelical co-operation: a symbol that England was assuming the leadership of a European movement threatened by Habsburg and papal reaction. However, the project was to be short-lived. The surviving Matthew fragment by Bucer and Cranmer already reveals problems. Bucer was a veteran of biblical commentary, including Matthew's Gospel, and he tackled the introduction and his section of commentary on chapters four to eight in his usual professional if verbose manner. Cranmer's section of commentary on chapters one to three is very different in character, written in what its German editor, with more accuracy than kindness, calls a '*Telegrammstil*'. With one or two significant exceptions noted below, its content (in a secretary's hand, with the Archbishop's corrections) is jejune, while the Latin style is elementary and the secretary has blemished the text with spelling mistakes. It is likely that Cranmer was rather hastily dictating to the writer as he looked at the biblical text, under the pressures of other business; he did not show himself at his best in what was for him an entirely new scholarly enterprise.[41]

Cranmer's text does provide further interesting clues about his doctrine of justification and election, as Dr Null's investigations have revealed. Once more these show him facing up to the consequences of a predestinarian theology, and this time not simply in a notebook which was to remain private, like the Great Commonplaces, but in a commentary whose eventual destination was intended to be publication. Cranmer decided to make a special comment on John the Baptist's discussion of the kingdom of heaven in Matthew 3, and described it in terms of arbitrary divine election to justification: 'here the kingdom of heaven is named, in which the Son of God preserves from the power of Satan *those given him by the Father*: purges, sanctifies, protects and leads [them] to him through the Holy Spirit all the way to that day on which he hands over this kingdom to God the Father.'[42]

In the detached fragment of commentary now tipped into Alexandre's commentary, the Archbishop further considered what this doctrine of election meant for the doctrine of baptism. It might seem to threaten both the validity of infant baptism to which all mainstream reformers were committed in opposition to the Anabaptists, and also the requirement which they

40 The commentary text is C.C.C.C. MS 104, pp. 1–131, published as *Bucer und Cranmer*, ed. Vogt; Cranmer's commentary is C.C.C.C. MS 104, pp. 17–34. Cheke's text is ibid., pp. 145–94. Pierre Alexandre on Mark, with a title-sheet in Cranmer's handwriting, is ibid., pp. 197–240; on the interpolated fragment (ibid., pp. 211–14), in the hand of the secretary of the main Cranmer commentary, see Null Ph.D., 'Cranmer's Doctrine of Repentance', pp. 24–5. On Cheke in May 1549 and his translation, see Strype, *Cheke*, pp. 39, 161–4; he was also one of the university visitation commissioners operating in Cambridge at this time.

41 *Bucer und Cranmer*, ed. Vogt, pp. 15–16.

42 My italics. Null Ph.D., 'Cranmer's Doctrine of Repentance', pp. 195; cf. *Bucer und Cranmer*, ed. Vogt, p. 45.

maintained that all should be brought to baptism. With these two problems in mind, Cranmer wrote, in a rather convoluted sentence, 'Therefore God is both the God of our children, and he also has among those elected to his kingdom, those for whom (since it is not for us to distinguish them from the others) we ought no less than the Early Church devoutly to seek and accept in good faith the grace offered in baptism, as for all our children; "for these too belong to the kingdom of God." Below, Matthew 19.'[43] Long before, Bucer had made a rather similar comment in the course of his many defences of the practice of infant baptism: 'If we are to pray to God for all men, should we not wish also to commit to God our children, to whom Christ acted with such kindness? Even if we baptise a few goats, whom Christ does not will to baptise with his spirit, it is only a matter of so much water and prayer.'[44] Baptism was therefore only a means of regeneration for those who were already elect; yet humanity must preserve a reverent agnosticism about who those might be, and hence all should be baptized.

One cannot emphasize enough the point first perceptible in Cranmer's debate with Henry VIII in 1538 about the revision of the Bishops' Book: predestination was a basic and central assumption for the Archbishop, as it was for Bucer or Martyr. Rare indeed was an English evangelical like John Hooper, who expressed his reservations on the subject. The radicals of south-eastern England who expressed their rejection of the doctrine in Edward's reign, and who for that reason were called the Freewillers, would be outcasts persecuted by the Archbishop himself. This may be a cause of embarrassment to later commentators who do not wish to see Cranmer as he was, but Thomas Cranmer, theologian, without the doctrine of predestination is *Hamlet* without the Prince of Denmark. We must also be careful with our terms: to be a predestinarian is not the same as being a Calvinist. Too often the description 'Calvinist' is lazily applied to the Edwardian Church and its formularies in the Forty-Two Articles of 1553, ignoring the fact that throughout the reign, Calvin was a middle-ranking theologian far away, who was consistently ill-informed about what was going on in England. He was respected by his English counterparts, but not in any sense central to their thinking. Nor should one look for the later full-blown double predestination of Theodore Beza or William Perkins in early statements of English evangelical faith, but these should not be understood as being outside the predestinarian tradition in Christian thinking simply because they do not conform to the rigidities produced by later debates.[45]

43 Null Ph.D., 'Cranmer's Doctrine of Repentance', p. 196: *Est ergo deus, et nostrorum infantium deus, et habet in his electis ad regnum suum, quos cum nostrum discernere non sit ab aliis debemus non minus quam veteres omnibus nostris infantibus oblatam gratiam baptismate religiose petere et bona fiducia recipere, pertinent enim et hi ad regnum dei. Infra* 19. I am offering a slightly different translation from Null, but the grammar remains awkward.

44 *Grund und Ursach*, qu. Stephens, *Holy Spirit in Bucer*, p. 224; and cf. ibid., p. 234.

45 For good analysis of early Tudor discussion on predestination, see Trueman, *Luther's Legacy*, passim, and in particular on Hooper, ibid., pp. 215–42. Cf. Stephens, *Holy Spirit in Bucer*, Ch. 1.

It is likely that the Bible translation scheme collapsed after little more than a month, because from May onwards the evangelical regime found itself facing a crisis of public order of which it nearly lost control, and which in the end proved the ruin of Protector Somerset. Throughout south and western England, late spring and summer 1549 was a time of popular 'commotion'. Both conservatives and evangelicals among the wider population outside the world of gentry politics took to direct mass action to express a variety of discontents and enthusiasms, and in large areas of the country these movements turned into rebellion, often thanks to inept crisis management by frightened leading politicians. As a result, Cranmer was forced to play his part in the government's efforts to contain the crisis; one aspect of this was that he and his literary team turned their energies to writing against the rebels, and the Bible project, which might have given England its place at the helm of Protestant progress, was never heard of again.

Already in early May, while the Archbishop was settling his guests into Croydon, trouble about the enclosure of common land had started breaking out in Wiltshire, Somerset and Bristol, and the protests were enlarged by crassly violent retaliation, particularly by Sir William Herbert of Wilton. A mark of how widespread and sudden they then became is that different contemporary commentators confidently ascribed their first beginnings variously to Hertfordshire, Northamptonshire, Suffolk or Kent, and there are further records of them in Hampshire, Surrey and elsewhere. Protector Somerset then frantically tried to undo the harm done through the initial harshness, by ostentatiously seeking conciliation with the protesters; his hand was evident in the proclamation at the end of the month promising redress of grievances, which may have been one factor in producing a temporary calm. However, even as the regime was nervously drafting a further proclamation in early June announcing royal pardons because the troubles had ended, a far more serious explosion in the far west, Devon and Cornwall, signalled a direct challenge to the whole evangelical programme.[46] In the previous year a Cornish mob at Helston had lynched a disreputable agent of official religious change, Archdeacon William Body; now it was actually Cranmer's Prayer Book which became the centre-piece for protest in what was (in contrast to the May stirs elsewhere) a conscious full-scale rebellion.

The chronology of the early stages of this Western Rebellion is vague, but it appears that there was trouble in Cornwall some time after Easter (21 April), perhaps when the deadline for the Prayer Book's use was announced at Easter visitations or synods, with armed crowds converging on Bodmin. One piece of evidence that the trouble may have started rather later than Easter is

46 For the May stirs, see Davies, 'Boulogne and Calais from 1545 to 1550', p. 61; P.R.O., E. 101/76/35 f.74, P.R.O., S.P. 10/9 ff. 91–2 (*C.S.P. Domestic Edward VI* no. 418, and cf. no. 231); Hudd, 'Two Bristol Calendars', p. 132; *Wriothesley's Chronicle* 2, p. 13; *T.R.P.* 1 nos 333–4 (333 misdated: it should be 22 May); Strype, *Ecclesiastical Memorials* 2 i, p. 259; *Chronicle of Henry VIII*, pp. 170–71; Clark, *Kent*, p. 80, qu. Godwin, *Annals*; Foxe 6, p. 245.

that there is no hint of official alarm in London until after the outbreak in Devon of protests at Sampford Courtenay on 9 and 10 June, when the parish priest introduced the use of the new book to his parishioners on the final deadline date of Whitsunday. Immediately he was forced to abandon the book, and the defiant reintroduction of the old rite sparked widespread enthusiasm throughout Devon; soon the combined forces of Devon and Cornwall were seizing control of their counties, their momentum only stalling when they settled down to a siege of loyalist Exeter from 2 July.[47] When the rebels produced successive versions of the articles of their grievances, it was religious matters which overwhelmingly dominated the list, and which produced the famous description of Cranmer's liturgical masterpiece as 'a Christmas play' or 'a Christmas game' – the phrase changed in successive versions of the articles, but it was there right from the earliest which can be identified. Arthur Couratin plausibly suggested that what inspired this memorable piece of scorn was the rubric of the 1549 Prayer Book ordering that when the congregation came up to receive communion, they should divide into groups of men and women on opposite sides of the chancel; this suggested to the rebels the opening of a feast-day dance! Although in fact segregation of seating was a widespread traditional custom, the new frequency of communion may indeed have produced the feeling of unwelcome novelty when people left their pews for the altar, and noticeably this rubric requirement was dropped in 1552. There may have been truth in the claim added in the second and third versions of the articles that not all Cornishmen understood enough English to be able to follow the new service. Bucer later told a foreign correspondent of his that the rebels gathered up all the copies of the Prayer Book which they could find and burnt them in their camp.[48]

The government, with no military force immediately to hand, was thrown into panic by the Sampford Courtenay demonstration and its results. The initial response in mid-June to the Western Rebellion was to continue the policy of promising pardon, in line with the proclamation which had been aimed at the very different stirs outside the far west, while casting round for military forces to stem any further rebel advance eastward.[49] Meanwhile, throughout June, southern England outside the new Devon–Cornwall rebellion remained in what the Earl of Arundel in Surrey graphically described as 'a quavering quiet', but this peace suddenly and dramatically collapsed at the beginning of July. On 1 July the government had summoned a long list of nobility and gentry from the Thames Valley and the home counties (Cranmer heading the list for Kent) to meet at or send representives to Windsor,

47 Beer, *Rebellion and Riot*, pp. 45–59; Youings, 'South-Western Rebellion', p. 99.

48 Rose-Troup, *Western Rebellion*, pp. 213, 218, 221. Couratin, 'The Holy Communion 1549', p. 159, n. 7; cf. Brightman, *English Rite* 2, pp. 662–3, and Aston, 'Segregation in Church'. Bucer to Johannes Praetorius, qu. Vinay, 'Riformatori e lotte contadine', p. 244.

49 Cf. the royal letter to the Devon county leadership, 20 June, ibid. no. 281, and Russell to Somerset, ibid. no. 288).

32 Anonymous portrait of Edward Seymour, Duke of Somerset, from original by Holbein.

probably in order to create an army to go westward. It may have been observation of these agitated preparations among the better sort that precipitated what happened next. With astonishing speed from 7 July and during the following week, mass uprisings swept through precisely the areas from which gentry had been summoned and also north to the furthest reaches of East Anglia.[50] A measure of how unexpected all this was is that in the first week of July, Cranmer had sent Martin Bucer into what would be the heartland of the stirs, to begin his academic duties at Cambridge. Bucer arrived in the University on 8 July, only to wake up the following day to find the colleges abuzz with the news of commotion; he scurried on to Ely to shelter with Bishop Goodrich, only to find himself deeper into rebel territory. In vain a royal proclamation of 8 July abused and threatened rumour-mongers and leaders of assemblies, and claimed that such assemblies were dispersing.

50 *C.S.P. Domestic Edward VI*, nos 292, 297–8, 308. For the timing of the stirs in East Anglia, see D. MacCulloch in Slack (ed.), *Rebellion, Popular Protest and the Social Order*, pp. 42–3. Some clues about timing in Kent are provided by a list of posts in Kent, P.R.O., E. 101/76/35, 1st foliation, ff. 6–8. It is noticeable that there was no apparent difficulty for a business journey from Oundle to Sandwich via Hertfordshire and London between 10 and 13 June 1549: cf. P.R.O., S.P. 46/5 pt 2 f. 11rv.

Large areas of the heartland of the kingdom fell helplessly under the control of great assemblies of people who formed 'camps' at traditional open-air meeting-places.[51]

For the most part, the commotions outside Devon and Cornwall seem to have been devoid of hostility to the government's religious changes, with the exception of the stirs in Oxfordshire: here conservative priests were said to be behind the troubles and some were eventually executed, while Peter Martyr found himself driven out of Oxford and forced to flee to London, because of the insurgents' hatred for what he represented.[52] The further east one goes, the more positive enthusiasm for the new religion one finds among the camps, despite the clear sense of anger which their yeoman and merchant leadership expressed against the irresponsible conduct of the governing élite, whatever its religious complexion, over the previous decade. Indeed, south of the Thames in Kent, Surrey and Sussex, the insurgent leader Latimer (not Bishop Hugh Latimer!) styled himself 'the Commonwealth of Kent' and the commotions there were subsequently known as the Rebellion of Commonwealth. Equally the word 'commonwealth' resounded through the Norwich stirs, attracting the scorn of Sir John Cheke (newly turned during August from Cranmer's Bible project to the pressing work of writing a government tract on obedience, *The Hurt of Sedition*). This talk of commonwealth had been pioneered by Thomas Cromwell's circle in the 1530s; now it had spread down the social scale, and had become the property of humble people who were excited by it and yearned for justice and fairness in society. Their enthusiasm presented members of the evangelical establishment, such as Somerset, Cranmer and Cheke, with an agonizing problem; their own careers, after all, had flourished as a result of the era of Thomas Cromwell. It was quite clear to them that they now faced two different sorts of rising. One shared their rhetoric and was not generally hostile to their own plans for restructuring the Church; the other was as determined to destroy everything that they had achieved as the northern Pilgrims had been in 1536. How could they devise distinct strategies for the two phenomena while still maintaining the normal cliché of early modern government that all rebellion was a sin?[53]

Evangelical perplexity can be gauged by the remarkable efforts which Somerset and Cranmer's circle made to reach out to the eastern camps and start a dialogue with them. J.D. Alsop has drawn our attention to Somerset's efforts throughout the summer to conciliate Latimer 'the Commonwealth of

51 C.C.C.C. MS 106, recto of 3rd unfoliated folio after f. 490; *T.R.P.* 1 no. 337.

52 Martyr, *Loci Communes* 1, sig. cii; *E.T.* p. 258 (*O.L.* p. 391); Beer, *Rebellion and Riot*, pp. 149–51; *Troubles connected with the Prayer Book*, p. 26.

53 For detailed discussion cf. MacCulloch in Slack (ed.), *Rebellion, Popular Protest and the Social Order*, pp. 47–61. On the southeastern commotions, see esp. Davies, 'Boulogne and Calais from 1545 to 1550', p. 60; Alsop, 'Latimer, the "Commonwealth of Kent" and the 1549 rebellions', and P.R.O., E. 133/6/815; E. 134/30,31 ELIZ/Mich. 19. Cf. Cheke on commonwealth, Holinshed, ed. Ellis, 3, pp. 989–90, and on evangelicals in the rebellion, ibid., pp. 1005, 1008–9.

Kent'. Despite the fury which this strategy aroused among the Kentish gentry establishment, it seems to have prevented the situation in Kent degenerating like the tragic official mishandling of the camps in Norfolk, which turned the stirs there towards full-scale rebellion, military clashes and massacre. Also in Kent, a later joke of Cranmer's reveals that his long-suffering clerical protégé Richard Turner preached twice in the camp at Canterbury, 'for the which the rebels would have hanged him'; much else might be revealed by the survival of other chance strays of evidence.[54] Equally striking are evangelical links with Robert Kett's rebels in Norfolk. Just like Turner at Canterbury, the leading Cambridge don (and Norwich local boy made good) Dr Matthew Parker preached to the assembled camp at Mousehold; later as Elizabeth's Archbishop of Canterbury, he told a good story about his escape from their anger at his rebukes to them. Also manning the sermon rota at Mousehold was the popular Norwich preacher on the Cathedral staff, Dr John Barret, a former Carmelite and Cambridge contemporary of Cranmer and John Bale. Barret's spiritual journey had been oddly similar to Cranmer's: an evangelical conversion about 1533 and a later rejection of Luther's eucharistic theology for spiritual presence belief.[55]

At the centre of the rebel counsels at Norwich was a third preacher, one Robert Watson, a man whose mystery deepens the more that one learns about him. John Strype says, without giving his sources, that Watson was Cranmer's steward under Henry VIII, and he was certainly described officially as a priest of the Archbishop's household when Cranmer gave him a plum Kentish benefice in 1550.[56] Under Henry VIII he had been a belligerent and effective opponent of the conservative Bishop Rugge of Norwich; his long-established leading role in Norwich as a charismatic popular preacher, in the same mould as his old friend John Barret, was confirmed on the very eve of the commotion in Norfolk, when on 28 June 1549 he was granted a prebend in Norwich Cathedral despite not being a priest 'and even twice married' – a startling clause to find in royal letters patent. His equally intriguing later career need not detain us here, but in the 1549 Norwich commotions he was one of the trio of leading Norwich worthies (including the mayor) who were chosen by popular vote as respectable figureheads for the stirs, and whose role in the whole affair remains prominent even in the sanitized narrative written later by Nicholas Sotherton. Watson and his fellows were only the most exalted examples of local office-holders hastening to join the rebel ranks, with a general sense that this was the best of way of aiding the King and his commonwealth against the misrule of local magnates. The official rationale

54 Alsop, 'Latimer, the 'Commonwealth of Kent' and the 1549 rebellions'; Cox 2, p. 439.

55 For Barret's spiritual odyssey, see Watson, *Aetiologia* ff. 29v–30r; cf. Foxe's anecdote about him and Cranmer, Foxe 8, p. 5, and for the facts of his role in Norwich albeit with misleading comment, Sheppard, 'Reformation and the Citizens of Norwich', p. 51. Cf. also Fines, *Register*, s.v. Barret, John.

56 Strype, *Cranmer* 2, p. 181; Cranmer's Register, f. 412v.

that they transmitted to posterity for their behaviour was that they co-operated 'to keep the people in better order during answer from the Prince what else they might further do'. Certainly they fell out with Kett as events escalated out of control, and were then imprisoned by him, but their actions attracted scornful comment during the rising itself in Cheke's *Hurt of Sedition*, and subsequently needed a good deal of explaining.[57]

One should not expect Cranmer personally to be involved in such probings of the rebel camps; he was a member of the government, and naturally he returned from Croydon to Lambeth to take his part in Privy Council action in the crisis. He was much involved in government business and a frequent signatory of Council letters from Richmond and Westminster during July and August; at the end of that period, Bucer noted that because of the rebellions the Archbishop was still far too busy to have time to further the career prospects of another young foreigner, who had so far been kicking his heels at Lambeth Palace for several weeks.[58] By the middle of July Cranmer and his colleagues were beginning to recover their nerve after their initial shock at the general explosion; between 16 and 18 July they launched a major initiative to make official contacts with the various rebel camps from Canterbury to Norwich, and to seize the propaganda offensive. Commissioners were sent with offers of pardon and a proclamation promising redress for grievances but also issuing solemn threats. For the most part their contacts succeeded in stilling trouble: the home counties and Sussex were quiet by the beginning of August, and only in East Anglia did the ineptitude of government representatives provoke a confrontation which turned into a rebellion to match the carnage in the West Country, leaving the label Kett's Rebellion to posterity.[59]

In London the issue of the royal proclamation formed part of a declaration of martial law on 18 July, of which the liturgical counterpart followed on the Sunday (21 July). The contrast with Cranmer's invisibility during the Pilgrimage of Grace thirteen years before is striking. In effect, he took over as Bishop of London; by spring and summer 1549 Bishop Bonner was increas-

57 For Watson's role in Sotherton's narrative, see 'Commoyson', ed. Beer, pp. 82, 88. Prebend grant: *C.P.R. Edward VI 1548–9*, p. 178. Early in Edward's reign Watson was given a national preaching licence, being vaguely styled 'Professor of Divinity' rather than being attributed a university degree: P.R.O., S.P. 10/2/34 f. 116 (*C.S.P. Domestic Edward VI* no. 74). Cf. also Elton, *Policy & Police*, pp. 138–9. On office-holders in the rebellion, see MacCulloch in Slack (ed.), *Rebellion, Popular Protest and the Social Order*, pp. 48–52. Cheke: Holinshed, ed. Ellis, 3, pp. 997–8.

58 *E.T.* pp. 353–4 (*O.L.* pp. 541–2); cf. C.C.C.C. MS 113 pp. 1–3, and evidence of Cranmer's consultations with Petre at Lambeth during August: Emmison, *Tudor Secretary*, p. 73.

59 *T.R.P.* 1 no. 339; for negotiations at Canterbury, P.R.O., E. 101/76/35, 1st foliation, f. 6v, and H.M.C. *Hatfield* 1, p. 54 (18 July 1549, there misdated to 1548); cf. also E. 101/76/35, 2nd foliation f. 111 for notes of payments in negotiations with rebels. On pacification generally, see Sir John Markham to the Earl of Rutland, H.M.C. *12th Report* 4, pp. 41–2.

ingly withdrawing from presiding at public events that, in less controversial times, he might have been expected to lead, and the vacuum had to be filled. As he had done for the inauguration of the new Prayer Book on Whitsunday, the Archbishop brusquely commandeered St Paul's Cathedral (Bonner's comments on either event are not recorded), and he proceeded vigorously to use the occasion both to launch the official Church line on the current rebellions, and also to restate the agenda for liturgical change contained in the new Prayer Book. After preaching to a crowd which included the city leadership, he personally led the singing of his litany, ending it with a freshly composed collect taking up the theme of repentance for the plague of rebellion which had dominated his sermon. Then he celebrated communion, pointedly wearing a cope and silk cap rather than eucharistic vestments, not even emphasizing his episcopal rank with a mitre or traditional crozier; afterwards his chaplain, John Joseph, repeated the gist of the sermon to an overflow crowd at Paul's Cross. Cranmer again hijacked Bonner's episcopal stall, on Saturday 10 August, to celebrate Lord Russell's relief of Exeter, preaching a blistering attack on the papistry of the western rebels; he had appointed himself again for Saturday 31 August, but in the end he sent Joseph instead, with much the same message.[60]

Cranmer's great demonstration of 21 July may be considered a success, since his sermon drew the frank admiration of the chronicler Charles Wriothesley, not normally an enthusiast for evangelical antics, and the even less susceptible Greyfriars Chronicler was at least impressed by the Archbishop's personal control of events. It was a reward for effort: Cranmer had put an extraordinary degree of preparation into this address, because of the vital task which it had to perform. As with the abortive biblical translation, it was to his chief Continental allies that he turned for help and ideas, not just for this sermon, but also for other material to combat the commotions: Bucer and Bernardino Ochino were also set to work to write about rebellion and sedition.[61] For the 21 July sermon, it was Ochino's compatriot Peter Martyr, who had accompanied him to England in 1547, who was Cranmer's principal collaborator. The sequence of evolution seems to have been that Cranmer first scribbled some still surviving notes in his own hand, other notes were prepared and a translation of all these was handed over to Martyr (who, it will be remembered, had just taken to his heels from Oxford for the safety of London). Martyr produced two sermons in Latin on the theme of rebellion; Cranmer drastically modified Martyr's efforts and turned them into the existing unified text, which bears a clear relationship to Wriothesley's description of the 21 July sermon. It represents the nearest remaining approximation to the text of a sermon preached by the Archbishop which we possess from his entire preaching career. With the collect added as a tailpiece

60 *Greyfriars Chronicle*, pp. 59–62; *Wriothesley's Chronicle* 2, pp. 16–18. Foxe 5, p. 745 sees Bonner's withdrawal from public events as deliberate.

61 See McNair, 'Ochino on sedition', passim.

for use either with the sermon itself or with the litany, it was intended for subsequent general publication as an extra *ad hoc* homily.[62] Although no version survives in print, there is no reason to suppose that it was not given wide circulation, and indeed it may have formed the basis of some of the preaching which Cranmer's associates took to the rebel camps.

Cranmer's final text, which evolved from his notes and Martyr's drafts, reflected the agonizing which the evangelicals were experiencing about what was happening, and indeed it was punctuated dialogue-style with Cranmer's answers to current worries, such as to the proposition that 'the gentlemen have done the commons great wrong, and things must needs be redressed'. Throughout, Cranmer made no effort to address the western rebels. His earliest notes on rebellion had already pictured the westerners as a hostile force external to his godly but misled audience, and he had also followed the initial official line about the July stirs by attempting to pin the blame for them on the west: 'these tumults first were excitated by the papists and others which came from the western camp, to the intent, that by sowing division among ourselves, we should not be able to impeach them'. The Archbishop thought better of leaving this divisive message in the final sermon text, perhaps sensing that in any case in eastern England it was proving too wide of the mark as an explanation to be convincing.[63] Instead he concentrated on creating a unified national atmosphere of sorrow. He represented himself as duty-bound to break through his most natural impulse, which like Job at the lowest of his troubles would be to keep a blank silence: the preacher was forced to take on the mantle of a prophet for the sake 'not only of a worldly kingdom and most noble realm, but also the eternal damnation of innumerable souls'.

After this, Cranmer's message of repentance must be addressed both to governors and governed, using an image of the rebellion as a retributive plague sent by God: a delicate task for an official sermon even in Edwardian England, where something of a genre of criticizing magisterial conduct was already developing among evangelical preachers. Cranmer avoided possible pitfalls by the nature of his first criticism to himself and his fellow-magistrates: we had been at fault for being too soft in punishing crime and sin! Immediately he widened the attack to a sin which affected both rulers and ruled: greed. This was a bold move, since as he acknowledged in his rhetorical questions greed among the wealthy and powerful was one of the themes of the protests; Cranmer did not shirk specifying the evils of unjust enclosures of land, which Protector Somerset's circle had already made a central theme of

62 On the surviving documents, see C.C.C.C. MS 102, pp. 483–541, some of which is published in Cox 2, pp. 188–202 (where the text discussed in succeeding paragraphs can be found); there is further material in CC.C.C. MS 340. Useful discussion of them, and of Cranmer's answer to the Western rebels, is in Vinay, 'Riformatori e lotte contadine'.

63 Cf. on the accusation of conservative involvement, MacCulloch in Slack (ed.), *Rebellion, Popular Protest and the Social Order*, pp. 60–61, and *C.S.P. Domestic Edward VI*, nos 327–8.

its attempt to mollify popular discontents. His answer was to shift the ground by pleading still greater themes: national security and the obedience demanded by God to rulers. The greed of the lower orders was worse than the admitted evil of their superiors, because it was covetousness yoked to disobedience, which was a revolt against God: here he coloured his case with an abusive caricature of the rebel leadership which was largely reworked material from a royal proclamation of 8 July.[64]

Having established this point to his own satisfaction, the entire second half of Cranmer's sermon was addressed to those of his audience who regarded themselves as evangelicals. Although Cranmer also acknowledged that 'the gospel of God now set forth to the whole realm is of many so hated, that it is reject, refused, reviled and blasphemed', it is a significant comment on his positive estimate of the impact of the Reformation that he felt able to adopt this strategy. He called evangelicals to see the implications of their faith, which could so easily be proclaimed yet so easily be skin-deep, and compared them to the chosen people of ancient Israel who had had the same experience, leading to repeated catastrophes. Interestingly, he then updated the historical parallels to the present day, by pointing his audience to the example of evangelical Germany, which as a result of its superficial religion was suffering the disaster of Charles V's Interim: a current allusion which he left hanging in the air unnamed but unmistakeable.[65] All this was the prelude to the final call to repentance, which could lead into the penitential rite of the litany, and his specially composed collect.

Altogether there is much to confuse posterity in the governing classes' attempts to find the right method of dealing with the 1549 stirs outside Devon and Cornwall, particularly in the developed crisis which government mishandling provoked in Norfolk during August. We have already considered some evangelical interventions in the rebel camps: it is worth noting that conservative Norfolk magnates like Bishop Rugge, Sir Richard Southwell and even the King's half-sister, the Lady Mary, vied with the evangelicals in trying their hand at manipulating the baffling act of self-assertion by the lower orders which the camps represented. Neither élite faction could claim success in its efforts, and the resulting military catastrophes, first in the city of Norwich on 31 July, and later on Mousehold Heath on 27 August, meant death for hundreds if not thousands of well-meaning demonstrators.[66] The painful ambiguity for the evangelicals shows through in their comments on

64 Cf. Cox 2, p. 194, with *T.R.P.* 1 no. 337.

65 Cox 2, p. 199 and cf. n. 1 there, which has promulgated the idea that the allusion is to the 1524–5 German peasant rebellions. The Interim is indicated by the phrasing and the context; the 1524–5 rebellions are mentioned later in the text, ibid. pp., 199–200.

66 On Rugge, 'Scudamore', ed. Brigden, pp. 90–91. On Southwell, B.L. Additional MS 48023 f. 351r; P.R.O., E. 351/221; Strype, *Ecclesiastical Memorials* 2 i, p. 536; MacCulloch in Slack (ed.), *Rebellion, Popular Protest and the Social Order*, pp. 74–5. On Mary, ibid., pp. 60–61.

the commotions of eastern England. Ochino's tract on the rebellions among Cranmer's papers, a lively dialogue in his own Tuscan dialect and with an equally lively English translation, is noticeably sympathetic to the grievances of those who had raised the stirs, despite its exclamations about sedition, and presumably this acute observer was reflecting what his English evangelical friends told him.

Likewise one notes the unhappy evasiveness of Cranmer's chaplain, Thomas Becon, about conservative charges that the eastern risings were all the fault of the evangelicals themselves, and that this was what one should expect from such subversive religion. Writing in a treatise of 1550, dedicated to the Norfolk magnate Sir John Robsart, whose daughter that same year married the son of the man who had massacred the Mousehold rebels, the best that Becon could do was the nervously strident assertion 'I am sure the very rebels themselves will confess . . . that the preachers were not *the authors nor provokers* of their commotion'. This was not the same as saying that the likes of Turner, Parker, Barret and Watson had not been involved in what had happened. It was common also for evangelicals, commenting in retrospect on 1549, to build on Cranmer's point in his rebellion homily and admit, like Ochino, that the commotions had been at least understandable, given the greed and injustice exhibited by many magistrates and gentlemen; this admission went significantly beyond preachers' propensity in every age to identify sin and to be against it.[67]

By comparison, the Western Rebellion was a relatively straightforward matter for Cranmer and fellow-clergy to define, even though it was a major military headache for his colleagues in government; it simply represented the sin and ignorance which one expects from agents of Antichrist. Cranmer turned his hand to writing an answer to one of the final versions of the Westerners' articles drawn up at the end of July, taking each rebel demand in turn and refuting it in detail.[68] In its final form, prepared for publication, this work can be dated quite precisely to November 1549–January 1550 because of its references to two rebel leaders being poised between condemnation and execution, but the content was probably more or less complete during the summer. It is uncertain whether an earlier version of it had ever reached the rebels, whose articles had already received extensive bombardment by the evangelical establishment. Protector Somerset himself had produced a brief answer, and a longer vituperative piece had been provided by the Devon evangelical Philip Nichols, probably at the request of the leading Devon

67 McNair, 'Ochino on sedition', esp. pp. 44–5; *Becon's Works* 2, pp. 596, 598–9 (my italics); cf. remarks by Philip Gerrard, B.L. Royal MS 17B XL f. 7r, and by Anthony Gilby and Robert Crowley, qu. Davies, 'Commonwealth', pp. 353, 379. Contrast also the frontal assault on conservative charges by Hooper, *Early Writings*, pp. 459–61, with Hooper's comments during the troubles, *E.T.* p. 42 (*O.L.* p. 66); for an example of charges by Richard Smith, Strype, *Ecclesiastical Memorials* 2 i p. 65.

68 Cox 2, pp. 163–87; C.C.C.C. MS 102, pp. 337f is the original corrected draft.

activist against the rebels, Sir Peter Carew. Nichols's work, certainly composed and issued in the summer, shows a relationship to Cranmer's work, sharing with his tract the same format of article and response, and also some citations on the subject of reception of communion. However, it is generally much more polite, even wheedling, since it was published before the rebels had been defeated, with conciliation or persuasion in mind; in any case Nichols was addressing his own countrymen, many of whom he had known for years.[69]

By contrast, it must be said that the Archbishop's relief at addressing a rebellion meriting unambiguous condemnation resulted in a document which, from the moment of its opening address to the 'ignorant men of Devonshire and Cornwall', is monotonous and unattractive in its shrill hostility. The surviving copy of Cranmer's tract is marked up ready for the printer, but it seems never to have been put into print at the time, which may reflect a recognition that six months after the suppression of the Western Rebellion it might do more harm than good. One notes, for instance, the frank personal abuse which the Archbishop directed towards the rebels' clerical heroes, Dr Moreman and Dr Crispin, and also the relish of his final contemptuous condemnation of rebel leaders under sentence of execution; this contrasts with circumspect remarks on these individuals by Nichols while the rebellion was still running its course, a stage at which such abuse might have been even more counter-productive.[70] Perhaps the rebels' curt dismissal of his liturgical endeavours particularly aroused Cranmer's annoyance; certainly his treatment of their 'Christmas game' article is a fine piece of abuse which turns round the jibe on to the old Latin service-books, and which indeed descends to a scatological joke about St Martin and the Devil which the Archbishop's Victorian editor found too appalling to print in full.[71] However, one of the main themes of his tract was a much more long-standing – indeed lifelong – concern of his: the importance of true councils of the Church and the medieval Church's misuse of its development of canon law. This was prompted by the first of the rebel articles, which demanded that 'all the general councils, and holy decrees of our forefathers' should be 'observed, kept and performed'.

For Cranmer, who had spent so many hours poring over and annotating his copy of Merlin's great compendium on the councils, *Quattuor Conciliorum Generalium*, this demand was a red rag to a bull, although his rush to deal with it also got his tract off to a rather spluttering and untidy start. Here was

69 For discussion of the date of both Articles and Cranmer's Answer, see Rose-Troup, *Western Rebellion*, pp. 219–23; comparison with the tract printed ibid., Appendix K, which likewise omits discussion of a sixteenth rebel article, suggests a composition date in July. For links between Nichols's and Cranmer's text, cf. *Troubles connected with the Prayer Book*, pp. 157–8 with Cox 2, p. 174. For Nichols's authorship rather than the traditional ascription to Nicholas Udall, see Youings, 'South-Western Rebellion', p. 115, and for his links to Carew, Garrett, *Marian Exiles*, p. 237.

70 Cf. *Troubles connected with the Prayer Book*, pp. 179–80 with Cox 2, pp. 183–4, 187.

71 Cox 2, p. 180.

ignorance indeed! How many of them knew what the councils actually said? As far back as February 1536 Cranmer had used papal canon law to make the then very precocious claim that the Pope was Antichrist, so he was saying nothing very novel in 1549 when he told the rebels that most of canon law had been constructed for the Pope's 'own advancement, glory and lucre, and to make him and his clergy governors of the whole world, and to be exempted from all princes' laws, and to do what they list'. Just as in the 1530s, he had no hesitation in labelling the papacy as a source of heresy, not merely of error, and he returned to the systematized collections of extracts from canon law which he had prepared in the early 1530s to collect ammunition for his pamphlet.[72] Repeatedly in the text he returned to these themes. It was a useful weapon against those who appealed to tradition, to keep reminding them how the details of authentically ancient tradition betrayed them: so Cranmer delighted in listing ancient sources, and even a papal decree, which demanded more frequent communion than the single yearly Easter communion in one kind which their fifth article stipulated.[73]

Given the bitter remarks about papistry which ran through all the government responses to the western rebel articles, it was not surprising that the position of Bishop Bonner of London was now becoming untenable. It was no coincidence that on 10 August, the day on which Cranmer used St Paul's to preach on the theme of popish priests after the defeat of the western rebels, Bonner was also haled before the Privy Council and given a set of 'private injunctions' which included the demand that three weeks afterwards he should preach at Paul's Cross 'exhorting the people to obedience'; a similar order to Stephen Gardiner to preach a set-piece sermon had precipitated Gardiner's downfall in June 1548. A second demand was that on the next ensuing feast-day Bonner should celebrate communion in his cathedral according to the new rite. This he did the following Sunday, but the fact that his presidency at eucharist and litany was done 'discreetly and sadly', in the opinion of the very conservative Greyfriars Chronicler, is a fairly sure indicator of the way in which he fulfilled the government's requirement: Bonner would muster whatever traditional splendour the Cathedral could import to the new book in order to subvert its evangelical purpose.[74]

Bonner was therefore being perfectly consistent in the strategy of his Paul's Cross sermon on 1 September: he used the occasion to condemn rebellion, but also to commend attendance at the new communion by the back-handed means of a robust affirmation of the real presence in the eucharist, claiming that neglect of this doctrine was the reason for widespread resistance to

72 On the collections, see above, Ch. 3, p. 54. For marginal notes on Cranmer's 1549 use of this MS, see Strype, *Cranmer*, Oxford edn 3, pp. 746, 754, 768, 772, 780, 784, 786, 788, 792, 802, 808, 830, 834, 836, 838, 840, 844, 856, 870. On Antichrist, cf. above, Ch. 4, pp. 150–51, and on Merlin, MacCulloch, 'Two dons in politics', pp. 8–9.

73 Cox 2, pp. 163, 174.

74 *Greyfriars Chronicle*, p. 62; cf. Foxe 5, pp. 728–30.

attendance. He also remained silent on the requirement that he should affirm that King Edward's authority was as complete during his childhood as during his adult years. It was equally predictable that the government should have expected trouble after his previous liturgical performance, and that they stationed two reliable observers to monitor his sermon: John Hooper, currently resident in Somerset's household, and Anne Boleyn's former chaplain, William Latimer. Bonner's efforts were sufficiently aggressive to cause evangelicals not in the know about the government's intentions to 'much marvel that he is not committed to the Tower'; the impact of his sermon was all the greater because earlier that day Hooper's lecture in the City had presented a very different theology of the eucharist. Hooper and Latimer duly denounced Bonner, and the machinery ground into operation for his deprivation.[75]

The Archbishop began this not uncongenial duty at Lambeth within nine days, and the highly contentious proceedings remained a prominent focus for London gossip and entertainment for the rest of September. Cranmer's fellow-commissioners, apart from the two Principal Secretaries, were his close colleagues Nicholas Ridley and William May, the Dean of Bonner's own cathedral. True to form, Bonner was not going down without a fight.[76] Even on his first day of examination, he began a robust performance by bringing the matter back to his affirmation of the eucharist, and he struck Cranmer on his weakest point, his involvement in the 1548 Justus Jonas Catechism: 'you have written very well of the sacrament, I marvel you do no more honour it', Bonner remarked with infuriating *faux-naif* courtesy. The eucharistic question would be at the centre of Bonner's strategy for the rest of his trial: it was an approach which was both bold and shrewd. 'I say and believe that there is the very true presence of the body and blood of Christ' – he said on that same first day – 'What believe *you*, and how do *you* believe, my Lord?' – a question which clearly nettled Cranmer and which did not produce a straightforward answer. Foxe's version of the story in his 1563 edition picks up a note of annoyance and embarrassment which significantly he later modified in later editions: Cranmer 'said "Our being here now is not to dispute that matter", and so passed over that matter and communication.'[77]

It sounds almost as if Bonner had acutely picked up the language of 'true presence' which we have identified as being Cranmer's way of expressing his views in the later 1530s (see above, Ch. 6). He would remorselessly repeat the phrase through the ensuing proceedings, and he repeatedly denounced his two principal accusers, Hooper and Latimer, as sacramentarian heretics. Moreover, at the third trial session on 16 September, he gleefully exploited

75 'Scudamore', ed. Brigden, p. 87 (including quotation); Foxe 5, pp. 746–7; *E.T.* p. 363 (*O.L.*, pp. 557–8).

76 *Greyfriars Chronicle*, pp. 63–4; the proceedings are described in Foxe 5, pp. 748–800.

77 Cf. text in 1563 edition of Foxe, p. 1699, with Foxe 5, pp. 752–3: italics provided by Cattley and Townsend.

the contradiction in eucharistic teaching between the first and the revised editions of the 1548 catechism: 'My Lord of Canterbury, I have here a note out of your books that you made touching the blessed sacrament, wherein you do affirm the verity of the body and blood of Christ to be in the sacrament, and I have another book also of yours of the contrary opinion; which is a marvellous matter.' The previous day Bonner had ostentatiously walked out of a sermon at St Paul's because of 'the heretic prater's uncharitable charity', following it up with a letter to the Lord Mayor regretting that he had not done the same.[78]

Bonner's subsidiary tactic, brilliantly employing his legal expertise, was to throw doubt on the fairness and legality of the proceedings. For instance, he objected to the subsidiary witnesses against him: an easy target, for out of five names, two were identifiable chaplains and one a close friend of Cranmer's and another was a friend of Hooper. Bonner's first requirement was that they should all be examined as to those 'by whom they have been found and maintained' for the previous twelve years. His disruption succeeded to the extent that a week into the trial, the government was forced to issue a new royal commission to the judges to quell the doubts which he had raised. This was by no means the end of his rearguard action; Bonner continued to play on the faults of the original trial proceedings. By 18 September Cranmer was sufficiently provoked that he took the tactically unwise step of an angry and schoolmasterly rebuke to Bonner for his behaviour; characteristically, he regarded the Bishop as having persistently given 'the multitude an intolerable example of disobedience' by calling into question the royal commission. 'You show yourself to be a meet judge', sneered Bonner triumphantly, and went on to accuse William Latimer of orchestrating crowd noise at the trial, rather like a modern studio broadcast manager with audience applause. Later he accused William Cecil of an angry outburst on the same occasion, similar to Cranmer's on the subject of obedience; since Cecil was supposed merely to be a witness, this did not reflect well on the proceedings.[79] Finally, on 20 September Bonner decided to bring matters to a showdown and make a martyr of himself. He made a point of turning up at Lambeth Palace in episcopal scarlet and rochet, openly challenged Sir Thomas Smith's right to sit as judge against him, as 'a notorious and manifest enemy of me the said Edmund', and he produced a formal appeal to the King. Earlier that day he had solemnly and sarcastically admonished a pair of Cranmer's gentlemen to denounce any sacramentarian preachers whom they might happen to hear, 'and also advertise my Lord your master of the same, and these my sayings'.[80]

The day's performance was the last straw for the commissioners. Bonner did not cross the Thames to return to his palace that night, but instead found

78 Foxe 5, pp. 749, 752, 765, 791.

79 Foxe 5, pp. 770 (the witnesses were John Cheke, Henry Markham, John Joseph, John Douglas and Richard Chambers), 773–6, 781.

80 Foxe 5, pp. 781–8; *Greyfriars Chronicle*, p. 63, for this and the next paragraph.

himself in the Marshalsea Prison. This would provide him with fresh matter for expressing grievance in subsequent sessions. Apart from the arguments in the sessions themselves, the public propaganda offensive against Bonner and all that he stood for needed to be maintained; John Hooper was once more pressed into service against Bonner. Cranmer was not an enthusiast for Hooper, who was repeatedly harassing his friend Bucer over questions of eucharistic doctrine, even accusing him of Lutheran-style ubiquitarianism; a previous obliquely expressed sneer by Hooper about another old friend, Hugh Latimer, and his achievements as a bishop may also have rankled. However, the Archbishop could see the fiery preacher's usefulness against the common enemy, and it was Hooper whom he chose to preach a Paul's Cross sermon on 22 September denouncing Bonner.[81] The following week 'one Golde' kept up the same theme at St Paul's. The whole process culminated on 1 October, when Cranmer finally pronounced sentence of deprivation, and the see of London was formally vacant: Bonner was still defiantly pouring out a barrage of declaration, appeal and supplications, and there was of course no chance that he would now leave prison for freedom as a private individual.

So after much trouble, Bonner was finally removed out of harm's way; but even as his trial was drawing to its stormy conclusion, there were symptoms that something else was stirring. On Wednesday 25 September, the evangelical preacher John Cardmaker announced that his Friday lecture would be cancelled for his attendance at Bonner's trial, but Bonner was not taken to Lambeth that day; the planned session of the trial was suddenly cancelled because 'divers urgent causes' took the commissioners elsewhere.[82] The crisis which was now beginning to unfold was an event wholly contrary to Bonner's downfall: it was to turn into a *coup d'état* of Privy Councillors which brought the overthrow of Protector Somerset. By now Somerset had raised fury among his colleagues for the flamboyant egocentricity of his rule. His playing the Renaissance prince was tolerable while his regime appeared to be achieving results, but the turmoil of England since May could be directly blamed on him, and his efforts to bring the commotions to an end by conciliating the rebels of eastern England had been bitterly resented by many local rulers. Somerset's adviser William Paget, for once in his life playing an unambiguous role as a candid friend, had repeatedly urged him through the time of commotions to avoid antagonizing or intimidating the powerful in the interests of the powerless, but not even Paget had been able to penetrate the Protector's self-regard.[83] The return of the Earl of Warwick, from the bloodsoaked aftermath of Kett's Norfolk rebellion, provided a convincing

81 On Cranmer's improved view of Hooper, see *E.T.* p. 363 (*O.L.* p. 557). NB Hooper's oblique cattiness about Latimer's explanations of ceremonies, *Early Works of Hooper*, pp. 30–31 (cf. *Sermons and Remains of Latimer*, p. 294). On Bucer and Hooper, cf. e.g. Gorham, *Gleanings*, p. 99.

82 *Greyfriars Chronicle*, p. 63; Foxe 5, p. 792.

83 Gammon, *Statesman and Schemer*, Ch. 7.

leader for the party among the Councillors who were now determined to restore collegiality to the young King's government: an incongruous combination of evangelicals and conservatives, united only by their conviction that Somerset must go.

Matters were brought to a head by the loss to French raids at the end of August of various forts around Boulogne, that potent symbol of national pride and of old King Henry's victory over the hereditary national enemy. There were even strong rumours that after this defeat Somerset was willing to hand back the whole of Henry's great prize to France.[84] The significant contrast with Warwick's simultaneous success in ending the impasse in Norfolk might not have proved fatal by itself, if late in September Somerset had not made the bad mistake of quarrelling with Warwick. He brusquely refused extra rewards above their wages to the English and foreign troops who had been operating in East Anglia; he had already annoyed Warwick by the tight financial rein which he had kept over the expedition. This was coupled with a proclamation in the name of King, Protector and Council on 30 September, peremptorily ordering all the soldiers out of London to various assigned posts now that their wages had been paid. Within a day or two, Warwick had summoned dissident Councillors to meet without Somerset, and he had also ensured that if necessary he would have the backing of the foreign mercenaries whom he had brought from East Anglia.[85]

Sensing the build-up of forces against him, Somerset panicked, and in the end it was he rather than the dissident Councillors who escalated the situation and openly tried to use force. On 5 October he issued a proclamation under the King's name, summoning all loyal subjects to Hampton Court to defend Edward and the Protector against a most dangerous conspiracy; he began a frantic round of letter-writing to provincial magnates to help him, and he or his supporters once more tried the dangerous tactic of appealing to ordinary people, using inflammatory flysheets, at least one of which identified his enemies with the gentry who had oppressed the poor before the summer commotions. Meanwhile the conspirator councillors consolidated their hold on London, including seizing the Tower with its national arsenal before Somerset's agents could do so; they also took the extraordinary step of summoning to the Council Board, on their own initiative, four politicians who had been sidelined by Somerset from the administration of Henry VIII's will or from Council business.[86]

84 *C.S.P. Spanish 1547–9*, p. 463.

85 *Chronicle of Henry VIII*, pp. 185–6, on this occasion a trustworthy source, since its information comes from mercenaries involved; 'Eye-witness account', pp. 603–5, and cf. *C.S.P. Domestic Edward VI*, no. 373. *T.R.P.* 1 no. 350; *Wriothesley's Chronicle* 2, p. 22

86 *C.S.P. Domestic Edward VI*, nos 368–81. The account in *Chronicle of Henry VIII*, pp. 186–90, is convincing; see also 'Eye-witness account', pp. 606–7 and *Wriothesley's Chronicle* 2, pp. 24–8. On the new Councillors, Hoak, *King's Council*, pp. 53–5.

Was Cranmer included in the flurry of preparations against the Protector? He was the one Councillor to rally to Somerset apart from Secretary Smith and William Paget, and it may be significant that the week before the crisis broke, on 24 September, he had similarly been alone at Hampton Court with Somerset and Smith to authorize a payment for the East Anglian expeditionary force as it was being stood down.[87] A note on one copy of the emergency royal summons to Hampton Court records the Archbishop's servant receiving it and forwarding it elsewhere on 6 October; likewise, according to the Spanish ambassador, Cranmer arrived at Hampton Court that day, and ordered a preacher to proclaim a message of loyalty to the King. He stayed with the royal party as it first moved towards London hoping to occupy the Tower, and then as it diverted to Windsor Castle, when Somerset learnt that the London Councillors had blocked that possibility.[88] It was true, of course, that Somerset and Cranmer had co-operated closely in religion since 1547, and especially (as we have seen) in Somerset's attempts to defuse the commotions of summer 1549. However, regardless of his feelings about the Protector, it was the Archbishop's duty to go to Hampton Court; he was King Edward's godfather, and he would be expected to seek access to him in a time of crisis. We also know that by now Paget had despaired of Somerset and seems to have been acting as a fifth columnist for the conspirators at Hampton Court. Given Paget's change of allegiance, one wonders how much even Cranmer was genuinely on Somerset's side by this stage, rather than acting to protect his godson and to prevent the Lord Protector's panic provoking open bloodshed. Even if he arrived at Hampton Court innocent of conspiratorial intentions, his old intimacy with Paget would no doubt soon initiate him into the attempt to stop Somerset falling into the abyss of tyranny. It was Tuesday 8 October before he, Paget and Smith joined the agitated flurry of letters which was passing between Windsor and the London Councillors; already by this time they had assumed the position of honest brokers and were distancing themselves from Somerset, stressing how they had 'communed' with him to hear his position and what he had to say to his fellow-Councillors. Their persuasions had indeed already brought the Protector back from the brink, and the same day he was offering to negotiate: as Secretary Smith wrote anxiously to Secretary Petre in London, the country must not have a double tragedy in one year, and become the scorn of the world.[89]

87 P.R.O., E. 101/76/35, f. 128.

88 P.R.O., S.P. 10/9/1, f. 1 (*C.S.P. Domestic Edward VI* no. 368); *C.S.P. Spanish 1547–9*, p. 157; 'Eye-witness account', p. 606. On Paget, see Gammon, *Statesman and Schemer*, pp. 160–67.

89 Cranmer and others to London Councillors, P.R.O., S.P. 10/9/26 f. 39 (*C.S.P. Domestic Edward VI* no. 396); poor text in Cox 2, pp. 520–22. The previous letter (1) which Cox identifies as from the Windsor Councillors is in fact from Somerset: cf. *C.S.P. Domestic Edward VI*, no. 383. Smith to Petre: ibid., no. 396.

There were still tensions over the next few days, as the two groups of Councillors tried to calm the continuing fears and smooth the ruffled feathers of their counterparts, but the worst of the crisis was over without a drop of blood being spilled. By 13 October, Somerset's Protectorship had been revoked, on the following day he was committed to the Tower, and on 17 October King Edward rode through London, to general relief at the peaceful outcome.[90] If Paget had been the man who liaised between the two groups, Cranmer had also played a masterly role at a time when one false move could have made matters infinitely worse: with his semi-detached role in secular politics and his habitual public even-temperedness, he was the one man who could act as a trusted mediator to the angry and frightened Somerset and the naturally alarmed boy-king. But now the coup had been successful, how should it be interpreted in wider terms of future policy? The enemies of Somerset began falling out as soon as the Protector was lodged in the Tower. Foreign observers, especially a delighted Van der Delft, the Imperial ambassador, assumed that the political upheaval would be a serious blow to the evangelical cause. Evangelicals at home were also very nervous: John Cardmaker in his St Paul's lecture on 9 October urged people not to abandon the godly cause for the mass, but to 'stick unto it', while on Sunday 13 October the Cathedral authorities kept their counsel in uncertain times by cancelling the sermon at Paul's Cross.[91]

Indeed, one powerful element backing the coup was a group of religiously conservative politicians whom Somerset had excluded from power in 1547, most notably the former Chancellor Thomas Wriothesley, the Earl of Southampton; these conservatives were determined to consolidate their power in the Catholic interest, probably with the aim of making the Lady Mary Regent for King Edward. However, Warwick knew that if this happened his chances of playing the leading role in the new regime were small. There was vigorous lobbying for the release of two symbols of the old faith from their imprisonment in the Tower, the Duke of Norfolk and the young Courtenay, Earl of Devon, and Bishop Gardiner also put in his bid for release with a letter to Warwick ornamented with well-honed compliments.[92] For the evangelical establishment, the whole point of bringing down Somerset was to protect their cause from association with his disastrous egotism: it was essential to stop the conservative bandwagon rolling on, and especially to prevent Mary becoming the figurehead for a Catholic comeback. Although the conservatives had an absolute majority among active councillors, Dale Hoak points out that

90 Cf. especially the letters, *C.S.P. Domestic Edward VI*, nos 407, 412 (*Troubles connected with the Prayer Book*, pp. 104–6; Cox 2, p. 522); Huntington Library, Ellesmere MS 1183. 13 October: *C.P.R. Edward VI* 3, p. 24. 14 October: *A.P.C. 1547–50*, p. 344. 17 October: *Greyfriars Chronicle*, pp. 64–5.

91 *C.S.P. Spanish 1547–9*, pp. 458–9, 462; *Greyfriars Chronicle*, p. 64. Cf. Hilles's comments on his feelings in October: *E.T.* p. 176 (*O.L.* p. 268).

92 'Scudamore', p. 97; *Gardiner's Letters*, p. 440.

this was not the decisive consideration. The body with overriding constitutional power, once Somerset's Protectorate was dissolved on 13 October, was not the whole body of twenty-four councillors, but the thirteen surviving executors of Henry VIII's will: among these, forces were much more evenly matched, with the evangelical executors including Cranmer and Warwick.[93] In the end, the evangelicals triumphed, and there is good evidence that at the heart of this rescue operation was Thomas Cranmer as chief assistant to the Earl of Warwick.

Straight away the evangelical politicians, with Warwick as their leader, set the pace. When Francis Dryander wrote to a nervous Heinrich Bullinger to reassure him about what had really happened during the coup against Somerset, he more or less told him that for those in the know the appearance of evangelical defeat had from the start been deceptive. Dryander himself had 'not only seen the outward and deplorable appearance of the change, but the purposes of the leading actors are well known to me', and he promised to acquaint Bullinger with the details in person when opportunity afforded.[94] There was some early window-dressing astutely calculated to please the conservatives. Van der Delft noted that the Earl of Warwick had ostentatiously enforced the Friday fasting rule in his household, as a gesture towards his conservative colleagues on the Council, and throughout early October Warwick kept the ambassador happy by mooting the possibility of sending his own son to serve at the Imperial Court. Equally with the Protector's fall, Somerset's chaplain John Hooper found his lecture-course at Court abruptly curtailed, a snub which neither Cranmer nor Latimer are likely to have regarded with particular sorrow.[95]

In contrast to such painless concessions to traditionalist hopes, the first step to assert evangelical dominance was taken as early as 15 October, when the full Council, including Cranmer, met at Hampton Court to appoint a new Privy Chamber entourage for the King, now that he was to return to the capital with them. The four Chief Gentlemen chosen included Warwick's brother Andrew Dudley, and the enthusiastic evangelicals Sir Thomas Wroth and Sir Edward Rogers; only one unambiguous conservative, the Earl of Arundel, was among the noblemen also appointed, and he was at this stage a political ally of Warwick.[96] The Archbishop would be the obvious person, as Edward's godfather, to reassure him that this was the best line-up for him. Thereafter Cranmer was noticeably constant in his attendance at the Council board throughout late October, and the next major setback for the conservatives on the Council came remarkably quickly. On 20 October (the day after the Council had appointed Warwick Admiral of England!) a letter went out

93 Hoak, *King's Council*, pp. 251–23
94 *C.S.P. Spanish 1547–9*, pp. 458–9, 462; *E.T.* p. 233 (*O.L.* p. 353).
95 Hooper to Bullinger, *E.T.* p. 44 (*O.L.* p. 70).
96 *A.P.C. 1547–50*, pp. 344–5. On Arundel and Warwick, see James, '1549 Coup', pp. 92–3; on Rogers and Wroth, *History of Parliament 1509–1558* 3, pp. 206–7, 667–8.

in the name of Edward VI to the city of Zürich, commending the bearer as a royal representative, and a similar letter to Berne probably went out on the same day. The reply to England from Berne reveals that the main business which this representative was authorized to discuss was the proposal which Cranmer had floated the previous year to various Continental reformers: a General Council to rival the false Council of Trent. The specific action of writing now may have been the end-result of a renewed initiative by Heinrich Bullinger, during summer 1549, to make official contact with England, following up his networking during the late 1530s; Bullinger had baited his trap by passing on the alarming information that the French were seeking help by treaty from their Swiss allies to recover Boulogne from the English.[97]

Even considering this military incentive, it is of the highest significance that the Council now agreed not only to pursue this Swiss alignment at such a time of political and religious flux, but also to revive the proposal for a General Council of evangelicals. The royal letter to Zürich of 20 October pointedly stressed 'the mutual agreement between us concerning the Christian religion and true godliness', and it named as the royal envoy the veteran evangelical agent of England in Germany, Christoff Mont; it is likely that the letters were carried abroad by the equally enthusiastic evangelical diplomat Sir Philip Hoby, who was back that month on a brief mission to England in October, and who now set out again for the Continent.[98] After his previous optimism about change, Ambassador Van der Delft felt the sudden chill in atmosphere, which he described to the Emperor when he wrote two days later: even the conservative Sir Thomas Cheyney, who came to see Van der Delft before setting out as envoy to the Imperial Court, was noticeably tight-lipped, and no one else on the Council (whom he described as very busy) had got in touch with him.[99] It was small wonder that, in the bundle of letters that went out overseas from Westminster on that fateful 20 October, there was a statement of cheery and well-informed optimism from John ab Ulmis to Bullinger. Writing to make up for a very brief letter to Bullinger from the royal tutor Richard Cox, who was that day 'occupied by matters of the highest importance', ab Ulmis told the Zürich leader:

> I am able to write to you as a most certain fact, that Antichrist in these difficult and perilous times is again cast down by the general decision of all the leading

97 *E.T.* p. 1 (*O.L.* p. 1); cf. Bullinger to Burcher, 28 June 1549, *E.T.* pp. 479–80 (*O.L.* pp. 739–40), and Richard Cox to Bullinger, 22 October 1549, *E.T.* p. 78 (*O.L.* pp. 119–20). The letter to Berne has not survived, but cf. Berne's reply, *E.T.* pp. 465–6 (*O.L.* pp. 717–18). On Warwick's admiralty, *A.P.C. 1547–50*, p. 347; and cf. remarks that day about the need to get the Emperor's help to defend Boulogne.

98 The embassy to Switzerland is not listed in *Handbook of Diplomatic Representatives*, pp. 280–81, but on Hoby, cf. ibid., p. 52. The Council meeting of 20 October (a Sunday) was not recorded in the Council book, but a Council warrant that day indicates a very full complement of Councillors at Westminster, not however including Cranmer: P.R.O., E. 101/76/35, f. 132.

99 *C.S.P. Spanish 1547–9*, p. 462.

men in all England; and that not only have they decided that the religion adopted last year is the true one, but a doubly severe penalty has now been imposed upon all who neglect it. There is nothing therefore for the godly to fear, and nothing for the papists to hope for, from the idolatrous mass.[100]

This was no idle rhetoric; what ab Ulmis meant became clear in England ten days later, with the issue of the first public policy statement at home by the new regime. This was a royal proclamation of 30 October, which was another emphatic reaffirmation that the evangelicals were in charge at Westminster. It ordered, on pain of imprisonment, an end to rumours that the Duke's arrest meant that 'the good laws made for religion should be now altered and abolished, and the old Romish service, mass and ceremonies eftsoons [a second time] renewed and revived'.[101] The proclamation brought to an end a period of seven days in which a temporary but total ban had been imposed on preaching, no doubt in preparation for this new official message. On the same day, John Stow preserves a fragment from the second of two baffled complaints from Bishop Gardiner about the increasing harshness of his treatment in the Tower of London; the atmosphere now prevailing in the Council may be gauged from the fact that Stow also records that 'they laughed very merrily thereat, saying he had a pleasant head', and the Council ignored his laments. The door had now been slammed shut not just on Gardiner's prison cell but also on a Catholic restoration.[102]

In the wake of the rapid sequence of events in October, it is difficult to get a picture of political developments during November. This may be more a reflection of calm in the wake of the evangelical triumph than simply a failure of the sources; Dryander recorded how he had come down from Cambridge with Bucer to join Cranmer at Lambeth on 5 November, the day after Parliament opened, and that all was then in a better state for the evangelical cause than it had been before the coup against Somerset.[103] Observers noted how little serious business was transacted in Parliament throughout the month, and it was nicknamed 'the still Parliament'. The one sign of Parliamentary controversy during November is difficult to interpret; this was the complaint, from a consortium of bishops (with Cranmer present), that their authority was being disregarded and undermined by proclamations and that this was one of the causes of popular disorder. The move could either have been a conservative assault on the late Protector's enthusiastic use of proclamations in religious matters, or a ploy in Cranmer's repeated efforts to resurrect the long-standing need for canon law reform. Either way, the secular

100 *E.T.* p. 261 (*O.L.* p. 395).

101 *A.P.C.* 1547–50, pp. 344–52 (cf. Hoak, *King's Council*, p. 249); *T.R.P.* 1 no. 352. Although Cranmer is not recorded as present on 30 October, he signed Council warrants on 28 and 29 October also without his presence being noted in the Council minute-book: P.R.O., E. 101/76/35 ff. 139–40.

102 On the preaching ban, *E.T.* p. 44 (*O.L.* p. 70). *Gardiner's Letters*, p. 442.

103 Dryander to Bullinger, *E.T.* p. 234 (*O.L.* p. 354).

Lords lost their initial sympathy for the complaint when they saw the draft proposal for legislation, drawn up by the bishops to strengthen their jurisdiction, and the House quickly sidelined the bill into a committee, from which it took three weeks to emerge.[104] One factor in the pause in politics was that Warwick's never very robust health had collapsed, perhaps as a result of strain in the dramatic events of October. Nevertheless, by the end of November Warwick was so obviously in charge of the Council that it was meeting at his house while he was indisposed. Worse still for the conservatives appointed to the Council in the crisis of the coup, they were now further counterbalanced by the appearance of two leading evangelicals: Cranmer's old friend, Bishop Goodrich of Ely, and Henry Grey, Marquess of Dorset. Goodrich had first attended a Council meeting on 6 November, Dorset on 28 November, and they were formally sworn in on 29 November: an event which one evangelical commentator described as putting 'all honest hearts in good comfort for the good hope that they have of the perseverance of God's word'. An anonymous Elizabethan reminiscence unambiguously put these events down once more to an alliance between Warwick and Cranmer.[105]

More significant still was what went on out of public view during December: nothing less than a plan for a further coup, this time unambiguously in the conservative interest, in a natural reaction to the seizing of the initiative by the evangelicals. The anonymous Elizabethan account of the new attempt cast Southampton as the leading figure; he had ceased to attend Council meetings after 22 October on the excuse of illness. Although there is no doubt that he was genuinely ill, even more seriously than Warwick, he had probably also been outraged at the moves which led up to the overtures to Switzerland and the 30 October proclamation, which seem to have caused fierce rows in the Council, if the Imperial ambassador's informants were correct. This was not what Southampton had envisaged when he had been readmitted to his position of honour on the Council, and his health may have been affected by his shock at the turn of events.[106] Now in December Southampton made a desperate bid against the evangelical triumph; he tried to exploit the opportunity provided by his appointment as one of the commissioners charged with examining Somerset in the Tower, on charges of treason. He aimed to implicate Warwick in Somerset's doings with the goal of having both men executed, and he is said to have won over the Earl of Arundel, Warwick's ally during the autumn, to give 'his consent that they were both worthy to die'. However, the third commissioner William Paulet (Lord St John) immediately warned Warwick of the plot against him. Warwick abandoned any support

104 'Scudamore', pp. 94, 97–8; *L.J.* 1, pp. 359–60, 367.

105 Hoak, *King's Council*, pp. 53–5; B.L. Additional MS 48126, ff. 15v–16r; *A.P.C. 1547–50* pp. 354, 362. Swearing-in, Warwick's illness and Council location: 'Scudamore', pp. 91, 93, 96; cf. *C.S.P. Spanish 1547–9*, p. 476.

106 Hoak, *King's Council*, p. 59; 'Scudamore', pp. 93, 95, and James, '1540 Coup', p. 92. *C.S.P. Spanish 1547–9*, p. 468 (7 November 1549).

which he had ever given to plans to put Somerset on trial for treason, 'and procured by the means of the Archbishop of Canterbury great friends about the King to preserve the Lord Protector, and joined together in the same all he could for his life'. The London gossip which reached the Spaniard who wrote the so-called 'Chronicle of Henry VIII' also portrayed the Archbishop as the leading figure in Somerset's escape from death.[107]

Dating this narrative suggests that the struggle lasted all through the month, as Southampton and Warwick both fought their illness as well as each other to gain the mastery; the examinations of Somerset which gave Southampton his chance were at their height in mid-December. A sign of an abrupt change of dynamics within the ruling clique which is probably a reflection of the sudden political commotion was the abandonment at some stage after 5 December of a whole series of planned promotions: Warwick to be Earl of Pembroke and Lord Treasurer, Arundel to be Lord Great Chamberlain and Paget to be Lord Chamberlain; by 15 December Richard Scudamore, who had recorded these prospective promotions, noted that they had been cancelled, and also described a good deal of agitated movement by royal lawyers between the Privy Council and Somerset in the Tower.[108] By the end of the month, Somerset was enjoying the liberty of the Tower and celebrating Christmas Day not only with a visit from his wife but with a godly sermon from his chaplain Hooper – perhaps Hooper's castigation on that occasion of 'governors that misordered their vocations' was not the most pastorally sensitive of Christmas presents, but his exhortation to Somerset to avoid revenge sounds as though his message had been guided by the government.[109] A few months later, the former Protector would be released and even readmitted to the Council on what amounted to probation. In rage and mortification, Southampton took to his bed again, but he was not going to be allowed to lie undisturbed in his chambers in Court; this was too close to the King. Late on 31 December, Warwick struck decisively, ordering Southampton out of the Court and likewise dismissing the Earl of Arundel, together with others who were probably involved in their conspiracy. Southampton never recovered his health: he died the following summer. Bizarrely, the preacher at his funeral was John Hooper.[110]

There is much which remains mysterious about the two coups of autumn 1549, in particular a cross-current from Kett's Rebellion which runs through events, involving Bishop Rugge of Norwich and the devious Norfolk magnate Sir Richard Southwell, who was accused on convincing evidence of

107 B.L. Additional MS 48126, f. 16r; *Chronicle of Henry VIII*, pp. 190–93.

108 'Scudamore', pp. 98, 101. On the dating of Somerset's examinations, see *C.S.P. Spanish 1547–9*, p. 489.

109 'Scudamore', pp. 103–4.

110 NB the sarcastic comment on Southampton's illness and likely reaction to Somerset's better fortune, 'Scudamore', p. 104; on the 31 December arrests, ibid., pp. 107–8. On the funeral, *Wriothesley's Chronicle* 2, p. 41.

aiding the Norfolk rebels with royal funds. This is not the place to unravel what is clearly a significant story, except to note that when John Ponet looked back on the events in 1556, he told a tale of Warwick's villainy and of a belated accusation of Southwell: the initial co-operation of Warwick with Wriothesley, Sir Thomas Arundel and Southwell was followed by the subsequent debacle in which Wriothesley was betrayed and Southwell 'confessed enough to be hanged for' after being placed in the Fleet. Southwell and Rugge's humiliation came at precisely the same time as the final fall of Southampton, at the turn of December and January, and it is quite likely that the supposed charges of treason which Wriothesley tried to fix on Warwick were to do with events in Norfolk during the summer.

Ponet was a *parti pris* observer of these machinations; a strong partisan for Somerset, he had been arrested in November 1549, probably for his work in translating a dialogue by Bernardino Ochino which was dedicated to Somerset and which contained flattering references to him.[111] However, he was also one of Cranmer's intimate chaplains. What should we make of his hostile account of Warwick's plotting as evidence for Cranmer's attitude to events? Probably little. Much happened between 1549 and 1556 to create the black legend of John Dudley, and everything else suggests that the Archbishop and Warwick were willing allies through the twists and turns of politics in the two coups. Once more, as in the first coup of October, there could have been no one better in December than Cranmer to supervise the crucial change of direction against Southampton represented by drawing back from an exemplary punishment for Somerset. The royal godfather was best placed to influence the boy Edward, who was clearly bewildered that the man whom he had been brought up to think of as his greatest friend was suddenly being treated as a traitor, and who was no doubt only too pleased to be told that matters were not that serious after all.

It was a mark of the frenzied activity now generated by the political situation that Parliament and Council officially ignored the Christmas season (although most MPs defiantly escaped home); even the Friday set aside each week for meetings of the Convocation of Canterbury was commandeered by the Lords from 27 December.[112] Even before the decisive eviction of Southampton and Arundel from the Court, a strong indication that the evangelicals had survived an exceptionally testing year came on Christmas Day 1549. On that day a royal letter was circulated to the bishops: the signatures of Councillors on the dorse were headed by Cranmer, as the Archbishop's scribe meticulously recorded, in registering the copy which was sent across the river

111 Ponet, *Treatise of politike power*, sig. I iii. On Ochino and Ponet, see Pocock, 'Preparations for the Second Prayer Book', pp. 141–4: *A.P.C. 1547–50*, p. 358. On Southwell, Hoak, *King's Council*, p. 58, and for his guilt, P.R.O., E. 351/221.

112 The question of Convocation meetings at this time is controversial; for evidence of meetings, see below, Ch. 11, p. 505 n112. I incline to think that there had been meetings in previous weeks, but that Convocation was now prorogued. The undateable prorogation which can be deduced from its renewal on 3 February 1550 may well have dated from December 1549: Cranmer's Register, f. 12v.

to Lambeth Palace.[113] This spelt out the message of the general proclamation of 30 October: all rumours that Somerset's overthrow meant a return to old-time religion were false. Not only was the *Book of Common Prayer* again commended by Cranmer and his fellow-Councillors as being 'grounded upon Holy Scripture, agreeable to the order of the primitive Church, and much to the edifying of our subjects'; now all competition would be eliminated, as the bishops were ordered to stage a rigorous diocesan campaign to destroy old service-books (pitilessly listed in all their variety). All opponents of the measure should be imprisoned, and continuing searches should be made in the future to make sure that destruction was complete. As an afterthought, the bishops were also ordered to punish those who refused to pay their share of provision for the financial burden of bread and wine for weekly communions according to the new liturgy: an interesting reflection of the frequency with which the new communion service was supposed to be celebrated. The measure would subsequently be confirmed by an Act of Parliament, and only three days after it was issued, on 28 December, Bishop Thirlby was already sending out an order to the diocese in which the Palace of Westminster stood, that it should be implemented. Curiously enough, Cranmer did not act in his own diocese on the order, which he himself had signed as a Councillor, until 14 February 1550; he was probably too preoccupied in Council and Parliament to hurry with a measure which would in any case secure ready compliance from his diocesan officials, headed by his own brother as Archdeacon.[114]

There is a distinct feeling of the calm after the storm in John Hooper's letter to Bullinger, written two days after the royal circular. Not only did he cautiously 'hope and expect better things' for his patron Somerset, but nationally 'God in his providence holds the ploughtail, and raises up in his Majesty's Council many more favourers of his word, who defend the cause of Christ with vigour and courage'. Hooper also noted that Cranmer was 'now very friendly' towards him. All his former doubts as to the Archbishop's eucharistic views were now stilled, and he especially approved of what Cranmer was saying about the eucharist in a series of doctrinal articles which were now being presented for subscription to all those seeking a licence to preach or teach theology. Rather condescendingly, Hooper commented that 'we desire nothing more for him than a firm and manly spirit. Like all the other bishops in this country, he is too fearful about what may happen to him'.[115] Given the commotions which he had survived during 1549, one may feel that the Primate of All England was entitled to his caution.

113 The letter is *T.R.P.* 1 no. 353, although strictly speaking it should not be regarded as a royal proclamation; an original copy is Cranmer's Register, ff. 55v–56r. On Parliamentary defections, 'Scudamore', p. 103.

114 Ayris and Selwyn (eds), *Cranmer*, p. 145.

115 *E.T.* pp. 45–7 (*O.L.* pp. 71–3). The 'articles' do not apparently survive, but were probably an early form of the Forty-Two Articles of 1553: see below, Ch. 11, pp. 503–4 and Ch. 12, p. 527.

CHAPTER 11

Building a Protestant Church: 1550–52

WINTER 1550 WAS A time for consolidating the gains of 1549 and healing the wounds among the evangelical establishment which the autumn stirs had produced. With Cranmer at the Council board, the Duke of Somerset was released from prison on bonds on 6 February; his first call after leaving the Tower was apparently on the Archbishop at Lambeth, before he went home with his wife to Syon House. He was restored to his place on the Council on 10 April. Nevertheless, his rehabilitation was at a price: two reliably evangelical bishops, Holbeach of Lincoln and Barlow of Bath and Wells, benefited from his fall by regrants of their principal estates, lately acquired by the Duke.[1] Indeed, one of the major themes of 1550 would be the remodelling of the episcopate. The day after Somerset had sworn to be of good behaviour, the Council rejected Bishop Bonner's appeal and confirmed Cranmer's sentence of deprivation on him. This opened the way for the translation of the Archbishop's old chaplain, Nicholas Ridley, from the minor see of Rochester, to put the diocese of London in safe evangelical hands; in the resulting shuffle of preferment, the bishopric of Rochester was filled by Cranmer's chaplain John Ponet, now completely rehabilitated after his brief entanglement in the autumn's political crises. Ponet was allowed to augment Rochester's rather meagre episcopal income by continuing to hold his other substantial preferment *in commendam*. This was an exceptional privilege for an English bishop, and the Privy Council permission for this stipulated that it should not happen again, suggesting that there was strong argument when the matter was raised; yet in the previous decade, the Archbishop's earlier protégés, Nicholas Heath and Ridley, had both enjoyed the same permission during their time at Rochester. Clearly Cranmer had long considered that his brother-diocesan of Rochester was under-rewarded, and he was not prepared to yield the point now.[2]

1 Cf. Alexandre's report of these events to Bucer, C.C.C.C. MS 119, p. 303. For Council actions detailed here, see *A.P.C. 1547–50*, pp. 384–8; episcopal grants at *C.P.R. Edward VI 1549–51*, pp. 178, 180. Somerset clawed back some of his losses from Bath and Wells: ibid., pp. 204–5.

2 For evidence of commendatory grants, see *Faculty Office Registers*, p. 214; Cranmer's Register, ff. 391v, 410r; *A.P.C. 1550–52*, p. 57; *C.P.R. Edward VI 1549–51*, p. 293.

What made Nicholas Ridley's promotion to the see of London all the more significant was that he would preside over a diocese restored to its old boundaries, since Thomas Thirlby's diocese of Westminster was now to be dissolved and reunited with London. During the vacancy in see, Cranmer had been acting as *de facto* Bishop of London, as he had begun to do during the emergency of summer 1549, even before the final showdown with Bonner. For instance, on behalf of the Privy Council he took over the choice of preachers at Paul's Cross, and he chose predictable establishment evangelicals.[3] He was also directly involved in a major initiative of moral discipline in co-operation with that year's Lord Mayor of London (Rowland Hill), on the very eve of Ridley's arrival in April 1550. An atmosphere of moral panic had been triggered in England, caused by upheavals such as the end of clerical celibacy and one or two highly publicized aristocratic marriage breakdowns, like that of William Parr. Cranmer arranged a high-profile sermon on national morality at Paul's Cross, attending it himself in company with the Lord Mayor; this was the signal for Hill to launch a rigorous campaign of inquisitions and prosecutions on sexual misdemeanours in London, with well-publicized backing from the Archbishop; victims came even from the upper strata of society in the capital.[4]

The results of the London campaign are unlikely to have been any more impressive than in any other official crackdown on sexual morality, but as is the way of such initiatives, it attracted a good deal of favourable comment, and made the respectable feel more secure. It was also a symbol of Cranmer's dominant position in the wake of the failure of the conservative coup attempt of December 1549. His power and influence were probably never greater than in the opening months of 1550. Although the year would present him with a serious challenge within the Church, from the more impatient evangelical John Hooper, that challenge was beaten off, and his position remained strong. A symbol of his continuing status as one of the chief magnates of the realm was his grant, in April 1550, of a licence to retain a hundred gentlemen and yeomen beside his domestic servants. This was also the first year since the death of King Henry that he resumed his old custom of spending most of the summer and autumn down in Kent; during his time there he staged a full-scale visitation of his cathedral.[5]

There were other symbols of a society purging itself of old wickedness besides London's moral crusade. All over England during winter 1550, the

3 Cf. his invitation to Matthew Parker to preach, B.L. Additional MS 19400, f. 19: this is dated 8 January 1550, and can be shown to refer to 1550 and not 1551 by its reference to Sunday 16 March.

4 The main account is in *Chronicle of Henry VIII*, pp. 167–9, which sounds bizarrely improbable until compared with *Wriothesley's Chronicle* 2, pp. 36–7, 'Two London Chronicles', ed. Kingsford, p. 45, and 'Scudamore', p. 130. Cf. also Brigden, *London*, p. 472.

5 Retainer licence is Lambeth MS Cart. Misc. XI 29. Visitation: Cox 2, pp. 159–62. For Cranmer's welcome to diplomats passing through Kent in September, cf. Ryan, *Ascham*, p. 120; he did not attend the Privy Council between 1 July and 16 November 1550.

bonfires of Latin service-books burned, as bishops followed the government order of Christmas Day 1549, even in a diocese like Worcester where Cranmer's old friend Bishop Heath must have been very unhappy at having to obey this instruction.[6] Indeed, as far as Heath was concerned, the order for destruction may have been the last straw, because he launched into immediate defiance of the government over its legislation to introduce a new Ordinal for the ordination of deacons and priests and the consecration of bishops. Heath first appeared before the Privy Council to answer for his obstinacy on 8 February, the day after the Council had rejected Bonner's appeal, and his opposition offered the prospect of removing another enemy of evangelical plans from a key diocese. On 2 March he was committed to the Fleet Prison, and although it would take more than a year to complete the process of his deprivation, the prospect opened up of delivering Worcester into reliable hands.[7]

Yet another important see, besides that of Bishop Heath, fell into evangelical clutches in winter 1550, thanks to the disgrace of Bishop Rugge of Norwich in the fall-out from Kett's Rebellion. Rugge had always been an annoyance to Cranmer; as an unmovable and vocal conservative in a large diocese which covered one of the regions of England most promising for evangelical advance, he was no better than his venerable predecessor Bishop Nix. Rugge's promotion to add the see of Norwich to his Broadland Abbey had occurred just at the time of the crisis which surrounded the fall of Queen Anne Boleyn, and one suspects that pressure from the Duke of Norfolk for a congenial diocesan had been too much for Cromwell, as he consolidated his position against possible political shipwreck. Rugge had remained true to the Howards all through King Henry's reign; he actually granted the Duke the reversion of the presentation to one of his Norfolk archdeaconries only a few days before the old man's arrest in December 1546. In 1537 Cranmer had expressed his impotent irritation about Rugge to Cromwell, when protesting that one of Rugge's chaplains was using East Anglian pulpits to harass an old Cambridge friend of his who was beneficed in Norfolk: the Bishop 'doth approve none to preach in his diocese that be of right judgement, as I do hear reported of credible persons'.[8] There was nothing that the Archbishop could do against the entrenched Norwich diocesan machine, beyond showing favour to Rugge's opponents like the redoubtable Robert Watson of Norwich, or using his archiepiscopal peculiars in the diocese as havens for the godly. The deanery of Bocking (largely consisting of the town of Hadleigh in Suffolk) continued through the 1540s to play the role of evangelical fifth column under the direction of Rowland Taylor. Cranmer duplicated this in 1548 by

6 On Worcester, H.W.R.O. 009:1-BA 2636/11 (no. 43701), f. 157r: for action in York diocese, 'Parkyn's Narrative', p. 72.

7 *A.P.C. 1547–50*, p. 404.

8 Presentation noted in *C.P.R. Edward VI 1550–3*, p. 288. Cranmer to Cromwell: P.R.O., S.P. 1/120 f. 198; Cox 2, p. 336 (*L.P.* 12 i, no. 1281).

engineering Taylor's appointment to a newly created post in another Suffolk peculiar, which had fallen into Crown hands through the monastic dissolutions: Taylor became Archdeacon of the town of Bury St Edmunds.[9]

Now the succession to Rugge could be carefully planned. As the old ex-abbot headed off for enforced retirement clutching a brace of royal pardons and a fat pension, Thomas Thirlby was designated as Norwich's new bishop, since he had been displaced from Westminster by the reconstruction of the old see of London. Thirlby may have needed the promise of an incentive in order to overcome his reluctance to move out of the capital to a large and poorly endowed see: immediately after he arrived at Norwich, his new diocese was given a substantial increase in estates, including an extra palace at Ipswich. Gifts of land to the Church were not common in the reign of Edward VI.[10] Christopher Hales the younger, one of Zürich's English friends, sourly said of Thirlby's translation that Norwich's new bishop would do less harm there than at the heart of politics in Westminster, and this may well have been the official intention.[11] Thirlby, like Nicholas Heath, was one of Cranmer's old Cambridge circle who had by now left behind his 1530s enthusiasm for the evangelical cause, but unlike Heath, he continued to be a reliable ambassador for the regime abroad; he was never prepared to make a final stand against the Edwardian programme in the Church, and his energies were increasingly diverted into foreign diplomacy. Thirlby was unlikely to be as troublesome at Norwich as Rugge, and he gave an earnest of his continuing loyalty to his old friend despite their growing theological estrangement, when as soon as he was translated in April, he granted the Archbishop the first nomination to an advowson in his new diocese: either an archdeaconry, a canonry or a lesser benefice.[12] In any case, Cranmer made sure that the future of Norwich would be safe: while preparations were made for Thirlby's appointment, a direction could be set for the diocese using the Archbishop's jurisdiction during a vacancy in see (*sede vacante*).

The Dean and Chapter of Norwich surrendered their authority to Cranmer on 31 January, and subsequent events suggest a continuing tussle between the conservative diocesan establishment and the Archbishop. The Dean and Chapter appealed to the agreement or composition about *sede vacante* jurisdiction for Norwich diocese which, after repeated rows, had been painfully created in the fourteenth century, and under its terms Cranmer nominated the Dean of Norwich, John Salisbury, to be his Official to visit in the diocese. A marginal note in Cranmer's Register, however, claims that this agreement

9 On Watson, see above, Ch. 10, pp. 433–4. On Taylor, MacCulloch, *Suffolk and the Tudors*, p. 168.

10 *C.P.R. Edward VI 1549–51*, pp. 287–8. For Rugge's pardons and pension, see *C.P.R. Edward VI 1548–9*, p. 385, *1549–50*, p. 163, *1550–3*, p. 14. Lyons, 'Resignation of Rugg', misses the dimension of Kett's Rebellion in Rugge's fall.

11 *E.T.* p. 122 (*O.L.* p. 185).

12 Cranmer's Register, f. 330r. It is not certain how Cranmer exploited this grant.

was now valueless, thanks to the inept way in which the Cathedral and diocesan establishment had been remodelled under Henry VIII. Indeed, Cranmer specifically said in his commission to Salisbury that it should not override a previous commission which he had already granted to two other men to be Keepers of the Spirituality in the diocese. Predictably, while Salisbury was an ex-monk of steadily more conservative religious outlook, these two were Rowland Taylor and another household chaplain of the Archbishop, William Wakefield. Even before all this complicated paperwork was complete, Cranmer was already instituting clergy to benefices in the vacant diocese.[13]

Juggling with the powers of commissions was far more than a piece of legal pedantry: compensating for Rugge's consistent defence of traditional religion, Cranmer's two agents outfaced Dean Salisbury and pushed forward what was the most advanced programme of change in any English diocese at that time. This is revealed by a circular letter which Bishop Thirlby sent out to his diocese in December 1550; prompted by the November letter from the King and Council which ordered the destruction of all stone altars in England, he ordered compliance in Norwich diocese, but he said that he knew that action would largely be unnecessary, 'knowing that the most part of all altars within this my diocese be already taken down by commandment of my Lord of Canterbury his grace's visitors in his late visitation in this diocese being void'. The diocese had been vacant less than two months from Taylor and Wakefield's formal appointment, because Thirlby was translated on 1 April 1550. Cranmer's visitors had clearly worked fast in their campaign, and they had anticipated the destruction of altars by Nicholas Ridley in London diocese during June, which historians have conventionally seen as the first such large-scale diocesan campaign.[14] Moreover, Taylor remained on the spot to keep an eye on progress after Thirlby had taken over. The latter, little relishing the programme of change which he was called upon to enforce, was not the most assiduous or resident of bishops in his time at Norwich, while Taylor seems to have regarded his East Anglian commitments as his main occupation among several other nominal offices.[15]

Rugge was not the only elderly bishop in the evangelicals' sights: 'it is openly spoken that there shall be more quondam bishops in England shortly', cheerfully reported the newsgatherer Richard Scudamore at the end of February, and one obvious name on the list was John Veysey of Exeter, whose

13 Cranmer's Register, ff. 107v–110r; Churchill, *Canterbury Administration* 1, pp. 196–8, 590–91. On Salisbury, MacCulloch, *Suffolk and the Tudors*, pp. 186–7.

14 For Thirlby's letter, see L'Estrange, 'Church goods of St Andrew and St Mary Coslany', pp. 72–3, and cf. Houlbrooke, *Church Courts*, pp. 165–6. On Ridley's destruction of altars in London, *Wriothesley's Chronicle* 2, p. 39. Robert Parkyn recorded the destruction of altars in southern England as taking place 'consequently after Easter' (6 April 1550): 'Parkyn's Narrative', p. 72.

15 On Taylor, MacCulloch, *Suffolk and the Tudors*, pp. 170–71, and on Thirlby, ibid., p. 78 and n.

diocese had been convulsed during 1549 by a rebellion even more serious than Rugge had experienced. Veysey's eventual successor, Miles Coverdale, was already marked down to succeed him and was exercising his talents as a preacher in the diocese in summer 1550, but it took a whole year more before the wily old survivor was satisfied with the terms of his retirement.[16] Another veteran administrator, and a much more formidable conservative theologian than Veysey, was Cuthbert Tunstall of Durham: he ceased to attend the Privy Council after 2 February 1550, another mark of the conservative reversal of the previous autumn, and from August 1550 he was removed from his diocese and transferred to house arrest in London, before being moved to the Tower in December 1551. The charges were in themselves fairly spurious allegations that he had been fomenting rebellion in the north, but the more general reality behind them was that Tunstall was a powerful symbol of resistance to religious change.[17]

A smaller-scale success for the process of uprooting incumbent conservatives can be noted in Cranmer's peculiar jurisdiction of South Malling, in the diocese of Chichester. The see was still at that stage in the uneasy possession of another champion of the old faith, Bishop George Day, who would not be ousted until the nationwide order to destroy all altars provoked him into defiance at the end of the year. A kindred spirit to Day was the elderly Dean of Malling, Robert Peterson, formerly Prior of the wealthy Cluniac house of Lewes; as long ago as 1542, Cranmer had given him a licence to be non-resident from Malling for the sake of his health. The Archbishop had always been scrupulous about non-residence in such livings as Malling which involved cure of souls, and in the heady atmosphere of 1550 his long patience with Peterson seems to have come to an end. Peterson was now forced into resigning his deanery, although up to his death in 1555 he clung on to a clutch of other profitable livings (both with and without cure of souls) which were beyond Cranmer's power of interference. Predictably, this Oxford graduate was replaced in May 1550 by a Cambridge man, a canon lawyer called Robert Taylor: Cranmer would make Taylor one of the *sede vacante* Custodians of the Spirituality in Chichester diocese when Day was finally ousted in 1551 to make way for an evangelical bishop. Although Taylor would conform to Roman Catholicism under Mary, and keep his offices in Chichester diocese, his arrival at South Malling in 1550 strongly suggests the same strategy of planting reliable men in peculiar jurisdictions by which Cranmer had placed Robert Taylor's namesake, Rowland, at Hadleigh in the days of Bishop Rugge of Norwich.[18]

16 'Scudamore', ed. Brigden, p. 122; on Coverdale, *E.T.* p. 318 (*O.L.* p. 483).

17 Hoak, *King's Council*, pp. 71–3.

18 Cranmer's Register, ff. 18r, 19r, 60rv, 61r–62r, 129v–130v, 373v. On Peterson, see also Emden, *Oxford to 1540*, p. 672, and his will, P.C.C. 25 More, P.R.O., PROB. 11/37 f. 184, and on Taylor, Venn, 4, p. 208, and O'Day and Heal, *Continuity and Change*, p. 235.

The Ordinal which had triggered Bishop Heath's downfall was the one major element of the liturgy which had not been provided for in the 1549 Prayer Book, and as has already been suggested (see above, Ch. 9, p. 397) it had probably been left out at that stage because in late 1548 and early 1549, the regime was not prepared to outface the conservative bishops on this explosive issue, which affected the very identity of the ministry. Now the balance among senior clergy was changing so rapidly, the omission could be remedied. In its final form, it represents the first season of co-operation and consultation between Cranmer and Bucer. Soon after Bucer had arrived in England, he wrote a treatise on the form of ordination (*De ordinatione legitima ministrorum ecclesiae revocanda*) which contributed materially to the completed ordinal, and also differed from it in a significant respect. Bucer provided the same service for all three acts of ordination, but he also rather vaguely suggested that the service ought to be 'attempered' to each grade to signify their distinction (characteristically, he felt that this should be done by increasing the length of the service for bishops). The English Ordinal took his proposed form of service as the basis for *The Form of ordering priests*, but it radically developed his subsidiary suggestion in a traditionalist direction in order to form three distinct services, one for each order. The Ordinal also ignored Bucer's rather uninspiring draft for words of commission at the crucial moment of the laying on of hands, and instead provided three entirely different sets of words for commissioning deacon, priest and bishop.[19]

The three services thus created also contained visual imagery which was not present in Bucer's rite: the delivery of symbolic instruments of their office to those being ordained. Such a delivery had been a feature of traditional ordinals, and although all three grades were now for the first time given a Bible to symbolize their calling to evangelical ministry (only the New Testament for deacons), a new bishop received his Bible in a remarkably traditional manner, laid 'upon his neck' as had been done in the old Sarum rite. Otherwise, a priest still received chalice and paten, and a bishop his pastoral staff; in the 1552 revision of the ordinal, these extras would be censored out, and the bishop would thereafter receive his Bible as a book to be read, rather than used in the manner of the blunt instrument in classic English detective novels. A provision in the Act that authorized the Ordinal allowed the creation of 'other ministers of the Church' besides the main scripturally attested three; this was probably not envisaged as an opportunity to continue the seven orders to be found in the medieval Western Church, but to allow for experiments such as the introduction of readers, briefly attempted by Archbishop Parker in the 1560s. The provision was not otherwise used, and not at all in Cranmer's time.

19 For the ordinal texts, their sources and later development, cf. Brightman, *English Rite*, pp. 928–1017. There is useful discussion of Bucer's role in Smyth, *Cranmer*, pp. 228–32 and Hopf, *Bucer*, pp. 88–94. A translation of Bucer's text is provided in *Bucer*, ed. Whitaker, pp. 176–83.

Overall it is doubtful whether one can greatly illuminate Cranmer's attitude to holy orders from the conservatism of this adaption of Bucer's draft. Since even Bucer was prepared to concede the historical value for discipline's sake of distinctions among the clergy, one can see the ordinal as another case of Cranmer's opportunist adoption of medieval forms for new purposes. There was no essential difference between having distinctive ordination rites for deacons, priests and bishops, and having distinctive royal commissions for sheriffs, justices of the peace and common law judges: indeed, both Bucer and Cranmer drew close analogies between the sacred ministry and secular office-holding. In an image which was striking, but which would only make its full impact in the context of city-states like Strassburg, Bucer once referred to the ministry of the first-century or apostolic church as 'the first senate and leaders of the city'.[20] Similarly, it was a secular analogy with an English flavour which came to Cranmer's mind when writing about the dignity of the ministry in his treatise the *Defence*, contemporary with the ordinal. 'If they are to be loved, honoured and esteemed that be the King's chancellors, judges, officers and ministers in temporal matters; how much then are they to be esteemed that be ministers of Christ's words and sacraments, and have to them committed the keys of heaven, to let in and shut out, by the ministration of his word and gospel!'[21]

Admittedly, one does note in the images developed by both men an emphasis on the special dignity of the ministry. Cranmer's question also contains an additional ambiguity characteristic of the man: were the ministers of the Church the ministers of the Crown or the ministers of Christ? Under Edward VI, it was still possible for the Archbishop to leave unresolved a question which would become of vital importance to him under Queen Mary. Nevertheless, Cranmer's receptionist views on the eucharist and his predestinarian interpretation of salvation forced a radical shift in his understanding of clerical ministry in the Church's central act of worship. Any real presence doctrine was calculated to stress the work of the priest in consecration of the eucharistic elements; by contrast, receptionist doctrine coupled with doctrines of election stressed the relationship of the elect believer to Christ, in which the role of priest or minister was distinctly secondary. As Cranmer put it in the same passage of the *Defence*, 'the priest and ministers prepare the Lord's Supper, read the Gospel, and rehearse Christ's words, but all the people say thereto, Amen'.

The *Defence* was Cranmer's second literary task besides the Ordinal in early 1550: the publication of a semi-official explanation of the eucharistic theology which lay at the heart of his Prayer Book. This was all the more necessary because of the failure of his efforts to do so in the 1548 *Catechism*, and because

20 Commentary on Romans, qu. Stephens, *Holy Spirit in Bucer*, p. 187. For Bucer's views on diversity in the ministry, ibid., pp. 188–9.

21 Cranmer, *Defence*, p. 456: NB the misleading repunctuation 'kings, chancellors' in Cox 1, p. 350.

of the way in which many conservatives were gleefully seizing on the ritual opportunities which the Archbishop had incautiously built into the 1549 liturgy. John Hooper was not simply displaying his usual hyper-sensitivity when he scornfully described, to Heinrich Bullinger, how the Prayer Book was being used as the basis for services which differed from the old mass only in being sung in English, observing the requirement to administer the elements in both kinds and avoiding the name of the mass itself. Quite apart from Privy Council concern at such behaviour by conservative staff at St Paul's Cathedral, an example of what Hooper was talking about can be found in the will of an elderly aristocratic lady of conservative outlook, Bridget Lady Marney, made on 16 September 1549. She left provision for what was clearly going to be an elaborate sung mass with a swarm of priests and choirmen, but using 'such service as is set out and appointed by the King's Book to be used at burials': by 'the King's Book', she meant the new Prayer Book.[22] The book itself had notably avoided any explanation of the sacramental theology which lay behind it, so that the short catechism which it provided for those coming to confirmation said not a word on the subject of sacraments until the Prayer Book revisers of 1604 cannibalized the Calvinist-inspired sacramental section of Alexander Nowell's catechisms from 1570–72.[23] No doubt this was part of the continuing effort in 1549 to keep conservative bishops and theologically aware laity from all-out rebellion, but the year's commotions ended that necessity: now it was time to remove all possibility of misunderstanding the official message.

The result was the first full-length book to bear Cranmer's name on the title-page: *A defence of the true and Catholic doctrine of the sacrament of the body and blood of our saviour Christ. . .*. The work seems to have been published in high summer 1550, since on 26 July the Imperial ambassador could send his master a copy together with an equally obnoxious publication by Hooper; on 28 August a very different commentator, the Flemish refugee Martin Micron, described the book as 'lately published'.[24] The gestation period is, however, likely to have been a long one. While common sense alone would suggest this, in view of the distracting upheavals which Cranmer had experienced in the previous year or two, there is one useful clue from the Archbishop himself: at his trial of September 1555, he referred in the course of a dispute about the eucharist to 'my book . . . made seven years before'. That takes us back to 1548. A careless reading of his remark would then take us to the wildly inappropriate context of the eucharistic theology so clumsily expressed in the Justus Jonas Catechism, but that is not how Cranmer's examiner, Bishop Brooks, understood what he said in 1555. When Brooks retorted that 'your book, which ye brag you made seven years ago, and no man answered it,

22 *E.T.* p. 46 (*O.L.* p. 72); cf. *A.P.C.* 1550–52, p. 138. Abstract of Lady Marney's will in *Testamenta Vetusta*, p. 727.

23 Brightman, *English Rite*, pp. clxxvii–clxxviii, clxxx–clxxxi, 786–90.

24 *C.S.P. Spanish* 1550–52, p. 140; *E.T.* p. 369 (*O.L.* p. 568).

Marcus Antonius hath sufficiently detected and confuted', he made it clear that he knew that Cranmer was talking about the *Defence*, which would be confuted by Stephen Gardiner; Gardiner's later pen-name against Cranmer's eucharistic writings was Marcus Antonius.[25]

We ought therefore to date the first drafts of the *Defence* to autumn 1548: in its conception, it formed part of that barrage of propaganda from the evangelical establishment, when the mysterious Richard Bonner was writing about the eucharist not a thousand miles from Lambeth Palace, and when preparations were being made for the December debate in the House of Lords. As with the 1549 Prayer Book, in preparation at the same time, Cranmer is not likely to have worked on the *Defence* exclusively on his own: one uncharacteristically racy passage about abuses of the mass, in a work which generally tries to maintain a dignified, devotional tone, has a direct echo in the later writings of Thomas Becon, who was always prepared to recycle a good phrase from one of his previous efforts, and this instance is not unique.[26] Such assistance does not alter the value of the *Defence* as an unambiguous statement of Cranmer's eucharistic views, and it further clarifies the chronology of their development: proof, if any more were needed, that both Prayer Books were written with the same eucharistic and general theological agenda behind them.

The *Defence* was divided into five sections, whose polemical architecture was dependent on the relatively brief first section. This set out the nature of the eucharistic sacrament, centring on a recitation of all the Gospel and Pauline texts which could be considered as directly referring to it. Cranmer took two principal points from these citations. First, when Christ referred to the bread as his body, this was precisely to be understood as a signification 'of Christ's own promise and testament' to the one who truly eats 'that he is a member of his body, and receiveth the benefits of his passion which he suffered for us upon the cross'; likewise Christ's description of the wine as his blood was a certificate of his 'legacy and testament, that he is made partaker of the blood of Christ which was shed for us'. Secondly, one must understand what was meant by the true eating of Christ's body: although both good and bad ate bread and drank wine as sacraments, Cranmer emphasized in a classic expression of the *manducatio impiorum* that 'none eateth the body of Christ and drinketh his blood, but they have eternal life', and that this could not include the wicked. All this can be closely paralleled in what he had said in the December 1548 debate.[27]

Having thus established, at least to his own satisfaction, that these were the ground-rules for his discussion, Cranmer enlarged on the devotional

25 Foxe 8, pp. 52, 60.
26 Cf. Cranmer, *Defence*, p. 442 with *Becon's Works* 3, pp. 270–71; also Cranmer, *Defence*, pp. 333–4 with *Becon's Works* 3, p. 426.
27 Cranmer, *Defence*, pp. 292–6. Cf. e.g. BL Royal MS 17 B XXXIX, ff. 3r, 4r, 15rv (Gasquet and Bishop, pp. 400–1, 418–19).

consequences of his view of the sacrament for the believer. He used a striking image deriving from Cyprian of Carthage, who in turn was enlarging on an image in 1 Corinthians 10: the eucharistic bread and wine were a peculiarly fitting metaphor for God's love and of mutual Christian love, because the bread was 'made of a great number of grains of corn, ground, baken and so joined together' in one loaf, and wine was similarly made from 'an infinite number of grapes . . . pressed together in one vessel': this was a sacramental symbol of the 'whole multitude of true Christian people spiritually joined, first to Christ, and then among themselves together' in the Church. The Cyprianic image had a great impact on the reformers, evidently impressing them as a powerful persuasion for the importance of the natural physical quality of the elements: it recurs in such writers as Miles Coverdale, Nicholas Ridley and Roger Hutchinson, and notably it was also used in the anonymous pamphlet which David Selwyn has suggested represents the 'book of doctrine' for the December 1548 eucharistic debate. Cranmer's preliminary discussion culminated in a chapter within his first section which was graphically summarized as affirming that 'the spiritual eating is with the heart, not with the teeth'.[28] Now he could turn to the 'confutation of sundry errors' which was announced on the book's title-page, and which all related to belief in the medieval Western Church. These were four in number: transubstantiation; other general misunderstandings about eucharistic presence, metaphor and sacrament; the belief that 'evil men eat and drink the very body and blood of Christ'; the assertion of a repeated daily sacrificial offering of Christ. The remaining four sections of the book, seven-eighths of the whole text, took each of these errors in turn and refuted them at length. Adoration and oblation, those chief points of controversy in autumn 1548, were dealt with as they arose in the fourth and fifth sections.

One of the crucial sections in the relatively brief Book 5 of the *Defence*, already echoed in the opening words of the book, was the definition and discussion of sacrifice: in effect an extended commentary on what had been intended by the prayer of consecration at the heart of Cranmer's 1549 eucharistic 'canon'. Basing his definitions on the Old Testament sacrifices as viewed through the prism of the Epistle to the Hebrews, Cranmer set up the contrast between the propitiatory sacrifice to pacify God's wrath, and the sacrifice of thanksgiving, 'to testify our duties unto God'. After the prophetic shadow sacrifices of the Old Testament, there has only been one propitiatory sacrifice in human history, that of Christ on the cross.[29] Later, in his 1551 *Answer* to Gardiner's attack, Cranmer would be provoked by Gardiner's mischievous

28 Cranmer, *Defence*, pp. 304–6. For uses of the Cyprianic image, mediated sometimes by Hugh of St Victor, cf. *Hutchinson*, p. 239, *Ridley*, p. 175, *Writings and Translations of Coverdale*, p. 420 (a work based on Zwingli's writings); and Selwyn, 'Vernacular tract', p. 228.

29 Cranmer, *Defence*, pp. 447–9 (Cranmer expressed no public doubts about the Pauline authorship of Hebrews); cf. ibid., pp. 291–2. Cf. Brightman, *English Rite*, pp. 692–3.

appeal to his own Prayer Book to give this contrast of sacrifices a liturgical context in Holy Week. In 1551 he spelt out his view that the propitiatory sacrifice of Christ is not the eucharistic work of Maundy Thursday, which is the institution of a remembrance, the holy communion: it is the work of Good Friday on the cross, 'our perfect redemption'.[30] To confuse these two sacrifices, especially to assert, as had been usual in the Western Church for four or five centuries, that the eucharist is a sacrifice propitiatory for sin, was the worst of modern errors.[31]

This, then, was the centre-piece of his animus against the old mass and its abuses, which the *Answer* of 1551 merely elaborated and clarified, in the face of assault from Stephen Gardiner and Richard Smith. For Cranmer, repetition of the propitiatory sacrifice was inconceivable: witness his repeated insistence of the once-for-all quality of the sacrifice of Christ on Calvary, already so prominent in the 1549 eucharistic rite. All the Church's sacraments, not merely the eucharist, look back to that, in symmetry with Old Testament ceremonies which had looked forward to it.[32] The pictures on the title-page of the *Defence*, putting the Last Supper in the context of the Hebrew Passover meal and the Mosaic miracles of manna from heaven and water from the rock, were designed to hammer home this message. We have already noticed one of the few points in the prose of the *Defence* where Cranmer's tone changed (or perhaps where he was prepared to unleash his assistant Thomas Becon): it was in the description of the multiplication of masses by the old Church, where he approached the later aggressiveness of the *Answer*. Elsewhere, there was no satire, but anger and sorrow in his discussion of repetition of sacrifice and of private masses. Cranmer could in 1551, for the purposes of debate with Richard Smith, still allow the word 'mass', as he had allowed it in the 1549 Prayer Book: the word itself was a matter of indifference, but the abuses behind it were not.[33]

Cranmer's eucharistic discussion places him firmly in the camp of those who wanted to make as clean a break as possible with the Church's tainted past: he would end his second eucharistic treatise, the *Answer*, as he began the preface of his Prayer Books, with a jaundiced discussion of the continual menace of corruption in the Church.[34] In this respect, as we shall see later in this chapter, his year-long struggle to bring John Hooper to conformity with the requirements of the Ordinal was a debate about the timing of change, not about its nature. One can understand his insistence at his 1555 trial that he had only ever held two eucharistic opinions, in other words, that his shift

30 Cox 1, pp. 83, 86. Cranmer in fact talked of Maundy Thursday originally in 1551 as 'a sacrament of his death', but clearly thought this ambiguous, and in subsequent editions it was changed to 'a remembrance of his death': see ibid., p. 86, n. 2.

31 Cranmer, *Defence*, pp. 291–2, and cf. Cox 1, pp. 349, 369.

32 Cranmer, *Defence*, p. 451.

33 Cranmer, *Defence*, pp. 442, 454, 460–61. Cf. Cox 1, p. 369.

34 Brightman, *English Rite*, pp. 34–5, and Cox 1, pp. 377–9.

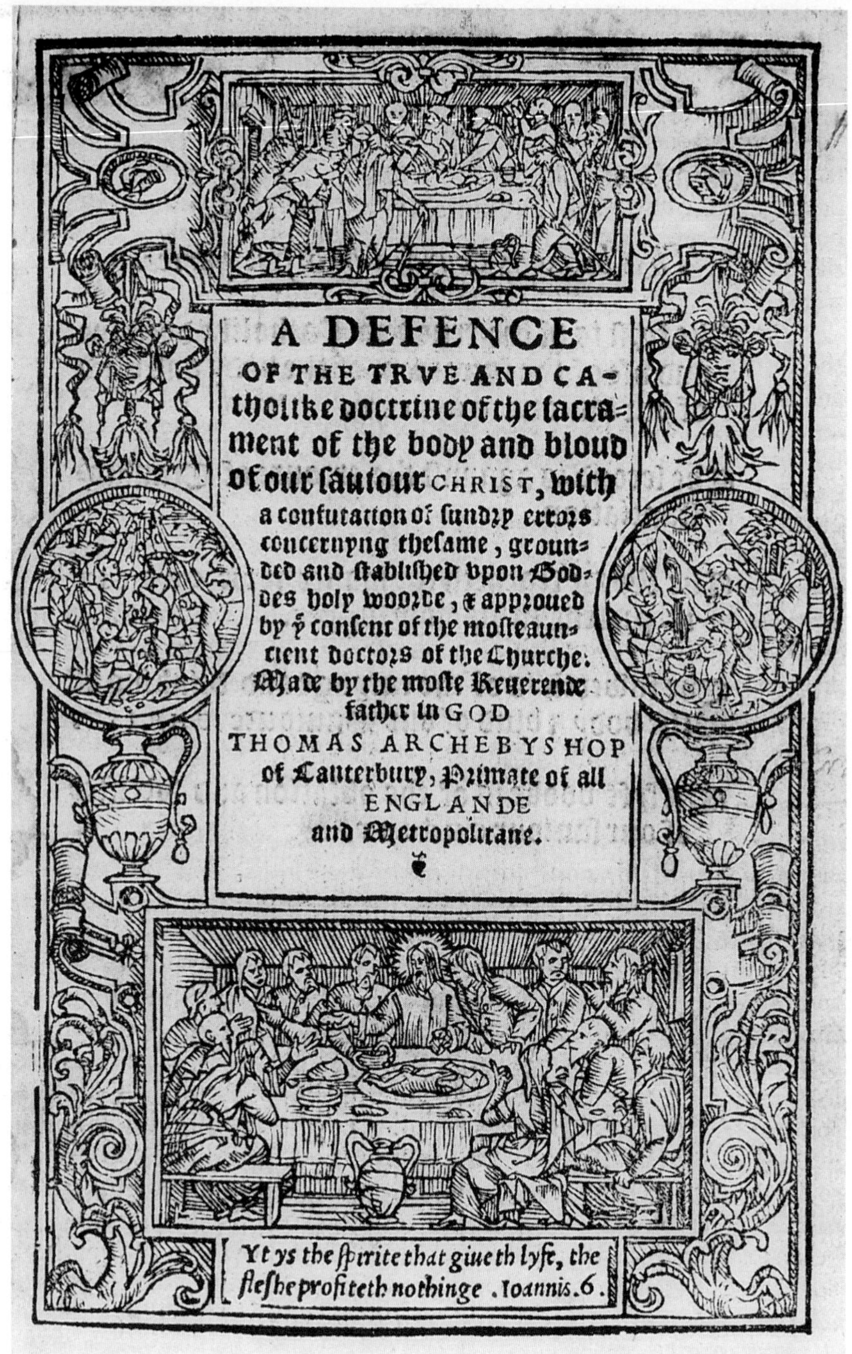

A DEFENCE
OF THE TRVE AND CA-
tholike doctrine of the sacrament of the body and bloud
of our sauiour CHRIST, with
a confutation of sundry errors
concernyng the same, grounded and stablished vpon Goddes holy woorde, & approued
by yͤ consent of the moste aun-
cient doctors of the Churche.
Made by the moste Reuerende
father in GOD
THOMAS ARCHEBYSHOP
of Canterbury, Primate of all
ENGLANDE
and Metropolitane.

Yt ys the spirite that giueth lyfe, the
fleshe profiteth nothinge. Ioannis.6.

33 Title-page of the 1550 edition of the *Defence*. It shows the Passover meal at the head, roundels depicting manna from heaven and water from the rock flank the sides, and the Last Supper is in the largest block at the foot.

from strict transubstantiation to a less closely defined realist position, in the 1530s, was not nearly as important as his shift, after 1546, to spiritual presence and the receptionist doctrine of the *manducatio impiorum*. When Gardiner in 1551 sought to embarrass him, with the memory of what he had said in defence of real presence in 1538 against John Lambert, Cranmer had no hesitation in admitting that he had then defended 'the untruth, which I then took for the truth . . . but praise be to the everliving God, who hath wiped away those Satanish scales from mine eyes!'[35]

A striking feature of the *Defence* was the confidence with which it brought the writers of the early Church as witnesses for its case: Augustine, as ever, and a ground-bass of the Latin fathers of the fourth and fifth centuries, with (as we have already noted) a considerable interest also in the third-century Cyprian. The Greeks were a long way behind, with the exception of Cranmer's perennial favourite John Chrysostom, especially the manuscript newly discovered by Peter Martyr in Florence: however, among other Greek writers, an important quotation from the second-century Justin Martyr put in an appearance late in the book's development, and Cranmer also drew on Peter Martyr's previous use of the *Dialogues* of Theodoret of Cyrrhus.[36] The agenda of the book, announced on the title-page, was that the case would be 'grounded and stablished upon God's holy word and approved by the consent of the most ancient doctors of the Church': in other words, the proof would come from scripture, but the most reliable post-scriptural traditions would vindicate the early Church's integrity by showing its agreement with the reformed understanding of the biblical message.

As Dr Walsh points out, Cranmer's use of the word 'doctors' on the title-page was not carried through to the rest of the work; neither was there much use of the term which would later be an Anglican favourite, 'the Fathers'. The term 'doctor' had connotations which the reformed Archbishop would not have relished: not just of the authority of the traditional Church, which had conveyed this reverential title on certain favoured writers, including Pope Gregory the Great (not one of Cranmer's favourites), but also of the fact that sets of Greek and Latin 'Doctors' made regular appearances in the ecclesiastical art which Cranmer had by now come to despise. Instead, he preferred to speak of 'authors', as he would have learnt to do in his years at Cambridge, where, as in universities for several centuries, this word would have been used to distinguish those writers whose antiquity gave their opinion a special right to be heard (*auctoritas*) over against the 'moderns'.[37] It must also be said that he generally used these 'authors' in a thoroughly medieval way, triumphantly flourishing the sentences which he captured from them like scalps, with little

35 Cox 1, pp. 240–41.

36 For Justin, Cranmer, *Defence*, pp. 320–21, and Selwyn, '"Book of Doctrine"', p. 469 and n. 106; on Theodoret, Cranmer, *Defence*, pp. 388–93, Walsh, 'Cranmer and the Fathers', p. 242, and Anderson, 'Martyr', pp. 461–3.

37 Walsh, 'Cranmer and the Fathers', pp. 237–8.

feel for their overall historical context. In this respect, he was not unique: few theologians within the sixteenth-century humanist world had really absorbed the lasting lessons of relativism in the practice of scientific history, which would be the ultimate legacy of humanism.

By now Cranmer's respect for, and easy familiarity with, ancient authority should cause the reader little surprise. Lying behind the work is a set of detailed notes compiling discussions on the eucharist from earlier writers: entitled '*de re sacramentaria*' and dateable to autumn 1547 at the earliest, these are now preserved at Corpus Christi, Cambridge.[38] They were prepared in Cranmer's habitual fashion, using the enviable resources of his great library: a clerk wrote the text to a prepared scheme, and Cranmer made his own additional annotations, additionally making cross-references to other notebooks so far not identified. The order of the citations and headings in the manuscript can be shown to be very close to that of the second, third and fourth sections of Cranmer's *Defence*. Besides these collections, in the later stages of his work, Cranmer could draw on the independent labours of his scholar-secretary, Pierre Alexandre, who during 1549 and early 1550 devoted himself to producing volumes of extracts from patristic sources, arranged with elaborate indices for easy reference.[39]

Dr Walsh's detailed comparison of the Corpus notebook with the published text reveals how Cranmer exploited his knowledge of the Fathers: he made good use of traditional collections of extracts, especially Gratian's standard twelfth-century compilation the *Decretum*, but he also recognized and corrected some of Gratian's faults and misattributions, because of his detailed knowledge of up-to-date humanist printed editions of the patristic writers. One modern humanist anthology which he much employed was the *Unio Dissidentium*: its authorship still remains mysterious, but it was a pioneering effort of the 1520s to enlist the Fathers in the reformers' cause, and its eucharistic stance was that of Strassburg and Switzerland: by 1550 very congenial to the author of the *Defence*. Sections of citations in the *Unio* still appear in the same order embedded in Cranmer's final published text.[40] There was nothing especially original in his research: why should there be? The job of dragooning the Fathers into supporting the spiritual presence view of the eucharist had mostly been done already by the *Unio* and by Johannes Oecolampadius of Basel. Peter Martyr added other important witnesses in his innovative use of Chrysostom and Theodoret, and indeed Cranmer had no hesitation in incorporating passages from the writings of Martyr himself in

38 C.C.C.C. MS 102, pp. 151–93; on the dating and good reasons for direct association with the *Defence*, Walsh, 'Cranmer and the Fathers', pp. 239, 241, 245. It is worth noting that this same volume contains the shorter version of the eucharistic tract discussed by Selwyn, 'Book of Doctrine', and above, Ch. 9, pp. 397–8.

39 C.U.L. MS Ee.2.8, finished on 28 April 1550; the statement of Anderson (*Martyr*, pp. 349–50), that Lambeth MS 1108 represents the other volume is a mistake.

40 Walsh, 'Cranmer and the Fathers', pp. 243; Anderson, 'Martyr', pp. 456–63.

his text. This was a book designed for polemical use, not to show off an archbishop's cleverness.[41]

Probably the last section of the *Defence* to be written was its preface. This was an outspoken attack on 'the Romish Antichrist' for a wilful distortion of eucharistic doctrine. After a paean of praise to Henry VIII and Edward VI for the removal of monks and friars and for the introduction of a vernacular liturgy, Cranmer went on in a now celebrated passage to the heart of his quarrel with the old world of devotion:

> many corrupt weeds be plucked up . . . But what availeth it to take away beads, pardons, pilgrimages and such other like popery, so long as two chief roots remain unpulled up? . . . the very body of the tree, or rather the roots of the weeds, is the popish doctrine of transubstantiation, of the real presence of Christ's flesh and blood in the sacrament of the altar (as they call it), and of the sacrifice and oblation of Christ made by the priest for the salvation of the quick and the dead. Which roots, if they be suffered to grow in the Lord's vineyard, they will spread all the ground again with the old errors and superstition.

This was the purpose of his book, and his duty and calling as Primate of all England: 'to cut down this tree, and to pluck up the weeds and plants by the roots'. Yet there is a contrast in the Preface (and in the *Defence* as a whole) with the unpleasing monotony of the anger in Cranmer's answer to the Western rebels of 1549: here, there is an obvious and urgent pastoral concern for the people entrusted to his care. He called 'all that profess Christ, that they flee far from Babylon'. 'Hearken to Christ, give ear unto his words, which shall lead you the right way unto everlasting life.' This was the language of the Prayer Book given a revolutionary edge.[42]

Now that the evangelical establishment had seen off the political challenge from Catholics and was consolidating its power, its problems came as much from its own side as from conservative opposition: those who felt that the careful pacing of evangelical change in Edward's Church was over-cautious, even a betrayal of the cause. This was a common concern among the émigrés; we have noted Cranmer trying to calm the worries of Bucer and Fagius as soon as they had arrived (see above, Ch. 10, p. 410). Although at first those two luminaries professed themselves happy with his explanations, by winter 1550 one can find disillusionment in Bucer's correspondence and an unmistakeable sense of grievance that the visitors were not being properly consulted on the pace of change. When he had first come to England, Bucer had been pleasantly overwhelmed by the demands which an excited Cranmer had made on him: a new biblical commentary, a guide for the Ordinal revision, contributions to the battery of literature to answer those involved in the 1549 commotions. Autumn 1549 had brought Bucer both the death of Fagius and

41 Walsh, 'Cranmer and the Fathers', p. 244.
42 Cranmer, *Defence*, pp. 288–90.

personal ill-health, which he would never again shake off; these blows left him intensely depressed, and he was additionally offended and anxious because of the time that it took the government to establish his official status in Cambridge. Perhaps the English backsliding over the final form of the Ordinal was a last straw, which stirred him to feeling that he and his fellow-experts, veterans of more fully reformed churches in Strassburg and elsewhere, were being underexploited. He was most frank about this when writing to Guillaume Farel of Geneva, on 12 January 1550. He repeated an earlier complaint to Farel that neither he, Peter Martyr, Bernardino Ochino nor any other of the exiles was given any chance to advise on the programme of reform, 'although we have not ceased to lobby our Patron [i.e. Cranmer] face to face and in writing about a true and firmly grounded restoration of the kingdom of Christ'.[43]

Cranmer was not disposed to eat humble pie in front of his friends; he might have pointed out to them that their presence in England as refugees was hardly a recommendation for the strategy of their own ministries, and indeed for nearly a decade before his flight, Bucer himself had been at odds with the city authorities of Strassburg precisely about the slowness of change in the city. Bucer gloomily reported to Farel the Archbishop's robust riposte that he 'gave the greatest thanks to God that they had achieved so much, even if vestments and other things of that sort had been kept; and he does not acknowledge that anything of Antichrist had been kept, since Christ's teaching is purely administered'. Cranmer had also shrewdly drawn his critics' attention to similar compromises in the Church of Saxony and elsewhere. What increased Bucer's frustration was the knowledge (conveyed for instance in a previous letter to him from John Calvin) that he himself was, in turn, being blamed for giving countenance to Edwardian compromise by his presence in England: 'Let those who falsely attack me because I am here where something of the old leaven is retained, consider how true charity prescribes brothers to be judged, and also that without charity we are nothing.' He continued with a prolonged wail of exhausted misery to Farel about the state of England, his many enemies, and his own troubles. Only the young King Edward – too young to be an immediate saviour – and support from that doyenne of evangelicals the Duchess of Suffolk provided much consolation. He repeated many of the same complaints four months later, in a letter to Calvin: the Geneva leadership was coming to represent for him almost the only reliable confidential counsellors in an unsympathetic world.[44]

43 Letter now at Neuchâtel pr. in Hopf, *Bucer*, pp. 253–6. For 'lobby' I am reading *movere* for *monere*, but in context the difference in meaning is not great. The letter appears to be in response to concerns expressed in Calvin's letter to Bucer, ?October 1549, pr. Gorham, *Gleanings*, pp. 114–18.

44 *E.T.* pp. 356–8 (*O.L.* pp. 545–8); see also his complaints to Brenz, *E.T.* p. 355 (*O.L.* pp. 542–4). On Bucer at Strassburg in the 1540s, see Abray, *People's Reformation*, p. 72.

Yet Cranmer could be confident that Bucer would not cause him any serious trouble. At the same time as he was bemoaning the shortcomings of the English Church tolerated by the Archbishop, the Strassburg reformer was self-consciously holding the line against what he regarded as unacceptable radicalism on eucharistic doctrine encouraged from Zürich. Bucer repeatedly deplored the unnecessary concessions which he felt that Peter Martyr had made in that direction, during the course of his 1549 Oxford disputation about the eucharist. 'I have as yet met with no real Christians who were not entirely satisfied with our simple view of the subject, as soon as it had been properly explained to them', he wrote to his former colleague Brenz, with blissful lack of self-awareness.[45] Nor was Bucer prepared to quit England, despite its dismal state; he busily made sure that he would not be recalled back to Strassburg by the collegiate Church of St Thomas (of which he was still nominally Dean), protesting that there was so much good work to be done in his new home.[46] Cranmer was careful in the wake of their frank exchange of views, at the turn of the year, that Bucer did not feel further alienated, and he kept in close touch with him at Cambridge: Pierre Alexandre faithfully and affectionately reported to Cambridge from Lambeth Palace, on the Archbishop's behalf, what was going on in national politics, and he emphasized Cranmer's concern that the German stove which would make the East Anglian climate bearable should soon be appearing in Cambridge.[47] This attention would pay off over the next year, during which Cranmer would find Bucer of considerable use against other reformers who were prepared to make a public issue of their unhappiness with the pace of change: principally John Hooper and the foreigner who emerged as his chief ally among the émigrés, Jan Laski.

Hooper had already expressed to various continental friends his disgust with the whole 1549 Prayer Book, but in spring 1550 he decided to take his stand on the same Ordinal revision which for different reasons had troubled Bishop Heath. Ironically, his opportunity was at least formally provided him by Cranmer, who was responsible for delivering the official invitation to preach a Lenten course of sermons at Court: Hooper took as his theme the book of Jonah, a suitable peg for diatribes against a wicked city. He waited until the publication of the Ordinal in March before making a two-pronged attack on it in his third sermon; he 'did not a little wonder' at the retention of the mention of saints in the oath of supremacy, and he also criticized the retention of vestments in the rite, since they were 'rather the habit and vesture of Aaron and the gentiles, than of the ministers of Christ'.[48] He also said, with

45 *E.T.* pp. 354–5 (*O.L.* p. 545).

46 Gorham, *Gleanings*, pp. 144–5; cf. *E.T.* pp. 358–9 (*O.L.* pp. 549–51; 26 December 1549, there misdated to 1550).

47 C.C.C.C. MS 119, p. 303.

48 *E.T.* p. 48 (*O.L.* p. 75); the passage (in his sermon of 5 March) is in Hooper, *Early Writings*, pp. 478–9.

elaborate puzzlement, that he could not imagine how the oath by the saints had been allowed 'or who is the author of that book': a common device of the time for legimitizing harsh words. This artifice did not spare Hooper from Cranmer's fury, and within four days the Archbishop had brought a charge against him in Star Chamber about what he had said about the supremacy oath, which could be construed as sedition. However, after much argument involving the judges and the bishops present (probably Goodrich and Cranmer), Hooper was able by the end of the month to report a triumphant result of this clash to Heinrich Bullinger.[49] Far from suffering harm from Cranmer's accusation, Hooper would soon be nominated to the diocese of Gloucester, which was yet another see newly liberated from conservative control, this time by the death of Bishop John Wakeman. Cranmer cannot have enjoyed attending the Privy Council meeting on Ascension Day (15 May) which confirmed the appointment, after Hooper had at first refused to accept the royal offer of the diocese. Hooper was already laying down his conditions for taking Gloucester: no formal address as 'my lord', no shaving off his long beard, no episcopal white rochet and black chimere, no anointing at his consecration – and more. Yet that day it seemed to him at least that all his demands would be met; he went off in triumph on holiday to his native Somerset, to a long-postponed reunion with a family whose continuing religious conservatism probably meant that they welcomed him with mixed emotions.[50]

The outcome of the confrontation about the oath was hardly surprising: once he had recovered from his natural annoyance at the attack on his liturgical handiwork, Cranmer knew that he was in a peculiarly awkward position about the saints in the oath of supremacy. In compiling the Ordinal, he could not possibly have unilaterally altered its wording from the form in which Henry VIII had cast it, but the saints were looking increasingly unwelcome guests in the official prose of Edward VI's regime. Their final ejection from the oath of supremacy came in an appropriately frivolous manner that summer, and to add to the sweetness of Hooper's victory, it was during the course of his own formal confirmation in the bishopric of Gloucester in July: in one of Edward's first acts of teenage self-assertion in government, the young king was alerted to the clause about the saints in the supremacy oath which the new bishop was about to take, and he angrily struck it out with his own pen. This was a Henry VIII in the making: seldom

49 *E.T.* p. 51 (*O.L.* p. 81). Hooper's mention of the judges indicates that this was a session of Star Chamber rather than of the Privy Council. Attendance of Goodrich and Cranmer nevertheless deduced from Privy Council attendance at this time: *A.P.C. 1547–50*, pp. 406–8.

50 *A.P.C. 1550–52*, pp. 30–31. Hooper's own account is *E.T.* p. 55 (*O.L.* p. 87); his conditions are described by Christopher Hales: *E.T.* p. 187 (*O.L.* p. 124). '*Radi*' is translated in *O.L.* as 'to receive the tonsure', but it is most unlikely by this stage that senior clergy were expected to be tonsured; whereas we know that Hooper ostentatiously sported an impressive beard. Cf. also *E.T.* pp. 364–6 (*O.L.* pp. 559–63).

has there been a more immediate demonstration of the meaning of the Royal Supremacy in the Tudor Church. Yet Edward could not have succeeded in his gesture if the adults in attendance had not recognized the logic of his action against the background of the previous four years of change.[51]

Less straightforward was the matter of clerical dress and ceremonies; in the end, as we pursue a complex story, we shall find that on this issue Hooper suffered a humiliating reverse, despite having won his point on the matter of the oath. Cranmer had consecrated John Ponet as Bishop of Rochester at the end of June, probably the first occasion on which the new episcopal Ordinal had been used: his Register made a particular point of recording the exact dress of those taking part. Now at the end of July, despite Hooper's confirmation before the King, Ridley and Cranmer between them blocked any further progress in Hooper's consecration if he would not wear the prescribed garments, and they were not intimidated by successive letters, first from the Earl of Warwick and then from the whole Council, ordering them to proceed. Instead, Ridley convinced the majority of members of the Council that Hooper was needlessly trouble-making over things indifferent by raising objections to clerical dress, in the face of a clear command from authority. Despite much lobbying and emphatic statements of his case, Hooper never regained the initiative in the affair.[52]

Why had Hooper suffered this sudden reverse? One possible reason was an immediate political consideration, the culmination of an entirely different episcopal drama: weeks of negotiations with Bishop Stephen Gardiner, to see whether he could be persuaded to conformity with the official religious programme in return for his rehabilitation, finally broke down on 19 July, the day before Hooper's confirmation by King Edward. The government was anxious to keep this breakdown secret for the time being, and Ridley could have represented to the Council that this was a bad moment to make an ostentatious gesture towards change: Hooper's consecration would have been turned into an aggressive evangelical demonstration if he were to have his way. Additionally, Hooper demonstrated his indifference to political timing and self-preservation when, at the height of his confrontation with Cranmer and Ridley in late July and August, he chose to preach about and also republish his radical views on divorce, which he maintained was necessary after irretrievable breakdown of a marriage.[53]

Hooper's outspokenness about divorce was a useful piece of evidence for his maverick status, on an issue which was arousing acute controversy, but

51 *E.T.* p. 274 (*O.L.* pp. 415–16): there is no reason to doubt the truth of this story.

52 Cranmer's Register, ff. 330v–331v; *E.T.* pp. 368–9 (*O.L.* pp. 566–7); Northumberland's and the Council's letters are pr. in Foxe 6, p. 641. The standard and reliable treatment of the whole affair is Primus, *Vestments Controversy*.

53 On the negotiations with Gardiner, see Muller, *Gardiner*, pp. 186–94. On Hooper and divorce, see *E.T.* pp. 274–5 (*O.L.* p. 416), *Early Writings of Hooper*, pp. 268–70, 379–84, and Gorham, *Gleanings*, p. 186.

Cranmer and Ridley could conjure up a still more profound fear. They managed to present the bishop-elect's continuing recalcitrance as a threat to all authority and due order, thus finding the Achilles heel of Hooper's position as surely as Hooper had found Cranmer's vulnerability over the oath. Their success reflected the acute nervousness about popular unrest that affected the government after the 1549 commotions. This was based on the reality of continual minor outbreaks of protest through 1550, but what deepened official fears, when Hooper pursued the goal of religious change, was the possibility that popular social and political protest might link up with the religious radicalism which affected much the same area of the country: London, and the surrounding counties in the south-east. We must therefore turn once more to consider the neurosis of the reformers about Anabaptists: those who outflanked them in theological and political radicalism, and who in their eyes perverted the work of reformation.

The radicals were just as troublesome in 1550 as they had been before, and the campaign against them now took on a new intensity. Even as round one of the Hooper-Cranmer confrontation was drawing towards Hooper's Ascension Day vindication at the Council board, on 2 May Joan Bocher was finally brought from prison to suffer death at the stake for heresy about the divine and human natures of Christ, a year after the royal tribunal presided over by the Archbishop had condemned her; she had been 'kept in hope of conversion', as the King put in his journal. She died utterly unrepentant, offending all the proprieties both as a woman and as a subject of punishment by 'raging and railing' against the Canterbury Six Preacher John Scory, who had been chosen, probably by Cranmer, to preach at her burning.[54] Before she died, frenzied efforts were made to get her to change her opinions as she lay in confinement at Lord Chancellor Rich's house. She must have been flattered, and probably strengthened in the proclamation of her faith, by repeated visits from the Primate of All England and the bishops of London and Ely. They were only chief among such luminaries of the evangelical establishment as Thomas Lever, David Whitehead and Roger Hutchinson, the latter being the author of *The Image of God*, an exercise in orthodox christological exposition dedicated to Cranmer, which was published less than two months after Bocher's death, and which paid specific attention to her views in the light of his final debate with her.[55]

Joan Bocher's burning was a significant moment for the Edwardian Reformation. In 1547 the government had ostentatiously secured the parliamentary repeal of all previous heresy legislation which had burnt heretics; now, as in the setting-up of the heresy tribunals against radicals in 1548 and 1549, it simply relied on the residual common-law powers of the Crown over heresy to

54 'Scudamore', p. 131; *Wriothesley's Chronicle* 2, pp. 37–8, which very misleadingly mistranscribes the preacher's name as Story. *Chronicle of Edward VI*, p. 28. Cf. the Catholic propagandist Miles Huggarde on Bocher: Knott, *Discourses of martyrdom*, p. 58.

55 Foxe 7, p. 631 (dated by *A.P.C. 1550–52*, p. 19); *Hutchinson*, pp. 145–6.

get its way, and in doing so, it reached the ultimate measure of persecution. Posterity has not been sympathetic, and has made the obvious comparison between the fiery deaths of Joan and of Cranmer himself. It is not surprising that the religious radicals immediately made this connection; a recurrent theme in their pronouncements on the established Protestant Church well into Elizabeth's reign was a reproach to the official hero-martyrs Ridley and Cranmer for the burning of Joan of Kent, even to the extent of seeing their deaths as a divine vengeance for hers.[56] Later, the most extreme statement of the same view came from a different variety of radical, William Cobbett, whose *History of the Protestant Reformation* (1829) won frequent grateful reprints from Roman Catholic presses: he said of Cranmer that his name could not be pronounced 'without almost doubting of the justice of God, were it not for our knowledge of the fact, that the cold-blooded, most perfidious man expired at last amidst those flames which he himself had been the chief cause of kindling'.[57]

What is more surprising is to find that writer so central to English Protestant identity, John Foxe, taking the same stance. Foxe was very unusual among English evangelicals in deploring all executions for religion, even of those who were clearly in error. He made clear his disapproval of what had happened to Bocher, in the 1559 Latin edition of his great work on Christian martyrs, in a passage reflecting on Cranmer's eventual death at the stake, which he then decided was too controversial and deleted from subsequent editions. Here he told an anecdote supposedly related to him by one of his readers, probably a thin disguise for Foxe himself: at the time when Joan was under condemnation, this man had lobbied Bishop Ridley's clerical protégé, John Rogers, to use his influence with Cranmer to get mercy for her. Rogers, however, refused to help, and he even defended burning as the most merciful form of execution for such a crime, despite its association with papal discipline. This provoked his friend to the furious riposte, 'Well then, maybe you will find out that on some occasion you yourself will have your hands full of this same gentle burning' – a remark which proved all too accurate, since Rogers was the first victim of Mary's burnings in 1555. Foxe followed this story with a similar prophetic remark from one of the radical Freewiller leaders facing imprisonment from Cranmer in 1552: it was extraordinary, and a proof of his strong feelings on the subject, that he should tell two such sympathic tales about enemies of the evangelical cause.[58] Even after he had decided on self-censorship and had excised this passage, Foxe remained so upset by the Bocher affair that, most uncharacteristically, he continued to tell a disapproving tale of his hero Cranmer: he said that

56 Knox, *Works* 5, p. 222; cf. *Rogers* p. 350, and Williams, *Radical Reformation*, pp. 789–90.
57 Cobbett, *Protestant Reformation*, para. 64.
58 The omitted passage was printed by the nineteenth-century editors as an appendix, Foxe, 5, p. 860; a translation of the first part is provided in Mozley, *Foxe*, pp. 35–6. On Foxe generally, see Elton, 'Persecution and Toleration', pp. 171–80.

the Archbishop bullied a reluctant Edward VI into signing Joan's death warrant.

The likelihood is that this story was exaggerated, but not as much as tender-hearted admirers of Cranmer have argued ever since the time of John Strype; it did little injustice to the Archbishop's position.[59] Cranmer was prepared to put a good deal of effort into argument and persuasion of the heretically inclined, and sometimes, as in the case of John Champneys, it succeeded, no doubt to his delight (see above, Ch. 10, pp. 424–5). However, when persuasion failed, there was no reason not to prescribe death. I have argued elsewhere that Cranmer saw erring evangelicals as far worse than papists, committing a double rather than a single offence. Conservatives were in error, but they might be part of the elect awaiting the words which would bring them the consciousness of gospel truth. When evangelicals taught wrong doctrine, their sin did not just affect themselves; their bad example could hinder these traditionalists who were making their painful journey towards true faith.[60] Cranmer would indeed have been the obvious person among the Privy Councillors in persuading the young King of his duty to burn his first heretic in 1550, but the Archbishop was hardly a disciplinary voice crying in the wilderness.

One has to realize how exceptional Foxe was in the mainstream of Tudor thought. Most evangelicals, like John Rogers, felt no problem in seeing the most obstinate heretics burnt: Roger Hutchinson in his *Image of God* coldly said that the evangelical preacher's responsibility was to excommunicate Anabaptist offenders, hand them over to the civil magistrate and then let the law take its course, whether death or otherwise. Likewise Bucer, in his last great work of 1550, *De Regno Christi*, which was specifically written with England in mind, had no problem with the death penalty; death inflicted by the civil power on obstinate heretics was also clearly envisaged in the reform of canon law which was completed in draft in 1553, in chapters including one heavily corrected by Cranmer himself.[61] Even the prospect of their own deaths in the fire during Mary's reign did not alter the opinion of mainstream evangelicals: Archdeacon John Philpot under examination in 1555, when he was well aware that his only fate would likewise be the stake, still asserted that Bocher was 'well worthy to be burnt'.[62] If one considers the most celebrated Continental analogy, the burning of the unitarian Miguel Servetus by the authorities at Geneva in 1553, it is notorious that if anything estab-

59 Foxe 5, p. 699. For sensible discussion of Cranmer, Edward VI and Bocher, Ridley, *Cranmer*, pp. 291–3.

60 MacCulloch, 'Archbishop Cranmer: consensus and tolerance' [forthcoming].

61 *Hutchinson*, p. 201. For a useful discussion of the relationship between the two documents, see Sachs, 'Cranmer's "Reformatio Legum Ecclesiasticarum"', pp. 111–16, and on heresy, p. 115. *Reformation of Laws*, ed. Cardwell, pp. 25, 27, 330.

62 Foxe 7, p. 631.

lished John Calvin's European-wide reputation as the doyen of Protestant theologians, it was that incident of retribution against a theological radical. England's last burning of a heretic would take place in the reign of that philosopher-king, James I, in 1612.

It was no coincidence that Bocher's burning came at the same time as the completion of moves to create a 'Stranger Church': that is, to give an officially recognized ecclesiastical status to the communities of refugees which were by now numbered in hundreds – primarily Dutch, but also including Germans, Italians and French. One major motive was to provide a structure of discipline for a group which, if left unregulated, would provide perfect cover for refugee radicals: Martin Micron noted this (linking the foundation specifically with Bocher's death), and so did King Edward in his journal, when in June he noted the grant to the Strangers of London's old Austin Friars church, 'for avoiding of all sects of Anabaptists and suchlike'. In the following year, the Stranger Church would demonstrate how effectively it could do this job, when it co-operated with Cranmer and a royal heresy commission in a second burning for heresy. This time the victim was a Fleming in the refugee congregation, George van Parris – again, his death caused John Foxe distress which he at first expressed in print, but then decided to censor out in the English editions of his work.[63] It was the hope of disciplining radicalism which explains the remarkable generosity of the Austin Friars grant.

The completion of the grant's formalities in July came only a day after John Hooper's triumphant confirmation as Bishop of Gloucester. For this reason, Andrew Pettegree's recent (and admirable) account of the London Stranger Church under Edward chooses to emphasize its partisan role in the continuing conflict between Hooper, on the one hand, and Cranmer and Ridley on the other, as a constant encouragement for root-and-branch reformation in the Church of England. There is no doubt of the importance of these thoroughly reformed congregations in the midst of a national Church which was half-reformed; they were a signpost to one version of the future. Their lively devotional and intellectual life soon attracted wide interest in London, and there is also no doubt that Ridley considered them a nuisance and did his best, as newly appointed Bishop of London, to harass their independent establishment.[64] However, the battle-lines in the Stranger Church's foundation were complicated by the Anabaptist background and the terror that radicalism had inspired among all evangelicals. Hooper had been at the forefront of the fight against the radicals from the moment of his return to England in 1549 (see above, Ch. 10, pp. 424–5); equally, as he continued to clash with Cranmer before the Council during summer 1550, one of the reasons for Hooper's enduring favour with the majority of Councillors was that he could be useful

63 *Chronicle of Edward VI*, p. 37; *E.T.* p. 365 (*O.L.* p. 560). On Van Parris, Cranmer's Register, f. 78rv; Pettegree, *Foreign Protestant Communities*, pp. 65–6; Mozley, *Foxe*, p. 36.

64 Pettegree, *Foreign Protestant Communities*, pp. 30–37.

against Anabaptists, and he was sent off to Essex and Kent to help Lord Chancellor Rich pursue the campaign against them in the wake of Bocher's burning.[65]

In this respect, Cranmer had no quarrel with the Bishop-elect of Gloucester. More cynically, he might have welcomed Hooper's departure into the home counties as a handy means of removing him from the London scene. Even so, because of the Anabaptist menace, there is no doubt that Hooper and Cranmer (if not Ridley) saw eye to eye on the creation of the Stranger Church as an essential curb on radicalism. The new superintendent-designate, the Polish exile Jan Laski, was much admired by Hooper, but equally Laski had been invited back to England by Cranmer himself, and he was the Archbishop's guest at Lambeth Palace after he arrived from Emden in May, until the technicalities of the foundation had been sorted out. Moreover, Cranmer as much as Hooper took a keen personal interest in the foundation, somewhat to the surprise of those who noted Ridley's obstructiveness; it was the Archbishop's secretary, Pierre Alexandre, who made sure that the francophone section of the congregation was given proper mention, alongside the Dutch, in the draft petition which secured the royal grant.[66]

Yet it cannot be denied that, in Jan Laski, Hooper gained an articulate and uninhibited ally in his crusade for drastic reformation. All the 'abuses' that Hooper was crusading against in the English Church were at a stroke removed in the practice and discipline of the Stranger Church, over which Laski presided with all the episcopal decisiveness that characterized John Calvin's version of presbyterian polity at Geneva. This no doubt came as an unpleasant shock to Cranmer, not simply because it would have seemed a poor reward for his hospitality to Laski at Lambeth Palace, but also because Laski's previous visit to England in 1548 had been an uncontroversial success. Hugh Latimer, for instance, had deplored the fact that Laski had quickly returned to Emden in 1549, and he had publicly referred to it in one of his sermons, as a stick to beat Somerset's government with, for its parsimony to the deserving godly. The great issue in the England of 1548 had been the nature of the eucharist, a subject on which Laski's views usefully coincided with the development of Cranmer's own thinking; likewise as far as that issue was concerned, when Laski came back, there was little chance of any argument between him and the author of the *Defence*.[67] Laski's 1548–9 visit had been part of Cranmer's masterplan to fulfil his vision of a true General Council, and there can be little doubt that together with the need to curb Anabaptism, this prospect was one

65 *E.T.* p. 55 (*O.L.* pp. 86–7).

66 Pettegree, *Foreign Protestant Communities*, pp. 36–7; on Cranmer's supportiveness, *E.T.* p. 369 (*O.L.* p. 568), and on his 1550 invitation to Laski, *Melanchthons Briefwechsel* 6, no. 5796. For contemporary popular admiration of the community, see Davies, 'Boulogne and Calais from 1545 to 1550', pp. 80–81.

67 *Latimer's Sermons*, p. 141. For the claim that Laski materially influenced Cranmer's eucharistic ideas, see *E.T.* p. 253 (*O.L.* p. 383). It is unlikely that Cranmer needed much prompting by autumn 1548: see above, Ch. 9.

of the two elements which fuelled the Archbishop's enthusiasm for the Stranger Church's foundation.

Yet quite apart from the entanglement with the Hooper controversy, the return of Laski failed to live up to Cranmer's expectations. One of the tasks which Laski was very concerned to fulfil on his second visit was the promulgation of a general agreed statement on the sacraments among the reformers exiled in England: a vital component of the attempt to keep alive the earlier hopes of creating an ecumenical front against Rome. Here the eucharist was still the problem, or to be more precise, the problem was Martin Bucer, with his habitual worry about the corruption of symbolist eucharistic ideas stemming from Zürich. Almost as soon as Laski had arrived at Lambeth Palace, he entered a long albeit reasonably eirenic wrangle on the subject, first with Pierre Alexandre and then with Bucer himself, a debate which remained unresolved at Bucer's death. This was the only obstacle to the preparation of the agreed statement, but as so often in such discussions in the Reformation, this one issue proved fatal to the conclusion of the whole enterprise.[68]

Rather than this parallel debate on the eucharist, the issues which led to a confrontation between Cranmer and Laski were those on which Hooper had decided to make his stand before accepting the bishopric of Gloucester: clerical dress and questions of ceremonial. Now that Hooper's struggle became directly linked to the struggles of the Stranger Church, Hooper and Laski almost certainly began co-ordinating their arguments: the essence of the case was that the ceremonies and garments under dispute were far from indifferent as Ridley maintained, but were offensive in a reformed Church.[69] Already in August Laski was finding himself cross-questioned by Paulet, the Lord Treasurer, about his reasons for not adopting the ceremonies of the *Book of Common Prayer* in the Stranger Church. Paulet had his own conservative religious agenda, but Martin Micron saw his attitude, and the delays which he caused in the handing-over of Austin Friars to Laski, as part of Ridley's harassment of the new congregations. Faced with this alarming change of official mood, Laski addressed a lengthy memorandum to Cranmer defending the independent practice and discipline of the Stranger Church; its content makes clear that it followed on earlier arguments between the two leaders.

Laski sought to refute Cranmer's arguments that, on the matter of clerical dress, the Stranger congregations ought to use what was commanded by authority, which exercised legitimate rights in things indifferent – these were, of course, precisely the points which Hooper and Ridley were now fighting out. Additionally, already Cranmer had expressed his unhappiness

68 For the opening stages of the eucharistic debate, see Gorham, *Gleanings*, pp. 148–50, and *E.T.* p. 368 (*O.L.* p. 566), and for crisp discussion on the dispute, *Bucer*, ed. Wright, pp. 385–7. On the ecumenical statement, cf. e.g. *E.T.* p. 372 (*O.L.* p. 572); Gorham, *Gleanings*, pp. 198–9, 235–6.

69 Pettegree, *Foreign Protestant Communities*, pp. 40–42, for this and the account of the Hooper affair which follows, where not otherwise referenced.

with the fact that Laski's congregation sat to receive communion, an issue which two years later would become an active issue in the national Church in England. As in that later clash, in response to Laski's assertion that sitting was the only biblical norm, the Archbishop expressed scepticism as to whether scripture offered any definite guidance; for the Archbishop, like vestments, this was something which could be regulated by the authority of the magistrate. Laski's refutation of these positions ended with scriptural illustration from Leviticus 10, emphasizing the need to avoid bad examples; the context necessarily raised the name of Aaron the priest, that name which had echoed through the year ever since Hooper's attack on the Ordinal in his fateful Court sermon back in March.[70]

Cranmer's response to Laski has not survived, but since neither he nor Ridley gave any ground to Hooper during the autumn, there is no likelihood that the Polish reformer got any greater sympathy from him. Laski turned to attempts to lobby those fellow-exiles who might have some influence with the English authorities, plunging first into long correspondence on the subject with Bucer, in which he tried to tie in the project for a joint doctrinal statement to the immediate dispute over ceremonies and clerical dress. This attempt did not pay off; despite the unhappiness which Bucer had felt in the previous winter about Cranmer's pragmatism, he now moved over to the Archbishop's stance in order to defend him. In the intervening months since Bucer had expressed his wounded feelings to foreign friends, the English evangelical establishment had made sure that Bucer and Peter Martyr did not feel excluded from the process of deciding on change, for instance punctiliously and genuinely consulting them about their views on revising the 1549 Prayer Book. As a result, little as they approved of traditional clerical garb, Bucer and Martyr were now determined to avoid being enlisted in support of Hooper.

Frustrated, isolated and also beset by family tragedy, with the chance of an agreed common statement on central matters of doctrine now increasingly remote, Laski made one positive response to the situation. Towards the end of the year he settled down to write the first version of what would later be published as the *Forma ac ratio tota ecclesiastici ministerii*. This ended up as a total description of the Stranger Church that he had created in the middle of these storms: its discipline, its liturgy and its views on doctrine. Basil Hall rightly calls this treatise unique in its comprehensiveness; in parallel with Calvin's monumental doctrinal statement in the *Institutes*, it provided a key text for the future of Reformed Christianity throughout Europe. Yet the *Forma* also had its moorings in a church on English soil, which had shown the way to root-and-branch reform; it would be an inspiration for all those who

70 The text is *Joannis a Lasco opera*, ed. Kuyper, pp. 655–62 (cf. Primus, *Vestments Controversy*, pp. 40–43): Kuyper's dating is to August 1551, but August 1550 is far more likely. The treatise is likely to correspond to that mentioned by Hardenberg in a letter to Bucer of 7 September 1550 as about to be presented to Cranmer by Laski: C.C.C.C. MS 119, p. 274.

sought to move the Church in England further and faster than Edwardian and Elizabethan Church leaders were prepared to go, in order to keep England tied into international Protestantism.[71]

Ridley and Cranmer were brilliantly successful in consistently keeping the spotlight on the question of authority, rather than on the issue of corruption and bad examples for weaker brethren which was the preferred ground for Laski and Hooper. This was how Cranmer placed the emphasis when, in December 1550, he wrote a short formal request in his own hand for Bucer's opinion on the matter: was the clerical dress prescribed by the magistrate offensive to God, and did someone refusing to wear it offend God and the magistrate? Two details stand out in Cranmer's note. First, having read some of Bucer's earlier pronouncements in the controversy, the Archbishop firmly stipulated 'a very brief response'! Second, this holograph letter is the one reference in all Cranmer's surviving correspondence to his own wife and family; when writing to this intimate friend, he passed on greetings from 'all mine to you and all yours'. Perhaps this is a hint that besides the friendship of the two men, Mrs Cranmer had enjoyed meeting a family of evangelicals with whom she could converse freely in her native German; the formidable Mrs Bucer was certainly someone who could hold her own with anyone on the subject of reformers, having married Bucer as the widow in succession of Johannes Oecolampadius and Wolfgang Capito. Mrs Proudie would probably have retired abashed from an encounter with these two ladies.[72]

Bucer's response to Cranmer's request showed that, as ever, he was incapable of obeying any instruction to be concise, but in every other respect it was just what Cranmer needed: in particular, buried amid his verbiage was the vital statement 'I think that such ministers of the English Churches may with the grace of God use those vestments which are prescribed at this day'. It was not that Bucer especially approved of vestments in themselves; in his almost contemporary comments on revising the Prayer Book, he made it clear that he wanted them abolished. However, evidently he had accepted Cranmer's arguments about timing and authority; he trusted his friend to choose the moment properly. Once more, Bucer showed that he had left behind his pique of the previous winter, when in his letter he generously acknowledged that 'piously has the tyranny of the Roman Antichrist been banished from this kingdom'.[73] It was virtually the last service which he would perform for the English Reformation: worn out by his exertions and defeated by ill-health, he died at Cambridge on 28 February 1551, still

71 Hall, *John à Lasco*, pp. 32–33; Leaver, *Goostly Songs*, pp. 155–6.

72 The Latin holograph original of his letter is New College Oxford MS 343 f. 41, illus. in Hopf, *Bucer*, facing p. 153, or cf. transcript, B.L. Additional MS 28571, f. 46: '*Mei omnes tibi tuisque omnibus plurimam salutem . . .*'. The English translation, Cox 2, p. 428, misses this phrase.

73 Gorham, *Gleanings*, pp. 216–17; for the comment on vestments in the *Censura*, see *Bucer*, ed. Whitaker, pp. 18–19.

working away to within a few days of his death. His funeral was a lavish and appropriate symbol of the bitter sense of loss felt by the evangelical establishment, both nationally and in Cambridge University.

By December, Canterbury and London were thus fully in control of events, and they could calibrate their action against Hooper very precisely: it was they who, in conjunction with the newly appointed Councillor, the Marquis of Dorset, interceded for him in the autumn, and postponed his committal to prison by the Council. Like Bucer, they made clear that they had no love for traditional clerical dress, but the essence of their position was that they were only prepared to see it abolished by 'the general consent of the whole kingdom, and not merely by the impulsiveness of an individual or of the Council'. This might be an indifferent matter, but it still warranted the sort of action in Parliament which had authorized the Prayer Book or the Ordinal.[74] Hooper, convinced of his own rightness, played into their hands by his continued noisy assertion of his position, even after he had been put under house arrest at home and forbidden to preach or publish. By mid-January 1551, this had brought him to imprisonment at Lambeth Palace, and a fortnight later his continuing intransigence provoked the ultimate humiliation for a bishop-elect: confinement in the Fleet prison, alongside the disgraced conservative bishops, Heath and Day. It was significant that on the same day that the Privy Council gave this order the major item of business on their agenda was an alarming new outbreak of radical assemblies in Essex and Kent: the constant antithesis of radicalism and due order did not cease to haunt Hooper's case.[75]

On 15 February, Hooper finally gave in, writing to Cranmer from prison to 'subject myself to the judgement of your clemency' in a letter which was still resonant with injured and sorrowful dignity. Laski's encouragement had prolonged his resistance, but the lack of support from any other major figure, particularly the positive disapproval of his stand by Bucer and Martyr, was in the end decisive; Martyr had not been afraid to tell Hooper to his face more than once that his stand was futile. The official account of Hooper's consecration in Cranmer's Register meticulously noted the wearing of the prescribed dress, and the new bishop also marked his capitulation by preaching before the King still dressed in the episcopal garments which he had first condemned from the Court pulpit twelve months before.[76] With his contentions past, he would prove himself the very model of a Reformed superintendent at Gloucester and Worcester, energetically carrying out the programme for which he had struggled over the twelve months of clashing with Cranmer and Ridley, and after his consecration it is doubtful whether his hated robes emerged frequently from his wardrobe.

74 *E.T.* p. 281 (*O.L.* p. 426).

75 *A.P.C. 1550–52*, pp. 198–200.

76 Cranmer's Register, f. 332r, *E.T.* pp. 178–9 (*O.L.* p. 271); on Martyr, Gorham, *Gleanings*, p. 231. Hooper's letter is B.L. Additional MS 28571 ff. 24–26, tr. Gorham, *Gleanings*, pp. 233–5.

Ridley's relations with Laski and the Stranger Church never really recovered from the affair, and it took the troubles of Mary's reign to persuade him fully to make his peace with Hooper, but as usual Cranmer was incapable of bearing a grudge. He immediately resumed his old friendship with Laski, consulting with him about the recruitment of more leading foreign divines, and inviting Laski and his wife to take refuge at Croydon Palace when in summer 1551 the terrible epidemic of sweating sickness hit London.[77] He also consistently supported Hooper in his work as a bishop, while Hooper in turn appears to have been happy to draw on the Archbishop's draft doctrinal articles when compiling a set of articles for his diocese (see below, p. 504). Both Hooper and Laski took their place in the commission for the revision of canon law when it was appointed in the autumn of 1551, probably because Cranmer wanted them both on it. It might seem, then, as if there had been a great deal of fuss over nothing.

Yet the struggle had not been a waste of energy; it had established a precedent of the highest significance for the future of the Reformation in England. Hooper and Laski between them had offered one vision for the future of the English Church: purged of all past corruption and moving straight to parity with the most thoroughly reformed of civic churches in Switzerland. There was little in the content of their programme to which Cranmer and Ridley objected: what made the two bishops put up such intransigent and ruthlessly pragmatic opposition was the source of the authority for the programme, and the pace which it sought to set. From the moment of old King Henry's death, the evangelical establishment of King Edward's England had known precisely what it wanted: a future of root-and-branch reform, set out with stark lack of compromise in the preface to Cranmer's *Defence*. However, that vision was to be accomplished in a strictly regulated series of steps taken with the authority of the Crown and the consent of Parliament: a series which was only brought to an abrupt and premature halt at the King's death, leaving the new Church still unfinished. The aim of this graduated progress was change accomplished with decency, order and the maximum possible degree of popular consent: it was the strategy which had lain behind the production of the interim rite of 1549, as Cranmer had told Bucer and Fagius on their arrival in England. Cranmer and Ridley maintained this principle against the achievement of immediate ideological purity, the governing criterion for Hooper and Laski. In the name of decency and order, they were prepared to see paradise postponed. The same struggle broke out again as a result of the eruption of John Knox on to the English scene in 1552; it would be resumed in the reign of Elizabeth, but with the added complication of a monarch who was content to restore only the

77 Gorham, *Gleanings*, pp. 245–8, 271–3; *E.T.* pp. 374–5 (*O.L.* pp. 575–6). Laski's views on vestments did not change: perhaps even while still at Croydon in 1551, he wrote a pamphlet attacking them, dated 20 September 1551 – cf. Primus, *Vestment Controversy*, p. 37. On Ridley and Hooper, see *Ridley's Works*, pp. 355–8.

Edwardian status quo of mid-1552 with minor modifications, and who ceased to take any further steps down the path which Edward's government had mapped out. The construction of a spirituality later styled Anglicanism, that peculiar hybrid which is the Church of England's legacy for world Christianity, became a possibility at the moment when Hooper reluctantly reached for his pen to write to Cranmer, admitting that the game was up.

Hooper's defeat was not the only success for the evangelical establishment during that winter: at the same time that his resistance was being worn down, more of the chief remaining conservative clergy were falling from office, fulfilling Richard Scudamore's earlier predictions about more quondam bishops. During December 1550, Bishop Day of Chichester crowned his increasing resistance to government plans by his refusal to co-operate with the national programme of demolition of altars: after fruitless discussions with Cranmer, Ridley and Goodrich, and angry confrontations with the Privy Council, he joined Bishop Heath in the Fleet prison.[78] However, the greatest showdown was with the chief symbol of resistance to religious change, Stephen Gardiner. Over the summer of 1550, tortuous negotiations to win over Gardiner to acquiescence in the destruction of everything that he had defended for so long, finally broke down with no result. The plan had been the particular enthusiasm of the Duke of Somerset, and it betrayed the naivety of his eagerness to bolster his re-entry into politics in the guise of a general peacemaker; not only was Somerset simultaneously a chief mainstay of Gardiner's *bête noire*, John Hooper, against Cranmer and Ridley, but it is difficult to see how profound or lasting Winchester's reconciliation could have been to a Church which spent the year systematically removing stone altars from places of worship.[79]

Although Cranmer had taken his official part in the discussions with Gardiner, he is unlikely to have felt much sorrow at their failure, after nearly twenty years of personal confrontation. Now, on 15 December 1550, Gardiner was summoned to Lambeth Palace for the first session of a trial before royal commissioners, headed by the Archbishop. This would last for another two months, and its proceedings were given much publicity as a show of evangelical strength; the government invested the best part of 300 marks in staging the proceedings, for which Cranmer duly put in an invoice when everything was safely complete. In appointing the commissioners, the regime decided from the start to abandon the pretence of impartial investigation which had caused so much procedural trouble in Bonner's trial the year before: the royal commission outlined Gardiner's previous disobedience, and charged the commissioners with the principal aim of securing his conformity on pain of deprivation.[80]

78 *A.P.C. 1550–52*, pp. 167–70, 172, 174, 178.

79 For Somerset's support of Hooper, see *E.T.* p. 270 (*O.L.* p. 410).

80 The proceedings and allied documents are set out *in extenso* in Foxe 6, pp. 64–266; there is a useful summary in Muller, *Gardiner*, Ch. 26. Warrant for expenses: P.R.O., E. 101/76/36 ff. 85, 87.

Gardiner displayed all the legal skills which one would expect from him against the commission's major charge of disobedience and contempt of royal commandments, meticulously detailing his previous conformity with each successive change as it happened, up to the moment of his test sermon of 1548 and the imprisonment which had followed it. He could also point to his own outstanding contributions to Henry VIII's campaign against papal obedience, and like Bonner before him, he made good use of the eucharistic sections of the 1548 Justus Jonas Catechism with which to torment Cranmer. Naturally, none of this did him any good, although it impressed observers more than the government would have liked. On 14 February, in the Great Hall of Lambeth Palace, he made a last-minute formal appeal to the King, in which he declared war on his judges, affirming that Cranmer, Ridley and Bishop Holbeach of Lincoln 'teach and set forth the manifest and condemned error against the very true presence of Christ's body and blood in the sacrament of the altar'. Naturally this was set aside, and Cranmer read the final judgement in the case, declaring him deprived of the see of Winchester; Gardiner was then taken to stricter confinement in the Tower of London. His deprivation laid the way open for John Ponet to be propelled in the episcopal hierarchy to Winchester, from one of the most junior to one of the most senior dioceses, with another Cranmer protégé, John Scory, replacing Ponet at Rochester. Perhaps the news also persuaded Hooper the following day to write his letter of capitulation to the Archbishop: Gardiner's loss of his see, at long last, was certainly a powerful reason for accepting the arguments put forward by Bucer and Martyr that there was work to be done in the English Church, and that minor scruples should not be allowed to get in the way.[81]

During the course of his trial, on 26 January 1551, Gardiner triumphantly presented the commissioners with the manuscript text of a work which represented a direct attack on the presiding commissioner. This book, *An Explication and assertion of the Catholic Faith touching the most blessed sacrament of the altar* . . . , was a major refutation of Cranmer's *Defence*; Gardiner must have written it at considerable speed after the appearance of Cranmer's book, during late summer and autumn 1550, as one phase of an extensive programme of writing with which he kept his mind active through his years of imprisonment. With extraordinary ineptitude, the regime failed to stop him smuggling the text out of the Tower to get it printed abroad soon after the trial, probably in Rouen.[82] Naturally it was a robust assertion of the doctrine of real presence in the eucharist, and it adopted a bold strategy by replying to the five sections of Cranmer's work in a new order, tackling the general question of real presence before the particular problem of transubstantiation, in order to defend both more effectively. Edmund Grindal later said sourly that Gardiner's inversion of Cranmer's text was a fitting exhibition of charac-

81 For Gardiner's appeal, see Foxe 6, p. 263; on Martyr's stance on Hooper, *E.T.* pp. 320–21 (*O.L.* pp. 486–7).

82 For discussion of this and Gardiner's publications generally, Muller, *Gardiner*, Appendix 2.

ter from one 'who, all his life long has been, so to speak, the most preposterous inverter of all things human and divine'.[83]

The published version of Gardiner's book affected to be uncertain as to whether one of Cranmer's 'dignity and authority' could really have written the *Defence*; this rhetorical device may have infuriated the Archbishop all the more because Hooper had adopted it when criticizing his Ordinal a year before. It represented a shift in strategy from Gardiner's trial, when he had frankly attacked Cranmer's eucharistic theology in his final appeal; perhaps he had picked up the idea from Cuthbert Tunstall, who had adopted the same pretence of uncertainty about the authorship in his depositions in Winchester's favour at the trial. Clearly the stratagem was the result of last-minute thoughts before publication: Gardiner abandoned one draft manuscript preface to his book even though it was a rather effectively destructive review of Cranmer's changes of mind on the eucharist, because that would have meant recognizing authorship of the *Defence*. The gain for Wily Winchester was the mock-puzzled use which he could then make of the 1548 *Catechism* and the 1549 Prayer Book, proving their compatibility with his own assertion of real presence in the eucharist.[84] It had always been a favourite technique of Gardiner in debate with his opponents to quote from them in order to damage their case. In his *Explication*, he was only too pleased to exploit the real presence language which he could find in Lutheran writers when they clashed with the Swiss, and he zestfully lined up with Zwingli's assertion against Luther that belief in the real presence necessarily involved acceptance of transubstantiation. He could even draw on the possibilities offered by Martin Bucer's attempts to find a middle way on the eucharist.[85]

However, Gardiner's use of the 1549 *Book of Common Prayer* against Cranmer was the most damaging of all these devices; it has proved of lasting importance, providing theological fools' gold for those Anglo-Catholics who have sought to reinterpret the first Prayer Book and Cranmer's intentions within it.[86] Gardiner had been inspired to seize on the Prayer Book by his negotiations with the government during summer 1550: Somerset and his fellows had been extremely anxious to get Gardiner to issue approving statements about the book, and having read through it, on 14 June the Bishop had grudgingly agreed to say that 'that book he would not have made after that form, but, as it was, he could with his conscience keep it, and cause others in

83 *Grindal's Remains*, pp. 233, 235.

84 For the prefaces, *Gardiner's Letters*, pp. 446–50, and cf. Cranmer's angry remark about the change, Cox 1, p. 10. On Tunstall, see Foxe 6, p. 241.

85 For an early example of Gardiner's quotation of an opponent (Henry VIII!), *Gardiner's Letters*, p. 49. On Lutherans, cf. e.g. Cox 1, pp. 20, 137, 149, 365; on Zwingli, ibid., pp. 239, 241, 244–5, 279, 335; on Bucer, ibid., pp. 90–91, 223, 225.

86 For Gardiner's use of the Prayer Book, see Cox 1, pp. 79, 83–4, 229, and a useful summary discussion in Muller, *Gardiner*, pp. 215–16.

his diocese to keep it'. The reason was that 'touching the truth of the very presence of Christ's most precious body and blood in the sacrament, there was as much spoken in that book as might be desired'. He had even gone on to approve of the declaration 'of ceremonies' at the end of the 1549 Prayer Book.[87] This moment of agreement with his enemies had come to nothing, but it clearly left Gardiner with the idea of putting the superficial ambiguity of the 1549 rite to good use in a different way. Now the book would witness against its devisers, a strategy which would prove an added incentive for Cranmer and his colleagues to move on to replace it with a more comprehensive revision.

Besides the task of producing a new Prayer Book, which was already in hand before Gardiner dropped his literary bombshell, Cranmer decided that he must take direct action against this challenge to his authority from his most long-standing opponent. The result was his second venture into print on the subject of the eucharist, *An Answer to a crafty and sophistical cavillation devised by Stephen Gardiner*. To it was appended his brief but pungent answer to another attack on the *Defence*, which had been written by the former Regius Professor at Oxford, Richard Smith, now an exile for his Catholic beliefs, and references to Smith's work also littered the main text. The *Answer* was produced with the same speed and energy which Gardiner had expended on his own treatise. It can hardly have been started much before Gardiner had presented his treatise in court at the end of January, and it is more likely to have been inspired by the sudden appearance of the *Explication* in print some time after that; Peter Martyr noted Cranmer at work on it in April. Progress must have been threatened by two successive disasters: first, during May, the bizarre accident of an earthquake in Surrey, which caused chaos in Cranmer's main library at Croydon; later, from July, the far more serious menace caused by the national epidemic of sweating sickness, which affected Croydon Palace and nearly killed Mrs Laski and the Archbishop's doctor, John Herd.[88] Yet the work was in print by the end of September 1551, and Cranmer's printer, Reyner Wolfe, was immediately given an exclusive royal licence for it.[89] The *Answer* is a triumph of Wolfe's printing expertise, with three different typefaces to distinguish the text of the original *Defence*, Gardiner's *Explication* and Cranmer's answer to it – Cranmer had decided that since Gardiner's work was now in print, there was no option but to reprint it in full in his own text in order to refute it systematically. Unhappily, such typographical skill was very necessary for Reformation printers, now that such repetitive dialogues had become common.

87 Foxe 6, p. 114: for the calculation of the date, see Muller, *Gardiner*, p. 188.

88 On the earthquake, Gorham, *Gleanings*, p. 262. On the sweat, *E.T.* pp. 374–5 (*O.L.* pp. 575–6); Gorham, *Gleanings*, pp. 271–3; life of Herd, Bodley MS Lincoln Lat (e) 122 f. 84v (illness there misdated to July 1550).

89 Martyr to Bullinger, *E.T.* p. 325 (*O.L.* pp. 494–5). Publication: Cox 2, p. 429; *A.P.C. 1550–52* p. 375.

The contentious title was an immediate indication that the tone of the *Answer* was markedly different to that of the *Defence*: it could bear comparison with the most savage Edwardian polemicists, although it did not explore the murky sexual depths which John Bale could reach. The *Defence* had no more than a couple of glancing references to an earlier eucharistic tract by Gardiner, but now in response to a clear personal attack in the *Exposition*, Cranmer decided to settle old scores. He played persistently with a metaphor which had sprung into his mind in typical humanist style from Pliny's *Natural History*: Gardiner was a cuttle-fish trying to obscure the truth with his discharge of ink.[90] Whereas the *Defence* won consistent admiration from evangelicals, and was much quoted, not all sympathetic observers felt that Cranmer had been wise in the extremity of his language in the *Answer*. This was certainly the opinion of that future doyen of the godly cause under Elizabeth I, Edmund Grindal, who even amid Mary's persecution delicately told John Foxe of mutterings in English evangelical circles that occasionally Cranmer 'falsely attributes to the papists what they do not hold', and suggested that for a Latin translation of the *Answer*, some discreet advice from Peter Martyr on editing the text would not come amiss.[91]

One does not need to credit Cranmer's team of colourful ghost-writers with the flavour of the *Answer*; like many mild-mannered men, Cranmer had always shown himself capable of dipping his pen in vitriol when roused. His answer to the Western rebels the year before carried much the same shrillness of tone, though it had been more *de haut en bas* to an easier target. Now the intellectual snobbery which had characterized that work was rather more appropriately addressed by one former Cambridge don to another: Cranmer had a technical knowledge of theology and Church history, 'having exercised myself in the study of scripture and divinity from my youth', and Gardiner did not, 'being brought up from your tender age in other kinds of study', that is, civil law. Cranmer sneered that Gardiner's knowledge of the patristic material was derived at second-hand from collections compiled by Richard Smith, and that the information was subsequently mangled when Gardiner used it; at one point, particularly nettled by Gardiner's reference to his 'ignorance' and by persistent misinterpretation of his intentions in the 1549 Prayer Book, he snapped at Gardiner as 'this ignorant lawyer'. His brief

90 References to Gardiner in the *Defence*, pp. 339, 376. For the cuttle-fish, Cox 1, pp. 24, 116, 237, 284, 293. Cf. another slightly later and perhaps derivative evangelical use of this metaphor by Thomas Purye, minister of Reading, *Narratives of the Reformation*, p. 111n.

91 *Grindal's Remains*, pp. 233–4, 236; cf. Cox 1, pp. 52, 97. Nevertheless, cf. John Redman's commendation of the *Answer* on his death-bed in November 1551: *E.T.* p. 100 (*O.L.* p. 152). For admiration of the *Defence*, cf. e.g. *Bradford's Works* 2, pp. 274, 383–4; Knox, *Works* 3, p. 279.

answer to Smith's work is expressed in particularly personal terms to both Smith and Gardiner. Smith was a curious combination of great talent, time-serving, deep conservative convictions and large sexual appetites; he was an easy target for evangelical gibes and clearly inspired Cranmer with contemptuous anger.[92]

The trauma of the Reformation had shifted the terms in which theological debates could be conducted: in order to argue effectively, defenders of the traditional Church would have to meet the reformers such as the author of the *Defence* on their own ground. It was always possible to cite scripture in support of scripture, but after a straight disagreement on the meaning of scripture, both sides would have to fall back on the early Fathers and interpret them for their own purposes. The danger of circularity, of course, remained: disputes on the meaning of the Fathers would push the argument back to what meaning the Bible sanctioned, yet from Gardiner's or Smith's point of view, one former escape-route from this circularity was not open. Both pre-Reformation humanist prejudice and the circumstance of Henry VIII's break with Rome meant that the great medieval authorities had lost their value, for instance being formally discounted in debate in the University of Oxford by the Edwardian period. This meant that conservatives had to ignore the weight of support for their viewpoint in medieval commentators, and they were thus arguing with one hand tied behind their backs.

Evangelicals were pleasantly aware of the conservative handicap; Cranmer was noticeably much more cavalier in quoting from a medieval writer like Aquinas than from any of the early fathers, clearly not considering him of equal importance, and indeed we have already noted him taking this relaxed attitude to Aquinas's text as long ago as 1531 (see above, Ch. 3, p. 59).[93] His detailed knowledge of the fathers, built up over years of taking systematic notes, gave him one built-in advantage over Gardiner. For instance, both in the *Defence* and the *Answer*, he could gather together from various sources Augustine of Hippo's discussion of how to detect figurative language in scripture: this was admirable for his purposes, and left Gardiner reduced to inept verbal contortions, to which Cranmer drew delighted attention. Similar results followed from a contest over passages from Tertullian.[94] Sometimes Cranmer's knowledge both of current patristic scholarship and its medieval background enabled him to cast doubt on texts which made for the realist case, as in his justified scepticism about the authenticity of supplementary epistles attributed to the first-century Clement of Rome; equally, he could dismiss supposed quotations from the fourth-century Theophilus of Alexan-

92 Cox 1, pp. 163, 185, 223–4, 368.

93 On Aquinas, cf. Cox 1, pp. 64, 68, and Foxe 6, p. 468. On debate at Oxford, *E.T.* p. 272 (*O.L.* p. 412), and for a neat exchange on circularity in authority between Bishop Brooks and Archdeacon Philpot, Foxe 6, p. 619.

94 Cox 1, pp. 114–21.

dria as by the eleventh-century Bulgarian Theophylact, and he got considerable mileage out of Gardiner's discomfiture about this.[95]

Nevertheless, Gardiner was an older hand at controversial writing than Cranmer. For instance, he scored a hit of unnerving accuracy which suggests inside information, when he suggested that Cranmer's notebooks on sources for eucharistic discussion had been built up in order to combat transubstantiation rather than more general notions of real presence, in the years when the Archbishop had not yet embraced the notion of spiritual eucharistic presence only.[96] His ready mind, in alliance with Smith's notebooks, could occasionally gain the advantage over Cranmer's massive but rather plodding scholarship; out of the two opponents, it was probably Gardiner who had the more subtle understanding of the processes of history and the nature of evidence. He was able to stand back from particular passages under discussion to put them into context, and in that respect he was a better humanist than the Archbishop. It was Gardiner who saw the point that Irenaeus's second-century discussion of the eucharist was in the context of his debate with the spiritualizing gnostics, who had wished to separate the spiritual nature of the divine from the grossness of fleshly things. Irenaeus was therefore unlikely to be helpful in his basic assumptions for Cranmer's 'spiritual presence' arguments: a point which Cranmer's reply failed to tackle.[97]

Among such struggles over the 'authors', which meant so much to both sides, is an instructive contrast in a very technical discussion of an ancient controversy between monophysites and Nestorians. Cranmer's key witness was the sixth-century writer Vigilius who had attacked monophysite views, especially those of the fourth- to fifth-century monophysite Eutyches. Cranmer gave a crisp résumé in the *Defence* of a discussion by Vigilius on the clear distinction of the divine and human natures in Christ; this was clearly of use in the case for a clear distinction between the physical and spiritual presence in the eucharist, and it left Gardiner at first incapable of effective reply about its content, feebly protesting that the passage was 'out of purpose superfluous'. However, Gardiner returned later to a different work of Vigilius, and he used this as a peg for a more broadly based discussion, not only of Eutyches' heresy but the heresy of his Nestorian opponents. This was with the aim of catching Cranmer out in an over-simplified explanation of the nature of Nestorian and Eutychian belief, casting doubt on the subtlety of his whole view of the monophysite controversy. It provoked a predictably irritable but also rather wooden and embarrassed response from the Archbishop.[98]

95 On Clement, Cox 1, pp. 141–2, 144–5, and cf. MacCulloch, 'Two dons in politics', pp. 8–9, n. 31; on Theophilus/Theophylact, Cox 1, pp. 187–90. On this point, Henry VIII in the *Assertio Septem Sacramentorum* was more accurate than Gardiner, although not as accurate as Cranmer: cf. *Miscellaneous writings of Henry the eighth* . . . , ed. Macnamara, pp. 64–5.

96 Cox 1, p. 281, and cf. Brooks, *Cranmer's Doctrine of the Eucharist*, pp. 21–37.

97 Cox 1, pp. 337–9.

98 Cox 1, pp. 98–101; 289–91, 293–4.

Gardiner was also acute enough to pick up the partisan unreliability of the fifth-century Nestorian sympathizer Theodoret of Cyrrhus, in his contribution to the same monophysite controversy; he further insinuated that Cranmer had got himself in a complete tangle in understanding what was at stake in that affair. The first point was a very shrewd blow at Cranmer, who in the *Defence* had followed Peter Martyr in considering Theodoret an important rediscovery for eucharistic discussion; the second reduced him to rage which is still not altogether coherent on the printed page.[99]

At the end of such debates on detail, much of the argument between Cranmer, Gardiner and Smith resolved itself into fairly fruitless squabbling about how literally to take the realist language which, despite all reformers' commentaries, was clearly so common in patristic discussion of the eucharist. Cranmer was something of a gourmet in grammar, as is illustrated in the *Defence* by his meticulous and rather enjoyable discussion of negatives by comparison; one might attribute this to the nominalist element in his training at Cambridge, but attempts to produce a comprehensive interpretation of Cranmer's thinking in nominalist terms have not been especially successful.[100] It was both important for his case and congenial to his temperament continually to stress the grammatically figurative nature of the fathers' realist language. Rather like the radical spiritualist Cornelius Hoen, or Huldrych Zwingli, he took a bleakly utilitarian view of a figure or metaphor in theological discussion: it was there to do a job. It was not part of his mental furniture to suppose that the early Fathers were using their language as a poetry of devotion; their metaphors were there to be quarried by the Church as a source of precise theological information. Gardiner, with his more showman-like feel for words, could come closer to seeing the point of poetic language: 'no approved author hath this exclusive, to say an only sign, an only token, an only similitude, or an only signification' when they used metaphorical speech. He could also grasp the atmosphere of reverent agnosticism in patristic writings more sensitively than Cranmer, admiring 'the wondering and great marvelling that the old authors make, how the substance of this sacrament is wrought by God's omnipotency'. Cranmer had always exhibited a tendency to deride such woolly imprecision about vital matters of salvation.[101]

With such a precise attitude to figurative language, it was natural for Cranmer unself-consciously to use realist language for figurative purposes in discussion after his 'conversion' to spiritual-presence views; this was the reason that he could tolerate so much realist-sounding phraseology in the successive versions of the Prayer Book. It was also the reason why he was so

99 Cox I, pp. 299–301. On Theodoret, Cranmer and Martyr, Cranmer, *Defence*, pp. 388–93, Walsh, 'Cranmer and the Fathers', p. 242, and Anderson, 'Martyr', pp. 461–3.

100 Cranmer, *Defence*, pp. 342–6. See McGee, 'Cranmer and nominalism', and the effective criticism of his article by Courtenay, 'Cranmer as a nominalist'.

101 Cox I, pp. 123, 340–41. Cf. Cranmer's mockery of the conservative bishops' replies on the eucharist in 1547: above, Ch. 9, pp. 379–80.

slow to understand that not everyone else reacted in the same way, or that friend and foe alike could interpret his attitude to the use of figurative language as dissembling. 'And therefore in the book of the holy communion, we do not pray that the creatures of bread and wine may be the body and blood of Christ; but that they may be to us the body and blood of Christ', he explained wearily: what could be plainer?[102] 'I do as plainly speak as I can, that Christ's body and blood be given to us in deed, yet not corporally and carnally, but spiritually and effectually.' Was there any more discussion needed? Evidently there was, since this exasperated statement was followed by several hundred pages of text, and also by a number of last-minute efforts at clarification in the short preface.[103]

Cranmer assembled a list of points in which he claimed Gardiner differed from other 'papists': mostly trivial. One, for instance, was over the momentous question of whether dogs or cats could eat the body of Christ if they ate consecrated bread, on which Gardiner took a stance which had already been condemned by scholastic theologians in their criticisms of the Master of the Sentences. However, there was a significant point beyond such exotic examples and such obvious debating points as Cranmer's attacks on Gardiner's supposed inconsistency.[104] While he was still a Catholic without the Pope, Gardiner was as much exercised to find a consistent rule for deriving authority as were Protestants. He faced the dilemma of later Anglo-Catholics, and might even at this stage of his career be termed the first Anglo-Catholic; Cranmer did indeed anticipate that much later term by labelling him and his sympathizers 'English papists'. Bereft of the support of Henry VIII in his more conservative mood, Gardiner was having to think on his feet to produce reliable doctrinal statements for a province of the Church Universal. Cranmer put it with brutal accuracy: 'You stand post alone, after the fall of the papistical doctrine, as sometime an old post standeth when the building is overthrown.'[105] It is not surprising that by the end of his years of imprisonment, the author of *De Vera Obedientia* would emerge from the Tower in 1553 once more a convinced supporter of papal authority.

While the *Answer* took its place in the bookshops in the autumn, Cranmer was confronted by two crises, one personal, the other political. The first was the marital disaster of his former chaplain, John Ponet. In finding a wife, Ponet had achieved the distinction of triggering what may be the first routine administrative mention of clerical marriage in the English Church, when on 4 November 1548 (before Parliament had made clerical celibacy optional) he and his wife had jointly obtained from Cranmer's Faculty Office a dispensation to eat meat in Lent and other prohibited times.[106] Some years after this

102 Cox 1, p. 271, and cf. ibid., p. 79.
103 Cox 1, pp. 37, 3–4.
104 Cox 1, p. 67; cf. e.g. ibid., p. 80.
105 Cox 1, pp. 302, 196.
106 *Faculty Office Registers*, p. 319.

happy statement of an evangelical partnership, matters took a disastrous turn, and the marriage foundered with the couple arraigned on charges of bigamy. Ponet was not the only senior cleric whose belated release from clerical celibacy led him into perhaps over-hasty marriage and caused traditionalists much unkind amusement: Robert Holgate, Archbishop of York, also found himself embroiled in a bigamy scandal. However, Ponet compounded his offence by blundering across the social boundaries which should have been obvious to him, even despite the lack of a precedent for defining the social position of bishops' wives: the Bishop of Winchester found himself married to the wife of a Nottingham butcher. Their formal separation took place in the consistory court in St Paul's Cathedral at the end of July 1551.[107] Ponet was not allowed to remain long in the single state: on 25 October he was married once more, in circumstances which his old master the Archbishop had clearly designed to be fool-proof. Cranmer himself was the principal guest at a crowded ceremony in the parish church at his favourite home, Croydon, and the bride was Mary, daughter of Peter Hayman, one of Cranmer's leading financial officials and a solid Kentish gentleman, who had known Ponet for years.[108]

Cranmer played a less central role in the political crisis which now intervened, and which resulted in the final fall of the Duke of Somerset. The Archbishop's involvement in politics had dwindled during the summer of 1551, either because of his concentration on the final stages of the *Answer*, or because of the severity of the sweating sickness in his household at Croydon. After the beginning of July, when Croydon was first affected by the disease, he was only once in attendance at the Council, on 9 August. This was an occasion on which a linked pair of particularly important formal diplomatic statements needed to be made – first to the Princess Mary that her religious nonconformity would no longer be tolerated, and then to the Emperor that his refusal of religious reciprocity to English embassies was equally intolerable. It was hardly surprising that Cranmer was recalled on this occasion: such a solemn declaration of diplomatic intent required maximum Council authority, and two prominent conservative magnates, the earls of Arundel and Derby, were specially sworn in as extraordinary Councillors in order to lend bipartisan weight to the statements. After the set-piece meeting of 9 August, the Archbishop was back at Croydon, enjoying the holiday company not only of Jan Laski and his convalescent wife, but also of Peter Martyr; he communicated with his Council colleagues via William Cecil, now principal

107 *Machyn's Diary*, p. 8; *Greyfriars Chronicle*, p. 70. On Holgate, 'Parkyn's Narrative', p. 71, and *A.P.C. 1550–52*, pp. 421, 426–7.

108 Croydon parish register, qu. *Machyn's Diary*, p. 320; *Visitations of Kent 1530–1, 1574, 1592*, 1, p. 63. On Ponet and Hayman, see above, Ch. 8, pp. 324–5, and on Hayman, *History of Parliament 1509–1558* 2, pp. 325–6. Alarmingly, when the couple were granted a royal licence to eat flesh in Lent on 26 November 1551, Ponet's bride was named as Elizabeth: B.L. Royal MS 18 C XXIV, f. 159r.

secretary at the Council board, and a man whom Cranmer found increasingly congenial.[109]

Cranmer was therefore absent when, on 16 October, Somerset's frail rehabilitation in politics came to an abrupt end, two years after his first overthrow: the Duke was arrested on charges of treason and taken to the Tower, a mere five days after the Earl of Warwick had been created Duke of Northumberland. The following day, Cranmer appeared at the Council for the first time for a fortnight, and if he felt any regret for Somerset's passing, there is no trace of it in the bald administrative record of this and subsequent meetings as the Councillors sorted out various matters raised by the Duke's imprisonment. These included a summons to the preacher planned for Paul's Cross, no doubt to prime him as to what to say about the new situation; there was widespread popular cynicism about the official explanations of Somerset's fall.[110] The Imperial ambassador, trying to make sense of the antics of a set of politicians whom he loathed impartially, heard that Cranmer was going to be imprisoned as a scapegoat for the fact that the religious changes were not going well, but there is no other indication of this. Indeed, the concern of Northumberland and his clique seems to have been to make sure that the Archbishop remained on their side, for they continued the momentum of action on two of his pet schemes. On the day that the Council summoned the Paul's Cross preacher, the same day that it launched a full-scale propaganda offensive in London against Somerset, it signed a warrant to the Chancellor to constitute a small preliminary sub-committee to plan the revision of canon law, so that the momentum of action would not falter on the revision as had happened so often before. On 27 October a Council meeting at which the Archbishop was present showed its continuing concern for another of his favoured projects, the Stranger Church, when it issued orders for the welfare of Somerset's community of French Protestant weavers at Glastonbury: this was a remarkable piece of attention to detail in the middle of a political upheaval.[111]

There is, indeed, nothing to make one suppose that, at this stage of the conflict, Cranmer's attitude to Northumberland's move was anything other than benevolent neutrality or active support, as in the first attack on Somerset in autumn 1549. It was worrying enough for the future of the Reformation

109 For Cranmer and Cecil at this time, cf. Cox 2, pp. 429–30, and Sir George Somerset to Cecil, *C.S.P. Foreign 1547–53*, p. 355. For consecrations of bishops in the private chapel at Croydon on 30 August, Cranmer's Register, ff. 333–4, and for Martyr's presence with him on 9 September, A.S.T. 41 fos. 99, 103.

110 *A.P.C. 1550–52*, pp. 389, 392, 394. For the facts of the fall, although not interpretation, see Jordan, *Edward VI: the Threshold of Power*, pp. 73–92.

111 *A.P.C. 1550–52*, p. 400; *C.S.P. Spanish 1550–52*, p. 389. Cf. events on 22 October in *Machyn's Diary*, p. 10, and the warrant for the commission the same day, B.L. Royal MS 18 C XXIV, f. 150r; the commission was issued on 4 November, and further modified on 9/11 November (*C.P.R. Edward VI 1550–3*, p. 114; *A.P.C. 1550–52*, p. 410). For a further Council intervention for the Glastonbury congregation on a day when Cranmer attended, see *A.P.C. 1550–52*, pp. 510.

that the two magnates had never established a working relationship after Somerset had returned to the Council, but there was a more specific problem than that. The vital issue, which would have made Cranmer side with Northumberland and not Somerset, was Seymour's irresponsible intervention in the long-running crisis caused by the obstinacy of the Lady Mary over her retention of the mass. Somerset's conduct after his return to politics had much alarmed many former admirers in the evangelical leadership.[112] In his continuing eclectic search for allies, he had backed Mary during 1551 just as he had tried to conciliate Gardiner in 1550, and his support of Mary had provoked a furious outburst about the devilish quality of the mass from the Earl of Warwick.[113] Cranmer's attitude was not in doubt; he felt very strongly about Mary's defiance, as is not surprising in the author of the *Defence* and the *Answer*. He has often been given the credit for the long and sermon-like Privy Council letter which Mary received about her nonconformity at Christmas 1550; although there is no proof of that, unquestionably authentic is the stern advice which he gave in conjunction with Ridley and Ponet when the Council consulted them in March 1551, in the middle of Mary's face-to-face confrontation with her royal brother about the mass. The three bishops then sharply urged that 'to give license to sin was sin; to suffer and wink at it for a time might be borne, so [i.e. as long as] all haste possible might be used'. This lined up closely with Warwick's angry words to Somerset.[114]

Cranmer played another significant part in the March crisis, which is another indication of his close involvement against Somerset's dangerously conciliatory attitude to the Princess. Back in December 1550, Mary's two principal chaplains, Dr Mallet and Dr Barclay, had been indicted in Essex on Council orders for their part in Mary's resistance, but full action against them seems to have been postponed until the confrontation with Mary in the spring. Noticeably only one of the two chaplains, Mallet, was brought before the Council as continuing in his defiance; he was committed to the Tower.[115] It is clear that the other of the pair, the former friar Alexander Barclay, a distinguished poet and a veteran conservative spokesman, had now been detached from Mary and persuaded to complete conformity with the Edwardian Church. His reward was not simply a pardon in May 1551 for having said mass, but a grant a month later of a preaching licence, and in the next year, a comfortable city of London living in the gift of Canterbury Cathedral to add to his existing clutch of preferment. Barclay's will shows signs of drastic last-minute alteration to exclude mention of his former

112 E.g. Jan Laski: *E.T.* p. 476 (*O.L.* p. 734).

113 *E.T.* p. 290 (*O.L.* p. 439). For a narrative of the December 1550–51 stage of the crisis, see Loades, *Mary Tudor: a life*, pp. 158–68.

114 On the Christmas 1550 letter (Foxe 6, pp. 14–18), cf. e.g. Ridley, *Cranmer*, pp. 317–18. March statement: *Chronicle of Edward VI*, p. 56.

115 For the arrest order for Mary's chaplains Mallet and Barclay, Foxe 6, pp. 13–14, *A.P.C. 1550–52*, p. 171; for the commitment of Mallet alone to the Tower of London, ibid. p. 18, and *A.P.C. 1550–52*, p. 267.

colleagues in Mary's entourage; it was made at Croydon and he was also buried there. At that stage Croydon was Cranmer's chief summer home, which strongly suggests that Barclay's late rejection of a lifetime of traditional faith was a personal achievement of the Archbishop. Barclay was the only substantial defector from Princess Mary's household, which remained remarkably steadfast in the face of the continual pressure from the government.[116]

The confrontation with Mary was not simply a domestic matter; it was part of a very serious diplomatic crisis in which the Emperor was using the issue of Mary's mass to bring general pressure to bear on the English government. The link was made clear when the Privy Council extended the conflict to the issue of reciprocal rights of worship without interruption in Imperial and English embassies. The whole future of the English Reformation was at stake. We have already noted the one occasion during the summer when Cranmer came to the Council board: the government's solemn defiance of the Emperor's pressure and its show-down with Mary on 9 August 1551. It was probably also significant that Somerset did not sign the draft minute of this declaration, although he was recorded as attending the Council that day.[117] During September, in a tense meeting between Warwick and the Imperial ambassador, the ambassador raised a further question which had been a constant bone of contention between Stephen Gardiner and the evangelical establishment: the right of the young King Edward to decide the country's religious policy during his years of minority, in conjunction with his advisors. By October, Mary of Hungary was actually contemplating setting up an invasion under the pretext of liberating King Edward from his current governors. Add to all this the undoubted evidence that Somerset was not only seeking out malcontent politicians, but was also actively using his continuing popular following to undermine Warwick's position, and the former Lord Protector could only be seen as a dangerous loose cannon in a highly alarming situation.[118]

The continuing link-up between the crisis and Somerset's fall was evident when William Paget was put under house arrest at the same time as Somerset was arrested, simply because the Emperor was claiming that Paget had given him a face-to-face guarantee that Mary would not be harassed in her religion. On the day of Somerset's arrest, the Council wrote to their man in Brussels to

116 Barclay's pardon is B.L. Royal MS 18 C XXIV f. 103v, and his preaching licence ibid., f. 110v. His will is P.C.C. 17 Powell (25 July 1551, proved 10 June 1552), and he was admitted to All Hallows Lombard Street on 30 April 1552: Cranmer's Register, f. 420v. *D.N.B.* says that he died and was buried at Croydon.

117 *A.P.C. 1550–52*, pp. 328–30, 9 August; a surviving draft of the statements signed by most of those present is B.L. Exported MSS RP 1669, B1/906/78 (apparently to be identified with the Cowper MS, *H.M.C. 12th Report Appendix* 1, pp. 1–2). See Hoak, *King's Council*, pp. 66–70.

118 Hoak, *King's Council*, pp. 73–6; Brigden, *London*, pp. 506–11; Loades, *Mary Tudor: a life*, pp. 166–7; *C.S.P. Spanish 1550–52*, p. 377.

announce Paget's calamity, and to spell out the reason for it, specifically to show the Emperor that they meant business. In fact, this moment proved the high-point of confrontation both with the Emperor and with Mary. Charles V, suddenly faced in the autumn with a hostile treaty between France and the anti-Imperial princes of Germany, including his former ally Prince Moritz of Saxony, lost his taste for interference in England. Now that Somerset was a spent force, Mary had lost both her chief potential domestic ally and her mainstay abroad, while Northumberland turned away from confronting her much diminished threat to the chief priority of removing his great rival for good. The heat went out of the row with Mary, and she was given a tacit permission to carry on as before, as long as there was not too much publicity.[119]

Once the issue of Mary and the Emperor had subsided, then Cranmer probably began to change his mind about what was happening at the top of English politics. A significant and rather sinister moment came on 10 November 1551, a meeting attended by the Archbishop, when tacked on to the record of the Council's daily business, almost like an afterthought, came a resolution that from now on the King could sign bills on his own signature, without the necessity of any Councillor counter-signing them. Far from giving the teenage Edward any more real say in government, this gave Northumberland a greater chance to control affairs through his influence on the King at Court, thus giving him more scope to by-pass his fellow-Councillors. It was precisely the same possibility as had turned the Council against the Protectorate of Somerset, and the minuted decision had to incorporate the apprehensions of some present by providing for a docquet-book of such bills.[120] More worrying still for Cranmer than this shift in the political balance was the outcome of Somerset's trial by his peers for treason and felony, which opened in full session on 1 December; although the charges of treason were unconvincing and were dropped, the Duke was still condemned to die for felony. He was hurried to his death on 22 January 1552, the day before a long-postponed session of Parliament was due to convene; Northumberland was worried in case Somerset's enduring popularity would lead to awkward questions being raised in the two Houses, and indeed the execution was anything but a public relations success for the current regime.[121]

The Duke's beheading was a shocking step beyond the bloodless coup of autumn 1549; whatever Somerset's faults and political misjudgements, his personal commitment to the evangelical cause had never been in doubt, and the speed and cynical orchestration of events around his execution represented a new phase in Edwardian politics. Two very different observers later testified to Cranmer and Ridley's desperate efforts to save Somerset from death, and they also both noted the political outcome. In February 1552, the Imperial

119 *C.S.P. Foreign 1547–53*, p. 180; Brandi, *Charles V*, pp. 602–6.

120 *A.P.C. 1550–52*, pp. 410–11; Hoak, *King's Council*, pp. 27, 120–23, 154–5.

121 For the trial and execution, Jordan, *Edward VI: the Threshold of Power*, pp. 92–105.

ambassador said that Northumberland was ill-disposed to the Archbishop because he had done all he could to get a pardon for the Duke. Likewise Bishop Ridley, looking back from his prison under Mary in a thinly disguised piece of autobiography, said that he had earned Northumberland's 'high displeasure . . . for shewing his conscience secretly, but plainly and fully, in the Duke of Somerset's cause'.[122] To express protest against Somerset's death was necessarily done in private; it was vital not to provoke Northumberland against the evangelical cause by any public expression of dissent. The French refugee leader, Valerand Poullain, may have been acting on Cranmer's instructions when he wrote urgently to John Calvin in early March, begging him not to address a letter of protest about Somerset's death to Edward VI, 'by which either a fresh flame may be rekindled, or the minds of certain parties be aroused against the professors of the gospel'.[123]

This was the beginning of a breach between Cranmer and Northumberland which would widen in the coming year. Cranmer would already have had cause to note in 1550 and 1551 that two of his largest former Kentish palaces, Otford and Knole, were now in the hands of John Dudley; furthermore, the then Earl of Warwick's entry into Knole had involved an unceremonious ejection of the servants placed there by Cranmer's friend Lord Cobham, who had a claim there by a previous grant.[124] Now the rift first exposed by the destruction of Somerset was further widened by the process in Parliament intended to deprive Cuthbert Tunstall of his diocese. Tunstall's fall did not simply mean the removal of the greatest remaining conservative in the episcopate, something to which Cranmer would have no reason to object; it became linked to the design indicated in John Dudley's assumption of the title of Northumberland and his border office of Warden-General, of building up a new and unprecedented territorial power-base for himself on the north-east English frontier. This would be well served by dismemberment of Tunstall's palatinate bishopric of Durham.[125] It was a move with implications both for the future of Church lands and for the balance of power among the aristocracy.

Three bitterly contentious issues wound their way through Parliament in winter and spring 1552. First was the Act of Uniformity which would authorize Cranmer's new Prayer Book; second was the resolution of the Marquess of Northampton's long quest for a divorce and remarriage from Elizabeth Cobham, with which was coupled a bill to provide more general

122 *C.S.P. Spanish 1550–52*, p. 453; *Ridley*, p. 59, where the reference is ambiguously-phrased, but at this point appears to refer to 'the one' who is not Cranmer.

123 *E.T.* pp. 478–9 (*O.L.* p. 738).

124 Davies, 'Boulogne and Calais from 1545 to 1550', p. 86. Cf. grant of Knole to Northumberland, 26 July 1550, *C.P.R. Edward VI 1549–51*, pp. 364–6 (NB that Lord Cobham is there described as bailiff of Southfrith). On Otford (granted May 1551), Beer, *Northumberland*, p. 188.

125 Beer, *Northumberland*, pp. 181–2.

legalization for divorce (see above, Ch. 9, pp. 367–9); third was Tunstall's deprivation. On each, there was a small core of conservative aristocrats and one or two still surviving conservative bishops who consistently voted against the proposed legislation; they had no luck with the Uniformity bill or the Parr divorce, although the general divorce bill disappeared into oblivion, perhaps waiting for the further consideration which the proposed revision of canon law would offer. On the third issue, Cranmer made an unlikely combination with the ultra-conservative Lord Stourton as the only two recorded votes in the Lords against their third reading of the Tunstall bill on 31 March. Remarkably, although this vote by itself did not halt the progress of Northumberland's plans against Tunstall, the Commons succeeded in derailing his scheme by insisting that the Bishop meet his accusers face to face: this the government was reluctant to do, and the Parliamentary process against him was abandoned.[126] Northumberland would have to secure other ways of removing the veteran Bishop of Durham, and he would not forget Cranmer's part in thwarting his plans.

A serious quarrel between the two men is apparent in the letter which the Duke wrote to his fellow-Councillors soon after the end of Parliament, on the morning of 26 April 1552; unfortunately, the subject of the quarrel is unclear, largely thanks to Northumberland's habitual incoherence on paper. On the previous day, when one of his frequent bouts of illness made him unable to attend the Council, Northumberland received a message about a dispute between himself and Cranmer which was sufficiently important for the letter to have been brought to him from his fellow-Councillors by Lord Chancellor Goodrich and Secretary Cecil; it must have been an urgent matter, since Duke and Archbishop had been together at the Council board only the day before. Northumberland indignantly rejected the idea that the 'contention' was caused by any personal interest of his own, or that blame for it should fall more on him than on Cranmer: it was a matter 'touching as I take it divers ways most earnestly the King's Majesty and the most weighty affairs of his Highness which now you are in hand withal'. He left the resolution of the matter to his colleagues. One likely contention which at that time could have seemed so important was the business of the Bishop of Durham; alternatively it could have been the major policy decision about the sale of chantry lands (discussed below, Ch. 12, pp. 520–21).[127]

From winter 1552, therefore, a serious contradiction began to open up in government policy on religion: on the one hand, a growing tide of personal mistrust between Northumberland and Cranmer, and on the other, the continuing pursuit of the programme of evangelical revolution which had begun

126 *L.J.* 1, p. 417; Strype, *Cranmer* 1, pp. 416–18. Gilbert Burnet said that Cranmer spoke against the bill, but that is probably no more than an extrapolation from this vote: Burnet 2 i, p. 313.

127 Hatfield MS 151/33 (H.M.C. *Hatfield MSS* 1, no. 380): the previous neglect of this letter is curious.

in 1547. Both themes must be kept in balance as one considers the last eighteen months of the Edwardian regime. For all his political ruthlessness and personal ambition, Northumberland remained committed to the evangelical cause, and perhaps more importantly he promoted the growing monopoly of power in government by evangelicals. Prominent in his governing team was the cultured and enthusiastic promoter of reform William Cecil, who achieved the remarkable feat of retaining the full confidence not only of the Duke but of the Archbishop, until the collapse of the Northumberland regime in 1553. Cranmer evidently took a strong liking to the young Cambridge-educated administrator: his letters to Cecil have a relaxed quality and a frequency of jokes which is paralleled in his surviving correspondence only in his more informal letters to Thomas Cromwell. Cecil had shown his importance in, and commitment to, the process of change when in November 1551 he staged, in his own home, the first of two disputes about the nature of the eucharist, between heavyweight teams of evangelical and conservative theologians, with a select audience of some of the most prominent politicians in England; the second of these was held a week later in the home of that veteran humanist and former client of Thomas Cromwell, Richard Morison, and Cecil joined the team of evangelical disputants on both occasions.[128] Additionally, Cranmer's old friend Bishop Goodrich of Ely had become Lord Chancellor, in place of that slippery conservative politician Richard Rich, whose genuine illness came at an opportune moment to get rid of him; Goodrich was first created Keeper of the Seal in December and then, in January 1552, Lord Chancellor of England, thus becoming the first cleric since Cardinal Wolsey to hold England's senior legal office. There was a curious symmetry in Goodrich's appointment, since in November 1549 his arrival on the Privy Council had been the first evangelical addition to its membership, to prove that Dudley's plans in overthrowing Somerset had succeeded. Now he was promoted just as Somerset was eliminated.

Winter and spring 1552 also saw further progress on three more important stages of the reform programme, beginning even during the destruction of Somerset: Cranmer's cherished canon law revision project, the formation of a concise statement of doctrine (eventually issued as the Forty-Two Articles), and the revision of the Prayer Book to save it from conservative subversion and evangelical criticism. If all three designs had been completed, then everything would have been put in place for the formation of a church which at last we could call without qualification Protestant: a church which could hold its head up among the best reformed churches of the Continent, and even assume leadership among them. We must now consider each of these schemes in turn.

First, the canon law revision: the scheme which John Foxe would later christen the *Reformatio Legum* ('the reformation of laws'), when he belatedly

128 Strype, *Cheke*, pp. 69–86.

published the final draft in 1571 as part of the campaign to resurrect it. Work began in earnest on 12 December 1551, when the eight planners began meeting to prepare drafts: the full team of thirty-two designated by the Privy Council the previous October was formally appointed with minor variations of membership at the beginning of February 1552. Consisting of four groups made up of bishops (to provide the experience of working ecclesiastical administrators), academic theologians, civil lawyers and common lawyers, it was dominated by Cranmer's close associates (at least eighteen of the thirty-two were Cambridge men).[129] He had further succeeded in including among the theologians two distinguished foreign representatives, Jan Laski and Peter Martyr, and Martyr was one of the preliminary sub-committee of eight. In late January Laski and Cranmer were both too occupied to do more than send second-hand greetings to Calvin by a traveller setting off for Geneva, and in February Peter Martyr was reported to be hard at work at Lambeth Palace on the revision. Another honoured guest at Lambeth, and a fellow-commissioner on the revision, was Laski's soul-mate Bishop Hooper: a piece of hospitality which was a remarkable example of Cranmer's ability to forgive and forget.[130]

The presence of the refugee divines on the commission was not merely a graceful tribute to their scholarship, or even simply a desire to rally as much talent as possible to a daunting task: once more it was part of the master-plan which Cranmer had inaugurated in 1548, to draw together all the evangelical churches of Europe under England's leadership, in conscious opposition to the work of the Council of Trent. This agenda can be heard in the cry of Peter Martyr when writing to Bullinger from Lambeth, in March 1552, about the work of revision: 'May God therefore grant that such laws may be appointed by us here, that by their godliness and holy justice may render totally null the Tridentine canons in the faithful churches of Christ!'[131] If the law-code was successfully enacted by the English Parliament, it would thus have international significance, in the same way that Laski's description of life and polity of the London Stranger Church, his *Forma ac ratio* with its dedication to the King of Poland, was intended to speak to all Europe.

Cranmer shared Martyr's enthusiasm for this European-wide vision. This is apparent from the fact that in the middle of the activity on the law revision, he chose to send out the most explicit and high-level set of invitations so far, in order to gather his ecumenical council in England. Acting, as he said, on behalf of the King, he wrote to the three most important leaders in the strongholds of Continental reform: Bullinger at Zürich and Calvin at Geneva

129 For the appointment in February, see *A.P.C. 1550–52*, p. 471; *Chronicle of Edward VI*, p. 110; *C.P.R. Edward VI 1550–3*, p. 354. For the composition of the commission, see Sachs, '"Reformatio Legum Ecclesiasticarum"', pp. 91–2.

130 *E.T.* pp. 293, 295, 444 (*O.L.* pp. 447, 478, 737). Cf. Martyr to Gualter, 2 March 1552, Martyr, *Loci Communes*, p. 1091, and on Hooper's presence at Lambeth, Cox 2, pp. 430–31.

131 *E.T.* p. 331 (*O.L.* p. 503).

(both on 20 March), and a week later to Melanchthon at Wittenberg.[132] He let each of them know of the other invitations, and although each letter was tailored to the particular concerns of the recipient, the menace of Trent figured in all of them. Bullinger was assured that King Edward had never even considered sending a representative to Trent, and also that the unhappy affair with Hooper, over which Zürich had written in concern a year before, was now completely resolved. Calvin, the author of the *Institutes*, was tempted with the prospect of a gathering of divines which would 'hand down to posterity, by the weight of their authority, some work not only upon the subjects themselves, but upon the forms of expressing them'; in reaction to the deliberations of Trent upon the eucharist, Calvin was also reminded about the importance of an evangelical agreement on the matter. Melanchthon was rather tactlessly reminded how previous 'religious dissensions, especially in the matter of the Sacrament', had weakened the German Church and encouraged the Emperor to attack the evangelicals. All three were offered England as the perfect place for such a Council to create the perfect agreement.

In Chapter Twelve we will discover what a lukewarm response there was to this initiative. Likewise, it must be said that not all the commissioners for the revision felt the same way as Cranmer and his foreign friends: among the doubters were bishops Ridley and Goodrich. Goodrich should have been an unambiguous asset to the evangelical cause, but when Martin Micron commented on the canon law project in March, he saw both Ridley and Goodrich as obstructing progress 'with their worldly ways of thinking'.[133] This is predictable from Ridley, given his continuing frostiness towards Laski and his stranger congregations, but evidently Goodrich had decided to take the same stance: a serious nuisance for the more radical spirits, given his new position of legal influence as Lord Chancellor. Evidently the international dimension to the scheme did not appeal to these two. Certainly the surviving final draft of the law-code often has a flavour which might have suited a city-state like Strassburg or Zürich better than the fields and hamlets of rural England, although this is no doubt a reflection of an effort to legislate for the urban parishes of England, which were likely to have the most complex life to need regulation. One can imagine Ridley and Goodrich casting a sceptical eye over the long complex speeches which a penitent was required to make in the suggested service for reconciled excommunicates, and asking how illiterate countryfolk were expected to recite them; they might also sarcastically have enquired whether the classical Latin word meaning 'grape-harvest' was entirely appropriate to legislation touching on the English agricultural scene.[134] Perhaps they also raised the more profound question of the scope of the revision. Unusually for a document which sought to codify law, it also sought to lay down the boundaries of doctrine in the Church, so that even in

132 Cox 2, pp. 430–44.

133 *E.T.* p. 377 (*O.L.* p. 580).

134 Cf. *Reformation of Laws*, ed. Cardwell, pp. 89–93, 177–88, 281 ('*vindemiarum*').

the final draft, three of the first five sections set out matters of belief ranging from the nature of God and the Trinity through to a discussion of the sacraments. What were these doing here? Was this the most appropriate setting in which to define doctrine?

The question could be put all the more urgently because at the same time as the canon law revision went ahead, a second prong of reform was independently under consideration: drafts of articles were circulating which were concerned purely with creating an official doctrinal statement for the Church – the ancestors of the Forty-Two and Thirty-Nine Articles. The relationship between the two separate formulations of doctrine in law revision and Articles is puzzling. The process of formulating a statement of doctrine for the English Church, which would have comparable status to the Augsburg Confession, had proceeded through Edward's reign as slowly as the canon law revision, and much of the reluctance to make progress with it seems for a considerable time to have come from Cranmer himself. However, against the background of his ecumenical concerns, the delay is perfectly comprehensible: Cranmer did not want to make a definitive statement of what the Church of England believed which might compete with his cherished aim, so enthusiastically expressed to Calvin in March 1552, of getting a general agreed statement which might put Augsburg in the shade and provide a real alternative to the statements of Trent. It is interesting to find that one client of Cranmer's late Elizabethan successor as Archbishop of Canterbury, the controversial and doctrinal writer Thomas Rogers, perceived the connection precisely in this manner: Cranmer had 'employed a great part of his time and study for the effecting of . . . a joint and common consent of all the churches . . . containing and expressing the sum and substance of that religion, which they do all both concordably teach and uniformly maintain'. It was only when this proved 'a work of much difficulty' that it became apparent that there was only one feasible alternative: 'every kingdom and free state, or principality' which had abandoned the Roman obedience 'should divulge a brief of that religion, which among themselves was taught and believed', and in England, that work was principally Cranmer's.[135]

It was not as if Cranmer did not have doctrinal material prepared long before 1552: as early as December 1549 we have noted John Hooper observing that the Archbishop was demanding subscription to doctrinal articles from all new preachers and theological teachers (see above, Ch. 10, p. 453).[136] During 1550 there seem to have been formal discussions about a doctrinal statement among the bishops, to which Martin Bucer alluded at one of his gloomiest moments – not enough of the conservative bishops had then been dethroned to make agreement possible. In 1551, Cranmer presented the

135 *Rogers*, pp. 3–4.
136 *E.T.* p. 46 (*O.L.* pp. 71–2); cf. his similar remark again to Bullinger, 5 February 1550: *E.T.* p. 48 (*O.L.* p. 76).

modified line-up of bishops with a draft version of a statement.[137] Sections of this draft appear to be fossilized in articles which John Hooper issued for the diocese of Gloucester soon after he arrived, in April or May that year: there are several correspondences of content and wording between his articles and the final version of the Forty-Two Articles which would be published in 1553, and that makes it likely that Hooper was drawing on the Archbishop's work.

Yet the articles given to the bishops in 1551 were clearly not much publicized otherwise, and their status remained ambiguous; a year later, in May 1552, the Privy Council sent a request to Cranmer to ask for a copy and enquired whether they had been issued 'by any public authority or no'.[138] Clearly in the intervening year Cranmer had not been pursuing the matter of the articles with any urgency: his energies seem to have been transferred to the canon law revision project, with its rival doctrinal discussion. However, during summer 1552, not only did the canon law discussions stall, but Cranmer's hopes of a speedy ecumenical council faded; it was only at this stage that he began to show an interest in pursuing the formation of a public doctrinal statement for England alone. So just as Thomas Rogers later suggested, the canon law revision, with its ecumenical dimension, took precedence, but once the ecumenical possibilities began to look problematic, Cranmer turned his attention once more to the articles of religion. Yet even the final issuing of the Articles would be further bedevilled by the disagreements which embroiled Cranmer and his fellow-Councillors during the autumn of 1552; at least they did receive authorization, before King Edward's death, as the Forty-Two Articles, unlike the canon law revision.

A third great project was reaching completion in winter 1551–2: the comprehensive revision of the 1549 Prayer Book, which was presented to Parliament for authorization in a new Act of Uniformity, passed at the end of the session in April 1552. As in the original compilation of 1549, much remains obscure about the work of revising it, although Cranmer was in charge and steered its development. Clearly intended from the moment of the 1549 book's introduction, the revision had taken a great deal of time, for it had begun in earnest as long ago as winter 1549–50: meetings of the Convocation of Canterbury held during that Parliament had discussed various matters, such as the large number of surviving saints' days allowed in the book, the possible real-presence implications of the words of administration

137 *E.T.* p. 356 (*O.L.* p. 546); however, one cannot be sure from Bucer's wording whether he was merely recording the undoubted fact of theological diversity among the episcopate of 1550, rather than a formal discussion.

138 *A.P.C. 1552–54*, p. 33. Hooper's articles are Hooper, *Later Writings*, pp. 120–29. For correspondences of numbered articles in these with numbered articles of the Forty-Two, cf. e.g. 4H/20FA (the church); 8H/12FA (good works); 9H/23FA (purgatory); 14H/25FA (vernacular worship); 15H/30FA (oblation of Christ); 17H/24FA (private ministry); 18H/38FA (oaths); 22–24H/26FA; 34–37H/36FA. As is often the case, there are also correspondences between Hooper's articles and other sets of episcopal articles and injunctions.

at communion and nationwide variety in administering communion. We know frustratingly little about these discussions, which seem to represent the only occasion on which Convocation was given any say in the making of the English liturgy.[139]

No immediate result followed, but the need to revise was given new urgency in 1551 by Stephen Gardiner's masterly subversion of the 1549 book in his *Explication and assertion of the Catholic faith*. Even so, Gardiner's efforts were probably not yet in the public domain when, late in 1550, the government sought the opinions of the chief refugee theologians, Martyr and Bucer, as to how the liturgy might be improved. This consultation may have helped to dispel Bucer's previous sense of grievance that his expertise was being neglected. By early January 1551, at the request of his diocesan Bishop Goodrich, Bucer had formulated his critique of the faults of the 1549 book: the document which Conrad Hubert, the editor of his works, would later christen the *Censura*. Coming so soon after his support of Cranmer against Hooper in the vestments row, this was the last service that Bucer would perform for the Church of England before his death. Martyr also provided a paper about the revision, which is now lost, and he also provided the Latin text of a new exhortation to receive communion, which was the most substantial block of entirely new material to be incorporated in the revised book.[140]

The opinions of both Bucer and Martyr very significantly influenced the revision of the Prayer Book, although Cranmer did not slavishly follow their recommendations in all things. It is unlikely that Bucer would have approved of all the changes made in the communion service, and in more than one instance Cranmer ignored Bucer's recommendations for retaining phrases which Bucer felt expressed his own subtle notion of eucharistic presence.[141] There is one possible instance of a more radical foreign influence on the revision: the insertion at the beginning of the communion service of a recitation by the minister of the Ten Commandments, with a set of responses by the congregation. This is reminiscent of the liturgical usage in Valerand Poullain's French refugee congregation set up by the Duke of Somerset in Glastonbury, although there the recitation and responses were in a metrical

139 There can be little doubt about the authenticity of this reference to a meeting of Convocation, despite frequent doubts expressed e.g. by Gasquet and Bishop, p. 286: cf. Heylyn I, pp. 227–8, who saw documentation when it was already fragmentary. Heylyn describes the meeting as of 1550, but it is likely to have taken place in November/December 1549 (see above, Ch. 10, p. 452, n. 112).

140 Martyr to Bucer, 10 January 1551, transcript in Strasbourg, Bibliothèque Nationale et Universitaire, Thesaurus Baumianus 20, pp. 161–2, tr. from the original in C.C.C.C. by Gorham, *Gleanings*, pp. 227–31; Beesley, 'Unpublished source of the Book of Common Prayer'.

141 Hopf, *Bucer*, pp. 80, 97, and cf. ibid., p. 70, for a change in the baptismal service which Bucer made and Cranmer ignored. For thorough discussion of Bucer's *Censura*, see ibid., pp. 58–81, and for its text, *Bucer*, ed. Whitaker.

version. Poullain published this liturgy in 1552, but there is no reason why Cranmer would not have known of it before that; as we have already noted (p. 494) the government was much concerned for the Glastonbury congregation's continuing welfare after Somerset's fall. It is noticeable that that firm friend of the Stranger congregations, Bishop Hooper, also anticipated this insertion of the Ten Commandments into the communion rite in his diocesan injunctions of 1551: an interesting indication, incidentally, that he was involved in the discussions which were taking place about the purification of the 1549 book which he disliked so much.[142]

A further important (albeit negative) influence on the revision of the communion rite, was the barrage of mock-approving comment which Stephen Gardiner's *Explication* had made about the eucharistic theology which he claimed to find within it. All Gardiner's points were met by revision, in order to clarify the spiritual presence view of the eucharist which Cranmer had advanced in the *Defence* and the *Answer*. Most noticeable for communicants was the substitution of entirely different words when they were offered the eucharistic bread and wine: no longer statements that the elements should preserve their bodies and souls to everlasting life, but directions to think on the sacrifice of Christ on the cross. 'Take and eat this in remembrance that Christ died for thee, and feed on him in thy heart by faith, with thanksgiving . . . Drink this in remembrance that Christ's blood was shed for thee, and be thankful.' In his investigation of the liturgy's sources, the indefatigable Brightman could find no precedent for either of these formulae; they are likely to be brand-new.

Equally devastating in their theological effect, if communicants were as attentive as Gardiner had been to the small print of the communion service, were newly created rubrics at the end. In place of the troublesome rubric to which Gardiner had drawn attention, stating that in the communion wafers 'men must not think less to be received in part, than in the whole, but in each of them the whole body of our Saviour Jesu Christ', there was inserted an instruction that there was no need for any other bread than the best quality which was in everyday use. More striking still was the next sentence: 'And if any of the bread or wine remain, the Curate shall have it to his own use.' Here was no mention made of the consecration of the elements, so that one cannot argue that the reference was to bread and wine which had not been consecrated. Bread and wine there had been at the beginning of the service, and bread and wine there were at the end of it. Once they had served their purpose, and treated with the reverence which the solemnity of the service demanded, they could be taken home to the parsonage and used as the human creations which they were. This was actually putting into effect a recommendation of Bucer, which shows that despite all his dislike of what he saw as

142 Leaver, *Goostly Songs*, pp. 144–7, with texts accessibly presented in Proctor and Frere, *Book of Common Prayer*, pp. 86–8; discussion in Brightman, *English Rite*, pp. cxlvii–cxlix, clvii–clix is probably over-sceptical. Hooper, *Later Writings*, pp. 132–3.

radicalism emanating from Zürich, he was as concerned as any of his colleagues to remove all association of presence from the elements themselves. The 1662 revisers of the Prayer Book fully realized the implications of what Cranmer was saying in the rubric when they gave it a drastic overhaul, creating a reference to consecrated elements left over, and strictly stipulating that these should reverently be consumed in the church itself by the clergyman, who by then was once more referred to as the 'priest'. The restored Church of England in the reign of Charles II looked out on a different sacramental world from that of 1552.[143]

Consistent with the Edwardian agenda of change was the drastic treatment of the central prayers of the communion. No longer could these be referred to as a 'canon' and thus implicitly linked with the Sarum canon of the mass on which they had been based, as Cranmer had been prepared to do at one place in the 1549 book. The sequence of material was thoroughly rearranged, so that the prayers of intercession were completely removed from the former 'canon', and the narrative of the Saviour's words of institution was immediately followed (without even an 'Amen') by the distribution of bread and wine to the communicants, so that they would make their communion with these words still echoing in their minds. Those gospel words were there to instruct, not to effect any change in the elements distributed. Gone were the crosses printed in the text in the passage immediately before the institution narrative, which had presumably been intended to indicate a moment of consecration; gone, too, was any instruction to the minister to accompany the recitation of the words of institution by any symbolic holding of the bread or the cup – this, again, was a visual symbolism which the 1662 revisers felt compelled to restore.

Altogether, Colin Buchanan is justified in seeing the purpose of this liturgical surgery as an alteration in the dramatic shape of the rite: 'the only "moment" is reception – and the only point where the bread and wine signify the body and blood is at reception'.[144] When the faithful received the elements in the Lord's Supper, they were 'partakers of his most blessed body and blood' because they were remembering the 'one oblation of himself once offered' on the cross. Their action of reception created the 'Amen' which was deliberately missing in the text itself at the end of the institution narrative – we may recall the way that Cranmer had described the balance between minister and people in 1550, when he said of the communion that 'the priest and ministers prepare the Lord's Supper, read the Gospel, and rehearse Christ's words, but all the people say thereto, Amen'. Arthur Couratin

143 Brightman, *English Rite*, pp. cxlv, clvi, 700–701, 716–17; cf. *Bucer*, ed. Whitaker, pp. 40–41.

144 Buchanan, *What did Cranmer think he was doing?*, p. 23, and cf. ibid., pp. 23–5, for effective ripostes to arguments for seeing a continuing doctrine of consecration expressed in the 1552 rite. Couratin, 'The service of Holy Communion, 1552–1662', pp. 435–6, has a similar approach.

34 Hailes Church, Gloucestershire: the chancel, looking west. The rearrangement of a medieval chancel for use in a post-1552 communion service: the table in the centre has replaced the altar at the east end of the church, and around it are seats for the communicants. The medieval rood screen survives as a partition to separate this area from the preaching-space of the nave.

effectively captured the novelty of the approach in this communion service by calling the whole rite 'a series of communion devotions; disembarrassed of the Mass with which they were temporarily associated in 1548 and 1549'.[145]

Discussion of the radical nature of the changes in the 1552 rite usually centres on these questions of eucharistic theology, but equally revolutionary was the allied question of the book's treatment of death and the funeral service, which had not figured directly in the literary clash between Cranmer and Gardiner. One of the matters which had troubled Bucer from his first acquaintance with the 1549 rite was its retention of commemoration of the dead: a very natural worry for evangelicals, who could see the old Church's hold over the passage from death to life as one of its strongest suits in the struggle for the minds of the laity. Not all evangelicals were wholly hostile to prayers for the dead, even after King Henry's departure freed them to express themselves openly; Hugh Latimer, who often exercised the privilege of age in order to be disconcertingly old-fashioned, went on praying for the dead in his sermons until at least the end of 1550.[146] However, he had to perform some

145 Cranmer, *Defence*, p. 456; Couratin, 'The service of Holy Communion, 1552–1662', p. 433.

146 *Latimer's Sermons*, pp. 217, 284.

nimble theological footwork in order to do so; the association of the custom with the doctrine of purgatory, and with the fatal idea that in some way the living could influence the fate of the departed, flew in the face of the evangelical insistence on God's grace as the sole determinant of human salvation. One hardly needs by now to emphasize that this had been at the heart of Cranmer's theology since the 1530s. The 1552 book would bring an end to any possibility of officially praying for the dead, as was noted with fury by that alert conservative Robert Parkyn, although Parkyn also noted the move's intimate connection with the remodelling of eucharistic theology: 'all this was done and brought to pass only to subdue the most blessed sacrament of Christ [*sic*] body and blood under form of bread and wine'. Masses 'for the salvation of the quick and the dead' were in evangelical eyes a chief symbol of the corruption of the mass: as Cranmer had emphasized in his preface to the *Defence*, together with transubstantiation, they were one of the two chief roots of the weeds of Roman error.[147]

This double agenda was clear within the communion service, where the intercessions which had previously formed the first part of the 1549 canon were not only moved to an earlier point in the service but edited. In particular they now emphasized in their introduction that they were offered for the Church 'militant here in earth' and not for the Church in the next life. However, Parkyn also noted the transformation in the funeral service: 'no diriges or other devout prayers to be sung or said for such as was departed this transitory world'. The 1549 rite had retained the provision for a eucharist to be celebrated at a funeral, and as in the medieval services, there were psalms to be recited, and even still a direct address to the corpse by the priest: 'I commend thy soul to God the father almighty, and thy body to the ground . . .'. These were too redolent of the past to survive in 1552, and all were abolished, in order to destroy the sense of continuing communion between living and dead which had been such a striking feature of late medieval religion. Now the bulk of the service was a long scripture reading, designed to edify the living rather than to maintain a relationship with the deceased. The body alone was committed to the ground, prayers concerned the welfare of the mourners, and no attempt was made to commend the deceased's soul to God; instead, the charitable assumption was made that 'it hath pleased almighty God of his great mercy to take unto himself the soul of our dear brother here departed'. As Eamon Duffy says, 'the oddest feature of the 1552 rite is the disappearance of the corpse from it . . . at the moment of committal in 1552, the minister turns not towards the corpse, but away from it, to the living congregation around the grave.' The Church had surrendered its power over death back to the Lord of life and death in heaven: a move of perfect theological consistency, but one which has ceased to satisfy the pastoral needs of Anglicanism in the twentieth century.[148]

147 'Parkyn's Narrative', p. 76.

148 Brightman, *English Rite*, pp. 848–78; cf. Duffy, *Stripping of the Altars*, pp. 473–5, Rowell, *Liturgy of Christian Burial*, pp. 84–7.

So dirges and requiems were gone, and with them the power of the mass. One major consequence of this was unintended by the reformers, and one can see them in the 1552 book beginning to cope with the unpleasant surprise. Cranmer and his colleagues had intended their communion service to be the centre-piece of the regular weekly worship of the Church, but this was not happening; people did not want to make their communion on such a frequent basis. One problem may have been the fierce exhortations to self-examination which were already part of the prescribed rite in 1549: conscientious or shy potential communicants may have felt that they were not worthy to receive. A Venetian diplomatic representative in 1551 indeed noticed the way that London households were sending along a single representative, often a servant, to communion services, and that some merchants were indeed making fun of the government's new requirements.[149] People's reluctance suddenly to take up the custom of weekly communion may have combined with churchwardens' horror at the expense of providing bread and wine for an entire parish Sunday by Sunday to frustrate Cranmer's intentions.

Something would have to be done to fill the devotional vacuum, and this was achieved by giving a new prominence to the morning and evening offices of the Church, mattins and evensong, to bring them into the centre of a congregation's worship day by day. In the 1549 rite, these offices still retained much of their traditional ethos of services intended for the regular devotional life of clergy and a handful of extra-devout laity, rather than for the whole congregation. This is how Martin Bucer still envisaged them in his comments on the 1549 rite in January 1551, and the offices themselves were not couched in language which suggested a large congregation: for instance, the sequence of versicles and responses retained the traditional use of the first person singular – 'O Lord, open thou my lips. And my mouth shall shew forth thy praise . . .'. In 1552 these clauses were put into the plural, although interestingly when a new primer was issued in March 1553 for private devotion, the old singular form was retained.[150] It was also specified for the first time in the 1552 offices that the whole congregation should join in the recital of the creed.

Moreover, in 1552 the offices were expanded and enriched. Further material was added at the beginning of mattins to allow for an act of penitence at the service, with the suggestion that this could also be provided at evensong, and provision was made for the regular use of the litany three times a week. This gave an opportunity for intercession at greater length than the offices themselves allowed, and the specification in 1662 that the litany should follow the morning service probably formalized a custom which had developed very soon after this Edwardian order. Additionally, the shifting of the main intercessions in communion to the first half of the service made it

149 *C.S.P. Venetian 1534–54*, p. 348.

150 *Liturgical Services of Edward VI*, pp. 384 passim. Cf. *Bucer*, ed. Whitaker, pp. 84–5.

possible to use this first half as a separate service, without proceeding to the communion itself: a service known as ante-communion. This usage had been already ordered in the rubrics of the 1549 rite, and it is noticeable that Bucer disapproved of it, recommending its abolition as a relic of the mass. It is an instance where Cranmer ignored his advice, presumably seeing the pastoral usefulness as outweighing ideological danger.[151] The way was open to create a morning marathon of prayer, scripture reading and praise, consisting of mattins, litany and ante-communion, preferably as the matrix for a sermon to proclaim the message of scripture anew week by week, but in any case with the mandatory addition of one of the official homilies.

More significant still was the positive encouragement to the laity to attend the offices which appeared in the preface of the 1552 book. In the 1549 preface, by contrast, the emphasis had been on the fact that there was no compulsion on anyone to attend the offices apart from those with cure of souls or specific duties in the greater churches. Now not only were 'all priests and deacons' specifically ordered to say the offices daily, but the parish clergyman was told to say the service openly in church, and to 'toll a bell thereto, a convenient time before he begin, that such as be disposed may come to hear God's word, and to pray with him'.[152] The bells were indeed tolled, and the laity began arriving at their newly whitewashed churches. From this hint in the Prayer Book preface sprang a characteristic pattern of Sunday worship in the Church of England, morning and evening prayer; this dominated the mainstream devotional life of the Church for four centuries between the accession of two Queen Elizabeths, before the modern emphasis on restoring the central place of the eucharist changed the shape of worship once more.

One could go on enlarging on the radical features of the 1552 Prayer Book: its virtual abandonment of any provision for music, its drastic simplification of permissible clerical vestments, its acceptance of the replacement of stone altars by wooden tables which had been the particular preoccupation of the government during 1550. Even chancel screens, which had not come under official nationwide attack despite the destruction of the rood figures which they had supported, were nevertheless implicitly lined up for the scrap-heap when they lost the one function which they had retained in the 1549 rite, as a location for the rite of churching of women. Instead of coming 'nigh unto the quire door' in the screen, the woman was now to find some convenient place 'nigh unto the place where the [communion] table standeth' – wherever that might be in the rather uncertain new layout of English church interiors.[153] Yet for all this radicalism, it remains an open question as to whether Cranmer regarded the 1552 rite as his final word. Certainly he had settled scores with Gardiner, and he had banished the old communion between living and dead from the English Church. Yet in January 1551 Peter

151 Cf. *Bucer*, ed. Whitaker, pp. 20–21, and *Liturgical Services of Edward VI*, p. 97.
152 Brightman, *English Rite*, pp. 38–9.
153 Ibid., pp. 880–81.

Martyr confided to Martin Bucer as the redrafting of the book progressed that he felt that Cranmer was being held back by less thoroughgoing colleagues: 'I am persuaded that, if the business had been committed to his individual hand, purity of ceremonies would without difficulty have been attained by him; but he has colleagues who offer resolute opposition.' Later, in exile under Mary, the more radically inclined exiles maintained that Cranmer 'had drawn up a book of prayer a hundred times more perfect than this that we now have'. Probably the commentator meant 'would have drawn up' rather than 'did draw up', but even that implication indicates that given greater leisure and a reformation more firmly consolidated, Cranmer would have moved the liturgy of the Church of England closer to that of Farel and Calvin in Geneva, Poullain in Glastonbury or Laski in the Stranger Church.[154]

For the time being, however, the problem was simply to get the new rite into the public arena. The Act of Uniformity which authorized the 1552 rite specified quite a long period of adjustment before the new book would have to be used exclusively: right up to All Saints' Day, 1 November 1552, rather more than six months after the bill passed into law. This was sensible enough: the first 1549 Act of Uniformity had also allowed a few months of breathing-space before everyone had to use the new rite. Yet there is a significant contrast between the two events: in 1549 the Prayer Book was ready and published even before the Act had been passed. In 1552, it was ready in the spring, for naturally Parliament had scrutinized a completed draft while it considered the Uniformity Bill, and had sealed the manuscript copy, depositing it with the Clerk of Parliament. However, the book was not finally published until the very last moment in October: even then, delay was extended by a bitter disagreement over a significant point of detail, as we will see (below, Ch. 12). The embarrassment of the delay is patent in a sermon of a close associate of the Cranmer–Ridley circle, Roger Hutchinson, who at Eastertide (mid-April) 1552 was still having to explain away the continuing traditionalism of the order in the 1549 Prayer Book that communicants should receive the eucharistic bread in their mouths, not in their hands: clearly there was still official silence on what the new book would contain.[155] Likewise, there was a curious hiatus in 1552 about progress on the reform of the canon law, which had begun so energetically in the winter: work seems to have stopped in the spring and did not resume until the autumn. For the first time, the disagreements which were a perennial feature of high politics under Edward VI were seriously affecting the carefully controlled pace of religious

154 Martyr to Bucer: Gorham, *Gleanings*, p. 232; exile comment qu. in Couratin, 'The Holy Communion 1549', pp. 151–2.

155 *Hutchinson*, pp. 231–2; sermons preached at Eton (cf. ibid., pp. 210–12). On Hutchinson, see ibid., biographical notice: he dedicated his 1550 christological treatise to Cranmer, and one of Cranmer's former servants, Thomas Willett, was proctor for his executrix in 1555. For the Parliamentary sealed copy see P.R.O., S.P. 10/15/15, f. 34r (*C.S.P. Domestic Edward VI*, no. 725).

change. Even though Cranmer's chief conservative opponents in the Church had now all been removed, and even though a Protestant Church was at last taking complete shape, from spring 1552 the Archbishop would now find the Duke of Northumberland first an obstacle and then the cause of shipwreck to all his cherished plans.

Part IV

FINDING IMMORTALITY

Here is a good lesson for you, my friends; if ever you come in danger, in durance, in prison for God's quarrel, and his sake . . . I will advise you first, and above all things, to abjure all your friends, all your friendships; leave not one unabjured. It is they that shall undo you, and not your enemies. It was his very friends that brought Bilney to it.

(Hugh Latimer, 'Seventh Sermon before King Edward', 1549: *Latimer's Sermons*, p. 222)

Skeleton: Thomas, all your life you have sought Christ
in images, through deflections; how else can man see?
Plastic, you sought integrity, and timid, courage.
Most men, being dishonest, seek dishonesty;
You, among few, honest, such as you knew;
in corners of sin, round curves of deception,
honesty, the point where only the blessed live,
where only saints settle, the point of conformity.

(Charles Williams, *Cranmer of Canterbury* [Canterbury, 1936], p. 38)

CHAPTER 12

Paradise betrayed: 1552–3

SUPERFICIALLY ALL MIGHT HAVE seemed well as the 1552 Parliament broke up in April: the new Prayer Book was authorized and the canon law revision launched. A new phase of the reign seemed to be beginning, symbolized by the fact that this first Parliament of King Edward, in being since 1547, was now finally dissolved. The summer also proved to be the first since 1547 (and it would be the last until 1557) in which there was not some serious commotion or uprising somewhere in the kingdom. A sign of the regime's self-confidence and return to stability was the way that its leading figures now dispersed in different directions, with the indefatigable and peripatetic William Cecil acting as liaison between them. Northumberland spent the summer months from June to August touring the far north in his capacity as Warden-General of the Marches, no doubt meditating on his plans to benefit from the dismemberment of the bishopric of Durham. For the first time King Edward, now on the verge of manhood, went on a major progress, something which his father had done in his years of health and strength and which his half-sister Mary would never do during her reign; he was away in Hampshire, Sussex and Surrey from July until the beginning of September.

Cranmer, too, left to spend an extended period in his diocese, mostly at Croydon: he only attended the Privy Council once between 24 April and its departure on progress with the King, and thereafter he did not attend again until 11 October.[1] He completed his first major recorded schemes of building in the two decades since he had become Archbishop, a period otherwise marked more by the dispersal of ancient archiepiscopal property than anything constructive. Apart from rebuilding the Great Parlour at Lambeth, he carried out major improvements down in furthest Kent at Bekesbourne, the former country home of the Prior of Christchurch, Canterbury; he had unsuccessfully coveted the house for his servant Edward Isaac before the dissolution, but later he himself received it in an exchange.[2] His enlarged house, mostly destroyed in 1647 and thereafter, is sited in a pleasant sheltered spot below the little hill on which the village church stands: much of the gatehouse wing

1 *A.P.C. 1552–54*, pp. 24, 92, 140.

2 For Bekesbourne and Isaac, P.R.O., S.P. 1/129 f. 76, Cox 2, p. 458 (misdated; *L.P.* 31 i, no. 310).

remains, and reset in its fabric are stone plaques, one with the Archbishop's arms, the other with his initials, motto and the date 1552. As usual with decorative work associated with the Archbishop, the lettering is in the most up-to-date Renaissance style. At his fall, the inventory of his houses makes it clear that this had become his main headquarters in furthest Kent, with named chambers occupied by some of his chief servants.[3] Was it deliberate that Cranmer chose to spend his money on this new acquisition rather than the old palace at Canterbury itself or the great archiepiscopal house at Ford, relatively near Bekesbourne? Perhaps he saw it as a symbol of a new beginning in his diocese.

However, in hindsight much of this confidence would be betrayed by fate. Most importantly the King's health, on which all evangelical hopes depended, became fragile that spring after an attack of measles and smallpox, and it never fully recovered: he contracted his fatal tuberculosis in winter 1553. The royal progress was in the end cut short, on Council advice.[4] Besides this, it may be significant that of all three absences from the capital during 1552 – Northumberland's, the King's and the Archbishop's – it was Cranmer's which was the longest; significant also that it began immediately after his bitter row with the Duke in April. Cranmer and Northumberland cannot have been sorry to see the back of each other as they went their separate ways, and time did not heal the wound. It was surely not merely the dispersal of the great men of the realm which led to standstill, for months on end, in the canon law revision or in the publication of the new Prayer Book.

Particularly depressing for Cranmer was the meagre response to his invitations to Bullinger, Calvin and Melanchthon to join in an ecumenical council. By the autumn, no word at all had come from Melanchthon, apart from an oblique message via Bullinger that neither of them felt like leaving their churches at a time when Germany was riven by the war between the Emperor and his princes. Calvin had shown the most enthusiasm, writing twice to the Archbishop during the spring and summer, yet both his letters said the same thing underneath their warm phrasing – it was the wrong moment for a General Council, and he himself felt unable to come to England. 'I will have discharged my role, if I accompany with my prayers what shall be undertaken by others', he purred.[5] Cranmer's reply to him, written on 4 October amid many domestic battles, was a short and sad acknowledgement that for the

3 See Tatton-Brown, 'Bekesbourne', although it is unfortunate that apparently he did not know about the 1553 inventory, P.R.O., E. 154/2/39 f. 74v (cf. Tatton-Brown, 'Bekesbourne', pp. 31–2, 34). Description in Strype, *Cranmer* 1, p. 135, apparently based on a rather longer description by Nicholas Batteley to Strype, 28 November 1690: C.U.L. MS Additional 3, no. 24. Notes in Lambeth MS 959 f. 282v suggest that these building schemes were begun in 1551.

4 *C.S.P. Domestic Edward VI*, no. 711.

5 *E.T.* p. 463 (*O.L.* p. 713); Gorham, *Gleanings*, pp. 277–80 (possibly 4 July 1552, the date of a letter to Edward VI, *E.T.* pp. 463–4, *O.L.* pp. 714–15). Bullinger's letter to Cranmer is lost, but mentioned in Cranmer's letter to Calvin on 4 October.

35 Datestone of 1552 with Thomas Cranmer's initials and motto, Bekesbourne.

36 Heraldic plaque, Bekesbourne: Cranmer with pelicans (as Archbishop) quartering Aslockton and Newmarch, all with a crescent for difference.

time being nothing would happen. 'Meanwhile', the Archbishop said bravely, 'we will reform the English Church to the utmost of our ability and give our labour that both its doctrines and laws will be improved after the model of holy scripture'.[6]

Cranmer was writing this when there was indeed fresh activity in the various proposals for further reform in the Church, but it came at the end of half a year in which nothing had happened to any of them. In a letter written by Peter Martyr to Bullinger on 14 June 1552, one hears Martyr's disappointment about the canon law reform which had once formed such an important element in the ecumenical strategy: he told the Zürich reformer that 'that matter which was desired by all good men, and which the King's Majesty had not a little at heart, could not be accomplished'. The obstacle in this case was the discussion of sacraments in the doctrinal section of the revision. Martyr recorded the controversy about the question of how far the sacraments of baptism and eucharist conferred grace; he identified himself with those who were anxious to resist the affirmation of grace in the sacraments, because of the 'superstitions such a determination would bring with it'. As a theologian who gave a strong emphasis to predestination, he wanted to spell out that 'it was impossible that the Sacraments should be worthily received, unless those who receive them have beforehand that which is signified by them' – that is, the gift of grace by faith. It is doubtful whether the predestinarian Cranmer would have disagreed with him, and opposition of those 'otherwise not unlearned, nor evil', must have come from elsewhere – perhaps Bishops Goodrich and Ridley once more. In the event, the final draft of the canon law revision on the sacraments managed to avoid any use of the word 'grace' except in the sense to which Martyr had restricted it in his letter to Bullinger: the text indeed had no mention of the sacraments conferring grace.[7]

Conflict, however, was not confined to the reshaping of theology. The question of money and property was a source of increasing poison in the relations between Northumberland's governing clique and the clergy; in view of mounting evidence of dire financial crisis in the kingdom, it was natural for an evangelical government to consider further ways of relieving the Church of the wealth acquired in its days of popish error, but the Church's leadership could and did question the real motivation of this move. Two commissions

6 *Corpus Reformatorum* 42 (*Calvini Opera* 14) col. 370, no. 1657. This letter was probably carried by John Ab Ulmis, together with a letter written at Lambeth the same day by Martyr to Bullinger: Gorham, *Gleanings*, pp. 286–7, and cf. *E.T.* pp. 80–81 (*O.L.* pp. 123–4).

7 Gorham, *Gleanings*, pp. 280–83; Latin text and an inferior translation appended to *Bradford's Writings* 2, pp. 400–406; cf. this with the sacramental discussion in *Reformation of Laws*, ed. Cardwell, pp. 29–32. On Micron on Goodrich and Ridley in the revision, March 1552, see above, Ch. 11, pp. 502–3. One should not be misled by the fact that this is a discussion on doctrine into thinking that Martyr was talking about the drafting of the Forty-Two Articles.

were issued on 13 July 1552, nominally headed by Cranmer's colleagues Ridley, Thirlby and Goodrich, but in fact packed with government financial experts; one was to investigate all Crown revenues and debts and the other was to make sales of the confiscated chantry lands. The latter was the outcome of a fierce battle about what to do with the chantry windfall of 1547–8, a battle which had been resolved against the Archbishop's wishes at the beginning of May, when a preliminary commission for these sales was agreed on in order to pay royal debts.[8] One must remember that this was an issue over which Cranmer had temporarily broken ranks with his evangelical colleagues in the 1547 parliamentary session, when he had voted against one stage of the chantry dissolution legislation (see above, Ch. 9, p. 377).

Probably during the arguments at the end of April 1552 that led up to the May decision to set up the chantry sales commission, Cranmer 'offered to combat with the Duke of Northumberland . . . speaking then on the behalf of his prince for the staying of the chantries until his highness had come unto lawful age, and that specially for the better maintenance of his estate then'. Northumberland would have resented the clear implication: the politicians of Edward's minority were not to be trusted to spend the money wisely. The debate had in any case taken place against the background of a wider drive to seize Church wealth: besides partially implemented plans for amalgamation of some dioceses, a major scheme was launched for a round-up of Church goods, with the appointment of another set of commissioners to undertake the mammoth task of a national parish-by-parish survey. The clear if unpublicized aim was large-scale losses for the Church and gains for the government. We have the later testimony of Bishop Ridley that both he and Cranmer ('but specially Cranmer') were in 'high displeasure', not just because of earlier protests about Somerset's death, but now also for their objections to the Church goods confiscations, 'taken away only by commandment of the higher powers, without any law or order of justice, and without any request of consent of them to whom they did belong'.[9]

The subject of Church wealth emerges in painfully personal form in a letter of Cranmer to Cecil on 21 July. In the week before, the same week that the two financial commissions had been issued, Cecil visited Cranmer at Croydon, and they had evidently been in correspondence as a result. Perhaps after comment in government circles about the Archbishop's new building activities, Cecil had raised the question of covetousness in the Church, which evidently hit Cranmer on a raw nerve after what had happened in the previous few months. Despite his liking for Cecil, his tone was both injured and irritable when he defended himself and his episcopal colleagues: far from being threatened by temptations to enrich himself, he

8 *Narratives of the Reformation*, p. 247. For the July commissions, *C.P.R. Edward VI 1550–53*, pp. 354–6; for the May chantry initiative, *Chronicle of Edward VI*, pp. 121–2.

9 Diocesan amalgamations: *C.S.P. Domestic Edward VI*, no. 609. Church goods commissioners: *Chronicle of Edward VI*, p. 119, 'Parkyn's Narrative', p. 75. Cf. *Ridley*, p. 59.

said, 'stark beggary' was his main fear. He summed up his situation in a classic cry of the churchman faced by the dire economic effects of the English Reformation:

> For I took not half so much care for my living, when I was a scholar of Cambridge, as I do at this present. For although I have now much more revenue, yet I have much more to do withal; and have more care to live now as an archbishop, than I had at that time to live like a scholar. I have not so much as I had within ten years past by £150 of certain rent, beside casualties. I pay double for everything that I buy. If a good auditor have this account, he shall find no great surplusage to wax rich upon.[10]

He went on to enquire sarcastically if Cecil knew of any bishops who were covetous, so that their Primate could send them an appropriate admonition; for his part he knew of only one bishop who was even moderately wealthy. 'To be short, I am not so doted [foolish], to set my mind upon things here, which neither I can carry away with me, nor tarry long with them.'

Poverty is always a relative concept. As his complaints about his obligations indicate, Cranmer was one of the few English bishops still living like a great magnate, with a peripatetic lifestyle structured round his five well-kept palaces at Lambeth, Croydon, Canterbury, Ford and Bekesbourne. Ralph Morice has a well-known anecdote about the last years of Henry VIII's reign, when the dignified state of Cranmer's household defeated an ill-natured aristocratic attempt to show that he did not keep hospitality appropriate to his dignity. Cranmer's household ordinances also survive, slightly modified by Archbishop Parker, but still designed for regulation of an aristocratic magnificence which Archbishop Warham (despite his much greater resources) would have recognized.[11] It must also be noted that as a leading member of the evangelical establishment, his estates suffered not at all from the depredations of Edward VI's courtiers, in sharp contrast to drastic reorganization and trimming by Henry VIII in the decade from 1537. We have already witnessed the brave show of troops which he could mount in Henry's reign (see above, Ch. 8, p. 323), but his continuing military power under Edward VI may come as a surprise. He provided more light horse than any other politician except the Marquess of Northampton in 1547, and more light horse and demilances than anyone except the Duke of Somerset in 1548; his royal licence of retainer for one hundred men in 1550 was the equal in number to any other leading member of the Privy Council, and it was no empty formality, because the spectacular yellow kersey coats for ninety-nine of these hundred were revealed as stored at Canterbury Palace in 1553.[12] Moreover, this was only part of the formidable armoury, mostly stored in his palaces at Canterbury and Lambeth,

10 Cox 2, p. 437 (better text in Strype, *Cranmer* 2, pp. 404–5). For Cecil's previous visit, *C.S.P. Domestic Edward VI*, no. 688, p. 248.

11 Lambeth MS 884; *Narratives of the Reformation*, pp. 260–63, and cf. ibid., pp. 268–9. Heal, 'Archbishops of Canterbury and hospitality'.

12 P.R.O., S.P. 10/2 f. 1r, S.P. 10/5 f. 55r; retainer licence, *C.P.R. Edward VI 1550–53*, p. 7. Coats: P.R.O., E. 154/2/41, f. 5v

revealed by Mary's commissioners at the Archbishop's fall. One can also note in those inventories that the total cash value of his goods (exclusive of plate), then confiscated was calculated by government officials as £1214.4s 2d – his clothes were valued at £205.8s 2d.[13]

Yet these considerations should not lead us to dismiss his grievance as unwarranted. Lying behind his outburst of ill-temper was a profound sense of worry and disappointment, felt by the evangelical clergy about the consistent misuse of a great proportion of Church property since the time of Henry VIII: it had been liberated from the tyranny of Rome not for any good use, but merely to enrich secular politicians. In the circle around Cranmer, the complaints were led by the foreign divines; being less involved in politics than the Archbishop himself, they were in a better position to be outspoken on the subject, but there can be little doubt that he and his entourage prompted them in their views. Otherwise it is difficult to account for the fact that within four days of his arrival in England in 1549, and after only one night as Cranmer's guest at Lambeth, Paul Fagius could write knowledgeably to one of his Strassburg confidants that 'I hear that persons in authority are shamefully guilty of seizing on ecclesiastical property; and consequently the churches are miserably destitute of sound pastors'. There is a strong hint in a letter from Calvin to Farel in 1551 that Cranmer had urged the same agenda of complaint on Geneva when encouraging Calvin to write regularly to Edward VI, and certainly the spoliation of the English Church was a theme to which the Genevan leader repeatedly returned in his correspondence. The same grievance was a favourite motif of Bucer's, most notably in his extended farewell note to the King of England, the *De Regno Christi*, and in his very last gift to the English Church, the *Censura* on the 1549 *Book of Common Prayer*.[14]

In the aftermath of Somerset's fall in winter 1550, one or two native-born clergy briefly came out in the open with the same complaints about Church lands: this was perhaps in response to the official hint of a guilty conscience provided in February 1550, when a royal commission was issued to Sackville, the Chancellor of Augmentations, to examine (among other matters) how best to fulfil the promises by Henry VIII and Edward VI to benefit the Church and charitable causes by the monastic and chantry dissolutions. However, this critique by the home team seems to have been abruptly stilled when, after a particularly outspoken attack on the plunder of the Church in a Court sermon in March 1550, the royal chaplain James Courthope found himself in the Fleet prison.[15] Only at the end of 1552 does it seem that the clergy again

13 P.R.O., E. 154/2/39, ff. 62v, 63v, 64r; E. 154/2/41, ff. 5v, 7rv, 8r.

14 Fagius to Marbach, 26 April 1549: Gorham, *Gleanings*, p. 78. Calvin: ibid., p. 267 (15 June 1551); ibid., pp. 270–71 (original text in Strype, *Cranmer* 2, p. 395), 279. Bucer: ibid., pp. 209–12; Hopf, *Bucer*, pp. 105, 127–30; C.C.C.C. MS 113, pp. 5–11; *Bucer*, ed. Whitaker, pp. 154–7.

15 'Scudamore', pp. 127–8. Cf. Thomas Lever's sermon of 2 February, Strype, *Ecclesiastical Memorials* 2 i, p. 409 and Pocock, 'Preparations for the Second Prayer Book of Edward VI', pp. 147–8. Commission, 20 February 1550: *C.P.R. Edward VI 1549–51*, pp. 214–16.

became sufficiently angry about the situation to begin systematic criticism of those in charge of secular government – with drastic consequences, as we will see.

It is not surprising that squabbling between Cranmer and the Duke of Northumberland resumed as soon as Northumberland returned from the north. The contest was also taking on something of an ideological dimension, with the Duke backing the more angular evangelicals, including those associated with Laski and the Stranger Church, who might be useful to him in annoying Cranmer and members of his circle such as Bishop Ridley. One symptom of this alignment came in a tussle about printers. The Archbishop was noticeably reluctant on 19 September to turn to Northumberland for help in defending the privilege grant of his favourite printer/publisher Reyner Wolfe, and he asked William Cecil for advice as to who else could be approached among their political colleagues to secure Wolfe's position. This seems not merely to be a commercial or political dispute, but a clash between rival evangelical styles. Wolfe's rival in this affair, the printer John Day, was apparently being backed by the Duke.[16] Day never worked for Cranmer, and instead he printed the works of radicals like Hooper and even the Freewiller Henry Hart: his association with Hooper takes Day into the world of Laski and the Stranger Church. Wolfe, by contrast, was one of the few long-standing evangelical immigrants from abroad who stood entirely aloof from the Stranger Church: quite a remarkable decision for a Dutchman who had been a key agent in Cranmer's Continental communications for twenty years. It looks, in fact, as if the Duke was backing Day for the rights to print the planned new catechism: it also appears that Cecil had to mediate between the two patrons to achieve a compromise between Wolfe and Day.[17] Although Northumberland does not name the man he was backing, Day gained the privilege for printing both English and Latin catechisms, while Wolfe hung on to his privilege of printing Latin books and produced the Latin edition of the 1553 catechism, with the English edition coming out from Day's press.[18]

The continued skirmishing between Northumberland and Cranmer also threatened to have a much more serious consequence: further delays when progress resumed on producing the Church of England's doctrinal statement, canon law revision and new Prayer Book. By September 1552 the draft articles of doctrine were shuttling back and forth between Cranmer and Sir John Cheke, who had been commissioned to turn them into the best humanist Latin. By 4 October, Martyr was back at Lambeth Palace hard at work on the canon law revision, as he proudly told Heinrich Bullinger. Both

16 Strype, *Cranmer* 2, no. 66, p. 404, Cox 2, p. 440; cf. this with Northumberland's letter to Cecil, 7 September (*C.S.P. Domestic Edward VI*, no. 713).

17 For Cecil's memorandum, see H.M.C. *Hatfield* 1, p. 99. On Wolfe, Pettegree, *Foreign Protestant Communities*, pp. 93–4.

18 Day's privilege is B.L. Royal MS 18 C XXIV f. 254r, 13 September 1552.

these schemes attracted enthusiastic support from the young King in a memorandum which he prepared on Council business on 13 October.[19] As far as Cranmer was concerned, the long-delayed Prayer Book was ready for publication by the end of August, for Lord Chancellor Goodrich had already seen to a translation of it into French for use in the Channel Isles. However, even this enterprise produced another dispute about printers, with a parallel line-up of forces to those in the Day/Wolfe conflict. The Archbishop urged Cecil to head off an attempt, sponsored by Jan Laski, to destroy the commercial prospects of the original Prayer Book translators, by establishing a rival monopoly French-language press for a member of the French Stranger Church, Thomas Gualtier. Gualtier's Dutch partner in printing, Nicholas van den Berghe, was likewise intimately involved in the Stranger Church as one of its founding elders. In this instance, Laski won and Cranmer lost: Gualtier and van den Berghe printed the French translation of the 1552 Prayer Book. One might point the finger at the Duke of Northumberland to find an explanation for Laski's success.[20]

During September, Richard Grafton made good progress with printing the English Prayer Book from the sealed copy deposited with the Clerk of Parliament back in April. However, during Northumberland's time on the northern border, he had become seized with enthusiasm for a refugee Scots clergyman by the name of John Knox. Knox had been ministering for the English Church in Berwick and Newcastle, and as a reward for his fairly lonely work for the godly cause in a highly conservative region, he had been chosen as one of a special and well-paid team of royal chaplain-preachers late in 1551.[21] Now Northumberland brought him south to play an active role in fine-tuning both the liturgical and doctrinal projects. The role which he envisaged for Knox fits into the other tensions which we have surveyed during the spring and summer: Knox, like Hooper before him, was a soul-mate of Jan Laski and strongly approved of the godly example which the Stranger Church offered England's so far unsatisfactory Reformation. It was therefore unsurprising that the issue on which Knox seized, when he arrived in the capital, was one of the chief bones of contention which had exercised Jan Laski during his 1550 confrontation with Cranmer: kneeling at communion. The connection did not go unnoticed in Laski's circle.

Thanks to Northumberland, the Scotsman whom admirers called the

19 Strype, *Cranmer*, p. 404 (Cox 2, pp. 439–40); Martyr to Bullinger, Gorham, *Gleanings*, pp. 287–8; *Journal of Edward VI*, p. 179.

20 Strype, *Cranmer*, p. 494 (NB this is the first half of the letter of which the second half is printed at ibid., pp. 403–4, a confusion repeated in Cox 2, pp. 438–9. The error is sorted out in H.M.C. *Bath*, 2, pp. 13–14). For Laski's petition for a press, dated 24 August, two days before Cranmer's letter, Strype, *Cranmer*, p. 390; on Gualtier and van den Berghe, see Pettegree, *Foreign Protestant Communities*, pp. 55, 95–6. *R.S.T.C.* does not list a surviving French translation of the 1549 book: this 1552 translation is *R.S.T.C.* 16430.

21 For a successful reconstruction of the dating of Knox's appointment as royal chaplain, see Lorimer, *Knox*, pp. 79–81.

Duke's preacher was commissioned to deliver a sermon before the King and the Privy Council, which he used 'freely to attack kneeling at the Lord's Supper'. The Dutch Stranger Church leader Jan Utenhove, who reported this incident with much satisfaction (he was writing from Laski's house), said that Knox had made a great impact, from which results could soon be expected. He was right: on 27 September the Privy Council in Cranmer's absence wrote to order Grafton to stop work immediately on printing the Prayer Book 'until certain faults therein be corrected'. The main 'fault' was the directions which the book gave about kneeling to receive communion. A few days later the Council got in touch with the Archbishop to explain what they had done, and it asked him to consult with Ridley, Peter Martyr and others about revising the book.[22]

Cranmer's response was a long letter to his Council colleagues, which is a masterpiece of controlled fury. His primary point was the same as the argument that had eventually defeated Hooper in 1550–51; it was not for any private person or even for the Privy Council to alter the liturgy, but it was a matter for Parliament with the royal assent, and this had already been secured. Earlier in 1552, he had tried in vain to press the same argument about Parliamentary sanction on the question of the confiscation of Church goods, but he had lost on that point: this time he would have to dig deep in his strategic armoury to repeat his success in the vestments affair. First, he frankly declared war on Knox and his sympathizers. 'I know your Lordships' wisdom to be such that I trust ye will not be moved with these glorious [vainglorious!] and unquiet spirits, which can like nothing but that is after their own fancy, and cease not to make trouble and disquietness when things be most quiet and in good order. If such men should be heard, although the book were made every year anew, yet should it not lack faults in their opinion.' He then considered the proposition which had been the mainstay for Hooper and Laski two years before, and which was the same for Knox: 'Whatsoever is not commanded in the scripture, is against the scripture and utterly unlawful and ungodly.' Cranmer closed in for the kill on this: 'This samen [same] is the chief foundation of the error of the Anabaptists, and of diverse other sects. This saying is a subversion of all order as well in religion as in common policy.' At a time when the Council had just written another letter to him in one of its periodic bouts of paranoia about religious radicalism, this was a devastating connection to make. The final *coup de grâce*, after further arguments about liturgical logic, was to point out the consequences of a 'scripture alone' view of the problem: with subversive donnish humour, the Archbishop pointed out that scholarship conclusively showed that first-century dining practice was 'as the Tartars and Turks use yet at this day, to eat their meat lying upon the ground'. One can imagine some uneasy glances round the

22 Utenhove to Bullinger, *E.T.* pp. 384–5 (*O.L.* pp. 591–2), where the word wrongly translated as 'chaplain' in *O.L.* is *concionator*. *A.P.C. 1552–54*, p. 131: the Council's letter to Cranmer has not survived.

Council table at the thought of the consequences for English communion services.[23]

It was not surprising that the day after this broadside, the Council asked Cranmer over from Lambeth 'to confer' with them, and he duly appeared on 11 October. He was now in a strong position, having used precisely the right combination of arguments to wrong-foot Knox, just as Hooper had been wrong-footed earlier. Moreover, it would not do for Northumberland decisively to alienate Cranmer at this moment, for he needed backing for the matter on which the Archbishop had helped to defeat him earlier in the year: the deprivation of Bishop Tunstall, which was duly completed at the end of a remarkably speedy trial, four days after Cranmer had talked face-to-face with his Council colleagues.[24] Of course, it would have been humiliating in the extreme for Northumberland to desert his new protégé too obviously. Accordingly, Knox and the other five members of the team of special royal chaplains were invited on 21 October to give their opinions in writing on the matter, in the oblique form of comments on the statement of doctrine which would become the Forty-Two Articles – at that stage, forty-five in number. A paper arguing against kneeling at communion survives from Knox and one or two of his fellow-chaplains, taking the form of an extended critique of what would eventually become Article 35 commending the new *Book of Common Prayer*; this almost certainly represents his response to the Council's request. It must have been written with remarkable speed, unless Knox had prepared it beforehand, perhaps in consultation with Laski.

Within twenty-four hours, however, it became apparent that Knox had written in vain. On 22 October the Council took the decision to add what has become known as the 'black rubric' to the final version of the Prayer Book – so called because time was now rushing on so fast towards the All Saints' Day deadline that at first the rubric appeared only on slips tipped into the already printed volumes, rather than taking its place in red ink in the text like conventional rubrics.[25] This declaration, issued on Council authority alone, was an extended justification for kneeling at communion, as 'a signification of the humble and grateful acknowledging of the benefits of Christ given unto the worthy receiving, and to avoid the profanation and disorder which about the Holy Communion might ensue'. It went on to rule out any suggestion of idolatry by making it clear that no adoration was intended

23 P.R.O., S.P. 10/15/15, ff. 34–5 (*C.S.P. Domestic Edward VI*, no. 725), pr. Lorimer, *Knox*, pp. 103–5.

24 *A.P.C. 1552–54*, pp. 138, 140; *Journal of Edward VI*, p. 150. On Tunstall's trial, *Machyn's Diary*, p. 26; *Greyfriars Chronicle*, p. 75.

25 *A.P.C. 1552–54*, p. 148 (21 October); text of Knox's paper is Lorimer, *Knox*, pp. 267–74; for this and subsequent paragraphs, see ibid., pp. 110–11, and Bailey, *Becon*, pp. 70–76. The vital dating is by the Council decision of 22 October: B.L. Royal MS 18 C XXIV f. 262v. This overtakes the arguments of Lorimer, *Knox*, p. 121, and his argument for a dispute at Windsor (ibid., p. 122) is erroneous: cf. *C.S.P. Domestic Edward VI*, no. 691.

to the eucharistic elements by kneeling, or to any real presence within them; the elements remained 'in their very natural substances', and 'the natural body and blood of our Saviour Christ' remained in heaven; 'for it is against the truth of Christ's true natural body to be in more places than in one at one time'.

The idea that this addition to the text was a victory for Knox and a defeat for Cranmer started very early: one can find the Catholic Dr Hugh Weston already promulgating the legend at the Oxford disputation of April 1554, when he said that 'a runagate Scot did take away the adoration or worshipping of Christ in the sacrament, by whose procurement that heresy was put into the last Communion-book'.[26] However, it is mysterious why any less partisan observer has ever regarded this text as symbolizing a defeat for Cranmer. The rubric exactly represents his eucharistic theology as it had been openly expressed since 1548, particularly in his detestation of adoration of the elements. Its subsequent history may have obscured this obvious fact: omitted in 1559 apparently to placate the sensibilities or constitutional scruples of Queen Elizabeth, it was restored to the 1662 Prayer Book (in slightly modified form) in a concession to Puritan worries which was rare in that revision. Given that Elizabeth disliked the declaration and Puritans liked it, perhaps it becomes more understandable why posterity may lazily have assumed that it was more to the taste of Knox than Cranmer. In fact, it was a vindication of the Archbishop's stance which saved the practice of kneeling, and thus despite its lack of Parliamentary sanction, its effect was to defend the spirit of the book presented to Parliament. That was the main point: it is doubtful whether even in his earlier discussions with Laski, Cranmer was especially worried by sitting at communion as a practice in itself, and younger members of his circle, like Thomas Becon and Roger Hutchinson, would indeed commend the custom in their writings. Once more, as in the Hooper case, the principle at stake was uniformity: it was decisively established that reformation would proceed at the uniform pace represented by government consensus, and not on the basis of good ideas presented by individual clergy like rabbits out of a hat. It was probably no coincidence that in the aftermath of this affair, in early November 1552, Bishop Ridley resumed his harassment of Laski's Stranger congregations for their nonconformity to the new Prayer Book and non-attendance at their parish churches; there is no evidence before this that he had caused trouble to the Strangers since the end of the confrontation with Hooper.[27]

There was more to come: within a few days or weeks of the 'black rubric' decision, Knox and his five fellow-chaplains put their signatures to a Latin draft of the doctrinal articles, which in what would become Article 35, still included the fatal affirmation that the new Prayer Book and Ordinal were

26 Foxe 6, p. 510, although NB the misinterpretation of this remark in the footnote to refer to Alexander Alesius.

27 Strype, *Cranmer*, 2, pp. 386–7; *A.P.C. 1552–54*, pp. 160–61.

'godly as to truth of doctrine, and as to their propriety of ceremonies, in no way contrary to the wholesome freedom of the Gospel, if those ceremonies are judged according to their nature, but excellently agree, and especially promote the same in very many respects'. Knox's signature of assent was particularly remarkable since he was still apparently noising abroad his unhappiness with the new Prayer Book during November.[28] Game, set and match to Cranmer: by 24 November, he was able to express his satisfaction with the latest form of the articles which the Council had sent him, probably this very version, and he urged their speedy publication. At some stage before the Articles were finally published, the passage quoted was modified to excise the precise reference to ceremonies alongside the reference to doctrine, but there is no reason to give Knox the credit for this: his signature shows that he had already caved in, like Hooper before him. The likelihood is that the modification was thanks to second thoughts from the Archbishop.[29]

Northumberland was clearly annoyed by the outcome of Cranmer's stand-off with Knox. Six days after the Council decision to create the 'black rubric', he even urged Cecil that Knox should be considered for the vacant diocese of Rochester; his main thought was that in that setting, traditionally close to the Primate, the fiery Scots reformer 'would be a whetstone to quicken and sharp the Bishop of Canterbury, whereof he hath need'. However, the Duke went on to suggest rather too many birds to be killed with one stone by appointing Knox to Rochester; one of the subsidiary birds was the alarming argument that if Knox were appointed a southern bishop, at least he would not encourage liturgical deviations from the official Prayer Book in the north of England. Knox's prospects of making a Hooper-like fuss about wearing episcopal rochet and chimere receded for ever; later he would assert that he had himself refused an English bishopric, and perhaps it is true that in his aggrieved state at his defeat about kneeling, the initiative for turning down Rochester did come from him.

The Duke may still have been trying to back a further attempt to promote Knox in early February 1553. The Privy Council then applied some pressure to Cranmer, trying to secure Knox one of the plum archiepiscopal livings in London: this was All Hallows, Bread Street, which had already provided a stepping-stone to higher things for a couple of prominent evangelical clergy. However, once more, Knox's rugged individuality made him look this particular gift horse in the mouth, causing an extraordinary interview with the Council at which Cranmer was present: Knox told the nonplussed Councillors that one of his chief reasons for refusing All Hallows was his continuing anger

28 Articles signed by the chaplains, P.R.O., S.P. 10/15/28, ff. 64v–65r (*C.S.P. Domestic Edward VI*, no. 739). On Knox's complaints, *C.S.P. Spanish 1550–52*, p. 593.

29 Cf. *A.P.C. 1552–54*, p. 173, and Strype, *Cranmer*, 2, pp. 402–3 (Cox 2, p. 440). I argue here against Lorimer, *Knox*, pp. 125–7, who does not explain why the fair copy draft which he argues was later altered by Knox bears Knox's signature.

about kneeling at communion.[30] It was typical of the man: a rather admirable refusal to make the most of the role which Northumberland had originally intended for him as a catspaw within the Church. Indeed, by the time of Knox's meeting with the Council, probably later that same February, he said that Northumberland opposed his appointment to Bread Street; much had happened during the course of the month. Even before the Bread Street affair, on a Christmas visit to Newcastle, his violent language from the pulpit against conservative nonconformity had not done him any favours in English political circles, and he did not court popularity in winter 1553, as we will discover.[31]

As was apparent in his October letter to the Council on kneeling, Cranmer made use of the fact that he was waging his guerilla warfare with Knox and Northumberland amid a struggle against other more lurid varieties of religious radical: both Anabaptists and the engagingly undogmatic and loosely organized groups in Kent and Essex who gained the nickname 'Freewillers', from their rejection of the increasing evangelical commitment to predestination. The Archbishop headed an official heresy commission issued on 9 October; this was largely aimed at Kent, and it absorbed his full attention down in the county until early in 1553. One does not therefore need to agree with the Imperial ambassador in attaching a sinister political explanation for the Archbishop's absence from the Council between the October confrontation (which delayed his journey into Kent) and February 1553; Cranmer had always taken a keen interest in the suppression of radicalism, and this would be the fifth year in succession in which he had devoted time to the problem. The commission did give him one further reason to be irritable with Northumberland, when in November the Duke accused him of dragging his feet in the work; the delay, Cranmer told Cecil, was simply because of the absence of most of the commission's Kentish gentry members on business in London.[32]

Once Cranmer got started on the commission, there are scraps of evidence of his energy in carrying it out. One pleasant anecdote, for instance, is preserved by John Foxe. In the course of his investigations into radical religion at Ashford, the Archbishop did some classic detective work, and thus saved an evangelical couple who had been unjustly accused of fornication by

30 Letter to Cranmer: *A.P.C. 1552–54*, p. 212 (2 February). Lorimer, *Knox*, pp. 174–6, but the meeting cannot have taken place on 14 April: the attendance Knox records at the meeting is completely at odds with *A.P.C. 1552–54*, p. 254, and Laurence Saunders, who took the living instead of Knox, was collated to it on 28 March (Cranmer's Register, f. 423r). Cf. also Ridley, *Knox*, Appendix III. Previous parsons of All Hallows included Robert Horne and Thomas Sampson, who both departed to be deans.

31 P.R.O., S.P. 10/15/35 (*C.S.P. Domestic Edward VI*, no. 747); cf. Knox, *Works* 3, p. 297.

32 NB the Kentish bias of the membership in *C.P.R. Edward VI 1550–53*, p. 355; cf. also *A.P.C. 1552–54*, pp. 131, 138. Cranmer's letter, Strype, *Cranmer*, 2, pp. 494–5 (Cox 2, pp. 440–41), has been misinterpreted by Strype (ibid., 1, p. 422) to refer to a commission for church goods. Cf. *C.S.P. Spanish 1550–52*, p. 591.

conservatives. By testing out a hunch about how the phases of the moon would have lit the supposed crime, he revealed the accusation as fabricated. Less happily, we have already noted Foxe's self-censorship of a passage in which he recorded the imprisonment at Canterbury of the Freewiller leader Humphrey Middleton in this Kentish campaign. After being bitterly reproached by the Archbishop and the other commissioners, Middleton grimly prophesied that Cranmer would soon be in a similar case to himself (see above, Ch. 11, p. 475). At the end of the whole operation, the Archbishop was guest of honour at a major sermon on 19 February 1553, when the former Freewiller schoolmaster Thomas Cole, now a respectable Protestant clergyman, preached against his erstwhile fellow-believers in Maidstone parish church, with two of them on show as living sermon illustrations (was Middleton one of them?). Cole's script was published by Cranmer's printer Reyner Wolfe soon afterwards. Sitting in his pew at Maidstone, Cranmer heard a ringing defence of predestination, and he might also have thought of John Knox as Cole proclaimed that 'whosoever therefore, either in ceremonies or godly religion, doth not conform himself to the common order, but misliking the common order, choose ceremonies and doctrines of their own inventions, are authors of sects'.[33]

Cole's sermon was probably intended as the formal culmination of Cranmer's campaign against the Kentish radicals, as two days later the Archbishop was back at Westminster attending the Privy Council. His return was on the eve of another Parliament, which despite its short duration (exactly the month of March) would prove a troubled and unhappy occasion for him. The political atmosphere at Westminster had deteriorated sharply since his departure to Kent; the King's illness may have been partly to blame for the regime's growing neurosis, which led the Council to exert unprecedented pressure on several counties to elect reliable knights of the shire to the Commons, and also to issue a large number of licences for absence from the Lords to a number of conservative bishops and secular peers. In Kent, clumsy conciliar efforts to influence the elections caused much local ill-feeling, which would probably not have distressed Cranmer, since one of the butts of the county's anger was his old adversary Sir Thomas Cheyney.[34] However, the Archbishop had good cause to be apprehensive about the increasingly fraught relations between prominent evangelical clergy and the secular politicians on whom further progress depended: the clergy were now stepping up their criticisms of those in government to fever pitch. The background to this was the renewed campaign of confiscation of Church goods, which reached its

33 Foxe, 5, p. 860; 8, pp. 41–3; Cole, *A godlie and frutefull sermon*, sig. Cv verso (he goes on to countenance devotional freedom in private houses). On Cole, Penny, *Freewill or Predestination*, pp. 68ff; cf. *A.P.C. 1552–54*, p. 222.

34 B.L. Royal MS 18 C XXIV ff. 288v–290v, 294r, 298v-299r, 307r, 320r. On Kent, cf. Clark, *Kent*, p. 85, and for Cheyney's contemporary row with Cranmer, Strype, *Cranmer*, p. 495 (Cox 2, p. 441).

climax during January 1553, when a commission of Westminster officials was appointed to receive the returns of the county commissions and to begin gathering the spoils to royal use. Throughout the process of confiscation, it was noticeable that very few clergy had been named to the local commissions: virtually none in the counties, and not many more in the cities apart from bishops; the numbers of clergy named were actually cut down during the course of compiling the commissions. The bulk of the work had been done by prominent local gentry, as with any secular commission. Even the most enthusiastic destroyer of old superstition could see the symbolism in this.[35]

A harbinger of what was to come was provided on 8 January by the appearance in the Court pulpit of an eccentric northern preacher, Bernard Gilpin, who despite his rather confused theological beliefs was quite clear that the Church was in an appalling state, mainly thanks to the greedy depredations of the landed class. Gilpin was distinctly put out that the King and Council did not attend his sermon to hear this denunciation as had been promised, yet the kingdom's leading men were not going to escape whipping that easily.[36] It was the Lent sermons at Court, beginning in February and running on into the parliamentary session in March, which really caused uproar. Both Nicholas Ridley and John Knox looked back later on that memorable Lent course as something quite exceptional; it was an outburst of clerical vitriol in which evangelicals of very different backgrounds and temperaments combined their rhetoric in an attempt to shock and shame the country's governors. Moreover, the Court sermons were only the most high-profile example of clerical complaints whose echoes now reached as far as Cambridge, where university disputations included denunciations of the spoliation of the Church.[37]

During Lent, Latimer, Lever, Bradford, Grindal, Knox, Wilson and Haddon all denounced what Ridley later rounded up as the vices of 'insatiable covetousness, of filthy carnality and voluptuousness, of intolerable ambition and pride, of ungodly loathsomeness to hear poor men's causes, and to hear God's word'. Bradford breached all the proprieties by calling down the example of the Duke of Somerset as an awful warning to his erstwhile colleagues; Knox seems to have gone even further, by launching a scarcely veiled attack on the recently rehabilitated William Paget in the guise of a villain from the Old Testament. The reaction of the Council was not penitence but fury: '"they would hear no more of their sermons; they were but indifferent prating fellows" (yea and some of them shamed not to call them "prating knaves")' are phrases echoing out of Knox's later reminiscences.

35 For the issue of the commission, see B.L. Royal MS 18 C XXIV f. 288r; *C.P.R. Edward VI 1550–53*, pp. 392–7, especially note on p. 397.

36 Strype, *Ecclesiastical Memorials*, 2 i, pp. 25–9; see also Marcombe, 'Bernard Gilpin'.

37 For this and what follows, Knox, *Works* 3, pp. 175–9, 280–2, 4, p. 566; *Ridley*, p. 59. On Miles Wilson at Cambridge, Strype, *Cranmer*, 2, pp. 464–5.

Anthony Gilby also later recalled a blistering letter from the Duke of Northumberland to the newly consecrated Bishop Harley of Hereford, in which he had warned that 'the liberty of the preachers' tongues would cause the Council and nobility to rise up against them, for they could not suffer so to be intreated'.'

One cannot understand what happened next in Parliament without considering this background of a dreadful breakdown of relations between clergy and lay politicians; for the predicted uprising came straight away, and from Northumberland himself. The great disaster of the Parliamentary session for Cranmer was the loss of the whole canon law revision, now at last complete and ready for enactment. It had been one of his chief ambitions, the second fruit of his co-operation with his foreign friends after the 1552 Prayer Book. The one partial manuscript draft which survives, very near the final version but needing the addition of some sections to make it complete, is peppered with corrections and comments on points of detail from both the Archbishop and Peter Martyr.[38] Our knowledge of what happened comes from the Imperial ambassador, who described how during the debate on the canon law bill in the House of Lords Northumberland scornfully sabotaged the proposal, promising Cranmer 'that it should come to nothing, and warned him and his brother bishops to take good care what they were about, as Parliament had entrusted a charge to them, but could not stand judge [of their fidelity to the trust]'. Significantly, the ambassador then made the connection with the preaching that had just taken place: Northumberland had gone on to denounce 'certain agitators' who had lately dwelt on the issue of confiscated Church property and lands and the proposed reorganization of the bishoprics. This he denounced as 'scandalous behaviour, tending to foster disorders and sedition'. 'Let the bishops henceforth take care that the like should not occur again, and let them forbear calling into question in their sermons the acts of the Prince and his ministers, else they should suffer with the evil preachers.' Altogether, Scheyfve's account is a remarkable confirmation of the reminiscences of Ridley, Knox and Gilby about that troubled Lent.[39]

There were of course other reasons for the canon law debacle besides immediate pique. The Church lands issue would have been brought to a head if the draft's provisions had been implemented. It sought to put strict limits on any alienations of land; it even provided a restricted total of four reasons which could be regarded as legitimate for such alienations, one of which was to raise funds for Christians enslaved to non-Christians – not a frequent cause of Church land sales in sixteenth-century England. It would also have limited all Church leases to ten years, a policy of short leasing which Cranmer had been aiming at from the start of his archiepiscopate, albeit with very limited

38 B.L. Harley MS 426. In *J.Eccl.Hist.* 44 (1993), pp. 309–10, I give reasons why one should reject the theories of J.S. Spalding about this MS: cf. editor's introduction in *Reformation of Ecclesiastical Laws*, ed. Spalding.

39 *C.S.P. Spanish 1553*, p. 33.

success.[40] Indeed, the Church envisaged in the revision reflected to a remarkable degree the remaining structures inherited from the medieval Church in England, and so it would have remained notably clerical in its day-to-day administration or decision-making; for instance, the only laity who were to be present at the proposed revived diocesan synods were a select group who had been invited to be there by the Bishop. This was only the faintest of hints that the English Church might move to give lay elders a role in its government, as was already the case in many Reformed churches, including the Stranger Church in London.[41]

Northumberland, if he had been so inclined, might also have appealed to other worries: both about what the law revision would do to England's other legal systems, and what it would do to England's morality. The whole revision was phrased as if it were a giant royal proclamation; this was apparent straight away in the opening chapter, which talked about 'our subjects'.[42] What did this say about the status of common law, or of equity, and was it in any case a further strengthening of Church lawyers' power under the wings of the royal prerogative? In fact, the draft was very gingerly in its approach to the common law; already during drafting Cranmer himself deleted an assertion of absolute ecclesiastical rights in hearings of disputes about patronage and clerical stipends, and he also removed provision for ecclesiastical judges issuing inhibitions against lay judges. Nevertheless, a further deletion was an admonition to royal delegate judges to be bound by the law, even though the prince was above the law: altogether, this tidy, systematic package of decrees had a rather uncomfortable reminiscence of the law of ancient Rome decreed by the emperors, as was not surprising in a code to which civil lawyers had materially contributed.[43] On sexual morality, the draft demanded draconian penalties for adultery, the proposed norm being banishment or imprisonment for life, and it was equally radical about marriage: it condemned as unnatural the traditional legal possibility of a couple separating 'from board and bed' (*a mensa et thoro*), and instead it made provision for the introduction of absolute divorce on grounds of adultery. The penalties for adultery might have seemed absurdly harsh to the legislators in Parliament; praiseworthy in theory, but unworkable in practice. As far as divorce was concerned, only a year before they had allowed an attempt to secure a general provision for divorce to lapse, even when they had finally allowed the case of the Parr–Cobham remarriage.[44]

It does not sound, however, as if Northumberland bothered to appeal to such elevated considerations when he torpedoed the legislation. Cranmer's withdrawal from the Privy Council after the end of Parliament, much more

40 *Reformation of Laws*, ed. Cardwell, pp. 83–4.
41 Ibid., p. 180.
42 Ibid., p. 1.
43 Ibid., pp. 206, 209, 339–40.
44 Ibid., pp. 49–58.

clearly than his absence in the previous autumn, must be regarded as deliberate and a mark of his anger. When Parliament was over and the Convocation of Canterbury had been dissolved, he only returned to one Privy Council meeting before June. Yet in the characteristic schizophrenic fashion of the last eighteen months of Edward's reign, the programme of change was rolling on at the same time as this major setback occurred: two important new books appeared during March, both no doubt timed to come out for the beginning of Parliament, and a third would appear in May. Cranmer himself in mid-March was able to write a preface to a completed Latin translation of his 1550 *Defence*, a response to a new attack on it by Stephen Gardiner using his pen-name of Marcus Antonius Constantius. By using Latin, Gardiner had presented their debate to an international audience, and Cranmer felt obliged to respond in kind: he promised that fairly soon he would produce a translation of the *Answer* as well. Strong traditions indicate that he did not undertake the work of turning the main text into Latin himself; although we have no way of judging which of two Cambridge dons, Sir John Cheke or John Young (a strong Catholic under Mary), is the more likely candidate for responsibility.[45] This preface was dedicated to Edward VI, and there is a melancholy interest in Cranmer's description of himself as holding office under the King 'as under Moses' – the lawgiver. Evidently when he took up his pen, he was anticipating the imminent passage of the canon law reform.

Besides this semi-official work of propaganda, the government authorized two important works of public instruction that month, both replacing earlier works unsatisfactory from an evangelical viewpoint: a primer and a catechism. Dr Haugaard rightly called the primer's publication in March 'the high point of protestant influence on official devotional books in sixteenth-century England'.[46] Admittedly, its kalendar included many more obscure saints than the 1552 *Book of Common Prayer* had deigned to do, but this was no doubt to facilitate people's business transactions when they were looking at legal documents: the signs of the Zodiac were in the primer's kalendar as well, and its entry at the feast day of Thomas Becket bluntly noted 'Becket traitor'! The book's compilers were members of the Goodrich–Cranmer circle. Forty-three of the fifty-three prayers are drawn from Thomas Becon's works; the preparative for prayer asks for prayers for its compiler, Bishop Goodrich's chaplain Thomas Cottisford, and other prayers included one against famine previously only to be found in the 1552 Prayer Book revision of the litany – this may well have been the work of the Archbishop himself.[47]

The new catechism was not ready for a couple of months after its authorization in March; it served to consign the Justus Jonas embarrassment to

45 Cox 1, second pagination pp. 2, 12; Strype, *Cranmer*, 1, p. 367.

46 Haugaard, *Elizabeth and the English Reformation*, pp. 14–15. The primer was authorized by letters patent on 6 March 1553: *C.P.R. Edward VI 1553*, p. 50, a version of which is printed in *Liturgical Services of Edward VI*, p. 358.

47 Bailey, Becon, p. 55; cf. *Liturgical Services of Edward VI*, pp. 365–8, 377, 399.

oblivion and to supplement the very brief catechism in the Prayer Book (which had actually been included in the March primer). The story of its publication is yet another example of the tangled agendas and confusion which afflicted the Edwardian regime in its last eighteen months: the author was Bishop Ponet of Winchester, who besides being Cranmer's former chaplain had prepared this text partly at the request of Northumberland, as the Duke himself testified. Far from this joint interest in the catechism producing agreement, we have already noted the evidence for a tussle back in autumn 1552, between Cranmer and Northumberland, around the potentially very lucrative privilege for printing the catechism (see above, p. 524): would John Day manage to supplant the Archbishop's printer Reyner Wolfe? The end-result was a compromise, with the two men splitting the English and Latin versions between them, but before either printer could get to work, there was a long further delay. The catechism was clearly intended to appear in autumn 1552, yet it was apparently only during the meetings of Convocation in the course of the March 1553 Parliament that a consortium of bishops and trusted senior clerics examined the text in detail and made suggestions for improvement. Apart from the other battles which were raging in the intervening period, especially the struggle to get the Prayer Book out on time, the delay may have been caused by a decision to issue the catechism jointly with the final version of the Forty-Two Articles. The articles were also discussed by the theological consortium in Parliament time, and they appeared appended to both the Latin and English versions of the catechism when the book at last appeared in May 1553.

Even then, the troubles of the catechism and the Forty-two Articles were not over. Their exact origin and therefore their authority remained unclear, thanks to the inept action of the Privy Council or its agents in formulating the title-page of the joint work. This first announced the catechism, 'set forth by the King's Majesty's authority', and then described the appended articles as 'agreed upon by the bishops and other learned and godly men in the last Convocation at London . . . likewise published by the King's Majesty's authority'. A casual reader would have been forgiven for assuming that the whole Convocation had authorized the articles and indeed the whole book, but this was not so. Although we have no formal record of Convocation's proceedings beyond a note of the arrangements for its opening day, we can be sure that it was no more than an *ad hoc* committee of bishops and senior clergy which had examined either work. Both Ridley and Cranmer later admitted this at the 1554 Oxford disputation: there were good reasons for not letting the whole Convocation loose on the articles, for there were conservatives present who would have given them a rough ride if they had been offered the chance, possibly even the remaining conservative bishops who were still clinging to their dioceses.[48] The title-page's mistake was a gift to those who

48 Discussion in this and the next paragraph is based on Foxe 6, pp. 468, 487. Opening arrangements: Lambeth MS 751, p. 126.

would now want to cause trouble for the implementation of the articles. It was also a mark of how far communications had broken down between Cranmer and his fellow-councillors in the wake of the March Parliament: he had not been consulted about the description, and it is unlikely that this gaffe would have been perpetrated if he had been.

The Archbishop was appalled when he saw the unfortunate phrase on the title-page, and he immediately complained to the Council. He was given the lame answer 'that the book was so entitled because it was set forth in the time of the convocation': true in terms of the date of the discussions which had finalized it and the letters patent which licensed the printing at least of the catechism, but otherwise a rather childish evasion of the truth. The royal circular which went out to the bishops and other ordinaries ordering subscription (a text probably devised soon after Cranmer had made his complaint) was equally shifty: it described the articles as 'devised and gathered with great study, and by counsel and good advice of the greatest learned part of our bishops of this realm, and sundry others of our clergy'.[49] Sir John Cheke in a private letter to Bullinger of 7 June resorted to humanist Latin to come up with the phrase *synodi Londinensis* to describe the warranty for the articles. The same phrase appeared soon after in English translation as 'the synod at London' in the Council docquet book for warrants, an appearance which is hardly surprising, since Cheke had been sworn in as one of the secretaries to the Council at the beginning of the month. All these formulations could, or could not, be a description of the Convocation of Canterbury; the truth was that they were intended to hide official embarrassment.[50]

The authorization of catechism and articles merely by royal authority was in any case curiously at odds with Cranmer's earlier insistence that the Prayer Book derived its authority from its full parliamentary sanction; surely something so fundamental as a statement of doctrine was equally if not more entitled to such solemn backing. However, the Archbishop had immediate practical reasons for being angry: it was he who must now plunge straight away into leading the bishops' campaign to secure general subscription for the Forty-Two Articles, with plenty of conservative participants in the recent Convocation ready to point out the curious anomaly of the title-page. Despite being armed with the royal circular, the Archbishop hit trouble straight away when he began his sittings in London on 26 May, finding that there were

49 For Bishop Ridley's copy, see Strype, *Ecclesiastical Memorials*, 2 ii, pp. 105–7 (cf. *C.S.P. Domestic Edward VI*, no. 827); this is dated 9 June, but the letters were first given Council approval on 24 May, two days before Cranmer's first session (B.L. Royal MS 18 C XXIV f. 352v). This note contains a mysterious reference apparently to 'liiii articles'; this either refers to the number of copies of the text to be made, or is a simple error for the Forty-Two Articles. It is less likely to refer to some list now lost: *pace* Gasquet and Bishop, p. 304 and Pollard, *Cranmer*, pp. 237–8.

50 *E.T.* p. 93 (*O.L.* p. 142; 7 June 53); cf. B.L. Royal MS 18 C XXIV f. 356v (12 June 1553: Cheke was sworn as Secretary on 2 June). However, for an example of a Marian use of '*synodo Londoniensi*' [*sic*] to describe Convocation, cf. Strype, *Cranmer*, 2, no. 78, p. 430.

'divers that denied many of the articles'. The ring-leader of the opposition was the prominent London clergyman and Rector of Lincoln College, Oxford, Dr Hugh Weston, whom Cranmer would meet again in changed but equally fraught circumstances.[51]

Yet by the time that this battle over subscriptions began, there was much more to worry about. King Edward's health was now finally giving way as his tuberculosis took hold; he had been taken out of London to Greenwich on 11 April, not soon enough to avoid arousing the interest of the foreign ambassadors, and by early May, his Councillors had been told the terrible truth by the royal doctors. It was not long before the French ambassador Noailles had also heard of the fatal diagnosis. By the end of that month, the doctors were saying that the King would be dead by the autumn. When on 7 June Secretary Cheke joined the writing of the batch of letters going off to Bullinger in Zürich, the message that he sent (and which he also fed to the other correspondents) was that Edward was getting better; nevertheless, the summary list of the King's achievements which he included in his letter read uncannily like an obituary, either unconsciously, or as a broad hint.[52] The consequences of this were clear to all: the successor under the terms of Henry VIII's will was the King's half-sister Mary. Although probably few at this stage realized the depths of Mary's commitment to the papacy, there could be no doubt that she would restore the old religion, and it would be shipwreck for the evangelical revolution: shipwreck too for Northumberland's ascendancy in government. We do not have to analyse here the evolution of the great scheme to sideline Mary and provide for a Protestant succession through Lady Jane Grey: King Edward was both capable of conceiving of this plan for himself as an enthusiastic evangelical, and also as an enthusiastic teenager, eminently suggestible to Northumberland's promptings in the matter.

Events in May took on an hysterical quality as the young King and his courtiers scrambled to rearrange the future: the marriage of Lady Jane and Northumberland's son Guildford, the beginning of a desperately lavish shower of gifts of land on those who would be useful in securing the altered succession, or who needed to be bought off from objecting to it. With either unbelievably naive optimism or supreme Machiavellian purpose, there were even gifts to the Lady Mary, giving her the prospect of a major grant at Hertford. There were licences of retainer, too, to anticipate any crisis by building up military forces in the hands of magnates considered reliable.[53] What appears at first sight almost heroic in the midst of all this were some

51 *Greyfriars Chronicle*, pp. 76–7.

52 *C.S.P. Spanish 1553*, pp. 32, 35; *Machyn's Diary*, p. 33; *Noailles* 2, pp. 3, 24; Bindoff, 'A Kingdom at stake', p. 647. For the letters of Cheke, Utenhove and Laski, see *E.T.* pp. 92–3, 385–6 (*O.L.* pp. 142–7, 592–4) and Gorham, *Gleanings*, p. 295.

53 For Mary's grant, see B.L. Royal MS 18 C XXIV ff. 356r (6 June), and ibid. f. 360v for a sale of lands in Essex on 19 June to her confidante Susan Tong *alias* Clarenceux; cf. Scheyfve's comments on this, *C.S.P. Spanish 1553*, p. 49. All the grants and licences of retainer are also most conveniently followed using the B.L. Royal volume.

symbolic gestures of faith in a Protestant future. As the politicking reached fever-pitch and King Edward coughed up his life-blood, the Council found time in May to authorize nine letters of commendation in Latin, Hebrew and Syriac for a squadron of three ships 'now going to the new found lands', that is, Thomas Wyndham's expedition down the West African coast: this translation job was no doubt a handy little piece of pocket money for some Oxbridge academics. Less exotically but more significantly, the Council took the major decision to seek to fill the gap left by the death of Martin Bucer with a reformer of equal international stature: they issued a formal invitation to Philipp Melanchthon to come to England and take up the vacant Regius Chair at Cambridge. Such was their anxiety to succeed where Henry VIII and Cranmer had successively failed over two decades, that even though they were desperately short of cash, they resolved to send the *Praeceptor Germaniae* his travel expenses in advance: the very substantial sum of £100.[54]

The following day the formal invitation was sent off to Melanchthon, as part of a large batch of letters for Continental reformers from their London friends, all of which letters relentlessly repeated the message that Edward's health was now improving. The Archbishop had already let Melanchthon know of the invitation to come. The royal letter of 7 May has not survived, but Cranmer's covering note for it remains, expressing his urgent pleas for the Wittenberg reformer to make the journey.[55] The bearer was the London merchant John Abell, who had undertaken a precisely similar mission to bring back Peter Martyr from Strassburg to England in autumn 1547, in order that Martyr could take up an Oxbridge post. However, it seems that Melanchthon was too cautious to take the optimistic reports of Edward's health at face value. The only surviving letter of his to Cranmer dated after these approaches (4 July) does not even mention the invitation; it almost appears to be playing for time, conveying small presents of books for Cranmer and the King, plus general news, and making no mention of coming to England. By 20 July Melanchthon knew of the King's death, and already, obviously well-informed, he saw it as a triumph for the Holy Roman Emperor.[56]

Was the invitation to Melanchthon heroic faith, or calculation? It is significant that the Council's final authorization for Melanchthon's travel money on 6 June had come five days after Cranmer returned to the Council board, ending nearly two months of absence. Moreover, the £100 for Melanchthon's travel was to be paid by the Treasurer of Augmentations to the

54 B.L. Royal MS 18 C XXIV ff. 343v, 346v, 356r: cf. Beer, 'Philip Melanchthon and the Cambridge Professorship' and Alsop, 'Philip Melanchthon and England in 1553'. On the financial crisis at the time, see Jack, 'Northumberland, Queen Jane and the financing of the 1553 Coup'.

55 *Melanchthonis Epistolae*, ed. Bindseil, pp. 351–2 (*Melanchthons Briefwechsel* 7, no. 6852); cf. *Melanchthons Briefwechsel* 7, no. 6928.

56 *Melanchthons Briefwechsel* 7, nos 6884 (4 July: Gorham, *Gleanings*, pp. 297–8), 6905, 6907, 6916.

Archbishop himself – paid it duly was, on 21 June. Amid the welter of bribes to secure his plans, it must have been obvious to Northumberland that one man could not directly be bribed, even if their relationship had not been ruined by the canon law affair: Thomas Cranmer. However, here was a subtler form of persuasion than bribery. The prospect of Melanchthon becoming a second Bucer was a powerful incentive for the Archbishop to invest in the future of the new regime, the greatest potential triumph yet for his ecumenical vision. It was probably the means by which he was tempted back to the Council board; the implications of this charm offensive which won his return were perfectly clear to the Imperial ambassador.[57] Now, during June, Cranmer would have to be won to the plan now completed for the diversion of the succession to Lady Jane.

Quite when the Archbishop was first brought into the scheme to put Jane on the throne is not certain. He was notably absent when, in the middle of June, the Council took several days and a good deal of effort to win over Chief Justice Montagu and other leading judges, using the King in person as the ultimate voice of persuasion.[58] We are dependent on the observations of the French ambassador Noailles for exact dating for much of what otherwise remains in anecdotal form; from his account, the turning-point must have come after 17 June, on which day the King made his will leaving his throne to Jane Grey. After that a fierce tussle took place to persuade the remaining doubters on the Council to accept the *fait accompli*; Noailles names Lord Treasurer Winchester, and different partisan narratives retrospectively vied among the other participants for the honour of being the last to be persuaded. The main competition is between Cecil's own account and Cranmer's, as presented by his anonymous biographer.[59] Cranmer's own later story to Queen Mary (a story which he insisted could be verified by the Marquess of Northampton and Lord Darcy) was that he demanded to speak alone to his royal godson, in order to try and dissuade him from diverting the succession, but permission was refused; he had to speak to the King in the presence of his fellow-Councillors. He was then told that the judges had confirmed the legitimacy of Edward's action, and then the King himself sharply commented that he 'trusted that I alone would not be more repugnant to his will than the rest of the Council were'.

To say this was to penetrate Cranmer's defences at their weakest point: the organizing principle of his view of Church and commonwealth over twenty years had been obedience to his prince. There was in any case a certain logic to his signing a document which diverted the Crown from Mary and Elizabeth, two illegitimate children of Henry VIII: in both cases it was his own judicial decision about the nullity of their mothers' marriages to the King

57 *C.S.P. Spanish 1553*, pp. 50–51.

58 Fuller 4, pp. 137–45; cf. '*Vita Mariae*', p. 248.

59 *Noailles* 2, pp. 40–41, 49; for Cecil, see Strype, *Annals* 4, pp. 486–7 and B.L. Lansdowne MS 104 f. 1r.

which had made them illegitimate. He now signed 'unfeignedly and without dissimulation': his signature appears with the other Councillors' on their undated agreement to uphold the King's new device for the succession.[60] It was symptomatic of the careful manipulation of the Archbishop that Northumberland was not present to arouse his hostility during this tussle of wills. One can also note that in the subsidiary provisions which were drawn up for addition to the King's will, the second of sixteen items was an order to the executors not only 'not to suffer any piece of religion to be altered', but also the much more elaborately expressed command that 'they shall diligently travail to cause godly ecclesiastical laws to be made and set forth, such as may be agreeable with the reformation of religion now received within our realm, and that done shall also cause the canon laws to be abolished'. This was another promise held out to the Archbishop, of equal significance for his vision of the future to the invitation to Melanchthon: his defeat in the March 1553 Parliament would be undone. With such powerful incentives, and his loyalty to his sovereign called into question, it is no wonder that he gave way.[61]

Cranmer's capitulation must have come between 17 and 19 June, because on that latter day there came two royal orders which involved him: a commission to him to convene the Convocation of Canterbury for the following 19 September, to accompany a session of Parliament which would recognize the new succession, and a follow-up order to the Archbishop's peculiar parishes in London to attend on him at Lambeth Palace to subscribe the Forty-Two Articles.[62] The pace of Council action became ever more frenetic now: there was all the bureaucracy to prepare for the September Parliament, and an ever faster dispersal of favours to those who mattered. There was also the job of collecting as many signatures as possible to witness the letters patent about the succession, with Cranmer's name once more heading the list, followed by politicians, noblemen, lawyers, London notables and home counties sheriffs.[63] The Court was now crowded with great men; when the Council gave instructions to an embassy to France on 1 July, Cranmer's signature was followed by twenty-two other signatures. The Archbishop and other senior clergy were simultaneously still preoccupied with the campaign for subscription to the Articles: the clergy of his peculiars turned up the day after the witnessing of the letters patent. Paul Ayris has meticulously traced into the first days of July other evidence of the campaign for subscription in the diocese of London and the University of Cambridge; even Bishop Coverdale

60 Cox 2, pp. 443–4; *Chronicle of Queen Jane*, pp. 90–91.

61 *Chronicle of Queen Jane*, p. 101.

62 Cranmer's Register, ff. 14r, 65v. For Cranmer's passing on of the order about Convocation to Ridley, Strype, *Ecclesiastical Memorials* 2 ii, p. 114, quoting Ridley's Register.

63 *Chronicle of Queen Jane*, pp. 91–100; the account of Montagu, Fuller 4, pp. 143–5, gives the date 29 June for his signing of the letters patent, and it probably took several days to gather signatures. For grants, B.L. Royal MS 18 C XXIV ff. 364r–375r (end of the volume); on Parliament, ibid. and *C.P.R. Edward VI 1553*, p. 419.

down in the diocese of Exeter made a start, although the only signature to be gathered there was his own.[64]

The end for the King came on 6 July: far sooner than the doctors had been predicting. Yet at first all seemed well: all the legal paperwork had been completed before the King's death. Bishop Ridley, for instance, did his duty as provincial Dean of the Convocation of Canterbury on that very day, by issuing his order for Convocation's September meeting.[65] After that, the announcement of Edward's death and the proclamation of Queen Jane went ahead without a hitch. The proclamations began fanning out throughout the length of the kingdom and into the kingdom of Ireland; as was customary, the Queen took up residence at the Tower, to a noisy artillery welcome which usefully underlined to the city the regime's command of the kingdom's military hardware.[66] However, even the evangelicals in the capital were already showing signs of divisions about what was happening. Ridley's positive partisanship for Queen Jane was far more than merely formal, and indeed more high-profile than Cranmer's; on two successive Sundays after the King's death, he used his cathedral pulpits to preach vigorously for Jane and proclaim both Henry VIII's daughters bastards, a fact of considerable embarrassment to his admirers in later times. Even on the Sunday before the King's death, it was noticed that the suffragan bishop of Bedford omitted reference to the two royal half-sisters from his prayers at St Paul's; he was doubtless under instructions from Ridley.[67] William Cecil, by contrast, was now backing away from the whole enterprise, although probably not as openly as he later claimed. Similarly John Bradford wrote an overwrought preface (dated six days into the new reign) to one of his sermons on repentance. He prophesied civil war and noticeably did not mention the name of the new Queen; he even added material to the body of the sermon text suggesting that Edward's mind had given way before his death.[68]

Such voices of dissent would no doubt have been stilled if the government had not made one fatal mistake: it did not secure the person of the Lady Mary before the King's death. One can only explain this by supposing that Northumberland was taken by surprise by the speed with which Edward died, and various instances of incomplete planning and improvisation do indeed point to this explanation.[69] Mary exploited efficient intelligence at Court, with the

64 Council letter: Strype, *Ecclesiastical Memorials* 2 ii, pp. 100–102. On the peculiars' subscriptions, Cranmer's Register, ff. 65v–66r; I am very grateful to Dr Ayris for allowing me to see an advance copy of his article on the campaign, to be published in the *H.J.*

65 Strype, *Ecclesiastical Memorials* 2 ii, p. 114.

66 Bodl. MS Ashmole 861, p. 344.

67 *Greyfriars Chronicle*, p. 78; 'Two London Chronicles', ed. Kingsford, p. 26; *Wriothesley's Chronicle* 2, p. 88.

68 Cecil: B.L. Lansdowne MS 104, f. 1r; see also his self-justifying account in Strype, *Annals* 4, pp. 486–7. *Bradford* 1, pp. 38–42, 62, and cf. his undated preface to a treatise by Melanchthon, ibid., pp. 19–24.

69 Cf. especially Jack, 'Northumberland, Queen Jane and the financing of the 1553 Coup', pp. 145–7.

result that she was on the run from Hertfordshire and successfully installed in East Anglia within two days of Edward dying. Matters then resolved themselves into a battle of wills between central government and the provinces, which was resolved in favour of the provinces, a result almost without precedent in Tudor England. A wave of popular legitimist outrage swept Mary from her Norfolk estates to Framlingham Castle in Suffolk; carefully avoiding any mention of the religious issue and stressing her rights as Henry VIII's daughter, she and her Catholic henchmen were able to win over the East Anglian elites which had at first recognized Queen Jane, encouraging the people's spontaneous attacks on loyal Janeite notables while simultaneously fomenting a gentry-led rebellion in the Thames Valley. Northumberland's London expeditionary force, aiming to cut Mary off from any Midlands support, got as far as Bury St Edmunds before his nerve failed him, and he retreated to Cambridge, putting on an abject show of joy as he proclaimed Mary himself on 20 July. By then, it was exactly a fortnight since the death of King Edward: Jane was not the nine days' queen of later convention. Indeed, we should not make the common mistake of treating these events with hindsight. The proper perspective on what happened is to see them as a rebellion by an outsider, the Lady Mary, against the established Queen Jane; that is how foreign observers and astute English politicians experienced events, and only Mary's zealots correctly anticipated the outcome.[70]

Through this collapse of all the political probabilities, Cranmer stayed with the Council, which had started establishing itself in the Tower of London on the day after the King's death.[71] He is first visible there in the crucial letter of 11 July in which Jane's Council brutally rejected Mary's claim to the throne, pointing out that her mother's divorce was 'necessary to be had both by the everlasting laws of God, and also by the ecclesiastical laws, and by the most part of the noble and learned universities of Christendom': how appropriate that the Archbishop should head the signatures on this![72] His name also led the Councillors in the circulars sent out the next day, ordering the sheriffs of England to gather troops against the bastard Mary, who was stirring the common people and plotting to bring 'papists, Spaniards and other strangers' into the realm, 'to the great peril and danger of the utter subversion of God's holy word' – a bold attempt to move the agenda away from Mary's chosen emphasis on her legitimist claim back to the question of religion. It is of great interest that the only recorded private deed to bear a date by Jane's first regnal year comes from the parish of St Dunstan in Canterbury; if only the nineteenth-century writer who noted its existence had

70 The best sources for this reconstruction are *Chronicle of Queen Jane* and '*Vita Mariae*'. We await a full treatment of Mary's coup by Professor Eric Ives.

71 Bodl. MS Ashmole 861, p. 344.

72 Foxe 6, pp. 385–6; the letter is probably deliberately misdated 9 July, but cf. *Noailles* 2, p. 59. It is noticeable that Cecil's signature is on this letter, contrary to his later protestations in B.L. Lansdowne MS 104, f. 1r (cf. also Strype, *Annals* 4, p. 489).

recorded more about it, we might have ascertained whether this notable piece of Janeite loyalism was associated with the archiepiscopal staff.[73]

On 14 July, a week into the new reign, news first began to reach London of really serious provincial revolts in Mary's favour, and other members of the Council began to make their first attempts to slip away from the Tower, starting with the Earl of Pembroke and Cranmer's enemy Sir Thomas Cheyney; but there was no place for the Archbishop to go.[74] He showed his continuing determination to support Jane's regime by contributing at least twenty men to Northumberland's expeditionary force against Mary; there is good reason to identify some of them with his own household servants, and probably all of them were. It would be this action which would be one of the two charges against him at his treason trial.[75] On 19 July he headed the signatories of the letter sent to Lord Rich desperately trying to keep him and his Essex influence on Jane's side, but by then the game was almost up. Several Councillors who signed that same letter slipped away into London later in the day and proclaimed Queen Mary in Cheapside, to scenes of wild enthusiasm. Jane's father, the Duke of Suffolk, was then forced to proclaim Mary on Tower Hill.[76]

The following day, Cranmer and his Council colleagues (by now all installed in the city of London) were kept busy signing a flurry of letters and warrants in the name of a new Queen, including an order to Northumberland to disarm, which was by now redundant; their dinner with the Lord Mayor that day was a prolonged business meeting, and in any case can hardly have been a festive occasion, with the relentless ringing of the city churches' bells only the most insistent noise in the clamour outside proclaiming the world's contempt for their previous actions.[77] Down in Kent, Pierre Alexandre soldiered on at Canterbury Cathedral giving a course of lectures on matrimony (partly a defence against Catholic attacks by Richard Smith on clerical marriage); he sadly rounded them off a week later on 27 July 'after the death of King Edward the sixth of the most godly everlasting memory'. Like his master, he knew that the great six-year adventure was over: an

73 This reference (the deed was dated 15 July) and the text of the Nottinghamshire and Derbyshire copy of the circular are to be found in the *Retrospective Review*, 2nd series 1 (1827), pp. 504–5. Cf. the copy of the proclamation sent to Kent in H.M.C. *Finch MSS*, pp. 1–2, and once more NB Cecil's signature on that copy. Proclamations in London that day recorded in *Greyfriars Chronicle*, p. 80 and *Noailles* 2, p. 59.

74 Cf. *Noailles* 2, p. 71; '*Vita Mariae*', p. 257; *Chronicle of Queen Jane*, pp. 8–9.

75 *Deputy Keeper's Report* 4, App. 2, p. 237; the first-named soldier, Barnaby Byllet, sounds as if he is a relative of Cranmer's gentleman servant Robert Byllet (cf. Cranmer's lease to Robert, *C.P.R. Elizabeth 1572–75*, no. 395). On William Mansford, see below, Ch. 13, p. 556.

76 Bodl. MS Ashmole 861, p. 344; B.L. Harley MS 353, f. 139r; *Greyfriars Chronicle*, p. 80; *Wriothesley's Chronicle* 2, pp. 88–9.

77 *Wriothesley's Chronicle* 2, pp. 89–90. A surviving warrant of 20 July is now in the possession of Mr. Roger W. Barrett of Chicago; cf. H.M.C. *Exeter City*, p. 366 and the order to Northumberland, B.L. Harley MS 6069, ff. 43, 97.

attempt to build in England if not an earthly paradise, at least a greater Strassburg.[78]

From then on, the new regime of Mary could only find a few fairly feeble pockets of resistance to the general flood of support, notably in the dioceses of both Cranmer and Thomas Goodrich; these may owe something to the clientages which the kingdom's two most long-established evangelical bishops had built up. Until well into August there was a persistent problem in Cambridgeshire and the Fens, centring on troops previously raised by Goodrich's authority.[79] In Canterbury diocese, the situation was still not altogether certain in the marches of Calais on 26 July, and among other traces of trouble in Kent, Dover managed to delay proclaiming the new Queen until 29 July. That same day the Council ordered the arrest in Kent of Cranmer's servant, Peter Hayman, and Sir Thomas Palmer, who also seems to have been in the archiepiscopal household; later on, Hayman, Thomas Cole the preacher of Maidstone, and Cranmer's lessee Walter Mantel of Horton were among the fairly short list of those who were excepted from the pardon granted at Mary's coronation. A less culpable time-lag in acknowledging the new regime occurred in faraway Kilkenny, where Jane was proclaimed Queen on 27 July, and Mary not until 20 August![80]

On the last day of July, thirty suits of Cranmer's armour were retrieved and impounded at Puckeridge in Hertfordshire, where they had presumably been abandoned by his contingent of troops as Northumberland's expeditionary force against Mary disintegrated. The care taken to retrieve them was presumably connected with the fact that they would be evidence for a charge against him.[81] Such charges were inevitable: quite apart from his complicity in the abortive military campaign, it was Cranmer's signature which, thanks to the rules of precedence, headed so many of the crucial documents which had sought to relegate Mary to the sidelines. In view of all this, the time-lag in dealing with him is at first sight puzzling. By the end of July the Dudleys and Bishop Ridley were all in the Tower on charges of treason; and others, like the Duke of Suffolk and Secretary Cheke, had both been imprisoned and for the time being secured their release, yet no action at all had been taken against the Archbishop. The most plausible explanation is that he had his usefulness in expediting

78 C.C.C.C. MS 126, f. 155v.

79 On the fens, Tittler and Battley, 'The accession of Mary Tudor revisited', especially p. 139, and *A.P.C. 1552–54*, p. 310; cf. also reference on 7 September to Lord Fitzwalter attending to a recent renewed rising in Norfolk (probably meaning the Fens) by *Noailles* 2, p. 146.

80 On Guisnes, Strype, *Ecclesiastical Memorials* 3 ii, pp. 174–5; Dover, *T.R.P.* 2 no. 388. Palmer is wrongly described as Henry in *A.P.C. 1552–54*, p. 303: cf. his chest among Cranmer's goods, P.R.O., E. 154/2/39 f. 86r. Pardon: *T.R.P.* 2 no. 394 (24 October 1553). On Mantel's Horton lease, *C.P.R. Elizabeth 1566–69* no. 1892. Kilkenny: Bale, *Vocacyon*, pp. 56–8.

81 *A.P.C. 1552–54*, p. 309; cf. P.R.O., E. 154/2/41 f. 8r.

business in a situation where Protestantism was still officially the established religion.

There was a curious political and religious limbo during early August: there were proprieties to be observed around the burial of the young evangelical King, and the new Queen also kept up her low-profile strategy on the religious question. There were good reasons for this: the ploy had served her well during her coup, and the legal position in restoring the old religion was very dubious, quite apart from the even more profound question of how the Bishop of Rome's authority could be restored. It was difficult, for instance, to know how to deal with the prominent London evangelical John Rogers when, on 6 August, he made a vehement attack from the Paul's Cross pulpit on 'pestilent popery, idolatry and superstition', and exhorted the people to remain in King Edward's religion; the Council examined him, but at that stage could find no good reason for imprisoning him, and they were forced to dismiss him.[82] Similarly, a few days later, angry London evangelicals nearly lynched an old priest who tried to say mass; the Lord Mayor, far from siding with the priest, complained about his traditionalist demonstration to the Queen. Much to her annoyance, she even had to make a show of imprisoning the celebrant, although his sufferings were not great or prolonged.[83]

Even more publicized was the riot which broke out at Paul's Cross on 13 August when Gilbert Bourne, one of Mary's chaplains, tried to undo the harm done there the previous Sunday by John Rogers. Bourne had to be rescued from an evangelical mob by John Bradford because of his Catholic preaching, and later that day Bradford added to his moral superiority by condemning the seditious violence, using one of the pulpits of St Mary le Bow, one of Cranmer's London peculiar churches, to do so. The presence of Bishop Bonner, newly released from prison, and Bourne's extravagant praise of him, had probably provoked the crisis at Paul's Cross: apart from Wily Winchester, Bonner was the greatest embodiment of religious division in the capital. It was this culmination of incidents which, the same day, prompted Mary to issue a soothing declaration through the city authorities that 'albeit her Grace's conscience is stayed in matters of religion, yet she meaneth graciously not to compel or constrain other men's consciences otherwise than God shall (as she trusteth) put in their hearts a persuasion of the truth that she is in, through the opening of his Word unto them by godly, virtuous and learned preachers'.[84] The prospect of an unprecedented religious freedom briefly beckoned, even prompting a reissue of the March 1553 Primer from the press of William Seres with its evangelicalism unmodified, apart from the adroit

82 Foxe 6, p. 592.

83 B.L. Harley MS 353, f. 141r, pr. *Chronicle of Queen Jane*, p. 16; *Noailles* 2, pp. 110–11.

84 *'Vita Mariae'*, pp. 223–4, 272–3, 298–9 (with refs there); *A.P.C. 1552–54*, p. 317; *Wriothesley's Chronicle* 2, pp. 97–8; *Bradford* 1, pp. 485–6.

substitution of prayers for Queen Mary in place of those for King Edward and Thomas Cottisford.[85]

In the middle of this, the Archbishop moved through his accustomed duties with the parody of normality which occurs in nightmares: after a complete silence in July, his register takes up business in August and September as if nothing had happened.[86] Particularly poignant was Cranmer's task of presiding over the funeral of Edward VI, in Westminster Abbey on 8 August. Mary had been persuaded that it would be inappropriate to deny her brother a burial according to the rites of the Prayer Book which he had enthusiastically authorized, although she consoled herself by not attending and by staging three days of requiems for Edward in the Tower of London, including a guest appearance as celebrant from her Lord Chancellor-designate, Bishop Stephen Gardiner. The night before the funeral, Cranmer transferred the body from Whitehall to the Abbey, with none of the Catholic ceremony which had escorted Henry VIII to the grave.[87] In the church there gathered the ghost of Edward's Court to say farewell to the King in the context of the 1552 communion service, conducted by the Archbishop. No foreign ambassadors felt able to put in an appearance. The former royal tutor Richard Cox, now almoner and Dean of Westminster, appears to have been released from detention to attend, but among Edward's Privy Councillors headed by Cranmer, Northumberland was an involuntary absentee; the clerk counting up the cost of mourning blacks for the official mourners and their servants recorded with bureaucratic precision an expenditure of nil on the entourage of the Duke as Lord Great Master. Hugh Latimer headed the chaplains who received allowances (John Knox was pointedly not included among them), and Ralph Morice's brother William was among the royal Gentlemen Ushers; however, no evangelical bishops were present apart from Latimer the quondam and Cranmer himself. Bishop Day, newly released from Bishop Goodrich's custodial hospitality and designated to his old see of Chichester, had been chosen by the Queen to preach, undermining the spirit of the occasion by a sermon which an observer bitterly said 'prepared the way for papistry just like an advance raiding party'.[88]

This was not the last official duty for Cranmer in that surreal month; on 14 August not only did he receive his customary writ of summons to a new Parliament called for October, but he was ordered by the Queen to summon the Convocation of Canterbury to St Paul's for the parliamentary

85 *R.S.T.C.* 20374: cf. *Liturgical Services of Edward VI*, pp. ix–x.

86 Cf. e.g. archiepiscopal business from 3 August to 13 September: Cranmer's Register, ff. 423v–424r.

87 *Greyfriars Chronicle*, pp. 82–3; on Gardiner, *C.S.P. Spanish 1553*, p. 159.

88 [Philpot or Poullain], *Vera expositio*, f. 30v, which settles the doubt as to whether Day or Scory preached as Bishop of Chichester; likewise one should not mistake the date of the funeral, 8 August. The official accounts for it are P.R.O., L.C. 2/4/1. See also *Noailles* 2, pp. 108–9, despite his confusion about the date.

session.[89] He was even forced to appear at Court at Richmond a day or two before that, as is revealed when on the day that the summonses were issued, he sat down at Lambeth Palace to write a frightened letter to his old friend Cecil. The night before, Cranmer had heard that Secretary Cheke had been indicted for his part in Jane's regime. Still his thoughts as he wrote were to see whether Cheke and Lord Russell could be spared serious consequences, since they had not been deeply involved in the Jane adventure; but now he had no influence to put in a good word for them: there was nothing that he could offer except prayer. Mary apparently refused to see him at any stage after she took power, which cannot have made easier what must have been an exceedingly uncomfortable visit to Richmond – his impossible position is indicated by the fact that he had dared not talk to Cecil while he was there.[90] It was perhaps at this time that he ordered a clerk to go through his entire library and label his books uniformly with the inscription *'Thomas Cantuariensis'*. Perhaps he did this with some notion of keeping the collection intact; perhaps the initiative may have come from the government, already anticipating the seizure of the whole collection and determined to avoid embezzlement from one of the largest libraries in England, but one notices the defiant assertion of his metropolitical title.[91]

Dignified self-assertion is the keynote of Cranmer's actions in late summer and early autumn 1553. When criticisms are made of cowardice or timidity in his life, the significance of his actions during that period should be remembered. Unlike most of the chief actors in Jane's coup, he was left at liberty until his own defiance in early September precipitated his arrest. In this time, he could have done what so many other Protestant clerics and vulnerable laypeople did, and slip away to the Continent, living to fight another day as he had done by his adaptability under Henry VIII. At some date which remains uncertain but is probably after his arrival in Oxford in the following year, this was certainly the advice which he gave to one leading evangelical laywoman, Anne Boleyn's former silkwoman Jane Wilkinson. 'What can be so heavy a burden as an unquiet conscience, to be in such a place as a man cannot be suffered to serve God in Christ's true religion? . . . remember that Christ, when his hour was not yet come, departed out of his country into Samaria, to avoid the malice of the scribes and the Pharisees . . . that you will do, do it with speed, lest by your own folly you fall into the persecutors' hands.' In Wilkinson's case, the advice bore excellent fruit, because after her flight, this wealthy and well-connected sister of

89 Writ of summons: *Catalogue of MSS in the Library of the Honourable Society of the Inner Temple*, ed. J. Conway Davies, no. 530; summons for convocation, Cranmer's Register, f. 14r.

90 Strype, *Cranmer*, 2, no. 109, pp. 495–6 (Cox 2, pp. 441–2). The Queen moved from the Tower to Richmond on 12 August (*Noailles* 2, p. 110), and the Convocation summons of 14 August is dated from there.

91 A good discussion of the book signatures is Selwyn's in Ayris and Selwyn (eds), *Cranmer*, pp. 46–7.

Lord North became a mainstay of persecuted evangelicals at home and abroad; yet in summer 1553, Cranmer himself clearly did not feel that he should desert his post.[92] He cannot have been under much illusion about Mary's attitude towards him, the man who had humiliated her mother, ruined her own life and brought destruction on the religion she loved. He faced his likely fate with fear, but also with stoicism; unlike Mrs Wilkinson, his hour had come.

By mid-August, Mary was gradually recoiling from any prospect of a substantial toleration: she forbade unauthorized preaching first in evangelically inclined East Anglia on 16 August, and then generally a couple of days later, in a proclamation which despite its still conciliatory language was widely seen as giving her royal authority to the open celebration of the mass. It was not long before the tide of Latin masses and improvised stone altars was overwhelming those evangelicals in authority still prepared to put up a fight for the legal niceties.[93] Soon after this came the great shock of the apostasy of the Duke of Northumberland and close associates of his, like Sir John Gates and the Marquess of Northampton. Northumberland led the others in openly repudiating his attachment to the evangelical cause and going to mass with every sign of devotion before his execution, a *volte-face* whose completeness has never satisfactorily been explained. This betrayal must have been a great encouragement to the new government to think that with such a spectacular cave-in among the leading supporters of the Edwardian adventure, the rest would follow easily. Having dealt with the lay leadership, the clergy must now be purged.[94]

At the end of the month and the beginning of September preparations were made to remove the evangelical bishops from office and replace them with their deprived Catholic predecessors, or with reliable new men: this meant summoning up to London such obvious *bêtes noires* of the new regime as John Hooper from Gloucester. This would throw the spotlight on the Archbishop: it is unlikely that the Greyfriars Chronicler was the only conservative who saw him as directly responsible for the Catholic bishops' previous humiliation.[95] The most remarkable consequence of this dismissal of the evangelical bishops is revealed accidentally in a later chancery lawsuit, the documentary witness of which, with inevitable perversity, survives only in a mangled state. Immediately after Bishop Coverdale of Exeter had been

92 Strype, *Cranmer*, 2, no. 72, pp. 410–11 (Cox 2, pp. 444–5). The signature 'T. Cranmer' addded in the Coverdale version would date this letter to after his deprivation, but it does not appear in the version in Foxe 8, p. 100. Wilkinson's achievement is best measured by her will, P.C.C. 29 Chayney (P.R.O., PROB. 11/42B ff. 233–234v); Garrett, *Marian Exiles*, did not think to provide her with her own biography.

93 *A.P.C. 1552–54*, p. 321; *T.R.P.* 2 no. 390, and cf. 'Parkyn's Narrative', pp. 79–80. For an example of defiant evangelical upholding of the law from Cranmer's circle in Kent in the first week of September, see Foxe 7, p. 288.

94 *Chronicle of Queen Jane*, pp. 18–19.

95 *Greyfriars Chronicle*, p. 83.

deprived that September, Cranmer's officials asserted the Archbishop's right to supervise the vacancy in see, superseding the jurisdiction of diocesan officers and maintaining their rights in the name of the Dean and Chapter of Canterbury even after Cranmer was deprived. Apparently they were taking advantage of the uncertain title of that ancient survivor Bishop Veysey, who had after all freely resigned in the time of Edward VI. It was also a clear signal that Cranmer was not going to go down without a fight.[96]

At this stage Cranmer was buoyed up in his self-assertion by daily contacts with those leading evangelical clergy who were still at large. 'The bishop of Canterbury, Hooper, Lever, the bishop of London and divers other are together in disputation daily at their own houses, but what is done amongst them I cannot learn', recorded the London observer William Dalby on 1 September.[97] During the following week came the culmination of the hearing in which Bishop Bonner appealed against the 1549 verdict for his deprivation, and claimed back his rights in the see of London; not surprisingly, on 5 September, Bonner won his suit, but at least the 1549 commissioners Cranmer, Ridley and Dean May of St Paul's sent proctors to the consistory court in St Paul's to ensure that his claim did not go uncontested.[98] Cranmer does not seem to have appeared in the consistory in person; instead on the day of the verdict he was at the nearby house of Dean May, which had been commandeered by royal commissioners, one of whose tasks was to begin to prepare proceedings against him for his role in promoting Queen Jane. The commissioners gave him a schedule of questions for him to prepare an inventory of his possessions, an inevitable prior measure before his deprival. One of the commissioners, according to Foxe his old friend Nicholas Heath, later claimed that at this stage the intention was to allow him to retire to private life, on condition that he remain completely out of public affairs. Perhaps that was plausible in the context of the still tentative programme of change in early September, but the rapidly worsening atmosphere of confrontation narrowed the government's options. The Queen's strong personal dislike of Cranmer makes it unlikely that this solution would have proved long-lasting, and in any case, his actions now ruled it out of court.[99]

Edmund Bonner, writing to friends the day after his triumphant verdict, badly misjudged Cranmer's mood on the strength of his co-operation with the royal commissioners on 5 September. 'This day is looked that Mr Canterbury must be placed where is meet for him; he is become very humble and ready

96 P.R.O., C. 1/1429/29. The wording of the complaint and answer appear to rule out the possibility that the vacancy in see was after Veysey's resignation in 1551, but the case cries out for further investigation.

97 B.L. Harley MS 353, f. 143r. One cannot be certain whether 'the Bishop of London' is Bonner or Ridley, in a period of release from imprisonment otherwise unrecorded, perhaps because of the legal hearing into Bonner's restoration. Previously Dalby referred to Bonner as 'the old Bishop of London' (ibid., f. 141r).

98 Strype, *Ecclesiastical Memorials*, 3 i, pp. 35–7; Foxe 6, p. 538.

99 Foxe 8, p. 38; for Cranmer's appearance at the Deanery, cf. P.R.O., E. 154/2/41, f. 3r.

to submit himself in all things, but that will not serve', the new Bishop of London crowed.[100] Cranmer might be prepared to do his secular duty to the Supreme Head by preparing an inventory of his property, but his spiritual duty simultaneously took him in an entirely different direction. The Primate of All England now launched on studied defiance of the new religious policy: a public repudiation of the mass. It was this same first week in September when the unofficial revival of the mass throughout the country seems to have reached a critical point, with the former major feast of the Nativity of the Blessed Virgin on 8 September approaching and stimulating a moment of decision.[101] Cranmer's suffragan Bishop of Dover, Richard Thornden, who was resident in the Palace at Canterbury, resumed the mass in the Cathedral, thus giving rise to rumours that the Archbishop himself had given way on this central issue of the Edwardian Reformation. Cranmer first expressed his fury in a private letter to a friend about this insult to the cause of the eucharist with which by now he was particularly associated: this letter must have been accompanying a proposed draft of a public declaration, judging by what happened next.[102] On that busy 5 September the text of this declaration was distributed in Cheapside as a solemn protest against the mass, apparently copied by a friend and published before Cranmer himself was ready to go public with it; Foxe names the friend as the Archbishop's old protégé, Bishop Scory of Chichester.

Cranmer was at first annoyed; he had intended both to elaborate his declaration and also to give it more weight as his public manifesto by ordering it to be affixed to every church door in London with his official seal. However, he made the best of a bad job, and was soon himself promoting the further distribution of the text through the capital. It denounced the 'Latin satisfactory mass' as of the devil's devising, and denounced Thornden (who was not named) as 'a false flattering and dissembling monk'; Cranmer absolutely denied that he himself had offered to say mass before Queen Mary. Defending King Edward's service (as at the time he was legally bound to do), he offered to join with Peter Martyr and other evangelicals to defend the Prayer Book as 'more pure and according to God's Word than any other that hath been used in England this thousand years'; probably he was hoping that the meeting of Convocation which he had summoned for October would provide the venue for this disputation. Twice he stressed the Parliamentary status of the book, just as he had done against Knox the previous year.[103]

100 Burnet 2 ii, pp. 339–40 (part 2, book 2, no. 7).

101 Cf. 'Parkyn's Narrative', p. 80; B.L. Harley MS 353, f. 143r.

102 *Narratives of the Reformation*, p. 227. On Thornden's chamber in the Palace, see P.R.O., E. 154/2/39, f. 81r.

103 English text in C.C.C.C. MS 105, p. 321, although this is not in Cranmer's hand, *pace* Ayris and Selwyn (eds), *Cranmer*, p. 285; Latin version appended to [Philpot or Poullain], *Vera Expositio*, ff. 30–31, which at f. 31v first has the story of the surreptitious publishing by an unnamed friend. The first surviving printed version dates from 1557. Cf. Foxe 8, p. 38.

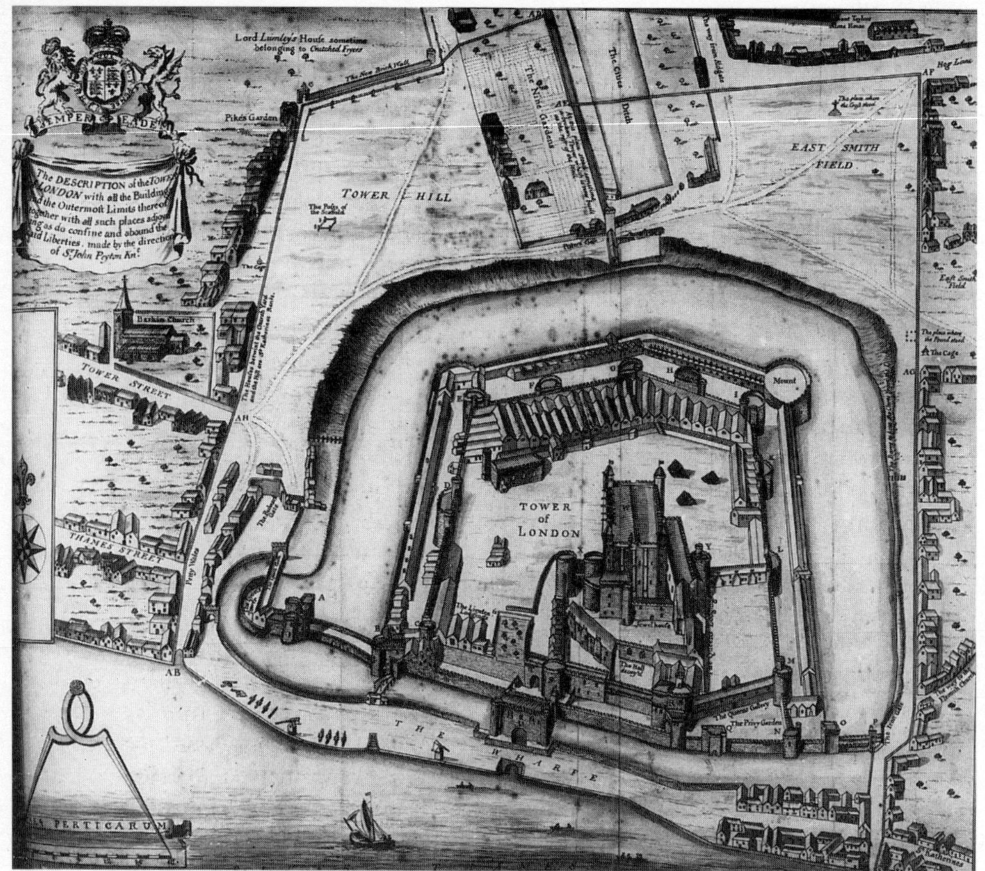

37 Panoramic view of the Tower of London as surveyed in 1597. The 'gate anenst [facing] the watergate' can be seen, with its round tower, in the inner curtain wall.

It was just at this moment that Martyr himself was at last allowed to leave an increasingly hostile Oxford, to negotiate his departure from England with the Privy Council. He got a warm welcome from the Archbishop at Lambeth, and far from resenting the *fait accompli* of the invitation to disputation, he was delighted at the thought of a chance to air their case in public: they occupied themselves with eager preparations for the debate. But in the following week, more copies of Cranmer's declaration spread around London, causing a sensation: it was the first boost to the morale of the evangelicals for a couple of months. 'The Bishop of Canterbury is the old man he was', commented one evangelical Londoner with relief when reporting the news of the declaration on 8 September.[104] It was hardly surprising that the government chose to regard Cranmer's action as tantamount to sedition. On Wednesday 13

104 B.L. Harley MS 353, f. 143v. For narrative of this and what follows, see accounts of Terentianus, *E.T.* pp. 242–7 (*O.L.* pp. 365–74), and Martyr, *E.T.* pp. 332–3 (*O.L.* pp. 505–7).

September, after examining and imprisoning Hugh Latimer, the Privy Council met the Archbishop, who arrived carrying the inventory of his possessions, as the royal commissioners had instructed him a week earlier. Cranmer found himself under the gaze of colleagues from Jane's Council, like Lord Treasurer Winchester and the Earl of Arundel, now model Marians, as well as his own former victims, bishops Gardiner and Tunstall. Either before or after this confrontation with the Council, he was transferred to the royal commissioners for examination. One of the commissioners, apparently Nicholas Heath, offered him a lifeline about his declaration on the mass, trying to get him to say that it was a private paper only: 'We do not doubt but you are sorry that it is gone abroad', the commissioner said meaningfully. Cranmer brushed aside the temptation: he spelt out the fact that even if the distribution of the declaration had been complicated by Scory, his only regret was that it had not received the more solemn official promulgation which he was planning for it. He gloried in his sedition, if sedition meant attacking the mass.[105]

It was therefore inevitable that the Archbishop should be ordered to return from Lambeth on the Thursday afternoon to see the Council in Star Chamber. He found time on that Wednesday to provide for the spiritual welfare of the parish which by now he seems to have regarded as home: he collated William Cooke to the vicarage of Croydon, and Cooke completed the formalities by compounding for his first fruits the following day, as Cranmer prepared for the Star Chamber appearance. It may have given the Archbishop some satisfaction to know that this last official piece of business of his public ministry saw the new Vicar of Croydon duly take the customary oath renouncing the Roman obedience.[106] On the Thursday, he had a final dinner with Martyr, and in a private interview after the meal, he called his friend to his chamber, and told him that a trial was inevitable; they would never meet again. If Martyr could not get a passport straight away, he said, he must take the initiative and flee – the option which Cranmer had conspicuously denied himself over the previous month and a half. Then he crossed the Thames to Star Chamber. The combination of his defiance over the declaration with his treason under Queen Jane ensured that he was now sent straight to the Tower, to join Hugh Latimer and Nicholas Ridley. Whether by accident in a crowded prison or by design, he was lodged in the last chamber that the Duke of Northumberland had occupied before his execution.[107] As he had predicted to Martyr, and in fulfilment of the prophecy of the Freewiller Humphrey Middleton, he would never be a free man again.

105 *A.P.C. 1552–54*, pp. 345–7; Foxe 8, p. 38. Heath is not actually recorded as present at any Privy Council meetings at this time, although he was sworn of the Council on 4 September: *A.P.C. 1552–54*, p. 340. Foxe places him among the commissioners who examined Cranmer.

106 Cranmer's Register, f. 424r; *Registra Gardiner/Poynet*, p. 151.

107 *Chronicle of Queen Jane*, p. 27.

CHAPTER 13

Condemned: 1553–6

FOR THE FIRST TIME in twenty years, the story of Thomas Cranmer becomes detached from the main political story of the kingdom of England and its Reformation. In his prison cell in the Tower, he was remote from the rapid march of events in October: the coronation, the meeting of Parliament and the stormy Convocation debates finally ending any sympathy which Mary's government might have had towards allowing free discussion of religious questions between Catholics and evangelicals. In his absence, Parliament overturned his annulment of the Aragon marriage, in a statute which contained inevitable comments about his conduct in the 'wicked device' which had culminated at Dunstable, as 'ungodly and against all laws, equity and conscience' – there was much more in the same vein.[1] His friends were either in prison like himself, had fled abroad or to remote parts of the kingdom, or had given way under the impact of the Catholic victory. Gone was the network of foreign clergy and laity, who for all their faults and frequent criticism of the English Reformation had been a sign of England's solidarity with the wider evangelical world: from Peter Martyr and Jan Laski downwards, they were unceremoniously told to leave the country or face the consequences. The new regime was triumphalist in its Catholicism, indeed consciously used the word 'Catholic' as a party term; and it is no coincidence that the word 'Protestant' also first became naturalized in England during the reign of Mary, to be used by conservatives and evangelicals alike.

Cranmer was only restored to the public world to stand trial for treason at Guildhall on 13 November, on charges of helping to seize the Tower for Jane and of levying troops for Northumberland's expeditionary force against Mary. With him on trial were the Dudley brothers Guildford, Henry and Ambrose, and Guildford's wife ex-Queen Jane. As always, it was an experience made deliberately humiliating and terrifying: the prisoners were made to walk from the Tower into the city, with the axe leading them: the Archbishop headed the procession.[2] There was no question of defence counsel being provided: the accused were on their own. To start with, Cranmer seems to have tried to

1 *C.J.* 1, pp. 26–7; Ridley, *Cranmer*, pp. 355–6.

2 *Chronicle of Queen Jane*, p. 32.

maintain the attitude of dignified defiance which had characterized him in the weeks before his arrest. When he appeared, he was the only one of the defendants to plead not guilty to the charges against him; this caused a delay in the government's smooth preparations for a quick trial within the day, for such a plea necessitated gathering and swearing in a petty jury.

The Archbishop's reasons for his plea have not survived, although his later letter to Queen Mary suggests that he would have maintained that he was only consenting to the will made by the previous sovereign monarch, Edward VI. However, before the jury decided its verdict, he changed his plea to one of guilty. One observer said that Cranmer 'was put to utter dismay after hearing [William] Staunford, the Queen's counsel, outline his treachery to him, and openly confessed his crime'; admittedly this is an unfriendly Catholic witness, but it is a plausible account. The charges as stated could hardly be denied, and they had nothing directly to do with Edward VI's will; they were presumably framed as they were to minimize the chances of the defendants pointing an accusing finger at other former supporters of Jane, who were now on Mary's Privy Council. A good lawyer could easily have played on what must already have been a very troubled conscience; Cranmer was confused and unhappy about the justification for what he had done, and later in more assertive mood he would say of his trial that he had 'confessed more . . . than was true'. By the end of the day, all five defendants had been found guilty and condemned to death, and from this moment the common law of England declared Cranmer deprived of his archiepiscopal see. An Act of Parliament would then attaint him and his fellow-accused of high treason, making him legally a dead man.[3]

It must have been in the following weeks that the Archbishop's establishment was finally dissolved, generating the inventories and accounts which partially survive, although these were based in turn on the inventory which Cranmer himself had made on the commissioners' orders of 5 September.[4] Dispersing and selling off his goods was a formidable task, which involved royal commissioners rounding up the contents of his five palaces and their supporting estates – even down to selling off, at the appropriate time of year, hay standing at Canterbury and Bekesbourne.[5] Already in the inventories there was much that was noted as 'lost and stolen away', notably equipment in the chapel; Cranmer's household presumably wanted to put this to better uses than papists would make of it.[6] The accounts reveal that the Archbishop had been allowed to make himself fairly comfortable when he was arrested in September; after all, he was still uncondemned. He had brought with him to

3 '*Vita Mariae*', pp. 225, 274. Cranmer to Queen Mary, Cox 2, pp. 442–4. On the trial, see *Deputy Keeper's Report* 4, App. 2, pp. 237–8; for his later doubts, Foxe 8, p. 51.

4 P.R.O., E. 117/14/59; E. 154/2/39; E. 154/2/41; E. 154/6/41. Croydon is the main omission from the surviving papers.

5 P.R.O., E. 117/14/59.

6 P.R.O., E. 154/2/39, ff. 64v–65r, 68v.

the Tower hangings, carpets for the tables, cushions, bedding, everyday dining plate and a range of clothing; in a rather poignant gesture of dignity, he had also taken with him to prison his scarlet and his black episcopal chimeres, no doubt to appear in his proper state at his trial. Optimistically, he had also taken a black velvet riding frock.[7]

Overall, there is evidence of a certain amount of humanity in the treatment of the fallen great household. Mrs Cranmer had presumably been living at Lambeth or Croydon after her husband's arrest, as she had a perfect right to do in the state of English law then current; in the accounts, she was given some of the Archbishop's curtains, linen, a table and some bedding, together with other domestic odds and ends: certainly a comprehensive enough selection to keep her in modest comfort.[8] Otherwise the goods were sold off to a range of courtiers – Mr Secretary Petre's private accounts detail the cost of shipping his acquisitions across the Thames from Lambeth – but also some went to Cranmer's own household, including his yeoman of the wardrobe and near relative John Cranmer. By one of history's ironic footnotes, one of the household purchasers was the Archbishop's servant, William Mansford; Mansford can almost certainly be identified with the man of the same name who appears in Cranmer's Guildhall indictment as marching off on his orders to fight with Northumberland, and who thus played an involuntary part in the Archbishop's destruction. Lord Chancellor Gardiner may also have reflected with satisfaction on Time's whirligig as Cranmer's great and little barges were rowed downstream to his Southwark palace to begin their new life in his service – a gift from the Queen.[9]

What is missing from the inventory is any mention of Cranmer's great library; as David Selwyn has concluded in a fine piece of detective work, this is probably because the normal home of the library was at Croydon Palace, the only one of Cranmer's homes for which the inventory does not survive. The first new owner of the book collection was the turncoat Earl of Arundel, Henry Fitzalan, Cranmer's former colleague on Jane's Privy Council, who may have received it by gift from Queen Mary as a reward for abandoning Queen Jane at a crucial moment. Arundel did not retain many of the books; only a few of the more sumptuous volumes tickled his refined aesthetic palate, for the library was designed for use rather than appearance. He passed the bulk of his gains on to his genuinely scholarly son-in-law John, Lord Lumley: very many of the Archbishop's remaining books, around 575 items, bear Lumley's signature. Arundel and Lumley (who also both bought luxury clothing and fabrics from the Archbishop's wardrobe) probably planned this division from

7 P.R.O., E. 154/2/39, ff. 64r, 65v; E. 154/2/41, f. 5r.

8 P.R.O., E. 154/2/39, ff. 64v, 66rv; E. 154/2/41, f. 6r; see also the full listing in E. 154/6/41, no. 7.

9 P.R.O., E. 154/2/39, f. 84v; E. 154/2/41, f. 11rv. On Mansford in the indictment, see *Deputy Keeper's Report* 4, App. 2, p. 237. On Petre's purchases, E. 154/2/41, f. 12r, and Emmison, *Tudor Secretary*, p. 168n.

the start, because the accounts for selling off Cranmer's goods include a reference to Lord Lumley buying a 'press', which was no doubt necessary to house the books which he obtained from the collection. Subsequent accidents of history which are only partly Lumley's fault mean that now the Cranmer library has to be chased through at least 65 different locations, which encompass 70 manuscripts and 586 printed books: it has been Dr Selwyn's achievement to take this reconstruction further than anyone else has managed.[10]

We ought to be grateful to the two noblemen for saving so much: it makes a remarkable contrast with the fate of another early Tudor library, conceived on a similar scale and dispersed in similar circumstances, that of John Fisher. All Richard Rex's searches have revealed only one book from Fisher's library which can be definitely identified with a copy surviving today.[11] However, there is one sinister and sad feature of what remains of the Cranmer collection: hardly any of the collection represents evangelical literature, indeed virtually nothing which bears Lumley's or Arundel's marks – perhaps in all, fourteen books remain from evangelical authors. A particular yawning gap is the substantial number of books which we know had strayed from Martin Bucer to Cranmer's collection, something which much concerned Bucer's Strassburg executors even before the disaster which befell the evangelical cause in 1553.[12] Evidently this side of the library was destroyed, with all the annotations in Cranmer's own hand, which according to his usual habit must have covered his volumes. Even with our knowledge of the greater human tragedies by fire to come during Mary's reign, this is a major and lamentable loss.

In view of the destruction of this material on a partisan basis, it is all the more remarkable that so many of Cranmer's manuscripts survive. It is likely that these were among the materials loyally 'lost and stolen away' by the household; certainly some of the most important items turned up in Elizabeth's reign in the hands of two former Cranmer servants, Stephen Nevinson and the Archbishop's former doctor, John Herd. Dr Selwyn is probably being too cautious in speculating that the eventual size of the printed book collection alone was around 700 books; if Cranmer had any interest in collecting the voluminous English evangelical literature in the vernacular produced in the two decades from the early 1530s (which surely he did), it may have totalled closer to a thousand volumes, outclassing any contemporary collection in the kingdom. Since the Archbishop was generous in allowing scholars of whom he approved to use his library (Roger Ascham and Hugh Latimer both

10 Lumley's purchase of press and forms: P.R.O., E. 154/2/39, f. 84v, and for purchases of clothing by Lumley and Arundel, E. 154/2/41, ff. 5r, 6r, 16v, 17v. For Arundel's part in Jane's government, see Loach, *Parliament and the Crown*, p. 5. For the definitive account of the library, Selwyn, in Ayris and Selwyn (eds), *Cranmer*, pp. 39–72.

11 Rex, *Theology of Fisher*, pp. 192–203, 271. One factor must be that Fisher cannot have annotated his books as Cranmer did.

12 A.S.T. 41 ff. 115, 117, 119.

testified to this), his household in its prime must have represented as great a scholarly resource as either university.[13]

The physical fate of the former Archbishop himself was still uncertain. Only a few days after the Guildhall trial, Ambassador Renard was reporting to the Emperor that Cranmer's fellow-accused at the trial, the Lady Jane, would be shown mercy, but that sentence would soon be executed on him. His parliamentary attainder for treason, in association with Northumberland and the other leading politicians singled out as conspirators, passed into law on the dissolution of Parliament on 5 December, yet by 17 December the Council were granting him a mark of favour, along with Lady Jane, by giving them both permission to walk in the garden of the Tower to recover their health after confinement indoors.[14] Equally hesitant was the treatment of the archdiocese. Five days after the Guildhall trial, the Dean and Chapter of Canterbury wrote to the Queen asking for a licence to elect a new Archbishop, but instead, after a month's interval, the only action taken was to guarantee the prosecution of routine administration and legal business. Henry Harvey, a senior official of the diocese of London, was given a round-up of powers as auditor, commissary general, official principal and keeper of the spirituality.[15]

This delay was inevitable, given the Queen's determination to restore the Roman obedience. Very quickly after her accession she had determined that her cousin, the newly appointed papal legate Reginald Pole, should be the next Archbishop of Canterbury, and she had sent a special messenger to him to put the request to him.[16] However, Pole was quick to point out that there was no chance of his agreeing before she had completed a much wider transformation of the relations between Rome and England; it might have occurred to her as a further minor embarrassment that under English law Pole himself was still as much an attainted person as the late Archbishop. As for Thomas Cranmer, whatever satisfaction the Queen might gain from seeing him die immediately for treason (and she was not especially vindictive in secular matters), he had committed a far more serious crime: he had led the whole realm into heresy. He must die for that, but only after due trial. So solemn a doctrinal condemnation as the former Primate deserved, demanded the proper restoration of papal authority – still a distant goal in December 1553. Foxe goes so far as to say that Mary actually pardoned Cranmer of his treason so that he could be tried for heresy, but it is doubtful whether she could reverse an attainder in this manner; pardon or no pardon, a heresy trial for a man already dead in law, under the terms of a parliamentary attainder,

13 On Ascham, Selwyn, in Ayris and Selwyn, *Cranmer*, pp. 39, 41–2; *Latimer's Sermons*, pp. 209–10.

14 *C.S.P. Spanish 1553*, p. 366; *A.P.C. 1552–54*, p. 379.

15 Ayris Ph.D., 'Cranmer's Register', pp. 225–6; Churchill, *Canterbury Administration* 2, pp. 226–8.

16 *C.S.P. Venetian 1555–56*, no. 22.

presented serious legal problems which the Privy Council found itself forced to tackle, not altogether conclusively, at a later stage of Cranmer's imprisonment, in May 1555. Given these tangles, for the time being Cranmer's life could be spared, and there was no harm in his taking the air within the walls of his prison.[17]

Cranmer may inadvertently have clarified the logic of the strategy for his destruction in a letter which he wrote some time in December, directly appealing to the Queen for a pardon for his 'heinous folly and offence'. In this, he confirmed that however complete his submission now was as a secular person, his religious integrity was unchanged. The first half of his letter was couched in secular terms. He wrote in the abject terms customary for a condemned prisoner, but he was trying to argue from his reluctance to sign his consent to the will of Edward VI that he was a suitable case for mercy. It was an irrelevant point, considering that he had not been tried and convicted for this offence, but for subsequent conduct which could not be denied. He also objected to the act of attainder describing him as part of the same conspiracy as the Duke of Northumberland to deprive Mary of her crown: an understandable reaction of annoyance given the eighteen months of hostility between the two men before Jane's accession, but again hardly a material argument.

Cranmer then shifted from asking for mercy to another request. He wanted to talk to the Queen on the dangerous subject of religion, which was now being officially altered by Act of Parliament: from 20 December all England was to be restored to the observances which had been in force at the death of Henry VIII. His letter did not contain any direct criticism of this decision; indeed, it would have been difficult for him to do so, since he had presided as Primate over precisely these observances in Henry's last years. However, he made his disapproval clear. While disclaiming any intention of being 'author of sedition' or of moving 'subjects from the obedience of their heads and rulers', he sought an interview with Mary simply to urge on her the duty 'to see the reformation of things that be amiss': he was in fact begging her to exercise the powers of the supreme headship which he knew she despised and wished to repudiate. He must have known also that his whole request was a futile gesture, but it was a necessary gesture for his own conscience. 'If I have uttered, I say, my mind unto your majesty, then I shall think myself discharged' – discharged, that is, of his duty as former Metropolitan, and thus discharged of any obligation to lead public resistance to the Queen's plans. 'To private subjects it appertaineth not to reform things, but quietly to suffer that they cannot amend.' Martin Luther and Martin Bucer would have said the same, and complete obedience had been Cranmer's consistent policy even

17 Foxe 8, p. 38; *A.P.C. 1554–56*, p. 17. For a discussion of Cranmer's attainder, see Bailey, 'A legal view of Cranmer's execution'.

when he had been a chosen officer of Henry VIII and not a private subject. Yet that obedience had never shifted him from his evangelical convictions, and Mary would now know that he was still his old self.[18]

Others did not share Cranmer's attitude to obedience. Outside London, his own adopted county of Kent was perhaps the area most resistant to the Catholic revival. John Bland, Cranmer's client clergyman at Adisham near his palace at Bekesbourne, resisted the coming of the mass right up to the last legal moment in December, and even on the following Sunday after that, Bland openly preached in his church against the mass until he was assaulted by parish officers. Bland's conduct that day was certainly going beyond Cranmer's principle of suffering quietly that which he could not amend. Similarly, a few days later, a clergyman who had celebrated mass in Canterbury appeared in the pulpit twenty-four hours afterwards, bitterly regretting what he had done, and asking his congregation's forgiveness.[19] It was perhaps not surprising, therefore, that when plans by dissident members of the Edwardian regime for a comeback through insurrection exploded into fatally premature action, in January and February 1554, only in Kent did their conspiracy become a serious challenge to Mary. Admittedly, Sir Thomas Wyatt's success in Kent owed much to the incompetent reaction of the government, but his rising did look for a moment as if it might topple the whole Marian enterprise. Although Wyatt's slogans emphasized the threat to the realm posed by Mary's plans for a Spanish marriage, this was window-dressing seeking as broad-based an appeal as possible: in her July *coup d'état* Mary had adopted the same strategy of downplaying religion and giving preference to a secular rallying-cry.[20] The leadership and many traceable activists in Wyatt's rebellion represented the evangelical faction in Kent which Cranmer had done so much to encourage, and the rebellion's defeat was therefore yet another hammer-blow to the evangelical cause, associating it still further with treachery and disloyalty. It can have done nothing to ease Cranmer's conscience about what he had done to Mary.

In the short term, the rising did have one useful accidental effect; at the end of January, when the government (for the time being mistakenly) believed that it had gained the upper hand in Kent and cleared the Tower to make room for the expected crowds of important prisoners, Cranmer was made to share a room or set of prison apartments with Nicholas Ridley and John Bradford. Soon afterwards, when Wyatt had indeed been defeated and the Tower filled up, they were joined by Hugh Latimer, who later recalled what a happy chance it was: 'there did we together read over the New Testament

18 Cox 2, pp. 442–4.

19 Foxe 7, pp. 290–91; 6, p. 542.

20 The standard account is Loades, *Two Tudor Conspiracies*, but for convincing arguments for the primarily religious motivation of the rebellion, see Thorp, 'Religion and the Wyatt Rebellion', and Clark, *Kent*, pp. 89–98.

with great deliberation and painful study', and one of their chief concerns was to reinforce their arguments about the nature of eucharistic presence.[21] This was a very necessary preparation, because soon they would be put to a public test. Throughout February, the political leaders of the Jane adventure who had been involved in the attempted comeback were executed at the Tower, together with Jane herself; in the provinces, many of their followers suffered death for their effort at rebellion. The government's next confrontation must be with the religious leaders of the Edwardian Reformation, and it would take the form of an effort to destroy their doctrine in the eyes of the people of England.

The trio of Cranmer, Ridley and Latimer would now be singled out as a representative symbol of everything that the new Catholic establishment hated. Between them they represented the whole span of the evangelical movement, from its beginnings in the 1520s while Henry VIII was still hostile, through the official break with Rome from 1533 and Henry's step-by-step assimilation of evangelical belief and practice, through to its full flowering in the reign of Edward. In the words of Cambridge University, when it chose its team to oppose them, they were 'the especial instigators and shock-troops' of the attack on the Church's unity.[22] The chosen venue for their trial was Oxford, because Mary had at first proposed to call her second Parliament to Oxford. She was then persuaded that the resentment which this would cause in London outweighed the possible security benefits of being away from a turbulent city. However, given the strong evangelical lobby which still remained in London, and which might cause embarrassing demonstrations in the evangelical bishops' favour, Oxford clearly had advantages for the theological debate.[23]

Accordingly, on 8 March the Privy Council gave the order for the removal of Cranmer, Ridley and Latimer to Oxford. On 11 or 12 March they were separated from John Bradford, told to leave behind everything except what they could carry, and were taken from the Tower. At Brentford in Middlesex they were handed over to Sir John Williams and conducted by him to Bocardo, the town prison in Oxford, over the north gate in the town walls; it was Williams's last major duty as Sheriff of Oxfordshire before he was given a peerage a month later.[24] Their transfer was the centre-piece of a concerted nationwide campaign throughout March against key evangelical clergy, a campaign which was made much easier by the publication on 4 March of a comprehensive set of royal injunctions extending the alteration of religion,

21 Foxe 8, p. 593; *Latimer's Remains*, pp. 258–9.

22 Strype, *Cranmer*, 2, no. 77, p. 429: '*praecipui authores et antisignani* [*sic*]'.

23 *Noailles* 3, p. 86; Cox 2, p. 558; Loach, *Parliament and the Crown*, p. 91.

24 *Machyn's Diary*, p. 57 suggests a date of 8 March, but the Council order for their removal is of that date, *A.P.C. 1552–54*, p. 406 (B.L. Additional MS 26748, f. 43). See discussion in Ridley, *Cranmer*, p. 362n pointing to 12 March. *Cranmer's Recantacyons*, pp. 16–17 gives 11 March. Cf. also *Ridley's Remains*, p. 390.

including the restoration of clerical celibacy. The injunctions were of course an exercise of Mary's powers as Supreme Head of the Church; a similarly uncomfortable use of the supremacy, in order to subvert the supremacy's chief supporters, resulted in the deprival of the remaining Edwardian bishops by royal commission.[25] In Canterbury Cathedral, the Marian majority in the chapter took advantage of the new legal situation to remove Cranmer loyalists among the canons and junior staff who had married; they declared deprived both absentees and those who had turned up to protest against this move. Among those ejected was Cranmer's brother Edmund, the Archdeacon of Canterbury; at some stage after this he quietly retired to the Continent. Edmund Cranmer was replaced as Archdeacon by Nicholas Harpsfield, a trusted lieutenant of Cardinal Pole: it was the first stage in asserting Pole's place in the realm, nine months before he was able to arrive in person. A similar operation a week earlier had flushed the Cranmerians out of Canterbury's peculiar parishes in the city of London. Elsewhere, there was a wave of arrests, provoked especially by conflicts over the observance of Holy Week, when the liturgical chasm between old and new learning was at its most obvious.[26]

At the turn of March and April, Bishop Ridley managed to get a letter to John Bradford, by now himself moved from the Tower to the King's Bench prison, to describe how the trio were being treated in Oxford in their 'college of quondams' – a veritable retirement home for former bishops. His tone was upbeat – 'we be merry in God' – although security in the prison had been tightened. At first conditions had not been draconian. The prisoners were sent comforts by the devoted and wealthy evangelical cousins by marriage Jane Wilkinson and Anne Warcup; they had brought their own servants with them, and through the servants' regular excursions into town, they had been able to keep up to date with current news such as the fracas at Hadleigh during Holy Week, which had resulted in the arrest of Cranmer's client clergyman Rowland Taylor. However, a visit from Bishop Heath to Oxford had worsened their situation (Ridley sarcastically noted that this former friend and protégé of Cranmer's had not deigned to visit them); now the prisoners could not take exercise on the adjacent stretch of town wall, their servants were similarly restrained, and even their copy of the Prayer Book was taken away from them. They had been completely isolated from the University, although they had heard reports of general hostility to them; Oxford was an easier target for the Catholic restoration than Cambridge. As yet they had no idea whether, like the Parliament, they would be transferred back from Oxford to London for their next test.[27]

25 *T.R.P.* 2 no. 407; a convenient listing of the episcopal deprivations is *Chronicle of Queen Jane*, pp. 177–8.

26 On the Canterbury and London deprivations, Strype, *Cranmer*, 2, pp. 36–7, 39–40. For arrests, MacCulloch, *Suffolk and the Tudors*, p. 171, and Foxe 6, p. 684.

27 *Ridley's Works*, pp. 358–60.

38 The north gate of the city of Oxford, with the tower of St Michael's Church behind it in Cornmarket within the city. Bocardo formed part of this gate, a prison so-called because it was supposed to be as difficult to escape from as the consequence of the logical figure called Bocardo. It was demolished in 1771.

In fact, by the time Ridley wrote, the necessary decisions had been taken; these were formalized when the Convocation of Canterbury opened in London the day after Parliament. Dr Hugh Weston, the Oxford don who had led the fight against the Forty-Two Articles in London a year before, was re-elected prolocutor of the Lower House. However, for this session it would be an honorary appointment, designed to give him prestige in a different task: at the first working session two days later he was elected as the head of a delegation of Convocation to act as a tribunal on the Oxford prisoners. A few days later, Cambridge University chose a team of seven, headed by its Vice-Chancellor, to join the investigation into the three Cambridge graduates.[28] What was about to happen was not exactly a trial: in the words of Mary when she wrote to the bailiffs of Oxford to authorize the daily movement of the prisoners, it was intended 'to hear in open disputations the said Cranmer,

28 Lambeth MS 751, pp. 128–9; Strype, *Cranmer*, 2, nos 77–8, pp. 428–31.

Ridley and Latimer; so as their erroneous opinions, being by the word of God justly and truly convinced, the residue of our subjects may be thereby the better established in the true catholic faith'. It was thus the successor of the disputations which had been staged in Oxford and Cambridge on the eucharist and on justification in the reign of Edward VI; but its purpose was more than to act as a giant theological seminar; it would provide material for a subsequent formal heresy trial once the Roman obedience had been properly re-established.[29]

The proceedings proper opened on the evening of Saturday 14 April in the University Church, when the three accused were each in turn presented with three questions about the mass, questions which had already been subscribed by Convocation members and which were now being subscribed by members of the University: was the natural body of Christ really in the elements by virtue of the words spoken by the priest? did any other substance remain after the words of consecration? was there a propitiatory sacrifice in the mass for the sins of the quick and the dead? Each prisoner would be asked to subscribe, or dispute on these questions; no one had any illusions that the subscriptions would be forthcoming from them, and indeed it would have been very disconcerting for the theatre of the occasion if they had been. The three confrontations were kept separate; it seems that already at the beginning of the proceedings, the prisoners had been split up. Cranmer appeared first, to be met with an introductory statement from Weston about the unity of the Church; the Prolocutor used this to give a rapid and unfavourable résumé of the ex-archbishop's career, designed to show how he had destroyed unity. Cranmer, who refused the offer of a stool and insisted on standing, made a good impression on observers and managed to reveal the confusion among his opponents about what their theological terms might mean; he was asked to put his opinions in writing for consideration on Sunday and for further disputation on Monday, and he agreed to both requests. Ridley was next, fighting off the old charges about his strongly realist language on eucharistic presence back in 1547, before he agreed to disputation. Then came Latimer, exploiting his genuine ill-health and playing the simple old man for all he was worth; using these as his reasons for refusing to play the game by the rules, he agreed only to make an informal statement of his belief.

The debate on Monday 16 April and for the rest of the week transferred to the Divinity School; proceedings there were recorded by notaries acting on behalf of Convocation, but the prisoners were allowed two sympathetic observers for their own side, the future bishop John Jewel and Gilbert Mounson, from whose notes together with Ridley's own reconstruction the fullest account survives. Observers were delighted by an unfortunate introductory slip of the tongue by Weston as moderator, in which he told the assembled company that they were met 'to confound the detestable heresy of

29 Foxe 6, pp. 531–2 (11 April 1554). The account which follows unless otherwise stated is conflated from Foxe 6, pp. 439–536, and Appendices 3–5, 8, and the official account, B.L. Harley MS 3642 (extracts from this are usefully footnoted in Cox 1, pp. 391–427).

the verity of the body of Christ in the sacrament'; this provoked much unfeeling laughter.[30] It was not a promising start to a thoroughly disorganized day, in which there was no proper formal consideration given to the three propositions under discussion. Cranmer was assailed by a barrage of arguments around the question of eucharistic presence from a variety of scholars besides Weston himself; the moderator did little to control the noise made by the highly partisan audience, and the arguments switched from Latin into English, an irregular procedure which revealed that this was far from the normal teaching exercise of the universities. Despite this, Cranmer was on strong ground: a debate on the eucharist would tackle material which he had made his own over the past few years. Indeed, his verbal arguments and his presentation of two written papers (one his brief answer from Sunday night) followed the lines that one would expect from the author of the *Defence* and the *Answer*. Cyprian's image of the grains coming together in the loaf was there, together with the comparison of the nature of the sacrament in eucharist and baptism, and the characteristic insistence that if strong realist language about the eucharist was to be found in the early fathers of the Church, it had a figurative or sacramental reference. Once more, as in the literary debate with Gardiner, the realist language of Bucer was brought in as a witness for the prosecution; once more, Cranmer could only give the irritated response that Bucer was a strange ally for a Romanist, and restate his own position.

The main achievement of the authorities on Monday was to cast a miasma of doubt on the accuracy of Cranmer's citations in his writings, and one Catholic commentator said that the prisoner was badly affected by these accusations.[31] Some of the examples did not matter from Cranmer's point of view; he freely admitted his fairly ruthless editing of medieval writers whose authority in his eyes was small. The accusations about his use of the early fathers were more serious. A clash about the interpretation and phrasing of a passage of Hilary of Poitiers, which Cranmer used in the *Defence*, produced a rather touching attempt at intervention that Monday evening, from a young scholar in the University called William Holcot. Having witnessed Cranmer being accused of falsification of his quotation, Holcot was excited to find Cranmer's interpretation was precisely paralleled in a tract by Stephen Gardiner (which may, indeed, have been the source of Cranmer's mistake); at the end of the day he naively tried to present the evidence to Cranmer in his prison. For his pains Holcot was arrested, examined and hauled up to London before Gardiner himself, where in a state of thorough fright he subscribed to the three articles – an anecdote which much later he passed on to John Foxe in order to purge his conscience. It was never going to be likely that an attempt to break Cranmer's isolation in the debate would be treated other than as subversion. Nevertheless, the incident cast a rather depressing light

30 Foxe 6, p. 444.
31 *Cranmer's Recantacyons*, p. 21.

on the cry with which Weston had brought Monday's proceedings to an end: '*Vicit veritas*' – the truth has prevailed.[32]

Ridley's turn came on Tuesday. From the start, there was more structure to the day's debate than on Monday; after an initial request from Weston for a quiet hearing, which seems to have had effect for most of the day, the prisoner was allowed to give proper academic consideration of all three propositions. Either the authorities were dissatisfied with Monday's chaos, or Ridley himself was more forceful and expert than Cranmer in imposing his own discipline on the proceedings – Foxe, indeed, more or less admitted the latter possibility in his retrospective consideration of the debates.[33] Although Weston made Ridley shorten the formidably long written text which he had prepared, and he did allow a certain amount of heckling which Ridley bitterly resented, generally he seems to have treated the ex-Bishop of London with more respect than he had done Cranmer. Latimer's appearance on Wednesday was an unsatisfactory attempt to get him to conform to the pattern of a formal disputation, which Weston in the end curtailed; it was a contest characterized by disorder and cheap point-scoring. One interesting detail of the discussion of the eucharist was Latimer's admission that he had come to his present view on the eucharist within the previous seven years, in other words, during 1547.[34] This was the same year in which we have found incontrovertible evidence of Cranmer's change of mind on the same matter (see above, Ch. 9).

Thursday 19 April brought a change of tone, with an occasion which brought a curious semblance of ordinary university business into the week: John Harpsfield was disputing for his grace to proceed to the degree of Doctor of Divinity, and Cranmer was called on to act as one of his disputants. The proceedings were not quite as innocent an interlude as they seemed. Harpsfield was Bishop Bonner's chaplain and he was on the eve of being made Archdeacon of London; he was familiar to Cranmer, having actually written one of the twelve official homilies of 1547, before his master had fallen from favour. One wonders whether it was Bonner or Harpsfield himself who had seized on the chance to symbolize the changed state of religion in this manner. The subject was a very technical discussion of the nature of the body of Christ in the sacrament, in which Dr Weston played the part of Peter Martyr to partner Cranmer as Harpsfield's opposer. Cranmer, despite his modest and quite unnecessary avowals of his rusty Latin, plunged with relish back into the distinctions of medieval scholasticism with which he had worked at the beginning of his academic career, raising a series of questions which provoked conflicting and confused answers from his opponents. One sympathetic evangelical observer felt that Cranmer had acquitted himself with unexpected

32 Foxe 8, pp. 708–9; cf. Cranmer, *Defence*, pp. 405–7, Cox 1, p. 414n and Foxe 6, pp. 460–61, 468. '*Vicit veritas*' is the reading in Foxe, *Rerum gestarum*, 1, p. 716. Later editions have it in the present tense: '*vincit veritas*'.

33 Foxe 6, p. 529.

34 Ibid., p. 505.

brilliance in this debate, to the extent that Weston felt obliged to ask him to draw his arguments to a close; by contrast, once more the Catholic commentator who wrote *Cranmer's Recantacyons* (very probably John Harpsfield's brother Nicholas) recorded him as routed in the discussion.[35] However, everyone kept their tempers on this occasion, and Weston paid Cranmer a graceful tribute after his contribution. This did not stop the disputation leading on to a collusive dialogue between Weston and Harpsfield in which they rapidly demolished, at least to their own satisfaction, the chief patristic witnesses that had been used by Cranmer and Martyr in their writings on the eucharist.

Friday brought a conclusion to the main disputation, in which Weston pronounced his verdict. He maintained that Cranmer had been overcome in argument, provoking an angry outburst from the ex-archbishop: how could he argue properly, he asked, when four or five interrupted him at a time? Ridley and Latimer were equally intransigent as they were asked what they would do, 'and so the sentence was read over them, that they were no members of the Church'. They were the only three in Oxford to refuse subscription to the three articles, whose otherwise unanimous reception even the Catholic commentator sarcastically noted was 'either an astonishing joy or a great dissembling'![36] Contemptuously refusing any final efforts at persuasion during the reading of the sentence, the prisoners had each prepared a comment of defiance which they were allowed to make after their condemnation. Cranmer chose a deliberate echo of the arguments about the presence of the body of Christ in heaven alone in Article 29 of the Forty-Two Articles on the Lord's Supper: 'From this your judgement and sentence, I appeal to the just judgement of God almighty, trusting to be present with him in heaven, for whose presence in the altar, I am thus condemned.'

Now they were carried off to be separated for the next few months: Cranmer, regarded as the greatest security risk, returned for the time being to Bocardo, Ridley to the Mayor's house and Latimer to the home of one of the bailiffs. They were to be deprived of contact with their own servants, and also of the use of pen and paper; Cranmer's conditions seem to have been most restrictive, to judge from a note which Ridley tried to send him at this time, enclosing scraps of news and urging him to find some way of circumventing his guard's rigorous restrictions as Ridley himself had been able to do. On Saturday 21 April there was a great procession of the sacrament through the town, which Cranmer was forced to watch from his prison; Dr Weston bore the Blessed Sacrament in the procession, and four doctors of both universities (including the bishops-elect of Bristol and Bangor) were the bearers of the canopy over Weston and his sacred burden. It was a triumphal and precise ceremonial statement that during the previous week scholarship had upheld

35 *Cranmer's Recantacyons*, p. 23.
36 Ibid., p. 25.

the truth of Catholic eucharistic teaching; its legal equivalent came during the following week, when a formal report of the proceedings by the Oxford University authorities was presented back in London to Convocation.[37]

There could be no pretence of fairness in a disputation which formed part of a rolling programme of religious revolution. The Edwardian disputations in the universities had been unbalanced enough, with the participants quite clear that their deliberations would have no effect on the direction of government policy, but at least all those then involved had been free men still holding university posts, and no lives depended on the outcome. Even at the time evangelicals pointed out the contrast between the Edwardian debates and what happened in April 1554: the atmosphere of the Marian disputation was unusually hysterical, both among the Catholic participants and the packed audiences, and Weston as moderator did not make much effort to control it. Moreover, as both Foxe and his Victorian editors were at some pains to point out, much of the technical framing of the arguments was fairly shoddy by the standards of university logic at the time. Latimer was wise in not agreeing to formal disputation, because his decision wrongfooted his opponents and enabled him to use his pugnacious wit in the form where it would be most effective, in an unregulated verbal dogfight. Ridley later noted that of the three propositions initially put to the prisoners, only the first one was given any proper consideration in the whole disputation, even though Weston at the end of proceedings denounced the trio as heretics in relation to all three. Overall, despite official claims of the occasion as a great success, it is probably significant that the regime did not think it worthwhile to publish any official version of the proceedings – equally significant that it abandoned plans to stage a similar event at Cambridge with Hooper, Ferrar, Rowland Taylor, Bradford and Philpot.[38]

Cranmer and Ridley both tried to get in touch with the capital on 23 April to present their protests at the way matters had been handled. While Ridley addressed his complaint to Convocation and in particular to the senior bishops who were his contemporaries and old acquaintances, Cranmer wrote as a former Councillor to the Privy Council. He began his letter with a short plea for mercy which echoed what he had said to the Queen the previous December: he had been a reluctant signatory of Edward VI's will, and he appealed to the witnesses among the Councillors for confirmation of this. When he had seen the contents of Cranmer's letter in the course of his journey back to Convocation in London, Weston refused to act the part of postboy, hardly surprisingly, since it was his conduct which was chiefly at fault; it is uncertain whether the letter was ever delivered, and its text now exists in two curiously

37 Foxe 6, pp. 534, 536; *Cranmer's Recantacyons*, pp. 26–7.

38 Foxe 6, App. 5. On the contrast between the disputations, see *R.S.T.C.* 21777, [attrib. Saunders, almost certainly incorrectly], *A trewe mirrour*, sigs. Aiii–Av. On the Cambridge disputation, Hooper, *Later Writings*, pp. 592–3.

different versions.[39] However, like Ridley, Cranmer's thoughts also turned to his old episcopal colleagues. He was visited by many distinguished scholars trying to change his opinion in the weeks after the disputation, but he stood on his dignity as a former Primate, and demanded discussions with the bishops, particularly Cuthbert Tunstall – the Catholic narrator of this incident, probably unfairly, said that he singled out Tunstall because he was too old to travel safely to Oxford. The Bishop of Durham turned down the opportunity: 'far from my being able to benefit Cranmer in the matter of the eucharist', he said, 'he is even confident that he will pass on his scruples about it to me'. This seems to have been a regretful reference to the fact that when during the disputation the Convocation delegate, Dr William Pye, had presented Cranmer with a copy of Tunstall's recently published treatise on the real presence in the eucharist, the prisoner had covered it with critical annotations. Tunstall's treatise was in any case remarkable for its admission that transubstantiation was a doctrine of quite late definition: a point which would delight Cranmer.[40]

As the excitement of the disputation subsided, conditions seem quickly to have eased for the former archbishop. He was removed from Bocardo to the home of one of the bailiffs of Oxford (Latimer was still the involuntary guest of the other bailiff); this was to be the pattern for the time being, with the new Mayor and bailiffs taking over the custodial responsibility from their predecessors when the town elected them at Michaelmas. In these conditions, up to the time of Cardinal Pole's arrival in England in November, Cranmer was able to talk with friends and take exercise in the bailiff's garden, and small comforts kept appearing for all three prisoners, even from people whom they did not know.[41] Despite careful watching, they also managed to get attendants whom they could trust to report news for them, and to communicate with the outside world when possible. Such attempts could be hazardous and sporadic; we have evidence from one letter of Ridley's how a messenger sent from the London prisoners to all three Oxford prisoners was prevented from seeing Ridley at least. Yet, they were assured constantly of a number of reliable attendants beyond the confines of their prisons: the Swiss Augustine Bernher, Latimer's old servant, was of great help to all of them as a messenger, Ridley had his relative William Punt, and Cranmer's doctor John Herd (preserver of many of the Archbishop's manuscripts) records that he was living in Oxford right up to the beginning of August 1555.[42]

39 Cox 2, pp. 445–6, which notes the variants.

40 *Cranmer's Recantacyons*, p. 24. This story is confirmed from a Protestant source: *Bradford* 1, p. 494 (and cf. ibid., pp. 511, 545). See also Pole's reference to Cranmer seeing Tunstall's book, Strype, *Cranmer*, 2, no. 89, p. 454.

41 *A.P.C. 1554–56*, p. 77; *Cranmer's Recantacyons*, p. 27; *Ridley's Works*, p. 365.

42 *Ridley's Works*, pp. 376–7; cf. ibid., pp. 363–6. On Herd, Bodley MS Lincoln Lat (e) 122 f. 84v; on Bernher, Loades, *Oxford Martyrs*, pp. 171–2.

Otherwise, during this period almost complete silence descends about Cranmer. Although Ridley claimed that his own confinement was the most strict of the three, we have a flow of surviving letters and other writings from him and also fragments from Hugh Latimer, including one substantial tract dated 15 May 1555.[43] By contrast, very little survives of Cranmer's writings or letters after his arrival in Oxford; however, he was able to beat the security for one major enterprise at least. We know that he was able to revise the Latin version of his *Defence* in order to cover more of the points raised against it by Stephen Gardiner, and to tackle the criticism of his citations at the April 1554 disputation; later he managed to get it smuggled out of Oxford. Edmund Grindal, in exile in Frankfurt, wrote to Ridley in May 1555 listing a series of works then awaiting publication which included *Antoniana objecta cum responsione*: this was simply Cranmer's revised version of the *Defensio* with marginal references to 'Marcus Antonius's' work.[44] A new Latin preface was written for the book, possibly by Sir John Cheke, some time before autumn that year, but there were complications about publishing a controversial work on sacramental theology in Frankfurt, and in the end it had to wait to be published after Cranmer's death: the new edition by the former London printer Nicholas van den Berghe came out at Emden in 1557.[45]

The prisoners' circumstances were bound to change when Reginald Pole finally overcame the tangles of national and international politics which had kept him out of the realm. At the end of November 1554 the Cardinal solemnly reconciled England to the papal obedience, amid joyfully emotional scenes in the Parliament House; the day (30 November, St Andrew's Day) was later ordered to be kept as a national feast of thanksgiving in perpetuity, a decision which was not destined to endure longer than Queen Mary herself.[46] One can see the mills of ecclesiastical justice beginning to turn once more when, on 28 December, Hugh Weston for a second time certified Convocation of the decision which had been taken about the prisoners at Oxford back in April.[47] As a result, there came a flurry of activity for the trio: at first in December the rumour was that they would each be transferred into separate colleges of the university, but a little while later they were all taken back to Bocardo, from where Ridley was writing towards the end of December. By mid-January 1555, he wrote to Bradford that the three were fully aware of the

43 *Latimer's Remains*, pp. 435–44, and cf. ibid., pp. 429–34, 444. *Ridley's Works*, pp. 391–2.

44 *Grindal's Remains*, pp. 238–40. For corrections and additions relating to Hilary, see Cox 1, 2nd pagination, pp. 53, 69, for an addition on Duns Scotus, p. 35, and for a clarification on Theophylact, p. 75 (cf. Cranmer, *Defence*, pp. 372, 405–6, 334, 419).

45 Cox 1, second pagination p. 8; the date of the preface is established by various references, especially to Gardiner as still alive. On van den Berghe, cf. Pettegree, *Foreign Protestant Communities*, p. 89n, and see Pettegree, 'Latin polemic of the Marian exiles', pp. 311–12.

46 *C.S.P. Spanish 1554–58*, no. 127; Burnet 2 i, p. 470.

47 Lambeth MS 751, p. 129. This is distinct from the certificate of 27 April 1554 recorded in *Concilia*, ed. Wilkins, 4, p. 94.

significance of the new situation, particularly the fact that the bishops now had full power once more to enquire into heresy: the persecution proper could begin. Bradford and the other chief London prisoners replied to this letter as a group, telling their Oxford colleagues that 'it is commonly thought your staff standeth next to the door', and they encouraged them with words from the Book of Revelation about the joy of martyrdom, 'to the which society God with you bring me also in his mercy, when it shall be his good pleasure'.[48]

In fact, it was some of those London prisoners who first suffered, beginning with the burning of John Rogers on 4 February. This delay in dealing with the Oxford trio is not as surprising as it seems: it is a tribute to their significance as symbolic of everything that had gone wrong in England in the previous thirty years. Their destruction could not be allowed prematurely. Cardinal Pole may have wished to involve himself personally in their fate when he had more leisure to do so; certainly there were rumours that he planned to have a conference with them.[49] More importantly, the delay attests to the determination shared by both the Cardinal and the Queen that when Mary reversed the national disobedience unleashed by her father and brother, everything should be done in due form and with proper obedience to the papacy. Pole referred punctiliously to Cranmer as 'the present Archbishop' when writing to his old friend Cardinal Morone in March 1555; for the time being the Cardinal could only exercise power in the Province of Canterbury by virtue of his general authority as papal legate, although as a matter of convenience he took up his lodging in Lambeth Palace. Pole's scruples were shared by a foul-mouthed evangelical from Ashford in Kent, who as late as 16 August 1555, when brought before Bishop Thornden of Dover on heresy charges, rejected his authority and pointed out that the imprisoned Archbishop of Canterbury was his diocesan.[50]

Mary, likewise, needed satisfaction about her persistent doubt as to whether Cranmer had been properly deprived of his see during the continuing schism of 1553–4, given that he had originally been provided by the papacy. With that extreme conscientiousness which was one of her most notable characteristics, from the moment that Pole had set foot in England, she never spoke to him directly about her previous invitations to him to become Archbishop of Canterbury, despite having twice officially raised the matter while he was still on the Continent. It was just as important to the Queen to get Cranmer properly deprived by papal authority as to get fresh recognition

48 *Ridley's Works*, pp. 366–7, 371–3; *Bradford* 1, pp. 169–71. For the dating, see the edition of this sequence of letters in *Bradford* 1, pp. 158–68, but NB that a printing error in the heading at ibid., p. 161, has undone the accurate dating by Bradford's editor to December 1554.

49 *E.T.* p. 113 (*O.L.* p. 171). Cf. *Bradford* 1, pp. 190–91.

50 *C.S.P. Venetian 1555–56*, nos 22–3, for this and the following paragraph. For Pole's residence at Lambeth, see *C.S.P. Spanish 1554–58*, p. 119, and for his action as legate in mid-February, Strype, *Cranmer*, 2, nos 80–81, pp. 432–7. On William Stere of Ashford, Foxe 7, p. 341.

from the Pope of her title to the island of Ireland, after Henry VIII's unilateral assumption of the title of King in 1541–2. Accordingly, both these points were to be presented to Pope Julius III by the first English embassy for twenty years, but the ambassadors only started out from England at the beginning of March. They carried with them an application signed by both Philip and Mary for the deprivation of Cranmer on account of his evil life; with a sad turn of fate, it was penned by Roger Ascham, who had once enjoyed Cranmer's financial and literary patronage.[51]

The Oxford prisoners themselves were well aware that the eyes of the world were upon them as the leaders of the whole evangelical cause. Ridley's explanation for the delay in their deaths was that the authorities thought that they would be able more easily to break the resolve of second-rank figures like Rogers and Saunders once they were isolated from the leadership of the Oxford trio: 'the subtle policy of the world, setting us apart, first assaulted them by whose infirmity they thought to have more advantage; but God disappointed their subtle purpose. For whom the world esteemed weakest (praised be God), they have found most strong, sound and valiant, in Christ's cause, unto the death.'[52] Ironically, even as the heresy trials of Bradford and his fellows began, and on the eve of those first burnings, the prospective London martyrs themselves were conducting their own struggle against heresy. Predictably, they attempted to enlist the authority of the Oxford prisoners. Bradford was the chief stirrer in the prison controversy between members of the former evangelical establishment and the Freewillers led by Henry Hart; he tried to draw on the continuing status of Cranmer, Ridley and Latimer 'as the chief captains . . . of Christ's Church here' to get backing for his assertion of predestination. Ridley became involved in this sufficiently to write a treatise on predestination, and smuggle it out of Bocardo, despite the new strict watch which was being kept; however, we have no evidence of Cranmer's involvement, despite his activity in Kent against the Freewillers in the last year of his power.[53] Far away in Strassburg, too, Cranmer was a touchstone in the row which was developing about how the English exile congregation there should worship. Some regarded even the 1552 rite as unacceptably over-ceremonial, but their opponents were for remaining faithful to the form of the book principally 'because the Archbishop of Canterbury defends it as good doctrine'.[54]

It is a measure of the secure confinement in which Cranmer was kept that the most plausible date for the last document surviving in his own hand is from this period, the opening two months of 1555, more than a year before his death. It is a short note to Peter Martyr Vermigli, who was by then safe in a

51 *Wriothesley's Chronicle* 2, p. 133n (NB the old-style date of 1554).

52 *Ridley's Works*, p. 370 (probably late February 1555).

53 *Bradford* 1, pp. 169–71, *Ridley's Works*, p. 379; Penny, *Freewill or Predestination*, pp. 130–37.

54 *E.T.* pp. 112–13 (*O.L.* pp. 170–71).

lecturer's post in Strassburg. One has to admit that the dating is unhappily open to question, because it depends on the rather insecure supposition that it was carried into exile by John Jewel, who had now finally ceased to try to live within the new Church, and who seems to have arrived in Strassburg towards the end of February 1555. For security reasons the bearer (whom Martyr knew) was simply referred to in the letter as 'of signal discretion, most faithful in all matters entrusted to him, exceedingly attached to us both, and possessing an entire acquaintance with the circumstances of our country'.[55] The little scrap of paper was appropriately treasured by Martyr, and since he ended his days at Zürich, it was laid up in the archives there with an explanatory inscription written by Heinrich Bullinger himself. Cranmer explained that he was under very strict guard; he had written to no one else, and he dared not sign it himself in case it was discovered and a signature drew attention to it; Martyr would know his very distinctive hand well enough. Most of what he had to say was entrusted to the bearer, and the main subject of what he wrote was his conviction, borne out of his sufferings, that the desperate situation of the Church was a proof of its imminent deliverance by God: 'surely raising them up if they think he is bringing them down, and laying them low; surely glorifying them if he is thought to be confounding them; surely making them live, if he is thought to be destroying them.' It was an eloquent testimony to the power of predestinarian belief in God's care for the elect: one can see why the evangelicals were so angry with the Freewillers for questioning such a strengthening doctrine. 'I pray that God may grant that we may endure to the end!' And he finally regretted that his lack of books and freedom prevented him from writing the definitive version of the *Answer*, promised long before in his 1553 preface to the *Defence*, so that the 'subtleties and juggling tricks and ravings' of Stephen Gardiner (under his pen name of Marcus Antonius) could finally be routed. It was appropriate that this last letter from the hand of Cranmer the unbowed evangelical should still be preoccupied with the man whose career had been so tangled with his own for a quarter of a century and more.

The first stirrings of the trial which would at last decide Cranmer's fate came far away in Rome on 19 June, when the mandate for it was issued, delegating the hearing from the Roman Inquisitor-General to the new Bishop of Gloucester, James Brooks. Added to the papal delegate were three proctors of the Crown, the civil lawyers Thomas Martin, John Story and David Lewis. Predictably, all four were Oxford men: Brooks was an old adversary of Cranmer's as one of the conservative grouping at Corpus Christi College during the 1530s, while Martin and Lewis were colleagues as Masters in Chancery. Lewis does not appear to have taken any part in the proceedings, an

55 Garrett, *Marian Exiles*, p. 198. The letter is Cox 2, pp. 457–8 (and see n. on Jewel there: I have altered the translation of the text). The fact that Martyr knew the bearer may slightly strengthen the case for Jewel, who was an Oxford don when Martyr was Professor there.

39 Cranmer's last letter to Peter Martyr, preserved at Zürich, in Cranmer's own hand. The signature is in another hand, and the explanatory inscription below is by Johann Heinrich Bullinger.

absence which no doubt helped his distinguished administrative career in Elizabeth's reign, but Martin and Story were both enthusiastic Catholics whose promotion had hung fire under Edward VI and who were now active diocesan administrators for bishops Gardiner and Bonner respectively.[56] The papal mandate was served on Cranmer on 7 September, and included the formal and fairly surreal requirement that he appear in Rome within eighty days; in fact, his trial before Brooks, Martin and Story opened in the familiar venue of the University Church in Oxford on 12 September. Latimer and Ridley would wait for a separate trial later in the month; the priority was to deal with the man who had become *legatus natus* in England when he was appointed Primate in 1533.[57]

Cranmer appears to have been transferred from prison to house arrest for the duration of the trial and for its aftermath, perhaps to give a semblance of judicial impartiality to the proceedings. The hearing was not empowered to judge, but only to report to Rome. The newly elected Pope Paul IV, that implacable defender of papal rights, was as determined as Pole and Mary that the hearing of Cranmer's crimes would be conducted entirely within the papal

56 Cox 2, pp. 543–4, 554; [Lambeth Film 3] Douai MS 922 vol. 4, f. 50v; for the careers of Lewis, Martin and Story, see *History of Parliament 1509–1558* 2, pp. 524–5, 578–80, 3, pp. 386–8. On Brooks at Corpus, P.R.O., S.P. 1/137, ff. 139–43, Cox 2, p. 383 (*L.P.* 13 ii, no. 561).

57 Loades, *Oxford Martyrs*, pp. 192–3. The formal account of the trial, Lambeth MS 1136, is pr. in Cox 2, pp. 541–62. What follows is conflated unless otherwise stated from this, and Foxe 8, pp. 44–69.

obedience, and so this was an entirely fresh process, procedurally distinct from the April 1554 disputation.[58] Nevertheless, the delegates did not propose to go in detail over the ground covered in April 1554, and indeed they used those findings as one of the principal exhibits to be confirmed in their interrogatories. This time it would be Cranmer's whole career which was on trial – his perjured papal oaths, his marriage, his public writings. This put the former Archbishop at a disadvantage: he had made himself the master of eucharistic theology, and even in the extremely unfavourable conditions of the earlier disputation, he had therefore been able to acquit himself creditably. Now the inconsistencies of a career which had opened amid a host of contradictions in the dying throes of King Henry's Roman obedience would be exposed for condemnation or justification, and to defend these twists and turns would not be an easy task.

To begin with, on his entrance to the church Cranmer made the careful distinction between his obedience to the Queen and his contempt for usurped ecclesiastical authority which had characterized his stance since the beginning of the reign; he made a great business of showing customary deference by taking off his cap to right and left to Martin and Story the royal proctors, but he would show no such courtesy to the central figure of Brooks, or to the other clerical dignitaries present clothed in the dress appropriate to their rank. His gesture was all the more pointed because the seating had been so set up in the chancel of the church that Brooks was sitting on a platform immediately under the hanging pyx containing the reserved sacrament: a deliberate symbol of the majesty of his authority and of the profound importance for Catholic doctrine of what was happening. The representative of the Vicar of Christ was presented below the body of Christ, charged with acting as its champion and defender; Cranmer scorned them both. It was an annoying start for Brooks, who decided to press ahead with an extended opening denunciation of the prisoner, even though Cranmer had not removed his cap.

The Bishop set out how unexpected Cranmer's disobedience had been when he had first been appointed to Canterbury: the Archbishop had then immediately betrayed the Pope's trust. He summed up the stages of Cranmer's apostasy through two reigns with the vivid phrase 'First your heart hath fallen, then your tongue and your pen'. Worse still, these lapses 'besides your own damage, have caused many more to fall'. Cranmer appears to have made an extended speech in reply at this, which was once more a careful distinction between the obedience which he owed to the Crown, and his complete rejection of the Pope. He said that it was the greatest grief of his life to see two royal proctors collaborating in an accusation of him before a foreign power. 'If I have transgressed the laws of the land, their Majesties have sufficient authority and power, both from God, and by the ordinance of the realm, to

58 *C.S.P. Venetian 1555–56*, no. 215. For Cranmer's confinement, *Cranmer's Recantacyons*, p. 36.

punish me.' He returned to an old favourite theme of his: the incompatibility of papal canon law with the law of the realm. 'Whosoever sweareth to both, must needs incur perjury to the one': a principle which cast a sad light on the oaths which Mary had sworn at her coronation. He went on to deal with accusations of heresy and schism: since he had devoted so many years to proving that the Pope was Antichrist (the particular mark of whom was usurped power over princes), he maintained that this was an absurd charge. By this speech he had discharged his conscience, and he announced his intention of writing to the Queen.

Martin's address seems to have followed this. He was more succinct than Brooks had been, and he concentrated on explaining the reason for the presence of a royal proctor by defining the relationship between secular and ecclesiastical power: this was a shrewd direction to take in a matter where Cranmer had already tried to stake out his territory in both gestures and words. Addressing himself again to Brooks, the prisoner then formally repudiated his authority before reciting the Lord's Prayer and Creed as a preliminary to his declaration that he would never accept Roman jurisdiction within the realm. He was still in aggressive form, cap on head: he ended his extended denunciation of the Pope ('unless he be Antichrist, I cannot tell what to make of him') by a direct and pertinent attack on Brooks for the inconsistency of his own career. It was Archbishop Warham, he pointed out, who had agreed to the submission of the clergy: 'it was three quarters of a year after ere ever I had the bishopric of Canterbury in my hands', and meanwhile Brooks as a member of Oxford University had given his consent to what had happened.

Brooks apparently let pass Cranmer's inaccurate reference to his having possessed a doctorate of divinity at the time of the schism, and it was Story's chance to make his opening attack. Although he did not directly engage in argument with Cranmer, he raised a point which would soon prove very damaging: the relationship of royal supremacy to the Church. 'Well, sir,' said Story, 'you will grant me that there was a perfect Catholic Church before any king was christened [i.e. became a Christian]'. Now in fact when Cranmer fifteen years before had last explicitly considered this question, this was precisely what he would not grant, at least in relation to the discipline of the Church. He had then stated that the Church's discipline was incomplete without a prince and that the early Christians formed their ministry willy-nilly, since 'they were constrained of necessity to take such curates and priests as either they knew themselves to be meet thereunto, or else as were commended unto them by other that were so replete with the Spirit of God . . . that they ought even of very conscience to give credit unto them'.[59] Cranmer's premise in 1540 was that the visible Church reached its perfection only in the era of the first Christian princes; Story's was that the initial state

59 Cox 2, p. 116; see also above, Ch. 7.

of the Church was perfect and therefore demonstrated the supremacy of the only authority extant after the Resurrection and Ascension: that of Peter.

After this, things started going rapidly downhill for the former Archbishop: John Foxe's explanation that the proceedings were distorted by partial reporting will not do. Martin jumped in after Story's speech to cross-question Cranmer with all a lawyer's ruthlessness. He pressed him hard on whether all oaths, good or bad, ought to be obeyed; he forced him into a defensive account of his reluctant acceptance – but acceptance nonetheless – of Henry's offer of the archbishopric. Then he began pushing him hard on his changing beliefs on the eucharist – not three phases, but two, protested Cranmer, since he now regarded all real presence doctrine as equally misguided. However, in doing so, he would have to repudiate his connivance at the death of John Lambert in 1538, the first really embarrassing admission. But there was worse to come from Martin: he raised the matter of the bungled translation of the Justus Jonas catechism and the alteration of its text between editions. Now at that distressing memory, Cranmer became really flustered. Who was supreme head of the Church? Martin asked. Christ, replied Cranmer. Not Henry VIII? enquired Martin. Cranmer hastily corrected himself: 'I mean not but every king in his own realm and dominion is supreme head.' 'Was it ever so in Christ's Church?' – the trap opened, and Cranmer, true to his beliefs expressed in 1540, walked straight in – 'It was so'. Martin slipped the trap shut: 'Then what say you by Nero? He was the mightiest prince of the earth after Christ was ascended: was he head of Christ's Church?' A verbal wriggle or two more, and Cranmer found himself saying that Nero was head of the Church. That did not say much for the Supreme Headship of Henry VIII, and the additional fragments of discussion which Foxe was able to resurrect do not make Cranmer's answers look any better.

It was a bad moment, but Cranmer's dignity returned when he was faced with sixteen interrogatories based on the charges against him.[60] The questions took his career right back to his first marriage to Joan in Cambridge: a cruel revival of a painful memory and hardly necessary, since he had been perfectly free to marry before his ordination. Yet Cranmer kept his nerve. His response to a sequence of questions about his second and uncanonical marriage was defiant self-assertion, which Foxe's additional notes suggest extended to a sharp riposte to Martin's pompously antiquarian suggestion that his children were bondmen to the see of Canterbury. Cranmer asked if the children of a priest's concubine were bondmen to his benefice, and nothing more was heard of this fossil from canon law. His self-possession continued as he was asked about responsibility for his controversial eucharistic works and the 1553 catechism. A curious mistake of the tribunal was to include in this list the

60 There are minor inconsistencies between the charges (Cox 2, pp. 557–8) and the interrogatories (Foxe 8, pp. 58–9), but if one adds the official account's first charge about taking the see of Canterbury, the differences are not great.

English account of Peter Martyr's 1549 Oxford disputation, which Cranmer simply denied seeing until after its publication.

When the questions moved once more to his breach of faith with the Pope in 1533, Martin brought out the notarial instruments which had been retrieved from the archives recording the Archbishop's oaths of loyalty to the papacy at the time of his consecration. This was the most damaging piece of inconsistency which the prosecution could bring; Cranmer had justified his marital conduct as a matter of personal integrity, but integrity did not shine out of the jurisdictional proceedings of 1533. Foxe rescued from another source Cranmer's long and circumstantial answer on this point which was not recorded by the Catholic account of the proceedings. We have examined it already when reconstructing the events of autumn 1532 (see above, Ch. 3); it is sufficiently tangled and unsatisfactory as a justification of what had happened to ring true, and as a defence, it adds little to the Catholic account's record of Cranmer's statement (both accurate and lame) 'that he did nothing but by the laws of the realm'.

A third source, however, gives a different emphasis in the prisoner's self-justification at this point: *Cranmer's Recantacyons* notes that he especially wanted those present at his trial to understand that he had done what he had done 'to improve the corrupt ways of the Church as Primate of the realm'. This is remarkably close to the persistent refrain of the oath which we have already heard Cranmer swearing to Henry during his 1533 consecration, immediately after and in modification of his oath of loyalty to the Pope. He had then promised not to obstruct 'the reformation of the Christian religion, the government of the English Church, or the prerogative of the Crown or the well-being of the same commonwealth', and moreover that he would 'prosecute and reform matters wheresoever they seem to me to be for the reform of the English Church'. Coming from a source bitterly hostile to Cranmer where one would least expect to hear it, this avowal of reforming idealism is of some significance, and it probably accurately reflects his motives in those confused months after he had returned from his German embassy.[61]

Overall, Cranmer had admitted virtually every fact which had been put to him, while denying all the negative implications of treachery, disobedience and heresy drawn from those facts. The long oration which Brooks now gave about his disobedience was wasted on him: it was a formal rebuttal of his arguments for the benefit of the rest of the audience. Notably, Brooks returned bitterly to Cranmer's point that he himself had sworn an oath against the Pope in his university career. 'I knew not then what an oath did mean, and yet to say the truth, I did it compulsed, compulsed I say by you, master Cranmer; and here were you the author and cause of my perjury.' Virtually every clergyman, civil lawyer and scholar present that day could say the same.

61 *Cranmer's Recantacyons*, p. 31; cf. Cox 2, p. 560. It is notable that Pole also commented on this reason of Cranmer's: Strype, *Cranmer*, 2, no. 89, p. 458.

On the next day a series of witnesses was brought to a room in New College formally to depose on the interrogatories. They were a procession of Oxford men; even the first witness, Richard Croke, whose degrees were from Cambridge, was an Oxford resident. He was the same Croke who two decades and more before in 1530 had tried to solicit Cranmer to help him against John Stokesley, when they were all colleagues on the mission to Rome.[62] The next witness, Robert Ward, rather unpleasantly said that he did not believe that Cranmer was sufficiently learned to have written all the books named by himself, even if he published them and said that they were his. He was succeeded by another hostile face from the past, Robert Serles, who was at last able to get his own back for his humiliations in the 1540s; indeed, virtually the only circumstantial evidence which he could provide was about Cranmer's expulsion of him from the Canterbury Six Preachers back in 1541, and about his two subsequent spells of imprisonment. Among the other witnesses, Richard Smith was not able to do anything more interesting than take his own revenge on the man who had savaged him in the *Answer*, by confirming the authorship of Cranmer's eucharistic writings. Serles's contribution was in fact about the only unusual testimony in a succession of dons who simply confirmed what the whole world knew: Cranmer was the symbol of everything that had changed in the Church between 1533 and 1553. The charges were proved, and from that moment, the eighty-day summons to Rome became fully operative. While that period ran, Cranmer's life would be spared.

Cranmer had no doubt drafted in advance much of his appeal to the Queen, a very substantial text; it was closely related to the speech which he had made at the trial in reply to Brooks and which had announced his intention of appealing, but it was also augmented with points which had been raised during the proceedings. He sent it up to Court via one of the Oxford bailiffs to await the arrival of Martin and Story to present it to the Queen, and he also presented the two proctors with further material, which seems to have been a version of his formal reply to Brooks.[63] Once more he declared his complete loyalty to the two monarchs and his grief at the imposition of a foreign power in the realm, and he took as his major theme the arbitrary tyranny of canon law: he must have been given access to reference books for the sake of this appeal during his temporarily more relaxed confinement, because he was able to make substantial quotations from a variety of sources. Most important among these were two citations from canon law which had first appeared long ago in his collections of extracts; these were used to hammer home again the theme of the incompatibility of canon law with English law.[64] Their message made it inevitable, said Cranmer, that Philip and Mary would be cursed by

62 On Croke's career, Emden, *Oxford to 1540*, pp. 151–2.

63 Cox 2, pp. 446–54. I suspect that Cranmer's second letter to the Queen, ibid., p. 454, is simply the ending of the main letter, which otherwise ends very abruptly.

64 Cf. Cox 2, p. 448 with Strype, *Cranmer*, Oxford edn 3, pp. 744, 870.

the Church as heretics for tolerating English laws which encroached on ecclesiastical liberties, and he cited examples of such laws right up to *praemunire*. It was a *reductio ad absurdum* logic, which like all such arguments ignored the compromises and complexities of history, but also contained a dangerous germ of truth: Philip and Mary would indeed find their jurisdiction deadlocked with that of Pope Paul IV after Cranmer's death, in the clash over whether Pole should be replaced as papal legate and recalled to Rome. There can be little doubt that Cranmer had been told of the accession of a rabidly anti-Spanish pope that summer; with two decades of knowledge of international affairs, he would not be slow to draw the conclusion that the implications were both sinister for the future of England and useful for his purpose.

The letter then broadened from a discussion of 'the laws of this realm' into a consideration of 'the laws of God': the purely theological crimes of the papacy. First there was a long consideration of Cranmer's great achievement, the liturgy in the vernacular, then a shorter attack on the Pope for taking away the administration of two kinds in communion, and then a return to the question of jurisdiction: the papacy's claim to universal monarchy. This claim was the proof, said Cranmer, of the Pope's identity with Antichrist. His case for rejecting papal obedience was complete, and now he launched into a defence of his belief in the eucharist. This was familiar ground, and phrased in familiar ways: he claimed that the Church of Rome for a thousand years had believed as he did, until the invention of transubstantiation. In an afterthought, the text then returned for a third time to the question of jurisdiction, with Cranmer making an inept effort to explain why he had not accepted Brooks as his judge during the trial: Brooks was twice perjured, he said, as having broken his oath against Rome by becoming a Roman judge, and by taking contradictory oaths to the Queen and to the Pope when he became a bishop. That was rich, coming from a man whose own career involved the mirror-image of Brooks's actions. His final plea to the Queen, in what seems to be the last section of the same letter, asked her to consider the similar contradictions of her own two coronation oaths, and he asked also for long-term access to writing materials and research tools before making his journey to Rome.

It is difficult to know what Cranmer expected the Queen to make of this undeferential document, rather more intransigent than his previous approach in late 1554: she consulted Martin as to whether she should even read it. Her response was swift and drastic: within a few days of the delegates leaving Oxford, Cranmer was returned to strict confinement, and for the time being he was forbidden all contact with the outside world. His reappearance in the world had sparked an unhealthy degree of interest, and too many people were getting in touch with him.[65] One curious confirmation that the Oxford trio

65 *Cranmer's Recantacyons*, pp. 35–6.

were indeed a nationwide sensation at this time, and were considered as likely to be accessible, comes from as far away as Essex: about Michaelmas 1555, a traveller from Cambridgeshire, Henry Orinel, had arguments in a Colchester tavern with an Anabaptist proselytizer, and was so upset by the discussion of the divinity of Christ which followed that he would have gone to Oxford to consult with Ridley and Latimer, had he not met with someone locally 'to satisfy [his] conscience in the mean season'. Orinel was no Cambridge don, but an ordinary evangelical husbandman or yeoman, who still looked to the leaders of his faith to help him out with a theological problem.[66]

The trials of Latimer and Ridley came at the end of the month and the beginning of October; neither man gave any more ground than Cranmer, and they managed to avoid the loss of face which he had suffered in his cross-examination by Thomas Martin.[67] At the same time, a fresh attempt was made to bring them to their senses by private conference. It actually seems to have been Cranmer, in his September appeal to the Queen, who signalled to the government that the effort might be worthwhile. Towards the end of the surviving copy, the text seems to have been subsequently tampered with: it now reads as a scatological joke which was unlikely to be a success with the devout and straitlaced Queen, in which Cranmer said that if he could be persuaded of the papal case in any of these matters, he would submit himself to the Pope, 'not only to kiss his feet, but another part also'. This would have been a disastrous and undignified sally in an appeal to a monarch; to judge from the text subsequently quoted back to Cranmer by Cardinal Pole, it seems to have read originally as a genuine offer to discuss the issues and find the truth, an offer which was in fact now taken up by the authorities.[68] The man chosen was a theological expert who stood outside the English squabbles of the last thirty years, and so might command more respect from the prisoners than the array of former colleagues or academic juniors who had so far met them: he was the Spanish Dominican theologian, Pedro de Soto, a very able theologian and former confessor to the Holy Roman Emperor, who would go on to have an international scholarly reputation. However, de Soto had little luck in this first phase of his Oxford task. He started with Cranmer, who after his initial characteristically courteous reception of a foreigner, moved from being 'a student, to a very troublesome audience, and finally an open enemy'. Ridley and Latimer proved even less receptive; indeed one of them refused to speak to de Soto.[69]

Ridley and Latimer therefore went defiant to their deaths, which were staged on 16 October, after ceremonies the previous day to disgrade them from the priesthood: Ridley made sure that his disgrading lacked any

66 Marsh, *Family of Love*, pp. 54–5, 285–6.
67 Loades, *Oxford Martyrs*, pp. 204–14.
68 Cf. text at Cox 2, p. 454 with Strype, *Cranmer*, 2, no. 89, p. 451. Pole would not have let pass this gross joke if it had been in the original text.
69 *Cranmer's Recantacyons*, p. 43; *C.S.P. Venetian 1555–56*, no. 256.

liturgical decorum. The two men were to be burnt outside the city gate in Broad Street, in front of Balliol College; they were led to the stake past Cranmer's prison, hoping to catch a glimpse of him and to shout a greeting, but at that moment he was arguing once more with de Soto's team. Once the ceremony was under way, however, Cranmer was brought to a tower of the gatehouse to watch what was going on: the author of *Cranmer's Recantacyons* says that a major aim of the day in the government's eyes was to frighten him out of his defiance, and as many eyes in the crowd were on him as on the two victims at the stake. He witnessed the perfunctory sermon from Richard Smith, and the peculiarly unfortunate prolonging of Ridley's agony as his brother-in-law George Shipside inadvertently stemmed the progress of the flames in his desperate efforts to pile on more fuel. According to the Catholic commentator, Cranmer was very publicly traumatized by the awful sight, tearing off his cap, falling to his knees and desperately bewailing what was happening. Latimer, by contrast to Ridley, had died fairly quickly, having bequeathed the English Reformation the last of his many memorable phrases: 'Be of good comfort, Master Ridley, and play the man. We shall this day light such a candle, by God's grace, in England, as I trust shall never be put out.' Cranmer would not have been able to hear these words, and it is doubtful whether they were ever reported to him in his hour of need.[70]

It was Cardinal Pole and not the Queen who eventually wrote from Court to Cranmer, first in a letter which *Cranmer's Recantacyons* rather ruefully said approached the size of a complete book – the Cardinal was never inclined to use two words where twenty would do. It was indeed a full-scale pamphlet, which was later put into print; Pole, who at this stage does not seem to have read the appeal to the Queen, enlarged in reproachful terms on the material of the sixteen interrogatories, but he concentrated in particular on refuting Cranmer's eucharistic errors. No doubt Pole had been long in preparing this first direct address to an adversary of more than two decades' standing, just as Cranmer had mulled over his address to the Queen.[71] He did not send the text to its subject straight away, but in his shock in the aftermath of the burnings, Cranmer seemed again receptive, this time imploring conference with Pole himself. On 23 October Pole finally sent a copy to 'that wretched man', a move which he almost immediately regretted when he received the news that in fact Pedro de Soto had failed to move Cranmer in any respect. What was the point of giving medicine to the terminally ill? he gloomily asked an

70 This account is conflated from Foxe 7, pp. 542–51 and *Cranmer's Recantacyons*, pp. 48–50. Latimer's last words were first recorded in the 1570 edition of Foxe, possibly on the authority of his old servant Augustine Bernher.

71 *Cranmer's Recantacyons*, pp. 36–43; the full text is Lambeth MS 2007, ff. 245–58. Ridley, *Cranmer*, p. 382, dates this letter to summer 1554, from Strype, *Cranmer*, 2, p. 118, where it is merely described as written 'a little after the disputation at Oxford'; that could equally well mean September 1555, a date which fits all the other evidence better.

Italian friend – and then hastily corrected himself. A different rule applied to diseases of the soul, and he must persevere.[72]

The Cardinal's chance to try again came quite soon, when Queen Mary decided to hand over to him the responsibility for responding to Cranmer's two September appeals. Rather than give Cranmer the benefit of the face-to-face conference which he had requested, Pole wrote from Court on 6 November combining a reply on the Queen's behalf with an attempt 'by reason to show you the error of your opinion'; this letter, written once more at considerable length, survives only in mutilated form.[73] There was little that could be said by now that was new, and it cannot be said that Pole's tone was one of detached reason: the first section once more bitterly reproached Cranmer for his history of disobedience, the next answered Cranmer's favourite theme of the incompatibility of papal and royal law, and the next dismissed his views on the eucharist. Pole made great play with Cranmer's perjury in his accepting the see of Canterbury, which was an effective counterblast to his attempt to criticize Bishop Brooks on the same grounds. He ended with a desperate plea to the prisoner to save himself at this last moment: 'I say if you be not plucked out by the ear, you be utterly undone both body and soul.'

For the moment Cranmer remained deaf to this entreaty. At some point in mid-November, he managed to smuggle out of his prison a letter to a sympathetic Oxford lawyer, possibly Richard Lyell, a Fellow of All Souls who had been Dean of most of his archiepiscopal peculiars since 1538, and who had been more positive than many civil lawyers to the religious changes of the reign of Edward VI.[74] It had suddenly occurred to the ex-Archbishop that he ought to follow in Luther's footsteps and appeal to a General Council: this seemed to him only logical, since 'the lawsuit is between the Roman Pontiff and me, and no man may be an indifferent judge in his own case'. However, he needed legal advice as to how such an appeal ought to be framed, and at what moment it was best to spring it on the Church's legal system: it was a matter which required the utmost secrecy. His main reason now for the appeal was to buy time so that he could finish his extended reply to 'Marcus Antonius Constantius', the cause which had been preoccupying him at intervals ever since 1553, and on which now at last he was working. One wonders whether the news of Stephen Gardiner's fatal illness had reached him; the Lord Chancellor died on 12 November. It was ironic that at the moment when Cranmer would know that he had physically survived his old enemy, his

72 *C.S.P. Venetian* 1555–56, nos. 255, 256 (which must be just before 255 in date).

73 Strype, *Cranmer*, 2, no. 89, pp. 450–61 (Cox 2, pp. 534–41); some of the missing sections are reflected in the summary in *Cranmer's Recantacyons*, pp. 43–7.

74 Cox 2, pp. 455–6, and cf. Foxe 8, pp. 760–61. On Lyell, see Emden, *Oxford to 1540*, p. 368, and H.M.C. *Hatfield MSS* 1, p. 97. Another possible candidate is Anthony Hussey, but he has no definite Oxford connection (cf. Emden, *Oxford to 1540*, p. 684).

consistent and careful preservation of his integrity over two and a half years of mental assault began to crumble.

Two sources illuminate Cranmer's last months. One is an oddity indeed: a detailed financial account from 30 September 1555 by the last pair of Oxford bailiffs who had to house, feed and eventually burn Latimer and Cranmer (Ridley was the responsibility of the Mayor's deputy, Edmund Irish). It survives thanks to the accident that Mary did not complete the bailiffs' reimbursement, paying them only £20 out of the £63 and more which they had spent; they had to wait until Elizabeth's reign in 1566 to claim the difference, and they then petitioned Archbishop Parker for help. He organized a whip-round among his episcopal colleagues, with the bizarre result that the Protestant bishops of Elizabeth's Church ended up paying for the faggots, stakes, posts and labour which had gone into burning Latimer, Ridley and Cranmer: 'the case is miserable, the debt is just', as Laurence Humphrey wrote in perplexity to Archbishop Parker from Oxford. One wonders whether Mary's bishops would have had such a highly developed sense of fairness. However, it is interesting that Parker and his colleagues accepted the accounts as accurate and realistic, and we ought to take them seriously as a record that whatever psychological pressure and humiliation the Marian authorities visited on their star prisoners, at least they fed them well. Cranmer's diet was more lavish than Latimer's, either because of his higher rank or because it was Latimer's decision to eat more sparsely; boiled meat, roast beef, goose, rabbit, fresh salmon and fruit appeared at the former Archbishop's table, with appropriate adjustments for the Advent and Lenten fasts, and there was beer to drink during the day. The daily bill for him during the autumn was between 4s and 3s 6d, and besides his two guards he also had the accommodation of a personal servant allowed for. The man was almost certainly not an evangelical sympathizer; he may have already been that Nicholas Woodson who was soon to play a fateful part in the prisoner's life. With the knowledge that Latimer and Ridley had finally gone, Cranmer was left to preserve his spiritual identity with no human help to hand.[75]

The second source, already occasionally used above, comes into its own as Cranmer entered his last turbulent months: the Latin account entitled *Bishop Cranmer's Recantacyons*. This virulently Catholic manuscript from the Bibliothèque Nationale in Paris was only put into print in 1885, and then in an obscure setting; opinions about its value have varied. A.F. Pollard in his life of Cranmer sneered at it, but rather undermined his case by dismissing its 'strange stories of attempted rescues, the appearance of comets, etc.': the appearance of a comet was in fact one of the authentic events of Cranmer's last days.[76] In fact, it is a circumstantial and scholarly narrative, and it has close

75 C.C.C.C. MS 128, ff. 367–401. Cf. the order for payment to the previous Mayor and bailiffs, *A.P.C. 1554–56*, p. 233.

76 Pollard, *Cranmer*, pp. 361–2n. On the comet, cf. *Noailles* 5, p. 320; *C.S.P. Venetian 1555–56*, no. 429.

associations with the circle of Pole and Bonner, the people most likely to be accurately informed about the events in Oxford. It was found among the papers of Nicholas Harpsfield, Marian Archdeacon of Canterbury and trusted aide to Cardinal Pole; Nicholas's brother John (Bonner's Archdeacon of London) was intimately involved in Cranmer's last days, and Pole was naturally keenly interested in the fate of his predecessor.[77] The narrative exhibits Nicholas Harpsfield's characteristically convoluted style, and often overlaps in its content with works which are definitely his; there is really no good reason to deny its authorship to him. Naturally the tract is viciously biased, and it has the clear purpose of discrediting Cranmer in the light of the dramatic events of his last day of life, but it has as good a claim to be trusted as the accounts of Foxe which have the opposite polemical aim in mind; wherever its statements and chronology can be cross-checked, it proves to be accurate. It will be treated with the respect which it deserves – that is, with equal respect to Foxe's testimony – as we follow the sudden change in Cranmer's circumstances and morale.

Cranmer's Recantacyons tells us that Cranmer had a sister who was still a devout Catholic, and who despite their religious disagreements was now doing all she could for him, lobbying Queen Mary and Pole. This sister is usually thought to be Alice Cranmer, the former Cistercian nun whom the Archbishop had made Prioress of Minster in Sheppey twenty years before, but it is not certain that Alice was still alive at this time.[78] Ex-nun or not, the Queen was notoriously susceptible to appeals for help from women. It may therefore indeed have been the sister's intervention and promise to work on her brother which inspired a radical change of policy with the prisoner, transferring him from Bocardo to confinement in a college of the University; however, one notes that this was the same policy which had been contemplated for the three prisoners twelve months before and not then put into effect. From Bocardo, Cranmer was taken to the Deanery at Christ Church, a move which can be precisely dated to 11 December, the day on which the bailiffs' accounts show that they were given a respite from their prison catering responsibilities until mid-February. His host as Dean was Dr Richard Marshall, who was also Vice-Chancellor of the University. Marshall had come up to Oxford from Kent in the days of Archbishop Warham, and it is noticeable that when he gave evidence against Cranmer at the September trial, he said that their acquaintance stretched back only sixteen years. Cranmer's episcopal regime had not offered Marshall any preferment in his native diocese; his Kent was that of the Maid of Kent and of the Prebendary Plotters. He would now have charge of the prisoner for the next two months.[79]

77 For testimony that Harpsfield had principal authority in Canterbury diocese under Pole, even outranking Bishop Thornden, see Foxe 7, p. 297.

78 Baskerville, 'A sister of Archbishop Cranmer', p. 288; *Cranmer's Recantacyons*, pp. 51, 93.

79 Emden, *Oxford to 1540*, pp. 380–81, and Cox 2, p. 552.

Christ Church was a startlingly different environment after more than two years of prison cells. If Cranmer was still a prisoner, it was now in the midst of a large academic community which centred on the life of England's newest cathedral foundation. He was treated as a guest, if a rather odd variety of guest, and was given the chance of exercise in the open air, even playing bowls; around him, in contrast to the isolation of his Bocardo cell, there moved the busy world of a college and cathedral caught up in the gathering liturgical drama of Advent and Christmas. It seems to have been at least a fortnight before a serious effort was made to work on him. Once more the strategy was to approach him through an outsider to the English ecclesiastical scene, Fray Juan de Villagarcia, like Pedro de Soto a highly talented Spanish Dominican friar; he had recently been chosen as Regius Professor of Divinity in the University. Villagarcia was initially reluctant to meet Cranmer, but was eventually persuaded and began discussions with him on 31 December.[80]

Initial arguments were on papal primacy, the issue which had dominated Cranmer's clashes with his opponents in the September trial and its aftermath; after two hours came the first sign of a chink in the defences of a thoughtful man used to weighing matters up carefully, when Cranmer conceded that he would not be so hostile to the notion of papal primacy if he did not plainly see the papacy defend manifest errors. Discussion then shifted to new ground: purgatory, hardly a matter which had entered at all into English public debate since Parliament had abolished the chantries in 1547. The two men argued in detail about the patristic evidence, congenial territory for the old scholar. Villagarcia was a worthy opponent; having mulled over their discussion, he returned from his afternoon lecture on 1 January 1556 triumphantly flourishing texts from Augustine, whose implications Cranmer admitted that he had not previously considered. Under the influence of a good dinner with a man whose scholarship he clearly respected, he went so far as to say that he could freely admit that the Church had always allowed prayer for the dead, but that was all. This was not really much of a concession: Bucer had said exactly the same in his *Censura* on the 1549 Prayer Book, while showing no enthusiasm for the practice; the admission implied nothing about purgatory. The argument reached deadlock.[81]

At Cranmer's request, the two men shifted their debate back to the role of the papacy, and Cranmer's cherished view of the General Council as the ultimate decision-maker in the Catholic Church – Villagarcia would not have known of the plans which the prisoner was secretly nurturing for an appeal to just such a Council. Cranmer felt on safe ground in scorning Villagarcia's claim that all General Councils had been called by papal authority: how could one say this of the first Oecumenical Council of Nicaea in 325? If that could be proved, he said flatly, 'I will indeed openly affirm the Pope to have been

80 *Cranmer's Recantacyons*, pp. 53–5; Foxe 8, p. 80.

81 *Bucer*, ed. Whitaker, pp. 50–53; *Cranmer's Recantacyons*, pp. 55–8.

and to be now head of the Church'. Villagarcia sniffed a possible victory. Calling up Dr Marshall as witness, he got Cranmer to sign an undertaking embodying his words; if the case could not be proved, it concluded, Brother Juan would be taken to be a liar. After a night of concentrated reading, Villagarcia came back with a handful of extracts from the *Chronica Maiora* of Isidore and the standard patristic text known as the Tripartite History; these stated that Nicaea ought to have been called by the then Pope, Sylvester I, and that Councils ought to be called by papal authority. Cranmer angrily and scornfully said that these were texts in a recent edition corrupted by papists, which resulted in an ill-tempered contest leafing through piles of various editions, and a systematic search in the college libraries throughout the University. None of them proved his contention. It was a bad moment, and he had been trapped.[82]

This may sound a trivial incident over a piece of pedantry, but in fact it provides a good rationale for the subsequent events which would nearly capsize Cranmer's sense of self-worth over the next three months. Cranmer's whole strategy after the disaster of his involvement in Queen Jane's regime was to separate out the questions of obedience to the Crown and obedience to the Pope. He had come freely to admit his crime against royal authority: distressing enough for a man who had devoted twenty years of his life to proclaiming the vital God-given nature of that authority. However, some consolation had been his unswerving commitment to the idea that the Pope was Antichrist. Mary might have provoked Cranmer to grief when she perverted the Royal Supremacy in the interest of restoring the Pope, but she had also given him back a cause. He could make a careful distinction in his various public statements between his legitimate obedience to her and the duty laid on him by his old master Henry VIII to oppose Rome and all its errors: it was a stand which held more consistency than the Marian regime's own unhappy position up to the reconciliation of the realm to Rome in November 1554. Now, however, if there was even the slightest trace of evidence in early sources that Roman authority was part of the fabric of God's purpose, his whole case stood in peril. If the Pope was not Antichrist, what did that say about his other beliefs? Were the King and Queen right when they ordered him to obey the Pope? Was the unity of the Church more important than its corruption? The questions would soon begin to flood in on him.

As the first cracks in Cranmer's spiritual self-confidence appeared in Oxford, far away in Rome his deprivation and condemnation had at last been completed. Progress was reasonably swift after the account of the Oxford proceedings reached the papal Consistory at the end of November. The Consistory was treated to a reading by Cardinal Puteo, the Inquisitor-General, of translations from selected highlights of Cranmer's heretical writings; the thought of his evangelical sentiments echoing through the Vatican might

82 *Cranmer's Recantacyons*, pp. 58–62.

have amused the prisoner in Oxford, but it is doubtful whether he ever had the chance to hear about it.[83] To make absolutely sure of the legal niceties, Cranmer was not declared deprived until 4 December, the day after the expiry of eighty days not from his initial citation, but from the end of the Oxford trial proceedings. Ten days later the paperwork was completed, and Pole was declared to be Archbishop of Canterbury; despite the great applause in the Consistory, behind the scenes there remained long-standing tensions which would soon produce a total and open breach between the Cardinal and Pope Paul IV. Nevertheless, the process for deposing and degrading Cranmer was launched on its long journey; on 27 December 1555 Somerset Herald set out for England with it and with Pole's bulls for Canterbury.[84] He arrived in London on 22 January, at the same time as a major delegation led by Pole's secretary, the Abbot of San Saluto, which was entrusted with the vital task of establishing peace between the Empire and France.[85]

It may have been this important conjunction of missions which prompted Juan de Villagarcia to go to London on business; in his absence, he assigned the business of disputation with Cranmer to others. Cranmer was still holding out about papal power, and indeed he was reported in London in late January as more obstinate than ever, yet he had complained before Villagarcia's departure that he felt under too much pressure to do himself justice.[86] The clash about patristic editions and papal authority may have badly jolted his self-confidence in an area of scholarship where he had long felt the master, and it must have been significant that he was now meeting a different quality of opponent. For two decades, Cranmer had argued from a position of strength against the English representatives of a Catholic Church in decay: a Church which had been on the defensive and continually losing ground to the revolution of which he was one of the spearheads. Now he was meeting scholars from Spain, where Catholicism had never ceased to be a vigorous and aggressively self-confident faith, just at the moment when the Roman Church as a whole was regaining its nerve and ceasing to look like a spent force. Besides this culture-shock, he was under terrible emotional strain: he had always relied much on a small intimate circle of trusted friends, and they had all been taken from him. Not surprisingly, his health was now frail; the author of *Cranmer's Recantacyons* would later suggest that soon before his death he was suffering from an advanced heart condition.[87] In an isolation which was spiritual rather than physical, he cast in the role of friend and confidant the attendant who was guarding him, a simple but devout traditionalist Catholic

83 *C.S.P. Venetian 1555–56*, no. 295; P.R.O., S.P. 69/7, f. 132 (*C.S.P. Foreign 1553–58*, no. 440).

84 *C.S.P. Venetian 1555–56*, nos 303, 312, 319; P.R.O., S.P. 69/8 f. 8 (*C.S.P. Foreign 1553–58*, no. 455). Papal commission to delegates, 14 December, Foxe 8, pp. 69–71.

85 *C.S.P. Venetian 1555–56*, nos 360, 363.

86 *Cranmer's Recantacyons*, p. 62; *C.S.P. Venetian 1555–56*, no. 363.

87 *Cranmer's Recantacyons*, pp. 109–10.

called Nicholas Woodson. Woodson's friendship came to be his only emotional support, and to please Woodson he began giving way to everything that he had fought for twenty years and more.

Cranmer's fall first came on the question of worship. This may be a sign of the loneliness of a man who was isolated in the midst of a community going about its daily approaches to God with order and solemnity: the strain of nonconformity became too much. While Villagarcia was still away, Cranmer took the plunge and appeared in the Cathedral, participated in liturgical processions and attended mass: this was his capitulation to the rite that he hated and had demolished so effectively in his two main polemical works. So sudden was the surrender that Villagarcia was not even aware of it when he returned from London, and straight away confronted Cranmer aggressively about what he now thought about the primacy of the Pope. Cranmer was still trying to hold out on this matter, and a bitter shouting-match ensued. This proved a crucial moment, because Woodson was furious when he heard of Cranmer's continuing obstinacy about the Pope: he had been much encouraged when he saw his prisoner reject heresy in terms of his behaviour by going to mass, and had confidently expected that soon Cranmer's words would match his actions. Woodson showed his feelings by storming out of the house and breaking off all contact.[88]

Cranmer was appalled at the loss. Very early on 28 January, he called Woodson to ask the reason for the breach, and begged him to spend the day with him. Woodson agreed, on condition that 'you pull yourself together and choose to be counted among us'. Still Cranmer begged for time – hardly surprisingly, for if he were to give way to the brutally simple request, he would be rejecting the whole of his public ministry. His continuing hesitations as late as breakfast-time provoked another furious walk-out from Woodson, and Cranmer was alone. He fainted with the strain; his physical collapse was total. It was only his subsequent bitter weeping that alerted another attendant in the next room that his spiritual capitulation was well-advanced as well.[89] Woodson was overjoyed, and Cranmer was ready to sign his first recantation. Nevertheless, he was still desperately fighting to preserve his past: he tried to cast the statement in language which would save his old concerns for Parliamentary authority and divine commands. 'Forasmuch as the King and Queen's Majesties, by consent of their Parliament, have received the Pope's authority within this realm, I am content to submit myself to their laws herein, and to take the Pope for chief head of this Church of England, so far as God's laws and the laws and customs of this realm will permit.' He must have remembered that long before, in 1531, it was by the same qualification 'insofar as the law of Christ allows' that the bishops and clergy of Convocation had tried to safeguard their independence from Henry VIII; and he ought to

88 Ibid., pp. 62–5.
89 Ibid., pp. 65–8, and cf. ibid., pp. 109–10.

have realized that the formula had won those churchmen no more than a temporary respite.[90]

Cranmer's turmoil was now desperate: the government would later describe it as a moment of 'inconstancy and unstableness'. His first statement was sent off to the Queen and Privy Council, but once it was gone, he cancelled it, and within twenty-four hours he tried to produce a text which would give even less ground; this has not survived. By contrast, it was not long before he had swung back in the direction of capitulation, with a statement which made no mention of Parliament, simply submitting himself 'to the Catholic Church of Christ, and to the Pope, supreme head of the same Church, and unto the King and the Queen's Majesties, and unto all their laws and ordinances'. In this there was now no hint that canon law and the kingdom's law could clash, the point to which he had clung all through the previous autumn, and which was still implicit in his first statement. The text of this second step towards the Pope's Church was again rapidly forwarded to the Privy Council, and it must have come at much the same time as a new public proof of his descent into abject obedience: his devout attendance at the first major liturgical event after the Christmas season, the feast of the Purification of Our Lady or Candlemas (2 February). Eight years before, Cranmer's 'Homily of Good Works annexed to Faith' had scorned the Candlemas ceremonies even before they had officially been declared illegal; now it must have been a sensation when he appeared to take a candle in traditional fashion. Soon after that, he even consented to take part in the singing of a requiem mass.[91]

However, now Cranmer again drew back from capitulation. The legal process of destroying him, set in motion by the Roman documentation, was not halted just because he had apparently admitted defeat, and this may have persuaded him to return to defiance: in the knowledge that he was now going to face formal disgrading from the ministry, he secretly planned to make his mark on the occasion by presenting the formal appeal to Rome which he had begun contemplating in November. He may have been strengthened in his resolve by the clear evidence that his major concession had gained him no advantage; quite the reverse. The public excitement caused by his behaviour had led to rumours that he was about to be discharged, and in order to scotch these stories, he was transferred back from Christ Church to Bocardo; the bailiffs started paying for his keep again from Friday 14 February.[92] This was also the day appointed for his disgrading in Christ Church Cathedral; the delegates commissioned by the Pope were Edmund Bonner

90 The first and second surviving recantations are pr. Cox 2, p. 563; see also *Cranmer's Recantacyons*, p. 68.

91 *Cranmer's Recantacyons*, p. 63, where these attendances are related out of sequence in order to group them with his earlier attendances at the liturgy. Cf. official comment on the two statements, pr. Cox 2, p. 563.

92 Ibid., p. 68; C.C.C.C. MS 128, p. 393.

and Thomas Thirlby, and John Harpsfield, Archdeacon of London, travelled down from London with them as the principal member of Bonner's entourage. Bonner and Harpsfield were predictable choices, but it was a cruel addition to the many uncongenial duties which Thirlby had been forced to perform in his career to be responsible for the ritual humiliation of his old Cambridge friend.

To begin with, the prisoner was placed dramatically high up in the Cathedral rood-loft beside the figure of the rood itself, as if in a show-case, while John Harpsfield preached on his crimes. At the end of this first attack, the prisoner turned to the rood beside which he was standing and said that he made it the sole judge of his fortunes – an irony, commented *Cranmer's Recantacyons*, coming from the man whose iconoclastic orders had destroyed so many roods. However, it was also not a promising sign for those who were expecting a humble penitent in the mould of the previous few weeks. A prisoner who trusted in the cross of Christ alone and not in the justice of the holy father in Rome sounded uncomfortably like an evangelical. Worse was to come. Cranmer's defiance became more explicit after he had been led down from the rood-loft and up to the high altar for the reading of the bishops' papal commission, which he interrupted with protests that he had not been able to defend himself at Rome.[93]

Foxe and the Catholic narrator concur that the formal disgrading which followed was a highly uncomfortable pantomime. Before it could get under way, Cranmer added his own carefully staged contribution of drama to the proceedings: he pulled out his prepared paper, and shouted out 'I do appeal to the next General Council', first in English and then in Latin. He called on those standing by to witness his actions, especially and meaningfully singling out Dr James Courthope, who had testified against him at the September trial, and whose apparent evangelical enthusiasm in the previous reign had won him a royal chaplaincy. After some hesitation and a downright refusal to accept the document from Bonner's registrar, the principal notary, Thirlby agreed to take it: the Bishop of Ely became very upset as the disgrading ritual was set in motion and Bonner's officials began solemnly dressing Cranmer up in mocked-up versions of the archiepiscopal robes to which he was entitled, in order to strip them from him. Bonner, savouring a chance to revenge himself for past humiliations, relentlessly went over a similar litany of accusation to Harpsfield's previous address, with Cranmer breaking in on the recitation with protests. Thirlby, thoroughly embarrassed at the tone of the proceedings, tried to curtail Bonner's diatribe, and Foxe claims that later the two bishops were embroiled in a row which marred their dinner. Cranmer, however, also broke the rules of the occasion; he treated the whole ceremony with deliberate flippancy, and questioned the right of the two delegates to exercise

93 My account of the disgrading is conflated from *Cranmer's Recantacyons*, pp. 68–73, Foxe 8, pp. 71–80, and the official account in Bonner's Register, pr. ibid., Appendix 2. Cox 2, pp. 224–7, collates variants in the text of Cranmer's appeal given by Foxe.

legatine powers over him. He was not going to suffer the ceremony passively any more than had Ridley before him.

Although the full appeal to a General Council was not heard that day, the text which Foxe has preserved provides a precious snapshot of the position to which Cranmer had returned. It was an attempt to extricate himself from the morass into which he had strayed over the previous few weeks, beginning with a solemn protestation that he meant to speak nothing 'against one holy catholic and apostolical Church, or the authority thereof'. To be admissible as an appeal, his statement would have to acknowledge papal authority, but Cranmer did so with careful qualification: 'although the Bishop of Rome (whom they call Pope) beareth the room of Christ on earth, and hath authority of God, yet by that power or authority he is not become unsinnable, neither hath he received that power to destroy, but to edify the congregation'. The 'law of nature' allowed appeal from his authority, and the natural final appeal was to a General Council.[94] Cranmer, the life-long sympathizer with conciliarism, now unequivocally stated that 'it is openly enough confessed, that a holy General Council, lawfully gathered together in the Holy Ghost, and representing the holy Catholic Church, is above the Pope, especially in matters concerning faith'. This argument was clearly modelled on that of Martin Luther's appeal back in November 1518; one wonders whether Cranmer remembered his former indignation at Luther's cavalier attitude to general councils, in the tranquillity of Cambridge so long ago. Now came the appeal proper, in which the prisoner styled himself 'Thomas Cranmer, Archbishop of Canterbury, or in time past ruler of the metropolitan church of Canterbury, Doctor in Divinity'.

Six reasons for the appeal followed. The first three were about procedure: his being prevented from making his appearance at Rome within eighty days, his being deprived of counsel during the proceedings before Brooks or of copies of his answers. The second trio returned to his own history and necessarily contradicted his earlier statements about papal authority: he cited his previous oath to Henry VIII against papal authority in England, the financial ruin which should follow for England if papal obedience was admitted, and the damage which should also be done to royal jurisdiction and to 'the most holy decrees of councils'. There followed a brief history of the position of Rome in the Church: at first 'the mother of other churches' and a shining example, then an example of corruption. From the see of Rome as it now existed, no reformation of abuses could be expected, particularly in his own case, so he repeated his appeal to what he now called 'a free General Council, that shall hereafter lawfully be, and in a sure place'. Martin Luther had used a similar phrase in 1518, but Luther's whole text was less comprehensive in its denunciation of papal error than this uncompromising docu-

94 Cf. a similar ambiguity of attitude in Melanchthon: Gerrish, *Continuing the Reformation*, pp. 24–5.

ment. In a final section, Cranmer bluntly reaffirmed his adherence to his Edwardian views on the eucharist, saying that he was accused of heresy merely because he sought to discuss sacramental theology exclusively in the terminology used by the early Fathers 'in their treatises on the sacrament', and because he would not allow 'the doctrine lately brought in' – in other words, transubstantiation.

After the disgrading ceremony, Cranmer was taken back to Bocardo, which he would not now leave until the day of his death. However, he was not left alone: his unexpected defiance had ruined the impact of what ought to have been an edifying show of repentance, and Bonner was determined to undo the damage. Noticeably Thirlby was not present when the Bishop of London, John Harpsfield and Juan de Villagarcia returned to the attack, taking up the matter of the eucharist which Cranmer had raised in his appeal. Very quickly the old man, probably exhausted by the drama of 14 February and probably in poor health, began giving ground, trying to find a way of avoiding further conflict. In reply to Villagarcia's sarcastic enquiry as to whether all the saints who disagreed with his eucharistic theology would perish because they were ignorant of his 'new faith', Cranmer did not try to correct the slur on the novelty of his views as he would readily have done in earlier days, but said feebly 'Indeed I think that you can attain salvation through your faith and likewise I can in mine' – a statement which would sound unexceptionable in modern ecumenical discussions, but in the polemical atmosphere of the sixteenth-century Reformation was a gift to a ruthless interrogator. So, said Villagarcia triumphantly, the matter of corporal presence was not a question of the essence of the faith! What, then, of Paul's claim in 1 Corinthians 11 that his narrative of the eucharist was 'received from the Lord'? Cranmer made no attempt to expound what he understood by 'This is my body', but seemed disturbed, and tugging at his beard in his distress, declared that he had no answer.[95]

It was the perfect moment in which to force yet another written statement out of the prisoner. Yet in fact the affirmation which he now wrote out for Bonner with his own hand gave no ground at all from the position set out in his appeal; he took refuge once more in his loyalty to the Crown, promising to submit himself to Philip and Mary 'and to all their ordinances, as well concerning the Pope's supremacy as others'. Otherwise, the statement simply commended his 'book' – that is, his appeal – 'to the judgement of the Catholic Church, and of the next General Council'. However, Bonner quickly made it quite clear that this would not do. Cranmer should have no illusions that he could play for time; his appeal would not be allowed. So he tried again, presenting the Bishop of London on 16 February with the fourth of his surviving statements. If anything, this stonewalled even more. Dropping all reference to the abortive appeal, it simply affirmed his belief 'in all articles

95 *Cranmer's Recantacyons*, pp. 72–3.

and points of the Christian religion and Catholic faith, as the Catholic Church doth believe, and hath ever believed from the beginning. Moreover' – reaffirming against Villagarcia the authentic original character of his eucharistic doctrine – 'as concerning the sacrament of the Church, I believe as the said Catholic Church doth and hath believed from the beginning of Christian religion.' This was an answer answerless: it said no more than the *Defence* and the *Answer* had said in the reign of Edward VI. Bonner must have left Oxford a disappointed and angry man.[96]

Once more stalemate, therefore: Cranmer was still anxious to talk with his opponents, but he had yielded nothing of any use to them, and Villagarcia's continued remorseless arguments produced little result. However, within ten days, a dramatic shift took place, the trigger for which was brutally simple. On 24 February the writ was issued to the Mayor of Oxford for Cranmer's burning, and it was brought up from Westminster to Oxford probably the following day; the accompanying messengers announced that the date set for the execution was 7 March.[97] Suddenly the reality of his position hit Cranmer: no more postponement of reality, just the same awful death which he had witnessed for Ridley and Latimer, and which had then so profoundly affected him. It is not necessary to speculate that he was physically tortured into his change of heart.[98] After the miserable history of brain-washing and interrogation in the twentieth century, we are better placed than historians in the heyday of Victorian liberalism to understand the sort of pressures to which Cranmer had been subjected. There was good reason for a simple collapse in his morale, after it had rallied in such an equivocal way, fatally compromised by his yearning to conciliate while retaining his integrity.

Cranmer's Recantacyons now reports a man 'trembling in every limb' who assured Villagarcia of his wish to return to what the friar would understand by the Catholic faith. The result on 26 February was a statement which can truly be called a recantation. It is unlikely that he wrote it himself; the Catholic account merely says that Cranmer was ordered to sign it, and later Cranmer would make a distinction in the writings after his degradation between those which he had 'written' and those merely 'signed with my hand'.[99] The fact that this was the first of his statements to be written in Latin and not English suggests that its author was a foreigner, and there can be no more likely candidate than Villagarcia himself. Cranmer affirmed in this fifth document that he anathematized Luther and Zwingli and any heresy contrary

96 Cox 2, p. 563; *Cranmer's Recantacyons*, pp. 73–4.

97 *Cranmer's Recantacyons*, p. 75. *C.P.R. Philip and Mary 1556–58*, p. 53; text in Burnet 2 ii, pp. 412–14 (Bk. 2, no. 27); English translation in Brooks, *Cranmer in Context*, p. 111.

98 Brooks, *Cranmer in Context*, p. 98, appears to suggest that Cranmer was physically tortured.

99 Foxe 8, p. 88. Syddall (the statement's second witness) is named as Vice-Dean in Foxe, *Rerum gestarum*, 1, p. 725; cf. also Emden, *Oxford to 1540*, p. 551.

to sound doctrine; he not only acknowledged the Pope's power on earth, but also his position as the vicar of Christ. In precise detail he acknowledged the doctrine of transubstantiation, the full complement of seven sacraments and the doctrine of purgatory – in all things, indeed, that he believed in no other fashion than the Catholic and Roman Church, and that he repented his previous contrary belief. He begged for prayers, and begged that those who had been seduced by his example should return to the unity of the Church, repeating also his submission to the King and Queen and their laws, as in his fourth statement. The witnesses were Villagarcia himself and Henry Syddall, Vice-Dean of Christ Church.[100]

Still in a highly emotional state, Cranmer received the congratulations of Pedro de Soto, who had never managed to achieve anything like this result, and begged for his prayers. Naturally by now, the only service-books or primers available to him were those of the traditional Church. The liturgical season had by now moved on to Lent, and the penitential tone of the prayers which he used played dangerously on his sense of guilt and confusion, producing frequent outbursts of tears. In this mood, Cranmer asked for sacramental absolution: a vital capitulation to Roman authority. Pole was happy to grant authority for this, but after some hesitations from de Soto and Villagarcia about whether Cranmer could really be trusted, the task was performed by another friar, Richard. It was a moment of great emotional release, and in its aftermath he repeatedly bewailed his former disobedience to the Pope, and announced his joy at returning to the Catholic faith.

Now Cranmer was given Thomas More's *Dialogue of Comfort* to read: how appropriate for a penitent Roman Catholic convert. More had written this moving defence of the human soul against desolation and despair in the Tower of London under sentence of death: nothing could be better for Cranmer in his new-found faith, facing a similar fate. It was a work which although conceived against the background of the tragedy which had befallen the Catholic Church, breathed a serenity which was in sharp contrast to the tedious bitterness of More's earlier controversial writings; those might well have brought back unhelpful memories to the ex-archbishop. The book had first been put into print at the time of Cranmer's trial in November 1553, having been smuggled out of the Tower in 1535 and successfully concealed from King Henry's officials; it probably came as a startling revelation to Cranmer about his former adversary. Commenting on the choice of the *Dialogue*, he praised More's talent, and observed that he himself had opposed his execution. From there it was a short step to hearing mass, celebrated specially for him by Friar Richard, with the gaoler and his household present. It may even have been possible that his Catholic sister was present; she had

100 *Cranmer's Recantacyons*, pp. 75–9; text in Cox 2, pp. 563–4, but cf. the dated version from Bonner's Register, Foxe 8, Appendix 2. Cf. Brooks, *Cranmer in Context*, pp. 98–100.

certainly come to Oxford to be near him. At last Cranmer had found friends again, who loved him for his new-found faith.[101]

All this was spectacularly good news for the authorities in Church and commonwealth. The story was rapidly reported first to Lord Williams of Thame (who seems to have exercised a semi-formal royal lieutenancy in Oxfordshire through these events) and then to the Queen and Privy Council. Yet the exploitation of the coup was curiously botched and hesitant: the first sign of this was the mess which was made of printing Cranmer's new recantation. The friars were so excited at their spiritual conquest that they rushed out the text in a printed edition from the London press of William Ryddall and William Copland. Yet by 13 March, the Council had summoned the printers, put them under bond for their obedience and ordered them to surrender all copies for destruction (too late to prevent de Noailles, the French ambassador, acquiring one and sending it on to his royal master); a couple of booksellers followed some days later. According to the Venetian ambassador, the publication had caused uproar in London because it bore the signatures of two foreigners, de Soto and Villagarcia: a very plausible explanation, given the build-up of anti-Spanish feeling in the city over the previous two years. The scorn of Londoners decidedly undermined the value of the document and made it imperative that Cranmer should sign a further recantation before he died.[102]

The government had good reason not to ignore such forceful expressions of public opinion in the capital; it was now facing serious unrest. From January it had been worried about the appearance of broadsheets in London announcing that King Edward VI was in reality still alive in France, and although many of those involved were hanged in February, the Council received even more alarming revelations around 4 March of a really serious conspiracy between political exiles in France and evangelicals and political malcontents in England. The plot even involved plans for a major robbery at the Exchequer.[103] For the time being, this sensational news was kept from the public, but it was particularly unfortunate from the official standpoint that a spectacular comet now appeared over southern England and remained visible throughout the first half of the month; this caused the usual excitement and speculation about its meaning. Cranmer himself climbed on to the roof of his gatehouse prison at night to view it (he had used his new status as a good Catholic to persuade his gaoler's wife to arrange secretly for access to be

101 *Cranmer's Recantacyons*, pp. 80–81. The narrative's discussion of the *Dialogue of Comfort* is yet another link between it and the circle of More's biographer Nicholas Harpsfield. For a brilliant account of the *Dialogue*, see Fox, *More: History and Providence*, pp. 223–42. November 1553 edition: R.S.T.C. 18082.

102 *A.P.C. 1554–56*, pp. 247–9; *Noailles* 5, p. 319; *C.S.P. Venetian 1555–56*, no. 434. On London and the Spaniards, Loades, *Mary Tudor: a life*, pp. 256–7.

103 Loades, *Two Tudor Conspiracies*, pp. 148–9, 176–217, and see *C.S.P. Venetian 1555–56*, no. 434.

opened up). Elsewhere, agitators used its appearance to play on the widespread worries about England's political future as a Habsburg dependency, and there was wild talk of defending the kingdom's liberties; in London, twelve men (probably religious radicals) were arrested for proclaiming the imminence of the Last Judgement. The planned death of the former Primate of All England would be grist to the mill of such apocalyptic fears, and there were indeed reports of rowdy night-time gatherings outside his prison, supposedly with the intention of setting him free. Mary was alarmed enough to send out circular letters to provincial magistrates about the security situation nationwide.[104]

Against this background of acute political uncertainty, Cranmer's burning was now postponed from the original date on the first full weekend in March. Cranmer himself seems to have made an appeal for postponement of his death 'hoping that God might inspire him in the meantime', as the French ambassador put it: the government seized on the offer with hope, because once it was clear that the fifth recantation had proved a public relations fiasco, some other statement was needed from the penitent.[105] Cranmer had every reason for expecting last-minute clemency; he was, after all, now fully repentant of his heresy, shriven, and once more in perfect communion with the Church. By the normal practice of canon law, he should have won his life. Yet Mary was implacable. For her, Cranmer's crimes had transcended the norms; the line which she peddled to foreign observers (as reported back to her by her ambassador in Venice, Peter Vannes) was that 'his iniquity and obstinacy was so great against God and your Grace that your clemency and mercy could have no place with him, but you were constrained to minister justice'. She now sent the Provost of Eton, Dr Henry Cole, with the news that there was no hope of any further postponement of Cranmer's fate; the date for this mission of 17 March, supplied from London gossip by Girolamo Zanchi in Strassburg, fits exactly with the narrative of *Cranmer's Recantacyons*.[106]

At first Cranmer took the appalling and unexpected news with his habitual outward calm; he said that he had never been afraid of dying, but felt oppressed by the weight of all his sins. He then asked Cole to try to make sure that the personal estates left him by King Henry were passed on to his son Thomas, since he had lost them himself by his attainder and his heresy, but the thought of the boy was too much for him; he broke down in tears. Cole, an austere celibate who had never known what it was to feel the visceral depth of a father's love for his son, implacably retorted that Cranmer ought to be concentrating on his loyalty to the Catholic cause, and he left the prisoner in a state of nervous collapse. Cranmer was by now so exhausted that sleep was

104 *Noailles* 5, pp. 319–21; *C.S.P. Venetian 1555–56*, no. 429. On Cranmer, the comet and the disturbances, *Cranmer's Recantacyons*, p. 91.

105 *Noailles* 5, p. 319.

106 Vannes to Mary, P.R.O., S.P. 69/8 f. 156 (*C.S.P. Foreign 1553–58*, no. 499). Zanchi: Gorham, *Gleanings*, pp. 355–6, and cf. *Cranmer's Recantacyons*, p. 83.

not a problem, but it brought him no respite. That night, between 17 and 18 March, he is said to have had a terrifying dream, which although only reported by the author of *Cranmer's Recantacyons*, has considerable psychological plausibility.

Cranmer the scholar dreamt in terms of a book which he would have known throughout his academic career: Augustine's *City of God*, with its theme of the strong clash of two realms, of God and of the self. Equally, his dream structured itself around the central polemical point which he had hammered home in so many of his public statements over the previous two-and-a-half years: the clash of incompatible jurisdictions, royal and ecclesiastical, now transformed by his deep sense of guilt and failure. He saw two kings. 'He had sought the goodwill of one of them in a life which was often chasing after power; from the other he pleaded for help after death' – for they were Henry VIII and Christ. The horror of the situation was that they both now rejected him: Henry would say not a word, pushed him from his Court, and would not allow him to remain alive, while Christ too turned away from him and closed the gate of heaven. Cranmer, shut off from both life and the afterlife, could turn only to the mouth of hell. There could be no more eloquent parable or expression of his torment. He had now rejected the Royal Supremacy, but something told him that his self-abasement was not yet adequate or complete: the entrance guarded by the Apostle Peter and his successors on the papal throne was still not his. It was a message hammered home to him by Cole and his colleagues when the prisoner reported what had happened. It was not enough to whisper his sins to a priest under the seal of confession; he must make a proper public statement of the crimes which had been so publicly committed.[107]

Accordingly, on 18 March Cranmer embarked on the sixth, longest and most wretched of his successive statements.[108] We have no way of knowing whether he wrote it himself, except that it seems over-elaborate for a man in a state of physical and mental exhaustion, and the style does not altogether sound like him; perhaps Cole had brought with him from London a draft composed in the circle of Cardinal Pole. The opening, however, did echo the terms of his dream, confessing that he had offended 'against heaven and the realm of England, indeed against the universal Church of Christ'; he was a more savage and wicked persecutor than Saul who became Paul. Although this Pauline image recurred in the text, together with mention of the other great symbol of penitence, Mary Magdalene, the dominant reference throughout the document was to the Gospel story of the penitent thief on the cross who was given the promise of paradise by Christ just before his death. Several useful parallels could be drawn out of this: apart from the imminent death which faced both thief and former primate, neither the attainted Cranmer nor

107 *Cranmer's Recantacyons*, pp. 83–4.

108 Ibid., pp. 85–90; Cox 2, pp. 564–5 (English text in Brooks, *Cranmer in Context*, pp. 113–14).

the condemned thief could offer any material recompense for their crimes, but only their hearts and lips. Moreover, by his recantation, Cranmer was rebuking the thief who had died impenitent – that is, his fellow-criminals Latimer and Ridley. Perhaps also Cranmer, or the hand who guided his pen, might have remembered that in his 'Homily of Good Works annexed to Faith' (a world away now!) the example of the penitent thief had been put to a very different use: to show that faith alone can save without good works.[109]

Cranmer's confessions of specific crimes followed: first his masterminding of the divorce, which had betrayed the spiritual welfare of Henry VIII, injured Catherine of Aragon, and had ushered in all manner of heresies. Then came the crime 'which bitterly tortures my soul', the denial in his published works of real presence in the eucharist, with all the consequences that followed: so many souls deprived of 'supersubstantial food' (not a very Cranmerian phrase), and the endangering of the souls of the dead by the abolition of requiem masses. He implored forgiveness of the Pope and pardon of the King and Queen – presumably the mention of pardon was simple stylistic variation; he no longer had hope of a legal escape from death. Notably, the government did not risk listing the witnesses to this document; almost inevitably they would have included one or other of the foreign friars who were attendant on his conversion, and which had ruined the credibility of the previous version. As far as the prisoner was concerned, once he had signed, he had now said everything necessary; it only remained for him to ask for requiem masses from all the colleges of the University.[110]

20 March was Cranmer's last full day on earth, and an oddly tranquil day. He spent it planning how he would present himself on the day of his burning, particularly at the service in the University Church which would precede the execution. He composed a final discourse, which at first he intended to learn and recite by heart; but then he changed his mind, and decided to commit it to paper. This would mean that a text would be available to the officials, and could also be used for printing afterwards. His last recorded menu for his evening meal was as ample as one could expect for a Friday in Lent: spice cakes and bread, fruit and nuts and a dish of stewed prunes which ensured that the prisoner would not suffer on a trying occasion with a bad digestion. With wine and ale at the table, he prolonged conversation with his companions into the night before getting some sound sleep. It might seem that all was now straightforward; his conscience was clear. Yet the narrator of *Cranmer's Recantacyons* picked up a curious detail: Cranmer gave a small coin to a servant-girl to pray for him, saying that he thought more of the prayers of a good man who was a layperson than those of a bad priest. This was not exactly unorthodox, but in retrospect it seemed significant.[111]

109 Bond, *Homilies*, p. 105.
110 *Cranmer's Recantacyons*, p. 90.
111 C.C.C.C. 128, p. 400; *Cranmer's Recantacyons*, pp. 92–3.

In the morning Cranmer made some edifying remarks to the assembled prison staff, recited the litany, and despite his previous resolution to avoid any additions to his sixth recantation, signed some fourteen additional copies of it with minor alterations. He was interrupted by a messenger from another of his sisters – this time, says *Cranmer's Recantacyons* meaningfully, not the Catholic sister – who sent him a ring with certain instructions not recorded; it may have started the rot. Yet Cranmer was still playing the devout Catholic: he asked the faithful Nicholas Woodson to arrange special prayers for him in the Cathedral, the two colleges of which as Archbishop he had been founder (Magdalen and All Souls), and the symbolically appropriate foundation of Corpus Christi. Just before being taken to the University Church, he reassured Woodson that God would finish what he had begun. It was a statement which could be taken in two ways, as became apparent in what happened next.[112]

Once more, Foxe and *Cranmer's Recantacyons* corroborate or complement each other's highly dramatic narratives. These may be compared with the account (also exploited by Foxe) which came from a Catholic witness who, despite his religious views, found much to admire in Cranmer's last hours; unfortunately, we only know this third source by his initials, J.A.[113] Cranmer processed on a rainy morning flanked by Villagarcia and de Soto reciting psalms antiphonally. He was led to a specially prepared stand in a packed and excited church: in addition to the assembled majesty of the Church, the Crown was represented by Lord Williams, together with the brother of Lord Chandos and a host of JPs and other local dignitaries. First came a sermon from Dr Cole, originally intended to be delivered beside the stake, if the weather had permitted. This had the job of explaining why a repentant sinner should still be burnt at the stake for heresy; a problem in canon law which Cole had little choice but to acknowledge openly. He adduced the somewhat dubious parallel of King David the sinner, who accepted that he needed punishment, but then found that God decided to remit only half of it, and then he gave three reasons why the half which remained in Cranmer's case should include burning.

The first two reasons were drawn straight from the sixth recantation: Cranmer's involvement in the Aragon divorce and the openness and normative character of his heresy in England. The third was so bizarre that one would think that Foxe had made it up, were it not confirmed by *Cranmer's Recantacyons*. The University Church now heard the preacher say that 'it seemed meet, according to the law of equality, that as the death of the Duke of Northumberland of late made even with Thomas More Chancellor . . . so there should be one that should make even with Fisher of Rochester; and because that Ridley, Hooper, Ferrar, were not able to make even with that

112 *Cranmer's Recantacyons*, pp. 93–4.

113 These main sources for the following paragraphs are *Cranmer's Recantacyons*, pp. 94–110; Foxe 8, pp. 84–90; B.L. Harley MS 422, ff. 48–52.

man, it seemed meet that Cranmer should be joined to them to fill up their part of equality'. The law of blood-feud was a startlingly new legal principle to be created by a civil lawyer, and it was rather lamely followed by reference to 'other just and weighty causes . . . which were not meet at that time to be opened to the common people'.[114] The rest of his sermon was not quite so surprising; there were conventional exhortations to the people to profit by the example of the fragility of human fortunes, and a predictable return to the text of the sixth recantation when Cole reminded Cranmer of the story of the penitent thief. He finished with promises to organize 'mass and dirige' for the prisoner throughout Oxford, and asked all priests present to pray for Cranmer, little realizing that by now this was wasted effort.[115] For now Cranmer would have his chance. Gathering his strength out of the bitter tears with which he had listened to Cole's words, he took out his text, and amid an atmosphere of intense concentration, began to speak and pray.[116]

He opened by asking the spectators to pray to God for forgiveness of his sins, but mysteriously added that 'yet one thing grieveth my conscience more than all the rest, whereof, God willing, I intend to speak more hereafter'. The speech proceeded conventionally; even on this last day of his life, Cranmer was still exercising his literary skill in the composition of his prayers. One curiosity occurred early on: Cranmer had been due to recite the Angelus after the Lord's Prayer, but it did not appear.[117] Still, by itself, that need not especially worry the authorities: perhaps this omission of the angelic salutation to Our Lady was an oversight. There followed exhortations to three forms of love: of God, Crown and neighbour. These ended with an elaborated plea to the rich to avoid covetousness. It was far from a formal recitation; Cranmer bowed low when he mentioned the King and Queen, and his tears welled up again when he spoke of the contemporary situation, in which the poor were starving as food prices soared. After a recitation of the creed, and his affirmation of the basics of the faith (although he omitted a prepared reference to his trust in General Councils of the Church), he finally embarked on explaining 'the great thing, which so much troubleth my conscience'. The authorities had the text, so they knew what was coming: a denunciation in the fashion of the sixth recantation of his 'untrue books and writings, contrary to the truth of God's word', which in an artfully constructed separate clause he had explained as 'the books which I wrote against the sacrament of the altar sith the death of King Henry the eight'; there would then follow a declaration of his belief in transubstantiation. But suddenly they realized that this was not

114 Foxe 8, p. 85; *Cranmer's Recantacyons*, pp. 96–7.

115 B.L. Harley MS 422, f. 49.

116 There are distinct textual traditions for the speech: (1) B.L. Harley MS 422, ff.50rv, 52r, B.L. Cotton MS Titus A XXIV, f. 88 (2) Foxe 8, pp. 87–8, largely from *Narratives of the Reformation*, pp. 231–3 (3) Lambeth 3152 ff. 114–15 (4) *Cranmer's Recantacyons*, pp. 98–106 (5) the official version printed by Cawood.

117 This point is only recorded in *Cranmer's Recantacyons*, p. 99.

40 Cranmer being plucked from the pulpit of the University Church, as portrayed in Foxe, *Acts and Monuments* (1563).

41 A probable alternative depiction of Cranmer being plucked from the pulpit of the University Church. This is to be found illustrating a later volume from John Day's press: Stephen Bateman's *A Christall Glasse of Christian Reformation*, 1569. It is clearly ill-fitted to the use to which it is put in that setting, and may have been a rejected version of the scene from the 1563 volume.

what they were hearing. The 'writing', which Cranmer said was written 'contrary to the truth which I thought in my heart, and written for fear of death', consisted of 'all such bills and papers which I have written or signed with my hand since my degradation'. One version of the text makes him refer to the rumours which had gone through London about these papers, but it was now becoming difficult for everyone to hear what was going on.[118]

Commotion (joy and rage) was breaking out in the church; yet through the hubbub, Cranmer persevered in shouting; it was vital to get two more messages across. He was deadly pale, but a surge of energy had taken away his tears. 'And as for the Pope, I refuse him, as Christ's enemy, and Antichrist, with all his false doctrine.' He was on his old course again. Lord Williams yelled out to ask him if he remembered what he was supposed to do, but Cranmer did not waste many words in defying him, and then across the din there floated his words 'and as for the sacrament, I believe as I have taught in my book against the Bishop of Winchester' – and there the enraged officials stopped him. It no longer mattered. He had thrown down the gauntlet to Gardiner his dead rival; and he had succeeded in his task. He was pulled from his stage, in a scene immortalized in an engraving for John Day's 1563 edition of Foxe's Book of Martyrs, and he was hurried out to the stake through the streets of Oxford. It would be a long and tangled journey amid scenes of chaos, which means that it is possible to accept both Foxe's and *Cranmer's Recantacyons*' accounts of the various snatches of conversation on the way. Juan de Villagarcia followed him all the way, according to J.A., and he must have been the Spanish friar whom Foxe records as dazedly repeating over and over again '*Non fecisti?*' – 'You didn't do it?' The Catholic narrator records a more coherent exchange between Villagarcia and his victim: Villagarcia said bitterly that Cranmer would have declared the Pope to be head of the Church if it would have saved his own head, and Cranmer, astonishingly, agreed. Villagarcia browbeat him: he pointed out that that same day he had confessed to a priest. 'What if the confession is no good?' Cranmer retorted contemptuously.[119]

The crowd arrived at the place where Latimer and Ridley had suffered six months before. Fire was put to the wood. In the flames, Cranmer achieved a final serenity; and he fulfilled the promise which he had made in his last shouts in the church: 'forasmuch as my hand offended, writing contrary to my heart, my hand shall first be punished there-for.' He stretched it out into the heart of the fire, for all the spectators to see. He repeated while he could 'his unworthy right hand', 'this hand hath offended', and also while he could, the dying words of the first martyr, Stephen, 'Lord Jesus, receive my spirit . . . I see the heavens open and Jesus standing at the right hand of God.' 'He was

118 *Cranmer's Recantacyons*, p. 105. The official text (cf. Cox 2, p. 566) notes that he was supposed to make a declaration of the Queen's title to the throne, but he does not seem to have done this: not a material point, after his earlier exhortation to obedience.

119 Foxe 8, p. 89; *Cranmer's Recantacyons*, p. 107.

very soon dead', said J.A. It was said that in the ashes of the fire his heart was found unburnt, and the Catholic narrative could do no more to destroy the story than to suggest that its condition was thanks to some form of heart disease.[120]

It is at these last and most vital few hours of Cranmer's life that the historian retires defeated in trying to unravel the motives of a sorely tried man facing a horrible death. Yet some attempt at assessment is inevitable. The effect was to make maximum use for the evangelical cause of a piece of theatre which had been geared to showing off the Catholic Church's most important prize since 1553 – perhaps the most important reconversion of the whole European Reformation so far. If Cranmer had made it clear beforehand that he was going to the stake with the defiance of a Ridley or a Latimer, then one can be sure that he would not have been given such a unique chance to plead his cause. Was this, then a Machiavellian plan, brilliantly executed? Catholics said that his last betrayal was the action of a man who was cheated of his pardon by the Queen, and therefore apostasized out of sheer spite. This was the explanation which the government put out, and which the Venetian ambassador retailed to his masters; we have already seen that *Cranmer's Recantacyons* provided circumstantial evidence with its anecdote set in the streets of Oxford on the way to the stake, when Cranmer told Villagarcia that he would have changed his mind if he had been able to save his life.[121] There is no reason to disbelieve the report of his words, but we cannot hear the bitter self-lacerating irony which may have accompanied them, the last evangelical confession of an honest man who knew himself to be a contemptible sinner in a world of sinners.

The problem with both the simple Catholic explanation and the picture of Cranmer as Machiavellian hero is that they fit badly with the course of events from 17 March onwards. From that day Cranmer knew that he could not escape the stake. There is no possibility that what happened between 17 and 20 March – his passionate rejection of his evangelical past, his deep repentance and his embrace of the Roman obedience – was mere play-acting; no one, particularly an elderly and infirm man, can counterfeit grief on such a scale. We should look to the day of sudden tranquillity on 20 March: that change of mood must be significant. As we have seen, *Cranmer's Recantacyons* is fairly clear that this was when the first hints of trouble occurred, and it speculates that Cranmer's contact with his Protestant sister on the morning of his death on 21 March was the next vital stage; from at least that moment, Cranmer was playing a double game with Mary's Church. When he finally decided to cheat the Catholic Church of its prize, it was after the experience of falling to his lowest depths of despair, being accepted back by the Church and being enfolded in its pastoral care in the hour of his death. That experience in the

120 *Cranmer's Recantacyons*, pp. 108–10; Parker, *De Antiquitate*, p. 403.

121 *C.S.P. Spanish 1554–58*, no. 266, pp. 261–2; *C.S.P. Venetian 1555–56*, no. 434; *Cranmer's Recantacyons*, p. 107.

end was not enough. Cranmer needed another form of forgiveness, which would make sense of his public career and rebuild his personal integrity. In his dream, Henry VIII and Christ had both turned away from him and spurned the chance of fighting for his soul; yet he knew at the last that the battle for his soul was indeed being waged among his own flesh and blood, between his two sisters. He chose to give the victory to the Protestant sister, and to leave the Catholic without her triumph.

CHAPTER 14

Aftermath and retrospect

THE REPERCUSSIONS OF THE rainy Saturday on which Cranmer died have spread through the centuries like ripples from a stone thrown into a pool, from immediate unfinished business through to the creation of religious and cultural identities for England and for the English-speaking world. To begin with: the aftermath in March 1556. The death of a great man will always leave matters to be tidied up, but the sensational and controversial circumstances of Cranmer's execution were exceptionally difficult. The Catholic Church's publicity coup lay in ruins: even the skies seemed to mock it, with popular opinion linking the March comet to the death of the former archbishop. The best that could be done was to mount a damage limitation exercise, and Dr Cole began the process the day after the burning, Passion Sunday, by preaching in the church still haunted by Cranmer's cries. His sermon listed a series of examples throughout Church history of how the devil had worked by stealth within the Christian community after failing to achieve his aim through the pre-Constantinian persecutions; the devil, he said, fomented varieties of opinion, and could turn himself into the appearance of an angel of light. All this led up to a comprehensive indictment of Cranmer's career, and a quotation of his last exchange of words with Villagarcia to show his conscious perfidy. Once more Cole returned to the theme of John Fisher and Thomas More, rather less egregiously than the day before, in order to contrast the consistency of their witness in life and death with the tangle of Cranmer's last days. It would not be the last time that this comparison would be made.[1]

In London, the government hastened to pre-empt the news of the fiasco, and also to remedy the earlier false start in printing the recantations, by bringing out a printed edition of all six of Cranmer's recantations, plus the text of the speech which he ought to have made in the University Church; all these were certified by Bishop Bonner, and this time they were printed by Cawood the royal printer. The pamphlet did not acknowledge that Cranmer had withdrawn his recantations, or that 'the prayer and saying . . . all written with his own hand' did not represent reality; the official record in Bonner's

1 *Cranmer's Recantacyons*, pp. 110–14.

register was necessarily more honest in admitting that Cranmer had died 'persisting in his errors and heresies'.[2] In any case, what had actually happened was soon common knowledge – within a fortnight the news was delighting Protestants in Antwerp and Strassburg. The pamphlet simply looked foolish, although it was conscientiously circulated by pious Catholics (at least, by those closely linked to the government).[3]

The Venetian ambassador, no friend to Protestants or admirer of what Cranmer had done, commented only three days after the burning that the double botch of printing the recantations, 'coupled with the execution, will cause greater commotion, as demonstrated daily by the way in which the preachers are treated, and by the contemptuous demonstrations made in the churches'. Together with the revelation of the plot to rob the Exchequer, it was an unhappy background to what ought to have been a joyful event for Catholics: the day after Cranmer's burning, Reginald Pole had finally proceeded beyond his deacon's orders, first to be ordained priest and then immediately consecrated as Archbishop of Canterbury. The ceremony took place in the presence of Queen Mary and in the powerfully symbolic setting of the newly restored church of the Friars Observant at Greenwich, that centre of resistance to the annulment of Catherine of Aragon's marriage; the following day, Pole received the papal *pallium* in the main church of the peculiar parishes of Canterbury diocese within the city of London, St Mary-le-Bow, since Mary did not consider that the security situation made it wise for him to travel down to Canterbury itself.[4]

The story of Cranmer's death was really so complex that it was difficult to rush out an accurate account of it for either side and be certain that it would be effective propaganda. This is surely the reason why Nicholas Harpsfield left his account of *Cranmer's Recantacyons* in manuscript, when the tract was probably intended as an expansion of Cawood's brief treatment of the documents. Similarly, the Strassburg community considered putting out their version of events very soon after the execution: Edmund Grindal wrote to John Foxe telling him that Peter Martyr had received 'an entire and exact account of my Lord of Canterbury's death' which he gathered was 'elegantly and faithfully written', although a decision had not been taken about whether to publish it by itself. In the end it probably found a place among the accounts which Foxe used from 1559 onwards in his general history of the martyrs, but it is significant that it did not immediately take its place among the output of exile propaganda.[5]

2 The pamphlet (*R.S.T.C.* 5590) is pr. in Cox 2, pp. 563–6. Bonner's Register: Foxe 8, App. 2.

3 *E.T.* pp. 114–15 (*O.L.* pp. 173–4); Gorham, *Gleanings*, pp. 355–7. For James Winnington's Catholic reference to the pamphlet, see P.R.O., S.P. 46/162/174 (6 May 1556).

4 *C.S.P. Venetian 1555–56*, no. 434; Bodl. MS Ashmole 861, p. 349.

5 *Grindal's Remains*, pp. 219–21.

Instead the exiles concentrated on getting out various specimens of Cranmer's writings: the Emden press of Giles van der Erve quickly rushed out a slim edition of his letters to Queen Mary and Martin and Story, written in autumn 1555.[6] The last project on which he was working in prison, a revised Latin version of the *Answer*, was gone for ever. The Latin translation of the *Answer* which does exist is not Cranmer's but was undertaken by John Foxe, and it has never appeared in print. However, as already outlined (see above, Ch. 13, p. 570), a revised Latin edition of Cranmer's *Defence* appeared from an Emden press in 1557, and it proved a great publishing success: copies can be found scattered through libraries across Europe as far as away as Sibiu in Romania. It was probably a Wesel printer who during 1556 brought out a brave, if not altogether successful, attempt to turn part of Cranmer's Great Commonplaces into a readable work of propaganda, the *Confutation of Unwritten Verities*.[7]

On the return of Elizabeth it was possible to gather together the scattered remains of Cranmer's papers. Perhaps the most important item from his former archive was his official archiepiscopal Register, which had been kept out of the hands of Cardinal Pole by its custodian, Cranmer's former registrar Anthony Hussey; this was very fortunate, because such a central witness to the entire early Reformation might otherwise have perished in the general round-up of objectionable records from various archives ordered by Mary's government at the end of 1556.[8] Hussey's career under Mary was exceptionally odd; previously already prominent in both ecclesiastical and maritime law, he remained active in his posts as registrar in the Court of Arches and in St Paul's Cathedral until the end of 1555, when he concentrated on his role of Governor of the Muscovy Company, also spending some time in Antwerp as Governor of the English merchants there. In both his ecclesiastical and commercial capacities, there is contradictory evidence about his religious stance after 1553, and a strong suspicion that he used his connections in Church and commonwealth to do good for at least some of his evangelical friends in trouble.[9]

One fruit of Hussey's slippery career was the preservation of the formidable unbound bundle of the Register, intact except for a few folios about the trial

6 *R.S.T.C.* 5999; Pettegree, *Marian Protestantism: six studies* [forthcoming], Ch. 1, and on the possible Emden connection with Cranmer's anonymous biographer via John Olde, see below, Appendix I.

7 *Grindal's Remains*, pp. 224–8, 238–40; Pettegree, 'Latin polemic of the Marian exiles', pp. 311–12, 320, and Pettegree, *Marian Protestantism: six studies* [forthcoming], Ch. 1. A MS version of Foxe's translation is B.L. Harley MS 418. On the *Confutation* and its possible authorship by Stephen Nevinson, see below, Appendix 1.

8 *C.P.R. Philip and Mary 1556–58*, pp. 555–6 (English tr. in Burnet 2 ii, pp. 414–16) and cf. C.P.R. *Philip and Mary 1556–58*, pp. 81, 282.

9 For some of the strands in Hussey's Marian career and sympathies, see his will (below, following note); Churchill, *Canterbury Administration* 2, pp. 226–8; *Narratives of the Reformation*, p. 216; Foxe 7, p. 656 and 8, p. 729.

and burning of Joan Bocher in 1550 – either Hussey or some later individual may have decided that these were discreditable to Cranmer's memory. In his will, made while Mary was still alive at the beginning of 1558, Hussey directed that his assistant in his Church offices, John Incent, should 'bind up in due form the Register of the late Archbishop Cranmer together with all books as belonging to the Archbishop as to the Dean and Chapter of Canterbury'. This was probably done after Hussey's death in 1560.[10] The Register, so belatedly bound, remains an anomalous though treasured item in Lambeth Palace Library; despite its significance in the story of the English Reformation, it is still without a proper class-mark in the sequence of all the other archiepiscopal registers of Cranmer's predecessors and successors, and with bewildering obstinacy it has avoided publication until overcome by Dr Paul Ayris's heroic persistence in the mid-1990s.[11]

Cranmer's private papers also gradually surfaced in substantial quantities after Mary's death. The story has been well told by Pamela Black; it was a quest spearheaded by Archbishop Matthew Parker, who had the incentive of already having been Martin Bucer's executor in Cambridge and therefore of inheriting much of Bucer's incoming and outgoing correspondence. Two former servants of Cranmer, his doctor John Herd and Stephen Nevinson, the cousin of his diocesan commissary, were each hoarding Cranmer material, and both were reluctant to yield what they may have taken considerable risks in saving from destruction under Mary. If my suggestion about Nevinson's role as Cranmer's biographer and creator of the *Confutation of Unwritten Verities* is correct, then it may be that he had a good motive for hanging on to Cranmer's theological notebooks; he may have been contemplating taking further the work of publishing their contents which he had begun in the *Confutation* (see Appendix I). Instead, both Herd and Nevinson reluctantly yielded to pressure from Cecil, Parker and the Privy Council; Parker reassembled the material in his own collection, much of which, alongside Bucer's papers, formed part of his magnificent manuscript bequest to Corpus Christi College, Cambridge. Yet two of the most important volumes, the Great Commonplaces preserved by Nevinson, seem to have been given by Parker to that enigmatic turncoat and Master of Peterhouse, Cambridge, Andrew Perne.[12]

The other task of preservation, besides Cranmer's literary heritage, was to look after his family. This trust was undertaken by the evangelical printers of London, led by Cranmer's favourite publishers Reyner Wolfe and Edward Whitchurch, although more exposed and exalted former friends of Cranmer, like William Cecil, may have done what they could in secret. The young son, Thomas, was taken to the Continent, probably under the care of his uncle Edmund until the former Archdeacon died about 1557; he was still in

10 P.C.C. 51 Mellershe (P.R.O., PROB. 11/43 ff. 402v–403). In Cranmer's Register, the foliation jumps from f. 75 to f. 78. The foliation is early.

11 We look forward to Dr Ayris's edition, to be published by Boydell in 1997.

12 Black, 'Written Books'.

Strassburg in the opening months of Elizabeth's reign, entrusted to the English merchant John Abell, a trusted former agent of the Archbishop.[13] While Thomas was abroad, steps were taken to retrieve his landed property; Cranmer's last-minute plea to Dr Henry Cole to safeguard his son's forfeit inheritance was heeded. The year after the burning, the lands centring on Kirkstall and Arthington Priories in Yorkshire, which had been granted to the Archbishop as part of the settlement of Henry VIII's will and were forfeited by his attainder, were regranted out to Reyner Wolfe and John Gawen, a former servant of Cranmer's.[14] The royal grant did not make it explicit that this had been done in the interest of Cranmer's son, but this is apparent from subsequent litigation, and from the grant to Thomas junior, in December 1559, of the rent reserved on the property by Philip and Mary two years before; Edward Whitchurch made it clear in his will that this redemption of the reserved rent was his achievement.[15] However, Thomas's restitution in blood after his father's attainder had to wait on a special act of Parliament in 1562–3.[16]

Like the saving of Cranmer's papers, the saving of his wife and children became a family affair in more senses than one. Not only did Reyner Wolfe become the father-in-law of Stephen Nevinson, but Edward Whitchurch married the widow Margaret Cranmer, at a date which remains uncertain. Whitchurch also negotiated a marriage for Mrs Cranmer's daughter Margaret to Thomas Norton, an energetic lawyer who in 1562 gained a professional interest in the printing industry as counsel to the Stationers' Company, probably thanks to his Whitchurch connection. Norton moved in with his parents-in-law in London, and while living there, he translated Calvin's *Institutes* into English; Reyner Wolfe was its joint publisher in 1561. As a former servant of the Duke of Somerset, Norton continued the tradition of thoroughgoing Edwardian evangelicalism into more equivocating times; besides his family tie to Whitchurch, he was an enthusiastic admirer of the long service given to the evangelical cause by the printer and chronicler Richard Grafton.[17] He was also very proud of his link to the old Archbishop.

In the 1571 Parliament Thomas Norton took a good deal of trouble, in collusion with John Foxe and William Strickland, over a plan to revive and authorize Cranmer's revision of the canon law. Norton was the custodian of the original complete manuscript of this work, which he had allowed Foxe to oversee through the press in preparation for its consideration by Parliament.

13 *Zürich Letters*, 1, p. 8. For Abell's role in escorting Martyr and Ochino to England in 1547, and his proposed role in escorting Melanchthon in 1553, see above, Ch. 9, pp. 380–1, Ch. 12, p. 539.

14 *C.P.R. Philip and Mary 1556–58*, pp. 483–4. Gawen had his own chamber at Bekesbourne in 1553: P.R.O., E. 154/2/39, f. 74v.

15 Black, 'Written Books', p. 317, and P.R.O., C. 3/169/6; cf. also B.L. Lansdowne MS 107, f. 121; *C.P.R. Elizabeth 1558–59*, p. 417. Whitchurch's will is P.C.C. 31 Streate.

16 *L.J.* 1, pp. 595, 597, 611.

17 Graves, *Thomas Norton*, pp. 29–30, 35–7. On the marriage negotiation, P.C.C. 31 Streate.

Their effort may have been covertly backed by Archbishop Parker and Norton's patron Lord Burghley, but it aroused no sympathy in Queen Elizabeth. By now the reform scheme was a symbol of dissatisfaction with her Church settlement, and it was a sure sign of the cast of mind which was now labelled Puritanism; significantly, Scots Protestant politicians and church leaders, including John Knox, took a lively interest in its republication.[18] Norton's enthusiasm for the Cranmers further led him, on his first wife's death, to marry her cousin Alice, daughter of Archdeacon Cranmer. When in 1581–2 he was thrown into the Tower of London for outspoken opposition to Queen Elizabeth's Catholic marriage plans to the Duke of Anjou, he tried with some success to use the magic name of Cranmer on Burghley for old times' sake, in order to shorten his imprisonment.[19]

In 1562, the last year of Edward Whitchurch's life, he and his wife retired to a rented property in the suburban Surrey village of Camberwell, leased from an old friend of his, Edward Scott; the couple shared the house with Scott (just as they had shared with Norton in London), and Margaret farmed the eight acres attached to it, including a herd of cattle. Whitchurch's will was made there. Margaret, not inclined to live an unprotected widow on his death, swiftly married Bartholomew Scott, a close relative of Edward Scott's (possibly a brother): these details have been preserved to us because the newly formed Scott *ménage à trois* fell out over the question of rent and Edward sued his relatives in Chancery.[20] To complicate matters still further, Bartholomew had given up hope of children to be his heirs, and he had long invested his hopes for the future in his nephew, Peter Scott, who did indeed succeed to his property. It is to be hoped that all this did not create a coda of bitterness to one of the more adventurous marital histories of the sixteenth century; the former wife of the Primate of All England finally died some time during the later 1570s, far from her native Nuremberg, having endured much. Her third husband married again twice and was buried in Camberwell in 1582, 'a valiant, wise and religious gentleman', according to his epitaph, which also made appropriate mention of the first Mrs Scott's unusual distinction.[21]

The adult life of the Archbishop's son Thomas was certainly not happy; charitably, one might blame the dismal story on a traumatic childhood and legal troubles which were beyond his control. Despite all the effort to which the evangelical printers had gone on his behalf, his inheritance remained contested, and in the early 1570s he was still having severe problems claiming his rights in Kirkstall, both against the Crown and against neighbouring

18 Graves, *Thomas Norton*, pp. 292–5, although I do not agree entirely with Graves's interpretation of events. Cf. *History of Parliament 1558–1603* 3, pp. 145–9; Hartley, *Proceedings in Parliament* 1, pp. 200–201. On Scottish interest in the lawcode, Donaldson, *The Scottish Reformation*, p. 178.

19 Graves, *Thomas Norton*, pp. 123–5, 400–403.

20 P.R.O., C. 3/170/81.

21 Strype, *Cranmer*, Oxford edn 3, pp. 729–30.

Yorkshire gentlemen.[22] Living either in Yorkshire or in London (for a while at Lincoln's Inn), he can be found involved in a series of lawsuits which remain a complex accumulation, even when one has disentangled those involving his various cousins also called Thomas Cranmer, and he never seems to have got the full benefit out of the Yorkshire properties which his father had intended.[23] Whatever the external factors in his misfortunes, one cannot help contrasting his career with that of his workaholic and deeply religious brother-in-law Thomas Norton: Thomas Cranmer cannot be traced in any public office, which however minor should have been his for the asking, given the goodwill attaching to his name, if he had shown the slightest capacity for responsibility. It is as well, moreover, that the Archbishop did not live to see his son summoned by Church courts on successive charges of fornication and adultery in York diocese. Thomas junior's widow was the sister of the Elizabethan Bishop of Dover, Richard Rogers, a member of the Cranmer penumbra of relatives, and her first husband Hugh Vaughan may also have had family links. She survived Thomas's death in London in 1598 to marry for a third time, but the end of her life was passed in poverty, which required a charitable collection in the parish of St Olave, Old Jewry in 1607. Neither of the Archbishop's children produced heirs to carry on his line.[24]

The wider aftermath of Cranmer's death is the history of the later English Reformation, and through it the whole history of religion and culture in the English-speaking world. To assess it involves considering in retrospect the story of Cranmer's career, and even indulging in the luxury of a little counterfactual speculation. He was brought up in the pious milieu of the late medieval Church at its best: the ultra-devout Clifton family, the conscientiously-reformed Premonstratensian community at Welbeck, the little Cistercian house at Stixwold where his sister became a nun; yet it is unsurprising that the clergy from this conservative world, and from his early years at Cambridge, played so little part in his life after 1529. We have noted the way in which even the long years at Jesus left little apparent mark of affection on Cranmer in his public career; there is a sense of a sharp break in his views, with strong evidence that this break took place in 1531. It was a remarkable step to take in middle life, from a man who was temperamentally and habitually disposed to caution; Cranmer was troubled all his life with short-sight, and short-sight is a powerful incentive to walk carefully.[25] From his earlier life, there remained his large network of relatives, who staffed his household as Archbishop and provided some of the new generation of evangelical clergy whom he patronized; there also remained a few friends from

22 B.L. Lansdowne MS 107, f. 121.

23 P.R.O., REQ. 2/78/45; P.R.O., C. 66/1232 m. 14; P.R.O., C. 2 ELIZ C22/18; C. 2 ELIZ C10/30; *C.P.R. Elizabeth 1566–69*, nos. 1810, 2640; *C.P.R. Elizabeth 1575–78*, no. 678; *C.P.R. Elizabeth 1578–80*, no. 422(ii).

24 Ridley, *Cranmer*, pp. 152–3; Pollard, *Cranmer*, pp. 326–7, and pedigree facing p. 384.

25 Morice said that he was 'purblind': *Narratives of the Reformation*, p. 240.

school or undergraduate days whose spiritual development followed the same path as his – Thomas Goodrich, William Benson, John Whitwell, Sir John Markham.

Otherwise, from 1529 the major influence in Cranmer's life became King Henry, the man whose scorn he dreaded even in his dreams in the last days of his life. It seems strange that anyone could have so loved and respected such a monster, but then Stalin was sincerely mourned too; there was a power about Henry transcending the cruelty, selfishness and injustice which were constant themes of high politics as directed by the King. Cranmer really came to believe that the Supreme Headship as exercised by this tyrant expressed God's will better than the traditional headship of the Western Church. It meant that he was prepared to do the King's will while he lived, to the extent of collaborating in the condemnation and burning of Frith and Lambert, evangelical theologians whose theology resembled his own in most respects. However, Henry could hardly be a spiritual mentor for the learned academic theologian, since the King's own theology became a moving target during the 1530s. In England, Cranmer's circle was formed by the Cambridge academics who, like him, gravitated to the bounty of Anne Boleyn's Court, plus the first great partner of his public career in royal service, Thomas Cromwell; William Cecil, though a far younger man, was beginning to play a similar role in his life to Cromwell at the end of Edward VI's reign. Internationally, from 1531 he was in warm personal touch first with the humanist Reformation of central Europe and then with the different impulse of Martin Luther, who structured his thoughts about how to replace the system of the old faith which he had discarded. It was unfortunate for him that he could never persuade Henry VIII to share his enthusiasm. If Philipp Melanchthon had overcome his natural reluctance to meet the alarming King of England face to face, matters might have taken an easier course for evangelical reformation in England.

We can never know the specific issue which propelled Cranmer out of four decades of quiet conformity with the Church of his fathers; we can only trace the bitterness against that Church which is apparent in his writings from 1533 onwards, and describe the shape which it took. How did this bitterness against the papacy arise in a cautious, gentle man, and persist so strongly that he felt that the Supreme Headship of the monarch was God's sole true provision for ordering the Church? We find the Reformation disputes about the eucharist baffling because the meaning of the service has shifted for Catholic and Protestant alike. For modern Western Christians it is primarily the service of the living, when those who love the Lord gather to give thanks, to make offering and to celebrate with him. For the late medieval Church, the mass had become as much something for the dead as for the living; it had broken down the barrier between life and death in a very particular, concrete sense. Behind the crowds of the faithful in a medieval parish church, convent church or cathedral jostled invisible crowds, the crowds of the dead. And they crowded in because the Church maintained a model of the afterlife in which the mass could speed the souls of the faithful departed through purgatory. A gigantic consumer demand of the dead fuelled the services of the Church.[26]

It was to change this that the reformers struggled. Insisting that the just shall live by faith alone, they believed that the medieval Church, with the papacy as its evil genius, had played a gigantic confidence trick on the living by claiming to aid the dead in this way. They sought to banish the dead, and to banish the theology which had summoned them into the circle of the living faithful gathered round the Lord's table. To do this they must humble the clergy – for in the late Middle Ages, one of the clergy's chief liturgical activities had become masses for the dead – and they must end what they saw as the superstition of the mass. We have seen this not merely in Cranmer's new communion rites, where the name of 'mass' was only grudgingly given house-room in 1549 and cut altogether in 1552, but also in the drastic reordering of the 1552 burial service, which was revised to remove any suggestion that liturgical acts could achieve anything further for the dead (see above, Chs 10, 11). Such an aggressive piece of liturgical hatchet-work was designed precisely to hit the old Church where its hold was strongest on the faithful: in their contemplation of death. This was an all-or-nothing confrontation; all the old devotional ways could be seen as part of the great confidence trick on the faithful. It was easy for Cranmer to feel that it was vital to destroy things which may seem to modern Anglicans harmless or even pleasing and useful aids to devotion. It was easy to move from saying that such and such a practice – saying rosary beads, or going on pilgrimages, for instance – had been abused so much as to become undesirable, to affirming that the practice was by its nature wrong and antichristian.

However, Cranmer moved from what is quite recognizable Lutheranism in the 1530s and early 1540s on the central question of eucharistic belief; discussions during 1546 or 1547 with Nicholas Ridley and Martin Bucer proved decisive in his abandoning any idea of real eucharistic presence. One should not reduce his new position any more than Bucer's to Zwinglian memorialism (indeed, one should not reduce Zwingli's mature eucharistic theology to mere memorialism!). Among the Reformed theologians there was a spectrum of belief about the significance of symbol in the sacraments, which B.A. Gerrish has very usefully reduced to three main varieties of outlook: symbolic memorialism, symbolic parallelism and symbolic instrumentalism. In all three, as he makes clear, there is the common notion 'that a sign or symbol "points to" something else'. What distinguishes the three is the reference of the sign: symbolic memorialism, the emphasis of Zwingli, points to 'a happening in the past', symbolic parallelism, the emphasis of Zwingli's successor in Zürich Heinrich Bullinger, to 'a happening that occurs simultaneously in the present' through the work of God alongside the sign itself. Symbolic instrumentalism emphasizes 'a present happening that is actually

26 Duffy, *Stripping of the Altars*, is a brilliant treatment of this devotional world.

brought about through the signs'. This third approach is that of John Calvin, whenever he can speak without the constraint of seeking to conciliate his fellow-Reformers in Switzerland.[27]

The stance taken by Cranmer in the *Answer* and the *Defence* comes closest to the symbolic parallelism of Bullinger. It is perhaps best expressed in an extended passage which forms the culmination of the *Answer*, when for a moment his polemical bitterness against Stephen Gardiner deserts him, and he contemplates the sacraments in a mood which is almost mystical:

> And furthermore, when we hear Christ speak unto us with his own mouth, and shew himself to be seen with our eyes, in such sort as is convenient for him of us in this mortal life to be heard and seen; what comfort can we have more? The minister of the Church speaketh unto us God's own words, which we must take as spoken from God's own mouth, because that from his mouth it came, and his word it is, and not the minister's. Likewise, when he ministereth to our sights Christ's holy sacraments, we must think Christ crucified and presented before our eyes, because the sacraments so represent him, and be his sacraments, and not the priest's; as in baptism we must think, that as the priest putteth his hand to the child outwardly, and washeth him with water, so must we think that God putteth to his hand inwardly, and washeth the infant with his holy Spirit; and moreover, that Christ himself cometh down upon the child, and appareleth him with his own self: and as at the Lord's holy table the priest distributeth wine and bread to feed the body, so we must think that inwardly by faith we see Christ feeding both body and soul to eternal life. What comfort can be devised any more in this world for a Christian man?[28]

More concisely, earlier in the *Answer*, he expresses the same parallelism:

> And although Christ be not corporally in the bread and wine, yet Christ used not so many words, in the mystery of his holy supper, without effectual signification. For he is effectually present, and effectually worketh not in the bread and wine, but in the godly receivers of them, to whom he giveth his own flesh spiritually to feed upon, and his own blood to quench their great inward thirst.[29]

However, just as Bullinger and Calvin were able to come together through the Zürich Agreement (*Consensus Tigurinus*) of 1549 in a statement which respected their mutual concerns and fears of misunderstanding, Cranmer and Calvin would find much common ground. Both were predestinarians, and belief in predestination shaped what they were able to say about both eucharist and baptism: the 'we' of Cranmer's passage above means the elect

27 Gerrish, *Grace and Gratitude*, esp. pp. 166–7; and cf. also Gerrish, 'Lord's Supper in the Reformed confessions', esp. p. 128; on Zwingli, Gerrish, *Continuing the Reformation*, pp. 64–75.

28 Cox 1, p. 366.

29 Ibid., pp. 34–5.

people of God. Within the framework of predestinarian belief, Cranmer can approach Calvin's view of the sacraments, both baptism and the eucharist, 'efficacious signs' in Gerrish's phrase, or 'effectual signification' in the passage just quoted from Cranmer. Calvin would also enjoy Cranmer's emphasis on the complementary ministry of word and sacrament, for the Genevan reformer was clear that (as Gerrish puts it) 'the indispensable component in a sacramental action is not the sign but the word, which the sign confirms and seals; and we are not to imagine that a sacrament adds to the word an efficacy of a totally different order'.[30]

Calvin would probably therefore have been able to concur with a plain statement of Cranmer, made during the Lords' debate in December 1548, 'The eating of the body is to dwell in Christ, and this may be though a man never taste the sacrament'. Yet because Stephen Gardiner as part of his polemical strategy emphasized that a sacramental sign could not be 'an only sign, an only token, an only similitude, or an only signification', so Cranmer was driven to give primacy to the role of a sacrament as a metaphor constructed in words and actions.[31] Words and actions were the important parts of the metaphor, which effectively gave meaning and shape to people's lives, just as a purposeful arrangement of sounds and linked images effectively shaped an idea in the metaphors of spoken or written language. He would be prepared to maintain that the communion was 'an only signification', if that was the only way of saying that the physical elements themselves were the least significant part of the metaphor.

Only with such constant stress on metaphor or sign could Cranmer go as far as to say in 1551, 'I do as plainly speak as I can, that Christ's body and blood be given to us in deed, yet not corporally and carnally, but spiritually and effectually'. In his writings, he needed constantly to maintain the parallelism between spirit and flesh, and his discussion tends to sound negative because of his concern to pull his Church away from error. He would not have enjoyed the language which Calvin in self-assertive mood could use, that the sacraments 'confer' or 'contain' grace.[32] Hence his hatred of devotion to the physical elements, and his insistence, encouraged by Bucer, that his 1552 rite should emphatically indicate in its structure and rubrics that outside the context of the communion service itself, the elements remained unchanged in their nature and were not holy of themselves. This emphasis, so necessary in his eyes to end the follies of the mass and of the idea of a repeated sacrifice of Christ, led him to lay much stress on the memorial aspect of the communion. However, one must also remember his positive insistence that communion was a liturgical event which was only complete when a congregation made an experience of God's grace effectual by its act of willing acceptance in faith: 'the priest and ministers prepare the Lord's Supper, read the Gospel, and

30 Gerrish, *Grace and Gratitude*, pp. 162–3.

31 Cox 1, p. 123.

32 Cox 1, p. 37; cf. Gerrish, *Grace and Gratitude*, p. 168.

rehearse Christ's words, but all the people say thereto, Amen'.[33] For 'people', once more one should understand the reference as meaning the elect.

Standing as he did in the developing Reformed tradition of Europe in the 1550s, Cranmer's conception of a 'middle way' or *via media* in religion was quite different from that of later Anglicanism. In the nineteenth century, when the word 'Anglicanism' first came into common use, John Henry Newman said of the middle way (before his departure for the Church of Rome) that 'a number of distinct notions are included in the notion of Protestantism; and as to all these our Church has taken a *Via Media* between it and Popery'.[34] Cranmer would violently have rejected such a notion: how could one have a middle way between truth and Antichrist? The middle ground which he sought was the same as Bucer's: an agreement between Wittenberg and Zürich which would provide a united vision of Christian doctrine against the counterfeit being refurbished at the Council of Trent. For him, Catholicism was to be found in the scattered churches of the Reformation, and it was his aim to show forth their unity to prove their Catholicity.

To define Cranmer as a reformed Catholic is to define all the great Continental reformers in the same way: for they too sought to build up the Catholic Church anew on the same foundations of Bible, creeds and the great councils of the early Church. Rather than the later notion of an Anglican Church walking between extremes, and hospitably and sympathetically listening out in either direction for good ideas, Cranmer was guiding the Church of England to a renewed Catholicity through thickets of wicked deceit which must be avoided at all costs: on the one hand, papistry, and on the other, Anabaptism, both equally 'sects' in his eyes. During the 1530s and early 1540s he had shared and perhaps shaped Henry VIII's rhetoric of the middle way, but although the two men had a common hatred of Rome and both felt that they were steering England through error, they became well aware that they had different opinions on the errors to be avoided. Henry's ragbag of opinions contained ideas which Cranmer felt were part of the Roman package, although gratifyingly the King shed more of these relics of the past as time went on; contrariwise, Cranmer's middle ground included Lutheranism, which for Henry remained an object of considerable suspicion.

In the end, the faith in the Royal Supremacy as defence of the middle way which King Henry had taught Cranmer failed him. In 1553, the unexpected reversal of events cast Cranmer in the role of a rebel against the Crown, a role which he came to accept at his first trial that November. He had thus betrayed his central belief in the Royal Supremacy which had guided him through treacherous political waters for twenty years, and to add to his bewilderment and agony, the Supreme Head herself also went on to betray that belief. Now

33 Cranmer, *Defence*, p. 456.
34 Newman, *Via Media of the Anglican Church*, 2, p. 33.

he could see that the Royal Supremacy had its limits; and he had also doomed himself. The government, and Queen Mary in particular, were determined to destroy him, to try him not merely as a traitor, but as a heretic. In him, the whole of the English Reformation was put on trial; and in his last ordeal in prison, his spirit broken by the muddles of his beliefs about Church and Commonwealth, he nearly gave way to those who sought a recantation of his Protestant faith. But in the end, he found a way of keeping his integrity, and of reaffirming what he loved and what he hated. Precisely because of his agonizings in those last months, leading up to the flames in front of Balliol College, Oxford, Cranmer deserves to stand alongside other hesitant, reluctant martyrs who have found that they must abandon the assumptions of a lifetime and resist apparently triumphant worldly powers: Dietrich Bonhoeffer, Archbishop Janani Luwum of Uganda, Archbishop Oscar Romero of San Salvador.

What would the Church of England have looked like if, instead of Queen Mary's triumph, Queen Jane's quite reasonable hereditary claim to the throne had succeeded in establishing her regime? The Lady Mary would have had to have been effectively neutralized before Edward's death, and one fears that neutralizing her for good would have involved the block, in a return to Henrician savagery. The Lady Elizabeth could have been married off to Lord Robert Dudley, a good catch for a royal bastard, and a good chance for them both of a happy love-match. Archbishop Cranmer, living to his allotted three-score years and ten or beyond, could have produced the third version of his Prayer Book, in the light of friendly criticism from Continental reformers whom he respected, like Martyr, Bullinger and Calvin; he would have been succeeded as Archbishop by Nicholas Ridley or Robert Holgate, with energetic younger reformers like Edmund Grindal ready to make their mark and pick up good ideas from the best reformed churches of Europe. John Knox, mellowed by an increasingly successful career in the Church of England, would have been appointed Bishop of Newcastle, benevolently taking no notice of the advanced congregations in his diocese who received communion sitting; this was a practice in any case increasingly common throughout Jane's Church, despite Archbishop Cranmer's grumbles. The reform of canon law would have been achieved, the 1553 primer and catechism would have become the standard, the Forty-Two Articles would have been unmodified by Elizabethan sacramentalist hesitations.

Out in the parishes, metrical psalms in the style of Geneva would quickly have spread: these were the best secret weapon of the English Reformation, making its public worship and private devotional practice genuinely popular throughout increasing areas of the kingdom. This congregational music would also have taken over in the cathedrals, now devoid of choirs or polyphony, and with their organs (where they survived) used mainly for entertainment, in the Dutch fashion. The conservative nobility would have continued the sullen public compliance with religious change which they had shown under Edward VI, their private celebration of ceremonial worship

42 The communion area in Deerhurst Church, Gloucestershire. An elaborate and expensive re-equipping of the church in the early seventeenth century, evidently assuming that the communicants will sit around the holy table to receive the elements.

tolerated as eccentricity, like the Lady Elizabeth's patronage of choral music in her own chapel. The traditionalist higher clergy would have died off in senior Church offices and in the universities, with no possibility of like-minded replacement: since the universities produced no major haemorrhage of exiles in the 1560s, the Jesuits and other religious orders would have found it difficult to recruit potential clergy to train for their attempt to treat Jane's England as a mission field. England would have become the most powerful political player in the Reformed camp, with Cranmer a cordial if geographically distant partner with John Calvin. There is a potent symbolism in the fact that it was Cranmer's son-in-law who translated Calvin's *Institutes* into

English, and Cranmer's veteran printer who published it. With a Cranmer–Calvin axis, the profile of Reformed religion across the whole Continent would have been changed, and with the help and encouragement of Bishop Knox, the Reformation in Scotland might have followed a close path to that in the Reformed Church of England.

That is the history that never happened. Instead, in 1558 Queen Elizabeth had to cope with the consequences of Mary's steadily more successful effort to integrate a traditionalist comeback with the new dynamism of the Counter-Reformation. At home, Elizabeth wanted to conciliate conservative interests, which were newly militant after the polarization produced by Mary's regime; on the diplomatic front, she wanted to conciliate the suspicious Catholic powers of Spain and France, and also to win friends among the Lutheran princes of Germany and Scandinavia, who were increasingly hostile to the Reformed Churches to their south. At the same time, however, she was identified with the Protestant cause by her birth, she had a team of advisers who were senior administrators from Northumberland's regime, and she faced a triumphalist Protestant grouping which was already creating a mythology of glorious resistance to evil in the deaths of so many martyrs. Of these martyrs, Cranmer's name headed the list. Elizabeth herself shows signs of having preferred his discredited first Prayer Book of 1549 to his second of 1552, but virtually no one at the time would have agreed with her: to reintroduce 1549 was not practical politics.[35]

Elizabeth's solution to her dilemmas was remarkable: quite deliberately, she established a version of the Edwardian Church which proved to be a snapshot, frozen in time, of the Church as it had been in September 1552, ignoring the progress made in further changing the Church of England after that date. This meant that the 1559 Prayer Book was the 1552 rite devoid of the 'black rubric' on adoration of the eucharistic elements; no government sympathy was offered to attempts in 1559 and 1571 to revive Cranmer's 1553 scheme of wholesale replacement for canon law. The 1553 catechism and primer were set aside, the primer in favour of a modified version of that issued in 1551 – itself a reworking of Henry VIII's primer of 1545.[36] In one respect, the 1559 settlement in fact lurched slightly earlier back, in a famously ambiguous rubric placed at the beginning of mattins. This paragraph, which in its 1662 version would be a much fought-over battlefield during the nineteenth century, specified that the minister should use 'such ornaments in the church, as were in use by authority of Parliament in the second year of the reign of King Edward the VI according to the Act of Parliament set in the beginning of this book'.

35 We await the publication of Roger Bowers's work on the evidence for Elizabeth's use of the 1549 book.

36 Haugaard, *Elizabeth and the English Reformation*, Chs 3, 4, and on the primers, ibid., pp. 144–7. The arguments put forward by Sir John Neale on the creation of the Elizabethan Settlement should be dismissed: see Jones, 'Elizabeth's first year'.

No one has ever satisfactorily explained the intention behind this puzzling instruction. The second year of Edward VI, 28 January 1548 to 27 January 1549, actually ended before assent had been given to the first Edwardian Act of Uniformity, which in any case was not the Act referred to in the 1559 rubric: the text may incorporate a simple mistake in dating, but it clearly ruled out a return to the *status quo ante* of 1553.[37] A paradox, indicated (however clumsily) in the rubric itself, was that Cranmer himself had established the principle which made possible these steps back from his vision of continued progress towards the best reformed churches. In his clashes with Hooper and Knox over ceremony and usage, he had won the point that the Crown in Parliament alone had authority to determine the pace at which change should come in the Church. Elizabeth chose to exercise this power of change only once in her reign, in 1559. Probably not even her chief architects of the 1559 settlement, William Cecil and Nicholas Bacon, realized for some years that this was the future for what they had achieved.

One of the most striking features of Elizabeth's 1559 Settlement was that it began the Church of England's long march away from Cranmer's eucharistic theology, if only in small details. The clarity of Cranmer's sacramental intentions was undermined by restoring to the communion service the 1549 formula of administering bread and wine to communicants which he had replaced in 1552, simply shackled to the later formula: was the communicant receiving the body and blood of Christ, or taking the elements in remembrance that Christ had died for human salvation? This and the omission of the 'black rubric' were the only modifications of significance to the 1552 book. Similarly, the most material alterations made by the 1563 Convocation to the Forty-Two Articles concerned eucharistic doctrine. Although advocates of Lutheran-style real presence views were virtually non-existent in the higher ranks of the Church, the 1563 deliberations seem to have had one eye on Lutheranism abroad: most significantly, the article statement on the *manducatio impiorum*, 'of the wicked which do not eat the body of Christ', was omitted in 1563 to spare Lutheran sensibilities, and it was only restored in 1571 when this was no longer an important diplomatic consideration. The argument of 1553 that Christ's body could not be on earth because he was locally present in heaven (the argument which had so distressed Bucer) was left out for ever. It was true that the replacement wording still emphasized spiritual presence: 'the body of Christ is given, taken and eaten in the supper only after an heavenly and spiritual manner; and the mean whereby the body of Christ is received and eaten in the supper is faith'. However, Edmund Guest, the architect of this phrase and one of the bishops on Elizabeth's bench farthest from the Reformed ethos, gave it a spin which would not have appealed greatly to Cranmer: it 'did not exclude the presence of Christ's body

37 *First Prayer Book of Edward VI*, pp. 64–5.

from the sacrament, but only the grossness and sensibleness in the receiving thereof'.[38]

One should not exaggerate the extent of the drift at this early stage. Those of the Edwardian evangelical establishment who had survived the Marian holocaust, either through exile or some form of discreet invisibility at home, resumed their careers in Elizabeth's Church. To men like Bishop Edmund Grindal, who had been a major help to John Foxe in compiling his collections on the Marian persecutions, Cranmer, Latimer and Ridley were shining examples whose work needed to be upheld and extended. Even the more radical evangelicals who had clashed with Cranmer under Edward VI could forget their differences in view of what had happened under Mary: John Knox was generous in his comments on the three Oxford prisoners' 'lenity, sincere doctrine, pure life, godly conversation, and discreet counsel' and he called the martyred Cranmer 'the mild man of God'.[39] Yet the plain fact was that the Supreme Governor would not allow the Edwardian Reformation to proceed on its path, at least not if it meant bringing structural change to her Church. Famously, she would confront Archbishop Grindal (a great admirer of Martin Bucer): she ruined Grindal's ministry in the Church because of his refusal to suppress the 'prophesyings' – gatherings of clergy for the improvement of their preaching, and much more useful and much less dramatic occasions than their name implied.[40] The generation of Parker and Sandys found themselves defending this fossilized version of the Edwardian Church in the face of criticism from those who had been their companions in resisting popish tyranny under Mary, and increasingly also from a new generation who had no such personal links to restrain their expression of anger at the bewildering immobilism of the Church establishment.

In the face of this unexpected turn of events, the memory of the Oxford martyrs became as much the property of those who deplored the Elizabethan Church's half-reformed polity as of those who were Cranmer's former colleagues; a tussle, indeed, took place for the honour of being the heirs of Cranmer, Latimer and Ridley between the groups within the Church which from the late 1560s can be distinguished as Puritan and conformist. Both sides claimed the myth-making of Foxe's Book of Martyrs for their own, and both sides chose what they wanted from the myth. For conformists, Cranmer's legacy was his Prayer Book, so that he was the symbol of their defence of the liturgy against Puritans, just as he had been in the disputes among the Marian exiles about how far they could depart from the 1552 book. For Puritans, this

38 Horie, 'Lutheran influence', *passim*; Litzenberger, 'Cheyney', pp. 580–81. See Articles text in Bray, *Documents of the English Reformation*, pp. 302–303, and cf. Gerrish's comments on the modified eucharistic article 28: Gerrish, 'Lord's Supper in the Reformed Confessions', p. 126. On Parker and Guest, see Graves, *Thomas Norton*, pp. 310–11.

39 Knox, *Works*, 3, p. 299, 4, p. 419.

40 See Collinson, 'The Reformer and the Archbishop', and the extended treatment in Collinson, *Grindal*.

43 and 44 The burning of Cranmer. (43) From the Latin 1559 edition of John Foxe, *Rerum in ecclesia gestarum commentarii* (Basel, 1559). (44) From John Day's 1563 English edition of Foxe, *Acts and Monuments*.

was a distortion of the Cranmer legacy, which had been tragically cut off before it could be completed. Notoriously, for John Field and Thomas Wilcox, the authors of the *Admonition to the Parliament* in 1572, the Prayer Book was 'an unperfect book, culled and picked out of that popish dunghill, the mass-book full of all abominations'. However, even John Foxe, in his 1571 introduction to the published text of Cranmer's canon law revision, felt compelled to point out the one serious flaw in this document prepared by his hero, that it ordered the exclusive use of the Prayer Book:

> Indeed we acknowledge that the Word of God alone is the final arbiter of divine worship, when however it is certain that there are several matters in this book which seem too little exactly to correspond to complete reformation of the Church, and which perhaps might radically be changed for the better.[41]

Foxe's collaborator, William Strickland, likewise attacked certain aspects of the Prayer Book when bringing the campaign for the adoption of the canon law revision into Parliament, and it is hard to believe that Cranmer's son-in-law Thomas Norton felt any differently in his collusion with Strickland about this initiative.[42] The way to avoid the seeming contradiction of attacking Cranmer's Prayer Book while regarding him as an example to all good Protestants was the quite reasonable supposition that his work had been interrupted: the tradition (discussed in Ch. 12, p. 512) that in time he would have 'drawn up a book of prayer a hundred times more perfect than this that we now have'.

The separatists who emerged on the fringe of the Puritan movement were much more equivocal towards Cranmer than mainstream Puritans, but they were by no means totally hostile; they too could use the Oxford martyrs as sticks with which to beat the Elizabethan hierarchy. Robert Browne, the Cambridge Puritan who had taken the rare step beyond the official Church into separatism, sneered about Elizabeth's bishops that 'neither Cranmer nor Latimer, nor Hooper, nor Ridley were so meet for the prison houses, as these are for their bishoprics'. He regarded the Marian persecution as God's way of trying to save Edwardian establishment evangelicals from repeating the follies of the old Church: 'They had got the popish tools, but they could not hold them. God was merciful by the rod of Queen Mary, and did beat such evil weapons out of their hands', but the Elizabethan hierarchy had not learned from Cranmer's and Ridley's mistakes, and 'these have got again that false popish government'. John Greenwood, a separatist who bitterly detested the Prayer Book that Cranmer had created, coupled his rather condescending view of the Oxford trio's 'ignorance' in borrowing a liturgy from Antichrist with the affirmation that 'I reverence those good men as much as I may by the word of God'. 'In that they knew, they shewed themselves faithful unto the

41 *Reformation of Laws*, ed. Cardwell, p. xxvii; cf. Graves, *Thomas Norton*, pp. 299–301.

42 For Strickland, see Hartley, *Proceedings in Parliament* 1, pp. 200–201. For a different opinion on Norton, Graves, *Thomas Norton*, pp. 295, 297.

death; therefore they [were] gatherers with Christ and not with antichrists.' 'God did pardon Cranmer for making that vile book, and his being metropolitan', he affirmed confidently.[43] Only among the real radicals, those who were conscious heirs of the Anabaptist martyrs of Edward VI's reign, was there a consistent tradition which had no admiration for the Oxford martyrs, and which had scorned them even amid the Marian troubles.[44]

Another less positive view of Cranmer would emerge from the 1580s in a different quarter, among members of the established Church who wished to lay greater stress on its sacramental life. Most of the first important figures (like so many Puritan leaders), were Cambridge dons for some or all of their careers, notably Lancelot Andrewes, the Master of Pembroke: later the movement would widen, until under the patronage of the two first Stuart monarchs it gained an edgy self-confidence and a leading role in the Church, with William Laud becoming Archbishop of Canterbury, and Richard Neile Archbishop of York. It is difficult to find a satisfactory general label for the grouping, except for the vague and variable description 'High Church'. At first without much public group identity, by the second decade of the seventeenth century these sacramentalists were being given the nickname 'Arminians', by comparison with the movement in the Netherlands pioneered by the maverick Calvinist theologian Jacobus Arminius. The common factor was their revolt against the orthodoxy established by the great figures of the Reformation, of whom Calvin was the most obvious reference-point.

However, the English 'Arminians' predated Arminius's emergence as a disruptive force in Dutch Calvinism, and they had other priorities: a predisposition to emphasize continuity rather than discontinuity in the English Church through the Reformation struggles, and a willingness to appreciate afresh the devotional traditions of the medieval West. Often this led them to an interest in – indeed, fascination with – Eastern Orthodoxy: the Orthodox world had the advantage of not having been directly involved in Reformation bitterness, and (perhaps fortunately) it was also not so readily to hand for detailed contemporary scrutiny as was the Roman Church.[45] Above all, the sacramentalists wished to restore the notion of real presence in the eucharist to what they regarded as its rightful key place in Christian doctrine.

For sacramentalists or Arminians, Cranmer's 1552 Prayer Book as lightly revised in 1559 was not promising territory; nor did they enjoy contemplating the work of the Edwardian Church over which the Archbishop had presided. For most of them, there was no question of open criticism; Arminians after all made much of their loyalty to the established Church, and they were fond of citing the homilies to prove controversial points which were

43 *Writings of Harrison and Browne*, p. 218; *Writings of Greenwood 1587–1590*, pp. 4–6; cf. Knott, *Discourses of martyrdom*, pp. 123–4.

44 On the radicals, above, Ch. 11, pp. 474–7, and cf. Knott, *Discourses of martyrdom*, p. 116.

45 For an entertaining treatment of the politics of English moves towards the Orthodox, see Trevor-Roper, 'The Church of England and the Greek Church'.

often far from the intentions of the homilies' original compilers. Rather, their disapproval manifested itself in a discreet lack of comment about the virtues of the Edwardian Church, and also an increasing interest in the 1549 Prayer Book, for the very reason that Cranmer had revised it, because of the possibilities that it offered of reinstating a more extrovert Catholic practice and devotion than was possible with the 1559 rite. Lancelot Andrewes, once he had become a bishop, set an example in his private chapel by rearranging the order of material in the 1559 communion service and multiplying the accompanying ceremonial to suit his theological predilections, an interesting action for a bishop who always emphasized uniformity and obedience to the Church in his public statements. When in 1637 the sacramentalists had the chance to create an entire new liturgy for the kingdom of Scotland (alas, a liturgy which was not appreciated by the recipients), it was to 1549 and not to 1559 that they looked for a model.[46]

Matters were made worse when the Arminians' growing ascendancy in the early Stuart Church, and their frequently aggressive promotion of their remoulding of its life and practice, met with opposition from the older Church establishment. One of the best examples of how Cranmer could now be used to embarrass the Arminians comes from the bitter dispute between William Laud and Bishop John Williams of Lincoln over the correct positioning of the communion table, and the symbolism or lack of it which the positioning might imply. In his 1637 justification of the general practice of the Elizabethan Church, *Holy Table: name and thing*, Williams naturally drew heavily on the phraseology and rubrics of the 1559 *Book of Common Prayer* and on the homilies. He also appealed directly to Cranmer's arguments as presented in the *Defence* and the *Answer*, since Cranmer was 'the most learned in this theme of our late divines'. The 'theme' was eucharistic sacrifice, and Cranmer's usefulness to Williams was in order to restrict the idea of sacrifice, oblation or offering in the communion to the 'sacrifice of laud and thanksgiving', so that the holy table could not be regarded as a place of sacrifice, an altar.[47]

Cranmer indeed became powerfully symbolic for all Laud's enemies. William Dowsing has entered history books (to a limited extent) as the man who turned iconoclasm into, if not a fine art, then at least a careful bureaucratic duty. He was an East Anglian Puritan who in the Civil War would gain a commission from Parliament to wreck churches, and he carried it out with zeal and thoroughness within his own home territory from Cambridge to Great Yarmouth. He was also an admirer of Thomas Cranmer and the Oxford martyrs; he owned three different editions of Foxe's Book of Martyrs, and he covered his books with cross-references to Foxe in the same way as he added biblical references. He possessed both Cranmer's *Defence* and his *Answer*: his surviving copy of the *Answer*, bought in 1637 at the height of the confronta-

46 I am indebted to my former research student, Marianne Dorman, for our discussions of Andrewes, and to John Morrill for our conversations about the Scottish rite.

47 *Work of Williams*, 2nd pagination, pp. 76, 104–6, 108–9.

tion with Laud and now far from home in St Andrews, is filled with his usual lavish marginal annotations. Having read Cranmer's book, Dowsing summed it up admiringly by reference to a scriptural verse, 2 Timothy 2:7, 'Consider what I say; and the Lord give thee understanding in all things'. He drew particular attention to what he called 'Cranmer's prayer', the acrid rebuke to Gardiner which began with the phrase 'I pray God that we, being called to the name of lords, have not forgotten our own baser estates, that once we were simple squires'. The passage culminated with the ringing call 'I pray God, that we have not rather been figures of bishops, bearing the name and title of pastors and bishops before men, than that we have in deed diligently fed the little flock of Christ with the sweet and wholesome pasture of his true and lively word.' Dowsing summed this passage up as Cranmer's 'desire he may answer his call of bishop'. Here was an archbishop after his own heart: a sad contrast to the contemporary occupant of the office in 1637.[48]

From 1641, as England came to split equally between royalists and parliamentarians, rather than unequally between the Laudian clique around the King and the vast majority of the political nation, attitudes to the Marian prelate-martyrs became more divided. William Prynne, for instance, can be found re-evaluating the deaths of Cranmer and Ridley, whom like Dowsing he had previously seen as symbolic allies in his campaigns against Laudian prelacy. Most hostile of all was John Milton, in his bitter attacks on the whole notion of episcopacy during the Interregnum. Cranmer and Ridley became 'halting and time-serving prelates' who were only brought to a better understanding of truth by the persecution which they endured, although it must be said that Milton's opinion of the tyranny of Genevan Church government was no higher! Conversely, moderate defenders of the pre-war established Church redoubled their praise of bishops who could be seen as redeeming episcopacy from Laud's follies.[49]

However, perhaps the most impressive Interregnum verdict on the memory of the martyred archbishop was spoken more quietly, throughout the parishes of England. That verdict was neither one of Laudian embarrassment nor of antagonism from those who had come to despise episcopacy. It was the unobtrusive continuing use of the *Book of Common Prayer* at a time when it was illegal and officially replaced by the Westminster Assembly's *Directory of Public Worship*. The Prayer Book itself had attracted little open hostility during the course of the Civil War, while bishops were abolished and church furnishings and ornaments were destroyed by the likes of Dowsing. In the years after the war, through all the turbulence of Commonwealth and Protec-

48 St Andrews University Library Typ. BL B51 WC, title-page and pp. 329, 459 (cf. Cox 1, p. 275). See Morrill, 'Dowsing', esp. pp. 180, 182.

49 Knott, *Discourses of martyrdom*, pp. 134–6, 152–5; Dickens and Tonkin, *Reformation in Historical Thought*, pp. 103–4. Judith Maltby's forthcoming *Prayer Book and People: religous conformity before the Civil War* will provide valuable further detail on attitudes to the Edwardian martyrs in the 1640s.

torate, its use continued in very many churches, adapted to local needs in the way sought by Elizabethan Puritans. After a century of use, as John Morrill concludes in his seminal reassessment of Interregnum religion, it had become part of 'a rhythm of worship, piety, practice, that had earthed itself into the Englishman's consciousness and had sunk deep roots in popular culture'.[50]

Given this testimony to the Prayer Book's place in the fabric of English Protestantism, the nature of Charles II's Restoration Settlement of 1660–62 with its startling triumph of militant Anglicanism becomes more comprehensible; Cranmer played his part in that victory. Whether he would have been happy with the aftermath of the triumph is less certain. Perhaps he would have understood the need to modify his liturgy after a century of use; after all, he had only been given four years in which to experiment with its practice in the reign of Edward VI. However, the author of the *Defence* and the *Answer* might have looked askance at the delicate subversion of his sacramental outlook by the 1662 revisers. Likewise, he is unlikely to have been happy that the new, more narrowly drawn identity of Anglicanism in 1662 excluded many Protestants who would have found a home in the pre-Laudian Church: almost single-handed, the triumphalist Anglicanism of the Restoration created that phenomenon which is so distinctive in the English religious tradition, large-scale Protestant nonconformity. At the moment in the eighteenth century when that 'Old Dissent' seemed to be fading in strength, a new outburst of energy within the established Church burst its banks and formed a family of Methodist churches. Particularly in the Wesleyan Connexion which lay at the heart of the Methodist phenomenon, this was a rebellion which remained true to the spirit of Cranmer's Prayer Book, and which was sustained by the spirituality of the English Reformation. As archivist for many years of the library of English Methodism's oldest surviving theological college, Wesley College, Bristol, I had in my custody the two quarto copies of the *Book of Common Prayer* used in the College's original chapel from its opening in Manchester: they were worn frail with regular use in leading the community's communal worship.

Jasper Ridley has ably outlined the later divisions in the attitude to Cranmer among historians and biographers. On the one hand, there has been a tradition of praise, of a godly father of the English Church, exemplified in the historical labours of John Strype and Gilbert Burnet; on the other, a tradition of blame, which stemmed naturally from Catholic sources, but which found some unexpected adherents during the nineteenth century.[51] Most bizarre was the virulent stance taken by William Cobbett, whose view of the Reformation as an act of deliberate plunder inflicted on the helpless poor needed a villain, duly provided by Thomas Cranmer. Besides this, however, there came a revival of coldness towards Cranmerian religion among

50 Morrill, 'The Church in England, 1642–9', esp. p. 113.

51 Ridley, *Cranmer*, pp. 1–12; cf. also Dickens and Tonkin, *Reformation in Historical Thought*, Part 2.

those who regarded themselves as the heirs of Laud and the Arminian tradition: the Tractarians and churchmen of the Oxford Movement, whose ideas would be absorbed into the wider Anglican movement known as Anglo-Catholicism. A characteristic attitude among nineteenth-century High Churchmen to the Reformation in which Cranmer played the central role was that of an anonymous reviewer in 1891, 'It has been well said that almost the only real reform that remained to be carried out at the death of Henry VIII, was the translation of the new services into English.'[52] Besides being in fact untrue about the dating of Cranmer's experiments in English (as we have seen in Chs 6–8), this comment defied the reality that the Church of England was in fact permanently shaped by the reign of Edward VI; and the responsibility for that shaping was in the hands of the one man who remained at the centre of religious policy throughout Edward's reign, Thomas Cranmer.

There was at least one escape-route for Tractarians and Anglo-Catholics from the worst consequences of the reign of Edward VI. As the Arminians and Laudians had done two centuries before, they could (quite mistakenly) see Cranmer's first Prayer Book as a welcome refuge from the theological implications of his second. Towards the end of the nineteenth century, reorderings of the eucharistic rite in the mould of 1549 became common in Anglo-Catholic parishes and convents, particularly in dioceses beyond the British Isles which had been created by the world-wide spread of Anglicanism in the wake of the successive British empires. Yet the 1549 Prayer Book's compiler remained loved more for his prose than for his theology. There are not many statues to him in the beautiful churches built in the Anglo-Catholic tradition. In the Anglican shrine of Our Lady at Walsingham in Norfolk, for instance, Charles I, King and martyr for the cause of the Church of England, stands in his niche with votive candles before him. Cranmer, a much less equivocal martyr for the Church of England, does not.

In an ecumenical age, and in a Western culture which honours honest doubt and hesitancy as a lesser evil than clear-eyed ideological certainty, Cranmer may win admirers and sympathizers, and take his due place in the history of Anglicanism. He would not have known what Anglicanism meant, and he would probably not have approved if the meaning had been explained to him, but without his contribution the unending dialogue of Protestantism and Catholicism which forms Anglican identity would not have been possible. Perhaps the most widespread use of his original texts in pure form remains Anglican evensong, where twentieth-century forms have failed to win admirers away from the majestic rhythms of his prose. One of the glories of the Anglican tradition is the choral performance of this evensong in the setting of great churches such as cathedrals: again a situation replete with irony. Cranmer had little affection for cathedrals, and no discernible love of complex choral music. He would have deplored the long-term survival of the

52 [Anon., possibly Brightman], 'Cranmer's Liturgical Projects', p. 459.

Anglican cathedral tradition which Elizabeth I's obstinate traditionalism made possible. At a deeper level, he would have been appalled at the spirituality which may be represented in the love of evensong. This is the exploration of religion by those who have decided to remain on the fringe of the Church, genuinely concerned to pursue their encounter with God, yet not prepared to demonstrate the degree of commitment demanded by the eucharist. For them, the encounter with the Anglican offices, however infrequent, can provide a spiritual home: a place where they can show that they still wish to look beyond the surface of events and say that there is more to human life and creation than the obvious, the everyday. That home has been bequeathed them by Archbishop Cranmer.

Cranmer could hardly complain about adaptability to different times, since the consistent evangelical drive apparent in his career from 1532 was coupled with a remarkable penchant for temporary adaptations to circumstances, and adaptations of alien means to evangelical ends. No one has made a very satisfactory defence of his conduct in taking the archbishopric, and his part in the annulment of the Aragon and Boleyn marriages is not inspiring. Yet to sneer at these three events as proving his craven wish to advance or preserve himself is a bad misjudgement. The thread running through them all, exemplified especially in his letter to Henry VIII about Anne Boleyn's conduct (see above, Ch. 5), is his fierce determination to promote the evangelical reform of the Church. With this as his guiding principle, there is no doubt that he cut legal corners. In 1532 he married Margarete in Nuremberg; in 1544 he smiled on his brother's diversion of the estates of the doomed Wingham College into safe evangelical hands (see above, Ch. 8, p. 323); in 1547 he took his part in the marriage feoffment of the evangelical grandee William Parr, which broke all the rules of current canon law (see above, Ch. 9, pp. 367–9). Equally, he captured the Devil's best tunes for the Lord's service. He cannibalized the writings of Cardinal Quiñones for his liturgical reforms, and the prose of Cardinal Cajetan for his homilies, without the slightest respect for the theology which underlay their work; he redirected some of the riches of the Church's liturgical heritage for his Prayer Book, and only gradually discovered that this was a risky thing to do. In all this, the comparison should be made with another great metropolitan of the Church Universal who failed where Cranmer succeeded, and whom Cranmer clearly regarded as following the same policy: Hermann von Wied of Cologne. With archbishops like these, Calvin need never have turned Calvinism into a presbyterian system, and Andrew Melville need not have waged his long war against bishops in the Church of Scotland.

The widest aftermath of Cranmer's life and work is to be found in the realm of language and of cultural identity. Cranmer could not know in 1552 that he was providing a vehicle for English worship which would remain almost unchanged for four hundred years; with his natural modesty and restraint, he might have been appalled by the responsibility if he had known. Yet it was the happiest of accidents that this ecclesiastical functionary, propelled into high office by the accidents of politics, had a natural feel for English prose. We have seen that his genius was limited to prose, and we can be grateful that, ever-practical, Cranmer knew his limitations. Doggerel verse was as bad in Tudor England as it is in modern England, and it might easily have become embedded in the Prayer Book if Cranmer had versified the old hymns. As it is, we forget that from the reign of Elizabeth down to the nineteenth century, the only liturgical expression in most English parish churches alongside the Prayer Book was the type of metrical psalm popularized by Sternhold and Hopkins after 1562. The surviving verses of the Old Hundredth show metrical psalmody at its best; at its worst, it was dismal. The Church of England was spared the official canonization of such efforts in its liturgy; and so the nineteenth-century Church could leave all but the best metrical psalms behind.

By contrast, Cranmer's prose has done much to guide the direction of the English language. He was a connoisseur who had demonstrated his feeling for the use of language straight away in his earliest surviving vernacular efforts on the translation for the *Determinations* in 1531. However, as a connoisseur, he was not ashamed to borrow what he liked from other people's efforts at translation into English; so what we think of as Cranmer's Prayer Book English is in fact a patchwork of his adaptations of other writers, such as Miles Coverdale, George Joye and Richard Taverner. If he were writing liturgy today, he would face crippling lawsuits for breach of copyright. However, his motive was not sinister; it was an expression of his natural modesty and practicality, and his alterations of existing texts were almost invariably improvements. And it came at a crucial time, for Cranmer was doing his work at a time when English, like all Western European languages, was facing a double challenge: the effect of the universities' enthusiasm for humanist Latin and the standardization and centralization caused by the coming of the printing-press. Every Western European language has certain key texts of literature from this era, and for English-speakers one of that handful of texts is the *Book of Common Prayer*. Millions who have never heard of Cranmer or of the muddled heroism of his death have echoes of his words in their minds.

It was inevitable that the Prayer Book would have a key role in deciding what was good English: it was destined to be one of the most frequently printed and oftenmost heard texts in the language. Whatever its content, it would have become decisive; as it was, the Prayer Book's language was created by an individual with a natural ear for formal prose: for sound and sentence construction. For this reason, Cranmer deserves the gratitude not merely of the Church of England, but of all English speakers throughout the world. Through his connoisseurship, his appreciative pilfering of other people's words and his own adaptations, he created a prose which was self-consciously formal and highly crafted, intended for repeated use until it was polished as smooth as a pebble on the beach. Yet he spared the users of the Prayer Book the worst pomposities of humanism and the sprawling sentence constructions which are only too common in the English prose writers of the sixteenth

APPENDIX I

Was Stephen Nevinson Cranmer's anonymous biographer?

The anonymous 'Life and death of Thomas Cranmer, late Archbishop of Canterbury' is one of our best sources for Cranmer's life; together with the biographical notes by Ralph Morice, it lies behind John Foxe's account of Cranmer in *Acts and Monuments*, and it was used by Foxe as early as the first Latin version of his masterpiece, the 1559 *Rerum . . . Gestarum*. It has been in print since 1859.[1] Unfortunately, it offers no direct clue about its author, and the one surviving manuscript, in Foxe's papers (B.L. Harley 417, ff. 90–93), appears to be a copy of some lost original, for it is written in two different hands. The phrase 'late Archbishop of Canterbury' suggests a date of composition during the time of the next Archbishop Reginald Pole (1556–8), and this date is also suggested by the marginal note about Cranmer's and Pole's suffragan bishop Richard Thornden, referring to an insult to Thornden in the text: 'These words following were not in the Archbishop's letters but they [*sic*] very true and added by the writer of this history who knoweth his condition very well.' This sounds to be phrased in the present tense, and Thornden died in 1557.

The text is linked with another anonymous text concerning Cranmer, printed probably at Wesel in 1556 as *A Confutation of Unwritten Verities*: this attempt to make a usable text out of a section of Cranmer's source-notebooks (the 'Great Commonplaces' as they are styled by Ashley Null) was republished in London in 1582, and there is a modern edition in Cox 2, pp. 1–67.[2] The two writings have in common a passage about the Bishops' Book of 1537 and the Six Articles; the *Confutation* reworks and expands material from the biography in a manner which can only have been the work of the same writer (cf. *Narratives of the Reformation*, pp. 223–4 with Cox 2, pp. 15–16). The *Confutation* announces itself on its 1556 title-page as having been written by 'E.P.', but no suitable candidate has been found to fill these initials. It is quite likely that they have no especial significance, except to link the *Confutation* to an anti-Spanish Protestant tract of 1554, published in Strassburg by W. Rihel and also in London possibly by John Day: *A faithful admonition of a certain true pastor and prophet, sent unto the Germans at such time as certain great princes went about to bring aliens into Germany . . . with a preface*

1 *Narratives of the Reformation*, pp. 218–33; Foxe, *Rerum Gestarum*, 1, pp. 708–26.
2 *R.S.T.C.* 5996–7.

of M. Philip Melanchthon.[3] This translates a tract by Martin Luther, but its first preface, by the translator, before Melanchthon's preface, has very much the style of anti-Marian invective and reproach to England's rulers which is found in the *Confutation*, and its translator calls himself 'Eusebius Pamphilus' after the fourth-century historian of the Church. It is more than likely that this Eusebius Pamphilus and E.P. of the *Confutation* are one and the same, necessarily preserving anonymity in a time of crisis, possibly because the writer was still living in England and was thus vulnerable.

What indirect clues about identity does the author of the anonymous biography and the *Confutation* provide? The compiler of the *Confutation* has access to Cranmer's notebooks which now form B.L. Royal 7 B XI and XII; he has selected and rearranged material from sections 2–17 to form the core of his English text. The biographer also knows about Cranmer's notebooks, describing in some detail the way in which Cranmer annotated his books and took notes, and later referring to the 'old collections of the new Archbishop' on the powers of Rome: here he is probably talking specifically of the collections on canon law which now form Lambeth MS 1107.[4] The *Confutation* editor has a strong Canterbury connection (also suggested in the anonymous biography by the reference to Bishop Thornden); he tells the story of Elizabeth Barton the Maid of Kent with original details concerning Nicholas Heath at Canterbury, and he also records a sermon at the beginning of Mary's reign in Canterbury Cathedral. He gives us his own age in 1557 as a little less than forty, since he talks of 'my memory, which is above thirty years'; this suggests a date of birth in the 1520s. He knows of and advertises the English translation by John Olde of Rodolf Gualter's sermons on Antichrist, published by Giles van der Erve at Emden in 1556; indeed, in the opening pages of his preface to the *Confutation*, he makes much of a text from Psalm 80 about a wild boar spoiling the vineyard, which is the text dominating the title-page of Olde's translation.[5] Olde was the agent in exile who arranged the printing in Emden of various documents of the persecution, including Nicholas Ridley's dialogues with his enemies in Oxford, and possibly also the edition of selections from Cranmer's prison letters which appeared in 1556. This may indicate that Olde was working in collusion with the biographer to get these documents out of England.[6] The biographer also has a particular interest in printing: he reminisces in his preface about the good days of Edward VI's reign, when with the word of God 'were all pulpits filled, churches garnished, printers' shops furnished, and every man's house decked'. He contrasts this with the proclamation of popish falsehoods under Mary: 'every street soundeth of these; yea, every printer's house is filled with such ungodly baggage'.[7]

3 *R.S.T.C.* 16980–81.

4 On B.L. Royal MS 7 B XI, XII, see the list of topic headings conveniently printed in Cox 2, pp. 7–8. *Narratives of the Reformation*, pp. 219, 221–2.

5 Cox 2, pp. 65–6, 38, 63. Olde's work is *R.S.T.C.* 25009.

6 Pettegree, *Marian Protestantism: six studies* [forthcoming], Ch. 1.

7 Cox 2, pp. 9–10.

One person who fits these data very well is Dr Stephen Nevinson. He was from a Westmorland family, the son of Richard Nevinson of Newby, and first cousin of Cranmer's servant and Commissary of Canterbury, Christopher Nevinson, who mentioned him in his will; he matriculated pensioner from Christ's College, Cambridge, in 1544 as a scholar from King's School, Canterbury, which suggests a date of birth in the late 1520s. He took his BA in 1544/5 and became a fellow of Trinity College in 1547; he took his MA in 1548 and his LL.D. in 1553.[8] He was also serving as one of Cranmer's junior estate officials, as assignee of Christopher Nevinson's son, Thomas, at Wingham in Kent, during 1551–2. Enjoying several ecclesiastical offices in Canterbury diocese under Elizabeth, in 1562 he succeeded Cranmer's old secretary Pierre Alexandre in a Canterbury prebend, and later on he was Chancellor of the diocese of Norwich; he died in summer 1580.[9]

Of particular significance is that Nevinson was strongly associated with Cranmer's publisher, the printer Reyner Wolfe, and also that Nevinson actually had custody of many of Cranmer's papers after the Archbishop's arrest and death, probably thanks to Wolfe. Wolfe published the first Latin edition of Cranmer's *Defensio* in 1553; the publisher of the second edition of the *Defensio* at Emden in 1556 was the same Giles van der Erve who published John Olde's translation of the Antichrist sermons by Gualter, referred to in the text of the *Confutation*. Van der Erve also published some of Cranmer's letters from prison; he would have known Wolfe when he was one of the Dutch exile community in London in Edward VI's reign, and his partner Nicholas van den Berghe (Nicholas Hill) had published most editions of Cranmer's version of the Justus Jonas Catechism.[10] Stephen Nevinson married Wolfe's daughter Elizabeth, and in 1574 Wolfe's widow Joan made Nevinson her supervisor and bequeathed him a chamber in her London house.[11] In 1570, in the course of a complex dispute over Nevinson's benefice of Stiffkey in Norfolk (he seems to have been a quarrelsome man), his resignation of the benefice was witnessed at Wolfe's house by Wolfe himself, and this document was written by a veteran servant of the Canterbury and vice-gerential administration back to the 1530s, William Say.[12]

Previously Nevinson had been at the centre of a rather embarrassing dispute with the Elizabethan government because of his reluctance to surrender Cranmer's notebooks in his possession; in 1563 Archbishop Parker had to call in William Cecil to bring pressure to bear on Nevinson, who was hoarding the books in his study and denying that he possessed them. The Archbishop

8 *Visitation of Kent 1619–21*, p. 146; Venn 3, p. 245. Christopher Nevinson's will is P.C.C. 4 Powell.

9 Black, 'Written Books', pp. 313–14; on his office at Wingham, P.R.O., S.C. 6/Edw VI/ 240.

10 *R.S.T.C.* 5992.5–5994, 5999, 6004–5. On van der Erve (Ctematius) and van den Berghe (Hill), see Pettegree, *Emden and the Dutch Revolt*, pp. 37, 39n, 88–90, 93–6, and Pettegree, *Foreign Protestant Communities*, 55, 56, 86, 88–90, 92.

11 Black, 'Written Books', p. 313.

12 *Bacon Papers* 1, p. 14 (12 June 1570).

expressed himself in a discreet manner, but said the rightful owner had complained that Nevinson had 'conveyed [the MSS] away from him the said owner'; it is more than likely that this rightful owner was either Nevinson's father-in-law, Reyner Wolfe, or Wolfe's close associate and fellow-printer, Edward Whitchurch, who had married Cranmer's widow Margaret. In the end it took a strong letter from the Privy Council to secure the books from Nevinson. We know precisely that the volumes possessed by Nevinson included BL Royal 7 B XI, XII, the source of the *Confutation* text, because the correspondence about the matter is pasted into the front of the first volume.[13]

The likelihood is, then, that Nevinson undertook at least two and possibly three works of propaganda during the Protestant disaster of Mary's reign; the two associated works, the biography and the *Confutation*, were precisely intended to glorify the memory of his first patron the Archbishop. He may well have been reluctant to surrender the volumes of Cranmer's collections in 1563 because he intended continuing the mammoth (and probably impossible) task of turning the notebooks into publishable form. Neither he nor his father-in-law Wolfe appear to have left England during Mary's reign, so they were ideally placed to preserve Cranmer's writings in England, while still exploiting Wolfe's lifetime of Continental contacts to keep in touch with the Marian exiles and get works printed abroad at Strassburg, Wesel and Emden. The subsequent failure of Elizabethan commentators to identify either the writer of the anonymous biography or of the *Confutation* may have owed something to the sour taste left by Nevinson's over-acquisitive attitude towards the precious relics of the man whom he sought to honour.

13 It is conveniently printed in *Narratives of the Reformation*, pp. 338–40. NB that the reference to Serjeant Manwood is irrelevant to the MSS, despite the note in *Narratives*; the 'good intent' to which Parker refers in his final sentence was Manwood's plan to found a school at Sandwich.

APPENDIX II

The Date of Henry VIII's marriage to Anne Boleyn

The consensus among modern commentators is that the first marriage of Henry VIII and Anne Boleyn took place on 24 or 25 January 1533. This is the opinion of E.W. Ives (*Anne Boleyn*, p. 202n, relying on the arguments of Friedmann 2 pp. 338–9), and J.J. Scarisbrick concurs (*Henry VIII*, p. 309). The evidence comes from two witnesses, neither of whom, admittedly, was present at the ceremony. Eustace Chapuys said that it took place 'on the day of St Paul's conversion', i.e. 25 January 1533, and about the time that Dr 'Bonart', i.e. Edmund Bonner, came back from Rome, which, as Bonner told his colleague William Benet, was also on 25 January.[1] Thomas Cranmer himself, writing to Nicholas Hawkins in June 1533, seems to agree, saying that Anne 'was married much about St Paul's day last', although 'I myself knew not thereof a fortnight after it was done'.[2]

Nicholas Harpsfield, in his attack on the *Determinations*, gives a very circumstantial account of the marriage and makes Rowland Lee the reluctant officiant; however, in another part of the same work he gives a series of dates which do not make complete sense. After describing the creation of Anne as Marchioness of Pembroke (September 1532), he correctly notes that Henry 'passing to Calais the October following to speak with the French King, took the said lady with him', but he then mysteriously says 'and after his return in the end of April did privily marry with her, and about a year after, perceiving her to be great with child, caused her to be proclaimed Queen, and at Whitsuntide following caused her to be crowned'.[3] Neither 'the end of April' nor 'about a year after' make good sense. Henry returned from Calais on 13 November 1532.[4] Even if one repunctuates the sentence to dissociate the end of April from the return from Calais (after his return, in the end of April did privily marry . . . '), one is left with an approximate 'year' which is in fact only six and a half months in total from mid-November to the Whitsun coronation. If the April date means anything, it refers to Anne's public proclamation as Queen, which preceded her coronation, being recorded for instance by a London chronicler as 12 April 1533.[5]

1 *C.S.P. Spanish 1531–3*, no. 1072, p. 674; *St.P.* 7, p. 410.
2 Cox 2, p. 246.
3 Harpsfield, *Pretended Divorce*, pp. 234–5, 198.
4 Hall 2, p. 221.
5 'Two London Chronicles', ed. Kingsford, p. 7.

There is, however, a different tradition of a wedding in mid-November 1532, rather than January 1533. Hall says that 'the King after his return [from Calais] married privily the Lady Anne Boleyn on Saint Erkenwald's Day, which marriage was kept so secret, that very few knew it, till she was great with child, at Easter after', in other words, at the time of her proclamation as Queen – Easter in 1533 fell on 13 April. The feast of the Translation of St Erkenwald, Bishop of London, is 14 November, which is indeed the day after Henry's return from Calais. Nicholas Sander picks up this date of 14 November, and combines with it Harpsfield's story of Rowland Lee being persuaded to officiate at the wedding.[6] Nicholas Pocock, in his edition of Harpsfield's *Pretended Divorce*, suggested that Cranmer's 'St Paul's day' referred to this feast of the Translation of St Erkenwald; this was indeed a St Paul's day because it was a grand occasion in the life of St Paul's Cathedral.[7] Attractive though this idea is as a reconciliation of the two dates, it seems a little strained.

Nevertheless, there is a compelling case that some sort of marriage ceremony took place in mid-November 1532. The single fact which points to it is Anne Boleyn's pregnancy, which must have begun early in December 1532 to have produced Princess Elizabeth on 7 September 1533. After all that Henry had been through to get a legitimate heir, he would surely not have jeopardized the future of the realm by fathering a child without some sort of ceremony which he considered to be a marriage. He was, of course, in his own eyes free to marry; moreover he would know that in canon law, a second marriage during annulment proceedings was considered valid if the first was declared null.[8] By November, Henry had a strategy for making sure that he would have an annulment within the realm, with the first drafts of the legislation in restraint of appeals already prepared, and he was sure that he would have an Archbishop who would grant him the annulment that he wanted. I am persuaded, then, that there were two ceremonies which witnessed to the marriage of Anne and Henry, one in November 1532 and one in January 1533. The November ceremony may have been the couple's impulsive reaction when they finally completed a slow and potentially hazardous crossing of the Channel back to the English mainland from Calais; they would then have begun full sexual intercourse leading to the pregnancy.[9] The repeat ceremony in January may have been the first occasion on which a priest was present.

6 Hall 2, p. 222; Sander, *Schism*, pp. 92–4, 348.
7 Harpsfield, *Pretended Divorce*, p. 327.
8 Kelly, *Matrimonial Trials*, p. 40n.
9 Cf. Ives, *Anne Boleyn*, pp. 201–2.

APPENDIX III

University connections among close relatives, servants and households of Thomas Cranmer and Stephen Gardiner

Close relatives, household and servants of Thomas Cranmer: Cambridge arranged by college

UNKNOWN

Bigg, William (chaplain, ?relative)
Devenish, Willam (relative)
Drum, Michael
?Ferrar, John
Lawney, Thomas (chaplain)
Morice, James
Nevinson, Christopher (nephew by marriage? servant)
Ridley, Robert
Thorpe, John (kinsman)
Vaughan, Hugh (chaplain)
Wakefield, Thomas (chaplain)
Wakefield, William (chaplain)

BLACKFRIARS

Scory, John (chaplain)

BURDEN HOSTEL

Taylor, Rowland

CHRIST'S/GODSHOUSE

Gunthorpe, Robert (friend)
Heath, Nicholas
Morice, Ralph (servant)
Nevinson, Stephen (servant)
Tamworth, Christopher (relation)

CLARE HALL

Heath, Nicholas
Ridley, Lancelot
Wakefield, Robert (servant)

CORPUS CHRISTI

Goodrich, John (servant)
Goodrich, Thomas (friend)
Sowode, William (steward)

GONVILLE HALL

Butts, Dr
Hoore, Richard (chaplain)

JESUS

Basset, Francis (servant)
?Cranmer, Edmund (brother)
Goodrich, Thomas (friend)
Langley, Thomas (chaplain)
Ramsey, John (chaplain)
Warner, John (chaplain)
?Whitwell, John (chaplain, servant)

KING'S

?Barnard, Thomas (chaplain)
Darell, Humphrey (chaplain)
Herd, John (servant)
Leigh, Dr (chaplain)
?Marshal, John (servant)

PEMBROKE

Ridley, Nicholas

QUEENS'

Mallet, Francis (chaplain)
Newman, John (friend)
Ponet, John (chaplain)

ST JOHN'S

Becon, Thomas (chaplain)
Bland, John (associate)
?Collier (chaplain)
Ramsey, John (chaplain)
Wakefield, Robert (servant)

Total individuals 44

Close relatives, household and servants of Thomas Cranmer: Oxford arranged by college

UNKNOWN

Butler, John (commissary)
Garrett, Robert (chaplain)
Gittings, Maurice (chaplain)
?Hussey, Anthony (servant)
Molyneux, Anthony (relative)
Twyne, John (agent)

ALL SOULS

Barber, John (chaplain)
Bullingham, Nicholas (chaplain)

BALLIOL

Markham, Henry (friend)

CANTERBURY

Drum, Michael

CARDINAL, THE KING'S COLLEGE, CHRIST CHURCH

Best, John (protégé)
Garrett, Thomas (chaplain)
Lawney, Thomas (chaplain)
Turner, Richard II

CORPUS

Garrett, Thomas (chaplain)

FRANCISCAN CONVENT

Glazier, Hugh (servant)
Joseph, John (chaplain)

LINCOLN

?Champion, Richard (chaplain)

MAGDALENE

Drum, Michael
Smith, Thomas (chaplain)
Turner, Richard I

MERTON

Devenish, Willam (relative)

NEW COLLEGE

Talbot, Robert (chaplain)

ORIEL

Carden, Thomas (chaplain)

ST MARY HALL

Ferrar, Robert (chaplain)

Total individuals 23

Close relatives, household and servants of Stephen Gardiner: Cambridge arranged by college

UNKNOWN

Cheston, Stephen
Cooke, John

CLEMENT'S HOSTEL

?Alexander, Robert (servant)

GONVILLE

Medowe, William (servant)
?Walker, Henry (witnesses will)

KING'S HALL

?Eden, Richard (patron)

ST JOHN'S

Seton, John (chaplain)
Watson, Thomas (chaplain)

TRINITY

Cheston, John

TRINITY HALL

Allen, Francis (secretary)
Cheston, Thomas
Cheston, William
Eden, Thomas (servant)
?Gardiner, Jermyn (servant)
Gawdy, Bassingbourn (witnesses will)
Gawdy, Thomas (brother of Bassingbourn)

Total individuals 16

Close relatives, household and servants of Stephen Gardiner: Oxford arranged by college

UNKNOWN

Burton, Robert (chaplain)
Cheston, Stephen
Cooke, John
Levet, William

BALLIOL

Brooks, James (chaplain)

CORPUS

Brooks, James (chaplain)

MERTON

Smith, Richard (assistant)

NEW COLLEGE

Clyffe, John (servant)
Copinger, William (servant)
Hampden, Richard (servant)
Harding, Thomas (chaplain)
?Payne, Robert
?Potinger, John (servant)
White, John (chaplain)

Total individuals 13

Bibliography

I have not provided a comprehensive list of Cranmer's writings in manuscript and in print, as that task has already been excellently performed by Drs Ayris and Selwyn, in *Thomas Cranmer: Churchman and Scholar*, Appendices 1–4.

Manuscripts and individual contemporary printed books

CAMBRIDGE: CORPUS CHRISTI COLLEGE

MS 102: Cranmer papers
MS 104: Cranmer papers
MS 105: miscellaneous collections
MS 106: miscellaneous collections, history of Cambridge University, by Matthew Parker
MS 113: letters, mainly correspondence of Martin Bucer
MS 115: discourse on predestination by Pierre Alexandre
MS 119: letters, mainly correspondence of Martin Bucer
MS 126: lectures on matrimony by Pierre Alexandre
MS 128: papers on the Prebendaries' Plot and other collections on Cranmer
MS 298: rhyming life of Becket and collections on Canterbury
MS 301: MS formerly of St Augustine's Abbey, Canterbury

CAMBRIDGE: UNIVERSITY LIBRARY

Additional MSS 3, 10: Strype papers
Ee.2.8: theological collections by Pierre Alexandre
UA [University Archives] Wills: Wills proved in the Vice-Chancellor's Court, Books 1, 2
Printed books from Cranmer's library

CRACOW, MUZEUM NARODOWE W KRAKOWIE

Bibl. Czartoryskich MS 1595, pp. 9–12, 13–16: Cranmer's correspondence with Johannes Dantiscus

DOUAI, MUNICIPAL ARCHIVES: SEE LONDON, LAMBETH PALACE

HATFIELD HOUSE, HERTFORDSHIRE

Cecil papers

HEREFORD AND WORCESTER RECORD OFFICE, ST HELEN'S, WORCESTER

OO9:1 and b.009:1-BA 2636: Ecclesiastical Commission papers relating to the diocese of Worcester

b.716.093-BA 2648/8(i)(ii), 9(i)(ii): Bishops' Registers, diocese of Worcester, Silvestro de Gigli to Hugh Latimer

HUNTINGTON LIBRARY: SEE SAN MARINO

LONDON: BRITISH LIBRARY

Additional MSS
Cottonian MSS
Harleian MSS and Charters
Lansdowne MSS and Rolls
Royal MSS
Sloane Charters
Stowe MSS

Printed books from Cranmer's library

LONDON: LAMBETH PALACE LIBRARY

Cartae Miscellanae
Cranmer's Register (no class reference)
MSS, General Series
MS Film 3: microfilm of Cardinal Pole's Legatine Register, Douai Municipal Archives 922
MS Film 205: microfilm of Merlin, *Quatuor Concilium* (Paris, 1524; q.v., Contemporary Printed Sources below), Karpeles MS, California

Printed books from Cranmer's library

LONDON: PUBLIC RECORD OFFICE

C. 1: Early Chancery Proceedings
C. 2 ELIZ: Chancery Proceedings, Series I, Elizabeth I
C. 3: Chancery Proceedings, Series II
C. 66: Patent Rolls
D.L. 1: Duchy of Lancaster, Court Proceedings
E. 101: Exchequer, King's Remembrancer, Various Accounts
E. 117: Exchequer, King's Remembrancer, Inventories of church goods
E. 133: Exchequer, King's Remembrancer, Barons' Depositions
E. 154: Exchequer, King's Remembrancer, Inventories of goods and chattels
E. 315: Court of Augmentations, Miscellaneous Books and Proceedings
E. 321: Court of Augmentations, Proceedings
E. 326: Court of Augmentations, Ancient Deeds, Series B
E. 334: Court of First Fruits and Tenths, Composition Book
E. 371: Exchequer, Lord Treasurer's Remembrancer: Originalia Rolls
REQ. 2: Court of Requests, Proceedings
S.C. 6: Ministers' and Receivers' Accounts
S.P. 1; S.P. 2; S.P. 3; S.P. 6; S.P. 10; S.P. 11; S.P. 12; S.P. 15; S.P. 46: State Papers, Domestic, Henry VIII–Elizabeth I

S.P. 69: State Papers, Foreign
STA.C. 1–4: Star Chamber, Proceedings, Henry VII-Philip and Mary

LONDON: WESTMINSTER ABBEY

W.A.M. 43047: letter from Cranmer to Dean and Chapter

NOTTINGHAMSHIRE RECORD OFFICE, NOTTINGHAM

DDWN 2: pedigree of Rosell and Cranmer authenticated by Peter Le Neve, 1715
Microfilm: Whatton Parish Registers (originals retained in the parish)

OXFORD: ALL SOULS COLLEGE

MS CTM p. 303, no. 21: Cranmer to Warden and Fellows

OXFORD: BODLEIAN LIBRARY

MS Ashmole 861: Ashmole's transcripts from the Chronicle of Anthony Anthony
MS Bodley 261, 262: writings by Thomas Netter from Cranmer's library
MS Jesus 74: collections by Thomas Master for Lord Herbert's *Life of Henry VIII* [q.v.]
MS Lincoln Lat. (e) 122: medical collections of John Smith (I am most grateful to Dr David Crankshaw for letting me know of this MS)
MS Tanner: collections of Bishop Thomas Tanner
Folio Δ 624: Edward, Lord Herbert of Chirbury, *The Life and Raigne of King Henry the Eighth* (London: E.G. for Thomas Whitaker, 1649: see also Secondary Printed Works below), interleaved with extracts from the Chronicle of Anthony Anthony
Quarto M.9.Th. (5,6): J. Eck, *Apologia . . . adversus mucores et calumnias Buceri* (Ingolstadt, 1542), with annotations by Cranmer. Bound with text of Interim, 1548
Quarto Rawl. 245: the *Institution of a Christian Man*, 1537, with Henry VIII's emendments

PARIS: BIBLIOTHÈQUE STE-GENEVIÈVE

MS 1458: transcripts of letters

ROME: VATICAN ARCHIVES

Vatican Archivo Secreto Vaticano, Brevi Clemente VII, Arm. 40 vol. 30: papal correspondence and business (I am very grateful to Dr Maria Dowling for alerting me to this crucial document)

ST ANDREWS UNIVERSITY LIBRARY

BL B51 WC: copy of Cranmer's *Answer* (Reynold Wolfe, 1551), owned by William Dowsing the iconoclast (see *Dictionary of National Biography*)
GS B30 XL: Francis Lambert, *Commentarii*, Strasbourg, ?1525 or ?1530, a gift from Cranmer to Thomas Garbrand

SAN MARINO, CALIFORNIA: HENRY E. HUNTINGTON LIBRARY

Ellesmere MSS

STRASBOURG: ARCHIVES MUNICIPALES

MSS Archives du Chapitre de St Thomas de Strasbourg vols 40, 41, 153, 157: collected letters and transcripts

STRASBOURG: BIBLIOTHÈQUE NATIONALE ET UNIVERSITAIRE

Thesaurus Baumianus: transcripts of letters of the Reformers

UPPSALA, UNIVERSITETSBIBLIOTEKET

MS H.155 ff. 30r–31v, 208–10: correspondence of Dantiscus and Cranmer

ZÜRICH, STAATSARCHIV

E II 343a, ff. 381; E II 345a, ff. 422: correspondence between John Hooper and Heinrich Bullinger (I am very grateful to Dr Hirofumi Horie for supplying me with these references, and to Dr Bruce Gordon for arranging for copies to be sent to me)

Contemporary printed sources, and primary sources in print

(NB: the keyword used in footnotes is capitalized. Individual books owned by Cranmer surviving in various collections are not listed (but see listings above). Place of publication is London unless otherwise stated)

ACTS *of the Privy Council of England*, ed. J.R. Dasent (32 vols, 1890–1907)

A. ALANE [ALES], *Of the auctorite of the word of God agaynst the bisshop of London* . . . (?Leipzig, ?1537, *R.S.T.C.* 292)

[ANON.], *The life off the 70. Archbishopp off Canterbury presentlye sitting Englished* . . . (n.p., 1574; *R.S.T.C.* 19292A)

[ANON.], ed., 'Kentish Wills. Genealogical extracts from sixteenth-century wills in the Consistory Court at Canterbury', *Miscellanea Genealogica et Heraldica*, ed. A.W. Hughes Clarke, 5th ser. 5 (1923–5), pp. 26, 54, 87, 119, 146, 177, 213, 247, 273, 301, 329, 364

Select works of John BALE, D.D. . . . , ed. H. Christmas (P.S., 1849)

J. BALE, *The Epistle exhortatorye of an Englyshe Christiane* (?Antwerp, 1544, *R.S.T.C.* 1291)

J. BALE, *A mysterye of inquityе contayned within the heretycall Genealogy of Ponce Pantolabus* (Geneva: M. Wood, 1545, *R.S.T.C.* 1303)

J. BALE, *The vocacyon of Johan Bale*, ed. P. Happé and J.N. King *(Medieval and Renaissance Texts and Studies* 70, Renaissance English Text Society 7th ser. 14, 1989)

Bishop BARLOWE'S Dialogue on the Lutheran Factions . . . , ed. J.R. Lunn (Ellis and Keene, 1897)

The Works of Thomas BECON, ed. J. Ayre (3 vols, P.S., 1843–4)

The Letter Book of Thomas BENTHAM, Bishop of Coventry and Lichfield, 1560–1561, ed. R. O'Day and J. Berlatsky, *Camden Miscellany* 27 (C.S. 4th ser. 22, 1979), pp. 113–237

R. BONNER [probably a pseudonym], *A treatyse of the ryght honourynge and wourshyppyng of our saviour Jesus Christe in the sacrament of breade and wyne* . . . (W. Lynne, 1548; *R.S.T.C.* 3287)

N. BOURBON, *Nugarum libri octo* (Lyon: S. Gryphius, 1538): B.L. shelfmark 1213 b. 24

The Writings of John BRADFORD, M.A. . . . , ed. A. Townsend (2 vols, P.S., 1848, 1853)

M. BUCER, *Metaphrases et enarrationes perpetuae Epistolarum D. Pauli Apostoli . . . Tomus Primus continens metaphrasim et enarrationem in Epistolam ad Romanos* (Strasbourg: W. Rihel, 1536) Bodley shelfmark A.3.9 Th.

The Gratulation of the mooste famous Clerke M. Martin BUCER. . . . , tr. and with preface by T. Hoby (R. Jugge, 1548, *R.S.T.C.* 3963)

Common Places of Martin BUCER, ed. D.F. Wright (Appleford: Courtenay Library of Reformation Classics 4, 1972)

Martin BUCER and the Book of Common Prayer, ed. E.C. Whitaker (A.C.C. 55, 1974)

Martini BUCERI Opera Latina IV: Consilium Theologicum privatim conscriptum, ed. P. Fraenkel (Leiden: E.J. Brill, Studies in Medieval and Reformation Thought 42, 1988)

Martin BUCER und Thomas CRANMER: Annotationes in octo priora capita evangelii secundum Matthaeum, Croydon 1549, ed. H. Vogt (Frankfurt: Athenäum Verlag, 1972)

Heinrich BULLINGERS Diarium (Annales Vitae) der Jahre 1504–1574, ed. E. Egli (Basel: Quellen zur Schweizerischen Reformationsgeschichte . . . 2, 1904)

Heinrich BULLINGER Werke (Theologischer Verlag, Zürich, 1972f.; in progress) (I am most grateful to Dr Bruce Gordon for obtaining copies of items from volumes still in preparation)

The BYBLE in Englyshe . . . (R. Grafton and E. Whitchurch, 1539, *R.S.T.C.* 2068)

The BYBLE in Englyshe . . . with a prologe therinto, made by the reverende father in God Thomas Archbysshop of Cantorbury (E. Whitchurch, 1540, *R.S.T.C.* 2070)

CALENDAR of State Papers Domestic, Edward VI, Philip and Mary, Elizabeth (9 vols, H.M.S.O., 1856–72. A supplementary volume ed. by C.S. Knighton, 1992, replaces the older Calendar for Edward VI, 1547–53)

CALENDAR of State Papers, Foreign (23 vols, H.M.S.O., 1863–1950)

CALENDAR of State Papers . . . Milan, ed. A.B. Hinds (H.M.S.O., 1912)

CALENDAR of State Papers, Spanish, ed. P. de Gayangos, G. Mattingly, M.A.S. Hume and R. Tyler (15 vols in 20, H.M.S.O., 1862–1954)

CALENDAR of State Papers, Venetian, ed. R. Brown, C. Bentinck and H. Brown (9 vols, H.M.S.O., 1864–98)

W. CAMDEN, *The History of the most renowned and victorious Princess Elizabeth* (C. Harper and J. Amery, 3rd edn 1675)

CANTERBURY COLLEGE, Oxford, ed. W.A. Pantin (Oxford Historical Society, 6–8, 30, 1947–50, 1985)

Correspondance Politique de Mm. de CASTILLON et de MARILLAC . . ., ed. J. Kaulek (Paris, 1885)

A CATECHISM set forth by Thomas Cranmer from the Nuremberg Catechism translated into Latin by Justus Jonas, ed. D.G. Selwyn (Appleford: Courtenay Library of Reformation Classics 6, 1978). NB that this has two separate paginations, one for the introduction and one for the main text.

CATECHISMUS, That is to say a shorte instruction into Christian Religion . . . (W. Lynne, 1548, *R.S.T.C.* 5993, 5994)

G. CAVENDISH, *The Life of Cardinal Wolsey . . . and metrical visions* . . ., ed. S.W. Singer (2 vols, Harding, Triphook and Lepard, 1825)

De obitu doctissimi et sanctissimi theologi Doctoris Martini Buceri, ed. J. CHEKE (Reynold Wolfe, 1551, *R.S.T.C.* 5108). Publ. in enlarged form as C. Hubert and J. Cheke, *Historia Vera de vita M. Buceri et P. Fagii; item historia Catharinae Vermiliae* (1561, *R.S.T.C.* and Strasbourg, 1562)

The CHRONICLE OF CALAIS, in the reigns of Henry VII and Henry VIII to the year 1540, ed. J. Gough Nichols (C.S. 1st ser. 35, 1846)

The CHRONICLE and political papers of King EDWARD VI, ed. W.K. Jordan (George Allen and Unwin, 1966)

CHRONICLE OF King HENRY VIII of England . . . , tr. and ed. M.S. Hume (George Bell & Sons, 1889)

The CHRONICLE of Queen Jane, and of Two Years of Queen Mary, ed. J. Gough Nichols (C.S. 1st ser. 48, 1850)

CHURCH Life in Kent, being Church Court Records of the Canterbury Diocese 1559–1565, ed. A.J. Willis (London and Chichester: Phillimore, 1975)

'Letters of the CLIFFORDS, Lords Clifford and Earls of Cumberland', ed. R.W. Hoyle, *Camden Miscellany* 31 (C.S. 4th ser. 44, 1992), pp. 1–189

Scopa Joannis COCHLAEI Germani, in Aranea Ricardi Morysini Angli (Leipzig: Nicholas Wolrab, 1538)

T. COLE, *A godly and frutefull sermon, made at Maydestone* . . . (London, Reyner Wolfe, 1553, *R.S.T.C.* 5539; copy in library of Emmanuel College, Cambridge, MS 4.4.1 (3)

'Transcript of an original manuscript, containing a memorial from George CONSTANTINE to Thomas Lord Cromwell', ed. T. Amyot, *Archaeologia* 23 (1831), pp. 50–78

Journals of the House of COMMONS, 1547ff (17 vols, s.a.)

'"The COMMOYSON in Norfolk, 1549": a narrative of popular rebellion in 16th century England', ed. B.L. Beer, *Journal of Medieval and Renaissance Studies* 6 (1976), pp. 73–99.

CORPUS REFORMATORUM, ed. C.G. Bretschneider *et al.* (101 vols to date, 1834–present)

Writings and Translations of Myles COVERDALE . . . , ed. G. Pearson (P.S., 1844)

Remains of Myles COVERDALE . . . , ed. G. Pearson (P.S., 1846)

Remains of Thomas CRANMER, D.D. . . . , ed. H. Jenkyns (4 vols, Oxford, 1833)

Works of Archbishop CRANMER, ed. J.E. Cox (2 vols, P.S., 1844 [Vol. 1 in two paginations], 1846)

T. CRANMER, *A Defence of the true and catholike doctrine of the sacrament* . . . (R. Wolfe, 1550, *R.S.T.C* 6000, 6001). References in the text are specified as taken from *Remains of CRANMER*, ed. Jenkyns, as above, vol. 2, or as embedded in the text of the *Answer*, pr. *Works of CRANMER*, ed. Cox, vol. 1.

All the submissyons, and recantations of Thomas CRANMER, late Archebyshop of Canterburye, truely set forth both in Latyn and Englysh . . . (J. Cawood, 1556, *R.S.T.C.* 5590)

T. CRANMER, *A Confutation of unwritten verities* (T. Purfoote, 1582, *R.S.T.C.* 5997)

The Work of Thomas CRANMER, ed. G.E. Duffield, with introd. by J.I. Packer (Appleford: Courtenay Library of Reformation Classics 2, 1964)

Cranmer: see also BONNER; *BUCER und CRANMER; CATECHISM*

[?Harpsfield, N.], *Bishop CRANMER'S RECANTACYONS*, ed. Lord Houghton with introd. by J. Gairdner (Philobiblon Society Miscellanies 15, 1877–84)

Fourth Report of the DEPUTY KEEPER of the Public Records (February 28, 1843) . . . (H.M.S.O., 1843)

The DIVORCE TRACTS of Henry VIII, eds E. Surtz and V. Murphy (Angers: Moreana, 1988)

DOCUMENTS OF THE ENGLISH REFORMATION, ed. G. Bray (Cambridge: James Clarke and Co., 1994)

Four Political Treatises: the Doctrinal of Princes (1533); Pasquil the Playne (1533); The Banquette of Sapience (1534); The Image of Governance (1541) by Sir Thomas ELYOT, ed. L. Gottesman (Gainesville, Florida: Scolars' Facsimiles and Reprints, 1967)

ENGLISH HISTORICAL DOCUMENTS 1485–1558, ed. C.H. Williams (Eyre and Spottiswoode, 1967)

EPISTOLAE TIGURINAE de rebus potissimum ad ecclesiae Anglicanae Reformationem pertinentibus . . . (P.S., 1848)

Opus EPISTOLARUM Des. ERASMI Roterodami . . . , eds P.S. Allen, H.M. Allen and H.W. Garrod (12 vols, Oxford, 1906–58)

'An EYE-WITNESS'S ACCOUNT of the *coup d'état* of October 1549', ed. A.J.A. Malciewicz, *E.H.R.* 70 (1955), pp. 600–609

FACULTY OFFICE REGISTERS 1534–1549, ed. D.S. Chambers (Oxford: Clarendon Press, 1966)

The FIRST PRAYER BOOK of Edward VI compared with successive revisions of the Book of Common Prayer (Oxford and James Parker, 1877)

J. FOXE, *Acts and Monuments of these latter and perilous days* . . . (London: J. Day, 1563, *R.S.T.C.* 11222)

The Acts and Monuments of John FOXE, ed. G. Townshend and S.R. Cattley (8 vols, 1837–41)

J. FOXE, *Rerum in ecclesia gestarum commentarii* (2 vols, Basel: Nicholas Brylinger and Johannes Oporinus, 1559–63)

Obedience in Church and State: three political tracts by Stephen GARDINER, ed. P. JANELLE (Cambridge U.P., 1930)

The Letters of Stephen GARDINER, ed. J.A. Muller (Cambridge U.P., 1933)

Notitia Cestriensis . . . by the Right Rev. Francis GASTRELL . . . , ed. F.R. Raines (Chetham Society, 4 vols, Old Ser. 8, 19, 21, 24, 1845, 1849–50)

Scrinium Antiquarium, ed. D. GERDES (Groningen and Bremen: Corn. Barlingkhof and G.W. Rump, 1749–65)

Gleanings of a few scattered ears, during the period of the Reformation in England . . . , ed. G.C. GORHAM (Bell and Daldy, 1857)

GRACE BOOKS, ed. S.M. Leathes et al. (5 vols, Cambridge Antiquarian Soc., Luard Memorial Ser. 1, 1897–1910)

The Writings of John GREENWOOD 1587–1590, ed. L.H. Carlson (George Allen and Unwin; Elizabethan Nonconformist Texts 4, 1962)

The Writings of John GREENWOOD and Henry BARROW 1591–1593, ed. L.H. Carlson (George Allen and Unwin; Elizabethan Nonconformist Texts 6, 1970)

Chronicle of the GREY FRIARS of London, ed. J. Gough Nichols (C.S. 1st Ser. 53, 1852)

The Remains of Edmund GRINDAL, D.D. . . . , ed. W. Nicholson (P.S., 1843)

Simonis GRYNAEI . . . Epistolae, ed. G.T. Streuber (Basel, 1847)

E. HALL, *The Triumphant Reigne of Kyng Henry the VIII*, ed. C. Whibley (2 vols, T.C. and E.C. Jack, 1904)

HANDLIST of British Diplomatic Representatives 1509–1688, ed. G.M. Bell (Royal Historical Society, 1990)

A treatise on the pretended divorce between Henry VIII and Catherine of Aragon, by Nicholas HARPSFIELD . . . , ed. N. Pocock (C.S. 2nd ser. 21, 1878)

HARPSFIELD'S narrative of the Divorce of Henry VIII and Catherine of Aragon, ed. Lord Acton (1880?) (narrative portions of Harpsfield ed. Pocock, 1878, from a different MS)

Archdeacon HARPSFIELD'S Visitation, 1557, ed. L.E. Whatmore (Catholic Record Society 45/46, 1950–51)

[?Harpsfield, N.], see *Bishop CRANMER'S RECANTACYONS*

The Writings of Robert HARRISON and Robert BROWNE, ed. A. Peel and L.H. Carlson (George Allen and Unwin; Elizabethan Nonconformist Texts 2, 1953)

William HARRISON, *The Description of England*, ed. G. Edelen (Ithaca: Cornell U.P., 1968)

Miscellaneous writings of HENRY THE EIGHTH . . . , ed. F. Macnamara (Golden Cockerel, 1924)

HISTORICAL Manuscripts Commission, Reports:

Manuscripts of . . . the Marquess of BATH (5 vols, ser. 58, 1904–80)

Manuscripts of . . . Earl COWPER (3 vols, ser. 23, 1888–9)

Records of the City of EXETER (ser. 73, 1916)

FIFTH Report (ser. 6, 1876)

Manuscripts of . . . Allan George FINCH (4 vols, 5th in preparation, ser. 71, 1913–65)

FOURTEENTH Report, Appendix 8 (ser. 37, 1895)

FOURTH Report (ser. 3, 1874)

Manuscripts . . . preserved at HATFIELD House (24 vols, ser. 9, 1883–1976)

NINTH Report (ser. 10, 1884)

Manuscripts of . . . the Duke of RUTLAND (4 vols, ser. 24, 1888–1905)

SEVENTH Report (ser. 6, 1879)

SIXTH Report (ser. 5, 1877–8)

TENTH Report, Appendix 6 (ser. 15, 1887)

THIRD Report (ser. 2, 1872)

Manuscripts in VARIOUS COLLECTIONS 1 (8 vols, ser. 55, 1901–14)

Manuscripts of WELLS Cathedral (Tenth Report, Appendix 3, 1885)

The travels and life of Sir Thomas HOBY . . . , ed. E. Powell (*Camden Miscellany* 10, C.S. 3rd ser. 4, 1902)

R. HOLINSHED, *Chronicles, &c.* . . . , ed. H. Ellis (6 vols, 1807–8)

Certain Sermons or HOMILIES (1547) and A Homily against Disobedience and Wilful Rebellion (1570), ed. R.B. Bond (Toronto U.P., 1987)

Early Writings of Bishop HOOPER . . . , ed. S. Carr (P.S., 1843)

Later Writings of Bishop HOOPER . . . , ed. C. Nevinson (P.S., 1852)

Hubert, C.: see Cheke, J.

The Works of Roger HUTCHINSON . . . , ed. J. Bruce (P.S., 1842)

The INSTITUTION of a Christen Man . . . (1537, *R.S.T.C.* 5163; B.L. C.38 f. 21)

'INVENTORIES of parish church goods in Kent, A.D. 1552', ed. M.E.C. Walcott, R.P. Coates and W.A. Scott Robertson, *A.C.* 8 (1872), pp. 74–163; 14 (1882), pp. 289?–312

The Letter Book of Robert JOSEPH . . . , ed. [J.] H. Aveling and W.A. Pantin (Oxford Historical Society N.S. 19, 1967)

G. JOYE, *The Letters whyche Johan Ashwell Priour of Newnham Abbey . . . sente . . . wherin the sayde pryour accuseth George Joye . . . wyth the answere of the sayde George . . .* (Strasbourg, ?1527, *R.S.T.C.* 844)

The Visitation of KENT, taken in the years 1619–1621. By John Philipot, Rouge Dragon . . ., ed. R. Hovenden (Harleian Society 42, 1898)

The Visitations of KENT, taken in the years 1530–1 by Thomas Benolte, Clarenceux and 1574 by Robert Cooke, Clarenceux, Pt. 1, ed. W.B. Bannerman (Harleian Society 74, 1923)

The Visitations of KENT, taken in the years 1574 and 1592 by Robert Cooke, Clarenceux, Pt. 2, ed. W.B. Bannerman (Harleian Society 75, 1924)

Johannes KESSLERS 'Sabbata' mit kleineren schriften und briefen, ed. E. Egli and R. Schoch (Historischen Verein des Kantons St Gallen, 1902)

The Works of John KNOX, ed. D. Laing (6 vols, Edinburgh, 1846–64)

Joannis a LASCO opera tam edita quam inedita, ed. A. Kuyper (2 vols, Amsterdam, 1866)

Sermons by Hugh LATIMER . . . , Sermons and Remains of Hugh Latimer . . ., ed. G.E. Corrie (P.S., 1844, 1845)

'William LATYMER'S Chronickille of Anne Bulleyne', ed. M. Dowling, *Camden Miscellany* 30 (C.S. 4th ser. 39, 1990), pp. 23–66

LELAND's Itinerary in England and Wales, ed. L. Toulmin Smith (G. Bell and Sons, 5 vols, 1906–8, repr. with introd. by T. Kendrick, Centaur Press, 1964)

J. LE NEVE, *Fasti Ecclesiae Anglicanae* (revised edn, Athlone Press, 1962-date): *1300–1541* (12 vols); *1541–1857* (4 vols, in progress)

LETTERS AND PAPERS, Foreign and Domestic, of the reign of Henry VIII, 1509–47, ed. J.S. Brewer *et al.* (H.M.S.O., 21 vols and 2 vols addenda, 1862–1932)

Chapter Acts of the Cathedral Church of St Mary of LINCOLN A.D. 1536–1547, 1547–1559, ed. R.E.G. Cole (Lincoln Record Soc. 13, 15, 1913, 1917)

LINCOLNSHIRE Pedigrees, ed. A.R. Maddison (4 vols, Harleian Society 51–3, 55, 1902–4, 1906: continuous pagination)

The LISLE Letters, ed. M. St C. Byrne (6 vols, 1980)

The Two LITURGIES . . . set forth by authority in the reign of King Edward VI . . ., ed. J. Ketley (P.S., 1844)

Formularies of Faith put forth by authority during the reign of Henry VIII, ed. C. LLOYD (Oxford, 1825)

'A LONDON Chronicle during the Reigns of Henry the Seventh and Henry the Eighth', ed. C. Hopper (*Camden Miscellany* 4, C.S. Old Ser. 73, 1859), pp. 1–21

LONDON and Middlesex Chantry Certificate 1548, ed. C.J. Kitching (London Record Society 16, 1980)

Journals of the House of LORDS, 1509ff (10 vols, s.a.)

LUTHER AND ERASMUS: Free Will and Salvation, ed. E.G. Rupp, A.N. Marlow, P.S. Wilson and B. Drewery (S.C.M. Press: *Library of Christian Classics* 17, 1969)

The Diary of Henry MACHYN, citizen and merchant-taylor of London, 1550–63, ed. J.G. Nichols (C.S. 1st ser. 42, 1848)

MARILLAC: see CASTILLON

P. MARTYR VERMIGLI, *Loci Communes* (1583, *R.S.T.C.* 24668)

MELANCHTHONS BRIEFWECHSEL: Kritische und Kommentierte Gesamtausgabe, ed. H. Scheible, W. Thüringer and R. Wetzel (7 vols and 1 vol of texts, Stuttgart-Bad Cannstatt: Fromann-Holzboog, 1977–93, in progress)

Philippi MELANCHTHONIS EPISTOLAE, iudicia, consilia, testimonia aliorumque ad eum epistolae quae in Corpore Reformatorum desiderantur . . . , ed. H.E. Bindseil (Halle: G. Schwetschke, 1874)

[MERLIN], *Quatuor conciliorum generalium. Quadraginta septem conciliorum provincialium authenticorum* . . . (4 vols, Paris, 1524)

The Correspondence of Sir Thomas MORE, ed. E.F. Rogers (1947)

R. MORISON, *Apomaxis calumniarum convitiorumque quibus Joannes Cochlaeus . . . in regis invidiam epistola studuit* (1537, *R.S.T.C.* 18109)

NARRATIVES of the Reformation, ed. J.G. Nichols (C.S. 1st ser. 77, 1859)

A NECESSARY DOCTRINE and erudition for any Christen man . . . (T. Bertelet, 1543; *R.S.T.C.* 5168, B.L. C. 37 e.12(1))

Ambassades de Messieurs NOAILLES en Angleterre, ed. A. de Vertot d'Anbeuf and C. Villaret (5 vols, Leyden, 1763)

The Visitations of the County of NOTTINGHAM in the Years 1569 and 1614 . . . , ed. G.W. Marshall (Harleian Society 4, 1871)

The Visitation of NOTTINGHAMSHIRE begun in 1662 and finished in 1664 made by William Dugdale . . . , ed. G.D. Squibb (Harleian Society New Ser. 5, 1986)

ORIGINAL Letters relative to the English Reformation . . . , ed. H. Robinson (2 vols, P.S., 1846–7)

ORIGINAL Letters illustrative of English History . . . from autographs in the British Museum and . . . other collections, ed. H. Ellis (11 vols in 3 series: Harding, Triphook and Lepard, 1824, 1827, 1846)

Andreas OSIANDER d. ä. Gesamtausgabe, ed. G. Müller and G. Seebass (8 vols, Güterslohe: Gerd Mohn, 1975–90; in progress)

'A critique of the Protectorate: an unpublished letter of Sir William PAGET to the Duke of Somerset', ed. B.L. Beer, *Huntington Library Quarterly* 34 (May 1971), pp. 277–83

'The Letters of William, Lord PAGET of Beaudesert, 1547–1563', ed. B.L. Beer and S.M. Jack (*Camden Miscellany* 25, Camden 4th ser. 13, 1974), pp. 1–142

M. PARKER, *De Antiquitate Britannicae Ecclesiae* . . . (1572, *R.S.T.C.* 19292)

Correspondence of Matthew PARKER, D.D. . . . , ed. J. Bruce and T.T. Perowne (P.S., 1853)

'Robert PARKYN'S narrative of the Reformation', ed. A.G. Dickens, *E.H.R.* 62 (1947), pp. 58–83

The Examinations and Writings of John PHILPOT . . . , ed. R. Eden (P.S., 1842)

[J. PHILPOT or V. Poullain], *Vera Expositio disputationis institutae mandato D. Mariae Reginae* . . . (Cologne, 1554, *R.S.T.C.* 19891)

PILKINGTON, James: see TUNSTALL

J. PONET, *A shorte treatise of politike power* (1556, *R.S.T.C.* 20178)

Poullain: see Philpot

PRIVATE PRAYERS put forth by authority during the reign of Queen Elizabeth, ed. W. Keatinge Clay (P.S., 1851)

PROCEEDINGS and Ordinances of the Privy Council of England VII: 32 Henry VIII MDXL to 33 Henry VIII MDXLII, ed. H. Nicolas (1837)

PROCEEDINGS in the Parliaments of Elizabeth I: I. 1558–1581, ed. T.E. Hartley (Leicester U.P., 1981)

George RAINSFORD'S Ritratto d'Ingliterra (1556), ed. P.S. Donaldson (*Camden Miscellany* 27, C.S. 4th ser. 22, 1979), pp. 49–111

The RATIONALE *of Ceremonial 1540–1543 with Notes and Appendices and an essay on the Regulation of Ceremonial during the Reign of Henry VIII*, ed. C.S. Cobb (*A.C.C.* 18, 1910)

RECORDS *of Early English Drama: Cambridge*, ed. A.H. Nelson (2 vols, Toronto U.P., 1989)

RECORDS *of the Reformation: the Divorce, 1527–33*, ed. N. Pocock (2 vols, Oxford, 1870)

The REFORMATION *of the Ecclesiastical Laws as attempted in the Reigns of King Henry VIII, King Edward VI, and Queen Elizabeth*, ed. E. Cardwell (Oxford, 1850)

The REFORMATION *of the Ecclesiastical Laws of England, 1552*, ed. J.C. Spalding (Sixteenth Century Essays and Studies 19, 1992)

REGISTRA *Stephani* GARDINER *et Johannis* POYNET, ed. H. Chitty with introd. by idem and H.E. Malden (Canterbury and York Society 37, 1930)

REGISTRUM *Johannis* WHYTE . . . , ed. W.H. Frere (Canterbury and York Society 16, 1914; bound with vol. 37)

U. RHEGIUS, *A Declaration of the Twelve Articles . . . and the righte foundation and principall common places of the hole godly scripture*, ed. W. Lynne (R. Jugge, 1548, *R.S.T.C.* 20843)

The Works of Nicholas RIDLEY, *D.D.* . . . , ed. H. Christmas (P.S., 1843)

The Catholic Doctrine of the Church of England, an Exposition of the Thirty-Nine Articles by Thomas ROGERS . . . , ed. J.J.S. Perowne (P.S., 1853)

'ST. MARTIN'S CHURCH, NEW ROMNEY: records relating to its removal in A.D. 1550', ed. H. Bacheler Walker and W.L. Rutton, *A.C.* 20 (1893), pp. 155–60

N. SANDER, *Rise and growth of the Anglican Schism* (Burns and Oates, 1877)

'The Letters of Richard SCUDAMORE to Sir Philip Hoby, September 1549–March 1555', ed. S. Brigden, *Camden Miscellany* 30 (C.S. 4th ser. 39, 1990), pp. 67–148

Correspondance Politique de Odet de SELVE . . . , ed. G. Lefèvre-Pontalis (Paris, 1888)

'The SERMON against the Holy Maid of Kent and her adherents, delivered at Paul's Cross, November the 23rd, 1533, and at Canterbury, December the 7th', ed. L.E. Whatmore, *E.H.R.* 58 (1943), pp. 463–75.

A SHORT TITLE CATALOGUE *of Books printed in England, Scotland, and Ireland and of English Books Printed Abroad before the year 1640*, ed. A.W. Pollard and G.R. Redgrave, rev. W.A. Jackson and F.S. Ferguson and completed by K.F. Pantzer (The Bibliographical Society, 3 vols, 1976–91)

The Life and illustrious martyrdom of Sir Thomas More by Thomas STAPLETON, tr. P.E. Hallett, ed. E.E. Reynolds (New York: Fordham U.P., 1966)

Thomas STARKEY, *A Dialogue between Pole and Lupset*, ed. T.F. Mayer (C.S. 4th ser. 37, 1989)

The Papers of Nathaniel Bacon of STIFFKEY, ed. A.H. Smith and G.M. Baker (4 vols, Centre of East Anglian Studies, University of East Anglia, 1979–93, in progress)

STATE *Papers published under the authority of His Majesty's Commission, King Henry VIII* (11 vols, 1830–52)

Three Chapters of Letters relating to the SUPPRESSION *of Monasteries*, ed. T. Wright (C.S. 1st ser. 26, 1843)

TESTAMENTA *Eboracensia* . . . , Part 4, ed. J. Raine jun. (Surtees Society 53, 1869)

TESTAMENTA *Vetusta* . . . , ed. N.H. Nicolas, (2 vols [continuous pagination], 1826)

TREVELYAN PAPERS prior to A.D. 1558, ed. J. Payne Collier (C.S. 1st ser. 67, 1856)

TROUBLES connected with the Prayer Book of 1549 . . ., ed. N. Pocock (C.S. 1st ser. 37, 1884)

TUDOR ROYAL PROCLAMATIONS, ed. P.L. Hughes and J.F. Larkin (2 vols, New Haven and Yale U.P., 1964, 1969)

TUDOR TRACTS 1532–1588, with introd. by A.F. Pollard (Archibald Constable, 1903)

The Registers of Cuthbert TUNSTALL Bishop of Durham 1530–59 and James Pilkington Bishop of Durham 1561–76, ed. G. Hinde (Surtees Society 161, 1946)

W. TURNER, *The Huntyng and Fyndyng out of the Romish Fox . . .*, ed. and abridged R. Potts (Cambridge, 1851)

'TWO LONDON Chronicles from the collections of John Stow . . .', ed. C.L. Kingsford, *Camden Miscellany* 4 (C.S. 3rd ser. 18, 1910), pp. iii–59

Doctrinal Treatises and introductions to different portions of the Holy Scriptures. By William TYNDALE . . ., ed. H. Walter (P.S., 1848)

Expositions and Notes on sundry portions of the Holy Scriptures together with the Practice of Prelates. By William TYNDALE . . ., ed. H. Walter (P.S., 1849)

An Answer to Sir Thomas More's Dialogue, the Supper of the Lord . . . and William Tracy's Testament expounded. By William TYNDALE . . ., ed. H. Walter (P.S., 1850)

P.V., Historical Narration of certain events that took place in the Kingdom of Great Britain in the month of July, in the year of our Lord, 1553, ed. J.P. Berjeau (Bell and Daldy, 1865)

Die VADIANISCHE Briefsammlung der Stadtbibliothek St Gallen, ed. E. Arbenz and H. Wartmann (7 vols, St Gallen, 1890–1913)

VISITATIONS in the Diocese of Lincoln 1517–1531, ed. A. Hamilton Thompson (3 vols: Lincoln Record Society 33, 35, 37, 1940, 1944, 1947)

'The *VITA MARIAE Angliae Reginae* of Robert Wingfield of Brantham', ed. D. MacCulloch (*Camden Miscellany* 28, C.S. 4th ser. 29, 1984), pp. 181–301

R. WATSON, *Aetiologia Roberti Watsoni Angli . . .* ([Emden], 1556; *R.S.T.C.* 25111)

The Autobiography of Thomas WHYTHORNE, ed. J.M. Osborn (Oxford: Clarendon Press, 1961)

Concilia Magnae Britanniae et Hiberniae, ed. D. WILKINS (4 vols, 1737)

The Work of Archbishop John WILLIAMS, ed. B. Williams (Appleford: Sutton Courtenay Press, Courtenay Library of Reformation Classics 14, 1980)

'WOLSEY'S and Cranmer's visitations of the Priory of Worcester', ed. J.W. Wilson, *E.H.R.* 31 (1926), pp. 418–23

A Chronicle of England . . . by Charles WRIOTHESLEY, Windsor Herald, ed. W.D. Hamilton (2 vols, C.S. 2nd ser. 11, 20, 1875, 1877)

The Papers of George WYATT Esquire . . ., ed. D.M. Loades (C.S. 4th ser. 5, 1968)

The ZÜRICH Letters . . ., ed. H. Robinson (2 vols, P.S., 1842, 1845)

Secondary printed works: books and articles

ABRAY, L.G., *The People's Reformation: Magistrates, Clergy and Commons in Strassburg 1500–1598* (Oxford: Basil Blackwell, 1985)

ADAIR, E.R., 'William Thomas: A forgotten clerk of the Privy Council', in R.W. Seton-Watson (ed.), *Tudor Studies Presented . . . to Albert Frederick Pollard . . .* (Longman, 1924; repr. New York, 1970), pp. 133–60

ALEXANDER, G., 'Victim or spendthrift? The Bishop of London and his income in the sixteenth century', in E.W. Ives, R.J. Knecht and J.J. Scarisbrick (eds), *Wealth and Power in Tudor England* (Athlone Press, 1978)

ALSOP, J.D., 'Thomas Argall, Administrator of Ecclesiastical Affairs in the Tudor Church and State', *Recusant History* 15 (1979–81), pp. 227–38

——, 'Cromwell and the Church in 1531; the case of Waltham Abbey', *J.Eccl.Hist.* 31 (1980), pp. 327–30

——, 'Latimer, the "Commonwealth of Kent" and the 1549 rebellions', *H.J.* 28 (1985), pp. 379–83

——, 'Philip Melanchthon and England in 1553', *N.Q.* N.S. 37 (June 1990), pp. 164–5

ANDERSON, M., *Peter Martyr: A Reformer in Exile (1542–1562): A Chronology of Biblical Writings in England and Europe* (Nieuwkoop: B. de Graaf, *Bibliotheca Humanistica et Reformatorica* 10, 1975)

——, 'Rhetoric and reality: Peter Martyr and the English Reformation', *S.C.J.* 19 (1988), pp. 451–69

[Anon., possibly F.E. Brightman], 'Cranmer's liturgical projects', *C.Q.R.* 31 (1891), pp. 446–62

[Anon.], 'The true history of the Edwardine Ordinal', *C.Q.R.* 44 (1897), pp. 123–47

ASTON, M., 'Gold and images', in W.J. Sheils and D. Wood (eds), *The Church and Wealth* (*St.Ch.Hist.* 24, 1987), pp. 189–208

——, *England's Iconoclasts. I. Laws against Images* (Oxford: Clarendon Press, 1988)

——, 'Segregation in church', in W.J. Sheils and D. Wood (eds), *Women in the Church* (*St.Ch.Hist.* 27, 1990), pp. 237–94

ASTON, T.H., DUNCAN G.D., and EVANS, T.A.R., 'The medieval alumni of the University of Cambridge', *P.P.* 86 (Feb 1980), pp. 9–86

AVIS, P.D.L., *The Church in the Theology of the Reformers* (Marshall, Morgan and Scott, 1981)

AWTY, B.G., 'The Continental origins of Wealden ironworkers, 1451–1544', *Economic History Review* 34 (1981), pp. 524–39

AYRIS, P., and SELWYN, D., (eds), *Thomas Cranmer: Churchman and Scholar* (Woodbridge: Boydell Press, 1993)

AYRIS, P., 'Thomas Cranmer and "devotion" money: the collections of 1543', *J.Eccl.H.*, forthcoming, 1997. I am grateful to Dr Ayris for allowing me to see an advance copy of his article.

BACKHUIZEN, J.N., van den Brink, 'Ratramn's eucharistic doctrine and its influence in 16th century England', in G.J. Cuming (ed.), *St.Ch.Hist.* 2 (1965), pp. 54–77

BAILEY, A., 'A legal view of Cranmer's execution', *E.H.R.* 7 (1892), pp. 466–70

BAILEY, D.S., 'Robert Wisdom under persecution, 1541–1543', *J. Eccl. Hist.* 2 (1951), pp. 180–89

——, *Thomas Becon and the Reformation of the Church of England* (Edinburgh, 1952)

BARTLETT, K., 'Papal policy and the English Crown, 1563–1565: The Bertano correspondence', *S.C.J.* 23 (1992), pp. 643–59

BASKERVILLE, E.J., 'John Ponet in exile: A Ponet letter to John Bale', *J.Eccl.Hist.* 37 (1986), pp. 442–7

BASKERVILLE, G., 'A sister of Archbishop Cranmer', *E.H.R.* 51, pp. 287–9

BATLEY, J.Y., *On a Reformer's Latin Bible: Being an Essay on the 'Adversaria' in the Vulgate of Thomas Bilney* (Cambridge, 1940)

BEDOUELLE, G., and LE GAL, P., *Le 'Divorce' du Roi Henry VIII: Etudes et Documents* (Geneva: *Travaux d'Humanism et Renaissance* 221, 1987)

BEER, B.L., *Northumberland: The Political Career of John Dudley, Earl of Warwick and Duke of Northumberland* (Kent State U.P., 1973)

——, *Rebellion and Riot: Popular Disorder in England during the Reign of Edward VI* (Kent State U.P., 1982)

——, 'London parish clergy and the Protestant Reformation, 1547–1559', *Albion* 18 (1986), pp. 375–93

——, 'Philip Melanchthon and the Cambridge Professorship', *N.Q.* 232 (1987), p. 185

BEESLEY, A., 'An unpublished source of the Book of Common Prayer: Peter Martyr Vermigli's *Adhortatio ad Coenam Domini Mysticam*', *J.Eccl.Hist.* 19 (1968), pp. 83–8

BEHRENS, B., 'A note on Henry VIII's divorce project of 1514', *B.I.H.R.* 11 (1933–4), pp. 163–4

BERNARD, G.W., 'The Pardon of the Clergy reconsidered', with comment by J. Guy, *J.Eccl.Hist.* 37 (1986), pp. 258–87

——, 'The fall of Anne Boleyn', *E.H.R.* 106 (1990), pp. 584–610

——, 'Anne Boleyn's religion', *H.J.* 36 (1993), pp. 1–20

BEVAN, A., 'Justices of the Peace, 1509–47: An additional source', *B.I.H.R.* 58 (1985), pp. 242–48.

BINDOFF, S.T., 'A kingdom at stake, 1553', *History Today* 3 (1953), pp. 642–8

DE BIRCH, G.W., *A Catalogue of Seals in the Department of MSS in the British Museum* (6 vols; British Museum, 1887–1900)

BLACK, P.M., 'Matthew Parker's search for Cranmer's "Great Notable Written Books"', *The Library*, 5th ser. 29 (1974), pp. 312–22.

BLENCH, J.W., *Preaching in England in the late 15th and 16th Centuries* (Oxford: Basil Blackwell, 1964)

BLOCK, J., *Factional Politics and the English Reformation 1520–1540* (R.H.S.St.Hist. 66, 1993)

BLOMEFIELD, F., and PARKIN, C., *A Topographical History of . . . Norfolk* (11 vols; 1805–10)

BOONE PORTER, H., 'Hispanic influences on worship in the English tongue', in J.N. Alexander (ed.), *Time and Community* (Washington: Pastoral Press, 1990), pp. 171–84

BOWKER, M., 'Lincolnshire 1536: Heresy, schism or religious discontent?' in D. Baker (ed.), *Schism, Heresy and Religious Protest* (*St.Ch.Hist.* 9, 1972), pp. 195–212

——, 'The Supremacy and the episcopate: The struggle for control, 1534–40', *H.J.* 18 (1975), pp. 227–43

——, *The Henrician Reformation: The Diocese of Lincoln under John Longland 1521–1547* (Cambridge U.P., 1981)

BRADSHAW, B., and DUFFY, E. (eds), *Humanism, Reform and the Reformation: The Career of Bishop John Fisher* (Cambridge U.P., 1989)

BRANDI, K., *The Emperor Charles V* (Jonathan Cape, 1965)

BRIGDEN, S., 'Tithe controversy in Reformation London', *J.Eccl.Hist.* 32 (1981), pp. 285–301

——, *London and the Reformation* (Oxford and New York: Clarendon Press, 1989)

——, 'Henry Howard, Earl of Surrey and the "Conjured League"', *H.J.* 37 (1994), pp. 507–37

[BRIGHTMAN, F.E., writing anonymously], 'Capitulum Coloniense: An episode in the Reformation', *C.Q.R.* 31 (1890–91), pp. 419–37

——, 'The Litany under Henry VIII', *E.H.R.* 24 (1909), pp. 101–4

——, *The English Rite* (2 vols; Rivingtons, 1915)

BRIGHTMAN, F. E.: see also Anon.

BROMILEY, G.W., *Thomas Cranmer, Theologian* (Lutterworth, 1956)

BROOKE, C., *A History of Gonville and Caius College* (Woodbridge: Boydell, 1985)

BROOKS, P.N., 'Cranmer studies in the wake of the quatercentenary', *Historical Magazine of the Protestant Episcopal Church* 31 (1962), pp. 365–74

——, (ed.) *Cranmer, Primate of All England* (British Library, 1989)

——, *Cranmer in Context: Documents from the English Reformation* (Cambridge: Lutterworth Press, 1989)

——, *Thomas Cranmer's Doctrine of the Eucharist. An Essay in Historical Development* (2nd edn Macmillan, 1992, superseding 1965 Macmillan edn); 1st edn reviewed by D.G. Selwyn, *J.T.S.* N.S. 17 (1966), pp. 229–32

BROWN, D.H., 'Abortive attempts to codify English criminal law', *Parliamentary History* 11 (1992), pp. 1–39

BROWN, W.J., *The Life of Rowland Taylor* (Epworth, 1959)

BUCHANAN, C., *What did Cranmer think he was doing?* (Bramcote: Grove Liturgical Study 7, 1976)

BUCKINGHAM, C., 'The movement of clergy in the diocese of Canterbury, 1552–1562', *Recusant History* 14 (1978), pp. 219–41

BURNET, G., *History of the Reformation of the Church of England* (3 vols in 6; 1820)

BUSH, M.L., *The Government Policy of Protector Somerset* (Edward Arnold, 1975)

BUTLER, J., *The Quest for Becket's Bones: The Mystery of the Relics of St Thomas of Canterbury* (New Haven and London: Yale U.P., 1995)

BUTTERWORTH, C.C., *The English Primers (1529–1545): Their Publication and Connection with the English Bible and the Reformation in England* (Philadelphia: Univ. of Pennsylvania Press, 1953)

BUTTERWORTH, C.C., and CHESTER, A.G., *George Joye 1495?–1553: A Chapter in the History of the English Bible and the English Reformation* (Philadelphia: Univ. of Pennsylvania Press, 1962)

BUXTON, R.F., *Eucharist and Institution Narrative* (*A.C.C.* 58, 1976)

CAMERON, A., 'Sir Henry Willoughby of Wollaton', *Tr.Thoroton Soc.* 74 (1970), pp. 10–21

——, 'Meering and the Meryng family', *Tr.Thoroton Soc.* 77 (1973), pp. 41–52

CAMERON, E., *The European Reformation* (Oxford: Clarendon Press, 1991)

CARGILL THOMPSON, W.D.J., 'Who wrote "The Supper of the Lord"?', in Thompson, *Studies in the Reformation: Luther to Hooker*, ed. DUGMORE, C.W. (Athlone Press. 1980), pp. 83–93, repr. from *H.T.R.* 53 (1960), pp. 77–91

CARLSON, E.J., 'Clerical marriage and the English Reformation', *Journal of British Studies* 31 (1992), pp. 1–31

——, *Marriage and the English Reformation* (Oxford and Cambridge, MA: Blackwell, 1994)

CHALLIS, C.E., *The Tudor Coinage* (Manchester U.P., 1978)

CHAMPION, J.A.I., *The Pillars of Priestcraft Shaken: The Church of England and its Enemies 1660–1730* (Cambridge U.P: Cambridge studies in early modern British history, 1992)

CHETTLE, H.F., 'The Burgesses for Calais, 1536–1558', *E.H.R.* 50 (1935), pp. 492–501

CHIBI, A., 'Henry VIII and his Marriage to his brother's wife: The sermon of Bishop John Stokesley of 11 July 1535', *H.R.* 67 (1994), pp. 40–56

CHURCHILL, I.J., *Canterbury Administration* (2 vols; SPCK for Church Historical Society, 1933)

CLARK, P., *English Provincial Society from the Reformation to the Revolution: Religion, Politics and Society in Kent 1500–1640* (Hassocks: Harvester, 1977)

CLEBSCH, W.A., *England's Earliest Protestants* (New Haven: Yale U.P., 1964)

COBBAN, A.B., *The King's Hall within the University of Cambridge in the Late Middle Ages* (Cambridge U.P., 1969)

——, *The Medieval English Universities: Oxford and Cambridge to c. 1500* (Aldershot: Scolar Press, 1988)

COBBETT, W., *A History of the Protestant Reformation in England and Ireland* (repr. Burns Oates and Washbourne, 1925)

C[OKAYNE], G.E., *Complete Peerage of England, Scotland, Ireland, etc., Extant, Extinct, or Dormant*, rev. V. Gibbs, (13 vols; St Catherine Press 1910–49)

COLLINSON, P., *Archbishop Grindal 1519–1583: The Struggle for a Reformed Church* (London: Jonathan Cape, 1979)

——, 'The Reformer and the Archbishop: Martin Bucer and an English Bucerian', *Journal of Religious History* 6 (1971), pp. 305–30; repr. P. Collinson, *Godly People: Essays in English Puritanism and Protestantism* (Hambledon Press, 1983), pp. 19–44

——, 'Thomas Cranmer', in G. Rowell (ed.), *The English Religious Tradition and the Genius of Anglicanism* (Wantage: Ikon Productions, 1993), pp. 79–104

COLLINSON, P., RAMSAY, N. and SPARKS, M. (eds), *A History of Canterbury Cathedral* (Oxford U.P., 1995)

CONSTANT, G., 'Formularies of faith during the reign of Henry VIII', *Downside Review* 54 (1936), pp. 155–64

COURATIN, A.H., 'The service of Holy Communion, 1552–1662', *C.Q.R.* 163 (1962), pp. 431–42; 'The Holy Communion of 1549', *C.Q.R.* 164 (1963), pp. 148–59

COURTENAY, W.J., 'Cranmer as a nominalist *Sed Contra*', *H.T.R.* 57 (1964), pp. 367–80 [see also McGee]

CRAIG, J., 'The marginalia of Dr Rowland Taylor', *H.R.* 64 (1991), pp. 411–20

CRAWFORD, P., *Women and Religion in England 1500–1720* (London and New York: Routledge, 1993)

CRAWLEY, C., *Trinity Hall: The History of a Cambridge College 1350–1975* (Cambridge: Trinity Hall, 1976)

CROSS, C., 'Continental students and the Protestant Reformation in England in the sixteenth century', in D. Baker (ed.), *Reform and Reformation: England and the Continent c. 1500–c. 1750* (Ecclesiastical History Society: *St.Ch.Hist.* Subsidia 2, 1979), pp. 35–58

CUMING, G.J., *The Godly Order: Texts and Studies relating to the Book of Common Prayer* (*A.C.C.* 65, 1983)

CUTTLER, C.D., 'Holbein's inscriptions', *S.C.J.* 24 (1993), pp. 369–82

DAVIES, C.S.L., 'Popular religion and the Pilgrimage of Grace', in A. Fletcher and J. Stevenson (eds), *Order and Disorder in Early Modern England* (Cambridge U.P., 1985), pp. 58–91

DAVIES, M.B., 'Suffolk's expedition to Montdidier 1523'; 'The "Enterprises" of Paris and Boulogne'; 'Boulogne and Calais from 1545 to 1550', *Bulletin of the Faculty of Arts, Fouad I University, Cairo* 7 (1944), pp. 33–44; 11 (1949), pp. 37–96; 12 (1950), pp. 1–90

DAVIS, J., 'Joan of Kent, Lollardy and the English Reformation', *J.Eccl.Hist.* 33 (1982), pp. 225–33

DEMAUS, R., *William Tindale: A Biography*, ed. R. Lovett (Religious Tract Society, 1904)

DENIS, P., 'John Veron: The first known French Protestant in England', *Proc. Huguenot Society of London* 22 (1973), pp. 130–34

DEVEREUX, J.A., 'Reformed doctrine in the collects of the first *Book of Common Prayer*', *H.T.R.* 58 (1965), pp. 48–68

DICKENS, A.G., *Lollards and Protestants in the Diocese of York 1509–1558* (Oxford: University of Hull, 1959, revised edn Hambledon Press, 1982)

——, *Late Monasticism and the Reformation* (London and Rio Grande: Hambledon Press, 1994)

——, and TONKIN, J.M. with POWELL, K., *The Reformation in Historical Thought* (Oxford: Basil Blackwell, 1985)

DOBSON, R.B., 'The English monastic cathedrals in the fifteenth century', *T.R.H.S.* 6th ser. 1 (1991), pp. 151–72

DONALDSON, G., *The Scottish Reformation* (Cambridge U.P., 1960)

DOWLING, M. and SHAKESPEARE, J., 'Religion and politics in mid Tudor England through the eyes of an English Protestant woman: The recollections of Rose Hickman', *B.I.H.R.* 55 (1982), pp. 94–102

DU BOULAY, F.R.H., *The Lordship of Canterbury: An Essay on Medieval Society* (Nelson, 1966)

DUFFY, E., *The Stripping of the Altars: Traditional Religion in England 1400–1580* (New Haven and London: Yale U.P., 1992)

DUGMORE, C.W., *The Mass and the English Reformers* (Macmillan, 1958), reviewed by T.M. Parker, *J.T.S.* N.S. 12 (1961), pp. 132–46

ELTON, G.R., *Star Chamber Stories* (Methuen, 1958)

——, *Policy and Police: The Enforcement of the Reformation in the Age of Thomas Cromwell* (Cambridge U.P., 1972)

——, *Reform and Reformation* (Edward Arnold, 1977)

——, *Reform and Renewal: Thomas Cromwell and the Commonweal* (Cambridge U.P., 1973)

——, *Studies in Tudor and Stuart Politics and Government* (4 vols; Cambridge U.P., 1974–92)

——, *The Tudor Constitution* (Cambridge U.P., 2nd edn 1982)

——, 'Persecution and toleration in the English Reformation', in W.J. Sheils (ed.), *Persecution and Toleration* (*St.Ch.Hist.* 21, 1984), pp. 164–71

EMDEN, A.B., *A Biographical Register of the University of Cambridge to 1500* (Cambridge U.P, 1963)

——, *A Biographical Register of the University of Oxford A.D. 1501 to 1540* (Oxford: Clarendon Press, 1974)

EMMISON, F.G., *Tudor Secretary: Sir William Petre at Court and Home* (Longman, 1961)

FAIRFIELD, L., 'John Bale and the development of Protestant hagiography in England', *J.Eccl.Hist.* 24 (1973), pp. 145–60

FICARO, B., 'Canterbury's first Dean', *S.C.J.* 18 (1987), pp. 343–6

FINES, J., *A Biographical Register of Early English Protestants and Others Opposed to the Roman Catholic Church 1525–1558: Part 1, A–C* (Abingdon: Sutton Courtenay Press, 1981). I am also very grateful to Dr Fines for supplying me with the remainder of his Register (D–Z) in typescript, together with his unpublished monograph drawing on material from the Register.

FIRTH, K.R., *The Apocalyptic Tradition in Reformation Britain 1530–1645* (Oxford U.P., 1979)

FOSTER, J. (ed.), *Alumni Oxonienses: The Members of the University of Oxford 1500–1714* . . . (4 vols; Oxford and London: James Parker and Co., 1891–2)

FOX, A., *Thomas More: History and Providence* (Oxford: Blackwell, 1982)

FOX, A. and GUY, J., *Reassessing the Henrician Age: Humanism, Politics and Reform 1500–1550* (Oxford: Blackwell, 1986)

FRIEDMANN, P., *Anne Boleyn: A Chapter of English History* (2 vols; Macmillan, 1884)

FULLER, T., *The Church History of Britain*, ed. J.S. Brewer (6 vols; Oxford U.P, 1845)

GAIRDNER, J., 'Cranmer and the Boleyn family', *N.Q.* 10th ser. 4 (1905), p. 201

GAMMON, S.R., *Statesman and Schemer: William, First Lord Paget – Tudor Minister* (Newton Abbot: David and Charles, 1973)

GARRETT, C.H., *The Marian Exiles: A Study in the Origins of Elizabethan Puritanism* (Cambridge U.P., 1938)

GARRETT, C., 'John Ponet and the confession of the banished ministers', *C.Q.R.* 137 (1943–4), pp. 47–74, 181–204

GASQUET, F.A. and BISHOP, E., *Edward VI and the Book of Common Prayer* (1890); and see anonymous review article, 'Cranmer's liturgical projects', *C.Q.R.* 31 (1891), pp. 446–62

GERRISH, B.A., 'Sign and reality: The Lord's Supper in the reformed confessions', in Gerrish, *The Old Protestantism and the New* (Chicago U.P. and Edinburgh: T. & T. Clark, 1982), pp. 118–30

——, *Continuing the Reformation: Essays on Modern Religious Thought* (Chicago U.P., 1993)

——, *Grace and Gratitude: The Eucharistic Theology of John Calvin* (Minneapolis, Fortress Press, and Edinburgh: T. & T. Clark, 1993)

GIRAUD, F.F., 'Faversham town accounts during the reign of Henry VIII', *A.C.* 10 (1876), pp. 233–41

GOULD, I.C., 'Some Nottinghamshire strongholds', *Journal of the British Archaeological Association* N.S. 13 (1907), pp. 51–64

GRAVES, M.A.R., *Thomas Norton the Parliament Man* (Oxford: Basil Blackwell, 1994)

GREENSLADE, S.L. (ed.), *The Cambridge History of the Bible: The West from the Reformation to the Present Day* (Cambridge U.P., 1963)

GUNN, S.G., *Charles Brandon Duke of Suffolk c.1484–1545* (Oxford: Blackwell, 1988)

——, and LINDLEY, P.G. (eds), *Cardinal Wolsey: Church, State and Art* (Cambridge U.P., 1991)

GUTH, DEL.J. and MCKENNA, J.W., (eds), *Tudor Rule and Revolution: Essays for G.R. Elton from his American Friends* (Cambridge U.P., 1982)

GUY, J., *The Public Career of Sir Thomas More* (Brighton: Harvester, 1980)

——, 'Henry VIII and the *praemunire* manoeuvres of 1530–31', *E.H.R.* 97 (1982), pp. 481–503

HAAS, S.W., 'The *Disputatio inter Clericum et Militem:* Was Berthelet's 1531 edition the first Henrician polemic of Thomas Cromwell?', *Moreana* 14 (Dec. 1977) pp. 65–72

——, 'Henry VIII's *Glasse of Truthe*', *History* 64 (1979), pp. 353–62

——, 'Martin Luther's "Divine Right" kingship and the royal supremacy: Two tracts from the 1531 Parliament and Convocation of the Clergy', *J.Eccl.Hist.* 31 (1980), pp. 317–25

HAIGH C. (ed.), *The English Reformation Revised* (Cambridge U.P., 1987)

HALL, B., *John à Lasco 1499–1560: A Pole in Reformation England* (Friends of Dr Williams Library Lecture 25, 1971)

——, 'The colloquies between Catholics and Protestants, 1539–41', in G.J. Cuming and D. Baker (eds), *Councils and Assemblies* (*St.Ch.Hist.* 7, 1971), pp. 235–66

——, 'The early rise and gradual decline of Lutheranism in England', in D. Baker (ed.), *Reform and Reformation: England and the Continent c. 1500–c. 1750* (*St.Ch.Hist.* Subsidia 2, 1979), pp. 103–32

HAREN, M.J., 'A suit of the Duke of Norfolk for papal favour, July 1531', *B.I.H.R.* 60 (1987), pp. 107–8

HARMER, A., [H. Wharton], *A Specimen of some Errors and Defects in the History of the Reformation of the Church of England wrote by Gilbert Burnet, D.D., now Lord Bishop of Sarum* (1693)

HARRINGTON, J., *A Brief View of the Church of England as it stood in Q. Elizabeths and King James his Reigne, to the Yeere 1608 . . .* (1653)

HAUGAARD, W.J., 'Katherine Parr: The religious convictions of a Renaissance queen', *Renaissance Quarterly* 22 (1969), pp. 346–59

——, *Elizabeth and the English Reformation: The Struggle for a Stable Settlement of Religion* (Cambridge U.P., 1968)

HEAL, F., 'The Archbishops of Canterbury and the practice of hospitality', *J.Eccl.Hist.* 33 (1982), pp. 544–63

HELMHOLZ, R.H., *Roman Canon Law in Reformation England* (Cambridge U.P., 1990)

HERBERT, E. [Lord Herbert of Chirbury], *The Life and Raigne of King Henry the Eighth* (E.G. for Thomas Whitaker, 1649)

HEYLYN, P., *Ecclesia Restaurata; or, the History of the Reformation of the Church of England* ed. J.C. Robertson (2 vols; Cambridge: Ecclesiastical History Society, 1859)

History of Parliament: The House of Commons 1509–1558, ed. S.T. Bindoff (3 vols; Secker and Warburg, 1982); *The History of Parliament: The House of Commons 1558–1603*, ed. P.W. Hasler (3 vols; Her Majesty's Stationery Office, 1982)

HOAK, D.E., *The King's Council in the Reign of Edward VI* (Cambridge U.P., 1976)

HOLMES, P., 'The last Tudor Great Councils', *H.J.* 33 (1990), pp. 1–22

HOPF, C., 'Bishop Hooper's "Notes" to the King's Council, 3 October 1550', *J.T.S.* 44 (1943), pp. 194–9

——, *Martin Bucer and the English Reformation* (Oxford: Basil Blackwell, 1946)

HORIE, H., 'The Lutheran influence on the Elizabethan Settlement, 1558–1563', *H.J.* 34 (1991), pp. 519–38

HORST, I.B., *The Radical Brethren: Anabaptism and the English Reformation to 1558* (Nieuwkoop: B. de Graaf, 1972)

HOULBROOKE, R.A., *Church Courts and the People during the English Reformation 1520–1570* (Oxford: Clarendon Press, 1979)

HOULBROOKE, R.A., see also E.W. Ives

HOUSE, S.B., 'Cromwell's message to the Regulars: The Biblical trilogy of John Bale,

1537', *Renaissance and Reformation/Renaissance et Réforme*, N.S. 15 (1991), pp. 123–38

HUDD, A.E., 'Two Bristol calendars', *Tr.Bristol & Glos.Arch.Soc.* 19 (1894–5), pp. 105–41

HUDSON, W.S., *The Cambridge Connection and the Elizabethan Settlement of 1559* (Durham, NC: Duke U.P., 1980)

HUGHES, C., 'Two sixteenth century northern Protestants: John Bradford and William Turner', *Bulletin of the John Rylands Library* 66 (1983), pp. 104–38

HUGHES, P., *The Reformation in England* (3 vols; Hollis and Carter, 1950–4)

HUNT, E.W., *The Life and Times of John Hooper (c. 1500–1555) Bishop of Gloucester* (Lewiston/Queenston/Lampeter: Edwin Mellen Press, 1992)

HUSSEY, A., 'Chapels in Kent', *A.C.* 29 (1911), pp. 217–67

HUTTON, R., *The Rise and Fall of Merry England* (Oxford: Clarendon Press, 1994)

IVES, E.W., *Anne Boleyn* (Oxford: Basil Blackwell, 1986)

——, 'Stress, faction and ideology in early-Tudor England', *H.J.* 34 (1991), pp. 193–202

——, 'Henry VIII's will: A forensic conundrum', *H.J.* 35 (1992), pp. 779–804, with following debate: R.A. Houlbrooke, 'Henry VIII's wills: A comment, *H.J.* 37 (1994), pp. 891–900, and Ives, 'Henry VIII's will: The protectorate provisions of 1546–7', ibid., pp. 901–13

——, 'Anne Boleyn and the early Reformation in England: The contemporary evidence', *H.J.* 37 (1994), pp. 389–400

——, 'The Queen and the painters: Anne Boleyn, Holbein and Tudor royal portraits', *Apollo* (July 1994), pp. 36–45

JACK, S.M., 'Northumberland, Queen Jane and the financing of the 1553 Coup', *Parergon* N.S. 6 (1988), pp. 137–48

JAMES, H., 'The aftermath of the 1549 coup and the Earl of Warwick's intentions', *H.R.* 62 (1989), pp. 91–5

JANELLE, P., 'An unpublished poem on Bishop Stephen Gardiner', *B.I.H.R.* 6 (1928–9), pp. 12–25, 89–96, 167–74

JAYNE, S. and JOHNSON, F.R. (eds), *The Lumley Library: The Catalogue of 1609* (British Museum, 1956)

JEANES, G., 'A Reformation treatise on the sacraments', *J.T.S.* N.S. 46 (1995), pp. 149–90

JOHNSON, M. (ed.), *Thomas Cranmer: Essays in Commemoration of the 500th Anniversary of his Birth* (Durham: Turnstone, 1990)

JONES, M.K. and UNDERWOOD, M.G., *The King's Mother: Lady Margaret Beaufort, Countess of Richmond and Derby* (Cambridge U.P., 1992)

JONES, N., 'Elizabeth's first year: The conception and birth of the Elizabethan political world', in C. Haigh (ed.), *The Reign of Elizabeth I* (Basingstoke: Macmillan, 1984), pp. 27–54

JONES, W.R.D., *William Turner: Tudor Naturalist, Physician and Divine* (Routledge, 1988)

KEISER, G., 'The mystics and the early English printers: The economics of devotionalism', in M. Glasscoe (ed.), *The Medieval Mystical Tradition* (Exeter Symposium IV: Papers Read at Dartington Hall, 1987)

KELLY, H.A., *The Matrimonial Trials of Henry VIII* (Stanford U.P., 1976)

KING, J.N., *English Reformation Literature: The Tudor Origins of the Protestant Reformation* (Princeton U.P., 1982)

KITCHING, C., 'Broken angels: The response of English parishes to the Turkish threat to Christendom, 1543–4', in W.J. Sheils and D. Wood (eds), *The Church and Wealth* (*St.Ch.Hist.* 24, 1987), pp. 209–18

KNOTT, J.R., *Discourses of Martyrdom in English Literature, 1563–1694* (Cambridge U.P., 1993)

KNOWLES, D.E., *The Religious Orders in England* (3 vols; Cambridge U.P., 1948–59)

KOENIGSBERGER, H.G., 'Prince and States General: Charles V and the Netherlands (1506–1555)', *T.R.H.S.* 6th ser. 4 (1994), pp. 127–51

KREIDER, A., *English Chantries: The Road to Dissolution* (Cambridge, MA: Harvard U.P., 1979)

L'ESTRANGE, J., 'The Church goods of St Andrew and St Mary Coslany in the City of Norwich', *Norfolk Archaeology* 7 (1879), pp. 45–78

RIEHL LEADER, D., *A History of the University of Cambridge 1: The University to 1546* (Cambridge: Cambridge U.P., 1988)

LEAVER, R.A., *'Goostly Psalmes and Spirituall Songes': English and Dutch Metrical Psalms from Coverdale to Utenhove 1535–1566* (Oxford: Clarendon Press, 1991)

LEHMBERG, S.E., *The Reformation Parliament 1529–1536* (Cambridge U.P., 1970)

——, *The Later Parliaments of Henry VIII 1536–1547* (Cambridge U.P., 1977)

——, *The Reformation of Cathedrals: Cathedrals in English Society, 1485–1603* (Princeton U.P., 1988)

LEVY, L.W., *Treason against God: A History of the Offense of Blasphemy* (New York: Schocken Books, 1981)

LITZENBERGER, C., 'Richard Cheyney, Bishop of Gloucester: An infidel in religion', *S.C.J.* 25 (1994), pp. 567–84

LOACH, J., *Parliament and the Crown in the Reign of Mary Tudor* (Oxford: Clarendon Press, 1986)

——, 'The function of ceremonial in the reign of Henry VIII', *P.P.* 142 (February 1994), pp. 43–68

LOADES, D.M., 'The Essex Inquisitions of 1556', *B.I.H.R.* 35 (1962), pp. 87–97

——, *Two Tudor Conspiracies* (Cambridge U.P., 1965)

——, *The Oxford Martyrs* (Batsford, 1970)

——, 'Anabaptism and English sectarianism in the mid-sixteenth century', in D. Baker (ed.), *Reform and Reformation: England and the Continent c. 1500–c. 1750* (Ecclesiastical History Society: *St.Ch.Hist.* Subsidia 2, 1979), pp. 59–70

——, *Mary Tudor: A Life* (Oxford and Cambridge, MA: Basil Blackwell, 1989)

——, *The Reign of Mary Tudor* (2nd edn, London and New York: Longman, 1991)

LOCKWOOD, S., 'Marsilius of Padua and the case for the royal ecclesiastical supremacy', *T.R.H.S.* 6th ser. 1 (1991), pp. 89–119

LOGAN, F.D., 'The Henrician canons', *B.I.H.R.* 48 (1974), pp. 99–103

——, 'The origins of the so-called regius professorships: An aspect of the Renaissance in Oxford and Cambridge', in D. Baker (ed.), *Renaissance and Renewal in Christian History* (*St.Ch.Hist.* 14, 1977), pp. 271–8

——, 'Thomas Cromwell and the vicegerency in spirituals: A revisitation', *E.H.R.* 103 (1988), pp. 658–67

LORIMER, J., *John Knox and the Church of England* (H.S. King & Co., 1875)

LYONS, S.M., 'The resignation of William Rugg: A reconsideration', *Catholic Historical Review* 73 (1987), pp. 23–40

MACCULLOCH, D., *Suffolk and the Tudors: Politics and Religion in an English County* (Oxford: Clarendon Press, 1986)

——, 'Two dons in politics: Thomas Cranmer and Stephen Gardiner, 1503–1533', *H.J.* 37 (1994), pp. 1–22

——, (ed.), *The Reign of Henry VIII: Politics, Policy and Piety* (Basingstoke: Macmillan, 1995)

——, 'Worcester', in P. Collinson and J. Craig (eds), *The Reformation in the English Towns* (forthcoming, Basingstoke: Macmillan, 1996)

——, 'Archbishop Cranmer: Consensus and tolerance in a changing Church', in O. Grell and R. Scribner (eds), *Tolerance and Intolerance in the European Reformation* (forthcoming, Cambridge U.P., 1996)

MCFARLANE, I.D., 'Religious verse in French neo–Latin poetry until the death of Francis I and Marguerite of Navarre', in J. Kirk (ed.), *Humanism and Reform: The Church in Europe, England, and Scotland, 1400–1643: Essays in Honour of James K. Cameron* (*St.Ch.Hist.* Subsidia 8, 1991), pp. 171–86

MCGEE, E.K., 'Cranmer: Nominalist', *H.T.R.* 57 (1964), pp. 189–216; 59 (1966), pp. 192–6 [see also Courtenay]

MCGRATH, A., *Iustitia Dei* (2 vols, Cambridge U.P., 1986)

MCINTOSH, M.K., 'Sir Anthony Cooke: Tudor humanist, educator and religious reformer', *Proceedings of the American Philosophical Society* 119 (1975), pp. 233–49

MCLEAN, A.M., '"A noughty and a false lyeng boke": William Barlow and the *Lutheran Factions*', *Renaissance Quarterly* 31 (1978), pp. 173–85

MCLELLAND, J.C., 'Calvinism perfecting Thomism? Peter Martyr Vermigli's question', *Scottish Journal of Theology* 31 (1978), pp. 571–8

MCNAIR, P., 'Ochino on sedition: An Italian dialogue of the sixteenth century', *Italian Studies* 15 (1960), pp. 36–49

——, 'Ochino's apology: Three Gods or three wives?', *History* 60 (1975), pp. 353–73

MARC'HADOUR, G., 'Lord, the Lord, our Lord, good Lord', *Moreana* 11 (1966), pp. 87–90

MARCOMBE, D., 'Bernard Gilpin: Anatomy of an Elizabethan legend', *Northern History* 16 (1980), pp. 20–39

MARCOMBE, D. and KNIGHTON, C.S. (eds), *Close Encounters: English Cathedrals and Society since 1540* (University of Nottingham Studies in Local and Regional History 3, 1991)

MARIUS, R., *Thomas More* (Collins, 1984)

MARKHAM, C., *Markham Memorials* (2 vols; Spottiswoode and Co., 1913)

MARSH, C., *The Family of Love in English Society, 1550–1630* (Cambridge U.P., 1994)

MATTINGLY, G., *Catherine of Aragon* (Jonathan Cape, 1950)

MAYER, T.F., 'A fate worse than death: Reginald Pole and the Parisian theologians', *E.H.R.* 103 (1988), pp. 870–91

——, 'If martyrs are to be exchanged with martyrs: The kidnappings of William Tyndale and Reginald Pole', *A.R.G.* 81 (1990), pp. 286–307

MERRIMAN, R.B., *The Life and Letters of Thomas Cromwell* (2 vols; Oxford: Clarendon Press, 1902)

MORANT, P., *The History and Antiquities of the County of Essex* (2 vols; 1763, 1768 [repr. Wakefield: EP Publishing, 1978])

MORETON, C.E., *The Townshends and their World: Gentry, Law and Land in Norfolk c. 1450–1551* (Oxford: Clarendon Press, 1992)

MORRILL, J., 'The Church in England, 1642–9', in J. Morrill (ed.), *Reactions to the English Civil War, 1642–1649* (London and Basingstoke: Macmillan, 1982), pp. 89–114

——, 'William Dowsing, the bureaucratic Puritan', in J. Morrill, P. Slack and D. Woolf, *Public Duty and Private Conscience in Seventeenth-century England: Essays presented to G.E. Aylmer* (Oxford: Clarendon Press, 1993), pp. 173–204

MOZLEY, J.F., *William Tyndale* (SPCK, 1937)

——, *John Foxe and his Book* (SPCK, 1940, repr. New York: Octagon Books, 1970)

MOYES, J., 'Warham, an English primate on the eve of the Reformation', *Dublin Review* 104 (1894), pp. 390–420

MULLER, J.A., *Stephen Gardiner and the Tudor Reaction* (1926)

MURPHY, V., 'The literature and propaganda of Henry's divorce', in MacCulloch (ed.), *Reign of Henry VIII* (q.v.), Ch. 6

NEAME, A., *The Holy Maid of Kent: The Life of Elizabeth Barton 1506–1534* (Hodder and Stoughton, 1971)

NEWMAN, J.H., *The Via Media of the Anglican Church* (2 vols; B.M. Pickering, 2nd edn 1877)

NICHOLSON, G., 'The Act of Appeals and the English Reformation', in C. Cross, D. Loades and J.J. Scarisbrick (eds), *Law and Government under the Tudors* (Cambridge U.P., 1988), pp. 19–30

OBERMAN, H.A., *Masters of the Reformation: The Emergence of a New Intellectual Climate in Europe* (Cambridge U.P., 1981)

O'DAY, R., *The Debate on the English Reformation* (London and New York: Methuen, 1986)

——, and HEAL, F. (eds), *Continuity and Change: Personnel and Administration of the Church in England 1500–1642* (Leicester U.P., 1976)

——, and HEAL, F. (eds), *Princes and Paupers in the English Church 1500–1800* (Leicester U.P., 1981)

OSWALD, A., 'Stephen Gardiner and Bury St Edmunds', *Proceedings of the Suffolk Institute of Archaeology* 26 (1952), pp. 54–57

OVERELL, M.A., 'Peter Martyr in England 1547–1553: An alternative view', *S.C.J.* 15(1) (1984), p. 104

PAGE, W., 'The First Book of Common Prayer and the Windsor Commission', *C.Q.R.* 98 (1924), pp. 51–64

PAPWORTH, J.W. and MORANT, A.W. (eds), *An Alphabetical Dictionary of Coats of Arms . . . Being an Ordinary of British Armorials . . .* (T. Richards, 1874, repr. with introduction by G.D. Squibb and A.R. Wagner, Tabard, 1961)

PARKER, T.M., see Dugmore

PAYLING, S.J., 'Law and arbitration in Nottinghamshire 1399–1461', in J. Rosenthal and C. Richmond (eds), *People, Politics and Community in the later Middle Ages* (Gloucester: Alan Sutton, 1987), pp. 140–60

——, *Political Society in Lancastrian England: The Greater Gentry of Nottinghamshire* (Oxford: Clarendon Press, 1991)

PENNY, D.A., *Freewill or Predestination: The Battle over Saving Grace in mid-Tudor England* (R.H.S.St.Hist. 61, 1990)

PETTEGREE, A., *Foreign Protestant Communities in Sixteenth Century London* (Oxford: Clarendon Press, 1986)

PETTEGREE, A., 'The Latin polemic of the Marian exiles', in J. Kirk (ed.), *Humanism and Reform: The Church in Europe, England, and Scotland, 1400–1643: Essays in Honour of James K. Cameron* (*St.Ch.Hist.* Subsidia 8, 1991), pp. 305–35

——, *Emden and the Dutch Revolt: Exile and the Development of Reformed Protestantism* (Oxford: Clarendon Press, 1992)

——, *Marian Protestantism: Six Studies* (Leicester: Scolar Press, St Andrews Studies in Reformation History 4, forthcoming, 1996)

PIEPHO, L., 'Mantuan's Eclogues in the English Reformation', *S.C.J.* 25 (1994), pp. 623–31.

[POCOCK, N.], 'Preparations for the first Prayer Book of Edward VI', *C.Q.R.* 35 (1892–93), pp. 33–68; idem, 'Preparations for the second Prayer Book of Edward VI', *C.Q.R.* 37 (1893–94), pp. 137–66

——, 'The condition of moral and religious belief in the reign of Edward VI', *E.H.R.* 10 (1895), pp. 417–44

POLLARD, A.F., *Thomas Cranmer and the English Reformation 1489–1556* (Frank Cass & Co., 1905)

POLLET, J.V., *Martin Bucer: Etudes sur la correspondance* (2 vols; Paris: Presses Universitaires, 1958–62)

PORTER, H.C., *Reformation and Reaction in Tudor Cambridge* (Cambridge U.P., 1958)

POWELL, K.G., 'The beginnings of Protestantism in Gloucestershire', *Tr.Bristol & Glos. Arch.Soc.* 90 (1971), pp. 141–57

——, *The Marian Martyrs and the Reformation in Bristol* (Bristol Hist. Assoc., 1972)

PRICE, F.D., 'Gloucester diocese under Bishop Hooper', *Tr.Bristol & Glos. Arch.Soc.* 60 (1938), pp. 51–151

PRIMUS, J.H., *The Vestments Controversy* (Kampen: J.H. Kok, 1960)

PROCTOR, F. and FRERE, W.H., *The Book of Common Prayer, with a Rationale of its Offices* (Macmillan, 1958)

PRUETT, G.E., 'Thomas Cranmer's progress in the doctrine of the eucharist, 1535–1548', *Historical Magazine of the Protestant Episcopal Church* 45 (1976), pp. 439–58

PRZYCHOCKI, G., 'Richard Croke's search for patristic MSS in connexion with the divorce of Catherine', *J.T.S.* 12 (1912), pp. 285–95

RATCLIFF, E.C., 'Liturgical work of Archbishop Cranmer', *J.Eccl.Hist.* 7 (1956), pp. 189–203, repr. in A.H. Couratin and D.H Tripp (eds), *Liturgical Studies* (SPCK, 1976), pp. 184–202

——, 'The English usage of eucharistic consecration 1548–1662', *Theology* 60 (1957), pp. 229–36, 273–80, repr. in idem, *Liturgical Studies*, pp. 203–21

REARDON, B.M.G., *Religious thought in the Reformation* (London and New York: Longman, 1981)

REDWORTH, G., 'A study in the formulation of policy: The genesis and evolution of the Act of Six Articles', *J.Eccl.Hist.* 37 (1986), pp. 42–67

——, *In Defence of the Church Catholic: The Life of Stephen Gardiner* (Oxford: Basil Blackwell, 1990)

REX, R., 'The English campaign against Luther in the 1520s', *T.R.H.S.* 5th ser. 39 (1989), pp. 85–106

——, 'The execution of the Holy Maid of Kent', *H.R* 64 (1991), pp. 216–20

——, *The Theology of John Fisher* (Cambridge: Cambridge U.P., 1991)

RICHARDSON, C.C., 'Cranmer and the analysis of eucharistic doctrine', *J.T.S.* 16 (1965), pp. 421–37

RICHARDSON, W.C., *Stephen Vaughan, Financial Agent of Henry VIII* (Baton Rouge: Louisiana State University, 1953)

RIDLEY, J.G., *Nicholas Ridley: A Biography* (Longman, Green and Co., 1957)

——, *Thomas Cranmer* (Oxford: Clarendon Press, 1962)

——, *John Knox* (Oxford: Clarendon Press, 1968)

ROSE-TROUP, F., *The Western Rebellion of 1549* (Smith, Elder and Co., 1913)

ROWELL, G., *The Liturgy of Christian Burial* (*A.C.C.* 59, 1977)

Royal Commission on Historical Monuments, *An Inventory of the Historical Monuments in the City of Cambridge* (2 parts and vol. of plans, 1959)

RUPP, E.G., *Studies in the Making of the English Protestant Tradition* (Cambridge U.P., 1947)

——, *Patterns of Reformation* (Epworth Press, 1969)

S.F. RYLE, 'Joannes Dantiscus and Thomas Cranmer: new light on the early career of an English Churchman', in *Joannes Dantiscus (1485–1548): Polish Ambassador and Humanist* (Brussels: Centre for European Culture, Koninklijke Academie voor Wetenschappen, Letteren en Schone Kunsten van België, *Studia Europaea*, 2, 1996: forthcoming)

SAWADA, P.A., 'Two anonymous Tudor treatises on the General Council', *J.Eccl.Hist.* 12 (1961), pp. 197–214

SCARISBRICK, J.J., 'Clerical taxation in England, 1485 to 1547', *J.Eccl.Hist.* 11 (1960), pp. 41–53

——, *Henry VIII* (Eyre and Spottiswoode, 1968)

DE SCHICKLER, F., *Les Eglises du refuge en Angleterre* (3 vols; Paris: Librarie Fischbacher, 1892)

SEEBASS, G., 'The importance of the Imperial city of Nuremberg in the Reformation', in J. Kirk (ed.) *Humanism and Reform: The Church in Europe, England, and Scotland, 1400–1643: Essays in Honour of James K. Cameron* (*St.Ch.Hist.* Subsidia 8, 1991), pp. 113–27

SELWYN, D.G., 'A neglected edition of Cranmer's Catechism', *J.T.S.* N.S 15 (1964), pp. 76–90

——, 'A new version of a mid-sixteenth century vernacular tract on the eucharist: A document of the early Edwardian Reformation?', *J.Eccl.Hist.* 39 (1988), pp. 217–29

——, 'The Book of Doctrine, the Lords' debate and the first Prayer Book of Edward VI: An abortive attempt at doctrinal consensus?', *J.T.S.* N.S. 40 (1989), pp. 446–80

SELWYN, D.G., see also P.N. Brooks

SHEPPARD, E.H., 'The Reformation and the citizens of Norwich', *N.A.* 38 (1981–83), pp. 44–58

SKEETERS, M.C., *Community and Clergy: Bristol and the Reformation c. 1530–c. 1570* (Oxford: Clarendon Press, 1993)

SLACK P. (ed.), *Rebellion, Popular Protest and the Social Order in Early Modern England* (Cambridge U.P., 1984)

SLAVIN, A.J., 'Cromwell, Cranmer and Lord Lisle, a study in the politics of reform', *Albion* 9 (1977), pp. 316–36

——, 'Defining the divorce: A review article', *S.C.J.* 20 (1989), pp. 105–11

SMITH, L.B., *Tudor Prelates and Politics* (Princeton U.P., 1953)

——, *A Tudor Tragedy: The Life and Times of Catherine Howard* (Jonathan Cape, 1961)

SMYTH, C.H., *Cranmer and the Reformation under Edward VI* (SPCK, 1926; 2nd edn 1973)

——, 'Studies in Bucer', *Cambridge Review*, 18 October 1947, p. 54

SPRUYT, B.J., '"En Bruit d'estre bonne luterine": Mary of Hungary (1505–58) and religious reform', *E.H.R.* 109 (1994), pp. 275–307

STARKEY, D., *The Reign of Henry VIII: Personalities and Politics* (George Philip, 1985)

——, (ed.), *Henry VIII: A European Court in England* (Collins and Brown, 1991)

STEPHENS, W.P., *The Holy Spirit in the Theology of Martin Bucer* (Cambridge U.P., 1970)

STOYEL, A.D., 'The lost buildings of Otford Palace', *A.C.* 100 (1984), pp. 259–80

STRYPE, J., *Annals of the Reformation . . . during Queen Elizabeth's Happy Reign* . . . (4 vols in 7; Oxford: Clarendon Press, 1820–40)

——, *Ecclesiastical Memorials* . . . (3 vols in 6; Oxford: Clarendon Press, 1822)

——, *The Life of the Learned Sir John Cheke* . . . (Oxford: Clarendon Press, 1821)

——, *The Life of the Learned Sir Thomas Smith* . . . (Oxford: Clarendon Press, 1820)

——, *Memorials . . . of . . . Thomas Cranmer* . . . (3 vols; Ecclesiastical History Society, Oxford, 1848–54)

——, *Memorials . . . of . . . Thomas Cranmer* . . ., ed. P.E. Barnes (2 vols; George Routledge and Co., 1853). I have referred to this edition of Strype in the text.

SWENSEN, P., 'Patronage from the Privy Chamber: Sir Anthony Denny and religious reform', *J.B.S.* 27 (1988), pp. 25–44

SYKES, N., RATCLIFF, E.C. and WILLIAMS, A.T.P., *Thomas Cranmer 1489–1556: Three Commemorative Lectures delivered in Lambeth Palace* (Church Information Office, 1956)

TAIT, H., 'The girdle-prayerbook or "tabelett"', *Jewellery Studies* 2 (1985), pp. 29–57

TATTON-BROWN, T., 'Excavations at the "Old Palace", Bekesbourne, near Canterbury', *A.C.* 96 (1980), pp. 27–58

THOMAS, M., 'Tunstal – trimmer or martyr?', *J.E.H.* 24 (1973), pp. 337–55

THORP, M.R., 'Religion and the Wyatt Rebellion of 1554', *Ch. Hist.* 47 (1978), pp. 363–80

THURSTON, H., 'The canon law of the divorce', *E.H.R.* 19 (1904), pp. 632–45

TITTLER, R. and BATTLEY, S.L., 'The local community and the Crown in 1553: The accession of Mary Tudor revisited', *B.I.H.R.* 57 (1984), pp. 131–9

TJERNAGEL, N.S., *Henry VIII and the Lutherans: A Study in Anglo-Lutheran Relations from 1521 to 1547* (St Louis: Concordia, 1965)

TONKIN, J.M., see A.G. Dickens

TREVOR-ROPER, H.R., 'The Church of England and the Greek Church in the time of Charles I', *St.Ch.Hist.* 15 (1978); repr. in Trevor-Roper, *From Counter-Reformation to Glorious Revolution* (Secker and Warburg, 1992), pp. 83–111

TRUEMAN, C., *Luther's Legacy: Salvation and English Reformers 1525–1556* (Oxford: Clarendon Press, 1994)

TUDOR, P., '"All youthe to learne the Creade and Tenne commaundementes": Unpublished draft injunctions of Henry VIII's Reign', *H.R.* 63 (1990), pp. 211–17

TUDOR-CRAIG, P., 'Henry VIII and King David', in D. Williams (ed.), *Early Tudor England* (Woodbridge: Boydell Press, 1989), pp. 183–206

ULLMANN, W., '"This realm of England is an Empire"', *J.Eccl.Hist.* 30 (1979), pp. 175–203

VENN, J. and S.A. (eds), *Alumni Cantabrigienses* (4 vols; Cambridge, 1922–27)

Victoria County Histories: *Cambridgeshire*; *Lincolnshire*; *Nottinghamshire*; *Surrey*

VINAY, V., 'Riformatori e lotte contadine. Scritti e polemiche relative all ribellione dei contadini nella Cornovaglia e nel Devonshire sotto Edoardo VI', *Rivista di Storia e Letteratura religiosa* 3 (1967), pp. 203–51

VIRGOE, R., 'Sir John Risley (1443–1512), courtier and councillor', *N.A.* 38 (1981–3), pp. 140–48

WABUDA, S., 'Equivocation and recantation during the English Reformation: The "subtle shadows" of Dr Edward Crome', *J.Eccl.Hist.* 44 (1993), pp. 224–42

WALSH, K.J., 'Cranmer and the fathers, especially in the *Defence*', *Journal of Religious History* 11 (1980), pp. 227–47

WEEVER, J., *Antient Funeral Monuments* . . . (2nd edn, 1767)

WHARTON, A., see A. Harmer

WHATMORE, L.E., 'A sermon of Henry Gold, Vicar of Ospringe, 1525–7, preached before Archbishop Warham', *Archaeologia Cantiana* 57 (1944), pp. 34–43

WIEDERMANN, G., 'Alexander Alesius's lectures on the Psalms at Cambridge, 1536', *J.Eccl.Hist.* 37 (1986), pp. 15–41

WILLEN, D., *John Russell, First Earl of Bedford: One of the King's Men* (R.H.S.St.Hist. 23, 1981)

WILLIAMS, G.H., *The Radical Reformation* (Weidenfeld and Nicolson, 1962)

WOOD, A.C., 'Notes on the early history of the Clifton family', *Tr.Thoroton Soc.* 37 (1933), pp. 24–40

——, *A History of Nottinghamshire* (Nottingham, 1947)

EVELEIGH WOODRUFF, C., 'Extracts from original documents illustrating the progress of the Reformation in Kent', *A.C.* 31 (1915), pp. 92–120

YOST, J.K., 'Hugh Latimer's reform program 1529–1536, and the intellectual origins of the Anglican *Via Media*', *Anglican Theological Review* 53 (1971), pp. 103–14

YOUINGS, J., *The Dissolution of the Monasteries* (George Allen and Unwin, 1971)

——, 'The South-Western Rebellion of 1549', *Southern History* 1 (1979), pp. 99–122

ZELL, M.L., 'The personnel of the clergy of Kent, in the Reformation period', *E.H.R.* 89 (1974), pp. 513–33

——, 'The Prebendaries' Plot of 1543: A reconsideration', *J.Eccl.Hist.* 27 (1976), pp. 241–53

Unpublished dissertations

AYRIS, P., 'Thomas Cranmer's Register: A record of archiepiscopal administration in diocese and province' (Cambridge Ph.D., 1984)

DAVIES, C.M.F., 'Towards a Godly Commonwealth: The public ideology of Protestantism, *c.* 1546–1553' (London Ph.D., 1988)

EDWARDS, A.J., 'The sede vacante administration of Archbishop Thomas Cranmer 1533–53' (London Univ. M. Phil., 1968)

MCENTEGART, R., 'England and the League of Schmalkalden 1531–1547: Faction, foreign policy and the English Reformation' (London School of Economics Ph.D., 1992)

MURPHY, V.M., 'The debate over Henry VIII's first divorce: An analysis of the contemporary treatises' (Cambridge Ph.D., 1984)

NICHOLSON, G., 'The nature and function of historical argument in the Henrician Reformation' (Cambridge Ph.D., 1977)

NULL, A., 'Thomas Cranmer's Doctrine of Repentance' (Cambridge Ph.D., 1994)

SACHS, L.R., 'Thomas Cranmer's "Reformatio Legum Ecclesiasticarum" of 1553 in the context of English Church law from the later Middle Ages to the canons of 1603' (Catholic Univ. America J.C.D., 1982)

SAMMAN, N., 'The Henrician Court during Cardinal Wolsey's ascendancy, *c.* 1514–1529' (Univ. Wales Ph.D., 1988)

SWENSEN, P.C., 'Noble hunters of the Romish Fox: Religious reform at the Tudor Court, 1543–1564' (Univ. California, Berkeley, Ph.D., 1981)

Index